Recommended by Teachers
Trusted by Toppers

AF819993

All in One®

Mathematics

CBSE Class 9

Focused Theory ▪ Practice Exercises ▪ Sample Papers

Authors
Rakesh Pandey
Sunil Rathore

arihant
SUCCESS AND NOTHING LESS

ARIHANT PRAKASHAN

(School Division Series)

卐 *ADMINISTRATIVE & PRODUCTION OFFICES*

Regd. Office

'Ramchhaya' 4577/15, Agarwal Road, Darya Ganj, New Delhi -110002
Tele: 011- 47630600, 43518550; Fax: 011- 23280316

卐 *Head Office*

Kalindi, TP Nagar, Meerut (UP) - 250002, Tel: 0121-7156203, 7156204

卐 *SALES & SUPPORT OFFICES*

Agra, Ahmedabad, Bengaluru, Bareilly, Chennai, Delhi, Guwahati, Hyderabad, Jaipur, Jhansi, Kolkata, Lucknow, Nagpur & Pune.

PO No : TXT-XX-XXXXXXX-X-XX

Published By Arihant Publications (India) Ltd.

For further information about the books published by Arihant, log on to www.arihantbooks.com or e-mail at info@arihantbooks.com

Follow us on

卐 *PRICE* ₹415.00

PRODUCTION TEAM

Publishing Managers
Mahendra Singh Rawat & Keshav Mohan

Cover Designer
Salman Shaikh

Inner Designer
Ankit Tyagi

Project Head
Ashwani

Page Layouting
Shivam Prajapati

Proof Reader
Mukul Kaushik

Index *cum* Study Planner

One Book- Endless Features

to Help you Succeed

Chapter Intro

A quick information about the coverage of the chapter to explain students about what they are going to study.

CHAPTER 1

Number Systems

In earlier classes, we have already study about the various types of numbers (i.e. natural numbers, integers and rational numbers) and their representation on the number line. Now, in this chapter, we will study rational numbers as recurring/terminating decimals and the existence of irrational numbers. We will also study the representation of irrational numbers on the number line.

TOPIC 01 Basics of Number Systems

A number is a mathematical object used to count, label and measure.

Natural Numbers

Numbers, which are used for counting i.e. 1, 2, 3, 4, ..., are called natural numbers, which is denoted by N.

Whole Numbers

All natural numbers together with 0 form the whole numbers, which is denoted by W.

Complete Theory

Each chapter has Complete, Easy to Understand and Simplified theory covering latest syllabus and rationalized NCERT Textbook.

Example 1. State whether the following statements are true or false. Give reasons for your answers.

(i) 0 is a rational number.

(ii) Every rational number is an integer.

Sol. (i) True, 0 is a rational number, since we can write $0 = \frac{0}{1}$

(ii) False, $\frac{1}{2}$ is a rational number but not an integer.

Equivalent Rational Numbers

Two rational numbers are said to be equivalent. If their standard form is equal.

e.g. $\frac{1}{2} = \frac{2}{4} = \frac{10}{20} = \frac{25}{50} = \frac{49}{98}$

Solved Examples

Solved Examples have been solved in step-by-step manner, so that students can learn the problem solving process completely.

Try These 1.1

1. State whether the following statements are true or false. Give reasons for your answers.
   (i) Every whole number is a natural number.
   (ii) Zero is neither a negative nor a positive integer.
   (iii) There are finitely many rational numbers between any two given rational numbers.
   (iv) Every real number is either irrational or rational.
   (v) $\sqrt{7}$ is an irrational number but not a real number.
   (vi) 4 is real but not irrational.

Try These

A set of Questions given after topic end, helps students to remain connected with topic while studying. They can instantly assess themselves for their understanding.

One Book- Endless Features

to Help you Succeed

Illustrative Figures

To make the concepts completely visible, illustrative diagrams have been given at various place.

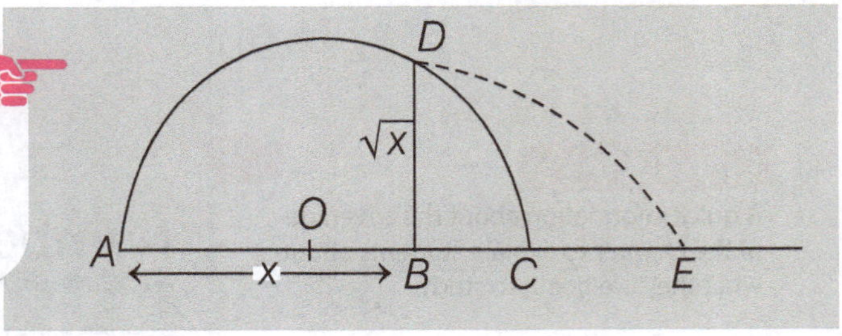

8. Find three rational numbers between 10 and 12.

9. Classify the following numbers as rational or irrational with justification. **NCERT Exemplar**

(i) $3\sqrt{18}$ (ii) $(1+\sqrt{5})-(4+\sqrt{5})$

(iii) 1.030030003... (iv) $\sqrt{\frac{9}{27}}$ (v) 0.3796

10. Insert a rational number and an irrational number between the following. **NCERT Exemplar**

(i) $-\frac{2}{5}$ and $\frac{1}{2}$ (ii) 0.15 and 0.16

NCERT Exemplar

Each chapter has selected problems from NCERT Exemplar, the best problem books for School/Board Exams.

Competency based Questions

Each chapter has sufficient number of Competency based Questions of all types.

13. $p(x) = ax^2 - 8x + 3$, where a is a non-zero re

One zero of $p(x)$ is 3 times the other zero.

(i) Find the value of a. Show your work.

(ii) What is the shape of the graph of $p(x)$? Give a reason for your answer. **Competency Based Question**

17. If the zeroes of the cubic polynomial $x^3 - 6x^2 + 3x + 10$ are of the form $a, a+b$ and $a+2b$ for some real numbers a and b, then find the values of a and b. **NCERT Exemplar**

NCERT Folder

Complete explanations of all the questions of NCERT Exercises.

NCERT FOLDER

Complete Solutions of All Exercises of NCERT Textbook

EXERCISE 1.1 (NCERT Page 5)

Q1. **Is zero a rational number? Can you write it in the form $\frac{p}{q}$, where p, q are integers and $q \neq 0$?**

Sol. Yes, zero is a rational number, because we can write $0 = \frac{0}{1}$ (where, 0, 1 are integers and $q = 1 \neq 0$).

Q2. **Find six rational numbers between 3 and 4.**

Sol. Here, $4 > 3$, so let $x = 3$, $y = 4$ and $n = 6$

Then, $d = \frac{y-x}{n+1} = \frac{4-3}{6+1} = \frac{1}{7}$

So, the six rational numbers between 3 and 4 are $(x+d), (x+2d), (x+3d), (x+4d) (x+5d)$ and $(x+6d)$

i.e. $\left(3+\frac{1}{7}\right), \left(3+\frac{2}{7}\right), \left(3+\frac{3}{7}\right), \left(3+\frac{4}{7}\right), \left(3+\frac{5}{7}\right)$ and $\left(3+\frac{6}{7}\right)$

or $\left(\frac{21+1}{7}\right), \left(\frac{21+2}{7}\right), \left(\frac{21+3}{7}\right), \left(\frac{21+4}{7}\right), \left(\frac{21+5}{7}\right)$ and $\left(\frac{21+6}{7}\right)$

(i) Every natural number is a whole number.

(ii) Every integer is a whole number.

(iii) Every rational number is a whole number.

Sol. (i) True, because every natural number i.e. 1, 2, 3,... belongs to the collection of whole numbers.

(ii) False, because negative integers are not considered in whole numbers.

(iii) False, because numbers like 3/2 is a rational number but not a whole number.

EXERCISE 1.2 (NCERT Page 8)

Q1. **State whether the following statements are true or false. Justify your answers.**

(i) Every irrational number is a real number.

(ii) Every point on the number line is of the form $\sqrt{m}$, where m is a natural number.

(iii) Every real number is an irrational number.

Sol. (i) True, because real numbers are the collection of rational numbers and irrational numbers.

One Book- Endless Features
to Help you Succeed

Review Exercise

Chapter exercise having all types of questions; MCQs, Assertion-Reason, True-False, Fillers, Matching, Case based, VSA, SA, LA.

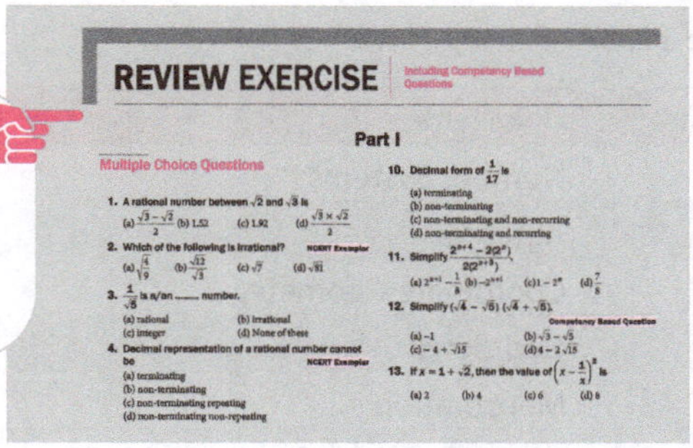

Sample Question Papers

There are 5 Sample Question Papers at the end. All these Sample Questions Papers are exactly prepared on the latest syllabus & pattern of examination.

Mind Map

A quick revision visual tool for the complete chapter.

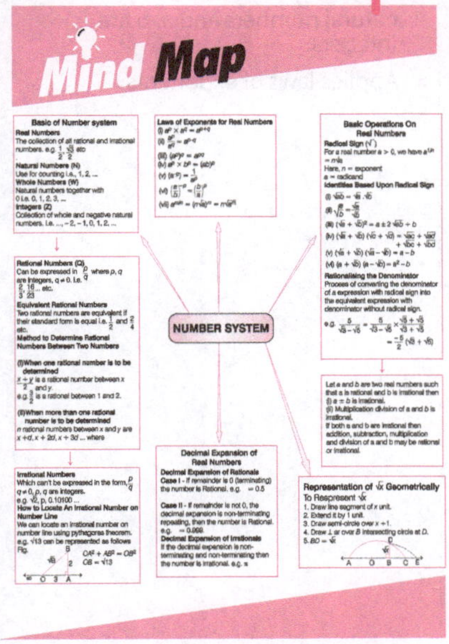

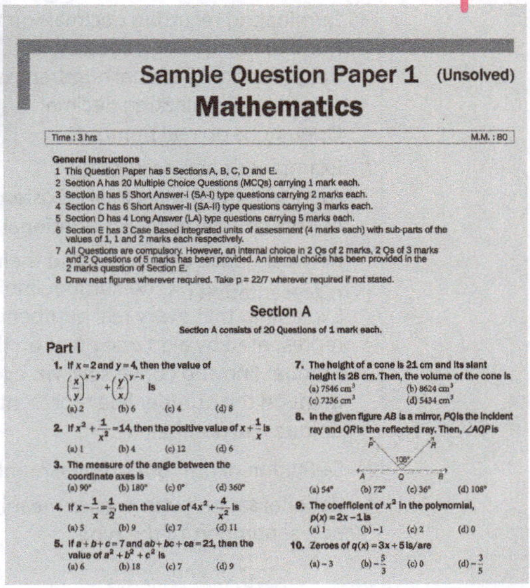

Latest Course *Structure*

Time: 3 Hrs

Total Marks : 80

Units	Unit Name	Marks
I	Number Systems	10
II	Algebra	20
III	Coordinate Geometry	04
IV	Geometry	27
V	Mensuration	13
VI	Statistics & Probability	06
	Total	**80**

S. No.	Content	Competencies	Explanation
	Unit 1: Number Systems		
1.	**Real Numbers** 1. Review of representation of natural numbers, integers and rational numbers on the number line. Representation of terminating/non-terminating recurring decimals on the number line through successive magnification. Rational numbers as recurring/ terminating decimals. Operations on real numbers. 2. Examples of non-recurring /non-terminating decimals. Existence of non-rational numbers (irrational numbers) such as $\sqrt{2}$, $\sqrt{3}$ and their representation on the number line. Explaining that every real number is represented by a unique point on the number line and conversely, *viz.* every point on the number line represents a unique real number. 3. Definition of *n*th root of a real number. 4. Rationalisation (with precise meaning) of real numbers of the type $\frac{1}{a+b\sqrt{x}}$ and $\frac{1}{\sqrt{x}+\sqrt{y}}$ (and their combinations), where *x* and *y* are natural numbers and *a*, *b* are integers. 5. Recall of laws of exponents with integral powers. Rational exponents with positive real bases (to be done by particular cases, allowing learner to arrive at the general laws.)	Develops a deeper understanding of numbers, including the set of real numbers and its properties. • Recognizes and appropriately uses powers and exponents. • Computes powers and roots and applies them to solve problems.	Differentiates rational and irrational numbers based on decimal representation. • Represents rational and irrational numbers on the number line. • Rationalizes real number expressions such as $\frac{1}{a+b\sqrt{x}}$ and $\frac{1}{\sqrt{x}+\sqrt{y}}$, where x, y are natural numbers and a, b are integers. • Applies laws of exponents

S. No.	Content	Competencies	Explanation
	Unit II : Algebra		
1.	**Polynomials** 1. Definition of a polynomial in one variable with examples and counter examples, Coefficients of a polynomial, terms of a polynomial and zero polynomial. 2. Degree of a polynomial. 3. Constant, linear, quadratic, cubic polynomials; monomials, binomials, trinomials. Factors and multiples. 4. Zeroes of a polynomial. 5. Motivate and state the remainder theorem with examples. 6. Statement and proof of the Factor Theorem. Factorisation of $ax^2 + bx + c$, $a \neq 0$, where a, b and c are real numbers and of cubic polynomials using the Factor Theorem. 7. Recall of algebraic expressions and identities. Verification of identities $(x + y + z)^2 = x^2 + y^2 + z^2 + 2xy + 2yz + 2zx$, $(x \pm y)^3 = x^3 \pm y^3 \pm 3xy(x \pm y)$, $x^3 \pm y^3 = (x \pm y)(x^2 \quad xy + y^2)$, $x^3 + y^3 + z^3 - 3xyz = (x + y + z)(x^2 + y^2 + z^2 - xy - yz - zx)$ and their use in factorisation of polynomials.	Learns the art of factoring polynomials.	Defines polynomials in one variable. • Identifies different terms and different types of polynomials. • Finds zeros of a polynomial • Proves factor theorem and applies the theorem to factorize polynomials. • Proves and applies algebraic identities up to degree three.
2.	**Linear Equations in Two Variables** 1. Recall of linear equations in one variable. Introduction to the equation in two variables. 2. Focus on linear equations of the type $ax+by+c = 0$. Explain that a linear equation in two variables has infinitely many solutions and justify their being written as ordered pairs of real numbers, plotting them and showing that they lie on a line. Explain that a linear equation in two variables has infinitely many solutions and justify their being written as ordered pairs of real numbers, plotting them and showing that they lie on a line.	Visualizes solutions of a linear equation in two variables as ordered pair of real numbers on its graph	Describes and plot a linear equation in two variables.

S. No.	Content	Competencies	Explanation
	Unit III : Coordinate Geometry		
1.	**Coordinate Geometry** 1. The Cartesian plane, coordinates of a point 2. Names and terms associated with the coordinate plane, notations.	Specifies locations and describes spatial relationships using coordinate geometry.	Describes cartesian plane and its associated terms and notations
	Unit IV : Geometry		
1.	**Introduction to Euclid's Geometry** 1. History - Geometry in India and Euclid's geometry. Euclid's method of formalising observed phenomenon into rigorous Mathematics with definitions, common/obvious notions, axioms/postulates and theorems. 2. The five postulates of Euclid. Equivalent versions of the fifth postulate. Showing the relationship between axiom and theorem, for example: (a) Given two distinct points, there exists one and only one line through them. (Axiom) (b) (Prove) Two distinct lines cannot have more than one point in common. (Theorem)	• Proves theorems using Euclid's axioms and postulates– for triangles, quadrilaterals, and circles and applies them to solve geometric problems.	• Understands historical relevance of Indian and Euclidean Geometry. • Defines axioms, postulates, theorems with reference to Euclidean Geometry.
2.	**Lines and Angles** 1. (Motivate) If a ray stands on a line, then the sum of the two adjacent angles so formed is 180° and the converse. 2. (Prove) If two lines intersect, the vertically opposite angles are equal. 3. (Motivate) Lines which are parallel to a given line are parallel.	• Derives proofs of mathematical statements particularly related to geometrical concepts, like parallel lines by applying axiomatic approach and solves problems using them.	• Visualizes, explains and applies relations between different pairs of angles on a set of parallel lines and intersecting transversal. • Solves problems based on parallel lines and intersecting transversal.
3.	**Triangles** 1. (Motivate) Two triangles are congruent if any two sides and the included angle of one triangle is equal to any two sides and the included angle of the other triangle (SAS Congruence). 2. (Prove) Two triangles are congruent if any two angles and the included side of one triangle is equal to any two angles and the included side of the other triangle (ASA Congruence). 3. (Motivate) Two triangles are congruent if three sides of one triangle are equal (respectively) to three sides of the other triangle (SSS Congruence).	• Describe relationships including congruency of two-dimensional geometrical shapes (lines, angle, triangles) to make and test conjectures and solve problems. • Derives proofs of mathematical statements particularly related to geometrical concepts triangles by applying axiomatic approach and solves problems using them.	• Visualizes and explains Congruency properties of two triangles • Applies Congruency Criteria to solve problems

	4. (Motivate) Two right angled triangles are congruent if the hypotenuse and a side of one triangle are equal (respectively) to the hypotenuse and a side of the other triangle. (RHS Congruence) 5. (Prove) The angles opposite to equal sides of a triangle are equal. 6. (Motivate) The sides opposite to equal angles of a triangle are equal.		
4.	**Quadrilaterals** 1. (Prove) The diagonal divides a parallelogram into two congruent triangles. 2. (Motivate) In a parallelogram, opposite sides are equal and conversely. 3. (Motivate) In a parallelogram, opposite angles are equal and conversely. 4. (Motivate) A quadrilateral is a parallelogram, if a pair of its opposite sides is parallel and equal. 5. (Motivate) In a parallelogram, the diagonals bisect each other and conversely. 6. (Motivate) In a triangle, the line segment joining the mid-points of any two sides is parallel to the third side and is half of it and (motivate) its converse.	• Derives proofs of mathematical statements particularly related to geometrical concepts of quadrilaterals by applying axiomatic approach and solves problems using them.	• Visualizes and explains properties of quadrilaterals • Solves problems based on properties of quadrilaterals.
5.	**Circles** 1. (Prove) Equal chords of a circle subtend equal angles at the centre and (motivate) its converse. 2. (Motivate) The perpendicular from the centre of a circle to a chord bisects the chord and conversely, the line drawn through the centre of a circle to bisect a chord is perpendicular to the chord. 3. (Motivate) Equal chords of a circle (or of congruent circles) are equidistant from the centre (or their respective centres) and conversely. 4. (Prove) The angle subtended by an arc at the centre is double the angle subtended by it at any point on the remaining part of the circle. 5. (Motivate) Angles in the same segment of a circle are equal. 6. (Motivate) If a line segment joining two points subtends equal angle at two other points lying on the same side of the line containing the segment, the four points lie on a circle. 7. (Motivate) The sum of either of the pair of the opposite angles of a cyclic quadrilateral is 180° and its converse.	• Proves theorems about the geometry of a circle, including its chords and subtended angles	• Visualizes and explains properties of circles. • Solves problems based on properties of circle.

Unit V : Mensuration

1.	**Areas** 1. Area of a triangle using Heron's formula (without proof).	• Visualizes, represents and calculates the area of a triangle using Heron's formula.	• States and applies Heron's Formula to find area of a triangle.
2.	**Surface Areas and Volumes** 1. Surface areas and volumes of spheres (including hemispheres) and right circular cones.	• Visualizes and uses mathematical thinking to discover formulas to calculate surface areas and volumes of solid objects (spheres, hemispheres and right circular cones)	• Solves problems based on surface areas and volumes of three-dimensional shapes (spheres/hemi-sphere, right circular cones).

Unit VI : Statistics

1.	**Statistics** 1. Bar graphs 2. Histograms (with varying base lengths) 3. Frequency polygons.	• Draws and interprets bar graph, histogram and frequency polygon	• Represents data using Bar Graph, Histogram and frequency polygon.

Topic/Chapters to be Assessed Formatively

The following topics are included in the syllabus but will be assessed only formatively to reinforce understanding without adding to summative assessments. This reduces academic stress while ensuring meaningful learning. Schools can integrate these with existing chapters as they align well. Relevant NCERT textual material is enclosed for reference.

S. No.	Content	Competencies	Explanation
	Unit II: Algebra		
1.	**Linear Equations In Two Variables** 1. Graph of linear equations in two variables. 2. Examples, problems from real life, including problems on Ratio and Proportion and with algebraic and graphical solutions being done simultaneously.	• Visualizes solutions of a linear equation in two variables as ordered pair of real numbers on its graph.	Describes and plot a linear equation in two variables. • Exemplifies a linear equation in two variables and its possible solutions using real life examples.
	Unit III: COORDINATE GEOMETRY		
1.	**Coordinate Geometry:** 1. Plotting points in the plane.	• Specifies locations and describes spatial relationships using coordinate geometry, e.g., plotting points in a plane	• Plots/locates points in the plane.
	Unit IV: Geometry		
1.	**Lines and Angles** 1. (State without proof) Results on corresponding angles, alternate angles, interior angles when a transversal intersects two parallel lines. 2. (Prove) The sum of the angles of a triangle is 180°. 3. (State without proof) If a side of a triangle is produced, the exterior angle so formed is equal to the sum of the two interior opposite angles.	• Derives proofs of mathematical statements particularly related to geometrical concepts, like parallel lines by applying axiomatic approach and solves problems using them.	• Visualizes, explains and applies relations between different pairs of angles on a set of parallel lines and intersecting transversal. • Solves problems based on parallel lines and intersecting transversal. • Visualizes the relation between exterior and interior angles of a triangle.
2.	**Triangles** 1. (State without proof) Triangle inequalities and relation between 'angle and facing side' inequalities in triangles.	• Derives proofs of mathematical statements particularly related to geometrical concepts in triangles by applying axiomatic approach and solves problems using them.	• Defines and applies triangle inequalities with reference to angles and sides
3.	**Areas Of Parallelograms And Triangles** 1. (Prove) Parallelograms on the same base and between the same parallels have equal area. 2. (State without proof) Triangles on the same base (or equal bases) and between the same parallels are equal in area.	• Find areas of all types of triangles by using appropriate formulae and apply them in real life situations	• Finds area of rectangle, parallelogram and triangle.

4.	**Circles** 1. Through examples, arrive at definition of circle and related concepts-radius, circumference, diameter, chord, arc, secant, sector, segment, subtended angle. 2. (State without proof) There is one and only one circle passing through three given non-collinear points.	• Proves theorems about the geometry of a circle, including its chords and subtended angles	• Solves problems based on properties of circle.
5.	**Constructions** 1. Construction of bisectors of line segments and angles of measure 60°, 90°, 45° etc., equilateral triangles. 2. Construction of a triangle given its base, sum/difference of the other two sides and one base angle.	• Constructs different geometrical shapes like bisectors of line segments, angles and their bisectors and triangles satisfying given constraints.	• Constructs line-segments, bisectors of line-segments, angles and triangle with given conditions.
	Unit V: Mensuration		
1.	**Areas** 1. Application of heron's formula in finding the area of a quadrilateral	• Visualizes, represents and calculates the area of a triangle using Heron's formula.	• States and applies Heron's Formula to find area of a quadrilateral.
2.	**Surface Areas And Volumes** 1. Surface areas and volumes of cubes, cuboids and right circular cylinders.	• Visualizes and uses mathematical thinking to discover formulas to calculate surface areas and volumes of solid objects (cubes, cuboids and right circular cylinders)	• Solves problems based on surface areas and volumes of three-dimensional shapes (cube, cuboid and right circular cylinders).
	Unit VI: Statistics		
1.	**Statistics** 1. Introduction to Statistics: Collection of data, presentation of data — tabular form, ungrouped / grouped data. 2. Mean, median and mode of ungrouped data.	• Applies measures of central tendencies such as mean, median and mode of ungrouped data.	• Organizes raw data in tabular form. • Calculates mean, median, mode of ungrouped data
2.	**Probability** 1. History, Repeated experiments and observed frequency approach to probability. Focus is on empirical probability. (A large amount of time to be devoted to group and to individual activities to motivate the concept); 2. The experiments to be drawn from real - life situations, and from examples used in the chapter on statistics).	• Applies concepts from probability to solve problems on the likelihood of everyday events.	• Conceptualizes probability using repeated experiments and observed frequencies.

CHAPTER 1

Number Systems

In earlier classes, we have already study about the various types of numbers (i.e. natural numbers, integers and rational numbers) and their representation on the number line. Now, in this chapter, we will study rational numbers as recurring/terminating decimals and the existence of irrational numbers. We will also study the representation of irrational numbers on the number line.

TOPIC 01 Basics of Number Systems

A number is a mathematical concept used for counting, labeling and measuring.

Natural Numbers

Numbers, which are used for counting

i.e. 1, 2, 3, 4, ..., are called natural numbers, which is denoted by N.

Whole Numbers

All natural numbers together with 0 form the whole numbers, which is denoted by W.

Integers

The collection of all whole numbers and negative of natural numbers are called integers.

The collection of integers is denoted by Z

i.e. $Z = \{ \ldots, -4, -3, -2, -1, 0, 1, 2, 3, 4, \ldots \}$

Rational Numbers

The numbers, which can be expressed in the form of p/q, where p, q are integers and $q \neq 0$, are known as rational numbers.

The collection of rational numbers is denoted by Q.

i.e. $Q = \left\{ \frac{p}{q} : p, q \text{ are integers and } q \neq 0 \right\}$

e.g. $\frac{0}{1}, \frac{-1}{2}, \frac{1}{2}, \frac{3}{2}, \frac{5}{2}, \frac{-3}{2}, -2, 2$, etc., are rational numbers.

Note it

- Every natural number is a whole number but every whole number is not a natural number.
- Every natural number is an integer.
- Every whole number is an integer.
- Zero is neither a negative nor a positive integer.
- Zero is a rational number, since we can write $0 = 0/1$.
- Every natural number, whole number and integer is a rational number. e.g. $1 = 1/1$ or $5 = 5/1$.

Example 1. **State whether the following statements are true or false. Give reasons for your answers.**

(i) 0 is a rational number.

(ii) Every rational number is an integer.

Sol. (i) True,

0 is a rational number, since we can write $0 = \frac{0}{1}$

(ii) False,

$\frac{1}{2}$ is a rational number but not an integer.

Equivalent Rational Numbers

Two rational numbers are said to be equivalent, if their standard form is equal.

e.g. $\frac{1}{2} = \frac{2}{4} = \frac{10}{20} = \frac{25}{50} = \frac{49}{98}$

To represent a rational number $\frac{p}{q}$ on number line, first convert it into standard or simplest form i.e. make p and q co-prime by dividing them with their HCF and then represent the resulting rational number on number line.

In above example, we will choose 1/2 to represent all of them.

Method to Determine Rational Numbers between Two Numbers

There are infinitely many rational numbers between any two given rational numbers.

For determining one or more than one rational numbers between two given numbers, we use the following methods.

When One Rational Number is to be Determined

Let x and y be two rational numbers.

Then, $\frac{x+y}{2}$ is a rational number lying between x and y.

Example 2. **Find a rational number lying between 3 and 4.**

Sol. We know that if x and y are two rational numbers.

Then, $\frac{x+y}{2}$ is a rational number between x and y.

So, a rational number between 3 and 4 $= \frac{3+4}{2} = \frac{7}{2}$

When More than One Rational Numbers are to be Determined

Let x and y be two rational numbers, such that $y > x$ and we want to find n rational numbers between x and y. Then, n rational numbers lying between x and y are

$(x+d), (x+2d), (x+3d), \ldots, (x+nd)$,

where $d = \frac{y-x}{n+1}$.

Example 3. **Find four rational numbers between − 5 and − 6.**

Sol. Here, $-5 > -6$, so let $x = -6$, $y = -5$ and $n = 4$

Now, $d = \frac{y-x}{n+1} = \frac{-5-(-6)}{4+1} = \frac{-5+6}{5} = \frac{1}{5}$

So, four rational numbers between − 5 and − 6 are $(x+d)$, $(x+2d)$, $(x+3d)$ and $(x+4d)$,

i.e. $\left(-6+\frac{1}{5}\right), \left(-6+\frac{2}{5}\right), \left(-6+\frac{3}{5}\right)$ and $\left(-6+\frac{4}{5}\right)$

$= \left(\frac{-30+1}{5}\right), \left(\frac{-30+2}{5}\right), \left(\frac{-30+3}{5}\right)$ and $\left(\frac{-30+4}{5}\right)$

$= -\frac{29}{5}, -\frac{28}{5}, -\frac{27}{5}$ and $-\frac{26}{5}$

Hence, the above numbers are the required rational numbers lie between −5 and −6.

Alternative solution

To find all four rational numbers between − 5 and − 6 in one step.

We write − 5 and − 6 as rational numbers with denominator 4 + 1 = 5 (since, we have to find 4 rational numbers)

−5 and −6 can be written as

$-5 \times \frac{5}{5}$ and $-6 \times \frac{5}{5}$

$\frac{-25}{5}$ and $\frac{-30}{5}$

Therefore, $\frac{-26}{5}, \frac{-27}{5}, \frac{-28}{5}, \frac{-29}{5}$ are the four rational number between −5 and −6.

Example 4. **Find four rational numbers lying between $\frac{3}{5}$ and $\frac{2}{3}$.**

Sol. Here, $\frac{2}{3} > \frac{3}{5}$, so let $x = \frac{3}{5}$, $y = \frac{2}{3}$ and $n = 4$

Since, $d = \frac{y-x}{n+1}$

$\therefore \quad d = \frac{\frac{2}{3}-\frac{3}{5}}{4+1} = \frac{\frac{10-9}{15}}{5} = \frac{1}{15 \times 5} = \frac{1}{75}$

Now, $x + d = \frac{3}{5} + \frac{1}{75} = \frac{45+1}{75} = \frac{46}{75}$

$x + 2d = \frac{3}{5} + \frac{2}{75} = \frac{45+2}{75} = \frac{47}{75}$

$x + 3d = \frac{3}{5} + \frac{3}{75} = \frac{45+3}{75} = \frac{48}{75} = \frac{16}{25}$

and $x + 4d = \frac{3}{5} + \frac{4}{75} = \frac{45+4}{75} = \frac{49}{75}$

Hence, the required four rational numbers lying between $\frac{3}{5}$ and $\frac{2}{3}$ are $\frac{46}{75}, \frac{47}{75}, \frac{16}{25}$ and $\frac{49}{75}$.

Alternative solution

To find four rational numbers between $\frac{3}{5}$ and $\frac{2}{3}$ in one step.

First change the denominators of $\frac{3}{5}$ and $\frac{2}{3}$ to 15

i.e. LCM of 5 and 3.

We have, $\dfrac{3\times3}{5\times3}$ and $\dfrac{2\times5}{3\times5}$ i.e. $\dfrac{9}{15}$ and $\dfrac{10}{15}$

Now, to find four rationals between $\dfrac{9}{15}$ and $\dfrac{10}{15}$.

We multiply both the numerators and denominator by $4+1=5$

$$\frac{9\times5}{15\times5} \text{ and } \frac{10\times5}{15\times5} \text{ i.e. } \frac{45}{75} \text{ and } \frac{50}{75}$$

Therefore, $\dfrac{46}{75}, \dfrac{47}{75}, \dfrac{48}{75}, \dfrac{49}{75}$ are four rationals between $\dfrac{3}{5}$ and $\dfrac{2}{3}$.

Example 5. **Find nine rational numbers between 0 and 0.1.**

Sol. Here, $0.1 > 0$, so let $x = 0, y = 0.1$ and $n = 9$

Now, $d = \dfrac{y-x}{n+1} = \dfrac{0.1-0}{9+1} = \dfrac{0.1}{10} = 0.01$

So, the nine rational numbers between 0 and 0.1 are

$$(x+d), (x+2d), (x+3d), (x+4d), (x+5d),$$
$$(x+6d), (x+7d), (x+8d) \text{ and } (x+9d)$$

i.e. $(0+0.01), (0+2\times0.01), (0+3\times0.01),$
$(0+4\times0.01), (0+5\times0.01), (0+6\times0.01),$
$(0+7\times0.01), (0+8\times0.01)$ and $(0+9\times0.01)$

$= 0.01, 0.02, 0.03, 0.04, 0.05, 0.06, 0.07, 0.08$ and 0.09

$= \dfrac{1}{100}, \dfrac{2}{100}, \dfrac{3}{100}, \dfrac{4}{100}, \dfrac{5}{100}, \dfrac{6}{100}, \dfrac{7}{100}, \dfrac{8}{100}$ and $\dfrac{9}{100}$

$= \dfrac{1}{100}, \dfrac{1}{50}, \dfrac{3}{100}, \dfrac{1}{25}, \dfrac{1}{20}, \dfrac{3}{50}, \dfrac{7}{100}, \dfrac{2}{25}$ and $\dfrac{9}{100}$

Irrational Numbers

The numbers, which cannot be expressed in the form p/q, where p, q both are integers and $q \neq 0$, are called irrational numbers.

e.g. $\sqrt{2}, \sqrt{3}, \pi, 0.10110111011110\ldots$ etc.

Note It

- When we use the symbol '$\sqrt{\ }$', we assume that it is the positive square root of the number. So, $\sqrt{4} = 2$, though both 2 and -2 are square roots of 4.
- There are infinitely many irrational numbers between any two given irrational numbers.

Real Numbers

The collection of all rational and irrational numbers together form a collection of real numbers which is denoted by R.

Every real number can be represented by a unique point on the number line. Also, every point on the number line represents a unique real number.

Locate an Irrational Number on the Number Line

We can explain how to locate some irrational numbers of the form $\sqrt{n}$, where n is a positive integer on the number line with the help of following example.

Example 6. **Locate $\sqrt{3}$ on the number line.**

Sol. Here, $3 = 2+1 = (\sqrt{2})^2 + 1^2$

[sum of square of two natural numbers]

Draw a number line and mark a point O, representing zero on it. Suppose, point A represents one unit distance from O

i.e. $OA = 1$.

Now, draw a right ΔOAB such that $AB = OA = 1$.

By Pythagoras theorem, we get

$$OB^2 = OA^2 + AB^2$$
$$\Rightarrow \quad OB^2 = 1^2 + 1^2$$
$$\Rightarrow \quad OB^2 = 1+1 = 2$$
$$\Rightarrow \quad OB = \sqrt{2}$$

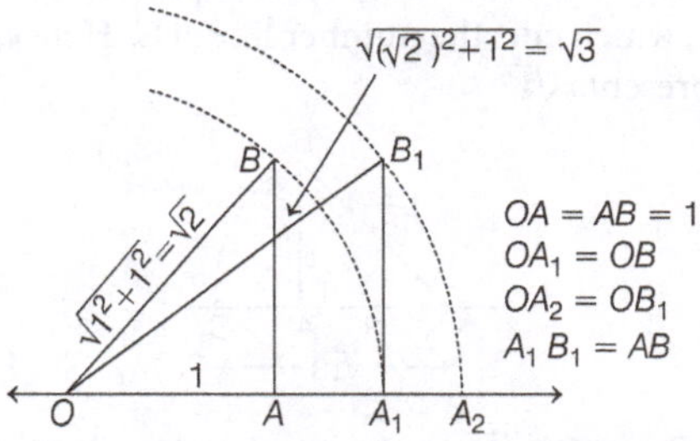

Now, draw a circle with centre O and radius OB. We find that the circle cuts the number line at A_1.

Clearly, $OA_1 = OB =$ Radius of the circle $= \sqrt{2}$

Thus, A_1 represents $\sqrt{2}$ on the number line.

But we have seen that $\sqrt{2}$ is not a rational number.

Now, we draw again right ΔOA_1B_1 such that $A_1B_1 = AB = 1$.

Again, by Pythagoras theorem, we get

$$OB_1^2 = OA_1^2 + A_1B_1^2$$
$$\Rightarrow \quad OB_1^2 = (\sqrt{2})^2 + 1^2$$
$$\Rightarrow \quad OB_1^2 = 3$$
$$\Rightarrow \quad OB_1 = \sqrt{3}$$

Now, again draw a circle with centre O and radius $OB_1 = \sqrt{3}$.

This circle cuts the number line at A_2 as shown in the figure.

$$OA_2 = OB_1 = \sqrt{3}$$

Hence, OA_2 represents $\sqrt{3}$ on the number line.

Example 7. **Locate $\sqrt{13}$ and $1+\sqrt{13}$ on the number line.**

Sol. (i) Here, $13 = 9 + 4 = 3^2 + 2^2$

[sum of square of two natural numbers]

So, we take $a = 3$ and $b = 2$

Draw $OA = 3$ units on number line and then draw $AB = 2$ units, such that $AB \perp OA$.

Join OB.

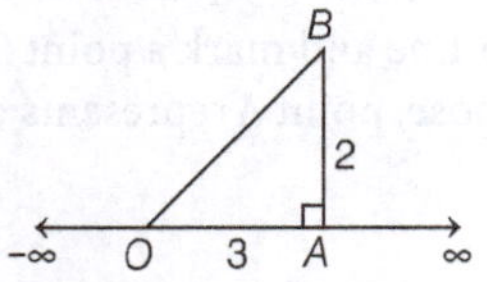

By Pythagoras theorem in ΔOAB,

$$OB = \sqrt{OA^2 + AB^2}$$

$$= \sqrt{3^2 + 2^2}$$

$$= \sqrt{9+4} = \sqrt{13}$$

Taking O as centre and radius equal to OB, draw an arc, which cuts the number line at C. Hence, OC represents $\sqrt{13}$.

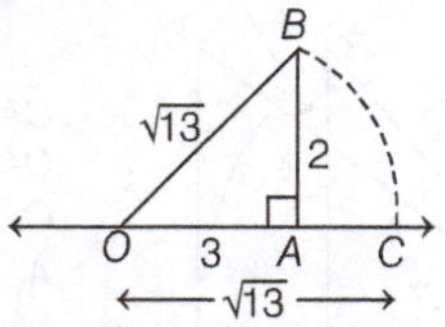

(ii) To locate $1+\sqrt{13}$ on the number line, firstly we mark a 1 unit distance from origin. On the number line, say A and further apply the same procedure as use in part (i).

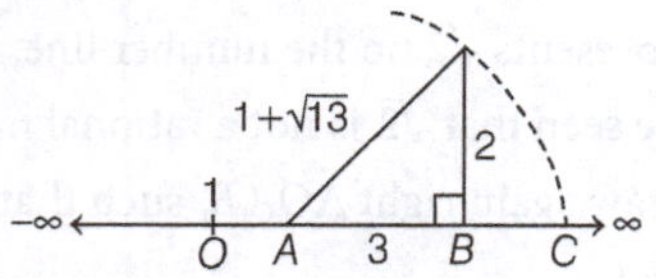

Try These 1.1

1. **State whether the following statements are true or false. Give reasons for your answers.**
   (i) Every whole number is a natural number.
   (ii) Zero is neither a negative nor a positive integer.
   (iii) There are finitely many rational numbers between any two given rational numbers.
   (iv) Every real number is either irrational or rational.
   (v) $\sqrt{7}$ is an irrational number but not a real number.
   (vi) 4 is real but not irrational.

2. **Find a rational number lying between the following numbers**
   (i) 8 and 9 (ii) $\frac{1}{9}$ and $\frac{2}{9}$
   (iii) –3 and –4 (iv) 0.75 and 1.2

3. **Find the following rational numbers between the numbers.**
   (i) Four rational numbers lying between 4 and 5.
   (ii) Five rational numbers lying between 2/5 and 3/4.
   (iii) Five rational numbers lying between 1 and 2.
   (iv) Eight rational numbers lying between 0 and 0.5.
   (v) Three rational numbers lying between $-\frac{2}{5}$ and 2.
   (vi) Three rational numbers lying between – 2 and – 3.

4. **Represent the following numbers on the number line.**
   (i) $\sqrt{26}$ (ii) $\sqrt{10}$ (iii) $\sqrt{2}$ (iv) $1+\sqrt{17}$
   (v) $\sqrt{6}$ (vi) $\sqrt{7}$ (vii) $\sqrt{12}$

5. **Are the square roots of all positive integers irrational? Why or why not ?**

Hints & Answers

1. (i) False, because 0 is not a natural number.
   (ii) True, because 0 is non-negative and non-positive integer.
   (iii) False, because there are infinitely many rational numbers between two rational numbers.
   (iv) True
   (v) False, because irrational numbers are a part of real numbers.
   (vi) True as 4 is a real and a rational number but not irrational number.

2. **Hint** Solve as Example 2.
   Ans. (i) $\frac{17}{2}$ (ii) $\frac{1}{6}$ (iii) $-\frac{7}{2}$ (iv) $\frac{39}{40}$

3. (i) **Hint** Solve as Example 3. **Ans.** $\frac{21}{5}, \frac{22}{5}, \frac{23}{5}, \frac{24}{5}$
   (ii) **Hint** Solve as Example 4. **Ans.** $\frac{11}{24}, \frac{31}{60}, \frac{23}{40}, \frac{19}{30}, \frac{83}{120}$
   (iii) **Hint** Solve as Example 3. **Ans.** $\frac{7}{6}, \frac{4}{3}, \frac{3}{2}, \frac{5}{3}, \frac{11}{6}$
   (iv) **Hint** Solve as Example 5. **Ans.** $\frac{1}{18}, \frac{1}{9}, \frac{1}{6}, \frac{2}{9}, \frac{5}{18}, \frac{1}{3}, \frac{7}{18}, \frac{4}{9}$
   (v) **Hint** Solve as Example 4. **Ans.** $\frac{1}{5}, \frac{4}{5}, \frac{7}{5}$
   (vi) **Hint** Solve as Example 3. **Ans.** $-\frac{11}{4}, -\frac{5}{2}, -\frac{9}{4}$

4. **Hint** Solve as Example 6 and Example 7.

5. **Hint** No, the square root of all positive integer is not always an irrational.
   e.g. $\sqrt{4} = 2$, which is a rational number.

TOPIC 02 Decimal Expansions of Real Numbers

A real number can be expressed as a decimal. The decimal expansion of real numbers can be either **terminating** or **non-terminating repeating** or **non-terminating non-repeating.**

With the decimal expansion of real numbers, we can check whether it is rational or irrational.

Decimal Expansions of Rational Numbers

For rational numbers in the form of p/q, where $q \neq 0$, on dividing p by q, two main cases occur either the remainder becomes zero after a certain stage or never becomes zero and we get a repeating string of remainders.

Case I The remainder becomes zero

On dividing p by q, if remainder becomes zero after some steps, then decimal expansion terminates or ends after a finite number of steps. Such decimal expansion is called terminating decimal expansion.

$\frac{639}{250}$

$$\begin{array}{r|l} 250 & 639 \;(2.556 \\ & \underline{500} \\ & 1390 \\ & \underline{1250} \\ & 1400 \\ & \underline{1250} \\ & 1500 \\ & \underline{1500} \\ & 0 \end{array}$$

$\therefore \frac{639}{250} = 2.556$

On dividing 639 by 250, we get the exact value 2.556 i.e. remainder is zero. So, 639/250 has the **terminating decimal** expansion.

Case II The remainder never becomes zero

On dividing p by q, if remainder never becomes zero and set of digits repeats periodically (or in same interval), then decimal expansion is called **non-terminating repeating decimal** expansion. It is also known as **non-terminating recurring decimal** expansion.

The block of repeated digits is denoted by the bar (–) over it.

e.g. (i) $\frac{2}{3}$

$$\begin{array}{r|l} 3 & 2.0 \;(0.66 \\ & \underline{18} \\ & 20 \\ & \underline{18} \\ & 2 \end{array}$$

$\therefore \quad \frac{2}{3} = 0.666\ldots$ or $\frac{2}{3} = 0.\bar{6}$

On dividing 2 by 3, we get the block of repeated number 6 again and again i.e. remainder never becomes zero. So, 2/3 has a non-terminating repeating decimal expansion.

(ii) $\frac{1}{7}$

$$\begin{array}{r|l} 7 & 10 \;(0.142857142857 \\ & \underline{7} \\ & 30 \\ & \underline{28} \\ & 20 \\ & \underline{14} \\ & 60 \\ & \underline{56} \\ & 40 \\ & \underline{35} \\ & 50 \\ & \underline{49} \\ & 10 \\ & \underline{7} \\ & 30 \\ & \underline{28} \\ & 20 \\ & \underline{14} \\ & 60 \\ & \underline{56} \\ & 40 \\ & \underline{35} \\ & 50 \\ & \underline{49} \\ & 1 \end{array}$$

$\therefore \quad \frac{1}{7} = 0.1428571428571\ldots$

or $\frac{1}{7} = 0.\overline{142857}$

On dividing 1 by 7, we get the block of repeated numbers 142857 again and again i.e. remainder never becomes zero.

So, 1/7 has a non-terminating repeating decimal expansion.

The decimal expansion of a rational number is either terminating or non-terminating recurring. In other words, a number whose decimal expansion is terminating or non-terminating recurring, is a rational number.

Example 1. Write the following in decimal form and say, what kind of decimal expansion each has? NCERT Exemplar

(i) $\frac{39}{100}$ (ii) $5\frac{1}{8}$ (iii) $\frac{4}{13}$ (iv) $\frac{2}{15}$ (v) $\frac{329}{500}$

Sol. (i) $\frac{39}{100} = 0.39$, so it has terminating decimal expansion.

(ii) $5\frac{1}{8} = \frac{41}{8} = 5.125$, so it has terminating decimal expansion.

(iii) $\frac{4}{13} = 0.\overline{307692}$, so it has non-terminating repeating decimal expansion.

(iv) $\frac{2}{15} = 0.1\overline{3}$, so it has non-terminating repeating decimal expansion.

(v) $\frac{329}{500} = 0.658$, so it has terminating decimal expansion.

Example 2. What can the maximum number of digits be in the repeating block of digits in the expansion of $\frac{2}{13}$? Perform the division to check your answer.

Sol. To find the repeating block of digits in the expansion $\frac{2}{13}$.

Divide 2 by 13

$$\begin{array}{r|l} 13 & 20 \;(0.1538461 \\ & \underline{13} \\ & 70 \\ & \underline{65} \\ & 50 \\ & \underline{39} \\ & 110 \\ & \underline{104} \\ & 60 \\ & \underline{52} \\ & 80 \\ & \underline{78} \\ & 20 \\ & \underline{13} \\ & 7 \end{array}$$

$\therefore \frac{2}{13} = 0.\overline{153846}$

Therefore, maximum number of digits in the repeating block of digits of $\frac{2}{13}$ are 6.

Method to Convert Non-terminating Recurring Decimal Expansion in the Form of *p*/*q*

Suppose the number in the form of $x = a \cdot b\bar{c}$, we have to transform the given number in the form of $\frac{p}{q}$. The following steps are given below.

Step I Firstly, transform the non-repeated digit(s) between decimal point and recurring number to the left side of decimal by multiplying both sides by 10^r i.e. where r is the number of digits between decimal point and recurring number i.e. $y = a \cdot b\bar{c}$, here we see that one digit 'b' exist between decimal point and recurring number. So, we multiply both sides by 10^1, we get

$$10y = ab \cdot \bar{c} \quad \text{...(i)}$$

Step II Count the number of digit in recurring number (say R) and then multiply Eq. (i) by that power of 10 (i.e. 10^R) and the equation becomes

$$10(10y) = abc \cdot \bar{c} \quad \text{... (ii)}$$

Step III Lastly, subtract Eq. (i) from Eq. (ii), we get the required result as

$$100y - 10y = abc \cdot \bar{c} - ab \cdot \bar{c}$$

$$\Rightarrow \quad y = \frac{abc \cdot \bar{c} - ab \cdot \bar{c}}{90} = \frac{abc - ab}{90}$$

This method can be easily understand with the help of following example.

Example 3. Show that $0.\bar{7}$ can be expressed in the form $\frac{p}{q}$, where p and q are integers such that $q \neq 0$.

Sol. Assume the given decimal expansion as x.

Let $x = 0.\bar{7}$

$$\Rightarrow \quad x = 0.777... \quad \text{...(i)}$$

Here, only 1 digit is repeating. On multiplying both sides of Eq. (i) by 10, we get

$$10x = 7.77... \quad \text{...(ii)}$$

On subtracting Eq. (i) from Eq. (ii), we get

$$10x - x = 7.777... - 0.777...$$

$$\Rightarrow \quad 9x = 7$$

$$\Rightarrow \quad x = \frac{7}{9}$$

Hence, $0.\bar{7} = \frac{7}{9}$

Example 4. **Express $0.2\overline{25}$ in the $\frac{p}{q}$ form, where p and q are integers and $q \neq 0$.**

Sol. Let $x = 0.22525...$ ...(i)

Here, we see that one digit (i.e. 2) exist between decimal point and recurring number.

So, we multiply both sides of Eq. (i) by 10, we get

$$10x = 2.2525... \quad ...(ii)$$

Here, we see that two digits are repeated in recurring number, so we multiply Eq. (ii) by 100, we get

$$1000x = 225.2525... \quad ...(iii)$$

On subtracting Eq. (ii) from Eq. (iii), we get

$$990x = 223 \Rightarrow x = \frac{223}{990}$$

Hence, $0.2\overline{25} = \frac{223}{990}$

Example 5. **Express $0.00323232...$ in the form of $\frac{p}{q}$.**

Sol. Let $x = 0.00323232... = 0.00\overline{32}$ ...(i)

On multiplying Eq. (i) by 100, we get

$$100x = 0.323232... \quad ...(ii)$$

Again, on multiplying Eq. (ii) by 100, we get

$$10000x = 32.3232... \quad ...(iii)$$

On subtracting Eq. (ii) from Eq. (iii), we get

$$10000x - 100x = 32.3232 .... - 0.3232.......$$

$$\Rightarrow \quad 9900x = 32 \Rightarrow x = \frac{32}{9900} = \frac{8}{2475}$$

Hence, $0.003232....... = \frac{8}{2475}$

Decimal Expansions of Irrational Numbers

The decimal expansion of an irrational number is non-terminating non-recurring. In other words, **a number whose decimal expansion is non-terminating non-recurring is irrational.**

e.g. Let $\sqrt{2}$ and π be two irrational numbers, then their decimal expansions are

$$\sqrt{2} = 1.41421356237309504880168872420 96...$$

and $\pi = 3.14159265358979323846264338327950...$

We often take value of π as $\frac{22}{7}$, which is a rational number but $\pi \neq \frac{22}{7}$.

Note it There are infinitely many irrational numbers exist between two distinct real numbers.

Example 6. **The decimal expansion of the number $\sqrt{3}$ is repeating. Is it true?**

Sol. No, because $\sqrt{3}$ is an irrational number and every irrational number is always non-terminating non-recurring.

Example 7. **Find an irrational number between $\frac{1}{7}$ and $\frac{1}{3}$.**

Sol. To find irrational number, firstly we will divide 1 by 7 and 1 by 3.

$$\therefore \quad \frac{1}{7} = 0.142857... = 0.\overline{142857}$$

[see Case II of decimal expansion of rational numbers]

Now,

$$\begin{array}{r|l} 3 & 10 \; (0.33... \\ & \underline{9} \\ & 10 \\ & \underline{9} \\ & 1 \end{array}$$

Thus, $\frac{1}{3} = 0.333... = 0.\overline{3}$

That means the required irrational numbers will lie between $0.\overline{142857}$ and $0.\overline{3}$. Also, the irrational numbers have non-terminating non-repeating decimals. Hence, the required irrational number between 1/7 and 1/3 is 0.2101001000... .

Note it Students can write other number also as per their choice. There is no specification in it.

Example 8. **Find two irrational numbers between $\frac{1}{7}$ and $\frac{2}{7}$, when it is given that $\frac{1}{7} = 0.142857142857...$**

Sol. We have,

$$\frac{1}{7} = 0.\overline{142857}$$

$$\Rightarrow \quad \frac{2}{7} = 0.\overline{285714}$$

Above rational numbers have non-terminating recurring decimal.

So, two irrational numbers between $\frac{1}{7}$ and $\frac{2}{7}$ may be

0.1430143001430001... and 0.254025400254...

Note it In this question, we can write infinite number of such irrational numbers.

Try These 1.2

1. The decimal expansion of the number $\sqrt{5}$ is repeating. Is it true?
2. Write the following in decimal form and also find the nature of the decimal expansion.
   (i) $\frac{56}{1000}$ (ii) $\frac{2}{11}$ (iii) $3\frac{6}{7}$ (iv) $\frac{4}{13}$
   (v) $\frac{13}{25}$
3. Find the number of repeating digits in the decimal expansion of $\frac{3}{7}$.
4. You know that $\frac{1}{11} = 0.\overline{09}$. Can you predict, what the decimal expansion of $\frac{3}{11}, \frac{4}{11}, \frac{5}{11}, \frac{6}{11}$ are without actually doing the long division method? If so, how?
5. Express the following numbers in the form of $\frac{p}{q}, q \neq 0$.
   (i) $0.\overline{4}$ (ii) $0.\overline{8}$ (iii) $0.\overline{68}$ (iv) $1.3\overline{2}$
   (v) $0.\overline{12}$ (vi) $18.\overline{48}$ (vii) $0.1\overline{7}$ (viii) $0.12\overline{3}$
6. Find the following.
   (i) Two irrational numbers between $\frac{2}{3}$ and $\frac{8}{9}$.
   (ii) An irrational number between $\frac{1}{9}$ and $\frac{1}{7}$.
   (iii) Three irrational numbers between $\sqrt{3}$ and $\sqrt{5}$.
7. Classify the following numbers as rational or irrational with justification.
   (i) 0.5918 (ii) 1.010010001... (iii) $\sqrt{289}$ (iv) $\sqrt{19}$
8. Write two numbers whose decimal expansion are non-terminating, non-recurring.

Hints & Answers

1. No, because $\sqrt{5}$ is an irrational number and every irrational number is always non-terminating non-recurring.
2. **Hint** Solve as Example 1.
   Ans. (i) 0.056, terminating
   (ii) $0.\overline{18}$, non-terminating repeating decimal expansion.
   (iii) $3.\overline{857142}$, non-terminating repeating decimal expansion.
   (iv) $0.\overline{307692}$, non-terminating repeating decimal expansion.
   (v) 0.52, terminating
3. $\frac{3}{7} = 0.\overline{428571}$. So, number of repeating digits is 6.
4. **Hint** We have, $\frac{1}{11} = 0.\overline{09}$
   $\frac{3}{11} = 3 \times \frac{1}{11} = 3 \times 0.\overline{09} = 0.\overline{27}$; $\frac{4}{11} = 4 \times \frac{1}{11} = 4 \times 0.\overline{09} = 0.\overline{36}$
   $\frac{5}{11} = 5 \times \frac{1}{11} = 5 \times 0.\overline{09} = 0.\overline{45}$; $\frac{6}{11} = 6 \times \frac{1}{11} = 6 \times 0.\overline{09} = 0.\overline{54}$
5. **Hint** Solve as Example 3 and Example 4.
   Ans. (i) $\frac{4}{9}$ (ii) $\frac{8}{9}$ (iii) $\frac{68}{99}$ (iv) $\frac{119}{90}$
   (v) $\frac{4}{33}$ (vi) $\frac{610}{33}$ (vii) $\frac{8}{45}$ (viii) $\frac{111}{900}$
6. **Hint** Solve as Example 7 and Example 8.
   Ans. (i) 0.6868868886... and 0.7070070007...
   (ii) 0.1303003000...
   (iii) 1.8010010001..., 1.9010010001... and 2.010010001...
7. (i) **Hint** Given, decimal number is terminating, so it is a rational.
   (ii) **Hint** Given, number is non-terminating non-recurring, so it is an irrational.
   (iii) **Hint** $\sqrt{289} = 17$, rational.
   (iv) **Hint** 4.35889894..., irrational.
8. **Ans.** 7.303003000 ..., 5.871087100871000 ...

TOPIC 03 Representation of Rational Number on the Number Line

Here, we will explain, how to represent rational numbers on number line. A rational number will either be an integer or a decimal, so the representation of both integer and decimal will be studied separately.

For Integers

Draw a line *XY*, which extends endlessly in both the directions, as indicated by arrowheads.

Take any point *O* on this line. Let this point represents the integer 0 (zero). Now, taking a fixed length, called unit length, set off equal distance to the right as well as to the left of *O*.

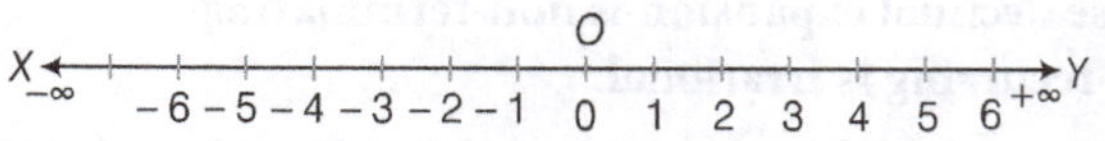

On the right hand side of *O*, the points at distance of 1 unit, 2 units, 3 units, 4 units etc. Hence, from *O* denote respectively the integers 1, 2, 3, 4, ... etc.

Similarly, on the left hand side of *O*, the points at a distance of 1 unit, 2 units, 3 units, 4 units etc. Hence, from *O* denote respectively the integers −1, − 2, −3, − 4, ... etc.

Since, the line *XY* can be extended endlessly on both sides of *O*, it follows that we can represent each and every integer by a point on this line. Thus, each and every integer can be represented by a point on this line.

For Decimals

We know that, there are many real numbers (decimal numbers) between two integers. So, decimal numbers can also be represented on a number line (between two integers). The representation of decimal number on number line is a complex process.

The process of visualisation of representation of decimal number on number line through a magnifying glass is known as **process of successive magnification**.

This process to visualise the position (or representation of a real number) with a non-terminating recurring decimal expansion on the number line can be understand with the help of an example which is given below:

Example 1. **Visualise the representation of $6.3\overline{7}$ on the number line upto 4 decimal places.**

Sol.

Step I Here, the number $6.3\overline{7}$ lies between 6 and 7. First, draw the number line and look the portion between 6 and 7 by a magnifying glass.

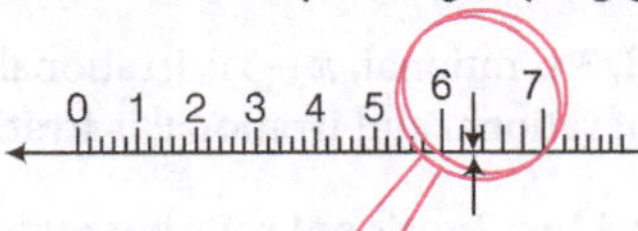

Step II Divide the above part into 10 equal parts and mark first point to the right of 6 as 6.1, the second 6.2 and so on.

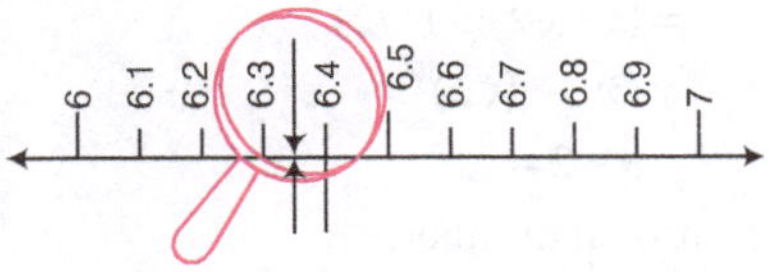

Step III Now, 6.37 lies between 6.3 and 6.4. So, focus on this portion and again divide it into 10 equal parts and mark first point to the right of 6.3 as 6.31, the second 6.32 and so on.

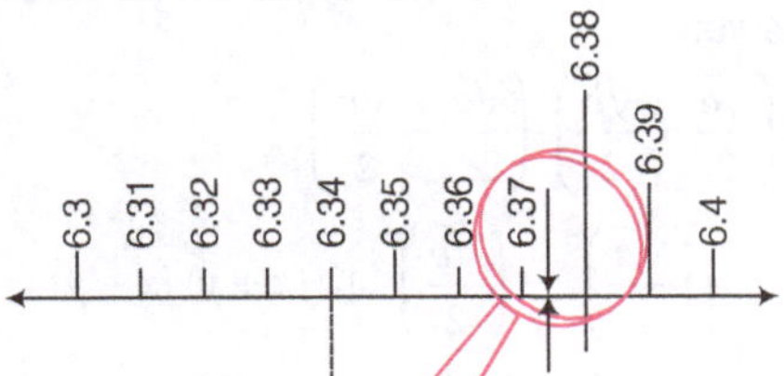

Step IV Now, 6.377 lies between 6.37 and 6.38. So, focus on this portion and again divide it into 10 equal parts and mark first point to the right of 6.37 as 6.371, the second 6.372 and so on.

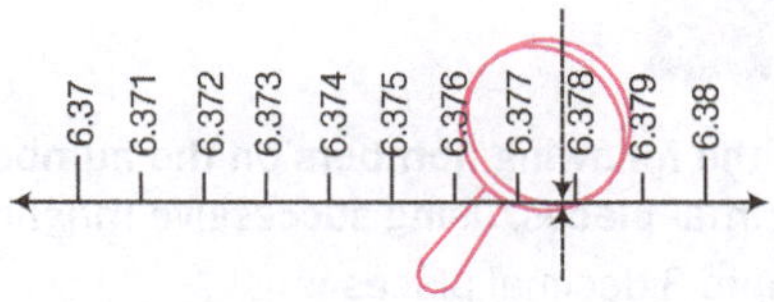

Step V To visualise $6.3\overline{7}$ more accurately, again divide the portion between 6.377 and 6.378 into 10 equal parts and visualise the representation of $6.3\overline{7}$ as in figure given below :

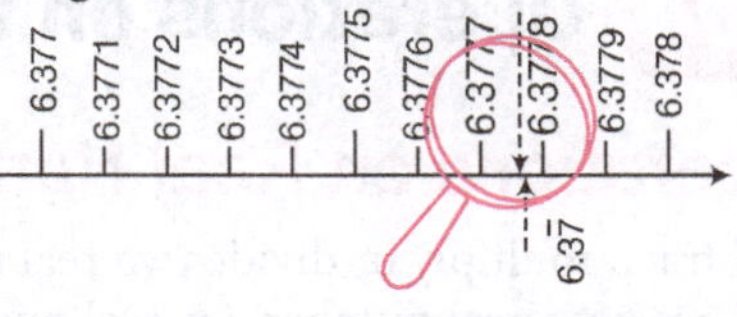

We can proceed endlessly in this manner. Thus, 6.3777 is the 7th mark in these subdivisions.

Example 2. **Visualise 4.575 on the number line, using successive magnification.**

Sol. We know that, 4.575 lies between 4 and 5. So, let us divide the part of the number line between 4 and 5 into 10 equal parts and look at the portion between 4.5 and 4.6 through a magnifying glass.

Now, 4.575 lies between 4.5 and 4.6 [Fig. (i)]. Now, we imagine to divide this again into 10 equal parts. The first mark will represent 4.51, the next 4.52 and so on. To see this clearly, we magnify this as shown [Fig. (ii)].

Again, 4.575 lies between 4.57 and 4.58 [Fig. (ii)].

So, let us focus on this portion of the number line and imagine to divide it again into 10 equal parts [Fig. (iii)].

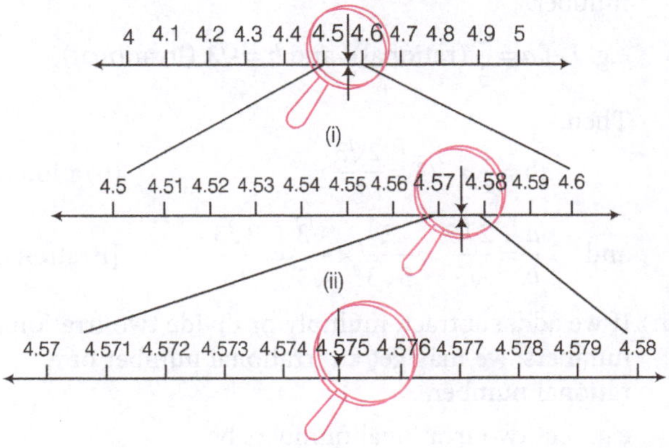

We call this process, visualisation of representation of numbers on the number line through a magnifying glass as we do successive magnification in it.

Thus, we can visualise that 4.571 is the first mark and 4.575 is the fifth mark in these subdivisions.

Try These 1.3

1. **Visualise the following numbers on the number line upto given decimal places, using successive magnification.**
   (i) $6.\overline{15}$ upto 3 decimal places
   (ii) $2.\overline{35}$ up to 4 decimal places
   (iii) $3.\overline{98}$ upto 4 decimal places
   (iv) $3.\overline{12}$ upto 4 decimal places
   (v) $4.\overline{18}$ upto 3 decimal places
   (vi) 5.38 upto 3 decimal places
2. **Visualise the following numbers on the number line, using successive magnification.**
   (i) 4.65 (ii) 3.256 (iii) 5.235
   (iv) 13.625 (v) 10.28

TOPIC 04 Operations on Real Numbers

Basic Operations on Real Numbers

If we add, subtract, multiply or divide two real numbers (except zero), we get a real number, i.e. real numbers are closed with respect to addition, subtraction, multiplication or division. Further more, we get the following facts about real numbers which are also true.

(i) The sum or difference of a rational number and an irrational number is an irrational number.

e.g. Let $a=\frac{2}{3}$ (rational) and $b=\sqrt{3}$ (irrational),

Then,

$$a+b=\frac{2}{3}+\sqrt{3}=\frac{2+3\sqrt{3}}{3} \quad \text{[irrational]}$$

and $a-b=\frac{2}{3}-\sqrt{3}=\frac{2-3\sqrt{3}}{3}$ [irrational]

(ii) The multiplication or division of a non-zero rational number with an irrational number is an irrational number.

e.g. Let $a=\frac{2}{5}$ (rational) and $b=\sqrt{3}$ (irrational),

Then,

$$ab=\frac{2}{5}\times\sqrt{3}=\frac{2\sqrt{3}}{5} \quad \text{[irrational]}$$

and $\frac{a}{b}=\frac{2/5}{\sqrt{3}}=\frac{2}{5\sqrt{3}}\times\frac{\sqrt{3}}{\sqrt{3}}=\frac{2\sqrt{3}}{15}$ [irrational]

(iii) If we add, subtract, multiply or divide two irrational numbers, we may get an irrational number or a rational number.

e.g. Let two irrational numbers be

$$a=1+\sqrt{2} \text{ and } b=1-\sqrt{2}, \text{ then}$$

$$a+b=(1+\sqrt{2})+(1-\sqrt{2})=2 \quad \text{[rational]}$$

or let two irrational numbers be

$$a=\sqrt{2}+1 \text{ and } b=\sqrt{2}-1, \text{ then}$$

$$a+b=\sqrt{2}+1+\sqrt{2}-1=2\sqrt{2} \quad \text{[irrational]}$$

Example 1. **Check whether $8\sqrt{3}$, $\frac{18}{\sqrt{3}}$, $\sqrt{3}+22$, $\pi-3$ are irrational numbers or not.**

Sol. We know that 8 is rational and $\sqrt{3}$ is irrational, so $8\sqrt{3}$ is irratonal as multiplication of non-zero rational by irrational is irrational.

Now, again 18 is rational, $\sqrt{3}$ is irrational, so $\frac{18}{\sqrt{3}}$ is irrational as division of non-zero rational and irrational is irrational.

For $\sqrt{3}+22$, 22 is rational, $\sqrt{3}$ is irrational, so $22+\sqrt{3}$ is also irrational as addition of rational and irrational is irrational.

π is irrational, 3 is rational, $\pi-3$ is irrational as subtraction of rational and irrational is irrational.

Example 2. **Find two irrational numbers whose product is a rational number.**

Sol. Let two irrational numbers be $3-\sqrt{2}$ and $3+\sqrt{2}$.
Now, product of two irrational numbers

$$=(3-\sqrt{2})(3+\sqrt{2})$$
$$=(3)^2-(\sqrt{2})^2$$
$$=9-2=7,$$

which is a rational number.

Example 3. **If a and b are natural numbers, then $\left(\frac{\sqrt{a}}{2}+\frac{\sqrt{b}}{2}\right)\left(\frac{\sqrt{a}}{2}-\frac{\sqrt{b}}{2}\right)$ is rational or irrational. Solve to find the answer.**

Sol. Given, $\left(\frac{\sqrt{a}}{2}+\frac{\sqrt{b}}{2}\right)\cdot\left(\frac{\sqrt{a}}{2}-\frac{\sqrt{b}}{2}\right)$

$$=\left(\frac{\sqrt{a}}{2}\right)^2-\left(\frac{\sqrt{b}}{2}\right)^2 \quad [\because (x+y)(x-y)=x^2-y^2]$$

$$=\frac{a}{4}-\frac{b}{4}=\frac{a-b}{4}$$

The number $\frac{a-b}{4}$ is rational number because $a-b$ is an integer and 4 is an integer such that $4\neq 0$.

Therefore, $\left(\frac{\sqrt{a}}{2}+\frac{\sqrt{b}}{2}\right)\left(\frac{\sqrt{a}}{2}-\frac{\sqrt{b}}{2}\right)$ is rational.

Example 4. **Add** $\left(\frac{2}{3}\sqrt{7}-\frac{1}{2}\sqrt{2}+6\sqrt{11}\right)$ **and** $\left(\frac{1}{3}\sqrt{7}+\frac{3}{2}\sqrt{2}-\sqrt{11}\right)$.

Sol. $\frac{2}{3}\sqrt{7}-\frac{1}{2}\sqrt{2}+6\sqrt{11}+\frac{1}{3}\sqrt{7}+\frac{3}{2}\sqrt{2}-\sqrt{11}$

$$=\left(\frac{2}{3}+\frac{1}{3}\right)\sqrt{7}+\left(\frac{-1}{2}+\frac{3}{2}\right)\sqrt{2}+(6-1)\sqrt{11}$$

$$=\left(\frac{3}{3}\right)\sqrt{7}+\left(\frac{2}{2}\right)\sqrt{2}+5\sqrt{11}=\sqrt{7}+\sqrt{2}+5\sqrt{11}$$

Example 5. **Multiply $2\sqrt{3}$ by $3\sqrt{3}$.**

Sol. $2\sqrt{3}\times 3\sqrt{3}=6\times\sqrt{3}\times\sqrt{3}=6\times 3=18$

Example 6. **Divide $4\sqrt{21}$ by $2\sqrt{3}$.**

Sol. $4\sqrt{21}\div 2\sqrt{3}=\dfrac{4\sqrt{21}}{2\sqrt{3}}=\dfrac{4\times\sqrt{7}\times\sqrt{3}}{2\times\sqrt{3}}=2\sqrt{7}$

Representation of $\sqrt{x}$ Geometrically

To find $\sqrt{x}$, where x is positive real number. We follow the below listed steps.

(i) Draw a line segment AB such that $AB = x$ unit.

(ii) Draw $BC = 1$ unit and find the mid-point of AC.

(iii) Mark mid-point of AC as O.

(iv) Draw a semi-circle using O as a centre.

(v) Draw a line perpendicular to AC passing through B and intersecting the semi-circle at D.

Then, $BD=\sqrt{x}$ unit.

[$\because$ using Pythagoras theorem in ΔOBD]

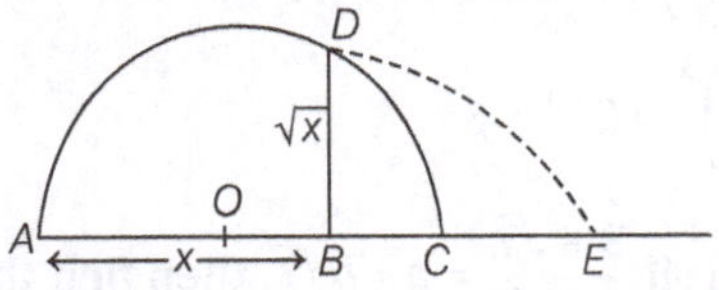

(vi) Draw an arc with B as a centre and BD as radius which intersect the number line at E.

Then, E represents $\sqrt{x}$.

For better understanding let's take an example.

Example 7. **Represent $\sqrt{4.5}$ on number line.**

Sol. (i) Draw a line segment $AB = 4.5$

(ii) Draw $BC = 1$ unit

(iii) The mid-point of AC is O.

(iv) Draw a semi-circle using O as a centre.

(v) Draw a line perpendicular to AC passing through B and intersecting the semi-circle at D.

Here, $BD=\sqrt{4.5}$ unit.

(vi) Draw an arc with centre B and radius BD, which intersect the number line in E. Then, E represent $\sqrt{4.5}$.

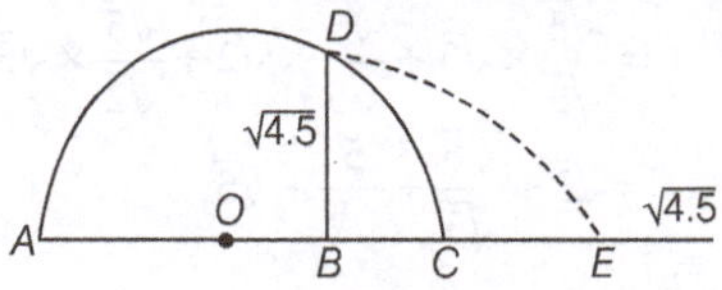

Radical Sign

Let $a\,(>0)$ be a real number and n be a positive integer, such that $a^{1/n}=\sqrt[n]{a}$ is a real number, then n is called **exponent**, a is called **radicand** and '$\sqrt{\ }$' is called **radical sign.**

Here, the expression $\sqrt[n]{a}$ is called surd.

If $n=2$, then $a^{1/2}=\sqrt[2]{a}$ is called **square root of a.**

Let a and b be positive real numbers. Then,

(i) $\sqrt{ab}=\sqrt{a}\cdot\sqrt{b}$ (ii) $\sqrt{\frac{a}{b}}=\frac{\sqrt{a}}{\sqrt{b}}$

(iii) $(\sqrt{a}+\sqrt{b})(\sqrt{a}-\sqrt{b})=a-b$

(iv) $(a+\sqrt{b})(a-\sqrt{b})=a^2-b$

or $(\sqrt{a}+b)(\sqrt{a}-b)=a-b^2$

(v) $(\sqrt{a}\pm\sqrt{b})^2=a\pm 2\sqrt{ab}+b$

(vi) $(\sqrt{a}+\sqrt{b})(\sqrt{c}+\sqrt{d})=\sqrt{ac}+\sqrt{ad}+\sqrt{bc}+\sqrt{bd}$

Example 8. **Simplify each of the following :**

(i) $\sqrt[4]{27}\times\sqrt[4]{3}$ **(ii)** $\dfrac{\sqrt[6]{256}}{\sqrt[6]{4}}$

Sol. (i) We know that $\sqrt[n]{a}\times\sqrt[n]{b}=\sqrt[n]{ab}$

$\therefore$ $\sqrt[4]{27}\times\sqrt[4]{3}=\sqrt[4]{27\times 3}$

$=\sqrt[4]{81}=\sqrt[4]{3^4}=(3^4)^{1/4}=3$

(ii) We know that $\dfrac{\sqrt[n]{a}}{\sqrt[n]{b}}=\sqrt[n]{\dfrac{a}{b}}$

$\therefore$ $\dfrac{\sqrt[6]{256}}{\sqrt[6]{4}}=\sqrt[6]{\dfrac{256}{4}}$

$=\sqrt[6]{64}=\sqrt[6]{2^6}=(2^6)^{1/6}=2$

Example 9. **Solve the following questions :**

(i) Find the product of $(8+3\sqrt{2})$ and $(8-3\sqrt{2})$.

(ii) Find the square of $(8+5\sqrt{3})$.

(iii) Find the product of $\left(\sqrt{\frac{3}{5}}+\sqrt{\frac{5}{2}}\right)$ and $(\sqrt{5}+\sqrt{2})$.

Sol. (i) $(8+3\sqrt{2})(8-3\sqrt{2})$

$=(8)^2-(3\sqrt{2})^2$ [$\because (a+b)(a-b)=a^2-b^2$]

$=64-18=46$

(ii) $(8+5\sqrt{3})^2=(8)^2+2\times 8\times 5\sqrt{3}+(5\sqrt{3})^2$

[$\because (a+b)^2=a^2+2ab+b^2$]

$=64+80\sqrt{3}+75=139+80\sqrt{3}$

(iii) $\left(\sqrt{\frac{3}{5}}+\sqrt{\frac{5}{2}}\right)(\sqrt{5}+\sqrt{2})$

$$=\frac{\sqrt{3}}{\sqrt{5}}\times\sqrt{5}+\frac{\sqrt{3}}{\sqrt{5}}\times\sqrt{2}+\frac{\sqrt{5}}{\sqrt{2}}\times\sqrt{5}+\frac{\sqrt{5}}{\sqrt{2}}\times\sqrt{2}$$

$$=\sqrt{3}+\frac{\sqrt{6}}{\sqrt{5}}+\frac{5}{\sqrt{2}}+\sqrt{5}$$

Rationalising the Denominator

If the denominator of an expression contains a term with a square root (or a number under a radical sign), then the process of converting it into an equivalent expression whose denominator is a rational number, is called rationalising the denominator.

Example 10. **Rationalise the denominator of $\frac{5}{\sqrt{3}-\sqrt{5}}$.**

Sol. Let $y=\frac{5}{\sqrt{3}-\sqrt{5}}$ and its denominator $=\sqrt{3}-\sqrt{5}$

Here, rationalisation of the denominator $(\sqrt{3}-\sqrt{5})$ is $(\sqrt{3}+\sqrt{5})$.

Multiply and divide $\frac{5}{\sqrt{3}-\sqrt{5}}$ by $\frac{\sqrt{3}+\sqrt{5}}{\sqrt{3}+\sqrt{5}}$

Then, $$y=\frac{5}{\sqrt{3}-\sqrt{5}}\times\frac{\sqrt{3}+\sqrt{5}}{\sqrt{3}+\sqrt{5}}=\frac{5(\sqrt{3}+\sqrt{5})}{(\sqrt{3})^2-(\sqrt{5})^2}$$

$[\because (a-b)(a+b)=a^2-b^2]$

$$=\frac{5(\sqrt{3}+\sqrt{5})}{3-5}=-\frac{5}{2}(\sqrt{3}+\sqrt{5})$$

Example 11. **Simplify $\frac{(\sqrt{3}-\sqrt{5})(\sqrt{5}+\sqrt{3})}{7-2\sqrt{5}}$.**

Sol. $$\frac{(\sqrt{3}-\sqrt{5})(\sqrt{3}+\sqrt{5})}{7-2\sqrt{5}}=\frac{(\sqrt{3})^2-(\sqrt{5})^2}{7-2\sqrt{5}}$$

$[\because (a-b)(a+b)=a^2-b^2]$

$$=\frac{3-5}{7-2\sqrt{5}}\times\frac{7+2\sqrt{5}}{7+2\sqrt{5}}$$ [by rationalising]

$$=\frac{-2(7+2\sqrt{5})}{(7)^2-(2\sqrt{5})^2}$$ $[\because (a-b)(a+b)=a^2-b^2]$

$$=\frac{-2(7+2\sqrt{5})}{49-20}=\frac{-2(7+2\sqrt{5})}{29}=\frac{-14-4\sqrt{5}}{29}$$

Example 12. **If $\sqrt{2}=1.4142$, then find the value of $\sqrt{\frac{\sqrt{2}-1}{\sqrt{2}+1}}$.**

NCERT Exemplar

Sol. Given, $\sqrt{2}=1.4142$

Now, $$\sqrt{\frac{\sqrt{2}-1}{\sqrt{2}+1}}=\sqrt{\frac{(\sqrt{2}-1)}{(\sqrt{2}+1)}\times\frac{(\sqrt{2}-1)}{(\sqrt{2}-1)}}$$ [by rationalising]

$$=\sqrt{\frac{(\sqrt{2}-1)^2}{2-1}}=\sqrt{\frac{(\sqrt{2}-1)^2}{1}}$$

$[\because (a+b)(a-b)=a^2-b^2]$

$$=\sqrt{2}-1=1.4142-1$$ $[\because \sqrt{2}=1.4142]$

$$=0.4142$$

Example 13. **Rationalise $\frac{4\sqrt{3}+5\sqrt{2}}{\sqrt{48}+\sqrt{18}}$.**

Sol. We have, $$\frac{4\sqrt{3}+5\sqrt{2}}{\sqrt{48}+\sqrt{18}}=\frac{4\sqrt{3}+5\sqrt{2}}{4\sqrt{3}+3\sqrt{2}}\times\frac{4\sqrt{3}-3\sqrt{2}}{4\sqrt{3}-3\sqrt{2}}$$

[by rationalising]

$$=\frac{(4\sqrt{3}+5\sqrt{2})(4\sqrt{3}-3\sqrt{2})}{(4\sqrt{3})^2-(3\sqrt{2})^2}$$ $[\because (a-b)(a+b)=a^2-b^2]$

$$=\frac{4\sqrt{3}(4\sqrt{3}-3\sqrt{2})+5\sqrt{2}(4\sqrt{3}-3\sqrt{2})}{48-18}$$

$$=\frac{48-12\sqrt{6}+20\sqrt{6}-30}{30}=\frac{18+8\sqrt{6}}{30}=\frac{9+4\sqrt{6}}{15}$$

Example 14. **If $x=1+\sqrt{2}$, then find the value of $\left(x-\frac{1}{x}\right)^3$.**

Sol. Given, $x=1+\sqrt{2}$

Now, $$\frac{1}{x}=\frac{1}{1+\sqrt{2}}=\frac{1}{1+\sqrt{2}}\times\frac{1-\sqrt{2}}{1-\sqrt{2}}$$ [by rationalising]

$$=\frac{1-\sqrt{2}}{1^2-(\sqrt{2})^2}$$ $[\because (a-b)(a+b)=a^2-b^2]$

$$=\frac{1-\sqrt{2}}{1-2}=\frac{1-\sqrt{2}}{-1}=\sqrt{2}-1$$

and $$\left(x-\frac{1}{x}\right)=(1+\sqrt{2})-(\sqrt{2}-1)=1+\sqrt{2}-\sqrt{2}+1=2$$

$$\therefore \left(x-\frac{1}{x}\right)^3=(2)^3=8$$

Example 15. **If $\frac{3+\sqrt{7}}{3-\sqrt{7}}=a+b\sqrt{7}$, then find the values of a and b.**

Sol. Given, $a+b\sqrt{7}=\frac{3+\sqrt{7}}{3-\sqrt{7}}$

$$\Rightarrow a+b\sqrt{7}=\frac{3+\sqrt{7}}{3-\sqrt{7}}\times\frac{3+\sqrt{7}}{3+\sqrt{7}}$$ [by rationalising]

$$\Rightarrow a+b\sqrt{7}=\frac{(3+\sqrt{7})^2}{(3)^2-(\sqrt{7})^2}$$ $[\because (a-b)(a+b)=a^2-b^2]$

$$=\frac{9+7+6\sqrt{7}}{9-7}$$ $[\because (a+b)^2=a^2+b^2+2ab]$

$$\Rightarrow a+b\sqrt{7}=\frac{16+6\sqrt{7}}{2}=8+3\sqrt{7}$$

On comparing the coefficients of a and b both sides, we get

$$a=8 \text{ and } b=3$$

Example 16. Show that

$$\frac{1}{(3-\sqrt{8})}-\frac{1}{(\sqrt{8}-\sqrt{7})}+\frac{1}{(\sqrt{7}-\sqrt{6})}-\frac{1}{(\sqrt{6}-\sqrt{5})}+\frac{1}{(\sqrt{5}-2)}=5.$$

Sol. $\text{LHS}=\frac{1}{(3-\sqrt{8})}-\frac{1}{(\sqrt{8}-\sqrt{7})}+\frac{1}{(\sqrt{7}-\sqrt{6})}-\frac{1}{(\sqrt{6}-\sqrt{5})}+\frac{1}{(\sqrt{5}-2)}$

$$=\frac{1}{(3-\sqrt{8})}\times\frac{3+\sqrt{8}}{3+\sqrt{8}}-\frac{1}{(\sqrt{8}-\sqrt{7})}\times\frac{\sqrt{8}+\sqrt{7}}{\sqrt{8}+\sqrt{7}}+\frac{1}{(\sqrt{7}-\sqrt{6})}\times\frac{\sqrt{7}+\sqrt{6}}{\sqrt{7}+\sqrt{6}}-\frac{1}{(\sqrt{6}-\sqrt{5})}\times\frac{\sqrt{6}+\sqrt{5}}{\sqrt{6}+\sqrt{5}}+\frac{1}{\sqrt{5}-2}\times\frac{\sqrt{5}+2}{\sqrt{5}+2}$$ [by rationalising]

$$=\frac{3+\sqrt{8}}{(3)^2-(\sqrt{8})^2}-\frac{(\sqrt{8}+\sqrt{7})}{(\sqrt{8})^2-(\sqrt{7})^2}+\frac{(\sqrt{7}+\sqrt{6})}{(\sqrt{7})^2-(\sqrt{6})^2}-\frac{(\sqrt{6}+\sqrt{5})}{(\sqrt{6})^2-(\sqrt{5})^2}+\frac{(\sqrt{5}+2)}{(\sqrt{5})^2-(2)^2}$$

[$\because (a-b)(a+b)=a^2-b^2$]

$$=\frac{3+\sqrt{8}}{9-8}-\frac{(\sqrt{8}+\sqrt{7})}{8-7}+\frac{(\sqrt{7}+\sqrt{6})}{7-6}-\frac{(\sqrt{6}+\sqrt{5})}{6-5}+\frac{(\sqrt{5}+2)}{5-4}$$

$$=3+\sqrt{8}-\sqrt{8}-\sqrt{7}+\sqrt{7}+\sqrt{6}-\sqrt{6}-\sqrt{5}+\sqrt{5}+2$$

$$=3+2=5=\text{RHS}$$ **Hence proved.**

Example 17. If $x=\frac{\sqrt{3}+\sqrt{2}}{\sqrt{3}-\sqrt{2}}$ and $y=\frac{\sqrt{3}-\sqrt{2}}{\sqrt{3}+\sqrt{2}}$, then find the value of $(x+y)^2$.

Sol. Given, $x=\frac{\sqrt{3}+\sqrt{2}}{\sqrt{3}-\sqrt{2}}=\frac{\sqrt{3}+\sqrt{2}}{\sqrt{3}-\sqrt{2}}\times\frac{\sqrt{3}+\sqrt{2}}{\sqrt{3}+\sqrt{2}}$ [by rationalising]

$$=\frac{(\sqrt{3}+\sqrt{2})^2}{(\sqrt{3})^2-(\sqrt{2})^2}\quad[\because (a+b)(a-b)=a^2-b^2]$$

$$=\frac{(\sqrt{3})^2+(\sqrt{2})^2+2\cdot\sqrt{3}\cdot\sqrt{2}}{3-2}\quad[\because (a+b)^2=a^2+b^2+2ab]$$

$$=\frac{3+2+2\sqrt{6}}{1}$$

$$=3+2+2\sqrt{6}$$

$$\therefore\quad x=5+2\sqrt{6}\qquad \text{...(i)}$$

Also given, $y=\frac{\sqrt{3}-\sqrt{2}}{\sqrt{3}+\sqrt{2}}=\frac{1}{x}=\frac{1}{5+2\sqrt{6}}$ [from Eq. (i)]

$$=\frac{1}{5+2\sqrt{6}}\times\frac{5-2\sqrt{6}}{5-2\sqrt{6}}\quad\text{[by rationalising]}$$

$$=\frac{5-2\sqrt{6}}{(5)^2-(2\sqrt{6})^2}\quad[\because (a-b)(a+b)=a^2-b^2]$$

$$=\frac{5-2\sqrt{6}}{25-24}\Rightarrow y=\frac{5-2\sqrt{6}}{1}=5-2\sqrt{6}$$

Now, $x+y=5+2\sqrt{6}+5-2\sqrt{6}=10$

On squaring both sides, we get

$$(x+y)^2=(10)^2=100$$

Try These 1.4

1. Classify the following numbers as a rational or an irrational.
   (i) $7+2\sqrt{3}$ (ii) $(4+\sqrt{32})+\sqrt{64}-4\sqrt{2}$
   (iii) $\frac{\sqrt{80}}{\sqrt{720}}$ (iv) $8\sqrt{2}$ (v) $\frac{6}{\sqrt{2}}$
2. Multiply $4\sqrt{5}$ by $6\sqrt{5}$.
3. Divide $21\sqrt{7}$ by $7\sqrt{7}$.
4. Represent $\sqrt{3.9}$ on number line.
5. If a and b are natural numbers, then $(\sqrt{a}+\sqrt{b})(\sqrt{a}-\sqrt{b})$ is rational. Is it true?
6. Simplify
   (i) $\sqrt{72}+\sqrt{800}-\sqrt{18}$ (ii) $3\sqrt{45}-\sqrt{125}+\sqrt{200}-\sqrt{50}$
7. Simplify each of the following.
   (i) $\sqrt[3]{4}\times\sqrt[3]{16}$ (ii) $\frac{\sqrt[4]{243}}{\sqrt[4]{3}}$
8. Simplify the following
   (i) $(\sqrt{3}-\sqrt{2})^2$ (ii) $(\sqrt{5}+\sqrt{7})(\sqrt{5}-\sqrt{11})$
   (iii) $\left(\sqrt{\frac{2}{5}}+\sqrt{\frac{3}{2}}\right)(\sqrt{2}+\sqrt{3})$ (iv) $(\sqrt{5}-\sqrt{3})^2$
9. Rationalise the denominator of the following
   (i) $\frac{2}{\sqrt{3}-\sqrt{5}}$ (ii) $\frac{1}{\sqrt{5}-\sqrt{4}}$ (iii) $\frac{5\sqrt{3}+3\sqrt{5}}{5\sqrt{3}-3\sqrt{5}}$
   (iv) $\frac{(\sqrt{2}-\sqrt{5})(\sqrt{2}+\sqrt{5})}{6-2\sqrt{5}}$
10. If $\sqrt{3}=1.732$ and $\sqrt{2}=1.414$, then find the value of $\frac{1}{\sqrt{3}-\sqrt{2}}$.
11. Find the value of $\frac{8}{\sqrt{3}+\sqrt{5}}$, where it is given that $\sqrt{3}=1.732$ and $\sqrt{5}=2.236$.
12. If $x=1-\sqrt{2}$, then find the value of $\left(x-\frac{1}{x}\right)^3$.

13. In the following equations, find the values of a and b.

(i) $\dfrac{2+\sqrt{3}}{2-\sqrt{3}} = a + b\sqrt{3}$ (ii) $\dfrac{\sqrt{5}+\sqrt{3}}{\sqrt{5}-\sqrt{3}} = a + b\sqrt{15}$

(iii) $\dfrac{5+2\sqrt{3}}{7+4\sqrt{3}} = a + b\sqrt{3}$ (iv) $\dfrac{\sqrt{2}+\sqrt{3}}{3\sqrt{2}-2\sqrt{3}} = (a + b\sqrt{6})$

14. Prove that $\dfrac{1}{2+\sqrt{3}} + \dfrac{2}{\sqrt{5}-\sqrt{3}} + \dfrac{1}{2-\sqrt{5}} = 0.$

15. Simplify $\dfrac{1}{2+\sqrt{5}} + \dfrac{1}{\sqrt{5}+\sqrt{6}} + \dfrac{1}{\sqrt{6}+\sqrt{7}} + \dfrac{1}{\sqrt{7}+\sqrt{8}}.$

Hints & Answers

1. **Hint** Solve as Example 1.
   (i) Irrational
   (ii) $4+\sqrt{32}+\sqrt{64}-4\sqrt{2} = 4+4\sqrt{2}+8-4\sqrt{2} = 12 =$ rational
   (iii) Rational (iv) Irrational (v) Irrational
2. **Hint** Solve as Example 5. **Ans.** 120
3. **Hint** Solve as Example 6. **Ans.** 3
4. **Hint** Solve as Example 7.
5. True; **Hint** $(\sqrt{a}+\sqrt{b})(\sqrt{a}-\sqrt{b}) = (\sqrt{a})^2 - (\sqrt{b})^2 = a - b$
6. (i) **Hint** $\sqrt{72}+\sqrt{800}-\sqrt{18} = 6\sqrt{2}+20\sqrt{2}-3\sqrt{2} = 23\sqrt{2}$
   (ii) **Hint** $3\sqrt{45}-\sqrt{125}+\sqrt{200}-\sqrt{50} = 9\sqrt{5}-5\sqrt{5}+10\sqrt{2}-5\sqrt{2}$
   $= 4\sqrt{5}+5\sqrt{2}$
7. **Hint** Solve as Example 8. **Ans.** (i) 4 (ii) 3
8. **Hint** Solve as Example 9. **Ans.** (i) $5-2\sqrt{6}$
   (ii) $5-\sqrt{55}+\sqrt{35}-\sqrt{77}$ (iii) $\dfrac{2}{\sqrt{5}}+\sqrt{\dfrac{6}{5}}+\sqrt{3}+\dfrac{3}{\sqrt{2}}$
   (iv) $8-2\sqrt{15}$
9. **Hint** Solve as Example 10.
   Ans. (i) $-(\sqrt{3}+\sqrt{5})$ (ii) $\sqrt{5}+\sqrt{4}$ (iii) $4+\sqrt{15}$
   (iv) $\dfrac{-3(3+\sqrt{5})}{8}$
10. **Hint** Solve as Example 12. **Ans.** 3.146
11. **Hint** Solve as Example 12. **Ans.** 2.02
12. **Hint** Solve as Example 14. **Ans.** 8
13. **Hint** Solve as Example 15. **Ans.** (i) $a=7$ and $b=4$
    (ii) $a=4, b=1$ (iii) $a=11$ and $b=-6$ (iv) $a=2$ and $b=\dfrac{5}{6}$
14. **Hint** Solve as Example 16.
15. **Hint** Solve as Example 16. **Ans.** $-2+\sqrt{8}$

TOPIC 05 Laws of Exponents for Real Numbers

Let $a\,(>0)$ be a real number and p, q be the numbers. Then,

(i) $a^p \times a^q = a^{p+q}$, e.g. $(3)^{\frac{1}{5}} \times (3)^{\frac{1}{7}} = (3)^{\frac{1}{5}+\frac{1}{7}} = (3)^{12/35}$

(ii) $(a^p)^q = a^{pq}$, e.g. $(5^{\frac{1}{3}})^{\frac{1}{5}} = (5)^{\frac{1}{15}}$

(iii) $\dfrac{a^p}{a^q} = a^{p-q}$, e.g. $\dfrac{(3)^{\frac{1}{7}}}{(3)^{\frac{1}{5}}} = (3)^{\frac{1}{7}-\frac{1}{5}} = (3)^{\frac{-2}{35}} = \left(\dfrac{1}{3}\right)^{\frac{2}{35}}$

(iv) $a^p \times b^p = (ab)^p$, e.g. $(2)^{\frac{1}{3}} \times (3)^{\frac{1}{3}} = (2\times 3)^{\frac{1}{3}} = (6)^{\frac{1}{3}}$

(v) $a^{-p} = \dfrac{1}{a^p}$, e.g. $3^{-\frac{1}{5}} = \dfrac{1}{(3)^{\frac{1}{5}}}$

(vi) $\left(\dfrac{a}{b}\right)^{-p} = \left(\dfrac{b}{a}\right)^{p}$, e.g. $\left(\dfrac{3}{5}\right)^{\frac{1}{-6}} = \left(\dfrac{5}{3}\right)^{\frac{1}{6}}$

(vii) $a^{m/n} = (\sqrt[n]{a})^m = \sqrt[n]{a^m}$, where $m, n \in N$

e.g. $4^{3/2} = (\sqrt{4})^3$
$= 2\times 2\times 2 = 8$

or $4^{3/2} = \sqrt{4^3}$
$= \sqrt{4\times 4\times 4} = 8$

Note It The value of zero exponent i.e. $a^0 = 1$.

Example 1. Simplify

(i) $3^{3/2} \cdot 3^{1/2}$ (ii) $(2^{1/5})^{10}$ (iii) $\dfrac{5^{1/7}}{5^{1/3}}$ (iv) $14^{1/5} \cdot 5^{1/5}$

Sol. (i) We have, $3^{3/2} \cdot 3^{1/2} = 3^{3/2+\frac{1}{2}} = 3^{4/2} = 3^2$

$= 9$ $\quad [\because a^p \times a^q = a^{p+q}]$

(ii) We have, $(2^{1/5})^{10} = 2^{10\times\frac{1}{5}} = 2^2 = 4$ $\quad [\because (a^p)^q = a^{pq}]$

(iii) We have, $\dfrac{5^{1/7}}{5^{1/3}} = 5^{\frac{1}{7}-\frac{1}{3}} = 5^{\frac{3-7}{21}} = 5^{\frac{-4}{21}}$ $\quad \left[\because \dfrac{a^p}{a^q} = a^{p-q}\right]$

(iv) We have, $14^{\frac{1}{5}} \cdot 5^{\frac{1}{5}} = (14\times 5)^{\frac{1}{5}} = 70^{\frac{1}{5}}$ $[\because a^p \times b^p = (ab)^p]$

Example 2. Find the value of $[(16)^{1/2}]^{1/2}$.

Sol. $[(16)^{1/2}]^{1/2} = [(2^4)^{1/2}]^{1/2} = [2^{4\times 1/2}]^{1/2}$ $\quad [\because (a^m)^n = a^{mn}]$

$= [2^2]^{1/2} = [2^{2\times 1/2}] = 2^1 = 2$

Example 3. Simplify the expression $[\{(81)^{-1/2}\}^{-1/4}]^2$.

Sol. $(81)^{-\frac{1}{2}\times\left(-\frac{1}{4}\right)\times 2} = (81)^{1/4}$

$= [(3)^4]^{1/4} = (3)^{4\times\frac{1}{4}} = 3$

$[\because (a^m)^n = (a)^{mn}$ and $81 = (3)^4]$

Example 4. Simplify the expression $\left[\left(\frac{5}{6}\right)^{1/5}\right]^{-1/6}$.

Sol. $\left[\left(\frac{5}{6}\right)^{1/5}\right]^{-1/6}=\left(\frac{5}{6}\right)^{\frac{1}{5}\times\left(\frac{-1}{6}\right)}=\left(\frac{5}{6}\right)^{-1/30}$

$=\left(\frac{6}{5}\right)^{1/30}$ $\left[\because \left(\frac{a}{b}\right)^{-m}=\left(\frac{b}{a}\right)^{m}\right]$

Example 5. Find the value of

$$\left(\frac{81}{16}\right)^{-3/4}\times\left[\left(\frac{9}{25}\right)^{3/2}\div\left(\frac{5}{2}\right)^{-3}\right]$$

Sol. $\left[\left(\frac{3}{2}\right)^{4}\right]^{-3/4}\times\left[\frac{\left\{\left(\frac{3}{5}\right)^{2}\right\}^{3/2}}{\left(\frac{5}{2}\right)^{-3}}\right]$

$=\left(\frac{3}{2}\right)^{4\times(-3/4)}\times\left[\left(\frac{3}{5}\right)^{2\times 3/2}\right]\times\left(\frac{5}{2}\right)^{3}$

$=\left(\frac{3}{2}\right)^{-3}\times\left(\frac{3}{5}\right)^{3}\times\left(\frac{5}{2}\right)^{3}$

$=\frac{2^3}{3^3}\times\frac{3^3}{5^3}\times\frac{5^3}{2^3}$ $\left[\because \left(\frac{a}{b}\right)^{-m}=\left(\frac{b}{a}\right)^{m}\right]$

$=1$

Example 6. Evaluate $\sqrt[4]{12}\times\sqrt[7]{6}$.

Sol. $\sqrt[4]{12}\times\sqrt[7]{6}=(2\times2\times3)^{1/4}\times(2\times3)^{1/7}$ $[\because \sqrt[n]{a}=a^{1/n}]$

$=2^{1/4}\times2^{1/4}\times3^{1/4}\times2^{1/7}\times3^{1/7}$

$=2^{1/4+1/4+1/7}\times3^{1/4+1/7}=2^{1/2+1/7}\times3^{1/4+1/7}$

$[\because a^m\times a^n=a^{m+n}]$

$=2^{9/14}\times3^{11/28}$

$=\sqrt[14]{2^9}\times\sqrt[28]{3^{11}}$

$=\sqrt[28]{2^{18}}\times\sqrt[28]{3^{11}}$

$=\sqrt[28]{2^{18}\times3^{11}}$ $[\because \sqrt[n]{a}\times\sqrt[n]{b}=\sqrt[n]{ab}]$

Example 7. Simplify $\sqrt{m^2n^2}\times\sqrt[6]{m^2n^2}\times\sqrt[3]{m^2n^2}$.

Sol. $\sqrt{m^2n^2}\times\sqrt[6]{m^2n^2}\times\sqrt[3]{m^2n^2}$

$=(m^2n^2)^{1/2}\times(m^2n^2)^{1/6}\times(m^2n^2)^{1/3}=(m^2n^2)^{\frac{1}{2}+\frac{1}{6}+\frac{1}{3}}$

$[\because (a)^m\times(a)^n=(a)^{m+n}]$

$=(m^2n^2)^{\frac{3+1+2}{6}}$

$=(m^2n^2)^{6/6}=m^2n^2$

Example 8. Simplify $\frac{6^{2/3}\times\sqrt[3]{6^7}}{\sqrt[3]{6^6}}$.

Sol. $\frac{6^{2/3}\times\sqrt[3]{6^7}}{\sqrt[3]{6^6}}=\frac{\sqrt[3]{6^2}\times\sqrt[3]{6^7}}{\sqrt[3]{6^6}}=\frac{\sqrt[3]{6^2\times6^7}}{\sqrt[3]{6^6}}$

$[\because \sqrt[n]{a}\times\sqrt[n]{b}=\sqrt[n]{a\times b}]$

$=\frac{\sqrt[3]{6^9}}{\sqrt[3]{6^6}}$ $[\because a^m\times a^n=(a)^{m+n}]$

$=\sqrt[3]{\frac{6^9}{6^6}}=\sqrt[3]{6^{9-6}}$

$\left[\because \frac{\sqrt[n]{a}}{\sqrt[n]{b}}=\sqrt[n]{\frac{a}{b}}\text{ and }a^m\div a^n=(a)^{m-n}\right]$

$=\sqrt[3]{6^3}=6$ $[\because \sqrt[m]{a^m}=a]$

Example 9. If $125^x=\frac{25}{5^x}$, then find the value of x.

Sol. Given, $125^x=\frac{25}{5^x}\Rightarrow(5^3)^x=\frac{5^2}{5^x}\Rightarrow5^{3x}=5^{2-x}$

On equating powers from both sides, we get

$3x=2-x\Rightarrow4x=2$

$\therefore\quad x=\frac{2}{4}=\frac{1}{2}$

Example 10. Find the value of x, if $\left(\frac{6}{5}\right)^x\left(\frac{5}{6}\right)^{2x}=\frac{125}{216}$.

Sol. Given, $\left(\frac{6}{5}\right)^x\left(\frac{5}{6}\right)^{2x}=\frac{125}{216}$

$\Rightarrow\left(\frac{5}{6}\right)^{-x}\times\left(\frac{5}{6}\right)^{2x}=\left(\frac{5}{6}\right)^{3}$ $\left[\because\left(\frac{a}{b}\right)^{m}=\left(\frac{b}{a}\right)^{-m}\right]$

$\Rightarrow\left(\frac{5}{6}\right)^{-x+2x}=\left(\frac{5}{6}\right)^{3}$ $[\because (a)^m\times(a)^n=(a)^{m+n}]$

$\Rightarrow\left(\frac{5}{6}\right)^{x}=\left(\frac{5}{6}\right)^{3}$

On comparing the powers from both sides, we get

$x=3$

Example 11. Show that

$$(x^{a-b})^{a+b}\cdot(x^{b-c})^{b+c}\cdot(x^{c-a})^{c+a}=1.$$

Sol. LHS $=(x^{a-b})^{a+b}\cdot(x^{b-c})^{b+c}\cdot(x^{c-a})^{c+a}$

$=x^{a^2-b^2}\cdot x^{b^2-c^2}\cdot x^{c^2-a^2}$

$[\because (A-B)(A+B)=A^2-B^2]$

$=x^{a^2-b^2+b^2-c^2+c^2-a^2}=x^0$ $[\because A^m\times A^n=A^{m+n}]$

$=1=$ RHS **Hence proved.**

Example 12. If $x = 5$ and $y = 2$, find the value of

(i) $(x^y + y^x)^{-1}$ (ii) $(x^x + y^y)^{-1}$

Sol. We have, $x = 5$ and $y = 2$

(i) $(x^y + y^x)^{-1} = (5^2 + 2^5)^{-1} = (25 + 32)^{-1} = (57)^{-1} = \frac{1}{57}$

(ii) $(x^x + y^y)^{-1} = (5^5 + 2^2)^{-1} = (3125 + 4)^{-1}$

$= (3129)^{-1} = \frac{1}{3129}$

Example 13. Prove that

$$\left(\frac{x^{a^2}}{x^{b^2}}\right)^{\frac{1}{a+b}} \cdot \left(\frac{x^{b^2}}{x^{c^2}}\right)^{\frac{1}{b+c}} \cdot \left(\frac{x^{c^2}}{x^{a^2}}\right)^{\frac{1}{c+a}} = 1.$$

Sol. LHS $= \left(\frac{x^{a^2}}{x^{b^2}}\right)^{\frac{1}{a+b}} \cdot \left(\frac{x^{b^2}}{x^{c^2}}\right)^{\frac{1}{b+c}} \cdot \left(\frac{x^{c^2}}{x^{a^2}}\right)^{\frac{1}{c+a}}$

$= (x^{a^2-b^2})^{\frac{1}{a+b}} \cdot (x^{b^2-c^2})^{\frac{1}{b+c}} \cdot (x^{c^2-a^2})^{\frac{1}{c+a}}$

$\left[\because \frac{A^m}{A^n} = A^{m-n}\right]$

$= [x^{(a-b)(a+b)}]^{\frac{1}{a+b}} \cdot [x^{(b-c)(b+c)}]^{\frac{1}{b+c}} \cdot [x^{(c-a)(c+a)}]^{\frac{1}{c+a}}$

$[\because A^2 - B^2 = (A-B)(A+B)]$

$= (x^{a-b}) \cdot (x^{b-c}) \cdot (x^{c-a})$ $[\because (A^m)^n = A^{mn}]$

$= x^{a-b+b-c+c-a}$ $[\because A^m \times A^n = A^{m+n}]$

$= x^0 = 1 =$ RHS $[\because x^0 = 1]$

Hence proved.

Example 14. Evaluate $\frac{2^{40} + 2^{39} + 2^{38}}{2^{41} + 2^{40} - 2^{39}}$.

Sol. $\frac{2^{40} + 2^{39} + 2^{38}}{2^{41} + 2^{40} - 2^{39}} = \frac{2^{38}(2^2 + 2^1 + 1)}{2^{39}(2^2 + 2^1 - 1)}$

[taking 2^{38} common from numerator and 2^{39} from denominator]

$= 2^{38-39}\left(\frac{4+2+1}{4+2-1}\right)$ $\left[\because \frac{a^p}{a^q} = a^{p-q}\right]$

$= 2^{-1} \times \frac{7}{5} = \frac{1}{2} \times \frac{7}{5} = \frac{7}{10}$

Example 15. If $2^x = 3^y = 6^z$, prove that

$$\frac{1}{x} + \frac{1}{y} - \frac{1}{z} = 0 \text{ or } z = \frac{xy}{x+y}.$$

Sol. Let $2^x = 3^y = 6^z = k$

$\Rightarrow 2^x = k,\ 3^y = k$ and $6^z = k$

$\Rightarrow 2 = k^{1/x},\ 3 = k^{1/y}$ and $6 = k^{1/z}$

Now, $6 = (k)^{1/z} \Rightarrow 2 \times 3 = (k)^{1/z}$

$\Rightarrow (k)^{1/x} \times (k)^{1/y} = (k)^{1/z} \Rightarrow (k)^{1/x+1/y} = (k)^{1/z}$

On equating the power from both sides, we get

$$\frac{1}{x} + \frac{1}{y} = \frac{1}{z}$$

$\therefore \frac{1}{x} + \frac{1}{y} - \frac{1}{z} = 0$

Now, $\frac{1}{z} = \frac{1}{x} + \frac{1}{y} \Rightarrow \frac{1}{z} = \frac{x+y}{xy}$

or $z = \frac{xy}{x+y}$ **Hence proved.**

Try These 1.5

1. Simplify the following expression.

(i) $\sqrt{3^{-2}}$ (ii) $(243)^{1/5}$ (iii) $\left[\left(\frac{3}{5}\right)^{1/4}\right]^{-1/5}$

(iv) $(14641)^{0.25}$ (v) $\left(\frac{3125}{243}\right)^{-4/5}$

(vi) $\frac{4}{(125)^{-2/3}} - \frac{1}{(16)^{-3/4}}$

(vii) $[9(64^{1/3} + 125^{1/3})^3]^{1/4}$

2. Find the value of $\left(\frac{625}{1296}\right)^{-3/4} \times \left[\left(\frac{16}{9}\right)^{3/2} \div \left(\frac{5}{3}\right)^{-2}\right]$.

3. If $z = 0.0064$, then find the value of $\left(\frac{1}{z}\right)^{1/2}$.

4. If $81^x = \frac{9}{3^x}$, then find the value of x.

5. Prove that $\frac{a^{-1}}{a^{-1} + b^{-1}} + \frac{a^{-1}}{a^{-1} - b^{-1}} = \frac{2b^2}{b^2 - a^2}$.

6. If $a^2 - b^2 = 1$, then find the value of $[(\mu)^{a-b}]^{a+b}$

7. Find the value of x, if $2^{9x} \div 2^{2x} = \sqrt[7]{2^{14}}$.

8. If $a = 2$ and $b = 3$, then find the value of the following.

(i) $(a^b + b^a)^{-1}$ (ii) $(a^a + b^b)^{-1}$

9. Prove that $\frac{2^{30} + 2^{29} + 2^{28}}{2^{31} + 2^{30} - 2^{29}} = \frac{7}{10}$.

10. Find the value of $\sqrt[5]{\sqrt[4]{3^2}}$.

11. Find the value of $\sqrt[4]{\sqrt[3]{2^2}}$. NCERT Exemplar

12. If $a = \frac{2^{x-1}}{2^{x-2}}$, $b = \frac{2^{-x}}{2^{x+1}}$ and $a - b = 0$, then find the value of x.

Hints & Answers

1. (i) **Hint** $\sqrt{3^{-2}}=(3^{-2})^{1/2}=3^{-1}$ **Ans.** $\frac{1}{3}$

   (ii) **Hint** $(243)^{1/5}=(3^5)^{1/5}$ **Ans.** 3

   (iii) **Hint** $\left[\left(\frac{3}{5}\right)^{1/4}\right]^{-1/5}=\left(\frac{3}{5}\right)^{\frac{1}{4}\times\frac{-1}{5}}$ **Ans.** $\left(\frac{5}{3}\right)^{1/20}$

   (iv) **Hint** $(14641)^{0.25}=(14641)^{\frac{25}{100}}=(14641)^{\frac{1}{4}}$

   $=[(11)^4]^{1/4}$ **Ans.** 11

   (v) **Hint** $\left(\frac{3125}{243}\right)^{-\frac{4}{5}}=\left(\frac{243}{3125}\right)^{\frac{4}{5}}=\left[\left(\frac{3}{5}\right)^5\right]^{\frac{4}{5}}$ **Ans.** $\frac{81}{625}$

   (vi) **Hint** $4\times(125)^{2/3}-(16)^{3/4}$ **Ans.** 92

   (vii) **Hint** $[9\{(4^3)^{1/3}+(5^3)^{1/3}\}^3]^{1/4}$ **Ans.** 9

2. **Hint** Do same as Example 5. **Ans.** $\frac{512}{45}$

3. **Hint** $\left(\frac{1}{0.0064}\right)^{1/2}=\left(\frac{10000}{64}\right)^{1/2}$ **Ans.** 12.5

4. **Hint** $3^{4x}=3^{2-x}$ **Ans.** $x=\frac{2}{5}$

5. **Hint** $a^{-1}=\frac{1}{a}, b^{-1}=\frac{1}{b}$

6. **Hint** $[\mu]^{a^2-b^2}$ **Ans.** μ

7. **Hint** $2^{9x-2x}=2^{14/7}\Rightarrow 2^{7x}=2^2$ **Ans.** $x=\frac{2}{7}$

8. **Hint** Solve as Example 12. **Ans.** (i) $\frac{1}{17}$ (ii) $\frac{1}{31}$

9. **Hint** LHS $=\frac{2^{28}(2^2+2^1+2^0)}{2^{29}(2^2+2^1-2^0)}$ **Ans.** $\frac{7}{10}$

10. **Hint** $\sqrt[5]{\sqrt[4]{3^2}}=[(3^2)^{1/4}]^{1/5}$ **Ans.** $3^{1/10}$

11. **Hint** $\sqrt[4]{\sqrt[3]{2^2}}=\sqrt[4]{2^{2/3}}$ **Ans.** $2^{1/6}$

12. **Hint** $\frac{2^{x-1}}{2^{x-2}}-\frac{2^{-x}}{2^{x+1}}=0\Rightarrow 2^{x-1-x+2}-2^{-x-x-1}=0$

    $\Rightarrow 2^1-2^{-2x-1}=0\Rightarrow 2^{-2x-1}=2^1$

    $\Rightarrow\ -2x-1=1$ **Ans.** $x=-1$

NCERT FOLDER

Complete Solutions of All Exercises of NCERT Textbook

EXERCISE 1.1 (NCERT Page 5)

Q1. Is zero a rational number? Can you write it in the form $\frac{p}{q}$, where p, q are integers and $q \neq 0$?

Sol. Yes, zero is a rational number because we can write $0 = \frac{0}{1}$ (where, 0, 1 are integers and $q = 1 \neq 0$).

Q2. Find six rational numbers between 3 and 4.

Sol. Here, $4 > 3$, so let $x = 3$, $y = 4$ and $n = 6$

Then, $d = \frac{y-x}{n+1} = \frac{4-3}{6+1} = \frac{1}{7}$

So, the six rational numbers between 3 and 4 are

$(x+d), (x+2d), (x+3d), (x+4d)$ $(x+5d)$ and $(x+6d)$

i.e. $\left(3+\frac{1}{7}\right), \left(3+\frac{2}{7}\right), \left(3+\frac{3}{7}\right), \left(3+\frac{4}{7}\right), \left(3+\frac{5}{7}\right)$ and $\left(3+\frac{6}{7}\right)$

or $\left(\frac{21+1}{7}\right), \left(\frac{21+2}{7}\right), \left(\frac{21+3}{7}\right), \left(\frac{21+4}{7}\right), \left(\frac{21+5}{7}\right)$ and $\left(\frac{21+6}{7}\right)$

or $\frac{22}{7}, \frac{23}{7}, \frac{24}{7}, \frac{25}{7}, \frac{26}{7}$ and $\frac{27}{7}$

Q3. Find five rational numbers between 3/5 and 4/5.

Sol. Here, $\frac{4}{5} > \frac{3}{5}$, so let $x = \frac{3}{5}$, $y = \frac{4}{5}$ and $n = 5$

Then, $d = \frac{y-x}{n+1} = \frac{\frac{4}{5}-\frac{3}{5}}{5+1} = \frac{\frac{1}{5}}{6} = \frac{1}{30}$

So, the five rational numbers between $\frac{3}{5}$ and $\frac{4}{5}$ are

$(x+d), (x+2d), (x+3d), (x+4d)$ and $(x+5d)$

i.e. $\left(\frac{3}{5}+\frac{1}{30}\right), \left(\frac{3}{5}+\frac{2}{30}\right), \left(\frac{3}{5}+\frac{3}{30}\right), \left(\frac{3}{5}+\frac{4}{30}\right)$ and $\left(\frac{3}{5}+\frac{5}{30}\right)$

or $\left(\frac{18+1}{30}\right), \left(\frac{18+2}{30}\right), \left(\frac{18+3}{30}\right), \left(\frac{18+4}{30}\right)$ and $\left(\frac{18+5}{30}\right)$

or $\left(\frac{19}{30}\right), \left(\frac{20}{30}\right), \left(\frac{21}{30}\right), \left(\frac{22}{30}\right)$ and $\left(\frac{23}{30}\right)$

or $\frac{19}{30}, \frac{2}{3}, \frac{7}{10}, \frac{11}{15}$ and $\frac{23}{30}$

Q4. State whether the following statements are true or false. Give reason for your answers.

(i) Every natural number is a whole number.

(ii) Every integer is a whole number.

(iii) Every rational number is a whole number.

Sol. (i) True, because every natural number i.e. 1, 2, 3,... belongs to the collection of whole numbers.

(ii) False, because negative integers are not considered in whole numbers.

(iii) False, because numbers like 3/2 is a rational number but not a whole number.

EXERCISE 1.2 (NCERT Page 8)

Q1. State whether the following statements are true or false. Justify your answers.

(i) Every irrational number is a real number.

(ii) Every point on the number line is of the form $\sqrt{m}$, where m is a natural number.

(iii) Every real number is an irrational number.

Sol. (i) True, because real numbers are the collection of rational numbers and irrational numbers.

(ii) False, because no negative number can be the square root of any natural number.

(iii) False, because rational numbers are also present in the collection of real numbers, which is not present in irrational number.

Q2. Are the square roots of all positive integers, irrational? If not, give an example of the square root of a number that is a rational number.

Sol. No, the square root of every positive integer is not always an irrational.

e.g. (i) $\sqrt{4} = 2$, which is a rational number.

(ii) $\sqrt{9} = 3$, which is a rational number.

Q3. Show how $\sqrt{5}$ can be represented on the number line?

Sol. We have, $\sqrt{5}$

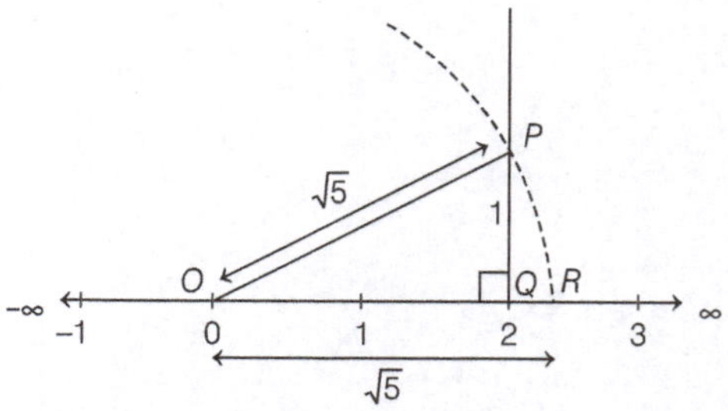

Now, 5 can be written as $5 = 4 + 1 = (2)^2 + (1)^2$

So, we take $OQ = 2$ and $PQ = 1$

Draw $OQ = 2$ units on the number line and then draw $PQ = 1$ unit, such that $PQ \perp OQ$. Join OP.

Now, by Pythagoras theorem in right angled ΔOQP, we get

$$OP^2 = OQ^2 + PQ^2$$

On taking positive square root, we get

$$OP = \sqrt{OQ^2 + PQ^2} = \sqrt{2^2 + 1^2} = \sqrt{4+1} = \sqrt{5}$$

On taking O as centre and $OP = \sqrt{5}$ as radius, draw an arc, which intersects the number line at point R.

Hence, OR represents $\sqrt{5}$.

Q4. Classroom activity (constructing the 'square root spiral').

Sol. Take a large sheet of paper and construct the 'square root spiral' in the following pattern.

Start with a point O and draw a line segment OP_1 of unit length.

Draw a line segment P_1P_2, perpendicular to OP_1 of unit length (see figure) and join OP_2.

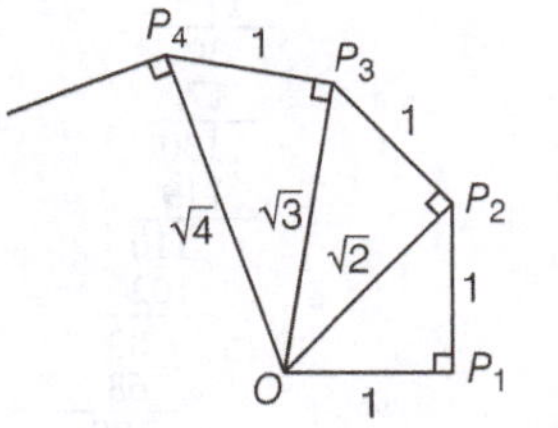

Now, draw a line segment P_2P_3, perpendicular to OP_2 of unit length and join OP_3. Then, draw a line segment P_3P_4, perpendicular to OP_3 of unit length and join OP_4.

Continuing in this manner, you can get the line segment $P_{n-1}P_n$ by drawing a line segment of unit length perpendicular to OP_{n-1}. Thus, you have created the points $P_2, P_3, \ldots, P_n$ and join them to create a spiral depicting $\sqrt{2}, \sqrt{3}, \sqrt{4}, \ldots$.

EXERCISE 1.3 (NCERT Page 14)

Q1. Write the following in decimal form and say what kind of decimal expansion each has?

(i) $\frac{36}{100}$ (ii) $\frac{1}{11}$ (iii) $4\frac{1}{8}$

(iv) $\frac{3}{13}$ (v) $\frac{2}{11}$ (vi) $\frac{329}{400}$

Sol. (i) $\frac{36}{100} = 0.36$

On dividing 36 by 100, we get the exact value 0.36 and set of remainder becomes zero. So, 36 / 100 has a terminating decimal expansion.

(ii) $\frac{1}{11} = 0.\overline{09}$

```
11) 100 (0.0909
     99
    ----
    100
     99
    ----
      1
```

On dividing 1 by 11, we get 09 again and again, i.e. remainder never becomes zero and set of digits repeats periodically.

So, 1/11 has a non-terminating repeating decimal expansion.

(iii) **Hint** Solve as part (i).

Ans. 4.125, Terminating decimal expansion

(iv) **Hint** Solve as part (ii).

Ans. $0.\overline{230769}$, Non-terminating repeating decimal expansion

(v) **Hint** Solve as part (ii).

Ans. $0.\overline{18}$, Non-terminating repeating decimal expansion

(vi) **Hint** Solve as part (i).

Ans. 0.8225, Terminating decimal expansion

Q2. We know that, $\frac{1}{7} = 0.\overline{142857}$. Can you predict, what the decimal expansions of $\frac{2}{7}, \frac{3}{7}, \frac{4}{7}, \frac{5}{7}, \frac{6}{7}$ are without actually doing the long division? If so, how?

Sol. Yes, we can predict the decimal expansions without actually doing long division.

According to the question,

$$\frac{1}{7} = 0.\overline{142857}$$

$$\frac{2}{7} = 2 \times \frac{1}{7} = 0.\overline{285714}$$

$$\frac{3}{7} = 3 \times \frac{1}{7} = 0.\overline{428571}$$

$$\frac{4}{7} = 4 \times \frac{1}{7} = 0.\overline{571428}$$

$$\frac{5}{7} = 5 \times \frac{1}{7} = 0.\overline{714285}$$

$$\frac{6}{7} = 6 \times \frac{1}{7} = 0.\overline{857142}$$

Q3. Express the following in the form p/q, where p, q are integers and $q \neq 0$.

(i) $0.\overline{6}$ (ii) $0.4\overline{7}$ (iii) $0.\overline{001}$

Sol. (i) Let $x = 0.\overline{6} = 0.666\ldots$ ...(i)

Here, only one digit is repeating, so multiply by 10 on both sides of Eq. (i), we get

$$10x = 10 \times 0.666\ldots$$

$$\Rightarrow \quad 10x = 6.6666\ldots \quad \ldots\text{(ii)}$$

On subtracting Eq. (i) from Eq. (ii), we get

$$10x - x = (6.666\ldots) - (0.666\ldots)$$

$$\Rightarrow \quad 9x = 6$$

$$\Rightarrow \quad x = \frac{6}{9} = \frac{2}{3}$$

Hence, $0.\bar{6} = \dfrac{2}{3}$

(ii) Let $x = 0.4\bar{7} = 0.4777\ldots$ ...(i)

Here, after decimal 4 is not repeating, to shift 4 to the left of decimal point multiply Eq. (i) by 10, we get

$$10x = 4.777\ldots \quad \ldots\text{(ii)}$$

Now, only one digit is repeating, so multiply Eq. (ii) by 10, we get

$$100x = 47.777\ldots \quad \ldots\text{(iii)}$$

On subtracting Eq. (ii) from Eq. (iii), we get

$$(100x - 10x) = (47.777\ldots) - (4.777\ldots)$$

$$\Rightarrow \quad 90x = 43$$

$$\Rightarrow \quad x = \frac{43}{90}$$

Hence, $0.4\bar{7} = \dfrac{43}{90}$

(iii) Let $x = 0.\overline{001} = 0.001001001\ldots$ ...(i)

On multiplying Eq. (i) by 1000, we get

$$1000x = 1.001001001\ldots \quad \ldots\text{(ii)}$$

On subtracting Eq. (i) from Eq. (ii), we get

$$(1000x - x) = (1.001001001\ldots) - (0.001001001\ldots)$$

$$\Rightarrow \quad 999x = 1$$

$$\Rightarrow \quad x = \frac{1}{999}$$

Hence, $0.\overline{001} = \dfrac{1}{999}$

Q 4. Express 0.99999... in the form *p/q*. Are you surprised by your answer? With your teacher and classmates, discuss why the answer makes sense?

Sol. Let $x = 0.99999\ldots$ ...(i)

On multiplying Eq. (i) by 10, we get

$$10x = 9.99999\ldots \quad \ldots\text{(ii)}$$

On subtracting Eq. (i) from Eq. (ii), we get

$$(10x - x) = (9.99999\ldots) - (0.99999\ldots)$$

$$\Rightarrow \quad 9x = 9$$

$$\Rightarrow \quad x = \frac{9}{9} = 1$$

Yes, we are surprised to get an integer 1 because after decimal 9 is repeating infinitely and this will tend to an integer.

Q 5. What can the maximum number of digits be in the repeating block of digits in the decimal expansion of $\frac{1}{17}$? Perform the division to check your answer.

Sol. The maximum number of digits in the repeating block of digits in the decimal expansion of $\frac{1}{17}$ is 16. We have,

$$
\begin{array}{r}
17\,)\,100\,(0.0588235294117647\ldots\ldots \\
85 \\ \hline
150 \\
136 \\ \hline
140 \\
136 \\ \hline
40 \\
34 \\ \hline
60 \\
51 \\ \hline
90 \\
85 \\ \hline
50 \\
34 \\ \hline
160 \\
153 \\ \hline
70 \\
68 \\ \hline
20 \\
17 \\ \hline
30 \\
17 \\ \hline
130 \\
119 \\ \hline
110 \\
102 \\ \hline
80 \\
68 \\ \hline
120 \\
119 \\ \hline
1
\end{array}
$$

Thus, $\dfrac{1}{17} = 0.\overline{0588235294117647}$, a block of 16-digits is repeated.

Q 6. Look at several examples of rational numbers in the form $p/q\ (q \neq 0)$, where *p* and *q* are integers with no common factors other than 1 and having terminating decimal representations (expansions). Can you guess what property *q* must satisfy?

Sol. Let us consider $\frac{1}{2}, \frac{1}{4}, \frac{5}{8}, \frac{36}{25}, \frac{7}{125}, \frac{19}{20}, \frac{29}{16}$ etc.

In each case, the denominator of the rational numbers can be changed into power of 10 by multiplying with suitable integer.

$$\frac{1}{2} = \frac{1 \times 5}{2 \times 5} = \frac{5}{10} = 0.5$$

$$\frac{1}{4} = \frac{1 \times 25}{4 \times 25} = \frac{25}{100} = 0.25$$

$$\frac{5}{8}=\frac{5\times125}{8\times125}=\frac{625}{1000}=0.625$$

$$\frac{36}{25}=\frac{36\times4}{25\times4}=\frac{144}{100}=1.44$$

$$\frac{7}{125}=\frac{7\times8}{125\times8}=\frac{56}{1000}=0.056$$

$$\frac{19}{20}=\frac{19\times5}{20\times5}=\frac{95}{100}=0.95$$

$$\frac{29}{16}=\frac{29\times625}{16\times625}=\frac{18125}{10000}=1.8125$$

From the above, we find that the decimal expansions of the above numbers are terminating. Along with it, we see that the denominators of above numbers are in the form $2^m\times5^n$, where m and n are whole numbers.

So, q will be of the form $2^m\times5^n$, where m and n are whole numbers. In other words, the prime factorisation of q has only power of 2 or power of 5 or both.

Q7. Write three numbers whose decimal expansions are non-terminating non-recurring.

Sol. The three numbers whose decimal expansions are non-terminating non-recurring are

0.01001000100001..., 0.202002000200002...,

0.003000300003...

In these examples, remainder never becomes zero and digits are non-repeating after some interval. So, the numbers are non-terminating non-recurring.

Note it Students can write other numbers also as per their choice. There is no specification in it.

Q8. Find three different irrational numbers between the rational numbers 5 / 7 and 9/11.

Sol. To find irrational numbers, first we will divide 5 by 7 and 9 by 11.

Thus, $\frac{5}{7}=0.714285...=0.\overline{714285}$ and $\frac{9}{11}=0.8181...=0.\overline{81}$

That means the required irrational numbers will lie between $0.\overline{714285}$ and $0.\overline{81}$

Also, the irrational numbers have non-terminating non-repeating decimals.

$\therefore$ The required numbers are

0.73073007300073000073...,

0.76507650076500076500000...

and 0.80800800080000...

Q9. Classify the following numbers as rational or irrational.

(i) $\sqrt{23}$ (ii) $\sqrt{225}$ (iii) 0.3796

(iv) 7.478478... (v) 0.101001000100001...

Sol. (i) $\sqrt{23}=4.795831523...$, so it has non-terminating non-recurring decimal expansion.

Hence, it is an irrational number.

Alternate The square root of any prime number is an irrational number.

So, $\sqrt{23}$ is an irrational number.

(ii) $\sqrt{225}=15$, so it is a rational number.

(iii) 0.3796 has terminating decimal expansion.

Hence, it is a rational number.

(iv) 7.478478... 478 has non-terminating repeating decimal expansion.

Hence, it is a rational number.

(v) 0.101001000100001..., has non-terminating non-recurring decimal expansion.

Hence, it is an irrational number.

EXERCISE 1.4 (NCERT Page 20-21)

Q1. Classify the following numbers as a rational or an irrational.

(i) $2-\sqrt{5}$ (ii) $(3+\sqrt{23})-\sqrt{23}$

(iii) $\frac{2\sqrt{7}}{7\sqrt{7}}$ (iv) $\frac{1}{\sqrt{2}}$ (v) 2π

Sol. (i) Here, 2 is a rational number and $\sqrt{5}$ is an irrational number. We know that subtraction of a rational number and an irrational number is always an irrational number.

Hence, $2-\sqrt{5}$ is an irrational number.

(ii) We have, $(3+\sqrt{23})-\sqrt{23}=3+\sqrt{23}-\sqrt{23}=3$

Hence, it is a rational number.

(iii) We have, $\frac{2\sqrt{7}}{7\sqrt{7}}=\frac{2}{7}$

Hence, it is a rational number.

(iv) Here, 1 is a rational number and $\sqrt{2}$ is an irrational number. We know that division of a non-zero rational number and an irrational number is always an irrational number.

Hence, $\frac{1}{\sqrt{2}}$ is an irrational number.

(v) Here, 2 is a rational number and π is an irrational number. We know that product of a non-zero rational number and an irrational number is always an irrational number.

Hence, 2π is an irrational number.

Q2. Simplify each of the following expressions.

(i) $(3+\sqrt{3})(2+\sqrt{2})$ (ii) $(3+\sqrt{3})(3-\sqrt{3})$

(iii) $(\sqrt{5}+\sqrt{2})^2$ (iv) $(\sqrt{5}-\sqrt{2})(\sqrt{5}+\sqrt{2})$

Sol. (i) $(3+\sqrt{3})(2+\sqrt{2}) = 3(2+\sqrt{2})+\sqrt{3}(2+\sqrt{2})$
$= 6+3\sqrt{2}+2\sqrt{3}+\sqrt{6}$

(ii) $(3+\sqrt{3})(3-\sqrt{3}) = (3)^2-(\sqrt{3})^2 = 9-3 = 6$
$[\because (a-b)(a+b) = a^2-b^2]$

(iii) $(\sqrt{5}+\sqrt{2})^2 = (\sqrt{5})^2+(\sqrt{2})^2+2\times\sqrt{5}\times\sqrt{2}$
$[\because (a+b)^2 = a^2+b^2+2ab]$
$= 5+2+2\sqrt{10} = 7+2\sqrt{10}$

(iv) $(\sqrt{5}-\sqrt{2})(\sqrt{5}+\sqrt{2}) = (\sqrt{5})^2-(\sqrt{2})^2 = 5-2 = 3$
$[\because (a-b)(a+b) = a^2-b^2]$

Q3. Recall, π is defined as the ratio of the circumference (say c) of a circle to its diameter (say d) i.e. $\pi = \frac{c}{d}$.

This seems to contradict the fact that π is an irrational. How will you resolve this contradiction?

Sol. When we measure the length with a scale or with any other device, we only get an approximate rational value, so we may not realise that in c and d which one is an irrational.

So, either c or d is an irrational and hence, c/d is an irrational i.e. π is an irrational. Hence, there is no contradiction in saying that π is an irrational.

Q4. Represent $\sqrt{9.3}$ on the number line.

Sol. Firstly, we draw $AB = 9.3$ units. Now, from B, mark a distance of 1 unit. Let this point be C. Let O be the mid-point of AC. Now, draw a semi-circle with centre O and radius OA.

Let us draw a line perpendicular to AC passing through point B and intersecting the semi-circle at point D.

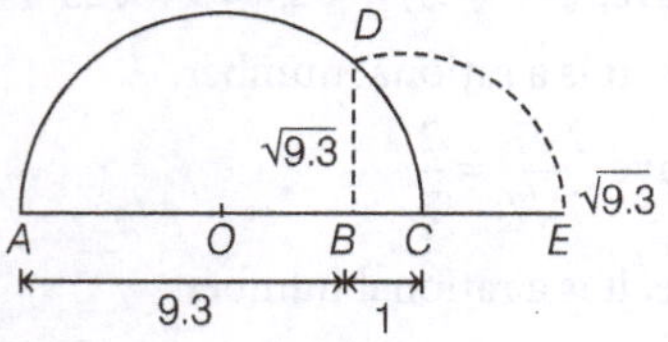

$\therefore$ Distance, $BD = \sqrt{9.3}$

Draw an arc with centre B and radius BD, which intersects the number line at point E. So, point E represents $\sqrt{9.3}$.

Q5. Rationalise the denominators of the following:

NCERT Exemplar

(i) $\frac{1}{\sqrt{7}}$ (ii) $\frac{1}{\sqrt{7}-\sqrt{6}}$ (iii) $\frac{1}{\sqrt{5}+\sqrt{2}}$ (iv) $\frac{1}{\sqrt{7}-2}$

Sol. (i) We have, $\frac{1}{\sqrt{7}}$

On multiplying both numerator and denominator by $\sqrt{7}$, we get

$$\frac{1}{\sqrt{7}}\times\frac{\sqrt{7}}{\sqrt{7}} = \frac{\sqrt{7}}{7}$$

(ii) We have, $\frac{1}{\sqrt{7}-\sqrt{6}}$

On multiplying both numerator and denominator by $\sqrt{7}+\sqrt{6}$, we get

$$\frac{1}{\sqrt{7}-\sqrt{6}}\times\frac{(\sqrt{7}+\sqrt{6})}{(\sqrt{7}+\sqrt{6})} = \frac{\sqrt{7}+\sqrt{6}}{(\sqrt{7})^2-(\sqrt{6})^2}$$
$[\because (a-b)(a+b) = a^2-b^2]$
$$= \frac{\sqrt{7}+\sqrt{6}}{7-6} = \frac{\sqrt{7}+\sqrt{6}}{1} = \sqrt{7}+\sqrt{6}$$

(iii) **Hint** Solve as part (ii). **Ans.** $\frac{\sqrt{5}-\sqrt{2}}{3}$

(iv) **Hint** Solve as part (ii). **Ans.** $\frac{\sqrt{7}+2}{3}$

EXERCISE 1.5 (NCERT Page 23)

Q1. Find

(i) $(64)^{1/2}$ (ii) $(32)^{1/5}$ (iii) $(125)^{1/3}$

Sol. (i) $(64)^{1/2} = (8^2)^{1/2} = 8$ $[\because (a^m)^n = (a)^{mn}]$

(ii) $(32)^{1/5} = (2^5)^{1/5} = 2$

(iii) $(125)^{1/3} = (5^3)^{1/3} = 5$

Q2. Find

(i) $9^{3/2}$ (ii) $32^{2/5}$ (iii) $16^{3/4}$ (iv) $125^{-1/3}$

Sol. (i) $(9)^{3/2} = (3^2)^{3/2} = (3)^3 = 27$ $[\because (a^m)^n = (a)^{mn}]$

(ii) $(32)^{2/5} = (2^5)^{2/5} = (2)^2 = 4$

(iii) $(16)^{3/4} = (2^4)^{3/4} = (2)^3 = 8$

(iv) $(125)^{-1/3} = \frac{1}{(125)^{1/3}} = \frac{1}{(5^3)^{1/3}} = \frac{1}{5}$

$\left[\because (a)^{-n} = \frac{1}{a^n} \text{ and } (a^m)^n = (a)^{mn}\right]$

Q3. Simplify

(i) $2^{2/3}\cdot 2^{1/5}$ (ii) $\left(\frac{1}{3^3}\right)^7$ (iii) $\frac{(11)^{1/2}}{(11)^{1/4}}$ (iv) $7^{1/2}\cdot 8^{1/2}$

Sol. (i) $(2)^{2/3}\cdot(2)^{1/5} = (2)^{2/3+1/5} = (2)^{\frac{10+3}{15}} = (2)^{\frac{13}{15}}$

$[\because (a)^m\cdot(a)^n = a^{m+n}]$

(ii) $\left(\frac{1}{3^3}\right)^7 = \frac{1}{(3^3)^7} = \frac{1}{(3)^{21}} = 3^{-21}$

$\left[\because (a^m)^n = (a)^{mn} \text{ and } \frac{1}{a^m} = a^{-m}\right]$

(iii) $\frac{(11)^{1/2}}{(11)^{1/4}} = (11)^{1/2-1/4} = (11)^{\frac{2-1}{4}} = (11)^{1/4}$

$\left[\because \frac{(a)^m}{(a)^n} = (a)^{m-n}\right]$

(iv) $7^{1/2}\cdot 8^{1/2} = (7\cdot 8)^{1/2} = (56)^{1/2}$ $[\because (a)^p(b)^p = (ab)^p]$

REVIEW EXERCISE

Including Competency Based Questions

Part I

Multiple Choice Questions

1. A rational number between $\sqrt{2}$ and $\sqrt{3}$ is

(a) $\frac{\sqrt{3}-\sqrt{2}}{2}$ (b) 1.52

(c) 1.92 (d) $\frac{\sqrt{3}\times\sqrt{2}}{2}$

2. Which of the following is irrational? NCERT Exemplar

(a) $\sqrt{\frac{4}{9}}$ (b) $\frac{\sqrt{12}}{\sqrt{3}}$ (c) $\sqrt{7}$ (d) $\sqrt{81}$

3. $\frac{1}{\sqrt{5}}$ is a/an .... number.

(a) rational (b) irrational

(c) integer (d) None of these

4. Decimal representation of a rational number cannot be NCERT Exemplar

(a) terminating

(b) non-terminating

(c) non-terminating repeating

(d) non-terminating non-repeating

5. Which of the following is irrational?

(a) 0.14 (b) $0.14\overline{16}$

(c) $0.\overline{1416}$ (d) 0.4014001400014

6. The value of 1.999... in the form of $\frac{p}{q}$, where p and q are integers and $q \neq 0$, is NCERT Exemplar

(a) $\frac{19}{10}$ (b) $\frac{1999}{1000}$ (c) 2 (d) $\frac{1}{9}$

7. 1.272727......can be expressed in rational form as

(a) $\frac{14}{99}$ (b) $\frac{14}{11}$ (c) $\frac{11}{14}$ (d) $\frac{99}{14}$

8. The value of $2.\overline{6} - 0.\overline{9}$ is

(a) $\frac{4}{3}$ (b) $\frac{1}{3}$

(c) $\frac{5}{3}$ (d) $\frac{7}{3}$

9. If 0.142857142857 ... express in the form of $\frac{m}{n}$, then the value of $2m + n$ is

(a) 1 (b) 2

(c) 7 (d) 9

10. Decimal form of $\frac{1}{17}$ is

(a) terminating

(b) non-terminating

(c) non-terminating and non-recurring

(d) non-terminating and recurring

11. Simplify $\frac{2^{n+4}-2(2^n)}{2(2^{n+3})}$.

(a) $2^{n+1}-\frac{1}{8}$ (b) -2^{n+1}

(c) $1-2^n$ (d) $\frac{7}{8}$

12. Simplify $(\sqrt{4}-\sqrt{5})(\sqrt{4}+\sqrt{5})$. Competency Based Question

(a) -1 (b) $\sqrt{3}-\sqrt{5}$

(c) $-4+\sqrt{15}$ (d) $4-2\sqrt{15}$

13. If $x = 1+\sqrt{2}$, then the value of $\left(x-\frac{1}{x}\right)^2$ is

(a) 2 (b) 4 (c) 6 (d) 8

14. After rationalisation, $\frac{1}{\sqrt{5}+\sqrt{3}}$ is equal to

(a) $\frac{\sqrt{5}-\sqrt{3}}{2}$ (b) $\sqrt{5}-\sqrt{3}$ (c) $\sqrt{5}+\sqrt{3}$ (d) $\frac{\sqrt{5}+\sqrt{3}}{2}$

15. If $\sqrt{5} = 2.2361$, then $\sqrt{\frac{\sqrt{5}-1}{\sqrt{5}+1}}$ is equal to

(a) 2.2361 (b) 4.4722 (c) 0.61805 (d) 1.2361

16. $\sqrt[4]{\sqrt[3]{3^2}}$ equals

(a) $3^{-\frac{1}{4}}$ (b) 3^{-4} (c) $3^{\frac{1}{4}}$ (d) 3^4

17. $\sqrt[8]{(81)^{-2}}$ is equal to

(a) $\frac{1}{81}$ (b) 9 (c) $\frac{1}{3}$ (d) $\frac{1}{9}$

18. If $2^{4x} = 16^2$, then x is equal to

(a) 2 (b) 3 (c) 1 (d) 4

19. The value of $7^{15} \times 7^{20}$ is

(a) 7^5 (b) 7^{-5} (c) 7^{35} (d) 7^{-35}

20. The value of $x^{p-q} \cdot x^{q-r} \cdot x^{r-p}$ is equal to

(a) x^{pqr} (b) 0 (c) x (d) 1

Assertion-Reason Type Questions

21. **Assertion** The decimal value of $\frac{437}{999}$ is 0.437437..., which is rational.

Reason A non-terminating repeating decimal number is a rational number.

(a) Both Assertion and Reason are correct and Reason is the correct explanation of Assertion.

(b) Both Assertion and Reason are correct but Reason is not the correct explanation of Assertion.

(c) Assertion is correct but Reason is incorrect.

(d) Assertion is incorrect but Reason is correct.

22. **Assertion** If $a = 3$ and $b = 4$, then the value of b^a is 64.

Reason If $a = 4$ and $b = 5$, then the value of $a^2 + b^2$ is 41.

(a) Both Assertion and Reason are correct and Reason is the correct explanation of Assertion.

(b) Both Assertion and Reason are correct but Reason is not the correct explanation of Assertion.

(c) Assertion is correct but Reason is incorrect.

(d) Assertion is incorrect but Reason is correct.

23. **Assertion** If $\sqrt{2} = 1.414$ and $\sqrt{3} = 1.732$, then the simplified value of $\frac{2-\sqrt{3}}{\sqrt{3}}$ upto three decimal place is 0.354.

Reason If $\sqrt{2} = 1.414$, $\sqrt{5} = 2.236$ and $\sqrt{10} = 3.162$, then the simplified value of $\frac{\sqrt{2}+1}{\sqrt{5}}$ is 1.079.

(a) Both Assertion and Reason are correct and Reason is the correct explanation of Assertion.

(b) Both Assertion and Reason are correct but Reason is not the correct explanation of Assertion.

(c) Assertion is correct but Reason is incorrect.

(d) Assertion is incorrect but Reason is correct.

Case Study Based Questions

24. To support helpless people and orphans is the collective responsibility of the whole society. To measure this spirit a survey was conducted in a city. It was found that 7 out of every 13 households are donating some amount of their income to an orphanage or old age home or institutions for physically handicapped.

On the basis of this information, answer the following questions.

(i) Write the fraction of households, which are donating their income?

(ii) Write the fraction of households, which are not donating their income?

(iii) (a) Write the decimal form of the fraction of households, which are donating their income?

Or (b) Write the decimal form of the fraction of households, which are not donating?

25. To judge the preparation of students of Class IX on topic 'Number System', Mathematics teachers write two numbers on blackboard (as shown in figure).

He asks some questions about the two members, which are following, then answer the questions.

(i) Write the decimal form of $\frac{2}{11}$.

(ii) Write the $\frac{p}{q}$ form of $0.\overline{38}$.

(iii) (a) Is $\frac{2}{11}$ a terminating, non-terminating repeating, non-terminating non-repeating.

Or (b) If $\frac{p}{q}$ form of $0.\overline{38}$ is $\frac{m}{n}$, then find the value of $m + n$.

26. Two friends, Neha and Rohan, were discussing how to simplify complex expressions.

Neha simplified the expression $\frac{\sqrt{8}-\sqrt{2}}{\sqrt{8}+\sqrt{2}}$ by rationalising the denominator.

Rohan worked on evaluating $(\sqrt{6}-\sqrt{2})(\sqrt{6}+\sqrt{2})$ using an identity.

Based on the above information, answer the following questions.

(i) What is the rationalise form of $\frac{\sqrt{8}-\sqrt{2}}{\sqrt{8}+\sqrt{2}}$?

(ii) By rationalising the denominator, Neha will get the numerator as

(iii) (a) What identity did Rohan use to simplify $(\sqrt{6}-\sqrt{2})(\sqrt{6}+\sqrt{2})$?

Or (b) What is the simplified value of $(\sqrt{6}-\sqrt{2})(\sqrt{6}+\sqrt{2})$?

Part II

Very Short Answer Type Questions

1. Irrational numbers can provide more precision on measuring scale. What can be the possible arguments in favour and against this statement?

Competency Based Question

2. If $x = (7 + 4\sqrt{3})$, then what is the value of the expression $x + \frac{1}{x}$?

3. Simplify the expression $(4\sqrt{5} - 3\sqrt{2})(3\sqrt{5} + 5\sqrt{2})$.

4. Find the value of $(256)^{0.16} \times (256)^{0.09}$.

5. Simplify $(25)^{1/3} \times (5)^{1/3}$.

6. Find the value of $\frac{\sqrt[4]{16}}{\sqrt[4]{81}}$.

7. Show that $\frac{1}{1 + x^{a-b}} + \frac{1}{1 + x^{b-a}} = 1$.

Short Answer Type Questions

8. Find three rational numbers between 10 and 12.

9. Classify the following numbers as rational or irrational with justification. **NCERT Exemplar**

(i) $3\sqrt{18}$ (ii) $(1 + \sqrt{5}) - (4 + \sqrt{5})$

(iii) 1.030030003... (iv) $\sqrt{\frac{9}{27}}$ (v) 0.3796

10. Insert a rational number and an irrational number between the following. **NCERT Exemplar**

(i) $-\frac{2}{5}$ and $\frac{1}{2}$ (ii) 0.15 and 0.16

11. Let x and y be rational and irrational numbers, respectively. Is $(x + y)$ necessarily an irrational number? Give an example in support of your answer. **NCERT Exemplar**

12. Deep draws the spiral of irrational numbers below on a paper.

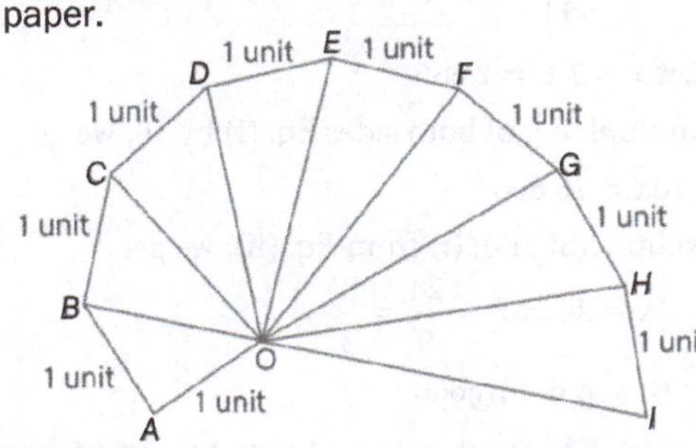

Based on the above information, answer the following question.

What is the length of OE in the spiral?

Competency Based Question

13. Express $32.12\overline{35}$ in the form of $\frac{p}{q}$.

14. Find the sum of 0.0333... and 0.444... .

15. Find the sum of $2.\overline{3}$ and $4.\overline{15}$.

16. Simplify $\frac{1}{\sqrt{5} + \sqrt{3}} + \frac{1}{2}(\sqrt{5} - \sqrt{3})$.

17. Evaluate $\{\sqrt{5 + 2\sqrt{6}}\} + \{\sqrt{8 - 2\sqrt{15}}\}$

18. Rationalise the denominator of $\frac{1}{\sqrt{3} + \sqrt{2}}$ and evaluate by taking $\sqrt{2} = 1.414$ and $\sqrt{3} = 1.732$.

19. If $\frac{(\sqrt{3} + 1)}{(\sqrt{3} - 1)} = a + b\sqrt{3}$, then find the values of a and b.

20. If $\sqrt{2} = 1.414$ and $\sqrt{3} = 1.732$, then find the value of $\frac{4}{3\sqrt{3} - 2\sqrt{2}} + \frac{3}{3\sqrt{3} + 2\sqrt{2}}$. **NCERT Exemplar**

21. If $\sqrt{3} = 1.73205$, what is the value of $\sqrt{\frac{2(\sqrt{3} - 1)}{\sqrt{3} + 1}}$?

22. If $a = 9 - 4\sqrt{5}$, then find the value of $a^2 + \frac{1}{a^2}$.

23. Simplify $\frac{4 - \sqrt{5}}{4 + \sqrt{5}} + \frac{4 + \sqrt{5}}{4 - \sqrt{5}}$.

24. Rationalise the denominator of $\frac{4}{2 + \sqrt{3} + \sqrt{7}}$.

25. Find the value of $\frac{6}{\sqrt{5} - \sqrt{3}}$, if $\sqrt{3} = 1.732$ and $\sqrt{5} = 2.236$. **NCERT Exemplar**

26. If a and b are rational numbers and $\frac{2 + \sqrt{3}}{2 - \sqrt{3}} = a + b\sqrt{3}$, find the value of $a^2 + b^2$.

27. If $x = 3 + \sqrt{8}$, then find the value of $\left(x^2 + \frac{1}{x^2}\right)$.

28. Simplify $\sqrt[3]{27} - 7\sqrt[3]{216} + 10\sqrt[6]{64} + \sqrt[2]{121}$.

29. Simplify $\frac{16 \times 2^{n+1} - 4 \times 2^n}{16 \times 2^{n+2} - 2 \times 2^{n+2}}$.

30. If x and y are positive real numbers, then find the value of $\sqrt[3]{xy^2} \div x^2y$.

31. If $(5)^{x-3} \times (3)^{2x-8} = 225$, then find the value of x.

32. Simplify $\frac{\sqrt{25}}{\sqrt[3]{64}} + \left(\frac{256}{625}\right)^{-1/4} + \frac{1}{\left(\frac{64}{125}\right)^{2/3}}$.

33. Evaluate $\dfrac{(243)^{n/5}\cdot 3^{2n+1}}{9^n \times 3^{n-1}}$.

34. If x, y and z are positive real numbers, then show that $\sqrt{x^{-1}y}\cdot\sqrt{y^{-1}z}\cdot\sqrt{z^{-1}x} = 1$.

35. Find the value of x, if $2^{7x} \div 2^{2x} = \sqrt[5]{2^{15}}$.

36. Show that $\dfrac{x^{a(b-c)}}{x^{b(a-c)}} \div \left(\dfrac{x^b}{x^a}\right)^c = 1$.

Long Answer Type Questions

37. Express $0.6 + 0.\bar{7} + 0.4\bar{7}$ in the form of $\dfrac{p}{q}$, where p, q are integers and $q \neq 0$. **NCERT Exemplar**

38. Simplify $\dfrac{3^{30}+3^{29}+3^{28}}{3^{31}+3^{30}-3^{29}} + \dfrac{2^{30}+2^{29}+2^{28}}{2^{31}+2^{30}-2^{29}}$.

39. If a and b are rational numbers and $\dfrac{\sqrt{11}-\sqrt{7}}{\sqrt{11}+\sqrt{7}} = a - b\sqrt{77}$, then find the values of a and b.

40. Find the values of a and b, if
$$\frac{7+3\sqrt{5}}{3+\sqrt{5}} - \frac{7-3\sqrt{5}}{3-\sqrt{5}} = a + \sqrt{5}b$$

41. If $a = \dfrac{1}{7-4\sqrt{3}}$ and $b = \dfrac{1}{7+4\sqrt{3}}$, then find the values of the following.

(i) $a^2 + b^2$ (ii) $a^3 + b^3$

42. If $x = (5 + 2\sqrt{6})$, then show that $\sqrt{x} + \dfrac{1}{\sqrt{x}} = 2\sqrt{3}$.

43. Simplify $\dfrac{-3}{\sqrt{3}+\sqrt{2}} - \dfrac{3\sqrt{2}}{\sqrt{6}+\sqrt{3}} + \dfrac{4\sqrt{3}}{\sqrt{6}+\sqrt{2}}$.

44. Rationalise $\dfrac{1}{\sqrt{7}+\sqrt{3}-\sqrt{2}}$.

45. If $a = \dfrac{3^{x-2}}{3^{x-5}}, b = \dfrac{3^x}{3^{-x-2}}$ and $a - b = 0$, then find the value of x.

46. Find the value of
$$\frac{4}{(216)^{-2/3}} + \frac{1}{(256)^{-3/4}} + \frac{2}{(243)^{-1/5}}.$$
NCERT Exemplar

HINTS & ANSWERS

Part I

1. (b) **Hint** $\sqrt{2} = 1.41421......$ and $\sqrt{3} = 1.73205......$
1.52 lies between $\sqrt{2}$ and $\sqrt{3}$.

2. (c) $\because \sqrt{\dfrac{4}{9}} = \dfrac{2}{3}$ (rational),

$\dfrac{\sqrt{12}}{\sqrt{3}} = \dfrac{2\sqrt{3}}{\sqrt{3}} = 2$ (rational),

$\sqrt{81} = 9$ (rational)

but $\sqrt{7}$ is an irrational number.

Hence, $\sqrt{7}$ is an irrational number.

3. (b) **Hint** $\sqrt{5}$ is irrational, so $\dfrac{1}{\sqrt{5}}$ is also irrational.

4. (d) Decimal representation of a rational number cannot be non-terminating non-repeating because the decimal expansion of rational number is either terminating or non-terminating recurring (repeating).

5. (d) An irrational number is non-terminating non-recurring which is 0.4014001400014....
Here, 0.14 is terminating and $0.14\overline{16}$, $0.\overline{1416}$ are non-terminating recurring, so they are rational numbers.

6. (c) Let $x = 1.999...$ ...(i)

Now, $10x = 19.999...$ ...(ii)

On subtracting Eq. (i) from Eq. (ii), we get

$10x - x = (19.999...) - (1.9999...)$

$\Rightarrow 9x = 18$

$\therefore x = \dfrac{18}{9} = 2$

7. (b) Let $x = 1.2727...$ ...(i)

Then, multiplying both sides of Eq. (i) by 100, we get

$100x = 127.2727$ ...(ii)

On subtracting Eq. (i) from Eq.(ii), we get

$99x = 126$

$\Rightarrow x = \dfrac{14}{11}$

8. (c) Let $x = 2.\bar{6} = 2.666$ ...(i)

On multiplying of both sides Eq. (i) by 10, we get

$10x = 26.666$ ...(ii)

On subtracting Eq. (i) from Eq. (ii), we get

$9x = 24 \Rightarrow x = \dfrac{24}{9} = \dfrac{8}{3}$ ...(iii)

Let $y = 0.\bar{9} = 0.9999$ ...(iv)

On multiplying both sides of Eq. (iv) by 10, we get

$10y = 9.999$ ...(v)

On subtracting Eq. (iv) from Eq. (v) we get

$10y - y = 9 \Rightarrow y = 1$ ...(vi)

$\therefore \quad 2.\bar{6} - 0.\bar{9} = x - y$ [using Eqs. (i) and (iv)]

$= \frac{8}{3} - 1$ [using Eqs. (iii) and (vi)]

$= \frac{5}{3}$

9. (d) Let $x = 0.142857142857...$ ...(i)

On multiplying both sides of Eq.(i) by 1000000, we get

$1000000x = 142857.142857...$ ...(ii)

On subtracting Eq. (i) from Eq. (ii), we get

$1000000x - x = (142857.142857...) - (0.142857...)$

$\Rightarrow \quad 999999x = 142857$

$\Rightarrow \quad x = \frac{142857}{999999}$

$\Rightarrow \quad x = \frac{1}{7}$

Here, $m = 1$ and $n = 7$

$\therefore \quad 2m + n = 2 \times 1 + 7 = 9$

10. (d) **Hint** $\frac{1}{17} = 0.058823529411764705 \ldots\ldots$

$= 0.\overline{0588235294117647}$

11. (d) We have, $\frac{2^{n+4} - 2(2^n)}{2(2^{n+3})} = \frac{2^{n+4} - 2^{n+1}}{2^{n+4}}$

$= 1 - \frac{2^{n+1}}{2^{n+4}} = 1 - 2^{n+1-n-4}$

$= 1 - 2^{-3}$

$= 1 - \frac{1}{8} = \frac{7}{8}$

12. (a) Use algebraic expression $(a + b)(a - b) = a^2 - b^2$

$\therefore (\sqrt{4} - \sqrt{5})(\sqrt{4} + \sqrt{5}) = (\sqrt{4})^2 - (\sqrt{5})^2$

$= 4 - 5$

$= -1$

13. (b) Given, $x = 1 + \sqrt{2}$

Now, $\frac{1}{x} = \frac{1}{1+\sqrt{2}} = \frac{1}{1+\sqrt{2}} \times \frac{1-\sqrt{2}}{1-\sqrt{2}}$ [rationalising]

$= \frac{1-\sqrt{2}}{1^2 - (\sqrt{2})^2}$ $[\because (a-b)(a+b) = (a^2 - b^2)]$

$= \frac{1-\sqrt{2}}{1-2} = \frac{1-\sqrt{2}}{-1} = \sqrt{2} - 1$

and $x - \frac{1}{x} = (1+\sqrt{2}) - (\sqrt{2} - 1)$

$= 1 + \sqrt{2} - \sqrt{2} + 1 = 2$

$\therefore \quad \left(x - \frac{1}{x}\right)^2 = (2)^2 = 4$

14. (a) **Hint** $\frac{1}{\sqrt{5}+\sqrt{3}} \times \frac{\sqrt{5}-\sqrt{3}}{\sqrt{5}-\sqrt{3}} = \frac{\sqrt{5}-\sqrt{3}}{5-3} = \frac{\sqrt{5}-\sqrt{3}}{2}$

15. (c) **Hint** $\sqrt{\frac{\sqrt{5}-1}{\sqrt{5}+1}} = \sqrt{\frac{\sqrt{5}-1}{\sqrt{5}+1} \times \frac{\sqrt{5}-1}{\sqrt{5}-1}} = \sqrt{\frac{(\sqrt{5}-1)^2}{(\sqrt{5})^2 - 1^2}}$

$= \frac{(\sqrt{5}-1)}{2} = \frac{2.2361 - 1}{2} = \frac{1.2361}{2}$

$= 0.61805$

16. (c) $\sqrt[4]{\sqrt[2]{3^2}} = (\sqrt[2]{3^2})^{1/4} = [(3^2)^{1/2}]^{1/4}$ $[\because \sqrt[n]{a} = a^{1/n}]$

$= [3^{2/2}]^{1/4} = 3^{1/4}$ $[\because (a^m)^n = a^{mn}]$

17. (c) **Hint** $\sqrt[8]{81^{-2}} = \left(\frac{1}{81^2}\right)^{1/8} = \left(\frac{1}{81}\right)^{1/4} = \frac{1}{3}$

18. (a) **Hint** $2^{4x} = 16^2$

$2^{4x} = (2^4)^2 \Rightarrow x = 2$

19. (c) **Hint** $7^{15} \times 7^{20} = 7^{15+20} = 7^{35}$

20. (d) We have, $x^{p-q} \cdot x^{q-r} \cdot x^{r-p}$

$= x^{p-q+q-r+r-p}$ $[\because x^m \cdot x^n = x^{m+n}]$

$= x^0 = 1$

21. (a) **Assertion** When we divide 437 by 999, we get 0.437437...

Here, we see that decimal number is a non-terminating but it is repeated, so it is a rational number. Hence, Assertion is correct.

Reason It is correct, that a non-terminating repeating decimal number is a rational number. And it is a correct explanation of Assertion.

22. (b) **Assertion** We have, $a = 3$ and $b = 4$

$\therefore b^a = (4)^3 = 64$, which is correct.

Reason We have, $a = 4$ and $b = 5$, then

$a^2 + b^2 = (4)^2 + (5)^2 = 16 + 25 = 41$, which is correct.

Hence, we conclude that both Assertion and Reason are correct but Reason is not the correct explanation of Assertion.

23. (d) **Assertion** We have, $\sqrt{2} = 1.414$, $\sqrt{3} = 1.732$

Now, $\frac{2-\sqrt{3}}{\sqrt{3}} = \frac{2-\sqrt{3}}{\sqrt{3}} \times \frac{\sqrt{3}}{\sqrt{3}} = \frac{2\sqrt{3} - 3}{3}$

$= \frac{2 \times 1.732 - 3}{3} = \frac{3.464 - 3}{3}$

$= \frac{0.464}{3} = 0.154,$

which is incorrect.

Reason $\frac{\sqrt{2}+1}{\sqrt{5}} = \frac{\sqrt{2}+1}{\sqrt{5}} \times \frac{\sqrt{5}}{\sqrt{5}} = \frac{\sqrt{10}+\sqrt{5}}{5}$

$= \frac{3.162 + 2.236}{5} = \frac{5.398}{5} = 1.0796,$

which is correct.

24. (i) Total households = 13

Number of households which are donating their income = 7

$\therefore$ Fraction of household which are donating = $\dfrac{7}{13}$

(ii) Total households = 13

Number of houses which are not donating their income = 13 − 7 = 6

$\therefore$ Fraction of households which are not donating = $\dfrac{6}{13}$

(iii) (a) We have, $\dfrac{7}{13}$

13) 70 (0.53846153
65
50
39
110
104
60
52
80
78
20
13
70
65
50
39
11

$\therefore \dfrac{7}{13} = 0.\overline{538461}$

Or

(b) We have, $\dfrac{6}{13}$

13) 60 (0.46153846
52
80
78
20
13
70
65
50
39
110
104
60
52
80
78
2

$\therefore \dfrac{6}{13} = 0.\overline{461538}$

25. (i) We have, $\dfrac{2}{11}$

11) 20 (0.1818
11
90
88
20
11
90
88
2

$\therefore 2 = 0.\overline{18}$

(ii) (b) Let $x = 0.3\overline{8} \Rightarrow x = 0.3888\ldots$ ...(i)

$10x = 3.888\ldots$

$100x = 38.888\ldots$ ...(ii)

On subtracting Eq. (ii) from Eq. (i), we get

$\Rightarrow (100x - 10x) = (38.888\ldots) - (3.888\ldots)$

$\Rightarrow \quad 90x = 35$

$\therefore \quad x = \dfrac{35}{90} = \dfrac{7}{18}$

(iii) (a) $\because \dfrac{2}{11} = 0.\overline{18}$

$\therefore \dfrac{2}{11}$ has non-terminating repeating decimal expansion.

Or (b) $\because \dfrac{m}{n} = \dfrac{7}{18}$

$\therefore m + n = 25$

26. (i) The rationalise form of $\dfrac{\sqrt{8}-\sqrt{2}}{\sqrt{8}+\sqrt{2}}$ is

$$\frac{\sqrt{8}-\sqrt{2}}{\sqrt{8}+\sqrt{2}} \times \frac{\sqrt{8}-\sqrt{2}}{\sqrt{8}-\sqrt{2}}$$

(ii) To rationalise $\dfrac{\sqrt{8}-\sqrt{2}}{\sqrt{8}+\sqrt{2}}$, multiply numerator and denominator by the conjugate $(\sqrt{8}-\sqrt{2})$, we get

$$\frac{\sqrt{8}-\sqrt{2}}{\sqrt{8}+\sqrt{2}} = \frac{\sqrt{8}-\sqrt{2}}{\sqrt{8}+\sqrt{2}} \times \frac{\sqrt{8}-\sqrt{2}}{\sqrt{8}-\sqrt{2}}$$

$$= \frac{(\sqrt{8}-\sqrt{2})^2}{(\sqrt{8})^2-(\sqrt{2})^2} = \frac{(\sqrt{8}-\sqrt{2})^2}{6}$$

$\therefore$ Numerator after rationalising the denominator of $\left(\dfrac{\sqrt{8}-\sqrt{2}}{\sqrt{8}+\sqrt{2}}\right)$ is $(\sqrt{8}-\sqrt{2})^2$.

(iii) (a) Rohan used the identity $(a-b)(a+b) = a^2 - b^2$

Or

(b) Using the identity, we get

$$(\sqrt{6}-\sqrt{2})(\sqrt{6}+\sqrt{2}) = (\sqrt{6})^2 - (\sqrt{2})^2$$

$$= 6 - 2 = 4$$

Part II

1. Irrational numbers are non-terminating with more number of decimals so precision on measuring scale can be more. But they are non-terminating, so fixing their exact location on a measuring scale is not possible.

2. Hint $\frac{1}{x} = \frac{1}{7+4\sqrt{3}} \times \frac{7-4\sqrt{3}}{7-4\sqrt{3}}$ [by rationalising]

$$= \frac{7-4\sqrt{3}}{(7)^2-(4\sqrt{3})^2} = 7-4\sqrt{3}$$

$$\therefore\ x + \frac{1}{x} = 7+4\sqrt{3}+7-4\sqrt{3} = 14$$

3. Hint Solve as Example 9 (i) of Topic 4.

Ans. $30+11\sqrt{10}$

4. Hint $(256)^{0.16} \times (256)^{0.09}$

$$= (256)^{0.16+0.09} \quad [\because (a)^m \times (a)^n = (a)^{m+n}]$$

$$= (256)^{0.25} = (256)^{\frac{25}{100}} = (256)^{1/4}$$

$$= [(4)^4]^{1/4} = 4 \quad [\because (a^m)^n = (a)^{mn}]$$

5. This expression can be written as $(5^2)^{1/3} \times 5^{1/3}$

Use law $a^p \times a^q = a^{p+q}$ **Ans.** 5

6. Hint We know that $\frac{\sqrt[n]{a}}{\sqrt[n]{b}} = \sqrt[n]{\frac{a}{b}}$

$$\therefore\ \frac{\sqrt[4]{16}}{\sqrt[4]{81}} = \sqrt[4]{\frac{16}{81}} = \left(\frac{16}{81}\right)^{1/4} = \left(\frac{2^4}{3^4}\right)^{1/4} = \frac{2}{3}$$

7. Hint LHS $= \frac{1}{1+x^{a-b}} + \frac{1}{1+x^{b-a}}$

$$= \frac{1}{1+\frac{x^a}{x^b}} + \frac{1}{1+\frac{x^b}{x^a}}$$

$$= \frac{x^b}{x^b+x^a} + \frac{x^a}{x^a+x^b} = 1 = \text{RHS}$$

8. Hint Solve as Example 3 of Topic 1 **Ans.** $\frac{21}{2}, 11, \frac{23}{2}$

9. (i) $3\sqrt{18} = 9\sqrt{2}$, irrational number as product of a non-zero rational number and an irrational number is always an irrational number.

(ii) $1+\sqrt{5}-4-\sqrt{5} = -3$, rational number.

(iii) Non-terminating non-repeating, irrational number.

(iv) $\sqrt{\frac{1}{3}} = \frac{1}{\sqrt{3}}$, irrational number as division of a non-zero rational number and an irrational number is always an irrational number.

(v) Terminating, rational number.

10. Hint (i) A rational number between $\frac{-2}{5}$ and $\frac{1}{2}$ is 0.

An irrational number between $\frac{-2}{5}$ and $\frac{1}{2}$

i.e. between $-$ 0.4 and 0.5 is 0.151151115... .

(ii) A rational number between 0.15 and 0.16 is 0.151.
An irrational number between 0.15 and 0.16 is 0.1515515551... .

11. Yes,

Hint e.g. Let $x = 2$ and $y = \sqrt{3}$

Then, $x + y = 2 + \sqrt{3}$

If possible, let $x + y = 2+\sqrt{3}$ be a rational number.

Consider $a = 2+\sqrt{3}$

On squaring both sides, we get $a^2 = (2+\sqrt{3})^2$

$$\Rightarrow\quad a^2 = 2^2 + (\sqrt{3})^2 + 2(2)\cdot(\sqrt{3})$$

$$\Rightarrow\quad a^2 = 4+3+4\sqrt{3} \Rightarrow \frac{a^2-7}{4} = \sqrt{3}$$

Since, a is rational.

$\therefore\ \frac{a^2-7}{4}$ is rational. $\Rightarrow \sqrt{3}$ is rational.

But this contradicts the fact that $\sqrt{3}$ is an irrational number. Thus, our assumption is wrong.

Hence, $(x + y)$ is an irrational number.

12. Hint In the spiral, we use Pythagoras theorem.

$\therefore\quad OE = \sqrt{5}$ units

13. Hint Let $x = 32.12353535...$

$\therefore\quad 100x = 3212.353535...$

and $10000x = 321235.3535...$

$\therefore 10000x - 100x = (321235.3535...) - (3212.353535...)$

$$\Rightarrow\quad 9900x = 318023 \Rightarrow x = \frac{318023}{9900}$$

14. Let $x = 0.0333$

$\Rightarrow\quad 10x = 0.333$ ......

$\Rightarrow\quad 100x = 3.333$

$\therefore\quad 100x - 10x = 3.333... - 0.333...$

$\Rightarrow\quad 90x = 3 \Rightarrow x = \frac{3}{90}$

Again, let $y = 0.444...$

$\Rightarrow\quad 10y = 4.444...$

$\therefore\quad 10y - y = 4.444... - 0.444...$

$\Rightarrow\quad 9y = 4$

$\Rightarrow\quad y = \frac{4}{9}$

$\therefore$ Sum of 0.0333... and 0.444... $= x + y = \frac{3}{90} + \frac{4}{9} = \frac{43}{90}$

15. Hint Solve as Q. 14. **Ans.** $\frac{214}{33}$

16. Hint Solve as Example 16 of Topic 4. **Ans.** $\sqrt{5}-\sqrt{3}$

17. $\sqrt{5+2\sqrt{6}} = \sqrt{3+2+2\sqrt{6}}$

$$= \sqrt{(\sqrt{3})^2+(\sqrt{2})^2+2\sqrt{3}\sqrt{2}}$$

$$= \sqrt{(\sqrt{3}+\sqrt{2})^2} = \sqrt{3}+\sqrt{2}$$

Also, $\sqrt{8-2\sqrt{15}} = \sqrt{5+3-2\sqrt{5}\sqrt{3}}$

$$= \sqrt{(\sqrt{5})^2+(\sqrt{3})^2-2\sqrt{5}\sqrt{3}}$$

$$= \sqrt{(\sqrt{5}-\sqrt{3})^2} = \sqrt{5}-\sqrt{3}$$

$\therefore$ Required sum $= (\sqrt{3}+\sqrt{2})+(\sqrt{5}-\sqrt{3}) = \sqrt{2}+\sqrt{5}$

18. Hint $\frac{1}{\sqrt{3}+\sqrt{2}}$

$$= \frac{1}{\sqrt{3}+\sqrt{2}} \times \frac{\sqrt{3}-\sqrt{2}}{\sqrt{3}-\sqrt{2}} \quad \text{[by rationalising]}$$

$$= \frac{\sqrt{3}-\sqrt{2}}{(\sqrt{3})^2-(\sqrt{2})^2} = \frac{\sqrt{3}-\sqrt{2}}{3-2}$$

$$= \sqrt{3}-\sqrt{2} = 1.732-1.414 = 0.318$$

19. Hint Solve as Example 15 of Topic 4.
Ans. $a=2, b=1$

20. Hint $\frac{4}{3\sqrt{3}-2\sqrt{2}}+\frac{3}{3\sqrt{3}+2\sqrt{2}}$

$$= \frac{4(3\sqrt{3}+2\sqrt{2})+3(3\sqrt{3}-2\sqrt{2})}{(3\sqrt{3}-2\sqrt{2})(3\sqrt{3}+2\sqrt{2})}$$

$$= \frac{21\sqrt{3}+2\sqrt{2}}{27-8} = \frac{21\times 1.732+2\times 1.414}{19}$$

$$= \frac{36.372+2.828}{19} = \frac{39.2}{19} = 2.06316 \approx 2.063$$

21. Hint $\sqrt{\frac{2(\sqrt{3}-1)}{\sqrt{3}+1}} = \sqrt{\frac{2(\sqrt{3}-1)}{(\sqrt{3}+1)}\times\frac{(\sqrt{3}-1)}{(\sqrt{3}-1)}}$

$$= \sqrt{\frac{2(\sqrt{3}-1)^2}{(\sqrt{3})^2-(1)^2}} = \sqrt{(\sqrt{3}-1)^2} = \sqrt{3}-1$$

$$= 1.73205-1 = 0.73205$$

22. $a = 9-4\sqrt{5}, \frac{1}{a} = \frac{1}{9-4\sqrt{5}} = \frac{9+4\sqrt{5}}{9^2-(4\sqrt{5})^2}$

$$= 9+4\sqrt{5}$$

$\therefore$ $$a+\frac{1}{a} = (9-4\sqrt{5})+(9+4\sqrt{5}) = 18$$

Now, use $\left(a+\frac{1}{a}\right)^2 = a^2+\frac{1}{a^2}+2\times a\times\frac{1}{a}$

$$\left(a+\frac{1}{a}\right)^2 = a^2+\frac{1}{a^2}+2$$

$$(18)^2 = a^2+\frac{1}{a^2}+2$$

$$a^2+\frac{1}{a^2} = 322$$

23. Hint Solve as Example 17 of Topic 4. **Ans.** $\frac{42}{11}$

24. Hint $\frac{4}{2+\sqrt{3}+\sqrt{7}}$

$$= \frac{4}{(2+\sqrt{3})+\sqrt{7}} \times \frac{(2+\sqrt{3})-\sqrt{7}}{(2+\sqrt{3})-\sqrt{7}}$$

$$= \frac{8+4\sqrt{3}-4\sqrt{7}}{(2+\sqrt{3})^2-(\sqrt{7})^2}$$

$$= \frac{8+4\sqrt{3}-4\sqrt{7}}{4+3+4\sqrt{3}-7} = \frac{8+4\sqrt{3}-4\sqrt{7}}{7+4\sqrt{3}-7}$$

$$= \frac{8+4\sqrt{3}-4\sqrt{7}}{4\sqrt{3}} \times \frac{\sqrt{3}}{\sqrt{3}}$$

$$= \frac{8\sqrt{3}+12-4\sqrt{21}}{12}$$

$$= \frac{2\sqrt{3}}{3}+1-\frac{\sqrt{21}}{3}$$

25. Hint $\frac{6}{\sqrt{5}-\sqrt{3}} = \frac{6}{\sqrt{5}-\sqrt{3}} \times \frac{\sqrt{5}+\sqrt{3}}{\sqrt{5}+\sqrt{3}} = \frac{6(\sqrt{5}+\sqrt{3})}{(\sqrt{5})^2-(\sqrt{3})^2}$

On putting the value of $\sqrt{5}$ and $\sqrt{3}$, we get

$$= 11.904$$

26. Hint Solve as Example 15 of Topic 4. **Ans.** 65

27. Hint Given, $x = 3+\sqrt{8}$

$\therefore$ $$\frac{1}{x} = \frac{1}{3+\sqrt{8}}$$

$$= \frac{1}{3+\sqrt{8}} \times \frac{(3-\sqrt{8})}{(3-\sqrt{8})} = \frac{3-\sqrt{8}}{(3)^2-(\sqrt{8})^2}$$

$[\because (a-b)(a+b) = a^2-b^2]$

$$= \frac{3-\sqrt{8}}{9-8} = 3-\sqrt{8}$$

Now, $\left(x+\frac{1}{x}\right) = 3+\sqrt{8}+3-\sqrt{8} = 6$

On squaring both sides, we get

$$x^2+\frac{1}{x^2}+2 = (6)^2$$

$\therefore$ $$x^2+\frac{1}{x^2} = 36-2 = 34$$

28. Hint $\sqrt[3]{27} - 7\sqrt[3]{216} + 10\sqrt[6]{64} + \sqrt[2]{121}$

$$= \sqrt[3]{3^3} - 7\sqrt[3]{6^3} + 10\sqrt[6]{2^6} + \sqrt[2]{11^2}$$
$$= (3^3)^{1/3} - 7(6^3)^{1/3} + 10(2^6)^{1/6} + (11^2)^{1/2}$$
$$= 3^1 - 7\times 6^1 + 10\times 2^1 + 11^1$$
$$= 3 - 42 + 20 + 11 = 34 - 42 = -8$$

29. Hint $\dfrac{16\times 2^{n+1} - 4\times 2^n}{16\times 2^{n+2} - 2\times 2^{n+2}}$

$$= \frac{2^4\times 2^{n+1} - 2^2\times 2^n}{2^4\times 2^{n+2} - 2\times 2^{n+2}} = \frac{2^{n+5} - 2^{n+2}}{2^{n+6} - 2^{n+3}}$$
$$= \frac{2^{n+5} - 2^{n+2}}{2\cdot 2^{n+5} - 2\cdot 2^{n+2}} = \frac{2^{n+5} - 2^{n+2}}{2(2^{n+5} - 2^{n+2})} = \frac{1}{2}$$

30. Hint $\sqrt[3]{xy^2} \div x^2y = \dfrac{\sqrt[3]{xy^2}}{x^2y} = \dfrac{(xy^2)^{1/3}}{x^2y} = \dfrac{x^{1/3}y^{2/3}}{x^2y}$

$$= x^{\frac{1}{3}-2} \cdot y^{\frac{2}{3}-1} = x^{\frac{1-6}{3}} \cdot y^{\frac{2-3}{3}}$$
$$= x^{-5/3}y^{-1/3} = \frac{1}{x^{5/3}y^{1/3}}$$

31. Hint $5^{x-3} \times 3^{2x-8} = 5^2 \times 3^2$. **Ans.** 5

32. Hint $\dfrac{\sqrt{25}}{\sqrt[3]{64}} + \left(\dfrac{256}{625}\right)^{-1/4} + \dfrac{1}{\left(\dfrac{64}{125}\right)^{2/3}}$

$$= \frac{\sqrt{5\times 5}}{\sqrt[3]{4\times 4\times 4}} + \left(\frac{625}{256}\right)^{1/4} + \left(\frac{125}{64}\right)^{2/3}$$
$$= \frac{5}{4} + \left(\frac{5^4}{4^4}\right)^{1/4} + \left(\frac{5^3}{4^3}\right)^{2/3}$$
$$= \frac{5}{4} + \frac{5}{4} + \left(\frac{5}{4}\right)^2$$
$$= \frac{5}{4} + \frac{5}{4} + \frac{25}{16}$$
$$= \frac{20 + 20 + 25}{16} = \frac{65}{16}$$

33. Hint $\dfrac{(243)^{n/5}\cdot(3)^{2n+1}}{9^n\times(3)^{n-1}}$

$$= \frac{(3^5)^{n/5}\times(3)^{2n+1}}{(3^2)^n\times(3)^{n-1}}$$
$$= \frac{3^n\times(3)^{2n+1}}{3^{2n}\times(3)^{n-1}}$$
$$= \frac{(3)^{3n+1}}{(3)^{3n-1}}$$
$$= (3)^{3n+1-(3n-1)}$$
$$= (3)^2 = 9$$

34. Hint LHS $= \sqrt{x^{-1}y}\cdot\sqrt{y^{-1}z}\cdot\sqrt{z^{-1}x}$

$$= \sqrt{\frac{y}{x}}\cdot\sqrt{\frac{z}{y}}\cdot\sqrt{\frac{x}{z}} = \left(\frac{y}{x}\right)^{1/2}\left(\frac{z}{y}\right)^{1/2}\left(\frac{x}{z}\right)^{1/2}$$
$$= \frac{(y)^{1/2}}{(x)^{1/2}}\cdot\frac{(z)^{1/2}}{(y)^{1/2}}\cdot\frac{(x)^{1/2}}{(z)^{1/2}} = 1 = \text{RHS}$$

35. Hint Given, $2^{7x} \div 2^{2x} = \sqrt[5]{2^{15}}$

$\Rightarrow\quad (2)^{7x-2x} = \sqrt[5]{2^{15}}$

$\Rightarrow\quad (2)^{5x} = (2)^{15\times 1/5}\quad [\because (a^m)^n = a^{mn}]$

$\Rightarrow\quad 2^{5x} = 2^3$

On comparing the power of 2 from both sides, we get

$$5x = 3$$

$\therefore\quad x = \dfrac{3}{5}$

36. Hint LHS $= \dfrac{x^{a(b-c)}}{x^{b(a-c)}} \div \left(\dfrac{x^b}{x^a}\right)^c = \dfrac{(x)^{ab-ac}}{(x)^{ab-bc}} \div \dfrac{(x)^{bc}}{(x)^{ac}}$

$$= (x)^{ab-ac-(ab-bc)} \div (x)^{bc-ac}$$
$$= (x)^{ab-ac-ab+bc} \div (x)^{bc-ac}$$
$$= (x)^{bc-ac} \div (x)^{bc-ac} = (x)^{bc-ac-bc+ac}$$
$$= (x)^0 = 1 = \text{RHS}$$

37. Hint $\therefore\ 0.6 + 0.\overline{7} + 0.4\overline{7} = \dfrac{6}{10} + \dfrac{7}{9} + \dfrac{43}{90}$

$$= \frac{54 + 70 + 43}{90} = \frac{167}{90}$$

38. Hint Solve as Example 14 of Topic 5. **Ans.** $\dfrac{361}{330}$

39. Hint Solve as Example 15 of Topic 4.

Ans. $a = \dfrac{9}{2}$ and $b = \dfrac{1}{2}$

40. Hint $\dfrac{7+3\sqrt{5}}{3+\sqrt{5}} - \dfrac{7-3\sqrt{5}}{3-\sqrt{5}} = a + \sqrt{5}b$

$$\Rightarrow \frac{(7+3\sqrt{5})(3-\sqrt{5}) - (7-3\sqrt{5})(3+\sqrt{5})}{(3+\sqrt{5})(3-\sqrt{5})} = a + \sqrt{5}b$$
$$\Rightarrow \frac{21 - 7\sqrt{5} + 9\sqrt{5} - 15 - (21 + 7\sqrt{5} - 9\sqrt{5} - 15)}{9-5} = a + \sqrt{5}b$$

$\Rightarrow \sqrt{5} = a + \sqrt{5}b \Rightarrow a = 0$ and $b = 1$

41. Hint Given,

$$a = \frac{1}{7-4\sqrt{3}} = \frac{1}{7-4\sqrt{3}} \times \frac{7+4\sqrt{3}}{7+4\sqrt{3}}$$

[by rationalising]

$$= \frac{7+4\sqrt{3}}{(7)^2 - (4\sqrt{3})^2} = 7 + 4\sqrt{3}$$

and $b = \frac{1}{7+4\sqrt{3}} = \frac{1}{7+4\sqrt{3}} \times \frac{7-4\sqrt{3}}{7-4\sqrt{3}}$

$= \frac{7-4\sqrt{3}}{7^2-(4\sqrt{3})^2}$

$= 7-4\sqrt{3}$

$\therefore \quad a+b = 7+4\sqrt{3}+7-4\sqrt{3} = 14$

and $ab = (7+4\sqrt{3})(7-4\sqrt{3})$

$= (7)^2 - (4\sqrt{3})^2 = 49 - 48 = 1$

(i) $\because \quad (a+b)^2 = a^2+b^2+2ab$

$\Rightarrow \quad (14)^2 = a^2+b^2+2$

$\therefore \ a^2+b^2 = 196-2 = 194$

(ii) $\because \quad (a+b)^3 = a^3+b^3+3ab(a+b)$

$\therefore \quad a^3+b^3 = (a+b)^3 - 3ab(a+b)$

$= (14)^3 - 3\times 1\times 14$

$= 2744 - 42$

$= 2702$

42. Hint We have,

$x = 5+2\sqrt{6}$

Now, $\frac{1}{x} = \frac{1}{5+2\sqrt{6}} \times \frac{5-2\sqrt{6}}{5-2\sqrt{6}}$

$= \frac{5-2\sqrt{6}}{(5)^2-(2\sqrt{6})^2} = 5-2\sqrt{6}$

$\therefore \quad x+\frac{1}{x} = 5+2\sqrt{6}+5-2\sqrt{6} = 10$

$\Rightarrow \quad x+\frac{1}{x}+2 = 12$

$\Rightarrow \left(\sqrt{x}+\frac{1}{\sqrt{x}}\right)^2 = (2\sqrt{3})^2$

$\Rightarrow \quad \sqrt{x}+\frac{1}{\sqrt{x}} = 2\sqrt{3}$

43. Hint $\frac{-3}{\sqrt{3}+\sqrt{2}} - \frac{3\sqrt{2}}{\sqrt{6}+\sqrt{3}} + \frac{4\sqrt{3}}{\sqrt{6}+\sqrt{2}}$

$= \frac{-3}{\sqrt{3}+\sqrt{2}} \times \frac{\sqrt{3}-\sqrt{2}}{\sqrt{3}-\sqrt{2}} - \frac{3\sqrt{2}}{\sqrt{6}+\sqrt{3}} \times \frac{\sqrt{6}-\sqrt{3}}{\sqrt{6}-\sqrt{3}}$

$+ \frac{4\sqrt{3}}{\sqrt{6}+\sqrt{2}} \times \frac{\sqrt{6}-\sqrt{2}}{\sqrt{6}-\sqrt{2}}$

$= \frac{-3(\sqrt{3}-\sqrt{2})}{(\sqrt{3})^2-(\sqrt{2})^2} - \frac{3\sqrt{2}(\sqrt{6}-\sqrt{3})}{(\sqrt{6})^2-(\sqrt{3})^2}$

$+ 4\sqrt{3} \times \frac{(\sqrt{6}-\sqrt{2})}{(\sqrt{6})^2-(\sqrt{2})^2}$

$= \frac{-3(\sqrt{3}-\sqrt{2})}{1} - \frac{3\sqrt{2}(\sqrt{6}-\sqrt{3})}{6-3}$

$+ \frac{4\sqrt{3}(\sqrt{6}-\sqrt{2})}{6-2}$

$= -3(\sqrt{3}-\sqrt{2}) - \sqrt{2}(\sqrt{6}-\sqrt{3})$

$+ \sqrt{3}(\sqrt{6}-\sqrt{2})$

$= -3\sqrt{3}+3\sqrt{2}-\sqrt{12}+\sqrt{6}+\sqrt{18}-\sqrt{6}$

$= -3\sqrt{3}+3\sqrt{2}-2\sqrt{3}+\sqrt{6}+3\sqrt{2}-\sqrt{6}$

$= 6\sqrt{2}-5\sqrt{3}$

44. Hint $\frac{1}{\sqrt{7}+\sqrt{3}-\sqrt{2}}$

$= \frac{1}{[(\sqrt{7}+\sqrt{3})-\sqrt{2}]} \times \frac{(\sqrt{7}+\sqrt{3})+\sqrt{2}}{(\sqrt{7}+\sqrt{3})+\sqrt{2}}$

$= \frac{\sqrt{7}+\sqrt{3}+\sqrt{2}}{[(\sqrt{7}+\sqrt{3})^2-(\sqrt{2})^2]}$

$= \frac{\sqrt{7}+\sqrt{3}+\sqrt{2}}{(\sqrt{7})^2+(\sqrt{3})^2+2\sqrt{7}\sqrt{3}-2} = \frac{\sqrt{7}+\sqrt{3}+\sqrt{2}}{7+3+2\sqrt{21}-2}$

$= \frac{\sqrt{7}+\sqrt{3}+\sqrt{2}}{2(4+\sqrt{21})} \times \frac{4-\sqrt{21}}{4-\sqrt{21}}$

$= \frac{4\sqrt{7}+4\sqrt{3}+4\sqrt{2}-7\sqrt{3}-3\sqrt{7}-\sqrt{42}}{2(16-21)}$

$= \frac{3\sqrt{3}-4\sqrt{2}+\sqrt{42}-\sqrt{7}}{10}$

45. Hint $a = b \Rightarrow 3^3 = 3^{2x+2} \Rightarrow x = \frac{1}{2}$

46. Hint $\frac{4}{(216)^{-2/3}} + \frac{1}{(256)^{-3/4}} + \frac{2}{(243)^{-1/5}}$

$= 4\times(216)^{2/3} + (256)^{3/4} + 2\times(243)^{1/5}$

$= 4\times(6^3)^{2/3} + (4^4)^{3/4} + 2\times(3^5)^{1/5}$

$= 4\times(6)^2 + (4)^3 + 2\times(3)^1$

$= 4\times 36 + 64 + 6 = 144 + 64 + 6 = 214$

Mind Map

NUMBER SYSTEM

Basics of Number System

Natural Numbers *(N)*
Used for counting i.e. 1, 2, ...

Whole Numbers *(W)*
Natural numbers together with 0 i.e. 0, 1, 2, 3, ...

Integers *(Z)*
Collection of whole and negative natural numbers i.e. ..., – 2, – 1, 0, 1, 2, ...

Rational Numbers *(Q)*
These can be expressed as $\frac{p}{q}$ where p and q are integers, $q \neq 0$
e.g. $\frac{2}{3}, \frac{16}{23}$ ... etc.

Equivalent Rational Numbers
Two rational numbers are equivalent if their standard form are equal
e.g. $\frac{1}{2}$ and $\frac{2}{4}$ etc.

Method to Determine Rational Numbers Between Two Rational Numbers

(i) When one rational number is to be determined
$\frac{x+y}{2}$ is a rational number between x and y.
e.g. $\frac{3}{2}$ is a rational number between 1 and 2.

(ii) When more than one rational number is to be determined
n rational numbers between x and y are
$x + d, x + 2d, x + 3d$ ...
where $d = \frac{y-x}{n+1}$

Irrational Numbers
Those which can't be expressed in the $\frac{p}{q}$, form, where $q \neq 0$, p and q are integers.
e.g. $\sqrt{2}, \pi$, 0.10100 ...

How to Locate an Irrational Number on Number Line
We can locate an irrational number on number line using Pythagoras theorem.
e.g. $\sqrt{13}$ can be represented as follows

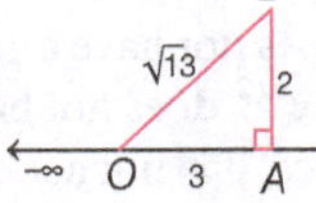

$OA^2 + AB^2 = OB^2$
$OB = \sqrt{13}$

Real Numbers
The collection of all rational and irrational numbers.
e.g. $\frac{1}{2}, \frac{\sqrt{3}}{2}$ etc

Laws of Exponents for Real Numbers

(i) $a^p \times a^q = a^{p+q}$
(ii) $\frac{a^p}{a^q} = a^{p-q}$
(iii) $(a^p)^q = a^{pq}$
(iv) $a^p \times b^p = (ab)^p$
(v) $(a^{-p}) = \frac{1}{a^p}$
(vi) $\left(\frac{a}{b}\right)^{-p} = \left(\frac{b}{a}\right)^p$
(vii) $a^{m/n} = \left(\sqrt[n]{a}\right)^m = \sqrt[n]{a^m}$

Basic Operations on Real Numbers

Radical Sign ($\sqrt{\ }$)
For a real number $a > 0$, we have
$a^{1/n} = \sqrt[n]{a}$
Here, n = Exponent
a = Radicand
$\sqrt{\ }$ = Radical sign

Identities Based Upon Radical Sign
(i) $\sqrt{ab} = \sqrt{a}\sqrt{b}$
(ii) $\sqrt{\frac{a}{b}} = \frac{\sqrt{a}}{\sqrt{b}}$
(iii) $(\sqrt{a} \pm \sqrt{b})^2 = a \pm 2\sqrt{ab} + b$
(iv) $(\sqrt{a} + \sqrt{b})(\sqrt{c} + \sqrt{d}) = \sqrt{ac} + \sqrt{ad} + \sqrt{bc} + \sqrt{bd}$
(v) $(\sqrt{a} + \sqrt{b})(\sqrt{a} - \sqrt{b}) = a - b$
(vi) $(a + \sqrt{b})(a - \sqrt{b}) = a^2 - b$

Let a and b be two real numbers such that a is rational and b is irrational. Then,
(i) $a \pm b$ is irrational.
(ii) Multiplication and division of a and b is irrational.
If both a and b are irrational, then addition, subtraction, multiplication and division of a and b may be rational or irrational.

Rationalising the Denominator
Process of converting the denominator of an expression with radical sign into the equivalent expression with denominator without radical sign.

e.g. $\frac{5}{\sqrt{3}-\sqrt{5}} = \frac{5}{\sqrt{3}-\sqrt{5}} \times \frac{\sqrt{3}+\sqrt{5}}{\sqrt{3}+\sqrt{5}}$
$= \frac{-5}{2}(\sqrt{3}+\sqrt{5})$

Decimal Expansion of Real Numbers

Decimal Expansion of Rational Numbers
Case I If remainder is 0 (terminating) the number is rational.
e.g. $\frac{1}{2} = 0.5$
Case II If remainder is not 0, the decimal expansion is non-terminating repeating, then the number is rational.
e.g. $\frac{1}{3} = 0.999......$

Decimal Expansion of Irrationals
If the decimal expansion is non-terminating and non-repeating. Then, the number is irrational.
e.g. π

Representation of $\sqrt{x}$ Geometrically

To respresent $\sqrt{x}$
1. Draw a line segment of x unit.
2. Extend it by 1 unit.
3. Draw semi-circle over $x + 1$.
4. Draw perpendicular over B intersecting circle at D.
5. $BD = \sqrt{x}$
6. Draw an arc with B as a centre and BD as redius which intersects the number line at E. Then, E represent $\sqrt{x}$

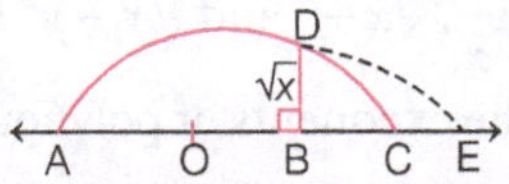

CHAPTER 2

Polynomials

In earlier classes, we have studied algebraic expression and their operations (i.e. addition, subtraction, multiplication and division) and some algebraic identities used in factorisation [i. e. $(x+y)^2 = x^2 + y^2 + 2xy$, $x^2 - y^2 = (x-y)(x+y)$ etc]. But in this chapter, we will study about a particular type of algebraic expression called polynomial and the terminologies related to it.

Here, we also study about zeroes of polynomials, factor theorem and their use in factorisation of a polynomial, alongwith some more algebraic identities.

Let us begin with the general definition of variables and constants.

Variables usually denoted by the letters x, y, z etc., can take various numerical values, i.e. the value of a variable is not fixed. e.g. xy, x^2 etc.

While **constants** generally denoted by the letters a, b, c etc. have a fixed numerical value throughout a particular solution. e.g. -4, 3, π etc. are all constants.

A combination of constants and variables, connected by the four fundamental arithmetical operations $+$, $-$, $\times$ and $\div$, is called an **algebraic expression.**

e.g. $6x^2 - 5y^2 + 2xy$ is an algebraic expression, where x and y are variables and 6, -5, 2 are constants.

An algebraic expression in which the variables involved only non-negative integral power, is called a **polynomial.**

TOPIC 01 Polynomials in One Variable and Their Classifications

An algebraic expressions involving single variable, which have only whole numbers (or non-negative integers) as the exponent of the variable, are called **polynomials in one variable.**

If the variable in a polynomial is x, then we denote the polynomial by $p(x)$ or $q(x)$ or $r(x)$ etc.

A polynomial in one variable x is an algebraic expression of the form

$$p(x) = a_n x^n + a_{n-1}x^{n-1} + a_{n-2}x^{n-2} + \cdots + a_2 x^2 + a_1 x + a_0$$

where, $a_0, a_1, a_2, \ldots, a_n$ are constants and $a_n \neq 0$.

e.g. $p(x) = 3x^3 + 2x^2 - 7x + 5$ is a polynomial in the variable x (one variable).

While $x + \frac{1}{x}$, $\sqrt{x+3}$ and $\sqrt[3]{y} + y^2$ are not polynomials because the exponents of polynomials are not whole number.

Example 1. **Which of the following are polynomials? Justify your answer.**

(i) $x^3 + 3x^2 + 2$ **(ii)** $\sqrt{x^5} + 4x + 2$ **(iii)** $\dfrac{x^4 + x^3 + 3x^2 + 2x}{x^2}$

Sol. (i) Given expression is $x^3 + 3x^2 + 2$.

Here, we see that a variable has all non-negative integer powers. Hence, it is a polynomial.

(ii) Given expression is $\sqrt{x^5} + 4x + 2$ or $x^{5/2} + 4x + 2$.

Here, we see that the variable x does not have a non-negative integer powers, i.e. $x^{5/2}$ does not have a non-negative integer power. Hence, it is not a polynomial.

(iii) Given expression is

$$\frac{x^4 + x^3 + 3x^2 + 2x}{x^2} \text{ or } x^2 + x + 3 + \frac{2}{x}.$$

Here, we see that the variable x does not have all non-negative integer powers. Hence, it is not a polynomial.

Example 2. **Which of the following expressions are polynomials in one or more variable(s)? State reasons for your answer.**

(i) $3x^2 - 5x$ (ii) $5y^2 + 8x$

(iii) $\sqrt{t} + 3y$ (iv) $x^3 + x^2 + \frac{1}{x}$

Sol. (i) Given expression is $3x^2 - 5x$.
Here, expression is in one variable and all powers of the variable are non-negative integers.
Hence, it is a polynomial in one variable.

(ii) Given expression is $5y^2 + 8x$.
Here, expression is in two variables and all powers of variables are non-negative integers.
Hence, it is a polynomial in two variables.

(iii) Given expression is $\sqrt{t} + 3y$ or $t^{1/2} + 3y$ and all powers of variables are not non-negative integers. Hence, it is not a polynomial.

(iv) Given expression is $x^3 + x^2 + \frac{1}{x}$ or $x^3 + x^2 + x^{-1}$.
Here, the expression is in one variable and all powers of the variable are not non-negative integers.
Hence, it is not a polynomial.

Term and Coefficient of a Polynomial

The part of a polynomial separated by '+' or '–' sign is called a **term** of the polynomial. Each term of a polynomial has a **coefficient**, which is the constant associated with that term.

e.g. In polynomial $x^2 - 4x + 7$, the expressions x^2, $4x$ and 7 are called terms of the polynomial and here coefficient of x^2 is 1, coefficient of x is – 4 and coefficient of x^0 i.e. constant term is 7.

Example 3. **Find the coefficient of x^2 in $(3x + x^3)\left(x + \frac{1}{x}\right)$.**

Sol. We have, $(3x + x^3)\left(x + \frac{1}{x}\right)$

$$= 3x \times x + 3x \times \frac{1}{x} + x^3 \times x + x^3 \times \frac{1}{x}$$

$$= 3x^2 + 3 + x^4 + x^2 = x^4 + 4x^2 + 3$$

So, the coefficient of x^2 is 4.

Degree of a Polynomial

Highest power of the variable in a polynomial is known as the degree of that polynomial.

Degree of a Polynomial in One Variable

For a polynomial in one variable, the highest power of the variable is called the degree of a polynomial.

Example 4. **Find the degree of the following polynomials.**

(i) $2x^4 - 6x^3 + 4x + 1$ (ii) $\frac{4}{3} + \frac{3}{5}x - 5x^2 + \frac{1}{2}x^3 + x^5$

(iii) $6x + \sqrt{3}$ (iv) $7x^2 + 2x + 5$

(v) $2z + 5$ (vi) 4

Sol. (i) We have, $2x^4 - 6x^3 + 4x + 1$.
Here, the highest power of x is 4, so its degree is 4.

(ii) We have, $\frac{4}{3} + \frac{3}{5}x - 5x^2 + \frac{1}{2}x^3 + x^5$.
Here, the highest power of x is 5, so its degree is 5.

(iii) We have, $6x + \sqrt{3}$.
Here, the highest power of x is 1, so its degree is 1.

(iv) We have, $7x^2 + 2x + 5$
Here, the highest power of x is 2, so its degree is 2.

(v) We have, $2z + 5$
Here, the highest power of z is 1, so its degree is 1.

(vi) We have, 4 i.e $4x^0$.
Here, the exponent of x is 0, so its degree is 0.

Note It The degree of a non-zero constant polynomial is zero. The degree of a zero polynomial is not defined.

Classifications of Polynomials

On the Basis of Number of Terms

(i) **Monomial** A polynomial containing one non-zero term, is called a monomial ('mono' means 'one').
e.g. $5x$, 7, $3x^3$, $-7x^2$ and u^4 are all monomials.

(ii) **Binomial** A polynomial containing two non-zero terms, is called a binomial ('bi' means 'two').
e.g. $(5 + 7x)$, $(7x^2y + 3y)$, $y^{30} + 1$ and $z^{23} - z^2$ are binomials.

(iii) **Trinomial** A polynomial containing three non-zero terms, is called a trinomial ('tri' means 'three').
e.g. $(8 + 3x + x^2)$, $(7 + 5xy + 6xy^2)$ and $(\sqrt{2} + x - x^2)$ are trinomials.

On the Basis of Degree of Variables

(i) **Constant Polynomial** A polynomial of degree zero, is called constant polynomial.
Or A polynomial containing only one constant term, is called a constant polynomial.
e.g. 3, -7 and $\frac{7}{4}$ are constant polynomials.

(ii) **Linear Polynomial** A polynomial of degree 1, is called a linear polynomial.
e.g. $2x + 5$ is a linear polynomial in x.

Thus, we observe that a linear polynomial in x will have atmost two terms. So, standard form of a linear polynomial in x will be $ax+b$, where a, b are constants and $a \neq 0$.

(iii) **Quadratic Polynomial** A polynomial of degree 2, is called a quadratic polynomial.

e.g. $3x^2 + 7x + 9$ is a quadratic polynomial in x.

Thus, we observe that a quadratic polynomial in x will have atmost 3 terms. So, a quadratic polynomial in x is of the form $ax^2 + bx + c$, where a, b, c are constants and $a \neq 0$.

(iv) **Cubic Polynomial** A polynomial of degree 3, is called a cubic polynomial.

e.g. $6y^3 + 7y^2 - 5y + 1$ is a cubic polynomial in y.

Thus, we observe that a cubic polynomial in y will have atmost 4 terms. So, a cubic polynomial in x is of the form $ax^3 + bx^2 + cx + d$, where a, b, c, d are constants and $a \neq 0$.

(vi) ***n* Degree Polynomial** A polynomial of degree n in x is an expression of the form

$$p(x) = a_n x^n + a_{n-1}x^{n-1} + a_{n-2}x^{n-2} + \dots + a_2x^2 + a_1x + a_0$$

where, $a_n, a_{n-1}, \dots, a_2, a_1, a_0$ are constants and $a_n \neq 0$.

Here, $a_n x^n, a_{n-1}x^{n-1}, a_{n-2}x^{n-2}, \dots, a_2x^2, a_1x, a_0$ are known as the terms of the polynomial $p(x)$ and $a_n, a_{n-1}, a_{n-2}, \dots, a_2, a_1, a_0$ are known as their coefficients.

(vii) **Zero Polynomial** If $a_0 = a_1 = a_2 = \dots = a_n = 0$ (all constants are zero), then we get the zero polynomial, which is denoted by 0.

If $p(x) = 0$, then it is called the zero polynomial. But the degree of zero polynomial is not defined, as $p(x)$ can be written as $p(x) = 0 = 0 \cdot x = 0 \cdot x^2 = 0 \cdot x^3 = \dots$

The constant polynomial 0 is also known as zero polynomial.

Example 5. **Identify the types of polynomials on the basis of terms from the following.**

(i) $4y + 3y^2 + 6$ (ii) $3x + 2$ (iii) $6t$

Sol. (i) We have, $4y + 3y^2 + 6$

Here, number of terms in given polynomial is 3.

Hence, it is a trinomial.

(ii) We have, $3x + 2$

Here, number of terms in given polynomial is 2.

Hence, it is a binomial.

(iii) We have, $6t$

Here, number of terms in given polynomial is 1.

Hence, it is a monomial.

Example 6. **Identify the types of polynomials, on the basis of degree from the following.**

(i) $3x^2 + 5$ (ii) $z^3 + 4z + 1$ (iii) $4t$

Sol. (i) We have, $3x^2 + 5$

Here, degree of polynomial $3x^2 + 5$ is 2.

Hence, it is a quadratic polynomial.

(ii) We have, $z^3 + 4z + 1$

Here, degree of polynomial $z^3 + 4z + 1$ is 3.

Hence, it is a cubic polynomial.

(iii) We have, $4t$

Here, degree of polynomial $4t$ is 1.

Hence, it is a linear polynomial.

Example 7. **Given an example of polynomial, which is (i) monomial of degree 3? (ii) binomial of degree 15? (iii) trinomial of degree 7?**

Sol. (i) $2x^3$ (ii) $x^{15} + 12x$ (iii) $y^7 + y^5 + y^3$

Try These 2.1

1. **Which of the following are polynomials? Justify your answer.** NCERT Exemplar

(i) $\sqrt{2x} - 1$ (ii) $x^2 + \frac{3x^{3/2}}{\sqrt{x}}$ (iii) $\frac{x-1}{x+1}$

(iv) $\frac{(x-2)(x-4)}{x}$ (v) $\frac{1}{5x^{-2}} + 5x + 7$

2. **Which of the following expressions are polynomials in one or more variable(s)? State reasons for your answers.**

(i) $5x^{3/2} + 2y + 1$ (ii) $x^4 + 2y + 1$

(iii) $\frac{x^4 + x^3 + x}{x}$ (iv) $\sqrt{y^3} + y^2 + 3$

3. **Find the coefficient of x^2 in the following polynomials.**

(i) $(x-4)(x-4)$ (ii) $1 - x^2 - x^3 + 2x^7$

(iii) $(x+4)(x+4)(x+4)$ (iv) $(2x-5)(2x^2 - 3x + 1)$

(v) $(3x^2 + 2x - 4)(x^2 - 3x - 2)$ (vi) $(x+3)^3$

4. **Find the degree of the following polynomials.** NCERT Exemplar

(i) $\frac{\sqrt{5}}{9}$ (ii) $1 - x^2 - x^3 + 2x^7$

(iii) $(x-1)(x+1)$ (iv) $4x^4 + 0 \cdot x^3 + 0 \cdot x^5 + 5x + 7$

(v) $2x - 3$

5. **Identify the types of following polynomials on the basis of terms.**

(i) $20y^3 + 3y + 8$ (ii) $4x$ (iii) $x^2 + 5x$

6. **Identify the types of following polynomials on the basis of their degree.**

(i) $\sqrt{5}$ (ii) $2x - 3$

(iii) $2t^3 - 3t^2 + 5t - 4$ (iv) $3y^2 - 4y + 5$

7. If $p=10$, then find the degree of the polynomial $g(x)=(p-x)^3+14$.

8. Give an example of a polynomial, which is
   (i) monomial of degree 1? (ii) binomial of degree 22?
   (iii) trinomial of degree 5?

9. For the polynomial $\frac{x^3+2x+1}{5}-\frac{7}{2}x^2-x^6$, find NCERT Exemplar
   (i) the degree of the polynomial.
   (ii) the coefficient of x^3.
   (iii) the coefficient of x^6.
   (iv) the constant term.

Hints & Answers

1. **Hint** Solve as Example 1.
   Ans. (i) No (ii) Yes (iii) No (iv) No (v) Yes
2. **Hint** Solve as Example 2. **Ans.** (i) No (ii) Yes (iii) Yes (iv) No
3. **Hint** Solve as Example 3.
   Ans. (i) 1 (ii) −1 (iii) 12 (iv) −16 (v) −16 (vi) 9
4. **Hint** Solve as Example 4. **Ans.** (i) 0 (ii) 7 (iii) 2 (iv) 4 (v) 1
5. **Hint** Solve as Example 5.
   Ans. (i) Trinomial (ii) Monomial (iii) Binomial
6. **Hint** Solve as Example 6.
   Ans. (i) Constant (ii) Linear (iii) Cubic (iv) Quadratic
7. **Hint** $g(x)=(10-x)^3+14=10^3-300x+30x^2-x^3+14$
   $=-x^3+30x^2-300x+1014$ **Ans.** 3
8. **Hint** Solve as Example 7.
   (i) $4t$ (ii) $5x^{22}+3$ (iii) $2x^5+6x+7$
9. (i) 6 (ii) $\frac{1}{5}$ (iii) −1 (iv) $\frac{1}{5}$

TOPIC 02 Zeroes of a Polynomial

Value of a Polynomial

The value of a polynomial obtained on putting a particular value of the variable is called the value of a polynomial. The value of a polynomial $p(x)$ at $x=a$ (say) is denoted by $p(a)$.

Example 1. **Find the value of each of the following polynomials at the indicated value of variables.**
(i) $p(x)=5x^3-2x^2+3x-2$ at $x=1$.
(ii) $q(y)=3y^3-4y+\sqrt{11}$ at $y=2$.
(iii) $p(t)=4t^4+5t^3-t^2+6$ at $t=a$.

Sol. (i) We have, $p(x)=5x^3-2x^2+3x-2$

On putting $x=1$ in $p(x)$, we get

$$p(1)=5(1)^3-2(1)^2+3(1)-2$$
$$=5-2+3-2=8-4=4$$

which is the required value of $p(x)$ at $x=1$.

(ii) We have, $q(y)=3y^3-4y+\sqrt{11}$

On putting $y=2$ in $q(y)$, we get

$$q(2)=3(2)^3-4(2)+\sqrt{11}=3\times 8-8+\sqrt{11}$$
$$=24-8+\sqrt{11}=16+\sqrt{11}$$

which is the required value of $q(y)$ at $y=2$.

(iii) We have, $p(t)=4t^4+5t^3-t^2+6$

On putting $t=a$ in $p(t)$, we get

$$p(a)=4(a)^4+5(a)^3-(a)^2+6=4a^4+5a^3-a^2+6$$

which is the required value of $p(t)$ at $t=a$.

Zero of a Polynomial

Zero of a polynomial $p(x)$ is a number α, such that $p(\alpha)=0$. Zero of a polynomial is also called the **root** of polynomial equation $p(x)=0$.

Example 2. **Find the zero of a polynomial**
(i) $5x+7$ **(ii) $2x+4$**

Sol. (i) Let $p(x)=5x+7$

On putting $p(x)=0$, we get

$$5x+7=0$$
$$\Rightarrow \quad 5x=-7$$
$$\Rightarrow \quad x=\frac{-7}{5}$$

Hence, $x=\frac{-7}{5}$ is the zero of the polynomial $5x+7$.

(ii) Let $p(x)=2x+4$ ...(i)

On putting $p(x)=0$, we get

$$2x+4=0$$
$$\Rightarrow \quad 2x=-4 \Rightarrow x=-\frac{4}{2}=-2$$

Hence, $x=-2$ is the zero of the polynomial $2x+4$.

Method to Check Whether the Given Value is a Zero of a Polynomial or Not

If a polynomial in one variable (say x) is given to us and a value of variable at $x=c$ (say) is also given, then to check that given value of x is a zero of given polynomial or not, we use the following steps

Step I Firstly, consider the given polynomial say $p(x)$.

Step II Put $x=c$ in given polynomial $p(x)$ and find the value of $p(c)$.

Step III If $p(c)=0$, then $x=c$ will be a zero of given polynomial and if $p(c)\neq 0$, then $x=c$ will not be a zero of given polynomial.

Example 3. **Verify that whether –2 and –3 are zeroes of the polynomial x^2+5x+6.**

Sol. Let $p(x)=x^2+5x+6$ ...(i)

On putting $x=-2$ in Eq. (i), we get

$$p(-2)=(-2)^2+5(-2)+6=4-10+6=0$$

Again, on putting $x=-3$ in Eq (i), we get

$$p(-3)=(-3)^2+5(-3)+6=9-15+6=0$$

Here, $p(-2)=0$ and $p(-3)=0$

So, $x=-2$ and $x=-3$ are zeroes of the given polynomial.

Example 4. **If $x=3$ is a zero of the polynomial $2x^2+kx-12$, find the value of k.**

Sol. Let $p(x)=2x^2+kx-12$

Since, $x=3$ is a zero of the polynomial.

$\therefore$ $p(3)=0$

$\Rightarrow 2(3)^2+k(3)-12=0$

$\Rightarrow$ $18+3k-12=0 \Rightarrow 3k+6=0 \Rightarrow k=-2$

Hence, the value of k is – 2.

Example 5. **If $x=3$ and $x=0$ are zeroes of the polynomial $2x^3-8x^2+ax+b$, then find the values of a and b.**

Sol. Let $p(x)=2x^3-8x^2+ax+b$

Since, $x=3$ is a zero of the polynomial.

$\therefore$ $p(3)=0$

$\Rightarrow$ $2(3)^3-8(3)^2+a\times 3+b=0$

$\Rightarrow$ $2\times 27-8\times 9+3a+b=0$

$\Rightarrow$ $54-72+3a+b=0$

$\Rightarrow$ $-18+3a+b=0$

$\Rightarrow$ $3a+b=18$ ...(i)

Also, $x=0$ is a zero of the polynomial.

$\therefore$ $p(0)=0$

$\Rightarrow$ $2(0)^3-8(0)^2+a\times 0+b=0$

$\Rightarrow$ $0-0+0+b=0 \Rightarrow b=0$ ... (ii)

On putting $b=0$ in Eq. (i), we get

$3a+0=18 \Rightarrow 3a=18$

$\therefore$ $a=\dfrac{18}{3}=6$

Hence, $a=6$ and $b=0$.

Important Points on Zeroes of a Polynomial

(i) Zero may be a zero of a polynomial.

(ii) Every linear polynomial has one and only one zero.

(iii) A non-zero constant polynomial has no zero.

(iv) Every real number is a zero of the zero polynomial.

(v) The number of zeroes of a zero polynomial is infinite.

(vi) Maximum number of zeroes of a polynomial is equal to its degree.

Try These 2.2

1. If $p(x)=x^2-2\sqrt{2}x+1$, find the value of $p(2\sqrt{2})$. NCERT Exemplar

2. Evaluate the following value.
   (i) If $f(x)=x-9$, find $f(2)-f(-2)$.
   (ii) If $p(x)=4x^5-3x^4-5x^3+x^2-8$, then find $p(1)$.
   (iii) If $q(x)=x^3+3x^2+3x+1$, then find $q(-2)+q(-3)+q\left(\dfrac{1}{2}\right)$.

3. If $f(t)=4t^2-3t+6$, find
   (i) $f(4)$ (ii) $f(-5)$.

4. What is the zero of the polynomial $p(x)=a^2x$, $a\neq 0$?

5. Find the zero of the following polynomials.
   (i) $p(x)=6-4x$ (ii) $p(t)=2t-\dfrac{5}{2}$
   (iii) $q(y)=2y-\dfrac{1}{2}$ (iv) $r(z)=\dfrac{z}{3}-5$

6. Verify whether the following are zeroes of the polynomial indicated against them.
   (i) $p(y)=2y^2+5y-3$ at $y=\dfrac{1}{2}$.
   (ii) $p(z)=z^2+z-6$ at $z=-3$.
   (iii) $p(x)=4x^3-3x$ at $x=1$.
   (iv) $p(t)=2x^3-9x^2+x+12$ at $x=\dfrac{3}{2}$.
   (v) $p(x)=2x^3-13x^2+17x+12$ at $x=2,3$.
   (vi) $p(x)=2x^3-3x^2+7x+6$ at $x=1,\dfrac{1}{2}$.

7. If $x=2$ and $x=1$ are zeroes of the polynomial $2x^3-5x^2+ax+b$, find the values of a and b.

Hints & Answers

1. **Hint** Solve as Example 1 (ii). **Ans.** 1
2. (i) **Hint** $f(2)-f(-2)=(2-9)-(-2-9)=4$
   (ii) **Hint** $p(1)=4(1)^5-3(1)^4-5(1)^3+(1)^2-8=-11$
   (iii) **Hint** $q(-2)+q(-3)+q\left(\dfrac{1}{2}\right)$
   $=[(-2)^3+3(-2)^2+3(-2)+1]+[(-3)^3+3(-3)^2+3(-3)+1]+\left[\left(\dfrac{1}{2}\right)^3+3\left(\dfrac{1}{2}\right)^2+3\left(\dfrac{1}{2}\right)+1\right]=-\dfrac{45}{8}$
3. **Hint** Solve as Example 1. **Ans.** (i) 58 (ii) 121
4. **Hint** $P(x)=0$
   $\Rightarrow$ $a^2x=0 \Rightarrow x=0$
5. **Hint** Solve as Example 2. **Ans.** (i) $\dfrac{3}{2}$ (ii) $\dfrac{5}{4}$ (iii) $\dfrac{1}{4}$ (iv) 15
6. **Hint** Solve as Example 3.
   Ans. (i) No (ii) Yes (iii) No (iv) Yes (v) No, Yes (vi) No, No
7. **Hint** Solve as Example 5. **Ans.** $a=1, b=2$

TOPIC 03 Remainder Theorem

To understand the remainder theorem clearly, firstly we should know about factors and multiples, long division algorithm.

Factors and Multiples

If x divides y exactly (without leaving any remainder), then x is a **factor** of y and y is a **multiple** of x.

e.g. 2, 3 and 4 divide 12 exactly, so 2, 3 and 4 are factors of 12 and 12 is a multiple of 2, 3 and 4.

Suppose we divide $(2x^3+x^2+x)$ by x, we get

$$\frac{(2x^3+x^2+x)}{x}=\frac{2x^3}{x}+\frac{x^2}{x}+\frac{x}{x}=(2x^2+x+1)$$

$$\Rightarrow \quad (2x^3+x^2+x)=x(2x^2+x+1)$$

Here, remainder is zero, so x divides $(2x^3+x^2+x)$ exactly. Thus, x is a factor of $(2x^3+x^2+x)$ and $(2x^3+x^2+x)$ is a multiple of x. So, $(2x^2+x+1)$ is also a factor of $(2x^3+x^2+x)$. Hence, x and $2x^2+x+1$ are factors of $2x^3+x^2+x$ and $2x^3+x^2+x$ is a multiple of x as well as $2x^2+x+1$.

Long Division Algorithm

If $p(x)$ and $g(x)$ be any two polynomials, such that degree of $p(x) \geq$ degree of $g(x)$ and $g(x) \neq 0$, then we can find polynomials $q(x)$ and $r(x)$, such that $p(x)=g(x)q(x)+r(x)$

i.e. **Dividend = (Divisor × Quotient) + Remainder**

where, $r(x)=0$ or degree of $r(x)<$ degree of $g(x)$.

Here, we can say that when $p(x)$ divided by $g(x)$ gives $q(x)$ as quotient and $r(x)$ as remainder.

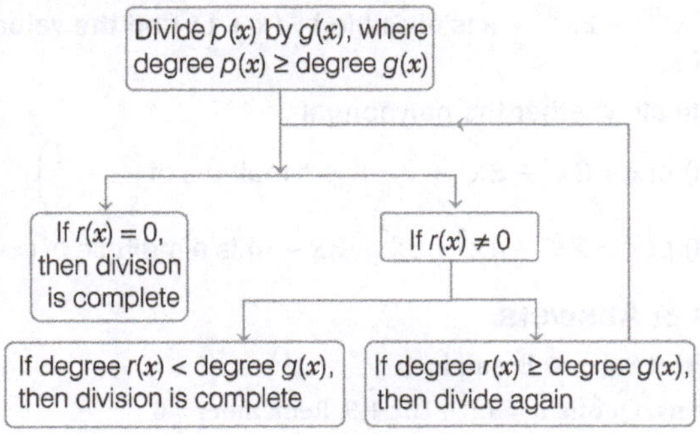

Example 1. **By actual division, find the quotient and the remainder when x^4+1 is divided by $x-1$.**

Sol. Using long division method,

$$\begin{array}{r|l} & x^3+x^2+x+1 \\ \hline x-1 & x^4+1 \\ & x^4-x^3 \\ & \underline{-\quad +} \\ & x^3+1 \\ & x^3-x^2 \\ & \underline{-\quad +} \\ & x^2+1 \\ & x^2-x \\ & \underline{-\quad +} \\ & x+1 \\ & x-1 \\ & \underline{-\quad +} \\ & 2 \end{array}$$

Hence, quotient $=x^3+x^2+x+1$ and remainder $=2$.

Example 2. **Show by long division that $(x-3)$ is a factor of $2x^4+3x^3-26x^2-5x+6$.**

Sol. We have to show that remainder is zero, while divide $2x^4+3x^3-26x^2-5x+6$ by $(x-3)$.

$$\begin{array}{r|l} & 2x^3+9x^2+x-2 \\ \hline x-3 & 2x^4+3x^3-26x^2-5x+6 \\ & 2x^4-6x^3 \\ & \underline{-\quad +} \\ & 9x^3-26x^2 \\ & 9x^3-27x^2 \\ & \underline{-\quad +} \\ & x^2-5x \\ & x^2-3x \\ & \underline{-\quad +} \\ & -2x+6 \\ & -2x+6 \\ & \underline{+\quad -} \\ & 0 \end{array}$$

Hence, $(x-3)$ is a factor of $2x^4+3x^3-26x^2-5x+6$.

Remainder Theorem

Let $p(x)$ be a polynomial of degree n greater than or equal to 1 (i.e. $n \geq 1$) and a be any real number. If $p(x)$ is divided by the linear polynomial $(x-a)$, then the remainder is $p(a)$.

Proof Let $p(x)$ be any polynomial with degree $n \geq 1$.

Suppose that when $p(x)$ is divided by $(x-a)$, the quotient and remainder are respectively $q(x)$ and $r(x)$.

Then, Dividend = (Divisor × Quotient) + Remainder

i.e. $p(x) = [(x-a) \times q(x)] + r(x)$ ...(i)

Since, degree of $r(x) <$ degree of $(x-a)$.

$\therefore$ Degree of $r(x) < 1$ [$\because$ degree of $(x-a) = 1$]

i.e. Degree of $r(x) = 0$

Here, $r(x)$ is a constant, equal to r (say).

For every value of x, $r(x) = r$.

On putting $r(x) = r$ in Eq. (i), we get

$$p(x) = (x-a) \times q(x) + r$$

In particular, if $x = a$, then from above equation,

$$p(a) = (a-a) \times q(a) + r$$

$\Rightarrow$ $p(a) = 0 \times q(a) + r \Rightarrow p(a) = r$

Thus, the remainder is $p(a)$.

In other words, we can say that the value of the polynomial $p(x)$ at the zero of the polynomial $(x-a)$ i.e. a gives the remainder obtained on dividing $p(x)$ by $(x-a)$.

Hence proved.

Example 3. **Using remainder theorem, find the remainder when $x^4 - 3x^3 + 2x^2 + x - 1$ is divided by $(x-2)$.**

Sol. Let $p(x) = x^4 - 3x^3 + 2x^2 + x - 1$ ...(i)

and $g(x) = x - 2$

Then, $p(x)$ is divided by $g(x)$.

For finding the zero of $g(x)$, put $g(x) = 0$

$\therefore$ $x - 2 = 0 \Rightarrow x = 2$

So, it is the zero of $g(x)$.

On putting $x = 2$ in Eq. (i), we get

$$p(2) = (2)^4 - 3(2)^3 + 2(2)^2 + 2 - 1$$
$$= 16 - 24 + 8 + 1 = 1$$

Hence, the value of $p(2)$ is 1, which is the required remainder obtained on dividing $x^4 - 3x^3 + 2x^2 + x - 1$ by $(x-2)$.

Example 4. **Find k, if $x^{51} + 2x^{60} + 3x + k$ is divisible by $x+1$.**

Sol. Let $p(x) = x^{51} + 2x^{60} + 3x + k$ ...(i)

and $g(x) = x + 1$

Then, $p(x)$ is divided by $g(x)$.

For finding the zero of $g(x)$, put $g(x) = 0$.

$\therefore$ $x + 1 = 0 \Rightarrow x = -1$

So, it is a zero of $g(x)$.

On putting $x = -1$ in Eq. (i), we get

$$p(-1) = 0$$

$\Rightarrow (-1)^{51} + 2(-1)^{60} + 3(-1) + k = 0$

$\Rightarrow$ $-1 + 2 - 3 + k = 0$

$\Rightarrow$ $k - 4 + 2 = 0$

$\Rightarrow$ $k - 2 = 0 \Rightarrow k = 2$

Example 5. **Check whether the polynomial $q(t) = 4t^3 + 4t^2 - t - 1$ is a multiple of $2t+1$ or not.**

Sol. Given polynomial is $q(t) = 4t^3 + 4t^2 - t - 1$ ...(i)

Let $g(t) = 2t + 1$

For finding the zero of $g(t)$, put $g(t) = 0$.

$\therefore$ $2t + 1 = 0$

$\Rightarrow$ $t = -1/2$

On putting $t = -\frac{1}{2}$ in Eq. (i), we get

$$q\left(\frac{-1}{2}\right) = 4\left(\frac{-1}{2}\right)^3 + 4\left(\frac{-1}{2}\right)^2 - \left(\frac{-1}{2}\right) - 1$$
$$= 4\left(\frac{-1}{8}\right) + 4\left(\frac{1}{4}\right) + \frac{1}{2} - 1$$
$$= -\frac{1}{2} + 1 + \frac{1}{2} - 1 = 0$$

Hence, $(2t+1)$ is a factor of $q(t)$ i.e. $q(t)$ is a multiple of $(2t+1)$.

Try These 2.3

1. **Find the quotient and the remainder if the polynomial $4x^3 + 20x^2 + 33x + 18$ is divided by $x + 2$.**
2. **Find the remainder,**
   (i) when $p(x) = 4x^3 - 12x^2 + 11x - 5$ is divided by $g(x) = 2x - 1$.
   (ii) when $x^{51} + 51$ is divided by $x + 1$.
   (iii) when $p(x) = x^3 - ax^2 + x$ is divided by $(x - a)$.
3. **If $x^{100} + 2x^{99} + k$ is divisible by $(x+1)$, find the value of k.**
4. **Check whether the polynomial**
   (i) $p(x) = 9x^3 - 3x^2 + x - 5$ is a multiple of $\left(x - \frac{2}{3}\right)$.
   (ii) $p(x) = 2x^4 - 4x^3 + 5x^2 - 3x - 14$ is a multiple of $(x+1)$.

Hints & Answers

1. **Hint** Solve as Example. 1.
   Ans. Quotient $= 4x^2 + 12x + 9$, Remainder $= 0$
2. **Hint** Solve as Example 3. **Ans.** (i) −2 (ii) 50 (iii) a
3. **Hint** Solve as Example 4. **Ans.** $k=1$
4. **Hint** Solve as Example. 5. **Ans.** (i) No (ii) Yes

TOPIC 04 Factorisation of the Polynomials

Factor Theorem

Let $p(x)$ be a polynomial of degree $n \geq 1$ and a be any real number.

(i) If $p(a) = 0$, then $(x - a)$ is a factor of $p(x)$.

(ii) If $(x - a)$ is a factor of $p(x)$, then $p(a) = 0$.

Example 1. **Examine whether $x - 2$ is a factor of $x^3 - 3x^2 + 5x - 6$ and $2x - 4$.**

Sol. The zero of $x - 2$ is 2.

Let $p(x) = x^3 - 3x^2 + 5x - 6$ and $S(x) = 2x - 4$

Then, $p(2) = (2)^3 - 3 \times (2)^2 + 5 \times (2) - 6$

$= 8 - 12 + 10 - 6 = 0$

So, by factor theorem, $x - 2$ is a factor of $x^3 - 3x^2 + 5x - 6$.

Again, $S(2) = 2 \times 2 - 4 = 0$

So, $x - 2$ is a factor of $2x - 4$.

Example 2. **Use the factor theorem to determine, whether $g(x) = x - 3$ is a factor of $p(x) = x^3 - 3x^2 + 6$.**

Sol. If $x - 3$ is a factor of $p(x)$, then

$$x - 3 = 0 \Rightarrow x = 3$$

$\therefore \quad p(3) = 3^3 - 3(3)^2 + 6 = 27 - 27 + 6 = 6 \neq 0$

Hence, $x - 3$ is not a factor of $x^3 - 3x^2 + 6$.

Example 3. **If $(x - a)$ is a factor of $4x^2 - mx - na$, prove that $a = \dfrac{m+n}{4}$.**

Sol. Let $p(x) = 4x^2 - mx - na$.

If $(x - a)$ is a factor of $p(x)$, then $p(a) = 0$.

$\therefore \quad 4a^2 - ma - na = 0$

$\Rightarrow \quad a(4a - m - n) = 0$

$\Rightarrow \quad 4a - m - n = 0 \qquad [\because a \neq 0]$

$\Rightarrow \quad 4a - (m + n) = 0$

$\Rightarrow \quad 4a = m + n$

$\therefore \quad a = \dfrac{m+n}{4}$ **Hence proved.**

Example 4. **Find the value of p, if $(2x - 1)$ is a factor of $2x^3 + px^2 + 11x + p + 3$.**

Sol. Let $q(x) = 2x^3 + px^2 + 11x + p + 3 \qquad \ldots(i)$

If $(2x - 1)$ is a factor of $q(x)$, then

$$2x - 1 = 0 \Rightarrow x = \frac{1}{2}$$

Since, $(2x - 1)$ is a factor of $q(x)$.

$\therefore q\left(\dfrac{1}{2}\right) = 0$

On putting $x = \dfrac{1}{2}$ in Eq. (i), we get

$$q\left(\frac{1}{2}\right) = 2 \times \left(\frac{1}{2}\right)^3 + p\left(\frac{1}{2}\right)^2 + 11 \times \frac{1}{2} + p + 3 = 0$$

$\Rightarrow \quad 2 \times \dfrac{1}{8} + p \times \dfrac{1}{4} + \dfrac{11}{2} + p + 3 = 0$

$\Rightarrow \quad \dfrac{1}{4} + \dfrac{p}{4} + \dfrac{11}{2} + p + 3 = 0$

$\Rightarrow \quad \dfrac{1 + p + 22 + 4p + 12}{4} = 0$

$\Rightarrow \quad 5p + 35 = 0$

$\Rightarrow \quad 5p = -35 \Rightarrow p = -7$

Thus, the given polynomial is divisible by $2x - 1$, if $p = -7$.

Example 5. **Find m and n, if $(x + 2)$ and $(x + 1)$ are the factors of $x^3 + 3x^2 - 2mx + n$.**

Sol. Let $f(x) = x^3 + 3x^2 - 2mx + n$

Since, $(x + 2)$ and $(x + 1)$ are the factors of $f(x)$.

$\therefore \quad f(-2) = 0$ and $f(-1) = 0$

$\Rightarrow (-2)^3 + 3(-2)^2 - 2m(-2) + n = 0$

and $(-1)^3 + 3(-1)^2 - 2m(-1) + n = 0$

$\Rightarrow \quad -8 + 12 + 4m + n = 0$

and $\quad -1 + 3 + 2m + n = 0$

$\Rightarrow \quad 4m + n = -4 \qquad \ldots(i)$

and $\quad 2m + n = -2 \qquad \ldots(ii)$

On multiplying Eq. (ii) by 2 and then subtracting Eq. (i) from Eq. (ii), we get

$$4m + 2n - (4m + n) = -4 - (-4)$$

$\Rightarrow \quad n = 0$

On putting $n = 0$ in Eq. (i), we get

$$4m + 0 = -4 \Rightarrow m = -1$$

Hence, $m = -1$ and $n = 0$.

Example 6. **Using factor theorem, show that $(x + 1)$ is a factor of $x^{19} + x^{18} + x^{17} + 1$.**

Sol. Let $p(x) = x^{19} + x^{18} + x^{17} + 1 \qquad \ldots(i)$

and $q(x) = x + 1$

On putting $q(x) = 0$, we get

$$x + 1 = 0 \Rightarrow x = -1$$

On putting $x = -1$ in Eq. (i), we get

$$p(-1) = (-1)^{19} + (-1)^{18} + (-1)^{17} + 1$$

$$= -1 + 1 + (-1) + 1 = 0$$

Hence, by factor theorem, $(x + 1)$ is a factor of $x^{19} + x^{18} + x^{17} + 1$.

Factorisation of a Quadratic Polynomial

Quadratic polynomial of the type ax^2+bx+c, where a, b, c are constants and $a \neq 0$, can be factorised by different methods like splitting the middle term and by factor theorem, both of these are discussed below.

1. By Splitting the Middle Term

Let factors of the quadratic polynomial ax^2+bx+c be $(px+q)$ and $(rx+s)$.

Then, $ax^2+bx+c=(px+q)(rx+s)$

$$=prx^2+(ps+qr)x+qs$$

On comparing the coefficients of x^2, x and constant terms from both sides, we get

$$a=pr, b=ps+qr \text{ and } c=qs$$

Here, b is the sum of two numbers ps and qr, whose product is $(ps)(qr)=(pr)(qs)=ac$.

Thus, to factorise ax^2+bx+c, write b as the sum of two numbers, whose product is ac.

Note it To factorise ax^2+bx-c and ax^2-bx-c, write b as the sum of two numbers whose product is $(-ac)$.

Example 7. Factorising $2x^2-5x+3$ by splitting the middle term.

Sol. Given polynomial is $2x^2-5x+3$.

On comparing with ax^2+bx+c, we get

$a=2, b=-5$ and $c=3$

Now, $ac=2\times 3=6$

So, all pairs of factors of 6 are 1 and 6, 2 and 3.

Clearly, 2 and 3 gives $-2-3=-5=b$

$$\therefore \ 2x^2-5x+3=2x^2-2x-3x+3$$
$$=2x(x-1)-3(x-1)$$
$$=(2x-3)(x-1)$$

2. By Factor Theorem

Write the given polynomial $p(x)=ax^2+bx+c$ in the form

$$p(x)=a\left(x^2+\frac{b}{a}x+\frac{c}{a}\right)=a\,g(x) \qquad \text{...(i)}$$

where, $g(x)=x^2+\frac{b}{a}x+\frac{c}{a}$

i.e. firstly make the coefficient of x^2 equal to one if it is not one.

Find all the possible factors of constant term $\left(\frac{c}{a}\right)$ of $g(x)$.

Using trial method, find the factors at which $g(x)=0$ say, $x=\alpha$ and $x=\beta$. Further, write $g(x)$ as the product of factors, then $g(x)=(x-\alpha)(x-\beta)$ and put this value of $g(x)$ in Eq. (i) to get required factors of $p(x)$.

Example 8. Factorise x^2-5x+6 by factor theorem.

Sol. Let given polynomial be $f(x)=x^2-5x+6$.

Here, coefficient of x^2 is 1, so we do not need to write it in the form $a\,g(x)$.

Now, constant term is 6 and all factors of 6 are $\pm 1, \pm 2, \pm 3$ and ± 6.

At $x=2$, $f(2)=2^2-5\times 2+6$

$$=4-10+6=10-10=0$$

At $x=3$, $f(3)=3^2-5\times 3+6=9-15+6=15-15=0$

Hence, $(x-2)$ and $(x-3)$ are the factors of given quadratic polynomial.

$\therefore x^2-5x+6=(x-2)(x-3)$

Factorisation of a Cubic Polynomial

To factorise a cubic polynomial, we use the following steps:

Step I Write the given cubic polynomial $p(x)=ax^3+bx^2+cx+d$ in the form

$$p(x)=a\left(x^3+\frac{b}{a}x^2+\frac{c}{a}x+\frac{d}{a}\right)=ag(x) \qquad \text{...(i)}$$

where, $g(x)=x^3+\frac{b}{a}x^2+\frac{c}{a}x+\frac{d}{a}$

i.e. first make the coefficient of x^3 equal to one if it is not one and then find the constant term.

Step II Find all the possible factors of constant term $\left(\frac{d}{a}\right)$ of $g(x)$.

Step III Check at which factor of constant term, $p(x)$ is zero by using trial method and get one factor of $p(x)$, (i.e. $x-\alpha$).

Step IV Write $p(x)$ as the product of this factor and a quadratic polynomial,

i.e. $p(x)=(x-\alpha)(a_1x^2+b_1x+c_1)$

Step V Apply splitting the middle term method or factor theorem in quadratic polynomial to get another two factors. Thus, we get all the three factors of given cubic polynomial.

Example 9. Using factor theorem, factorise $x^3-6x^2+3x+10$.

Sol. Let $p(x)=x^3-6x^2+3x+10$

Here, constant term = 10 and coefficient of x^3 is one.

All possible factors of 10 are $\pm 1, \pm 2, \pm 5$ and ± 10.

At $x=-1$, $p(-1)=(-1)^3-6(-1)^2+3(-1)+10$

$$=-1-6-3+10=0$$

So, $(x+1)$ is a factor of $p(x)$.

On dividing $p(x)$ by $(x+1)$, we get

Quotient $=x^2-7x+10$

So, $p(x) = (x+1)(x^2 - 7x + 10)$

By splitting the middle term, we get

$$p(x) = (x+1)\{x^2 - (5+2)(x) + 10\}$$

$[\because 2 + 5 = 7 \text{ and } 2 \times 5 = 10]$

$$= (x+1)\{x^2 - 5x - 2x + 10\}$$

$$= (x+1)\{x(x-5) - 2(x-5)\} = (x+1)(x-2)(x-5)$$

Example 10. **Factorise $2x^3 - 5x^2 - 19x + 42$.**

Sol. Let $p(x) = 2x^3 - 5x^2 - 19x + 42$

Here, we see that coefficient of x^3 is not one, so firstly we make the coefficient of x^3 is one.

i.e. $p(x) = 2\left(x^3 - \frac{5}{2}x^2 - \frac{19}{2}x + \frac{42}{2}\right) = 2g(x)$ ...(i)

where, $g(x) = x^3 - \frac{5}{2}x^2 - \frac{19}{2}x + 21$

Here, constant term is 21 and its all factors are

$\pm 1, \pm 3, \pm 7, \pm 21.$

At $x = 1$, $g(1) = (1)^3 - \frac{5}{2}(1)^2 - \frac{19}{2}(1) + 21$

$$= 1 - \frac{5}{2} - \frac{19}{2} + 21$$

$$= -12 + 22 = 10 \neq 0$$

So, $(x-1)$ is not a factor of $g(x)$.

At $x = -3$, $g(-3) = (-3)^3 - \frac{5}{2}(-3)^2 - \frac{19}{2}(-3) + 21$

$$= -27 - \frac{5}{2} \times 9 + \frac{57}{2} + 21 = 0$$

So, $(x+3)$ is a factor of $g(x)$.

On dividing $g(x)$ by $(x+3)$, we get

Quotient $= \left(x^2 - \frac{11}{2}x + 7\right)$

$\therefore \quad g(x) = (x+3)\left(x^2 - \frac{11}{2}x + 7\right)$

From Eq. (i), $p(x) = 2(x+3)\left(\frac{2x^2 - 11x + 14}{2}\right)$

$$= (x+3)(2x^2 - 11x + 14)$$

$$= (x+3)(2x^2 - 4x - 7x + 14)$$

$$= (x+3)[2x(x-2) - 7(x-2)]$$

$$= (x+3)(x-2)(2x-7)$$

Example 11. **If $p(x) = x^3 - 4x^2 + x + 6$, then show that $p(3) = 0$ and hence factorise $p(x)$.**

Sol. Given, $p(x) = x^3 - 4x^2 + x + 6$ ...(i)

On putting $x = 3$ in Eq. (i), we get

$$p(3) = (3)^3 - 4(3)^2 + 3 + 6$$

$$= 27 - 36 + 9 = 0$$

Since, $p(3) = 0$, therefore $x - 3$ is a factor of $p(x)$.

On dividing $p(x)$ by $(x-3)$, we get

Quotient $= (x^2 - x - 2)$

$\therefore \quad p(x) = (x-3)(x^2 - x - 2) = (x-3)(x^2 - 2x + x - 2)$

$[\because -2 + 1 = -1 \text{ and } -2 \times 1 = -2]$

$$= (x-3)[x(x-2) + 1(x-2)]$$

$$= (x-3)(x+1)(x-2)$$ **Hence proved.**

Try These 2.4

1. **If $x^2 + px - 30 = (x - 15)(x + 2)$, $\forall$ x, find the value of p.**
2. **If both $x - 2$ and $x - \frac{1}{2}$ are factors of $px^2 + 5x + r$, show that $p = r$.**
3. (i) Using factor theorem, show that $(x-2)$ is a factor of the polynomial $2x^3 - 3x^2 - 17x + 30$.
   (ii) Show that $(x-1)$ is a factor of $4x^3 + 3x^2 - 4x - 3$ by using factor theorem.
4. **Determine whether $(x-1)$ is a factor of the polynomial $3x^4 + 4x^3 - 10x^2 - 5x - 28$.**
5. **Check whether $(-2x - 5)$ is a factor of the polynomial $p(x) = 3x^4 + 5x^3 - 2x^2 - 4$ or not.**
6. **If $(x^2 - 1)$ is a factor of $ax^3 + bx^2 + cx + d$, then show that $a + c = 0$.**
7. (i) Find the value of k, if $x - 3$ is a factor of $k^2x^3 - x^2 + 3x - 1$.
   (ii) If $(x+2)$ is a factor of $x^3 + 6x^2 + 4x + k$, then find the value of k.
8. **Find the value of k, if $(x - 2)$ is a factor of $8x^3 + 4x^2 - 3x + k$.**
9. **If $x^3 - 5x^2 - px + 24 = (x - 4) \cdot q(x)$, then what is the value of p?**
10. **If $(ax^3 + bx^2 + x - 6)$ has $(x+2)$ as a factor and leaves remainder 4, when divided by $(x-2)$, then find the values of a and b.**
11. **Show that $x + 5$ is a factor of the polynomial $f(x) = x^3 + x^2 + 3x + 115$.**
12. **Factorise the following by using splitting the middle terms.**
    (i) $x^2 + 2x - 3$ (ii) $3x^2 + 7x - 6$
    (iii) $2\sqrt{5}x^2 + 3\sqrt{5}x - 5\sqrt{5}$
13. **Factorise the following.**
    (i) $ab(x^2 + 1) + x(a^2 + b^2)$ (ii) $x^2 - (a + b)x + ab$
    (iii) $\sqrt{2}\,x^2 + 3x + \sqrt{2}$ (iv) $x^2 - 24x - 180$
    (v) $5\sqrt{5}\,x^2 + 20x + 3\sqrt{5}$ (vi) $x^2 + x - 6$
    (vii) $3x^2 - x - 4$ (viii) $x^2 - 4x + 4$
14. **Factorise the following using factor theorem.**
    (i) $x^2 + 5x - 66$ (ii) $3x^2 - 11x - 4$
    (iii) $x^2 + \frac{12}{35}x + \frac{1}{35}$
15. **Factorise the following**
    (i) $x^3 + 13x^2 + 32x + 20$ (ii) $3u^3 - 4u^2 - 12u + 16$
    (iii) $x^3 + 2x^2 - 5x - 6$

Hints & Answers

1. **Hint** $x^2 + px - 30 = x^2 - 13x - 30 = 0 \Rightarrow px = -13x$

   Ans. $p = -13$

2. **Hint** For $x = 2, 4p + r = -10$ ...(i)

   For $x = \frac{1}{2}, p + 4r = -10$ ...(ii)

   On solving above equations, we get

   $p = r$

3. **Hint** Solve as Example 2.
4. **Hint** Solve as Example 2. **Ans.** No
5. **Hint** Solve as Example 2. **Ans.** Not
6. **Hint** Solve as Example 3.
7. **Hint** Solve as Example 4. **Ans.** (i) $\left[k = \pm\frac{1}{3\sqrt{3}}\right]$ (ii) -8
8. **Hint** Solve as Example 4. **Ans.** $k = -74$
9. **Hint** $r(x) = 0$, where $r(x) = x^3 - 5x^2 - px + 24$

   Since, $(x-4)$ is a factor of $r(x)$.

   Put $x = 4$ in equation $r(x) = 0$ **Ans.** $p = 2$

10. **Hint** Let $p(x) = ax^3 + bx^2 + x - 6$. Put $p(-2) = 0$ and $p(2) = 4$.

    Ans. $a = 0,\ b = 2$

11. **Hint** Solve as Example 6.
12. **Hint** Solve as Example 7.

    Ans. (i) $(x+3)(x-1)$

    (ii) $(x+3)(3x-2)$

    (iii) $(2x+5)(\sqrt{5}x - \sqrt{5})$

13. **Hint** Solve as Example 7.

    Ans. (i) $(ax+b)(bx+a)$ (ii) $(x-a)(x-b)$

    (iii) $(x+\sqrt{2})(\sqrt{2}x+1)$ (iv) $(x+6)(x-30)$

    (v) $(5x+3\sqrt{5})(\sqrt{5}x+1)$ (vi) $(x+3)(x-2)$

    (vii) $(x+1)(3x-4)$ (viii) $(x-2)(x-2)$

14. **Hint** Solve as Example 8. **Ans.** (i) $(x+11)(x-6)$

    (ii) $(x-4)(3x+1)$ (iii) $\left(x+\frac{1}{7}\right)\left(x+\frac{1}{5}\right)$

15. **Hint** Solve as Example 9.

    Ans. (i) $(x+2)(x+1)(x+10)$ (ii) $(u-2)(u+2)(3u-4)$

    (iii) $(x+1)(x-2)(x+3)$

TOPIC 05 Algebraic Identities

An identity is an equality, which is true for all values of its variables i.e. an identity is a universal truth. Some useful algebraic identities are given below:

(i) $(x+y)^2 = x^2 + 2xy + y^2$

(ii) $(x-y)^2 = x^2 - 2xy + y^2$

(iii) $x^2 - y^2 = (x-y)(x+y)$

(iv) $(x+a)(x+b) = x^2 + (a+b)x + ab$

(v) $(x+y+z)^2 = x^2 + y^2 + z^2 + 2xy + 2yz + 2zx$

(vi) $(x+y)^3 = x^3 + y^3 + 3xy(x+y)$

$= x^3 + y^3 + 3x^2y + 3xy^2$

(vii) $(x-y)^3 = x^3 - y^3 - 3xy(x-y)$

$= x^3 - y^3 - 3x^2y + 3xy^2$

(viii) $x^3 + y^3 + z^3 - 3xyz$

$= (x+y+z)(x^2 + y^2 + z^2 - xy - yz - zx)$

$= (x+y+z)[(x+y+z)^2 - 3(xy+yz+zx)]$

If $(x+y+z) = 0$, then $x^3 + y^3 + z^3 = 3xyz$

Problems Based on Algebraic Identities

We can use these identities to solve many problems, such as to factorise the algebraic expression, to find product without multiplying directly and to evaluate the value of a number having exponent.

Example 1. Using appropriate identity factorise the following.

(i) $4a^2 + 12ab + 9b^2$ (ii) $x^2 + 4x + 4$

Sol. (i) $4a^2 + 12ab + 9b^2 = (2a)^2 + 2 \times 2a \times 3b + (3b)^2$

$= (2a+3b)^2$

$[\because (x+y)^2 = x^2 + y^2 + 2xy]$

$= (2a+3b)(2a+3b)$

(ii) $x^2 + 4x + 4 = (x)^2 + 2 \times 2 \times x + (2)^2$

$= (x+2)^2$ $[\because (x+y)^2 = x^2 + y^2 + 2xy]$

$= (x+2)(x+2)$

Example 2. Using appropriate identity factorise the following.

(i) $9x^2 - 6xy + y^2$ (ii) $9x^2 - 30x + 25$

Sol. (i) $9x^2 - 6xy + y^2 = (3x)^2 - 2 \times 3x \times y + y^2$

$= (3x-y)^2$

$[\because (x-y)^2 = x^2 - 2xy + y^2]$

$= (3x-y)(3x-y)$

(ii) $9x^2 - 30x + 25 = (3x)^2 - 2 \times 5 \times 3x + (5)^2$

$= (3x-5)^2$

$[\because (x-y)^2 = x^2 - 2xy + y^2]$

$= (3x-5)(3x-5)$

Example 3. Using appropriate identity, factorise the following.

(i) $4x^2 - \frac{x^2}{9}$ (ii) $x^2 - 4$

Sol. (i) $4x^2 - \frac{x^2}{9} = (2x)^2 - \left(\frac{x}{3}\right)^2$

$= \left(2x - \frac{x}{3}\right)\left(2x + \frac{x}{3}\right)$

$[\because a^2 - b^2 = (a-b)(a+b)]$

(ii) $x^2 - 4 = x^2 - (2)^2$

$= (x-2)(x+2)$ $[\because a^2 - b^2 = (a-b)(a+b)]$

Example 4. Evaluate 103×102 without multiplying directly.

Sol. Write $103 = 100 + 3$ and $102 = 100 + 2$

$\therefore$ $103 \times 102 = (100+3) \times (100+2)$

$= (100)^2 + (3+2) \times 100 + 3 \times 2$

$[\because (x+a)(x+b) = x^2 + (a+b)x + ab]$

$= 10000 + 500 + 6 = 10506$

Example 5. Use suitable identity to find the following product.

(i) $(x+4)^2$ (ii) $(x-10)^2$

(iii) $(3x-5)(3x+5)$ (iv) $(y+1)(y+5)$

Sol. (i) $(x+4)^2 = x^2 + 2 \times x \times 4 + (4)^2$

$= x^2 + 8x + 16$ $[\because (x+y)^2 = x^2 + y^2 + 2xy]$

(ii) $(x-10)^2 = x^2 - 2 \times x \times 10 + (10)^2$

$[\because (x-y)^2 = x^2 + y^2 - 2xy]$

$= x^2 - 20x + 100$

(iii) $(3x-5)(3x+5) = (3x)^2 - (5)^2$

$[\because (x-y)(x+y) = x^2 - y^2]$

$= 9x^2 - 25$

(iv) $(y+1)(y+5) = (y)^2 + (1+5)y + 1 \times 5$

$[\because (x+a)(x+b) = x^2 + (a+b)x + ab]$

$= y^2 + 6y + 5$

Example 6. Expand $\left(x - \frac{1}{2}y + \frac{1}{3}z\right)^2$.

Sol. $\left(x - \frac{1}{2}y + \frac{1}{3}z\right)^2 = (x)^2 + \left(-\frac{1}{2}y\right)^2 + \left(\frac{1}{3}z\right)^2$

$+ 2x\left(-\frac{1}{2}y\right) + 2\left(-\frac{1}{2}y\right)\left(\frac{1}{3}z\right) + 2\left(\frac{1}{3}z\right)(x)$

$[\because (a+b+c)^2 = a^2 + b^2 + c^2 + 2ab + 2bc + 2ca]$

$= x^2 + \frac{1}{4}y^2 + \frac{1}{9}z^2 - xy - \frac{yz}{3} + \frac{2zx}{3}$

Example 7. Factorise $25x^2 + 4y^2 + 9z^2 - 20xy - 12yz + 30zx$ using suitable identity.

Sol. We have, $25x^2 + 4y^2 + 9z^2 - 20xy - 12yz + 30zx$

We can rewrite the given expression as

$(5x)^2 + (2y)^2 + (3z)^2 - 2 \times 5x \times 2y$

$- 2 \times 2y \times 3z + 2 \times 3z \times 5x$

$= (5x)^2 + (-2y)^2 + (3z)^2 + 2(5x)(-2y)$

$+ 2(-2y)(3z) + 2(3z)(5x)$

$= (5x - 2y + 3z)^2$

$[\because a^2 + b^2 + c^2 + 2ab + 2bc + 2ca = (a+b+c)^2]$

Example 8. Write the cubes in expanded form

(i) $(x+1)^3$

(ii) $(3a-2b)^3$

Sol. (i) $(x+1)^3 = x^3 + 1^3 + 3 \times x \times 1(x+1)$

$[\because (x+y)^3 = x^3 + y^3 + 3xy(x+y)]$

$= x^3 + 1 + 3x(x+1)$

$= x^3 + 1 + 3x^2 + 3x$

(ii) $(3a-2b)^3 = (3a)^3 - (2b)^3 - 3 \times 3a \times 2b[3a - 2b]$

$[\because (x-y)^3 = x^3 - y^3 - 3xy(x-y)]$

$= 27a^3 - 8b^3 - 18ab[3a - 2b]$

$= 27a^3 - 8b^3 - 54a^2b + 36ab^2$

Example 9. Factorise $\frac{x^3}{8} - 64 - 3x^2 + 24x$ by using suitable identity.

Sol. We can rewrite the given expression as

$\left(\frac{x}{2}\right)^3 - (4)^3 - 3 \times \frac{x}{2} \times 4\left(\frac{x}{2} - 4\right)$

$= \left(\frac{x}{2} - 4\right)^3$ $[\because a^3 - b^3 - 3ab(a-b) = (a-b)^3]$

$= \left(\frac{x}{2} - 4\right)\left(\frac{x}{2} - 4\right)\left(\frac{x}{2} - 4\right)$

Example 10. Evaluate $(101)^3$ by using suitable identity.

Sol. First write $101 = 100 + 1$

$\therefore$ $(101)^3 = (100+1)^3$

$(100+1)^3 = (100)^3 + (1)^3 + 3 \times 100 \times 1(100+1)$

$[\because (x+y)^3 = x^3 + y^3 + 3xy(x+y)]$

$= 1000000 + 1 + 300(101)$

$= 1000000 + 1 + 30300$

$= 1030301$

Example 11. **Simplify**

$$(x+y)^3-(x-y)^3-6y(x+y)(x-y).$$

Sol. $(x+y)^3-(x-y)^3-6y(x+y)(x-y)$

$$=(x+y)^3-(x-y)^3-3(x+y)(x-y)[(x+y)-(x-y)]$$

$$=[x+y-(x-y)]^3 \quad [\because a^3-b^3-3ab(a-b)=(a-b)^3]$$

$$=(2y)^3=8y^3$$

Example 12. **Without actually calculating the cubes, find the value of $(-11)^3+(6)^3+(5)^3$.**

Sol. We know that

$$x^3+y^3+z^3-3xyz$$

$$=(x+y+z)(x^2+y^2+z^2-xy-yz-zx)$$

When $x+y+z=0$,

$$x^3+y^3+z^3=3xyz$$

Now, $(-11)^3+(6)^3+(5)^3=3\times(-11)\times6\times5$

$$[\because (-11)+6+5=0]$$

$$=-990$$

Hence, $(-11)^3+(6)^3+(5)^3=-990$

Example 13. **Factorise $x^3+8y^3+64z^3-24xyz$**

Sol. We have,

$$x^3+8y^3+64z^3-24xyz$$

$$=(x)^3+(2y)^3+(4z)^3-3\times x\times2y\times4z$$

$$=(x+2y+4z)[x^2+(2y)^2+(4z)^2-x\times2y-2y\times4z-x\times4z]$$

$$[\because x^3+y^3+z^3-3xyz=(x+y+z)(x^2+y^2+z^2-xy-yz-zx)]$$

$$=(x+2y+4z)[x^2+4y^2+16z^2-2xy-8yz-4xz]$$

Example 14. **If $a+b=5$ and $ab=6$, then find the value of a^3+b^3.**

Sol. We know that

$$a^3+b^3=(a+b)(a^2-ab+b^2)$$

$$=(a+b)(a^2+2ab+b^2-2ab-ab)$$

[adding and subtracting $2ab$]

$$=(a+b)\{(a+b)^2-3ab\}$$

$$=5\{(5)^2-3\times6\} \quad [\text{given, } a+b=5, ab=6]$$

$$=5(25-18)=5\times7=35$$

Hence, $a^3+b^3=35$

Example 15. **Find the product**

$$(8a-6b)(64a^2+48ab+36b^2)$$

Sol. We have, $(8a-6b)(64a^2+48ab+36b^2)$

$$=(8a-6b)[(8a)^2+6b\times8a+(6b)^2]$$

$$=(8a)^3-(6b)^3=512a^3-216b^3$$

$$[\because a^3-b^3=(a-b)(a^2+ab+b^2)]$$

Hence, $(8a-6b)(64a^2+48ab+36b^2)$

$$=512a^3-216b^3$$

Some Special Identities

(i) $x^3-y^3=(x-y)(x^2+xy+y^2)$

(ii) $x^3+y^3=(x+y)(x^2-xy+y^2)$

(iii) $x^2+y^2+z^2-xy-yz-zx$

$$=\frac{1}{2}[(x-y)^2+(y-z)^2+(z-x)^2]$$

Example 16. **Expand $\frac{1}{2}[(2a-3b)^2+(3b-4c)^2+(4c-2a)^2]$ using suitable identity.**

Sol. We know that $\frac{1}{2}[(x-y)^2+(y-z)^2+(z-x)^2]$

$$=x^2+y^2+z^2-xy-yz-zx$$

Here, $x=2a, y=3b$ and $z=4c$

So, $\frac{1}{2}[(2a-3b)^2+(3b-4c)^2+(4c-2a)^2]$

$$=(2a)^2+(3b)^2+(4c)^2-2a\times3b-3b\times4c-4c\times2a$$

$$=4a^2+9b^2+16c^2-6ab-12bc-8ca$$

Example 17. **If $a+b+c=9$ and $ab+bc+ca=40$, then find the value of $a^2+b^2+c^2$.**

Sol. Given that $a+b+c=9$

On squaring both sides, we get

$$(a+b+c)^2=(9)^2$$

$$\Rightarrow a^2+b^2+c^2+2ab+2bc+2ca=81$$

$$\Rightarrow a^2+b^2+c^2+2(ab+bc+ca)=81$$

On putting $ab+bc+ca=40$, we get

$$a^2+b^2+c^2+2\times40=81$$

$$\therefore \quad a^2+b^2+c^2=81-80=1$$

Example 18. **If $x^2+\frac{1}{x^2}=7$, then find the value of $x^3+\frac{1}{x^3}$, using only the positive value of $x+\frac{1}{x}$.**

Sol. Given, $$x^2+\frac{1}{x^2}=7$$

$$\Rightarrow \quad x^2+\frac{1}{x^2}+2=7+2 \quad [\text{adding both sides by 2}]$$

$$\Rightarrow \quad \left(x+\frac{1}{x}\right)^2=(3)^2$$

On taking positive square root, we get

$$x+\frac{1}{x}=3 \quad \dots(i)$$

Now, on cubing both sides, we get

$$x^3+\left(\frac{1}{x}\right)^3+3x\times\frac{1}{x}\left(x+\frac{1}{x}\right)=(3)^3$$

$$\Rightarrow \quad x^3+\frac{1}{x^3}+3(3)=27 \quad [\text{from Eq. (i)}]$$

$$\therefore \quad x^3+\frac{1}{x^3}=27-9=18$$

Example 19. **Find the following product using suitable identity.**

$$(3x-5y-4)(9x^2+25y^2+15xy+12x-20y+16)$$

Sol. $(3x-5y-4)(9x^2+25y^2+15xy+12x-20y+16)$

$= [3x+(-5y)+(-4)][(3x)^2+(-5y)^2+(-4)^2$
$-(3x)(-5y)-(-5y)(-4)-(-4)(3x)]$

$= (3x)^3+(-5y)^3+(-4)^3-3\times 3x\times(-5y)\times(-4)$

$[\because a^3+b^3+c^3-3abc=(a+b+c)$
$(a^2+b^2+c^2-ab-bc-ca)]$

$= 27x^3-125y^3-64-180xy$

Problems Based on Geometrical Figure

Sometimes the problem is given in the form of an area and volume of some geometrical figure (square, cube etc.) in polynomial form.

For this, firstly we determine all the factors of the given polynomial and proceed according to the question.

Example 20. **Give possible expression for the length and breadth of the rectangle whose area is given by $4a^2+4a-3$.**

NCERT Exemplar

Sol. Given, area of rectangle $= 4a^2+4a-3$

$= 4a^2+6a-2a-3$ [by splitting the middle term]

$= 2a(2a+3)-1(2a+3)=(2a-1)(2a+3)$

Hence, possible expression for length/breadth $= (2a-1)$
and possible expression for breadth/length $= (2a+3)$

Example 21. **What are the possible expressions for the dimensions of a cuboid, whose volume is $36kx^2y-21kxy^2+3ky^3$?**

Sol. $\because$ Volume $= 36kx^2y-21kxy^2+3ky^3$

$= 3ky[12x^2-7xy+y^2]$

$= 3ky[12x^2-4xy-3xy+y^2]$

$= 3ky[4x(3x-y)-y(3x-y)]$

$= 3ky(4x-y)(3x-y)$

Hence,
possible expression for length/breadth/height $= 3ky$,
possible expression for breadth/height/length $= 4x-y$
and possible expression for height/length/breadth $= 3x-y$.

Try These 2.5

1. **Factorise the following using suitable identities**
   (i) $4y^2+4xy+x^2$
   (ii) x^2+6x+9
2. **Factorise the following using suitable identities**
   (i) $4z^2-4zy+y^2$ (ii) $4x^2-12x+9$
3. **Factorise the following using suitable identities**
   (i) $y^2-\frac{z^2}{25}$ (ii) x^2-16
4. **Evaluate the following product without multiplying directly.**
   (i) 77×79
   (ii) 109×105
   (iii) 108×100
5. **Use suitable identity to find the following product**
   (i) $(x+6)^2$ (ii) $(x-9)^2$
   (iii) $(x-1)(x+1)$ (iv) $(x+2)(x+3)$
6. **Expand each of the following by using suitable identities.**
   (i) $(x-2y-3z)^2$
   (ii) $(a+2b+5c)^2$
   (iii) $(-2x+5y-3z)^2$
   (iv) $\left(\frac{1}{2}a-\frac{1}{3}b+c\right)^2$
7. **Factorise the following by using suitable identities.**
   (i) $4a^2+9b^2+16c^2+12ab-24bc-16ca$
   (ii) $x^2+4y^2+z^2-4xy-4yz+2xz$
8. **Write the following cubes in expanded form.**
   (i) $\left(\frac{3}{2}x+1\right)^3$ (ii) $\left(\frac{x}{2}-\frac{y}{3}\right)^3$
9. **Factorise the following using suitable identities.**
   (i) $x^3-8y^3-6x^2y+12xy^2$
   (ii) $27a^3+\frac{1}{64b^3}+\frac{27a^2}{4b}+\frac{9a}{16b^2}$
10. **Using suitable identities, evaluate the following.**
    (i) $(997)^3$ (ii) $(103)^3$
11. **Simplify $(2a+b)^3-(2a-b)^3-6b(2a+b)(2a-b)$.**
12. **Without actually calculating the cubes, find the following value.**
    (i) $(0.2)^3-(0.3)^3+(0.1)^3$
    (ii) $(7)^3-(4)^3-(3)^3$
13. **Factorise each of the following using identities.**
    (i) $125x^3+y^3$ (ii) $8x^3-(2x-y)^3$
14. **Using suitable identity, simplify**
    $(a-b-1)(a^2+b^2+1+ab+a-b)$
15. **Expand $\frac{1}{2}[(a-b)^2+(b-c)^2+(c-a)^2]$ using suitable identity.**
16. **If $a+b=12$ and $ab=27$, then find the value of a^3+b^3.**
17. **If $x-\frac{1}{x}=2$, then find $x^4+\frac{1}{x^4}$.**

18. If $y^2+\frac{1}{y^2}=23$, then find the value of $y^3+\frac{1}{y^3}$, using only the negative value of $y+\frac{1}{y}$.

19. If $a+b+c=5$ and $ab+bc+ca=10$, then prove that $a^3+b^3+c^3-3abc=-25$. NCERT Exemplar

20. Give possible expression for the length and breadth of the rectangle having $35y^2+8y-16$ as its area.

21. What are the possible expressions for the dimensions of the cuboid, whose volume is $x^3-6x^2+11x-6$?

Hints & Answers

1. **Hint** Solve as Example 1.
   Ans. (i) $(2y+x)(2y+x)$ (ii) $(x+3)(x+3)$
2. **Hint** Solve as Example 2.
   Ans. (i) $(2z-y)(2z-y)$ (ii) $(2x-3)(2x-3)$
3. **Hint** Solve as Example 3.
   Ans. (i) $\left(y-\frac{z}{5}\right)\left(y+\frac{z}{5}\right)$
   (ii) $(x-4)(x+4)$
4. (i) **Hint** $77\times79=(78-1)(78+1)=(78)^2-(1)^2=6084-1$
   Ans. 6083
   (ii) **Hint** $(100+9)(100+5)$ **Ans.** 11445
   (iii) **Hint** $(100+8)(100+0)$ **Ans.** 10800
5. **Hint** Solve as Example 5
   Ans.
   (i) $x^2+12x+36$ (ii) $x^2-18x+81$
   (iii) x^2-1 (iv) x^2+5x+6.
6. **Hint** Solve as Example 6.
   Ans. (i) $x^2+4y^2+9z^2-4xy+12yz-6zx$
   (ii) $a^2+4b^2+25c^2+4ab+20bc+10ac$
   (iii) $4x^2+25y^2+9z^2-20xy-30yz+12zx$
   (iv) $\frac{a^2}{4}+\frac{b^2}{9}+c^2-\frac{ab}{3}-\frac{2bc}{3}+ac$
7. **Hint** Solve as Example 7.
   Ans. (i) $(2a+3b-4c)(2a+3b-4c)$
   (ii) $(x-2y+z)(x-2y+z)$
8. **Hint** Use identity $(a+b)^3$ and $(a-b)^3$.
   Ans. (i) $\frac{27}{8}x^3+\frac{27}{4}x^2+\frac{9}{2}x+1$ (ii) $\frac{x^3}{8}-\frac{x^2y}{4}+\frac{xy^2}{6}-\frac{y^3}{27}$
9. **Hint** Solve as Example 9.
   Ans. (i) $(x-2y)^3$ (ii) $\left(3a+\frac{1}{4b}\right)^3$
10. (i) **Hint** $(997)^3=(1000-3)^3$
    $=(1000)^3-9000000+27000-27=991026973$
    (ii) **Hint** $(103)^3=(100+3)^3=1092727$
11. **Hint** Solve as Example 11. **Ans.** $8b^3$
12. **Hint** Use the identity, if $a+b+c=0$,
    then $a^3+b^3+c^3=3abc$ **Ans.** (i) −0.018 (ii) 252
13. (i) **Hint** Using identity $x^3+y^3=(x+y)(x^2-xy+y^2)$
    Ans. $(5x+y)(25x^2-5xy+y^2)$
    (ii) Use identity $x^3-y^3=(x-y)(x^2+xy+y^2)$,
    $(2x)^3-(2x-y)^3=[2x-(2x-y)][(2x)^2+(2x-y)^2+2x(2x-y)]$
    Ans. $y(12x^2+y^2-6xy)$
14. **Hint** Use identity
    $a^3+b^3+c^3-3abc=(a+b+c)(a^2+b^2+c^2-ab-bc-ca)$
    Ans. $a^3-b^3-1-3ab$
15. $a^2+b^2+c^2-ab-bc-ca$
16. **Hint** $(a+b)^3=a^3+b^3+3ab(a+b)$
    $\therefore$ $(12)^3=a^3+b^3+3\times27\times12$ [given $a+b=12$, $ab=27$]
    $\Rightarrow a^3+b^3=756$
17. $\left(x-\frac{1}{x}\right)^2=2\Rightarrow x^2+\left(\frac{1}{x}\right)^2-2x\times\frac{1}{x}=4$
    $\Rightarrow x^2+\frac{1}{x^2}=6$
    $\Rightarrow (x^2)^2+\left(\frac{1}{x^2}\right)^2+2(x^2)\left(\frac{1}{x^2}\right)=36$
    $\Rightarrow x^4+\frac{1}{x^4}=34$
18. **Hint** Solve as Example 18. **Ans.** 110
19. **Hint** Use identity
    $a^3+b^3+c^3-3abc=(a+b+c)(a^2+b^2+c^2-ab-bc-ca)$
    $=(a+b+c)[(a+b+c)^2-3(ab+bc+ca)]$
20. **Hint** Solve as Example 20.
    Ans. Length/breadth $=7y-4$ and breadth/length $=5y+4$
21. **Hint** Solve as Example 21.
    Ans. Length/breadth/height $=x-1$,
    Breadth/height/length $=x-2$,
    Height/length/breadth $=x-3$

NCERT FOLDER

Complete Solutions of All Exercises of NCERT Textbook

EXERCISE 2.1 (NCERT Page 29)

Q1. Which of the following expressions are polynomials in one variable and which are not? State reasons for your answer.

(i) $4x^2 - 3x + 7$ (ii) $y^2 + \sqrt{2}$ (iii) $3\sqrt{t} + t\sqrt{2}$

(iv) $y + 2/y$ (v) $x^{10} + y^3 + t^{50}$

Sol. (i) Given expression is $4x^2 - 3x + 7$.
Here, expression is in one variable and all powers of the variable x are non-negative integers.
Hence, it is a polynomial in one variable.

(ii) Given expression is $y^2 + \sqrt{2}$.
Here, the expression is in one variable and the power of the variable y is a non-negative integer.
Hence, it is a polynomial in one variable.

(iii) Given expression is $3\sqrt{t} + t\sqrt{2}$.
Here, the expression is in one variable but all powers of the variable are not non-negative integers.
Hence, it is not a polynomial in one variable.

(iv) Given expression is $y + \frac{2}{y}$.
In the above expression, all powers of variable y are not non-negative integer.
Hence, it is not a polynomial in one variable.

(v) Given expression is $x^{10} + y^3 + t^{50}$.
Here, expression has three variables.
Hence, it is not a polynomial in one variable.

Q2. Write the coefficients of x^2 in each of the following

(i) $2 + x^2 + x$ (ii) $2 - x^2 + x^3$

(iii) $\frac{\pi}{2}x^2 + x$ (iv) $\sqrt{2}\,x - 1$

Sol. (i) The coefficient of x^2 in $2 + x^2 + x$ is 1.

(ii) The coefficient of x^2 in $2 - x^2 + x^3$ is -1.

(iii) The coefficient of x^2 in $\frac{\pi}{2}x^2 + x$ is $\frac{\pi}{2}$.

(iv) The coefficient of x^2 in $\sqrt{2}\,x - 1$ is 0.

Q3. Give one example each of a binomial of degree 35 and of a monomial of degree 100.

Sol. (i) We know that a binomial contains two non-zero terms. So, $3x^{35} - 5$ is a binomial of degree 35.

(ii) A monomial contains one non-zero term. So, $5y^{100}$ is a monomial of degree 100.

Q4. Write the degree of each of the following polynomials.

(i) $5x^3 + 4x^2 + 7x$ (ii) $4 - y^2$

(iii) $5t - \sqrt{7}$ (iv) 3

Sol. (i) In the polynomial $5x^3 + 4x^2 + 7x$, the highest power of variable x is 3. Hence, the degree of polynomial is 3.

(ii) Solve as part (i). **Ans.** 2

(iii) Solve as part (i). **Ans.** 1

(iv) Solve as part (i). **Ans.** 0

Q5. Classify the following as linear, quadratic and cubic polynomials :

(i) $x^2 + x$ (ii) $x - x^3$ (iii) $y + y^2 + 4$

(iv) $1 + x$ (v) $3t$ (vi) r^2

(vii) $7x^3$

Sol. (i) The degree of polynomial $x^2 + x$ is 2. Hence it is a quadratic polynomial.

(ii) The degree of polynomial $x - x^3$ is 3. Hence, it is a cubic polynomial.

(iii) The degree of polynomial $y + y^2 + 4$ is 2. Hence, it is a quadratic polynomial.

(iv) The degree of polynomial $1 + x$ is 1. Hence, it is a linear polynomial.

(v) The degree of polynomial $3t$ is 1. Hence, it is a linear polynomial.

(vi) The degree of polynomial r^2 is 2. Hence, it is a quadratic polynomial.

(vii) The degree of polynomial $7x^3$ is 3. Hence, it is a cubic polynomial.

EXERCISE 2.2 (NCERT Page 31-32)

Q1. Find the value of the polynomial $5x - 4x^2 + 3$ at

(i) $x = 0$.

(ii) $x = -1$.

(iii) $x = 2$.

Sol. Let $p(x) = 5x - 4x^2 + 3$

(i) On putting $x = 0$, we get

$$p(0) = 5 \times 0 - 4 \times (0)^2 + 3 = 3$$

(ii) Solve as part (i). **Ans.** -6

(iii) Solve as part (i). **Ans.** -3

Q 2. Find $p(0)$, $p(1)$ and $p(2)$ for each of the following polynomials.

(i) $p(y)=y^2-y+1$

(ii) $p(t)=2+t+2t^2-t^3$

(iii) $p(x)=x^3$

(iv) $p(x)=(x-1)(x+1)$

Sol. (i) Given, $p(y)=y^2-y+1$

On putting $y=0$, we get

$p(0)=(0)^2-0+1=1$

On putting $y=1$, we get

$p(1)=(1)^2-1+1=1$

On putting $y=2$, we get

$p(2)=(2)^2-2+1=4-2+1=3$

(ii) Solve as part (i). **Ans.** 2, 4, 4

(iii) Solve as part (i). **Ans.** 0, 1, 8

(iv) Solve as part (i). **Ans.** – 1, 0, 3

Q 3. Verify whether the following are zeroes of the polynomial, indicated against them.

(i) $p(x)=3x+1,\ x=-\dfrac{1}{3}$

(ii) $p(x)=5x-\pi,\ x=\dfrac{4}{5}$

(iii) $p(x)=x^2-1,\ x=1,-1$

(iv) $p(x)=(x+1)(x-2),\ x=-1,2$

(v) $p(x)=x^2,\ x=0$

(vi) $p(x)=lx+m,\ x=-\dfrac{m}{l}$

(vii) $p(x)=3x^2-1,\ x=-\dfrac{1}{\sqrt{3}},\dfrac{2}{\sqrt{3}}$

(viii) $p(x)=2x+1,\ x=1/2$

Sol. When we put the given value of x in corresponding $p(x)$, if we get zero, then that value of x will be the zero of that $p(x)$, otherwise not.

(i) Given, $p(x)=3x+1$ and $x=-\dfrac{1}{3}$

On putting $x=-\dfrac{1}{3}$, we get

$$p\left(-\frac{1}{3}\right)=3\times\left(-\frac{1}{3}\right)+1=-1+1=0$$

Hence, $x=-\dfrac{1}{3}$ is zero of the polynomial $p(x)$.

(ii) Solve as part (i). **Ans.** No

(iii) Solve as part (i). **Ans.** Both are zeroes

(iv) Solve as part (i). **Ans.** Both are zeroes

(v) Solve as part (i). **Ans.** Yes

(vi) Solve as part (i). **Ans.** Yes

(vii) Solve as part (i). **Ans.** Yes, for $x=-\dfrac{1}{\sqrt{3}}$, No for $x=\dfrac{2}{\sqrt{3}}$

(viii) Solve as part (i). **Ans.** No

Q 4. Find the zero of the polynomial in each of the following cases

(i) $p(x)=x+5$

(ii) $p(x)=x-5$

(iii) $p(x)=2x+5$

(iv) $p(x)=3x-2$

(v) $p(x)=3x$

(vi) $p(x)=ax,\ a\neq 0$

(vii) $p(x)=cx+d,\ c\neq 0$; c and d are real numbers.

Sol. (i) Given, $p(x)=x+5$

On putting $p(x)=0$, we get,

$$x+5=0\Rightarrow x=-5$$

Hence, $x=-5$ is the zero of the polynomial $p(x)$.

(ii) Solve as part (i). **Ans.** 5

(iii) Solve as part (i). **Ans.** $-\dfrac{5}{2}$

(iv) Solve as part (i). **Ans.** $\dfrac{2}{3}$

(v) Solve as part (i). **Ans.** 0

(vi) Solve as part (i). **Ans.** 0

(vii) Solve as part (i). **Ans.** $-\dfrac{d}{c}$

EXERCISE 2.3 (NCERT Page 35-36)

Q 1. Determine which of the following polynomials has $(x+1)$ as a factor

(i) x^3+x^2+x+1

(ii) $x^4+x^3+x^2+x+1$

(iii) $x^4+3x^3+3x^2+x+1$

(iv) $x^3-x^2-(2+\sqrt{2})\,x+\sqrt{2}$

Sol. If $(x+1)$ is a factor of given polynomial say $p(x)$, then at $x=-1$, $p(x)$ will become zero, otherwise it is not a factor of given polynomial.

(i) Let $p(x)=x^3+x^2+x+1$

On putting $x=-1$, we get

$p(-1)=(-1)^3+(-1)^2+(-1)+1=-1+1-1+1=0$

Hence, $(x+1)$ is a factor of x^3+x^2+x+1.

(ii) Solve as part (i). **Ans.** No

(iii) Solve as part (i). **Ans.** No

(iv) Solve as part (i). **Ans.** No

Q 2. Use the Factor theorem to determine, whether $g(x)$ is a factor of $p(x)$ in each of the following cases

(i) $p(x)=2x^3+x^2-2x-1,\ g(x)=x+1$

(ii) $p(x)=x^3+3x^2+3x+1,\ g(x)=x+2$

(iii) $p(x)=x^3-4x^2+x+6,\ g(x)=x-3$

Sol. (i) Given, $p(x)=2x^3+x^2-2x-1$ and $g(x)=x+1$

Zero of $g(x)$ is $x=-1$. $[\because x+1=0 \Rightarrow x=-1]$

On putting $x=-1$ in $p(x)$, we get

$$p(-1)=2\times(-1)^3+(-1)^2-2\times(-1)-1$$
$$=-2+1+2-1=0$$

Hence, $g(x)$ is the factor of $p(x)$.

(ii) Solve as part (i). **Ans.** No

(iii) Solve as part (i). **Ans.** Yes

Q3. **Find the value of k, if $(x-1)$ is a factor of $p(x)$ in each of the following cases**

(i) $p(x)=x^2+x+k$

(ii) $p(x)=2x^2+kx+\sqrt{2}$

(iii) $p(x)=kx^2-\sqrt{2}x+1$

(iv) $p(x)=kx^2-3x+k$

Sol. (i) If $(x-1)$ is a factor of $p(x)=x^2+x+k$.

Then, putting $x=1$ in $p(x)$, we get

$p(1)=0$ [since, zero of $x-1$ is 1]

$\Rightarrow (1)^2+1+k=0 \Rightarrow 2+k=0$

$\therefore k=-2$

(ii) Solve as part (i). **Ans.** $-2-\sqrt{2}$

(iii) Solve as part (i). **Ans.** $\sqrt{2}-1$

(iv) Solve as part (i). **Ans.** $\frac{3}{2}$

Q4. **Factorise**

(i) $12x^2-7x+1$ (ii) $2x^2+7x+3$

(iii) $6x^2+5x-6$ (iv) $3x^2-x-4$

Sol. (i) We have, $12x^2-7x+1=12x^2-(3+4)x+1$

[by splitting the middle term]

$$=12x^2-3x-4x+1=3x(4x-1)-1(4x-1)$$
$$=(4x-1)(3x-1)$$

(ii) Solve as part (i). **Ans.** $(x+3)(2x+1)$

(iii) Solve as part (i). **Ans.** $(3x-2)(2x+3)$

(iv) Solve as part (i). **Ans.** $(x+1)(3x-4)$

Q5. **Factorise**

(i) x^3-2x^2-x+2 (ii) x^3-3x^2-9x-5

(iii) $x^3+13x^2+32x+20$ (iv) $2y^3+y^2-2y-1$

Sol. (i) Solve as Example 9 of Topic-4.

Ans. $(x-1)(x+1)(x-2)$.

(ii) Solve as Example 9 of Topic-4.

Ans. $(x+1)(x+1)(x-5)$

(iii) Solve as Example 9 of Topic-4.

Ans. $(x+1)(x+2)(x+10)$

(iv) Solve as Example 10 of Topic-4.

Ans. $(y-1)(y+1)(2y+1)$

EXERCISE 2.4 (NCERT Page 40-42)

Q1. **Use suitable identities to find the following products**

(i) $(x+4)(x+10)$ (ii) $(x+8)(x-10)$

(iii) $(3x+4)(3x-5)$ (iv) $\left(y^2+\frac{3}{2}\right)\left(y^2-\frac{3}{2}\right)$

(v) $(3-2x)(3+2x)$

Sol. (i) $(x+4)(x+10)=x^2+(4+10)x+4\times10$

$[\because (x+a)(x+b)=x^2+(a+b)x+ab]$

$$=x^2+14x+40$$

(ii) Solve as part (i). **Ans.** $x^2-2x-80$

(iii) Solve as part (i). **Ans.** $9x^2-3x-20$

(iv) $\left(y^2+\frac{3}{2}\right)\left(y^2-\frac{3}{2}\right)=(y^2)^2-\left(\frac{3}{2}\right)^2=y^4-\frac{9}{4}$

$[\because (a-b)(a+b)=a^2-b^2]$

(v) Solve as part (iv). **Ans.** $9-4x^2$

Q2. **Evaluate the following products without multiplying directly.**

(i) 103×107 (ii) 95×96 (iii) 104×96

Sol. (i) $103\times107=(100+3)\times(100+7)$

$$=(100)^2+(7+3)\times100+7\times3$$

$[\because (x+a)(x+b)=x^2+(a+b)x+ab]$

$$=10000+1000+21=11021$$

(ii) Solve as part (i). **Ans.** 9120

(iii) $104\times96=(100+4)\times(100-4)$

$$=(100)^2-(4)^2 \quad [\because (a-b)(a+b)=a^2-b^2]$$
$$=10000-16=9984$$

Q3. **Factorise the following using appropriate identities**

(i) $9x^2+6xy+y^2$

(ii) $4y^2-4y+1$

(iii) $x^2-\frac{y^2}{100}$

Sol. (i) $9x^2+6xy+y^2=(3x)^2+2\times3x\times y+(y)^2$

$$=(3x+y)^2 \quad [\because (a+b)^2=a^2+2ab+b^2]$$
$$=(3x+y)(3x+y)$$

(ii) Solve as part (i). **Ans.** $(2y-1)(2y-1)$

(iii) $x^2-\frac{y^2}{100}=(x)^2-\left(\frac{y}{10}\right)^2=\left(x-\frac{y}{10}\right)\left(x+\frac{y}{10}\right)$

$[\because a^2-b^2=(a-b)(a+b)]$

Q4. **Expand each of the following using suitable identities.**

(i) $(x+2y+4z)^2$ (ii) $(2x-y+z)^2$

(iii) $(-2x+3y+2z)^2$ (iv) $(3a-7b-c)^2$

(v) $(-2x+5y-3z)^2$ (vi) $\left(\frac{1}{4}a-\frac{1}{2}b+1\right)^2$

Sol. (i) $(x+2y+4z)^2 = (x)^2 + (2y)^2 + (4z)^2 + 2 \times x \times 2y + 2 \times 2y \times 4z + 2 \times 4z \times x$

$[\because (a+b+c)^2 = a^2 + b^2 + c^2 + 2ab + 2bc + 2ca]$

$= x^2 + 4y^2 + 16z^2 + 4xy + 16yz + 8zx$

(ii) Solve as part (i).

Ans. $4x^2 + y^2 + z^2 - 4xy - 2yz + 4xz$

(iii) Solve as part (i).

Ans. $4x^2 + 9y^2 + 4z^2 - 12xy + 12yz - 8xz$

(iv) Solve as part (i).

Ans. $9a^2 + 49b^2 + c^2 - 42ab + 14bc - 6ac$

(v) Solve as part (i).

Ans. $4x^2 + 25y^2 + 9z^2 - 20xy - 30yz + 12xz$

(vi) Solve as part (i).

Ans. $\frac{a^2}{16} + \frac{b^2}{4} + 1 - \frac{1}{4}ab - b + \frac{1}{2}a$

Q5. Factorise

(i) $4x^2 + 9y^2 + 16z^2 + 12xy - 24yz - 16xz$

(ii) $2x^2 + y^2 + 8z^2 - 2\sqrt{2}\,xy + 4\sqrt{2}\,yz - 8xz$

Sol. (i) $4x^2 + 9y^2 + 16z^2 + 12xy - 24yz - 16xz$

$= (2x)^2 + (3y)^2 + (-4z)^2 + 2 \times (2x) \times (3y) + 2 \times (3y) \times (-4z) + 2 \times (-4z) \times 2x$

$= (2x + 3y - 4z)^2$

$[\because (a+b+c)^2 = a^2 + b^2 + c^2 + 2ab + 2bc + 2ca]$

$= (2x + 3y - 4z)(2x + 3y - 4z)$

(ii) Solve as part (i).

Ans. $(-\sqrt{2}x + y + 2\sqrt{2}z)(-\sqrt{2}x + y + 2\sqrt{2}z)$

Q6. Write the following cubes in expanded form

(i) $(2x+1)^3$ (ii) $(2a-3b)^3$

(iii) $\left(\frac{3}{2}x+1\right)^3$ (iv) $\left(x-\frac{2}{3}y\right)^3$

Sol. (i) $(2x+1)^3 = (2x)^3 + (1)^3 + 3 \times 2x \times 1(2x+1)$

$[\because (a+b)^3 = a^3 + b^3 + 3ab(a+b)]$

$= 8x^3 + 1 + 6x(2x+1) = 8x^3 + 12x^2 + 6x + 1$

(ii) $(2a-3b)^3 = (2a)^3 - (3b)^3 - 3 \times (2a)(3b)(2a-3b)$

$[\because (x-y)^3 = x^3 - y^3 - 3xy(x-y)]$

$= 8a^3 - 27b^3 - 18ab(2a-3b)$

$= 8a^3 - 27b^3 - 36a^2b + 54ab^2$

(iii) Solve as part (i). **Ans.** $\frac{27}{8}x^3 + \frac{27}{4}x^2 + \frac{9}{2}x + 1$

(iv) Solve as part (i). **Ans.** $x^3 - \frac{8}{27}y^3 - 2x^2y + \frac{4}{3}xy^2$

Q7. Evaluate the following using suitable identities.

(i) $(99)^3$ (ii) $(102)^3$ (iii) $(998)^3$

Sol. (i) $(99)^3 = (100-1)^3$

$= (100)^3 - (1)^3 - 3 \times 100 \times 1(100-1)$

$[\because (a-b)^3 = a^3 - b^3 - 3ab(a-b)]$

$= 1000000 - 1 - 300(100-1)$

$= 1000000 - 1 - 300 \times 99$

$= 1000000 - 29701 = 970299$

(ii) $(102)^3 = (100+2)^3$

$= (100)^3 + (2)^3 + 3 \times 100 \times 2(100+2)$

$[\because (a+b)^3 = a^3 + b^3 + 3ab(a+b)]$

$= 1000000 + 8 + 600(102)$

$= 1000000 + 8 + 61200 = 1061208$

(iii) Solve as part (i).

Ans. 994011992

Q8. Factorise each of the following.

(i) $8a^3 + b^3 + 12a^2b + 6ab^2$

(ii) $8a^3 - b^3 - 12a^2b + 6ab^2$

(iii) $27 - 125a^3 - 135a + 225a^2$

(iv) $64a^3 - 27b^3 - 144a^2b + 108ab^2$

(v) $27p^3 - \frac{1}{216} - \frac{9}{2}p^2 + \frac{1}{4}p$

Sol. (i) $8a^3 + b^3 + 12a^2b + 6ab^2$

$= (2a)^3 + (b)^3 + 3 \times 2a \times b(2a+b)$

$= (2a+b)^3$ $[\because (a+b)^3 = a^3 + b^3 + 3ab(a+b)]$

$= (2a+b)(2a+b)(2a+b)$

(ii) $8a^3 - b^3 - 12a^2b + 6ab^2$

$= (2a)^3 - (b)^3 - 3 \times (2a) \times (b)(2a-b)$

$= (2a-b)^3$ $[\because (x-y)^3 = x^3 - y^3 - 3xy(x-y)]$

$= (2a-b)(2a-b)(2a-b)$

(iii) Solve as part (ii). **Ans.** $(3-5a)(3-5a)(3-5a)$

(iv) Solve as part (ii). **Ans.** $(4a-3b)(4a-3b)(4a-3b)$

(v) Solve as part (ii). **Ans.** $\left(3p-\frac{1}{6}\right)\left(3p-\frac{1}{6}\right)\left(3p-\frac{1}{6}\right)$

Q9. Verify

(i) $x^3 + y^3 = (x+y)(x^2 - xy + y^2)$

(ii) $x^3 - y^3 = (x-y)(x^2 + xy + y^2)$

Sol. (i) RHS $= (x+y)(x^2 - xy + y^2)$

$= x(x^2 - xy + y^2) + y(x^2 - xy + y^2)$

$= x^3 - x^2y + xy^2 + x^2y - xy^2 + y^3$

$= x^3 + y^3 =$ LHS

(ii) Solve as part (i).

Q 10. Factorise each of the following.

(i) $27y^3 + 125z^3$ (ii) $64m^3 - 343n^3$

Sol. (i) $27y^3 + 125z^3 = (3y)^3 + (5z)^3$

$= (3y + 5z)[(3y)^2 - 3y \times 5z + (5z)^2]$

$[\because x^3 + y^3 = (x + y)(x^2 - xy + y^2)]$

$= (3y + 5z)(9y^2 - 15yz + 25z^2)$

(ii) Use formula $x^3 - y^3 = (x - y)(x^2 + xy + y^2)$ and solve it. [**Ans.** $(4m - 7n)(16m^2 + 28mn + 49n^2)$]

Q 11. Factorise $27x^3 + y^3 + z^3 - 9xyz$

Sol. $27x^3 + y^3 + z^3 - 9xyz$

$= (3x)^3 + (y)^3 + (z)^3 - 3 \times 3xyz$

$= (3x + y + z)[(3x)^2 + (y)^2 + (z)^2 - 3xy - yz - 3xz]$

$[\because x^3 + y^3 + z^3 - 3xyz = (x + y + z)(x^2 + y^2 + z^2 - xy - yz - zx)]$

$= (3x + y + z)(9x^2 + y^2 + z^2 - 3xy - yz - 3xz)$

Q 12. Verify that $x^3 + y^3 + z^3 - 3xyz = \frac{1}{2}(x + y + z)[(x - y)^2 + (y - z)^2 + (z - x)^2]$.

Sol. We have, $x^3 + y^3 + z^3 - 3xyz$

$= (x+y+z)(x^2 + y^2 + z^2 - xy - yz - zx)$

$= \frac{1}{2}(x+y+z)(2x^2 + 2y^2 + 2z^2 - 2xy - 2yz - 2zx)$

$= \frac{1}{2}(x+y+z)[(x^2 + y^2 - 2xy) + (y^2 + z^2 - 2yz) + (z^2 + x^2 - 2zx)]$

$= \frac{1}{2}(x+y+z)[(x-y)^2 + (y-z)^2 + (z-x)^2]$

Q 13. If $(x + y + z) = 0$, show that $x^3 + y^3 + z^3 = 3xyz$

Sol. We know that $x^3 + y^3 + z^3 - 3xyz$

$= (x + y + z)(x^2 + y^2 + z^2 - xy - yz - zx)$

Given, $x + y + z = 0$. Then, $x^3 + y^3 + z^3 - 3xyz$

$= 0 \times (x^2 + y^2 + z^2 - xy - yz - zx) = 0$

$\therefore x^3 + y^3 + z^3 = 3xyz$ **Hence proved.**

Q 14. Without actually calculating the cubes, find the value of each of the following :

(i) $(-12)^3 + (7)^3 + (5)^3$

(ii) $(28)^3 + (-15)^3 + (-13)^3$

Sol. (i) We know that $x^3 + y^3 + z^3 - 3xyz$

$= (x+y+z)(x^2 + y^2 + z^2 - xy - yz - zx)$

Also, we know that if $x + y + z = 0$

Then, $x^3 + y^3 + z^3 = 3xyz$

Given expression is $(-12)^3 + (7)^3 + (5)^3$.

Here, $-12 + 7 + 5 = 0$

$\therefore (-12)^3 + (7)^3 + (5)^3 = 3 \times (-12) \times 7 \times 5 = -1260$

(ii) Solve as part (i). **Ans.** 16380

Q 15. Give possible expressions for the length and the breadth of each of the following rectangles, in which their areas are given :

(i) Area $= 25a^2 - 35a + 12$

(ii) Area $= 35y^2 + 13y - 12$

Sol. (i) We have,

Area of rectangle $= 25a^2 - 35a + 12$

$= 25a^2 - (20 + 15)a + 12$

[by splitting the middle term]

$= 25a^2 - 20a - 15a + 12$

$= 5a(5a - 4) - 3(5a - 4)$

$= (5a - 4)(5a - 3)$

Hence, possible expression for length/breadth $= (5a - 3)$ and possible expression for breadth/length $= (5a - 4)$

(ii) Solve as part (i).

Ans. Possible expression for length/breadth $= (7y - 3)$ and possible expression for breadth/length $= (5y + 4)$

Q 16. What are the possible expressions for the dimensions of the cuboids whose volumes are given below?

(i) Volume $= 3x^2 - 12x$

(ii) Volume $= 12ky^2 + 8ky - 20k$

Sol. (i) We have, volume of cuboid $= 3x^2 - 12x = 3x(x - 4)$

So, the possible expressions for the dimensions of the cuboid are 3, x and $x - 4$.

[$\because$ Volume of cuboid = Length × Breadth × Height]

(ii) We have, volume of cuboid

$= 12ky^2 + 8ky - 20k$

$= 12ky^2 + (20 - 12)ky - 20k$

[by splitting the middle term]

$= 12ky^2 + 20ky - 12ky - 20k$

$= 4ky(3y + 5) - 4k(3y + 5)$

$= (3y + 5)(4ky - 4k)$

$= (3y + 5)4k(y - 1)$

$= 4k(3y + 5)(y - 1)$

So, the possible expressions for the dimensions of the cuboid are $4k$, $3y + 5$ and $y - 1$.

REVIEW EXERCISE

Including Competency Based Questions

Part I

Multiple Choice Questions

1. Which one of the following algebraic expressions is a polynomial in variable x?

(a) $x^2 + \frac{2}{x^2}$ (b) $\sqrt{x} + \frac{1}{\sqrt{x}}$

(c) $x^2 + \frac{3x^{3/2}}{\sqrt{x}}$ (d) None of these

2. The coefficient of x^2 in the expansion of $(2x-1)^2$ is

(a) 2 (b) 4 (c) 1 (d) 3

3. $\sqrt{2}$ is a polynomial of degree **NCERT Exemplar**

(a) 2 (b) 0 (c) 1 (d) $\frac{1}{2}$

4. $x^{29} + 12x^{28} + 4$ is a

(a) monomial (b) binomial

(c) trinomial (d) None of these

5. How many zeroes does a zero polynomial have?

(a) 1 (b) 2 (c) 0 (d) Infinite

6. If $p(1) = 0$ for a polynomial $p(x)$, then by factor theorem one of the factor of $p(x)$ is

(a) $(x-1)$ (b) $(x+1)$ (c) x (d) $-x$

7. A polynomial is divided by $(x-1)$. The quotient obtained is $3x^3 - x^2 - x - 4$ and the remainder is -5. Which polynomial meets these conditions? **Competency Based Question**

(a) $3x^3 - x^2 - x - 9$ (b) $3x^3 - x^2 - x - 4$

(c) $3x^4 - 4x^3 - 3x + 4$ (d) $3x^4 - 4x^3 - 3x - 1$

8. What is the common factor of $x^3 - x^2$ and $-22x^2 + 142x - 120$? **Competency Based Question**

(a) x (b) $(x-1)$ (c) x^2 (d) 1

9. If $(2x+1)$ is a factor of $4x^2 + kx + 3$, then the value of k is

(a) 8 (b) -8 (c) 4 (d) -4

10. $x^9 + 100$ is divided by $(x-1)$, then the remainder is

(a) 99 (b) 100 (c) 101 (d) 0

11. If $49x^2 - b = \left(7x + \frac{1}{2}\right)\left(7x - \frac{1}{2}\right)$, then the value of b is **NCERT Exemplar**

(a) 0 (b) $\frac{1}{\sqrt{2}}$ (c) $\frac{1}{4}$ (d) $\frac{1}{2}$

12. One of the dimensions of the cuboid whose volume is $12Kx^2y - 7Kxy^2 + Ky^3$, can be

(a) Ky (b) $4x - y$

(c) $3x - y$ (d) All of these

Assertion-Reason Type Questions

13. Assertion The degree of the polynomial $(x-2)(x-3)(x+4)$ is 4.

Reason The number of zeroes of a polynomial is the degree of that polynomial.

(a) Both Assertion and Reason are correct and Reason is the correct explanation of Assertion.

(b) Both Assertion and Reason are correct but Reason is not the correct explanation of Assertion.

(c) Assertion is correct but Reason is incorrect.

(d) Assertion is incorrect but Reason is correct.

14. Assertion The remainder when $p(x) = x^3 - 6x^2 + 2x - 4$ is divided by $3x - 1$ is $-\frac{107}{27}$.

Reason If a polynomial $p(x)$ is divided by $ax - b$, the remainder is the value of $p(x)$ at $x = \frac{b}{a}$.

(a) Both Assertion and Reason are correct and Reason is the correct explanation of Assertion.

(b) Both Assertion and Reason are correct but Reason is not the correct explanation of Assertion.

(c) Assertion is correct but Reason is incorrect.

(d) Assertion is incorrect but Reason is correct.

15. Assertion The value of $a^2 + b^2 + 2ab + 2bc + 2ca$ when $a + b = 10$, $c = 5$ is 200.

Reason The value of $x^2 + \frac{1}{x^2} + 2 - 2x - \frac{2}{x}$ when $x = 2 - \sqrt{3}$ is 8.

(a) Both Assertion and Reason are correct and Reason is the correct explanation of Assertion.

(b) Both Assertion and Reason are correct but Reason is not the correct explanation of Assertion.

(c) Assertion is correct but Reason is incorrect.

(d) Assertion is incorrect but Reason is correct.

Case Study Based Questions

16. Charity is the humanitarian act of giving something good to the needy people. While doing charity, we should not expect anything in return. As, an act of charity to distribute fruits in an orphanage, Kishan buys x kg apples at the rate of ₹ 80 and orange at the rate of ₹ 40 per kg for charity. Along that he buy 10 kg pomegranate at the rate of ₹ 120 per kg. The quantity of oranges is equal to the square of the apple quantity. On the above information answer the following questions.

(i) Find the equation of the total cost of the quantity.

(ii) Find the equation of the total quantity of fruits.

(iii) (a) Find the degree of an equation of total cost of quantity.

Or (b) Find the coefficient of x^2 in equation of the total quantity.

17. A company produces square tiles whose sides are represented by the polynomial $(7x+5)$ cm. The cost of producing one tile is proportional to area of the tile.

(i) Write an expression for the area of tile in terms of x.

(ii) If the cost per square centimetre is ₹ 5, write an expression for total cost of producing one tile.

(iii) (a) If $x = 3$ cm, then find side length, area and cost of producing one tile.

Or (b) If the length of one side is increased by 1 cm, then write new area of the tile.

Part II

Very Short Answer Type Questions

1. Determine the degree of each of the following polynomial.

(i) $3x-2$ (ii) -20

(iii) $x^3(2-x^3)$

2. Find the factors of the expression $ab+bc+ax+cx$.

3. Find the value of 401×407 by using suitable identity.

4. Factorise $(25x^2-1)+(1+5x)^2$. **NCERT Exemplar**

5. What are the factors of $(x+y)^3-(x^3+y^3)$? **NCERT Exemplar**

6. If $x^2+\frac{1}{x^2}=51$, then find $x+\frac{1}{x}$.

7. If $\frac{x}{y}+\frac{y}{x}=-1$, $x \neq 0, y \neq 0$, then find the value of x^3-y^3. **NCERT Exemplar**

8. If the volume of a cuboid is $3x^2-27$, then find its possible dimensions.

9. The area of a rectangle is $(3x^2+x-2)$ sq unit. Its width is $(1+x)$ units. What is the length of the rectangle? **Competency Based Question**

Short Answer Type Questions

10. Find $p(0), p(1)$ and $p(-2)$ for the following polynomials.

(i) $p(x)=10x-4x^2-3$

(ii) $p(y)=(y+2)(y-2)$

11. If $(x-3)$ is a factor of the polynomial $x^3-x^2-14x+24$, find its other factors.

12. Factorise

(i) $2x^2+13x+15$ (ii) $84-2r-2r^2$

13. Factorise

(i) $2x^2-\frac{5}{6}x+\frac{1}{12}$.

(ii) $7\sqrt{2}\,x^2-10x-4\sqrt{2}$.

14. Factorise $5(3x+y)^2+6(3x+y)-8$.

15. Factorise the following $x^3-x^2+ax+x-a-1$.

16. Factorise $2x^3-3x^2-17x+30$. **NCERT Exemplar**

17. A polynomial is expressed as

$$p(x)=x^3+x^2-x-1.$$

At what values of x is the polynomial $p(x)=0$? **Competency Based Question**

18. Simplify $\sqrt{2a^2+2\sqrt{6}\,ab+3b^2}$.

19. Factorise $x^2+\frac{1}{x^2}-2-3x+\frac{3}{x}$.

20. If $\sqrt{u}+\sqrt{v}-\sqrt{w}=0$, then find the value of $(u+v-w+2\sqrt{uv})$.

21. Factorise $(x^2+4)-2a-a^2-5$.

22. Find the product $\left(a-\frac{1}{a}\right)\left(a+\frac{1}{a}\right)\left(a^2+\frac{1}{a^2}\right)\left(a^4+\frac{1}{a^4}\right)$ using a suitable identity.

23. Find the zeroes of the polynomial

$$p(x)=(x-2)^2-(x+2)^2.$$ **NCERT Exemplar**

24. Factorise x^4-7x^2+6.

25. Factorise the following expressions.

(i) $25x^2 + 9y^2 + 9z^2 - 30xy - 18yz + 30xz$

(ii) $9x^2 + 16y^2 + 4z^2 - 24xy + 16yz - 12xz$

(iii) $9x^2 + 4y^2 + 16z^2 + 12xy - 16yz - 24xz$

(iv) $16x^2 + 4y^2 + 9z^2 - 16xy - 12yz + 24xz$

26. Simplify the following expressions.

(i) $(x+y+z)^2 + (x+y-z)^2$

(ii) $(2x+p-c)^2 - (2x-p+c)^2$

27. Factorise $24\sqrt{3}\,x^3 - 125y^3$.

28. Factorise the following. **NCERT Exemplar**

(i) $1 - 64a^3 - 12a + 48a^2$

(ii) $8p^3 + \frac{12}{5}p^2 + \frac{6}{25}p + \frac{1}{125}$

29. Simplify $27x^3 - (3x-y)^3$.

30. Factorise $a^7 - ab^6$.

31. Factorise $a^3(b-c)^3 + b^3(c-a)^3 + c^3(a-b)^3$

32. Evaluate

$(2x - y + 3z)(4x^2 + y^2 + 9z^2 + 2xy + 3yz - 6xz)$.

NCERT Exemplar

33. Factorise the following

(i) $3a^3b - 243ab^3$. (ii) $x^4 - 625$.

(iii) $a^3 + b^3 + a + b$. (iv) $x(x-y)^3 + 3x^2y(x-y)$.

34. If $a^2 + \frac{9}{a^2} = 31$, what is the positive value of $a - \frac{3}{a}$?

35. Find $y^2 + \frac{1}{y^2}$ and $y^4 + \frac{1}{y^4}$, if $y - \frac{1}{y} = 9$.

36. If $x^2 + \frac{1}{x^2} = 14$, find $x^3 + \frac{1}{x^3}$.

Long Answer Type Questions

37. If $(x^3 + ax^2 + bx + 6)$ has $(x-2)$ as a factor and leaves a remainder 3 when divided by $(x-3)$, then find the values of a and b.

38. The polynomial $p(x) = ax^3 - 3x^2 + 4$ and $g(x) = 2x^3 - 5x + a$ when divided by $(x-2)$ and $(x-3)$ leave the remainders p and q, respectively. If $p - 2q = 4$, then find the value of a.

39. Let A and B be the remainders, when the polynomials $y^3 + 2y^2 - 5ay - 7$ and $y^3 + ay^2 - 12y + 6$ are divided by $(y+1)$ and $(y-2)$, respectively. If $2A + B = 6$, find the value of a.

40. Without actual division, prove that $(2x^4 - 6x^3 + 3x^2 + 3x - 2)$ is exactly divisible by $(x^2 - 3x + 2)$.

41. One-fourth of a herd of camels was seen in the forest. Twice the square root of the herd had gone to mountains and the remaining 15 camels were seen on the bank of a river. Find the total number of camels.

42. Find the square root of $(x^2 - 4x + 4)(x^2 - 6x + 9)$.

43. If $x = (2+\sqrt{5})^{1/2} + (2-\sqrt{5})^{1/2}$ and $y = (2+\sqrt{5})^{1/2} - (2-\sqrt{5})^{1/2}$, evaluate $x^2 + y^2$.

44. Factorise $a^{12}y^4 - a^4y^{12}$.

45. Factorise $p(x) = 9x^2 + y^2 + z^2 - 6xy + 2yz - 6xz$. Also, determine the value of $p(x)$, when $x = 1, y = 2$ and $z = 1$.

46. If a, b and c are all non-zero and $a + b + c = 0$, prove that $\frac{a^2}{bc} + \frac{b^2}{ca} + \frac{c^2}{ab} = 3$.

NCERT Exemplar

47. Prove that

$$(a+b+c)^3 - a^3 - b^3 - c^3 = 3(a+b)(b+c)(c+a).$$

NCERT Exemplar

48. Simplify $\frac{(a^2-b^2)^3 + (b^2-c^2)^3 + (c^2-a^2)^3}{(a-b)^3 + (b-c)^3 + (c-a)^3}$.

HINTS & ANSWERS

Part I

1. (c) $x^2 + \frac{3x^{3/2}}{\sqrt{x}}$ can be written as $x^2 + 3x$, which is a polynomial in x.
2. (b) **Hint** $(2x-1)^2 = 4x^2 + 1 - 4x$
   Coefficient of $x^2 = 4$.
3. (b) $\sqrt{2} = \sqrt{2}x^0$.
   Hence, $\sqrt{2}$ is a polynomial of degree 0, becaucse exponent of x is 0.
4. (c) **Hint** A trinomial have 3 terms.
5. (d) **Hint** The number of zeroes of a zero polynomial is infinite.
6. (a) **Hint** $p(1) = 0 \Rightarrow x = 1 \Rightarrow x - 1 = 0$
7. (d) We know that,
   Dividend = Divisor × Quotient + Remainder
   $= (x-1) \times (3x^3 - x^2 - x - 4) - 5$
   $= 3x^4 - 4x^3 - 3x - 1$
8. (b) **Hint** $-22x^2 + 142x - 120 = -2(x-1)(11x-60)$
   and $x^3 - x^2 = x^2(x-1)$
   ∴ The common factor = $(x-1)$ **Ans.** $(x-1)$
9. (a) **Hint** We have, $2x + 1 = 0$
   $\Rightarrow \quad x = -\frac{1}{2}$
   Here, $x = -\frac{1}{2}$ is a zero of $4x^2 + kx + 3$.
   $\therefore \quad 4 \times \left(\frac{-1}{2}\right)^2 + k\left(-\frac{1}{2}\right) + 3 = 0$
   $\Rightarrow \quad 4 \times \frac{1}{4} - \frac{k}{2} + 3 = 0 \Rightarrow 1 - \frac{k}{2} + 3 = 0$
   $\Rightarrow \quad k = 8$
10. (c) **Hint** Remainder of $x^9 + 100$ when divided by $x - 1$ is given by $(1)^9 + 100 = 1 + 100 = 101$ $\quad [\because x - 1 = 0 \Rightarrow x = 1]$
11. (c) Given, $(49x^2 - b) = \left(7x + \frac{1}{2}\right)\left(7x - \frac{1}{2}\right)$
   $\Rightarrow \quad [49x^2 - (\sqrt{b})^2] = \left[(7x)^2 - \left(\frac{1}{2}\right)^2\right]$
   $\Rightarrow \quad 49x^2 - (\sqrt{b})^2 = 49x^2 - \left(\frac{1}{2}\right)^2$
   $\Rightarrow \quad -(\sqrt{b})^2 = -\left(\frac{1}{2}\right)^2 \Rightarrow (\sqrt{b})^2 = \left(\frac{1}{2}\right)^2$
   [multiplying both sides by −1]
   $\therefore \quad b = \frac{1}{4}$
12. (d) Volume $= 12Kx^2y - 7Kxy^2 + Ky^3$
   $= Ky[12x^2 - 7xy + y^2]$
   $= Ky[12x^2 - 4xy - 3xy + y^2]$
   $= Ky[4x(3x-y) - y(3x-y)]$
   $= Ky(4x-y)(3x-y)$
   Hence, according to the given options, possible expression for the length/breadth/height is Ky or $4x - y$ or $3x - y$.
13. (d) **Assertion** $p(x) = (x-2)(x-3)(x+4)$
   $= (x-2)(x^2 + x - 12)$
   $= x^3 + x^2 - 12x - 2x^2 - 2x + 24$
   So, degree of $p(x)$ is 3.
   ∴ Assertion is not correct.
   Reason It is correct that the number of zeroes of a polynomial is the degree of that polynomial.
14. (a) **Assertion** $p(x) = x^3 - 6x^2 + 2x - 4$
   To find the remainder, put $x = \frac{1}{3}$ in $p(x)$, we get
   $p\left(\frac{1}{3}\right) = \left(\frac{1}{3}\right)^3 - 6\left(\frac{1}{3}\right)^2 + 2\left(\frac{1}{3}\right) - 4$
   $= \frac{1}{27} - \frac{6}{9} + \frac{2}{3} - 4 = \frac{1 - 18 + 18 - 108}{27} = -\frac{107}{27}$
   Reason By definition of remainder theorem, it is correct and it is the correct explanation of Assertion.
15. (b) **Assertion** $a^2 + b^2 + 2ab + 2bc + 2ca$
   $= (a+b)^2 + 2c(b+a)$
   $= (10)^2 + 2 \times 5 \times 10$
   $= 100 + 100 = 200$
   So, Assertion is correct.
   Reason We have, $x = 2 - \sqrt{3}$
   Now, $\frac{1}{x} = \frac{1}{2-\sqrt{3}} \times \frac{2+\sqrt{3}}{2+\sqrt{3}}$
   $= \frac{2+\sqrt{3}}{(2)^2 - (\sqrt{3})^2}$
   $= \frac{2+\sqrt{3}}{4-3} = 2 + \sqrt{3}$
   $\therefore x + \frac{1}{x} = 2 - \sqrt{3} + 2 + \sqrt{3} = 4$
   Now, $x^2 + \frac{1}{x^2} + 2 - 2x - \frac{2}{x} = \left(x + \frac{1}{x}\right)^2 - 2\left(x + \frac{1}{x}\right)$
   $= (4)^2 - 2(4) = 16 - 8 = 8$
   So, Reason is also correct but it is not the correct explanation for Assertion.

16. (i) According to the question, an equation of the total cost of quantity in terms of x is

$$p(x) = 80x + 40x^2 + 10 \times 120$$
$$= 80x + 40x^2 + 1200$$

(ii) An equation of the total quantity of fruits in terms of x is $g(x) = x + x^2 + 10$

(iii) (a) The degree of $p(x)$ is 2.

Or (b) Coefficient of x^2 in $x^2 + x + 10$ is 1.

17. (i) Let $A(x)$ denote the area of tile.

Since, tile is in the square shape.

$\therefore$ Area, $A(x) = (\text{side})^2$

$\Rightarrow \quad A(x) = (7x+5)^2 \quad [\because \text{side} = (7x+5)\text{ cm}]$

$\Rightarrow \quad A(x) = 49x^2 + 2 \times 7x \times 5 + 5^2$

$= (49x^2 + 70x + 25)\text{ cm}^2$

(ii) Since, cost of per square centimetre is ₹ 5.

Let $C(x)$ denote the cost of one tile.

$\therefore \quad C(x) = 5(49x^2 + 70x + 25)$

$C(x) = 245x^2 + 350x + 125$

(iii) (a) If $x = 3$, then side length $= 7 \times 3 + 5 = 26$ cm

Area, $A(x) = 49 \times 3^2 + 70 \times 3 + 25$

$= 676\text{ cm}^2$

Cost of one tile, $C(x) = 5 \times 676 =$ ₹ 3380

Or

(b) If length is increased by 1 cm, then new area $A'(x)$ of the tile is

$A'(x) = (7x + 5 + 1)^2 = (7x+6)^2$

$= 49x^2 + 2 \times 7x \times 6 + 6^2$

$= 49x^2 + 84x + 36\text{ cm}^2$

Part II

1. Hint Solve as Example 4 of Topic 1.

(i) 1 (ii) 0 (iii) 6

2. Hint $ab + bc + ax + cx = b(a+c) + x(a+c)$

$= (a+c)(b+x)$

3. Hint $401 \times 407 = (400+1)(400+7) = 163207$

4. Hint $(25x^2 - 1) + (1+5x)^2 = 25x^2 - 1 + 1 + 25x^2 + 10x$

$= 50x^2 + 10x = 10x(5x+1)$

5. Hint $(x+y)^3 - (x^3 + y^3)$

$= x^3 + y^3 + 3xy^2 + 3x^2y - x^3 - y^3$

$= 3xy^2 + 3x^2y = 3xy(x+y)$

6. Hint $\because \left(x + \frac{1}{x}\right)^2 = x^2 + \frac{1}{x^2} + 2$

$\therefore \quad \left(x+\frac{1}{x}\right)^2 = 51 + 2 = 53 \Rightarrow x + \frac{1}{x} = \pm\sqrt{53}$

7. Hint Given, $\frac{x}{y} + \frac{y}{x} = -1$

$\Rightarrow \quad \frac{x^2+y^2}{xy} = -1 \Rightarrow x^2 + y^2 = -xy$

Now, $x^3 - y^3 = (x-y)(x^2 + xy + y^2)$

$= (x-y)(-xy+xy) = (x-y)\,0 = 0$

8. Hint $3x^2 - 27 = 3(x^2 - 9) = 3(x-3)(x+3)$

Ans. 3, $(x-3)$ and $(x+3)$.

9. The area of rectangle = Length × Breadth

$= (3x^2 + x - 2)$

$= (3x^2 + 3x - 2x - 2)$

$= 3x(x+1) - 2(x+1)$

$= (3x-2)(x+1)$

On comparing, $l = (3x-2)$, $b = (x+1)$

Ans. $(3x-2)$ units

10. Hint Solve as Q. 2 of NCERT Exercise 2.2.

Ans. (i) -3, 3 and -39. (ii) -4, -3 and 0.

11. Hint $x^3 - x^2 - 14x + 24 = (x-3)(x^2 + 2x - 8)$

$= (x-3)(x-2)(x+4)$

Hence, other factors are $(x-2)$ and $(x+4)$.

12. (i) **Hint** $2x^2 + 13x + 15 = 2x^2 + 10x + 3x + 15$

$= 2x(x+5) + 3(x+5)$

$= (2x+3)(x+5)$

(ii) Solve as part (i). **Ans.** $2(6-r)(r+7)$

13. (i) **Hint** $2x^2 - \frac{5}{6}x + \frac{1}{12} = \frac{24x^2 - 10x + 1}{12}$

$= \frac{1}{12}[24x^2 - (6+4)x + 1]$

$= \frac{1}{12}[24x^2 - 6x - 4x + 1]$

$= \frac{1}{12}[6x(4x-1) - 1(4x-1)]$

$= \frac{1}{12}(4x-1)(6x-1)$

(ii) **Hint** Solve as part (i). **Ans.** $(x - \sqrt{2})(7\sqrt{2}\,x + 4)$

14. Hint Let $(3x + y) = p$, then the given expression becomes $5p^2 + 6p - 8 = (p+2)(5p-4)$

On putting $p = 3x + y$ in

$5(3x+y)^2 + 6(3x+y) - 8$, we get

$= (3x + y + 2)(15x + 5y - 4)$

15. Hint $x^3 - x^2 + ax + x - a - 1 = x^3 - x^2 + ax - a + x - 1$

$= x^2(x-1) + a(x-1) + 1(x-1)$

$= (x-1)(x^2 + a + 1)$

16. Hint Solve as Example 10 of Topic 4.

Ans. $(x-2)(x+3)(2x-5)$

17. Hint By factor theorem, find the factors of polynomial equation.

$$x^3+x^2-x-1=0$$

$$\Rightarrow \quad x^2(x+1)-1(x+1)=0$$

So, 1 and -1 are zeroes of $p(x)$. **Ans.** 1, -1, -1

18. Hint $\sqrt{2a^2+2\sqrt{6}\,ab+3b^2}$

$$=\sqrt{(\sqrt{2}\,a+\sqrt{3}\,b)^2}=\sqrt{2}\,a+\sqrt{3}\,b$$

19. Hint $x^2+\frac{1}{x^2}-2-3x+\frac{3}{x}$

$$=\left(x^2+\frac{1}{x^2}-2\right)-3\left(x-\frac{1}{x}\right)$$

$$=\left(x-\frac{1}{x}\right)^2-3\left(x-\frac{1}{x}\right)=\left(x-\frac{1}{x}\right)\left(x-\frac{1}{x}-3\right)$$

20. Hint $\sqrt{u}+\sqrt{v}=\sqrt{w} \Rightarrow (\sqrt{u}+\sqrt{v})^2=(\sqrt{w})^2$

$$\Rightarrow \quad u+v+2\sqrt{uv}=w$$

$$\Rightarrow \quad u+v-w=-2\sqrt{uv}$$

$$\Rightarrow u+v-w+2\sqrt{uv}=0$$

21. Hint $(x^2+4)-2a-a^2-5$

$$=x^2-2a-a^2-1=x^2-(1+2a+a^2)$$

$$=x^2-(1+a)^2=[x-(1+a)][x+(1+a)]$$

$$=(x-1-a)(x+1+a)$$

22. Hint Using identity

$(x-y)(x+y)=x^2-y^2$,

$$\left(a-\frac{1}{a}\right)\left(a+\frac{1}{a}\right)\left(a^2+\frac{1}{a^2}\right)\left(a^4+\frac{1}{a^4}\right)$$

$$=\left[\left(a^2-\frac{1}{a^2}\right)\left(a^2+\frac{1}{a^2}\right)\right]\left(a^4+\frac{1}{a^4}\right)$$

$$=\left[(a^2)^2-\frac{1}{(a^2)^2}\right]\left[a^4+\frac{1}{a^4}\right]$$

$$=\left(a^4-\frac{1}{a^4}\right)\left(a^4+\frac{1}{a^4}\right)=a^8-\frac{1}{a^8}$$

23. Hint Given, $p(x)=(x-2)^2-(x+2)^2$

$$=[(x-2)+(x+2)][(x-2)-(x+2)]$$

$$=(2x)(-4)=-8x \quad \textbf{Ans. } 0$$

24. Hint Let $p(x)=x^4-7x^2+6$

On putting $x^2=y$, then the given expression becomes

$$p(y)=y^2-7y+6=y^2-6y-y+6$$

$$=y(y-6)-1(y-6)=(y-1)(y-6)$$

On putting $y=x^2$, we get

$$p(x)=(x^2-1)(x^2-6)$$

$$=(x^2-1)(x^2-(\sqrt{6})^2)$$

$$=(x-1)(x+1)(x-\sqrt{6})(x+\sqrt{6})$$

25. Hint Solve as Example 7 of Topic 5.

Ans.

(i) $(5x-3y+3z)^2$ (ii) $(-3x+4y+2z)^2$

(iii) $(3x+2y-4z)^2$ (iv) $(4x-2y+3z)^2$

26. (i) **Hint** $(x+y+z)^2+(x+y-z)^2$

$$=(x^2+y^2+z^2+2xy+2yz+2zx)+(x^2+y^2+z^2+2xy-2yz-2zx)$$

$$=2x^2+2y^2+2z^2+4xy$$

(ii) **Hint** Use identity $x^2-y^2=(x+y)(x-y)$

Ans. $8x(p-c)$

27. Hint $24\sqrt{3}\,x^3-125y^3=(2\sqrt{3}\,x)^3-(5y)^3$

$$=(2\sqrt{3}\,x-5y)(12x^2+25y^2+10\sqrt{3}\,xy)$$

28. (i) **Hint** $1-64a^3-12a+48a^2$

$$=(1)^3-(4a)^3-3\times1^2\times4a+3\times1\times(4a)^2$$

$$=(1-4a)^3$$

(ii) **Hint** $8p^3+\frac{12}{5}p^2+\frac{6}{25}p+\frac{1}{125}$

$$=(2p)^3+3\times(2p)^2\times\frac{1}{5}+3\times(2p)\times\left(\frac{1}{5}\right)^2+\left(\frac{1}{5}\right)^3$$

$$=\left(2p+\frac{1}{5}\right)\left(2p+\frac{1}{5}\right)\left(2p+\frac{1}{5}\right)=\left(2p+\frac{1}{5}\right)^3$$

29. Hint $27x^3-(3x-y)^3$

$$=(3x)^3-(3x-y)^3$$

$$=[3x-(3x-y)][(3x)^2+(3x-y)^2+3x\times(3x-y)]$$

$$=y(9x^2+9x^2+y^2-6xy+9x^2-3xy)$$

$$=27x^2y+y^3-9xy^2$$

30. Hint $a^7-ab^6=a(a^6-b^6)=a[(a^3)^2-(b^3)^2]$

$$=a(a^3+b^3)(a^3-b^3)$$

$$=a(a+b)(a^2-ab+b^2)(a-b)(a^2+ab+b^2)$$

31. Hint $a^3(b-c)^3+b^3(c-a)^3+c^3(a-b)^3$

$$=[a(b-c)]^3+[b(c-a)]^3+[c(a-b)]^3$$

On putting $a(b-c)=x, b(c-a)=y$ and $c(a-b)=z$, we get

$$x^3+y^3+z^3=3xyz \qquad [\because x+y+z=0]$$

$$=3[a(b-c)][b(c-a)][c(a-b)]$$

$$=3abc(a-b)(b-c)(c-a)$$

32. Hint $(2x-y+3z)(4x^2+y^2+9z^2+2xy+3yz-6xz)$

$$=(2x-y+3z)[(2x)^2+(-y)^2+(3z)^2-(2x)(-y)-(-y)(3z)-(2x)(3z)]$$

$$=(2x)^3+(-y)^3+(3z)^3-3(2x)(-y)(3z)$$

$$=8x^3-y^3+27z^3+18xyz$$

33. (i) **Hint** $3a^3b-243ab^3=3ab(a^2-81b^2)$

$$=3ab[(a)^2-(9b)^2]$$
$$=3ab(a-9b)(a+9b)$$

(ii) **Hint** $x^4-625=(x^2)^2-(25)^2=(x^2-25)(x^2+25)$

$$=[(x)^2-(5)^2](x^2+25)$$
$$=(x+5)(x-5)(x^2+25)$$

(iii) **Hint** $a^3+b^3+(a+b)$

$$=(a+b)(a^2-ab+b^2)+(a+b)$$
$$=(a+b)(a^2-ab+b^2+1)$$

(iv) **Hint** $x(x-y)^3+3x^2y(x-y)$

$$=(x-y)[x(x-y)^2+3x^2y]$$
$$=x(x-y)(x^2+y^2-2xy+3xy)$$
$$=x(x-y)(x^2+y^2+xy)$$

34. Hint Given, $a^2+\dfrac{9}{a^2}=31$ ...(i)

Now, $\left(a-\dfrac{3}{a}\right)^2=a^2+\dfrac{9}{a^2}-6$

$\Rightarrow$ $\left(a-\dfrac{3}{a}\right)^2=31-6 \Rightarrow \left(a-\dfrac{3}{a}\right)^2=25$

$\Rightarrow$ $a-\dfrac{3}{a}=5$

35. Hint Given, $y-\dfrac{1}{y}=9$

$\Rightarrow$ $y^2+\dfrac{1}{y^2}-2\times y\times\dfrac{1}{y}=81 \Rightarrow y^2+\dfrac{1}{y^2}=83$

$$\left(y^2+\frac{1}{y^2}\right)^2=(83)^2$$

$\Rightarrow y^4+\dfrac{1}{y^4}+2\times y^2\times\dfrac{1}{y^2}=6889$

$\Rightarrow$ $y^4+\dfrac{1}{y^4}=6887$

36. Hint $\left(x+\dfrac{1}{x}\right)^2=x^2+\dfrac{1}{x^2}+2$

$\Rightarrow$ $\left(x+\dfrac{1}{x}\right)^2=14+2=16 \Rightarrow x+\dfrac{1}{x}=\pm 4$

***Case* I** When $x+\dfrac{1}{x}=4$, then

$$\left(x+\frac{1}{x}\right)^3=x^3+\frac{1}{x^3}+3\left(x+\frac{1}{x}\right)$$

$\Rightarrow$ $(4)^3=x^3+\dfrac{1}{x^3}+3\times 4$

$\therefore$ $x^3+\dfrac{1}{x^3}=64-12=52$

***Case* II** When $x+\dfrac{1}{x}=-4$, then

$$\left(x+\frac{1}{x}\right)^3=x^3+\frac{1}{x^3}+3\left(x+\frac{1}{x}\right)$$

$\Rightarrow$ $(-4)^3=x^3+\dfrac{1}{x^3}+3(-4)$

$\therefore$ $x^3+\dfrac{1}{x^3}=-64+12=-52$

37. Hint Let $f(x)=x^3+ax^2+bx+6$ ...(i)

Since, $(x-2)$ is a factor of $f(x)$, then $f(2)=0$.

$\therefore$ $2^3+a\times 2^2+b\times 2+6=0 \Rightarrow 2a+b=-7$ ...(ii)

Since, $f(x)$ leaves remainder 3 when divided by $(x-3)$.

$\therefore$ $3=f(3)=(3)^3+a\times(3)^2+b\times 3+6$

$\Rightarrow$ $3=9a+3b+33 \Rightarrow 9a+3b=-30$ ...(iii)

On solving Eqs. (ii) and (iii), we get

$$a=-3,\ b=-1$$

38. Hint $\because$ $p(2)=p \Rightarrow a(2)^3-3(2)^2+4=p$

$\Rightarrow$ $8a-12+4=p$

$\Rightarrow$ $8a-8=p$ ...(i)

and $g(3)=q$

$\Rightarrow$ $2(3)^3-5(3)+a=q$

$\Rightarrow$ $54-15+a=q \Rightarrow 39+a=q$ ...(ii)

We have, $p-2q=4$

$\Rightarrow 8a-8-2(39+a)=4$ [from Eqs. (i) and (ii)]

$\Rightarrow$ $8a-8-78-2a=4$

$\Rightarrow$ $6a-86=4 \Rightarrow 6a=4+86=90$

$\Rightarrow$ $a=\dfrac{90}{6}=15$

39. Hint Let $f(x)=y^3+2y^2-5ay-7$

and $g(x)=y^3+ay^2-12y+6$

Now, $f(-1)=(-1)^3+2\times(-1)^2-5\times a\times(-1)-7$

$$=-1+2+5a-7=5a-6$$

and $g(2)=(2)^3+a\times(2)^2-12\times 2+6$ $[\because y=2]$

$$=8+4a-24+6$$
$$=14+4a-24=4a-10$$

But it is given that,

$$A=f(-1),\ B=g(2)$$

$\therefore$ $A=5a-6,\ B=4a-10$

Given, $2A+B=6$

$\Rightarrow 2(5a-6)+(4a-10)=6$

$\Rightarrow$ $10a-12+4a-10=6 \Rightarrow 14a=28$

$\Rightarrow$ $a=\dfrac{28}{14}=2$

40. Hint Let $f(x)=2x^4-6x^3+3x^2+3x-2$

and $g(x)=x^2-3x+2=(x-2)(x-1)$

Now, $f(x)$ will be exactly divisible by $g(x)$, if it is exactly divisible by $(x-2)$ as well as $(x-1)$.

For this, we must have $f(2)=0$ and $f(1)=0$.

41. Hint Let the total number of camels be x.

Then, number of herds of camels seen in the forest $= \frac{x}{4}$

Number of camels gone to mountains $= 2\sqrt{x}$

Number of camels on the bank of river = 15

$\therefore$ Total number of camels $= \frac{x}{4} + 2\sqrt{x} + 15$

$\Rightarrow \quad x = \frac{x}{4} + 2\sqrt{x} + 15$

$\Rightarrow \quad x - \frac{x}{4} - 2\sqrt{x} - 15 = 0$

$\Rightarrow \quad \frac{4x - x - 8\sqrt{x} - 15 \times 4}{4} = 0$

$\Rightarrow \quad 3x - 8\sqrt{x} - 60 = 0 \quad \ldots(i)$

Let $\sqrt{x} = y$, then Eq. (i) becomes

$3y^2 - 8y - 60 = 0$

$\Rightarrow \quad (3y + 10)(y - 6) = 0$

$\Rightarrow \quad 3y + 10 = 0$ and $y - 6 = 0$

$\Rightarrow \quad 3y = -10$ and $y = 6$

$\Rightarrow \quad y = \frac{-10}{3}$ and $y = 6$

When $y = -\frac{10}{3}$, then $\sqrt{x} = -\frac{10}{3}$ which is not possible. [put $y = \sqrt{x}$]

When $y = 6$, then $\sqrt{x} = 6$ [put $y = \sqrt{x}$]

$\Rightarrow \quad x = 6^2 = 36$

42. Hint $\because (x^2 - 4x + 4)(x^2 - 6x + 9) = (x-2)^2 (x-3)^2$

On taking square root both sides, we get

$\sqrt{(x^2 - 4x + 4)(x^2 - 6x + 9)} = \sqrt{(x-2)^2 (x-3)^2}$

$= (x-2)(x-3) = x^2 - 5x + 6$

43. Hint We know that $x^2 + y^2 = (x+y)^2 - 2xy$

Now, $(x+y)^2 = [(2+\sqrt{5})^{1/2} + (2-\sqrt{5})^{1/2} + (2+\sqrt{5})^{1/2} - (2-\sqrt{5})^{1/2}]^2$

$= [2(2+\sqrt{5})^{1/2}]^2 = 4(2+\sqrt{5}) = 8 + 4\sqrt{5}$

and $\quad 2xy = 2[(2+\sqrt{5})^{1/2} + (2-\sqrt{5})^{1/2}]$
$[(2+\sqrt{5})^{1/2} - (2-\sqrt{5})^{1/2}]$

$= 2[((2+\sqrt{5})^{1/2})^2 - ((2-\sqrt{5})^{1/2})^2]$

$= 2[2 + \sqrt{5} - 2 + \sqrt{5}]$

$= 4\sqrt{5}$

Hence, $x^2 + y^2 = (x+y)^2 - 2xy$

$= 8 + 4\sqrt{5} - 4\sqrt{5} = 8$

44. Hint $a^{12}y^4 - a^4y^{12} = a^4y^4(a^8 - y^8)$

$= a^4y^4[(a^4)^2 - (y^4)^2]$

$= a^4y^4[(a^4 + y^4)(a^4 - y^4)]$

$= a^4y^4[(a^4 + y^4)\{(a^2)^2 - (y^2)^2\}]$

$= a^4y^4[(a^4 + y^4)(a^2 + y^2)(a^2 - y^2)]$

$= a^4y^4[(a^4 + y^4)(a^2 + y^2)(a + y)(a - y)]$

45. Hint Given,

$p(x) = 9x^2 + y^2 + z^2 - 6xy + 2yz - 6xz$

$= (3x)^2 + (-y)^2 + (-z)^2 + 2(3x)(-y) + 2(-y)(-z) + 2(3x)(-z)$

$= (3x - y - z)^2$

On putting $x = 1$, $y = 2$ and $z = +1$, we get

$p(x) = [3 \times 1 - 2 - (+1)]^2$

$= (3 - 2 - 1)^2 = 0 = 0$

46. Hint Given, $a + b + c = 0$

$\therefore \quad a^3 + b^3 + c^3 - 3abc = 0$

$\Rightarrow \quad a^3 + b^3 + c^3 = 3abc$

$\Rightarrow \quad \frac{a^3 + b^3 + c^3}{abc} = 3$

$\Rightarrow \quad \frac{a^3}{abc} + \frac{b^3}{abc} + \frac{c^3}{abc} = 3$

$\Rightarrow \quad \frac{a^2}{bc} + \frac{b^2}{ac} + \frac{c^2}{ab} = 3$ **Hence proved.**

47. Hint To prove,

$(a+b+c)^3 - a^3 - b^3 - c^3 = 3(a+b)(b+c)(c+a)$

LHS $= [(a+b+c)^3 - a^3] - (b^3 + c^3)$

$= (a+b+c-a)[(a+b+c)^2 + a^2 + a(a+b+c)] - [(b+c)(b^2 + c^2 - bc)]$

$= (b+c)[a^2 + b^2 + c^2 + 2ab + 2bc + 2ca + a^2 + a^2 + ab + ac] - (b+c)(b^2 + c^2 - bc)$

$= (b+c)[b^2 + c^2 + 3a^2 + 3ab + 3ac - b^2 - c^2 + 3bc]$

$= (b+c)[3(a^2 + ab + ac + bc)]$

$= 3(b+c)[a(a+b) + c(a+b)]$

$= 3(a+b)(b+c)(c+a)$

48. Hint Here, $(a^2 - b^2) + (b^2 - c^2) + (c^2 - a^2) = 0$

$\therefore (a^2 - b^2)^3 + (b^2 - c^2)^3 + (c^2 - a^2)^3$

$= 3(a^2 - b^2)(b^2 - c^2)(c^2 - a^2)$

$3(a-b)(a+b)(b-c)(b+c)(c-a)(c+a)$

Similarly, $(a - b) + (b - c) + (c - a) = 0$

$\therefore \quad (a-b)^3 + (b-c)^3 + (c-a)^3$

$= 3(a-b)(b-c)(c-a)$

Now, $\frac{(a^2 - b^2)^3 + (b^2 - c^2)^3 + (c^2 - a^2)^3}{(a-b)^3 + (b-c)^3 + (c-a)^3}$

$= \frac{3(a-b)(a+b)(b-c)(b+c)(c-a)(c+a)}{3(a-b)(b-c)(c-a)}$

$= (a+b)(b+c)(c+a)$

Mind Map

POLYNOMIALS

Terms and Coefficients of a Polynomial

Terms

Parts of polynomial separated by '+' or '–' sign.

e.g. x^2, $-4x$, 7 are terms of $x^2 - 4x + 7$.

Coefficient

Constants associated with terms.

e.g. 1, – 4, 7 are coefficients for $x^2 - 4x + 7$.

Algebraic Identities

Identities are universal truth.

(i) $(x \pm y)^2 = x^2 \pm 2xy + y^2$

(ii) $x^2 - y^2 = (x - y)(x + y)$

(iii) $(x + a)(x + b) = x^2 + (a + b)x + ab$

(iv) $(x + y + z)^2$
$= x^2 + y^2 + z^2 + 2xy + 2yz + 2zx$

(v) $(x \pm y)^3 = x^3 \pm y^3 \pm 3xy(x \pm y)$

(vi) $x^3 + y^3 + z^3 - 3xyz$
$= (x + y + z)(x^2 + y^2 + z^2 - xy - yz - zx)$

Some Special Identities

(vii) $x^3 - y^3 = (x - y)(x^2 + xy + y^2)$

(viii) $x^3 + y^3 = (x + y)(x^2 - xy + y^2)$

(ix) $x^2 + y^2 + z^2 - xy - yz - zx$
$= \frac{1}{2}[(x - y)^2 + (y - z)^2 + (z - x)^2]$

Classification of Polynomials

On the Basis of Number of Terms

Monomial

Containing one non-zero term.

e.g. 5x, 7

Binomial

Containing two non-zero terms.

e.g. $z^{24} - z^2$.

Trinomial

Containing three non-zero terms.

e.g. $8 + 3x + x^2$

On the Basis of Degree of Variables

Constant Polynomial

Having zero degree i.e. have one constant term.

e.g. 7.

Linear Polynomial

Having degree 1.

e.g. $2x + 5$

Quadratic Polynomial

Having degree 2.

e.g. $3x^2 + 7x + 9$

Cubic Polynomial

Having degree 3.

e.g. $ax^3 + bx^2 + cx + d$

***n*-degree**

Having degree n.

e.g. $a_n x^n + a_{n-1} x^{n-1} + \dots$

Zero Polynomial

If $p(x) = 0$, then it is the zero polynomial.

Polynomial in One Variable

Variables

It can take various numerical values. Value of variable is not fixed.

Constant

Have fixed numeric values.

e.g. π

Algebraic Expression

Combination of variables and constants connected by four fundamental arithmetic operations.

e.g. $6x^2 - 5y^2$

Polynomial

Algebraic operation involved only non-negative integral power of variable.

e.g. $3x^2 + 2x^2 + 7x + 5$

Polynomial in One Variable

Polynomials involving single variable.

e.g. $5y^2 + 3y$, $4y^2$

Factorisation of the Polynomials

Factor Theorem

Let $p(x)$ be a polynomial of degree $n \geq 1$ and a be any real number.

(i) If $p(a) = 0$, then $(x - a)$ is a factor of $p(x)$.

(ii) If $(x - a)$ is a factor of $p(x)$, then $p(a) = 0$.

Factorisation of Quadratic Polynomials

(i) By Splitting the Middle Term

To factorise $ax^2 + bx + c$, write b as a sum of two numbers whose product is ac.

e.g. $p(x) = x^2 + 5x + 6$
$= x^2 + 3x + 2x + 6 = (x + 3)(x + 2)$

(ii) By Factor Theorem

Let $p(x) = ax^2 + bx + c$ write
$p(x) = ag(x)$, where $g(x) = x^2 + \frac{b}{a}x + \frac{c}{a}$

Find all factors of $\frac{c}{a}$ using trial method, then find a factor of $g(x)$.

Write $g(x) = (x - \alpha)(x - \beta)$

Factorisation of Cubic Polynomials

Write $p(x) = ag(x)$, find all factors of constant term write
$p(x) = (x - a)(a_1 x^2 + b_1 x + c_1)$ for quadratic factor apply splitting the middle term.

Degree of a Polynomial

In One Variable

The highest power of variable is called degree of polynomial.

e.g. Let $p(x) = 2x^4 - 6x^3 + 4x + 1$

Degree of $p(x) = 4$.

Zeroes of a Polynomial

Value of a Polynomial

The value of polynomial obtained on putting a particular value of the variable is called the value of a polynomial.

e.g. Let $p(x) = 5x^2 + 2$

Then, $p(1) = 5 \times 1^2 + 2 = 7$

Zeroes of a Polynomial

Also called roots of polynomial. It is the value of x for which $p(x) = 0$.

e.g. Let $p(x) = 2x - 1$, then $p\left(\frac{1}{2}\right) = 0$

So, $\frac{1}{2}$ is the zero of $p(x)$.

CHAPTER 3

Coordinate Geometry

Coordinate geometry is the branch of Mathematics in which we study the position of any object lying in a plane, with the help of two mutually perpendicular lines in the same plane. This study was initially developed by the French Philosopher and Mathematician Rene Descartes (1596-1650).

Cartesian System

In cartesian system, there are two perpendicular straight lines XX' (horizontal line) and YY' (vertical line) which intersect at point O, shown below:

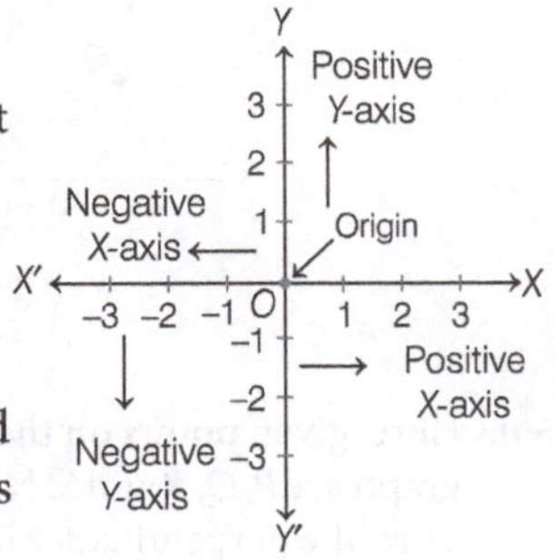

The point of intersection of these lines is called **origin** and it is denoted by O.

The horizontal line XOX' is called X-**axis** and the vertical line YOY' is called Y-**axis**.

Directions OX and OY are called the **positive directions** of X-axis and Y-axis, respectively.

Similarly, directions OX' and OY' are called the **negative directions** of X-axis and Y-axis, respectively.

Note It The X-axis and Y-axis is written in short as X and Y-axes.

Quadrant

The X and Y-axes divide the plane into four parts. These four parts are called **quadrant** $\left(\text{i.e.} \frac{1}{4}\text{th part}\right)$, numbered I, II, III and IV anti-clockwise from OX.

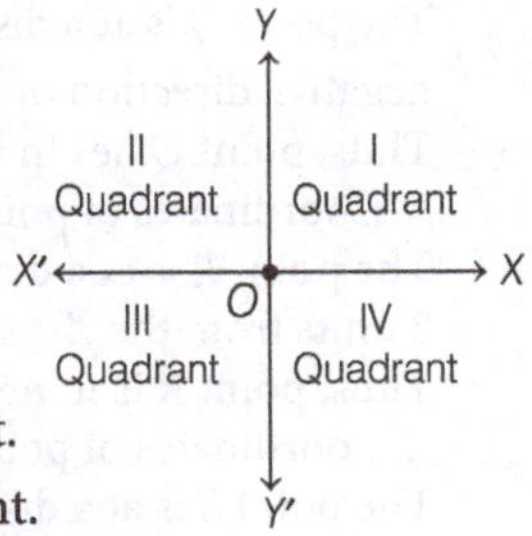

(i) XOY is called the I quadrant.

(ii) $X'OY$ is called the II quadrant.

(iii) $X'OY'$ is called the III quadrant.

(iv) XOY' is called the IV quadrant.

So, the plane consists of two axes and four quadrants. The plane is known as **XY-plane** or **Cartesian plane** or **coordinate plane** and the axes are known as the **coordinate axes.**

Coordinates of a Point in Cartesian Plane

To locate a point in the cartesian plane, its perpendicular distances from X-axis and Y-axis are required, these distances are called **coordinates of the point.** Each point in cartesian plane has two coordinates, x-coordinate and y-coordinate.

(i) The **x-coordinate** of a point is the perpendicular distance from the Y-axis measured along the X-axis (positive, along the positive direction of the X-axis and negative, along the negative direction of X-axis). The x-coordinate is also called the **abscissa.**

(ii) The **y-coordinate** of a point is the perpendicular distance from the X-axis measured along the Y-axis (positive, along the positive direction of the Y-axis and negative, along the negative direction of Y-axis). The y-coordinate is also called the **ordinate.**

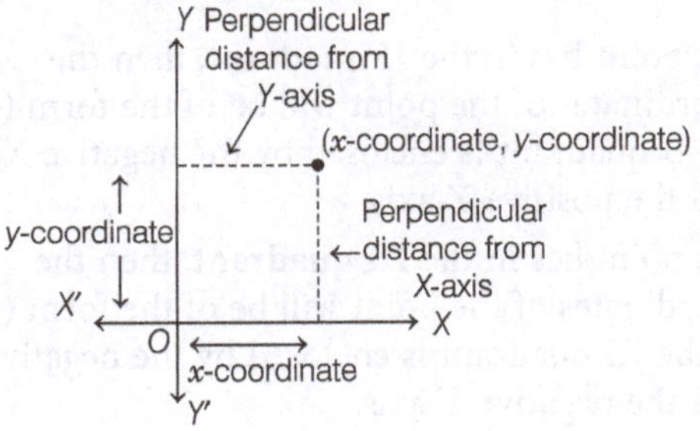

The x-coordinate and y-coordinate taken together are called **cartesian coordinates** or **coordinates of a point** and it is denoted by (x, y). Here, the x-coordinate comes first and y-coordinate comes second, so (x, y) is called an **ordered pair.**

Coordinates describe a point in the plane uniquely i.e. point (a, b) is not same as (b, a).

Important Points

(i) **Coordinates of a point on X-axis** Every point on the X-axis has zero perpendicular distance from the X-axis, so its ordinate is 0. Thus, the coordinates of every point on the X-axis are of the form $(x, 0)$.

(ii) **Coordinates of a point on Y-axis** Every point on the Y-axis has zero perpendicular distance from the Y-axis, so its abscissa is 0. Thus, the coordinates of every point on the Y-axis are of the form $(0, y)$.

(iii) **The coordinates of a point at origin** The coordinates of origin is (0, 0) because it has zero distance from both the axes. So, its abscissa and ordinate both are zero.

(iv) If x-coordinate of two or more points are same, then the line joining these points is parallel to Y-axis.

(v) If y-coordinate of two or more points are same, then the line joining these points is parallel to X-axis.

Convention of Signs of Coordinates in Different Quadrants

Useful rules to determine the signs of the coordinates of a point in a quadrant are given below:

(i) If a point lies in the **I quadrant**, then the coordinates of the point will be of the form (+, +), as the I quadrant is enclosed by the positive X-axis and the positive Y-axis.

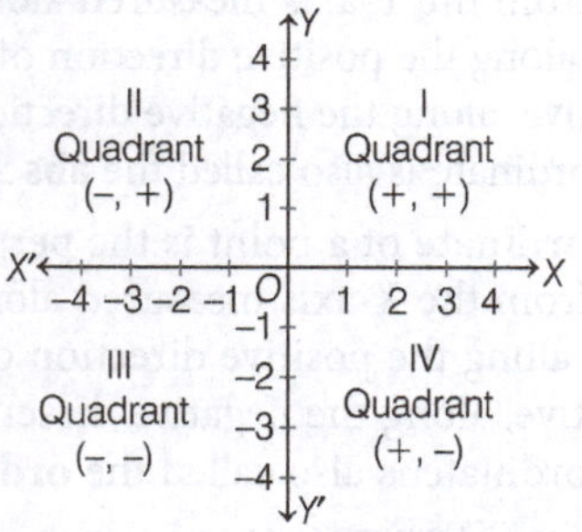

(ii) If a point lies in the **II quadrant**, then the coordinates of the point will be of the form (–, +), as the II quadrant is enclosed by the negative X-axis and the positive Y-axis.

(iii) If a point lies in the **III quadrant**, then the coordinates of the point will be of the form (–, –), as the III quadrant is enclosed by the negative X-axis and the negative Y-axis.

(iv) If a point lies in the **IV quadrant**, then the coordinates of the point will be of the form (+, –), as the IV quadrant is enclosed by the positive X-axis and the negative Y-axis (see figure).

Region	Quadrant	Nature of x and y coordinates	Sign of x-coordinate	Sign of y-coordinate	Sign of Coordinates of a point
XOY	I	$x > 0, y > 0$	+	+	(+, +)
$X'OY$	II	$x < 0, y > 0$	–	+	(–, +)
$X'OY'$	III	$x < 0, y < 0$	–	–	(–, –)
XOY'	IV	$x > 0, y < 0$	+	–	(+, –)

Example 1. **Write the coordinates of the point which lies at a distance of x units from X-axis and y units from Y-axis.**

Sol. Required point is $P(y, x)$.

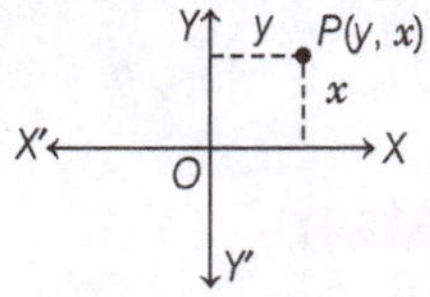

Example 2. **Write the coordinates of the points given in the following graph.**

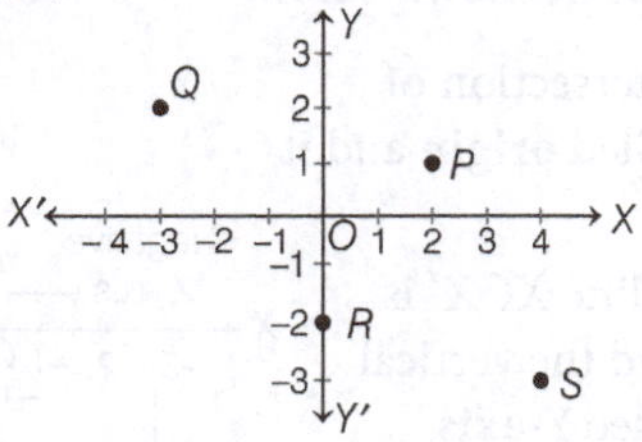

Sol. Here, given points on the graph are P, Q, R and S. Now, draw the perpendicular lines from points P, Q, R and S on the X-axis and Y-axis.

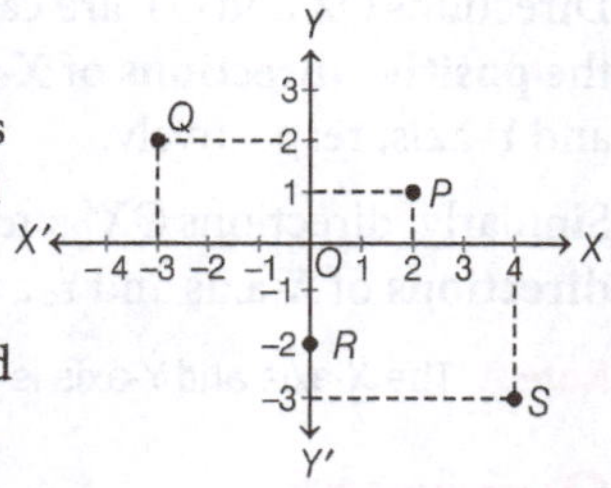

The point P is at a distance of 2 units from the Y-axis and 1 unit from the X-axis. Thus, point P lies in I quadrant.

$\therefore$ Coordinates of point P are (2, 1).

The point Q is at a distance of 3 units from the Y-axis in negative direction of X-axis and 2 units from the X-axis. Thus, point Q lies in II quadrant.

$\therefore$ Coordinates of point Q are (–3, 2).

The point R is at a distance of 0 unit from the Y-axis and 2 units from the X-axis.

Thus, point R is in negative direction of Y-axis.

$\therefore$ Coordinates of point R are (0, – 2).

The point S is at a distance of 4 units from the Y-axis and 3 units from the X-axis in the negative direction of Y-axis.

Thus, point S lies in IV quadrant.

$\therefore$ Coordinates of point S are (4, – 3).

Example 3. **In which quadrant or on which axis each of the following points lie?** NCERT Exemplar

(i) (–3, 5) (ii) (4, –1) (iii) (2, 0) (iv) (2, 2) (v) (–3, –6)

Sol. (i) For point (–3, 5), x-coordinate is negative and y-coordinate is positive, so it lies in II quadrant.

(ii) For point (4, – 1), x-coordinate is positive and y-coordinate is negative, so it lies in IV quadrant.

(iii) For point (2, 0), x-coordinate is positive and y-coordinate is zero, so it lies on X-axis.

(iv) For point (2, 2), x-coordinate and y-coordinate both are positive, so it lies in I quadrant.

(v) For point (–3, – 6), x-coordinate and y-coordinate both are negative, so it lies in III quadrant.

Example 4. **If the coordinates of two points are $A(3, 4)$ and $B(-2, 5)$, then find (Abscissa of A) – (Abscissa of B).**

Sol. Given, point A (3, 4) i.e. abscissa of $A = 3$

and point B (– 2, 5) i.e. abscissa of $B = -2$

$\therefore$ Abscissa of A – Abscissa of $B = 3 - (-2) = 3 + 2 = 5$

Example 5. **In the given figure, LM is a line parallel to the Y-axis at a distance of 3 units.**

(i) What are the coordinates of the points P, R and Q?

(ii) What is the difference between the abscissa of the points L and M? NCERT Exemplar

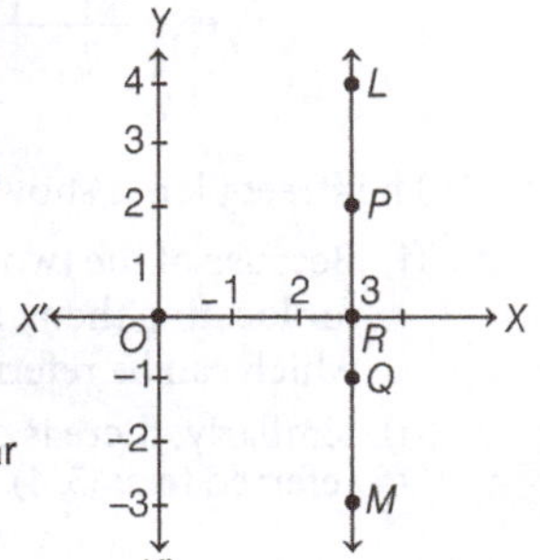

Sol. Given, LM is a line parallel to the Y-axis and its perpendicular distance from Y-axis is 3 units.

(i) Coordinates of point P are (3, 2).

[since, its perpendicular distance from X-axis is 2 units]

Coordinates of point Q are (3, – 1).

[since, its perpendicular distance from X-axis is 1, in the negative direction of Y-axis]

Coordinates of point R are (3, 0).

[since, it lies on X-axis, so its y-coordinate is zero]

(ii) Abscissa of point $L = 3$, abscissa of point $M = 3$

$\therefore$ Difference between the abscissa of points L and M
$= 3 - 3 = 0$

Example 6. **A point lies on X-axis at a distance of 9 units from Y-axis. What are its coordinates? What will be the coordinates of a point, if it lies on Y-axis at a distance of 9 units from X-axis in negative direction?**

Sol. We know that coordinates of any point lie on X-axis at the distance a from the Y-axis are $(a, 0)$ and $(-a, 0)$.

Since, the given point lies on X-axis at a distance of 9 units from Y-axis, so its coordinates are (9, 0) or (– 9, 0).

Now, if point lies on Y-axis at a distance of 9 units from X-axis in negative direction, then its coordinates is (0, –9).

Example 7. **Find the values of x and y, if two ordered pairs $(x-3, -6)$ and $(4, x+y)$ are equal.**

Sol. Given, ordered pairs are $(x-3, -6)$ and $(4, x+y)$.

Since, these ordered pairs are equal, so their corresponding coordinates are equal. Thus, first components are equal

$\therefore \quad x - 3 = 4 \Rightarrow x = 7$

and second components are also equal

$-6 = x + y \Rightarrow -6 = 7 + y \Rightarrow y = -13$

Hence, $x = 7$ and $y = -13$

Example 8. **In the following figure, O is the intersecting points of OA and OC and $OABC$ is a square of side 2 units. Find the position of points A, B and C.**

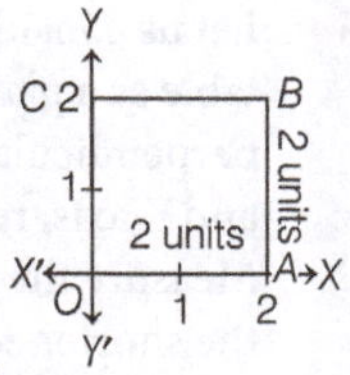

Sol. Here, position means the coordinates of the points. As the point A lies on positive X-axis, at a distance of 2 units from the intersection point O, so its position will be (2, 0). Point B lies in I quadrant and it is at a distance of 2 units from both the axes, so its position will be (2, 2) and point C lies on the positive Y-axis, at a distance of 2 units from the intersection point O, so its position will be (0, 2).

Example 9. **Write down the**

(i) abscissa

(ii) ordinate

(iii) coordinates and

(iv) quadrant

for the points P, Q, R and S.

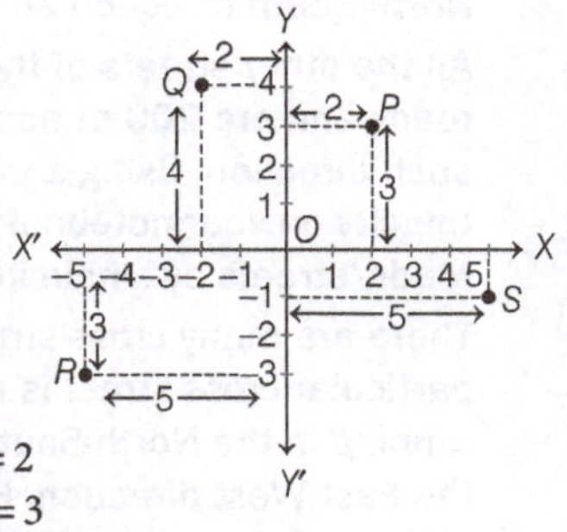

Sol. For Point P

(i) Abscissa of the point = 2

(ii) Ordinate of the point = 3

(iii) Coordinates of the point = (2, 3)

(iv) The point (2, 3) lies in the I quadrant.

For Point Q

(i) Abscissa of the point = – 2

(ii) Ordinate of the point = 4

(iii) Coordinates of the point = (–2, 4)

(iv) The point (–2, 4) lies in the II quadrant.

For Point R

(i) Abscissa of the point = – 5

(ii) Ordinate of the point = – 3

(iii) Coordinates of the point = (–5, – 3)

(iv) The point (–5, – 3) lies in the III quadrant.

For Point S

(i) Abscissa of the point = 5

(ii) Ordinate of the point = – 1

(iii) Coordinates of the point = (5, – 1)

(iv) The point (5, – 1) lies in the IV quadrant.

NCERT FOLDER

Complete Solutions of All Exercises of NCERT Textbook

EXERCISE 3.1 (NCERT Page 45-46)

Q1. How will you describe the position of a table lamp on your study table to another person?

Sol. Let us consider the lamp as a point and table as a plane. Take any two perpendicular edges of the table as X-axis and Y-axis, respectively.

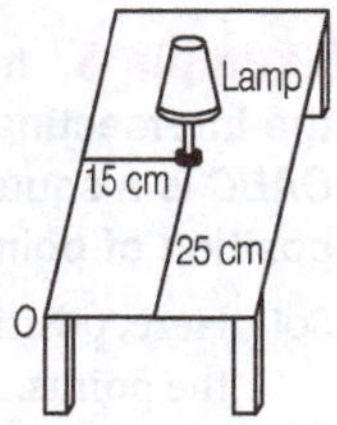

Measure the distance of the lamp from the shorter edge, let it be 25 cm. Again, measure the distance of the lamp from the larger edge, let it be 15 cm. Then, you can write the position of the lamp as (15, 25) or (25, 15) depending on the order you fix.

Q2. A city has two main roads which cross each other at the centre of the city. These two roads are along the North-South direction and East-West direction.

All the other streets of the city run parallel to these roads and are 200 m apart. There are 5 streets in each direction. Using 1 cm = 200 m, draw a model of the city on your notebook. Represent the roads/streets by single lines.

There are many cross-streets in your model. A particular cross-street is made by two streets, one running in the North-South direction and another in the East-West direction. Each cross-street is referred to in the following manner:

If the 2nd street running in the North-South direction and 5th in the East-West direction meet at some crossing, then we will call this cross-street (2, 5). Using this convention, find

(i) how many cross-streets can be referred to as (4, 3)?

(ii) how many cross-streets can be referred to as (3, 4)?

Sol. Let EW and NS be two main roads such that the road EW is along the East-West direction and road NS is along the North-South direction. Then, the angle between the two roads is 90°, i.e. the roads EW and NS are perpendicular to each other.

Let us consider EW along X-axis and NS along Y-axis and let the centre of city is O.

Here, the distance between two consecutive streets in same direction is 200 m and all the streets are parallel to the main roads.

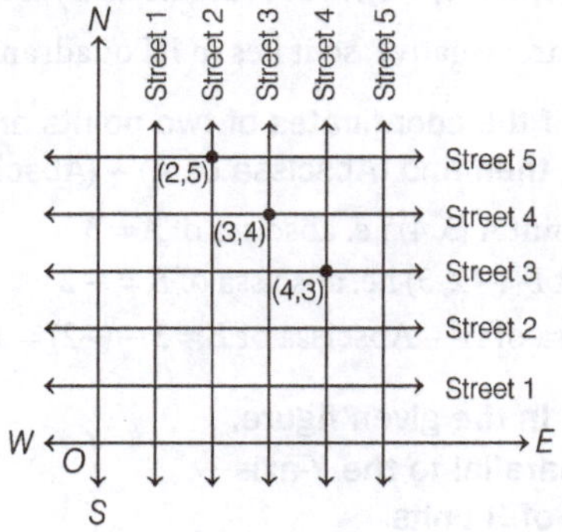

The street plan is shown in the above figure:

(i) Because of the two reference lines that we have used for locating them, there is only one cross-street which can be referred to as (4, 3).

(ii) Similarly, there is only one cross-street which can be referred to as (3, 4).

EXERCISE 3.2 (NCERT Page 52-53)

Q1. Write the answer of each of the following questions:

(i) What is the name of the horizontal and the vertical lines drawn to determine the position of any point in the cartesian plane?

(ii) What is the name of each part of the plane formed by these two lines?

(iii) Write the name of the point, where these two lines intersect.

Sol. (i) The horizontal line is called X-axis and vertical line is called Y-axis.

(ii) Each part of the plane formed by horizontal and vertical lines is known as quadrant.

(iii) The point where these two lines intersect is called the origin and it is denoted by O.

Q2. See figure and write the following

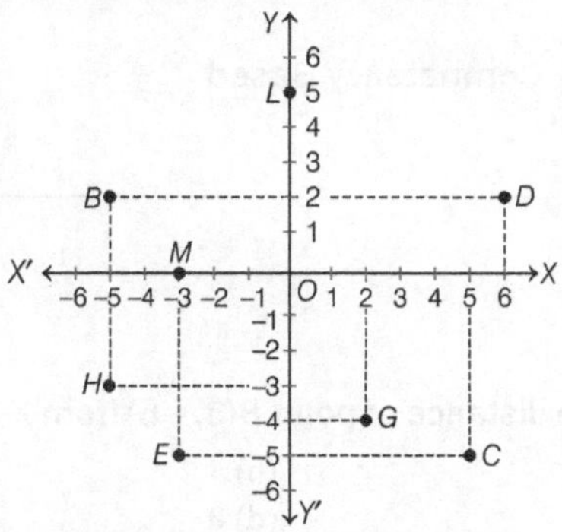

(i) The coordinates of the point *B*.

(ii) The coordinates of the point *C*.

(iii) The point identified by the coordinates (−3, −5).

(iv) The point identified by the coordinates (2, −4).

(v) The abscissa of the point *D*.

(vi) The ordinate of the point *H*.

(vii) The coordinates of the point *L*.

(viii) The coordinates of the point *M*.

Sol. (i) Point *B* is at a distance of 5 units from the *Y*-axis along negative *X*-axis and 2 units from the *X*-axis along positive *Y*-axis. Hence, the coordinates of the point *B* are (−5, 2).

(ii) Do same as part (i). **Ans.** (5, − 5)

(iii) Point, (−3, −5) which has distance of 3 units from the *Y*-axis along negative *X*-axis and 5 units from the *X*-axis along negative *Y*-axis is *E*.

(iv) Do same as part (iii). **Ans.** *G*

(v) Point *D* is at a distance of 6 units from the *Y*-axis along positive *X*-axis. Therefore, its abscissa is 6.

(vi) Point *H* is at a distance of 3 units from the *X*-axis along the negative *Y*-axis.

Therefore, its ordinate is −3.

(vii) Do same as part (i). **Ans.** (0, 5)

(viii) Do same as part (i). **Ans.** (−3, 0)

REVIEW EXERCISE

Including Competency Based Questions

Part I

Multiple Choice Questions

1. A point whose coordinates are both negative will lie in

(a) I quadrant (b) II quadrant
(c) III quadrant (d) IV quadrant

2. In which quadrant, the point (5, – 6) lies?

(a) I (b) II (c) III (d) IV

3. The point $A(a, b)$ lies in II quadrant. Find which of a or b is greater?

(a) a (b) b
(c) Both are equal (d) $a + b$

4. The perpendicular distance of a point from Y-axis is known as

(a) intersection point (b) origin
(c) abscissa (d) ordinate

5. Abscissa of all the points on the X-axis is NCERT Exemplar

(a) 0 (b) 1
(c) 2 (d) any number

6. The point whose ordinate is 4 and which lies on Y-axis is NCERT Exemplar

(a) (4, 0) (b) (0, 4) (c) (1, 4) (d) (4, 2)

7. The point which lies on Y-axis at a distance of 5 units in the negative direction of Y-axis is NCERT Exemplar

(a) (0, 5) (b) (5, 0) (c) (0, – 5) (d) (–5, 0)

8. If the coordinates of the two points are $P(-2, 3)$ and $Q(-3, 5)$, then (Abscissa of P) – (Abscissa of Q) is NCERT Exemplar

(a) – 5 (b) 1 (c) –1 (d) –2

9. If the coordinates of two points are $A(4, 5)$ and $B(-3, 6)$, then (abscissa of A) – (ordinate of B) is

(a) 3 (b) 5
(c) –2 (d) 9

10. If the coordinates of two points are $A(7, -3)$ and $B(7, -5)$, then (ordinate of A) – (ordinate of B) is

(a) 2 (b) –2 (c) 8 (d) –8

11. The coordinates of points P and Q are (– 5, 3) and (– 5, m), respectively. And if sum of abscissa and ordinate of both points are equal. Then, the possible value of m is

(a) – 5 (b) – 13 (c) – 10 (d) 3

12. Find the distance of point $B(3, -5)$ from X-axis.

(a) 3 (b) 5
(c) 4 (d) 8

13. Find the distance of point $C(8, 9)$ from Y-axis.

(a) 7 (b) 8
(c) 9 (d) 1

14. The perpendicular distance of the point $P(3, 4)$ from the Y-axis is NCERT Exemplar

(a) 3 (b) 4 (c) 5 (d) 7

15. Which of the following points lie on Y-axis?

(a) (6, 0) (b) (3, 0)
(c) (0, 7) (d) (3, 2)

16. If the perpendicular distance of a point P from the X-axis is 5 units and the foot of the perpendicular lies on the negative direction of X-axis, then the point P has

(a) x-coordinate = – 5
(b) y-coordinate = 5 only
(c) y-coordinate = – 5 only
(d) y-coordinate = 5 or – 5

17. From the figure given below, find the coordinates of point M. [Competency Based Question]

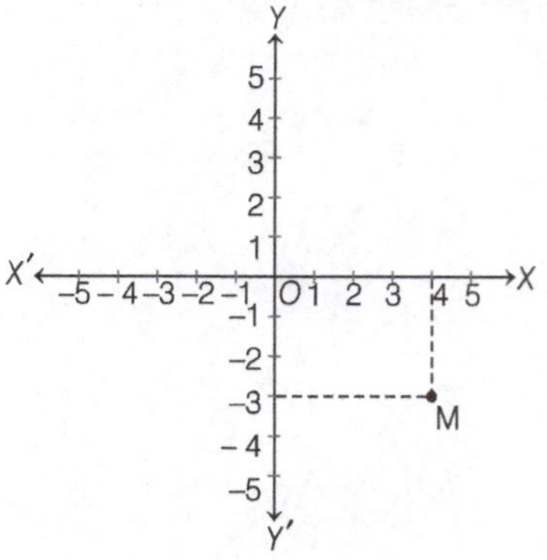

(a) (–4, – 3) (b) (4, – 3)
(c) (–4, 3) (d) (4, 3)

18. The point D lies at a distance of 3 units from X-axis and 6 units from Y-axis along the negative direction of X-axis. The coordinates of the point D are

(a) (–6, 3) (b) (6, 3)
(c) (3, – 6) (d) (–3, 6)

Assertion-Reason Type Questions

19. **Assertion** The point (–6, 0) lies on *Y*-axis and point (0, – 7) lies on *X*-axis.

Reason Every point on the *X*-axis has zero distance from *X*-axis and every point on the *Y*-axis has zero distance from *Y*-axis.

(a) Both Assertion and Reason are correct and Reason is the correct explanation of Assertion.

(b) Both Assertion and Reason are correct but Reason is not the correct explanation of Assertion.

(c) Assertion is correct but Reason is incorrect.

(d) Assertion is incorrect but Reason is correct.

20. **Assertion** The points (–3, 8) and (8, –3) are at different positions in the coordinate plane.

Reason If $x \neq y$, then position of (x, y) in the cartesian plane is different from the position of (y, x).

(a) Both Assertion and Reason are correct and Reason is the correct explanation of Assertion.

(b) Both Assertion and Reason are correct but Reason is not the correct explanation of Assertion.

(c) Assertion is correct but Reason is incorrect.

(d) Assertion is incorrect but Reason is correct.

21. **Assertion** In the following graph, the coordinates of points *P* and *Q* are (2, 2) and (–3, – 2), respectively.

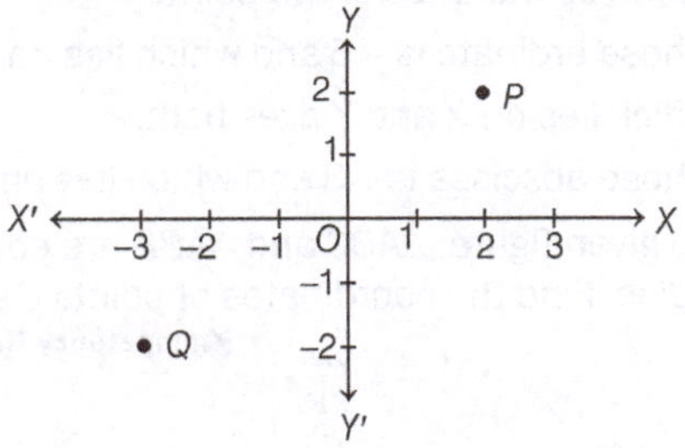

Reason Coordinates of any point can be determined by drawing a perpendicular line to the coordinate axes.

(a) Both Assertion and Reason are correct and Reason is the correct explanation of Assertion.

(b) Both Assertion and Reason are correct but Reason is not the correct explanation of Assertion.

(c) Assertion is correct but Reason is incorrect.

(d) Assertion is incorrect but Reason is correct.

Case Study Based Questions

22. Krisha is a class IX student residing in a village. One day, he went to a city hospital along with his grand father for general checkup. From there, he visited three places - school, library and police station. After returning to his village, he plotted a graph by taking hospital as origin and marked three places on the graph as per his direction of movement and distance. The graph is shown below

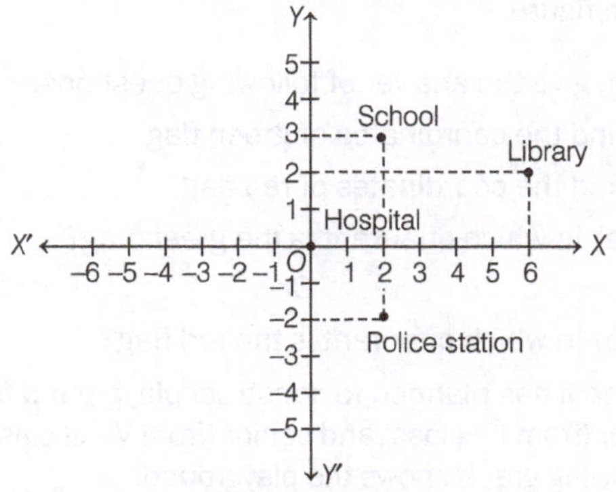

On the basis of above information, answer the following questions.

(i) What are the coordinates of police station?

(ii) What are the coordinates of school?

(iii) (a) What is the distance between school and police station?

Or

(b) In which quadrant the point (–3, 2) lie?

23. To raise the fund for cancer patients, a charity race was organised on rectangular school ground *ABCD*.

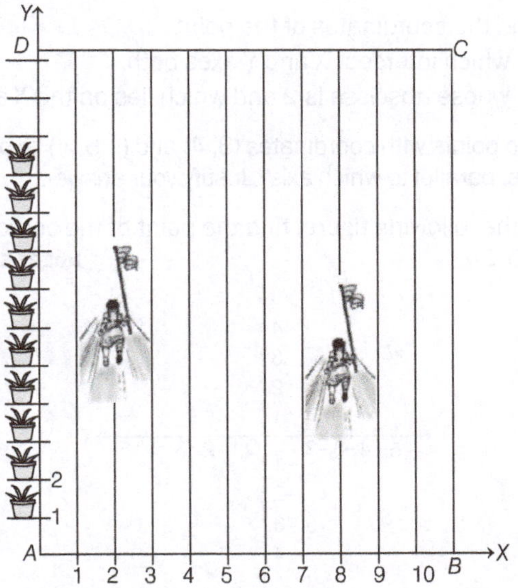

Lines have been drawn with chalk powder at a distance of 1 m each. 100 flower pots have been placed at a distance of 1 m from each other along *AD*.

Niharika runs $\frac{1}{4}$ of the distance *AD* on the second line and posts a green flag. Preeti runs $\frac{1}{5}$ of the distance *AD* on the 8th line and posts a red flag as shown in given figure.

Then, give the answer of following questions.

(i) Find the coordinates of green flag.

(ii) Find the coordinates of red flag.

(iii) (a) In which quadrant is the green flag?

Or

(b) In which quadrant is the red flag?

24. A school has planned to construct playground for junior (from I-V class) and senior (from VI-XII class). Following graph shows the playground.

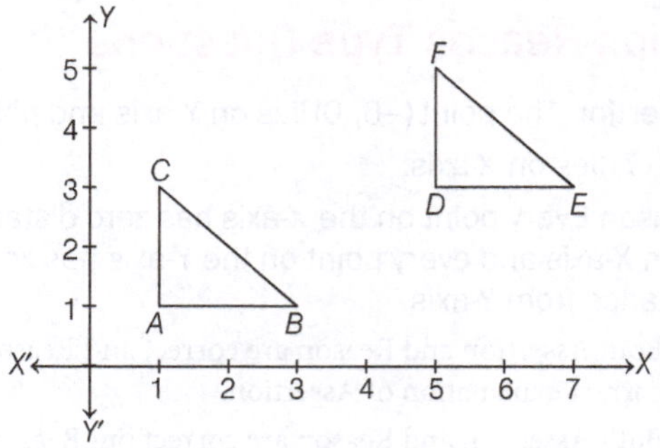

On the basis of above information, answer the following questions:

(i) Find the coordinates of *A*.

(ii) Find the coordinates of *F*.

(iii) (a) What is the area of playground *ABC*?

Or (b) What is the area of playground *DEF*?

Part II

Very Short Answer Type Questions

1. Find the maximum number of points on the *X*-axis and *Y*-axis.

2. In which quadrants do the given points lie?

(i) (4, −2) (ii) (−3, 7) (iii) (−1, −2) (iv) (3, 6)

3. Write the coordinates of a point on *X*-axis at a distance of 6 units from the origin in the positive direction of *X*-axis.

4. Find the coordinates of the point

(i) which intersect *X* and *Y*-axes both.

(ii) whose abscissa is 2 and which lies on the *X*-axis.

5. Two points with coordinates (3, 4) and (− 5, 4) lie on a line, parallel to which axis? Justify your answer.

6. In the following figure, find the point of the coordinates (−5, 3). **NCERT Exemplar**

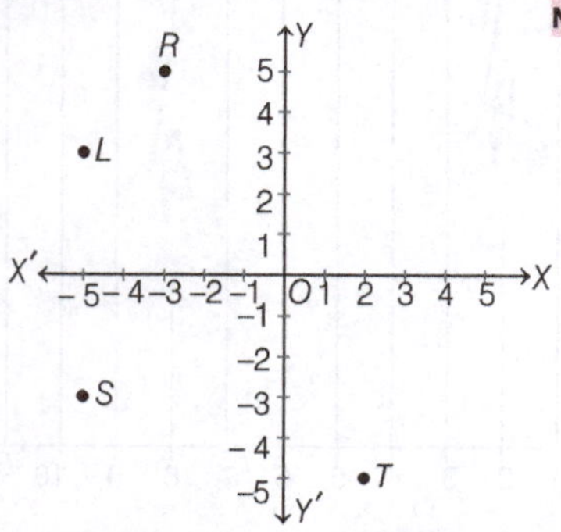

Short Answer Type Questions

7. Name the quadrant in which the graph of point *P*(*x*, *y*) lies when

(i) $x > 0$ and $y > 0$. (ii) $x < 0$ and $y < 0$.

8. Find the coordinates of two points on *X*-axis and two points on *Y*-axis which are at equal distance from the origin.

9. The perpendicular distance of a point from the *X*-axis is 2 units and the perpendicular distance from the *Y*-axis is 3 units. Write the coordinates of the point and find in which quadrant these points lie.

10. Write the coordinates of the point,

(i) whose ordinate is − 5 and which lies on *Y*-axis.

(ii) which lies on *X* and *Y*-axes both.

(iii) whose abscissa is − 3 and which lies on *X*-axis.

11. In the given figure, ΔABC and ΔABD are equilateral triangles. Find the coordinates of points *C* and *D*.

[Competency Based Question]

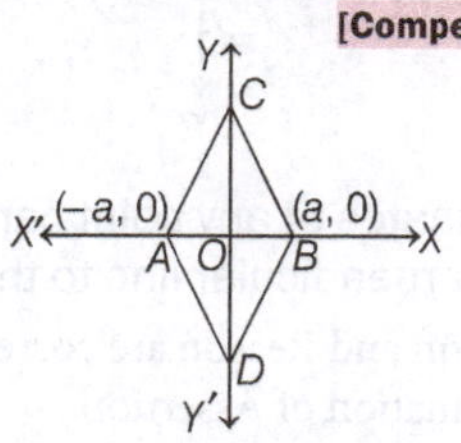

[**Hint** Altitude of an equilateral triangle,

$$OC = OD = \frac{\sqrt{3}}{2} \times \text{Side}]$$

12. Find the coordinates of the vertices of a rectangle placed in III quadrant, in the cartesian plane with length *p* units on *X*-axis and breadth *q* units on *Y*-axis.

13. In the adjoining figure, *PQR* is an equilateral triangle in which coordinates of *Q* and *R* are (0, 4) and (0, −4), respectively. Find the coordinates of the vertex *P*.

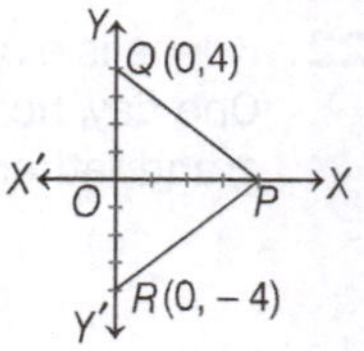

Long Answer Type Questions

14. From the given figure, answer the following questions.

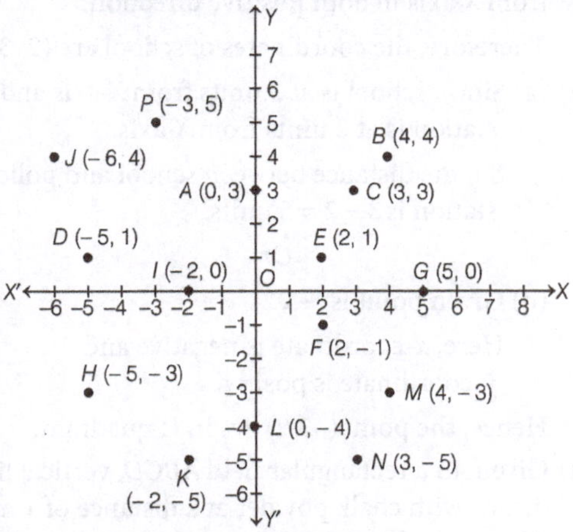

(i) Write the points whose abscissa is 0.

(ii) Write the points whose ordinate is 0.

(iii) Write the points whose abscissa is – 5.

(iv) Write the points whose ordinate is 4.

15. In the given figure, *ABCD* is a rhombus with diagonals *AC* = 16 cm and *BD* = 8 cm. **[Competency Based Question]**

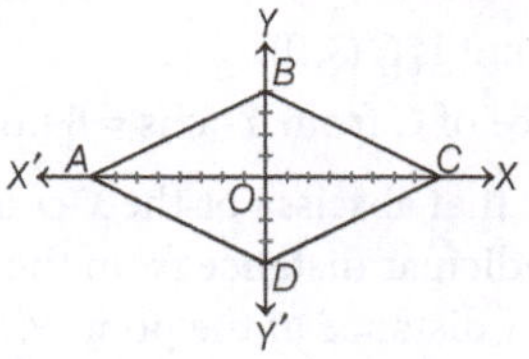

Find the coordinates of *A, B, C* and *D*.

16. Without plotting the points, indicate the quadrants in which they will lie, if

(i) ordinate is 5 and abscissa is –3.

(ii) abscissa is –5 and ordinate is –3.

(iii) abscissa is 5 and ordinate is –3.

(iv) ordinate is 5 and abscissa is 3.

17. Write the coordinates of the vertices of a rectangle, whose length and breadth are 6 units and 3 units respectively, one vertex at the origin, the longer side lies on the *Y*-axis and one of the vertices lies in the II quadrant. Also, find the area of the rectangle.

HINTS & ANSWERS

Part I

1. (c) A point both of whose coordinates are negative will lie in III quadrant because, in III quadrant x-coordinate and y-coordinate both are negative.

2. (d) In point $(5, -6)$, $x = 5 > 0$ and $y = -6 < 0$

$\therefore$ Point $(5, -6)$ lies in IV quadrant.

3. (b) The point $A(a, b)$ lies in II quadrant.

Thus, x-coordinate is negative i.e. a and y-coordinate is positive i.e. b.

$\therefore a < b$

Hence, b is greater.

4. (c) Perpendicular distance of a point from *Y*-axis is called abscissa or x-coordinate.

5. (d) Abscissa of all the points on the *X*-axis is any number because *X*-axis is a number line which contains many real numbers on it.

6. (b) Given, ordinate of the point is 4 and the point lies on *Y*-axis, so its abscissa is zero. Hence, the required point is (0, 4).

7. (c) Given, the point lies on *Y*-axis this shows that its x-coordinate is zero.

Also, it is at a distance of 5 units in negative direction of *Y*-axis, so its y-coordinate is negative. Hence, the required point is $(0, -5)$.

8. (b) We have, points $P(-2, 3)$ and $Q(-3, 5)$

Here, abscissa of P i.e. x-coordinate of P is –2 and abscissa of Q i.e. x-coordinate of Q is –3.

So, (Abscissa of P) – (Abscissa of Q) $= -2 - (-3)$

$= -2 + 3 = 1$

9. (c) Given, point is $A(4, 5)$ i.e. abscissa of $A = 4$ and point $B(-3, 6)$ i.e. ordinate of $B = 6$

$\therefore$ Abscissa of A – ordinate of $B = 4 - 6 = -2$

10. (a) Given, point is $A(7, -3)$ i.e. ordinate of $A = -3$ and point $B(7, -5)$ i.e. ordinate of $B = -5$

$\therefore$ Ordinate of A – Ordinate of $B = -3 - (-5)$

$= -3 + 5 = 2$

11. (b) Given, coordinates of $P = (-5, 3)$ and $Q = (-5, m)$

According to the question,

$$m + 3 = -5 - 5$$

$$\Rightarrow \quad m + 3 = -10$$

$$\Rightarrow \quad m = -10 - 3 = -13$$

12. (b) Given, point is $B(3, -5)$.

Thus, distance of B from X-axis = 5 units

13. (b) Given, point is $C(8, 9)$.

Thus, distance of C from Y-axis = 8 units

14. (a) We know that abscissa or the x-coordinate of a point is the perpendicular distance from the Y-axis. So, perpendicular distance of the point $P(3, 4)$ from Y-axis = Abscissa = 3

15. (c) If a point lies on Y-axis, then its x-coordinate is zero. Thus, the point (0, 7) lies on Y-axis.

16. (d) We know that the perpendicular distance of a point from the X-axis gives y-coordinate at that point. Here, the foot of perpendicular lies on the negative direction of X-axis, so perpendicular distance can be measure from II quadrant or III quadrant.

Hence, the point P has y-coordinate = 5 or -5.

17. (b) In the given figure, point M lies at a distance of 4 units from Y-axis and at a distance of 3 units from X-axis along the negative direction of Y-axis. x-coordinate is 4 and y-coordinate is -3. Thus, the coordinates of point M are $(4, -3)$.

18. (a) The point D lies at a distance of 3 units from X-axis, i.e. y-coordinate is 3 and at a distance of 6 units from Y-axis along the negative direction of X-axis i.e. x coordinate is -6.

Thus, the coordinates of point D are $(-6, 3)$.

19. (d) **Assertion** The point $(-6, 0)$ lies on X-axis and point $(0, -7)$ lies on Y-axis. So, Assertion is incorrect.

Reason It is correct that every point on the X-axis and Y-axis has zero distance from X-axis and Y-axis, respectively.

20. (a) **Assertion** $(-3, 8)$ and $(8, -3)$ are different points as $(-3, 8)$ lies in II quadrant and $(8, -3)$ lies in IV quadrant. So, Assertion is correct.

Reason It is correct that, if $x \neq y$, then position of (x, y) in the cartesian plane is different from the position of (y, x). And it is the correct explanation of Assertion.

21. (a) **Assertion** The coordinates of points P and Q are (2, 2) and $(-3, -2)$ respectively, which is correct.

Reason It is correct that the coordinates of any point can be determined by drawing perpendicular to the coordinate axes. It is also a correct explanation for Assertion.

22. (i) It is clear from the given figure, the police station is at 2 units from X-axis along the negative direction of Y-axis and 2 units from Y-axis in positive direction of X-axis.

$\therefore$ The coordinates of police station are $(2, -2)$.

(ii) The school is at 2 units from Y-axis and 3 units from X-axis in both positive direction.

Therefore, the coordinates of school are (2, 3).

(iii) (a) Since, school is at 3 units from X-axis and police station is at 2 units from X-axis.

So, the distance between school and police station is $3 + 2 = 5$ units.

Or

(b) Given point is $(-3, 2)$.

Here, x-coordinate is negative and y-coordinate is positive.

Hence, the point $(-3, 2)$ lies in II quadrant.

23. (i) Given, in a rectangular field $ABCD$, vertical lines are drawn with chalk powder at a distance of 1 m each. Also, placed 100 flower pots along AD at a distance of 1 m each, i.e. total length of AD is 100 m.

Now, we consider AB as X-axis and AD as Y-axis.

Since, Niharika runs $\frac{1}{4}$ of the distance AD on second line and posts a green flag.

$\therefore$ Position of green flag $= \left(2, \frac{1}{4} \times 100\right) = (2, 25)$

(ii) Since, Preeti runs $\frac{1}{5}$ of the distance AD on the 8th line and posts a red flag.

$\therefore$ Position of red flag $= \left(8, \frac{1}{5} \times 100\right) = (8, 20)$

(iii) (a) For point (2, 25), x-coordinate is positive and y-coordinate is also positive, so it lies in I quadrant.

Or

(b) For point (8, 20), x-coordinate and y-coordinate both are positive. So, it lies in I quadrant.

24. (i) From the given graph, we have coordinates of A are (1, 1).

(ii) From graph, we have coordinates of F are (5, 5).

(iii) (a) Area of playground ABC, $A_1 = \frac{1}{2} \times AB \times AC$

$= \frac{1}{2}(3 - 1) \times (3 - 1)$

$= \frac{1}{2} \times 2 \times 2 = 2$ sq units

Or (b) Area of playground DEF, $A_2 = \frac{1}{2} \times DE \times DF$

$= \frac{1}{2}(7 - 5)(5 - 3)$

$= \frac{1}{2} \times 2 \times 2 = 2$ sq units

Part II

1. Infinite
2. **Hint** Solve as Example 3.

   Ans. (i) IV quadrant. (ii) II quadrant.
   (iii) III quadrant. (iv) I quadrant.

3. **Hint** y-coordinate on the X-axis is zero.

   So, y-coordinate = 0

   $\therefore (x, y) = (6, 0)$ **Ans.** (6, 0)

4. (i) (0, 0) (ii) (2, 0)
5. 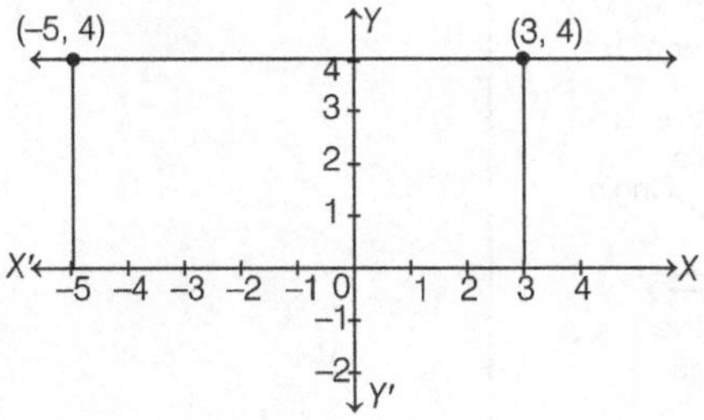

   From the graph, it is clear that the line with points (3, 4) and (–5, 4) is parallel to the X-axis.

6. For the point (–5, 3), x-coordinate is negative and y-coordinate is positive.

   So, it will lie in II quadrant. Also, its perpendicular distance from Y-axis is 5 units and from X-axis is 3 units. So, the required point is L.

7. (i) I quadrant (ii) III quadrant
8. Let a be the equal distance from origin on both axes.

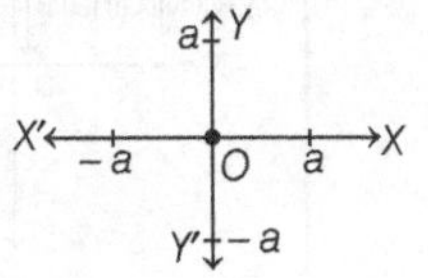

   Then, the coordinates of two points on X-axis are $(a, 0)$ and $(-a, 0)$ and the coordinates of two points on Y-axis are $(0, a)$ and $(0, -a)$.

9. (3, 2) or (–3, 2) or (–3, –2) or (3, –2); I or II or III or IV quadrant, respectively.
10. (i) (0, – 5) (ii) (0, 0) (iii) (– 3, 0)
11. Given ΔABC is equilateral.

$$\therefore \quad AB = BC = CA$$

$$\Rightarrow \quad AB = 2a$$

Since, $OC = OD = \dfrac{\sqrt{3}}{2} \times \text{side}$

$$= \frac{\sqrt{3}}{2} \times 2a = \sqrt{3}a$$

Therefore, the coordinates of point $C = (0, \sqrt{3}a)$ and the coordinates of point $D = (0, -\sqrt{3}a)$

12. Let $ABCO$ is a rectangle placed in III quadrant.

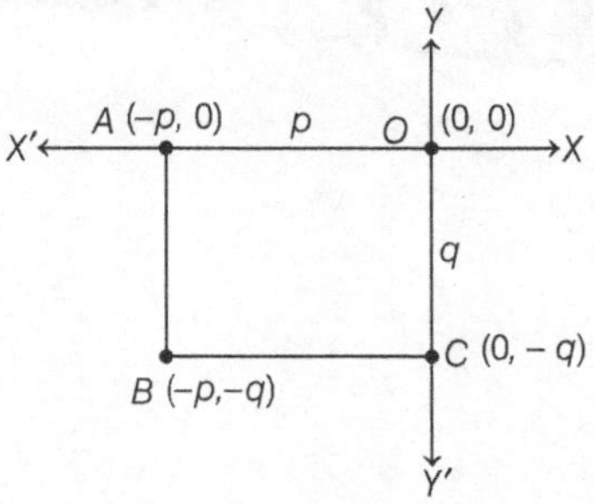

   Coordinates of its vertices are

   $O(0, 0), A(-p, 0), B(-p, -q)$ and $C(0, -q)$.

13. **Hint** By Pythagoras theorem in ΔPOQ,

$$OP^2 = PQ^2 - OQ^2 = 64 - 16 = 48$$

$$[\because OQ = 4, PQ = QR = 8]$$

$$\Rightarrow \quad OP = 4\sqrt{3}$$

   Ans. $(4\sqrt{3}, 0)$

14. (i) A, L and O (ii) G, I and O (iii) D and H
    (iv) B and J
15. Since, $AC = 16$ cm and $BD = 8$ cm

   So, $OA = OC = \dfrac{AC}{2} = \dfrac{16}{2}$ cm $= 8$ cm

   and $OB = OD = \dfrac{BD}{2} = \dfrac{8}{2}$ cm $= 4$ cm

   Thus, the coordinates of A, B, C and D are as follows

   $A = (-8, 0); B = (0, 4); C = (8, 0); D = (0, -4)$

16. (i) II quadrant (ii) III quadrant
    (iii) IV quadrant (iv) I quadrant
17. **Hint**

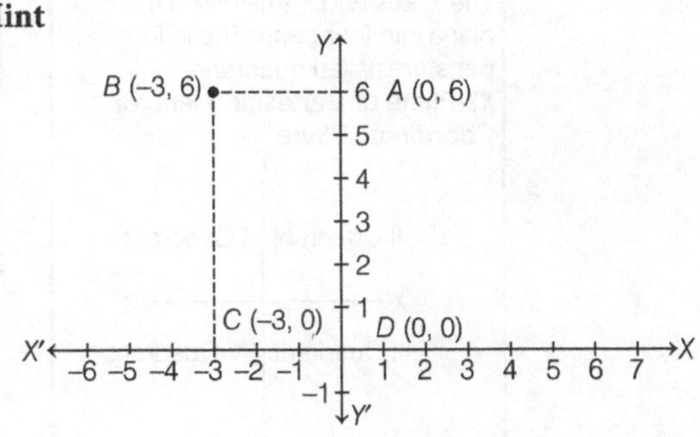

   Ans. $A(0, 6), B(-3, 6), C(-3, 0)$ and $D(0, 0)$;
   Area = 18 sq units

Mind Map

COORDINATE GEOMETRY

Cartesian System
It describes the position of a point in a plane.

Two Perpendicular Straight Lines
1. ***X*-axis** The horizontal line *XOX*'.
2. ***Y*-axis** The vertical line *YOY*'.

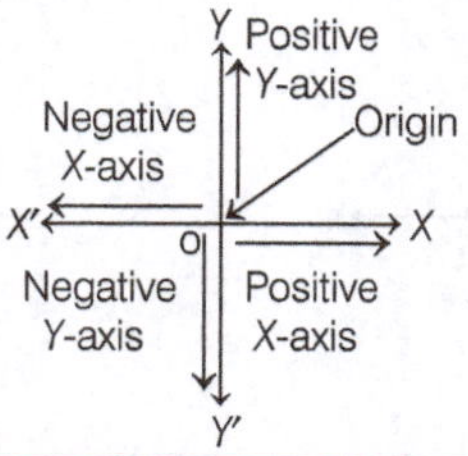

Origin
The point of intersection of *X*-axis and *Y*-axis. The coordinates of origin are denoted by *O*(0, 0).

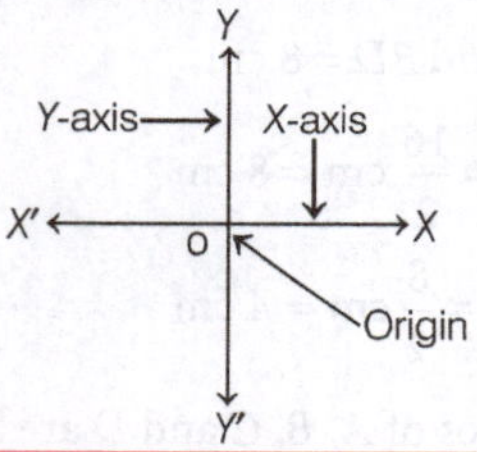

Coordinates of a Point
1. ***x*-coodinates** The perpendicular distance from the *Y*-axis measured along the *X*-axis. This is also called abscissa.
2. ***y*-coordinates** The perpendicular distance from the *X*-axis measured along *Y*-axis. This is also called ordinate.

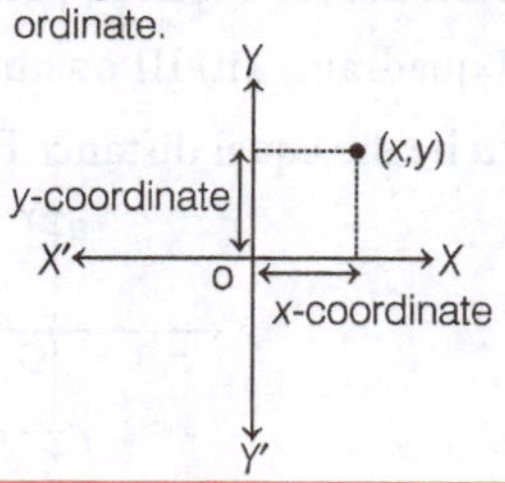

Quadrant
The *X*-axis and *Y*-axis divide the plane into four parts. These four parts are called quadrants.
***XY*-Plane or Cartesian Plane or Coordinate Plane**

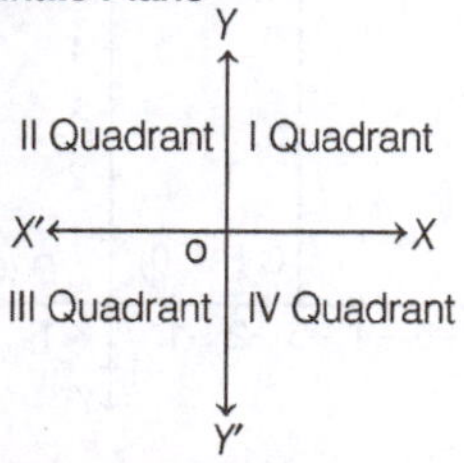

Convention of signs of Coordinates in different Quadrants

Region	Quadrant	Nature of *x* & *y*-coordinates	Sign of coordinates of a point	Example
XOY	I	$x > 0, y > 0$	(+,+)	(5, 3), (4, 4)
X'OY	II	$x < 0, y > 0$	(–,+)	(–4, 3), (–7, 8)
X'OY'	III	$x < 0, y < 0$	(–, –)	(–3, –2), (–4, –1)
XOY'	IV	$x > 0, y < 0$	(+,–)	(5, –3), (7, –4)

Topics to be Assessed Formatively

Plotting a Point in Cartesian Plane

Here, we will learn how to plot a point in cartesian plane, if its coordinates are given. This can be explained with the help of following example.

Example 1. Plot the points (3, 4), (−3, −3)(−7, 6) and (0,−6) on Cartesian plane and give their positions in quadrants/axes.

Sol. Let us draw mutually perpendicular axes XOX' and YOY' and choose a suitable units of distance on the axes. Let 1 cm = 1 unit

Here, Point $P(3, 4)$ is at a distance of 3 units from Y-axis and 4 units from X-axis. Point $Q(-3, -3)$ is at a distance of 3 units from negative Y-axis and 4 units from negative X-axis.

Point $R(-7, 6)$ is at a distance of 7 units from negative Y-axis and 6 units from positive X-axis.

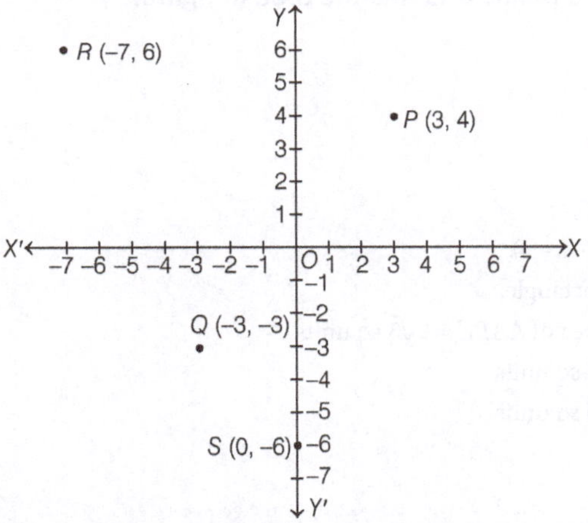

It is clear from the graph that point $P(3, 4)$ lies in I quadrant, point $R(-7, 6)$ lies in IInd quadrant, point $Q(-3, -3)$ lies in III quadrant and point $S(0, -6)$ lies on Y-axis.

Example 2. (i) Plot the points $P(1, 0)$, $Q(4, 0)$ and $S(1, 3)$. Find the coordinates of the point R such that $PQRS$ is a square. NCERT Exemplar

(*ii*) Determine the length of line segment SR in figure $PQRS$.

Sol. (*i*) Let us draw mutually perpendicular axes XOX' and YOY' and choose a suitable units of distance on the axes. Let 1 cm = 1 unit. For point $P(1, 0)$, y-coordinate is zero, so it lies on X-axis at a distance of 1 unit from Y-axis.

In point $Q(4, 0)$, y-coordinate is zero, so it lies on X-axis at a distance of 4 units from Y-axis.

The point $S(1, 3)$ is at a distance of 1 unit from Y-axis and 3 units from X-axis. On plotting these points, we get the below graph.

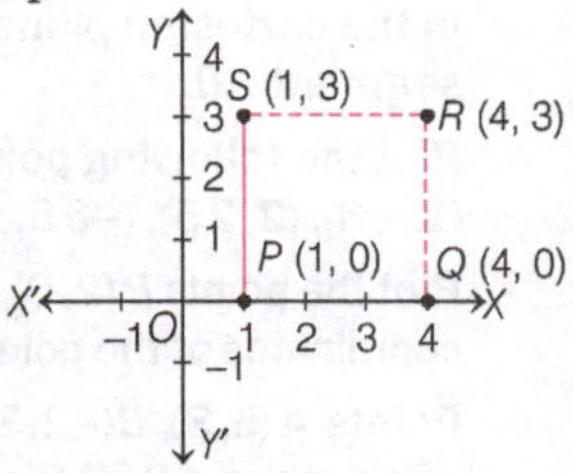

Now, we need to take a point R on the graph such that $PQRS$ is a square. For this, draw a line passing through Q and parallel to PS and draw a line passing through S and parallel to PQ. Both lines intersect each other at a point, say R. Thus, we get a square $PQRS$.

Clearly, abscissa of R will be equal to abscissa of Q, i.e. 4 and ordinate of R will be equal to ordinate of S, i.e. 3. Hence, the coordinates of point R are (4, 3).

(*ii*) We have, $S(1, 3)$ and $R(4, 3)$

Here, we see that y-coordinate of both points S and R are same.

$\therefore$ Length of the line segment SR

= Difference of x-coordinate of both points S and R

$= 4 - 1 = 3$ units

Example 3. Plot the points $P(1, 5)$, $Q(3, 2)$, $R(1, -1)$, and $S(-1, 2)$ on a cartesian plane and join them in order. Now, write the name of the figure obtained.

Sol. Let us draw mutually perpendicular axes XOX' and YOY' and choose a suitable units of distance on the axes. Let 1 cm = 1 unit. Then, the given points can be plotted as given below.

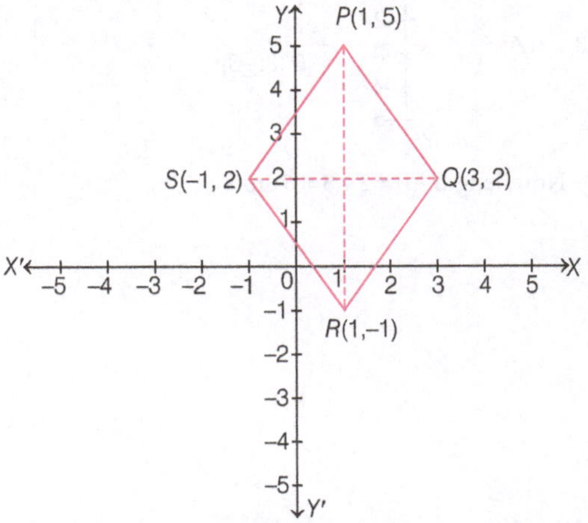

It is clear from the graph that all four sides are equal but diagonals are not equal, so it is a rhombus.

Exercise

1. If $P(0,-5)$, $Q(3,0)$, $R(0,7)$ and $S(5,-2)$ are plotted on the graph paper, then find the point(s) on the Y-axis.
2. Two points with coordinates (4, 3) and (4, – 2) lie on a line, parallel to which axis?
3. Plot the points $A(-3-3)$, $B(3,-3)$, $C(3,3)$ and $D(-3,3)$ in the cartesian plane. Also, find the length of line segment AB.
4. Plot the following points on the graph paper (1, –3), (2, 2.5), (–3.5, 1.5) and (0, 4).
5. Plot the points $P(2,0)$, $Q(5,0)$ and $S(2,4)$. Find the coordinates of the point R such that $PQRS$ is a rectangle.
6. Points $A(5,3)$, $B(-2,3)$ and $D(5,-4)$ are three vertices of a square $ABCD$. Plot these points on a graph paper and hence find the coordinates of the vertex C.
   NCERT Exemplar
7. Plot the points (3, 2), (– 2, 2), (– 2, – 2) and (3, – 2) in the cartesian plane. Join these points in order and name the figure, so formed.
8. Plot the points (x, y) given in the following table.

x	4	5.5	– 2	– 1	0	2.5
y	– 5	– 3	5	– 6	5	0

9. In the given figure, ABC is an equilateral triangle. The coordinates of vertices B and C are (3, 0) and (– 3, 0), respectively. Find the coordinates of its vertex A. Also, find its area.

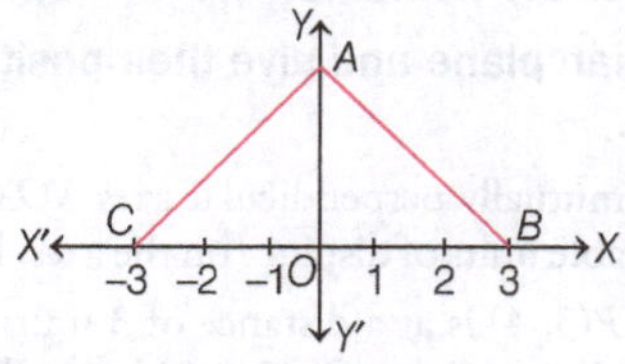

10. Plot the points $A(4,0)$, $B(4,4)$ and $C(-3,0)$. Join AB and AC. Find the area of ΔABC.
11. Plot the points (5, 4), (0, 0) and (5, 0). Join the points and find the area of figure.

Answers

1. P and R
2. Y-axis
3.

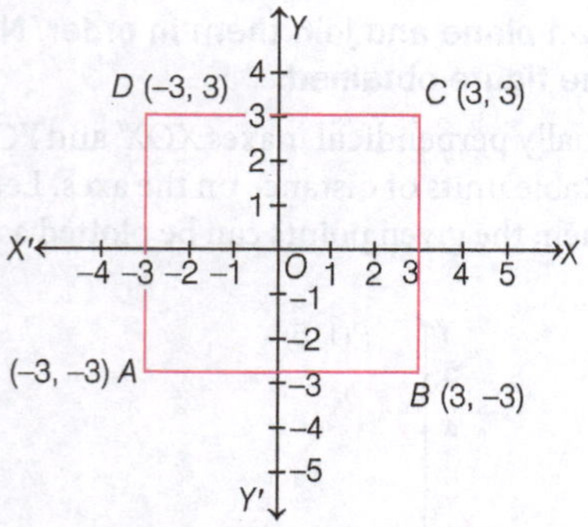

Now, length $AB = 3 + 3 = 6$ units

5. $R(5, 4)$.
6. $C(-2, -4)$.
7. Rectangle.
9. Area of $\Delta ABC = 9\sqrt{3}$ sq units
10. 14 sq units
11. 10 sq units

Linear Equations in Two Variables

CHAPTER 4

In earlier classes, we have studied linear equations in one variable, like $x + 2 = 0$, $z + \sqrt{3} = 0$, etc. We also know that such equations have a unique solution and solution of these equations can be represented on a number line.
In this chapter, we will study linear equations in two variables and their solutions.

Linear Equation in Two Variables

An equation of the form $ax + by + c = 0$, where a, b and c are real numbers (a and b are not both zero) and x, y are variables, is called a linear equation in two variables and it is also called standard form of linear equation in two variables.

e.g. (i) $3s + 4t = 10$ (ii) $\pi x + 4y = 3$

Note it It is customary to denote the variables in such equations by x and y, but other letters may also be used.

Example 1. **Write each of the following linear equations in the form $ax + by + c = 0$ and indicate the values of a, b and c in each case.**

(i) $3x + 4y = 4$ (ii) $x - 5 = \sqrt{3}y$ (iii) $x = 2y$

Sol. (i) $3x + 4y = 4$ can be written as $3x + 4y - 4 = 0$.
On comparing with $ax + by + c = 0$, we get
$$a = 3, b = 4 \text{ and } c = -4$$
(ii) $x - 5 = \sqrt{3}y$ can be written as $x - \sqrt{3}y - 5 = 0$.
On comparing with $ax + by + c = 0$, we get
$$a = 1, b = -\sqrt{3} \text{ and } c = -5$$
(iii) $x = 2y$ can be written as $x - 2y + 0 = 0$.
On comparing with $ax + by + c = 0$, we get
$$a = 1, b = -2 \text{ and } c = 0$$

To Write a Linear Equation in One Variable into Linear Equation in Two Variables

We can represent a linear equation in one variable (say x) as linear equation in two variables, by taking the coefficient of other variable (say y) as zero and thus writing the given equation in the form $ax + by + c = 0$.

e.g. $x = -5$ can be written as $x + 5 = 0$ or $x + 0 \cdot y + 5 = 0$.

Example 2. **Write each of the following equations as an equation in two variables.**

(i) $2y = 3$
(ii) $3x = -5$

Sol. (i) $2y = 3$ can be written as $0 \cdot x + 2y - 3 = 0$.
(ii) $3x = -5$ can be written as $3x + 0 \cdot y + 5 = 0$.

Method to Write A Given Statement as Linear Equation in Two Variables

To write a given statement or a word problem in the form of linear equation in two variables, first identify the variable quantities and assume them as x and y.

Then, write the given condition in terms of x and y and convert it in the form of $ax + by + c = 0$ which is the required linear equation in two variables.

Example 3. **A lending library has a fixed charge for the first three days and an additional charge for each day thereafter. Roshni paid ₹ 35 for a book kept for seven days. Write a linear equation which satisfies this data.**

Sol. Let the fixed charge be ₹ x and thereafter the additional charge be ₹ y per day.

Then, according to the question,

$$x+y(7-3)=35$$

$$\Rightarrow \quad x+4y-35=0,$$

which is the required linear equation in two variables.

Example 4. **The cost of a ball pen is ₹ 5 less than half of the cost of a fountain pen. Write this statement as a linear equation in two variables.**

Sol. Here, variable quantities are cost of ball pen and cost of fountain pen.

So, let cost of a ball pen = ₹ x

and cost of a fountain pen = ₹ y

According to the question,

Cost of a ball pen = Half of the cost of a fountain pen − 5

$$\Rightarrow \quad x=\frac{y}{2}-5$$

$$\Rightarrow \quad x=\frac{y-10}{2}$$

$$\Rightarrow \quad 2x=y-10$$

$$\Rightarrow \quad 2x-y+10=0,$$

which is the required linear equation in two variables.

Solution of a Linear Equation in Two Variables

Any pair of values of x and y which satisfies the given equation in x and y, is called its **solution**. This solution is written as an ordered pair (x, y).

In ordered pair, we first write the value of x and then the value of y. A linear equation in two variables has **infinitely many solutions.**

e.g. Linear equation $3x+2y=14$ is satisfied by $(x=0,\ y=7)$, $(x=2,\ y=4)$, $(x=4,\ y=1)$, $(x=-2,\ y=10)$ and $\left(x=5,\ y=\frac{-1}{2}\right)$ etc. So, these pairs are the solutions of given linear equation. But $(x=1,\ y=5)$ does not satisfy the given linear equation, so it is not the solution of the given linear equation.

Note It The solution of a linear equation is not affected, if

- The same number is added to (or subtracted from) both the sides of the equation.
- Both the sides of the equation are multiplied or divided by the same non-zero number.

Method of Finding the Solution of Linear Equation in Two Variables

Let the given linear equation in two variables be $ax+by+c=0$, where $a \neq 0$ and $b \neq 0$.

Then, for finding its solution, we use the following steps

Step I Put an arbitrary value of x (or y) in given equation and find the corresponding value of other variable.

Thus, we get one pair of solution of the given equation.

Step II Repeat Step I for another arbitrary value of x (or y) and get other pair of solution of given equation.

Note It For convenience, we put $x=0$ and get corresponding value of y to find one pair of solution. Also, we put $y=0$ and get corresponding value of x to find second pair of solution.

Example 5. **Find any four solutions of the equation $4x+3y=12$.**

Sol. Given equation is $4x+3y=12$ ...(i)

On putting $x=0$ in Eq. (i), we get

$$4(0)+3y=12$$

$$\Rightarrow \quad 3y=12$$

$$\Rightarrow \quad y=\frac{12}{3}=4$$

So, (0, 4) is a solution of given equation.

On putting $y=0$ in Eq. (i), we get

$$4x+3(0)=12$$

$$\Rightarrow \quad 4x=12$$

$$\Rightarrow \quad x=\frac{12}{4}=3$$

So, (3, 0) is a solution of given equation.

On putting $x=1$ in Eq. (i), we get

$$4(1)+3y=12$$

$$\Rightarrow \quad 3y=12-4=8$$

$$\Rightarrow \quad y=\frac{8}{3}$$

So, $\left(1, \frac{8}{3}\right)$ is another solution of the given equation.

Further, putting $x=2$ in Eq. (i), we get

$$4(2)+3y=12$$

$$\Rightarrow \quad 3y=12-8=4$$

$$\Rightarrow \quad y=\frac{4}{3}$$

So, $\left(2, \frac{4}{3}\right)$ is also a solution of the given equation.

Hence, the four solutions of given equation are (0, 4), (3, 0), $\left(1, \frac{8}{3}\right)$ and $\left(2, \frac{4}{3}\right)$.

Example 6. When 3 times the larger of two numbers is divided by the smaller, then the quotient and remainder are 2 and 7, respectively. Form a linear equation in two variables for above and give its two solutions.

Sol. Let the larger and smaller numbers be x and y, respectively.

According to the question,

$$3x = 2y + 7$$

$\Rightarrow 3x - 2y - 7 = 0,$

which is the required linear equation in two variables.

Now, putting $x = 0$, we get

$$0 - 2y - 7 = 0$$

$$\Rightarrow \quad y = -\frac{7}{2}$$

So, $\left(0, -\frac{7}{2}\right)$ is a solution of $3x - 2y - 7 = 0$.

Now, putting $x = \frac{1}{3}$, we get

$$3 \times \frac{1}{3} - 2y - 7 = 0 \Rightarrow y = -3$$

So, $\left(\frac{1}{3}, -3\right)$ is another solution of $3x - 2y - 7 = 0$.

Hence, two solutions are $\left(0, -\frac{7}{2}\right)$ and $\left(\frac{1}{3}, -3\right)$.

Method to Check Whether Given Pair of Values is a Solution of Given Equation or Not

Sometimes, a pair of values is given and we have to check whether this pair is a solution of given linear equation in two variables or not. For this, we put the given values in given linear equation.

If we get LHS = RHS, then this pair of values is a solution of given linear equation, otherwise not.

Example 7. Check whether $x = 2$ and $y = 1$ is a solution of the following equations or not.

(i) $2x + 5y = 9$ (ii) $x + y + 4 = 0$

(iii) $\frac{5}{2}x + 3y = 14$

Sol. Given, $x = 2$ and $y = 1$

(i) Given linear equation is $2x + 5y = 9$.

On putting $x = 2$ and $y = 1$ in LHS, we get

$\text{LHS} = 2x + 5y = 2(2) + 5(1) = 4 + 5 = 9 = \text{RHS}$

So, $x = 2$ and $y = 1$ is a solution of given equation.

(ii) Given linear equation is $x + y + 4 = 0$.

On putting $x = 2$ and $y = 1$ in LHS, we get

$\text{LHS} = x + y + 4 = 2 + 1 + 4 = 7 \neq 0$

$\Rightarrow \text{LHS} \neq \text{RHS}$

So, $x = 2$ and $y = 1$ is not a solution of given equation.

(iii) Given linear equation is $\frac{5}{2}x + 3y = 14$.

On putting $x = 2$ and $y = 1$ in LHS, we get

$$\text{LHS} = \frac{5}{2}x + 3y$$

$$= \frac{5}{2}(2) + 3(1)$$

$$= 5 + 3 = 8 \neq 14$$

$$\Rightarrow \quad \text{LHS} \neq \text{RHS}$$

So, $x = 2$ and $y = 1$ is not a solution of given equation.

Method of Finding the Value of Unknown When Solution of Equation is Given

To find the value of unknown (say k) when solution of the equation is given. Put the given solution (i.e. the values of variables x and y) in the given linear equation and simplify the equation for k.

Example 8. Find the value of k for each of the following equations, if $x = 1$ and $y = 1$ is its solution.

(i) $9kx + 12ky = 63$

(ii) $5x + 2ky = 3k$

Sol. (i) Given equation is $9kx + 12ky = 63$.

On putting $x = 1$ and $y = 1$ in this equation, we get

$$9k(1) + 12k(1) = 63$$

$$\Rightarrow \quad 9k + 12k = 63$$

$$\Rightarrow \quad 21k = 63$$

$$\Rightarrow \quad k = \frac{63}{21} = 3$$

Hence, the required value of k is 3.

(ii) Given equation is $5x + 2ky = 3k$.

On putting $x = 1$ and $y = 1$ in this equation, we get

$$5(1) + 2k(1) = 3k$$

$$\Rightarrow \quad 5 + 2k = 3k$$

$$\Rightarrow \quad 5 = 3k - 2k$$

$$\Rightarrow \quad k = 5$$

Hence, required value of k is 5.

NCERT FOLDER

Complete Solutions of All Exercises of NCERT Textbook

EXERCISE 4.1 (NCERT Page 57)

Q1. The cost of a notebook is twice the cost of a pen. Write a linear equation in two variables to represent this statement. (Take the cost of a notebook to be ₹ x and that of a pen to be ₹ y)

Sol. Let the cost of a notebook = ₹ x and the cost of a pen = ₹ y

According to the question,

Cost of a notebook = 2 (Cost of a pen)

$\Rightarrow \quad x = 2y \Rightarrow x - 2y = 0$

which is the required linear equation in two variables.

Q2. Express the following linear equations in the form $ax + by + c = 0$ and indicate the values of a, b and c in each case.

(i) $2x + 3y = 9.3\overline{5}$ (ii) $x - \frac{y}{5} - 10 = 0$

(iii) $-2x + 3y = 6$ (iv) $x = 3y$

(v) $2x = -5y$ (vi) $3x + 2 = 0$

(vii) $y - 2 = 0$ (viii) $5 = 2x$

Sol. (i) Given equation can be written as $2x + 3y - 9.3\overline{5} = 0$

On comparing with $ax + by + c = 0$, we get

$$a = 2, b = 3 \text{ and } c = -9.3\overline{5}$$

(ii) Solve as part (i).

Ans. $x - \frac{y}{5} - 10 = 0; a = 1, b = \frac{-1}{5}$ and $c = -10$

(iii) Solve as part (i).

Ans. $-2x + 3y - 6 = 0; a = -2, b = 3$ and $c = -6$

(iv) Solve as part (i).

Ans. $x - 3y = 0; a = 1, b = -3$ and $c = 0$

(v) Solve as part (i).

Ans. $2x + 5y = 0; a = 2, b = 5$ and $c = 0$

(vi) Solve as part (i).

Ans. $3x + 2 = 0; a = 3, b = 0$ and $c = 2$

(vii) Solve as part (i).

Ans. $y - 2 = 0; a = 0, b = 1$ and $c = -2$

(viii) Solve as part (i).

Ans. $-2x + 5 = 0; a = -2, b = 0$ and $c = 5$

EXERCISE 4.2 (NCERT Page 59)

Q1. Which one of the following options is true and why?

$y = 3x + 5$ has

(a) a unique solution

(b) only two solutions

(c) infinitely many solutions

Sol. (c) We know that a linear equation in two variables has infinitely many solutions. Here, given equation is a linear equation in two variables x and y, so it has infinitely many solutions.

Q2. Write four solutions for each of the following equations.

(i) $2x + y = 7$ (ii) $\pi x + y = 9$ (iii) $x = 4y$

Sol. (i) Given equation is $2x + y = 7$ ...(i)

On putting $x = 0$ in Eq. (i), we get

$$y = 7$$

So, (0, 7) is a solution of given equation.

Similarly, putting $y = 0$ in Eq. (i), we get

$$2x = 7 \Rightarrow x = \frac{7}{2}$$

So, $\left(\frac{7}{2}, 0\right)$ is a solution of given equation.

On putting $x = 1$ in Eq. (i), we get

$$2(1) + y = 7 \Rightarrow y = 5$$

Therefore, (1, 5) is also a solution of the given equation.

Again, putting $x = 2$ in Eq. (i), we get

$$2(2) + y = 7 \Rightarrow y = 7 - 4 = 3$$

So, (2, 3) is a solution of given equation.

Hence, four out of the infinitely many solutions of the given equation are (0, 7), $\left(\frac{7}{2}, 0\right)$, (1, 5) and (2, 3).

(ii) Solve as part (i).

Ans. (0, 9), $\left(\frac{9}{\pi}, 0\right)$, $(1, 9 - \pi)$ and $(-1, 9 + \pi)$

(iii) Solve as part (i). **Ans.** (0, 0), (4, 1), $\left(2, \frac{1}{2}\right)$ and $\left(1, \frac{1}{4}\right)$

Q3. Check which of the following are solutions of the equation $x - 2y = 4$ and which are not?

(i) (0, 2) (ii) (2, 0)

(iii) (4, 0) (iv) $(\sqrt{2}, 4\sqrt{2})$

(v) (1, 1)

Sol. (i) Given equation is $x - 2y = 4$.

On putting $x = 0$ and $y = 2$ in LHS, we get

$$\text{LHS} = x - 2y = 0 - 2 \times 2$$
$$= 0 - 4 = -4 \neq 4$$

$\Rightarrow$ LHS $\neq$ RHS

Hence, (0, 2) is not a solution of $x - 2y = 4$.

(ii) Given equation is $x - 2y = 4$.

On putting $x = 2$ and $y = 0$ in LHS, we get

$$\text{LHS} = x - 2y = 2 - 2 \times 0$$
$$= 2 - 0 = 2 \neq 4$$

$\Rightarrow$ LHS $\neq$ RHS

Hence, (2, 0) is not a solution of $x - 2y = 4$.

(iii) Given equation is $x - 2y = 4$.

On putting $x = 4$ and $y = 0$ in LHS, we get

$$\text{LHS} = x - 2y = 4 - 2 \times 0 = 4 - 0 = 4 = \text{RHS}$$

Hence, (4, 0) is a solution of $x - 2y = 4$.

(iv) Solve as part (i).

Ans. $(\sqrt{2}, 4\sqrt{2})$ is not a solution of $x - 2y = 4$.

(v) Solve as part (i).

Ans. (1, 1) is not a solution of $x - 2y = 4$.

Q4. Find the value of k, if $x = 2$ and $y = 1$ is a solution of the equation $2x + 3y = k$.

Sol. Given, equation is $2x + 3y = k$.

If $x = 2$ and $y = 1$ is a solution of given equation, then it must satisfy the given equation.

So, on putting $x = 2$ and $y = 1$ in given equation, we get

$$2(2) + 3(1) = k$$

$\Rightarrow$ $4 + 3 = k$

$\therefore$ $k = 7$

REVIEW EXERCISE

Including Competency Based Questions

Part I

Multiple Choice Questions

1. **The equation $x = 7$, in two variables can be written as** **NCERT Exemplar**

(a) $1 \cdot x + 1 \cdot y = 7$ (b) $1 \cdot x + 0 \cdot y = 7$
(c) $0 \cdot x + 1 \cdot y = 7$ (d) $0 \cdot x + 0 \cdot y = 7$

2. **The equation $y = k$ in two variables can be written as**

(a) $0 \cdot x + 0 \cdot y = k$ (b) $0 \cdot x + 1 \cdot y = 0$
(c) $1 \cdot x + 1 \cdot y = k$ (d) $0 \cdot x + 1 \cdot y = k$

3. **The parking charges of a car in a parking lot is ₹ 50 for the first two hours and ₹ 20 per hour for subsequent hours. The above statement can be expressed in a linear equation as**

(a) $5x - y + 5 = 0$ (b) $7x - y + 7 = 0$
(c) $20x - y + 10 = 0$ (d) $9x - y + 9 = 0$

4. **The equation $2x + 5y = 7$ has a unique solution, if x and y are** **NCERT Exemplar**

(a) natural numbers (b) positive real numbers
(c) real numbers (d) rational numbers

5. **The linear equation $3x + 6y = 9$ has**

(a) a unique solution (b) two solutions
(c) no solution (d) infinitely many solutions

6. **Any point on the line $y = -x$ is of the form** **Competency Based Question**

(a) (a, a) (b) $(-a, a)$
(c) $(0, -a)$ (d) $(-a, -a)$

7. **Any solution of the linear equation $4x + 0y + 10 = 0$ in two variables is of the form**

(a) $\left(0, \frac{-5}{2}\right)$ (b) $\left(0, \frac{5}{2}\right)$ (c) $\left(\frac{5}{2}, 0\right)$ (d) $\left(\frac{-5}{2}, 0\right)$

8. **If a linear equation has solutions $(-2, 2)$, $(0, 0)$ and $(2, -2)$, then it is of the form** **Competency Based Question**

(a) $y - x = 0$ (b) $x + y = 0$
(c) $-2x + y = 0$ (d) $-x + 2y = 0$

9. **$x = 3$ and $y = 1$ is a solution of the linear equation.**

(a) $3x + 4y = 10$ (b) $8x + 5y = 25$
(c) $8x + 5y = 29$ (d) $5x + 8y = 29$

10. **If $y = x + 4t$, then the value of t when $x = 4$ and $y = 12$ is**

(a) 2 (b) 4 (c) 8 (d) 12

11. **If $x = k^2$ and $y = k$ is a solution of the equation $x - 5y + 6 = 0$, then the values of k is**

(a) 2, 3 (b) 3, 4 (c) 1, 2 (d) 3, 5

12. **If (2, 0) is a solution of the linear equation $2x + 3y = k$, then the value of k is** **NCERT Exemplar**

(a) 4 (b) 6 (c) 5 (d) 2

Assertion-Reason Type Questions

13. **Assertion** These are infinite number of lines, which passes through (3, 15).

Reason A linear equation in two variables has infinitely many solutions.

(a) Both Assertion and Reason are correct and Reason is the correct explanation of Assertion.
(b) Both Assertion and Reason are correct but Reason is not the correct explanation of Assertion.
(c) Assertion is correct but Reason is incorrect.
(d) Assertion is incorrect but Reason is correct.

14. **Assertion** If $\left(-\frac{3}{2}, k\right)$ is a solution of the linear equation $2x + 3y = 0$. Then, $k = 1$.

Reason The linear equation $ax + b = 0$ can be expressed as a linear equation in two variables as $ax + y + b = 0$.

(a) Both Assertion and Reason are correct and Reason is the correct explanation of Assertion.
(b) Both Assertion and Reason are correct but Reason is not the correct explanation of Assertion.
(c) Assertion is correct but Reason is incorrect.
(d) Assertion is incorrect but Reason is correct.

Case Study Based Questions

15. Manisha distributed chocolates in an orphanage, on her birthday, she gave 5 chocolates to each child and 20 chocolates to adults. Taking number of children as x and total chocolates distributed as y.

(i) Write a linear equation, according to given question.
(ii) If she distributed 145 chocolates, then how many children are there in the orphanage?

(iii) (a) If she distributed 205 chocolates, then how many children are there in the orphanage?

Or

(b) If there are 15 children, then find the number of chocolates.

16. Car parking is a major problem in urban areas in both developed and developing countries. In the Jaipur City GT mall, the parking charges of a car in a parking lot is ₹ 30 for the first two hours and ₹ 10 per hour for subsequent hours, then answer the following questions.

(i) Taking total parking time to be x hour, and total charges as ₹ y, write a linear equation.

(ii) If $y = 20$, then find the value of x.

(iii) (a) If $x = 2$, then find the value of y.

Or

(b) If charges of a car in a parking lot is ₹ 50 for the first two hours, then find the linear equation.

17. India is the world's fourth largest consumer of energy. With an increasing number of private vehicles, the overall domestic consumption of petrol and petroleum products is on rise in India. Answer the following questions.

(i) Every six month, price of petrol increases at the rate of ₹ 5 per litre, taking price of petrol in December 2018 as x and present price of petrol as y, form a linear equation showing amount spent on petrol in December 2019.

(ii) Due to continuous rise in the petrol price, peoples are shifting towards CNG whose price increases at the rate of ₹ 5 per litre in a year. Form a linear equation taking price of CNG in December 2017 as a and in December 2018 as b.

(iii) (a) If in part (i), $y = 20$, then find the value of x.

Or

(b) If in part (ii), $b = 10$, then find the value of a.

18. On his birthday, Mr. Sharma planned that this time he will celebrate his birthday in a small orphanage centre. He bought apples to give to children and adults working there. Mr. Sharma donated 3 apples to each children and 2 apples to each adults working there along with birthday cake. He distributed 160 total apples.

On the basis of above information, answer the following questions.

(i) Represent the above situation in linear equation in two variables by taking the number of children as x and the number of adults as y.

(ii) If the number of children is 40, then find the number of adults.

(iii) (a) If the number of adults is 20, then find the number of children.

Or

(b) If $x = 5$ and $y = 0$ is a solution of the equation $3x + 5y = b$, then find the value of b.

Part II

Very Short Answer Type Questions

1. Express each of the following equations in the form $ax + by + c = 0$ and write the values of a, b and c in each case.

(i) $2x + 3y = 5$ (ii) $x = -5 + 3y$

(iii) $\pi y = 2x$ (iv) $y = 9$

(v) $\frac{x}{3} - \frac{y}{4} = 2$

(vi) $12y - \frac{1}{3} = x$

2. "The cost of a hen is 50 times the cost of its egg." Write the linear equation for the above statement, if x represents the cost of a hen and y represents cost of an egg. **Competency Based Question**

3. From a bus stand in Delhi, if we buy 2 tickets to Agra and 3 tickets to Mathura, the total cost is ₹ 440. Express this situation in linear equation. **Competency Based Question**

4. The cost of a book is ₹ 20 more than twice the cost of a pen. Express this statement as a linear equation.

5. 'Five years ago, Nuri was thrice as old as Sonu.' Express this information in linear equation.

6. If we add 1 to the numerator and subtract 1 from the denominator, a fraction reduces to 1. Form a linear equation for this information.

7. When 5 times the larger of the two numbers is divided by the smaller, the quotient and the remainder are 2 and 9, respectively. Form a linear equation in two variables. Write it in standard form.

Short Answer Type Questions

8. The cost of a toy telephone is the same as cost of 4 balls. Express the statement as a linear equation in two variables. Also, find the cost of getting 2 toy telephones packed, if cost of 1 ball is ₹ 5 and there is a fixed cost of ₹ 2 for packing a toy telephone.

9. The monthly hostel charges for Apeksha comprises ₹ 1000 per month as fixed boarding charges and remaining charges at the rate of ₹ 50 per day (for the number, for which the food has been availed by Apeksha).

(i) Form a linear equation in two variables to represent the above situation.

(ii) Find two solutions possible for equation formed.

(iii) What are the monthly charges to be paid by Apeksha who availed meals for 21 days in a given month?

Competency Based Question

10. Write any two solutions of $x = 2y$.

11. Write the four solutions of $2x + y = 7$.

12. Find whether $(\sqrt{3}, 0)$ is a solution of $3\sqrt{3}x - 3y = 9$ or not.

13. Check which of the following is (are) the solution of the equation $3y - 2x = 1$.

(i) $(4, 3)$ (ii) $(2\sqrt{2}, 3\sqrt{2})$ (iii) $\left(-\frac{1}{2}, 0\right)$

(iv) $(1, -1)$ (v) $(1, 1)$

14. If $(5, k)$ is a solution of the linear equation $2x + y - 6 = 0$, then find the value of k.

15. Find the value of a for each of the following, if $x = 1$ and $y = 1$ is its solution.

(i) $x - y = a$

(ii) $3x + ay = 6$

16. If $\pi x + 3y = 25$ and $y = 1$, then find x. [take $\pi = 22/7$]

17. The sum of a two-digit number and the number obtained by reversing the order of its digits is 121. If unit's and ten's digits of the number are x and y respectively, then write the linear equation representing the above statement.

18. Alka and Noori, two students of Class IX, together contributed ₹ 500 towards Prime Minister's Relief fund to help earthquake victims. Write a linear equation which satisfies this data.

19. Government has plan to make rainwater harvesting scheme in housing society. As we know that it is major source of water harvesting. To do this, we make a underground tank at the rate of 40 cm^3/s. Taking volume of water collected in x second as y cm^3.

(i) Form a linear equation.

(ii) Write it in standard form as $ax + by + c = 0$ and find the value of $a^2 + b^2 - c^2$.

Competency Based Question

20. Let y varies directly as x. If $y = 12$ when $x = 4$, then write a linear equation. What is value of y when $x = 5$?

NCERT Exemplar

21. For what value of c, the linear equation $2x + cy = 8$ has equal values of x and y for its solution?

NCERT Exemplar

Long Answer Type Questions

22. A player Rohan of Class X is unable to play football in the ground, due to fracture in his leg. Then, Mohan a student of Class IX replaces them. The sum of their ages is 24 yr.

Competency Based Question

(i) Write a linear equation for the above situation and find four solutions to the equations.

(ii) Find the age of Mohan when age of Rohan is 13 yr.

23. The bus fare in a city is charged ₹ 20 for first three kilometre and at ₹ 5 per km for subsequent distance covered. Write the linear equation to express the above statement and find 4 solutions to the equations.

24. Represent the equation $5x - 8y = 3(x + y) - 22$ in the form of $ax + by + c = 0$. Has the equation a unique solution? If not, then find two solutions of the given equation.

25. Given below a linear equation that converts Fahrenheit to Celsius and *vice-versa*.

$$F = \frac{9}{5}C + 32$$

(i) If the temperature is 40°C, then what is the temperature in Fahrenheit?

(ii) If the temperature is 104°F, then what is the temperature in Celsius?

(iii) If the temperature is numerically the same in both Fahrenheit and Celsius, then find it.

Competency Based Question

HINTS & ANSWERS

Part I

1. (b) Here, the coefficient of 'y' in the given equation $x = 7$ is 0. So, the equation can be written as

$$1 \cdot x + 0 \cdot y = 7$$

Hence, the required equation is $1 \cdot x + 0 \cdot y = 7$

2. (d) The equation $y = k$ in two variables can be written as

$$0 \cdot x + 1 \cdot y = k$$

3. (c) Given, parking charges for the first two hours = ₹ 50 and for subsequent hours = ₹ 20 per hour

Let total parking time = x hours and total charges = ₹ y

According to the question,

$$50 + 20(x - 2) = y$$
$$\Rightarrow \quad 50 + 20x - 40 = y$$
$$\Rightarrow \quad 20x - y + 10 = 0$$

which is the required linear equation in two variables.

4. (a) In natural numbers, there is only one pair i.e. (1, 1) which satisfy the given equation but in positive real numbers, real numbers and rational numbers there are many pairs to satisfy the given linear equation.

5. (d) Since, a linear equation in two variables has infinitely many solutions.

6. (b) Given equation is $y = -x$ ...(i)

When $x = -a$, then from Eq. (i), we get

$$y = -(-a) = a$$

$\therefore$ The required point is $(-a, a)$.

7. (d) For the equation,

$$4x + 0y + 10 = 0$$
$$\Rightarrow \quad 4x + 10 = 0 \Rightarrow 4x = -10$$
$$\Rightarrow \quad x = -\frac{10}{4} = -\frac{5}{2}$$

$\therefore$ Solution for given equation is $\left(\frac{-5}{2}, 0\right)$.

8. (b) Let us consider a linear equation

$$ax + by + c = 0 \quad \text{...(i)}$$

Since, $(-2, 2)$, $(0, 0)$ and $(2, -2)$ are the solutions of linear equation, therefore it satisfies the Eq. (i), we get

At point $(-2, 2)$,

$$-2a + 2b + c = 0 \quad \text{...(ii)}$$

At point $(0, 0)$, $\quad 0 + 0 + c = 0 \Rightarrow c = 0$ ...(iii)

and at point $(2, -2)$, $\quad 2a - 2b + c = 0$ ...(iv)

From Eqs. (ii) and (iii), we get

$$c = 0 \text{ and } -2a + 2b + 0 = 0,$$
$$\Rightarrow \quad -2a = -2b, a = \frac{2b}{2} \Rightarrow a = b$$

On putting $a = b$ and $c = 0$ in Eq. (i),

$$bx + by + 0 = 0 \Rightarrow bx + by = 0$$
$$\Rightarrow \quad b(x + y) = 0 \Rightarrow x + y = 0, b \neq 0$$

Hence, $x + y = 0$ is the required form of the linear equation.

9. (c) When $x = 3$ and $y = 1$,

For equation $3x + 4y = 10$, LHS $= 3x + 4y = 3(3) + 4(1) = 9 + 4 = 13 \neq 10$

For equation $8x + 5y = 25$, LHS $= 8x + 5y = 8(3) + 5(1) = 24 + 5 = 29 \neq 25$

For equation $8x + 5y = 29$, LHS $= 8x + 5y = 8(3) + 5(1) = 24 + 5 = 29 = 29$

For equation $5x + 8y = 29$, LHS $= 5x + 8y = 5(3) + 8(1) = 15 + 8 = 23 \neq 29$

Thus, $x = 3$ and $y = 1$ is the solution of $8x + 5y = 29$

10. (a) When $x = 4$ and $y = 12$, then

$$y = x + 4t$$
$$\Rightarrow \quad 12 = 4 + 4t$$
$$\Rightarrow \quad 4t = 12 - 4 = 8$$
$$\Rightarrow \quad t = \frac{8}{4} = 2$$

11. (a) It is given that $x = k^2$ and $y = k$ is a solution of the equation $x - 5y + 6 = 0$.

Therefore, $\quad k^2 - 5k + 6 = 0$

$$\Rightarrow \quad k^2 - 3k - 2k + 6 = 0$$
$$\Rightarrow \quad k(k - 3) - 2(k - 3) = 0$$
$$\Rightarrow \quad (k - 3)(k - 2) = 0$$
$$\Rightarrow \quad k - 2 = 0 \text{ or } k - 3 = 0$$
$$\Rightarrow \quad k = 2, k = 3$$

12. (a) Since, (2, 0) is a solution of the given linear equation $2x + 3y = k$, then put $x = 2$ and $y = 0$ in the equation.

$$\Rightarrow \quad 2(2) + 3(0) = k \Rightarrow k = 4$$

Hence, the value of k is 4.

13. (b) **Assertion** From the given point (3, 15), there are infinitely many lines passing through this point. Hence, Assertion is correct.

Reason It is also correct that linear equation in two variables has infinitely many solutions. But this is not a correct explanation of Assertion.

14. (c) **Assertion** Since, $\left(-\frac{3}{2}, k\right)$ is a solution of $2x + 3y = 0$.

$$\therefore \quad 2\left(-\frac{3}{2}\right) + 3k = 0 \Rightarrow -3 + 3k = 0 \Rightarrow k = 1$$

Hence, if $\left(-\frac{3}{2}, k\right)$ is a solution of $2x + 3y = 0$

Then, $k = 1$. So, it is correct.

Reason Also, $ax + b = 0$ can be expressed in linear equation in two variables as $ax + 0 \cdot y + b = 0$.

Hence, Reason is not correct.

15. (i) Given, number of children = x

and total number of chocolates distributed = y

Now, by given condition,

$$y = 5x + 20$$

(ii) Here, $y = 145$, then

$$145 = 5x + 20$$
$$\Rightarrow \quad 5x = 125$$
$$\Rightarrow \quad x = 25$$

(iii) (a) Here, $y = 205$, then

$$205 = 5x + 20$$
$$\Rightarrow \quad 5x = 185$$
$$\Rightarrow \quad x = 37$$

Or

(b) Here, $x = 15$

Now, $y = 15 \times 5 + 20$

$$\Rightarrow \quad y = 75 + 20$$
$$\Rightarrow \quad y = 95$$

16. (i) Total parking time = x h

and total charges = ₹y

Now, according to the question,

$$30 + 10(x - 2) = y$$
$$\Rightarrow \quad 30 + 10x - 20 = y$$
$$\Rightarrow \quad 10x - y + 10 = 0 \quad \text{...(i)}$$

(ii) Given, $y = 20$

On putting $y = 20$ in Eq. (i), we get

$$10x - 20 + 10 = 0$$
$$\Rightarrow \quad 10x = 10$$
$$\Rightarrow \quad x = 1$$

(iii) (a) $\because$ $x = 2$

$$\therefore 10 \times 2 - y + 10 = 0 \quad \text{[using Eq. (i)]}$$
$$\Rightarrow \quad y = 20 + 10 = 30$$

Or

(b) Let the total parking time = x h

and total charges = ₹ y

Now, according to the question,

$$50 + 10(x - 2) = y$$
$$\Rightarrow \quad 50 + 10x - 20 = y$$
$$\Rightarrow \quad 30 + 10x = y$$
$$\Rightarrow \quad 10x - y + 30 = 0$$

17. (i) Given, price of petrol in December 2018 is ₹ x and present price of petrol in December 2019 is ₹ y.

Since, every six months, price of petrol increases at the rate of ₹ 5 per litre.

Then, by given condition, $y = x + 10$.

(ii) Given, price of CNG in December 2017 = ₹ a

and price of CNG in December 2018 = ₹ b

Then, by given condition,

$b = a + 5$

(iii) (a) $\because$ $y = 20$

Then, $y = x + 10$

$$\Rightarrow \quad 20 = x + 10$$
$$\Rightarrow \quad x = 10$$

Or

(b) $\because$ $b = 10$

$$\therefore \quad 10 = a + 5$$
$$\Rightarrow \quad a = 10 - 5 = 5$$

18. (i) $\because$ The number of children be x

and the number of adults be y.

According to the question,

the required linear equation is

$$3x + 2y = 160 \quad \text{... (i)}$$

(ii) Given the number of children is 40 i.e. $x = 40$

On putting the value of x in Eq. (i), we get

$$3(40) + 2y = 160$$
$$\Rightarrow \quad 120 + 2y = 160$$
$$\Rightarrow \quad 2y = 160 - 120$$
$$\Rightarrow \quad 2y = 40$$
$$\Rightarrow \quad y = 20$$

$\therefore$ Hence, the number of adults is 20.

(iii) (a) Given, the number of adults is 20 i.e. $y = 20$

On putting the value of y in Eq. (i), we get

$$3x + 2(20) = 160$$
$$\Rightarrow \quad 3x = 160 - 40$$
$$\Rightarrow \quad x = \frac{120}{3} = 40$$

Hence, the number of children is 40.

Or

(b) On putting $x = 5$ and $y = 0$ in the equation $3x + 5y = b$, we get

$$3(5) + 5(0) = b$$
$$\Rightarrow \quad b = 15$$

Part II

1. **Hint** Solve as Example 1.

Ans.

(i) $2x+3y-5=0,\ a=2,\ b=3,\ c=-5$

(ii) $x-3y+5=0, a=1, b=-3, c=5$

(iii) $2x-\pi y+0=0, a=2, b=-\pi, c=0$

(iv) $0x+y-9=0, a=0, b=1, c=-9$

(v) $\frac{x}{3}-\frac{y}{4}-2=0, a=\frac{1}{3}, b=\frac{-1}{4}, c=-2$

(vi) $-x+12y-\frac{1}{3}=0,\ a=-1, b=12,\ c=\frac{-1}{3}$

2. Given, the cost of a hen $= x$

and the cost of an egg $= y$

Then, according to question,

$x=50y \Rightarrow x-50y=0$

3. Let cost of a ticket to Agra be ₹ x and cost of a ticket to Mathura be ₹ y.

According to question,

$$2x+3y=440$$

$$\Rightarrow\quad 2x+3y-440=0$$

4. **Hint** Do same as Example 4.

Ans. $x-2y-20=0$

5. **Hint** Let present ages of Nuri and Sonu be x and y years, respectively. Then, $(x-5)=3(y-5)$

Ans. $x-3y=-10$

6. **Hint** Let numerator and denominator be x and y, respectively. Then, $\frac{x+1}{y-1}=1$

Ans. $x-y+2=0$

7. **Hint** Solve as Example 6.

Ans. $5x-2y-9=0$

8. **Hint** Let the cost of a toy telephone and a ball be ₹ x and ₹ y, respectively. Then, $x=4y$

As $y=5$, therefore $x=4\times5=20$

$\therefore$ Cost of packing of two telephone toys

$$=2x+4=20\times2+4=44$$

Ans. $x=4y$, ₹ 44

9. (i) **Hint** Let the number of days for which the food has been availed by Apeksha be x and total charges be y.

Then, $1000+50x=y$

Ans. $50x-y+1000=0$

(ii) $(x=4,\ y=1200)$ and $(x=6,\ y=1300)$

(iii) **Hint** For 21 days, put $x=21$, then

$$y=1000+50\times21$$

Ans. ₹ 2050

10. **Hint** Solve as Example 5.

Ans. (2, 1), (– 4, – 2)

11. **Hint** Solve as Example 5.

Ans. (0, 7), (1, 5), (2, 3), (– 1, 9)

12. **Hint** Put $x=\sqrt{3}$ and $y=0$ in given equation

$3\sqrt{3}x-3y=9$.

Ans. Yes

13. **Hint** Do same as Q. 3 of NCERT FOLDER Exercise 4.2.

Ans. (i) Yes (ii) No (iii) Yes (iv) No (v) Yes

14. **Hint** Solve as Example 8. **Ans.** $k=-4$

15. **Hint** Solve as Example 8. **Ans.** (i) $a=0$ (ii) $a=3$

16. **Hint** Put $y=1$ and $\pi=\frac{22}{7}$ in given equation.

Ans. 7

17. Given, unit digit is x and tens digit is y.

Then, number $=10y+x$ and new number after reversing the digits $=10x+y$

According to the question,

$$10y+x+10x+y=121$$

$$\Rightarrow\quad 11x+11y=121$$

$$\Rightarrow\quad x+y=11$$

18. **Hint** Let the contribution of Alka be x and that of Noori be y.

Ans. $x+y=500$

19. (i) Given, volume of water collected in x second $= y$ cm^3

According to the question, $y=40x$, which is the required linear equation.

(ii) We have, $y=40x$

$\Rightarrow\quad 40x-y+0=0$,

this is the standard form of equation.

On comparing with $ax+by+c=0$, we get

$$a=40, b=-1 \text{ and } c=0$$

Now, $a^2+b^2-c^2=(40)^2+(-1)^2-(0)^2$

$$=1600+1-0=1601$$

20. **Hint** Given that y varies directly as x.

i.e. $\quad y\propto x$

$\Rightarrow\quad y=kx \quad$ ...(i)

where, k is an arbitrary constant.

Given, $\quad y=12$ and $x=4$

Then, from Eq. (i), $12 = 4k$

$\Rightarrow \quad k = 3$

From Eq (i), $\quad y = 3x \quad$ ...(ii)

When $x = 5$, then from Eq. (ii), we get

$$y = 3 \times 5 = 15$$

21. Hint Now, by given condition, the values of x and y for given linear equation are same, i.e. $x = y$.

Ans. $c = \dfrac{8-2x}{x}, x \neq 0$

22. Let the age of Rohan = x yr

and the age of Mohan = y yr

(i) According to the question, the linear equation for the above situation is

$$x + y = 24$$

or $\quad y = 24 - x \quad$ ... (i)

Now, to find four solutions of the given equations, we take the arbitrary values of x and y.

When $x = 0$, then from Eq. (i),

$$y = 24 - 0 = 24$$

When $y = 0$, then from Eq. (i),

$$0 = 24 - x \Rightarrow x = 24$$

When $x = 1$, then from Eq. (i),

$$y = 24 - x = 24 - 1 = 23$$

When $y = 2$, then from Eq. (i),

$$2 = 24 - x \Rightarrow x = 24 - 2 = 22$$

Thus, four solutions are (0, 24), (24, 0), (1, 23) and (22, 2).

(ii) Now, age of Rohan = 13 yr

i.e. $x = 13$ yr.

$\because \quad x + y = 24 \quad$ [from Eq. (i)]

$\Rightarrow \quad 13 + y = 24$

$\Rightarrow \quad y = 24 - 13 = 11$

Hence, Mohan's age = 11 yr.

23. Total distance covered = x km

Total fare = ₹ y

Fare for the first three kilometer = ₹ 20

Subsequent distance = $(x - 3)$ km

$\therefore$ Fare for the subsequent distance = ₹ $5(x - 3)$

According to the question,

$$y = 20 + 5(x - 3)$$

$\Rightarrow \quad y = 20 + 5x - 15$

$\Rightarrow \quad y = 5x + 5 \quad$ ...(i)

$\therefore$ Required linear equation is

$$y = 5(x + 1)$$

Now, we find the four solutions of the equations.

Let $x = 0$, then from Eq. (i), we get

$$y = 5(0) + 5 = 5$$

Let $y = 0$, then from Eq. (i), we get

$$0 = 5(x) + 5$$

$\Rightarrow \quad 5x = -5$

$\Rightarrow \quad x = -1$

Let $x = 2$, then from Eq. (i), we get

$$y = 5(2) + 5 = 10 + 5 = 15$$

Let $x = 1$, then from Eq. (i), we get

$$y = 5(1) + 5 = 5 + 5 = 10$$

Thus, 4 solutions for linear equation $y = 5x + 5$ represented as

x	0	− 1	2	1
y	5	0	15	10

24. Given equation is

$$5x - 8y = 3(x + y) - 22$$

$\Rightarrow \quad 5x - 8y = 3x + 3y - 22$

$\Rightarrow 5x - 3x - 8y - 3y + 22 = 0$

$\Rightarrow \quad 2x - 11y + 22 = 0 \quad$ ...(i)

Here, the solution for the above equation is not unique.

Now, we find the 2 solutions.

x	0	− 11
y	2	0

25. Hint $F = \dfrac{9}{5}C + 32$

(i) C = 40°

Ans. 104° F

(ii) F = 104°

Ans. 40° C

(iii) Let °C = °F = x

Now, $F = \dfrac{9}{5}C + 32$

$\Rightarrow \quad x = \dfrac{9}{5}x + 32$

Ans. −40°

Mind Map

LINEAR EQUATIONS IN TWO VARIABLES

Linear Equation in Two Variables
An equation which can be put in the form $ax + by + c = 0$, where a, b and c are real numbers (a & b together cannot be zero) and x, y are variables.
e.g. $4x + 5y = 7$

Solution of a Linear Equation in Two Variables
Any pair of values of x and y which satisfies the given equation in x and y is called its solution.
e.g., $6x + 3y = 24$, then solutions are (0, 8), (4, 0).
There can be some other solutions.

To Write a Linear Equation in One Variable into Linear Equation in Two Variables
We can write a linear equation in one variable (say x) as linear equation in two variables, by taking the coefficient of other variable (say y) as zero.
e.g. $2y = 3$ can be written as
$0 \cdot x + 2y - 3 = 0$

Method to Write a Given Statement as Linear Equation in Two Variables
First identify the variable quantities and assume them as x and y. Then, write the given condition in terms of x and y in the form of $ax + by + c = 0$

Linear Equation in One Variable
An equation with linear expression in one variable only.
The equation is of the form $ax + b = 0$, where $a \neq 0$ and b are real numbers.
e.g. $5x + 8 = 9$

Solution of a Linear Equation in One Variable
The value of the variable (say x) which satisfies the given equation in x, is called a solution of the linear equation in one variable.
e.g. $3x + 5 = 0$
$\Rightarrow$ Solution is $x = -\frac{5}{3}$

Method To Check Whether Given Pair of Values is a Solution of Given Equation or not
Put the given values in given linear equation. If LHS = RHS, then the given pair of values is a solution of given linear equation, otherwise not.

Method of Finding the Value Of Unknown When Solution of Equation is Given
Put the values of variables x and y in the given linear equation and simplify the equation to find the value of unknown (say k).

Topics to be Assessed Formatively

Graph of a Linear Equation in Two Variables

We know that a linear equation $ax + by + c = 0$ in two variables x and y has infinitely many solutions. If we plot these solutions on a graph paper, we see that each solution represents a point and on joining these points, we get a straight line, such a straight line is called the graph of the linear equation.

Thus, we can conclude that every point on the line satisfies the equation of the line i.e. every point on the line is a solution of the equation and every solution of the equation is a point on the line.

Method to Draw The Graph of Linear Equation in Two Variables

Let the linear equation in two variables be $ax + by + c = 0$, where $a \neq 0, b \neq 0$ and x, y are variables. Then, to draw its graph, we use the following steps

Step I Write given linear equation and express y in terms of x.

i.e. $$by = -(ax + c)$$

$$\Rightarrow \quad y = -\frac{(ax + c)}{b} \quad \text{...(i)}$$

Step II Put different arbitrary values of x in Eq. (i) and find the corresponding values of y.

Step III Form a table as follows, by writing the values of y below the corresponding values of x.

x	x_1	x_2	x_3	x_4
y	y_1	y_2	y_3	y_4

Step IV Draw the coordinate axes on graph paper and take a suitable scale to plot points $(x_1, y_1), (x_2, y_2), \ldots$ on graph paper.

Step V Join these points $(x_1, y_1), (x_2, y_2), \ldots$. Thus, we get a straight line and produce it on both sides.

Hence, the straight line, so obtained is the required graph of given linear equation. Similarly, we can draw the graph of more than one linear equation in two variables.

Note
- If possible, choose the integral values of x in step II in such a way that the corresponding values of y are also integers.
- It is enough to plot two points corresponding to two solutions and join them by a line. However, it is advisable to plot more than two such points, so that the correctness of the graph may be checked immediately.

Example 1. **Draw the graph of the equation $y - x = 2$.**

Sol. Given linear equation can be written as $y = 2 + x$ ...(i)

When $x = -2$, then from Eq. (i), we get $y = 2 - 2 = 0$

When $x = 0$, then from Eq. (i), we get $y = 2$

When $x = 1$, then from Eq. (i), we get $y = 2 + 1 = 3$

Thus, we get the table

x	0	−2	1
y	2	0	3

Draw the coordinate axes XOX' and YOY', and plot the points $A(-2, 0)$, $B(0, 2)$ and $C(1, 3)$ by taking a suitable scale.

On joining the points A, B and C, we get a straight line AC. Thus, the line AC represents the required graph of given linear equation in two variables.

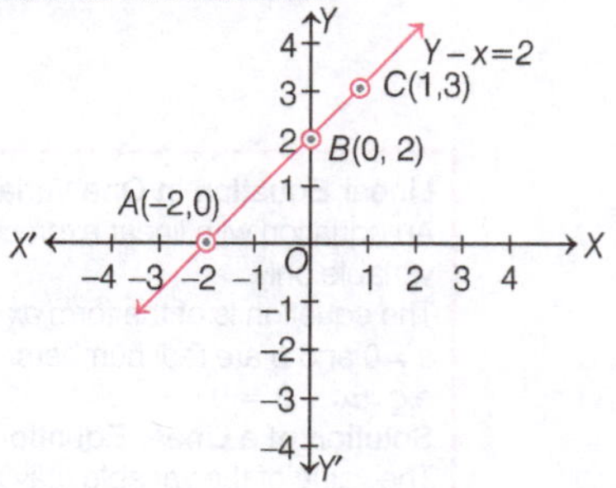

Note An equation of the type $y = mx$ always represents a line passing through the origin and the quadrants I and III, where m is a real number.

Example 2. **Draw the graph of $2x + y = 6$ and find the point where graph intersects Y-axis.**

Sol. When $x = 0$, then $y = 6 - 2(0) = 6$

When $x = 1$, then $y = 6 - 2(1) = 6 - 2 = 4$

When $x = 2$, then $y = 6 - 2(2) = 6 - 4 = 2$

So, we have the following table to draw the graph

x	0	1	2
y	6	4	2

Here, we have three points $A(0, 6)$, $B(1, 4)$ and $C(2, 2)$. Now, plot these points on the graph and join them by a straight line.

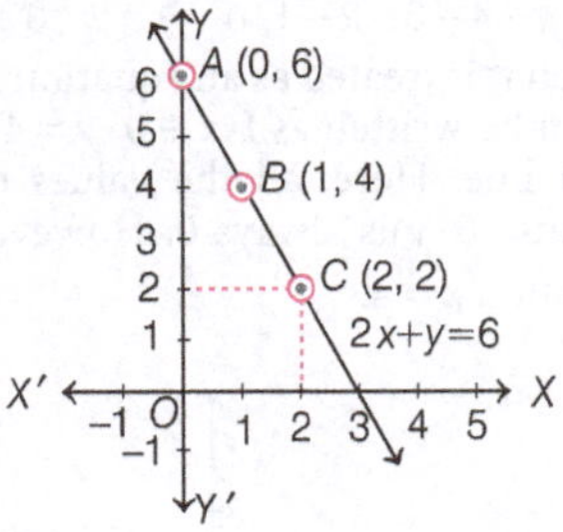

Thus, we get the straight line *AC*, which represents the required graph of given linear equation. Also, from the graph, it is clear that the graph intersects *Y*-axis at the point (0, 6).

Example 3. **The parking charges of a car in a parking lot is ₹ 30 for the first two hours and ₹ 10 per hour for subsequent hours. Taking total parking time to be x h and total charges as ₹ y, write a linear equation in two variables to express the above statement. Draw a graph for the linear equation and read the charges for five hours.**

Sol. Given, parking charges for the first two hours = ₹ 30 and for subsequent hours = ₹ 10

Total parking time = x h and total charges = ₹y

Then, according to the given condition,

$30 + 10(x - 2) = y \Rightarrow 30 + 10x - 20 = y$

$\Rightarrow \quad 10x - y + 10 = 0$

which is the required linear equation in two variables.

It can also be written as $y = 10x + 10$ ...(i)

Now, for drawing the graph, we need atleast two solutions of the equation.

When $x = -1$, then $y = -10 + 10 = 0$

When $x = 0$, then $y = 10(0) + 10 = 10$

When $x = 1$, then $y = 10(1) + 10 = 20$

So, we have the following table to draw the graph

x	−1	0	1
y	0	10	20

Here, we have three points $A(-1, 0)$, $B(0, 10)$ and $C(1, 20)$. By plotting these points on the graph paper and joining them, we get a straight line *AC*, which represents the required graph of linear equation. From the graph, charges for the hours 1, 2, 3, 4 and 5 are ₹ 20, ₹ 30, ₹ 40, ₹ 50 and ₹ 60, respectively.

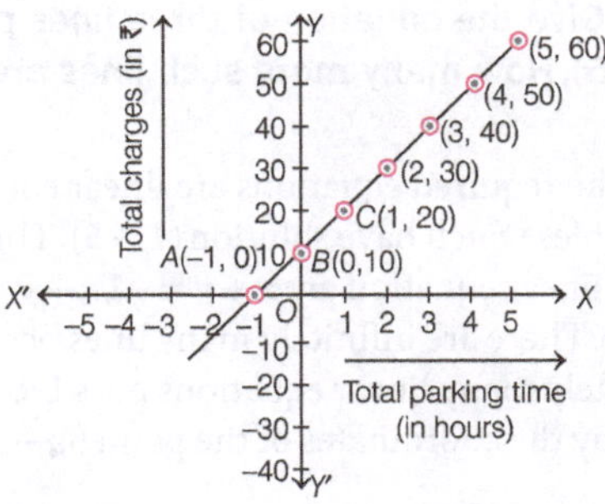

Example 4. **From the choices given below, choose the equation whose graph is shown in the figure.**

(i) $x + y = 2$ **(ii) $x - y = 2$**

(iii) $2x + 2y = 6$

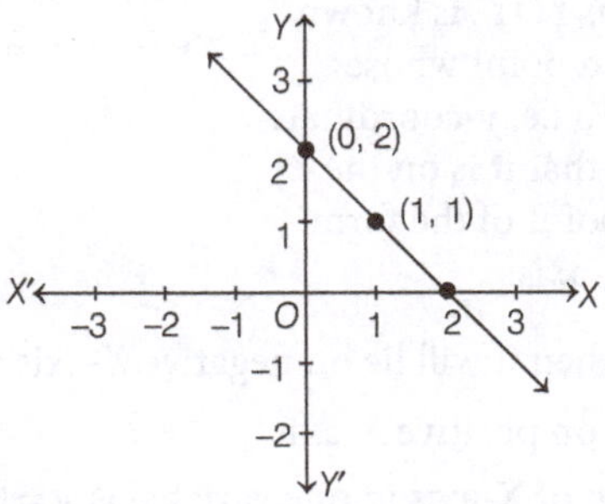

Sol. Now, consider the equation of given graph is $x + y = 2$.

Given points on the graph are (0, 2) and (1, 1). So, these points will satisfy the equation of line.

Now, at (0, 2), $x + y = 0 + 2 = 2$ and at (1, 1), $x + y = 1 + 1 = 2$

Thus, the points satisfy the equation $x + y = 2$.

Hence, the given graph is a graph of the equation $x + y = 2$.

Example 5. **If the point (2, 3) lies on the graph of the equation $2x + ay = 10$, find the value of a.**

Sol. Since, the point (2, 3) lies on the graph, then it will satisfy its equation.

On putting $x = 2$ and $y = 3$ in given equation, we get

$$2 \times 2 + a \times 3 = 10$$

$$\Rightarrow \quad 3a = 6 \Rightarrow a = 2$$

Example 6. **Find a point on X-axis from where graph of linear equation $2x = 1 - 5y$ will pass.**

Sol. Let the point be $(m, 0)$. [∵ on *X*-axis, *y*-coordinate is zero]

Since, the equation passes through this point, so put $x = m$ and $y = 0$ in $2x = 1 - 5y$, we get

$$2 \times m = 1 - 5 \times 0 \Rightarrow 2m = 1 \Rightarrow m = \frac{1}{2}$$

Hence, $\left(\frac{1}{2}, 0\right)$ is the required point.

Example 7. **Give the equation of three lines passing through (4, – 5). How many more such lines are there and why?**

Sol. Clearly, the required equations are linear equations in two variables which have solution (4, – 5). Three examples of such a linear equation are $x + y = -1$, $x - y = 9$ and $2x + y = 3$. There are infinitely many lines because there are infinitely many linear equations possible which are satisfied by the coordinates of the point (4, – 5).

Equations of Lines Parallel to Axes

Equation of X-axis and Y-axis

We know that in cartesian plane, axis XOX' is known as X-axis and axis YOY' is known as Y-axis. For a point whose ordinate is zero i.e. y-coordinate is zero we say that it is on the X-axis. So, a point of the form $(a, 0)$ lies on X-axis.

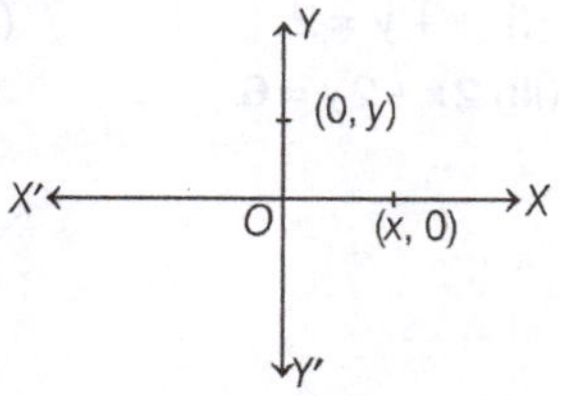

Also, if $a < 0$, then it will lie on negative X-axis and if $a > 0$, then it will lie on positive X-axis.

Thus, equation of X-axis in one variable is $y = 0$ and equation of X-axis in two variables is $0 \cdot x + 1 \cdot y = 0$. This equation shows that for each value of x, the corresponding value of y is zero i.e. the point corresponding to each solution of the linear equation lies on the X-axis. Similarly, a point of the form $(0, b)$ lies on Y-axis. Also, if $b < 0$, then it will lie on negative Y-axis and if $b > 0$, then it will lie on positive Y-axis.

Thus, equation of Y-axis in one variable is $x = 0$ and equation of Y-axis in two variables is $1 \cdot x + 0 \cdot y = 0$. This equation shows that for each value of y, the corresponding value of x is zero i.e. the point corresponding to each solution of the linear equation lies on the Y-axis.

Equation of Lines Parallel to Y-axis

Let $x - a = 0$ be an equation. Then,

(*i*) if it is treated as an equation in one variable x only, then it has a unique solution $x = a$, which is a point on the number line.

(*ii*) if it is treated as an equation in two variables x and y, then it can be written as $1 \cdot x + 0 \cdot y - a = 0$. It has infinitely many solutions of the form (a, r), where r is any real number. Also, we can say that every point of the form (a, r) will lie on given line. Thus, given equation represents a line parallel to Y-axis.

Note If $a > 0$, then $x = a$ represent the equation of a line parallel to Y-axis in the positive direction of X-axis and $x = -a$ in the negative direction of X-axis.

Example 1. **Give the geometric representation of**
(*i*) $x = 4$ (*ii*) $x + 1 = 0$
as an equation in one variable and in two variables.

Sol. (*i*) Given equation is $x = 4$.

When it is treated as an equation in one variable, then unique solution of this equation is $x = 4$. So, it is a point on number line.

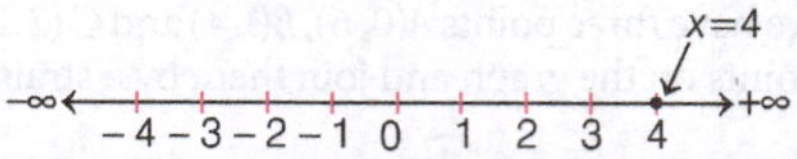

When it is treated as an equation in two variables, then it can be written as $1 \cdot x + 0 \cdot y = 4$ and it is represented by a line. Here, all the values of y are permissible, because $0 \cdot y$ is always 0. However, x must satisfy the equation $x = 4$.

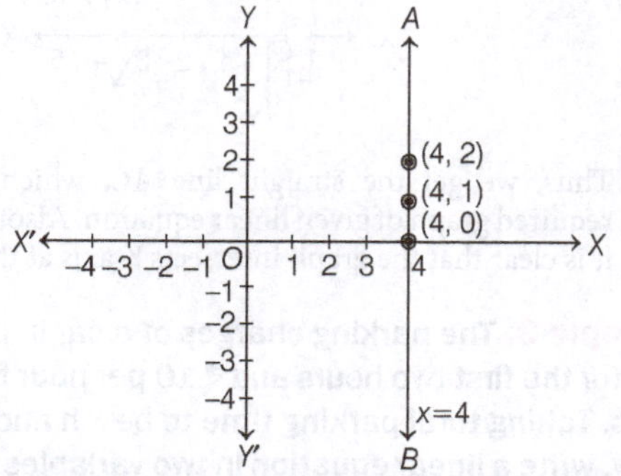

The graph AB is a line parallel to Y-axis at a distance of 4 units from Y-axis in positive direction of X-axis.

(*ii*) Given equation is $x + 1 = 0$.

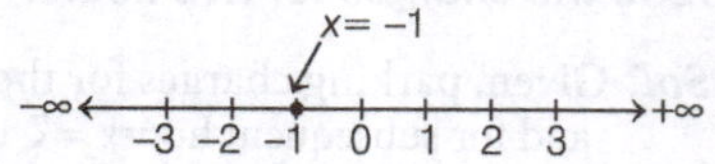

When it is treated as an equation in one variable, then unique solution of this equation is $x = -1$. So, it is a point on the number line.

When it is treated as an equation in two variables, then it can be written as $1 \cdot x + 0 \cdot y + 1 = 0$ and it is represented by a line.

Here, all the values of y are permissible, because $0 \cdot y$ is always 0. However, x must satisfy the equation $x + 1 = 0$.

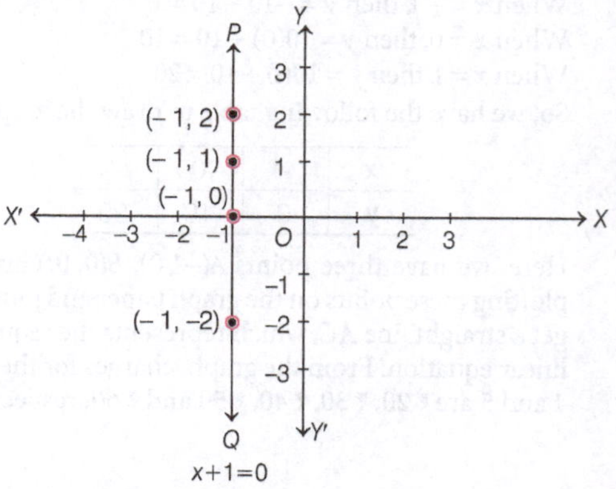

The graph PQ is a line parallel to Y-axis at a distance of 1 unit from Y-axis in the negative direction of X-axis.

Equation of Lines Parallel to *X*-axis

Let $y - b = 0$ be an equation. Then,

(*i*) if it is treated as an equation in one variable y only, then it has a unique solution $y = b$, which is a point on the number line.

(*ii*) if it is treated as an equation *in two variables* x and y, then it can be written as $0 \cdot x + 1 \cdot y - b = 0$. It has infinitely many solutions of the form (r, b), where r is any real number.

Also, we can say that every point of the form (r, b) will lie on this line. Thus, given equation represents a line parallel to *X*-axis.

Note If $b > 0$, then $y = b$ repersent the equation of a line parallel to *X*-axis in positive direction of *Y*-axis and $y = -b$ in the negative direction of *Y*-axis.

Example 2. **Solve the equation $3y - 3 = 13 - y$ and represent the solution**

(*i*) on the number line.

(*ii*) in the cartesian plane.

Sol. Given equation is $3y - 3 = 13 - y$

$\Rightarrow \quad 3y + y = 13 + 3 \Rightarrow 4y = 16$

$\therefore \quad y = \frac{16}{4} = 4$

(*i*) If we treated $y = 4$ as an equation in one variable only, then it has a unique solution $y = 4$. So, it is a point on number line.

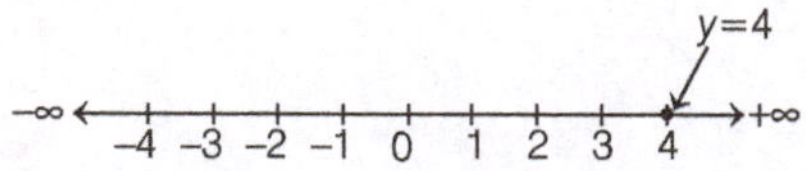

(*ii*) If we treated $y = 4$ as an equation in two variables, then it can be written as $0 \cdot x + 1 \cdot y = 4$ and it is represented by a line.

Here, all the values of x are permissible, because $0 \cdot x$ is always 0. However, y must satisfy the equation $y = 4$.

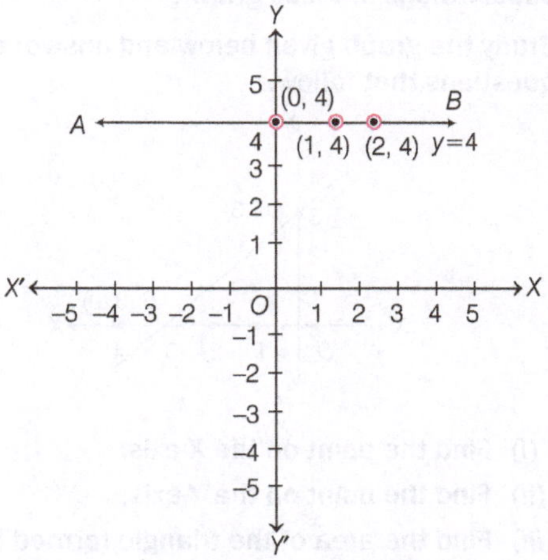

The graph *AB* is a line parallel to *X*-axis in cartesian plane at a distance of 4 units from *X*-axis in positive direction of *Y*-axis. It has infinitely many solutions as (0, 4), (1, 4), (2, 4), (3, 4), ...

Exercise

1. Draw the graph of $2x-3y+12=0$ in a cartesian plane and find the point where graph intersects at Y-axis.
2. Draw the graphs of the linear equations $y=x$ and $y=2x$ on the same cartesian plane. What is your observations in these graphs?
3. Study the graph given below and answer the questions that follow.

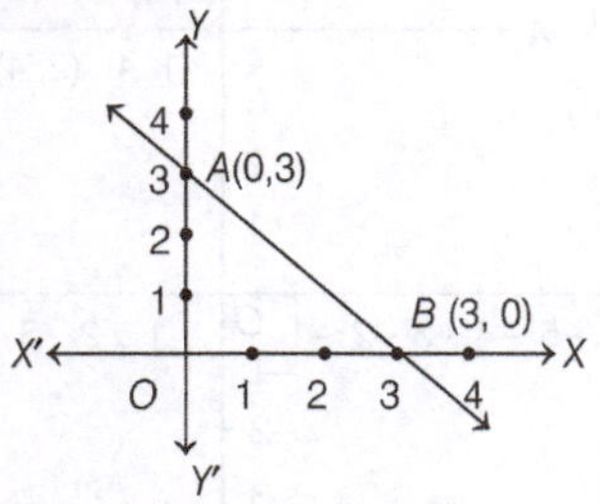

(i) Find the point on the X-axis.
(ii) Find the point on the Y-axis.
(iii) Find the area of the triangle formed by the line and the axes.

4. The price of 2 pens and 5 pencils is ₹ 60. Draw the graph after forming a linear equation.
5. The path of a train A is given by the equation $2x-3y=17$ and path of another train B is given by the linear equation $4x-6y=18$. Represent the above situations graphically and write your observation.
6. If $(1,-1)$ is a point on the line $2x-(2a+5)y=5$, then find the value of a.
7. (i) Find a point on X-axis, from where graph of linear equation $2x=1-5y$ will pass.
   (ii) Find a point on Y-axis, from where graph of linear equation $x-5y=3$ will pass.
8. Give the equations of two lines passing through $(2,10)$. How many more such lines are there and why?
9. Through which quadrant(s), the graph of the linear equation $x-2y=0$ will pass?
10. How many solutions of the equation $2x+1=x-3$ are there on the
    (i) number line?
    (ii) cartesian plane?
11. What is the distance between the graph of the equations $x=-4$ and $x=-1$?

Directions (Q. Nos. 12-17) *Give the geometric representations of following equations. And also identify the line parallel to which axis.*

(i) in one variable. (ii) in two variables.

12. $2x+1=5$
13. $3x+4=7+2x$
14. $-4-2x=x+5$
15. $2x+7=5x-5$
16. $3y+4=10$
17. $4y+3=2y+9$

Answers

1. (0, 4)
3. (i) (3,0) (ii) (0,3) (iii) $\frac{9}{2}$ sq unit
6. $a=-1$
7. (i) $\left(\frac{1}{2},0\right)$ (ii) $\left(0,-\frac{3}{5}\right)$
8. $5x-y=0$ and $x+y=12$, infinitely many lines
9. Third quadrant
10. (i) One (ii) Infinitely many
11. 3 units
12. Y-axis
13. Y-axis
14. Y-axis
15. Y-axis
16. X-axis
17. X-axis

Introduction to Euclid's Geometry

CHAPTER 5

The word 'Geometry' comes from the Greek words '*Geo*' means 'The Earth' and '*Metrein*' means 'To measure'. Geometry appears to have originated from the need for measuring land. Around 300 BCE, Euclid belongs to the greece. He was a teacher of Mathematics of Alexandria in Egypt. He collect all the known work and arranged in his famous treatise called 'Elements'. He divided the 'Elements' into thirteen chapters, each called a book. These books influenced the whole world's understanding of geometry for generations to come.

In this chapter, we shall discuss Euclid's approach to geometry and shall try to link it with present day geometry.

Euclid's Definitions

A solid has shape, size and position. Also, it can be moved from one place to another. Its boundaries are called **surfaces,** which separate one part of the space from another and are said to have no thickness. The boundaries of the surface are **curves or straight lines**. These lines end in **points.**

Thus, there are three steps from solids to points 'solids-surfaces-lines-points'. In each step, we lose one extension which is called a **dimension.** A solid has three dimensions, a surface has two dimensions, a line has one dimension and a point has no dimension.

Euclid summarised these statements as definitions and began his exposition by listing 23 definitions in Book 1 of the 'Elements'. Some of them are as follows:

(i) A **point** is that which has no part, i.e. a point is an exact location.

(ii) A **line** is breadthless length.

(iii) The ends of a line are points.

(iv) A **straight line** is a line which lies evenly with the points on itself.

(v) A **surface** is that which has length and breadth only.

(vi) The edges of a surface are **lines.**

(vii) A **plane surface** is a surface which lies evenly with the straight lines on itself.

In Euclid's definitions stated above, there are some terms like part, breadth, length, etc., which have not been explained. If we try to define these terms, then we will get a chain of definitions without an end, due to which some geometric terms have been left **undefined**.

Note It Euclid defined a point, a line and a place but these definitions are not accepted by Mathematician. So, in geometry, we take a point, a line and a plane, (in Euclid's words a plane surface) as **undefined terms.** We can only explain these terms with the help of physical models.

Euclid's Axioms and Postulates

Starting with his definitions, Euclid assumed certain properties, which were not to be proved as these were universal truths. He divided his assumptions into two types:

(i) **Postulate** The term postulate was used for the assumptions specific to geometry. Actually, postulate is a verb. If we say that 'Let us postulate', then we mean that firstly make some statement based on the observed phenomenon in the universe and then check its truth/validity. If it is true/valid, then it is accepted as a postulate, otherwise not.

(ii) **Axiom** The term axiom was used throughout Mathematics and not specifically linked to geometry.

Euclid's Axioms

Axiom 1 Things which are equal to the same things are equal to one another.

e.g. If $\overline{AB} = \overline{CD}$ and $\overline{CD} = \overline{EF}$, then $\overline{AB} = \overline{EF}$

Axiom 2 If equals are added to equals then the wholes are equal.

e.g. If $m\angle ABC = m\angle DEF$, then

$m\angle ABC + m\angle XYZ = m\angle DEF + m\angle XYZ$

Axiom 3 If equals are subtracted from equals then the remainders are equal.

e.g. If $4x = 5y$, then $4x - 2 = 5y - 2$.

Axiom 4 Things which coincide with one another are equal to one another.

e.g. If $\overline{AB}$ coincides with $\overline{PQ}$, such that A falls on P and B falls on Q, then $\overline{AB} = \overline{PQ}$.

Axiom 5 The whole is greater than the part.

e.g. If $x = y + z$ (where, $y, z \neq 0$), then $x > y$ and $x > z$.

Axiom 6 Things which are double of the same things are equal to one another.

e.g. If $y = 2x$ and $z = 2x$, then $y = z$.

Axiom 7 Things which are halves of the same things are equal to one another.

e.g. If $y = \frac{x}{2}$ and $z = \frac{x}{2}$, then $y = z$

Note it A system of axioms is called consistent, if it is impossible to deduce from these axioms a statement that contradicts any axiom or previously proved statements.

Example 1. **In the adjoining figure, it is given that $\angle 1 = \angle 4$ and $\angle 3 = \angle 2$. By which Euclid's axiom, it can be shown that, if $\angle 2 = \angle 4$, then $\angle 1 = \angle 3$?**

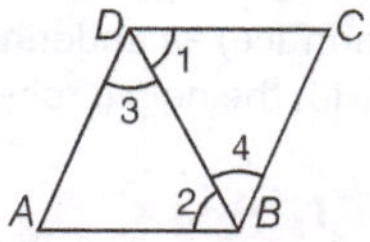

Sol. Given, $\angle 1 = \angle 4$ and $\angle 3 = \angle 2$ ...(i)

If $\angle 2 = \angle 4$

Then, $\angle 2 = \angle 1$ [$\because \angle 1 = \angle 4$, by axiom 1]...(ii)

$\Rightarrow$ $\angle 3 = \angle 1$ [$\because \angle 2 = \angle 3$]

Hence, Euclid's axiom 1 is used to show the above result.

Example 2. **Two salesmen make equal sales during the month of June. In July, each salesman doubles his sale of the month comparing to June. Compare their sales in July. State which axiom you use here. Also, give two more axioms other than the axiom used in the above situation.**

Sol. Let the equal sales of two salesmen in the month of June be x. In July, each salesman doubles his sale comparing to June. Therefore, sale of first salesman is $2x$ and sale of second salesman is $2x$.

According to Euclid's axiom 6, things which are double of the same things are equal to one another. So, in the month of July, their sales are again equal. The two more axioms other than the axiom 6 are axiom 2 and axiom 3.

Example 3. **In the adjoining figure,**

(i) If $AB = BC$, M is the mid-point of AB and N is the mid-point of BC. Show that $AM = NC$.

(ii) If $BM = BN$, M is the mid-point of AB and N is the mid-point of BC. Show that $AB = BC$. NCERT Exemplar

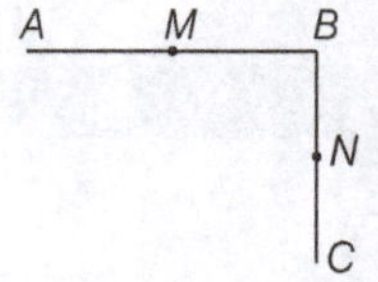

Sol. (i) Given, $AB = BC$ ...(i)

Since, M is the mid-point of AB.

$\therefore$ $AM = MB = \frac{1}{2}AB$ ...(ii)

Also, N is the mid-point of BC.

$\therefore$ $BN = NC = \frac{1}{2}BC$ ...(iii)

According to Euclid's axiom 7, things which are halves of the same things, are equal to one another.

On multiplying both sides of Eq. (i) by $\frac{1}{2}$, we get

$$\frac{1}{2}AB = \frac{1}{2}BC$$

$\Rightarrow$ $AM = NC$ [from Eqs. (ii) and (iii)]

(ii) Given, $BM = BN$ ...(i)

Since, M is the mid-point of AB.

$\therefore$ $AM = BM = \frac{1}{2}AB$

$\Rightarrow$ $2AM = 2BM = AB$ ...(ii)

Also, N is the mid-point of BC.

$\therefore$ $BN = NC = \frac{1}{2}BC$

$\Rightarrow$ $2BN = 2NC = BC$ ...(iii)

According to Euclid's axiom 6, things which are double of the same things are equal to one another.

On multiplying Eq. (i) by 2, we get

$$2BM = 2BN$$

$\Rightarrow$ $AB = BC$ [from Eqs. (ii) and (iii)]

Hence proved.

Example 4. **In the given figure, if $\angle DOB = 87°$, $\angle COA = 82°$ and $\angle BOA = 35°$, then find $\angle COB$ and $\angle COD$.**

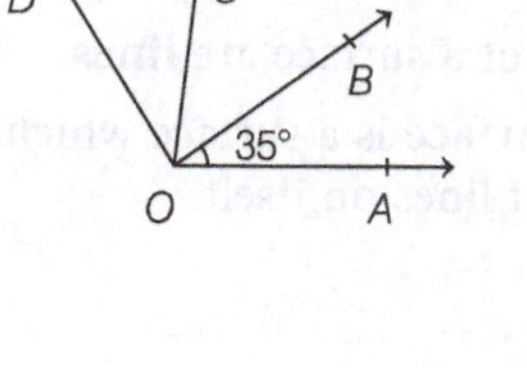

Sol. From figure, we have $\angle DOB = \angle DOC + \angle COB$

Given, $\angle DOB = 87°$

$\therefore$ $\angle DOC + \angle COB = 87°$ [by axiom 1] ...(i)

Similarly, $\angle COB + \angle BOA = \angle COA$

$\Rightarrow$ $\angle COB + \angle BOA = 82°$ ...(ii)

[$\because \angle COA = 82°$, given]

But $\angle BOA = 35°$ [given]

From Eq. (ii), $\angle COB + 35° = 82°$

$\Rightarrow$ $\angle COB + 35° - 35° = 82° - 35°$

[using axiom 3, subtracting equal thing, i.e. $\angle BOA = 35°$ from both sides]

$\Rightarrow$ $\angle COB = 47°$ ...(iii)

On subtracting equal thing, $\angle COB$ from both sides from Eq. (i), we get

$\angle DOC + \angle COB - \angle COB = 87° - \angle COB$ [using axiom 3]

$\Rightarrow$ $\angle DOC = 87° - \angle COB$

$\Rightarrow$ $\angle DOC = 87° - 47°$ [from Eq. (iii)]

$\therefore$ $\angle DOC = 40°$

Hence, $\angle COB = 47°$ and $\angle DOC$ or $\angle COD = 40°$

Euclid's Postulates

Euclid's five postulates are discussed below:

Postulate 1

A straight line may be drawn from any one point to any other point.

It means that atleast one straight line passes through two distinct points, but it does not say that there cannot be more than one such line. However, Euclid has frequently assumed that there is a unique line joining two distinct points.

This result can be stated in the form of an axiom given below:

Axiom

Given two distinct points, there is a unique line that passes through them.

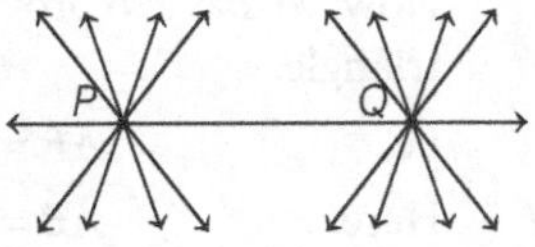

Note that in the given figure, the number of lines passing through P, which also pass through Q, is only one, i.e. PQ or the number of lines passing through Q, which also pass through P, is again only one, i.e. PQ. Thus, the above statement is self-evident and so, it is called an axiom.

Postulate 2

A terminated line can be produced indefinitely.

Euclid's terminated line is now called a line segment.

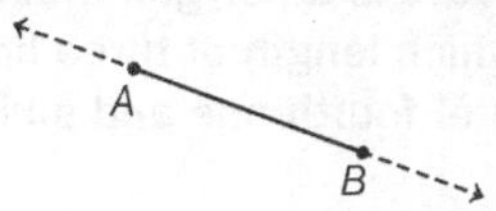

In other words, we can say that a line segment can be extended on either side to form a line.

Postulate 3

A circle can be drawn with any centre and any radius.

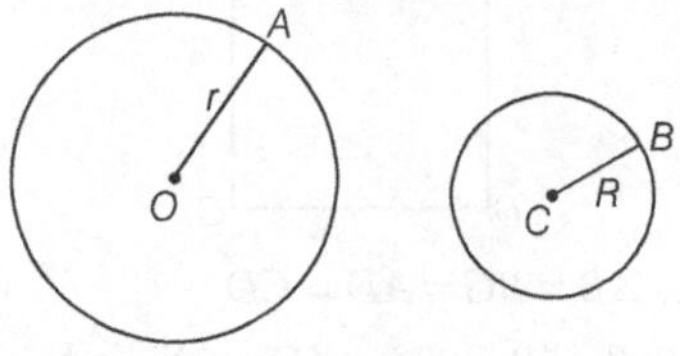

Postulate 4

All right angles are equal to one another.

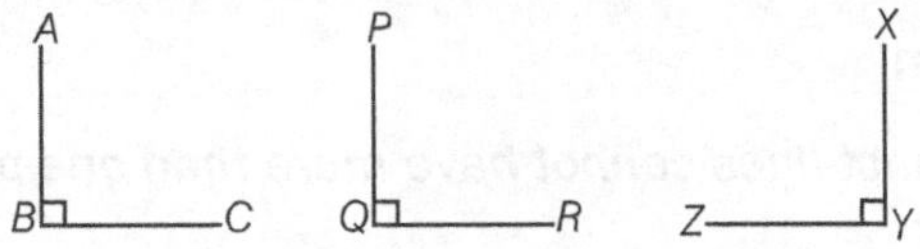

If $\angle ABC = 90°$, $\angle PQR = 90°$ and $\angle XYZ = 90°$, then

$\angle ABC = \angle PQR = \angle XYZ$

i.e. all the right angles are equal to each other.

Postulate 5

If a straight line falling on two straight lines makes the interior angles on the same side of it taken together less than two right angles, then the two straight lines, if produced indefinitely, meet on that side on which the sum of angles is less than two right angles.

e.g. A line PQ falls on lines AB and CD such that the sum of the interior angles $\angle 1 + \angle 2 < 180°$ on the left side of PQ.

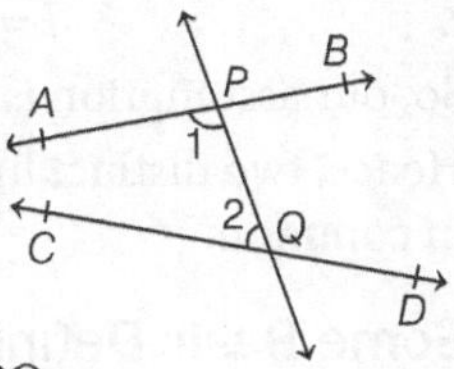

So, the lines AB and CD will eventually intersect on the left side of PQ.

Postulates 1 to 4 are simple and these are taken as self-evident truths.

Using these postulates and axioms, Euclid proved other results. Then, using these results, he proved some more results using deductive reasoning.

The statement that were proved, are called **propositions or theorems.** Euclid deduced 465 propositions in a logical chain using his axioms, postulates, definitions and theorems proved earlier in the chain.

Example 5. **"A square is a polygon made up of four line segments, out of which length of three line segments are equal to the length of fourth one and all its angles are right angles ".**
Using Euclid's, axiom/postulates, justify that all angles and sides of a square are equal.

Sol. Let $ABCD$ be a square. Then,

$$AB = CD, AD = CD \quad \text{and} \quad BC = CD$$

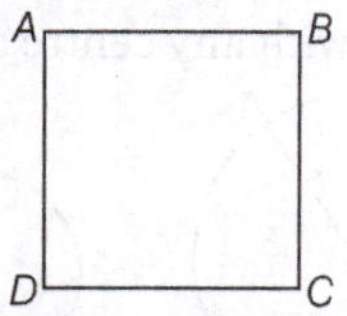

By axiom 1, $AB = BC = AD = CD$

Also, $\angle A = 90°$, $\angle B = 90°$, $\angle D = 90°$ and $\angle C = 90°$

By postulates 4, $\angle A = \angle B = \angle C = \angle D$.

Hence, all angles and sides of a square are euqal.

Theorem

Two distinct lines cannot have more than one point in common

This theorem can be proved in the following way:

Given Two distinct lines l and m.

To prove l and m have only one common point.

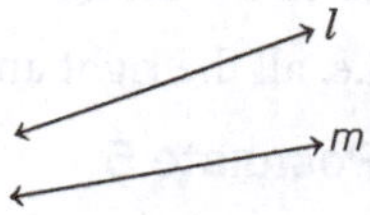

Proof Let us assume that the two lines l and m intersect at two distinct points, say P and Q.

Then, l contains both the points P and Q and m contains both the points P and Q. But from the axiom, we know that only one line can pass through two distinct points.

$\therefore \quad l = m$

So, our assumption is wrong.

Hence, two distinct lines cannot have more than one points in common. **Hence proved.**

Some Basic Definitions

- **Line segment** A part of a line which is bounded by two distinct points is called the line segment. It has two end points.
- **Interior point of a line segment** A point P is called an interior point of a line segment AB, if P lies between A and B but P is neither A nor B. Clearly, all points on the line segment AB are its interior points except the end points A and B.
- **Congruence of line segment** Two line segments AB and CD are congruent, if the trace-copy of one can be superposed on the other so as to cover it completely or exactly and it is denoted by $\overline{AB} \cong \overline{CD}$.
- **Ray** A line segment AB when extended infinitely in one direction, is called the ray and it is denoted as $\overrightarrow{AB}$.
- **Opposite rays** Two rays AB and AC are said to be opposite rays, if they are collinear and point A is the only common point of the two rays.
- **Collinear points** Three or more than three points are said to be collinear, if there is a line which contains all of them.
- **Intersecting lines** Two lines having a common point are called intersecting lines. The common point is called the point of intersection.
- **Concurrent lines** Three or more lines intersecting at the same point are said to be concurrent lines.
- A **pyramid** is a solid figure whose base is a triangle or square or some other polygon and its side faces are triangles converging to a point at the top.

Example 6. **In the given figure, if A, B and C are three points on a line and B lies between A and C, then prove that $AB + BC = AC$.**

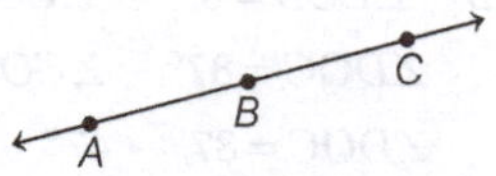

Sol. In the given figure, AC coincides with $AB + BC$.

Also, Euclid's axiom 4 says that things which coincide with one another are equal to one another. So, it can be deduced that

$$AB + BC = AC$$

Example 7. **Prove that an equilateral triangle can be constructed on any given line segment.**

Sol. A line segment, say AB of any length is given.

Using Euclid's postulate 3, we can draw a circle with point A as the centre and AB as the radius. Similarly, draw another circle with point B as the centre and BA as the radius. The two circles meet at a point, say C.

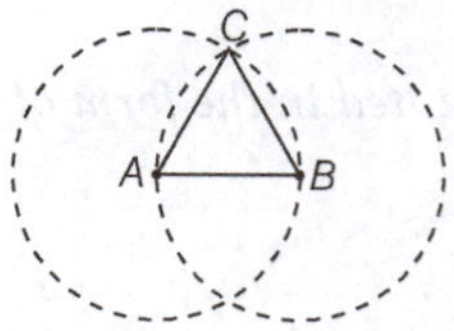

Now, draw line segments AC and BC to form ΔABC.

Now, we have to prove that this triangle is an equilateral triangle.

i.e. $\quad AB = BC = CA$

Here, $\quad AB = AC$ [radii of the same circle]

Similarly, $\quad AB = BC$ [radii of the same circle]

From these two facts and Euclid's axiom 1, i.e. things which are equal to the same things are equal to one another.

We can conclude that, $AB = BC = CA$

Hence, ΔABC is an equilateral triangle. **Hence proved.**

NCERT FOLDER

Complete Solutions of All Exercises of NCERT Textbook

EXERCISE 5.1 (NCERT Page 67-68)

Q1. Which of the following statements are true and which are false? Give reason for your answers.

(i) Only one line can pass through a single point.

(ii) There are an infinite number of lines which pass through two distinct points.

(iii) A terminated line can be produced indefinitely on both the sides.

(iv) If two circles are equal, then their radii are equal.

(v) In the given figure, if $AB = PQ$ and $PQ = XY$, then $AB = XY$.

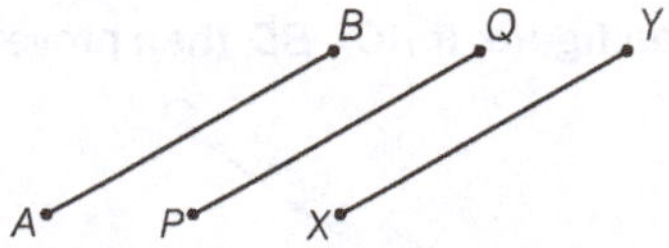

Sol. (i) False, because from a single point, infinite number of lines can pass.

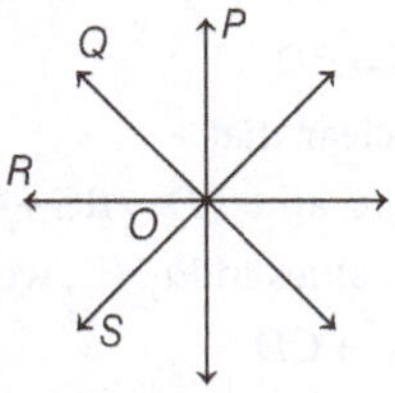

(ii) False, because from two distinct points, only one straight line can pass. [by postulate axiom]

(iii) True, it is Euclid's postulate 2.

(iv) True, because radii of congruent (equal) circles are always equal. In other words, if we superimpose the region bounded by one circle on the other circle, then they coincide. Then, their centres and boundaries also coincide. Therefore, their radii will be same.

(v) True, given that $AB = PQ$ ...(i)

and $PQ = XY$ ...(ii)

From Eqs. (i) and (ii), $AB = XY$ [by axiom 1]

Q2. Give a definition for each of the following terms. Are there other terms that need to be defined first? What are they and how might you define them?

(i) Parallel lines (ii) Perpendicular lines

(iii) Line segment (iv) Radius of a circle

(v) Square

Sol. (i) **Parallel lines** Two lines in a plane are said to be parallel, if they have no common point.

In figure, x and y are said to be parallel lines because they have no common point and we write them as $x \parallel y$.

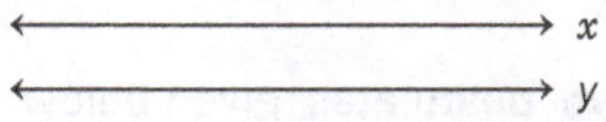

Here, the term point, line, plane is defined first.

Point A dimensionless dot which is drawn on a plane surface is called a point.

Line A collection of points having only length.

Plane Planes are the flat surfaces which lies evenly with the straight lines on itself.

(ii) **Perpendicular lines** Two lines in a plane are said to be perpendicular, if they intersect each other at right angle.

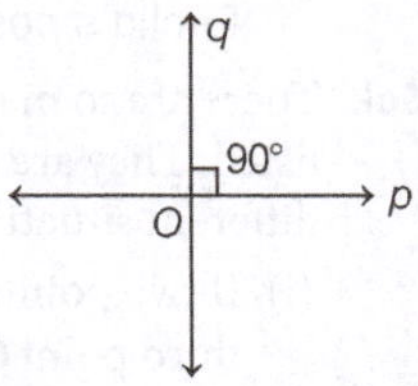

In the figure, p and q are perpendicular lines because they intersect each other at 90° and we write it as $q \perp p$.

Here, the term right angle is defined first.

Right angle An angle of 90° is called right angle.

(iii) **Line segment** The definite length between two points, is called the line segment.

In figure, the definite length between A and B is line segment and it is represented by $\overline{AB}$.

Here, the terms point and definite length are defined first.

Definite length The length between two stationary points of a line segment which can be determined.

(iv) **Radius of a circle** The distance from the centre to a point on the circle, is called the radius of the circle.

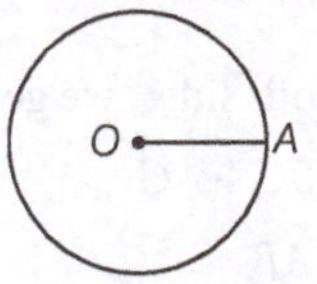

In the figure, OA is the radius of the circle.

Here, the terms point and centre are defined first.

Centre The centre of a circle is the mid-point, where all the radii meet.

(v) **Square** A square is a rectangle having same length and breadth.

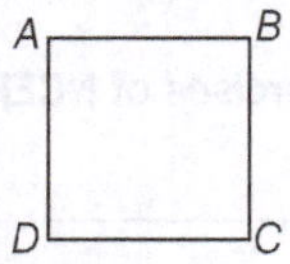

In the figure, AB, BC, CD and DA are equal.
Here, the terms length and breadth are defined first.
Length The longer side of rectangle is called length.
Breadth The shorter side of rectangle is called breadth.

Q3. Consider two 'postulates' given below

(i) Given any two distinct points A and B, there exists a third point C which is in between A and B.

(ii) There exist atleast three points that are not on the same line.

Do these postulates contain any undefined terms? Are these postulates consistent? Do they follow Euclid's postulates? Explain.

Sol. There are so many undefined terms which should be listed. They are consistent because they deal with two different situations which are as follows:

(i) If two points A and B are given, then there exists a third point C which is in between A and B.

(ii) If two points A and B are given, then we can take a point C which do not lie on the line passing through the points A and B. Thus, these points do not coincide with each other.

These postulates do not follow Euclid's postulates. However, they follow axiom. Euclid's postulate 1 axiom states that, through two distinct points, there is a unique line that passes through them.

Q4. If a point C lies between two points A and B such that $AC = BC$, then prove that $AC = \frac{1}{2} AB$. Explain by drawing the figure.

Sol. Given, a point C lies between two points A and B such that $AC = BC$.

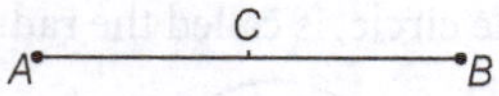

On adding AC to both sides, we get

$$AC + AC = BC + AC \quad \text{[by axiom 2]}$$

$$\Rightarrow \quad 2AC = AB$$

$$\Rightarrow \quad AC = \frac{1}{2} AB$$

Hence proved.

Q5. In question 4, point C is called a mid-point of line segment AB. Prove that every line segment has one and only one mid-point.

Sol. We have, C as the mid-point of line segment AB, so $AC = BC$.

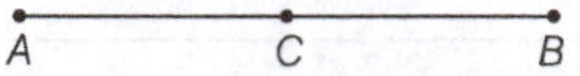

Let there be two mid-points C and C' of AB.

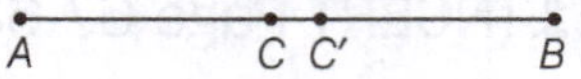

Then, $AC = \frac{1}{2} AB$

and $AC' = \frac{1}{2} AB$

$$\Rightarrow \quad AC = AC' \quad \text{[by axiom1]}$$

which is possible only when C and C' coincide.

So, point C' lies on C.

Hence, every line segment has one and only one mid-point.

Q6. In the given figure, if $AC = BD$, then prove that $AB = CD$.

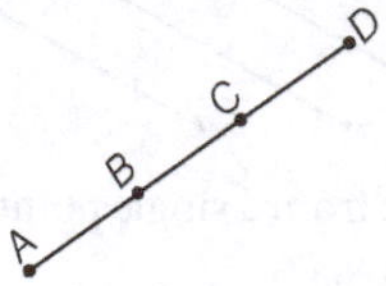

Sol. Given, $AC = BD$ ...(i)

From figure, it is clear that

$$AC = AB + BC \text{ and } BD = BC + CD$$

On putting these values in Eq. (i), we get

$$AB + BC = BC + CD$$

On subtracting BC from both sides, we get

$$AB + BC - BC = BC + CD - BC$$

$$\Rightarrow \quad AB = CD \quad \text{[by axiom 3]}$$

Hence proved.

Q7. Why is axiom 5, in the list of Euclid's axioms, considered a 'universal truth'?

Sol. According to axiom 5 we have, the whole is greater than the part, which is a universal truth. Let a line segment $PQ = 8$ cm. Consider a point R in its interior, such that $PR = 5$ cm.

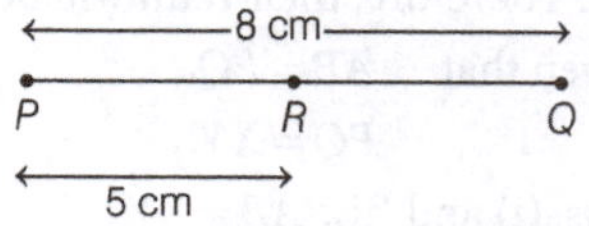

Clearly, PR is a part of the line segment PQ and R lies in its interior. So, PR is smaller than PQ.

Hence, the whole is greater than its part and this is true for anything in any part of the world.

REVIEW EXERCISE

Including Competency Based Questions

Part I

Multiple Choice Questions

1. John is of the same age as Mohan. Ram is also of the same age as Mohan. State the Euclid's axiom that illustrates the relative ages of John and Ram.

(a) First axiom (b) Second axiom
(c) Third axiom (d) Fourth axiom

2. Axioms are assumed

(a) Theorems
(b) Definitions
(c) Universal truths specific to geometry
(d) Universal truths in all branches of Mathematics

3. The number of Euclid's postulates are

(a) 3 (b) 4
(c) 5 (d) 6

4. The line drawn from the centre of the circle to any point on its circumference is called

(a) Radius (b) Diameter
(c) Sector (d) Arc

5. The three steps from solids to points are **NCERT Exemplar**

(a) solid-surfaces-lines-points
(b) solid-lines-surfaces-points
(c) lines-points-surfaces-solids
(d) lines-surfaces-points-solids

6. The number of dimensions, a solid has **NCERT Exemplar**

(a) 1 (b) 2
(c) 3 (d) 0

7. If equals be added to equals, then the wholes are

(a) equal (b) unequal
(c) twice of each other (d) half of the other

8. It is known that, if $x + y = 10$, then $x + y + z = 10 + z$. The Euclid's axiom that illustrates this statement is **NCERT Exemplar**

(a) first axiom
(b) second axiom
(c) third axiom
(d) fourth axiom

9. A number Y is greater than a number X and another number $Z < 0$. Which of the following relations can be true for a unique value of Z? **Competency Based Question**

(a) $X \times Z = Y \times Z$ (b) $X \div Z = Y \div Z$
(c) $X - Z = Y$ (d) $X + Z = Y$

10. The map shows three cities Conlen (C), Stratford (S) and Texhoma (T) on a straight highway.

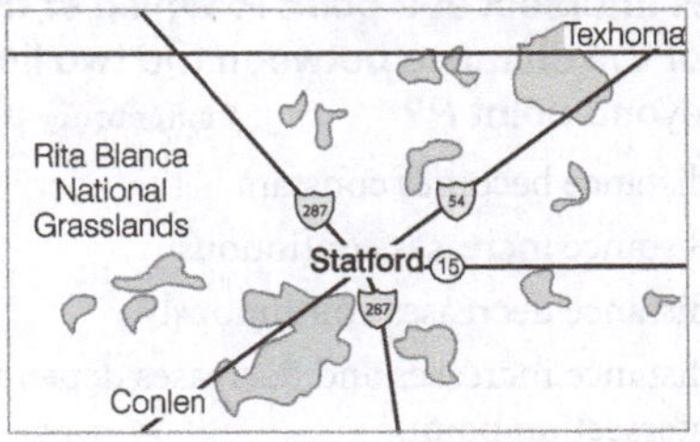

Which of the following is true for the length of the highway between them? **Competency Based Question**

(a) The length of the highway between C and S is equal to the length of the highway between S and T.
(b) The length of the highway between C and S is three-fourth of the length of the highway between S and T.
(c) The length of the highway between S and T is the sum of the lengths of the highway between CT and CS.
(d) The length of the highway between C and T is the sum of the lengths of the highway between CS and ST.

11. If A, B and C are three points on a line such that A lies in between B and C, then

(a) $BC = \frac{1}{2}AC$ (b) $AC = \frac{BC}{4}$
(c) $AC = BC$ (d) $AB + AC = BC$

12. If PQ is a line segment of length 12 cm and R is a point in its interior, then $PR^2 + QR^2 + 2PR \cdot QR$ equals **Competency Based Question**

(a) 12 (b) 13 (c) 144 (d) 169

13. In the given figure, C is the mid-point of the segment AB. P and Q are mid-points of the segments AC and BC respectively, then AP is equal to

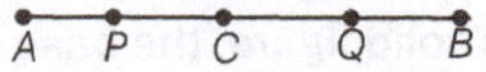

(a) $\frac{AB}{4}$ (b) $\frac{AB}{2}$ (c) $\frac{AB}{3}$ (d) AB

14. TAB is a straight line. C is the mid-point of AB. D is the mid-point of AC. Which of the following shows the relation between the line segments? **Competency Based Question**

(a) $AD = \frac{1}{2}AB$ (b) $AD = \frac{1}{2}CB$
(c) $AD = 2AC$ (d) $AD = 2DC$

15. Balan says, 'The measure of all right angles cannot be equal as their arms can be of different lengths.' Why is Balan's statement not true? **Competency Based Question**

(a) The measure of an angle depends upon its orientation.
(b) The measure of an angle depends upon the instrument used to measure it.
(c) The measure of an angle depends on the length of its angle arms.
(d) The measure of an angle depends upon the rotation of one arm on another.

16. Two lines intersect at a point *P*. Which of the following is true for the distance between the two lines as they travel beyond point *P*? **Competency Based Question**

(a) The distance becomes constant.
(b) The distance increases continuously.
(c) The distance decreases continuously.
(d) The distance increases and decreases depending upon the intersection point.

17. Which pair of angles have sum less than 180° according to Euclid's postulate

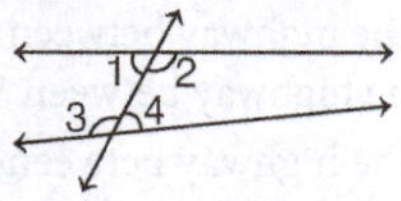

(a) $\angle 1$ and $\angle 4$ (b) $\angle 1$ and $\angle 3$
(c) $\angle 2$ and $\angle 4$ (d) $\angle 2$ and $\angle 3$

18. Greek's emphasised on **NCERT Exemplar**

(a) inductive reasoning (b) deductive reasoning
(c) Both (a) and (b) (d) practical use of geometry

19. Which of the following needs a proof? **NCERT Exemplar**

(a) Theorems (b) Axiom
(c) Definition (d) Postulate

20. Highways 20A and 56C run parallel to each other for 20 km in a state. Which of the following statements is most likely to be true regarding them? **Competency Based Question**

(a) Both highways are of the same length.
(b) There can be no link road between them.
(c) The highways make an angle 90° with each other.
(d) The distance between the two highways remains almost the same in the state.

21. A pyramid is a solid figure, the base of which is **NCERT Exemplar**

(a) only a triangle (b) only a square
(c) only a rectangle (d) any polygon

Assertion-Reason Type Questions

22. Assertion Given two distinct points, there is a unique line that passes through them.

Reason If *A*, *B* and *C* are three points on a line and *B* lies between *A* and *C*, then $AB + BC = AC$.

(a) Both Assertion and Reason are correct and Reason is the correct explanation of Assertion.
(b) Both Assertion and Reason are correct but Reason is not the correct explanation of Assertion.
(c) Assertion is correct but Reason is incorrect.
(d) Assertion is incorrect but Reason is correct.

23. Assertion If lines *AB*, *AC*, *AD* and *AE* are parallel to a line *l*, then points *A*, *B*, *C*, *D* and *E* are collinear.

Reason One and only one line can be drawn through *A* and parallel to *l*.

(a) Both Assertion and Reason are correct and Reason is the correct explanation of Assertion.
(b) Both Assertion and Reason are correct but Reason is not the correct explanation of Assertion.
(c) Assertion is correct but Reason is incorrect.
(d) Assertion is incorrect but Reason is correct.

Case Study Based Questions

24. Karan marks his city on the map as point *A*.

Based on the above information, answer the following questions.

(i) Savita's says, 'A dot is dimensionless, so your city is also dimensionless'. Why is Savita wrong? Justify your answer.
(ii) Which of the following is not true?
(a) A line has one dimension.
(b) A plane has two dimensions.
(c) A circle can be drawn with any radius and at any point.
(d) Two distinct lines can pass through a point in the same direction.

25. In last year, cyclone comes out in Odisha. Due to this cyclone, many peoples lost their lifes and property. Rahul and Kamal decided to contribute equal amounts to National Disaster Relief Fund, so that the suffered peoples get some relief.

(i) If Rahul contributed ₹ 25000,then how much was contributed by Kamal?
(ii) Write the statement of Euclid postulate 1.
(iii) (a) In this process, which axiom is used? Also, write its statements.
Or (b) If Kamal contributed ₹ 1000 more again, then how much was contributed by Rahul? And write which axiom is used.

Part II

Very Short Answer Type Questions

1. Solve the equation $y - 25 = 40$ and state which axiom will you use here?
2. P lies in the interior of $\angle BAC$. If $\angle BAC = 70°$ and $\angle BAP = 42°$, then determine the measure of $\angle PAC$.
3. The area of a triangle is equal to the area of a rectangle. The area of the rectangle is equal to the area of a parallelogram. Then, what is the relation between the area of the triangle and the area of the parallelogram? **Competency Based Question**
4. Define the condition of a line segment AB, such that point C is called the mid-point of AB.
5. If B lies between A and C, $AC = 19$ cm and $BC = 8$ cm. What is the measure of AB?
6. Raghvan claims that the magnitude of the $\angle ABC$ is greater than the magnitude of the area of the right ΔPQR. Is his claim corrcet? Why? **Competency Based Question**

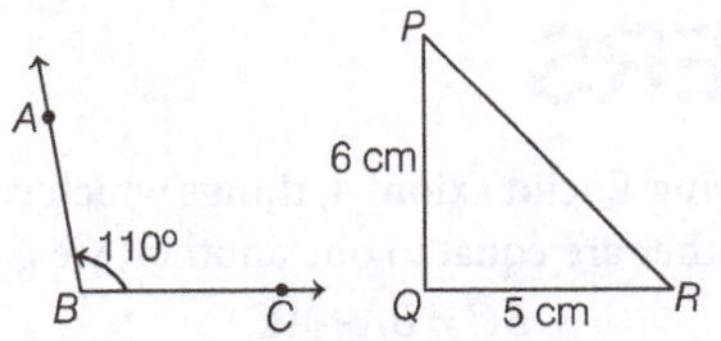

7. A point C is said to lie between the points A and B. Explain it.
8. If A, B and C are three collinear points, name all the line segments determined by them.
9. Given four collinear points A, B, C and D. List all the line segments determined by these.

Short Answer Type Questions

10. In the given figure, if $\angle 1 = \angle 3$, $\angle 2 = \angle 4$ and $\angle 3 = \angle 4$, then write the relation between $\angle 1$ and $\angle 2$.

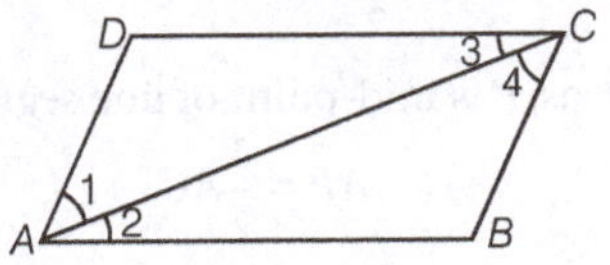

11. In the given figure, if P and Q are the centres of two intersecting circles, then prove that $PQ = QR = PR$.

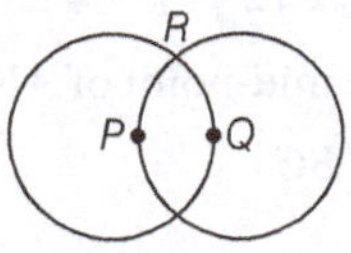

12. In the given figure, $\angle 2 = \angle 1$ and $\angle 3 = \angle 4$. Find $\angle\theta$. **Competency Based Question**

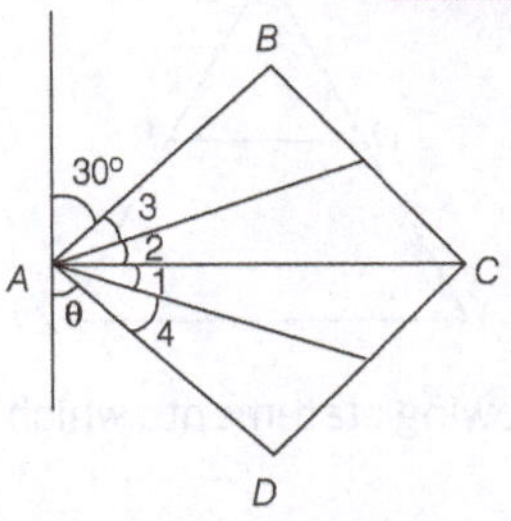

13. In the given figure, $PR = RS$ and $RQ = RT$. Show that $PQ = ST$ and write the Euclid's axiom to support this. **NCERT Exemplar**

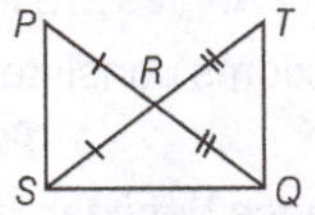

14. In the given figure, if $AC = DC$ and $CB = CE$, then show that $AB = DE$. **Competency Based Question**

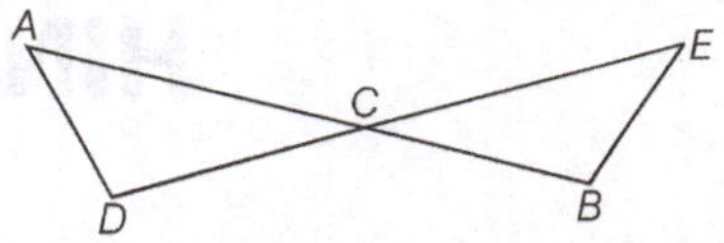

15. If $AB = (x + 3)$, $BC = 2x$ and $AC = (4x - 5)$, then for what value of x, B lies on AC?
16. If $x + y = 10$ and $x = z$, then show that $z + y = 10$. **NCERT Exemplar**
17. In the given figure, if $AB = BC$ and $BX = BY$, then show that $AX = CY$. **NCERT Exemplar**

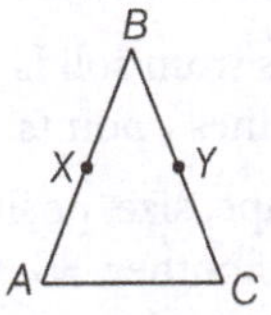

18. In the adjoining figure, if $AE = CB$ and $DE = CD$, then prove that D is the mid-point of the line segment AB.

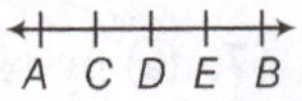

19. PQ is a line segment 12 cm long and R is a point in its interior such that $PR = 8$ cm. Then, find QR, $PQ^2 - PR^2$ and $PR^2 + QR^2 + 2PR \cdot QR$.
20. Look at the given figure. Show that length $AH >$ sum of lengths of $AB + BC + CD$. **Competency Based Question**

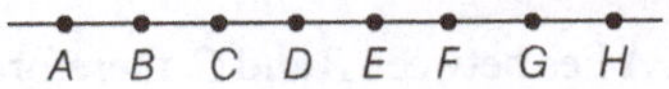

21. In the given figure, if $QX = \frac{1}{2}XY$, $PX = \frac{1}{2}XZ$ and $QX = PX$, then show that $XY = XZ$. **NCERT Exemplar**

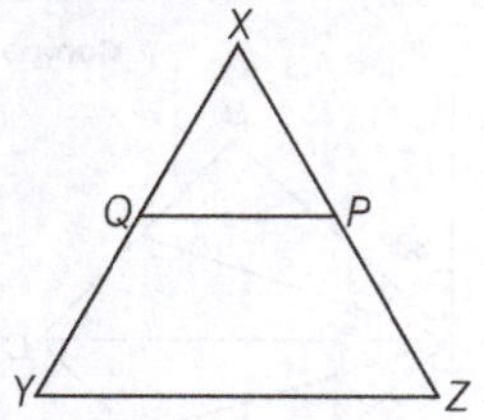

22. Read the following statements which are taken as axioms.

I. If a transversal intersects two parallel lines, then corresponding angles are not necessarily equal.

II. If a transversal intersects two parallel lines, then alternate interior angles are equal.

Is this system of axioms consistent? Justify your answer. **Competency Based Question**

23. What is the difference between a Euclid's postulates and an axioms?

Long Answer Type Questions

24. In the given figure, we have $\angle ABC = \angle ACB$ and $\angle 3 = \angle 4$. Show that $BD = DC$. **NCERT Exemplar**

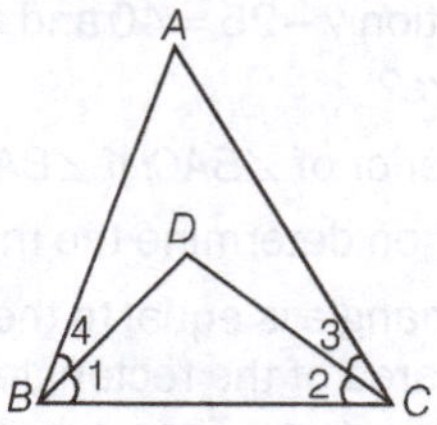

25. Read the following axioms.

(i) Things which are equal to the same things, are equal to one another.

(ii) If equals are added to equals, then wholes are equal.

(iii) Things which are double of the same things, are equal to one another.

Check whether the given system of axioms is consistent or inconsistent. **NCERT Exemplar**

HINTS & ANSWERS

Part I

1. (a) **Hint** Things which are equal to the same things are equal to one another.

2. (d) Axiom are assumed universal truth in all branches of Mathematics.

3. (c) The number of Euclid's Postulates are five.

4. (a) Radius is the length of line segment from centre to any point on circumference of circle.

5. (a) The three steps from solids to points are solids- surfaces - lines - points.

6. (c) A solid has shape, size, position and can be moved from one place to another. So, solid has three dimensions, e.g. Cuboid.

7. (a) By axiom 2

8. (b) The Euclid's axiom that illustrates the given statement is second axiom, according to which. If equals are added to equals, the wholes are equal.

9. (c) $X - Z = Y, Z < 0$

10. (d) By observing the map,

Length between C and T

= Length between C and S + Length between S and T

11. (d) Since, A lies between B and C, therefore BC coincides with $BA + AC$.

Now, using Euclid axiom 4, things which coincide with one another are equal to one another, we get

$$BC = BA + AC$$

12. (c) Here, point R lies in the interior of PQ.

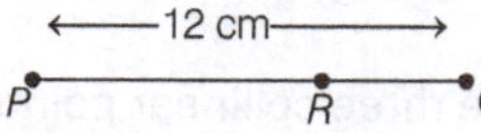

So, $PR + RQ = PQ = 12$ cm [by axiom 4]

Now, $PR^2 + QR^2 + 2PR \cdot QR = (PR + QR)^2 = (PQ)^2$

$= (12)^2 = 144$ cm

13. (a) Since, C is mid-point of the line segment AB.

$\therefore \quad AB = AC + CB$ [by axiom 4]

$\Rightarrow \quad AB = AC + AC$ [$\because AC = CB$]

$\Rightarrow \quad AC = \frac{1}{2}AB$ ...(i)

Similarly as, P is mid-point of line segment AC.

$\therefore \quad AP = \frac{1}{2}AC$ ...(ii)

From Eqs. (i) and (ii), we get

$$AP = \frac{1}{2}\left\{\frac{1}{2}AB\right\} = \frac{1}{4}AB$$

14. (b) Since, C is the mid-point of AB,

i.e. $\quad AC = BC$ ...(i)

$\because D$ is the mid-point of AC i.e. $AD = \frac{1}{2}AC$ ...(ii)

From Eqs. (i) and (ii), we get

$$AD = \frac{1}{2} BC$$

15. (d) The measure of an angle depends upon the rotation of one arm to another.

16. (b) Lines are travelling beyond P after intersecting. So, distance between them increases continuously.

17. (c) By postulate 5

18. (b) Greek's emphasised on deductive reasoning.

19. (a) The statements that were proved are called propositions or theorems.

20. (d) They run parallel to each other for 20 km. The distance between them remains almost the same in the state.

21. (d) A pyramid is a solid figure, the base of which is a triangle or square or some other polygon.

22. (b) Assertion is correct, also Reason is correct.

As,

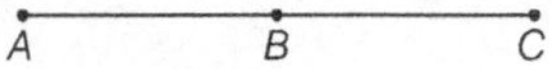

$$AB + BC = AC$$

But Reason is not correct explanation of Assertion.

23. (a) Through a point not on the line l, one and only one line can be parallel to l.

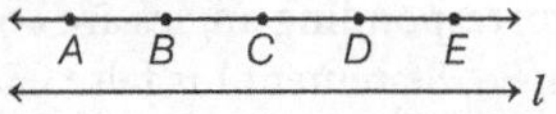

i.e. Through point A, AB, AC, AD and AE are parallel to l means they all should coincide.

$\Rightarrow A, B, C, D$ and E should be collinear.

Both Assertion and Reason are correct and Reason is the correct explanation of Assertion.

24. (i) She is wrong, because a dot is used in a map to show the location of city, not its area.

(ii) (d) Two distinct lines cannot pass through a point in the same direction.

25. (i) We have, Rahul and Kamal contribute equal amounts. Since, Rahul contributes ₹ 25000, so Kamal also contribute ₹ 25000.

(ii) **Postulate 1** A straight line may be drawn from any one point to any other point.

(iii) (a) In this process, axiom 1 is used i.e. things which are equal to the same things are equal to the one another.

Or (b) We have, Kamal contributes ₹ 1000 more again, i.e. he contributes ₹ 26000, then Rahul also contributes ₹ 26000.

Here, axiom 2 is used.

Part II

1. Euclid's axiom 2 is used in this question.

2. **Hint** $\angle PAC = \angle BAC - \angle BAP = 28°$ **Ans.** 28°

3. Since, both have equal area, therefore area of triangle is equal to area of parallelogram.

4. Mid-point is an interior point of a line which divides the line into two equal parts.

5. **Hint** $AB = AC - BC$ **Ans.** 11 cm

6. No, the measure of angle cannot be compared to the area of a triangle.

7. When three or more points lie in the line, then they are said to be collinear points.

8. Let A, B and C be three collinear points, then possible line segments are $\overline{AB}, \overline{BC}$ and $\overline{AC}$.

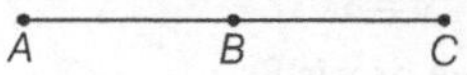

9. **Hint** Three or more points are said to be collinear, if there is a line which contains all of them.

All the line segments determined by A, B, C and D are

$$\overline{AB}, \overline{BC}, \overline{CD}, \overline{AC}, \overline{BD}, \overline{AD}$$

10. **Hint** Given, $\angle 1 = \angle 3, \angle 3 = \angle 4$ ...(i)

and $\angle 2 = \angle 4$ ...(ii)

According to Euclid's axiom 1, things which are equal to the same things, are equal to one another.

Therefore, from Eq. (i), $\angle 1 = \angle 4$ ...(iii)

Now, from Eqs. (ii) and (iii), $\angle 1 = \angle 2$ [by axiom 1]

11. **Hint** In the given figure,

$PR = PQ$ [radii of the same circle]...(i)

and $QP = QR$ [radii of the same circle] ...(ii)

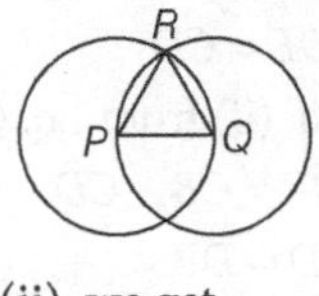

From Eqs. (i) and (ii), we get

$PR = QR$ [by axiom1]...(iii)

From Eqs. (i), (ii) and (iii), we get

$PQ = QR = PR$ [by axiom 1]

12. **Hint** Given, $\angle 2 = \angle 1$ and $\angle 3 = \angle 4$ ...(i)

Now, $\angle 2 = \angle 1$

$\angle 2 + \angle 3 = \angle 1 + \angle 3$ [by axiom 2]

$\Rightarrow \angle 2 + \angle 3 = \angle 2 + \angle 3$ [from Eq. (i)]

$\Rightarrow \angle 2 + \angle 3 + 30° = \angle 2 + \angle 3 + 30°$ [by axiom 2]

$\Rightarrow \angle 2 + \angle 3 + 30° = \angle 2 + \angle 3 + \theta$

Ans. 30°

13. Euclid's axiom 2.

14. Hint Given, $AC = DC$ and $CB = CE$

$\Rightarrow \quad AC + CB = DC + CE \Rightarrow AB = DE$

15. If B lies on AC, then

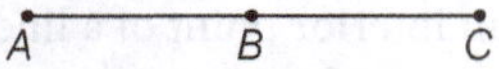

$$AC = AB + BC$$

$\Rightarrow \quad 4x - 5 = x + 3 + 2x$

$\Rightarrow \quad 4x - 5 = 3x + 3$

$\Rightarrow \quad 4x - 5 + 5 = 3x + 3 + 5$ [adding 5 both sides]

$\Rightarrow \quad 4x = 3x + 8$

$\Rightarrow \quad 4x - 3x = 3x + 8 - 3x$ [subtracting $3x$ from both sides]

$\Rightarrow \quad x = 8$ [by axiom 3]

Hence, the value of x is 8.

16. Given, $x + y = 10$ ...(i)

and $x = z$ ...(ii)

On subtracting y from both sides of Eq. (i), we get

$x + y - y = 10 - y$ [by axiom 3]

$\Rightarrow \quad z = 10 - y$ [from Eq. (ii)]

On adding y both sides, we get

$z + y = 10 - y + y$ [by axiom 2]

$\Rightarrow \quad z + y = 10$

17. Given, $AB = BC$ ...(i)

and $BX = BY$ ...(ii)

On subtracting Eq. (ii) from Eq. (i), we get

$AB - BX = BC - BY$ [by axiom 3]

$\Rightarrow \quad AX = CY$

18. In the given figure,

$AE = CB$ ...(i) [given]

and $DE = CD$ ...(ii) [given]

On subtracting Eq. (ii) from Eq. (i), we get

$AE - DE = CB - CD$

$\Rightarrow \quad AD = DB$

So, $AD + DB = AB$

Hence, D is the mid-point of the line segment AB.

19. Hint

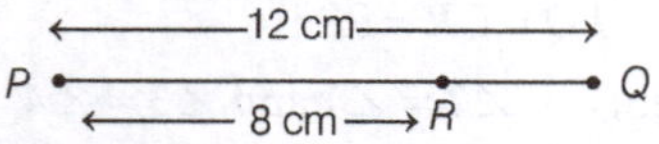

Here, point R lies in the interior of PQ.

So, $PR + QR = PQ$

$\Rightarrow \quad 8 + QR = 12$

On subtracting 8 from both sides, we get

$8 + QR - 8 = 12 - 8$ [by axiom 3]

$\Rightarrow \quad QR = 4$ cm

Now, $PQ^2 - PR^2 = (12)^2 - (8)^2 = 144 - 64 = 80$ cm

Also, $PR^2 + QR^2 + 2PR \cdot QR = (PR + QR)^2$

$= (8 + 4)^2 = (12)^2 = 144$ cm

20. Hint From the given figure,

$$AB + BC + CD = AD$$

$\because$ AD is a part of AH.

We know that by Euclid's Axiom 5,

"The whole is greater than the part" i.e. $AH > AD$

Hence, length $AH >$ sum of lengths of $AB + BC + CD$.

21. Hint Given, $QX = \frac{1}{2} XY$ ...(i)

$PX = \frac{1}{2} XZ$ ...(ii)

and $QX = PX$ ...(iii)

From Eqs. (i), (ii) and (iii), we get

$$\frac{1}{2} XY = \frac{1}{2} XZ$$

$\Rightarrow \quad XY = XZ$ [by axiom 6] **Hence proved.**

22. Hint

I. A system of axiom is called consistent, if there is no statement which can be deduced from these axioms such that it contradicts any axiom. We know that, if a transversal intersects two parallel lines, then each pair of corresponding angles are equal, which is a theorem. So, Statement I is false. Hence, it is not an axiom.

II. Also, we know that if a transversal intersects two parallel lines, then each pair of alternate interior angles are equal. It is also a theorem. So, Statement II is true. Hence, it is an axiom. Thus, in given statements, I is false and II is an axiom.Hence, given system of axioms is not consistent.

23. Hint Euclid used the term postulate for the assumptions that were specific to geometry and otherwise called axioms.

24. Given, $\angle ABC = \angle ACB$ ...(i)

and $\angle 4 = \angle 3$ ...(ii)

According to Euclid's axiom 3, if equals are subtracted from equals, then remainders are also equal.

On subtracting Eq. (ii) from Eq. (i), we get

$$\angle ABC - \angle 4 = \angle ACB - \angle 3$$

$\Rightarrow \quad \angle 1 = \angle 2$

Now, in ΔBDC, $\angle 1 = \angle 2$

$\Rightarrow \quad DC = BD$

$\therefore \quad BD = DC$

25. The given three axioms are consistent.

Mind Map

INTRODUCTION TO EUCLID'S GEOMETRY

Euclid's Definition

Point
A point is an exact location.

Line
It is breadthless length. Ends of a line are points.

Straight line
It is a line which lies evenly with the points on itself.

Surface A surface has length and breadth only.

Plane Surface
A surface which lies evenly with the straight lines on itself.

Euclid's Axioms

Axiom 1
Things which are equal to the same things, are equal to one another.

Axiom 2
If equals are added to equals then the wholes are equal.

Axiom 3
If equals are subtracted from equals then the remainders are equal.

Axiom 4
Things which coincide with one another are equal to one another.

Axiom 5
The whole is greater than the part.

Axiom 6
Things which are double of the same things are equal to one another.

Axiom 7
Things which are halves of the same things are equal to one another.

Euclid's Postulates

Postulate 1
A straight line may be drawn from any one point to any other point.

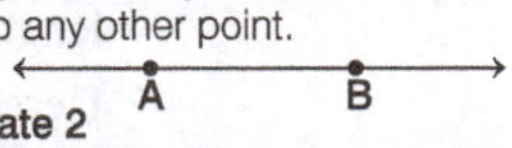

Postulate 2
A terminated line can be produced indefinitely.

Postulate 3
A circle can be drawn with any centre and any radius.

Postulate 4
All right angles are equal to one another.

Postulate 5
If a straight line falling on two straight lines makes the interior angles on the same side of it taken together less than two right angles, then the two straight lines, if produced indefinitely, meet on that side on which the sum of angles is less than two right angles.

Lines and Angles

CHAPTER 6

In this chapter, we will study the properties of the angles formed when two lines intersect each other and when a line intersects two or more parallel lines at distinct points.

Basic Terms and Definitions

Line

A line is a straight path, that is endless in both directions.

It is denoted by $\overleftrightarrow{AB}$ or $\overleftrightarrow{BA}$.

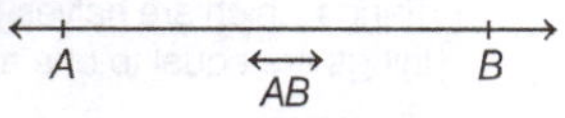

Ray

A part of a line with one end point, is called a ray. The ray AB is denoted by $\overrightarrow{AB}$.

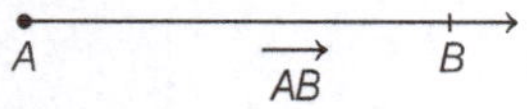

Line Segment

A part of a line with two end points, is called a line segment. Line segment AB is denoted by $\overline{AB}$.

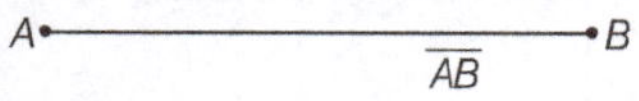

A line segment has a definite length, which can be measured. The $\overline{AB}$ is the same thing as the $\overline{BA}$.

Collinear and Non-collinear Points

If three or more than three points lie on the same line, then they are called collinear points otherwise they are called non-collinear points.

e.g. In the above figure, P, Q and R are collinear points.

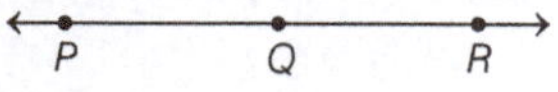

In the figure below, A, B and C are non-collinear points.

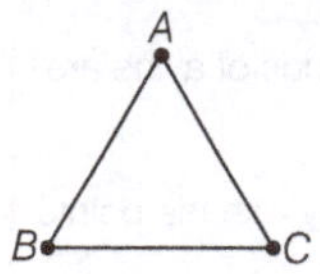

Example 1. **In the given figure, write the name of**
(i) line segments. **(ii) rays.**

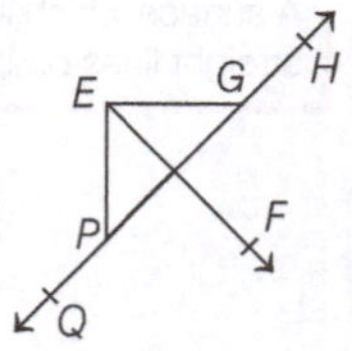

Sol. Use the property of a line segment and a ray (i.e. a line segment has a definite length and a ray has only one end point).
Here, $\overline{GE}$, $\overline{GP}$ and $\overline{EP}$ are line segments and $\overrightarrow{EF}$, $\overrightarrow{GH}$ and $\overrightarrow{PQ}$ are rays.

Intersecting Lines and Non-intersecting Lines

Lines PQ and RS are intersecting lines because they intersect each other at O.

Lines AB and CD are non-intersecting lines i.e. parallel lines because they never intersect each other.

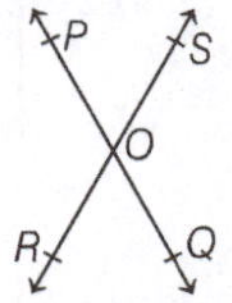

Intersecting lines

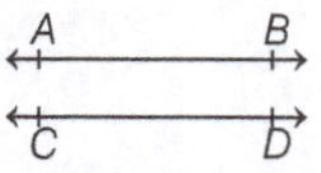

Non-intersecting (parallel) lines

The lengths of the common perpendicular at different points on these parallel lines is the same and this equal length is called the distance between two parallel lines.

Angle

The angle formed by two rays with the same initial point, is called an angle.

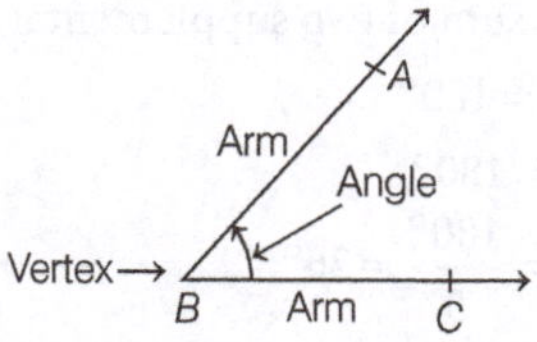

In the above figure, the common initial point B is known as the **vertex** of the angle and the rays ($\overrightarrow{BA}$ and $\overrightarrow{BC}$) forming the angle are called its **arms** or **sides**.

Types of Angles

1. Acute Angle

An angle whose measure is more than 0° but less than 90°, is called an acute angle.

In the given figure, $\angle AOB$ is an acute angle

i.e. $0° < \angle AOB < 90°$

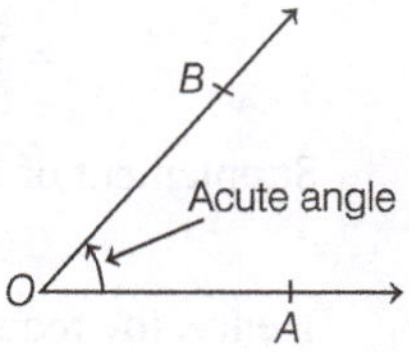

2. Right Angle

An angle whose measure is 90°, is called a right angle.

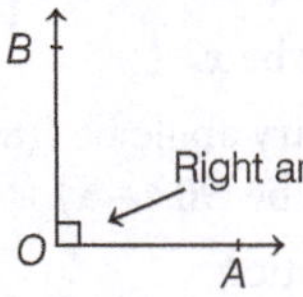

In the above figure, $\angle AOB$ is a right angle i.e. $\angle AOB = 90°$ and $BO \perp OA$.

3. Obtuse Angle

An angle whose measure is more than 90° but less than 180°, is called an obtuse angle.

In the given figure, $\angle AOB$ is an obtuse angle.

$90° < \angle AOB < 180°$

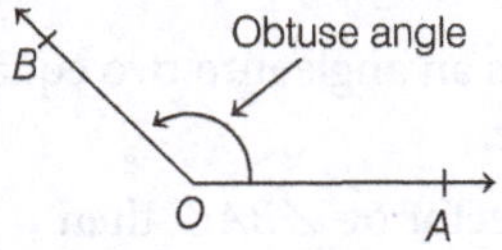

4. Straight Angle

An angle whose measure is 180°, is called a straight angle. In the given figure, $\angle AOB = 180°$ is a straight angle.

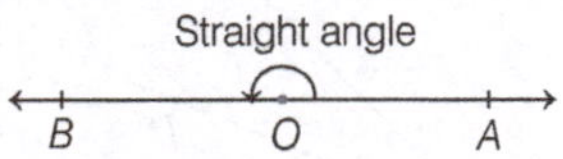

A straight angle has formed by joining two right angles.

5. Reflex Angle

An angle whose measure is more than 180° but less than 360°, is called a reflex angle.

In the given figure, $\angle AOB$ is a reflex angle.

$180° < \text{reflex } \angle AOB < 360°$

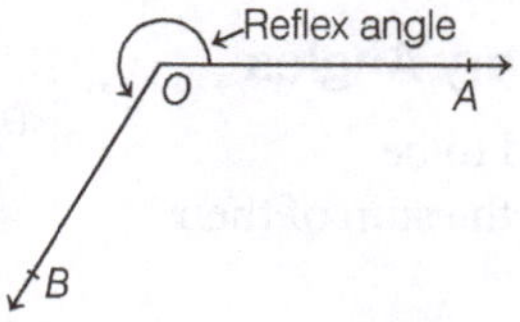

6. Complete Angle

An angle whose measure is 360°, is called a complete angle. In the given figure, $\angle AOA = 360°$ is a complete angle.

Example 2. Which type of angle is formed in the given figures?

(i)

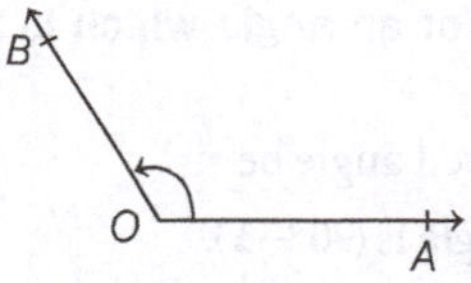

(ii)

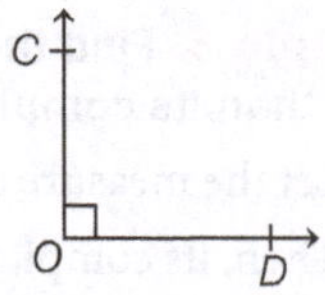

(iii)

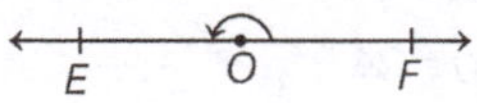

(iv)

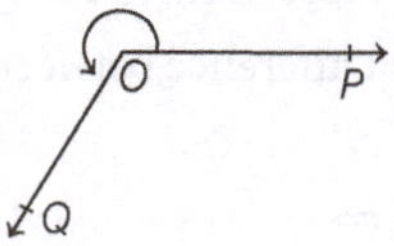

(v)

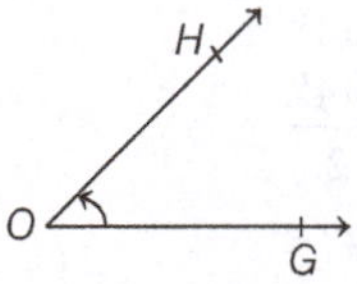

(vi)

Sol. (i) In the given figure, $\angle AOB$ is an obtuse angle. (i.e. $90° < \angle AOB < 180°$)

(ii) In the given figure, $\angle COD$ is a right angle. (i.e. $\angle COD = 90°$)

(iii) In the given figure, $\angle FOE$ is a straight angle. (i.e. $\angle FOE = 180°$)

(iv) In the given figure, $\angle POQ$ is a reflex angle. (i.e. $180° < \text{reflex } \angle POQ < 360°$)

(v) In the given figure, $\angle HOG$ is an acute angle. (i.e. $0° < \angle HOG < 90°$)

(vi) In the given figure, $\angle POP$ is a complete angle. (i.e. $\angle POP = 360°$)

Example 3. **In which angle, the measure is more than 180° but less than 360°?**

Sol. In a reflex angle, the measure is more than 180° but less than 360°.

Pair of Angles

1. Complementary Angles

Two angles are said to be complementary, if the sum of their measures is 90°.

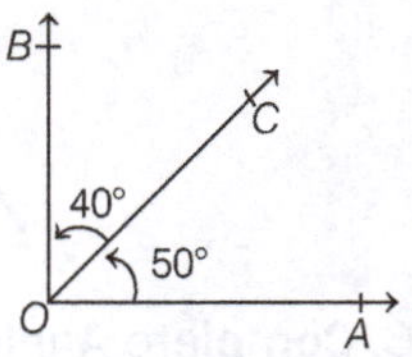

In the adjoining figure, $\angle COB$ and $\angle AOC$ are complementary angles.

$[\because \angle COB + \angle AOC = 90° \text{ i.e. } 40° + 50° = 90°]$

Example 4. **If two angles are complements of each other, then what is the type of each angle?**

Sol. We know that if the sum of two angles is 90°, then they are complementary angles. So, each angle will be an acute angle.

Example 5. **Find the measure of an angle which is 24° more than its complementary.**

Sol. Let the measure of the required angle be x.

Then, its complementary angle is $(90° - x)$.

According to the question,

Difference between both angles = 24°

$\therefore \quad x - (90° - x) = 24°$

$\Rightarrow \quad x - 90° + x = 24°$

$\Rightarrow \quad 2x = 114°$

$\Rightarrow \quad x = \frac{114°}{2}$

$\Rightarrow \quad x = 57°$

and $\quad 90° - x = 90° - 57° = 33°$

Hence, the measure of required angle is 57°.

2. Supplementary Angles

Two angles are said to be supplementary, if the sum of their measures is 180°.

In the given figure, $\angle BOC$ and $\angle AOC$ are supplementary angles.

$[\because \angle BOC + \angle AOC = 180° \text{ i.e. } 120° + 60° = 180°]$

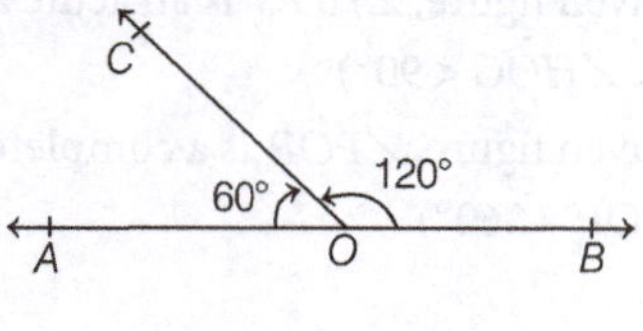

Example 6. **If two supplementary angles are in the ratio 3 : 2, then find their angles.**

Sol. Let the two supplementary angles be $3x$ and $2x$.

We know that sum of two supplementary angles is 180°.

$\therefore \quad 3x + 2x = 180°$

$\Rightarrow \quad 5x = 180°$

$\Rightarrow \quad x = \frac{180°}{5} = 36°$

So, one angle $= 3x = 3 \times 36° = 108°$

and its supplementary angle $= 2x = 2 \times 36° = 72°$

Hence, two supplementary angles are 108° and 72°.

Example 7. **Find the supplement of $\frac{3}{5}$ of a right angle.**

Sol. Given, angle $= \frac{3}{5}$ of a right angle

$= \frac{3}{5} \times 90° = 3 \times 18° = 54°$

Supplement of 54° = An angle of measure $(180° - 54°)$

= An angle of measure 126°

Hence, the required angle is 126°.

Example 8. **Find the measure of an angle, if six times its complement is 12° less than twice its supplement.**

Sol. Let the required angle be x.

Then, its supplementary angle be $(180° - x)$ and its complementary angle be $(90° - x)$.

According to the question,

$6(90° - x) = 2(180° - x) - 12°$

$\Rightarrow \quad 540° - 6x = 360° - 2x - 12°$

$\Rightarrow \quad 540° - 360° + 12° = -2x + 6x$

$\Rightarrow \quad 4x = 192°$

$\Rightarrow \quad x = 48°$

Hence, the required angle is 48°.

3. Bisector of an Angle

A ray which divides an angle into two equal parts, is called bisector of an angle.

If ray AD is the bisector of $\angle BAC$, then

$$\angle BAD = \angle CAD = \frac{1}{2} \angle BAC$$

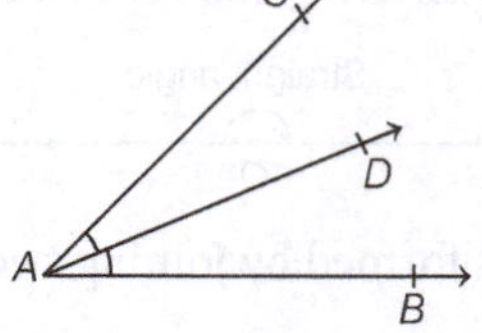

4. Adjacent Angles

Two angles are called adjacent angles, if

(i) they have a common vertex.

(ii) they have a common arm.

(iii) their non-common arms are on different sides of the common arm.

In the adjoining figure, $\angle AOC$ and $\angle COB$ are adjacent angles because these angles have a common vertex O, a common arm OC and non-common arms OA and OB are on different sides of the common ray OC.

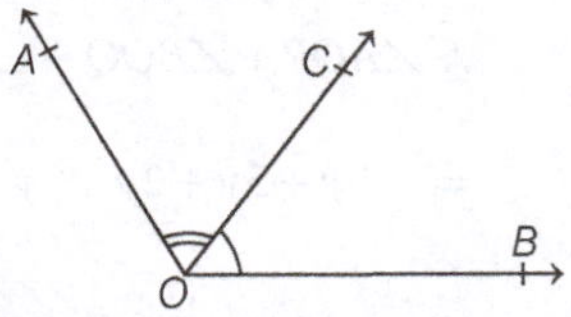

When two angles are adjacent, then their sum is always equal to the angle formed by the two non-common arms. So, here $\angle AOB = \angle AOC + \angle COB$.

Note it Here, $\angle AOB$ and $\angle AOC$ are not adjacent angles because their non-common arms OC and OB lie on the same side of the common arm OA.

5. Linear Pair of Angles

If the non-common arms of two adjacent angles form a line, then these angles are called linear pair of angles.

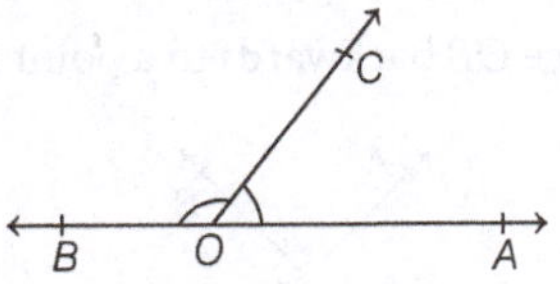

In the above figure, $\angle AOC$ and $\angle BOC$ form a linear pair of angles.

6. Vertically Opposite Angles

When two lines intersect each other at a point, then the opposite angles, formed due to intersection of lines are called vertically opposite angles. There are two pairs of vertically opposite angles.

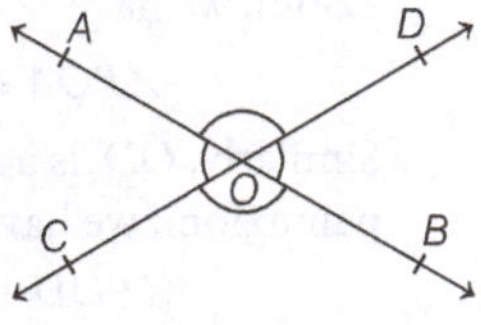

In the above figure, lines AB and CD intersect each other at O. So, $\angle AOC$ and $\angle BOD$ are vertically opposite angles and $\angle AOD$ and $\angle BOC$ are also vertically opposite angles.

Relations between Pairs of Angles

There are some relations between these angles which are given in the form of axioms and theorem as given below:

Axiom 1

If a ray stands on a line, then the sum of two adjacent angles so formed is 180° i.e. the sum of the linear pair is 180°.

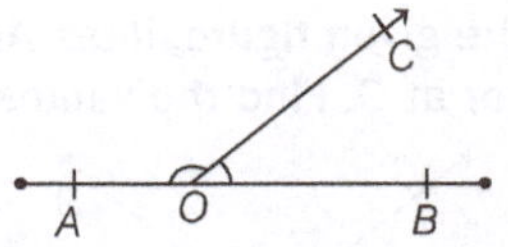

In the above figure, $\angle AOC + \angle BOC = 180°$ whereas, $\angle AOC$ and $\angle BOC$ are linear pair angles.

Axiom 2

If the sum of two adjacent angles is 180°, then the non-common arms of the angles form a line.

The two axioms given above together are called the **linear pair axioms.**

Theorem 1 If two lines intersect each other, then the vertically opposite angles are equal.

Given Two lines AB and CD intersect each other at a point O.

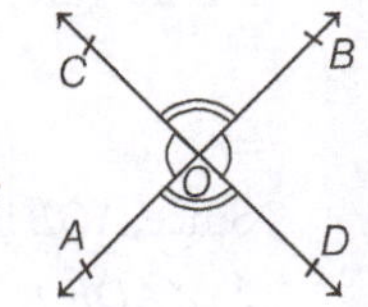

To prove The vertically opposite angles are equal

i.e.

(i) $\angle AOC = \angle BOD$

(ii) $\angle AOD = \angle BOC$

Proof

(i) Here, ray OC stands on line AB.

$\therefore \angle AOC + \angle BOC = 180°$ [by linear pair axiom] ...(i)

Again, ray OB stands on line CD.

$\therefore \angle BOC + \angle BOD = 180°$[by linear pair axiom] ...(ii)

From Eqs. (i) and (ii), we get

$$\angle AOC + \angle BOC = \angle BOC + \angle BOD$$

On subtracting $\angle BOC$ from both sides, we get

$$\angle AOC = \angle BOD$$

(ii) Similarly, we can prove that

$$\angle AOD = \angle BOC$$ **Hence proved.**

Example 9. In the given figure (as shown below), lines PQ and RS intersect each other at point O. If $\angle POR : \angle ROQ = 7:11$, then find all the angles.

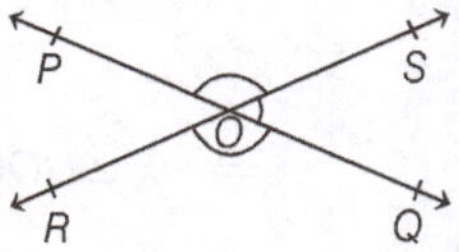

Sol. $\angle POR + \angle ROQ = 180°$ [linear pair of angles]

But $\angle POR : \angle ROQ = 7:11$ [given]

Therefore, $\angle POR = \frac{7}{7+11} \times 180° = 70°$

Similarly, $\angle ROQ = \frac{11}{7+11} \times 180° = 110°$

Now, $\angle POS = \angle ROQ = 110°$ [vertically opposite angles]

and $\angle SOQ = \angle POR = 70°$ [vertically opposite angles]

Example 10. In the given figure, lines AB and CD intersect each other at O. Find the values of x, y and z.

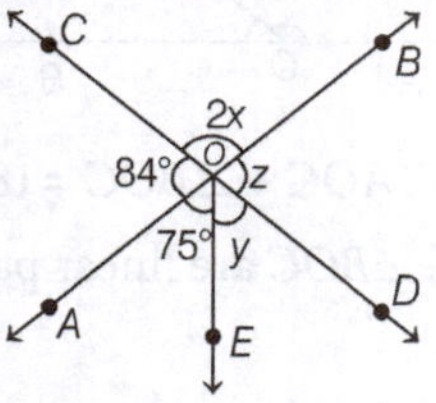

Sol. Here, AOB and COD are straight lines. So, by linear pair axiom, we have

$$\angle AOC + \angle BOC = 180°$$

$$\Rightarrow \quad 84° + 2x = 180°$$

$$\Rightarrow \quad 2x = 96° \Rightarrow x = 48°$$

From figure, $\angle COA = \angle BOD$ [vertically opposite angles]

$$\Rightarrow \quad 84° = z$$

Since, AOB is a straight line.

$$\therefore \angle AOE + \angle EOD + \angle DOB = 180°$$

$$\Rightarrow \quad 75° + y + z = 180°$$

$$\Rightarrow \quad 75° + y + 84° = 180°$$

$$\Rightarrow \quad y = 180° - 159°$$

$$\Rightarrow \quad y = 21°$$

Hence, $x = 48°$, $y = 21°$ and $z = 84°$.

Example 11. Prove that the bisectors of the angles of a linear pair are at right angles.

Sol. Consider $\angle AOC$ and $\angle BOC$ form a linear pair of angles, OD and OE are the bisectors of $\angle AOC$ and $\angle BOC$, respectively.

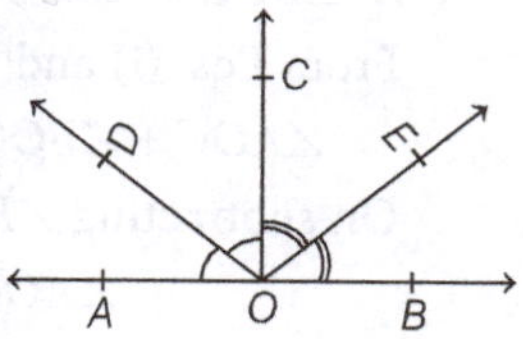

To prove $\angle DOE = 90°$

Proof Here, AOB is a straight line.

$$\therefore \quad \angle AOC + \angle BOC = 180° \text{ [by linear pair axiom]}$$

$$\Rightarrow \frac{1}{2}\angle AOC + \frac{1}{2}\angle BOC = 90°$$

[dividing both sides by 2]

$$\Rightarrow \quad \angle DOC + \angle COE = 90°$$

[since, OD is the bisector of $\angle AOC$ and OE is the bisector of $\angle BOC$]

$$\therefore \quad \angle DOE = 90°$$

Hence proved.

Example 12. In the given figure, AB, CD and PQ are three lines concurrent at O. If $\angle AOP = 5y$, $\angle QOD = 2y$ and $\angle BOC = 5y$, then find the value of y.

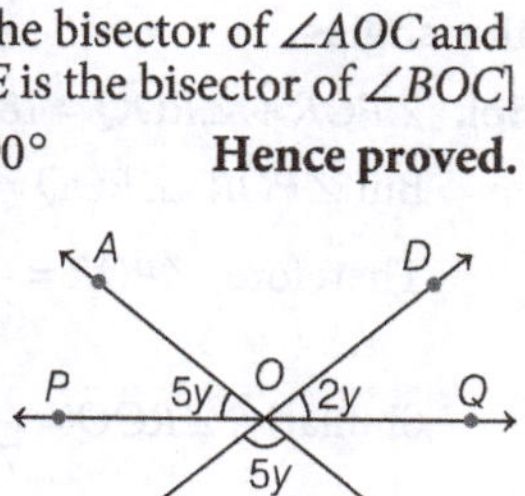

Sol. From the given figure, we have

$$\angle AOP = \angle BOQ = 5y$$

[vertically opposite angles]...(i)

$$\angle QOD = \angle COP = 2y$$

[vertically opposite angles]...(ii)

and $\angle BOC = \angle AOD = 5y$

[vertically opposite angles]...(iii)

We know that sum of angles around a point is 360°.

$$\therefore \angle AOP + \angle BOQ + \angle QOD + \angle COP + \angle BOC + \angle AOD = 360°$$

$$\Rightarrow \quad 5y + 5y + 2y + 2y + 5y + 5y = 360°$$

[from Eqs. (i), (ii) and (iii)]

$$\Rightarrow \quad 24y = 360°$$

$$\Rightarrow \quad y = \frac{360°}{24} = 15°$$

Example 13. In the given figure, OA, OB, OC and OD are four rays. Prove that

$$\angle AOB + \angle BOC + \angle COD + \angle AOD = 360°$$

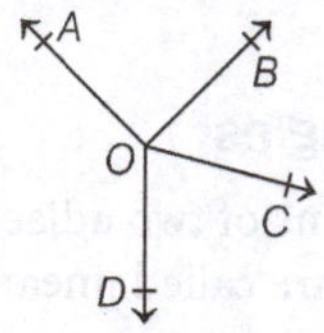

Sol. Let us produce OB backwards to a point P. Then, POB is a straight line.

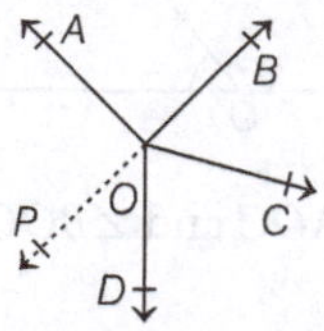

Now, OA is a ray on the line POB. Then, by linear pair axiom, we have

$$\angle POA + \angle AOB = 180° \quad \text{...(i)}$$

Similarly, OD is a ray on the line POB. Then, by linear pair axiom, we have

$$\angle POD + \angle DOB = 180° \quad \text{...(ii)}$$

Also, $\angle DOC + \angle BOC$ are adjacent angles.

$$\therefore \quad \angle DOB = \angle DOC + \angle BOC \quad \text{...(iii)}$$

On putting the value of $\angle DOB$ from Eq. (iii) in Eq. (ii), we get

$$\angle POD + \angle DOC + \angle BOC = 180° \quad \text{...(iv)}$$

Now, on adding Eqs. (i) and (iv), we get

$$\angle POA + \angle AOB + \angle POD + \angle DOC + \angle BOC = 180° + 180° \quad \text{...(v)}$$

But $\quad \angle POA + \angle POD = \angle AOD$

Then, from Eq. (v), we get

$$\angle AOD + \angle AOB + \angle DOC + \angle BOC = 360°$$

Hence proved.

Example 14. **In the given figure, AB, CD are straight lines and OP, OQ are respectively the bisectors of $\angle BOD$ and $\angle AOC$. Show that the rays OP and OQ are in the same line.**

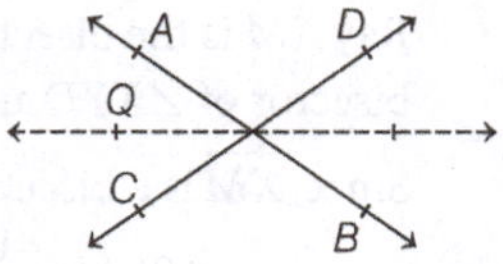

Sol. From the given figure, we have

$$\angle AOC = \angle BOD$$

[vertically opposite angles]

$$\Rightarrow \quad \frac{1}{2}\angle AOC = \frac{1}{2}\angle BOD$$

[dividing both sides by 2]

$$\Rightarrow \quad \angle COQ = \angle POD \quad \text{...(i)}$$

[since, OQ bisects $\angle AOC$ and OP bisects $\angle BOD$]

Now, CD is a straight line and OA stands on it.

$$\therefore \quad \angle COA + \angle DOA = 180^\circ$$

[by linear pair axiom]

$$\Rightarrow \quad \angle COQ + \angle QOA + \angle DOA = 180^\circ$$

$$\Rightarrow \quad \angle POD + \angle QOA + \angle DOA = 180^\circ \quad \text{[from Eq. (i)]}$$

$$\Rightarrow \quad \angle QOA + \angle DOA + \angle POD = 180^\circ$$

$$\Rightarrow \quad \angle QOP = 180^\circ$$

Hence, QOP is a straight line.

So, rays OP and OQ are in the same line. **Hence proved.**

Example 15. **In the given figure, lines AB and PQ intersect each other at O. If $\angle AOQ = 45^\circ$ and $a : b = 8 : 7$, then find c.**

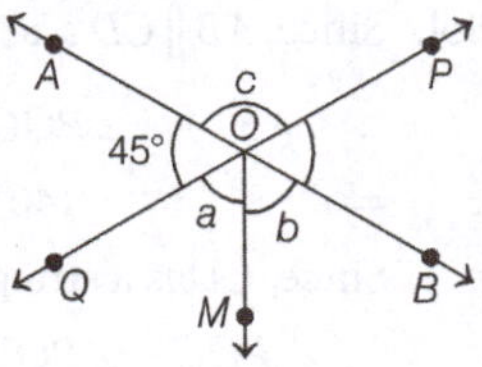

Sol. Since, AB is a line OQ and OM are rays.

Then, $\angle AOQ + \angle QOM + \angle BOM = 180^\circ$

[linear pair axiom]

$$\Rightarrow \quad 45^\circ + a + b = 180^\circ \quad \text{...(i)}$$

Since, $a : b = 8 : 7$

So, let $a = 8x$ and $b = 7x$.

Then, from Eq. (i), we get

$$45^\circ + 8x + 7x = 180^\circ$$

$$\Rightarrow \quad 45^\circ + 15x = 180^\circ$$

$$\Rightarrow \quad 15x = 180^\circ - 45^\circ = 135^\circ$$

$$\Rightarrow \quad x = \frac{135^\circ}{15} = 9^\circ$$

$\therefore \; a = 8x = 8 \times 9^\circ = 72^\circ, b = 7x = 7 \times 9^\circ = 63^\circ$

Now, $\angle AOP = \angle BOQ$

[vertically opposite angles]

$$\Rightarrow \quad c = a + b$$

$$\Rightarrow \quad c = 72^\circ + 63^\circ = 135^\circ$$

Lines Parallel to the Same Line

Theorem 2 Lines which are parallel to the same line, are parallel to each other.

Given Three lines a, b and c such that $a \parallel c$ and $b \parallel c$.

To prove $a \parallel b$

Construction Draw a transversal r cutting a, b and c at points P, Q and R, respectively.

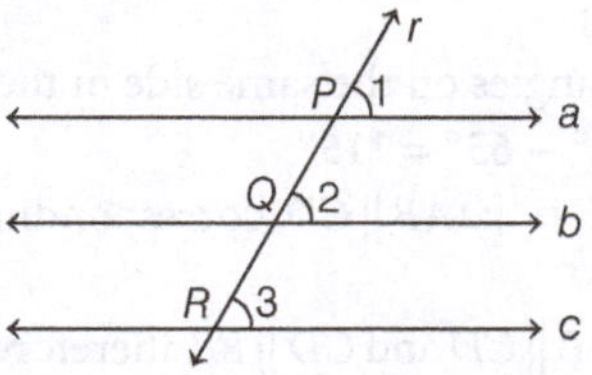

Proof Since, parallel lines a and c are intersected by the transversal r at points P and R, respectively.

$\therefore \quad \angle 1 = \angle 3$ [corresponding angles axiom] ...(i)

Again, parallel lines b and c are intersected by the transversal r at points Q and R, respectively.

$\therefore \quad \angle 2 = \angle 3$ [corresponding angles axiom] ...(ii)

From Eqs. (i) and (ii), we get

$\angle 1 = \angle 2$

But these are corresponding angles.

$\therefore \quad a \parallel b$ [by converse of corresponding angles axiom]

Hence proved.

Example 16. **If $AB \parallel PQ$ and $PQ \parallel CD$, $\angle MOQ = 55^\circ$ and $\angle OND = 140^\circ$, then find $\angle OMB$, $\angle CNO$ and $\angle NOQ$.**

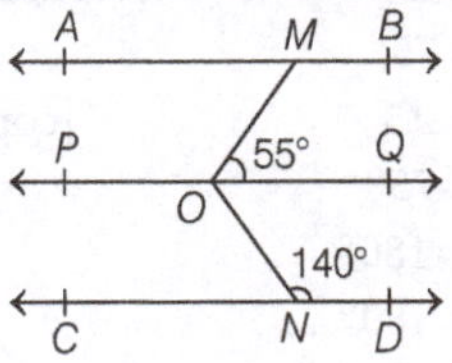

Sol. Here, $AB \parallel PQ$ and $PQ \parallel CD$

Therefore, $AB \parallel CD$ [using Theorem 2]

Now, $\angle OMB + \angle MOQ = 180^\circ$ [$\because AB \parallel PQ$, interior angles on the same side of the transversal OM]

But $\angle MOQ = 55^\circ$

So, $\angle OMB + 55^\circ = 180^\circ$

$\Rightarrow \quad \angle OMB = 180^\circ - 55^\circ = 125^\circ$

Now, CND is a line.

Therefore, $\angle CNO + \angle OND = 180^\circ$

$\Rightarrow \quad \angle CNO + 140^\circ = 180^\circ$

$\Rightarrow \quad \angle CNO = 180^\circ - 140^\circ = 40^\circ$

$\therefore \quad \angle CNO = 40^\circ$

Also, $\angle CNO = \angle NOQ$

[$\because PQ \parallel CD$, alternate angles]

$\therefore \quad \angle NOQ = 40^\circ$

Example 17. **In the given figure, $AB \parallel CD$ and $CD \parallel EF$. Also, $EA \perp AB$. If $\angle BEF = 65°$, then find the values of a, b and c.**

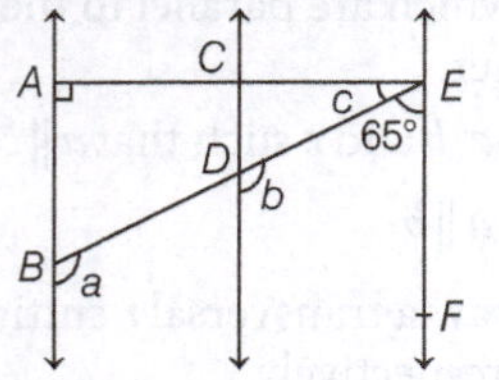

Sol. $b + 65° = 180°$

[interior angles on the same side of the transversal ED]

$\Rightarrow \quad b = 180° - 65° = 115°$

Again, $a = b$ [$\because AB \parallel CD$, corresponding angles axiom]

$\Rightarrow \quad a = 115°$

Now, since $AB \parallel CD$ and $CD \parallel EF$, therefore, $AB \parallel EF$.

So, $\angle EAB + \angle FEA = 180°$

[interior angles on the same side of the transversal EA]

Therefore, $90° + c + 65° = 180° \Rightarrow c = 25°$

Hence, $a = 115°, b = 115°$ and $c = 25°$.

Example 18. **In the given figure, $l \parallel m$ is cut by the transversal r. If $\angle 1 = 75°$, then find the measure of $\angle 3, \angle 5, \angle 4$ and $\angle 8$.**

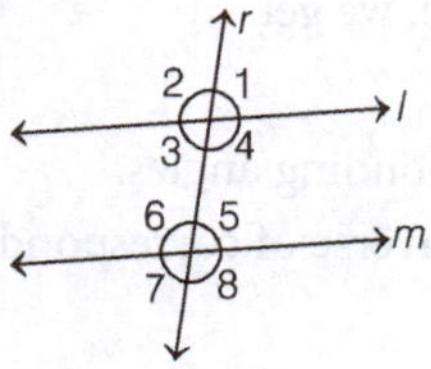

Sol. We have, $\angle 1 = 75°$

Now, $\angle 1 = \angle 3$ [vertically opposite angles]

$\therefore \quad \angle 3 = 75°$

Now, $\angle 1 = \angle 5$ [corresponding angles]

$\therefore \quad \angle 5 = 75°$

Now, $\angle 4 + \angle 5 = 180°$ [co-interior angles]

$\Rightarrow \quad \angle 4 + 75° = 180°$

$\Rightarrow \quad \angle 4 = 180° - 75° = 105°$

Also, $\angle 4 = \angle 8$ [corresponding angles]

$\therefore \quad \angle 8 = 105°$

Hence, $\angle 3 = 75°, \angle 5 = 75°, \angle 4 = 105°$ and $\angle 8 = 105°$

Example 19. **If a transversal intersects two lines such that the bisectors of a pair of corresponding angles are parallel, then prove that the two lines are parallel.**

Sol. In the given figure, a transversal PQ intersects two lines AB and CD at points X and Y, respectively.

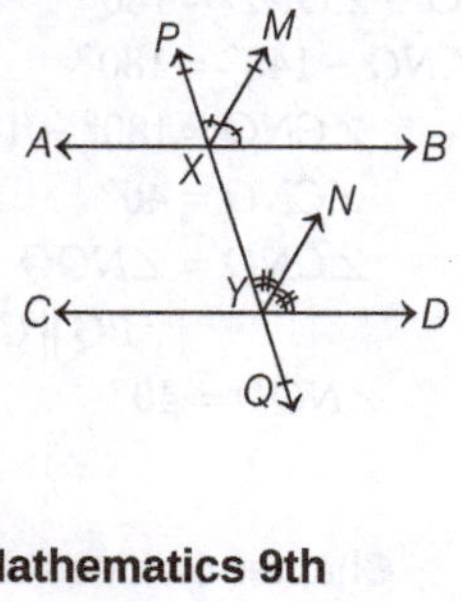

Ray XM is the bisector of $\angle PXB$ and ray YN is the bisector of $\angle XYD$ and $XM \parallel YN$.

Since, $\overrightarrow{XM}$ is a bisector at $\angle PXB$.

$\therefore \quad \angle PXM = \frac{1}{2} \angle PXB$ ...(i)

Also, $\overrightarrow{YN}$ is a bisector of $\angle XYD$.

$\therefore \quad \angle XYN = \frac{1}{2} \angle XYD$ ...(ii)

But $XM \parallel YN$ and PQ is the transversal.

$\therefore \quad \angle PXM = \angle XYN$ [corresponding angle axiom]

$\Rightarrow \quad \frac{1}{2} \angle PXB = \frac{1}{2} \angle XYD$ [from Eqs. (i) and (ii)]

$\Rightarrow \quad \angle PXB = \angle XYD$

Now, since these angles are corresponding angles formed by transversal PQ with AB and CD and both are equal.

$\therefore AB \parallel CD$.

Example 20. **In the given figure, $AB \parallel CD$, $\angle PQC = 140°$. Find x, y and z.**

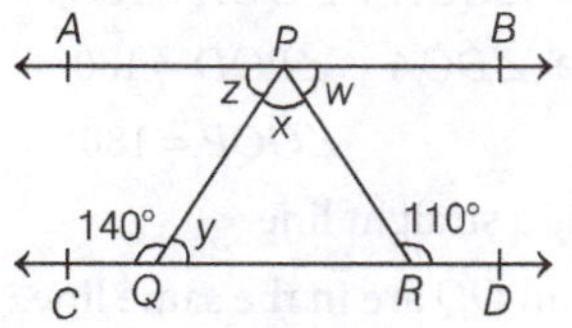

Sol. Since, $AB \parallel CD$ and PQ is a transversal.

$\therefore \quad \angle PQC = \angle QPB$ [alternate interior angles]

$\Rightarrow \quad 140° = x + w$ ...(i)

Since, CD is a straight line and ray PQ is stand on it.

$\therefore \quad \angle PQC + \angle PQR = 180°$ [linear pair axiom]

$\Rightarrow \quad 140° + y = 180°$

$\Rightarrow \quad y = 180° - 140° = 40°$

$\therefore \quad y = 40°$

And $\angle PQR = \angle APQ$ [alternate interior angles]

$\Rightarrow \quad y = z$

$\therefore \quad z = 40°$ [$\because y = 40°$]

Again, $\angle APR = \angle PRD$ [alternate interior angles]

$\Rightarrow \quad z + x = 110°$

$\Rightarrow \quad 40° + x = 110°$ [$\because z = 40°$]

$\Rightarrow \quad x = 110° - 40° = 70°$

$\therefore \quad x = 70°$

Now, from Eq. (i), we have

$x + w = 140°$

$\Rightarrow \quad 70° + w = 140°$

$\Rightarrow \quad w = 140° - 70° = 70°$

Hence, $x = 70°, y = 40°, z = 40°$ and $w = 70°$

NCERT FOLDER

Complete Solutions of All Exercises of NCERT Textbook

EXERCISE 6.1 (NCERT Page 76-77)

Q1. In the given figure, lines *AB* and *CD* intersect at *O*. If $\angle AOC + \angle BOE = 70°$ and $\angle BOD = 40°$, then find $\angle BOE$ and reflex $\angle COE$.

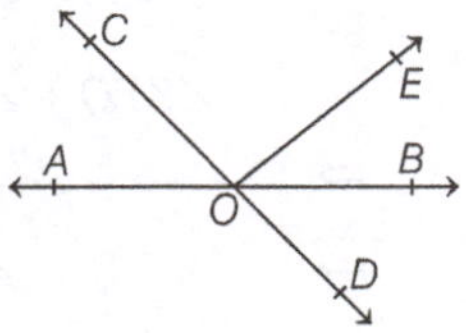

Sol. Given, $\angle AOC + \angle BOE = 70°$ ...(i)

and $\angle BOD = 40°$ ...(ii)

Also, lines *AB* and *CD* intersect each other at *O*.

So, $\angle AOC = \angle BOD$ [vertically opposite angles]

$\therefore$ $\angle AOC = 40°$ [from Eq. (ii)]

Then, from Eq. (i),

$40° + \angle BOE = 70°$

$\Rightarrow$ $\angle BOE = 70° - 40°$

$\therefore$ $\angle BOE = 30°$

Now, *OB* is a ray on *CD*.

So, $\angle BOD + \angle BOC = 180°$ [by linear pair axiom] ...(iii)

Also, $\angle COE$ and $\angle BOE$ are adjacent angles.

So, $\angle BOC = \angle COE + \angle BOE$

On putting the value of $\angle BOC$ in Eq. (iii), we get

$\angle BOD + \angle COE + \angle BOE = 180°$

$\Rightarrow$ $40° + \angle COE + 30° = 180°$

$\Rightarrow$ $\angle COE + 70° = 180°$

$\Rightarrow$ $\angle COE = 180° - 70° = 110°$

Also, $\angle COE$ + reflex $\angle COE = 360°$ [since, sum of angles at a point is 360°]

$\Rightarrow$ $110°$ + reflex $\angle COE = 360°$

$\therefore$ Reflex $\angle COE = 360° - 110° = 250°$

Q2. In the given figure, lines *XY* and *MN* intersect at *O*. If $\angle POY = 90°$ and $a : b = 2 : 3$, then find the value of *c*.

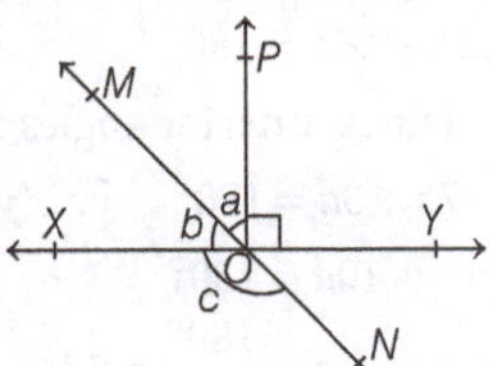

Sol. Here, *OP* is a ray on the line *XY*.

$\therefore$ $\angle POX + \angle POY = 180°$ [by linear pair axiom]

$\Rightarrow$ $b + a + 90° = 180°$

$\Rightarrow$ $a + b = 90°$ ...(i)

Let $a = 2x$ and $b = 3x$ [$\because a : b = 2 : 3$]

On putting the values of *a* and *b* in Eq. (i), we get

$x = 18°$

$\therefore$ $a = 2x = 2 \times 18° = 36°$

and $b = 3x = 3 \times 18° = 54°$

Now, *OX* is a ray on the line *MON*.

$\therefore$ $\angle XOM + \angle XON = 180°$ [by linear pair axiom]

$\Rightarrow$ $b + c = 180°$

$\Rightarrow$ $54° + c = 180° \Rightarrow c = 126°$

Q3. In the given figure, if $\angle PQR = \angle PRQ$, then prove that $\angle PQS = \angle PRT$.

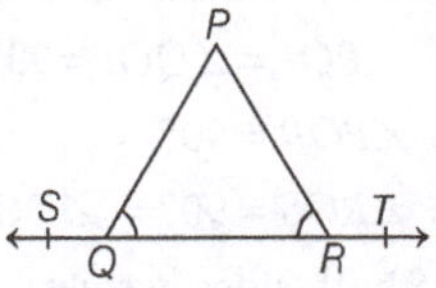

Sol. Given $\angle PQR = \angle PRQ$

To prove $\angle PQS = \angle PRT$

Proof Here, *SQR* is a straight line and *PQ* is a ray on it

$\Rightarrow$ $\angle PQS + \angle PQR = 180°$ [by linear pair axiom] ...(i)

Again, *QRT* is a straight line and *PR* is a ray on it

$\Rightarrow$ $\angle PRT + \angle PRQ = 180°$ [by linear pair axiom] ...(ii)

From Eqs. (i) and (ii), we get

$\angle PQS + \angle PQR = \angle PRT + \angle PRQ$

$\Rightarrow$ $\angle PQS + \angle PRQ = \angle PRT + \angle PRQ$ [$\because \angle PQR = \angle PRQ$, given]

$\Rightarrow$ $\angle PQS = \angle PRT$ **Hence proved.**

Q4. In the given figure, if $x + y = w + z$, then prove that *AOB* is a line.

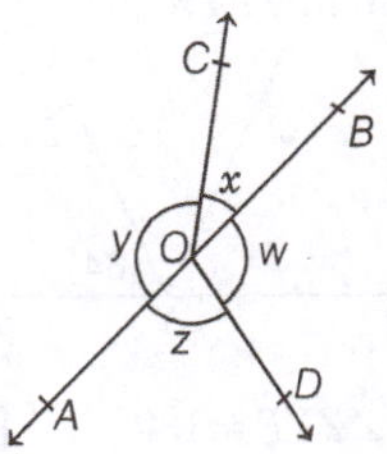

Sol. We know that the sum of all the angles around a point is 360°.

$\therefore \quad x+y+z+w=360°$ ...(i)

Now, given $\quad x+y=w+z$

Then, from Eq. (i), we get

$x+y+x+y=360°$

$\Rightarrow \quad 2x+2y=360°$

$\Rightarrow \quad x+y=180°$

$\Rightarrow \angle BOC+\angle AOC=180°$

Thus, AOB is straight line.

Q5. **In the given figure, *POQ* is a line. Ray *OR* is perpendicular to line *PQ*. *OS* is another ray lying between rays *OP* and *OR*.**

Prove that $\angle ROS=\frac{1}{2}(\angle QOS-\angle POS)$.

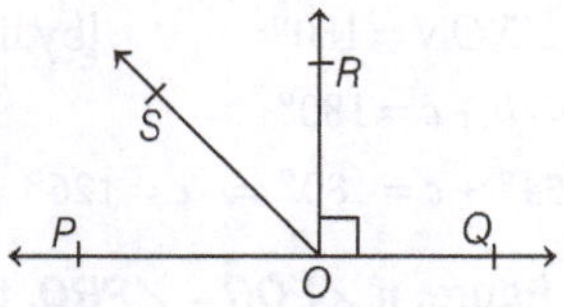

Sol. Given, POQ is a line and $OR \perp PQ$.

$\therefore \quad \angle POR=\angle QOR=90°$

Now, $\quad \angle POR=90°$

$\Rightarrow \quad \angle POS+\angle ROS=90°=\angle QOR$

On adding $\angle ROS$ both sides, we get

$\angle POS+\angle ROS+\angle ROS=\angle QOR+\angle ROS$

$\Rightarrow \quad \angle POS+2\angle ROS=\angle QOS$

$\Rightarrow \quad 2\angle ROS=\angle QOS-\angle POS$

$\therefore \quad \angle ROS=\frac{1}{2}[\angle QOS-\angle POS]$

Hence proved.

Q6. **It is given that $\angle XYZ=64°$ and *XY* is produced to point *P*. Draw a figure from the given information. If ray *YQ* bisects $\angle ZYP$, then find $\angle XYQ$ and reflex $\angle QYP$.**

Sol. Given, $\angle XYZ=64°$ and XY is produced to point P.

So, PYX is a straight line.

$\therefore \quad \angle PYX=180°$

Now, YZ is a ray on line PYX.

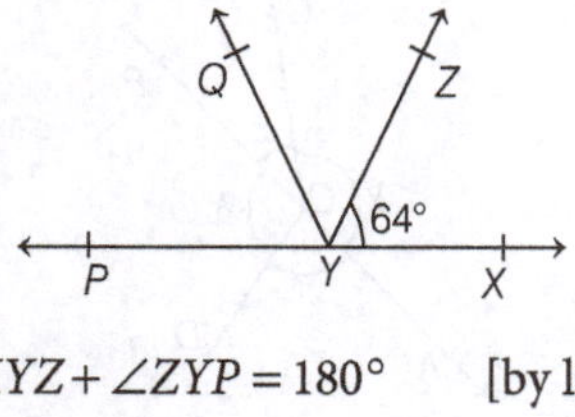

So, $\quad \angle XYZ+\angle ZYP=180°$ [by linear pair axiom]

$\Rightarrow \quad 64°+\angle ZYP=180°$

$\Rightarrow \quad \angle ZYP=180°-64°$

$\Rightarrow \quad \angle ZYP=116°$

$\Rightarrow \quad \angle ZYQ+\angle QYP=116°$ ...(i)

If ray YQ bisects $\angle ZYP$, then

$\angle QYP=\angle ZYQ$ ...(ii)

On putting the value of $\angle QYP$ from Eq. (ii) in Eq. (i), we get

$\angle ZYQ+\angle ZYQ=116°$

$\Rightarrow \quad 2\angle ZYQ=116°$

$\Rightarrow \quad \angle ZYQ=\frac{116°}{2}$

$\Rightarrow \quad \angle ZYQ=58°$ ...(iii)

From Eqs. (ii) and (iii), we get

$\angle QYP=58°$

Now, $\quad \angle XYQ=\angle XYZ+\angle ZYQ$

$=64°+58°=122°$

and $\quad$ reflex $\angle QYP=360°-\angle QYP$

$=360°-58°=302°$

$[\because \angle QYP=\angle ZYQ=58°]$

EXERCISE 6.2 (NCERT Page 80-81)

Q1. **In the given figure, if *AB* || *CD*, *CD* || *EF* and $y:z=3:7$, then find the value of *x*.**

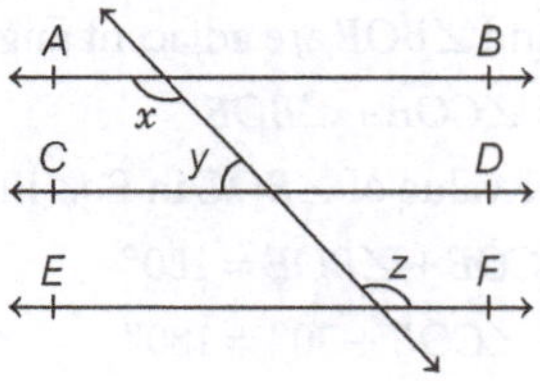

Sol. Given, $AB \parallel CD$ and $CD \parallel EF$

$\therefore \quad AB \parallel EF$ [since, lines which are parallel to the same line, are parallel to each other]

Then, $\quad \angle x=\angle z$ [alternate interior angles] ...(i)

Also, given that $\quad y:z=3:7$

$\Rightarrow \quad y:x=3:7$ [from Eq. (i)] ...(ii)

Let $\angle y=3a$ and $\angle x=7a$

Now, $\quad AB \parallel CD$

$\therefore \quad \angle x+\angle y=180°$

[since, interior angles are supplementary]

$\Rightarrow \quad 7a+3a=180°$ $[\because \angle y=3a$ and $\angle x=7a]$

$\Rightarrow \quad 10a=180°$

$\Rightarrow \quad a=\frac{180°}{10}=18°$

Hence, $\quad x=7a=(7\times 18)°=126°$

Q 2. In the given figure, if $AB \parallel CD$, $EF \perp CD$ and $\angle GED = 126°$, then find $\angle AGE$, $\angle GEF$ and $\angle FGE$.

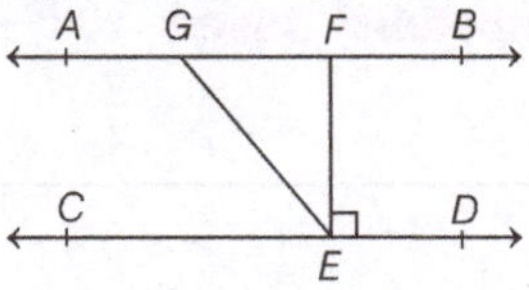

Sol. Here, $\angle AGE = \angle GED$ [alternate interior angles]

$\Rightarrow \angle AGE = 126°$ [$\because \angle GED = 126°$, given]

Now, $\angle GEF = \angle GED - \angle FED$

$\Rightarrow \angle GEF = 126° - 90° = 36°$

[$\because FE \perp CD \Rightarrow \angle FED = 90°$]

Also, AB is a straight line and EG is a ray on it.

So, $\angle FGE + \angle AGE = 180°$

$\Rightarrow \angle FGE = 180° - \angle AGE$

$= 180° - 126° = 54°$

Hence, $\angle AGE = 126°$, $\angle GEF = 36°$ and $\angle FGE = 54°$.

Q 3. In the given figure, if $PQ \parallel ST$, $\angle PQR = 110°$ and $\angle RST = 130°$, then find $\angle QRS$.

[Hint Draw a line parallel to ST through point R.]

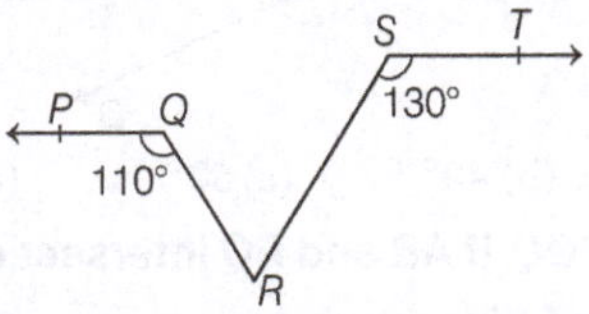

Sol. Draw a line parallel to ST through point R.

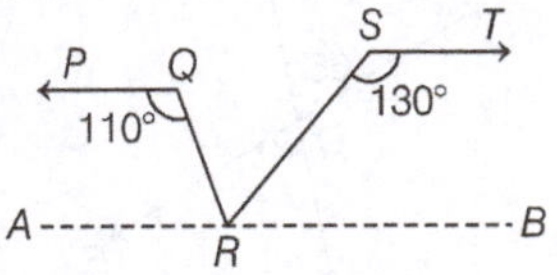

Since, $\angle RST + \angle SRB = 180°$ [cointerior angles]

$\Rightarrow \angle SRB = 50°$ ...(i)

and $\angle PQR + \angle QRA = 180°$ [cointerior angles]

$\Rightarrow \angle QRA = 70°$ ...(ii)

Now, ARB is a line.

$\therefore \angle QRA + \angle QRS + \angle SRB = 180°$ [by linear pair axiom]

$\Rightarrow 70° + \angle QRS + 50° = 180°$

$\Rightarrow \angle QRS = 60°$

Hence, $\angle QRS = 60°$

Q 4. In the given figure, if $AB \parallel CD$, $\angle APQ = 50°$ and $\angle PRD = 127°$, then find the values of x and y.

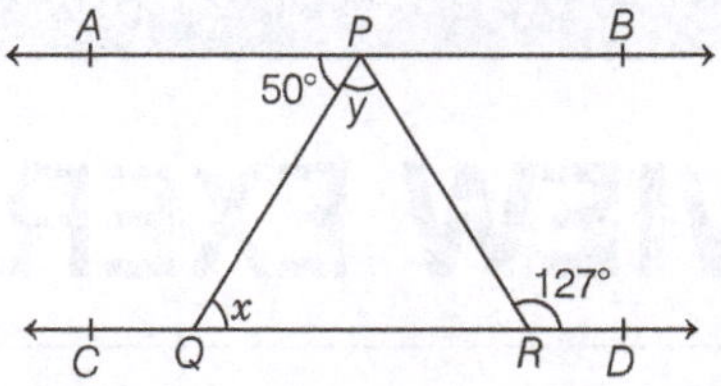

Sol. $\angle APQ + \angle PQC = 180°$ [co-interior angles]

$\Rightarrow 50° + \angle PQC = 180°$

$\angle PQC = 130°$

Also, $\angle PQC + \angle PQR = 180°$ [by linear pair axiom]

$\therefore x = 180° - 130° = 50°$

Also, $\angle APR = \angle PRD$

[alternate interior angles]

$\Rightarrow 50° + y = 127°$

$\Rightarrow y = 77°$

Hence, $x = 50°$ and $y = 77°$

Q 5. In the adjoining figure, PQ and RS are two mirrors placed parallel to each other. An incident ray AB strikes the mirror PQ at B, the reflected ray moves along the path BC and strikes the mirror RS at C and again reflects back along CD. Prove that $AB \parallel CD$.

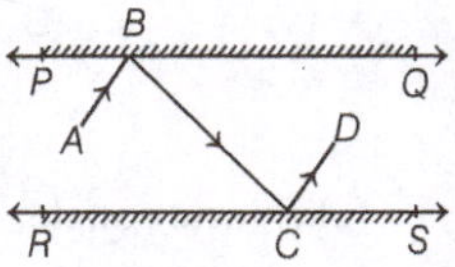

Sol. Draw $BE \perp PQ$ and $CF \perp RS$

$\Rightarrow BE \parallel CF$ [$\because PQ \parallel RS$]

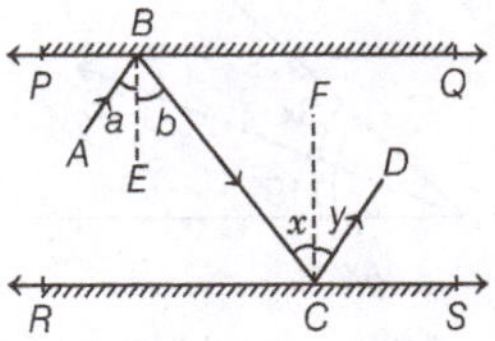

Also, $\angle a = \angle b$ ...(i)

[$\because$ Angle of incidence = Angle of reflection]

and $\angle x = \angle y$ ...(ii)

[$\because$ Angle of incidence = Angle of reflection]

Since, $BE \parallel CF$ and BC is a transversal.

$\therefore \angle b = \angle x$ [alternate interior angles]

$\Rightarrow 2\angle b = 2\angle x$ [multiplying by 2 both sides]

$\Rightarrow \angle b + \angle b = \angle x + \angle x$

$\Rightarrow \angle a + \angle b = \angle x + \angle y$ [from Eqs. (i) and (ii)]

$\Rightarrow \angle ABC = \angle DCB$

which are alternate interior angles.

Hence, $AB \parallel CD$ **Hence proved.**

REVIEW EXERCISE

Including Competency Based Questions

Part I

Multiple Choice Questions

1. Given lines are the example of

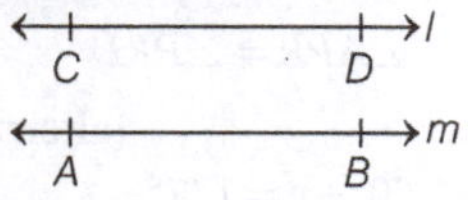

(a) transversal lines
(b) parallel lines
(c) intersecting lines
(d) non-parallel intersecting lines

2. Given angle is an example of

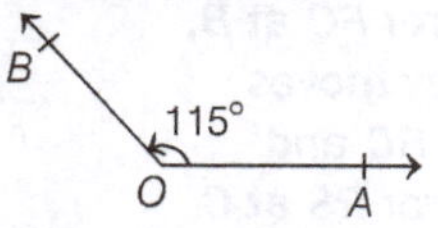

(a) an acute angle (b) an obtuse angle
(c) a reflex angle (d) a complete angle

3. In the given figure, $\angle AOB : \angle BOC = 3:4$. If $\angle AOC = 119°$, then the find the measure of $\angle BOC$.

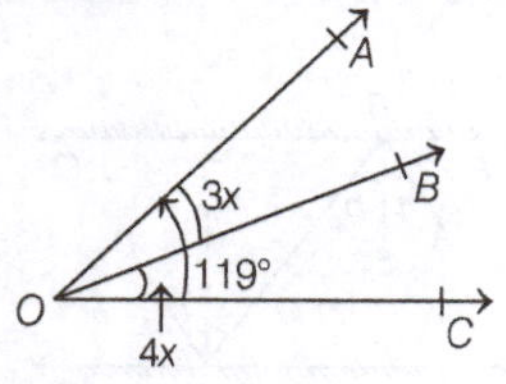

(a) 68° (b) 51° (c) 78° (d) 64°

4. Two complementary angles are in ratio $3:6$. Find the measure of smaller angle.

(a) 30° (b) 50° (c) 60° (d) 70°

5. What is the measure of an angle, which is complement of itself?

(a) 40° (b) 45° (c) 50° (d) 55°

6. If angles with measures x and y form a complementary pair, then which of the following measures of angles will form a supplementary pair?

Competency Based Question

(a) $(x+47°), (y+43°)$ (b) $(x-23°), (y+23°)$
(c) $(x-43°), (y-47°)$ (d) No such pair is possible

7. Two supplementary angles are in ratio $3:7$. Find the measure of largest angle.

(a) 54° (b) 56°
(c) 126° (d) 136°

8. If an angle is such that six times its complement is 32° less than twice its supplement, then the value of angle is

(a) 38° (b) 53° (c) 58° (d) 68°

9. If two supplementary angles are in the ratio $3:2$, then its angles are .... and ....

(a) 70° and 108° (b) 108° and 72°
(c) 70° and 110° (d) 72° and 110°

10. In the given figure, lines AB and CD intersect at O. If $\angle AOC + \angle BOE = 80°$ and $\angle BOD = 30°$, then $\angle BOE$ equals to

Competency Based Question

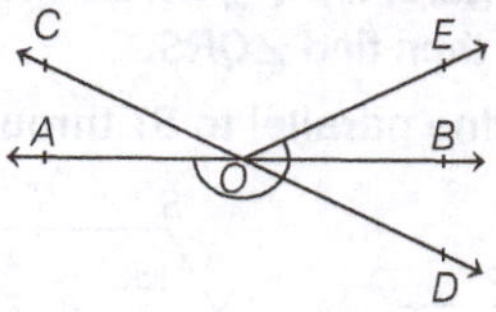

(a) 30° (b) 40° (c) 50° (d) 60°

11. Find the $\angle BOQ$, if AB and PQ intersect each other at O and $\angle POA = 65°$.

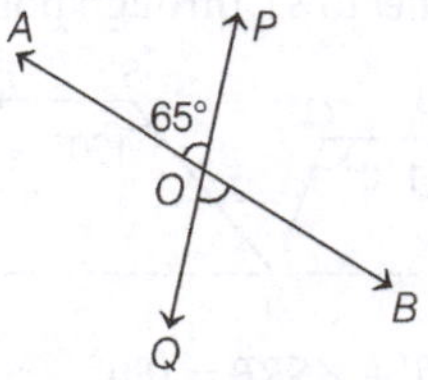

(a) 65° (b) 75° (c) 115° (d) 55°

12. The figure below, AOB is a straight line. Calculate the measure of $\angle POR - \angle POA$.

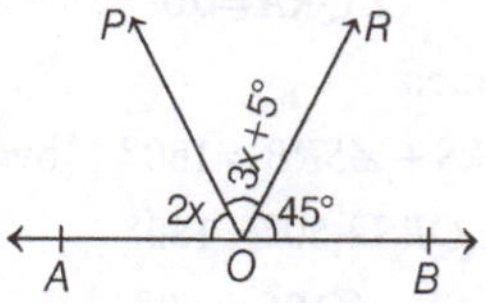

(a) 26° (b) 31° (c) 83° (d) 35°

13. In the figure, POQ is a line. The value of x is

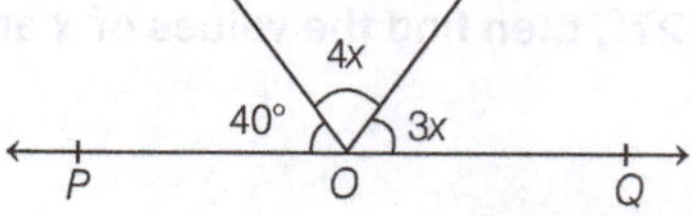

Competency Based Question

(a) 20° (b) 25° (c) 30° (d) 35°

14. In a ΔABC, if $3\angle A = 4\angle B = 6\angle C$, then the ratio of $A : B : C$ is ....

(a) 2 : 3 : 4 (b) 3 : 4 : 2

(c) 4 : 3 : 2 (d) 2 : 3 : 2

15. If lines l, m and n are parallel to each other and r is the transversal line. If $\angle PQC = 105°$, then find sum of $\angle DQR + \angle QRE$. **Competency Based Question**

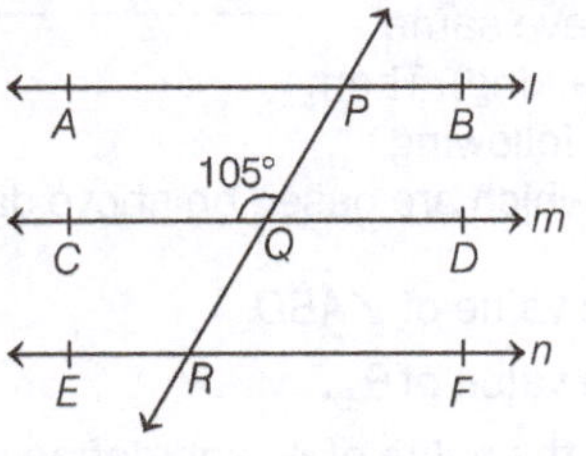

(a) 105° (b) 210° (c) 215° (d) 110°

Assertion-Reason Type Questions

16. Assertion The bisectors of the angles of a linear pair are at right angles.

Reason If the sum of two adjacent angles is 180°, then the non-common arms of the angles are in a straight line.

(a) Both Assertion and Reason are correct and Reason is the correct explanation of Assertion.

(b) Both Assertion and Reason are correct but Reason is not the correct explanation of Assertion.

(c) Assertion is correct but Reason is incorrect.

(d) Assertion is incorrect but Reason is correct.

17. Assertion Two adjacent angles always form a linear pair.

Reason In a linear pair of angles two non-common arms are opposite rays.

(a) Both Assertion and Reason are correct and Reason is the correct explanation of Assertion.

(b) Both Assertion and Reason are correct but Reason is not the correct explanation of Assertion.

(c) Assertion is correct but Reason is incorrect.

(d) Assertion is incorrect but Reason is correct.

18. Assertion If a line is perpendicular to one of the two given parallel lines, then it is also perpendicular to the other line.

Reason If two lines are intersected by a transversal, then the bisectors of any pair of alternate interior angles are parallel.

(a) Both Assertion and Reason are correct and Reason is the correct explanation of Assertion.

(b) Both Assertion and Reason are correct but Reason is not the correct explanation of Assertion.

(c) Assertion is correct but Reason is incorrect.

(d) Assertion is incorrect but Reason is correct.

Case Study Based Questions

19. During the maths class, teacher draws a straight line AB on the blackboard as per the following figure. Now, he told Ramesh to draw another line CD as in the figure and to mark $\angle AOD$ as $2x$. Again, he told Suraj to mark $\angle AOC$ and $\angle COE$ as $3z$ and 60°, respectively. After that he marks $\angle BOE$ and $\angle BOD$ as z and y, respectively.

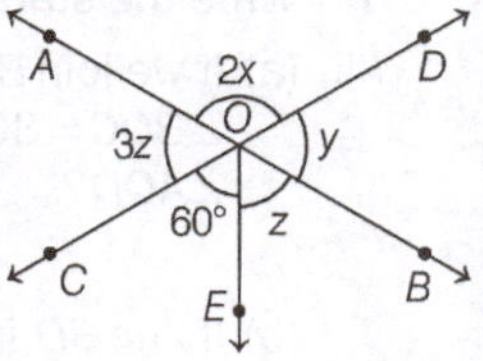

Based on the above information, answer the following questions.

(i) What is the value of z?

(ii) What is the value of y?

(iii) (a) Find the value of $2x + y$.

Or

(b) Find the relation between x and z.

20. A class teacher says to the students, make a banner for 'Swachh Bharat'. Which is defined such as l_1 and l_2 are two parallel lines and m is a transversal line, which intersects two lines l_1 and l_2 at A and B, respectively.

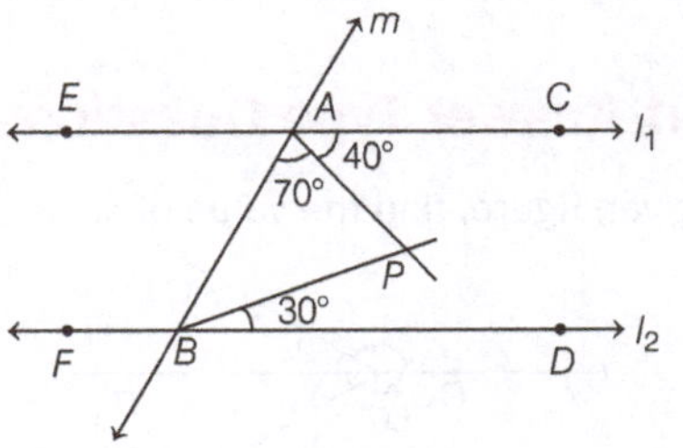

Based on the above information, answer the following questions.

(i) Find the $\angle ABP$. (ii) Determine $\angle EAB$.

(iii) (a) Find $\angle ABD$ and $\angle FBA$.

Or

(b) From the figure, we see that $\angle EAB = \angle ABD$. Which property of angle is shown by this result?

21. BSE stands for a disease called Bovine Spongiform Encepholopathy. This disease is commonly called "Mad cow disease" A farmer has a field $ABCD$ formed by two pair of paralled lines as shown below in which $l \parallel m$ and $p \parallel q$. His four cows suffering from BSE. Thus, he tied them at four corners of the field $ABCD$.

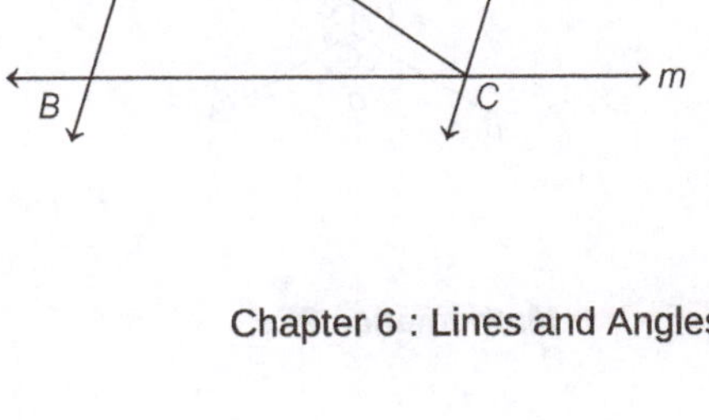

Based on the above information, answer the following questions.

(i) If $\angle BAC = 30°$, then find $\angle ACD$.

(ii) Write the statement why $\angle ABC + \angle BCD = 180°$?

(iii) (a) If we join BD' such that BD meet AC at O and $\angle BOC = 30°$, then what is the measure of $\angle AOD$?

Or

(b) If line BD intersects line AC at point O and $\angle AOB = 30°$, $\angle BDC = 45°$. Then, find the measure of $\angle COD$ and $\angle ABD$.

22. In game period, the teacher of Meerut Public School decided to play the puzzle game. For this game, firstly the teacher draw a geometrical figure on the ground, which is shown as below.

While drawing this figure, the teacher have no scale for measuring this length, but they know the side which is opposite to the smallest angle, is smaller and the side which is opposite to the largest angle, is larger.

In this game, the teacher invite the two students Vicky and Vishal and said them that Vicky stands on point A and Vishal stands on point B, respectively (assume that both have same space of walking). Then, answer the following questions, which are based on above data.

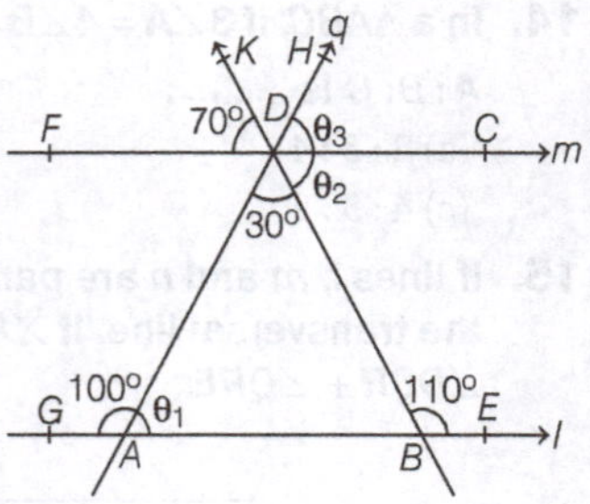

(i) Find the value of $\angle ABD$.

(ii) Find the value of θ_1.

(iii) (a) Find the value of θ_2 and define vertically opposite angles.

Or

(b) Find the value of θ_3 and define the linear pair axiom.

Part II

Very Short Answer Type Questions

1. In the given figure, find the value of x.

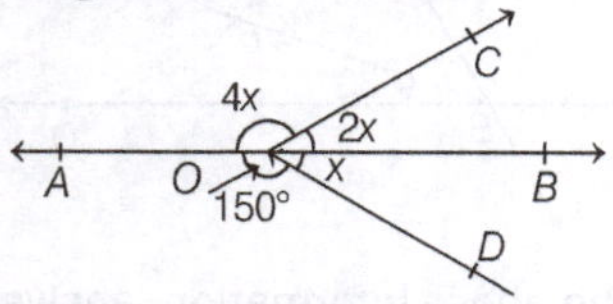

2. If two supplementary angles are in the ratio 13 : 5, then find the angles.

3. In the given figure, if POQ is a line, then find the value of x.

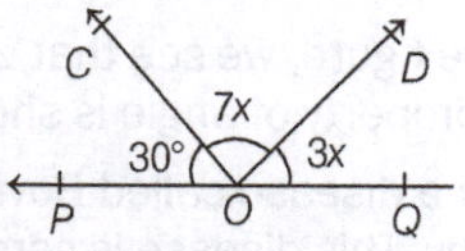

4. Two lines l and m are perpendicular to the same line n. Are l and m perpendicular to each other? Give reason for your answer. **Competency Based Question**

5. In the given figure, $a - c = d - b$, then prove that POQ is a line.

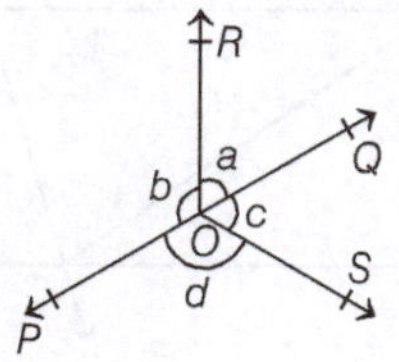

6. In the given figure, AOB is a line. Ray OP is perpendicular to line AB. OQ is another ray lying between rays OA and OP. Prove that

$$\angle POQ = \frac{1}{2}(\angle BOQ - \angle AOQ)$$

Competency Based Question

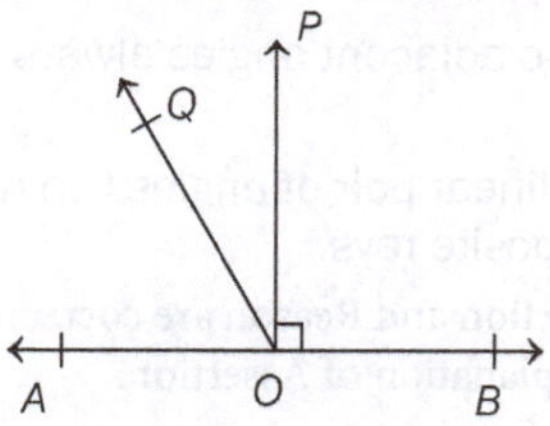

Short Answer Type Questions

7. If two complementary angles are such that two times the measure of one is equal to three times the measure of the other. Then, find the measure of the larger angle.

8. Find the value of x.

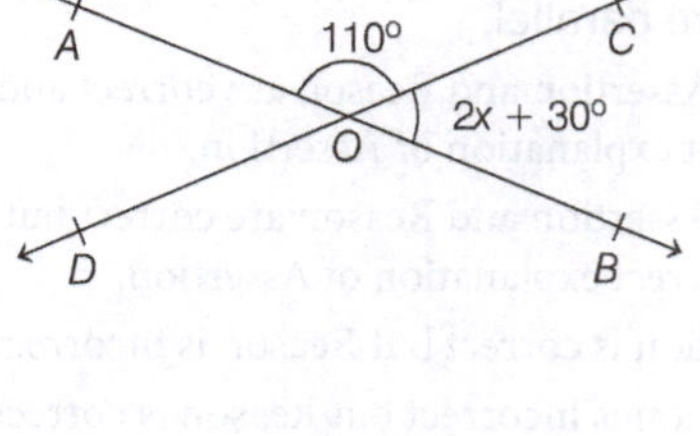

9. In the given figure, if $\angle PQR = \angle PRQ = 75°$ then prove that $\angle PQS = \angle PRT$. Find $\angle PQS$.

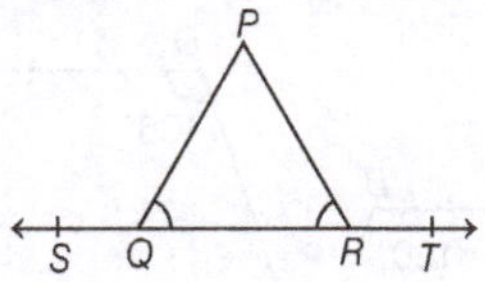

10. In the given figure, find the value of m and n, where $m = 2n$.

Competency Based Question

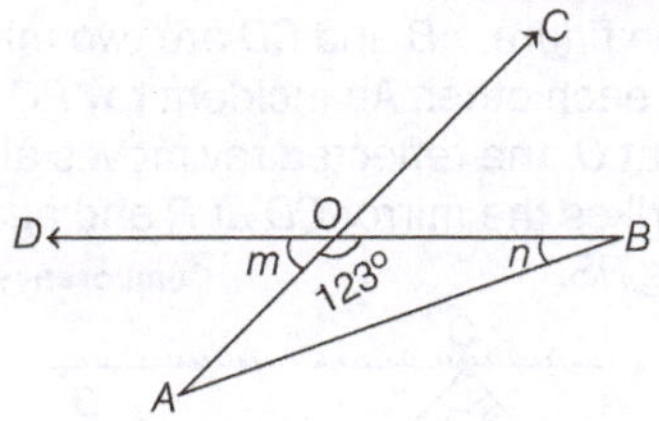

11. Find the value of $\angle ABC$, if $AC = AB$.

Competency Based Question

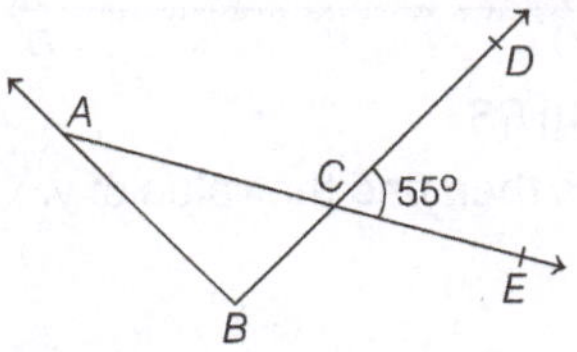

12. In the given figure, if $AC = AB$, then find the value of x.

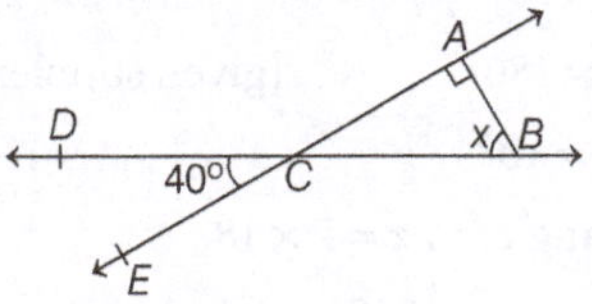

13. Three lines AB, CD and EF meet at a point O, forming angles as shown in the figure. Find the values of x, y, z and u.

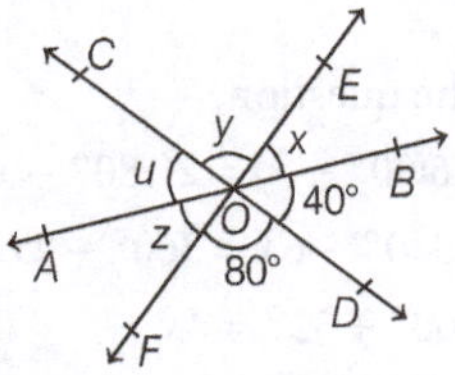

14. Find the values of $\angle GFA$, $\angle CDB$ and $\angle ABE$.

Competency Based Question

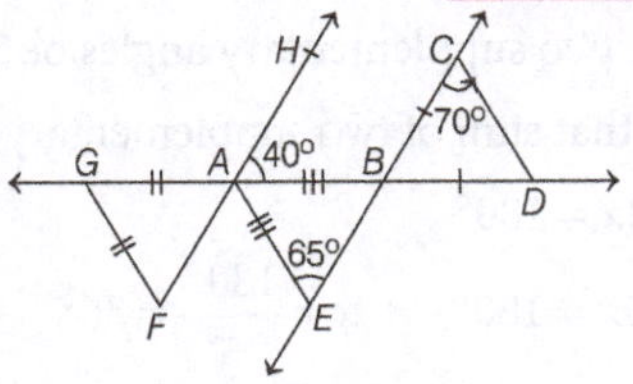

15. Prove that two lines that are respectively perpendicular to two intersecting lines intersect each other.

Competency Based Question

16. In the given figure, $AB \parallel CD$, $PQ \perp AB$ and $\angle RQD = 53°$, find $\angle PRQ$, $\angle APQ$ and $\angle BRQ$.

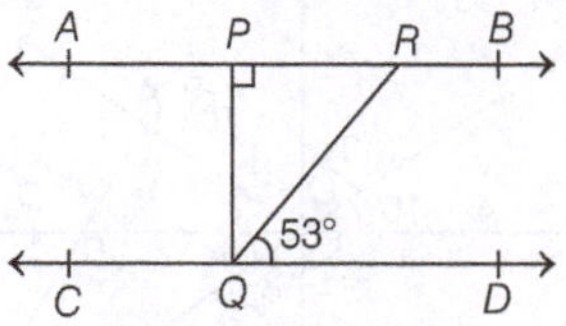

17. In the given figure (as shown below), if $PQ \parallel RS, RS \parallel TU$ and $y : z = 7 : 13$, then find the value of x.

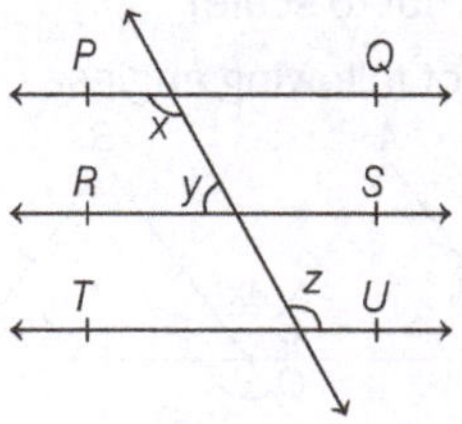

18. In the given figure, $AB \parallel CD$, $CD \parallel WY$, $PQ \perp CD$, $RS \perp AB$ and $\angle PRQ = 43°$. Find the values of x, y and z.

Competency Based Question

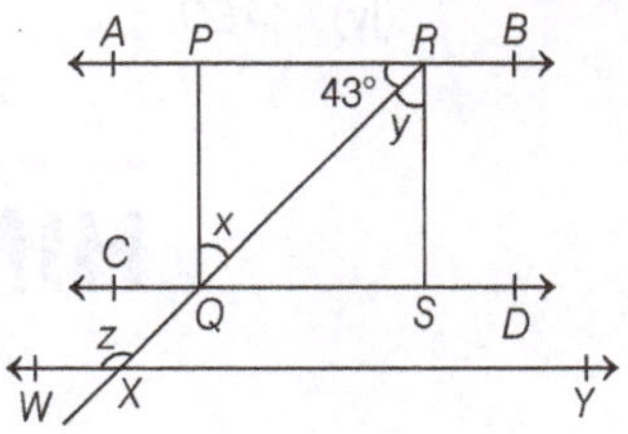

Long Answer Type Questions

19. If the arms of one angle are respectively parallel to the arms of another angle, then show that the two angles are either equal or supplementary.

Competency Based Question

20. Find the values of $\angle TRS$, $\angle TRU$ and $\angle PRQ$.

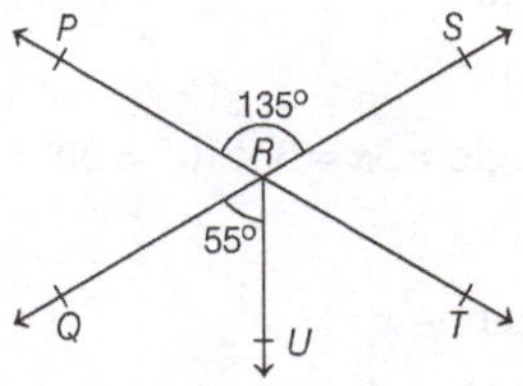

21. Find the values of x, y and z.

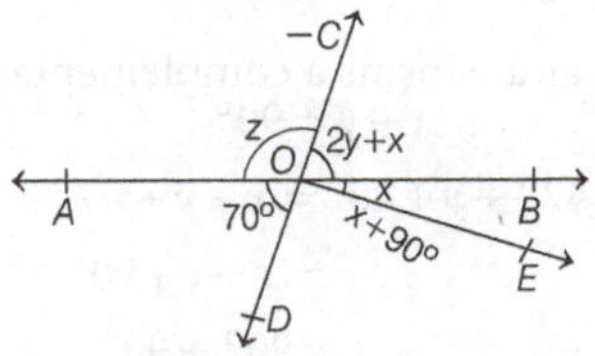

22. Find the value of $\angle DBC$, if $AB = AO$.

Competency Based Question

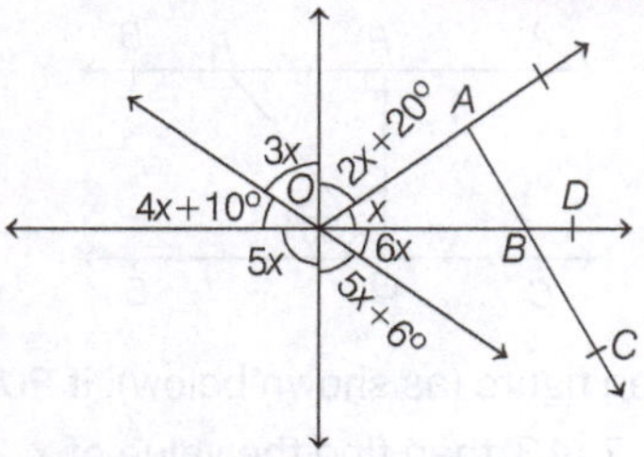

[**Note** Figure is not to scale]

23. Find the value of following angles

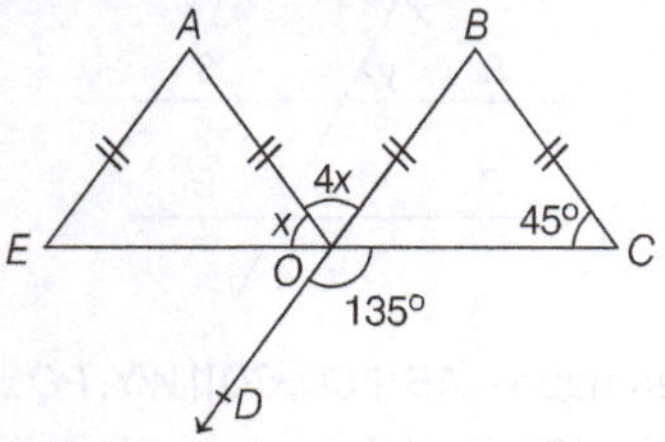

(i) $\angle BOC$ (ii) $\angle AOE$
(iii) $\angle AOB$ (iv) $\angle AEO$

24. In the given figure, if $AB \parallel DE$, $\angle ABC = 120°$ and $\angle CDE = 135°$, then find $\angle BCD$.

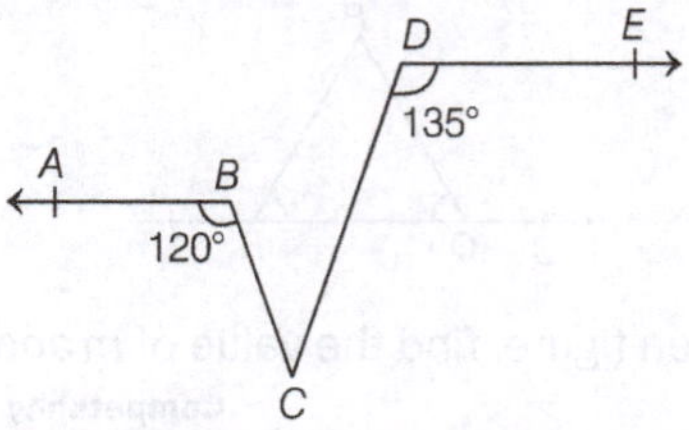

25. In the given figure, AB and CD are two mirrors placed parallel to each other. An incident ray PQ strikes the mirror AB at Q, the reflected ray moves along the path QR and strikes the mirror CD at R and again reflects back along RS.

Competency Based Question

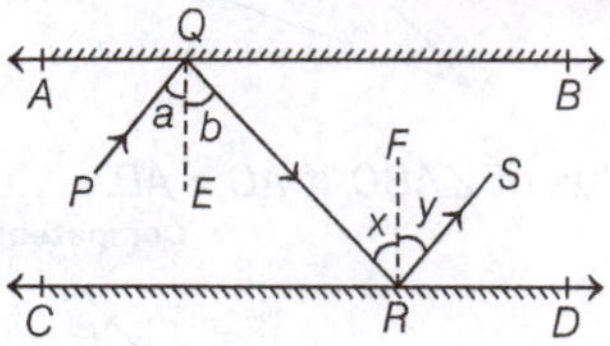

(i) Prove $PQ \parallel RS$.
(ii) If $a = 30°$, then find the value of y.

HINTS & ANSWERS

Part I

1. (b) Given lines are parallel lines.

2. (b) Given angle is an obtuse angle.

3. (a) $3x + 4x = 119°$

$\Rightarrow \quad 7x = 119°$

$\Rightarrow \quad x = 17°$

So, $\angle BOC = 4x = 4 \times 17° = 68°$

4. (a) $3x + 6x = 90°$

$\Rightarrow \quad x = 10°$

So, smaller angle $= 3x = 3 \times 10° = 30°$

5. (b) $x = 90° - x$

$\Rightarrow \quad 2x = 90°$

$\Rightarrow \quad x = 45°$

6. (a) Since, x and y forms a complementary pair.

$\therefore \quad x + y = 90° \quad \ldots$(i)

Now, $x + 47° + y + 43° = x + y + 47° + 43°$

$= x + y + 90°$

$= 90° + 90°$ [from Eq. (i)]

$= 180°$

$\therefore$ $(x + 47°)$ and $(y + 43°)$ forms a supplementary pair.

7. (c) $3x + 7x = 180°$ [given supplementary angles]

$x = 18°$

So, largest angle $= 7x = 7 \times 18°$

$= 126°$

8. (b) Let the required angle be x. Then, its supplementary angle be $180° - x$ and its complementary angle be $90° - x$.

According to the question,

$6(90° - x) = 2(180° - x) - 32°$

$\Rightarrow \quad 540° - 6x = 360° - 2x - 32°$

$\Rightarrow \quad 540° - 360° + 32° = 4x$

$\Rightarrow \quad 4x = 212°$

$\Rightarrow \quad x = 53°$

9. (b) Let the two supplementary angles be $3x$ and $2x$.

We know that sum of two supplementary angles is 180°.

$\therefore \quad 3x + 2x = 180°$

$\Rightarrow \quad 5x = 180° \Rightarrow x = \frac{180°}{5} = 36°$

So, one angle $= 3x = 3 \times 36° = 108°$

and its supplementary angle $= 2x = 2 \times 36° = 72°$

Hence, supplementary angles are 108° and 72°.

10. (c) Given, $\angle AOC + \angle BOE = 80°$ ...(i)

and $\angle BOD = 30°$ ...(ii)

Since, lines AB and CD intersect at O.

$\therefore \quad \angle AOC = \angle BOD$ [vertically opposite angles]

$\Rightarrow \quad \angle AOC = 30°$ [from Eq. (ii)]

Now, on putting the value of $\angle AOC$ in Eq. (i), we get

$30° + \angle BOE = 80°$

$\Rightarrow \quad \angle BOE = 80° - 30° = 50°$

11. (a) $\because$ AB and PQ intersect each other.

$\therefore \quad \angle POA = \angle BOQ$ [vertically opposite angles]

$\therefore \quad \angle BOQ = 65°$ [given, $\angle POA = 65°$]

12. (b) Since, AOB is a straight line.

$\therefore \angle AOP + \angle POR + \angle ROB = 180°$

$\Rightarrow \quad 2x + 3x + 5° + 45° = 180°$

$\Rightarrow \quad 5x = 180° - 50°$

$\Rightarrow \quad 5x = 130°$

$\Rightarrow \quad x = 26°$

So, $\angle POR - \angle POA = 3x + 5° - 2x$

$= x + 5°$

$= 26° + 5° = 31°$

13. (a) Since, POQ is a line segment.

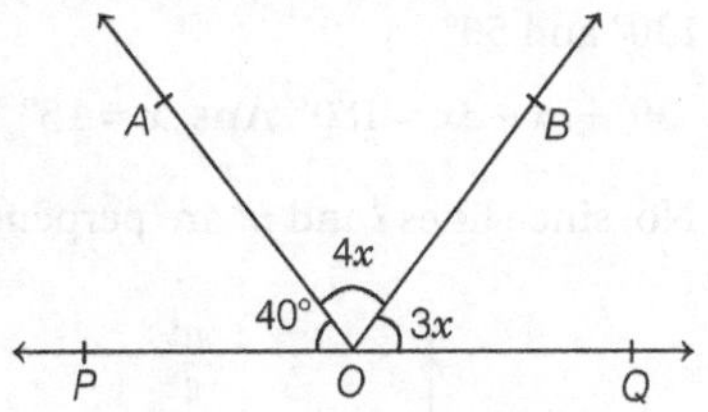

$\therefore \quad \angle POQ = 180°$

$\Rightarrow \quad \angle POA + \angle AOB + \angle BOQ = 180°$

$\Rightarrow \quad 40° + 4x + 3x = 180°$

[putting $\angle POA = 40°$, $\angle AOB = 4x$ and $\angle BOQ = 3x$]

$\Rightarrow \quad 7x = 180° - 40°$

$\Rightarrow \quad 7x = 140°$

$\Rightarrow \quad x = \dfrac{140°}{7}$

$\Rightarrow \quad x = 20°$

14. (c) Let $3\angle A = 4\angle B = 6\angle C = k$, then $\angle A = \dfrac{k}{3}$,

$\angle B = \dfrac{k}{4}$ and $\angle C = \dfrac{k}{6}$

$\therefore A : B : C = \dfrac{k}{3} : \dfrac{k}{4} : \dfrac{k}{6} = 4 : 3 : 2$

15. (b) Since, $l \parallel m$ and $m \parallel n$.

So, $\quad \angle PQC = \angle DQR$ [vertically opposite angles]

$\therefore \quad \angle DQR = 105°$ [given, $\angle PQC = 105°$]

Also, $\quad \angle PQC = \angle QRE$ [corresponding angles]

$\therefore \quad \angle QRE = 105°$

Thus, $\angle DQR + \angle QRE = 105° + 105° = 210°$

16. (b) **Assertion** Here, $\angle AOC + \angle BOC = 180°$

[linear pair]

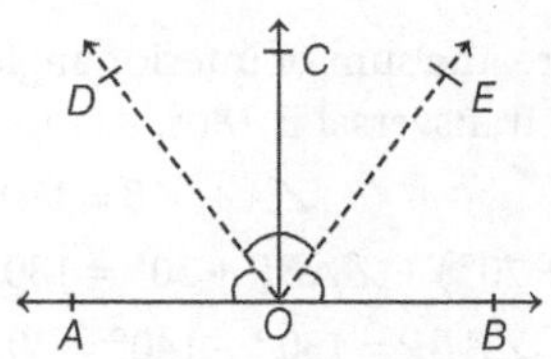

$\Rightarrow \quad \dfrac{1}{2}(\angle AOC + \angle BOC) = \dfrac{180°}{2}$

$\Rightarrow \quad \dfrac{\angle AOC}{2} + \dfrac{\angle BOC}{2} = 90°$

$\Rightarrow \quad \angle DOC + \angle EOC = 90°$

Thus, the bisectors of the angles of a linear pair are at right angle. So, Assertion is correct.

Also, Reason is true by linear pair axiom, but it is not the correct explanation for Assertion.

17. (d) **Assertion** Two adjacent angles do not always form a linear pair.

$\therefore$ Assertion is incorrect.

Reason In a linear pair of angles, two non-common arms are opposite rays.

Hence, Assertion is incorrect but Reason is correct.

18. (c) **Assertion** Let l and m be two parallel lines and $n \perp l$.

$\angle OAB = 90°$

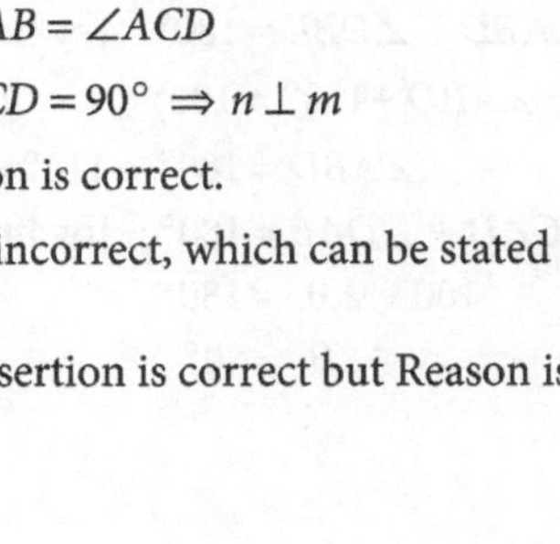

Since, $\quad l \parallel m$

$\Rightarrow \quad \angle OAB = \angle ACD$

$\Rightarrow \quad \angle ACD = 90° \Rightarrow n \perp m$

$\therefore$ Assertion is correct.

Reason is incorrect, which can be stated in the parallel lines.

Hence, Assertion is correct but Reason is not correct.

19. (i) $3z + 60° + z = 180°$ [linear pair]

$\Rightarrow 4z = 120° \Rightarrow z = 30°$

(ii) $y = 3z$ [vertically opposite angles]

$\Rightarrow y = 3 \times 30° = 90°$

(iii) (a) $2x + y = 180°$ [linear pair]

Or

(b) $2x + 3z = 180°$ [linear pair]

20. (i) Since, $l_1 \parallel l_2$ and m is a transversal line.

Therefore, the sum of interior angles on the same side of a transversal is 180°.

$\therefore \angle A + \angle B = 180°$

$\Rightarrow (40° + 70°) + \angle ABP + 30° = 180°$

$\Rightarrow \angle ABP = 180° - 140° = 40°$

(ii) Since, l_1 is a straight line.

$\therefore \angle EAB + 70° + 40° = 180°$

$\Rightarrow \angle EAB = 180° - 110° = 70°$

(iii) (a) $\angle ABD = \angle ABP + \angle PBD = 40° + 30° = 70°$

Since, $l_1 \parallel l_2$ and m is a transversal line.

$\therefore \angle FBA + \angle EAB = 180°$ [co-interior angles]

$\Rightarrow \angle FBA + 70° = 180°$

$\Rightarrow \angle FBA = 110°$

Or

(b) The result $\angle EAB = \angle ABD$ shows the property of alternate interior angles.

21. (i) **Hint** Alternate interior angles are equal. **Ans.** 30°

(ii) We know that the sum of the co-interior angles which are same side of the transversal line is 180°.

$\therefore \angle ABC + \angle BCD = 180°$

(iii) (a) Given, $\angle BOC = 30°$

We know that vertically opposite angles are equal, then $\angle AOD = \angle BOC$

$\Rightarrow \angle AOD = 30°$

Or

(b) **Hint** Vertically opposite angles and alternate interior angles are equal to each other.

Ans. 30° and 45°

22. (i) In the question figure,

$\angle ABD + \angle DBE = 180°$ [by linear pair axiom]

$\Rightarrow \angle ABD + 110° = 180°$ [$\because \angle DBE = 110°$]

$\Rightarrow \angle ABD = 180° - 110° = 70°$

(ii) $\angle GAD + \angle DAB = 180°$ [by linear pair axiom]

$\Rightarrow 100 + \angle\theta_1 = 180°$

$\Rightarrow \angle\theta_1 = 80°$

(iii) (a) $\angle FDK = \angle CDB$

[by vertically opposite angles]

$\Rightarrow \theta_2 = 70°$

If two lines intersect each other at a point, then opposite angles formed due to intersection are called vertically opposite angles.

Or

(b) Also, HDA is a straight line.

Therefore,

$\angle\theta_3 + \theta_2 + 30° = 180°$

$\Rightarrow \angle\theta_3 + 70° + 30° = 180°$

$\Rightarrow \angle\theta_3 = 180° - 100° = 80°$

If a ray stands on a line, then the sum of two adjacent angles, so formed is 180° i.e. the sum of the linear pair is 180°.

Part II

1. **Hint** $4x + 2x + x + 150° = 360°$

$\Rightarrow 7x + 150° = 360°$ **Ans.** $x = 30°$

2. **Hint** Let two supplementary angles be $13x$ and $5x$, respectively.

Then, $13x + 5x = 180° \Rightarrow x = 10°$

Therefore, angles are 130° and 50°.

Ans. 130° and 50°

3. **Hint** $30° + 7x + 3x = 180°$ **Ans.** $x = 15°$

4. **Hint** No, since lines l and m are perpendicular to the line n.

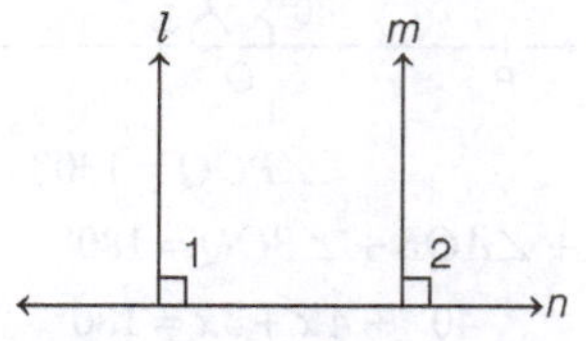

$\therefore \angle 1 = \angle 2 = 90°$ [$\because l \perp n$ and $m \perp n$]

It implies that these are corresponding angles.

Hence, $l \parallel m$

5. We know that sum of all the angles around a point is 360°.

$\therefore a + b + c + d = 360°$ ...(i)

Since, we have

$a - c = d - b$

$\Rightarrow a + b = c + d$ ...(ii)

From Eqs. (i) and (ii), we get

$2(a + b) = 360° \Rightarrow a + b = \frac{360°}{2}$

$\Rightarrow a + b = 180°$

$\therefore POQ$ is a straight line.

6. Given, AOB is a line and $OP \perp AB$.

$\therefore \quad \angle AOP = \angle BOP = 90°$

Now, $\quad \angle AOP = 90°$

$\Rightarrow \quad \angle AOQ + \angle POQ = 90° = \angle BOP$

On adding $\angle POQ$ both sides, we get

$\angle AOQ + \angle POQ + \angle POQ = \angle BOP + \angle POQ$

$\Rightarrow \quad \angle AOQ + 2\angle POQ = \angle BOQ$

$\Rightarrow \quad 2\angle POQ = \angle BOQ - \angle AOQ$

$\Rightarrow \quad \angle POQ = \frac{1}{2}(\angle BOQ - \angle AOQ)$

7. Let one of the angle be x.

Then, its complementary angle be $(90° - x)$.

According to the question,

$2x = 3(90° - x)$

$\Rightarrow \quad 2x = 270° - 3x$

$\Rightarrow \quad 5x = 270° \Rightarrow x = 54°$

$\therefore \quad 90° - x = 90° - 54° = 36°$

Thus, the measure of the larger angle is 54°.

8. In the given figure,

$\angle AOC + \angle COB = 180°$ [$\because AB$ is a straight line]

$\Rightarrow \quad 110° + 2x + 30° = 180°$

$\Rightarrow \quad 2x = 40° \Rightarrow x = 20°$

9. Given, $\angle PQR = \angle PRQ = 75°$ ...(i)

ST is a straight line, so

$\angle PQR + \angle PQS = 180°$ ...(ii)

and $\angle PRQ + \angle PRT = 180°$ ...(iii)

From Eqs.(ii) and (iii), we get

$\angle PQR + \angle PQS = \angle PRQ + \angle PRT$

$\Rightarrow \quad \angle PQR + \angle PQS = \angle PQR + \angle PRT$ [from Eq.(i)]

$\Rightarrow \quad \angle PQS = \angle PRT$

$\therefore \quad \angle PQR = \angle PRQ$

From Eq. (ii), we have

$\angle PQR + \angle PQS = 180°$

$\Rightarrow \quad 75° + \angle PQS = 180°$ [from Eq. (i)]

$\Rightarrow \quad \angle PQS = 180° - 75° = 105°$

10. In the given figure, DB is a straight line.

$\therefore \quad \angle AOD + \angle AOB = 180°$ ...(i)

$\Rightarrow \quad \angle AOD + 123° = 180°$

$\Rightarrow \quad m + 123° = 180°$

$\Rightarrow \quad m = 180° - 123°$

$\therefore \quad m = 57°$

Now, $m = 2n$

$\Rightarrow \quad n = \frac{m}{2} = 28.5°$

11. In the given figure,

$\angle ACB = \angle DCE$

[vertically opposite angles]

$\Rightarrow \quad \angle ACB = 55°$ [given, $\angle DCE = 55°$] ...(i)

Now, $\quad AC = AB$ [given]

$\Rightarrow \quad \angle ABC = \angle ACB$

$\Rightarrow \quad \angle ABC = 55°$ [from Eq. (i)]

12. Given, $\quad AC = AB$

i.e. $\quad \angle ACB = \angle ABC$

$\Rightarrow \quad \angle ACB = x$

$\Rightarrow \quad x = \angle DCE$

[vertically opposite angles]

$\Rightarrow \quad x = 40°$ [$\because \angle DCE = 40°$]

13. Since, AB intersect CD at O,

$\therefore \quad \angle u = 40°$ [vertically opposite angles]

Also, CD and EF intersect each other at O,

$\therefore \quad \angle y = 80°$

Now, since COD is a line,

$\therefore \quad \angle u + \angle z + 80° = 180°$

$\Rightarrow \quad 40° + \angle z + 80° = 180°$

$\Rightarrow \quad \angle z = 60°$

Now, since COD is a line.

$\therefore \quad \angle y + \angle x + 40° = 180°$

$\Rightarrow \quad 80° + \angle x + 40° = 180°$

$\Rightarrow \quad \angle x = 60°$

Hence, $x = 60°$, $y = 80°$, $z = 60°$ and $u = 40°$

14. In the given figure,

$\angle BCD = \angle CDB = 70°$ [$\because BC = BD$]

Now, $\quad \angle HAB = 40°$

$\Rightarrow \quad \angle GAF = \angle HAB$

[vertically opposite angles]

$\Rightarrow \quad \angle GAF = 40°$

$\therefore \quad \angle GAF = \angle GFA = 40°$ [$\because GA = GF$]

Again, $\angle ABE = \angle AEB = 65°$ [$\because AE = AB$]

15. **Hint** Consider lines l and m be two intersecting lines. Again, let n and p be another two lines which are perpendicular to the intersecting lines and meet each other at point D.

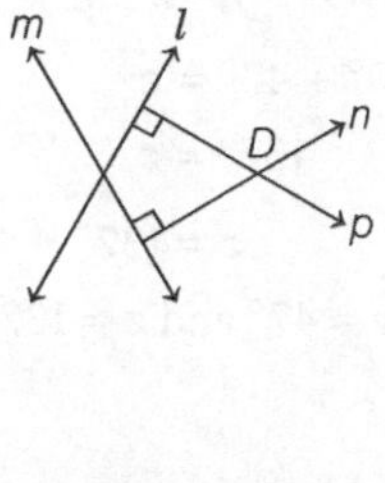

Suppose, we consider lines n and p are not intersecting, then it means they are parallel to each other

i.e. $n \parallel p$ ...(i)

Since, lines n and p are perpendicular to m and l, respectively.

But from Eq. (i), $n \parallel p$, which implies that $l \parallel m$.

This is a contradiction.

Thus, our assumption is wrong.

Hence, two perpendicular lines n and p drawn on two intersecting lines meet at a point D.

16. Since, $AB \parallel CD$, $PQ \perp AB$

$\therefore \quad \angle QPR = 90^\circ$

Now, $\angle APQ + \angle QPR = 180^\circ$ [linear pair axiom]

$\Rightarrow \quad \angle APQ = 180^\circ - 90^\circ = 90^\circ$

$\therefore \quad \angle APQ = 90^\circ$

Also, $\angle PRQ = \angle RQD$ [alternate interior angles]

$\therefore \quad \angle PRQ = 53^\circ$

Now, $\angle PRQ + \angle BRQ = 180^\circ$ [linear pair axiom]

$\Rightarrow \quad 53^\circ + \angle BRQ = 180^\circ$

$\Rightarrow \quad \angle BRQ = 180^\circ - 53^\circ = 127^\circ$

17. Hint Do same as Q. 1 NCERT Folder Exercise 6.2.

Ans. 117°

18. Since, $PQ \perp CD$ and $RS \perp AB$.

$\therefore \quad \angle PRS = 90^\circ$

$\Rightarrow \quad \angle PRQ + \angle QRS = 90^\circ$

$\Rightarrow \quad 43^\circ + \angle QRS = 90^\circ$ [given, $\angle PRQ = 43^\circ$]

$\Rightarrow \quad \angle QRS = 90^\circ - 43^\circ = 47^\circ$

$\therefore \quad y = 47^\circ$ ...(i)

Now, $\angle QRB = \angle RQC$ [alternate angles]

$\Rightarrow \quad y + 90^\circ = x + 90^\circ$

[$\because \angle PQC = \angle BRS = 90^\circ$]

$\Rightarrow \quad 47^\circ + 90^\circ = x + 90^\circ$ [form Eq. (i)]

$\Rightarrow \quad x = 47^\circ$ ...(ii)

Since, $AB \parallel CD$ and $CD \parallel WY$, therefore $AB \parallel WY$ and RX is a transversal.

$\therefore \quad \angle BRX = \angle WXR$ [alternate angles]

$\Rightarrow \quad \angle BRS + y = z$

$\Rightarrow \quad 90^\circ + 47^\circ = z$ [from Eq. (i)]

$\Rightarrow \quad 137^\circ = z$

$\therefore \quad z = 137^\circ$

Hence, $x = 47^\circ, y = 47^\circ$ and $z = 137^\circ$

19. The arms of the angles may be parallel in the same sense or in the opposite sense, so three cases arise.

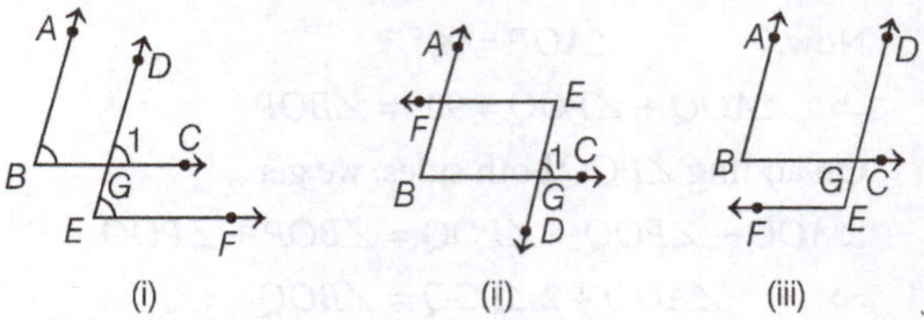

Case I When both pair of arms are parallel in same sense [Fig. (i)].

In this case, $BA \parallel ED$ and BC is the transversal.

$\therefore \quad \angle ABC = \angle 1$ ...(i)

Again, $BC \parallel EF$ and DE is the transversal.

$\therefore \quad \angle 1 = \angle DEF$ [by corresponding angle axiom]

Hence, $\angle ABC = \angle DEF$ [from Eq. (i)]

Case II When both pair of arms are parallel in opposite sense [Fig. (ii)].

In this case, $BA \parallel ED$ and BC is the transversal.

$\therefore \quad \angle ABC = \angle 1$

Again, $EF \parallel BC$ and ED is the transversal.

$\therefore \quad \angle DEF = \angle 1$ [alternate interior angles]

Hence, $\angle ABC = \angle DEF$

Case III When one pair of arms is parallel in same sense and the other is parallel in opposite sense [Fig. (iii)].

In this case, $BA \parallel ED$ and BC is the transversal.

$\therefore \angle EGB = \angle ABC$ [alternate interior angles] ...(ii)

Now, $BC \parallel EF$ and DE is the transversal.

$\therefore \angle DEF + \angle EGB = 180^\circ$

$\Rightarrow \angle DEF + \angle ABC = 180^\circ$ [from Eq. (ii)]

Hence, $\angle ABC$ and $\angle DEF$ are supplementary angles.

20. In the given figure,

QS is a straight line.

i.e. $\angle QRP + \angle PRS = 180^\circ$ [linear pair axiom]

$\Rightarrow \quad \angle QRP + 135^\circ = 180^\circ$ [given]

$\Rightarrow \quad \angle QRP = 180^\circ - 135^\circ = 45^\circ$

Now, $\angle PRQ = \angle TRS$

[$\because$ vertically opposite angles]

$\angle TRS = 45^\circ$ ...(i) [$\because \angle QRP = 45^\circ$]

$\therefore$ QS is a straight line.

$\Rightarrow \quad \angle QRU + \angle TRU + \angle TRS = 180^\circ$

$\Rightarrow \quad 55^\circ + \angle TRU + \angle TRS = 180^\circ$ [given]

$\Rightarrow \quad 55^\circ + \angle TRU + 45^\circ = 180^\circ$ [from Eq. (i)]

$\Rightarrow \quad \angle TRU = 80^\circ$

21. Lines AB and CD are intersect at the point O.

Then, $\angle AOD + z = 180°$

$\Rightarrow z = 110°$ $[\because \angle AOD = 70°]$

AB is a straight line.

$\therefore x + x + 90° + \angle AOD = 180°$

$\Rightarrow 2x + 90° + 70° = 180°$ $[\because \angle AOD = 70°]$

$\Rightarrow 2x = 20° \Rightarrow x = 10°$

In the given figure, $\angle AOD = 2y + x$

[$\because$ vertically opposite angles]

$\Rightarrow 70° = 2y + 10°$

$\therefore y = 30°$

22. As we know that

The sum of all the angles around a point is 360°

i.e. $x + 2x + 20° + 3x + 4x + 10° + 5x + 5x + 6° + 6x = 360°$

$\Rightarrow 26x + 36° = 360°$

$\Rightarrow 26x = 360° - 36°$

$\Rightarrow 26x = 324° \Rightarrow x = 12.5°$

$\therefore \angle ABO = \angle AOB = x$ $[\because AB = AO]$

$\Rightarrow \angle ABO = 12.5°$

By vertically opposite angles,

$\angle ABO = \angle DBC = 12.5°$

23. (i) In the given figure,

$BC = BO$

i.e. $\angle BCO = \angle BOC$

$\therefore \angle BOC = 45°$ [given, $\angle BCO = 45°$]

(ii) CE and DE intersect at the point O.

$\Rightarrow \angle AOE + \angle AOB = \angle COD$

[vertically opposite angles]

$\Rightarrow x + 4x = 135°$ $[\because \angle COD = 135°]$

$\Rightarrow 5x = 135°$

$\Rightarrow x = 27°$

$\therefore \angle AOE = 27°$

(iii) $\angle AOB = 4x = 4 \times 27°$ [from above part]

$= 108°$

(iv) Given, $AO = AE$

i.e. $\angle AOE = \angle AEO$

$\Rightarrow \angle AEO = 27°$ [from part (ii)]

24. Hint Do same as Q. 3 NCERT Folder Exercise 6.2.

Ans. 75°

25. Hint Do same as Q. 5 NCERT Folder Exercise 6.2.

Ans. (ii) 30°

Mind Map

LINES AND ANGLES

Basic Terms

1. Point

A point is an exact location and is represented by a fine dot.

2. Line

A line is a straight path, which is endless in both directions. It is denoted by $\overleftrightarrow{AB}$.

3. Ray

A part of line with one end point. It is denoted by $\overrightarrow{AB}$.

4. Line Segment

A part of line with two end points. It is denoted by $\overline{AB}$.

Types of Angles

1. Acute Angle

An angle whose measure is more than 0° but less than 90°.

$0 < \angle AOB < 90°$

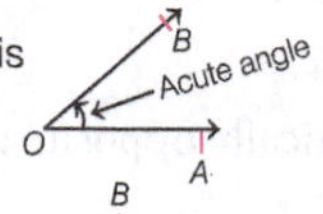

2. Right Angle

An angle whose measure is 90°.

$\angle AOB = 90°$

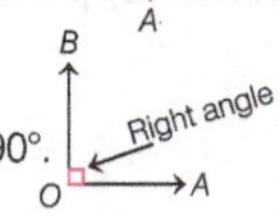

3. Obtuse Angle

An angle whose measure is more than 90° but less than 180°.

$90° < \angle AOB < 180°$

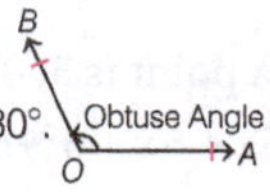

4. Straight Angle

An angle whose measure is 180°.

$\angle AOB = 180°$

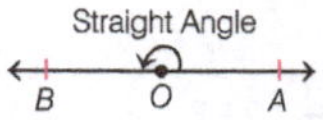

5. Reflex Angle

An angle whose measure is more than 180° but less than 360°.

$180° < \angle AOB < 360°$

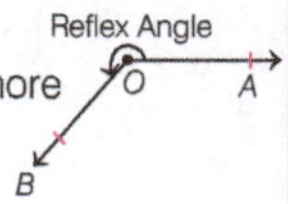

6. Complete Angle

An angle whose measure is 360°.

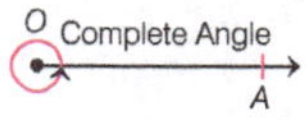

Angle

The angle formed by two rays with the same initial point. The common point *B* is known as vertex. The ray ($\overrightarrow{BA}$ and $\overrightarrow{BC}$) forming the angle are called arms.

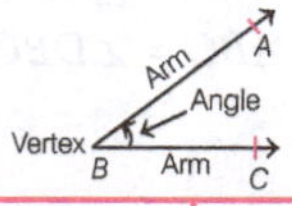

Collinear and Non-Collinear Points

Collinear Points

If three or more than three points lie on the same line.

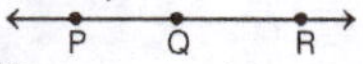

Non-Collinear Points

If three or more points do not lie on the same line.

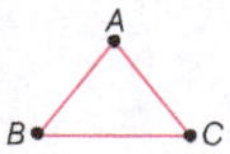

Intersecting and Non-Intersecting Lines

Intersecting Lines :

Lines *PQ* and *RS* are intersecting lines because they intersect each other at *O*.

Non-Intersecting Lines :

Lines which do not intersect each other. Here, *AB* and *CD* are non-intersecting (parallel) lines.

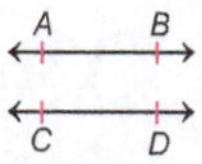

Relations between Pair of Angles

Axiom 1

If a ray stands on a line, then the sum of two adjacent angles is 180°.

i.e. $\angle AOC + \angle BOC = 180°$

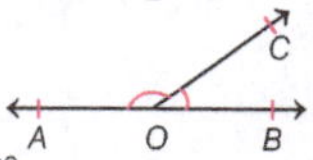

Axiom 2

If the sum of two adjacent angles is 180°, then the non-common arms of the angles form a line.

Theorem 1

If two lines intersect each other, then the vertically opposite angles are equal.

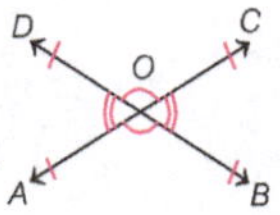

Theorem 2

Lines Parallel to the Same Line

Lines which are parallel to the same line, are parallel to each other

i.e. $a \| c$ and $b \| c$, then $a \| b$.

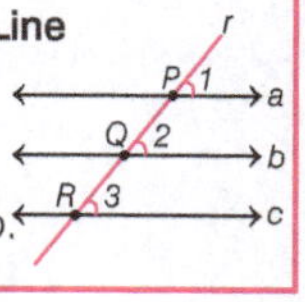

Pair of Angles

1. Complementary Angles

Two angles are complementary, if the sum of their angles is 90°.

$\angle BOC + \angle AOC = 90°$

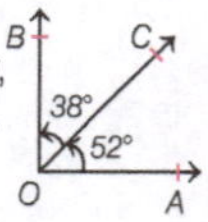

2. Supplementary Angles

Two angles are supplementary, if the sum of their angles is 180°.

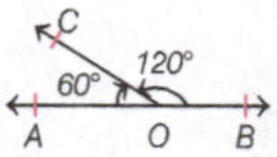

3. Bisector of an Angles

A ray which divides an angle into two equal parts.

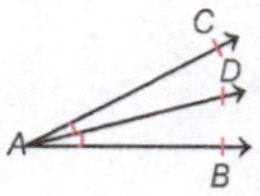

4. Adjacent Angles

Two angles are adjacent, if they have common vertex, common arm and their non-common arms are on different sides of the common arm.

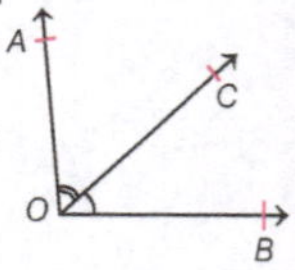

5. Linear Pair of Angles

If the non-common arms of two adjacent angles form a line, then $\angle AOC$ & $\angle BOC$ form a linear pair of angles.

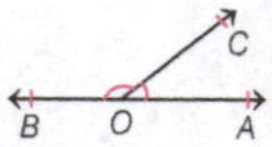

6. Vertically Opposite Angles

The opposite angles formed due to intersection of two lines. $\angle AOC$ & $\angle BOD$ are vertically opposite angles. Similarly, $\angle AOD$ & $\angle BOC$ are vertically opposite angles.

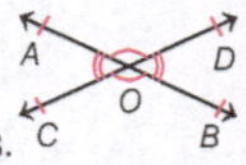

Topics to be Assessed Formatively

Parallel Lines and a Transversal Line

Parallel Lines

If two lines lie in the same plane and do not intersect when produced on either side, then such lines are said to be parallel to each other.

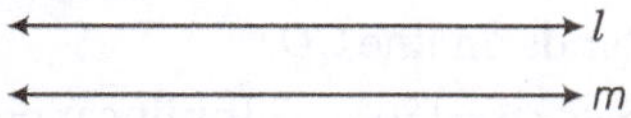

If l and m are two parallel lines, we write $l \parallel m$ and read it as l is parallel to m.

Clearly, when $l \parallel m$, then $m \parallel l$.

Transversal Line

A straight line which cuts two or more straight lines at distinct points, is called a **transversal line**.

In the figure given below, line l is a transversal of the lines m and n, respectively. If line l intersects m and n at points P and Q respectively, then four angles are formed at each of the points P and Q namely $\angle 1, \angle 2, \angle 3, \ldots, \angle 8$.

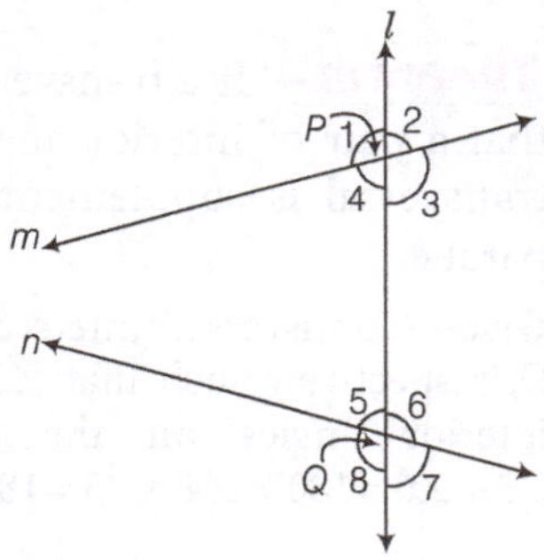

Angles $\angle 1$, $\angle 2$, $\angle 7$ and $\angle 8$ are called **exterior angles** while angles $\angle 3$, $\angle 4$, $\angle 5$ and $\angle 6$ are called **interior angles.**

Thus, we get some pairs of angles which are given below:

I. **Corresponding angles** The angles on the same side of a transversal are known as the corresponding angles, if both lie either above the two lines or below the two lines. In the above figure, pair of corresponding angles are

(*a*) $\angle 1$ and $\angle 5$ (*b*) $\angle 2$ and $\angle 6$

(*c*) $\angle 4$ and $\angle 8$ (*d*) $\angle 3$ and $\angle 7$

II. **Alternate angles** When two lines are crossed by another line, the pair of angles on opposite sides of the transversal, is called alternate angles.

(*i*) **Alternate interior angles** The following pair of angles are called alternate interior angles:

(*a*) $\angle 4$ and $\angle 6$ (*b*) $\angle 3$ and $\angle 5$

Note Sometimes, we simply use the word alternate angles for alternate interior angles.

(*ii*) **Alternate exterior angles** The following pair of angles are called alternate exterior angles:

(*a*) $\angle 1$ and $\angle 7$ (*b*) $\angle 2$ and $\angle 8$

III. **Interior angles on the same side of the transversal** The pair of interior angles on the same side of the transversal are called **consecutive interior angles** or **allied angles** or **cointerior angles.** In the given figure, pair of interior angles are

(*a*) $\angle 4$ and $\angle 5$ (*b*) $\angle 3$ and $\angle 6$

Some Axioms and Theorems

When line m is parallel to line n and a transversal l intersects them, then the relation between angles, thus formed are obtained as axioms and theorems which are given below:

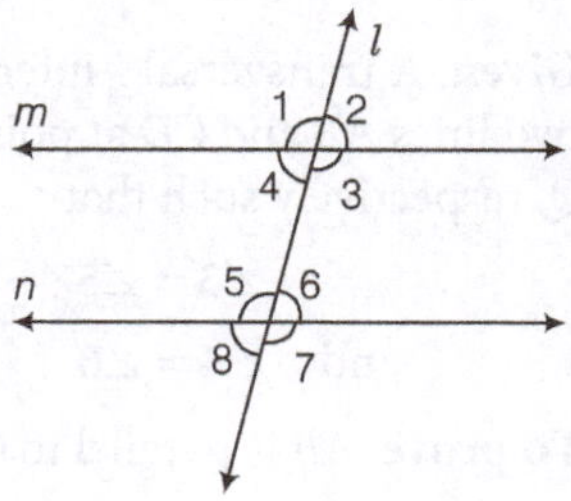

Axiom 1 If a transversal intersects two parallel lines, then each pair of corresponding angles is equal. This axiom is known as **corresponding angle axiom.**

Here, $\angle 1 = \angle 5, \angle 2 = \angle 6$

and $\angle 4 = \angle 8, \angle 3 = \angle 7$

Axiom 2 If a transversal intersects two lines such that a pair of corresponding angles is equal, then the two lines are parallel to each other (converse of axiom 1).

Theorem 1 If a transversal intersects two parallel lines, then each pair of alternate interior angles is equal.

Given $AB \parallel CD$ and a transversal r cuts AB at P and CD at Q and make two pairs of alternate interior angles ($\angle 3$, $\angle 5$) and ($\angle 4$, $\angle 6$).

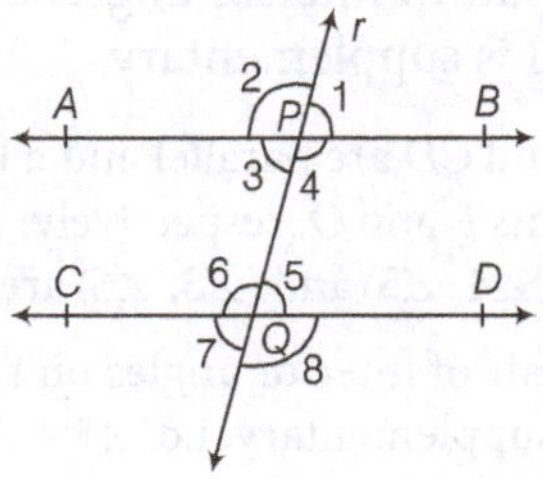

To prove $\angle 3 = \angle 5$ and $\angle 4 = \angle 6$

Proof We have,

$\angle 1 = \angle 3$ [vertically opposite angles] ...(i)

and $\angle 1 = \angle 5$ [corresponding angles] ...(ii)

From Eqs. (i) and (ii), we get

$\angle 3 = \angle 5$

Again, $\angle 2 = \angle 4$ [vertically opposite angles] ...(iii)

and $\angle 2 = \angle 6$ [corresponding angles] ...(iv)

From Eqs. (iii) and (iv), we get

$\angle 4 = \angle 6$

Hence, $\angle 3 = \angle 5$

and $\angle 4 = \angle 6$ **Hence proved.**

Theorem 2 If a transversal intersects two lines, such that a pair of alternate interior angles is equal, then the two lines are parallel. [Converse of theorem 1]

Given A transversal r intersects two lines AB and CD at points P and Q, respectively such that

$\angle 3 = \angle 5$

and $\angle 4 = \angle 6$

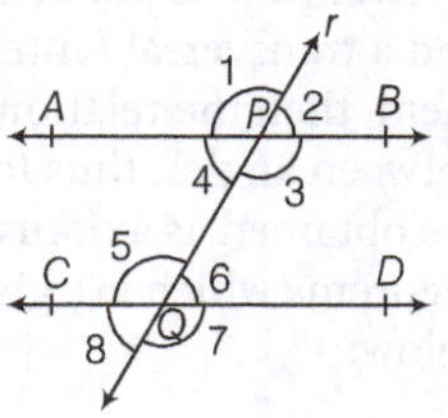

To prove AB is parallel to CD.

i.e. $AB \parallel CD$

Proof We have,

$\angle 3 = \angle 5$ [alternate interior angles] ...(i)

and $\angle 3 = \angle 1$ [vertically opposite angles]...(ii)

Then, from Eqs. (i) and (ii), we get

$\angle 1 = \angle 5$

But these are corresponding angles.

So, $AB \parallel CD$

[by converse of corresponding angles axiom]

Hence proved.

Theorem 3 If a transversal intersects two parallel lines, then each pair of interior angles on the same side of the transversal is supplementary.

Given Lines AB and CD are parallel and a transversal r cuts AB and CD at points P and Q, respectively. Thus, two pairs of interior angles ($\angle 4$, $\angle 5$) and ($\angle 3$, $\angle 6$) are formed.

To prove Each pair of interior angles on the same side of the transversal is supplementary, i.e. $\angle 3 + \angle 6 = 180°$ and $\angle 4 + \angle 5 = 180°$.

Proof Here, ray PQ stands on line AB.

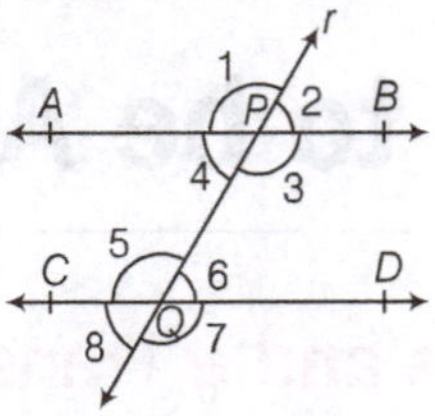

So, $\angle 4 + \angle 3 = 180°$ [by linear pair axiom] ...(i)

But $\angle 3 = \angle 5$ [alternate interior angles]

On putting $\angle 3 = \angle 5$ in Eq. (i), we get

$\angle 4 + \angle 5 = 180°$

Again, ray PQ stands on line CD.

Then, $\angle 5 + \angle 6 = 180°$ [by linear pair axiom]...(ii)

But $\angle 5 = \angle 3$ [alternate interior angles]

On putting $\angle 5 = \angle 3$ in Eq. (ii), we get

$\angle 3 + \angle 6 = 180°$

Hence, $\angle 3 + \angle 6 = 180°$ and $\angle 4 + \angle 5 = 180°$

Hence proved.

Theorem 4 If a transversal intersects two lines such that a pair of interior angles on the same side of the transversal is supplementary, then the two lines are parallel. [Converse of theorem 3]

Given A transversal r intersects two lines AB and CD at P and Q, respectively such that $\angle 3$, $\angle 6$ and $\angle 4$, $\angle 5$ are pairs of interior angles on the same side of r and $\angle 3 + \angle 6 = 180°$, $\angle 4 + \angle 5 = 180°$.

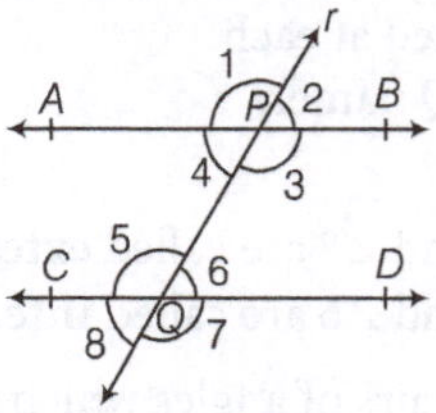

To prove $AB \parallel CD$

Proof Here, ray PB stands on line r.

$\therefore$ $\angle 2 + \angle 3 = 180°$ [by linear pair axiom] ...(i)

Also, $\angle 3 + \angle 6 = 180°$ [given]...(ii)

From Eqs. (i) and (ii), we get $\angle 2 + \angle 3 = \angle 3 + \angle 6$

On subtracting $\angle 3$ from both sides, we get

$\angle 2 = \angle 6$

But these are corresponding angles.

So, $AB \parallel CD$ [by converse of corresponding angles axiom]

Hence proved.

Problems Based on Axioms and Theorems

There are many types of problems which can be solved by using above axioms and theorems. There is no particular method to solve these problems but we can understand the way of using these axioms and theorems with the help of following examples:

Example 1. **In the given figure, it is given that $AB \parallel CD$ and r is a transversal. If $\angle 1 = (110° - x)$ and $\angle 5 = 4x$, then find the measures of $\angle 1$ and $\angle 5$.**

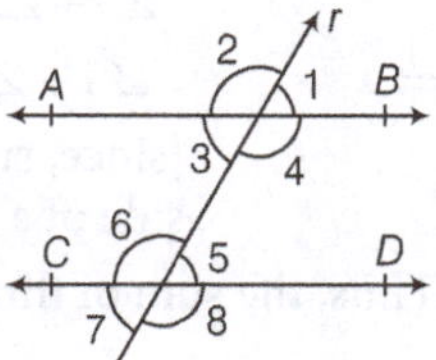

Using the property of corresponding angles, determine the value of x. Then, put the value of x in $\angle 1 = (110° - x)$ and $\angle 5 = 4x$, to get the measures of $\angle 1$ and $\angle 5$.

Sol. Given, $AB \parallel CD$, $\angle 1 = (110° - x)$ and $\angle 5 = 4x$

Here, $\angle 1 = \angle 5$ [corresponding angles axiom]

So, $110° - x = 4x \Rightarrow 4x + x = 110°$

$\Rightarrow 5x = 110° \Rightarrow x = \frac{110°}{5} = 22°$

$\therefore \angle 1 = 110° - x = 110° - 22° = 88°$

and $\angle 5 = 4x = 4 \times 22° = 88°$

Example 2. **In the given figure, $AB \parallel CD$. What is the value of y?**

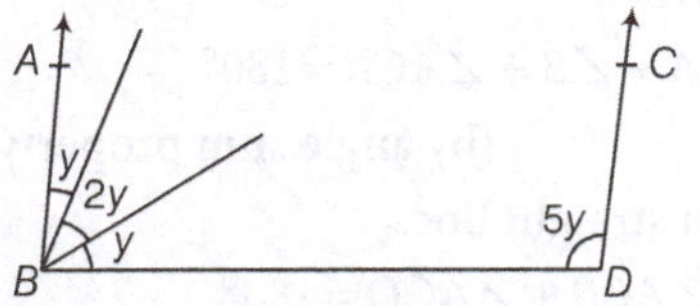

Sol. Given, $AB \parallel CD$ and BD is a transversal.

So, $\angle ABD + \angle CDB = 180°$ [cointerior angles]

$\Rightarrow y + 2y + y + 5y = 180°$

[$\because \angle ABD = y + 2y + y = 4y$ and $\angle CDB = 5y$]

$\Rightarrow 9y = 180° \Rightarrow y = \frac{180°}{9}$

$\Rightarrow y = 20°$

Hence, the value of y is $20°$.

Example 3. **In the given figure, $m \parallel n$ and $\angle 1$ and $\angle 2$ are in the ratio $3:2$. Determine all the angles from 1 to 8.**

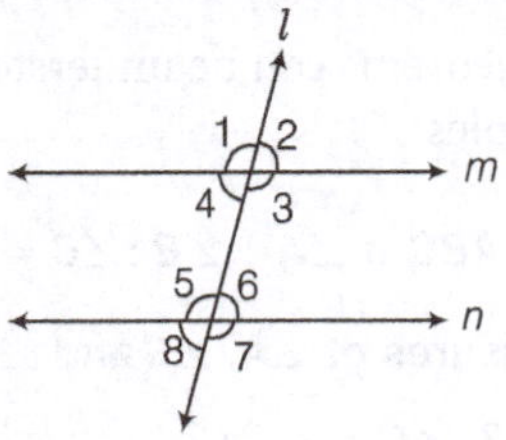

Sol. Given, $m \parallel n$ and ratio between $\angle 1$ and $\angle 2$ is $3 : 2$.

Let $\angle 1 = 3x$ and $\angle 2 = 2x$ ...(i)

Here, m is a line and ray l stands on it.

$\therefore \angle 1 + \angle 2 = 180°$ [by linear pair axiom]

$\Rightarrow 3x + 2x = 180° \Rightarrow 5x = 180°$

$\Rightarrow x = \frac{180°}{5} = 36°$

On putting the value of x in Eq. (i), we get

$\angle 1 = 3x = 3 \times 36° = 108°$

and $\angle 2 = 2x = 2 \times 36° = 72°$

Here, $m \parallel n$ and l is a transversal.

So, we know that, corresponding angles are equal.

$\therefore \angle 1 = \angle 5 = 108°$ and $\angle 2 = \angle 6 = 72°$

Also, we know that, alternate interior angles are equal.

$\therefore \angle 5 = \angle 3 = 108°$ and $\angle 6 = \angle 4 = 72°$

We know that, corresponding angles are equal.

$\therefore \angle 3 = \angle 7 = 108°$ and $\angle 4 = \angle 8 = 72°$

Hence, $\angle 1 = \angle 3 = \angle 5 = \angle 7 = 108°$

and $\angle 2 = \angle 4 = \angle 6 = \angle 8 = 72°$

Example 4. **In the given figure, if $\angle 2 = 120°$ and $\angle 5 = 60°$, then show that $a \parallel b$.**

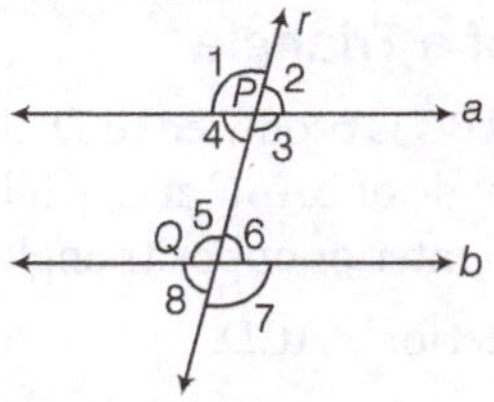

Sol. Given, $\angle 2 = 120°$ and $\angle 5 = 60°$

Also, transversal r intersects two lines a and b at P and Q, respectively.

Here, $\angle 2 = \angle 4$ [vertically opposite angles]

$\therefore \angle 4 = \angle 2 = 120°$

Now, $\angle 4 + \angle 5 = 120° + 60° \Rightarrow \angle 4 + \angle 5 = 180°$

So, $\angle 4$ and $\angle 5$ are supplementary angles.

Since, a is a straight line.

$\therefore \angle 4 + \angle 3 = 180°$ [by linear pair axiom]

$\Rightarrow 120° + \angle 3 = 180°$

$\Rightarrow \angle 3 = 180° - 120° = 60°$

Now, $\angle 7 = \angle 5 = 60°$ [vertically opposite angles]

Here, $\angle 7 + \angle 8 = 180°$ [by linear pair axiom]

$\therefore 60° + \angle 8 = 180°$

$\Rightarrow \angle 8 = 180° - 60° = 120°$

$\because \angle 6 = \angle 8 = 120°$ [vertically opposite angles]

$\therefore \angle 3 + \angle 6 = 60° + 120° = 180°$

So, $\angle 3$ and $\angle 6$ are supplementary angles.

Thus, transversal r intersects lines a and b such that pair of interior angles on the same side of the transversal is supplementary. Hence, lines a and b are parallel.

Hence proved.

Angles Sum Property of a Triangle

Triangle

A closed figure formed by three intersecting lines is called a triangle. A triangle has three sides, three angles and three vertices. We denote a triangle by the symbol Δ. The line segments AB, BC and CA form sides of ΔABC. A, B and C are vertices of the triangle and $\angle A$, $\angle B$ and $\angle C$ are three angles of ΔABC.

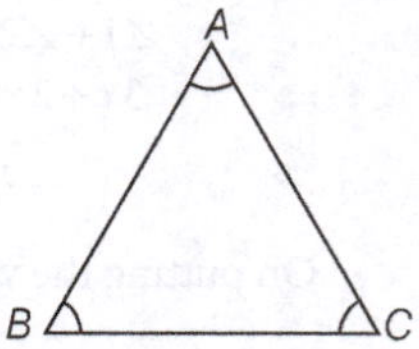

Interior Angles of a Triangle

In ΔABC, the angles A, B and C are called interior angles of ΔABC.

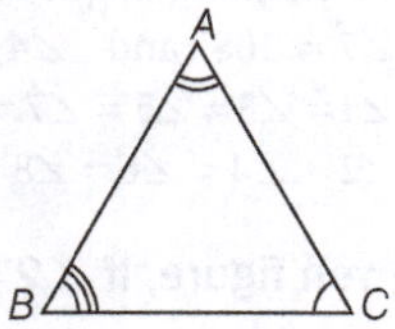

Exterior Angle of a Triangle

If the side BC of ΔABC is produced to D, then $\angle ACD$ is called an exterior angle of ΔABC at C, while $\angle BAC$ and $\angle ABC$ are called its interior opposite angles.

It is denoted by exterior $\angle ACD$.

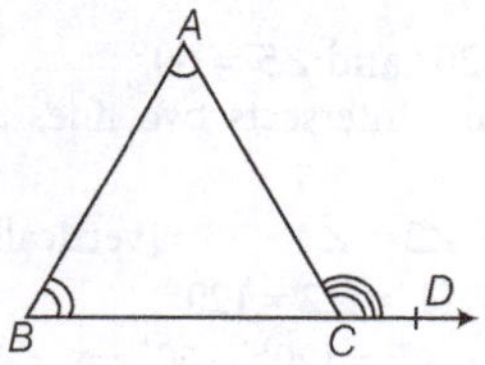

Theorem 1 The sum of the angles of a triangle is 180°.

Given A ΔABC whose angles are represented by 1, 2 and 3, i.e. $\angle B = \angle 1$, $\angle C = \angle 2$ and $\angle A = \angle 3$.

To prove Sum of the angles $= 180°$

i.e. $\angle 1 + \angle 2 + \angle 3 = 180°$

Construction Through A, draw a line PQ parallel to BC.

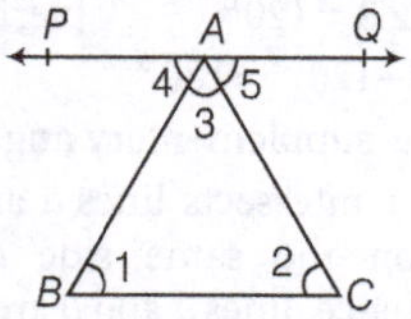

Proof Here, $PQ \parallel BC$ and AB is the transversal.

$\therefore \quad \angle 1 = \angle 4$ [alternate interior angles] ...(i)

Again, $PQ \parallel BC$ and AC is the transversal.

$\therefore \quad \angle 2 = \angle 5$ [alternate interior angles] ...(ii)

On adding Eqs. (i) and (ii), we get

$$\angle 1 + \angle 2 = \angle 4 + \angle 5$$

On adding $\angle 3$ in both sides, we get

$$\angle 1 + \angle 2 + \angle 3 = \angle 3 + \angle 4 + \angle 5$$

$\Rightarrow \quad \angle 1 + \angle 2 + \angle 3 = 180°$

[since, sum of all the angles formed on the same side of a line at a given point on the line is 180°]

Thus, the sum of three angles of a triangle is 180°.

Hence proved.

Theorem 2 If a side of a triangle is produced, then the exterior angle so formed is equal to the sum of the two interior opposite angles.

Given A ΔABC in which side BC is produced to D to form the exterior $\angle ACD$.

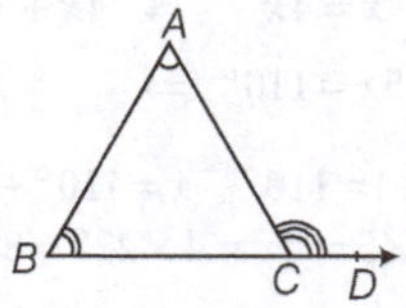

To prove $\angle A + \angle B = \angle ACD$

Proof In ΔABC,

$\angle A + \angle B + \angle ACB = 180°$ ...(i)

[by angle sum property of a triangle]

Here, BCD is a straight line.

$\therefore \quad \angle ACB + \angle ACD = 180°$ ...(ii)

From Eqs. (i) and (ii), we get

$$\angle A + \angle B + \angle ACB = \angle ACB + \angle ACD$$

$\Rightarrow \quad \angle A + \angle B = \angle ACD$ **Hence proved.**

Note

- A triangle cannot have more than one right angle.
- A triangle cannot have more than one obtuse angle.
- In a right angled triangle, the sum of two acute angles is 90°.
- An exterior angle of a triangle is greater than either of its interior opposite angles.

Problems Based on Theorems 1 and 2

The use of these theorems can be understood with the help of following examples:

Example 5. In ΔABC, if $\angle A : \angle B : \angle C = \frac{1}{2} : \frac{1}{3} : \frac{1}{6}$, then calculate the measures of $\angle A$, $\angle B$ and $\angle C$.

Sol. Given, $\angle A : \angle B : \angle C = \frac{1}{2} : \frac{1}{3} : \frac{1}{6}$

Then, let $\angle A = \frac{x}{2}$, $\angle B = \frac{x}{3}$ and $\angle C = \frac{x}{6}$

In ΔABC, we know that

$$\angle A+\angle B+\angle C=180°$$

[by angle sum property of a triangle]

$$\Rightarrow \quad \frac{x}{2}+\frac{x}{3}+\frac{x}{6}=180°$$

$$\Rightarrow \quad \frac{3x+2x+x}{6}=180°$$

$$\Rightarrow \quad 3x+2x+x=180°\times 6$$

$$\Rightarrow \quad 6x=180°\times 6$$

$$\Rightarrow \quad x=\frac{180°\times 6}{6}=180°$$

Now, $\angle A=\frac{x}{2}=\frac{180°}{2}=90°$

$$\angle B=\frac{x}{3}=\frac{180°}{3}=60°$$

and $\angle C=\frac{x}{6}=\frac{180°}{6}=30°$

Example 6. In ΔABC, if $\angle A=(2x-5°)$, $\angle B=(5x+5°)$ and $\angle C=(3x+50°)$ then find the values of x and $\angle C$.

Use the property that sum of all angles of a triangle is 180°, to find the value of x and then find the measures of $\angle A$, $\angle B$ and $\angle C$.

Sol. Given, $\angle A=(2x-5°)$, $\angle B=(5x+5°)$

and $\angle C=(3x+50°)$

In ΔABC, $\angle A+\angle B+\angle C=180°$

[by angle sum property of a triangle]

$$\Rightarrow \quad (2x-5°)+(5x+5°)+(3x+50°)=180°$$

$$\Rightarrow \quad 10x+50°=180°$$

$$\Rightarrow \quad 10x=180°-50°$$

$$\Rightarrow \quad x=\frac{180°-50°}{10}=\frac{130°}{10}=13°$$

Hence, $\angle A=(2x-5°)=(2\times 13°-5°)=26°-5°=21°$

$$\angle B=(5x+5°)=(5\times 13°+5°)=(65°+5°)=70°$$

and $\angle C=(3x+50°)=(3\times 13°+50°)=(39°+50°)=89°$

Example 7. How many triangles can be drawn having its angles 53°, 64° and 63°? Give reason. NCERT Exemplar

Sol. Here, sum of angles $=53°+64°+63°=180°$

Hence, one triangle can be drawn by the given angles.

Example 8. Can a triangle have all angles less than 60°? Give reason. NCERT Exemplar

Sol. No, a triangle cannot have all the angles less than 60° because if all the angles will be less than 60°, then their sum will not be equal to 180°. Hence, it will not be a triangle.

Example 9. An exterior angle of a triangle is 105° and its two interior opposite angles are equal. Find each of these equal angles. NCERT Exemplar

Sol. Let each interior opposite angle of a triangle be x.

Given, exterior angle of a triangle $=105°$

$$\therefore \quad x+x=105°$$

[$\because$ exterior angle = the sum of opposite interior angles]

$$\Rightarrow \quad 2x=105°$$

$$\Rightarrow \quad x=\frac{105°}{2}$$

$$\Rightarrow \quad x=52\frac{1}{2}°$$

Example 10. In the given figure, if $QT\perp PR$, $\angle TQR=40°$ and $\angle SPR=30°$, then find x and y.

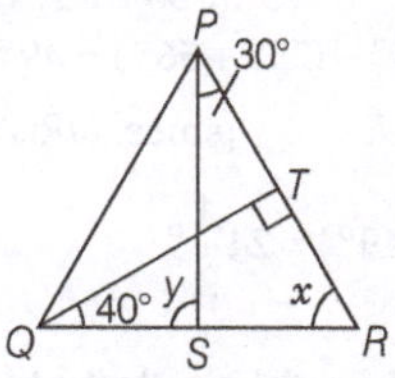

Sol. Given, $QT\perp PR$, $\angle TQR=40°$ and $\angle SPR=30°$

In ΔTQR, $\angle TQR+\angle QTR+\angle TRQ=180°$

[by angle sum property of a triangle]

$$\Rightarrow \quad 40°+90°+x=180°$$

$$\Rightarrow \quad 130°+x=180°$$

$$\Rightarrow \quad x=180°-130°$$

$$\Rightarrow \quad x=50°$$

Now, $\angle PSQ$ is an exterior angle for ΔPSR.

$$\therefore \quad \angle PSQ=\angle SPR+\angle SRP \quad \text{[by theorem 2]}$$

$$\Rightarrow \quad y=30°+x$$

$$\Rightarrow \quad y=30°+50° \quad [\because x=50°]$$

$$\Rightarrow \quad y=80°$$

Hence, $x=50°$ and $y=80°$

Example 11. In the given figure, find $\angle x$.

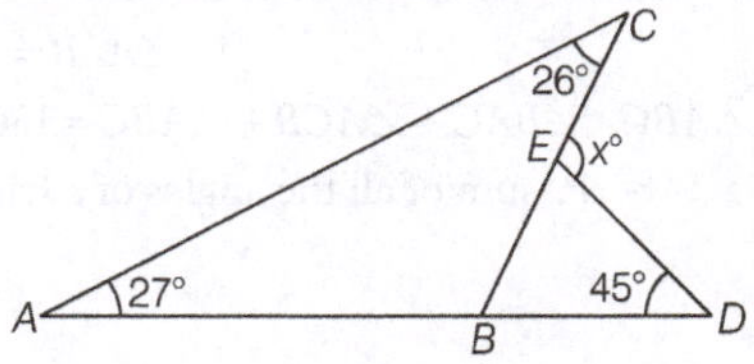

Use the property that sum of two interior opposite angles is equal to exterior angle of the triangle, then find the value of $\angle x$.

Sol. In ΔABC, $\angle CBD$ is an exterior angle.

$$\therefore \quad \angle CBD=\angle A+\angle C$$

[$\because$ exterior angle = sum of interior opposite angles]

$$\Rightarrow \quad \angle CBD=27°+26° \Rightarrow \angle CBD=53°$$

In ΔBED, $\angle CED$ is an exterior angle.

$$\therefore \quad \angle CED=\angle EBD+\angle EDB$$

[$\because$ exterior angle = sum of interior opposite angles]

$$\Rightarrow \quad \angle x=53°+45° \quad [\because \angle CBD=\angle EBD=53°]$$

$$\Rightarrow \quad \angle x=98°$$

Example 12. **In the given figure, QO and RO are the bisectors of Q and R, respectively. If $\angle QPR = 75°$ and $\angle PQR = 56°$ then find the measure of $\angle ORQ$.**

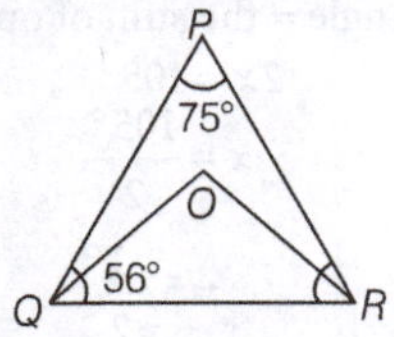

Sol. In ΔPQR, we have $\angle P + \angle Q + \angle R = 180°$

[$\because$ sum of all the angles of a triangle is 180°]

$\Rightarrow \quad 75° + 56° + \angle R = 180°$

$\Rightarrow \quad \angle R = 180° - (75° + 56°) = 49°$

But $\angle ORQ = \frac{1}{2}\angle R$ [since, OR is the bisector of $\angle R$]

$\therefore \quad \angle ORQ = \frac{1}{2}(49°) = 24\frac{1}{2}°$

Example 13. **ΔABC is right angled at A. L is a point on BC such that $AL \perp BC$. Prove that $\angle BAL = \angle ACB$.**

NCERT Exemplar

Sol. Given In ΔABC, $\angle A = 90°$ and $AL \perp BC$

To prove $\angle BAL = \angle ACB$

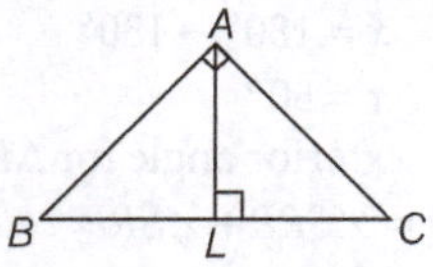

Proof In ΔABC and ΔABL,

$\angle BAC = \angle ALB$ [each 90°]...(i)

and $\angle ABC = \angle ABL$ [common angle]...(ii)

On adding Eqs. (i) and (ii), we get

$\angle BAC + \angle ABC = \angle ALC + \angle ABL$ ...(iii)

[$\because \angle ALB = \angle ALC = 90°$]

Again, in ΔABC, $\angle BAC + \angle ACB + \angle ABC = 180°$

[$\because$ sum of all the angles of a triangle is 180°]

$\Rightarrow \quad \angle BAC + \angle ABC = 180° - \angle ACB$ ...(iv)

In ΔABL, $\angle ABL + \angle ALB + \angle BAL = 180°$

[since, sum of all the angles of a triangle is 180°]

$\Rightarrow \quad \angle ABL + \angle ALC = 180° - \angle BAL$ ...(v)

[$\because \angle ALC = \angle ALB = 90°$]

On substituting the values from Eqs. (iv) and (v) in Eq. (iii), we get

$180° - \angle ACB = 180° - \angle BAL$

$\therefore \quad \angle ACB = \angle BAL$ **Hence proved.**

Example 14. **In the adjoining figure, if the bisectors of $\angle ABC$ and $\angle ACB$ of a triangle ABC meet at a point O, show that $\angle BOC = 90° + \frac{\angle A}{2}$.**

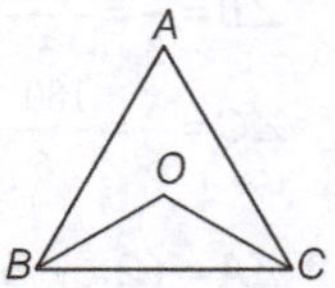

Sol. We know that the sum of all the angles of a triangle is 180°.

$\therefore \quad \angle A + \angle B + \angle C = 180°$

$\Rightarrow \quad \angle B + \angle C = 180° - \angle A$

On dividing both sides by 2, we get

$\frac{\angle B}{2} + \frac{\angle C}{2} = 90° - \frac{\angle A}{2}$ ...(i)

Again, in ΔBOC

$\angle OBC + \angle BCO + \angle BOC = 180°$

[angle sum property of a triangle]

$\Rightarrow \quad \frac{\angle B}{2} + \frac{\angle C}{2} + \angle BOC = 180°$

$\Rightarrow \quad 90° - \frac{\angle A}{2} + \angle BOC = 180°$ [from Eq. (i)]

$\therefore \quad \angle BOC = 90° + \frac{\angle A}{2}$

Hence proved.

Exercise

1. A transversal l intersects two lines m and n such that a pair of alternate interior angles is equal. Then, what can you say about the lines m and n?

2. In the given figure, what type of pair $\angle 2$ and $\angle 8$, is called?

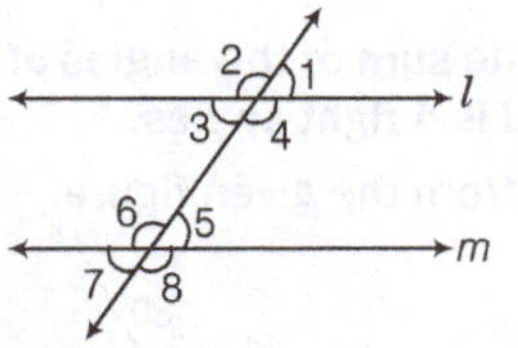

3. In the adjoining figure, if two parallel lines AB and CD are cut by a transversal EF at G and H and $\angle 1$ and $\angle 2$ are in the ratio of 3 : 2, then find $\angle 5$ and $\angle 6$.

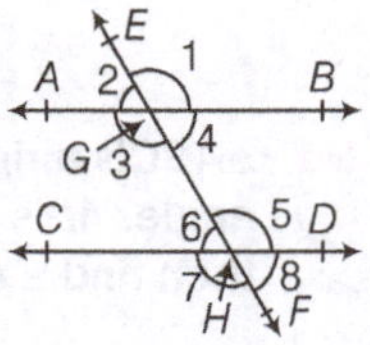

4. In the given figure, $m \parallel n$ and $\angle 1$ and $\angle 2$ are in the ratio 4 : 5. Determine all the angles.

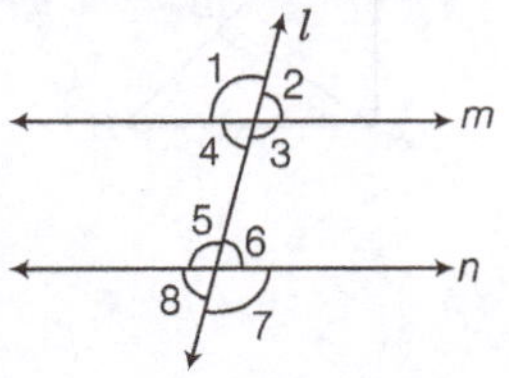

5. In the given figure, if $p \parallel q$, what is the value of b?

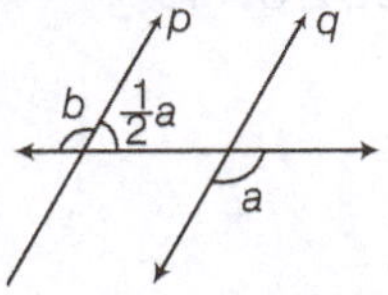

6. In the given figure, if $l \parallel m$, then find the value of $\angle x$.

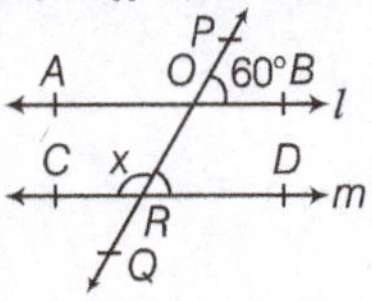

7. In the given figure, find the sum of a, c and e.

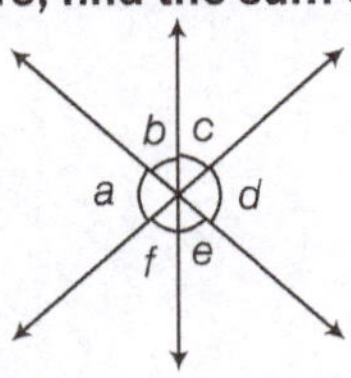

8. In the adjoining figure, transversal l intersects two lines m and n, such that $\angle 4 = 110°$ and $\angle 7 = 65°$. Is $m \parallel n$? Give reason.

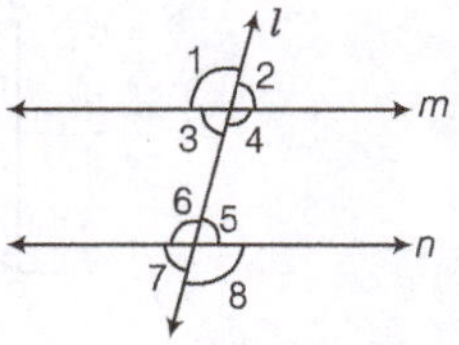

9. In the given figure $l \parallel m$ and n is a transversal such that $\angle 3 : \angle 8 = 1 : 2$. Find $\angle 4$ and $\angle 3$.

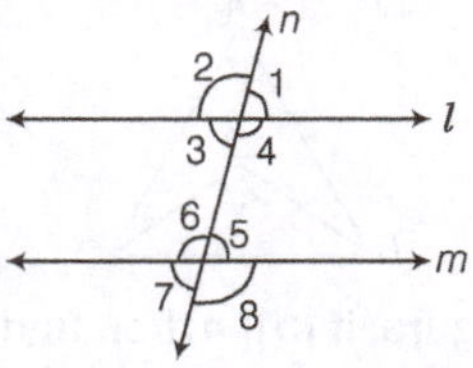

10. How many triangles can be drawn having its angles as 60°, 73° and 40°? Give reason for your answer.

11. If the angles of a triangle are in the ratio 1 : 2 : 3 then find the angles.

12. In $\triangle ABC$, if $\angle A : \angle B : \angle C = 2 : 4 : 4$ then find the measures of $\angle A$, $\angle B$ and $\angle C$.

13. Angles of a triangle are in the ratio 2 : 4 : 3. Find the smallest angle of the triangle.

14. The angles of a triangle are in the ratio 2 : 3 : 4. Then, find the angles of the triangle.

15. In the given figure, if $PQ \parallel RS$ then find the value of m.

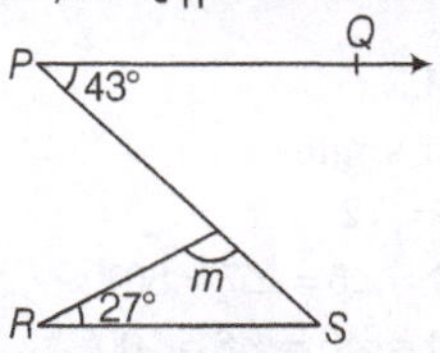

16. One of the angle of a triangle is 65°. If the difference of the remaining angles is 35°, then find remaining angles.

17. In the given figure, if $AB \parallel CD$ and $DE \parallel CF$ then find the value of x.

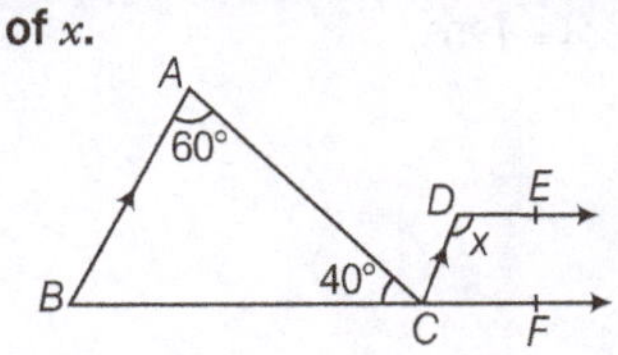

18. If one of the angles of a triangle is 130° then find the angle between the bisectors of the other two angles.

19. **In the figure, if $PS \perp l$ and $RQ \perp l$ then find the measure of y.**

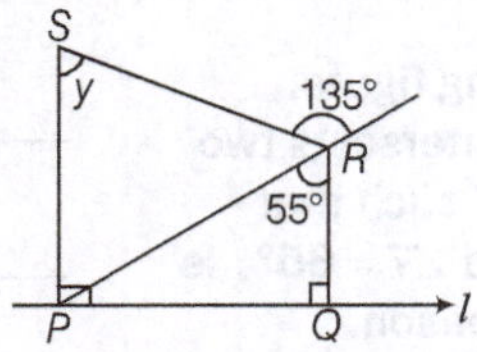

20. **In $\triangle ABC$ of the figure, BD and CD are internal bisectors of $\angle B$ and $\angle C$, respectively. Prove that $180° + y = 2x$.**

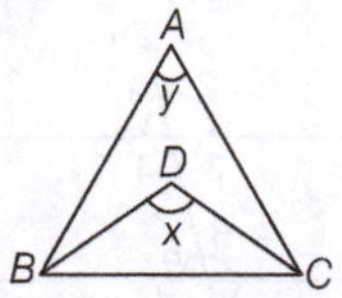

21. **In the given figure, if $m \parallel n$ then find the value of a.**

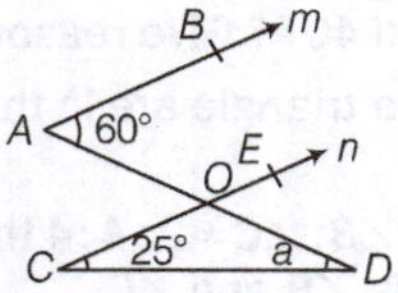

22. **In the given figure, find the value of x and y if $l \parallel m$ and $p \parallel q$.**

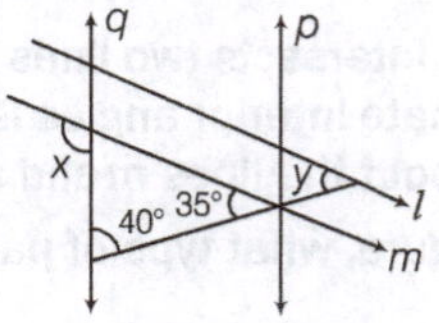

23. **Prove that the sum of the angles of a quadrilateral is 4 right angles.**

24. **Find $\angle ADC$ from the given figure.**

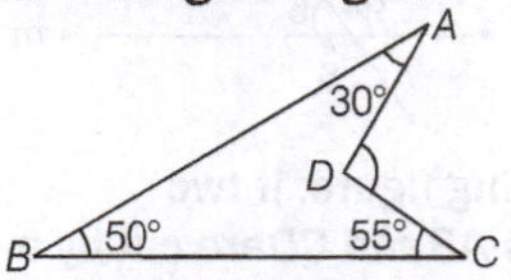

25. **ΔABC is a right angled triangle, in which $\angle A$ is a right angle. AL is drawn perpendicular to BC. If $\angle BAL = 35°$, then find $\angle ACB$.**

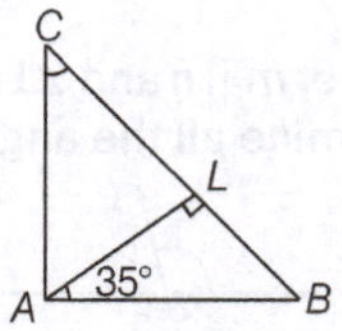

Answers

1. Lines are parallel.
2. Alternate exterior angles.
3. $\angle 5 = 108°$ and $\angle 6 = 72°$
4. $\angle 1 = \angle 3 = \angle 5 = \angle 7 = 80°$
   and $\angle 2 = \angle 4 = \angle 6 = \angle 8 = 100°$
5. $b = 120°$
6. 120°
7. $a + e + c = 180°$
8. No
9. $\angle 3 = 60°$ and $\angle 4 = 120°$
10. 0
11. 30°, 60°, 90°
12. $\angle A = 36°$, $\angle B = 72°$, $\angle C = 72°$
13. 40°
14. 40°, 60°, 80°
15. $m = 110°$
16. $x = 75°$, $y = 40°$
17. $x = 100°$
18. $\angle D = 155°$
19. $y = 80°$
21. $a = 35°$
22. $y = 35°$ and $x = 75°$
24. $\angle ADC = 135°$
25. $\angle ACB = 35°$

Triangles

CHAPTER 7

In previous classes, we have studied about triangles and their various properties such as angle sum property of a triangle etc. But in this chapter, we will study about the congruence of triangles and their rules, alongwith some more properties of triangles.

TOPIC 01 Basics of Triangles and Criteria for Congruence of Triangles

A plane figure closed by three intersecting lines is called a **triangle**, here 'Tri' means 'three'. A triangle has three sides, three angles and three vertices and it is denoted by the symbol Δ. A triangle ABC is shown in the figure.

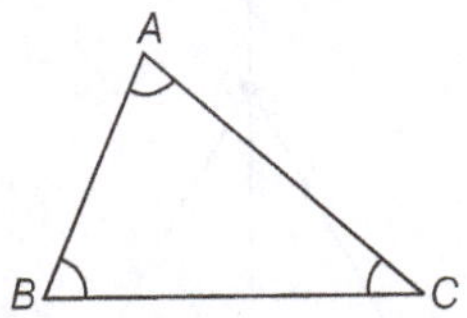

Triangle ABC can be denoted as ΔABC, where AB, BC, CA are three sides, $\angle A$, $\angle B$, $\angle C$ are the three angles and A, B, C are three vertices and the sum of all angles of a triangle is 180°.

Congruent Figures

Two figures are said to be congruent, if they are of same shape and of same size ('congruent' means 'equal in all respects or figures whose shapes and sizes are both same').

e.g. Two circles of the same radii and two squares of the same sides are congruent.

Congruence of Triangles

Two triangles are congruent, if sides and angles of one triangle are equal to the corresponding sides and angles of the other triangle.

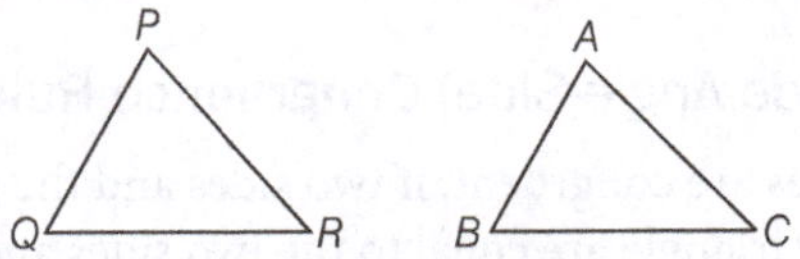

From the above definition, it is clear that

$$\angle P = \angle A,\ \angle Q = \angle B,\ \angle R = \angle C$$

and $$PQ = AB,\ QR = BC,\ RP = CA$$

If ΔPQR is congruent to ΔABC, then we write $\Delta PQR \cong \Delta ABC$. In congruent triangles, corresponding parts are equal and we write it in short 'CPCT' i.e. **Corresponding Parts of Congruent Triangles.**

Note it $\Delta PQR \cong \Delta ABC$ is not same as $\Delta PQR \cong \Delta CBA$ (or $\Delta QPR \cong \Delta ABC$), because the first statement says that $PQ = AB$, $QR = BC$, $PR = AC$, $\angle P = \angle A$, $\angle Q = \angle B$ and $\angle R = \angle C$. While the second statement says that $PQ = CB$, $QR = BA$, $PR = CA$, $\angle P = \angle C$, $\angle Q = \angle B$ and $\angle R = \angle A$ (or $QP = AB$, $PR = BC$, $QR = AC$, $\angle Q = \angle A$, $\angle P = \angle B$ and $\angle R = \angle C$). So, it is necessary to write the correspondence of vertices correctly for writing the congruence of triangles in symbolic form.

Example 1. **It is given that $\Delta ABC \cong \Delta RPQ$. Is it true to say that $BC = QR$? Why?** NCERT Exemplar

Sol. No, because we know that triangles are congruent, i.e. the sides and angles of one triangle are equal to the corresponding sides and angles of other triangle.

Here, $\Delta ABC \cong \Delta RPQ$

$\therefore$ $AB = RP, BC = PQ$ and $AC = RQ$

Hence, it is not true to say that $BC = QR$.

Example 2. **It is given that $\Delta ABC \cong \Delta FDE$. If $AB = 5$ cm, $\angle B = 40°$ and $\angle A = 80°$, then find the length of DF and also measurement of $\angle E$.**

Sol. Given, $AB = 5$ cm, $\angle B = 40°$ and $\angle A = 80°$

Since, $\Delta ABC \cong \Delta FDE$ [given]

$$\therefore \left.\begin{aligned} FD &= AB = 5 \text{ cm} \\ \angle D &= \angle B = 40° \\ \angle F &= \angle A = 80° \end{aligned}\right\} \text{[by CPCT]}$$

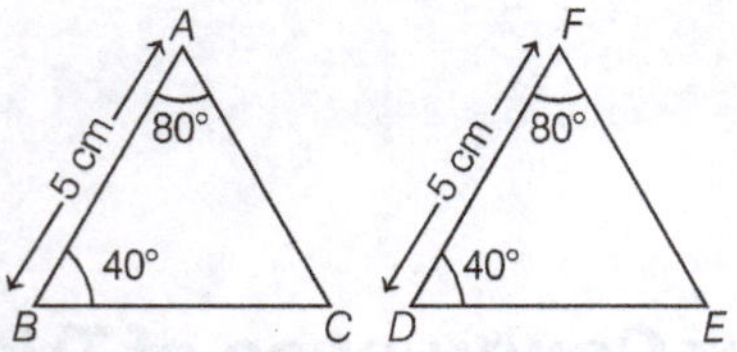

Now, in ΔFDE, $\angle F + \angle D + \angle E = 180°$

[by angle sum property of a triangle]

$\therefore \angle E = 180° - 40° - 80° = 60°$ [$\because \angle D = 40°$ and $\angle F = 80°$]

Hence, $DF = 5$ cm and $\angle E = 60°$

Criteria for Congruence of Triangles

1. SAS (Side-Angle-Side) Congruence Rule

Two triangles are congruent, if two sides and the included angle of one triangle are equal to the two sides and the included angle of the other triangle.

In ΔABC and ΔPQR,

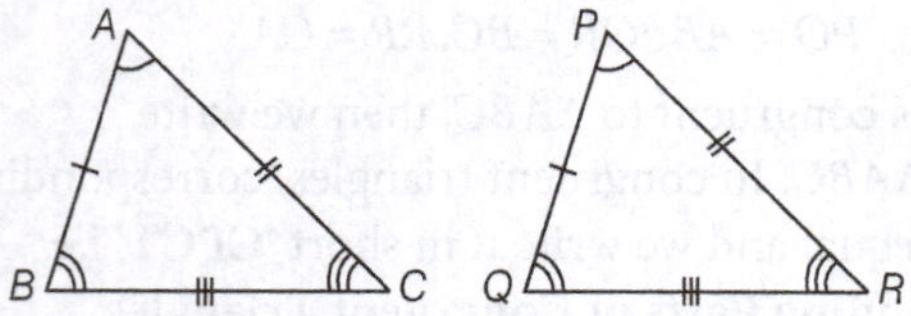

If $AB = PQ, \angle A = \angle P, AC = PR$

or $AC = PR, \angle C = \angle R, CB = RQ$

or $CB = RQ, \angle B = \angle Q, BA = QP$

Then, $\Delta ABC \cong \Delta PQR$

This result cannot be proved with the help of previously known results and so it is accepted true as an axiom.

Note it ASS or SSA rule do not hold.

Example 3. **In the given figure, find the measure of $\angle B'A'C'$.**

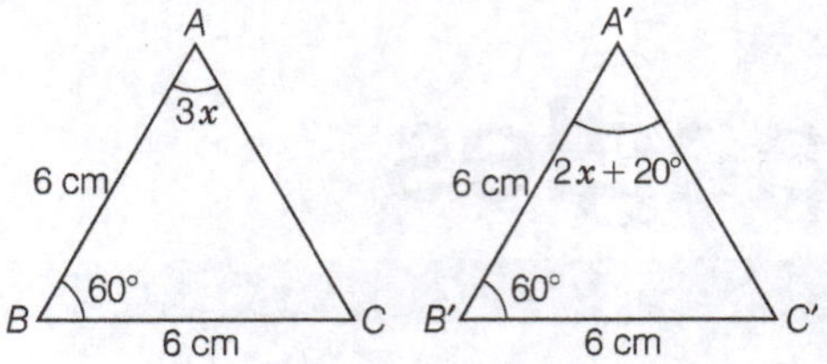

Sol. In ΔABC and $\Delta A'B'C'$,

$AB = A'B' = 6$ cm [given]

$\angle ABC = \angle A'B'C' = 60°$ [given]

and $BC = B'C' = 6$ cm [given]

$\therefore$ $\Delta ABC \cong \Delta A'B'C'$ [by SAS congruence rule]

Then, $\angle BAC = \angle B'A'C'$ [by CPCT]

$\Rightarrow$ $3x = 2x + 20°$ [from figure]

$\Rightarrow$ $3x - 2x = 20°$

$\Rightarrow$ $x = 20°$

$\therefore$ $\angle B'A'C' = 2x + 20°$

$= 2 \times 20° + 20°$

$= 60°$

Example 4. **PQ is a line segment and line l is a perpendicular bisector of PQ. If a point X lies on l, then show that $XP = XQ$.**

Sol. Given Line l is a perpendicular bisector of PQ.

$\therefore$ $PC = QC$ [since, C is the mid-point of PQ]

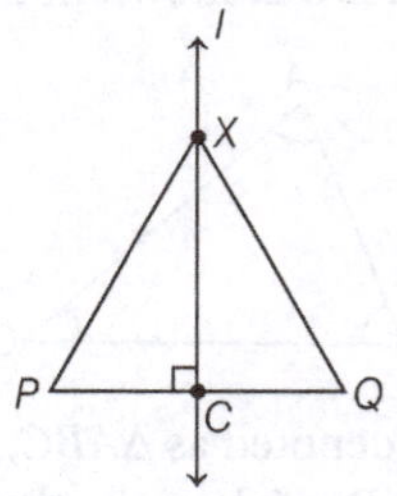

To prove X is equidistant from P and Q

i.e. $XP = XQ$

Proof Since, line l is perpendicular bisector of PQ.

$\therefore$ $\angle PCX = \angle QCX = 90°$ ... (i)

In ΔXCP and ΔXCQ,

$\angle XCP = \angle XCQ$ [each 90°, from Eq. (i)]

$PC = QC$ [given]

and $XC = XC$ [common side]

$\therefore$ $\Delta XCP \cong \Delta XCQ$ [by SAS congruence rule]

Then, $XP = XQ$ [by CPCT]

Hence proved

Example 5. **In the given figure, $AB \perp BE$ and $FE \perp BE$. If $BC = DE$ and $AB = FE$, then prove that ΔABD is congruent to ΔFEC.**

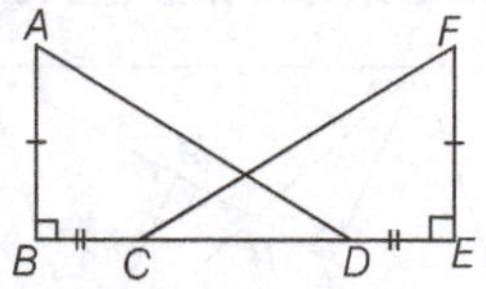

Sol. Given In ΔABD and ΔFEC, $AB \perp BE$ and $FE \perp BE$ in which $BC = DE$ and $AB = FE$.

To prove $\Delta ABD \cong \Delta FEC$

Proof In ΔABD and ΔFEC,

$AB = FE$ [given]

$BC = DE$ [given]

$\Rightarrow$ $BC + CD = DE + CD$ [adding CD both sides]

$\Rightarrow$ $BD = EC$

and $\angle ABD = \angle FEC$ [each 90°, since $AB \perp BE$ and $FE \perp BE$]

$\therefore$ $\Delta ABD \cong \Delta FEC$ [by SAS congruence rule]

Hence proved.

Example 6. **In the given figure, ΔPQR and ΔPQS are such that $PS = QR$, $\angle 1 = \angle 2$ and $\angle 3 = \angle 4$. Prove that $QS = PR$.**

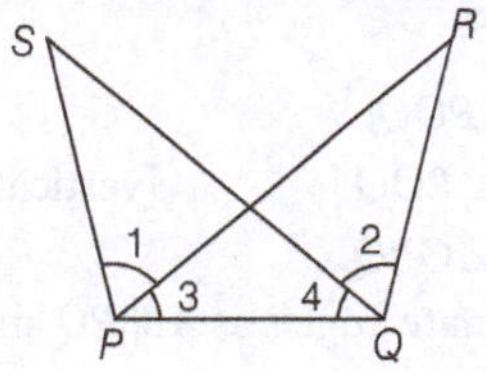

Sol. Given In ΔPQR and ΔPQS,

$PS = QR$,

$\angle 1 = \angle 2$

and $\angle 3 = \angle 4$

To prove $QS = PR$

Proof In ΔPQS and ΔPQR,

$\angle 1 = \angle 2$ and $\angle 3 = \angle 4$ [given]

$\Rightarrow$ $\angle 1 + \angle 3 = \angle 2 + \angle 4$

$\Rightarrow$ $\angle QPS = \angle PQR$

$PQ = PQ$ [common side]

and $PS = QR$ [given]

$\therefore$ $\Delta PQS \cong \Delta PQR$ [by SAS congruence rule]

Then, $QS = PR$ [by CPCT]

Hence proved.

2. ASA (Angle-Side-Angle) Congruence Rule

Two triangles are congruent, if two angles and the included side of one triangle are equal to two angles and the included side of other triangle.

In ΔABC and ΔPQR,

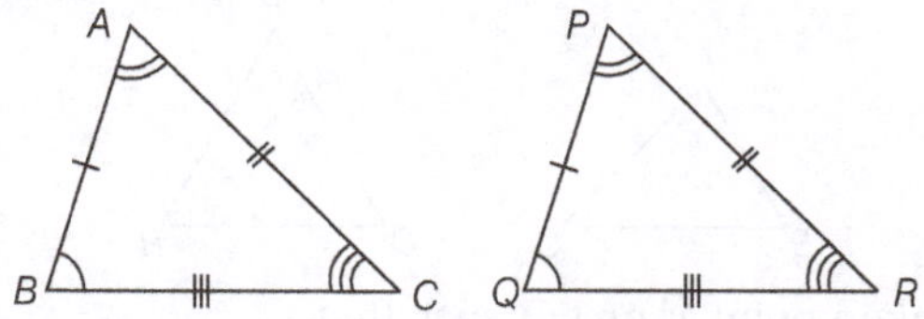

If $\angle B = \angle Q$, $BA = QP$, $\angle A = \angle P$

or $\angle A = \angle P$, $AC = PR$, $\angle C = \angle R$

or $\angle C = \angle R$, $CB = RQ$, $\angle B = \angle Q$

Then, $\Delta ABC \cong \Delta PQR$

This rule can be proved in the following way:

Given We are given two triangles ABC and PQR in which $\angle B = \angle Q$, $\angle C = \angle R$ and $BC = QR$.

To prove $\Delta ABC \cong \Delta PQR$

Proof There are three possibilities.

Case I When $AB = PQ$.

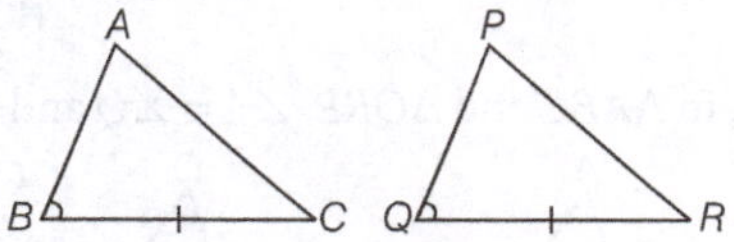

Then, in ΔABC and ΔPQR, $AB = PQ$

$\angle B = \angle Q$ [given]

and $BC = QR$ [given]

So, $\Delta ABC \cong \Delta PQR$ [by SAS congruence rule]

Case II When $AB > PQ$.

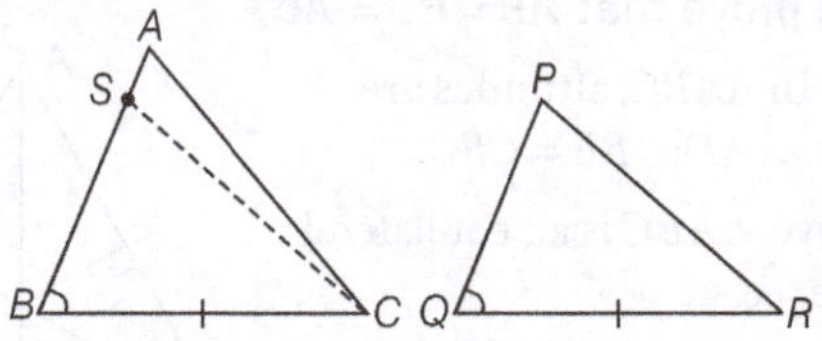

Then, take a point S on AB, such that $SB = PQ$

Now, in ΔSBC and ΔPQR,

$SB = PQ$

$\angle B = \angle Q$ [given]

and $BC = QR$ [given]

So, $\Delta SBC \cong \Delta PQR$ [by SAS congruence rule]

$\therefore$ $\angle SCB = \angle PRQ$ [by CPCT]

But $\angle ACB = \angle PRQ$ [given]

So, $\angle SCB = \angle ACB$

It is possible only if S coincides with A.

Then, $SB = AB = PQ$

So, $\Delta ABC \cong \Delta PQR$

Case III **When $AB < PQ$.**

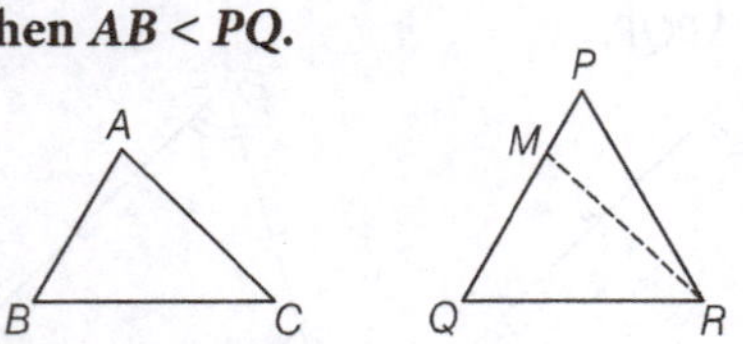

Then, take a point M on PQ, such that

$$MQ = AB$$

Now, proceed same as in Case II to get

$$MQ = AB = PQ$$

$\therefore \quad \Delta ABC \cong \Delta PQR$

Hence, in all three cases, we conclude that

$$\Delta ABC \cong \Delta PQR$$

Note it AAS congruence rule also holds. Two triangles are congruent, if any two pairs of angles and one pair of corresponding sides are equal and it is called AAS congruence rule.

Example 7. **In ΔABC and ΔQRP, $\angle A = \angle Q$ and $\angle B = \angle R$. Which side of ΔQRP should be equal to side AB of ΔABC, so that the two triangles are congruent? Give reason for your answer.** NCERT Exemplar

Sol. We have, in ΔABC and ΔQRP, $\angle A = \angle Q$ and $\angle B = \angle R$

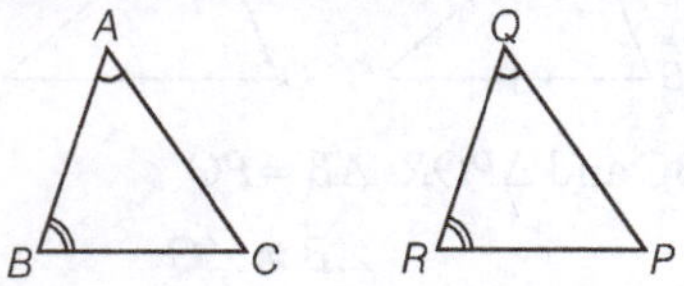

Since, sides AB and QR are included between equal angles. Hence, the side QR of ΔQRP should be equal to side AB of ΔABC, so that the triangles are congruent by the ASA rule.

Example 8. **If the altitudes AD, BE and CF of a ΔABC are equal, then prove that $AB = BC = AC$.**

Sol. **Given** In ΔABC, altitudes are equal, i.e. $AD = BE = CF$

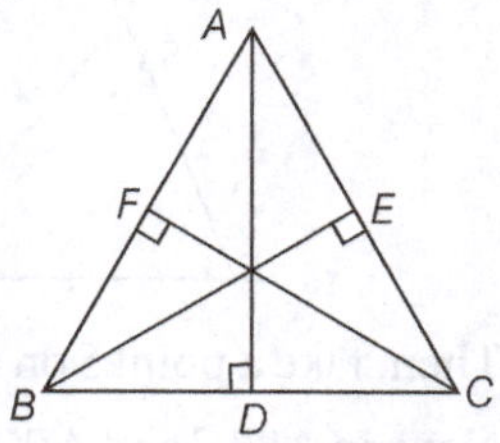

To prove ΔABC is an equilateral triangle, i.e.

$$AB = BC = CA$$

Proof In ΔADC and ΔBEC,

$\angle ADC = \angle BEC$ [each 90°]

$\angle ACD = \angle BCE$ [common angle]

and $AD = BE$ [given]

$\therefore \quad \Delta ADC \cong \Delta BEC$ [by AAS congruence rule]

Then, $AC = BC$ [by CPCT] ...(i)

Similarly, we can prove that $\Delta ADB \cong \Delta CFB$ [by AAS congruence rule]

Then, $AB = CB$ ...(ii)

From Eqs. (i) and (ii), we get

$$AB = BC = AC$$

Hence, ΔABC is an equilateral triangle. **Hence proved.**

Example 9. **In a quadrilateral $ABCD$, perpendiculars BM and DN are drawn to AC, such that $BM = DN$. If $BR = 8$ cm, then prove that $BD = 2BR$ and find the length of BD.**

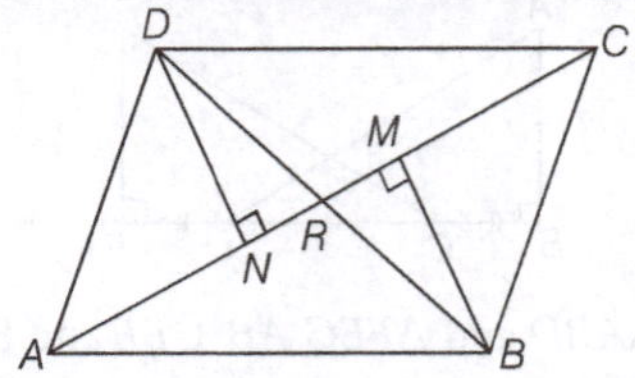

Sol. In ΔDNR and ΔBMR,

$DN = BM$ [given]

$\angle DNR = \angle BMR$ [each 90°, because $DN \perp AC$ and $BM \perp AC$]

and $\angle DRN = \angle BRM$ [vertically opposite angles]

$\therefore \quad \Delta DNR \cong \Delta BMR$ [by AAS congruence rule]

$\Rightarrow \quad DR = BR$ [by CPCT]

$\Rightarrow \quad 2DR = 2BR$ [multiplying both sides by 2]

$\Rightarrow \quad BD = 2BR$

$\therefore \quad BD = 2 \times 8 = 16$ cm [$\because BR = 8$ cm, given]

Example 10. **Line segment AB is parallel to another line segment PQ. O is the mid-point of AQ, show that O is the mid-point of BP.**

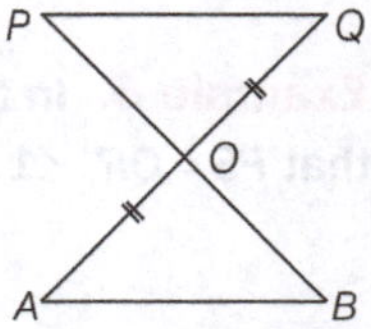

Sol. In ΔAOB and ΔPOQ,

$\angle AOB = \angle POQ$ [vertically opposite angles]

$\angle ABO = \angle OPQ$ [alternate angles as $AB \| PQ$ and BP is transversal]

$OA = OQ$ [given]

$\therefore \quad \Delta AOB \cong \Delta QOP$ [by AAS congruence rule]

$\therefore \quad OP = OB$ [by CPCT]

Thus, O is the mid-point of BP.

Example 11. **AD is a median and BL and CM are perpendiculars drawn from B and C, respectively on AD produced to M. Prove that $BL = CM$.**

Sol. **Given** AD is a median and BL, CM are perpendiculars drawn from B and C respectively on AD produced to M.

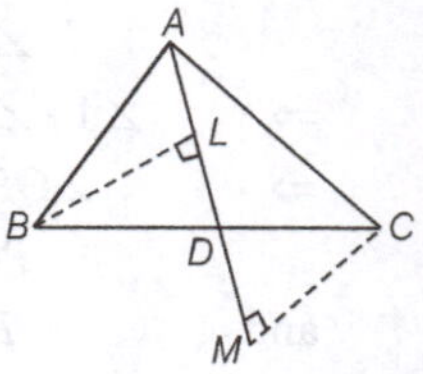

To prove $BL = CM$

Construction Join BL and CM.

Proof In ΔBDL and ΔCDM,

$\angle BLD = \angle CMD$ [each 90°]

$\angle BDL = \angle CDM$ [vertically opposite angles]

and $BD = CD$ [$\because AD$ is a median, so D is the mid-point of BC]

$\therefore \quad \Delta BDL \cong \Delta CDM$ [by AAS congruence rule]

Then, $BL = CM$ [by CPCT] **Hence proved.**

Some Properties of a Triangle

Theorem 1 ***Angles opposite to equal sides of an isosceles triangle are equal.***

Given An isosceles ΔABC, in which $AB = AC$.

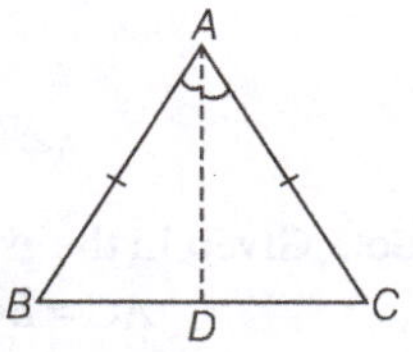

To prove $\angle B = \angle C$

Construction Draw the bisector of $\angle A$ which intersects the side BC at D.

Proof Since, AD is the angle bisector of $\angle A$.

$\therefore \quad \angle BAD = \angle CAD \quad$ ...(i)

In ΔBAD and ΔCAD,

$AB = AC$ [given]

$\angle BAD = \angle CAD$ [from Eq. (i)]

and $AD = AD$ [common side]

$\therefore \quad \Delta BAD \cong \Delta CAD$ [by SAS congruence rule]

Then, $\angle ABD = \angle ACD$ [by CPCT]

i.e. $\angle B = \angle C$ **Hence proved.**

Theorem 2 ***The sides opposite to equal angles of a triangle are equal. [Converse of theorem 1]***

Given A ΔABC in which $\angle B = \angle C$.

To prove $AB = AC$

Construction Draw the bisector of $\angle A$ and let D be the point of intersection of this bisector of $\angle A$ on BC.

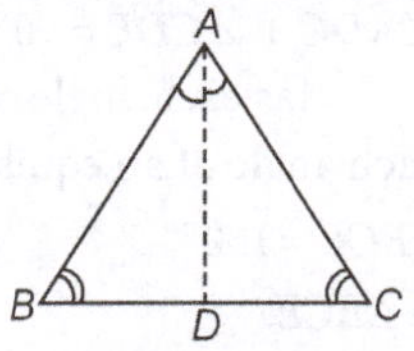

Proof Since, AD is the angle bisector of $\angle A$.

In ΔBAD and ΔCAD,

$\angle ABD = \angle ACD$ [given]

$AD = AD$ [common side]

$\angle BAD = \angle CAD$ [by construction]

So, $\Delta BAD \cong \Delta CAD$ [by AAS congruence rule]

$\therefore \quad AB = AC$ [by CPCT]

Hence proved.

Example 12. **In an isosceles ΔPQR with $PQ = PR$, A and B are the points on QR such that $QB = RA$. Show that $PA = PB$.**

Sol. ΔPQR is an isosceles triangle with

$PQ = PR$

and A and B are points on QR such that

$QB = RA \quad$ ... (i)

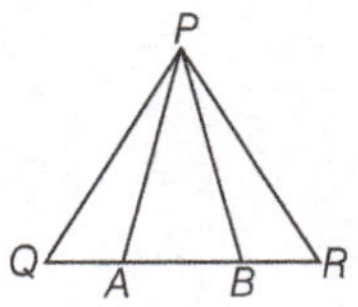

Since, $PQ = PR$

$\therefore \quad \angle PRQ = \angle PQR \quad$ ... (ii)

[$\because$ angles opposite to equal sides are also equal]

Now, $QB = RA$ [given]

$\Rightarrow \quad QB - AB = RA - AB$

[subtracting AB from both sides]

$\Rightarrow \quad QA = RB \quad$ ... (iii)

In ΔPQA and ΔPRB,

$\angle PQA = \angle PRB$ [from Eq. (ii)]

$PQ = PR$ [given]

$QA = RB$ [from Eq. (iii)]

$\therefore \quad \Delta PQA \cong \Delta PRB$ [by SAS congruence rule]

Then, $PA = PB$ [by CPCT] **Hence proved.**

Example 13. **In the given figure, ΔABC is an isosceles triangle in which $AB = AC$ and LM is parallel to BC. If $\angle A = 54°$, find $\angle LMC$.**

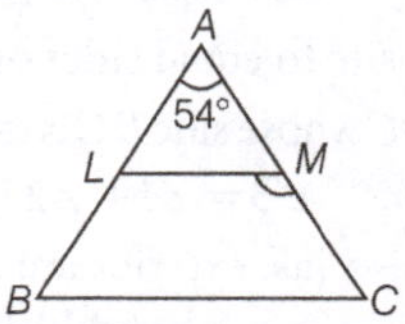

Sol. Given, ΔABC is an isosceles triangle having $AB = AC$.

$\therefore \quad \angle ACB = \angle ABC \quad$ ...(i)

[$\because$ angles opposite to equal sides of a triangle are equal]

By angle sum property of a triangle,

$\angle ABC + \angle ACB + \angle CAB = 180°$

$\Rightarrow \quad \angle ACB + \angle ACB + 54° = 180°$ [from Eq. (i)]

$\Rightarrow \quad 2\angle ACB = 126°$

$\Rightarrow \quad \angle ACB = 63°$

Since, lines $LM \parallel BC$

$\therefore \quad \angle LMC + \angle BCM = 180°$ [co-interior angles]

$\Rightarrow \quad \angle LMC + 63° = 180°$ [$\because \angle BCM = \angle ACB$]

$\Rightarrow \quad \angle LMC = 117°$

Example 14. **In a ΔABC, O and P are the points on AB and AC, respectively. If $OA = \frac{1}{2}AB$, $PA = \frac{1}{2}AC$ and $OA = PA$, show that ΔABC is an isosceles triangle.**

Sol. Given In a ΔABC,

$OA = \frac{1}{2}AB, PA = \frac{1}{2}AC$

and $OA = PA$

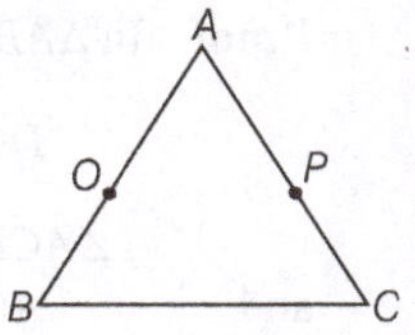

To prove $AB = AC$

Proof We have, $OA = AP$

Also, $BO = OA \quad \left[\because OA = \frac{1}{2}AB\right]$

$BO = AP$

$\therefore \quad AB = 2OB = 2AP$ ...(i)

Since, $PC = AP$ $\left[\because PA = \frac{1}{2}AC\right]$

$\therefore \quad AC = 2AP$ ...(ii)

From Eqs. (i) and (ii), $AB = AC$ **Hence proved.**

Example 15. In the given figure, $AB = BC$ and $AC = CD$. Prove that $\angle BAD : \angle ADB = 3:1$.

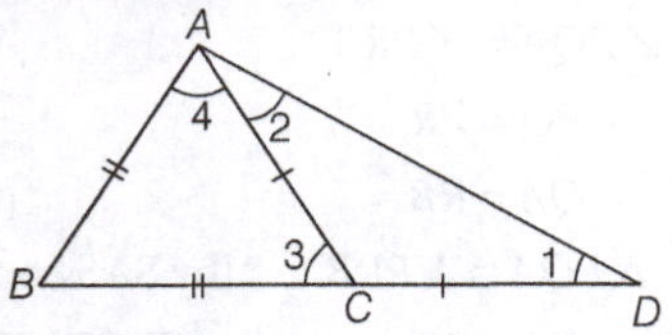

Sol. Given $AB = BC$ and $AC = CD$

To prove $\angle BAD : \angle ADB = 3:1$

Proof $CA = CD$ [given]

$\Rightarrow \quad \angle 1 = \angle 2 = x$ [say] ...(i)

[$\because$ angles opposite to equal sides of a triangle are equal]

Considering ΔADC whose side DC is extended to B, we have

$\angle 3 = \angle 1 + \angle 2$

[as, exterior angle is equal to the sum of interior opposite angles]

$\Rightarrow \quad \angle 3 = x + x = 2x$ ...(ii)

Also, $BA = BC$ [given]

$\Rightarrow \quad \angle 3 = \angle 4$ ...(iii)

[$\because$ angles opposite to equal sides of a triangle are equal]

From Eqs. (ii) and (iii), we get

$\angle 4 = 2x$ ...(iv)

Now, $\angle BAD = \angle BAC + \angle CAD = \angle 4 + \angle 2 = 2x + x = 3x$

[from Eqs. (i) and (iv)]

Now, $\angle BAD : \angle ADB = 3x : x$

$\therefore \quad \angle BAD : \angle ADB = 3:1$ **Hence proved.**

Example 16. Prove that the medians of an equilateral triangle are equal.

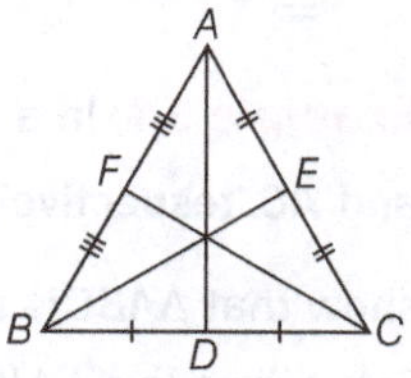

Sol. Consider a ΔABC in which sides $AB = BC = AC$; $\angle A = \angle B = \angle C = 60°$ and AD, BE and CF are its medians.

To prove $AD = BE = CF$

Proof In ΔADC and ΔBEA, we have

$DC = EA$ $\left[\because BC = AC \Rightarrow \frac{1}{2}BC = \frac{1}{2}AC\right]$

$\angle ACD = \angle BAE$ [each 60°]

and $AC = AB$ [given]

$\therefore \quad \Delta ADC \cong \Delta BEA$ [by SAS congruence rule]

Then, $AD = BE$ [by CPCT]

Similarly, $BE = CF$

$\therefore \quad AD = BE = CF$ **Hence proved.**

Example 17. In the given figure, if $AC = BC$, $\angle DCA = \angle ECB$ and $\angle DBC = \angle EAC$, prove that $DC = EC$.

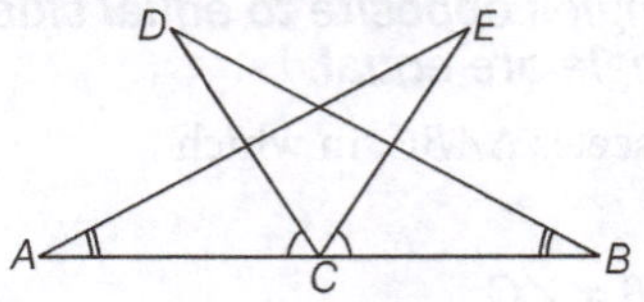

Sol. Given In the given figure,

$AC = BC$, $\angle DCA = \angle ECB$ and $\angle DBC = \angle EAC$

To prove $DC = EC$

Proof In ΔEAC and ΔDBC,

$AC = BC$ [given]

$\angle ECB = \angle DCA$ [given]

$\Rightarrow 180° - \angle ECA = 180° - \angle DCB$

$\Rightarrow \quad \angle ECA = \angle DCB$

and $\angle DBC = \angle EAC$ [given]

$\therefore \quad \Delta EAC \cong \Delta DBC$ [by ASA congruence rule]

$\Rightarrow \quad EC = DC$ [by CPCT] **Hence proved.**

Example 18. In the given figure, $ABCD$ is a square and ΔDEC is an equilateral triangle. Prove that

(i) $\Delta ADE \cong \Delta BCE$ (ii) $AE = BE$

(iii) $\angle AED = 15°$

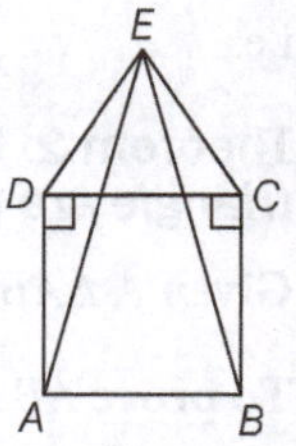

Sol. Given $ABCD$ is a square and ΔDEC is an equilateral triangle.

To prove (i) $\Delta ADE \cong \Delta BCE$ (ii) $AE = BE$ (iii) $\angle AED = 15°$

Proof From figure, we have

$\angle ADE = \angle ADC + \angle CDE = 90° + 60° = 150°$ ...(i)

[as each angle of a square is 90° and each angle of an equilateral triangle is 60°]

Similarly, $\angle BCE = 150°$ ...(ii)

(i) In ΔADE and ΔBCE,

$AD = BC$ [sides of a square]

$DE = CE$ [sides of an equilateral triangle]

and $\angle ADE = \angle BCE = 150°$ [from Eqs. (i) and (ii)]

$\therefore \quad \Delta ADE \cong \Delta BCE$ [by SAS congruence rule]

(ii) From part (i), $\Delta ADE \cong \Delta BCE$

Then, $AE = BE$ [by CPCT]

(iii) In ΔADE, $AD = DE$ [$\because AD = DC = DE$]

$\Rightarrow \quad \angle AED = \angle DAE$ ...(iii)

[as angles opposite to equal sides of a triangle are equal]

Now, $\angle DAE + \angle AED + \angle ADE = 180°$

[by angle sum property of a triangle]

$\Rightarrow \quad \angle AED + \angle AED + 150° = 180°$

[from Eqs. (i) and (iii)]

$\Rightarrow \quad 2\angle AED = 30°$

$\therefore \quad \angle AED = 15°$

Hence proved.

Try These 7.1

1. In quadrilateral $PQRS$, $PQ = PS$ and PR bisects $\angle P$. Show that $QR = RS$

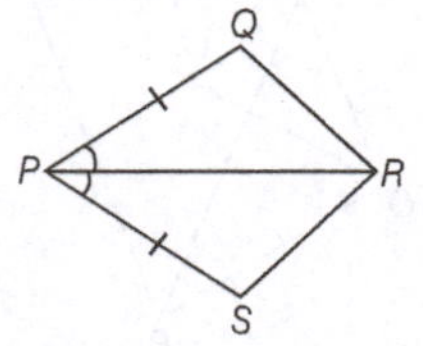

2. In the given figure, $AB = DE$, $BC = EF$ and $\angle ABC = \angle DEF$. Then, what is the possible relation between both triangles?

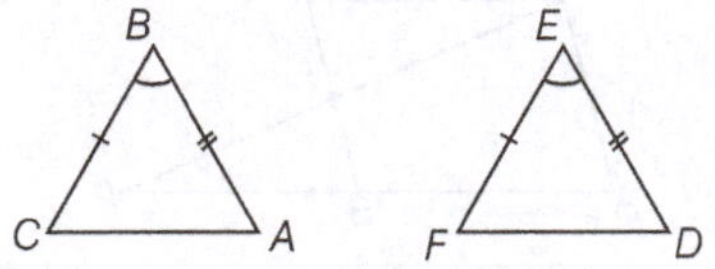

3. In the given figure, by which rule $\Delta ABC \cong \Delta DEF$?

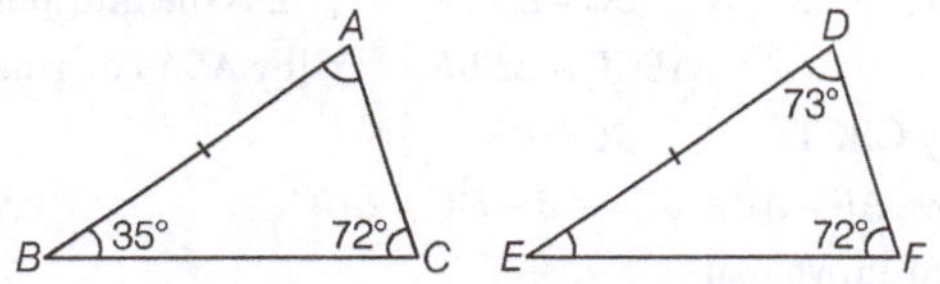

4. $PQRS$ is a quadrilateral in which $PS = QR$ and $\angle QPS = \angle PQR$. Prove that
   (i) $PR = QS$
   (ii) $\angle PQS = \angle QPR$

5. $ABCD$ is a parallelogram and E is the mid-point of side BC, DE and AB when produced meet at F. Prove that $AF = 2AB$.

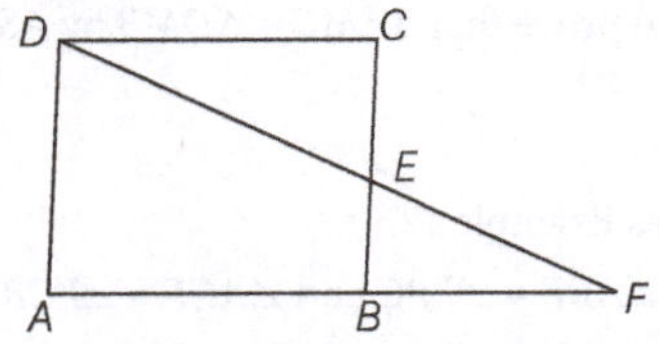

6. AB and CD are equal perpendicular to line segment BC. Show that $OC = OB$.

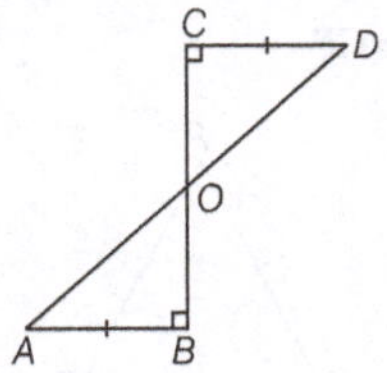

7. m and n are two parallel lines intersected by another pair of parallel lines r and s show that $\Delta PSR \cong \Delta RQP$.

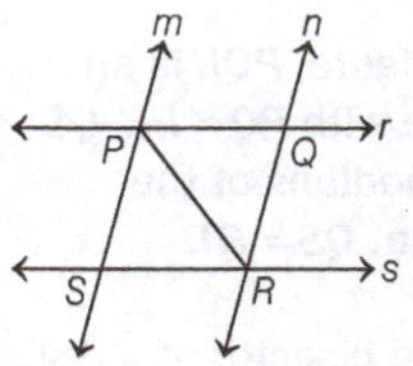

8. In the given figure, $l \parallel m$ and M is the mid-point of a line segment AB. Show that M is also the mid-point of any line segment CD having its end points on l and m, respectively.

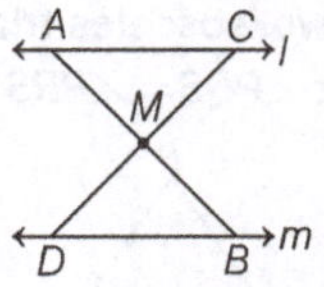

9. In the given figure, $AB = BC$ and $AD = EC$. Show that $\Delta ABE \cong \Delta CBD$.

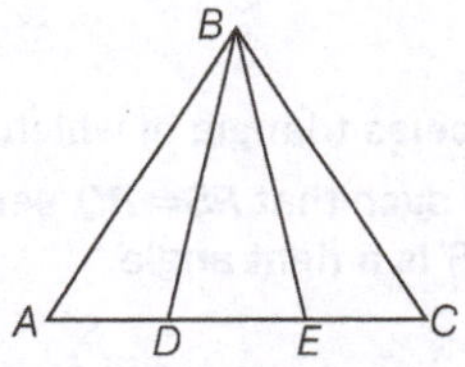

10. In the adjoining figure, $AB = AC$ and BE and CF are bisector of $\angle B$ and $\angle C$, respectively. Prove that
    (i) $\Delta EBC \cong \Delta FCB$
    (ii) $BE = CF$

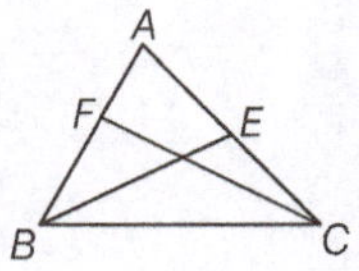

11. In a ΔPQR, X and Y are the points on PQ and QR, respectively. If $PQ = QR$ and $QX = QY$, show that $PX = RY$.

12. In ΔABC and ΔPQR, $\angle A = \angle Q$ and $\angle B = \angle R$. Which side of ΔPQR should be equal to side BC of ΔABC, so that the two triangles are congruent? Give reason for your answer. NCERT Exemplar

13. Line m is the bisector of $\angle P$ and Q is any point on m. QS and QR are perpendicular from Q to arms of $\angle P$. Show that Q is equidistant from the arms of $\angle P$.

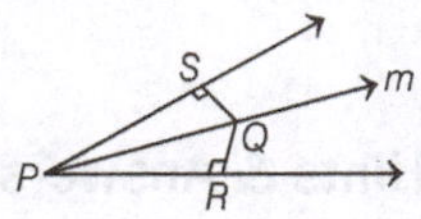

14. In the given figure, if $AB = AC$ and $\angle 1 = \angle 2$, then prove that $\angle PBC = \angle PCB$.

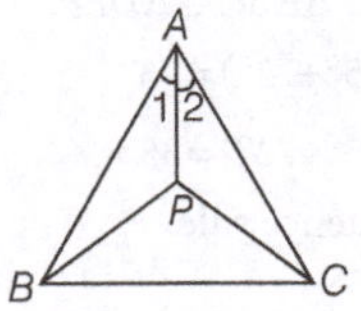

15. In ΔABC and ΔPQR, if $AB = AC$, $\angle C = \angle P$ and $\angle B = \angle Q$, prove that the two triangles are isosceles but not congruent. NCERT Exemplar

16. In the adjoining figure, PQR is an isosceles triangle with $PQ = PR$, QS and RT are two medians of the triangle. Prove that $QS = RT$.

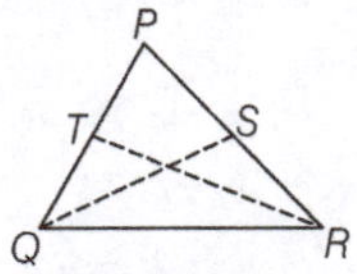

17. P is a point on the bisector of $\angle ABC$. If the line through P, parallel to BA meets BC at Q, prove that BPQ is an isosceles triangle. NCERT Exemplar

18. If the altitude from one vertex of a triangle bisects the opposite side, prove that the triangle is isosceles.

19. PQR and QRS are two isosceles triangle on the same base QR. Show that $\angle PQS = \angle PRS$

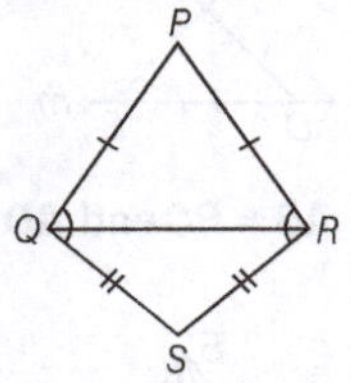

20. ΔPQR is an isosceles triangle in which $PQ = PR$. Side QP is produced to S such that $PS = PQ$, see figure, then prove that $\angle QRS$ is a right angle.

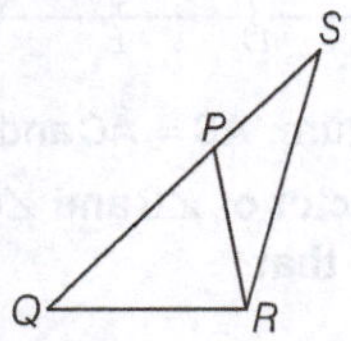

21. In the given figure, $AD = AE$ and $BD = EC$.

Prove that $AB = AC$.

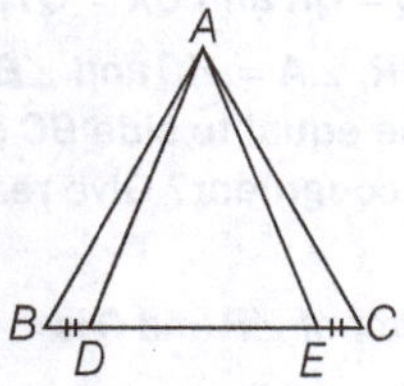

Hints & Answers

1. Hint Prove that $\Delta PQR \cong \Delta PSR$ [by SAS congruence rule]

Then, $QR = RS$ [by CPCT]

2. Hint By SAS congruence rule,

$\Delta ABC \cong \Delta DEF$.

3. Hint $\angle A = 180° - (35° + 72°) = 73°$

and $\angle E = 180° - (73° + 72°) = 35°$

ASA or AAS congruence rule.

4. Hint Prove that $\Delta PQS \cong \Delta QPR$ [by SAS congruence rule]

$\therefore$ $PR = QS$ [by CPCT]

$\angle PQS = \angle QPR$ [by CPCT]

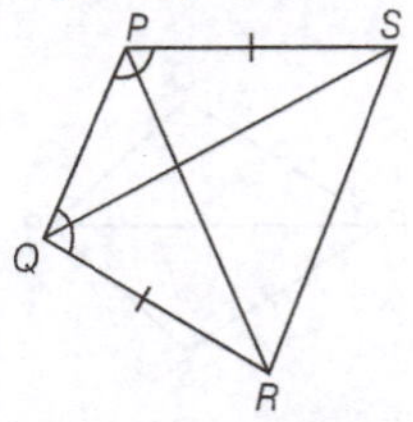

5. Hint In ΔECD and ΔEBF; $\angle DEC = \angle FEB$

[vertically opposite angles]

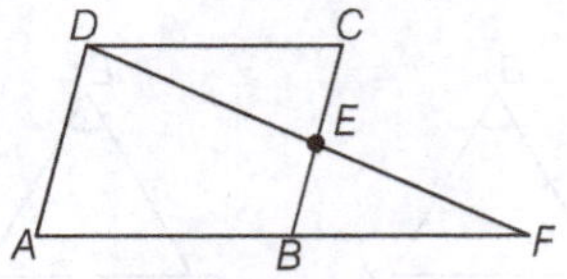

$\angle DCB = \angle EBF$ [alternate angles]

$\Rightarrow$ $\angle ECD = \angle EBF$ [$\because \angle DCB = \angle ECD$]

and $EC = EB$ [$\because E$ is the mid-point of BC]

$\therefore$ $\Delta ECD \cong \Delta EBF$ [by ASA congruence rule]

$\therefore$ By CPCT, $DC = BF$

Now, $AF = AB + BF = AB + DC = 2AB$ [$\because AB = DC$]

6. Hint Prove that

$\Delta OBA \cong \Delta OCD$ [by AAS congruence rule]

$\therefore$ $OB = OC$ [by CPCT]

7. Hint In ΔPSR and ΔRQP,

$\angle SPR = \angle QRP$ [alternate interior angles]

$\angle PRS = \angle RPQ$ [alternate interior angles]

$PR = PR$ [common]

$\therefore$ $\Delta PSR \cong \Delta RQP$ [by ASA congruence rule]

8. Hint Only to prove that $\Delta AMC \cong \Delta DMB$ by ASA congruence rule.

$\therefore MC = MD$ [by CPCT]

9. Hint Solve as Example 12.

10. Hint Here, $\angle ABE = \angle EBC$ and $\angle ACF = \angle FCB$

Since, $AB = AC \Rightarrow \angle C = \angle B$

$\therefore$ $\angle EBC = \angle FCB$

$\therefore$ $\Delta EBC \cong \Delta FCB$ [by ASA congruence rule]

$\therefore$ $BE = CF$ [by CPCT]

11. Hint

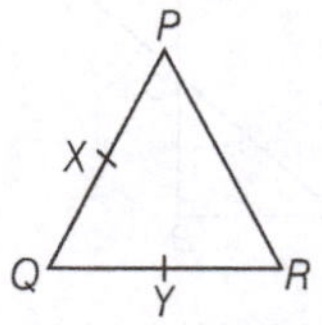

$PQ = QR$ [given]

$\Rightarrow PX + XQ = QY + YR$ [$\because QY = QX$]

$\Rightarrow$ $PX = YR$

12. Hint $BC = RP$

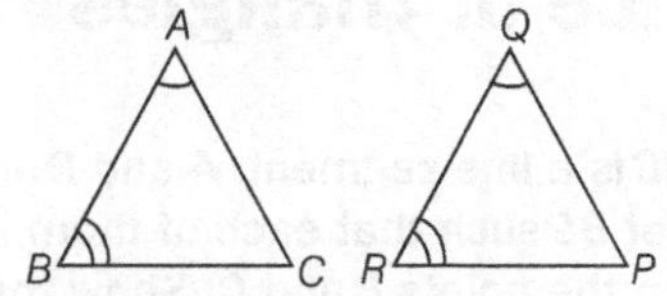

In ΔABC and ΔPQR,

$\angle A = \angle Q, \angle B = \angle R$ and $BC = RP$

$\Delta ABC \cong \Delta QRP$ [by AAS congruence rule]

13. Hint Prove that $\Delta PQS \cong \Delta PQR$ [by AAS congruence rule]

$\therefore\ QS = QR$ [by CPCT]

Thus, Q is equidistant from the arms of $\angle P$.

14. Hint In ΔAPB and $\Delta APC, AB = AC$ [given]

$\angle 1 = \angle 2$ [given]

and $AP = AP$ [common]

$\therefore$ $\Delta APB \cong \Delta APC$ [by SAS congruence rule]

Then, $\angle ABP = \angle ACP$ [by CPCT] ...(i)

In $\Delta ABC,\ AB = AC$

$\therefore$ $\angle ACB = \angle ABC$ ...(ii)

[$\because$ angles opposite to equal sides are equal]

On subtracting Eq. (i) from Eq. (ii), we get

$\angle PBC = \angle PCB$

15. Hint

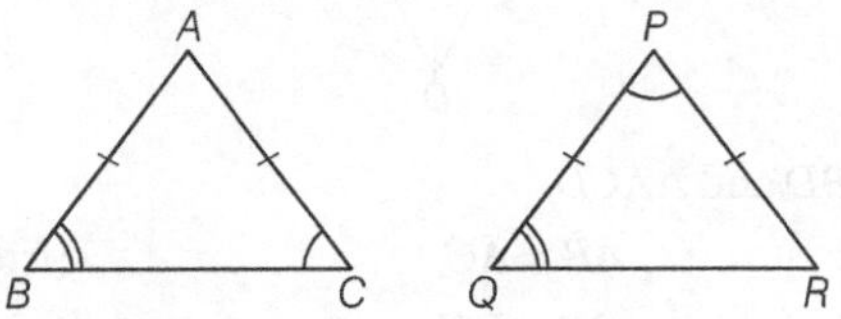

Since, $AB = AC$

$\Rightarrow$ $\angle C = \angle B$

But $\angle C = \angle P$ and $\angle B = \angle Q$

$\Rightarrow$ $\angle P = \angle Q$

$\therefore\ \Delta ABC$ and ΔPQR are isosceles.

But both triangles do not follow either SAS or ASA.

So, they are not congruent.

16. Hint $\because\ PQ = PR$

$\Rightarrow$ $\frac{1}{2}PQ = \frac{1}{2}PR \Rightarrow QT = RS$

Thus, $\Delta QRS \cong \Delta RQT$ [by SAS congruence rule]

So, $QS = RT$ [by CPCT]

17. Hint

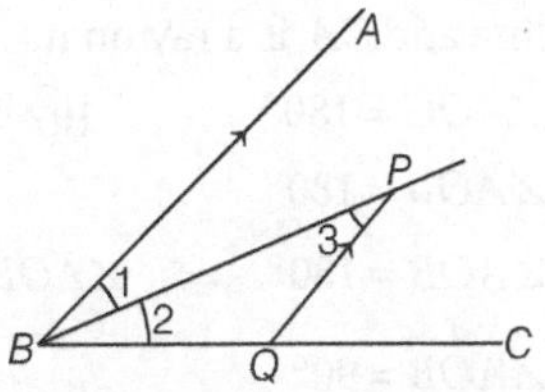

Since, $AB \parallel PQ \Rightarrow \angle 1 = \angle 3$ [alternate interior angles]

But $\angle 1 = \angle 2$ [given]

$\therefore$ $\angle 2 = \angle 3$

$\therefore \Delta BPQ$ is an isosceles triangle.

18. Hint Solve as Theorem 1.

19. To prove $\angle PQS = \angle PRS$

In ΔPQR, $PQ = PR$ [given]

$\Rightarrow$ $\angle PRQ = \angle PQR$ [$\because$ angles opposite to equal sides of a triangle are equal] ... (i)

In ΔQSR, $QS = RS$ [given]

$\Rightarrow$ $\angle QRS = \angle SQR$ ...(ii)

[$\because$ angles opposite to equal sides of a triangle are equal]

On adding Eqs. (i) and (ii), we get

$\angle PRQ + \angle QRS = \angle PQR + \angle SQR$

$\Rightarrow$ $\angle PRS = \angle PQS$

20. Given ΔPQR is an isosceles triangle in which $PQ = PR$

To prove $\angle QRS$ is a right angle.

Proof In the given figure,

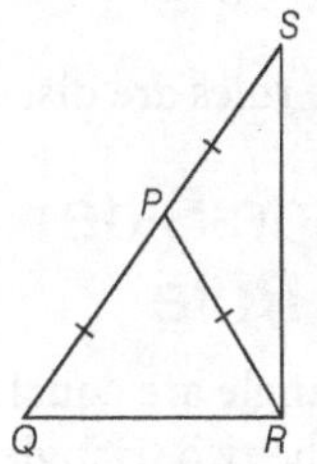

$PQ = PR$ [given]

and $PS = PQ$ [given]

$\therefore$ $PS = PR$ ... (i)

Since, $PQ = PR$

$\Rightarrow$ $\angle PRQ = \angle PQR$

[$\because$ angles opposite to equal sides of a triangle are equal] ... (ii)

From Eq. (i),

$PS = PR$

$\Rightarrow$ $\angle PRS = \angle PSR$

[$\because$ angles opposite to equal sides of a triangle are equal] ... (iii)

On adding Eqs. (ii) and (iii), we get

$\angle PQR + \angle PSR = \angle PRQ + \angle PRS$

$\Rightarrow$ $\angle PQR + \angle PSR = \angle QRS$ [$\because \angle QRS = \angle PRQ + \angle PRS$]

$\Rightarrow$ $\angle SQR + \angle QSR = \angle QRS$

In $\Delta\ QRS$,

$\angle SQR + \angle QRS + \angle QSR = 180°$

[by angle sum property of triangle]

$\Rightarrow$ $\angle QRS + \angle QRS = 180°$

$\Rightarrow$ $2\angle QRS = 180°$

$\Rightarrow$ $\angle QRS = 90°$

21. Hint Since, $AD = AE$

$\therefore$ $\angle AED = \angle ADE$

[$\because$ angles opposite to equal sides of a triangle are equal]

Now, $180° - \angle ADE = 180° - \angle AED$

$\Rightarrow$ $\angle ADB = \angle AEC$ ...(i)

Now, prove that $\Delta ADB \cong \Delta AEC$ with the help of Eq. (i), then by SAS congruence rule, then show that $AB = AC$ by CPCT.

TOPIC 02 Some More Criteria for Congruence of Triangles

We know that equality of three angles of one triangle to three angles of another triangle is not sufficient for the congruence of the two triangles. But equality of three sides of one triangle to three sides of another triangle is sufficient for the congruence of the two triangles.

e.g. In ΔABC and ΔPQR, $\angle A = \angle P$, $\angle B = \angle Q$ and $\angle C = \angle R$ but $\Delta ABC \not\cong \Delta PQR$.

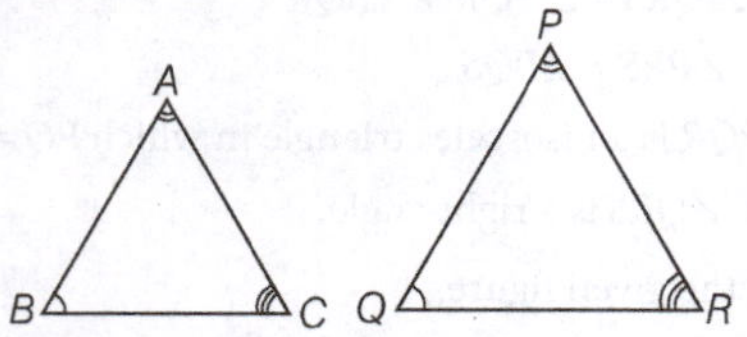

Some more congruence rules are discussed below:

1. SSS (Side-Side-Side) Congruence Rule

If three sides of one triangle are equal to the three sides of another triangle, then the two triangles are congruent.

In ΔABC and ΔPQR,

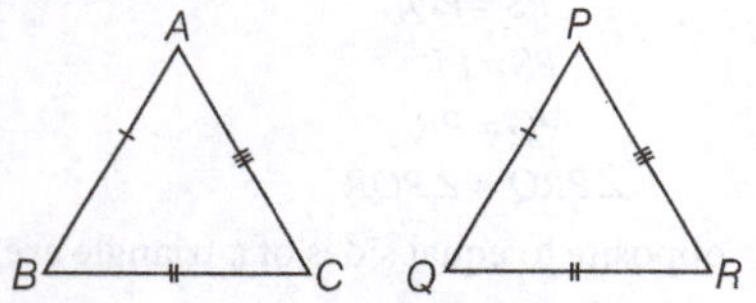

If $AB = PQ$, $BC = QR$ and $CA = RP$, then $\Delta ABC \cong \Delta PQR$.

Note it The right angled triangle is not the included angle in SSS congruence rule.

2. RHS (Right Angle-Hypotenuse-Side) Congruence Rule

In two right angled triangles, the hypotenuse and one side of one triangle are equal to the hypotenuse and one side of the other triangle, then the two triangles are congruent.

In right angled ΔPQR and ΔABC,

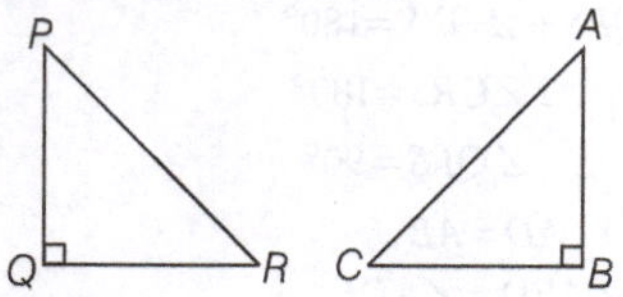

If $\quad PQ = AB, \angle Q = \angle B$

and $\quad PR = AC$

or $\quad QR = BC, \angle Q = \angle B$ and $PR = AC$

Then, $\Delta PQR \cong \Delta ABC$

Example 1. ***BC* is a line segment. *A* and *D* are points on opposite sides of *BC* such that each of them is equidistant from the points *B* and *C*. Show that the line *AD* is the perpendicular bisector of *BC*.**

Or

***ABC* and *DBC* are two triangles on the same base *BC* such that *A* and *D* lie on the opposite sides of *BC*, *AB* = *AC* and *DB* = *DC*. Show that *AD* is the perpendicular bisector of *BC*.**

NCERT Exemplar

Sol. Given, BC is a line segment. A and D are points on opposite sides of BC,

such that $\quad AB = AC \quad$ ...(i)

and $\quad DB = DC \quad$ ...(ii)

Here, AD bisects BC at point O.

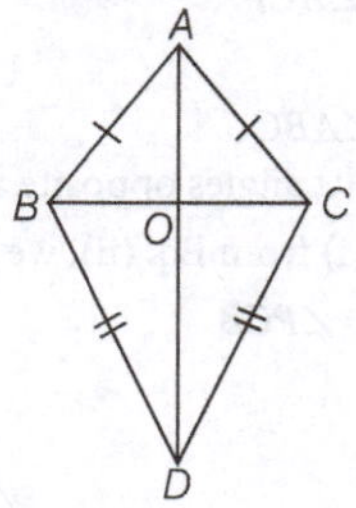

In ΔABD and ΔACD,

$AB = AC$ [from Eq. (i)]

$DB = DC$ [from Eq. (ii)]

and $AD = AD$ [common side]

$\therefore \Delta ABD \cong \Delta ACD$ [by SSS congruence rule]

Then, $\angle BAD = \angle CAD$ [by CPCT]

or $\angle BAO = \angle CAO$ ...(iii)

In ΔABO and ΔACO,

$AB = AC$ [from Eq. (i)]

$\angle BAO = \angle CAO$ [from Eq. (iii)]

and $AO = AO$ [common side]

$\therefore \Delta ABO \cong \Delta ACO$ [by SAS congruence rule]

Then, $BO = CO$ [by CPCT] ... (iv)

and $\angle AOB = \angle AOC$ [by CPCT] ...(v)

Since, BC is a line and OA is a ray on it.

$\therefore \angle AOB + \angle AOC = 180°$ [by linear pair axiom]

$\Rightarrow \angle AOB + \angle AOB = 180°$ [from Eq. (v)]

$\Rightarrow 2\angle AOB = 180° \Rightarrow \angle AOB = \dfrac{180°}{2}$

$\Rightarrow \angle AOB = 90°$

Thus, $BO = CO$ [from Eq. (iv)]

and $\angle AOB = 90° = \angle AOC$

Hence, AD is the perpendicular bisector of BC.

Hence proved.

Example 2. In the given figures, two sides AB, BC and the median AD of ΔABC are correspondingly equal to the sides PQ, QR and the median PM of ΔPQR. Prove that $\Delta ABC \cong \Delta PQR$.

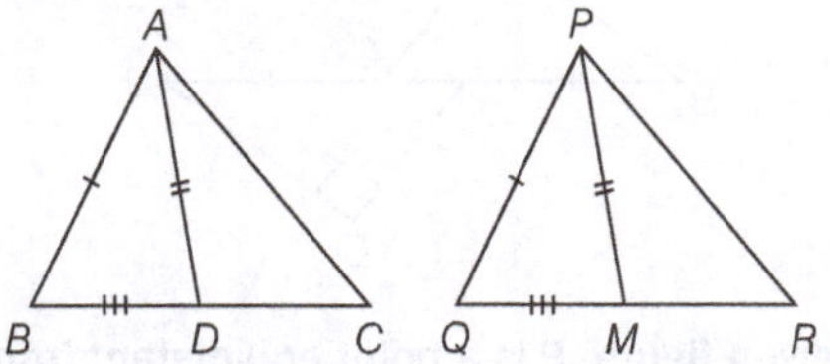

Sol. **Given** AD is median of ΔABC and PM is median of ΔPQR. Also, $AB = PQ$, $BC = QR$ and $AD = PM$.

To prove $\Delta ABC \cong \Delta PQR$

Proof In ΔABD and ΔPQM, $AB = PQ$ [given]

$AD = PM$ [given]

and $BD = QM$

$$\left[\because BC = QR \Rightarrow \frac{1}{2}BC = \frac{1}{2}QR \Rightarrow BD = QM\right]$$

$\therefore$ $\Delta ABD \cong \Delta PQM$ [by SSS congruence rule]

Then, $\angle B = \angle Q$ [by CPCT]

In ΔABC and ΔPQR, we have

$AB = PQ$ [given]

and $\angle B = \angle Q$ [proved above]

$BC = QR$ [given]

$\therefore$ $\Delta ABC \cong \Delta PQR$ [by SAS congruence rule]

Hence proved.

Example 3. In the given figure, ΔABC is an equilateral triangle. If altitude AD is drawn from the vertex A, then prove that $AB = AC = 2BD$.

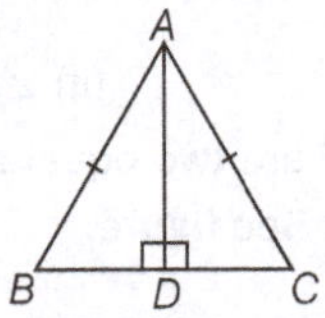

Sol. Given In ΔABC, $AB = AC = BC$ (equilateral triangle) and $AD \perp BC$ (altitude on base).

To prove $AB = AC = 2BD$

Proof In ΔADB and ΔADC,

$AB = AC$ [given]

$AD = AD$ [common side]

and $\angle ADB = \angle ADC$ [each 90°]

$\therefore$ $\Delta ADB \cong \Delta ADC$ [by RHS congruence rule]

Then, $BD = CD$ [by CPCT]

$\Rightarrow$ $BC = 2BD$

$\because$ $AB = AC = BC$

$\therefore$ $AB = AC = 2BD$ **Hence proved.**

Example 4. In the given figure, if AC is bisector of $\angle BAD$, such that $AD = AB = 3$ cm and $AC = 5$ cm. Show that $\Delta ABC \cong \Delta ADC$ and $BC = CD$.

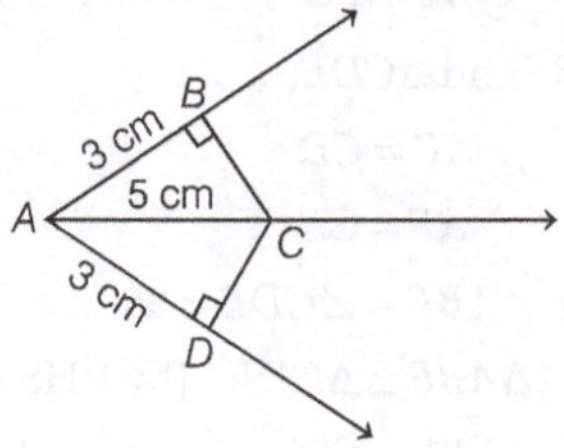

Sol. In ΔABC and ΔADC,

$\angle ABC = \angle ADC$ [each 90°]

$AB = AD$ [given]

and $AC = AC$ [common side]

$\therefore$ $\Delta ABC \cong \Delta ADC$ [by RHS congruence rule]

Then, $BC = DC$ [by CPCT]

Hence proved.

Example 5. In the given figure, $BA \perp AC$, $DE \perp DF$ such that $BA = DE$ and $BF = EC$. Show that $\Delta ABC \cong \Delta DEF$.

NCERT Exemplar

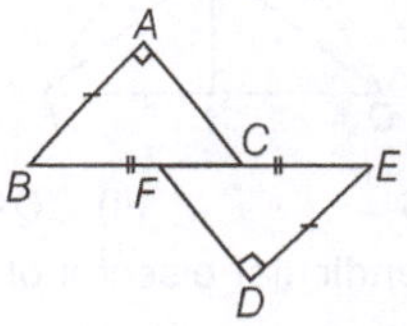

Sol. **Given** In figure, $BA \perp AC$, $DE \perp DF$ such that $BA = DE$ and $BF = EC$.

To prove $\Delta ABC \cong \Delta DEF$

Proof We have, $BF = EC$ [given]

On adding CF both sides, we get

$BF + CF = EC + CF$

$\Rightarrow$ $BC = EF$ ...(i)

In ΔABC and ΔDEF,

$\angle A = \angle D = 90°$ [$\because BA \perp AC$ and $DE \perp DF$]

$BC = EF$ [from Eq. (i)]

and $BA = DE$ [given]

$\therefore$ $\Delta ABC \cong \Delta DEF$ [by RHS congruence rule]

Hence proved.

Example 6. In the given figure, AB and CD are perpendiculars on BD. Also, $AB = CD$ and $AF = CE$. Prove that $BE = FD$.

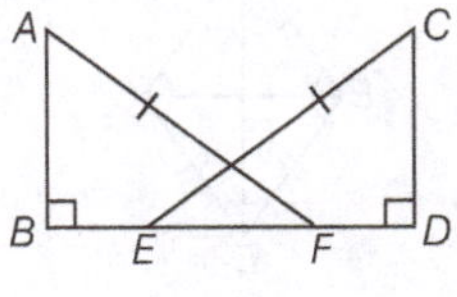

Sol. Given In ΔABF and ΔCDE, $AB \perp BD$ and $CD \perp BD$ in which $AB = CD$ and $AF = CE$.

To prove $BE = FD$

Proof In ΔABF and ΔCDE,

$AB = CD$ [given]

$AF = CE$ [given]

and $\angle ABF = \angle CDE = 90^\circ$

$\therefore$ $\Delta ABF \cong \Delta CDE$ [by RHS congruence rule]

$\Rightarrow$ $BF = ED$ [by CPCT]

$\Rightarrow$ $BF - EF = ED - EF$ [subtracting EF from both sides]

$\Rightarrow$ $BE = FD$ **Hence proved.**

Try These 7.2

1. ΔPQR and ΔAQR are two isosceles triangles on the same base QR and vertices P and A are on the same side of QR. If PA is extended to intersect QR at S, then show that

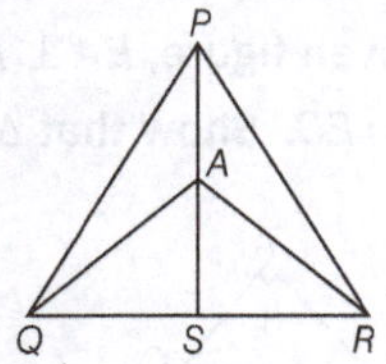

(i) $\angle QPS = \angle RPS$ (ii) $\angle QAS = \angle RAS$

(iii) PS is the perpendicular bisector of QR.

2. In the given figures, $AB = DE$, $BC = EF$ and median AP = median DQ. Prove that $\angle B = \angle E$.

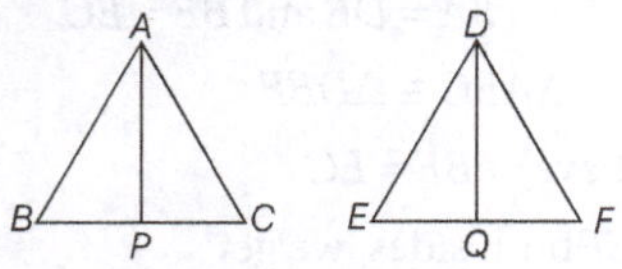

3. In the given figure, $AB = AC$, D is the point in the interior of ΔABC such that $\angle DBC = \angle DCB$. Prove that AD bisects $\angle BAC$ of ΔABC.

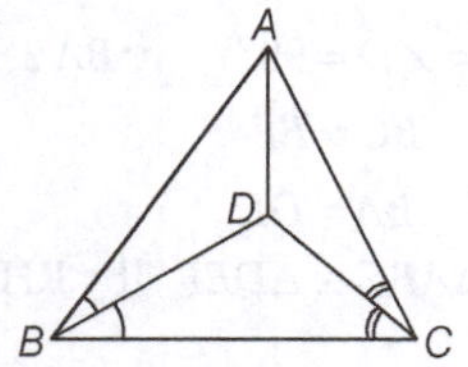

4. In the given figure, ΔABC and ΔDBC are two isosceles triangles on the same base BC. Show that $\Delta ABD \cong \Delta ACD$.

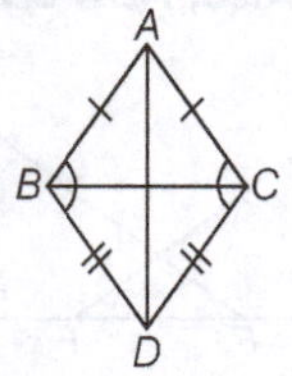

5. In the given figure, $BA \perp AC$ and $DE \perp EF$ such that $BA = DE$ and $BF = DC$. Prove that $AC = EF$.

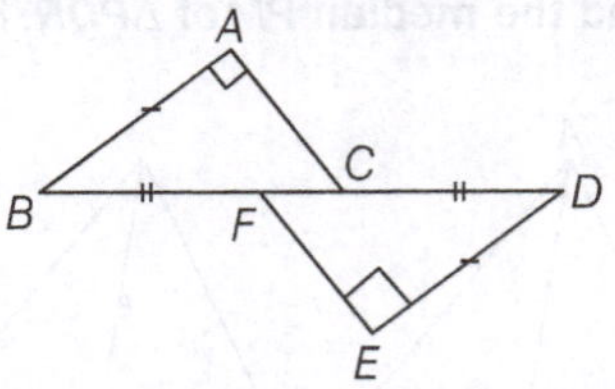

6. In the given figure, P is a point equidistant from two lines l and m intersecting at point A. Prove that ΔABP and ΔACP are congruent and length of AC is 8 cm.

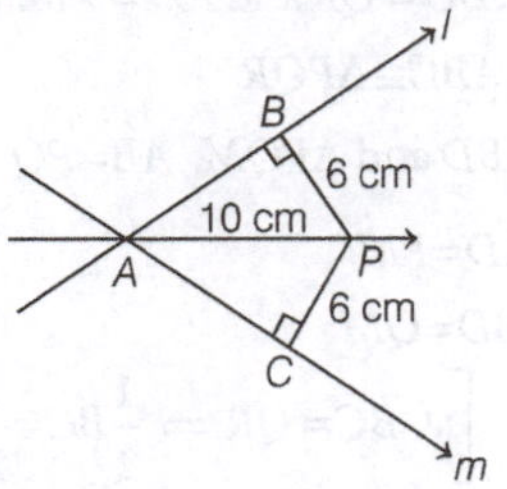

7. $ABCD$ is a square, X and Y are points on sides AD and BC, respectively such that $AY = BX$. Prove that $BY = AX$ and $\angle BAY = \angle ABX$.

8. It is given that $DE = EF$, $BE = EC$, $ED \perp AB$ and $EF \perp AC$. Prove that $AB = AC$.

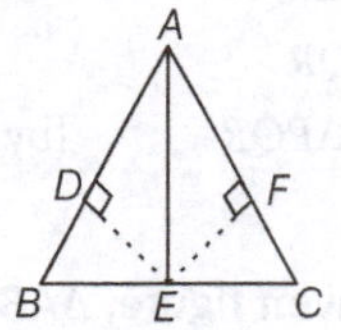

9. In isosceles ΔABC in which $AB = AC$ and AM is an altitude. Show that

(i) $BM = CM$ (ii) $\angle BAM = \angle CAM$

10. In ΔPQR, RE and QF are two equal altitude of ΔPQR. Prove that $PQ = PR$. See figure.

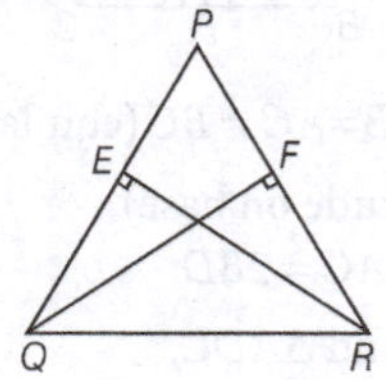

Hints & Answers

1. Hint

(i) Prove $\Delta QAP \cong \Delta RAP$ [by SSS congruence rule]

$\Rightarrow$ $\angle QPA = \angle RPA$

$\therefore$ $\angle QPS = \angle RPS$

(ii) We have,

$\Delta QAP \cong \Delta RAP$ [proved in part (i)]

$\Rightarrow$ $\angle QAP = \angle RAP$ ...(i) [by CPCT]

Now, $\angle QAS + \angle QAP = 180°$ [linear pair axiom] ...(ii)

and $\angle RAS + \angle RAP = 180°$ [linear pair axiom] ...(iii)

From Eqs. (ii) and (iii), we get

$\angle QAS + \angle QAP = \angle RAS + \angle RAP$

$\Rightarrow \angle QAS + \angle QAP = \angle RAS + \angle QAP$ [using Eq. (i)]

$\Rightarrow \angle QAS = \angle RAS$ **Hence proved**

(iii) $\Delta QAS \cong \Delta RAS$

Then, $QS = SR$ [by CPCT]

and $\angle ASQ = \angle ASR$ [by CPCT] ... (iii)

and $\angle ASQ + \angle ASR = 180°$ [by linear pair axiom]

$\Rightarrow \angle ASQ + \angle ASQ = 180°$ [from Eq. (iii)]

$\Rightarrow \angle ASQ = 90°$

Hence, PS is the perpendicular bisector of QR.

2. Hint First, prove that $\Delta APB \cong \Delta DQE$ by SSS congruence rule, then show that $\angle B = \angle E$ by CPCT.

3. Hint

$\because \angle DBC = \angle DCB$ [given]

$\Rightarrow DC = BD$ ...(i)

Now, prove that $\Delta ADB \cong \Delta ADC$ by SSS congruence rule, then show that $\angle BAD = \angle CAD$ by CPCT.

4. Hint Apply SSS congruence rule.

5. Hint Solve as Example 5.

6. Hint First, prove that $\Delta ABP \cong \Delta ACP$ by RHS and then show that $AC = 8$ cm by Pythagoras theorem.

7. Hint First, prove that $\Delta XAB \cong \Delta YBA$ by RHS congruence rule, then show that $BY = AX$ and $\angle BAY = \angle ABX$ by CPCT.

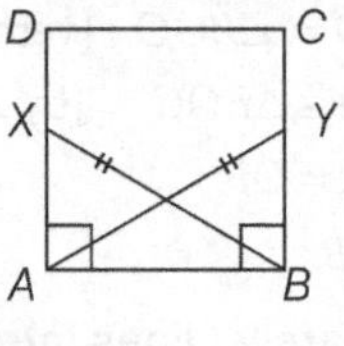

8. Hint In ΔBDE and ΔCFE,

$DE = FE$ [given]

$BE = CE$ [given]

$\angle EDB = \angle EFC = 90°$

$\therefore$ By RHS, $\Delta BDE \cong \Delta CFE$

$\therefore$ By CPCT, $\angle B = \angle C \Rightarrow AB = AC$

[$\because$ sides opposite to equal angles are equal]

9. Given ΔABC is an isosceles triangle and $AM \perp BC, AB = AC$

To prove

(i) $BM = CM$ (ii) $\angle BAM = \angle CAM$

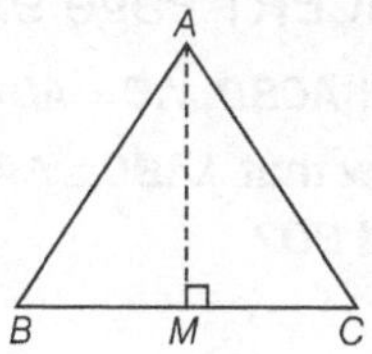

Proof

(i) In ΔAMB and ΔAMC,

$AB = AC$ [given]

$\angle AMB = \angle AMC$ [each 90°]

and $AM = AM$ [common side]

$\therefore \Delta AMB \cong \Delta AMC$ [by RHS congruence rule]

Then, $BM = CM$ [by CPCT]

(ii) $\because \Delta AMB \cong \Delta AMC$

$\therefore \angle BAM = \angle CAM$ [by CPCT] **Hence proved.**

10. Given $QF = RE, RE \perp PQ$ and $QF \perp PR$

To prove $PQ = PR$

Proof In ΔQFR and ΔREQ,

$\angle QFR = \angle REQ$ [each 90°]

$QF = RE$ [given]

$QR = QR$ [common side]

$\therefore \Delta QFR \cong \Delta REQ$ [by RHS congruence rule]

$\Rightarrow \angle RQE = \angle QRF$ [by CPCT]

$\Rightarrow \angle RQP = \angle QRP$

$\therefore PR = PQ$ [$\because$ sides opposite to equal angles of a triangle are equal]

NCERT FOLDER

Complete Solutions of All Exercises of NCERT Textbook

EXERCISE 7.1 (NCERT Page 92-94)

Q1. **In a quadrilateral $ACBD$, $AC = AD$ and AB bisects $\angle A$ (see figure). Show that $\Delta ABC \cong \Delta ABD$. What can you say about BC and BD?**

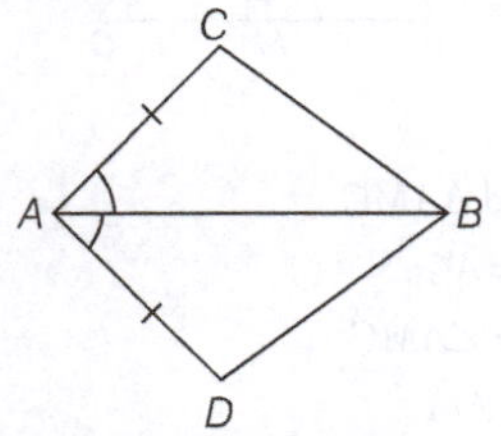

Sol. Given In quadrilateral $ACBD$,

$AC = AD$ and $\angle BAC = \angle BAD$

To prove $\Delta ABC \cong \Delta ABD$

Proof In ΔABC and ΔABD, $AC = AD$ [given]

$\angle BAC = \angle BAD$ [given]

and $AB = AB$ [common side]

Hence, $\Delta ABC \cong \Delta ABD$ [by SAS congruence rule]

Then, $BC = BD$ [by CPCT]

Thus, BC and BD are equal. **Hence proved.**

Q2. **$ABCD$ is a quadrilateral in which $AD = BC$ and $\angle DAB = \angle CBA$ (see figure). Prove that**

(i) $\Delta ABD \cong \Delta BAC$

(ii) $BD = AC$

(iii) $\angle ABD = \angle BAC$

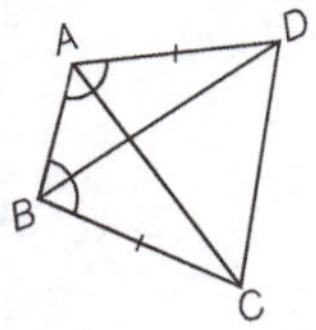

Sol. Given In a quadrilateral $ABCD$,

$AD = BC$ and $\angle DAB = \angle CBA$

To prove

(i) $\Delta ABD \cong \Delta BAC$ (ii) $BD = AC$

(iii) $\angle ABD = \angle BAC$

Proof

(i) In ΔABD and ΔBAC, $AD = BC$ [given]

$\angle DAB = \angle CBA$ [given]

and $AB = AB$ [common side]

$\therefore$ $\Delta ABD \cong \Delta BAC$

[by SAS congruence rule]

(ii) From part (i), $\Delta ABD \cong \Delta BAC$

Then, $BD = AC$ [by CPCT]

(iii) From part (i), $\Delta ABD \cong \Delta BAC$

Then, $\angle ABD = \angle BAC$ [by CPCT]

Hence proved.

Q3. **AD and BC are equal perpendiculars to a line segment AB (see figure). Show that CD bisects AB.**

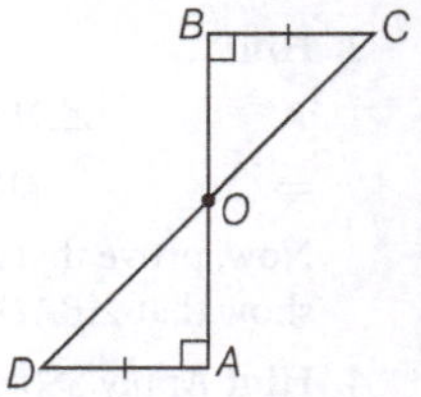

Sol. Given $AD \perp AB$ and $BC \perp AB$

To prove CD bisects AB.

i.e. $OA = OB$

Proof In ΔAOD and ΔBOC,

$AD = BC$ [given]

$\angle OAD = \angle OBC$ [each 90°]

and $\angle AOD = \angle BOC$ [vertically opposite angles]

$\therefore$ $\Delta AOD \cong \Delta BOC$ [by AAS congruence rule]

Then, $OA = OB$ [by CPCT]

Thus, CD bisects AB. **Hence proved.**

Q4. **l and m are two parallel lines intersected by another pair of parallel lines p and q (see figure). Show that $\Delta ABC \cong \Delta CDA$.**

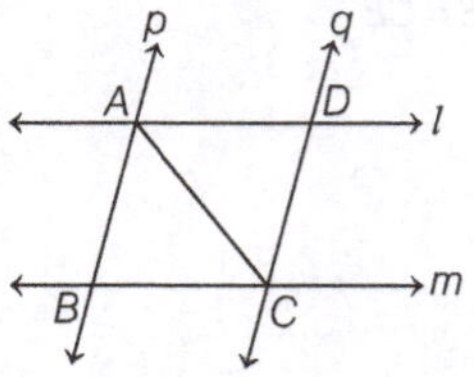

Sol. Given $l \parallel m$ and $p \parallel q$

To prove $\Delta ABC \cong \Delta CDA$

Proof In ΔABC and ΔADC,

$\angle BAC = \angle ACD$ [alternate interior angles as $p \parallel q$]

$\angle ACB = \angle DAC$ [alternate interior angles as $l \parallel m$]

and $AC = AC$ [common side]

$\therefore$ $\Delta ABC \cong \Delta CDA$ [by ASA congruence rule]

Hence proved.

Q5. **Line l is the bisector of $\angle A$ and B is any point on l. BP and BQ are perpendiculars from B to the arms of $\angle A$ (see figure).**

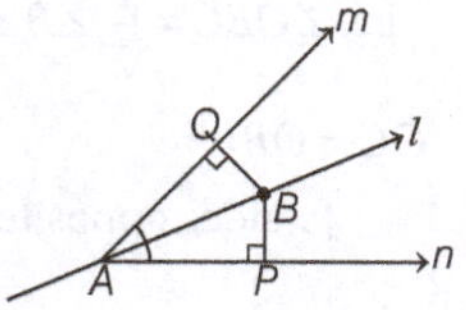

Show that

(i) $\Delta APB \cong \Delta AQB$

(ii) $BP = BQ$ or B is equidistant from the arms of $\angle A$.

Sol. Given l is the bisector of $\angle A$.

i.e. $\angle QAB = \angle PAB$ and $BP \perp n$ and $BQ \perp m$

To prove

(i) $\Delta APB \cong \Delta AQB$

(ii) $BP = BQ$ or B is equidistant from the arms of $\angle A$.

Proof (i) In ΔAQB and ΔAPB,

$\angle BQA = \angle BPA$ [each 90°]

$\angle QAB = \angle PAB$ [given]

and $AB = AB$ [common side]

$\therefore$ $\Delta AQB \cong \Delta APB$ [by AAS congruence rule]

(ii) From part (i),

$\Delta AQB \cong \Delta APB$

$\therefore$ $BQ = BP$ [by CPCT]

Hence, B is equidistant from the arms of $\angle A$.

Hence proved.

Q6. **In the given figure, $AC = AE$, $AB = AD$ and $\angle BAD = \angle EAC$. Show that $BC = DE$.**

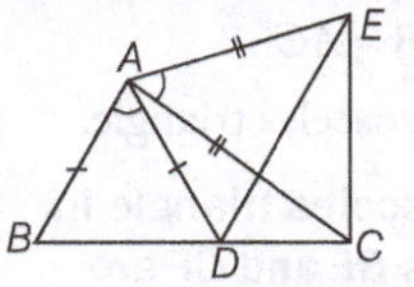

Sol. Given $AC = AE, AB = AD$ and $\angle BAD = \angle EAC$

To prove $BC = DE$

Proof We have, $\angle BAD = \angle EAC$

On adding $\angle DAC$ both sides, we get

$\angle BAD + \angle DAC = \angle EAC + \angle DAC$

$\Rightarrow$ $\angle BAC = \angle DAE$ ...(i)

In ΔABC and ΔADE, $AC = AE$ [given]

$AB = AD$ [given]

and $\angle BAC = \angle DAE$ [from Eq. (i)]

$\therefore$ $\Delta ABC \cong \Delta ADE$

[by SAS congruence rule]

Then, $BC = DE$ [by CPCT]

Hence proved.

Q7. **AB is a line segment and P is its mid-point. D and E are points on the same side of AB, such that $\angle BAD = \angle ABE$ and $\angle EPA = \angle DPB$ (see figure). Show that**

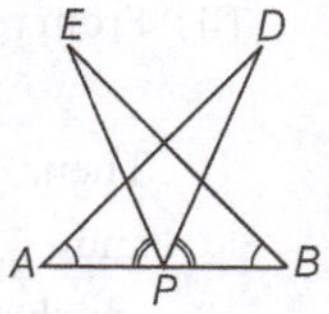

(i) $\Delta DAP \cong \Delta EBP$ (ii) $AD = BE$

Sol. Given P is the mid-point of AB, i.e. $AP = BP$,

$\angle BAD = \angle ABE$ and $\angle EPA = \angle DPB$

To prove (i) $\Delta DAP \cong \Delta EBP$ (ii) $AD = BE$

Proof

(i) We have, $\angle EPA = \angle DPB$

On adding $\angle EPD$ to both sides, we get

$\angle EPA + \angle EPD = \angle DPB + \angle EPD$

$\Rightarrow$ $\angle DPA = \angle EPB$

or $\angle EPB = \angle DPA$ ...(i)

In ΔDAP and ΔEBP,

$AP = BP$ [given]

$\angle PAD = \angle PBE$ [given]

and $\angle DPA = \angle EPB$ [from Eq. (i)]

$\therefore$ $\Delta DAP \cong \Delta EBP$ [by ASA congruence rule]

(ii) From part (i),

$\Delta DAP \cong \Delta EBP$

$\therefore$ $AD = BE$ [by CPCT] **Hence proved.**

Q8. **In right angled ΔABC, right angled at C, M is the mid-point of hypotenuse AB. C is joined to M and produced to a point D such that $DM = CM$. Point D is joined to point B (see figure). Show that**

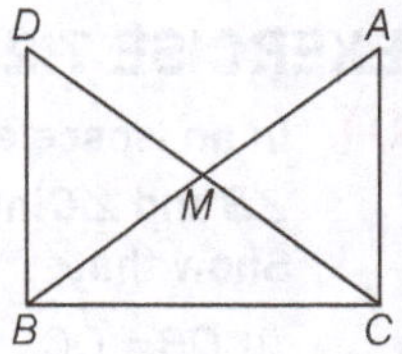

(i) $\Delta AMC \cong \Delta BMD$ (ii) $\angle DBC$ is a right angle.

(iii) $\Delta DBC \cong \Delta ACB$ (iv) $CM = \frac{1}{2} AB$

Sol. Given In right angled ΔABC, $\angle C = 90°$, M is the mid-point of AB, i.e. $AM = MB$ and $DM = CM$.

To prove (i) $\Delta AMC \cong \Delta BMD$

(ii) $\angle DBC$ is a right angle.

(iii) $\Delta DBC \cong \Delta ACB$

(iv) $CM = \frac{1}{2} AB$

Proof

(i) In ΔAMC and ΔBMD,

$AM = BM$ [given]

$MC = DM$ [given]

and $\angle AMC = \angle DMB$ [vertically opposite angles]

$\therefore$ $\Delta AMC \cong \Delta BMD$ [by SAS congruence rule]

(ii) From part (i),

$\Delta AMC \cong \Delta BMD$

Then, $AC = DB$ [by CPCT]

and $\angle ACM = \angle BDM$ [by CPCT]

which are alternate angles.

$\therefore BD \parallel CA$ and BC is a transversal.

Then, $\angle ACB + \angle DBC = 180°$

[sum of co-interior angles]

$\Rightarrow 90° + \angle DBC = 180°$ [$\because \angle C = 90°$, given]

$\Rightarrow \angle DBC = 90°$

Hence, $\angle DBC$ is a right angle.

(iii) In ΔDBC and ΔACB,

$DB = AC$ [proved above]

$BC = BC$ [common side]

and $\angle DBC = \angle BCA$ [each 90°]

$\therefore \Delta DBC \cong \Delta ACB$ [by SAS congruence rule]

(iv) From part (iii),

$\Delta DBC \cong \Delta ACB$

Then, $CD = AB$ [by CPCT]

$\Rightarrow CM + MD = AB$ [$\because CD = CM + MD$]

$\Rightarrow CM + CM = AB$ [$\because DM = CM$, given]

$\Rightarrow 2CM = AB$

$\therefore CM = \frac{1}{2} AB$ **Hence proved.**

EXERCISE 7.2 (NCERT Page 97-98)

Q1. In an isosceles ΔABC with $AB = AC$, the bisectors of $\angle B$ and $\angle C$ intersect each other at O. Join A to O. Show that

(i) $OB = OC$

(ii) AO bisects $\angle A$

Sol. Given ΔABC is an isosceles triangle with $AB = AC$

OB and OC are the bisectors of $\angle B$ and $\angle C$, respectively and intersect each other at O.

i.e. $\angle OBA = \angle OBC$ and $\angle OCA = \angle OCB$

To prove (i) $OB = OC$

(ii) AO bisects $\angle A$.

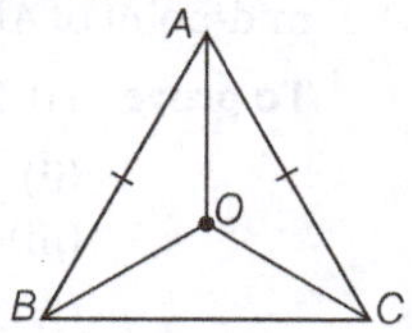

Proof

(i) In ΔABC, we have

$AB = AC$

[given]

$\Rightarrow \angle B = \angle C$

[$\because$ angles opposite to equal sides are equal]

$\Rightarrow \frac{1}{2}\angle B = \frac{1}{2}\angle C$ [dividing both sides by 2]

$\Rightarrow \angle OBC = \angle OCB$

and $\angle OBA = \angle OCA$ ...(i)

[$\because OB$ and OC are the bisectors of $\angle B$ and $\angle C$, i.e. $\angle OBC = \frac{1}{2}\angle B$ and $\angle OCB = \frac{1}{2}\angle C$]

$\Rightarrow OC = OB$ ...(ii)

[$\because$ sides opposite to equal angles of a triangle are equal]

(ii) In ΔABO and ΔACO, we have

$AB = AC$ [given]

$\angle OBA = \angle OCA$ [from Eq. (i)]

and $OB = OC$ [from Eq. (ii)]

$\therefore \Delta ABO \cong \Delta ACO$ [by SAS congruence rule]

Then, $\angle BAO = \angle CAO$ [by CPCT]

So, AO is the bisector of $\angle BAC$. **Hence proved.**

Q2. In ΔABC, AD is the perpendicular bisector of BC (see figure). Show that ΔABC is an isosceles triangle in which $AB = AC$.

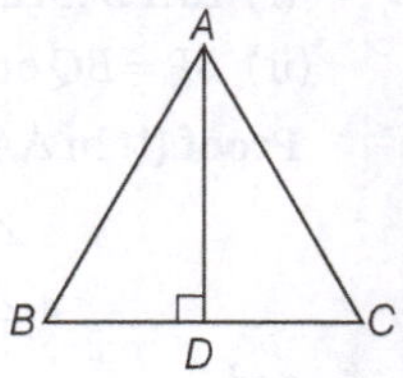

Sol. Given AD is the perpendicular bisector of BC.

To prove ΔABC is an isosceles triangle.

i.e. $AB = AC$

Proof In ΔADB and ΔADC,

$AD = AD$ [common side]

$BD = DC$ [given]

and $\angle ADB = \angle ADC$ [each 90°]

$\therefore \Delta ADB \cong \Delta ADC$ [by SAS congruence rule]

$\Rightarrow AB = AC$ [by CPCT]

So, ΔABC is an isosceles triangle. **Hence proved.**

Q3. ΔABC is an isosceles triangle in which altitudes BE and CF are drawn to equal sides AC and AB respectively (see figure). Show that these altitudes are equal.

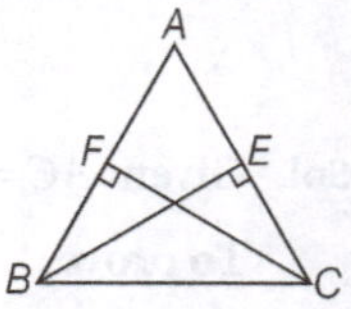

Sol. Given ΔABC is an isosceles triangle in which

$AB = AC$, $BE \perp AC$ and $CF \perp AB$

To prove $BE = CF$

Proof In ΔABE and ΔACF,

$AB = AC$ [given]

$\angle AEB = \angle AFC$

[each 90°, $BE \perp AC$ and $CF \perp AB$]

and $\angle BAE = \angle CAF$ [common angle]

$\therefore \Delta ABE \cong \Delta ACF$ [by AAS congruence rule]

Then, $BE = CF$ [by CPCT] **Hence proved.**

Q4. ***ABC* is a triangle in which altitudes *BE* and *CF* to sides *AC* and *AB* are equal (see figure).**

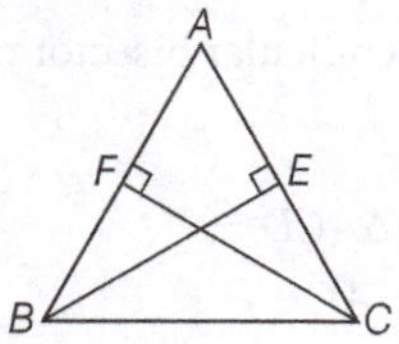

Show that

(i) $\Delta ABE \cong \Delta ACF$

(ii) $AB = AC$, i.e. ΔABC is an isosceles triangle.

Sol. Given ΔABC in which $BE \perp AC$ and $CF \perp AB$, such that $BE = CF$.

To prove (i) $\Delta ABE \cong \Delta ACF$ (ii) $AB = AC$

Proof

(i) In ΔABE and ΔACF,

$\angle AEB = \angle AFC$ [each 90°]

$\angle BAE = \angle CAF$ [common angle]

and $BE = CF$ [given]

$\therefore$ $\Delta ABE \cong \Delta ACF$

[by AAS congruence rule]

(ii) From part (i), $\Delta ABE \cong \Delta ACF$

$\therefore$ $AB = AC$ [by CPCT]

$\therefore$ ΔABC is an isosceles triangle.

Q5. ***ABC* and *DBC* are two isosceles triangles on the same base *BC* (see figure).**

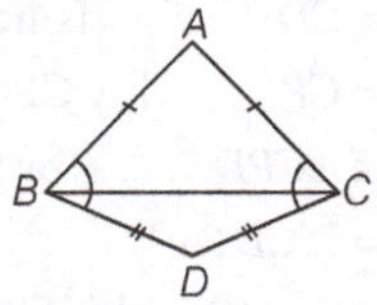

Show that $\angle ABD = \angle ACD$.

Sol. Given ΔABC and ΔDBC are two isosceles triangles in which $AB = AC$ and $BD = CD$.

To prove $\angle ABD = \angle ACD$

Proof In ΔABC, $AB = AC$ [given]

$\Rightarrow$ $\angle ACB = \angle ABC$ ...(i)

[$\because$ angles opposite to equal sides of a triangle are equal]

In ΔDBC, $DB = DC$ [given]

$\Rightarrow$ $\angle DCB = \angle DBC$ ...(ii)

[$\because$ angles opposite to equal sides of a triangle are equal]

On adding Eqs. (i) and (ii), we get

$\angle ACB + \angle DCB = \angle ABC + \angle DBC$

$\Rightarrow$ $\angle ACD = \angle ABD$ **Hence proved.**

Q6. **ΔABC is an isosceles triangle in which $AB = AC$. Side *BA* is produced to *D* such that $AD = AB$ (see figure). Show that $\angle BCD$, is a right angle.**

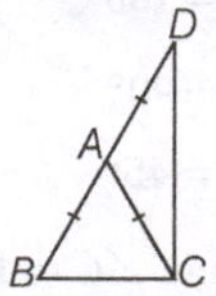

Sol. Given ΔABC is an isosceles triangle in which $AB = AC$ and $AD = AB$.

To prove $\angle BCD$ is a right angle.

Proof In the given figure,

$AB = AC$ [given] ...(i)

and $AB = AD$ [given] ...(ii)

Then, $AC = AD$ [from Eqs. (i) and (ii)]

As, $AC = AB$

$\Rightarrow$ $\angle ABC = \angle ACB$ ...(iii)

[since, angles opposite to equal sides of a triangle are equal]

Also, $AC = AD$

$\Rightarrow$ $\angle ADC = \angle ACD$ ...(iv)

[since, angles opposite to equal sides are equal]

On adding Eqs. (iii) and (iv), we get

$\angle ABC + \angle ADC = \angle ACB + \angle ACD$

$\Rightarrow$ $\angle ABC + \angle ADC = \angle BCD$

[$\because$ $\angle BCD = \angle ACB + \angle ACD$]

$\Rightarrow$ $\angle DBC + \angle BDC = \angle BCD$ ...(v)

[$\because$ $\angle ABC = \angle DBC$ and $\angle ADC = \angle BDC$]

In ΔBCD, we have

$\angle DBC + \angle BDC + \angle BCD = 180°$

[by angle sum property of a triangle]

$\Rightarrow$ $\angle BCD + \angle BCD = 180°$ [from Eq. (v)]

$\Rightarrow$ $2\angle BCD = 180° \Rightarrow \angle BCD = 90°$

So, $\angle BCD$ is a right angle. **Hence proved.**

Q7. **ΔABC is a right angled triangle in which $\angle A = 90°$ and $AB = AC$. Find $\angle B$ and $\angle C$.**

Sol. Given, ΔABC is a right angled triangle in which $\angle A = 90°$ and $AB = AC$.

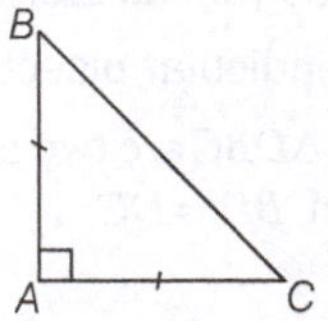

Then, $\angle C = \angle B$ ...(i)

[$\because$ angles opposite to equal sides of a triangle are equal]

Now, $\angle A + \angle B + \angle C = 180°$

[by angle sum property of a triangle]

$\Rightarrow \quad 90° + \angle B + \angle B = 180°$ [from Eq. (i)]

$\Rightarrow \quad 2\angle B = 90°$

$\therefore \quad \angle B = 45°$

Hence, $\angle B = 45°$ and $\angle C = 45°$

Q 8. Show that the angles of an equilateral triangle are 60° each.

Sol. Given ΔABC is an equilateral triangle.

To prove $\angle A = \angle B = \angle C = 60°$

Proof Since, all three sides of an equilateral triangle are equal.

$AB = BC = CA$

$\Rightarrow \quad \angle A = \angle B = \angle C$ ...(i)

$\therefore \quad \angle A + \angle B + \angle C = 180°$

[by angle sum property of a triangle]

$\Rightarrow \angle A + \angle A + \angle A = 180°$ [from Eq. (i)]

$\Rightarrow \quad 3\angle A = 180°$

$\Rightarrow \quad \angle A = \frac{180°}{3}$

$\Rightarrow \quad \angle A = 60°$

Hence, $\angle A = \angle B = \angle C = 60°$ **Hence proved.**

EXERCISE 7.3 (NCERT Page 102)

Q 1. ΔABC and ΔDBC are two isosceles triangles on the same base BC and vertices A and D are on the same side of BC (see figure). If AD is extended to intersect BC at P, show that

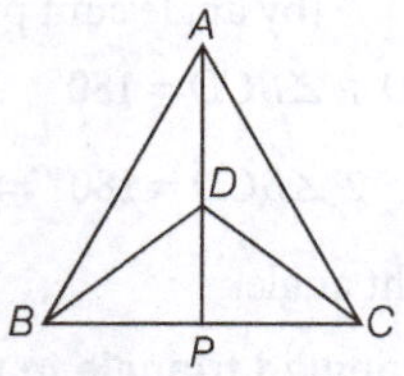

(i) $\Delta ABD \cong \Delta ACD$

(ii) $\Delta ABP \cong \Delta ACP$

(iii) AP bisects $\angle A$ as well as $\angle D$.

(iv) AP is the perpendicular bisector of BC.

Sol. Given ΔABC and ΔDBC are two isosceles triangles, in which $AB = AC$ and $BD = DC$.

To prove

(i) $\Delta ABD \cong \Delta ACD$

(ii) $\Delta ABP \cong \Delta ACP$

(iii) AP bisects $\angle A$ as well as $\angle D$.

(iv) AP is the perpendicular bisector of BC.

Proof

(i) In ΔABD and ΔACD,

$AB = AC$ [given]

$BD = DC$ [given]

and $AD = AD$ [common side]

$\therefore \quad \Delta ABD \cong \Delta ACD$ [by SSS congruence rule]

$\therefore \quad \angle BAD = \angle CAD$ [by CPCT]

(ii) In ΔABP and ΔACP,

$AB = AC$ [given]

$AP = AP$ [common side]

and $\angle BAP = \angle CAP$

[$\because \Delta ABD \cong \Delta ACD, \angle BAP$ or $\angle BAD$) $= \angle CAP$ or $\angle CAD$)]

$\therefore \quad \Delta ABP \cong \Delta ACP$ [by SAS congruence rule]

(iii) From part (ii),

$\Delta ABD \cong \Delta ACD$

$\Rightarrow \quad \angle BAD = \angle DAC$ [by CPCT]

or $\quad \angle PAB = \angle PAC$

Thus, AP bisect $\angle A$ ...(i)

Also, $\Delta BPD \cong \Delta CPD$ [by SSS congruence rule]

$PD = PD$ [common]

$BD = CD$ [since, ΔDBC is isosceles]

$BP = CP$ [by CPCT as $\Delta ABr \cong \Delta ACP$]

So, $\quad \Delta BPD \cong \Delta CPD$ [by SSS congruence rule]

$\Rightarrow \quad \angle BDP = \angle CDP$ [by CPCT] ...(i)

Now, by comparing (i) and (ii) it can be said that AP bisects $\angle A$ as will as $\angle D$.

(iv) From part (iii),

$\Delta DBP \cong \Delta DCP$

Then, $\quad BP = PC$

[$\because \Delta ABP \cong \Delta ACP \Rightarrow BP = PC$, by CPCT]

and $\quad \angle DPB = \angle DPC$ [by CPCT]...(iii)

Also, $\angle DPC + \angle DPB = 180°$ [by linear pair axiom]

$\Rightarrow \quad \angle DPC + \angle DPC = 180°$ [from Eq. (iii)]

$\Rightarrow \quad 2\angle DPC = 180°$

$\therefore \quad \angle DPC = 90°$

Hence, AP is the perpendicular bisector of BC.

Hence proved.

Q2. *AD* is an altitude of an isosceles ΔABC in which *AB* = *AC*. Show that

(i) *AD* bisects *BC*. (ii) *AD* bisects $\angle A$.

Sol. Given ΔABC is an isosceles triangle and $AD \perp BC$, $AB = AC$.

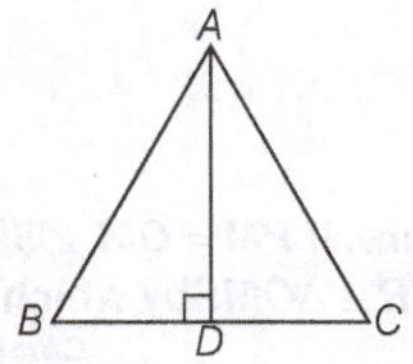

To prove

(i) *AD* bisects *BC*. (ii) *AD* bisects $\angle A$.

Proof

(i) In ΔADB and ΔADC,

$AB = AC$ [given]

$\angle ADB = \angle ADC$ [each 90°]

and $AD = AD$ [common side]

$\therefore$ $\Delta ADB \cong \Delta ADC$

[by RHS congruence rule]

Then, $BD = DC$ [by CPCT]

Hence, *AD* bisects *BC*.

(ii) As, $\Delta ADB \cong \Delta ADC$, then $\angle BAD = \angle CAD$

i.e. *AD* bisects $\angle A$. **Hence proved.**

Q3. Two sides *AB*, *BC* and median *AM* of ΔABC are respectively equal to sides *PQ*, *QR* and median *PN* of ΔPQR. Show that

(i) $\Delta ABM \cong \Delta PQN$

(ii) $\Delta ABC \cong \Delta PQR$

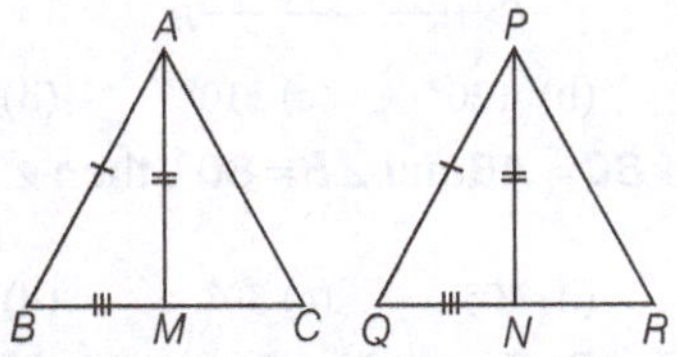

Sol. Given $AB = PQ, BC = QR$, *AM* is the median of ΔABC and *PN* is the median of ΔPQR.

i.e. $BM = MC$ and $QN = NR$

To prove (i) $\Delta ABM \cong \Delta PQN$

(ii) $\Delta ABC \cong \Delta PQR$

Proof Since, *AM* is the median of ΔABC.

$\therefore$ $BM = MC = \frac{1}{2}BC$ [$\because M$ bisects *BC*]...(i)

and *PN* is the median of ΔPQR.

$\therefore$ $QN = NR = \frac{1}{2}QR$ [$\because N$ bisects *QR*] ...(ii)

Now, $BC = QR$ [given]

$\Rightarrow$ $\frac{1}{2}BC = \frac{1}{2}QR$ [divide both sides by 2]

$\therefore$ $BM = QN$ [from Eqs. (i) and (ii)]...(iii)

(i) In ΔABM and ΔPQN, we have

$AB = PQ$ [given]

$AM = PN$ [given]

and $BM = QN$ [from Eq. (iii)]

$\therefore \Delta ABM \cong \Delta PQN$ [by SSS congruence rule]

(ii) In ΔABC and ΔPQR, we have

$AB = PQ$ [given]

$\angle B = \angle Q$ [by CPCT, $\because \Delta ABM \cong \Delta PQN$]

and $BC = QR$ [given]

$\therefore \Delta ABC \cong \Delta PQR$ [by SAS congruence rule]

Hence proved.

Q4. *BE* and *CF* are two equal altitudes of a ΔABC. Using RHS congruence rule, prove that the ΔABC is an isosceles.

Sol. Given $BE = CF$, $BE \perp AC$ and $CF \perp AB$

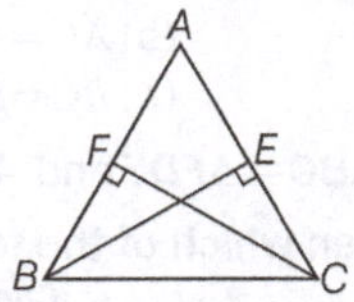

To prove ΔABC is an isosceles triangle.

Proof In ΔBEC and ΔCFB,

$\angle BEC = \angle CFB$ [each 90°]

$BE = CF$ [given]

and $BC = BC$ [common side]

$\therefore$ $\Delta BEC \cong \Delta CFB$ [by RHS congruence rule]

Then, $\angle BCE = \angle CBF$ [by CPCT]

or $\angle BCA = \angle CBA$

$\therefore$ $AB = AC$

[$\because$ sides opposite to equal angles of a triangle are equal]

Hence, ΔABC is an isosceles triangle.

Q5. ΔABC is an isosceles triangle with *AB* = *AC*. Draw $AP \perp BC$ to show that $\angle B = \angle C$.

Sol. Solve as Q. 2.

REVIEW EXERCISE

Including Competency Based Questions

Part I

Multiple Choice Questions

1. **If two triangles are congruent using two sides and the include angle of one triangles are equal to the sides and the included angle of the other triangle. Then, this rule is known as**

(a) SAS congruence rule (b) ASA congruence rule
(c) AAS congruence rule (d) SSS congruence rule.

2. **Which of the following is not well defined congruence rule?**

(a) SAS (b) SSS (c) AAA (d) ASA

3. **Which of the following is not a criterion for congruence of triangles?** Competency Based Question

(a) SAS (b) ASA (c) SSA (d) SSS

4. **In ΔABC and ΔDEF, $AB = FD$ and $\angle A = \angle D$. The two triangles will be congruent by SAS axiom, if** NCERT Exemplar

(a) $BC = EF$ (b) $AC = DE$
(c) $AC = EF$ (d) $BC = DE$

5. **It is given that $\Delta ABC \cong \Delta FDE$ and $AB = 5$ cm, $\angle B = 40°$ and $\angle A = 80°$, then which of the following is true?** Competency Based Question

(a) $DF = 5$ cm, $\angle F = 60°$ (b) $DF = 5$ cm, $\angle E = 60°$
(c) $DE = 5$ cm, $\angle E = 60°$ (d) $DE = 5$ cm, $\angle D = 40°$

6. **In ΔABC and ΔPQR, $AB = PQ$, $\angle A = \angle P$. What will be the condition in which the two triangles will be congruent by ASA axiom?**

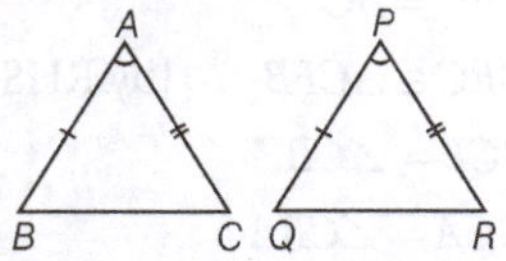

(a) $\angle B = \angle Q$ (b) $\angle B = \angle R$
(c) $\angle B = \angle P$ (d) $\angle C = \angle Q$

7. **In the given figure, if $AF = CD$ and $\angle AFE = \angle CDE$. If $EF = 5$ cm, then ED is**

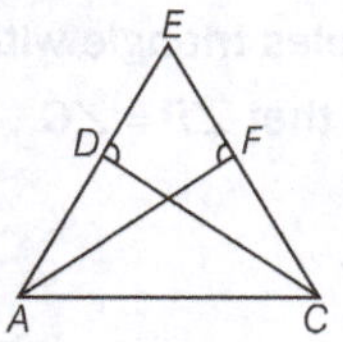

(a) 6 cm (b) 5 cm (c) 8 cm (d) 10 cm

8. **In the given figure, if $PM = QM$, $\angle SMP = \angle RMQ$. Therefore, $\Delta PMR \cong \Delta QMS$ by which congruence rule?** Competency Based Question

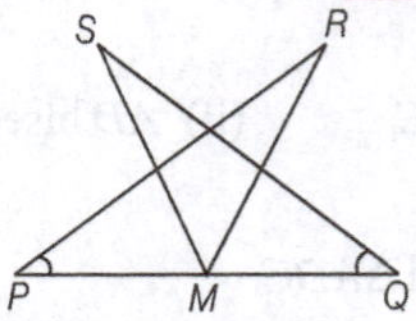

(a) SSS (b) AAS (c) ASA (d) SAS

9. **ΔPQR is an isosceles right angled triangle in which $\angle P = 90°$. Then, $\angle Q$ is equal to**

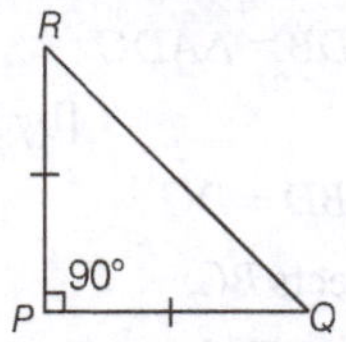

(a) 35° (b) 45° (c) 55° (d) 50°

10. **In the figure, ABC is an isosceles triangle in which $AB = AC$ and PQ is parallel to BC. If $\angle A = 40°$, then $\angle PQB$ is**

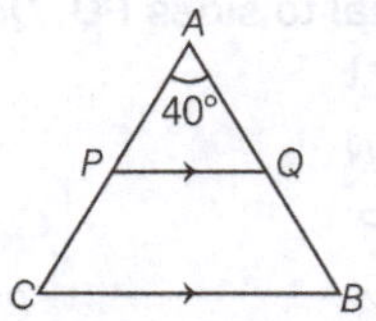

(a) 100° (b) 120° (c) 110° (d) 90°

11. **In ΔABC, if $BC = AB$ and $\angle B = 80°$, then $\angle A$ is equal to** NCERT Exemplar

(a) 80° (b) 40° (c) 50° (d) 100°

12. **In a ΔABC, $AB = 5$ cm, $AC = 5$ cm and $\angle A = 50°$, then $\angle B$ equals**

(a) 35° (b) 65° (c) 80° (d) 40°

13. **In the given figure, if $AB = AC$, $\angle ACM = 125°$ and $\angle PAB = x$, then the value of x is** Competency Based Question

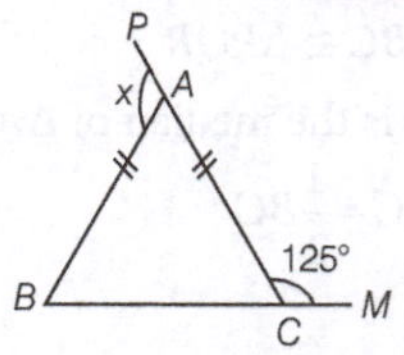

(a) 55° (b) 75° (c) 95° (d) 110°

14. **In the given figure, x and y are**

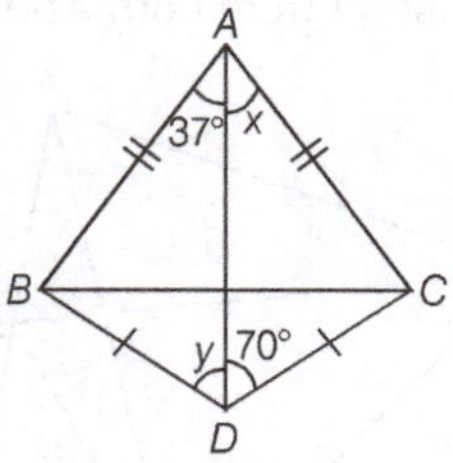

(a) $x=70°, y=37°$
(b) $x=37°, y=70°$
(c) $x=35°, y=60°$
(d) $x=60°, y=37°$

15. **In the given figure, $AD=BC$ and $BD=AC$. If $\angle DAB=45°$, then $\angle CBA$ is**

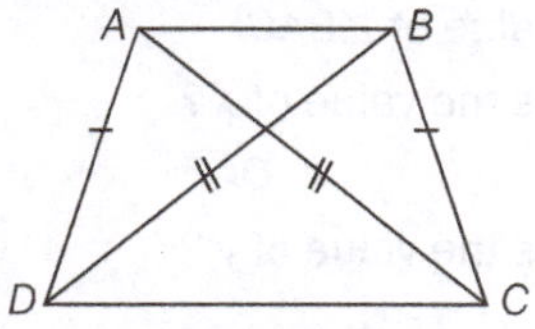

(a) 35° (b) 40°
(c) 43° (d) 45°

Assertion-Reason Type Questions

16. **Assertion** In ΔABC and ΔPQR, $AB=PQ$, $AC=PR$ and $\angle BAC=\angle QPR$.

$\therefore \Delta ABC \cong \Delta PQR$

Reason Both the triangles are congruent by ASA congruence.

(a) Both Assertion and Reason are correct and Reason is the correct explanation of Assertion.
(b) Both Assertion and Reason are correct but Reason is not the correct explanation of Assertion.
(c) Assertion is correct but Reason is incorrect.
(d) Assertion is incorrect but Reason is correct.

17. **Assertion** If we draw triangles with angles 30°, 70° and 80° and the length of the sides of one triangle be different than that of the corresponding sides of the other triangles, then they are not congruent.

Reason If two triangles are constructed, which have all corresponding angles equal but have a pair of unequal corresponding sides, then two triangles cannot be congruent to each other.

(a) Both Assertion and Reason are correct and Reason is the correct explanation of Assertion
(b) Both Assertion and Reason are correct but Reason is not the correct explanation of Assertion
(c) Assertion is correct but Reason is incorrect
(d) Assertion is incorrect but Reason is correct

Case Study Based Questions

18. In a park, there are two triangular flower beds. Flower bed ABC has sides $AB=10$ m, $BC=8$ m and $\angle ABC=60°$.

Flower bed PQR has sides $PQ=10$ m, $QR=8$ m.

On the based of above information answer the following questions

(i) If $\angle PQR=\angle ABC$, then prove that flower bed ABC is congruent to flower bed PQR.

(ii) If $\angle PQR=60°$, then find the sum of angle $\angle BAC$ and $\angle PRQ$.

(iii) (a) If in flower bed ABC, $\angle B=60°$ and $\angle C=80°$, then find $\angle QPR$ in flower bed PQR.

Or

(b) If in flower bed PQR, $\angle PQR=60°$, then what is the measure of $\angle PRQ$?

19. Rajeev and Amit sit together at B. Their work places are at A and C, respectively such that A, B and C form a triangle. BD is the bisector of $\angle ABC$, meets AC at right angle. Various distances are expressed in terms of x and y as shown in the figure.

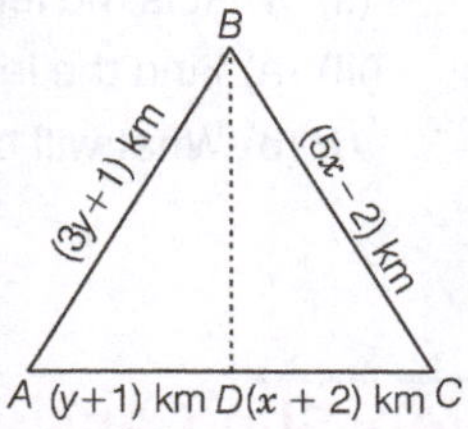

They used bicycles instead of bikes to go to their work places.

On the based of above information answer the following questions

(i) Show that ΔABD and ΔCBD are congruent.

(ii) By using bicycles instead of bikes, which values are depicted by Rajeev and Amit?

(iii) (a) Find the distance between A and C.

Or

(b) Find the distance between B and C.

20. Pavan is studying in IX standard. His father purchase a squared shape plot (shown in figure).

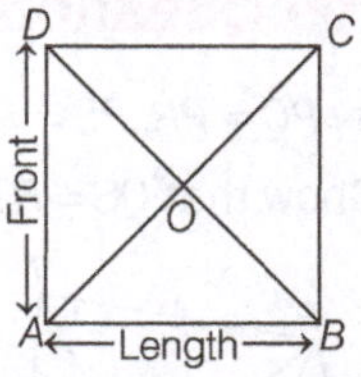

After visiting the land, few questions came in his mind, give answers to his questions by looking at the figure.

(i) What is the measure of $\angle AOB$?

(ii) If $OA=3$ cm, then find the value of OC.

(iii) (a) Which is the correct congruence rule applicable to prove $\Delta ABO \cong \Delta ADO$?

Or (b) If $OB=5$ cm, then find value of BD.

21. In the given figure, $\Delta AFB \cong \Delta AFG$, $\Delta ADE \cong \Delta AGE$ and $\angle EAF = 45°$.

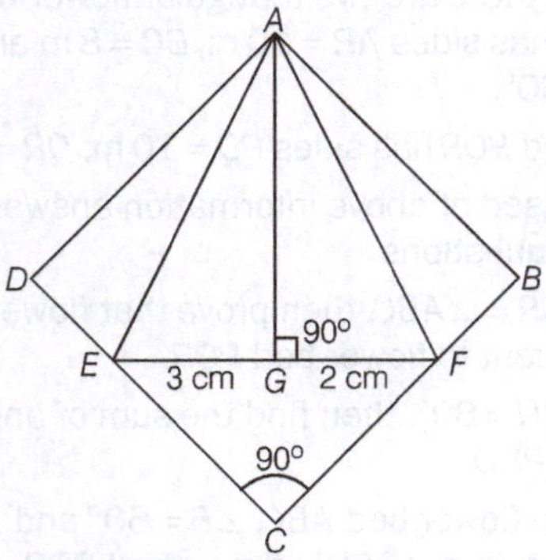

Based on the above information, answer the following questions.

(i) What is the measure of $\angle DAB$?

(ii) What is the length of AD?

(iii) (a) Find the length of AG.

Or (b) What will be the measure of AF?

22. In the given figure, the isosceles $\Delta ABC \cong \Delta EAD$. The point E is equidistant from both A and B.

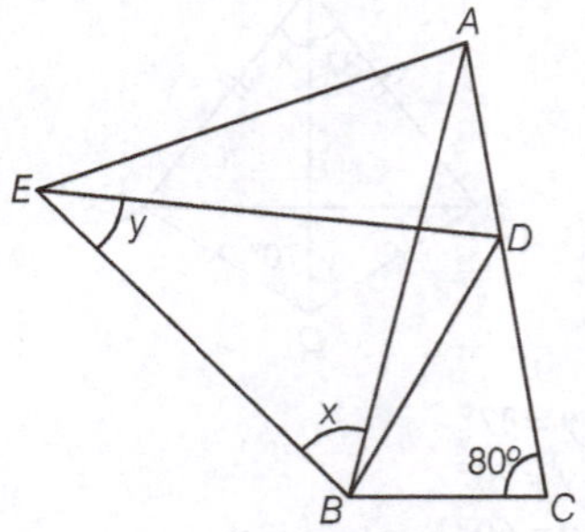

Based on the above information, answer the following questions.

(i) What is the measure of $\angle EAD$?

(ii) Find the value of $\angle BAC$.

(iii) (a) What is the value of x?

Or

(b) What is the value of y?

Part II

Very Short Answer Type Questions

1. If the altitudes from two vertices of a triangle to the opposite sides are equal, then what type of triangle will be formed?

2. In ΔABC, if $BC = AB$ and $\angle B = 70°$, find $\angle A$.

3. In ΔABC and ΔPQR, it is given that $\angle A = \angle R$, $\angle C = \angle P$ and $\angle B = \angle Q$. Find either both triangles are isosceles or congruent. **Competency Based Question**

4. In an isosceles triangle, prove that the altitude from the vertex bisects the base.

Short Answer Type Questions

5. In the given figure, $PQ = PR$, $PS = PT$ and $\angle QPR = \angle SPT$. Show that $QS = RT$

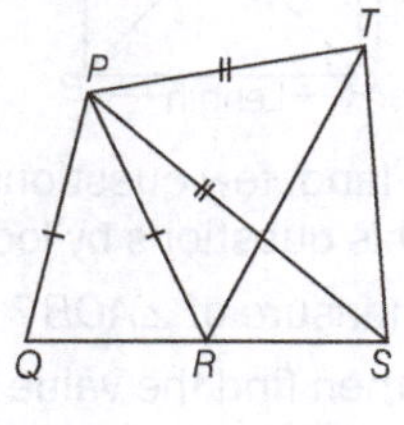

6. In the given figure, if $AB = AD$, $\angle x = \angle w$ and $\angle y = \angle z$, then prove that $AP = AQ$. **Competency Based Question**

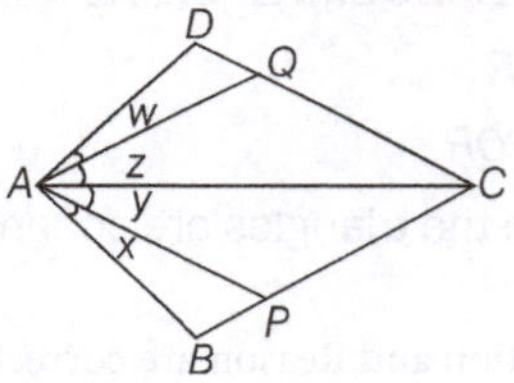

7. In right angled ΔABC, right angled at B, such that $\angle BCA = 2\angle CAB$, show that hypotenuse $AC = 2BC$. **NCERT Exemplar**

8. In right angled ΔABC, $\angle C = 90°$. M is the mid-point of hypotenuse AB. C is joined to M and produced to a point D such that $DM = CM$. Point D is joined to point B. Show that **Competency Based Question**

(i) $\Delta AMC \cong \Delta BMD$ (ii) $\angle DBC = \angle ACB$

9. If P is any point in the square $ABCD$ and $DPQR$ is another square, then prove that $AP = CR$. **Competency Based Question**

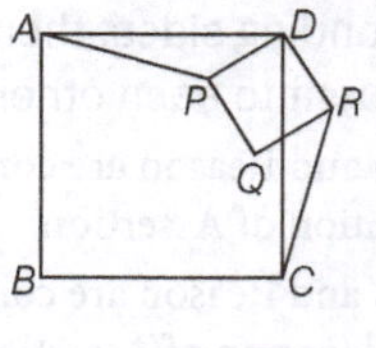

10. *ABCD* is a square. *M* is the mid-point of *AB* and $PQ \perp CM$ meets *AD* at *P* and *CB* produced at *Q*.

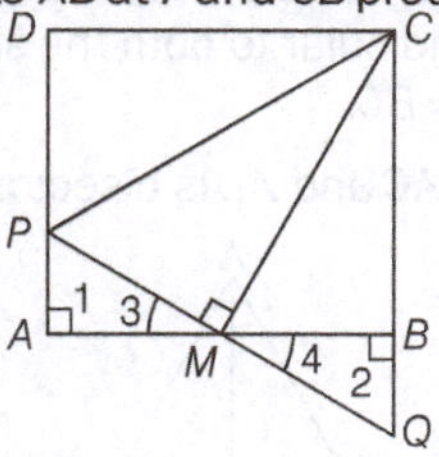

Prove that

(i) $PA = BQ$ (ii) $CP = AB + PA$

11. In the given figure, if $l \parallel m$, $\angle ABC = \angle ABD = 40°$ and $\angle BAC = \angle BAD = 90°$, then prove that ΔBCD is an isosceles triangle.

Competency Based Question

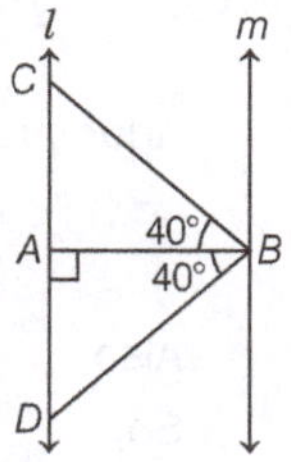

12. In the figure, the diagonal *AC* of a quadrilateral *ABCD* bisects $\angle A$ and $\angle C$. Prove that $AB = AD$ and $CB = CD$. If $AB = 10$ cm, find *AD*.

NCERT Exemplar

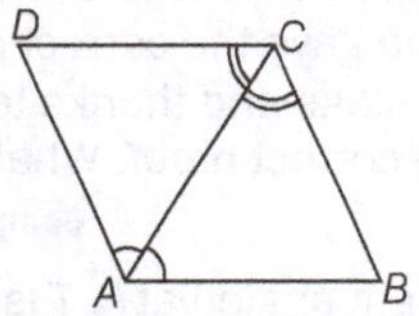

13. In the given figure, $\angle B = \angle E$, $BD = CE$ and $\angle 1 = \angle 2$. Show that $\Delta ABC \cong \Delta AED$.

Competency Based Question

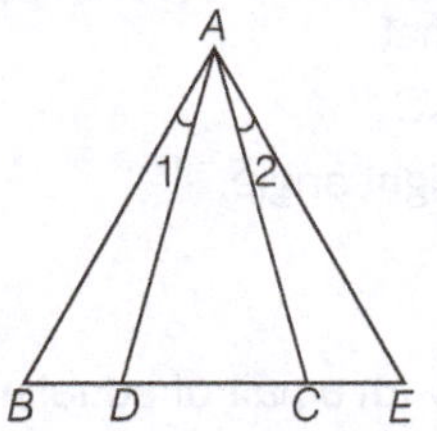

14. In the given figure, *ABCD* is a square. *M* is the mid-point of *AB* and $PQ \perp CM$ meets *AD* at *P* and *CB* introduced at *Q*. Prove that

(i) $\Delta PAM \cong \Delta QBM$

(ii) $CP = CQ$ **Competency Based Question**

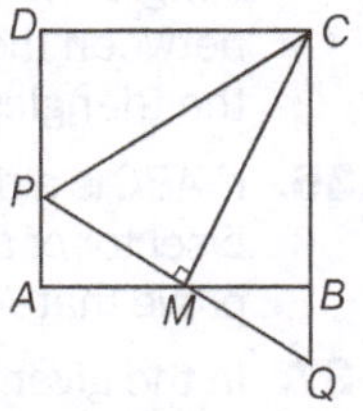

15. In the given figure, $AB = AC$ and $\angle x = \angle y$. Prove that $DC = BE$.

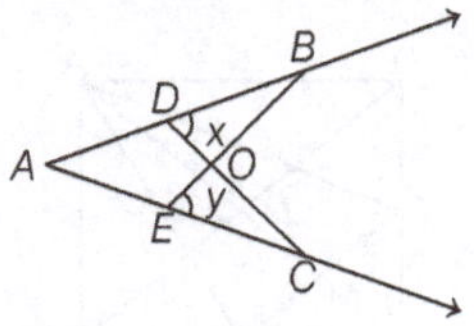

16. The image of an object placed at a point *A* before a plane mirror *LM* is seen at the point *B* by an observer at *D* as shown in figure. Prove that the image is as far behind the mirror as the object is in front of the mirror.

NCERT Exemplar

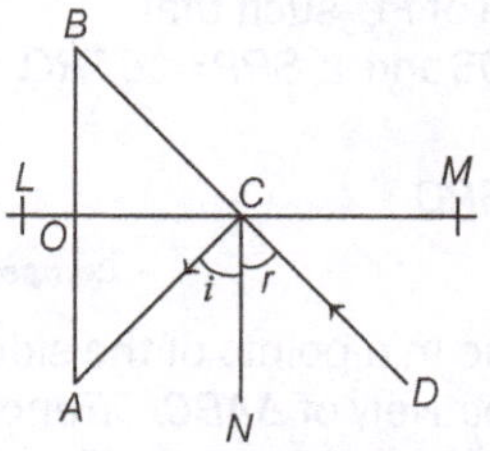

17. Prove that angles opposite to equal sides of a triangle are equal.

18. In ΔABC, the sides *AB*, *AC* are equal and the base *BC* is produced to any point *D*. From *D*, *DE* is drawn perpendicular to *BA* produced and *DF* perpendicular to *AC* produced. Prove that *BD* bisects $\angle EDF$.

19. In the given figure, if $AB = AC$, then prove that $\angle ABD = \angle ACE$. If $\angle ABD = 110°$; find $\angle ACE$.

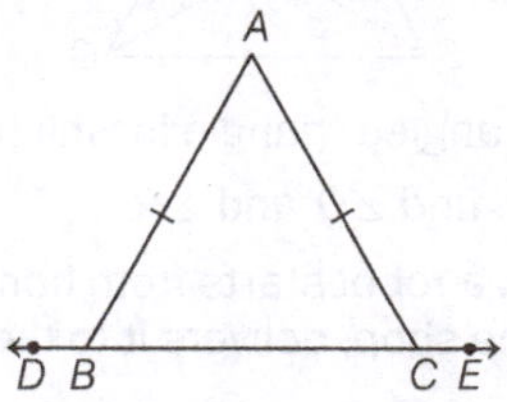

20. In the given figure, *PQRS* is a square and *M* is the mid-point of *PS*. *MR* and *MQ* are joined. Prove that $\angle MQR = \angle MRQ$.

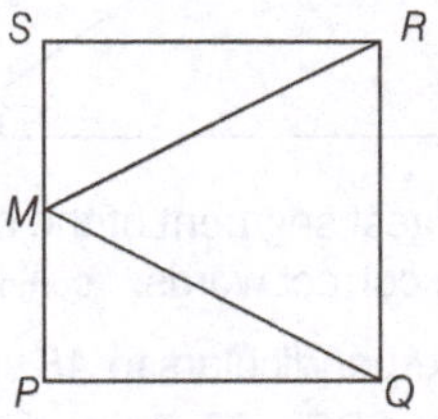

21. *ABC* is a triangle in which $\angle B = 2\angle C$. *D* is a point on *BC* such that *AD* bisects $\angle BAC$ and $AB = CD$. Prove that $\angle BAC = 72°$.

22. Bisectors of the angles *B* and *C* of an isosceles triangle with $AB = AC$ intersect each other at *O*. *BO* is produced to a point *M*. Prove that $\angle MOC = \angle ABC$. **NCERT Exemplar**

23. In the given figure, $\angle BAC = 80°$, $CA = CB$ and $BD = CD$. Find the measures of $\angle x$, $\angle y$ and $\angle z$.

Competency Based Question

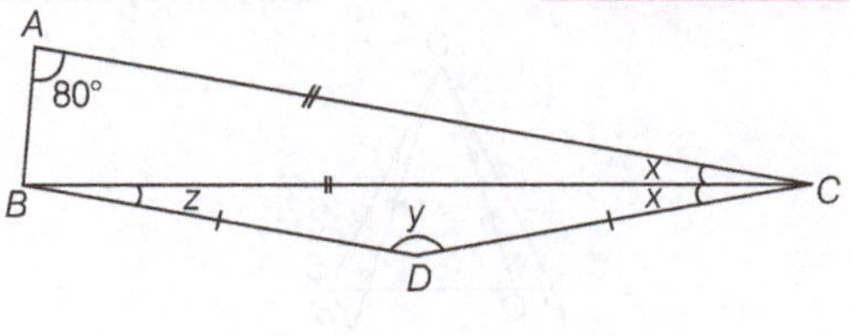

24. PQ is a line segment and R is its mid-point S and T are points on the same side of PQ such that $\angle QPT = \angle PQS$ and $\angle SRP = \angle TRQ$. Show that

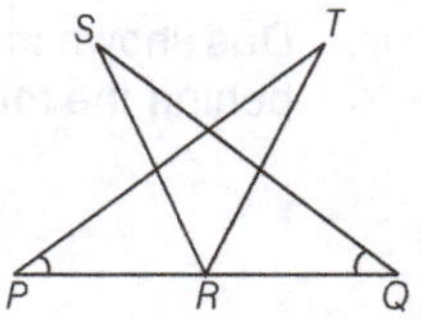

(i) $\Delta PRT \cong \Delta SRQ$

(ii) $PT = SQ$ **Competency Based Question**

25. E and F are the mid-points of the sides AB and AC, respectively of ΔABC. CE and BF are produced to X and Y respectively, so that $EX = CE$ and $FY = BF$. AX and AY are joined.

Prove that

(i) $\Delta AEX \cong \Delta BEC$ and $\Delta AFY \cong \Delta CFB$.

(ii) XAY is a straight line.

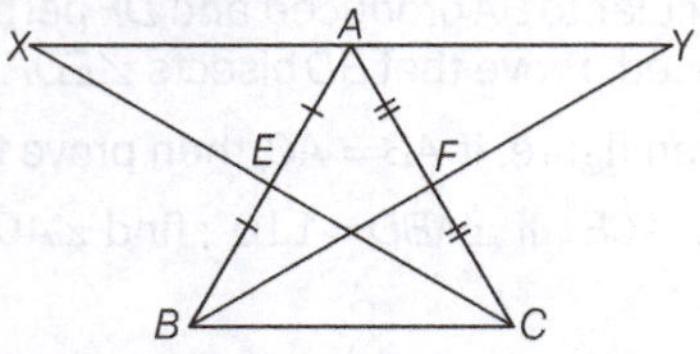

26. PQR is a right angled triangle in which $\angle P = 90°$ and $PQ = PR$, then find $\angle Q$ and $\angle R$.

27. In a toy game, a robot starts from home, picks an object from the shop, delivers it to the client and goes back home.

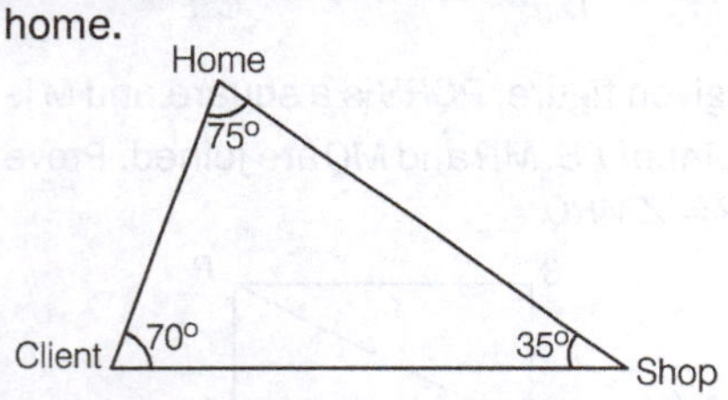

Which is the longest segment of the path travelled by the robot? Write the correct words. **Competency Based Question**

28. CE and BF are perpendiculars to AB and AC, respectively in ΔABC such that $BE = CF$. Prove that $\angle B = \angle C$.

29. PQR is an isosceles triangle with $PQ = PR$. Draw $PM \perp QR$ to show that $\angle Q = \angle R$.

Long Answer Type Questions

30. O is a point in the interior of a square $ABCD$ such that OAB is an equilateral triangle. Prove that $OC = OD$.

31. In the given figure, $OP = OR$, $OQ = OS$ and $\angle POR = \angle QOS$. Prove that $PQ = RS$. **Competency Based Question**

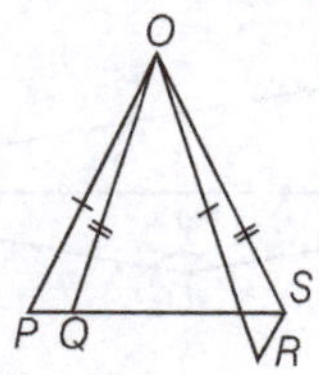

32. Line segment joining the mid-points M and N of parallel sides AB and DC, respectively of a trapezium $ABCD$ is perpendicular to both the sides AB and DC. Prove that $AD = BC$. **NCERT Exemplar**

33. In ΔABC, $AB = AC$ and AD is bisector of $\angle BAC$.

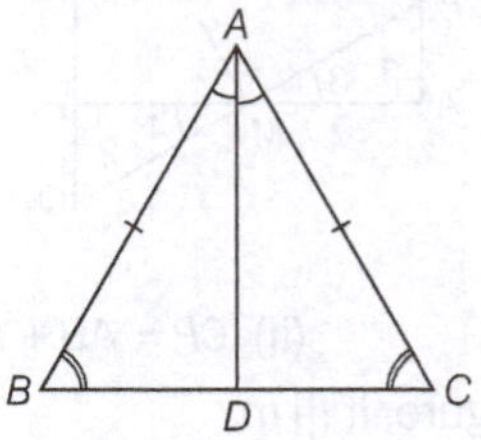

Arjun proved that $\Delta ABD \cong \Delta ACD$ as follows:

$AB = AC$ [given]

$\angle BAD = \angle CAD$ [given]

Also, $\angle B = \angle C$ [$\because AB = AC$]

So, $\Delta ABD \cong \Delta ACD$

[by ASA congruence rule]

His classmate Mansoor pointed to him that this proof is not correct and gave the correct proof. Arjun accepted his mistake and thanks to Mansoor for the same. Write the correct proof. What is the mistake in Arjun's proof? **Competency Based Question**

34. In right ΔPQR, right angled at R, T is the mid-point of hypotenuse PQ, R is joined to T and produced to a point S such that $ST = RT$. Point S is joined to point Q. Show that

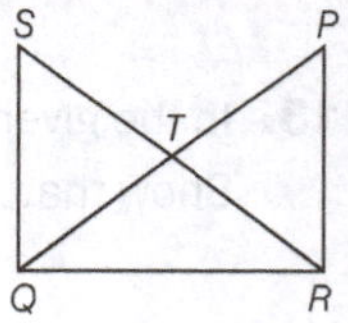

(i) $\Delta PTR \cong \Delta QTS$

(ii) $\angle SQR$ is a right angle.

(iii) $RT = \frac{1}{2} PQ$

35. 'Two triangles with a pair of equal angles are congruent.' Why is it necessary to have the side between the two angles be of the same length for both the triangles? **Competency Based Question**

36. If ABC is a right angled triangle such that $AB = AC$ and bisector of angle C intersects the side AB at D, then prove that $AC + AD = BC$. **NCERT Exemplar**

37. In the given figure, $ABCD$ is a square and EF is parallel to diagonal BD and $EM = FM$. **Competency Based Question**

Prove that

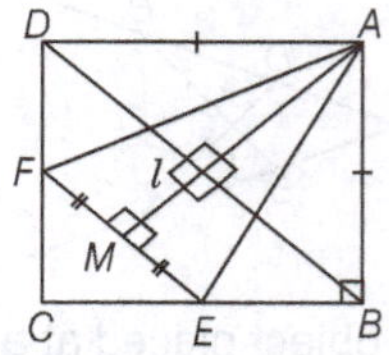

(i) $DF = BE$ (ii) $\angle DAM = \angle BAM$

38. Two lines l and m intersect at the point O and P is a point on a line n passing through the point O such that P is equidistant from l and m. Prove that n is the bisector of the angle formed by l and m. **NCERT Exemplar**

39. In the given figure, QX and RX are the bisectors of $\angle PQR$ and $\angle PRQ$, respectively of ΔPQR. If $XS \perp QR$ and $XT \perp PQ$, then prove that $\Delta XTQ \cong \Delta XSQ$ and PX bisects $\angle P$.

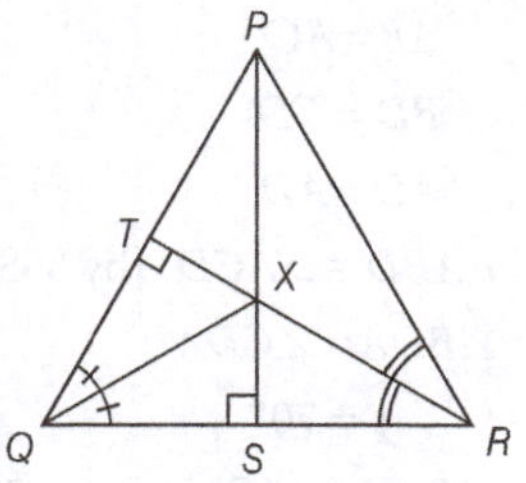

40. Rita says, 'For two triangles to be congruent, any three parameters of the six (3 sides and 3 angles) should be equal.' Give examples in favour of and against her statement. **Competency Based Question**

41. The picture below shows a staircase outside a house. Each step of the staircase is congruent and there are 25 steps in the staircase from the floor to the platform and 25 steps from the platform to the roof.

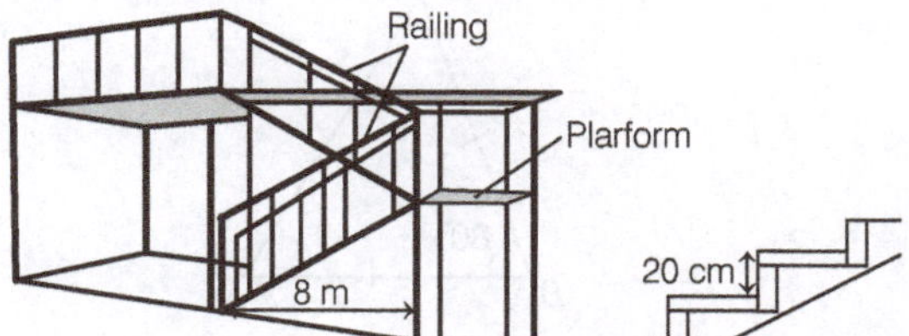

What is the length of the staircase railing? **Competency Based Question**

HINTS & ANSWERS

Part I

1. (a) This rule is known as SAS congruence rule.
2. (c) AAA is not well defined congruence rule.
3. (c) We know that two triangles are congruent, if the sides and angles of one triangle are equal to the corresponding sides and angles of the other triangle. Also, criterion for congruence of triangles are SAS (Side-Angle-Side), ASA (Angle-Side-Angle), SSS (Side-Side-Side) and RHS (right angle-hypotenuse-side). So, SSA is not a criterion for congruence of triangles.
4. (b) Given, in ΔABC and ΔDEF,
$$AB = DF \text{ and } \angle A = \angle D$$
We know that two triangles will be congruent by SAS rule, if two sides and the included angle of one triangle are equal to the two sides and the included angle of other triangle.
$\therefore \quad AC = DE$
5. (b) Given, $\Delta ABC \cong \Delta FDE$, $AB = 5$ cm, $\angle B = 40°$ and $\angle A = 80°$.
Since, $\Delta FDE \cong \Delta ABC$

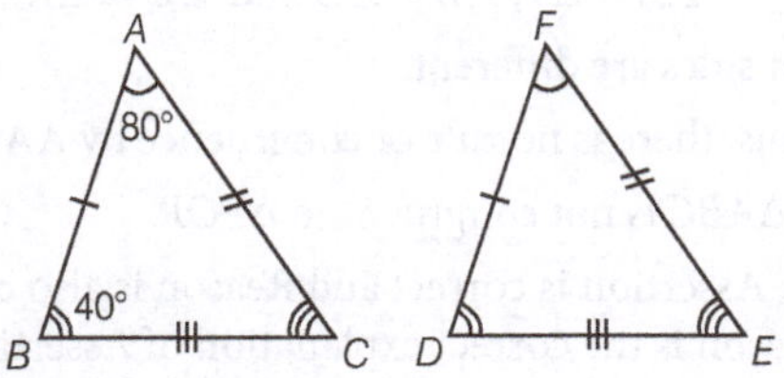

$\therefore \quad DF = AB$ [by CPCT]
$\Rightarrow \quad DF = 5$ cm
and $\quad \angle E = \angle C$ [by CPCT]
$\Rightarrow \quad \angle E = \angle C = 180° - (\angle A + \angle B)$
[by angle sum property of a ΔABC]
$\Rightarrow \quad \angle E = 180° - (80° + 40°)$
$\Rightarrow \quad \angle E = 60°$
6. (a) Since, $AB = PQ$, $\angle A = \angle P$
and $\Delta ABC \cong \Delta PQR$ [by ASA congruence rule]
$\therefore \quad \angle B = \angle Q$
7. (b) Prove that $\Delta AFE \cong \Delta CDE$ [by AAS congruence rule]
Then, by CPCT, $\quad EF = ED$
$\therefore \quad ED = 5$ cm
8. (c) Given, $\angle SMP = \angle RMQ$
On adding $\angle SMR$ to both sides, we get
$\angle SMP + \angle SMR = \angle RMQ + \angle SMR$
$\Rightarrow \quad \angle PMR = \angle SMQ$
Also, $\quad PM = QM$ [given]
$\therefore \quad \Delta PMR \cong \Delta SMQ$ [by ASA congruence rule]
9. (b) Since, $PR = PQ$
$\therefore \quad \angle PQR = \angle PRQ$ [angles opposite to equal sides]
Now, $\angle P + \angle Q + \angle R = 180°$
$\Rightarrow \quad 90° + \angle Q + \angle Q = 180°$
$\Rightarrow \quad 2\angle Q = 180° - 90° = 90°$
$\Rightarrow \quad \angle Q = 45°$
10. (c) $\angle C = \angle B$
[$\because AB = AC$, angles opposite to equal sides are equal]
$\therefore \quad \angle B = \angle C = 70°$
$PQ \parallel BC$

$\Rightarrow \angle PQB + \angle CBQ = 180°$ [co-interior angles]

$\Rightarrow \angle PQB + 70° = 180°$

$\Rightarrow \angle PQB = 110°$

11. (c) Given, ΔABC such that $BC = AB$ and $\angle B = 80°$

In ΔABC, $AB = BC \Rightarrow \angle C = \angle A$ ...(i)

[angles opposite to equal sides are equal]

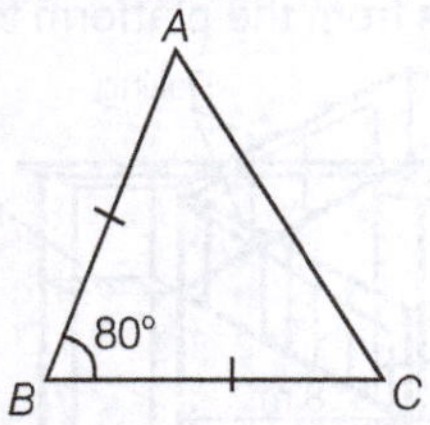

We know that the sum of all the angles of a triangle is 180°.

$\therefore \angle A + \angle B + \angle C = 180°$

$\Rightarrow \angle A + 80° + \angle A = 180°$ [from Eq. (i)]

$\Rightarrow 2\angle A = 180° - 80° = 100°$

$\Rightarrow \angle A = \frac{100°}{2}$

$\Rightarrow \angle A = 50°$

12. (b) Since, $AB = AC$ and the angles opposite to equal sides of a triangle are equal.

$\therefore \angle C = \angle B$

Let $\angle B = \angle C = x$

In ΔABC,

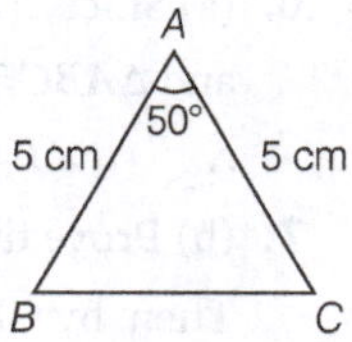

$\angle A + \angle B + \angle C = 180°$

$\Rightarrow 50° + x + x = 180°$

$\Rightarrow 2x = 130°$

$\Rightarrow x = 65°$

$\Rightarrow \angle B = \angle C = 65°$

13. (d) In the given figure, we have

$\angle ACB + \angle ACM = 180°$ [linear pair]

$\Rightarrow \angle ACB + 125° = 180°$

$\Rightarrow \angle ACB = 180° - 125°$

$\Rightarrow \angle ACB = 55°$ ...(i)

Also, we are given that in ΔABC,

$AB = AC$

$\Rightarrow \angle ACB = \angle ABC$

[$\because$ angles opposite to equal sides of a triangle are equal]

$\Rightarrow \angle ABC = 55°$ [using Eq. (i)]

Now, the exterior angle $\angle PAB$ is equal to the sum of the two opposite interior angles, $\angle ABC$ and $\angle ACB$.

Thus, we have

$\angle PAB = \angle ABC + \angle ACB$

$\Rightarrow x = 55° + 55°$

$\therefore x = 110°$

14. (b) In ΔABD and ΔACD,

$AB = AC$ [given]

$BD = CD$ [given]

$AD = AD$ [common]

$\therefore \Delta ABD \cong \Delta ACD$ [by SSS congruence rule]

$\Rightarrow \angle BDA = \angle CDA$ [by CPCT]

$\Rightarrow y = 70°$

Similarly, $\angle BAD = \angle CAD \Rightarrow x = 37°$ [by CPCT]

Hence, $x = 37°$ and $y = 70°$.

15. (d) **Hint** Prove $\Delta ABD \cong \Delta BAC$,

[by SSS congruence rule]

$\therefore \angle DAB = \angle CBA$ [by CPCT]

Thus, $\angle CBA = 45°$

16. (c) **Assertion** In ΔABC and ΔPQR,

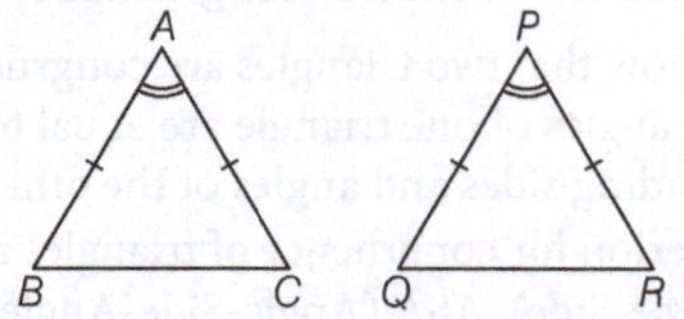

$AB = PQ, AC = PR$

and $\angle BAC = \angle QPR$

$\therefore \Delta ABC \cong \Delta PQR$ [by SAS congruence rule]

$\therefore$ Assertion is correct.

Reason is not correct.

17. (a) **Assertion** In ΔABC and ΔPQR,

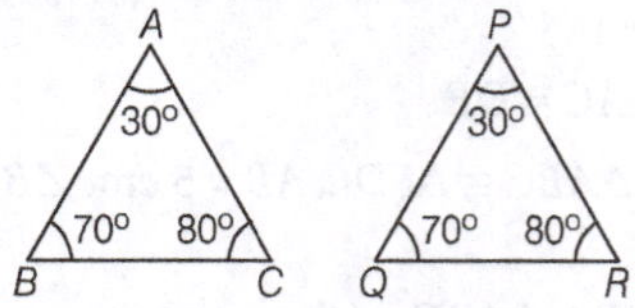

$\angle A = \angle P, \angle B = \angle Q$ and $\angle C = \angle R$

But sides are different.

Thus, there is no rule of congruence by AAA.

$\therefore \Delta ABC$ is not congruent to ΔPQR.

So, Assertion is correct and Reason is also correct and Reason is the correct explanation of Assertion.

18. (i) In ΔABC and ΔPQR,

$$AB = PQ = 10 \text{ m}$$

and $\angle BC = QR = 8 \text{ m}$

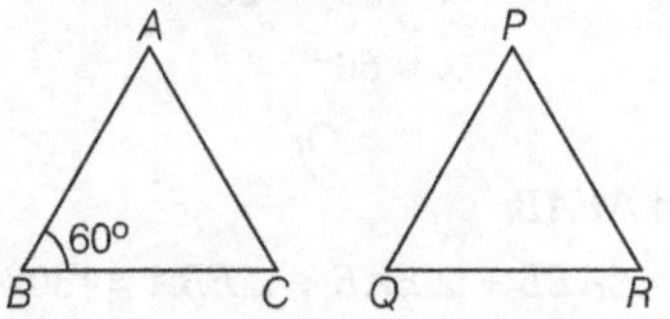

Also, given

$$\angle ABC = \angle PQR = 60°$$

Thus, $\Delta ABC \cong \Delta PQR$ [by SAS Congruence rule]

(ii) Given, $\angle PQR = 60°$

From part (i),

$$\Delta ABC \cong \Delta PQR$$

$\Rightarrow \angle BAC = \angle QPR$ ...(i) [by CPCT]

Now, in ΔPQR,

$$\angle PRQ + \angle PQR + \angle QPR = 180°$$

[by linear pair axiom]

$\Rightarrow \angle PRQ + 60° + \angle BAC = 180°$ [using Eq. (i)]

$\Rightarrow \angle PRQ + \angle BAC = 180° - 60°$

$\Rightarrow \angle BAC + \angle PRQ = 120°$

(iii) (a) We have,

$\Delta ABC \cong \Delta PQR$ [from part (i)]

$\Rightarrow \angle BAC = \angle QPR$ [by CPCT]

$\Rightarrow \angle QPR = \angle BAC$ ...(ii)

Now, in ΔABC,

$\angle A + \angle B + \angle C = 180°$ [by linear pair axiom]

$\angle A + 60° + 80° = 180°$

[given $\angle B = 60°, \angle C = 80°$]

$\Rightarrow \angle A = 180° - 140°$

Thus, $\angle BAC = 40°$

Then, from Eq (ii), we get

$$\angle QPR = 40°$$

Or

(b) From part (ii), we have

$\angle BAC + \angle PRQ = 120°$ ...(iii)

Also, we have, $\angle BAC = 40°$ [from part (iii) (a)]

Therefore, from Eq (iii), we get

$$40° + \angle PRQ = 120°$$

$\Rightarrow \angle PRQ = 120° - 40° = 80°$

19. (i) In the given figure, BD is perpendicular to AC.

$\therefore \angle 3 = \angle 4$ [each 90°]

Also, BD is the bisector of $\angle ABC$.

$\therefore \angle 1 = \angle 2$

In ΔABD and ΔCBD,

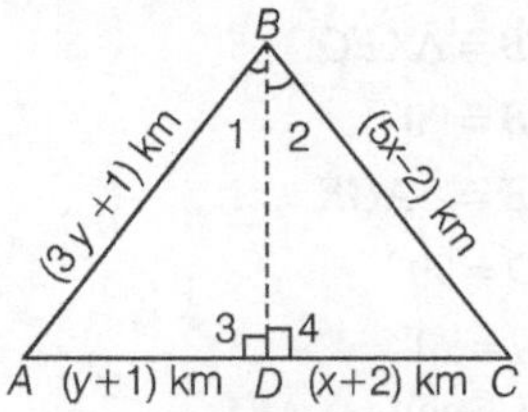

$\angle 1 = \angle 2$ [proved above]

$\angle 3 = \angle 4$ [proved above]

and $BD = BD$ [common side]

$\therefore \Delta ABD \cong \Delta CBD$ [by ASA congruence rule]

(ii) By using bicycles instead of bikes by Rajeev and Amit, values shown by them are making an effort towards reducing pollution which helps in protecting the environment and maintaining their physical fitness.

(iii) (a) We have, from part (i)

$$\Delta ABD \cong \Delta CBD$$

Then, $AB = CB$ [by CPCT]

$\Rightarrow 3y + 1 = 5x - 2 \Rightarrow 5x - 3y = 3$ ...(i)

and $AD = CD$ [by CPCT]

$\Rightarrow y + 1 = x + 2 \Rightarrow -x + y = 1$ ...(ii)

From Eqs. (i) and (ii), we get

$$x = 3, y = 4$$

$\because$ Distance between A and C

$= [(y + 1) + (x + 2)]$ km

$= [(4 + 1) + (3 + 2)]$ km $= 10$ km

Or (b) We have, $x = 3$ and $y = 4$.

$\because$ Distance between B and $C = (5x - 2)$ km

$= (5 \times 3 - 2)$ km $= 13$ km

20. (i) Since, given quadrilateral $ABCD$ is a square.

$\therefore AC \perp BD$

So, $\angle AOB = \angle AOD = 90°$

(ii) As we know that the diagonals of square bisect each others.

$\therefore OC = AO = 3$ cm

(iii) (a) In ΔABO and ΔADO,

$BO = OD$ [given]

$AO = AO$ [common]

$\angle AOB = \angle AOD = 90°$ [given]

$\therefore \Delta ABO \cong \Delta ADO$ [by SAS congruence rule]

Or

(b) Since, the diagonals of square bisect each others.

$\therefore OB = OD$

So, $OD = 5$ cm

$\therefore BD = 10$ cm [$\because BD = 2 \times OB$]

21. Hint

(i) $\Delta AFB \cong \Delta AFG$

$\therefore \quad \angle B = 90°$ [by CPCT]

$\Delta ADE \cong \Delta AGE$

$\therefore \quad \angle D = 90°$ [by CPCT]

$\angle C = 90°$ [given]

$\therefore \quad \angle A = 90°$

Ans. $\angle DAB = 90°$

(ii) $EG = 3$ cm

$\therefore ED = 3$ cm [by CPCT]

$GF = 2$ cm

$\therefore FB = 2$ cm [by CPCT]

$\because ABCD$ is a square.

Let the side be x cm.

$\therefore DE = 3$ and $EC = x - 3$

$BF = 2$ and $FC = x - 2$

Now, in ΔEFC, by Pythagoras theorem,

$$(x-3)^2 + (x-2)^2 = 25$$

$$x = -1, 6$$

Ans. Length of $AD = 6$ cm

(iii) (a) Since, $\Delta ADE \cong \Delta AGE$

$\therefore \quad AD = AG$ [by CPCT]

Thus, $\quad AG = 6$ cm

Or

(b) We have, $AG = 6$ cm and $GF = 2$ cm

Now, in right angled ΔAGF,

$$AF = \sqrt{(AG)^2 + (GF)^2}$$

$$= \sqrt{36 + 4} = 2\sqrt{10} \text{ cm}$$

22. (i) ΔABC is an isosceles triangle,

$\therefore \quad AB = AC \Rightarrow \angle ACB = \angle ABC = 80°$

[angles opposite to equal side of triangle are equal]

and ΔEAD is an isosceles triangle,

$\therefore \quad EA = ED \Rightarrow \angle EDA = \angle EAD$

[angles opposite to equal side of triangle are equal]

Since, $\Delta ABC \cong \Delta EAD$

$\angle ABC = \angle EAD = 80°$

(ii) Given that E is equidistant from A and B.

$\therefore \quad EA = EB \Rightarrow \angle EBA = \angle EAB = x$

[angles opposite to equal side of triangle are equal]

In ΔABC,

$\angle ABC + \angle BAC + \angle ACB = 180°$

$\Rightarrow \quad \angle BAC = 180° - (80° + 80°)$

$= 180° - 160° = 20°$

$\therefore \quad \angle BAC = 20°$

(iii) (a) **Hint** $\angle EAD = \angle EAB + \angle BAC$

$\Rightarrow \quad 80° = x + 20°$

$\Rightarrow \quad x = 80° - 20°$

$x = 60°$

Or

(b) In ΔEAB,

$\angle AEB + \angle EAB + \angle EBA = 180°$

$\Rightarrow \angle AED + \angle DEB + x + x = 180°$

$\Rightarrow \quad 20° + y + 60° + 60° = 180°$

$[\because \angle AED = 180° - 80 - 80°]$

$\Rightarrow \quad y + 140° = 180°$

$\Rightarrow \quad y = 180° - 140° = 40°$

Hence, the value of y is 40°.

Part II

1. Hint We know, if the altitudes from two vertices of a triangle to the opposite sides are equal, then the triangle is an isosceles triangle.

2. Hint

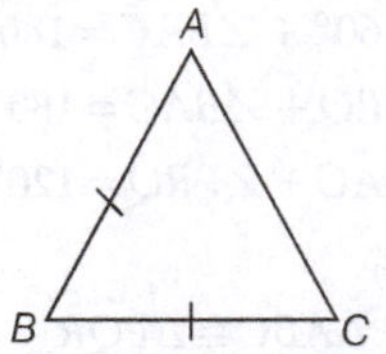

Angles opposite to equal sides are also equal.

Thus, $\angle A = \angle C$ **Ans.** 55°.

3. Both ΔABC and ΔPQR are neither congruent nor isosceles because there is no congruence rule related to all three angles.

4. Hint In ΔABD and ΔACD,

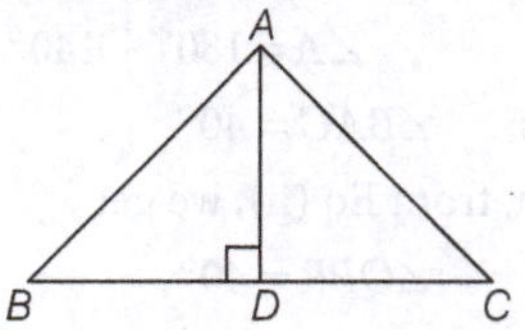

$AB = AC$

$\Rightarrow \quad AD = AD$ [common side]

$\angle ADB = \angle ADC = 90°$

$\therefore \quad \Delta ABD \cong \Delta ACD$ [by RHS congruence rule]

Hence, $BD = CD$ [by CPCT]

5. Given $PS = PT$, $PQ = PR$ and $\angle QPR = \angle SPT$.

To prove $\quad QS = RT$

Proof Since, $\angle QPR = \angle SPT$

On adding $\angle RPS$ to both sides, we get

$\angle QPR + \angle RPS = \angle SPT + \angle RPS$

$\Rightarrow \quad \angle QPS = \angle RPT$ ... (i)

In ΔPQS and ΔPRT, we have

$PS = RT$ [given]

$PQ = PR$ [given]

$\angle QPS = \angle RPT$ [from Eq. (i)]

$\therefore$ $PQS \cong \Delta PRT$ [by SAS congruence rule]

Then, $QS = RT$ [by CPCT]

6. Hint $\angle x = \angle w$ ...(i)

and $\angle y = \angle z$ ...(ii)

On adding Eqs. (i) and (ii), we get

$\angle x + \angle y = \angle z + \angle w$ ...(iii)

Now, take ΔADC and ΔABC and prove them congruent using SAS congruence rule. And prove $AP = AQ$. [by CPCT]

7. Hint Given In right angled ΔABC, right angled at B, $\angle BCA = 2\ \angle CAB$

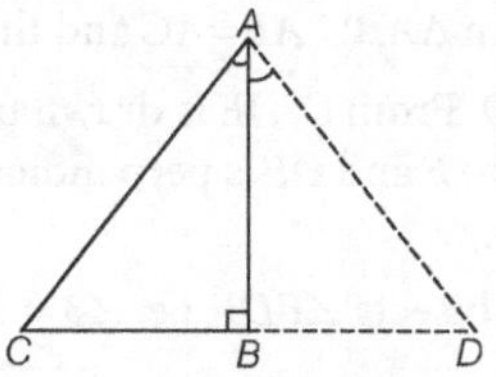

To prove $AC = 2BC$

Construction Produce a line CB to a point D such that $BC = BD$ and join AD.

Proof In ΔABC and ΔABD,

$AB = AB$ [common side]

$BC = BD$ [by construction]

and $\angle ABC = \angle ABD$ [each 90°]

$\Delta ABC \cong \Delta ABD$ [by SAS congruence rule]

$\Rightarrow$ $\angle CAB = \angle DAB$ [by CPCT] ...(i)

and $AC = AD$ [by CPCT] ...(ii)

Now, $\angle CAD = \angle CAB + \angle BAD$

$\Rightarrow$ $\angle CAD = \angle CAB + \angle CAB$ [from Eq. (i)]

$\Rightarrow$ $\angle CAD = 2\ \angle CAB = \angle BCA$

[$\because \angle BCA = 2\angle CAB$, given]

$\Rightarrow$ $\angle CAD = \angle DCA$ [$\because \angle DCA = \angle BCA$] ...(iii)

From Eq. (ii), we get $AC = AD$

$\Rightarrow$ $\angle ADC = \angle DCA$ ...(iv)

[$\because$ angles opposite to equal sides of a triangle are equal]

From Eqs. (iii) and (iv), $\angle CAD = \angle DCA = \angle ADC$

Thus, ΔACD is an equilateral triangle.

$\therefore$ $AC = CD$

$\Rightarrow$ $AC = 2BC$ [$\because BC = BD$] **Hence proved.**

8. Hint (i) In ΔAMC and ΔBMD,

$AM = BM$

$CM = DM$ [given]

and $\angle AMC = \angle BMD$ [vertically opposite angles]

$\Delta AMC \cong \Delta BMD$ [by SAS congruence rule]

(ii) $AC = BD$ [by CPCT]

$\angle CAM = \angle DBM$ [by CPCT]

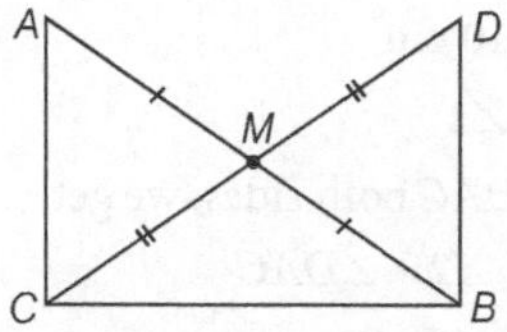

$\therefore$ $AC \parallel DB$

$\therefore$ $\angle C + \angle B = 180°$ [co-interior angles]

$\Rightarrow$ $\angle B = 90°$ [$\because \angle C = 90°$]

$\therefore$ $\angle B = \angle C = 90°$

9. Given P is any point in the square $ABCD$ and $DPQR$ is another square.

To prove $AP = CR$

Proof Let $\angle PDC = x$

Then, $\angle ADP = \angle ADC - \angle PDC = (90° - x)$ ...(i)

and $\angle CDR = \angle PDR - \angle PDC = (90° - x)$ ...(ii)

From Eqs. (i) and (ii), we get

$\angle ADP = \angle CDR$ ...(iii)

In ΔADP and ΔCDR, we have

$AD = CD$ [sides of a square]

$\angle ADP = \angle CDR$ [from Eq. (iii)]

and $DP = DR$ [sides of a square]

$\therefore$ $\Delta ADP \cong \Delta CDR$ [by SAS congruence rule]

Then, $AP = CR$ [by CPCT] **Hence proved.**

10. Hint

(i) Prove $\Delta PAM \cong \Delta QBM$ [by ASA congruence rule]

Then, $MP = MQ$ and $PA = QB$ [by CPCT]

(ii) In ΔCMP and ΔCMQ, we have

$MP = MQ$ [proved above]

$\angle CMP = \angle CMQ$ [each 90°]

and $CM = CM$ [common side]

$\therefore$ $\Delta CMP \cong \Delta CMQ$ [by SAS congruence rule]

Then, $CP = CQ$ [by CPCT]

$\Rightarrow$ $CP = CB + BQ$ [$\because CQ = CB + BQ$]

$\Rightarrow$ $CP = AB + PA$

[$\because CB = AB$, sides of a square and $BQ = PA$, proved above]

Hence proved.

11. Hint Prove $\Delta BAC \cong \Delta BAD$

[by ASA congruence rule]

Then, $BC = BD$ [by CPCT]

$\therefore$ ΔBCD is an isosceles triangle.

12. Hint Prove $\Delta ABC \cong \Delta ADC$ [by ASA congruence rule]

and then by CPCT

$AB = AD$ and $CB = CD$

$\therefore AB = AD = 10$ cm

13. Hint $\angle 1 = \angle 2$ [given]

On adding $\angle DAC$ both sides, we get

$\angle 1 + \angle DAC = \angle 2 + \angle DAC$

$\angle BAC = \angle EAD$ ...(i)

Also, $BD = CE$ [given]

On adding DC both sides, we get

$BD + DC = CE + DC \Rightarrow BC = ED$ ...(ii)

$\Rightarrow$ $\Delta ABC \cong \Delta AED$ [by AAS congruence rule]

14. Hint In ΔPAM and ΔQBM,

$AM = BM$ [given]

$\angle AMP = \angle BMQ$ [vertically opposite angles]

$\angle PAM = \angle QBM$ [each 90°]

$\Delta PAM \cong \Delta QBM$ [by ASA congruecne rule]

Hence proved.

$PM = QM$ [by CPCT] ...(i)

In ΔPCM and ΔQCM,

$CM = CM$ [common side]

$PM = QM$ [from Eq. (i)]

$\angle CMP = \angle CMQ$

$\Delta PCM \cong \Delta QCM$ [by SAS congruence rule]

$\Rightarrow$ $CP = CQ$ [by CPCT] **Hence proved.**

15. Hint In ΔADC and ΔAEB,

$AB = AC$ [given]

$\angle DAC = \angle EAB$ [common angle]

In ΔDOB and ΔCOE, $\angle x = \angle y$ [given]

$\angle DOB = \angle COE$

[vertically opposite angles]

$\therefore$ $\angle DBO = \angle ECO$ i.e. $\angle ABE = \angle ACD$

$\angle ACD = \angle ABE$

Then, $\Delta ADC \cong \Delta AEB$ [by ASA congruence rule]

$DC = BE$ [by CPCT]

16. Hint In ΔBOC and ΔAOC, we have

$\angle 1 = \angle 2$ [each 90°]

Also, $\angle i = \angle r$ [$\because$ incident angle = reflected angle]

On multiplying both sides by -1 and then adding $90°$ both sides, we get $90° - \angle i = 90° - \angle r$

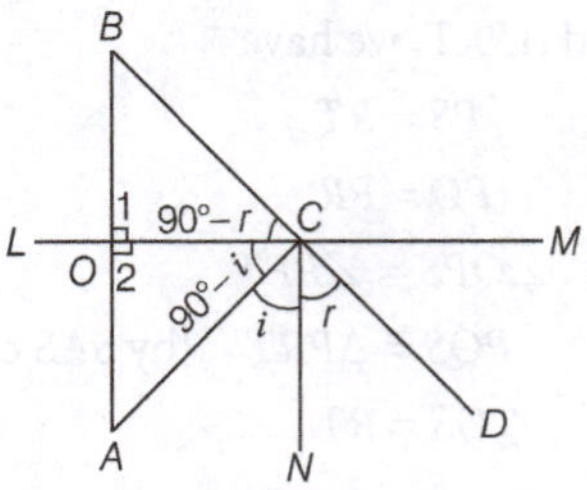

$\Rightarrow$ $\angle ACO = \angle BCO$ [$\because \angle BCO = 180° - \angle OCN - r$

$= 180° - 90° - r = 90° - r$]

and $OC = OC$ [common side]

$\therefore$ $\Delta BOC \cong \Delta AOC$ [by ASA congruence rule]

Then, $OB = OA$ [by CPCT]

Hence, the image is as far behind the mirror as the object is in front of the mirror.

17. Hint Isosceles triangle property.

18. Hint Given In ΔABC, $AB = AC$ and the base BC is produced to D. From D, DE is drawn perpendicular to BA produced to E and DF is perpendicular to AC produced to F.

To prove BD bisects $\angle EDF$, i.e. $\angle 3 = \angle 4$

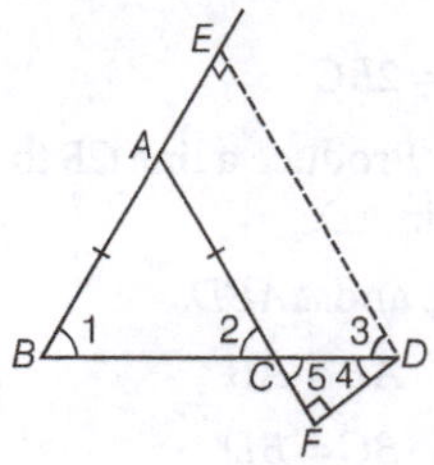

Proof In ΔABC, $AC = AB$ [given]

$\Rightarrow$ $\angle 1 = \angle 2$ ...(i)

[$\because$ angles opposite to equal sides of a triangle are equal]

In right angled ΔBED, we have

$\angle 1 + \angle 3 + \angle BED = 180°$

[by angle sum property of a triangle]

$\Rightarrow$ $\angle 1 + \angle 3 + 90° = 180°$

[$\because DE \perp BE \Rightarrow \angle BED = 90°$]

$\Rightarrow$ $\angle 3 = 90° - \angle 1$ ...(ii)

Similarly, in ΔCFD,

$\angle 4 = 90° - \angle 5$

$\Rightarrow$ $\angle 4 = 90° - \angle 2$ ...(iii)

[$\because \angle 2 = \angle 5$, vertically opposite angles]

From Eqs. (i), (ii) and (iii), $\angle 3 = \angle 4$

Hence, BD bisects $\angle EDF$. **Hence proved.**

19. Hint $\angle ABC = 180° - \angle ABD$

$= 180° - 110° = 70°$ [by linear pair axiom]

$\because \quad AB = AC$

$\therefore \quad \angle ACB = \angle ABC = 70°$

Then, $\angle ACE = 180° - \angle ACB = 180° - 70° = 110°$

20. Hint Take ΔSRM and ΔPQM, prove them congruent.

Then, using CPCT prove

$MR = MQ$

Now, use property of angles opposite to equal sides are also equal.

21. Hint In ΔABC, given

$\Rightarrow \angle B = 2\angle C \Rightarrow \angle B = 2y$ [$\because \angle C = y$]

Since, AD is the bisector of $\angle BAC$.

So, let $\angle BAD = \angle CAD = x$

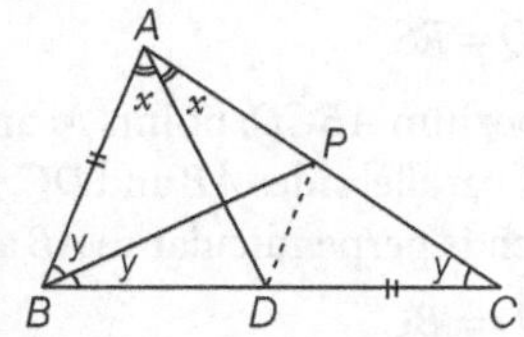

Let BP be the bisector of $\angle ABC$. Join PD.

In ΔBPC, $\angle CBP = \angle BCP = y \Rightarrow PC = BP$ ...(i)

[$\because$ sides opposite to equal angles of a triangle are equal]

In ΔABP and ΔDCP,

$\angle ABP = \angle DCP = y$

[$\because \angle ABP = \angle CBP = y$ and $\angle DCP = \angle BCP = y$]

$AB = DC$ [given]

and $BP = PC$ [from Eq. (i)]

$\therefore \quad \Delta ABP \cong \Delta DCP$ [by SAS congruence criterion]

$\Rightarrow \angle BAP = \angle CDP$ and $AP = DP$ [by CPCT]

$\Rightarrow \angle CDP = 2x$ [from figure]

and $\angle ADP = \angle DAP = x$ [$\because$ angles opposite to equal sides of a triangle are equal]

In ΔABD, $\angle ADC = \angle ABD + \angle BAD$

[$\because$ exterior angle of a triangle is equal to the sum of opposite interior angles]

$\Rightarrow \angle ADP + \angle PDC = \angle ABD + \angle BAD$

[$\because \angle ADC = \angle ADP + \angle PDC$]

$\Rightarrow \quad x + 2x = 2y + x \Rightarrow x = y$ ...(ii)

In ΔABC, $\angle A + \angle B + \angle C = 180°$

[by angle sum property of a triangle]

$\Rightarrow \quad 2x + 2y + y = 180°$

$\Rightarrow \quad 2x + 2x + x = 180°$ [from Eq. (ii)]

$\Rightarrow \quad 5x = 180° \Rightarrow x = 36°$

$\therefore \quad \angle BAC = 2x = 2 \times 36° = 72°$ **Hence proved.**

22. Given Lines OB and OC are respectively the angle bisectors of $\angle B$ and $\angle C$ of an isosceles ΔABC such that $AB = AC$ which intersect each other at O and BO is produced to M.

To prove $\angle MOC = \angle ABC$

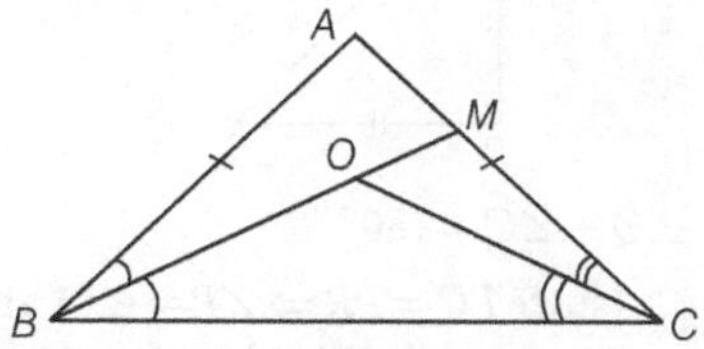

Proof In ΔABC, $AB = AC$ [given]

$\Rightarrow \quad \angle ACB = \angle ABC$

[$\because$ angles opposite to equal sides of a triangle are equal]

$\Rightarrow \quad \frac{1}{2}\angle ACB = \frac{1}{2}\angle ABC$ [dividing both sides by 2]

$\Rightarrow \quad \angle OCB = \angle OBC$ ...(i)

[$\because OB$ and OC are the bisectors of $\angle B$ and $\angle C$]

Now, $\angle MOC = \angle OBC + \angle OCB$

[$\because$ exterior angle of a triangle is equal to the sum of two opposite interior angles]

$\Rightarrow \quad \angle MOC = \angle OBC + \angle OBC$ [from Eq. (i)]

$\Rightarrow \quad \angle MOC = 2\angle OBC$

$\Rightarrow \quad \angle MOC = \angle ABC$

[$\because$ OB is the bisector of $\angle B$] **Hence proved.**

23. Hint Use angles opposite to equal sides are also equal.

Ans. $x = 20°$, $y = 140°$ and $z = 20°$

24. Hint (i) $\angle PRS = \angle TRQ$

On adding $\angle SRT$ to both sides, we get

$\angle PRS + \angle SRT = \angle TRQ + \angle SRT$

$\Rightarrow \quad \angle PRT = \angle SRQ$

$\therefore \quad \Delta PRT \cong \Delta SRQ$ [by ASA congruence rule]

(ii) $\because \Delta PRT \cong \Delta SRQ$

$\therefore \quad PT = SQ$ [by CPCT]

25. Hint

(i) In ΔAEX and ΔBCE,

$\angle AEX = \angle BEC$ [vertically opposite angles]

$AE = BE$ [$\because E$ is the mid-point]

$XE = EC$ [given]

$\therefore \quad \Delta AEX \cong \Delta BEC$ [by SAS congruence rule]

Similarly, $\Delta AFY \cong \Delta CFB$ [by SAS congruence rule]

(ii) Prove $AX \parallel BC$ and $AY \parallel BC$, instead of proving XAY as a straight line.

26. Hint $\angle P + \angle Q + \angle R = 180°$

[by angle sum property of a triangle]

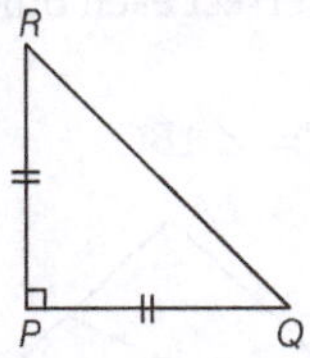

$\Rightarrow \angle P + \angle Q + \angle Q = 180°$

[since $PQ = PR \Rightarrow \angle R = \angle Q$, angles opposite to equal sides of a triangle are equal.]

$\Rightarrow \quad 90° + 2\angle Q = 180° \Rightarrow \angle Q = \dfrac{90°}{2} = 45°$

$\therefore \quad \angle Q = \angle R = 45°$

27. Hint We know that the path opposite to the longest angle of a triangle is longest path.

Here, at home, given angle = 75°, which is largest.

$\therefore$ The longest segment of the path travelled by the robot is from shop to client.

28. Hint In ΔBCE and ΔCBF,

$BC = BC$ [common side]

$\Rightarrow \quad BE = CF$ [given]

$\angle BEC = \angle CFB = 90°$

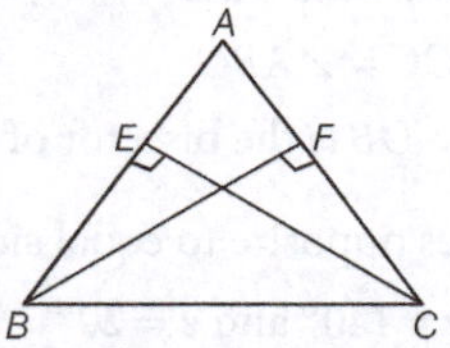

$\therefore \quad \Delta BCE \cong \Delta CBF$ [by RHS congruence rule]

$\therefore \quad \angle B = \angle C$

29. Hint $\Delta PMQ \cong \Delta PMR$ [by RHS congruence rule]

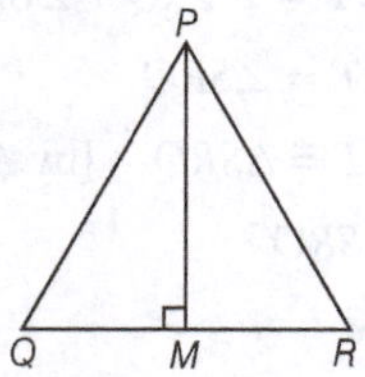

$\therefore \angle Q = \angle R$ [by CPCT]

30. Given O is a point in the interior of a square $ABCD$ such that ΔOAB is an equilateral triangle.

To prove ΔCOD is an isosceles triangle.

Construction Join OC and OD.

Proof As AOB is an equilateral triangle.

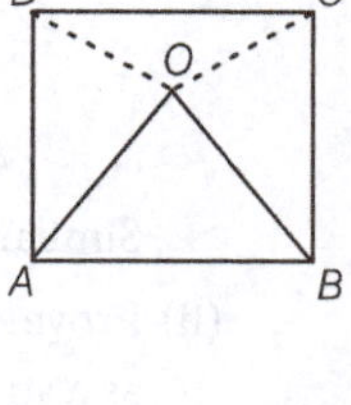

$\therefore \quad \angle OAB = \angle OBA = 60°$ ...(i)

Also, $\quad \angle DAB = \angle CBA = 90°$ ...(ii)

[each angle of a square $ABCD$ is 90°]

On subtracting Eq. (i) from Eq. (ii), we get

$\angle DAB - \angle OAB = \angle CBA - \angle OBA$

$= 90° - 60°$

i.e. $\quad \angle DAO = \angle CBO = 30°$

In ΔAOD and ΔBOC, $AO = BO$

[all the sides of an equilateral triangle are equal]

$\angle DAO = \angle CBO$ [proved above]

and $\quad AD = BC$ [sides of a square are equal]

$\therefore \quad \Delta AOD \cong \Delta BOC$ [by SAS congruence rule]

Hence, $\quad OD = OC$ [by CPCT]

31. Hint Use SAS to prove $\Delta POQ \cong \Delta ROS$

$PQ = RS$ [by CPCT]

32. Given In trapezium $ABCD$, points M and N are the mid-points of parallel sides AB and DC, respectively and join MN, which is perpendicular to AB and DC.

To prove $AD = BC$

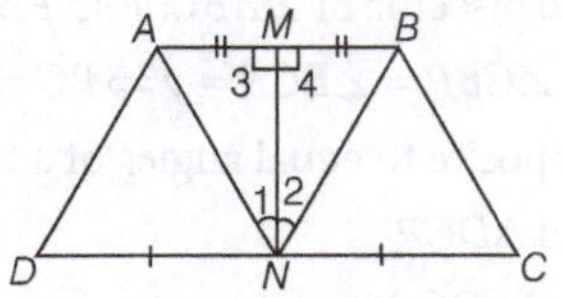

Proof As M is the mid-point of AB.

$\therefore \quad AM = MB$

Now, in ΔAMN and ΔBMN,

$AM = MB$ [proved above]

$\angle 3 = \angle 4$ [each 90°]

and $\quad MN = MN$ [common side]

$\therefore \quad \Delta AMN \cong BMN$ [by SAS congruence rule]

$\Rightarrow \quad \angle 1 = \angle 2$ [by CPCT] ...(i)

On multiplying both sides of Eq. (i) by -1 and then adding 90° both sides, we get

$90° - \angle 1 = 90° - \angle 2$

$\Rightarrow \quad \angle AND = \angle BNC$ ...(ii)

Now, in ΔADN and ΔBCN,

$\angle AND = \angle BNC$ [from Eq. (ii)]

$AN = BN$ [by CPCT, $\because \Delta AMN \cong \Delta BMN$]

and $\quad DN = NC$ [$\because N$ is the mid-point of CD]

$\therefore \quad \Delta ADN \cong \Delta BCN$ [by SAS congruence rule]

$\Rightarrow \quad AD = BC$ [by CPCT] **Hence proved.**

33. Hint In ΔABD and ΔACD,

$AB = AC$ [given]

$\angle BAD = \angle CAD$ [as AD is the bisector of $\angle BAC$]

and $AD = AD$ [common side]

So, $\Delta ABD \cong \Delta ACD$ [by SAS congruence rule]

Arjun has used $\angle B = \angle C$ for proving $\Delta ABD \cong \Delta ACD$ which is wrong because for proving $\angle B = \angle C$, we have to first prove that $\Delta ABD \cong \Delta ACD$.

34. Hint

(i) $\Delta PTR \cong \Delta QTS$ [by SAS congruence rule]

$\Rightarrow PR = SQ$ [by CPCT] ... (i)

(ii) From Eq. (i), we get $PR = SQ$

and $\angle PRT = \angle QSR$ [by CPCT]

which are alternate angles.

$\therefore SQ \parallel PR$ and SR is a transversal.

Then, $\angle SQR + \angle PRQ = 180°$ [co-interior angles]

$\Rightarrow 90° + \angle SQR = 180°$

$\Rightarrow \angle SQR = 90°$

$\therefore \angle SQR$ is a right angle.

(iii) $\Delta SQR \cong \Delta PRQ$ [by SAS congruence rule]

Then, $SR = PQ$ [by CPCT]

$\Rightarrow ST + RT = PQ$

$\Rightarrow RT + RT = PQ$ [$\because ST = RT$, given]

$\Rightarrow 2RT = PQ \Rightarrow RT = \frac{1}{2}PQ$

35. We know, two triangles are congruent, if two angles and the included side of one triangle are equal to two angles and the included side of another triangle.

e.g. Construct ΔABC with $\angle A = 30°$ and $\angle B = 60°$ and ΔPQR with $\angle P = 30°$ and $\angle Q = 60°$.

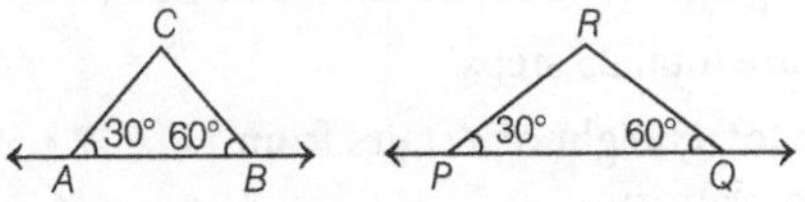

Here, AB and PQ are line segments.

Both triangles cannot be congruent as the measurement of line segment is not fixed.

But if constructed ΔABC and ΔPQR with

$\angle A = \angle P = 30°$, $\angle B = \angle Q = 60°$ and $AB = PQ = 8$ cm

i.e.

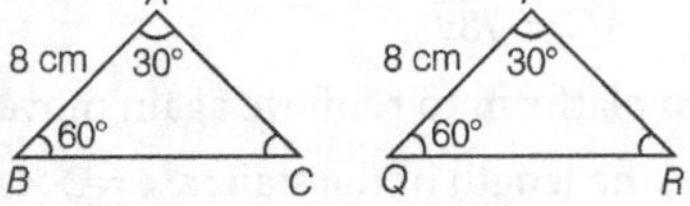

$\therefore$ Both are congruent and equal.

Because when specified angles are drawn at two end points of a line segment they meet at a unique point.

36. Given In right angled ΔABC, $AB = AC$ and CD is the bisector of $\angle C$.

To prove $AC + AD = BC$

Construction Draw $DE \perp BC$.

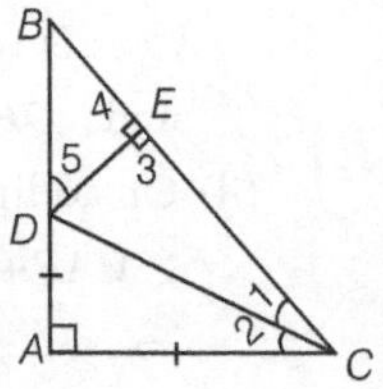

Proof In right angled ΔABC, $AB = AC$ and BC is a hypotenuse. [given]

$\therefore \angle A = 90°$

In ΔDAC and ΔDEC,

$\angle A = \angle 3 = 90°$

$\angle 1 = \angle 2$ [CD is the bisector of $\angle C$]

and $DC = DC$ [common side]

$\therefore \Delta DAC \cong \Delta DEC$ [by AAS congruence rule]

$\Rightarrow DA = DE$ [by CPCT]...(i)

and $AC = EC$ [by CPCT] ...(ii)

In ΔABC, $AB = AC$

$\angle C = \angle B$ ...(iii)

[$\because$ angles opposite to equal sides of a triangle are equal]

Again, in ΔABC, $\angle A + \angle B + \angle C = 180°$

$\Rightarrow 90° + \angle B + \angle B = 180°$

[$\because \angle A = 90°$ and using Eq. (iii)]

$\Rightarrow \angle B = 45°$

In ΔBED, $\angle 5 = 180° - (\angle B + \angle 4)$

[by angle sum property of a triangle]

$= 180° - (45° + 90°) = 180° - 135° = 45°$

$\therefore \angle B = \angle 5 \Rightarrow BE = DE$ ...(iv)

[$\because$ sides opposite to equal angles of a triangle are equal]

From Eqs. (i) and (iv), we get

$DA = DE = BE$ ...(v)

$\because BC = CE + EB = CA + DA$ [from Eqs. (ii) and (v)]

$\therefore AD + AC = BC$ **Hence proved.**

37. Hint

(i) In ΔAMF and ΔAME,

$MF = ME$ [given]

$AM = AM$ [common]

$\angle AMF = \angle AME$ [each 90°]

So, $\Delta AMF \cong \Delta AME$ [by SAS congruence rule]

$\therefore AF = AE$ [by CPCT]

and $\angle MAF = \angle MAE$ [by CPCT] ...(i)

In ΔAFD and ΔAEB,

$AF = AE$ [proved above]

$AB = AD$ [sides of square]

$\angle B = \angle D$ [each 90°]

$\therefore$ $\Delta AFD \cong \Delta AEB$ [by RHS congruence rule]

$\therefore$ $\angle DAF = \angle EAB$ [by CPCT] ...(ii)

and $DF = BE$ [by CPCT]

(ii) On adding Eqs. (i) and (ii), we get

$\angle MAF + \angle DAF = \angle MAE + \angle EAB$

$\Rightarrow$ $\angle DAM = \angle MAB$ **Hence proved.**

38. Hint Prove $\Delta PQO \cong \Delta PRO$ [by RHS congruence rule]

$\therefore$ $\angle POQ = \angle POR$

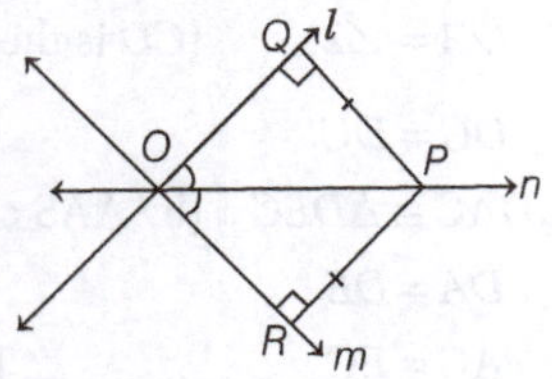

39. Hint Given QX and RX are the bisectors of $\angle PQR$ and $\angle PRQ$, respectively. Also, $XS \perp QR$ and $XT \perp PQ$.

To prove $\Delta XTQ \cong \Delta XSQ$ and PX bisects $\angle P$.

Construction Draw $XY \perp PR$

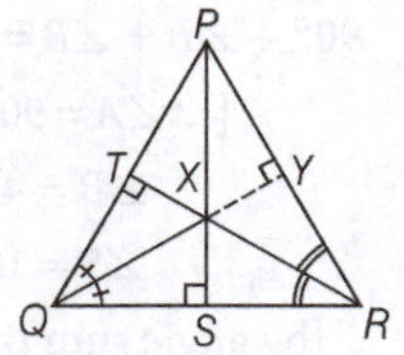

Proof In ΔXTQ and ΔXSQ, we have

$\angle TQX = \angle SQX$

[$\because$ QX is the bisector of $\angle PQR$]

$\angle XTQ = \angle XSQ$ [each 90°]

and $QX = QX$ [common side]

$\therefore$ $\Delta XTQ \cong \Delta XSQ$ [by AAS congruence rule]

Then, $XT = XS$ [by CPCT] ...(i)

Similarly, it can be proved that

$\Delta XSR \cong \Delta XYR$ [by AAS congruence rule]

Then, $XS = XY$ [by CPCT]...(ii)

From Eqs. (i) and (ii), we get

$XT = XY$

In right angled ΔXTP and ΔXYP, we have

$XT = XY$ [proved above]

$\angle XTP = \angle XYP$ [each 90°]

and $XP = XP$ [common side]

$\therefore$ $\Delta XTP \cong \Delta XYP$ [by RHS congruence rule]

Then, $\angle XPT = \angle XPY$ [by CPCT]

Therefore, PX bisects $\angle P$.

Hence, $\Delta XTQ \cong \Delta XSQ$ and PX bisects $\angle P$.

Hence proved.

40. Triangles are congruent on the basis of the following rules i.e.

1. SSS [Side-Side-Side]
2. SAS [Side-Angle-Side]
3. ASA [Angle-Side -Angle]
4. AAS [Angle-Angle-Side]
5. RHS [Right angle-Hypotenuse side].

But there are two rules of congruence that cannot be used to prove congruence of triangles.

That are

1. SSA [Side-Side-Angle]
2. AAA [Angle-Angle-Angle]

e.g.

1. In ΔABC, $AB = 5$ cm, $\angle A = 30°$ and $\angle B = 60°$ and in ΔPQR, $PQ = 5$ cm, $\angle P = 30°$, and $\angle Q = 60°$
   Thus, $\Delta ABC \cong \Delta PQR$ [by ASA congruence rule]
2. In ΔABC and ΔPQR,
   $\angle A = 40°$, $\angle B = 50°$
   and $\angle P = 40°$, $\angle Q = 50°$
   $\therefore$ Third angle $\angle C = \angle R = 90°$
   Though angles are equals but, sides are not.
   $\therefore$ AAA cannot be used to prove congruence.

41. The given difference from floor to platform at base is 8 m.

And height of 1 stair = 20 cm = 0.20 m

There are total 25 steps.

So, the total height of a stairs from floor to platform.

$= 25 \times 0.20 \text{ m} = 5 \text{ m}$

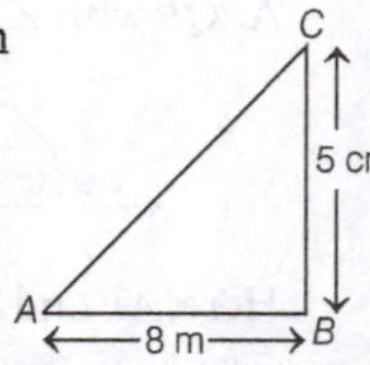

Thus, using Pythagoras theorem for ΔABC, we have

$$AC^2 = AB^2 + BC^2$$

$$= 8^2 + 5^2$$

$$= 64 + 25 = 89$$

$\therefore$ $AC = \sqrt{89}$

Also, from platform to roof, we again move 25 steps.

Therefore, the length of the staircase $= 2 \times AC$

$= 2\sqrt{89} = 18.86$ m.

Mind Map

TRIANGLES

Congruence of Triangles

Two triangles are congruent, if sides and angles of a triangle are equal to the corresponding sides and angles of the other triangle.

e.g.

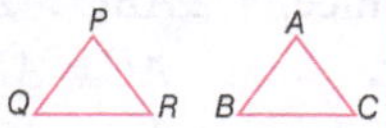

In ΔPQR and ΔABC

$\angle P = \angle A$, $\angle Q = \angle B$, $\angle R = \angle C$

and $PQ = AB$, $QR = BC$, $RP = CA$

Thus, $\Delta PQR \cong \Delta ABC$

Criteria for Congruence of Triangles

1. SAS (Side-Angle-Side) Congruence Rule

If two sides and the included angle of one triangle are equal to the two sides and the included angle of other triangle.

e.g.

If $AB = PQ$, $\angle A = \angle P$, $AC = PR$

or $AC = PR$, $\angle C = \angle R$, $CB = RQ$

or $CB = RQ$, $\angle B = \angle Q$, $BA = QP$

then, $\Delta ABC \cong \Delta PQR$

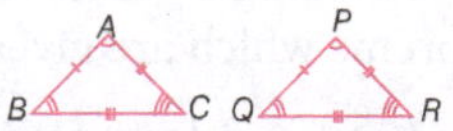

2. ASA (Angle-Side-Angle) Congruence Rule

If two angles and the included side of one triangle are equal to two angles and the included side of other triangle.

e.g.

If $\angle B = \angle Q$, $BA = QP$, $\angle A = \angle P$

or $\angle A = \angle P$, $AC = PR$, $\angle C = \angle R$

or $\angle C = \angle R$, $CB = RQ$, $\angle B = \angle Q$

then, $\Delta ABC \cong \Delta PQR$

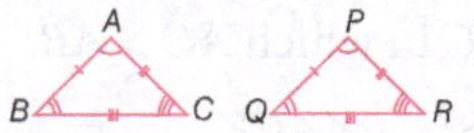

3. SSS (Side-Side-Side) Congruence Rule :

If three sides of one triangle are equal to the three sides of another triangle.

e.g.

If $AB = PQ$, $BC = QR$, $AC = PR$

then, $\Delta ABC \cong \Delta PQR$

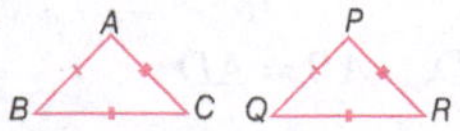

4. RHS (Right Angle-Hypotenuse-Side) Congruence Rule

If hypotenuse and one side of one triangle are equal to the hypotenuse and one side of another triangle.

e.g.

If $PQ = AB$, $\angle Q = \angle B = 90°$, $PR = AC$

or, $QR = BC$, $\angle Q = \angle B = 90°$, $PR = AC$

then, $\Delta PQR \cong \Delta ABC$

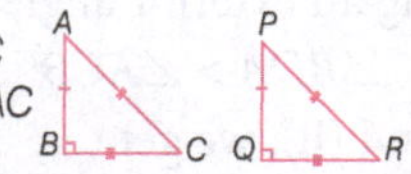

Note : AAS (Angle-Angle-Side) Congruence Rule

If any two pairs of angles and one pair of corresponding sides are equal, then it is called AAS Congruence Rule.

Some Properties of a Triangle

Theorem 1 Angles opposite to equal sides of an isosceles triangle are equal.

Theorem 2 The sides opposite to equal angles of a triangle are equal.

Topics to be Assessed Formatively

Inequalities in a Triangle

In previous topics, we have been mainly studying the equality of sides and angles of a triangle or triangles. Sometimes, we do come across unequal objects and we need to compare them.

e.g. The line segment PQ is greater than in length as compared to line segment RS and $\angle P$ is greater than $\angle Q$.

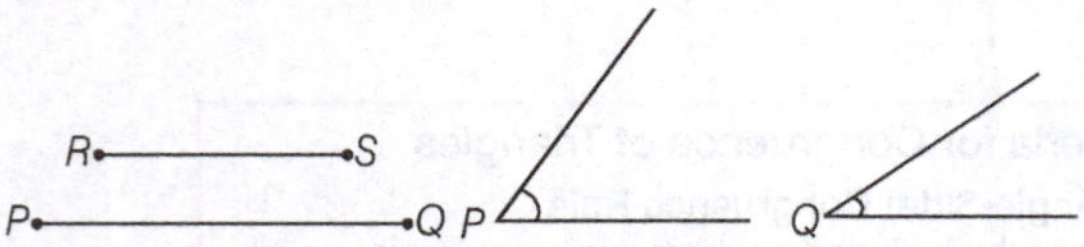

There are some relations between unequal sides and unequal angles of a triangle. These relations are stated in the form of theorems which are given below:

Theorem 1 If two sides of a triangle are unequal, then the angle opposite to the longer side is larger (or greater).

Given A ΔABC in which $AC > AB$.

To prove $\angle ABC > \angle ACB$

Construction Take a point D on AC such that $AB = AD$.

Join BD.

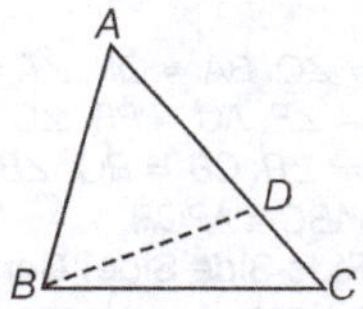

Proof In ΔABD, $AB = AD$ [by construction]

$\Rightarrow \quad \angle BDA = \angle ABD \quad$ ...(i)

[$\because$ angles opposite to equal sides of a triangle are equal]

But $\angle BDA$ being an exterior angle of ΔBCD, so we have

$\angle BDA > \angle ACB \quad$ ...(ii)

From Eqs. (i) and (ii), we get

$\angle ABD > \angle ACB$

$\Rightarrow \quad \angle ABC > \angle ABD > \angle ACB$

$\Rightarrow \quad \angle ABC > \angle ACB$

Hence proved.

Theorem 2 In any triangle, the side opposite to the larger (or greater) angle is longer.

Given A ΔABC in which $\angle ABC > \angle ACB$.

To prove $AC > AB$

Proof In ΔABC, we have the following three possibilities:

(i) $AC = AB$ (ii) $AC < AB$ (iii) $AC > AB$

Out of these three possibilities, exactly one must be true.

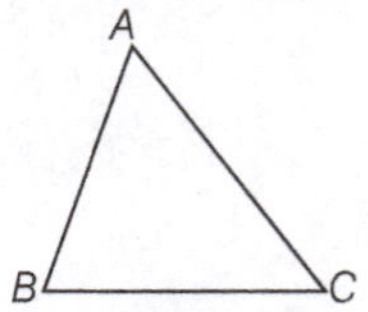

Case I When $AC = AB$, then

$\angle ABC = \angle ACB$

[$\because$ angles opposite to equal sides of a triangle are equal]

This is contradiction.

Since, $\angle ABC > \angle ACB$ [given]

$\therefore \quad AC \neq AB$

Case II When $AC < AB \Rightarrow \angle ACB > \angle ABC$

[$\because$ longer side has the greater angle opposite to it]

This also contradicts the given hypothesis.

Thus, we are left with the only possibility, $AC > AB$, which must be true.

Hence, $AC > AB$ i.e. case III. **Hence proved.**

Theorem 3 The sum of any two sides of a triangle is greater than the third side.

Given ABC is a triangle.

To prove (i) $AB + AC > BC$ (ii) $AB + BC > AC$ (iii) $BC + AC > AB$

Construction Produce side BA to D such that $AD = AC$.

Join CD.

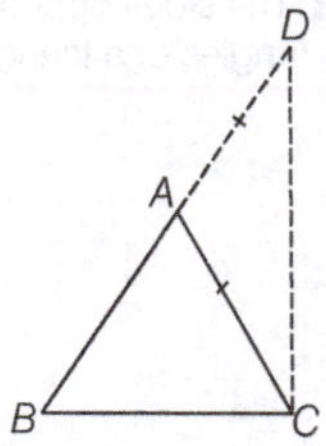

Proof In ΔACD,

$AC = AD$ [by construction]

$\Rightarrow \quad \angle ADC = \angle ACD$

[as, angles opposite to equal sides of a triangle are equal]

$\because \quad \angle ACD = \angle ADC$

From figure, $\angle BCA + \angle A\dot{C}D > \angle ACD$

$\therefore \quad \angle BCA + \angle ACD > \angle ADC \Rightarrow \angle BCD > \angle ADC$

$\Rightarrow \quad \angle BCD > \angle BDC \quad [\because \angle ADC = \angle BDC]$

$\Rightarrow \quad BD > BC$

[as, side opposite to greater angle in a triangle is greater]

$\Rightarrow \quad BA + AD > BC \Rightarrow BA + AC > BC$

$[\because AC = AD$, by construction]

Thus, $AB + AC > BC$

Similarly, $AB + BC > AC$ and $BC + AC > AB$

Hence proved.

Example 1. **If a, b and c are the sides of a triangle then write any one inequality of a triangle.**

Sol. The sum of two sides of a triangle is greater than the third side.

i.e. $a + b > c$ or $b + c > a$ or $c + a > b$

Example 2. **Is it possible to construct a triangle with lengths of its sides as 4 cm, 3 cm and 7 cm? Give reason for your answer.** NCERT Exemplar

Sol. No, it is not possible to construct a triangle with length of its sides as 4 cm, 3 cm and 7 cm, because here we see that sum of the lengths of two sides is equal to third side i.e. $4 + 3 = 7$.

We know that the sum of any two sides of a triangle is greater than its third side, so construction of given sides of triangle is not possible.

Example 3. **In ΔPQR, $\angle P = 70°$ and $\angle R = 30°$. Which side of this triangle is the longest? Give reason for your answer.** NCERT Exemplar

Sol. Given, in ΔPQR, $\angle P = 70°$ and $\angle R = 30°$

We know that sum of angles of a triangle is 180°.

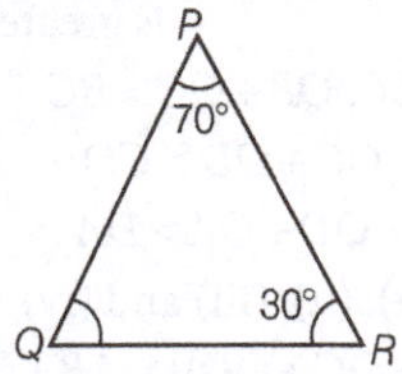

$\therefore \quad \angle P + \angle Q + \angle R = 180°$

$\Rightarrow \quad 70° + \angle Q + 30° = 180°$

$\Rightarrow \angle Q = 180° - (70° + 30°) = 80°$

Here, $\angle Q$ is greatest, so side PR is longest.

[as, side opposite to the greatest angle of a triangle is the longest]

Example 4. **Show that the sum of three altitudes of a triangle is less than the sum of the three sides of the triangle.**

Sol. Consider ABC is a triangle and AL, BM and CN are the altitudes an sides BC, AC and AB respectively.

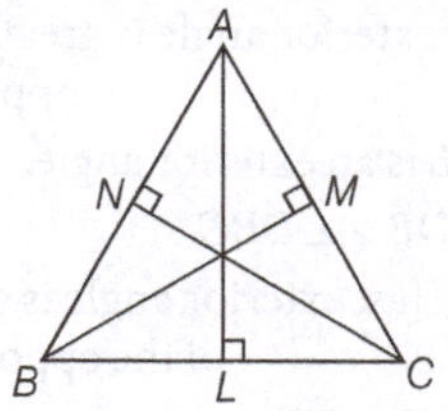

To prove $AL + BM + CN < AB + BC + AC$

Proof We know that the perpendicular AL drawn from the point A to the line BC is shorter than the line segment AB drawn from point A to the line BC.

$\therefore \quad AL < AB \quad \ldots(i)$

Similarly, $\quad BM < BC \quad \ldots(ii)$

and $\quad CN < AC \quad \ldots(iii)$

On adding Eqs. (i), (ii) and (iii), we get

$AL + BM + CN < AB + BC + AC$ **Hence proved.**

Example 5. **D is a point on side BC of ΔABC, such that $AD = AC$. Show that $AB > AD$.**

Sol. Given In ΔABC, $AD = AC$

To prove $AB > AD$

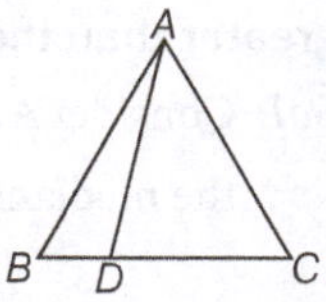

Proof Since, $AD = AC$

$\therefore \quad \angle ACD = \angle ADC \quad \ldots(i)$

[as, angles opposite to equal sides of a triangle are equal]

Now, $\angle ADC$ is an exterior angle of ΔABD.

i.e. $\quad \angle ADC > \angle ABD$

$\Rightarrow \quad \angle ACD > \angle ABD$ [from Eq. (i)]

$\Rightarrow \quad \angle ACB > \angle ABC$

$[\because \angle ABD = \angle ABC$ and $\angle ACD = \angle ACB]$

$\Rightarrow \quad AB > AC$ [as, side opposite to greater angle in a triangle is greater]

$\therefore \quad AB > AD \; [\because AD = AC$, given] **Hence proved.**

Example 6. **Show that the difference of any two sides of a triangle is less than the third side.**

Sol. Consider, ABC is a triangle.

To prove $AC - AB < BC$, $BC - AC < AB$

$BC - AB < AC$

Construction Take a point D on AC such that $AD = AB$ and join BD.

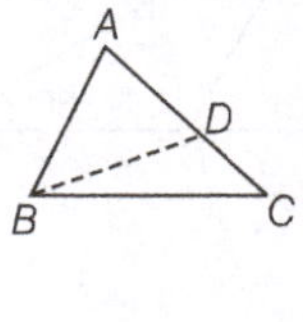

Proof In ΔABD, $\angle BDC$ is an exterior angle.

$\therefore \quad \angle BDC > \angle ABD \quad$ ...(i)

[as, exterior angle is greater than either of the opposite interior angle]

In ΔBDC, $\angle ADB$ is an exterior angle.

$\therefore \quad \angle ADB > \angle DBC \quad$ ...(ii)

[as, exterior angle is greater than either of the oppostive interior angle]

In ΔABD, $\quad AB = AD \quad$ [by construction]

$\Rightarrow \quad \angle ADB = \angle ABD \quad$ ...(iii)

[as, angles opposite to equal sides are also equal]

From Eqs. (i) and (iii),

$\angle BDC > \angle ADB \quad$ ...(iv)

$\Rightarrow \quad \angle BDC > \angle DBC \quad$ [from Eq. (ii)]

$\Rightarrow \quad BC > CD$

[as, side opposite to greater angle is larger]

$\Rightarrow \quad CD < BC \Rightarrow AC - AD < BC$

$\Rightarrow \quad AC - AB < BC \quad [\because AD = AB$, by construction]

Similarly, $BC - AC < AB$ and $BC - AB < AC$

Hence proved.

Example 7. **Prove that the perimeter of a triangle is greater than the sum of its three medians.**

Sol. Consider ABC is a triangle and AD, BE and CF are the medians of ΔABC.

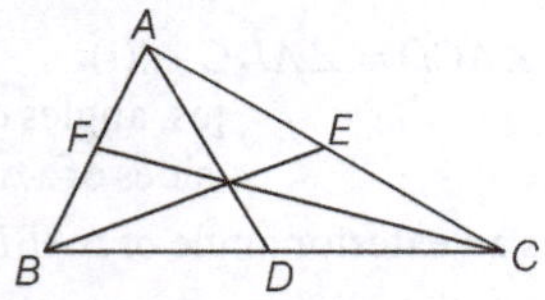

We know that, the sum of any two sides of a triangle is greater than twice the median drawn to the third side.

$\therefore \quad AB + AC > 2AD \quad$ ...(i)

$AB + BC > 2BE \quad$ ...(ii)

and $\quad BC + AC > 2CF \quad$ ...(iii)

On adding Eqs. (i), (ii) and (iii), we get

$$2(AB + BC + AC) > 2(AD + BE + CF)$$

$\therefore \quad AB + BC + AC > AD + BE + CF$

Hence, the perimeter of a triangle is greater than the sum of its three medians. **Hence proved.**

Example 8. **In the given figure, AD bisects $\angle A$. Then, find the relation between the sides AB, AC and DC.**

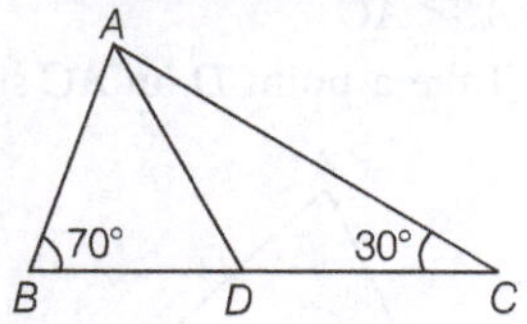

Sol. Given, AD is the bisector of $\angle BAC$.

In ΔABC, sum of three angles of a triangle is 180°.

$\therefore \quad \angle A = 180° - (\angle B + \angle C)$

$= 180° - (70° + 30°) = 80°$

$\Rightarrow \quad \angle BAD = \angle DAC = \dfrac{80°}{2} = 40°$

[as, AD is the bisector of $\angle A$]

In ΔABD, $\quad \angle ADB = 180° - (\angle BAD + \angle ABD)$

[as, sum of three angles of a triangle is 180°]

$= 180° - (40° + 70°) = 70°$

and $\quad \angle DBA = \angle ADB$

$\Rightarrow \quad AD = AB$

[as, sides opposite to equal angles of a triangle are equal]

In ΔADC,

$\angle ADC = 180° - (\angle DAC + \angle ACD)$

[as, sum of three angles of a triangle is 180°]

$= 180° - (40° + 30°) = 110°$

And $\angle DCA < \angle CAD < \angle ADC$

$[\because \angle DCA = 30°, \angle CAD = 40°$ and $\angle ADC = 110°]$

$\Rightarrow \quad AD < DC < AC$

But $\quad AB = AD$

Therefore, $AB < DC < AC$

Example 9. **Show that in a quadrilateral $ABCD$, $AB + BC + CD + DA < 2(BD + AC)$.**

Sol. ***Given*** $\quad ABCD$ is a quadrilateral.

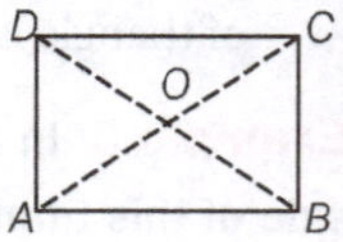

To prove

$AB + BC + CD + DA < 2(BD + AC)$

Construction $\quad$ Join diagonals AC and BD.

Proof $\quad$ In ΔOAB, $\; OA + OB > AB \quad$ ...(i)

[as, sum of any two sides of a triangle is greater than the third side]

Similarly, In ΔOBC, $OB + OC > BC \quad$ ...(ii)

In ΔOCD, $\quad OC + OD > CD \quad$ ...(iii)

and in ΔODA, $\quad OD + OA > DA \quad$ ...(iv)

On adding Eqs. (i), (ii), (iii) and (iv), we get

$$2[(OA + OB + OC + OD)] > AB + BC + CD + DA$$

$\Rightarrow \quad 2[(OA + OC) + (OB + OD)] > AB + BC + CD + DA$

$\Rightarrow \quad 2(AC + BD) > AB + BC + CD + DA$

$[\because OA + OC = AC$ and $OB + OD = BD]$

$\Rightarrow \quad AB + BC + CD + DA < 2(BD + AC) \quad$ **Hence proved.**

Example 10. **If AB and CD are the smallest and largest sides of a quadrilateral $ABCD$, out of $\angle B$ and $\angle D$ decide which is greater?**

Sol. Given In quadrilateral $ABCD, AB$ is the smallest side and CD is the largest side.

To prove $\angle B > \angle D$ or $\angle D > \angle B$

Construction Join BD.

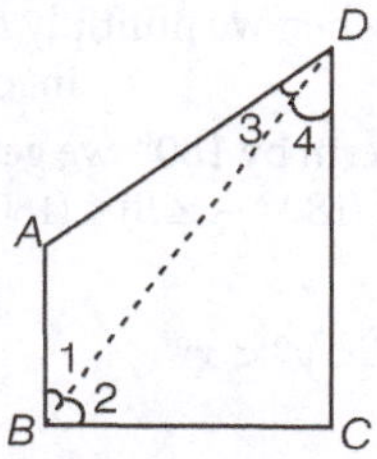

Proof Now, in ΔABD, $AD > AB$

[as, AB is the smallest side in quad. $ABCD$]

$\Rightarrow$ $\angle 1 > \angle 3$ ...(i)

[as, angle opposite to larger side of a triangle is greater]

In ΔBCD, $CD > BC$

[as, CD is the largest side in quad $ABCD$]

$\Rightarrow$ $\angle 2 > \angle 4$ ...(ii)

[as, angle opposite to larger side is greater]

On adding Eqs. (i) and (ii), we get

$$\angle 1 + \angle 2 > \angle 3 + \angle 4$$

$\Rightarrow$ $\angle B > \angle D$

Hence, $\angle B > \angle D$ **Hence proved.**

Example 11. ***S*** **is any point on side** ***QR*** **of a** ΔPQR**. Show that** $PQ + QR + RP > 2PS$**.** NCERT Exemplar

Sol. Given In ΔPQR, S is any point on side QR.

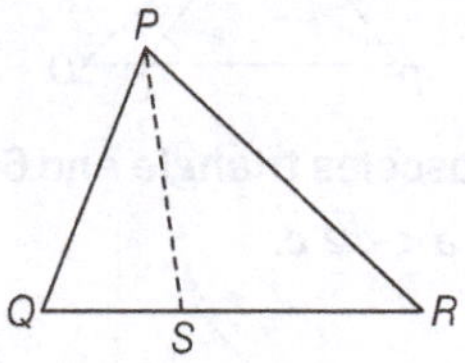

To prove $PQ + QR + RP > 2PS$

Construction Join PS.

Proof In ΔPQS, $PQ + QS > PS$ ...(i)

[as, sum of any two sides of a triangle is greater than the third side]

Similarly, in ΔPRS, $SR + RP > PS$ ...(ii)

[as, sum of two sides of a triangle is greater than the third side]

On adding Eqs. (i) and (ii), we get

$$PQ + QS + SR + RP > 2PS$$

$\Rightarrow$ $PQ + (QS + SR) + RP > 2PS$

$\Rightarrow$ $PQ + QR + RP > 2PS$ [$\because QR = QS + SR$]

Hence proved.

Example 12. In the given figure, $PQ > PR$**,** ***QS*** **and** ***RS*** **are the bisectors of** $\angle Q$ **and** $\angle R$ **respectively, then find the relation between the sides** ***SQ*** **and** ***SR*****.**

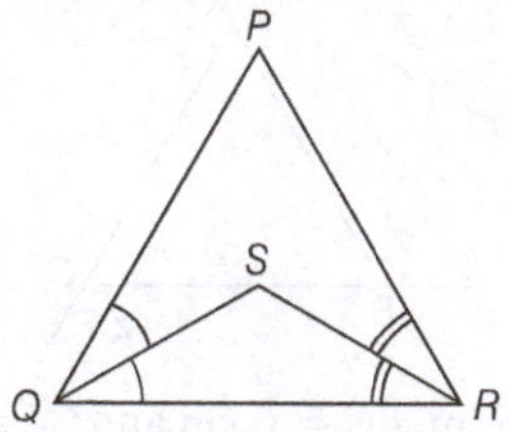

Sol. Given, $PQ > PR$

$\Rightarrow$ $\angle PRQ > \angle PQR$

[as, angle opposite to longer side is greater]

$\Rightarrow$ $\frac{1}{2}\angle PRQ > \frac{1}{2}\angle PQR$ [dividing by 2]

$\Rightarrow$ $\angle SRQ > \angle SQR$

[as, QS and RS are the bisectors of $\angle Q$ and $\angle R$, respectively]

$\therefore$ $SQ > SR$

[as, side opposite to greater angle of a triangle is longer]

Example 13. In the given figure, ***T*** **is a mid-point of side** ***QR*** **of** ΔPQR **and** ***S*** **is a point such that** $RT = ST$**. Prove that** $PQ + PR > QS$

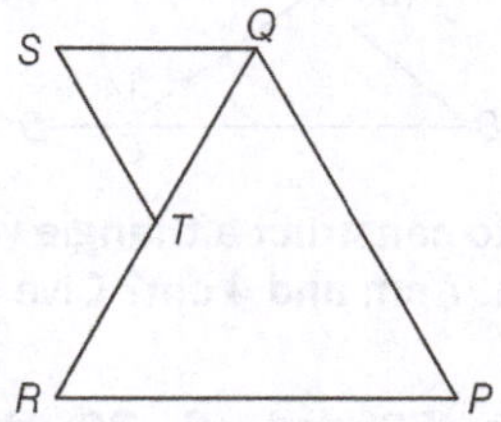

Sol. Given T is a mid-point of side QR of ΔPQR and S is a point such that $RT = ST$.

To prove $PQ + PR > QS$

Proof In ΔPQR,

$$PQ + PR > QR$$

[as, sum of any two sides of a triangle is greater than the third side]

$\Rightarrow$ $PQ + PR > QT + RT$ [$\because QR = QT + RT$]

$\Rightarrow$ $PQ + PR > QT + ST$ [$\because RT = ST$, given]...(i)

In ΔQST, $QT + ST > QS$ ...(ii)

[as, sum of any two sides of a triangle is greater than the third side]

From Eqs. (i) and (ii),

$PQ + PR > QS$ **Hence proved.**

Example 14. **In the given figure, $AB = 8.5$ cm, $BC = 6$ cm and $CA = 7.2$ cm. Write $x°$, $y°$ and $z°$ in ascending order.**

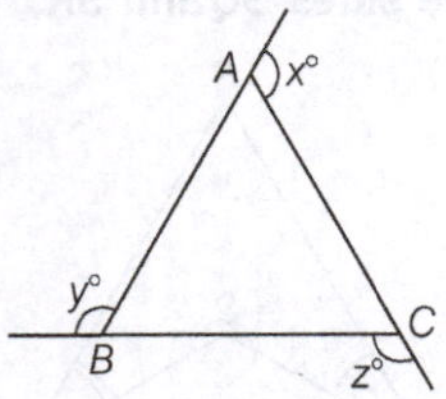

Sol. Given, $AB = 8.5$ cm, $BC = 6$ cm and $CA = 7.2$ cm

$\therefore \quad AB > CA > BC$

$\Rightarrow \quad \angle C > \angle B > \angle A$

[as, angle opposite to longer side is greater]

On multiplying each term of an inequality by -1, we get

$-\angle C < -\angle B < -\angle A$

[when we multiply the '–' sign, the sign of inequality will be reverse]

On adding each term by 180°, we get

$(180° - \angle C) < (180° - \angle B) < (180° - \angle A)$

[triangle inequalities]

$z° < y° < x°$

Exercise

1. **Is it possible to construct a triangle with lengths of its sides as 9 cm, 7 cm and 17 cm? Give reason for your answer.**

2. **In $\triangle ABC$, if $\angle A = 40°$ and $\angle B = 60°$, then find the longest side of $\triangle ABC$.**

3. **In the given figure, ABC is a triangle, having sides BC and CA produced to D and E, respectively. Then, $AC > BC$. Is it true?**

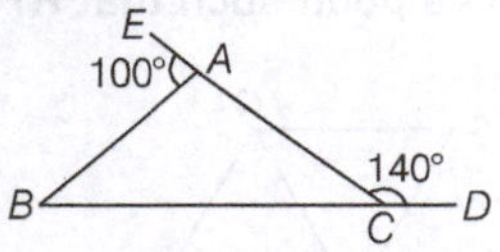

4. **Is it possible to construct a triangle with lengths of its sides as 8 cm, 7 cm and 4 cm? Give reason for your answer.**

5. **In $\triangle ABC$, if $\angle A = 50°$ and $\angle B = 30°$, then which side of the triangle is longest and which side is shortest?**

6. **In the given figure, $AB > AC$. Then, what is the relation between the sides AB and AD?**

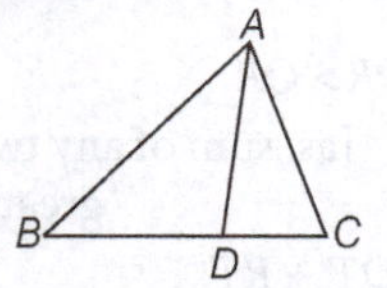

7. **O is any point in the interior of $\triangle ABC$. Show that $OB + OC < AB + AC$.**

8. **Show that in the quadrilateral $ABCD$, $AB + BC + CD + DA > AC + BD$.**

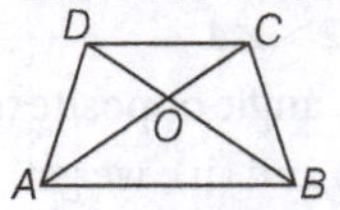

9. **In the figure of Q. 8, if AC is the bisector of $\angle A$, then show that**

(i) $AB > BD$ (ii) $AC > CD$

10. **In the given figure, if $\angle B = \angle C = 55°$ and $\angle D = 25°$, then show that $BC > CA$ and $CA < AD$.**

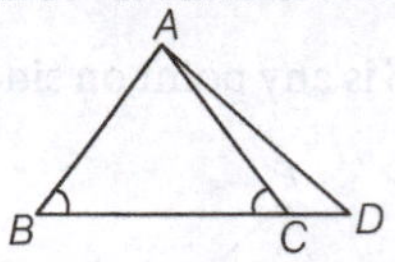

11. **If ABC is an isosceles triangle and $60° < A < 90°$, then show that $c < a < \sqrt{2}\,c$.**

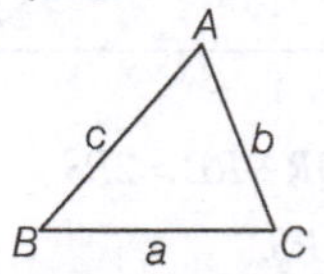

12. **In the given figure, $PQ = PR$. Prove that $PF > PE$.**

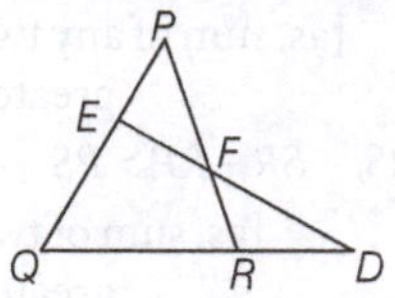

Answers

1. No
2. AB
3. No
4. Yes
5. AB = longest side and AC = shortest side
6. $AB > AD$

CHAPTER 8

Quadrilaterals

In the previous classes, we have studied quadrilaterals and their type. In this chapter, we will study parallelogram which is a quadrilateral having both pairs of opposite sides are parallel and equal.

TOPIC 01 Properties of a Parallelogram

A quadrilateral in which both pairs of opposite sides are parallel and equal, is called **parallelogram** and it is written as $\|_{gm}$.

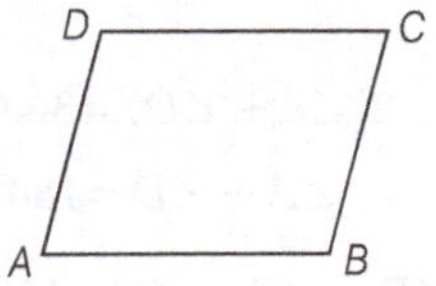

In the above figure, $ABCD$ is a parallelogram in which $AB \parallel DC$ and $BC \parallel AD$.

Now, let's learn the properties of a parallelogram with their proofs.

Theorem 1 *A diagonal of a parallelogram divides it into two congruent triangles.*

Given $ABCD$ is a parallelogram and AC is its one diagonal.

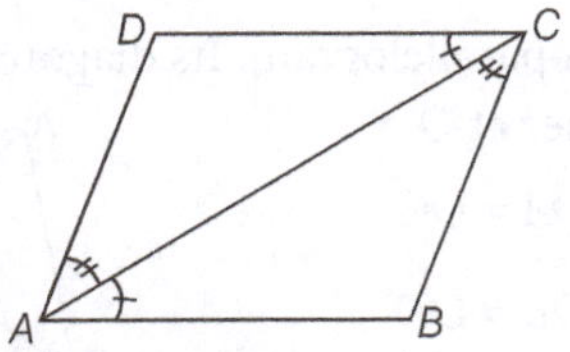

To prove $\Delta ABC \cong \Delta CDA$

Proof Since, $ABCD$ is a parallelogram.

$\therefore$ $AB \parallel DC$ and $BC \parallel AD$

In ΔABC and ΔCDA, $\angle BCA = \angle DAC$

[$\because BC \parallel AD$ and AC is transversal, so a pair of alternate angles are equal]

and $\angle BAC = \angle DCA$

[$\because AB \parallel DC$ and AC is transversal, so a pair of alternate angles are equal]

and $AC = AC$ [common sides]

$\therefore$ $\Delta ABC \cong \Delta CDA$ [by ASA congruence rule]

Similarly, we can prove that $\Delta ABD \cong \Delta CDB$

Hence, diagonal of a parallelogram divides it into two congruent triangles.

Theorem 2 *In a parallelogram, opposite sides are equal.*

Given $ABCD$ is a parallelogram.

To prove $AB = DC$ and $BC = AD$

Construction Join AC.

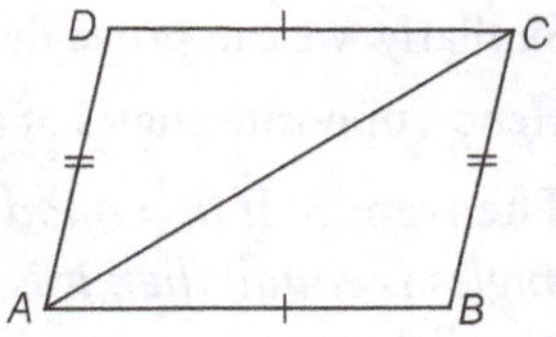

Proof We know that diagonal of a parallelogram divides it into two congruent triangles.

$\therefore$ $\Delta ABC \cong \Delta CDA$

Then, $AB = DC$ [by CPCT]

and $BC = AD$ [by CPCT]

Hence, opposite sides of a parallelogram are equal.

Theorem 3 *If each pair of opposite sides of a quadrilateral is equal, then it is a parallelogram.*

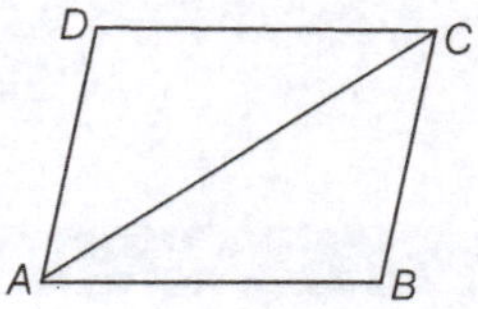

Given $ABCD$ is a quadrilateral in which opposite sides are equal

i.e. $AB = DC$ and $BC = AD$.

To prove $ABCD$ is a parallelogram,

i.e. $AB \parallel DC$ and $BC \parallel AD$.

Construction Join AC.

Proof In ΔABC and ΔCDA,

$$AC = AC \quad \text{[common sides]}$$
$$AB = DC \quad \text{[given]}$$
$$BC = AD \quad \text{[given]}$$

$\therefore$ $\Delta ABC \cong \Delta CDA$ [by SSS congruence rule]

Then, $\angle BAC = \angle DCA$

and $\angle BCA = \angle DAC$ [by CPCT]

But these are pairs of alternate angles.

$\therefore$ $AB \parallel DC$ and $BC \parallel AD$.

Hence, $ABCD$ is a parallelogram.

Theorem 4 *In a parallelogram, opposite angles are equal.*

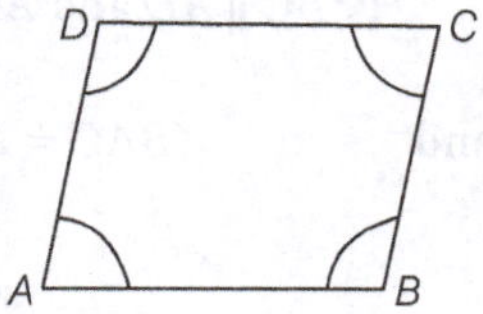

Given $ABCD$ is a parallelogram.

$\therefore$ $AB \parallel DC$ and $BC \parallel AD$.

To prove $\angle A = \angle C$ and $\angle B = \angle D$.

Proof Since, $AB \parallel DC$ and AD is a transversal, then $\angle A + \angle D = 180°$ ...(i)

[co-interior angles]

Similarly, $AD \parallel BC$ and CD is a transversal, then

$$\angle D + \angle C = 180° \quad \text{...(ii)}$$

[consecutive interior angles]

From Eqs. (i) and (ii), we get

$$\angle A + \angle D = \angle D + \angle C$$

$\Rightarrow$ $\angle A = \angle C$

Similarly, we can prove that $\angle B = \angle D$.

Hence, opposite angles of a parallelogram are equal.

Theorem 5 *If in a quadrilateral, each pair of opposite angles is equal, then it is a parallelogram.*

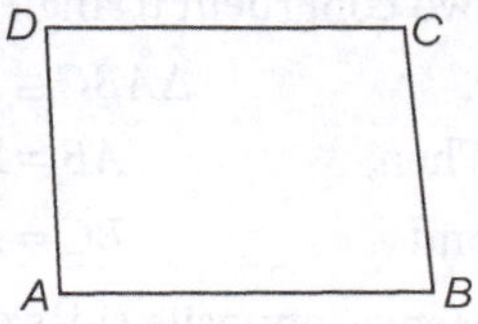

Given $ABCD$ is a quadrilateral in which $\angle A = \angle C$ and $\angle B = \angle D$.

To prove $ABCD$ is a parallelogram.

Proof In quadrilateral $ABCD$,

$$\angle A = \angle C \quad \text{[given] ...(i)}$$
$$\angle B = \angle D \quad \text{[given] ...(ii)}$$

On adding Eqs. (i) and (ii), we get

$$\angle A + \angle B = \angle C + \angle D \quad \text{...(iii)}$$

or $\angle A + \angle D = \angle B + \angle C$

[from Eqs. (i) and (ii)] ...(iv)

Now, by angle sum property of a quadrilateral, we have

$$\angle A + \angle B + \angle C + \angle D = 360° \quad \text{...(v)}$$

On putting the value of $\angle C + \angle D$ from Eq. (iii) in Eq. (v), we get

$$\angle A + \angle B + \angle A + \angle B = 360°$$

$\Rightarrow$ $2(\angle A + \angle B) = 360°$

$\Rightarrow$ $\angle A + \angle B = 180°$

$\therefore$ $\angle A + \angle B = \angle C + \angle D = 180°$ [from Eq. (iii)]

Since, line AB intersects AD and BC at points A and B, respectively, such that $\angle A + \angle B = 180°$

[consecutive interior angles]

$\therefore$ $AD \parallel BC$

Similarly, on putting the value $\angle B + \angle C$ from Eq. (iv) in Eq. (v), we get

$$2(\angle A + \angle D) = 360°$$

$\Rightarrow$ $\angle A + \angle D = 180°$

$\therefore$ $\angle A + \angle D = \angle B + \angle C = 180°$ [from Eq. (iv)]

Since, line AD intersects AB and DC at points A and D, respectively, such that

$\angle A + \angle D = 180°$ [consecutive interior angles]

$\therefore$ $AB \parallel DC$

Hence, $ABCD$ is a parallelogram.

Theorem 6 *The diagonals of a parallelogram bisect each other.*

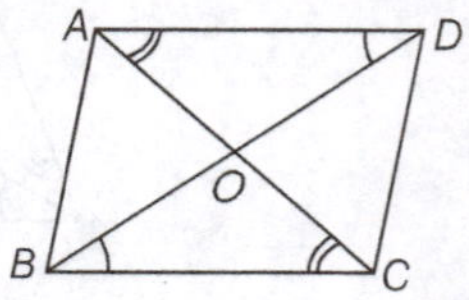

Given $ABCD$ is a parallelogram. Its diagonals AC and BD intersect each other at O.

To prove $OA = OC$

and $OB = OD$

Proof In ΔAOD and ΔCOB,

$$\angle ADO = \angle CBO$$

[$\because BC \parallel AD$ and BD is transversal, so alternate angles are equal]

$\angle DAO = \angle BCO$

[$\because BC \parallel AD$ and AC is transversal, so alternate angles are equal]

and $AD = BC$

[opposite sides of parallelogram $ABCD$ are equal]

$\therefore \Delta AOD \cong \Delta COB$ [by ASA congruence rule]

Then, $OA = OC$

and $OB = OD$ [by CPCT]

Hence, the diagonals of a parallelogram bisect each other.

Theorem 7 *If the diagonals of a quadrilateral bisect each other, then it is a parallelogram.*

Given $ABCD$ is a quadrilateral whose diagonals AC and BD bisect each other at O

i.e. $OA = OC$ and $OB = OD$

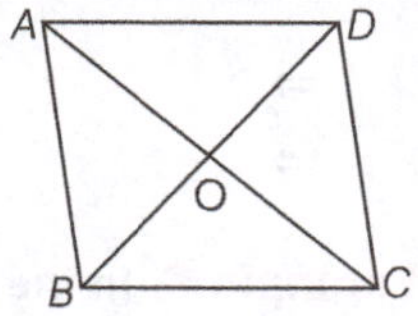

To prove $ABCD$ is a parallelogram.

Proof In ΔAOB and ΔCOD,

$OA = OC$ [given]

$OB = OD$ [given]

$\angle AOB = \angle COD$ [vertically opposite angles]

$\therefore \Delta AOB \cong \Delta COD$ [by SAS congruence rule]

Then, $\angle ODC = \angle OBA$ [by CPCT]

But these are alternate angles which are formed when transversal BD intersects lines AB and DC.

$\therefore AB \parallel DC$

Similarly, we can prove that $BC \parallel AD$.

Hence, $ABCD$ is a parallelogram.

Problems Based on Properties of Parallelogram

Example 1. ***ABCD* is a rectangle in which diagonal *BD* bisects ∠*B*. Show that *ABCD* is a square.** NCERT Exemplar

Sol. Given In a rectangle $ABCD$, diagonal BD bisects $\angle B$.

Construction Join AC.

To prove $ABCD$ is a square.

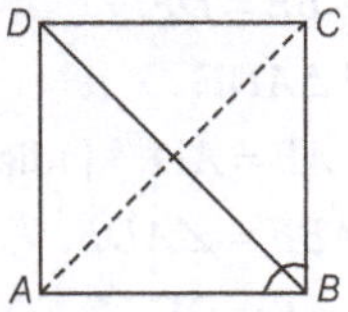

Proof In ΔBAD and ΔBCD, $\angle ABD = \angle CBD$ [given]

$\angle A = \angle C$ [each 90°]

and $BD = BD$ [common sides]

$\therefore \Delta BAD \cong \Delta BCD$ [by AAS congruence rule]

Then, $AB = BC$ [by CPCT] ...(i)

and $AD = DC$ [by CPCT] ...(ii)

But in rectangle $ABCD$, opposite sides are equal.

$\therefore AB = DC$ ...(iii)

and $BC = AD$ ...(iv)

From Eqs. (i), (ii), (iii) and (iv), we get

$AB = BC = CD = DA$

So, $ABCD$ is a square. **Hence proved.**

Example 2. **In the adjoining figure, *ABCD* is a quadrilateral such that *AC* = *BD* and *AC* and *BD* bisect each other at right angle. *O* is the intersection point of *AC* and *BD*. Show that the quadrilateral *ABCD* is a square.**

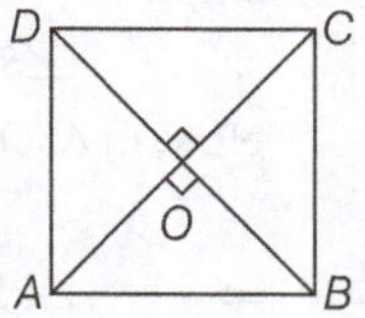

Sol. Given, $ABCD$ is a quadrilateral such that $AC = BD$ and AC and BD bisect each other at right angle at point O.

$\therefore OA = OB = OC = OD$ [$\because AC = BD$] ...(i)

and $\angle AOB = \angle BOC = \angle COD = \angle DOA = 90°$ ...(ii)

We have to show that quadrilateral $ABCD$ is a square.

Now, in ΔAOB, $OA = OB$ [given]

and $\angle AOB = 90°$ [given]

$\therefore \angle OAB = \angle OBA = 45°$

[angles opposite to equal sides are also equal]

Similarly, we can prove that

$\angle OAD = \angle ODA = 45°$

$\angle OBC = \angle OCB = 45°$

Then, $\angle A = \angle BAD = \angle BAO + \angle OAD$

$= 45° + 45°,$

$\angle A = 90°$

Similarly, $\angle B = \angle ABC$

$= \angle OBA + \angle OBC$

$= 45° + 45° = 90°$

Also, $\angle C = 90°$ and $\angle D = 90°$

In ΔAOB and ΔCOB, $OA = OC$ [given]

$OB = OB$ [common side]

and $\angle AOB = \angle BOC$ [given]

$\therefore \Delta AOB \cong \Delta COB$ [by SAS congruence rule]

Then, $AB = BC$ [by CPCT]

Similarly, we can prove that

$BC = CD$ and $CD = AD$

Thus, we get $AB = BC = CD = AD$

and $\angle A = \angle B = \angle C = \angle D = 90°$

Hence, quadrilateral $ABCD$ is a square. **Hence proved.**

Example 3. **In the adjoining figure, *PQRS* is a rhombus, *SQ* and *PR* are the diagonals of the rhombus intersecting at point *O*. If $\angle OPQ = 42°$, then find the value of $\angle ORS + \angle OQP$.**

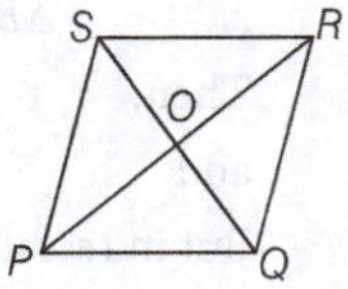

Sol. Given, $PQRS$ is a rhombus.

$\Rightarrow PQRS$ is a parallelogram.

Since, $PQ \| SR$ and PR is a transversal.

$\therefore \quad \angle ORS = \angle OPQ = 42°$ [alternate interior angles] ...(i)

Also, diagonals of rhombus bisect each other at right angle.

$\therefore \quad \angle SOR = 90°$ ...(ii)

Now, in ΔSOR, $\angle RSO + \angle SOR + \angle ORS = 180°$

[angle sum property of triangles]

$\Rightarrow \quad \angle RSO = 180° - \angle SOR - \angle ORS$

$\Rightarrow \quad \angle RSO = 180° - 90° - 42°$ [from Eqs. (i) and (ii)]

$\Rightarrow \quad \angle RSO = 48° \Rightarrow \angle OQP = 48°$ ...(iii)

[alternate interior angles, since $PQ \| SR$ and QS is a transversal]

From Eqs. (i) and (iii), we get

$$\angle ORS + \angle OQP = 42° + 48° = 90°$$

Example 4. **In the following figure, *ABCD* is a rhombus. If $\angle ABC = 54°$, then determine $\angle ACD$.**

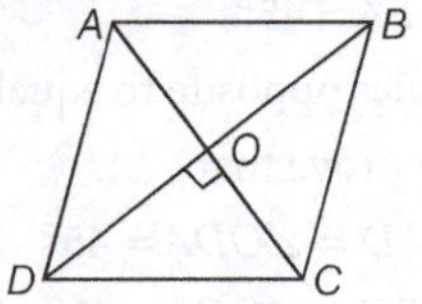

Sol. Given, $ABCD$ is a rhombus.

$\Rightarrow ABCD$ is a parallelogram.

$\Rightarrow \quad \angle ADC = \angle ABC = 54°$

[$\because$ opposite angles of a parallelogram are equal]

$$\angle ODC = \frac{1}{2} \angle ADC$$

[$\because$ diagonal DB of rhombus $ABCD$ bisects $\angle ABC$ and $\angle ADC$]

$\Rightarrow \quad \angle ODC = \frac{1}{2} \times 54° = 27°$

Now, in ΔOCD,

$$\angle OCD + \angle ODC + \angle COD = 180°$$

[angle sum property of a triangle]

$\Rightarrow \quad \angle OCD + 27° + 90° = 180°$

[$\because \angle COD = 90°$, diagonals of a rhombus bisect each other at right angles]

$\Rightarrow \quad \angle OCD + 117° = 180°$

$\Rightarrow \quad \angle OCD = 180° - 117°$

$\Rightarrow \quad \angle OCD = 63°$ or $\angle ACD = 63°$

Example 5. **In a parallelogram, show that the angle bisectors of two adjacent angles intersect at right angles.**

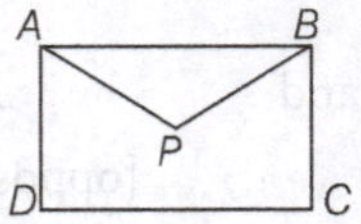

Sol. Given, $ABCD$ is a parallelogram such that angle bisectors of adjacent angles A and B intersect at point P.

We have to show that $\angle APB = 90°$

Here, $\quad \angle A + \angle B = 180°$

[$\because AD \| BC$ and $\angle A$ and $\angle B$ are consecutive interior angles]

$\Rightarrow \quad \frac{1}{2} \angle A + \frac{1}{2} \angle B = 90°$

[dividing by 2 on both sides] ...(i)

But in ΔAPB, $\frac{1}{2} \angle A + \frac{1}{2} \angle B + \angle APB = 180°$

[by angle sum property of a triangle]

$\Rightarrow \quad 90° + \angle APB = 180°$ [from Eq. (i)]

$\Rightarrow \quad \angle APB = 90°$ **Hence proved.**

Example 6. **In the given figure, *ABCD* is a square and *EF* || *BD*. *M* is the mid-point of *EF*. Prove that *AM* bisects $\angle BAD$.**

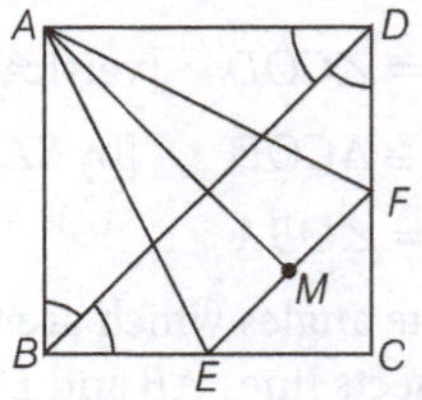

Sol. Given, $ABCD$ is a square and BD is a diagonal.

$\therefore \quad \angle CBD = \angle CDB = \frac{1}{2} \times 90° = 45°$

[$\because$ diagonal of a square bisect each angle at the vertex]

Also, $\quad EF \| BD$ [given]

So, $\quad \angle CEF = \angle CBD = 45°$ [corresponding angles]

and $\quad \angle CFE = \angle CDB = 45°$ [corresponding angles]

$\Rightarrow \quad CE = CF$

[$\because$ sides opposite to equal angles are equal]

$\Rightarrow \quad BC - CE = CD - CF$ [$\because BC = CD$]

$\Rightarrow \quad BE = DF$ ... (i)

Now, in ΔABE and ΔADF,

$AB = AD$ [adjacent sides of a square]

$\angle ABE = \angle ADF$ [each 90°]

$BE = DF$ [from Eq. (i)]

So, $\quad \Delta ABE \cong \Delta ADF$ [by SAS congruence rule]

Then, $\quad AE = AF$ [by CPCT] ... (ii)

and $\quad \angle BAE = \angle DAF$ [by CPCT] ... (iii)

Now, in ΔAEM and ΔAFM,

$AE = AF$ [from Eq. (ii)]

$ME = MF$ [M is mid-point of EF]

$AM = AM$ [common side]

$\therefore$ $\Delta AEM \cong \Delta AFM$ [by SSS congruence rule]

So, $\angle EAM = \angle FAM$ [by CPCT]...(iv)

On adding Eqs. (iii) and (iv), we get

$$\angle BAE + \angle EAM = \angle DAF + \angle FAM$$

$$\Rightarrow \quad \angle BAM = \angle DAM$$

i.e. AM bisects $\angle BAD$. **Hence proved.**

Example 7. Show that the bisectors of angles of a parallelogram form a rectangle.

Sol. Let P, Q, R and S be the points of intersection of the bisectors of $\angle A$ and $\angle B$, $\angle B$ and $\angle C$, $\angle C$ and $\angle D$, $\angle D$ and $\angle A$ respectively of parallelogram $ABCD$ (see figure).

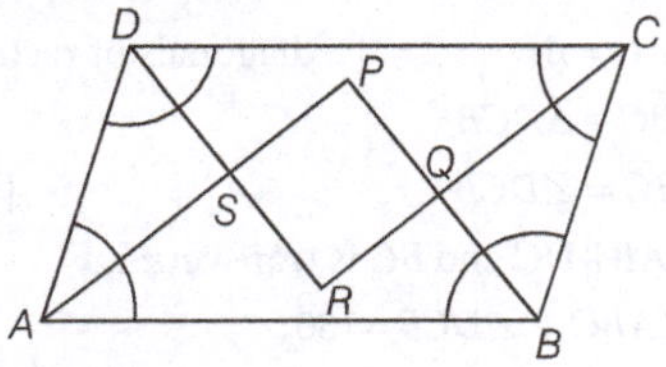

In ΔASD, we observe

DS bisects $\angle D$ and AS bisects $\angle A$, therefore

$$\angle DAS + \angle ADS = \frac{1}{2}\angle A + \frac{1}{2}\angle D$$

$$= \frac{1}{2}(\angle A + \angle D) = \frac{1}{2} \times 180^\circ$$

[$\angle A$ and $\angle D$ are interior angles on the same side of the transversal]

$$= 90^\circ$$

Also, $\angle DAS + \angle ADS + \angle DSA = 180^\circ$

[angle sum property of a triangle]

$\Rightarrow$ $90^\circ + \angle DSA = 180^\circ$

$\Rightarrow$ $\angle DSA = 90^\circ \Rightarrow \angle PSR = 90^\circ$

[vertically opposite angles $\angle DSA = \angle PSR$]

Similarly, it can be shown that $\angle APB = 90^\circ$ or $\angle SPQ = 90^\circ$ (as it was shown for $\angle DSA$). Similarly, $\angle PQR = 90^\circ$ and $\angle SRQ = 90^\circ$.

So, $PQRS$ is a quadrilateral in which all angles are right angles.

Therefore, $PQRS$ is a parallelogram in which one angle (in fact all angles) is 90° and so $PQRS$ is a rectangle.

Example 8. ABC is an isosceles triangle in which $AB = AC$. AD bisects exterior $\angle PAC$ and $DC \parallel AB$ (see the figure). Show that

(i) $\angle DAC = \angle BCA$ (ii) $ABCD$ is a parallelogram.

Sol. (i) Given, ABC is an isosceles triangle in which $AB = AC$.

So, $\angle ACB = \angle ABC$ [$\because$ angles opposite to equal sides are also equal]

Now, $\angle PAC = \angle ABC + \angle ACB$

[exterior angle property]

$\Rightarrow$ $\angle PAC = 2\angle ACB$ [$\because \angle ABC = \angle ACB$]...(i)

Since, AD bisects $\angle PAC$.

So, $\angle PAC = 2\angle DAC$ ...(ii)

From Eqs. (i) and (ii), we get

$$2\angle ACB = 2\angle DAC$$

$$\Rightarrow \quad \angle ACB = \angle DAC$$

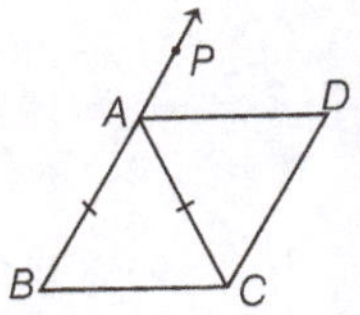

(ii) From part (i), we have

$$\angle DAC = \angle BCA$$

These angles form a pair of alternate angles, when line segments BC and AD are intersected by a transversal AC.

$\therefore$ $BC \parallel AD$

Also, $CD \parallel AB$ [given]

Since, both pairs of opposite sides of quadrilateral $ABCD$ are parallel. So, $ABCD$ is a parallelogram.

Hence proved.

Try These 8.1

1. Justify your answer for the following statements.

(i) Three angles of a quadrilateral $ABCD$ are equal. Is it a parallelogram? Why or why not?

(ii) Diagonal AC and BD of a quadrilateral $ABCD$ intersect each other at O such that $OA : OC = 3 : 2$. Is $ABCD$ a parallelogram?

(iii) $ABCD$ is a parallelogram. If its diagonals are equal, then find the value of $\angle ABC$. NCERT Exemplar

2. Show that each angle of a rectangle is a right angle.

3. Show that the diagonals of a rhombus are perpendicular to each other.

4. In the given figure, $ABCD$ is a parallelogram. E and F are points on opposite sides AD and BC, respectively such that $ED = \frac{1}{2}AD$ and $BF = \frac{1}{3}BC$. If $\angle ADF = 60^\circ$, then find $\angle BFD$.

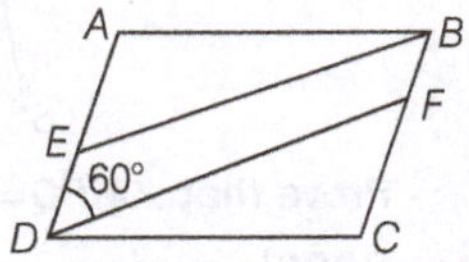

5. In the given figure, $PQRS$ is a parallelogram in which PQ is produced to T, such that $QT = PQ$. Prove that ST bisects RQ.

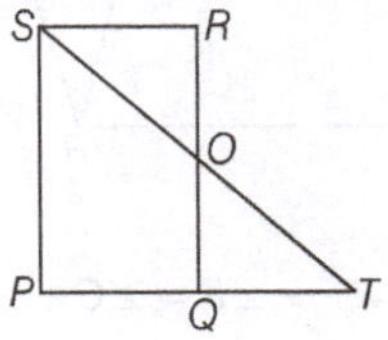

6. **In the given figure, $PQRS$ is a parallelogram, PO and QO are respectively, the angle bisectors of $\angle P$ and $\angle Q$. Line LOM is drawn parallel to PQ. Prove that**

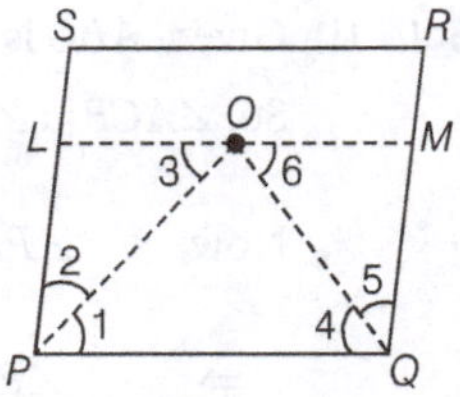

(i) $PL = QM$ (ii) $LO = OM$

7. **Diagonal BD of parallelogram $ABCD$ bisect $\angle B$. Show that it bisects $\angle D$.**

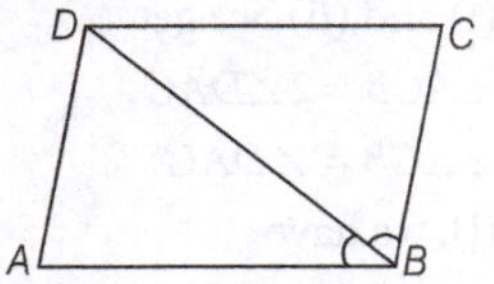

8. **Two parallel lines l and m are intersected by a transversal t. Show that the quadrilateral formed by the bisectors of interior angles is a rectangle.**

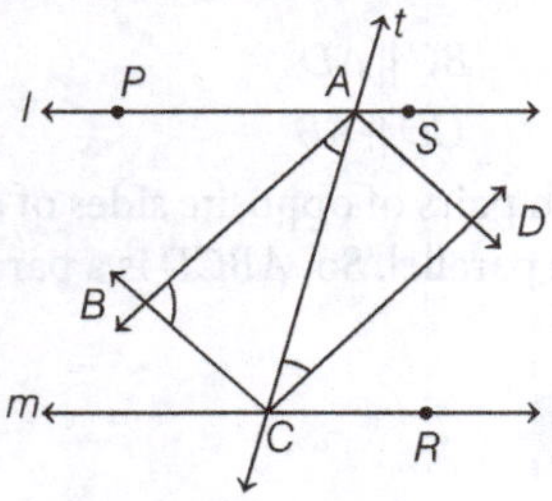

9. **$ABCD$ is a parallelogram in which P and Q are mid-points of opposite sides AB and DC. If AQ intersects DP at S and BQ intersect CP at R, show that**

(i) $APCQ$ is a parallelogram.

(ii) $DPBQ$ is a parallelogram.

10. **In parallelogram $PQRS$, two points M and N are taken on diagonal QS such that $QM = NS$ [see figure]**

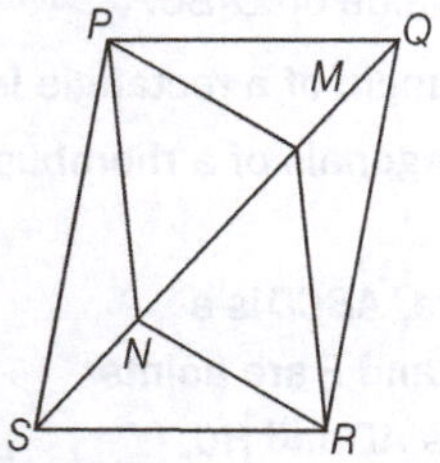

Prove that $\angle MPQ = \angle NRS$.

11. **$PQRS$ is a trapezium in which $PQ \parallel SR$ and $PS = QR$ [see figure].**

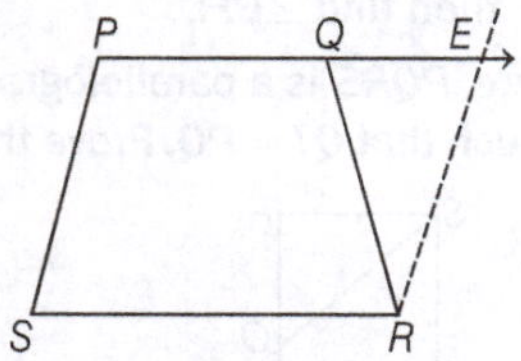

Show that

(i) $\angle P = \angle Q$ (ii) $\angle P + \angle R = \angle Q + \angle S$

Hints & Answers

1. **Hint**

(i) It need not be a parallelogram, because we may have $\angle A = \angle B = \angle C = 80°$ and $\angle D = 120°$.
Here, $\angle B \neq \angle D$.

(ii) $ABCD$ is not a parallelogram, because diagonals of a parallelogram bisect each other. But here, $OA \neq OC$.

(iii) As diagonals of the parallelogram $ABCD$ are equal, it is a rectangle. Therefore, $\angle ABC = 90°$

2. Let $ABCD$ be rectangle.

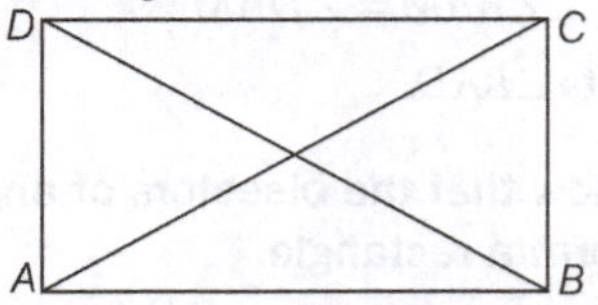

In ΔABC and ΔBCD,

$AB = DC$ [$\because$ opposite sides of rectangle are equal]

$BC = CB$ [common]

$AC = BD$ [$\because$ diagonals of rectangle are equal]

$\therefore$ $\Delta ABC \cong \Delta DCB$ [by SSS]

$\therefore$ $\angle ABC = \angle DCB$ [by CPCT] ...(i)

$\because$ $AB \parallel DC$ and BC is transversal.

$\therefore$ $\angle ABC + \angle DCB = 180°$

$\Rightarrow$ $\angle ABC + \angle ABC = 180°$ [from Eq. (i)]

$\Rightarrow$ $\angle ABC = 90° = \angle DCB$ ...(ii)

Similarly, $\angle ADC = \angle DAB = 90°$ ...(iii)

From Eqs. (ii) and (iii), we get

$\angle ABC = \angle BCD = \angle CDA = \angle DAB = 90°$ **Hence proved.**

3. **Hint** In ΔAOD and ΔCOD,

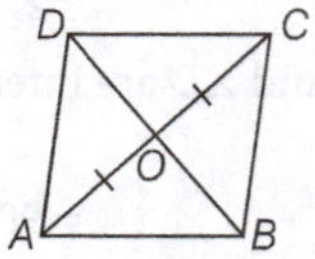

$OA = OC$

[diagonals of parallelogram bisect each other]

$OD = OD$ [common side]

$AD = CD$ [equal sides of rhombus]

$\Rightarrow$ $\Delta AOD \cong \Delta COD$ [by SSS]

$\angle AOD = \angle COD$ [by CPCT]

But $\angle COD + \angle AOD = 180°$ [linear pair]

$\Rightarrow$ $2\angle AOD = 180° \Rightarrow \angle AOD = 90°$

4. **Hint** $ABCD$ is a parallelogram.

$\therefore$ $AD \parallel BC \Rightarrow AD \parallel BF$

and DF is a transversal.

$\therefore$ $\angle ADF + \angle BFD = 180°$ [co-interior angles]

$\Rightarrow$ $\angle BFD = 180° - 60° = 120°$ **Ans.** $120°$

5. **Hint** $PQRS$ is a parallelogram.

$\therefore$ $PQ = SR$ ...(i)

Given, $PQ = QT$ ...(ii)

From Eqs. (i) and (ii), we get

$$PQ = SR = QT$$

$\angle ROS = \angle QOT$ [vertically opposite angles]

$\angle RSO = \angle QTO$ [alternate interior angles]

Now, $\Delta SOR \cong \Delta TOQ$ [by AAS congruence rule]

Then, $OQ = OR$ [by CPCT]

6. Hint

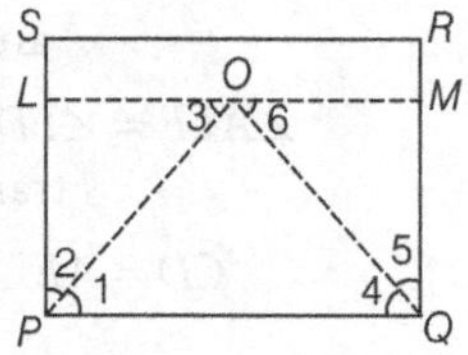

(i) $\angle 1 = \angle 2$ and $\angle 4 = \angle 5$

Now, $PS \| RQ \Rightarrow PL \| QM$

Also, $PQ \| SR \Rightarrow PQ \| LM$

$\therefore$ PQML is a parallelogram.

$\therefore$ $PL = QM$

[opposite sides of parallelogram are equal]... (i)

(ii) Now, $PQ \| LM$ and OP is transversal.

$\therefore$ $\angle 1 = \angle 3$ [alternate interior angles]

$\therefore$ $\angle 2 = \angle 3$ [$\because \angle 1 = \angle 2$]

In ΔOPL, $\angle 2 = \angle 3$

$\Rightarrow$ $OL = PL$ ...(ii)

[$\because$ opposite sides of equal angles are equal]

Also, $PL \| QM$ and OQ is transversal.

$\therefore$ $\angle 4 = \angle 6 \Rightarrow \angle 5 = \angle 6$

In ΔOQM, $\angle 5 = \angle 6$

$OM = QM$ ...(iii)

[$\because$ opposite sides of equal angles are equal]

$\therefore$ From Eqs. (i), (ii) and (iii), we get

$$OL = OM$$

7. Hint $\angle ABD = \angle DBC = \frac{1}{2} \angle ABC$ ...(i)

$AB \| DC$, so $\angle ADB = \angle DBC$ [alternate angles] ...(ii)

Also, $BC \| AD$,

$\angle BDC = \angle DBA$ [alternate angles] ...(iii)

From Eqs. (i), (ii) and (iii), we get

$$\angle ABD = \angle DBC = \angle ADB = \angle BDC$$

Now, $\angle ADC = \angle ADB + \angle BDC = \angle DBC + \angle ABD = \angle ABC$

Therefore, diagonal BD bisects $\angle D$ also.

8. Hint $PS \| CR$

$\angle PAC = \angle ACR$ [alternate angles]

$\Rightarrow$ $\frac{1}{2} \angle PAC = \frac{1}{2} \angle ACR$

$\Rightarrow$ $\angle BAC = \angle ACD$

[a pair of alternate angles for lines AB and CD]

So, $AB \| DC$

Similarly, $BC \| AD$

$\Rightarrow ABCD$ is a parallelogram.

$\Rightarrow$ $\angle PAC + \angle SAC = 180°$ [linear pair]

$\Rightarrow$ $\frac{1}{2} \angle PAC + \frac{1}{2} \angle SAC = \frac{1}{2} \times 180°$

$\Rightarrow$ $\angle BAC + \angle DAC = 90° \Rightarrow \angle BAD = 90°$

Thus, one angle of parallelogram $ABCD$ is a right angle.

Hence, $ABCD$ is a rectangle.

9. Hint

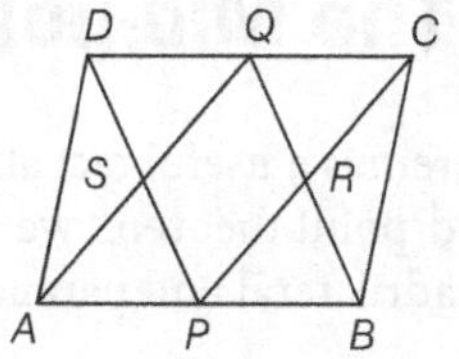

(i) In $APCQ$, $AP \| QC$ [$\because AB \| DC$]

$AP = \frac{1}{2} AB, QC = \frac{1}{2} DC$ [given]

Also, $AB = DC \Rightarrow \frac{1}{2} AB = \frac{1}{2} DC \Rightarrow AP = QC$

$\because AP \| QC$ and $AP = QC$

$\therefore$ APQC is a parallelogram.

(ii) Similarly, in $DPBQ$

$BP \| QD$ and $BP = QD$

$\therefore$ BPDQ is a parallelogram.

10. Hint Since, $PQRS$ is a parallelogram and M and N are points on QS such that $QM = NS$.

In ΔPMQ and ΔRNS, we have

$QM = SN$ [given]

$PQ = SR$ [opposite sides of parallelogram are equal]

$\angle PQM = \angle RSN$ [alternate interior angles]

$\therefore$ $\Delta MPQ \cong \Delta NRS$ [by SAS congruence rule]

$\therefore$ $\angle MPQ = \angle NRS$ [by CPCT]

11. Hint

(i) $PQRS$ is a trapezium in which $PQ \| SR$, $PS = QR$.

Now, extend PQ and draw a line through R parallel to PS intersecting extended PQ at E.

$\therefore$ $PS \| ER$

So, $PSRE$ is a parallelogram.

$\therefore$ $PS = ER$ and $PE = SR$

But $PS = QR$

$\therefore$ $PS = QR = ER$

Now, $\angle P + \angle E = 180°$

[interior angles on the same side of transversal PE]

$\Rightarrow$ $\angle E = 180° - \angle P$

Also, $QR = ER \Rightarrow \angle E = \angle RQE = 180° - \angle P$

But $\angle PQR = 180° - \angle RQE = 180° - 180° + \angle P = \angle P$

[$\because PQE$ is a straight line]

$\Rightarrow$ $\angle Q = \angle P$ ... (i)

(ii) Now, $\angle P + \angle S = 180°$ [co-interior angles]

$\Rightarrow$ $\angle S = 180° - \angle P = 180° - \angle Q$ ... (ii)

[from Eq. (i)]

Also, $\angle Q + \angle R = 180°$ [co-interior angles]

$\Rightarrow$ $\angle R = 180° - \angle Q$ ... (iii)

From Eqs. (ii) and (iii), we get

$\angle S = \angle R$ ... (iv)

On adding Eqs (i) and (iv), we get

$\angle Q + \angle S = \angle P + \angle R$ **Hence proved.**

TOPIC 02 The Mid-point Theorem

The mid-point theorem is a useful fact about a triangle. With the help of mid-point theorem, we can prove various results related to quadrilateral and parallelogram easily.

Mid-point Theorem

The line segment joining the mid-points of any two sides of a triangle is parallel to the third side and equal to half of it.

Given In a ΔABC, E and F are the mid-points of AB and AC, respectively.

To prove $EF \parallel BC$ and $EF = \frac{1}{2} BC$.

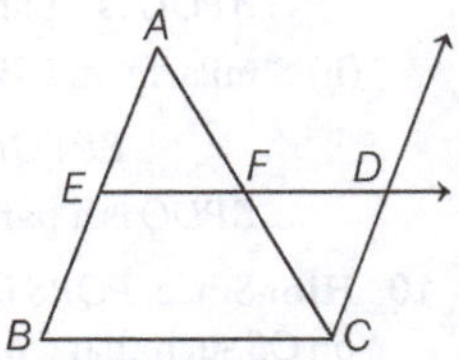

Construction Through vertex C, draw $CD \parallel BA$ and let it meets extended EF at D.

Proof Now, in ΔAEF and ΔCDF,

$\angle AFE = \angle CFD$ [vertically opposite angles]

$AF = CF$ [since, F is mid-point of AC]

and $\angle EAF = \angle DCF$

[$\because$ alternate angles between parallel lines BA and CD]

$\therefore$ $\Delta AEF \cong \Delta CDF$ [by ASA congruence rule]

Then, $AE = CD$ and $EF = FD$ [by CPCT]...(i)

Also, $AE = BE$ [since, E is the mid-point of AB]...(ii)

From Eqs. (i) and (ii), we get

$AE = BE = CD$ ...(iii)

and $BE \parallel CD$ [by construction]

So, $BCDE$ is a parallelogram.

[$\because$ one pair of opposite sides is parallel and equal]

Then, $ED \parallel BC$ or $EF \parallel BC$ and $ED = BC$

Now, $BC = ED = EF + FD = 2EF$

[from Eq. (i), $EF = FD$]

$\Rightarrow$ $EF = \frac{1}{2} BC$

Hence, the line segment joining the mid-points of two sides of a triangle is parallel to the third side and equal to half of it. **Hence proved.**

(Converse of mid-point Theorem) *The line drawn through the mid-point of one side of a triangle, parallel to another side bisect the third side.*

Given In a ΔABC, E is the mid-point of AB and $EF \parallel BC$.

To prove F is the mid-point of AC.

Construction Draw $CM \parallel BA$ and extend EF such that it intersects CM at D.

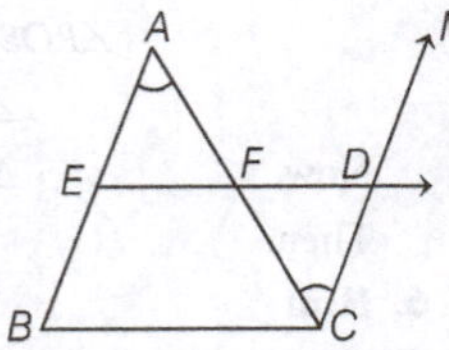

Proof In ΔAEF and ΔCDF,

$\angle FAE = \angle FCD$

[$\because AB \parallel CM$ and AC is a transversal, so alternate angles are equal]

$\angle AEF = \angle FDC$ [$\because AB \parallel CM$ and ED is a transversal, so alternate angles are equal]

$CD = AE$ [$\because BCDE$ is a parallelogram, so $CD = BE = AE$]

$\therefore$ $\Delta AEF \cong \Delta CDF$ [by ASA congruence rule]

Then, $AF = CF$ [by CPCT]

Hence, F is a mid-point of AC.

Alternate Method

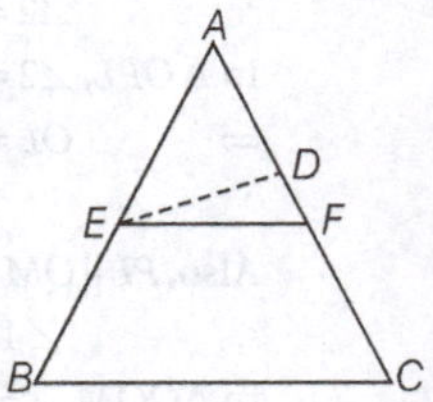

Let F not be the mid-point of AC and D be the mid-point of AC. Join ED.

In ΔABC, E is the mid-point of AB and D is the mid-point of AC, then by mid-point theorem,

$ED \parallel BC$ ...(i)

But $EF \parallel BC$ [given]...(ii)

From Eqs. (i) and (ii), we conclude that ED and EF both are parallel to BC.

But this is a contradiction to the parallel line axiom. So, our assumption that F is not the mid-point of AC is wrong.

Hence, F is the mid-point of AC. **Hence proved.**

Example 1. **ABC is an equilateral triangle and L, M and N are the mid-points of the sides AB, BC and CA, respectively. Prove that ΔLMN is an equilateral triangle.** NCERT Exemplar

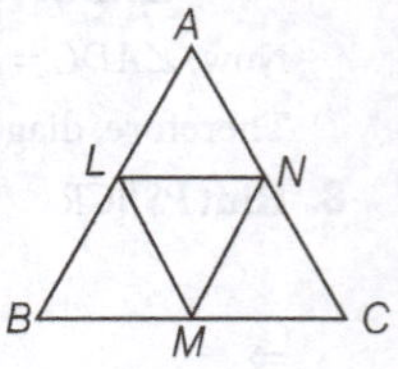

Sol. **Given** ΔABC is an equilateral triangle and L, M, N are the mid-points of the sides AB, BC and CA, respectively.

To prove ΔLMN is an equilateral triangle.

Proof Since, L and N are the mid-points of AB and AC, respectively.

$\therefore$ $LN = \frac{1}{2} BC$ [by mid-point theorem]

Similarly, $LM = \frac{1}{2} AC$ and $MN = \frac{1}{2} AB$

Now, ΔABC is an equilateral triangle.

$\therefore$ $AB = BC = CA$

$\Rightarrow$ $\frac{1}{2}AB = \frac{1}{2}BC = \frac{1}{2}CA \Rightarrow MN = LN = LM$

Hence, ΔLMN is an equilateral triangle. **Hence proved.**

Example 2. ***E* and *F* are respectively the mid-points of non-parallel sides *AD* and *BC* of a trapezium *ABCD*. Prove that *EF* || *AB* and $EF = \frac{1}{2}(AB + CD)$.**

NCERT Exemplar

Sol. Given *E* and *F* are respectively the mid-points of non-parallel sides of *AD* and *BC* of trapezium *ABCD*.

To prove $EF \parallel AB$ and $EF = \frac{1}{2}(AB + CD)$

Construction Join *CE* and produce it to meet *BA* at *P*.

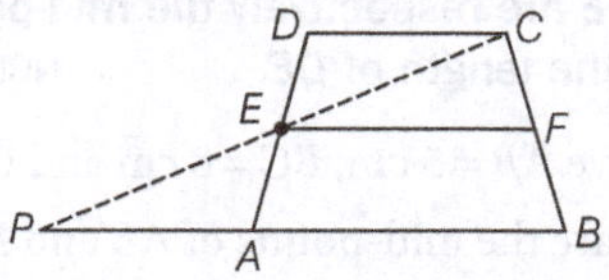

Proof In ΔDEC and ΔAEP, we have

$\angle DEC = \angle AEP$ [vertically opposite angles]

$\angle DCE = \angle APE$

[$\because DC \parallel PB$ and *PC* is transversal, so alternate angles are equal]

$DE = AE$ [$\because$ *E* is the mid-points of *AD*]

$\therefore$ $\Delta DEC \cong \Delta AEP$ [by AAS congruence rule]

Then, $CE = PE$ [by CPCT]

and $CD = PA$ [by CPCT]

Now, in ΔCPB, *E* is the mid-point of *CP*. [$\because CE = PE$]

and *F* is the mid-point of *BC*. [given]

So, by mid-point theorem,

$EF \parallel PB$ and $EF = \frac{1}{2} PB$

$\Rightarrow$ $EF \parallel AB$ and $EF = \frac{1}{2}(PA + AB) = \frac{1}{2}(CD + AB)$

[$\because PA = CD$]

Hence, $EF \parallel AB$ and $EF = \frac{1}{2}(AB + CD)$ **Hence proved.**

Example 3. ***l*, *m* and *n* are three parallel lines intersected by transversals *p* and *q* such that *l*, *m* and *n* cut-off equal intercepts *AB* and *BC* on *p*. Show that *l*, *m* and *n* cut-off equal intercepts *DE* and *EF* on *q* also.**

Sol. Given $l \parallel m \parallel n$ and $AB = BC$

To show $DE = EF$

Proof In ΔACF, *B* is the mid-point of *AC*

[$\because AB = BC$, given]

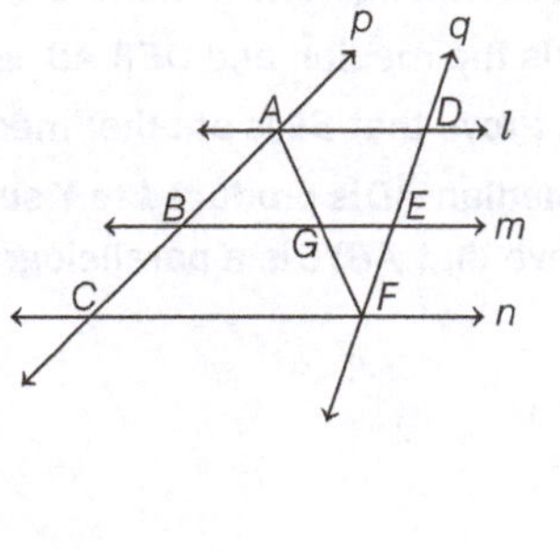

and $BG \parallel CF$ [$\because m \parallel n$, given]

By converse of mid-point theorem, *G* is the mid-point of *AF*.

Now, in ΔAFD, *G* is the mid-point of *AF*

and $GE \parallel AD$ [$\because l \parallel m$, given]

So, by converse of mid-point theorem, *E* is the mid-point of *DF*.

Then, $DE = EF$

Hence, *l*, *m* and *n* cut-off equal intercepts *DE* and *EF* on *q* also. **Hence proved.**

Example 4. ***ABCD* is a kite with *AB* = *AD* and *CD* = *CB*. Prove that the figure formed by joining the mid-points of the consecutive sides is a rectangle.**

Sol. We draw the figure as shown below.

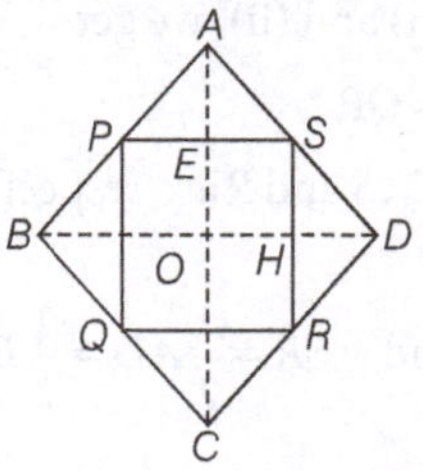

Let *P*, *Q*, *R* and *S* be the mid-points of the sides *AB*, *BC*, *CD* and *DA*, respectively. Join *AC* and *BD*. Which intersects each other at *O*.

Now, in ΔABC, $PQ \parallel AC$

and $PQ = \frac{1}{2} AC$ [by mid-point theorem] ...(i)

and in ΔACD, $RS \parallel AC$ and $RS = \frac{1}{2} AC$

[by mid-point theorem] ...(ii)

From Eqs. (i) and (ii), we get

$PQ \parallel RS$ and $PQ = RS$

Since, a pair of opposite sides equal and parallel.

So, *PQRS* is a parallelogram.

Also, $AB = AD$ [given] ...(i)

So, *A* lies on the perpendicular bisector of *BD* further

$CB = CD$ [given] ...(ii)

So, *C* lies on the perpendicular bisector of *BD*. ...(iii)

From Eqs. (ii) and (iii), *AC* is the perpendicular bisector of *BD*

i.e. $AC \perp BD$

$\Rightarrow$ $\angle AOD = 90°$

Now, clearly $HS \parallel OE$ and $SE \parallel OH$

So, *SEOH* is a parallelogram.

Hence, $\angle ESH = \angle EOH = 90°$

So, parallelogram *PQRS* is a rectangle. **Hence proved.**

Example 5. ***ABCD* is a trapezium in which *AB* || *DC* and *AD* = *BC*. If *P*, *Q*, *R* and *S* are respectively, the mid-points of *BA*, *BD*, *CD* and *CA*, then show that *PQRS* is a rhombus.**

Sol. In ΔABC, P and S are respectively the mid-points of sides AB and AC.

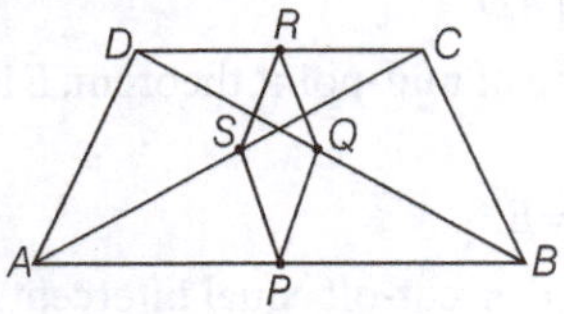

$\therefore \quad PS \parallel BC$ and $PS = \frac{1}{2} BC$

[using mid-point theorem] ...(i)

Similarly, $\quad QR \parallel BC$ and $QR = \frac{1}{2} BC$ ...(ii)

Now, from Eqs. (i) and (ii), we get

$PS \parallel QR$ and $PS = QR$ ...(iii)

Further, in ΔACD, S and R are respectively the mid-points of AC and CD.

$\therefore \quad SR \parallel AD$ and $\quad SR = \frac{1}{2} AD = \frac{1}{2} BC$ ... (iv)

Similarly, $PQ \parallel AD$ and $PQ = \frac{1}{2} AD = \frac{1}{2} BC$ ... (v)

Thus, from Eqs. (iv) and (v), we get

$PQ \parallel SR$ and $PQ = SR$ ... (vi)

From Eqs. (i), (ii), (iv) and (v), we get

$PS = QR = SR = PQ$

and from Eqs. (iii) and (vi), we get $PQ \parallel SR$ and $PS \parallel QR$.

Hence, $PQRS$ is a rhombus. **Hence proved.**

Example 6. **ΔABC is an isosceles triangle in which *AB* = *AC*. *D* and *E* are the mid-points of sides *AB* and *AC* and *DE* = 2.5 cm. Find the perimeter of ΔABC, when *AD* = 4.5 cm.**

Sol. Given, ΔABC in which $AB = AC$, D and E are the mid-points of AB and AC.

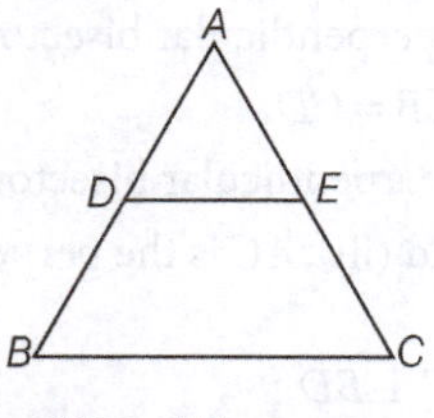

$AD = DB = 4.5$ cm

Then, $\quad AB = 2 \times 4.5 = 9$ cm

So, $\quad AB = AC = 9$ cm

Since, D and E are the mid-points of AB and AC, respectively.

So, by mid-point theorem, $DE \parallel BC$ and $DE = \frac{1}{2} BC$

Then, $BC = 2DE = 2 \times 2.5 = 5$ cm $\quad$ [$DE = 2.5$ cm, given]

Now, perimeter of $\Delta ABC = AB + BC + CA$

$= 9 + 5 + 9 = 23$ cm

Example 7. **In ΔABC, *AB* = 5 cm, *BC* = 8 cm and *CA* = 7 cm. If *D* and *E* are respectively the mid-point of *AB* and *BC*, determine the length of *DE*.** NCERT Exemplar

Sol. In ΔABC, we have $AB = 5$ cm, $BC = 8$ cm and $CA = 7$ cm.

Since, D and E are the mid-points of AB and BC, respectively.

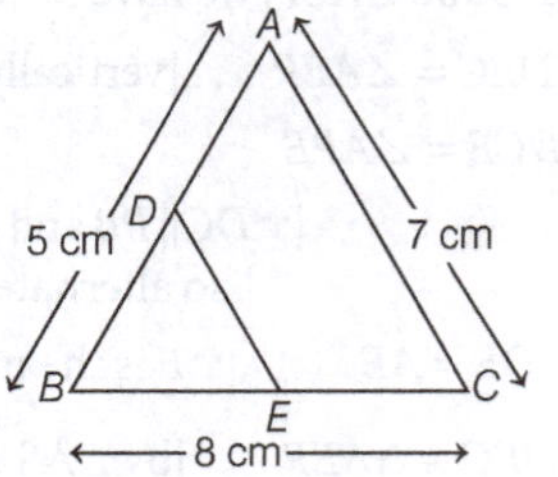

By mid-point theorem,

$DE \parallel AC$

and $\quad DE = \frac{1}{2} AC = \frac{7}{2} = 3.5$ cm

Hence, the length of DE is 3.5 cm.

Try These 8.2

1. ***D* and *E* are the mid-points of sides *AB* and *AC*, respectively of ΔABC. If the perimeter of ΔABC = 40 cm. Find the perimeter of ΔADE.**
2. **In ΔABC, *AB* = 13 cm, *BC* = 16 cm and *AC* = 8 cm. Find the perimeter of the triangle formed by joining the mid-points of the sides of the triangle.**
3. ***P*, *Q*, *R* and *S* are respectively the mid-points of the sides *AB*, *BC*, *CD* and *DA* of a quadrilateral *ABCD*, such that $AC \perp BD$. Prove that *PQRS* is a rectangle.**
4. ***P*, *Q*, *R* and *S* are respectively the mid-points of the sides *AB*, *BC*, *CD* and *DA* of a quadrilateral *ABCD* in which *AC* = *BD*. Prove that *PQRS* is a rhombus.** NCERT Exemplar
5. **In ΔABC, *AD* is the median and *DE* || *AB*, such that *E* is a point on *AC*. Prove that *BE* is another median.**
6. **In a ΔABC, median *AD* is produced to *Y* such that *AD* = *DY*. Prove that *ABYC* is a parallelogram.**

Hints & Answers

1. Hint $AB + BC + CA = 40$

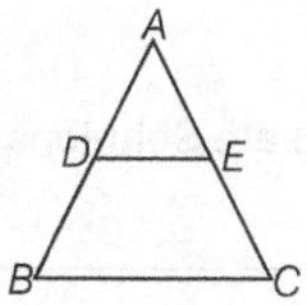

$$\Rightarrow \quad \frac{1}{2}AB + \frac{1}{2}BC + \frac{1}{2}CA = \frac{40}{2}$$

$$\Rightarrow \quad AD + DE + AE = 20 \text{ cm}$$

2. Hint $DF = \frac{1}{2}AC = \frac{8}{2} = 4 \text{ cm}$

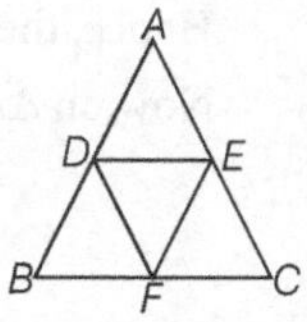

$$FE = \frac{1}{2}AB = \frac{13}{2} = 6.5 \text{ cm}$$

$$ED = \frac{1}{2}BC = \frac{16}{2} = 8 \text{ cm}$$

Ans. 18.5 cm

3. Hint $AC \perp BD$

$\therefore \angle COD = \angle AOD = \angle AOB = \angle COB = 90°$

In ΔADC, by mid-point theorem,

$$SR \parallel AC \text{ and } SR = \frac{1}{2}AC \qquad \ldots\text{(i)}$$

Similarly, in ΔABC,

$$PQ \parallel AC \text{ and } PQ = \frac{1}{2}AC \qquad \ldots\text{(ii)}$$

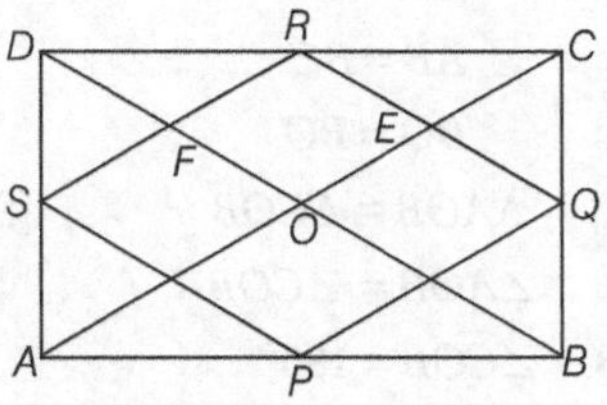

From Eqs. (i) and (ii),

$$PQ \parallel SR \text{ and } PQ = SR = \frac{1}{2}AC \qquad \ldots\text{(iii)}$$

Similarly, $SP \parallel RQ$ and $SP = RQ = \frac{1}{2}BD \qquad \ldots$(iv)

In quadrilateral $EOFR$, $OE \parallel FR$, $OF \parallel ER$

$\therefore \quad \angle EOF = \angle ERF = 90°$

Hence, $PQRS$ is a rectangle.

4. Hint Solve as Q. 3.

Here, $\quad AC = BD \qquad$ [given]

So, $\quad SR = PQ = SP = RQ$

$$= \frac{1}{2}AC = \frac{1}{2}BD$$

5. Hint AD is median, so D is the mid-point of BC.

Also, $DE \parallel AB$

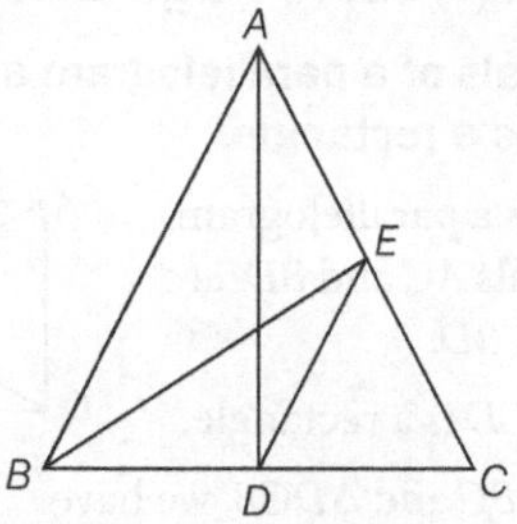

So, by converse mid-point theorem. E is mid-point of AC.

Hence, BE is median.

6. Hint AD is median.

$\therefore \qquad BD = DC$ and $AD = DY \qquad$ [given]

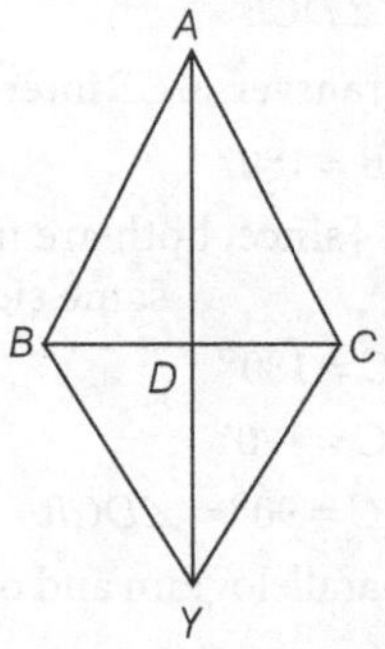

Then, $\quad \Delta ABD \cong \Delta YCD \qquad$ [by SAS congruence rule]

$\therefore \quad AB = CY$

Similarly, $\quad AC = BY$

So, $ABYC$ is a parallelogram.

NCERT FOLDER

Complete Solutions of All Exercises of NCERT Textbook

EXERCISE 8.1 (NCERT Page 110-111)

Q1. If the diagonals of a parallelogram are equal, then show that it is a rectangle.

Sol. **Given** $ABCD$ is a parallelogram, whose diagonals AC and BD are equal i.e. $AC = BD$.

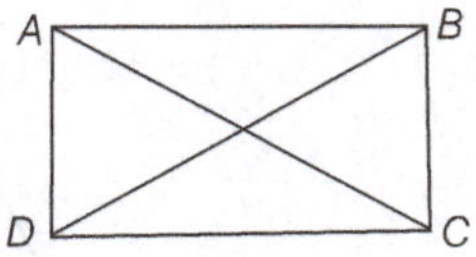

To prove $ABCD$ is a rectangle.

Proof In ΔABC and ΔDCB, we have

$AB = CD$ [opposite sides of parallelogram]

$BC = CB$ [common in both triangles]

and $AC = BD$ [given]

$\therefore$ $\Delta ABC \cong \Delta DCB$ [by SSS congruence rule]

So, $\angle ABC = \angle DCB$ [by CPCT] ...(i)

But $DC \parallel AB$ and transversal CB intersect them.

$\therefore$ $\angle ABC + \angle DCB = 180°$

[since, both are interior angles on the same side of the transversal]

$\Rightarrow \angle ABC + \angle ABC = 180°$ [from Eq. (i)]

$\Rightarrow$ $2\angle ABC = 180°$

$\Rightarrow$ $\angle ABC = 90° = \angle DCB$

Thus, $ABCD$ is a parallelogram and one of its angle is $90°$.

Hence, $ABCD$ is a rectangle. **Hence proved.**

Q2. Show that the diagonals of a square are equal and bisect each other at right angles.

Sol. **Given** $ABCD$ is a square.

Diagonal AC and BD intersect at O.

$AB = BC = CD = DA$,

$\angle ADC = \angle DCB = \angle CBA = \angle BAD = 90°$

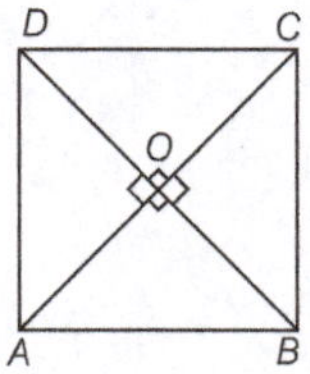

To Prove We need to prove three things

(i) $AC = BD$

(ii) $OA = OC$, $OD = OB$

(iii) $\angle AOB$, $\angle BOC$, $\angle COD$, $\angle AOD$ are $90°$.

Proof In ΔABC and ΔDCB,

$AB = CD$ [given]

$\angle ABC = \angle DCB$ [given]

$BC = BC$ [common]

So, $\Delta ABC \cong \Delta DCB$ [SAS congruence rule]

$\Rightarrow$ $AC = DB$ [by CPCT]

Hence, the diagonals of square are equal.

Now, in ΔAOB and ΔCOD,

$\angle AOB = \angle COD$

[vertically opposite angles]

$\angle ABO = \angle CDO$

[$AB \parallel CD$ and BD is transversal, so alternate angle are equal]

$AB = CD$ [given]

$\therefore$ $\Delta AOB \cong \Delta COD$ [AAS congruence rule]

$\therefore$ $AO = CO$ and $OB = OD$ [by CPCT] ...(i)

Hence, diagonals AC and BD bisect each other.

Again, in ΔAOB and ΔCOB,

$OA = OC$ [from Eq. (i)]

$AB = BC$ [given]

$BO = BO$ [common]

$\therefore$ $\Delta AOB \cong \Delta COB$ [SSS congruency]

$\therefore$ $\angle AOB = \angle COB$ [by CPCT] ...(ii)

Now, $\angle AOB + \angle COB = 180°$ [linear pair]

$\Rightarrow$ $\angle AOB + \angle AOB = 180°$

$\Rightarrow$ $2\angle AOB = 180° \Rightarrow \angle AOB = 90°$

Hence, AC and BD bisect each other at right angles.

Hence proved.

Q3. Diagonal AC of a parallelogram $ABCD$ bisects $\angle A$ (see the figure). Show that

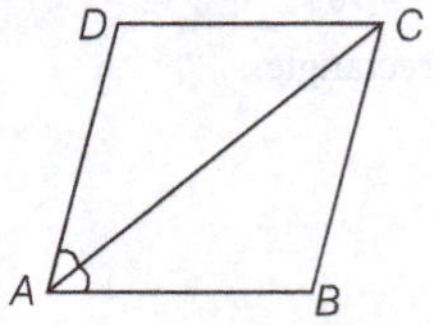

(i) it bisects $\angle C$ also. (ii) $ABCD$ is a rhombus.

Sol. (i) Given, diagonal AC of a parallelogram $ABCD$ bisects $\angle A$.

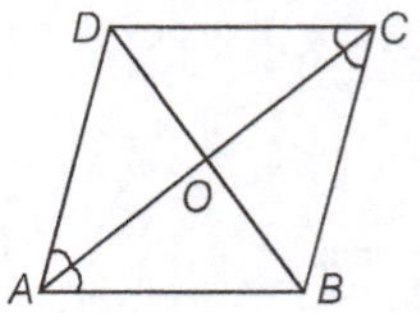

i.e. $\angle DAC = \angle BAC = \frac{1}{2} \angle BAD$ ...(i)

Here, $AB \parallel DC$ and AC is a transversal.

$\therefore \quad \angle DCA = \angle BAC$

[pair of alternate angles] ...(ii)

Similarly, $BC \parallel AD$ and AC is a transversal.

$\therefore \quad \angle BCA = \angle DAC$

[pair of alternate angles] ...(iii)

From Eqs. (i), (ii) and (iii), we get

$\angle DAC = \angle BCA = \angle BAC = \angle DCA$ ...(iv)

Hence, diagonal AC also bisects $\angle C$.

(ii) From Eq. (iv), $\angle DAC = \angle DCA \Rightarrow CD = DA$

[$\because$ sides opposite to equal angles are equal]

But $\quad AB = DC$ and $AD = BC$

[$\because ABCD$ is a parallelogram]

$\therefore \quad AB = BC = CD = DA$

Hence, $ABCD$ is a rhombus.

Q 4. *ABCD* is a rectangle in which diagonal *AC* bisects ∠*A* as well as ∠*C*. Show that

(i) *ABCD* is a square.

(ii) diagonal *BD* bisects ∠*B* as well as ∠*D*.

Sol. Given $ABCD$ is a rectangle.

$\therefore AB = DC$ and $BC = AD$, AC bisects $\angle A$ and $\angle C$. ...(i)

To prove

(i) $ABCD$ is a square

i.e. $AB = BC = CD = DA$

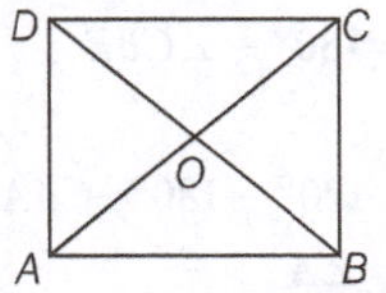

(ii) Diagonal BD bisects $\angle B$ as well as $\angle D$.

Proof

(i) $\because AC$ bisects $\angle A$ and $\angle C$

$\therefore \quad \angle DAC = \angle CAB$

and $\quad \angle DCA = \angle ACB$ ...(ii)

Now, $\quad \angle DAC = \angle BCA$

[$\because BC \parallel AD$ and AC is transversal]

$\angle DAC = \angle BCA = \angle CAB$

[from Eq. (ii)] ...(iii)

In ΔABC,

$\angle BCA = \angle CAB$ [From Eq. (iii)]

$\therefore \quad BC = AB$

[$\because$ sides opposite to equal angles are equal] ...(iv)

Similarly, $AD = CD$ ...(v)

From Eqs. (i), (iv) and (v), we get

$AB = BC = AD = CD$

So, $ABCD$ is a square.

(ii) In ΔAOB and ΔCOB, we have

$AB = BC$ [sides of a square]

$BO = OB$ [common side]

$OA = OC$

[since, diagonals of a square bisect each other]

$\therefore \quad \Delta AOB \cong \Delta COB$ [by SSS congruence rule]

Then, $\angle OBA = \angle OBC$ [by CPCT]

This shows that BO or BD bisects $\angle B$.

Similarly, in ΔAOD and ΔCOD, we have

$AD = CD$ [sides of a square]

$OD = DO$ [common side]

and $\quad OA = OC$

[since, diagonals of square bisect each other]

$\therefore \quad \Delta AOD \cong \Delta COD$ [by SSS congruence rule]

Then, $\angle ADO = \angle CDO$ [by CPCT]

This shows that DO or DB bisect $\angle D$.

Hence, BD bisects $\angle B$ as well as $\angle D$. **Hence proved.**

Q 5. In parallelogram *ABCD*, two points *P* and *Q* are taken on diagonal *BD* such that *DP* = *BQ*(see the figure).

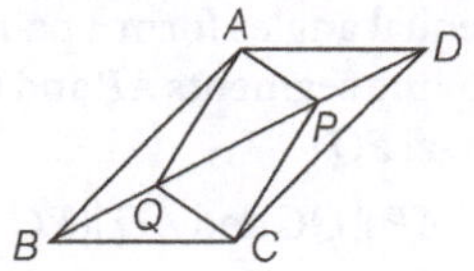

Show that

(i) Δ*APD* ≅ Δ*CQB* (ii) *AP* = *CQ*

(iii) Δ*AQB* ≅ Δ*CPD* (iv) *AQ* = *CP*

(v) *APCQ* is a parallelogram.

Sol. Given, $ABCD$ is a parallelogram and P and Q are points on BD such that $DP = BQ$ ...(i)

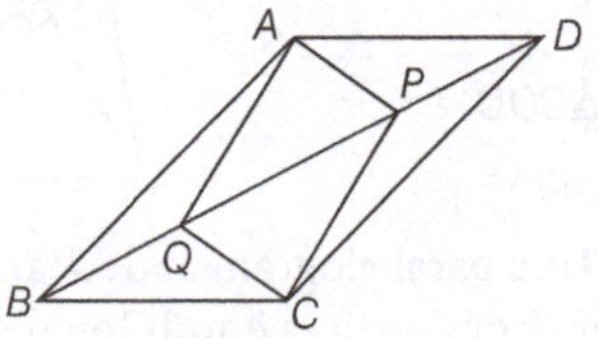

(i) We have to show,

$\Delta APD \cong \Delta CQB$

In ΔAPD and ΔCQB, we have

$DP = BQ$ [given]

$AD = BC$

[opposite sides of parallelogram are equal]

$\angle ADP = \angle CBQ$

[since, $AD \parallel BC$ and BD is a transversal, so alternate interior angles are equal]

$\therefore \quad \Delta APD \cong \Delta CQB$ [by SAS congruence rule]

(ii) Since, $\Delta APD \cong \Delta CQB \Rightarrow AP = CQ$ [by CPCT]

(iii) We have to show, $\Delta AQB \cong \Delta CPD$

Now, in ΔAQB and ΔCPD, we have

$BQ = DP$ [given]

$AB = CD$

[opposite sides of parallelogram are equal]

$\angle ABQ = \angle CDP$

[$\because AB \parallel CD$ and BD is a transversal, so alternate interior angles are equal]

So, $\Delta AQB \cong \Delta CPD$ [by SAS congruence rule]

(iv) Since, $\Delta AQB \cong \Delta CPD$

$\therefore$ $AQ = CP$ [by CPCT]

(v) We have to show, $APCQ$ is a parallelogram.

Now, in ΔAPQ and ΔCQP, we have

$AQ = CP$ [from part (iv)]

$AP = CQ$ [from part (ii)]

$PQ = QP$ [common side]

$\therefore$ $\Delta APQ \cong \Delta CQP$ [by SSS congruence rule]

Then, $\angle APQ = \angle CQP$ [by CPCT]

and $\angle AQP = \angle CPQ$ [by CPCT]

Now, these equal angles form a pair of alternate angles, when line segments AP and QC are intersected by a transversal PQ.

$\therefore$ $AP \parallel QC$ and $AQ \parallel PC$

Now, both pairs of opposite sides of quadrilateral $APCQ$ are parallel and equal.

Hence, $APCQ$ is a parallelogram. **Hence proved.**

Q 6. $ABCD$ is a parallelogram and AP and CQ are perpendiculars from vertices A and C on diagonal BD (see the figure).

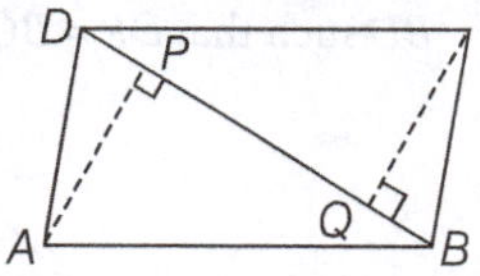

Show that

(i) $\Delta APB \cong \Delta CQD$

(ii) $AP = CQ$

Sol. Given, $ABCD$ is a parallelogram and AP and CQ are perpendiculars from vertices A and C on diagonal BD.

Since, $AB \parallel DC$ and BD is a transversal.

$\therefore$ $\angle CDB = \angle ABD$ ...(i)

(i) Now, in ΔCQD and ΔAPB, we have

$CD = BA$ [sides of a parallelogram]

$\angle CQD = \angle APB = 90^\circ$

[$\because AP \perp BD$ and $CQ \perp BD$, given]

$\angle CDQ = \angle ABP$ [from Eq. (i)]

$\therefore$ $\Delta CQD \cong \Delta APB$ [by AAS congruence rule]

(ii) Since, $\Delta APB \cong \Delta CQD$

$\therefore$ $AP = CQ$ [by CPCT] **Hence proved.**

Q 7. $ABCD$ is a trapezium in which $AB \parallel CD$ and $AD = BC$ (see the figure). Show that

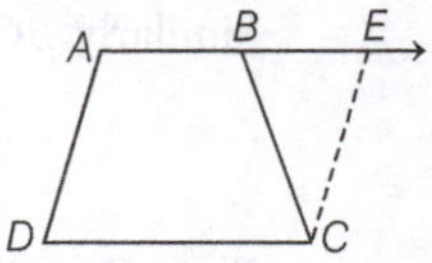

(i) $\angle A = \angle B$

(ii) $\angle C = \angle D$

(iii) $\Delta ABC \cong \Delta BAD$

(iv) Diagonal AC = Diagonal BD

[**Hint** Extend AB and draw a line through C parallel to DA intersecting AB produced at E]

Sol. Given, $ABCD$ is a trapezium in which

$AB \parallel CD$ and $AD = BC$

Now, extend AB and draw a line through C parallel to DA intersecting extended AB at E.

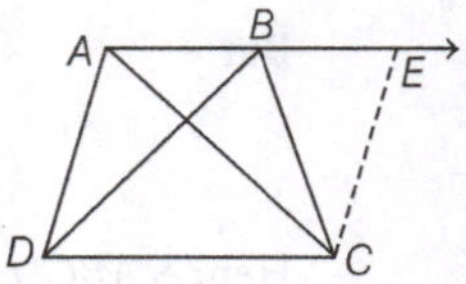

$\therefore AD \parallel EC$

So, $ADCE$ is a parallelogram.

$\therefore$ $AD = EC$ and $DC = AE$

But $AD = BC$ [given]

$\therefore$ $AD = BC = EC$

(i) We know that $\angle A + \angle E = 180^\circ$

[$\because$ interior angles on the same side of the transversal AE]

$\Rightarrow$ $\angle E = 180^\circ - \angle A$

Also, $BC = EC$

$\Rightarrow$ $\angle E = \angle CBE = 180^\circ - \angle A$

But $\angle ABC = 180^\circ - \angle CBE$

[$\because ABE$ is a straight line]

$= 180^\circ - 180^\circ + \angle A$

$\Rightarrow$ $\angle B = \angle A$ ...(i)

(ii) Now, $\angle A + \angle D = 180^\circ$

[$\because$ interior angles on the same side of the transversal AD]

$\Rightarrow$ $\angle D = 180^\circ - \angle A$

$\Rightarrow$ $\angle D = 180^\circ - \angle B$ ...(ii) [from Eq. (i)]

Also, $\angle C + \angle B = 180^\circ$

[$\because$ interior angles on the same side of the transversal BC]

$\Rightarrow$ $\angle C = 180^\circ - \angle B$ ...(iii)

From Eqs. (ii) and (iii), we get $\angle C = \angle D$

(iii) Now, in ΔABC and ΔBAD, we have

$AB = BA$ [common sides]

$AD = BC$ [given]

$\angle A = \angle B$ [from Eq. (i)]

$\therefore$ $\Delta ABC \cong \Delta BAD$ [by SAS congruence rule]

(iv) Since, $\Delta ABC \cong \Delta BAD$

$\therefore$ $AC = BD$ [by CPCT] **Hence proved.**

EXERCISE 8.2 (NCERT Page 113-114)

Q1. *ABCD* is a quadrilateral in which *P*, *Q*, *R* and *S* are mid-points of the sides *AB*, *BC*, *CD* and *DA*. *AC* is a diagonal. Show that

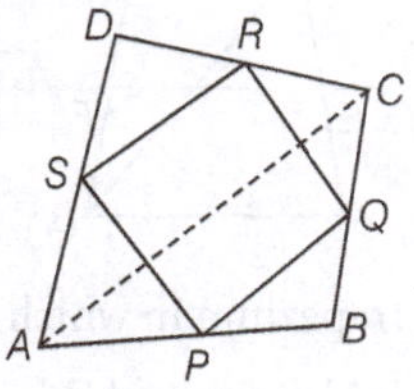

(i) $SR \parallel AC$ and $SR = \frac{1}{2} AC$.

(ii) $PQ = SR$.

(iii) *PQRS* is a parallelogram.

Sol. **Given** *P*, *Q*, *R* and *S* are the mid-points of the sides *AB*, *BC*, *CD* and *DA*, respectively.

$\therefore \quad AP = BP, \; BQ = CQ, \; CR = DR$

and $\quad AS = DS$

To prove

(i) $SR \parallel AC$ and $SR = \frac{1}{2} AC$

(ii) $PQ = SR$

(iii) *PQRS* is a parallelogram.

Proof

(i) In ΔADC, we have *S* is mid-point of *AD* and *R* is mid-point of *DC*.

We know that the line segment joining the mid-points of any two sides of a triangle is parallel to the third side and equal to half of it.

$\therefore \quad SR \parallel AC \quad \ldots(i)$

Also, $\quad SR = \frac{1}{2} AC \quad \ldots(ii)$

(ii) Similarly, in ΔABC, we have *P* is mid-point of *AB* and *Q* is the mid-point of *BC*.

$PQ \parallel AC \quad \ldots(iii)$

and $\quad PQ = \frac{1}{2} AC \quad \ldots(iv)$

Now, from Eqs. (ii) and (iv), we get

$SR = PQ = \frac{1}{2} AC \quad \ldots(v)$

(iii) From Eqs. (i) and (iii), we get

$PQ \parallel SR$ and from Eq. (v),

$PQ = SR$

Since, a pair of opposite sides of a quadrilateral *PQRS* is equal and parallel.

So, *PQRS* is a parallelogram. **Hence proved.**

Q2. *ABCD* is a rhombus and *P*, *Q*, *R* and *S* are the mid-points of the sides *AB*, *BC*, *CD* and *DA*, respectively. Show that the quadrilateral *PQRS* is a rectangle.

Sol. **Given** *ABCD* is a rhombus and *P*, *Q*, *R* and *S* are the mid-points of the sides *AB*, *BC*, *CD* and *DA*, respectively.

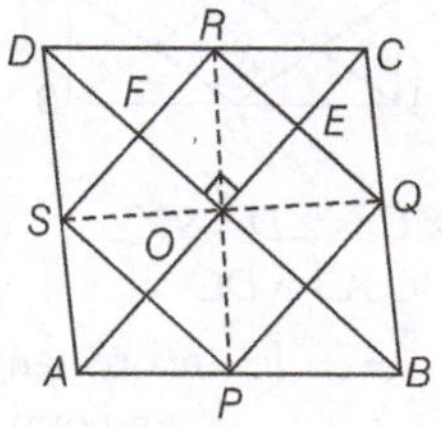

To prove Quadrilateral *PQRS* is a rectangle.

Proof By mid-point theorem.

In ΔADC, we have *S* and *R* are the mid-points of *DA* and *CD*, respectively.

$\therefore \quad SR \parallel AC$ and $SR = \frac{1}{2} AC \quad \ldots(i)$

In ΔABC, we have *P* and *Q* are the mid-points of *AB* and *BC*, respectively.

$\therefore \quad PQ \parallel AC$

and $\quad PQ = \frac{1}{2} AC \quad \ldots(ii)$

From Eqs. (i) and (ii), we get

$PQ \parallel SR$

and $\quad PQ = SR = \frac{1}{2} AC$

Since, a pair of opposite sides of a quadrilaterals *PQRS* is equal and parallel.

So, *PQRS* is a parallelogram.

We know that diagonals of a rhombus bisect each other at right angles.

$\therefore \quad \angle COD = \angle EOF = 90°$

Now, in ΔBCD, *R* and *Q* are the mid-points of *CD* and *BC*, respectively.

$RQ \parallel DB$ [by mid-point theorem]

$\Rightarrow \quad RE \parallel OF$

Also, $\quad SR \parallel AC$ [from Eq. (i)]

$\Rightarrow \quad FR \parallel OE$

So, *OERF* is a parallelogram.

$\therefore \quad \angle ERF = \angle EOF = 90°$

[opposite angles of a parallelogram are equal]

Thus, *PQRS* is a parallelogram with $\angle R = 90°$.

Hence, *PQRS* is a rectangle. **Hence proved.**

Q3. ***ABCD* is a rectangle and *P*, *Q*, *R* and *S* are mid-points of the sides *AB*, *BC*, *CD* and *DA*, respectively. Show that the quadrilateral *PQRS* is a rhombus.**

Sol. Given, $ABCD$ is a rectangle.

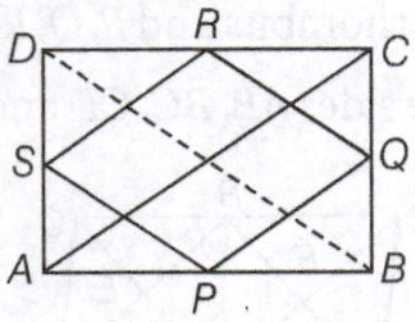

$\therefore \quad \angle A = \angle B = \angle C = \angle D = 90°$

and $\quad AD = BC, AB = DC$

[$\because$ in a rectangle each angle is 90° and opposite sides are equal]

Also, given P, Q, R and S are mid-points of AB, BC, CD and DA, respectively.

In ΔABD, P and S are the mid-points of AB and DA, respectively.

$\therefore \quad PS \parallel BD$ and $PS = \frac{1}{2} BD$

[by mid-point theorem]...(i)

and in ΔACD, R and S are the mid-points of DC and AD, respectively.

$\therefore \quad SR \parallel AC$ and $SR = \frac{1}{2} AC$

[by mid-point theorem]...(ii)

In rectangle $ABCD$, $AC = BD$

[since, diagonals of a rectangle are equal]

$\therefore \quad PS = SR \quad$ [from Eqs. (i) and (ii)] ...(iii)

Now, in ΔASP and ΔBQP,

$AP = BP \quad$ [$\because P$ is mid-point of AB]

$AS = BQ \quad$ [$\because AD = BC$ and S, Q are mid-points of AD and BC]

$\angle A = \angle B \quad$ [each 90°]

$\therefore \quad \Delta ASP \cong \Delta BQP \quad$ [by SAS congruence rule]

Then, $\quad SP = PQ \quad$ [by CPCT] ...(iv)

Similarly, in ΔRDS and ΔRCQ,

$SD = CQ$

[$\because AD = BC$ and S, Q are mid-points of AD and BC]

$DR = RC \quad$ [$\because R$ is mid-point of DC]

$\angle C = \angle D \quad$ [each 90°]

$\therefore \quad \Delta RDS \cong \Delta RCQ \quad$ [by SAS congruence rule]

Then, $\quad SR = RQ \quad$ [by CPCT] ...(v)

From Eqs. (iii), (iv) and (v), we get

$PS = SR = RQ = PQ$

Hence, quadrilateral $PQRS$ is a rhombus. **Hence proved.**

Q4. ***ABCD* is a trapezium in which *AB* || *DC*, *BD* is a diagonal and *E* is the mid-point of *AD*. A line is drawn through *E* parallel to *AB* intersecting *BC* at *F* (see the figure). Show that *F* is the mid-point of *BC*.**

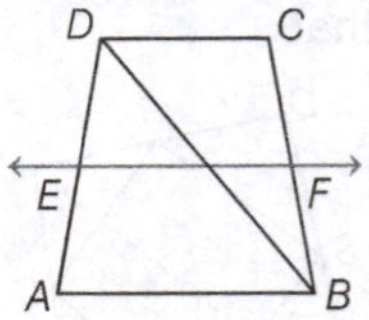

Sol. Given $ABCD$ is a trapezium in which $AB \parallel DC$, BD is a diagonal and E is mid-point of AD

$EF \parallel AB$

To prove F is the mid-point of BC.

Proof Let EF intersects BD at P.

In ΔABD, we have $EP \parallel AB$ [$\because EF \parallel AB$]

and E is mid-point of AD. [given]

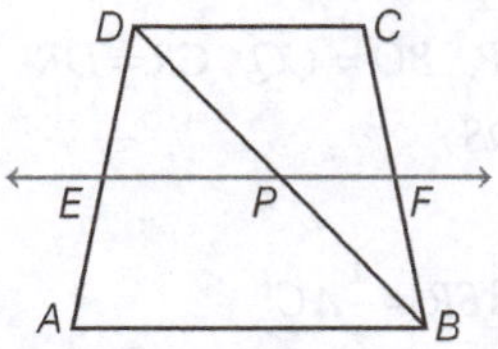

So, by converse of mid-point theorem, P is the mid-point of BD.

Similarly, in ΔBCD, we have $PF \parallel CD$

[$\because EF \parallel AB$ and $AB \parallel CD$]

and P is mid-point of BD.

So, by converse of mid-point theorem, F is mid-point of BC.

Hence proved.

Q5. **In a parallelogram *ABCD*, *E* and *F* are the mid-points of sides *AB* and *CD*, respectively (see the figure). Show that the line segments *AF* and *EC* trisect the diagonal *BD*.**

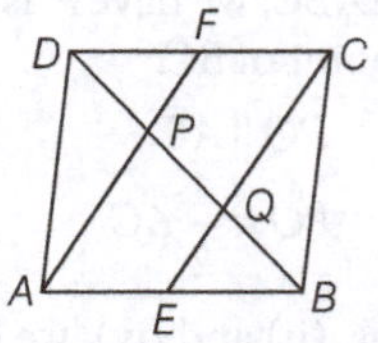

Sol. **Given** $ABCD$ is a parallelogram and E, F are the mid-points of sides AB and CD, respectively.

To prove Line segments AF and EC trisect the diagonal BD.

Proof Since, $ABCD$ is a parallelogram.

$\therefore \quad AB \parallel DC$ and $AB = DC$

[opposite sides of a parallelogram]

$\Rightarrow \quad AE \parallel FC$

and $\quad \frac{1}{2}AB = \frac{1}{2}DC$

$\Rightarrow \quad AE = FC$

[$\because$ E and F are the mid-points of AB and CD]

Since, a pair of opposite sides of a quadrilaterals AECF is equal and parallel.

So, AECF is a parallelogram.

Then, $\quad AF \parallel EC$

$\Rightarrow \quad AP \parallel EQ$

and $\quad FP \parallel CQ$

[$\because$ opposite sides of a parallelogram are parallel]

In ΔBAP, E is the mid-point of AB and $EQ \parallel AP$, so Q is the mid-point of BP.

[by converse of mid-point theorem]

$\therefore \quad BQ = PQ \quad \ldots(i)$

Again, in ΔDQC, F is the mid-point of DC and $FP \parallel CQ$.

So, P is the mid-point of DQ.

[by converse of mid-point theorem]

$\therefore \quad QP = DP \quad \ldots(ii)$

From Eqs. (i) and (ii), we get

$BQ = PQ = PD$

Hence, CE and AF trisect the diagonal BD. **Hence proved.**

Q6. *ABC* is a triangle right angled at *C*. A line through the mid-point *M* of hypotenuse *AB* and parallel to *BC* intersects *AC* at *D*.

Show that

(i) *D* is the mid-point of *AC*.

(ii) $MD \perp AC$.

(iii) $CM = MA = \frac{1}{2}AB$.

Sol. Given ABC is a right angled triangle, in which $\angle C = 90°$ and M is the mid-point of AB.

Also, a line through the mid-point M of hypotenuse AB and parallel to BC intersects AC at D such that $MD \parallel BC$.

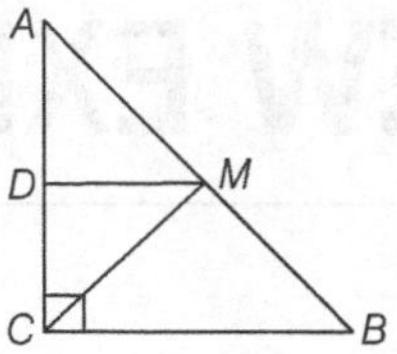

To prove

(i) D is the mid-point of AC.

(ii) $MD \perp AC$

(iii) $CM = MA = \frac{1}{2}AB$

Proof

(i) In ΔABC, $BC \parallel MD$ and M is mid-point of AB.

So, D is the mid-point of AC.

[by converse of mid-point theorem]

(ii) Given, $MD \parallel BC$ and CD is a transversal.

$\therefore \quad \angle ADM = \angle ACB$ [corresponding angles]

But $\quad \angle ACB = 90°$ [given]

$\therefore \quad \angle ADM = 90° \Rightarrow MD \perp AC$

(iii) Now, in ΔADM and ΔCDM, we have

$DM = MD$ [common side]

$AD = CD$ [since, D is the mid-point of AC]

$\angle ADM = \angle MDC$ [each equal to 90°]

$\therefore \quad \Delta ADM \cong \Delta CDM$ [by SAS congruence rule]

Then, $\quad CM = AM$ [by CPCT] ...(i)

Also, given M is the mid-point of AB.

$\therefore \quad AM = BM = \frac{1}{2}AB \quad \ldots(ii)$

From Eqs. (i) and (ii), we get

$CM = AM = \frac{1}{2}AB$ **Hence proved.**

REVIEW EXERCISE

Including Competency Based Questions

Part I

Multiple Choice Questions

1. **Three angles of a parallelogram are 85°, 95° and 85°. The fourth angle is**

(a) 90° (b) 95° (c) 105° (d) 120°

2. **A diagonal of a parallelogram divides into two triangles. The triangles formed are**

(a) congruent (b) similar

(c) does not have equal area (d) None of these

3. **If the perimeter of a parallelogram *ABCD* is 32 cm and one of its side *AD* = 7 cm, then what is the length of *AB*?** **Competency Based Question**

(a) 7 cm (b) 8 cm (c) 9 cm (d) 10 cm

4. ***ABCD* is a quadrilateral. *AC* and *BD* intersect each other at *O*. In which of the following case, *ABCD* is a parallelogram?** **Competency Based Question**

(a) $\angle A = 75°, \angle B = 75°, \angle C = 85°$

(b) $AB = 7$ cm, $BC = 7$ cm, $CD = 6$ cm, $DA = 6$ cm

(c) $AB = 7$ cm, $BC = 6$ cm, $CD = 7$ cm, $DA = 6$ cm

(d) $\angle A = 100°, \angle B = 100°, \angle C = 80°, \angle D = 80°$

5. **The measure of all the angles of a parallelogram, if an angle is 24° less than twice the smallest angle, are respectively**

(a) 37°, 143°, 37°, 143° (b) 108°, 72°, 108°, 72°

(c) 68°, 112°, 68°, 112° (d) None of these

6. **The value of *x* if *PQRS* is a parallelogram, is**

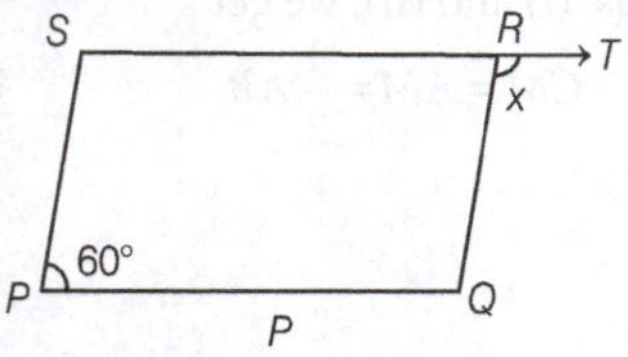

(a) 60° (b) 90° (c) 30° (d) 120°

7. **Which of the following is always true?** **Competency Based Question**

(a) A parallelogram is a square.

(b) A rectangle is a parallelogram.

(c) A rectangle is a square.

(d) A rhombus is a rectangle.

8. **Which of the following quadrilateral is not a square?**

(a) All four sides are equal.

(b) All four interior angles are equal.

(c) Diagonal bisect each other.

(d) One angle between the diagonals is 30°.

9. **The two diagonals are not always equal in**

(a) square (b) rectangle

(c) parallelogram (d) None of these

10. **The quadrilateral formed by joining the mid-points of the sides of a quadrilateral *PQRS*, taken in order, is a rectangle, if** **NCERT Exemplar**

(a) *PQRS* is a rectangle

(b) *PQRS* is a parallelogram

(c) diagonals of *PQRS* are perpendicular

(d) diagonals of *PQRS* are equal

11. **If *ABCD* is a parallelogram, *P* is a point on *AD* such that $AP = \frac{1}{3}$ *AD* and *Q* is a point on *BC* such that $CQ = \frac{1}{3}$ *BC*, then *APCQ* is a** **Competency Based Question**

(a) rhombus (b) rectangle

(c) parallelogram (d) square

12. ***ABCD* is a rhombus such that $\angle ACB = 60°$. Then, $\angle ADB$ is**

(a) 40° (b) 45° (c) 60° (d) 30°

13. **In ΔABC, *AB* = 5 cm, *BC* = 8 cm and *CA* = 7 cm. If *D* and *E* are respectively the mid-point of *AB* and *BC*, then the length of *DE* is**

(a) 4.5 cm (b) 3.5 cm (c) 5.5 cm (d) 6.5 cm

14. **ΔABC is an isosceles triangle in which *AB* = *AC*. *D* and *E* are the mid-points of sides *AB* and *AC*, respectively. If *AD* = 4.5 cm and *DE* = 3.5 cm, then the perimeter of ΔABC is** **Competency Based Question**

(a) 16 cm (b) 25 cm (c) 36 cm (d) 42 cm

15. **Which of the following relation is correct, if *S* is the mid-point of *PR* such that *TS* || *QR*?**

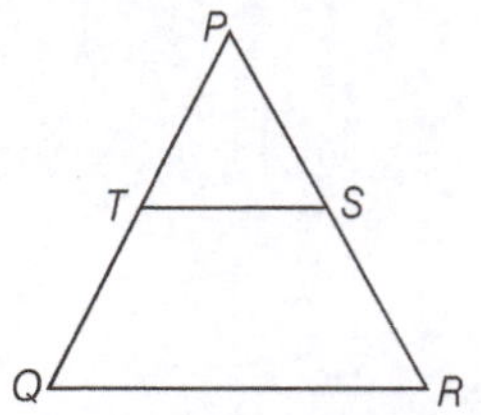

(a) $2QR = TS$ (b) $PT = 2TQ$

(c) $TS = \frac{1}{2}QR$ (d) $PS = TS$

Assertion-Reason Type Questions

16. Assertion If an angle of a parallelogram is two third the adjacent angle, then two angles of a parallelogram are 106° and 74°.

Reason Adjacent angles of a parallelogram are supplementary.

(a) Both Assertion and Reason are correct and Reason is the correct explanation of Assertion.

(b) Both Assertion and Reason are correct but Reason is not the correct explanation of Assertion.

(c) Assertion is correct but Reason is incorrect.

(d) Assertion is incorrect but Reason is correct.

17. Assertion In ΔABC, median AD is produced to X such that $AD = DX$. Then, $ABXC$ is a parallelogram.

Reason Diagonals of parallelogram bisect each other at right angle.

(a) Both Assertion and Reason are correct and Reason is the correct explanation of Assertion.

(b) Both Assertion and Reason are correct but Reason is not the correct explanation of Assertion.

(c) Assertion is correct but Reason is incorrect.

(d) Assertion is incorrect but Reason is correct.

18. Assertion In ΔABC, E and F are the mid-points of AC and AB, respectively. The altitude AP at BC intersects EF at Q. Then, $AQ = QP$.

Reason The line drawn through the mid-point of one side of a triangle parallel to another side bisects the third side.

(a) Both Assertion and Reason are correct and Reason is the correct explanation of Assertion.

(b) Both Assertion and Reason are correct but Reason is not the correct explanation of Assertion.

(c) Assertion is correct but Reason is incorrect.

(d) Assertion is incorrect but Reason is correct.

Case Study Based Questions

19. The figure below shows the side view of a shopping trolley. The metal plate is fixed on the side by the store keeper for advertisement.

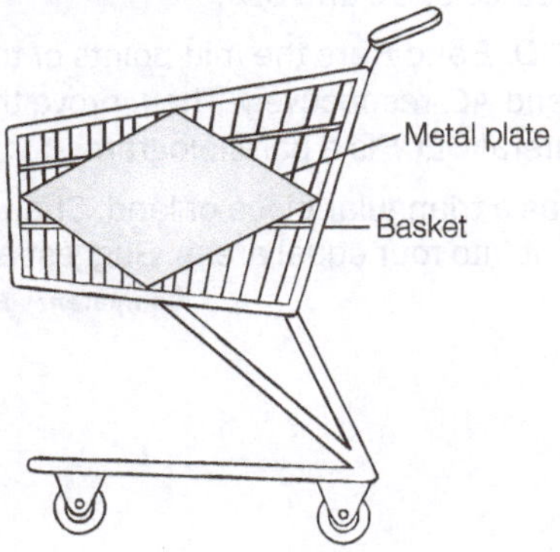

Based on the above information, answer the following questions.

(i) Three angles of the basket are obtuse. Which type of angle is the fourth?

(a) Acute (b) Obtuse (c) Right (d) Reflex

(ii) What is the shape of the metal plate?

(a) Square (b) Rectangle

(c) Rhombus (d) Parallelogram

20. Atul likes to observe the stars with his telescope. He likes to track the movements of stars in the sky. He took a picture of the night sky one day. On that day, Mars was equidistant from Saturn and Jupiter.

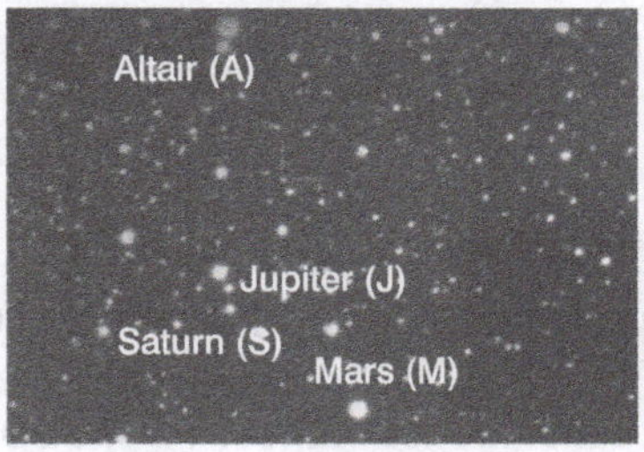

He draws a circle such that the dots showing the planets Mars (M), Jupiter (J), Saturn (S) and a star Altair (A) lies on the boundary of circle and $\angle SMJ = 150°$.

Based on the above information, answer the following questions.

(i) What is the measure of $\angle SAJ$?

(ii) Atul claims that the quadrilateral $MJAS$ is a kite. What additional information is required to confirm his claim?

(iii) (a) If $\angle ASM = 70$, then find the obtuse angle $\angle AJM$.

Or

(b) Join point S and J which make bisector of $\angle S$ and $\angle J$ respectively. Then, find the $\angle AJS$, given that $\angle ASM = 70°$.

21. There is a visit of Director of Education in Nirja Modi school. To welcome the guest, girls were asked to prepare a rangoli in triangular shape. Dimensions of ΔABC are 26 cm, 28 cm, 25 cm. Garland is to be placed along the side of ΔPQR, which is formed by joining mid-points of sides of ΔABC.

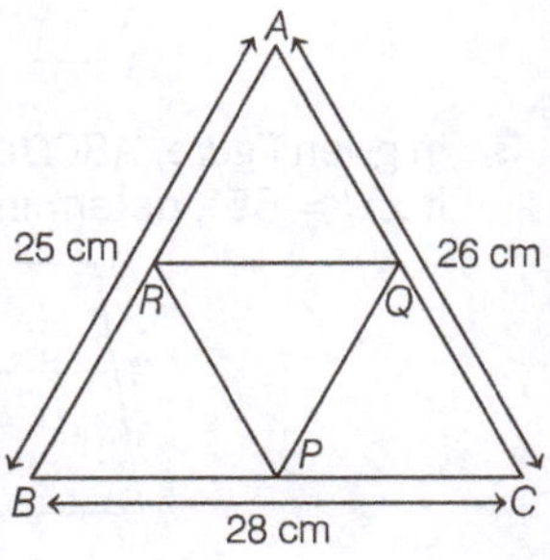

On the above information answer the following questions.

(i) Find the value of RQ.

(ii) Find the value of QP.

(iii) (a) Find the perimeter of triangular rangoli.

Or

(b) Find the length of garland.

22. The class teacher of Class IX gave students coloured papers made by recycling of waste products in shape of quadrilateral. She asked them to make a parallelogram by folding the papers.

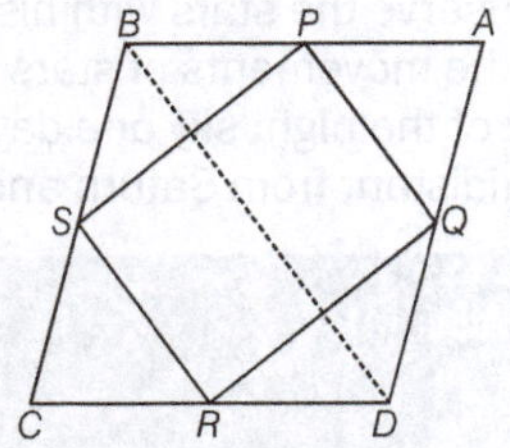

Then, teacher ask them some questions.

(i) How can a parallelogram be formed by using paper folding?

(ii) What condition lies between PQ and BD?

(iii) (a) Show that $SR = \frac{1}{2} BD$.

Or

(b) Show that PQ and SR are equal.

23. In the quadrilateral $ABCD$ given below, $\angle DAC = 90°$ and $AB = AC = AD = DE = EB$.

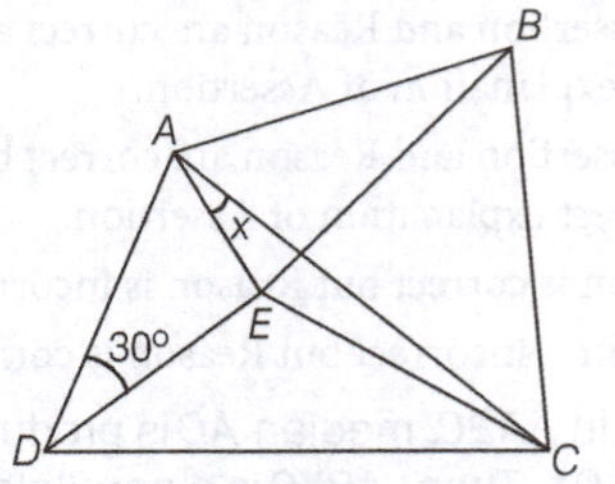

Based on the above information, answer the following questions.

(i) What is the value of $\angle EAC$?

(ii) Which type of quadrilateral is $ABED$?

(iii) (a) What is the value of $\angle ABE$?

Or

(b) Find the value of $\angle ACD$.

Part II

Very Short Answer Type Questions

1. Does joining four distinct points always produce a quadrilateral? Justify your answer.

Competency Based Question

2. $ABCD$ is a parallelogram in which $\angle ADC = 75°$ and side AB is produced to point E as shown in the figure. Find $x + y$.

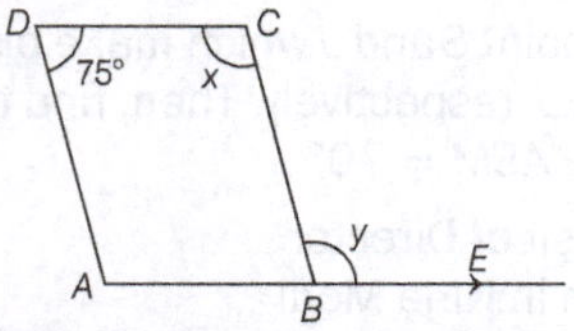

3. In given figure, $ABCD$ and $AEFG$ are two parallelograms. If $\angle C = 55°$, determine $\angle F$. **NCERT Exemplar**

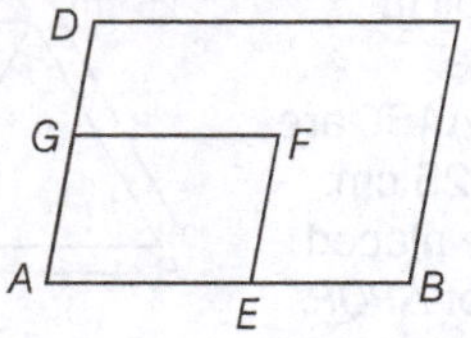

4. In the given figure, $ABCD$ is a parallelogram, what is the sum of the angles x, y and z?

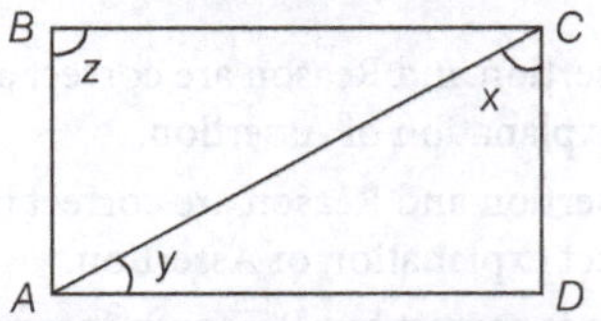

5. The diagonals AC and BD of a parallelogram $ABCD$ intersect each other at the point O.
If $\angle DAC = 42°$ and $\angle AOB = 90°$, then find the value of $\angle DBC$. **Competency Based Question**

6. In a parallelogram $ABCD$, diagonals AC and BD intersect at O and $AC = 6.8$ cm and $BD = 5.6$ cm. Find the measures of OC and OD.

7. In ΔABC, D, E and F are the mid-points of the sides AB, BC and AC, respectively. Then, prove that quadrilateral $DECF$ is a parallelogram.

8. Sanya has a triangular piece of land. She wants to divide it into four equal areas. Suggest a way to do so. **Competency Based Question**

Short Answer Type Questions

9. Prove that a diagonal of a parallelogram divides it into two congruent triangles.

10. Points X and Y lie on opposite sides AB and CD, respectively of a parallelogram $ABCD$ such that $AX = CY$. Show that AC and XY bisect each other. **Competency Based Question**

11. In the given figure, P is the mid-point of side BC of a parallelogram $ABCD$, such that $\angle BAP = \angle DAP$. Prove that $AD = 2\,CD$. **NCERT Exemplar**

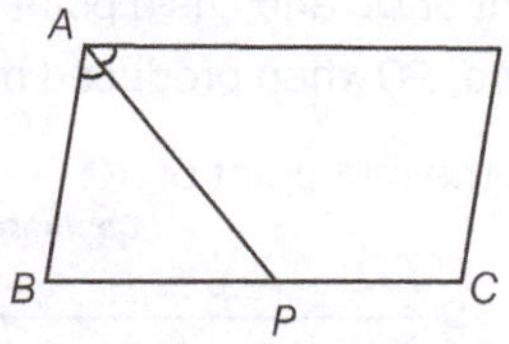

12. Sohan wants to give a card to his teacher made by him thanking for her support. He has three pieces of trapezium pasted one above the other as shown in the figure.

These pieces are arranged in a way that $AB \parallel HC \parallel GD \parallel FE$. Also, $BC = CD = DE$, $AF = BE$ and $GF = 6$ cm. He wants to decorate the card by putting up a coloured tape on non-parallel sides of a trapezium.

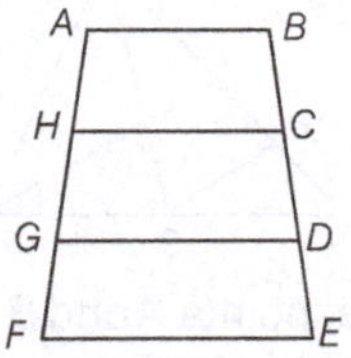

(i) Find the total length of coloured tape required.

(ii) Is $\angle AHC$ equals to $\angle AGD$? **Competency Based Question**

13. In the given figure, $ABCD$ is a parallelogram and E is the mid-point of side BC. DE and AB, when produced meet at F. Prove that $AF = 2AB$.

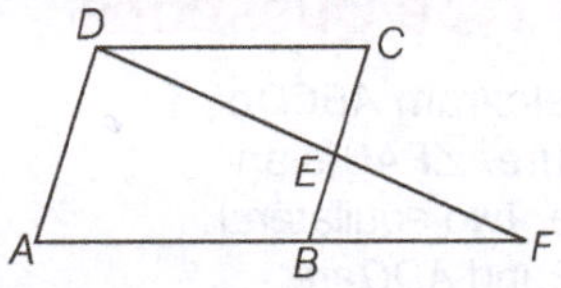

14. In the figure, $ABCD$ is a trapezium with $AB \parallel DC$. F is the mid-point of BC. DF and AB are produced to meet at E. Show that F is also the mid-point of DE. **Competency Based Question**

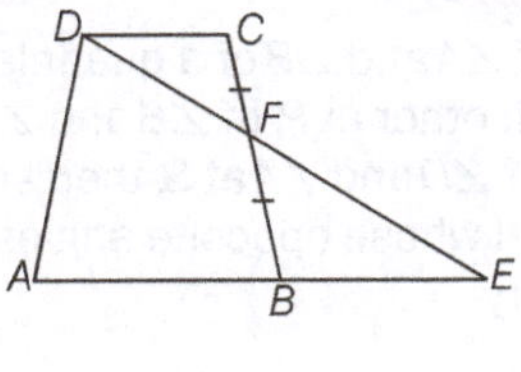

15. Through A, B and C, lines RQ, PR and QP has been drawn respectively parallel to sides BC, CA and AB of a ΔABC as shown in figure. Show that $BC = \frac{1}{2} QR$. **NCERT Exemplar**

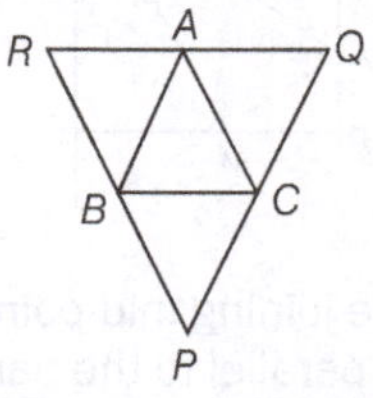

16. Opposite angles of a quadrilateral $ABCD$ are equal. If $AB = 4$ cm, then determine CD. **NCERT Exemplar**

17. The perimeter of a parallelogram is 32 cm. If the longer side measures 9.5 cm, then what is the measure of the shorter side?

18. $ABCD$ is a parallelogram. AM and BN are respectively the perpendiculars from A and B to DC and CD produced. Prove that $AM = BN$.

19. The angle between two altitudes of a parallelogram through the vertex of an obtuse angle of the parallelogram is $60°$. Find the angles of the parallelogram. **Competency Based Question**

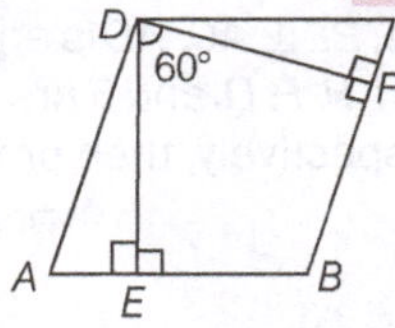

20. In the given figure, AX and CY are respectively the bisectors of the opposite $\angle A$ and $\angle C$ of a parallelogram $ABCD$. Show that $AX \parallel CY$. **NCERT Exemplar**

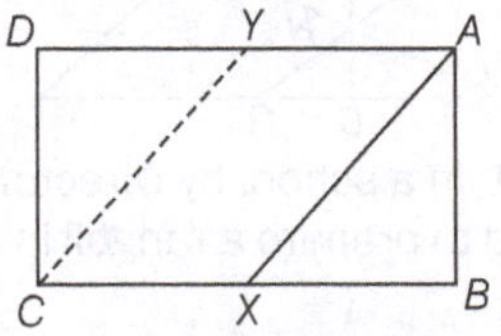

21. The adjacent sides of Quadrilateral A are equal to corresponding sides of Quadrilateral B. All angles of Quadrilateral A measure $90°$. The angles of Quadrilateral B are $120°$, $60°$, $120°$ and $60°$, respectively. Which quadrilateral has a greater area? Given reason? **Competency Based Question**

22. P and Q are points on opposite sides AD and BC of a parallelogram $ABCD$, such that PQ passes through the point of intersection O of its diagonals AC and BD. Show that PQ is bisected at O.

23. The diagonals of a quadrilateral $ABCD$ are perpendicular, show that quadrilateral formed by joining the mid-points of its sides, is rectangle.

24. A diagonal of a parallelogram bisects one of its angle. Show that it is a rhombus. **NCERT Exemplar**

25. In the following figure, $PQRS$ is a square. M is the mid-point of PQ and $RM \perp AB$. Prove that $RA = RB$.

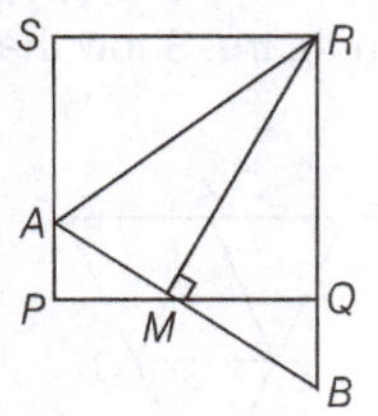

26. Prove that the line joining mid-points of the diagonals of a trapezium is parallel to the parallel sides of the trapezium. **NCERT Exemplar**

27. E is the mid-point of the side AD of the trapezium $ABCD$ with $AB \parallel DC$. A line through E drawn parallel to AB intersects BC at F. Show that F is the mid-point of BC.

28. In ΔABC, $AB = 5$ cm, $BC = 8$ cm and $CA = 7$ cm. If D and E are respectively the mid-points of AB and BC, then determine the length of DE.

29. D, E and F are respectively the mid-points of the sides AB, BC and CA of a ΔABC. Prove that by joining these mid-points D, E and F, the ΔABC is divided into four congruent triangles.

30. In the given figure, $BE \perp AC$. AD is any line from A to BC intersecting BE at H. P, Q and R are mid-points of AH, AB and BC respectively, then prove that $\angle PQR = 90°$. **Competency Based Question**

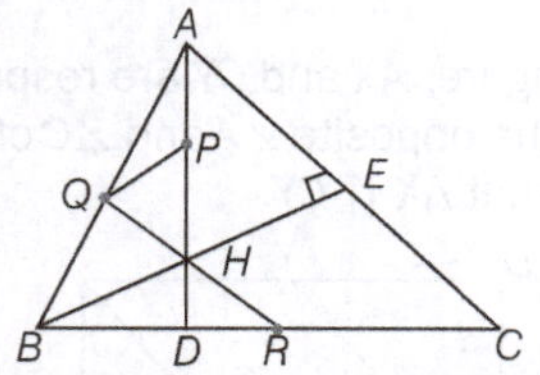

31. There is a visit in a school by Directorate of Education. Girls are asked to prepare a rangoli in triangular shape.

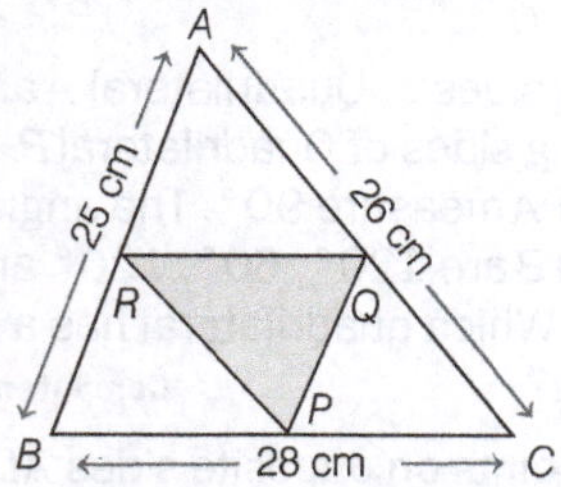

Dimensions of ΔABC are 26 cm, 28 cm and 25 cm. Garland is to be placed along the side of ΔPQR, which is formed by joining mid-points of sides of ΔABC.

(i) Prove that $\Delta BRP \cong \Delta QPR$.

(ii) Prove that ar $(\Delta QRP) = \frac{1}{3}$ ar (quad $BCQR$).

Competency Based Question

32. In the following figure, AD is a median of ΔABC and E is the mid-point of AD. Also, BE is produced to meets AC at F. Prove that $AF = \frac{1}{3} AC$.

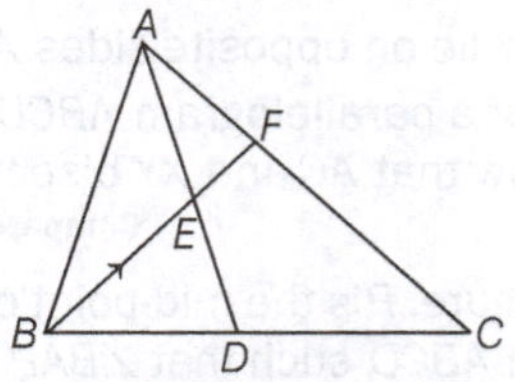

33. In the given figure, $ABCD$ is a parallelogram in which P is the mid-point of DC and Q is a point on AC, such that $CQ = \frac{1}{4} AC$. Also, PQ when produced meets BC at R.

Prove that R is the mid-point of BC.

Competency Based Question

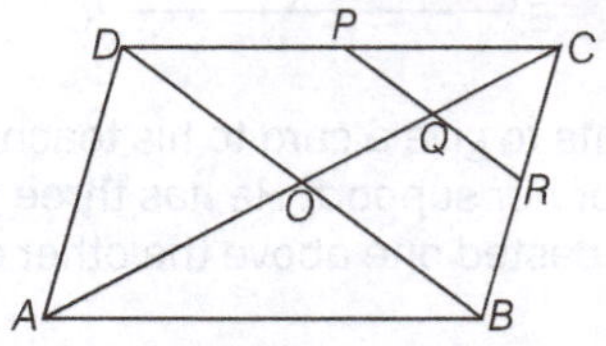

34. In the following figure, PS and RT are medians of ΔPQR and $SM \parallel RT$. Prove that $QM = \frac{1}{4} PQ$.

Competency Based Question

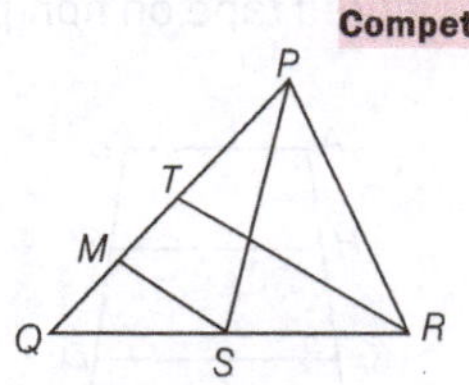

35. In the given figure, points A and B are on the same side of a line m, $AD \perp m$ and $BE \perp m$ and meet m at D and E, respectively. If C is the mid-point of AB, then prove that $CD = CE$.

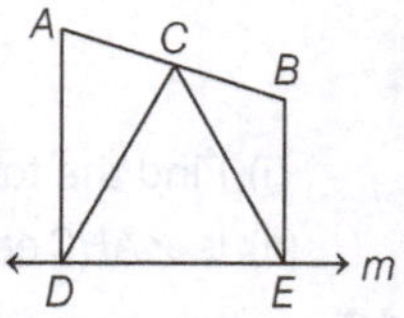

Long Answer Type Questions

36. In the parallelogram $ABCD$ of the given figure, $\angle PAQ$ is an obtuse angle. Two equilateral triangles ABP and ADQ are drawn outside the parallelogram.

Prove that ΔCPQ is also an equilateral triangle. **Competency Based Question**

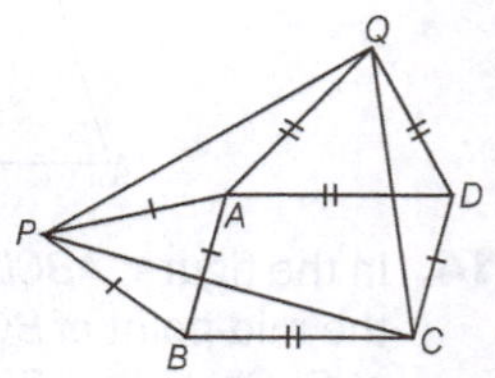

37. If bisectors of $\angle A$ and $\angle B$ of a quadrilateral $ABCD$ intersect each other at P, of $\angle B$ and $\angle C$ at Q, of $\angle C$ and $\angle D$ at R and of $\angle D$ and $\angle A$ at S, then show that $PQRS$ is a quadrilateral whose opposite angles are supplementary. **NCERT Exemplar**

38. PQ and RS are two equal and parallel line segments. Any point M not lying on PQ or RS is joined to Q and S and lines through parallel to QM and through R parallel to SM meet at N. Prove that line segments MN and PQ are equal and parallel to each other. **Competency Based Question**

39. In the given figure, $ABCD$ is a parallelogram and $\angle DAB = 60°$. If the bisectors AP and BP of angles A and B, respectively meets at P on CD. Prove that P is the mid-point of CD.

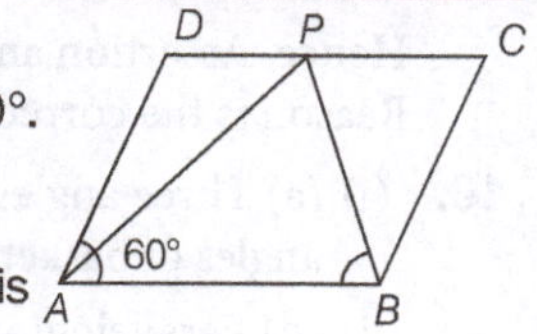

40. P and Q are the mid-points of the opposite sides AB and CD of a parallelogram $ABCD$. AQ intersects DP at S and BQ intersects CP at R. Show that $PRQS$ is a parallelogram. **NCERT Exemplar**

41. $ABCD$ is a square. E, F, G and H are points on AB, BC, CD and DA respectively, such that $AE = BF = CG = DH$. Prove that $EFGH$ is a square.

HINTS & ANSWERS

Part I

1. (b) The opposite angles of the given parallelogram are equal. Hence, the fourth angle is 95°.

2. (a) Congruent

Since, a diagonal of parallelogram divides it into two congruent triangle.

3. (c) Length of $AB = \dfrac{32-(2\times 7)}{2} = \dfrac{32-14}{2} = \dfrac{18}{2} = 9$ cm

Perimeter of parallelogram $ABCD = 2(AB + CD)$

4. (c) Opposite sides of a parallelogram are equal in length.

5. (c) Let $ABCD$ be a parallelogram with smallest angle $\angle A = x$ and $\angle B = (2x - 24)°$

Since, the adjacent angles of a parallelogram are supplementary.

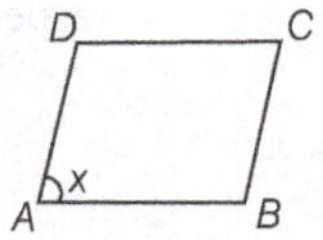

$\therefore \quad \angle A + \angle B = 180°$

$\Rightarrow \quad x + (2x - 24)° = 180°$

$\Rightarrow \quad 3x = 204 \Rightarrow x = 68$

$\therefore \quad \angle A = x = 68°$

and $\angle B = (2x - 24)° = (2 \times 68 - 24)° = 112°$

Since, the opposite angles of a parallelogram are equal.

So, $\angle A = \angle C = 68°$ and $\angle B = \angle D = 112°$.

6. (d) $\angle SRQ = 60°$

[$\because$ opposite angles in a parallelogram are equal]

$\angle SRQ + \angle TRQ = 180°$ [linear pair]

$\Rightarrow x = 180° - 60° = 120°$

7. (b) All the rectangles are parallelogram.

8. (d) Diagonals of square are perpendicular bisector.

9. (c)

10. (c) Since, the quadrilateral $ABCD$ formed by joining the mid-points of quadrilateral $PQRS$ is a rectangle.

$\therefore \quad AC = BD$ [$\because$ diagonals of a rectangle are equal]

$\Rightarrow \quad PQ = QR$

Thus, quadrilateral $PQRS$ is a rhombus.

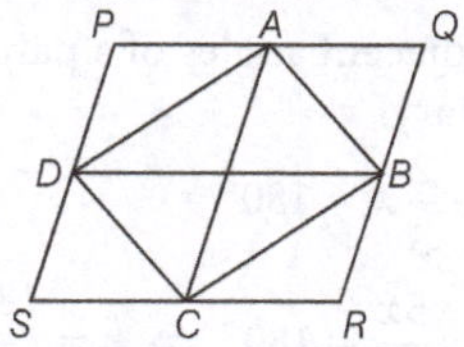

Hence, diagonals of $PQRS$ i.e. PR and QS are perpendicular. [$\because$ diagonals of rhombus are perpendicular to each other]

11. (c) Since, $ABCD$ is parallelogram.

$AD = BC$ and $AD \parallel BC$

$\Rightarrow \quad \dfrac{1}{3}AD = \dfrac{1}{3}BC$ and $AD \parallel BC$

$\Rightarrow \quad AP = CQ$ and $AP \parallel CQ$

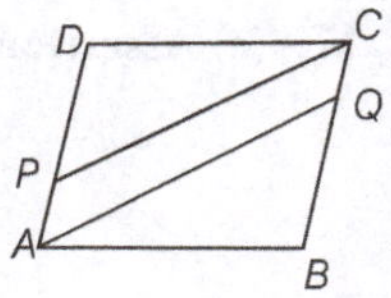

Thus, $APCQ$ is a quadrilateral such that one pair of opposite sides AP and CQ are parallel and equal. Hence, $APCQ$ is a parallelogram.

12. (d) Diagonals of rhombus bisect the angle, so

$$\angle ACD = 60°$$

Also, sum of adjacent angles is 180°.

$\therefore \quad \angle BCD + \angle ADC = 180°$

13. (b) In ΔABC, we have $AB = 5$ cm, $BC = 8$ cm and $CA = 7$ cm.

Since, D and E are the mid-points of AB and BC, respectively.

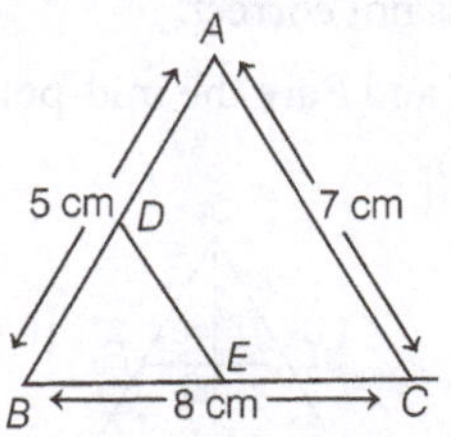

$\therefore$ By mid-point theorem,

$DE \parallel AC$ and $DE = \dfrac{1}{2}AC = \dfrac{7}{2} = 3.5$ cm

14. (b) Given, a ΔABC in which $AB = AC$, D and E are the mid-points of AB and AC, respectively.

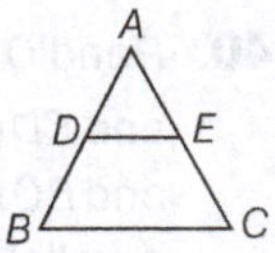

$\therefore \quad AD = DB = 4.5$ cm

$\Rightarrow AB = 2 \times 4.5 = 9$ cm

and $\quad AB = AC = 9$ cm

Since, D and E are the mid-points of AB and AC, respectively.

So, by mid-point theorem,

$$DE \parallel BC \text{ and } DE = \frac{1}{2}BC$$

Then, $BC = 2DE = 2 \times 3.5 = 7$ cm [$\because DE = 3.5$ cm, given]

Now, perimeter of $\Delta ABC = AB + BC + CA$

$= 9 + 7 + 9 = 25$ cm

15. (c) By mid-point theorem

16. (d) Since, adjacent angles of a parallelogram are supplementary.

$$\therefore \quad x + \frac{2}{3}x = 180°$$

$$\Rightarrow \quad \frac{5x}{3} = 180° \Rightarrow x = \frac{180° \times 3}{5} = 108°$$

$\therefore$ One angle is 108° and other angle is $180° - 108° = 72°$.

Hence, Assertion is not correct but Reason is correct.

17. (c) **Assertion** In quadrilateral $ABXC$, we have

$AD = DX$ [given]

$BD = DC$ [given]

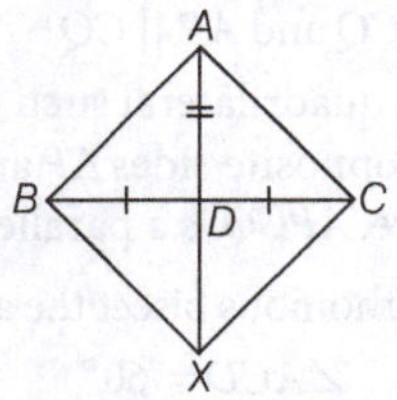

So, diagonals AX and BC bisect each other.

Therefore, $ABXC$ is a parallelogram.

Thus, Assertion is correct.

Reason In a parallelogram, diagonals does not bisect at right angles.

Thus, Reason is not correct.

18. (a) In ΔABC, E and F are the mid-point of sides AC and AB, respectively.

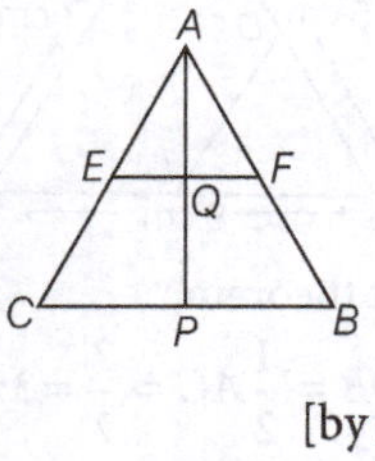

$\therefore \quad EF \parallel CB$ [by mid-point theorem]

Now, in ΔABP, F is the mid-point of AB and $FQ \parallel BP$.

Q is the mid-point of AP.

[by converse of mid-point theorem]

$\Rightarrow AQ = QP$

Hence, Assertion and Reason both are correct and Reason is the correct explanation of Assertion.

19. (i) (a) Three angles of the basket are obtuse. As, sum of angles of basket (a quadrilateral) is 360°.

(ii) (d) Parallelogram.

20. (i) $\quad \angle SAJ + \angle SMJ = 180°$

$MJAS$ is a cyclic quadrilateral. So, sum of opposite angles is 180°.

$\angle SAJ = 180° - 150° = 30°$

(ii) Pairs of adjacent sides are equal in case of kite.

(iii) (a) Given, $\angle ASM = 70°$.

$MJAS$ is a cyclic quadrilateral. So, sum of opposite angles is 180°

$\therefore \angle ASM + \angle AJM = 180°$

$\Rightarrow \quad \angle AJM = 180° - \angle ASM$

$= 180° - 70° = 110°$

Or

(b) **Hint** We know that bisector of an angle divides the angle into two equal parts

Ans. 55°

21. (i) Since, R and Q are the mid-point of AB and CA, respectively.

$$RQ \parallel BC \text{ and } RQ = \frac{1}{2} BC$$

[by mid-point theorem]

$\Rightarrow \quad RQ = \frac{1}{2} \times 28 = 14$ cm $\quad$ [$\because BC = 28$ cm]

(ii) Since, Q and P are the mid-points of AC and BC, respectively.

$\therefore \quad QP \parallel AB$ and $QP = \frac{1}{2}AB$

$\therefore \quad QP = \frac{1}{2} \times AB = \frac{1}{2} \times 25 = 12.5$ cm

(iii) (a) **Hint** Perimeter of triangular rangoli

= Perimeter of triangle ABC

Ans. 79 cm

Or

(b) $\because \quad RQ = 14$ cm, $QP = 12.5$ cm

and $PR = 13$ cm

$\therefore$ Length of garland = Perimeter of ΔPQR

$= RQ + QP + PR$

$= 14 + 12.5 + 13 = 39.5$ cm

22. (i) By joining the mid-points of sides of a quadrilateral $ABCD$.

(ii) In ΔABD, P and Q are the mid-points of AB and AD.

$\therefore \quad PQ \parallel BD$ and $PQ = \frac{1}{2} BD$

[by mid-point theorem]

(iii) (a) In ΔBCD, R and S are the mid-points of CD and BC, respectively.

$\therefore \quad RS \parallel BD$ and $RS = \frac{1}{2} BD$

[by mid-point theorem]

Or

(b) $\therefore$ $PQ \parallel BD$ and $PQ = \frac{1}{2} BD$ ...(i)

$RS \parallel BD$ and $RS = \frac{1}{2} BD$ ...(ii)

From Eqs. (i) and (ii), we get

$PQ \parallel SR$ and $PQ = SR$

23. (i) In ΔADE, $\angle ADE = 30°$, $AD = DE$

$\Rightarrow \quad \angle DAE = \angle DEA$

Let $\quad \angle DAE = \angle DEA = y$

$y + y + 30° = 180°$

[angle sum property of a triangle]

$\Rightarrow \quad 2y = 150°$

$\Rightarrow \quad y = 75°$

Also, $\angle DAC = 90°$ [given]

$\Rightarrow \quad x + y = 90°$

$\Rightarrow \quad x = 90° - 75° = 15°$

(ii) **Ans.** Rhombus

(iii) (a) In ΔADE and ΔABE,

$AE = AE$ [common]

$AB = AD$ [given]

$EB = ED$ [given]

$\Delta ADE \cong \Delta ABE$

$\therefore \quad \angle ADE = \angle ABE = 30°$ [by CPCT]

Or

(b) **Hint** In ΔACD, use angle sum property.

$\angle DAC + \angle ADC + \angle ACD = 180°$

and $\quad AD = AC$

Ans. 45°

Part II

1. No, quadrilateral is obtained, when we join 4 non-collinear point in an order.

2. **Hint** $\quad x + 75° = 180°$

$\Rightarrow \quad x = 105°$

and $y = 180° - 75° = 105°$ **Ans.** 210°

3. **Hint** Given, $ABCD$ is a parallelogram and $\angle C = 55°$

$\therefore \quad \angle A = \angle C = 55°$

[in a parallelogram, opposite angles are equal]

Also, $AEFG$ is a parallelogram.

$\therefore \quad \angle A = \angle F = 55°$

4. **Hint** In ΔADC, $x + y + \angle ADC = 180°$

[angle sum property of a triangle]

$\Rightarrow \quad \angle ADC = 180° - (x + y)$ ...(i)

$\because \quad \angle ABC = \angle ADC$

[opposite angles of a parallelogram]

$\therefore \quad z = 180° - (x + y)$ [from Eq. (i)]

$\Rightarrow \quad z + x + y = 180°$

5. **Hint** Use properties of parallelogram. **Ans.** 48°

6. **Hint** Diagonals of a parallelogram bisect each other.

$\therefore \quad OC = 3.4$ cm

$OD = 2.8$ cm

7. **Hint** In ΔABC, D and F are the mid-points of the sides AB and AC, respectively.

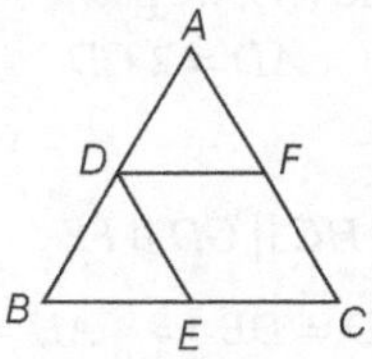

$\therefore$ By mid-point theorem,

$DF \parallel BC$ ...(i)

$\Rightarrow \quad DF \parallel EC$ and $DF = \frac{1}{2} BC$

$\Rightarrow \quad DF = EC$ ...(ii)

[since, E is mid-point of BC]

From Eqs. (i) and (ii), we get

$DF \parallel EC$ and $DF = EC$

Since, a pair of opposite sides of a quadrilateral $DECF$ are equal and parallel.

Hence, $DECF$ is a parallelogram. **Hence proved.**

8. **Hint** Sanya can apply mid-point theorem to divide the triangle into 4 triangles of equal areas.

9. **Hint** Use properties of parallelogram.

10. **Hint** In ΔAOX and ΔCOY,

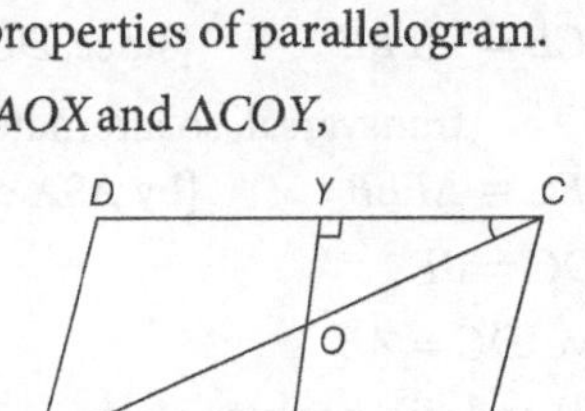

$AX = CY, \angle OAX = \angle OCY, \angle AXO = \angle CYO$

$\therefore$ $\Delta AOX \cong \Delta COY$ [by ASA congruence rule]

$\Rightarrow$ $OA = OC$ and $OX = OY$ [by CPCT]

11. Hint Given $ABCD$ is a parallelogram. P is the mid-point of BC i.e. $BC = 2BP$

$\Rightarrow$ $AD = 2BP$ [$\because BC = AD$]

and $\angle BAP = \angle DAP$

To prove $AD = 2\ CD$

Proof We have, $\angle BAP = \angle DAP$ [given] ...(i)

and $\angle DAP = \angle APB$ ...(ii)

[alternate interior angles]

$\Rightarrow$ $\angle BAP = \angle APB$ [from Eqs. (i) and (ii)]

$\Rightarrow$ $BP = AB$ [sides opposite to equal angles of a triangle are equal]

and $AB = CD$ [opposite sides of parallelogram]

$\Rightarrow$ $BP = CD$ [$\because BP = AB$] ...(iii)

Also, $BC = 2BP$ [given]

$\Rightarrow$ $AD = 2BP$ ...(iv)

[$\because BC = AD$, opposite sides of parallelogram]

From Eqs. (iii) and (iv), we get

$AD = 2\ CD$ **Hence proved.**

12. Hint

(i) Given, $AB \parallel HC \parallel GD \parallel FE$

and $BC = CD = DE \Rightarrow AH = HG = GF$

[$\because$ three parallel lines making equal intercepts on any transversal, then they will make equal intercepts on other transversal also]

$\therefore$ $AF + BE = 18 + 18 = 36$ cm

(ii) Yes, as $HC \parallel GD$ and AF is a transversal line.

$\therefore$ $\angle AHC = \angle AGD$ [by corresponding angles]

13. Hint Given $ABCD$ is a parallelogram.

$\therefore$ $AB = CD$ and $AD = BC$

and E is the mid-point of side BC, i.e. $BE = CE$

To prove $AF = 2AB$

Proof Now, in ΔDEC and ΔFEB, we have

$\angle DEC = \angle BEF$ [vertically opposite angles]

$BE = CE$ [given]

and $\angle DCE = \angle FBE$ [since, $DC \parallel AF$ and BC is transversal, so alternate interior angles]

$\therefore$ $\Delta DEC \cong \Delta FEB$ [by ASA congruence rule]

So, $DC = BF$ [by CPCT] ...(i)

Also, we have $DC = AB$ [given] ...(ii)

From Eqs. (i) and (ii), we get

$AB = BF$

$\therefore$ $AF = 2AB$ **Hence proved.**

14. Hint Firstly, prove $\Delta FCD \cong \Delta FBE$ using ASA congruence rule. further prove the required result.

15. Hint Given $PQ \parallel AB$ and $PR \parallel AC$ and $RQ \parallel BC$.

To prove $BC = \frac{1}{2} QR$

Proof In quadrilateral $BCAR$, $BR \parallel CA$ and $BC \parallel RA$

So, $BCAR$ is a parallelogram.

$\therefore$ $BC = RA$ ...(i)

Now, in quadrilateral $BCQA$, $BC \parallel AQ$ and $AB \parallel QC$

So, $BCQA$ is a parallelogram.

$\therefore$ $BC = AQ$ ...(ii)

On adding Eqs. (i) and (ii), we get

$2BC = AR + AQ \Rightarrow 2BC = RQ$

$\Rightarrow$ $BC = \frac{1}{2} QR$ **Hence proved.**

16. Hint $ABCD$ is a parallelogram. **Ans.** 4 cm

17. Hint Let the measure of shorter side be x cm.

Given, longer side measure = 9.5 cm

and perimeter = 32 cm

$\Rightarrow$ 2 (Longer side + Shorter side) = 32

[$\because$ in a parallelogram, opposite sides are equal.

$\Rightarrow$ Perimeter = Sum of four sides

= 2(longer side + shorter side)]

$\Rightarrow 9.5 + x = \frac{32}{2} \Rightarrow x = 16 - 9.5$

$\Rightarrow$ $x = 6.5$ cm

18. Hint $\Delta AMD \cong \Delta BNC$

$\therefore$ $AM = BM$

19. Hint The angles of the parallelogram are 60°, 120°, 60° and 120°, respectively.

20. Hint $\angle A = \angle C \Rightarrow \frac{1}{2} \angle A = \frac{1}{2} \angle C$

$\therefore$ $AX \parallel CY$ and $CX \parallel AY$

21. Hint Since, all angles of quadrilateral A measure 90°, so quadrilateral A is a rectangle.

The opposite angles of quadrilateral B are equal.

$\therefore$ Quadrilateral B is a parallelogram.

Therefore, area of Quadrilateral A is more than Quadrilateral B.

22. Hint Prove $\Delta ODP \cong \Delta OBQ$ using ASA congruence rule. Then, $OQ = OP$ [CPCT]

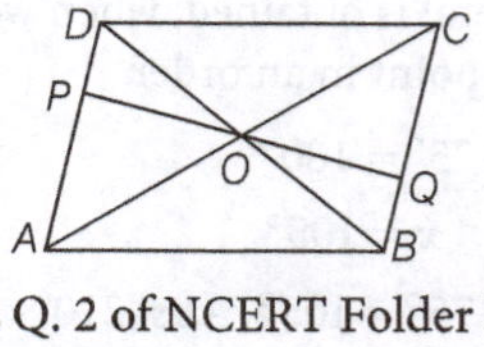

23. Hint Solve as Q. 2 of NCERT Folder Exercise 8.2.

24. Hint Use properties of parallelogram.

25. Hint Given *PQRS* is a square. *M* is the mid-point of *PQ*

i.e. $PM = MQ$ and $RM \perp AB$

$\therefore \quad \angle AMR = \angle BMR = 90°$

To prove $RA = RB$

Proof In ΔAMP and ΔBMQ, we have

$PM = MQ$ [given]

$\angle AMP = \angle BMQ$ [vertically opposite angles]

and $\angle APM = \angle BQM$ [each 90°]

$\therefore \quad \Delta AMP \cong \Delta BMQ$ [by ASA congruence rule]

So, $AM = MB$ [by CPCT] ...(i)

Now, in ΔRMA and ΔRMB, we have

$\angle AMR = \angle BMR = 90°$ [given]

$RM = RM$ [common side]

and $AM = MB$ [from Eq. (i)]

$\therefore \quad \Delta RMA \cong \Delta RMB$ [by SAS congruence rule]

So, $RA = RB$ [by CPCT] **Hence proved.**

26. Hint Given *ABCD* is a trapezium in which $AB \parallel DC$ and *M* and *N* are the mid-points of the diagonals *AC* and *BD*, respectively.

To prove $MN \parallel AB \parallel CD$

Construction Join *CN* and produce it to meet *AB* at *E*.

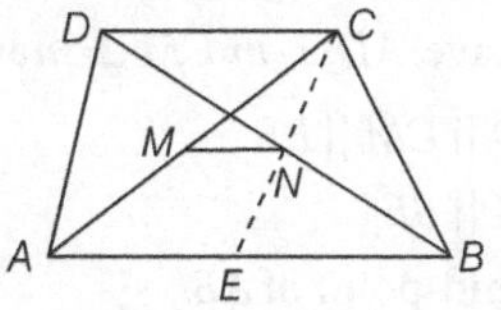

Proof In ΔCDN and ΔEBN, we have

$DN = BN$ [$\because$ *N* is mid-point of *BD*]

$\angle DCN = \angle BEN$ [alternate interior angles]

$\angle CDN = \angle EBN$ [alternate interior angles]

$\therefore \quad \Delta CDN \cong \Delta EBN$ [by AAS congruence rule]

So, $DC = EB$

and $CN = NE$ [by CPCT]

$\therefore$ *N* is the mid-point of *CE*.

Thus, in ΔCAE, the points *M* and *N* are the mid-points of *AC* and *CE*, respectively.

$\therefore \quad MN \parallel AE$ [by mid-point theorem]

$\Rightarrow \quad MN \parallel AB \parallel CD$ **Hence proved.**

27. Hint Use the mid-point theorem to prove *F* is the mid-point of *BC*.

28. Hint Use mid-point theorem. **Ans.** 3.5 cm

29. Hint Given *ABC* is a triangle and *D*, *E* and *F* are mid-points of sides *AB*, *BC* and *CA*, respectively.

To prove ΔABC is divided into four congruent triangles.

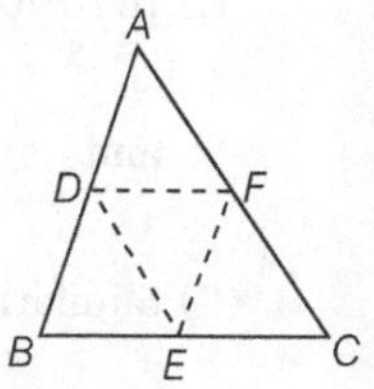

Construction Join *DE*, *EF* and *FD*.

Proof Given, *D*, *E* and *F* are the mid-points of sides *AB*, *BC* and *CA*, respectively.

Then, $AD = BD = \frac{1}{2}AB$

$BE = EC = \frac{1}{2}BC$ and $AF = CF = \frac{1}{2}AC$

Now, by mid-point theorem.

$EF \parallel BA$ and $EF = \frac{1}{2}AB = AD = BD$

$\Rightarrow \quad EF \parallel DA$ and $EF = DA$

$\Rightarrow$ *ADEF* is a parallelogram

$ED \parallel CA$ and $ED = \frac{1}{2}AC = AF = CF$

$\Rightarrow \quad ED \parallel CF$ and $ED = CF$

$\Rightarrow$ *EDFC* is a parallelogram.

and $DF \parallel BC$ and $DF = \frac{1}{2}BC = BE = CE$

$\Rightarrow \quad DF \parallel BE$ and $DF = BE$

$\Rightarrow$ *DFEB* is a parallelogram.

Now, in ΔADF and ΔEFD, $AD = EF$

[$\because$ opposite sides of a parallelogram *ADEF* are equal]

$AF = DE$

[$\because$ opposite sides of a parallelogram are equal]

and $DF = FD$ [common side]

$\therefore \quad \Delta ADF \cong \Delta EFD$ [by SSS congruence rule]

Similarly, $\Delta DEF \cong \Delta EDB$ and $\Delta DEF \cong \Delta CFE$

Thus, ΔABC is divided into four congruent triangles.

Hence proved.

30. Hint Since, *Q* and *R* are the mid-points of *AB* and *BC*, respectively.

$\therefore \quad QR \parallel AC$ ...(i)

and *Q* and *P* are the mid-points of *AB* and *AH*, respectively.

$\therefore \quad QP \parallel BH \Rightarrow QP \parallel BE$ ...(ii)

But $BE \perp AC$

$\therefore$ From Eqs. (i) and (ii),

$QP \perp QR \Rightarrow \angle PQR = 90°$

31. Hint Since, *R* and *P* are the mid-points of sides *AB* and *BC* of ΔABC, then by mid-point theorem, $RP \parallel AC$.

Similarly, $RQ \parallel BC$ and $PQ \parallel BA$.

$\therefore$ *BRQP*, *RQCP* and *ARPQ* are all parallelogram.

(i) In ΔBRP and ΔQPR,

$$BP = RQ,\ BR = PQ \quad [\because BRQP \text{ is } || \text{gm}]$$

and $RP = RP$ [common side]

$\therefore \quad \Delta BPR \cong \Delta QPR$ [by SSS congruency rule]

(ii) Similarly, $\Delta QRP \cong \Delta PCQ$

$\therefore \quad \Delta BRP \cong \Delta QRP \cong \Delta PCQ$

$\Rightarrow$ All three triangles have equal areas.

Now, ar(quad $BCQR$) = ar(ΔBRP) + ar(ΔQRP) + ar(ΔPCQ)

= 3 ar(ΔQRP)

$\Rightarrow \quad$ ar(ΔQRP) = $\frac{1}{3}$ ar(quad $BCQR$)

32. Hint Given In ΔABC, AD is a median and E is mid-point of AD.

To prove $\quad AF = \frac{1}{3}AC$

Construction Draw $DP \parallel BF$

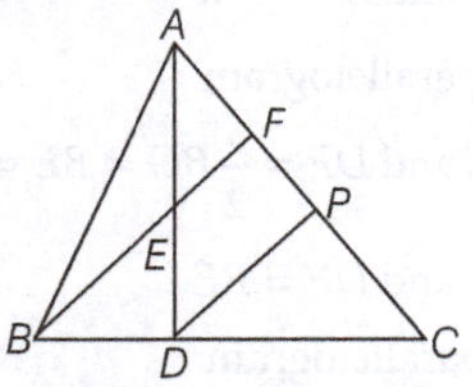

Proof In ΔADP, E is the mid-point of AD and $EF \parallel DP$. $[\because BF \parallel DP]$

$\therefore$ F is the mid-point of AP.

[by converse of mid-point theorem]

$\therefore \quad AF = FP$ ...(i)

In ΔFBC, D is the mid-point of BC and $DP \parallel BF$.

$[\because AD$ is a median of $\Delta ABC]$

$\therefore$ P is the mid-point of FC.

[by converse of mid-point theorem]

$\therefore \quad FP = PC$ ...(ii)

Thus, $\quad AF = FP = PC$ [from Eqs. (i) and (ii)]

$\therefore \quad AF = \left(\frac{1}{3}\right)AC$ **Hence proved.**

33. Hint In a parallelogram $ABCD$, $AO = OC$

[$\because$ diagonals of a parallelogram bisect each other]

$AC = AO + OC \Rightarrow AC = 2OC$

$\therefore \quad CQ = \frac{1}{4}AC = \frac{1}{4} \times (2OC) = \frac{1}{2}OC$

Thus, Q is the mid-point of OC.

Now, in ΔCDO, P and Q are the mid-points of CD and CO, respectively.

$\therefore \quad PQ \parallel DO$ and therefore, $QR \parallel OB$

$[\because PQ \parallel DO \Rightarrow PQR \parallel DOB]$

Now, in ΔCOB, Q is the mid-point of CO and $QR \parallel OB$.

So, R must be the mid-point of BC.

[by converse of mid-point] **Hence proved.**

34. Hint Given PS and RT are medians of ΔPQR, i.e. S and T are the mid-points of QR and PQ, respectively,

i.e. $SR = QS = \frac{1}{2}QR$ and $QT = PT = \frac{1}{2}PQ$ and $SM \parallel RT$.

To prove $\quad QM = \frac{1}{4}PQ$

Proof In ΔQTR, S is the mid-point of QR and $SM \parallel RT$.

So, by converse of mid-point theorem, M is mid-point of QT.

i.e. $\quad QM = MT = \frac{1}{2}QT$ ...(i)

Also, $\quad QT = \frac{1}{2}PQ$ [given] ...(ii)

From Eqs. (i) and (ii), we get

$$QM = \frac{1}{2}\left(\frac{1}{2}PQ\right) \Rightarrow QM = \frac{1}{4}PQ$$ **Hence proved.**

35. Hint Given In the given figure, $AD \perp m$ and $BE \perp m$.

Also, C is the mid-point of AB,

i.e. $\quad AC = BC$.

To prove $\quad CD = CE$

Construction Draw $CM \perp m$ and join AE.

Proof We have, $AD \perp m$, $CM \perp m$ and $BE \perp m$.

$\therefore \quad AD \parallel CM \parallel BE$

In ΔABE, $CG \parallel BE$ $[\because CM \parallel BE]$

and C is the mid-point of AB.

Thus, by converse of mid-point theorem, G is the mid-point of AE.

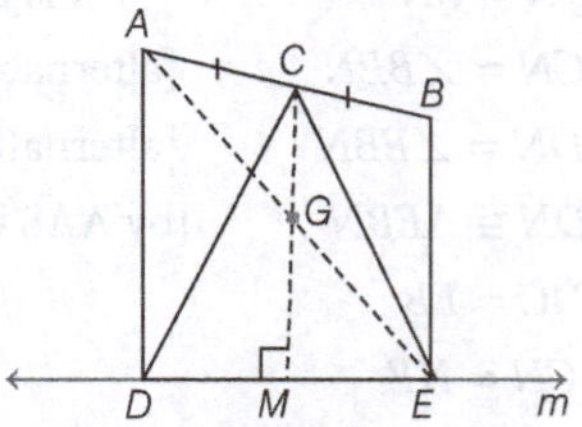

In ΔADE, G is the mid-point of AE and $GM \parallel AD$.

$[\because CM \parallel AD]$

Thus, by converse of mid-point theorem, M is mid-point of DE.

In ΔCMD and ΔCME,

$DM = EM$ [M is the mid-point of DE]

$CM = CM$ [common side]

$\angle CMD = \angle CME = 90°$

$\therefore \quad \Delta CMD \cong \Delta CME$ [by SAS congruence rule]

So, $\quad CD = CE$ [by CPCT] **Hence proved.**

36. Hint Let in given parallelogram $ABCD$, $\angle ABC = x$.

So, $\angle ADC = x$ and $\angle BCD = 180° - x$

[opposite angles of parallelogram are same]

So, $\angle PBC = x + 60°$ and $\angle QDC = x + 60°$ ...(i)

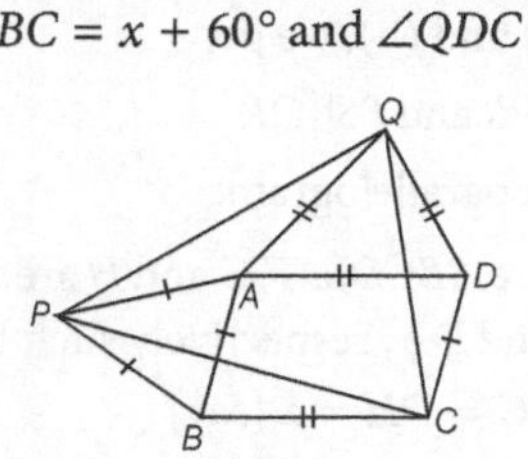

Now, in ΔPBC and ΔQDC,

$PB = CD$ [$\because PB = AB = CD$]

$BC = QD$ [$\because BC = AD = QD$]

and $\angle PBC = \angle QDC = x + 60°$ [from Eq. (i)]

So, $\Delta PBC \cong \Delta CDQ$ [by SAS congruence rule]

Hence, $CP = CQ$ [by CPCT] ...(ii)

At point A,

$\angle PAB + \angle BAD + \angle QAD + \angle PAQ = 360°$

$\Rightarrow$ $60° + 180° - x + 60° + \angle PAQ = 360°$

$\Rightarrow$ $\angle PAQ = 60° + x$

In ΔPAQ and ΔCDQ,

$AP = CD$, [$\because AP = AB = CD$]

$AQ = DQ$

and $\angle PAQ = \angle CDQ$ [each $(60 + x)°$]

Therefore, $\Delta PAQ \cong \Delta CDQ$ [by SAS congruency]

$\therefore$ $PQ = CQ$ ...(iii)

From Eqs. (ii) and (iii), we get

$PQ = CQ = CP$

i.e. ΔCPQ is an equilateral triangle. **Hence proved.**

37. Hint In quadrilateral $ABCD$, AS, BQ, CQ and DS are angle bisectors of $\angle A, \angle B, \angle C$ and $\angle D$.

Also, $\angle QPS = \angle APB$ [vertically opposite angles] ... (i)

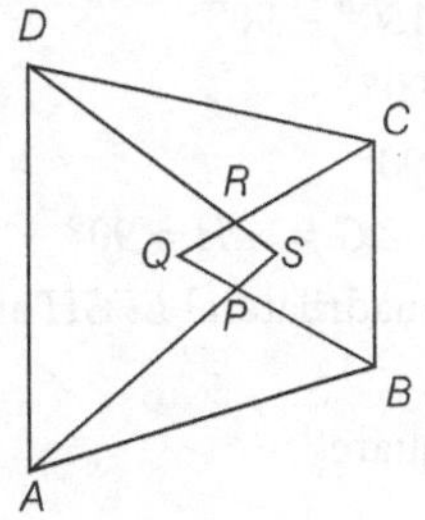

In ΔAPB,

$\angle APB + \angle PAB + \angle ABP = 180°$

$\Rightarrow$ $\angle APB + \frac{1}{2}\angle A + \frac{1}{2}\angle B = 180°$

$\Rightarrow$ $\angle APB = 180° - \frac{1}{2}[\angle A + \angle B]$ ... (ii)

From Eqs. (i) and (ii), we get

$$\angle QPS = 180° - \frac{1}{2}[\angle A + \angle B] \quad \text{... (iii)}$$

Similarly, $\angle QRS = 180° - \frac{1}{2}(\angle C + \angle D)$ ... (iv)

From Eqs. (iii) and (iv), we get

$$\angle QPS + \angle QRS = 360° - \frac{1}{2}[\angle A + \angle B + \angle C + \angle D]$$

$$= 360° - \frac{1}{2}[360°] = 180°$$

So, $PQRS$ is a quadrilateral whose opposite angles are supplementary.

38. Hint We draw the figure as per the given conditions.

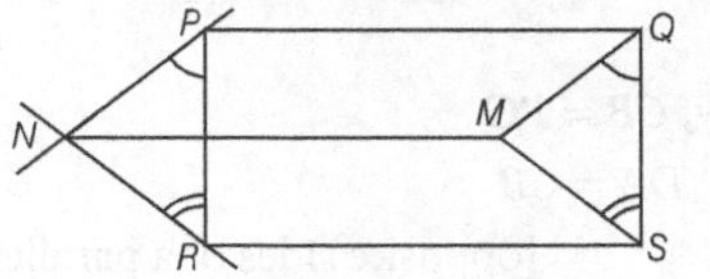

It is given that $PQ = RS$ and $PQ \parallel RS$.

Since, a pair of opposite side of a quadrilateral $PQSR$ is equal and parallel. Therefore, $PQSR$ is a parallelogram.

So, $PR = QS$ and $PR \parallel QS$ ...(i)

Now, $PR \parallel QS$

Therefore, $\angle RPQ + \angle PQS = 180°$

[interior angles on the same side of the transversal]

i.e. $\angle RPQ + \angle PQM + \angle MQS = 180°$ ... (ii)

Also, $PN \parallel QM$ [by construction]

Therefore, $\angle NPQ + \angle PQM = 180°$

i.e. $\angle NPR + \angle RPQ + \angle PQM = 180°$ ...(iii)

So, $\angle NPR = \angle MQS$

[from Eqs. (ii) and (iii)] ...(iv)

Similarly, $\angle NRP = \angle MSQ$ ...(v)

In ΔPNR and ΔQMS,

$PR = QS$ [from Eq. (i)]

$\angle NPR = \angle MQS$ [from Eq. (iv)]

$\angle NRP = \angle MSQ$ [from Eq. (v)]

Therefore, $\Delta PNR \cong \Delta QMS$ [by ASA congruence rule]

So, $PN = QM$ and $NR = MS$ [by CPCT]

As, $PN = QM$ and $PN \parallel QM$, we have $PQMN$ is a parallelogram. [$\because$ a pair of opposite side of a quadrilateral equal and parallel]

So, $NM = PQ$ and $NM \parallel PQ$.

39. Hint Given, $ABCD$ is a parallelogram i.e. $AB \parallel CD$ and $AD \parallel BC$ and $\angle DAB = 60°$. AP and BP are the bisectors of $\angle A$ and $\angle B$, respectively.

$\therefore \quad \angle PAB = \angle DAP = \frac{1}{2}\angle DAB = \frac{1}{2} \times 60° = 30°$

$\Rightarrow \quad \angle PAB = \angle DAP = 30°$

and $\quad \angle B = 180° - \angle A = 180° - 60° = 120°$

[co-interior angles of parallelogram]

$\Rightarrow \quad \angle PBA = \angle CBP = \frac{1}{2}\angle B = 60°$

We have, $AB \parallel DC$ and PA is a transversal.

$\therefore \quad \angle DPA = \angle PAB = 30°$ [alternate angle] ...(i)

Also, $\angle DAP = \angle PAB = 30°$ [given] ...(ii)

From Eqs. (i) and (ii), we get

$\angle DAP = \angle DPA \Rightarrow DP = DA$ ...(iii)

[sides opposite to equal angles of a triangle are also equal]

Similarly, $CB = PC$ ...(iv)

Also, $DA = CB$

[opposite sides of a parallelogram] ...(v)

From Eqs. (iii), (iv) and (v), we get

$DP = PC$

Hence, P is the mid-point of CD. **Hence proved.**

40. Hint Given In parallelogram $ABCD, P$ and Q are the mid-points of the opposite sides AB and CD, respectively.

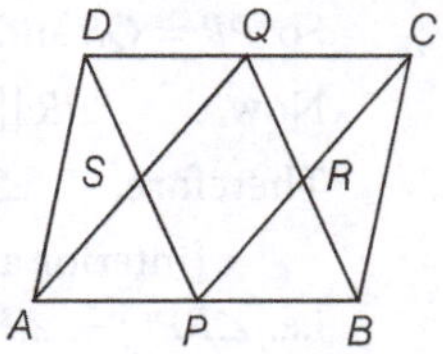

To show $PRQS$ is a parallelogram.

Proof Since, $ABCD$ is a parallelogram.

$AB \parallel CD \Rightarrow AP \parallel QC$

Also, $AB \parallel DC$

So, $\quad AB = DC$

$\Rightarrow \frac{1}{2}AB = \frac{1}{2}DC \Rightarrow AP = QC$

[$\because P$ and Q are the mid-points of AB and DC]

Now, $AP \parallel QC$ and $AP = QC$

$\therefore APCQ$ is a parallelogram.

$\therefore \quad AQ \parallel PC$ or $SQ \parallel PR$ ... (i)

Again, $AB \parallel DC$

$\Rightarrow \quad BP \parallel DQ$

and $\quad AB = DC \Rightarrow \frac{1}{2}AB = \frac{1}{2}DC$

$\Rightarrow \quad BP = QD$

So, $BPDQ$ is a parallelogram.

$\therefore \quad PD \parallel BQ$ or $PS \parallel QR$ ... (ii)

From Eqs. (i) and (ii), we get

$SQ \parallel PR$ and $PS \parallel QR$

So, $PRQS$ is a parallelogram.

41. Hint In square $ABCD, E, F, G$ and H are the points on AB, BC, CD and DA, respectively such that,

$AE = BF = CG = DH = x$ [say]

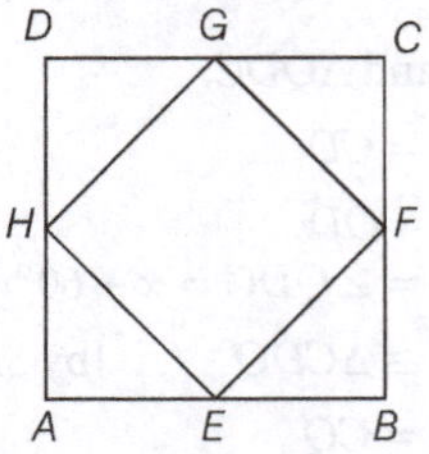

Then, $BE = CF = DG = HA = y$ [say]

Now, in ΔAEH and ΔBFE

$AE = BF$ [given]

$\angle A = \angle B = 90°$

$AH = BE = y$

$\therefore \quad \Delta AEH \cong \Delta BFE$ [SAS criterion]

$\therefore \quad \angle AEH = \angle BFE$ [by CPCT] ... (i)

$EH = FE$ [by CPCT]

and $\angle AHE = \angle BEF$ [by CPCT] ... (ii)

Now, $\angle AEH + \angle AHE = 90°$ [$\because \angle A = 90°$]

and $\quad \angle BFE + \angle BEF = 90°$ [$\because \angle B = 90°$]

Now, $\angle AEH + \angle AHE + \angle BFE + \angle BEF = 90° + 90°$

$\Rightarrow \quad \angle AEH + \angle BEF + \angle AEH + \angle BEF = 180°$

[from Eqs. (i) and (ii)]

$\Rightarrow \quad 2(\angle AEH + \angle BEF) = 180°$

$\Rightarrow \quad \angle AEH + \angle BEF = 90°$ ... (iii)

Now, $\angle HEF = 180° - \angle AEH - \angle BEF$

$= 180° - 90°$ [from Eq. (iii)]

$= 90°$

$\therefore \quad \angle E = 90°$

Similarly, $\angle F = \angle G = \angle H = 90°$

Since, sides of quadrilateral $EFGH$ are equal and each angle is $90°$.

$\therefore$ $EFGH$ is a square.

Mind Map

QUADRILATERALS

Parallelogram

A quadrilateral in which both pairs of opposite sides are parallel.

BC || AD

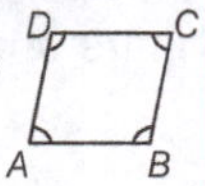

AB || DC

Properties of a Parallelogram

1. A diagonal of a parallelogram divides it into two congruent triangles.
   $\Delta ABC \cong \Delta CDA$

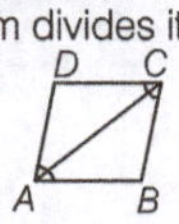

2. In a parallelogram, opposite sides are equal.
   $AB = DC$
   $BC = AD$

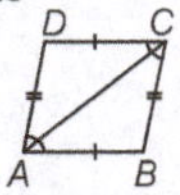

3. If each pair of opposite sides of a quadrilateral is equal, then it is a parallelogram.

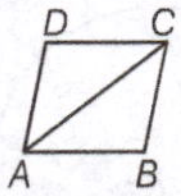

4. In a parallelogram, opposite angles are equal.
   $\angle A = \angle C$
   $\angle B = \angle D$

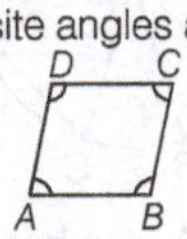

5. If in a quadrilateral, each pair of opposite angles are equal, then it is a parallelogram.

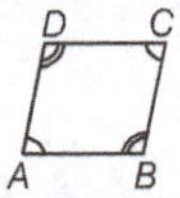

6. The diagonals of a parallelogram bisect each other.
   $OA = OC$
   $OB = OD$

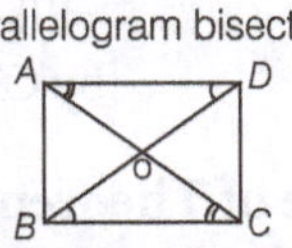

7. If the diagonals of a quadrilateral bisect each other, then it is a parallelogram.

Mid-Point Theorem

1. The line segment joining the mid-point of any two sides of a triangle is parallel to the third side and equal to the half of it.
   i.e $EF \parallel BC$
   and $EF = \frac{1}{2}BC$

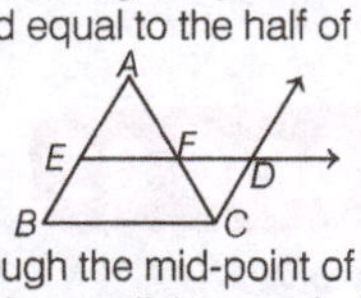

2. The line drawn through the mid-point of one side of a triangle, parallel to another side bisect the third side.
   F is the mid-point of AC.

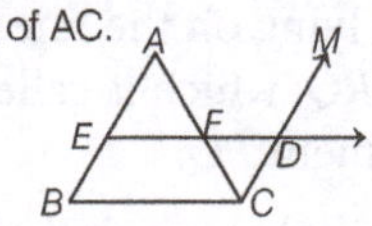

CHAPTER 9

Circles

The collection of all the points in a plane, which are at a fixed distance from a fixed point in the plane, is called a **circle**. The fixed point is called the **centre** of the circle and the fixed distance is called the **radius** of the circle or in other words, the line segment joining the centre and any point on the circle is called radius of circle.

TOPIC 01 Angle Subtended by a Chord at a Point

We know that, if we take a line segment PQ and a point R not lying on the line PQ, then by joining PR and RQ, we get $\angle PRQ$, which is called the angle subtended by the line segment PQ.

Similarly, in a circle with centre O, let AB be a chord and we take two points P and Q on the circle as shown in figure and join PA, PB, QA and QB. Then, we get $\angle APB$ and $\angle AQB$, which are called the angles subtended by the chord AB at the points P and Q, respectively. Also, $\angle AOB$ is the angle subtended by the chord AB at the centre O.

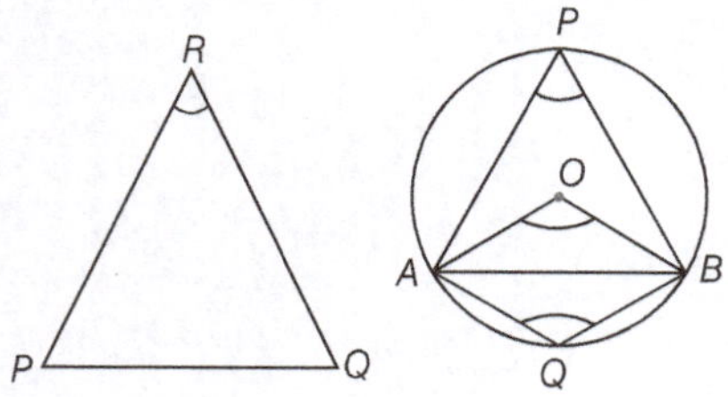

Theorem 1 ***Equal chords of a circle subtend equal angles at the centre.***

Given A circle with centre O. AB and CD are two equal chords of the circle which subtend $\angle AOB$ and $\angle COD$ at the centre O.

To prove $\angle AOB = \angle COD$

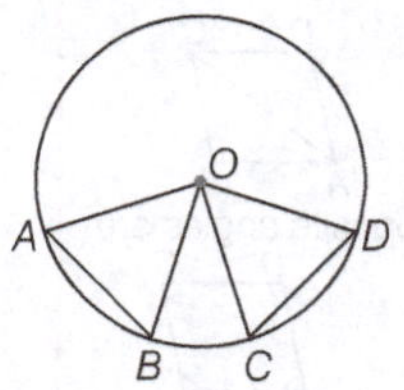

Proof In ΔAOB and ΔCOD, we have

$OA = OC$ [radii of same circle]

$OB = OD$ [radii of same circle]

$AB = CD$ [given]

$\therefore \Delta AOB \cong \Delta COD$ [by SSS congruence rule]

Then, $\angle AOB = \angle COD$ [by CPCT] **Hence proved.**

Theorem 2 (Converse of Theorem 1) ***If the angles subtended by the chords of a circle at the centre are equal, then the chords are equal.***

Given A circle with centre O.

Let AB and CD be two chords of a circle such that angles subtended by these chords at the centre O of a circle are equal

i.e. $\angle AOB = \angle COD$

To prove $AB = CD$

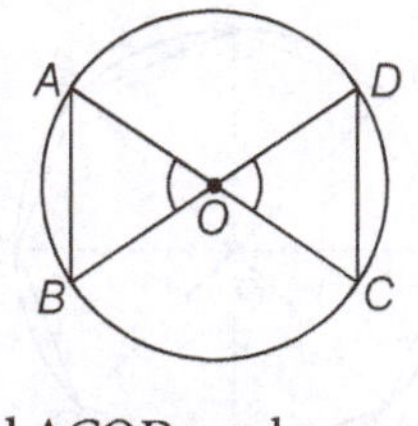

Proof In ΔAOB and ΔCOD, we have

$AO = CO$ [radii of same circle]

$\angle AOB = \angle COD$ [given]

and $OB = OD$ [radii of same circle]

$\therefore$ $\Delta AOB \cong \Delta COD$ [by SAS congruence rule]

So, $AB = CD$ [by CPCT]

Hence, chords are equal if they subtend equal angles at the centre of a circle.

Example 1. ***AB* is a chord of a circle having centre *O*. If $\angle AOB = 60°$, then prove that the chord *AB* is of radius length.**

Sol. Let O be the centre and r be the radius of the circle.

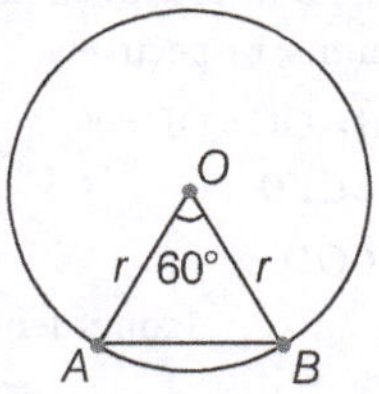

Chord AB subtends $\angle AOB = 60°$ at the centre of the circle.

Here, $OB = OA = r$ [radii of same circle]

$\Rightarrow$ $\angle OAB = \angle OBA$

i.e. $\angle A = \angle B$ ...(i)

[$\because$ angles opposite to equal sides of a triangle are also equal]

In ΔOAB,

$\angle O + \angle A + \angle B = 180°$ [angle sum property]

$\Rightarrow$ $60° + \angle A + \angle B = 180°$

$\Rightarrow$ $\angle A + \angle B = 120°$ ...(ii)

From Eqs. (i) and (ii), we get

$2\angle A = 120°$

$\Rightarrow$ $\angle A = \frac{1}{2} \times 120° = 60°$

and $\angle B = 60°$

Thus, $\angle O = \angle A = \angle B = 60°$

Hence, ΔOAB is an equilateral triangle.

$\therefore$ $AB = OA = OB = r$

i.e. $AB = r$ **Hence proved.**

Example 2. **If *A*, *B* and *C* are three points on a circle such that *AB* = *BC* = *CA* and *O* is the centre of the circle, then find the angle subtended by the chords *AB*, *BC* and *CA* at the centre *O*.**

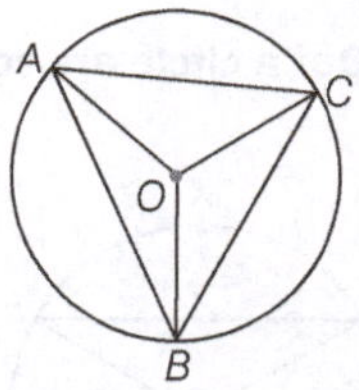

Sol. Given, three points A, B and C are on a circle such that, $AB = BC = CA$.

We know that equal chords of a circle subtend equal angles at the centre of circle.

So, $\angle AOB = \angle BOC = \angle AOC$ ...(i)

Now, $\angle AOB + \angle BOC + \angle AOC = 360°$

[$\because$ sum of angles at a point is 360°]

$\Rightarrow$ $3\angle AOB = 360°$ [from Eq. (i)]

$\Rightarrow$ $\angle AOB = \frac{360°}{3} = 120°$

Hence, angle subtended by the chords AB, BC and CA at the centre O is 120°.

Try These 9.1

1. **In the given figure, chords *AB* and *CD* are equal. If $\angle OBA = 55°$, then find the measure of $\angle COD$.**

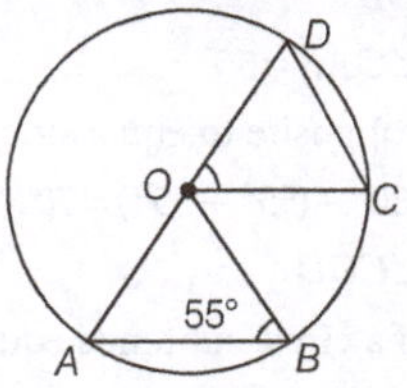

2. **In the figure given below, *O* is the centre of the circle and *CD* = *DE* = *EF* = *GF*. If the $\angle COD = 40°$, then find the reflex $\angle COG$.**

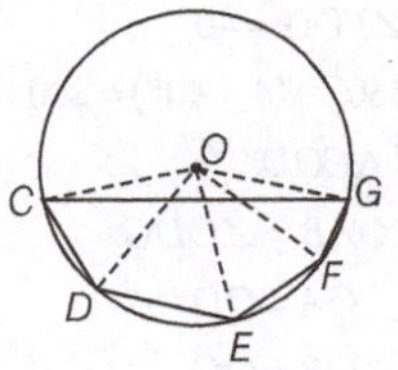

3. **In the given figure, *O* is the centre of the circle. If $\angle OAB = 65°$ and $\angle AOB = 50°$, then find $\angle COD$.**

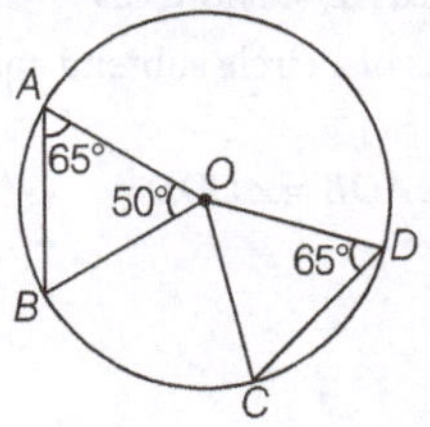

4. **If O is the centre of a circle and points A, B, C, D, E, F, G and H are on the circle such that**
$AB = BC = CD = DE = EF = FG = GH = HA$.
Find $\angle AOB, \angle AOC, \angle DOF$ and $\angle EOH$.

5. **If arcs AXB and CYD of a circle are congruent, find the ratio of AB and CD.**

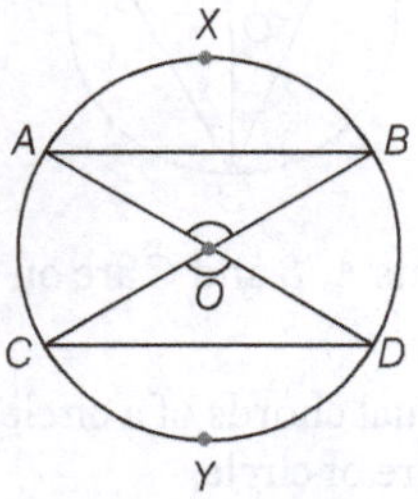

6. **In the given figure, the two chords AC and BC are equal and the radius OC intersects AB at M. Then, find the ratio $AM : BM$.**

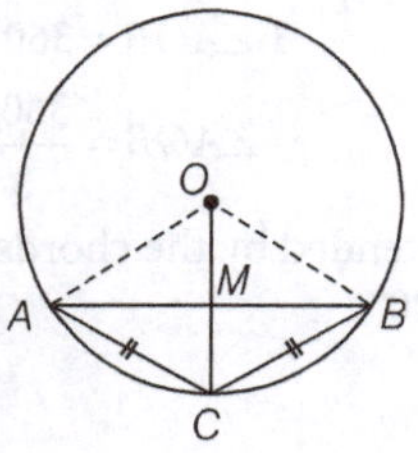

Hints & Answers

1. Hint Since, $OA = OB$

$\Rightarrow \quad \angle OBA = \angle OAB = 55^\circ$

[$\because$ angles opposite to equal sides of triangle are equal]

$\therefore \quad \angle AOB = 180^\circ - (55^\circ + 55^\circ) = 70^\circ$

$\therefore \quad \angle AOB = \angle COD$

[$\because$ equal chords of a circle subtends equal angles at the centre]

Ans. 70°

2. Hint Since, equal chords subtend equal angles.

$\therefore \quad \angle COD = \angle DOE = \angle EOF$
$= \angle FOG = 40^\circ$

$\therefore$ Reflex $\angle COG = 360^\circ - (4 \times 40^\circ) = 200^\circ$

3. Hint In ΔAOB and ΔCOD,

$\angle OAB = \angle ODC$

$OA = OD$ [radii of circle]

$OB = OC$ [radii of circle]

$\therefore \quad AB = CD$ [by CPCT]

i.e. Chord AB = Chord CD

Since, equal chords of a circle subtend equal angles at the centre.

$\therefore \quad \angle AOB = \angle COD$

Ans. 50°

4. Hint We know that the equal chords subtends equal angles.

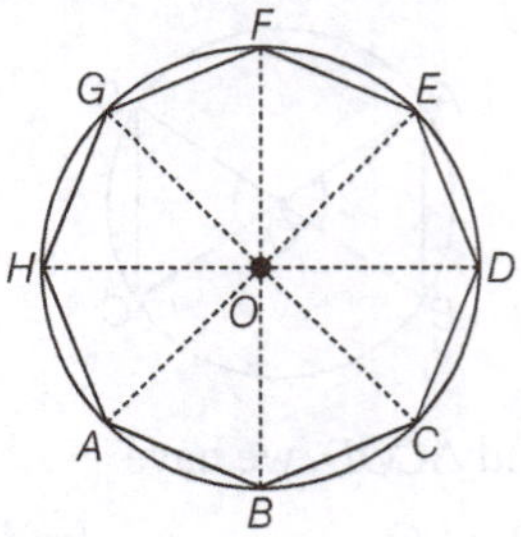

Given, $AB = BC = CD = DE = EF = FG = GH = HA$

$\Rightarrow \quad \angle AOB = \angle BOC = \angle COD = \angle DOE$
$= \angle EOF = \angle FOG$
$= \angle GOH = \angle AOH$ ...(i)

$\therefore \quad 8 \times \angle AOB = 360^\circ$

[$\because$ sum of angles at a point is 360° and from Eq. (i)]

$\Rightarrow \quad \angle AOB = 45^\circ$

Now, $\quad \angle AOC = \angle AOB + \angle BOC$
$= 45^\circ + 45^\circ = 90^\circ$

Similarly, $\quad \angle DOF = 90^\circ$

and $\quad \angle EOH = \angle EOF + \angle FOG + \angle GOH = 135^\circ$

5. Hint Let AXB and CYD be arcs of circle whose centre and radius are O and r units, respectively.

So, $\quad OA = OB = OC = OD = r$ ...(i)

$\because \quad$ arc $AXB \cong$ arc CYD

$\therefore \quad \angle AOB = \angle COD$ ...(ii)

[congruent arcs of a circle subtend equal angles at the centre]

In ΔAOB and ΔCOD,

$AO = CO$ [from Eq. (i)]

$BO = DO$ [from Eq. (i)]

and $\quad \angle AOB = \angle COD$ [from Eq. (ii)]

$\therefore \quad \Delta AOB \cong \Delta COD$ [by SAS congruence rule]

$\Rightarrow \quad AB = CD$ [by CPCT]

$\Rightarrow \quad \dfrac{AB}{CD} = \dfrac{1}{1}$

6. Hint Since, chords AC and BC are equal.

$\therefore \quad \angle AOC = \angle BOC$

[equal chords of a circle subtend equal angles at the centre]

$\Rightarrow \quad \angle AOM = \angle BOM$

In ΔAOM and ΔBOM,

$\angle AOM = \angle BOM$ [Proved above]

$AO = BO$ [$\because$ radii of sames circle]

$OM = OM$ [common]

$\therefore \quad \Delta AOM \cong \Delta BOM$ [by SAS congruence rule]

$\Rightarrow \quad AM = BM$ [by CPCT]

$\therefore$ Ratio $AM : BM = 1:1$

TOPIC 02 Perpendicular from Centre to the Chord

In a circle, the property of a perpendicular drawn from the centre to a chord in the form of a theorem is given below

Theorem 1 ***The perpendicular from the centre of a circle to a chord bisects the chord.***

Given AB is a chord of a circle with centre O and $OM \perp AB$.

To prove OM bisects AB i.e. $AM = MB$.

Construction Join OA and OB.

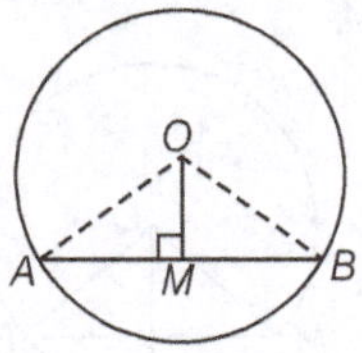

Proof In ΔAMO and ΔBMO, we have

$OA = OB$ [radii of same circle]

$\angle AMO = \angle BMO$ [each 90°]

and $OM = OM$ [common sides]

$\therefore$ $\Delta AMO \cong \Delta BMO$ [by RHS congruence rule]

Then, $AM = MB$ [by CPCT] **Hence proved.**

Theorem 2 **(Converse of Theorem 1)** ***The line drawn through the centre of a circle to bisect a chord is perpendicular to the chord.***

Given AB is a chord of a circle with centre O. A line OM is drawn through the centre O to chord AB such that M is the mid-point of AB, i.e. $AM = MB$.

To prove $OM \perp AB$.

Construction Join OA and OB.

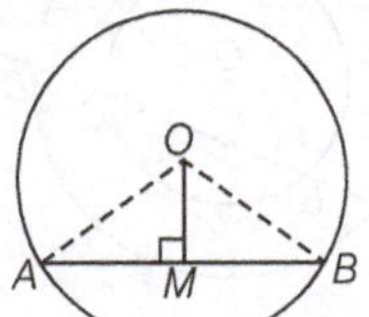

Proof In ΔOAM and ΔOBM, we have

$AM = MB$ [$\because M$ is the mid-point of AB]

$OA = OB$ [radii of same circle]

$OM = OM$ [common sides]

$\therefore$ $\Delta OAM \cong \Delta OBM$ [by SSS congruence rule]

Then, $\angle OMA = \angle OMB$ [by CPCT] ...(i)

Now, AB is a straight line. So, by linear pair axiom,

$\angle OMA + \angle OMB = 180° \Rightarrow 2\angle OMA = 180°$ [using Eq. (i)]

$\Rightarrow$ $\angle OMA = \frac{180°}{2} = 90°$

Thus, $\angle OMA = \angle OMB = 90°$

Then, $OM \perp AB$ **Hence proved.**

Problems Based on Perpendicular from Centre to the Chord

With the help of given theorems, we can find the length of chord/distance of chord from centre/radius of circle. To solve such problems, we use the Pythagoras theorem also.

Example 1. **The radius of a circle is 13 cm and the length of one of its chords is 10 cm. Find the distance of the chord from the centre.**

Sol. Let AB be a chord of the given circle with centre O.

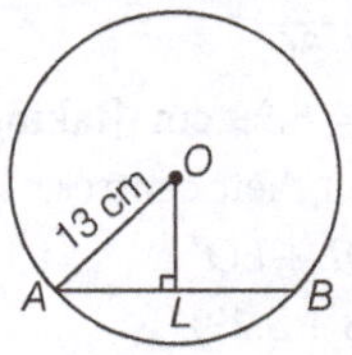

Given, radius, $OA = 13$ cm and $AB = 10$ cm

From O, draw $OL \perp AB$.

We know that the perpendicular drawn from the centre of a circle to a chord bisects the chord.

$\therefore$ $AL = \frac{1}{2}AB = \frac{1}{2} \times 10 = 5$ cm

Now, from the right angled ΔOLA,

$OA^2 = OL^2 + AL^2$ [by Pythagoras theorem]

$\Rightarrow$ $13^2 = OL^2 + 5^2$

$\Rightarrow$ $OL^2 = 13^2 - 5^2 = 169 - 25 = 144$

$\Rightarrow$ $OL = 12$ cm [taking positive square root]

Hence, the distance of the chord from the centre is 12 cm.

Example 2. **Two circles of radii 10 cm and 8 cm intersect and the length of the common chord is 12 cm. Find the distance between their centres.**

Sol. Let O and O' be the centres of the circles of radii 10 cm and 8 cm, respectively and PQ be their common chord of length 12 cm.

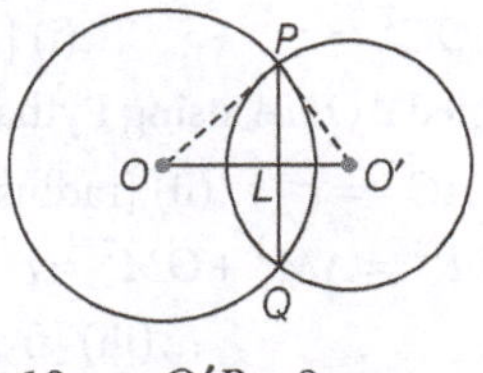

We have, $OP = 10$ cm, $O'P = 8$ cm

and $PQ = 12$ cm

$\therefore$ $PL = \frac{1}{2}PQ = 6$ cm

[$\because$ when two circles intersect at two points, then their centres lie on the perpendicular bisector of the common chord]

In right angled ΔOLP,

$$OP^2 = OL^2 + LP^2 \quad \text{[by Pythagoras theorem]}$$

$$\Rightarrow \quad OL = \sqrt{OP^2 - LP^2}$$

$$= \sqrt{10^2 - 6^2}$$

$$= \sqrt{100 - 36}$$

$$= \sqrt{64} = 8 \text{ cm} \quad \text{[taking positive square root]}$$

Now, in right angled $\Delta O'LP$,

$$O'P^2 = O'L^2 + LP^2 \quad \text{[by Pythagoras theorem]}$$

$$\Rightarrow \quad O'L = \sqrt{O'P^2 - LP^2}$$

$$= \sqrt{8^2 - 6^2}$$

$$= \sqrt{64 - 36}$$

$$= \sqrt{28} = 5.29 \text{ cm} \quad \text{[taking positive square root]}$$

$\therefore$ Distance between their centres,

$$OO' = OL + LO'$$

$$= (8 + 5.29)$$

$$= 13.29 \text{ cm}$$

Example 3. ***AB* and *CD* are two chords of a circle such that *AB* = 6 cm, *CD* = 12 cm and *AB* || *CD*. If the distance between *AB* and *CD* is 3 cm, find the radius of the circle.**

Sol. We have, $AB = 6$ cm, $CD = 12$ cm and $PM = 3$ cm

Let the radius of the circle be r cm.

Draw $OM \perp AB$ and $OP \perp CD$.

$\therefore \quad AM = MB = 3$ cm and $CP = PD = 6$ cm

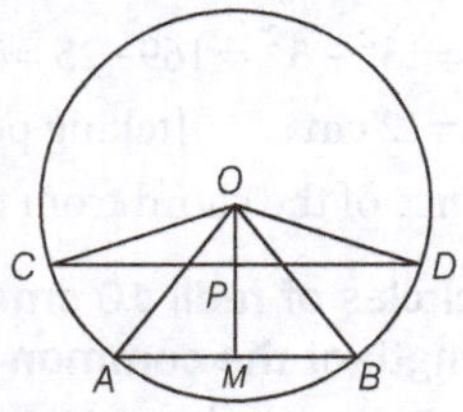

Let $\quad OP = y$

Also, $\quad PM = 3$ cm $\quad$ [given]

$\therefore$ In right angled ΔOPC, using Pythagoras theorem,

$$CP^2 + OP^2 = OC^2 = r^2 \quad \text{...(i) [radius of circle} = r\text{]}$$

and in right angled ΔOMA, using Pythagoras theorem,

$$AM^2 + OM^2 = AO^2 = r^2 \quad \text{...(ii) [radius of circle} = AO = r\text{]}$$

$$\therefore \quad CP^2 + OP^2 = AM^2 + OM^2 = r^2$$

...(iii) [from Eqs. (i) and (ii)]

$$\Rightarrow \quad 6^2 + y^2 = 3^2 + (3 + y)^2$$

$$\Rightarrow \quad 36 + y^2 = 9 + 9 + y^2 + 6y$$

$$\Rightarrow \quad 6y = 18 \Rightarrow y = 3 \text{ cm}$$

$$\therefore \quad r^2 = 6^2 + y^2 = 36 + 9 = 45 \quad \text{[using Eq. (i)]}$$

$$\Rightarrow \quad r = 3\sqrt{5} \text{ cm}$$

$$= 6.708 = 6.71 \text{ cm}$$

Try These 9.2

1. **In the shown figure, perpendicular is drawn from centre *O* to the chord *AB*. If *AB* = 8 cm, then find *AP* and *PB*.**

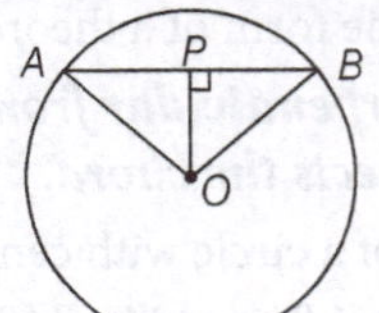

2. **In the shown figure, if *MP* = *PN*, then find the values of ∠*OPN* and ∠*OPM*.**

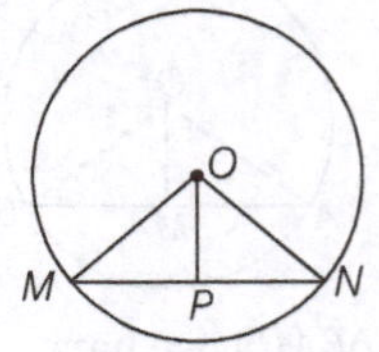

3. **In the given figure, chord *AB* = chord *CD*, *AP* = 8 cm and *PC* = 3 cm, radius *OP* = 4 cm. Find the length of chords *AB* and *CD*.**

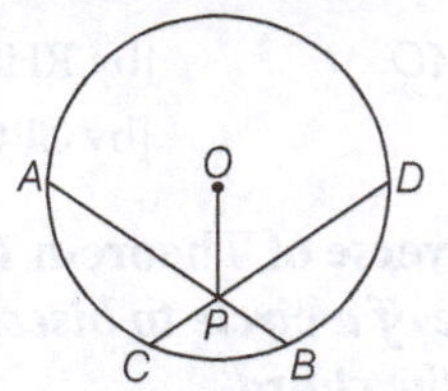

4. **Two concentric circles with centre *O* have *A*, *B*, *C* and *D* as points of intersection with a line *l* as shown in the figure. If *AD* = 12 cm and *BC* = 8 cm, then find the lengths of *AB* and *CD*.**

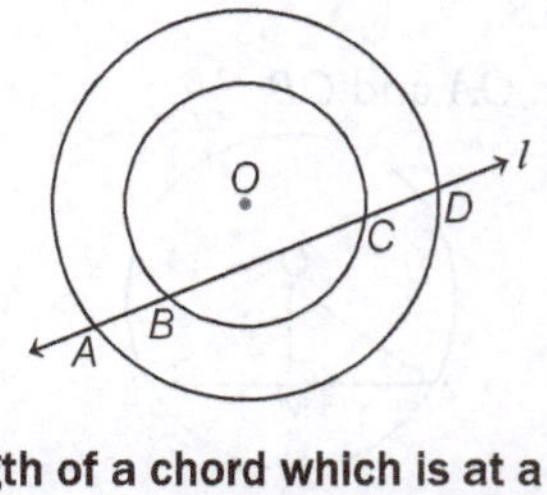

5. **Find the length of a chord which is at a distance of 5 cm from the centre of a circle of radius 10 cm.**
6. **The radius of a circle is 5 cm and the length of a chord in the circle is 8 cm. Find the distance of the chord from the centre of the circle.**
7. **In the given figure, *O* and *O′* are the centres of circles of radii 20 cm and 37 cm. If *AB* = 24 cm, then find the distance *OO′*.**

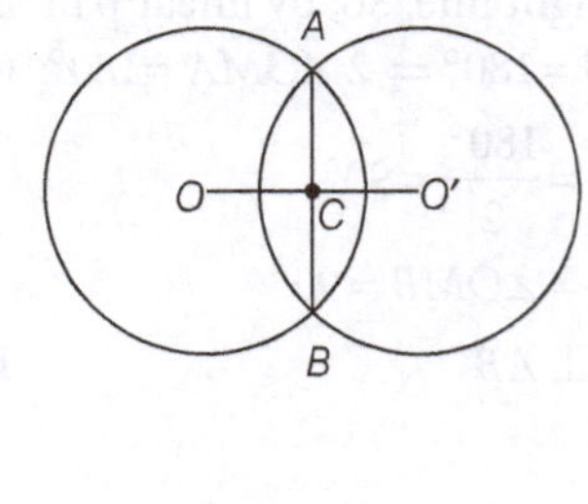

8. **Two parallel chords of a circle whose diameter is 13 cm, are 5 cm and 12 cm, respectively. Find the distance between them if they lie on opposite sides of the centre.**

9. **The lengths of two parallel chords of a circle are 8 cm and 14 cm. If the smaller chord is at a distance of 2 cm from the larger chord, then what is the distance of the other chord from the centre?**

10. **In the given figure, O is the centre of a circle of radius r cm, OP and OQ are perpendiculars to AB and CD, respectively and $PQ = 1$ cm if $AB \parallel CD$, $AB = 6$ cm and $CD = 8$ cm, then find radius r.**

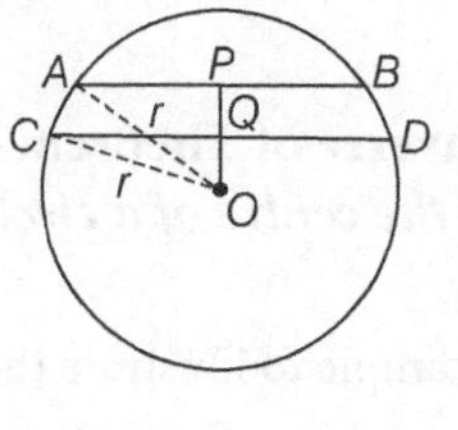

Hints & Answers

1. **Hint** $AP = PB = 4$ cm

2. **Hint** Since, $MP = PN$ and MN is a chord.

Therefore, line OP bisects the chord.

We know that, if line drawn through the centre of a circle bisects a chord, then it is perpendicular to the chord.

$\therefore$ Line OP is perpendicular to the chord MN

$\therefore \quad \angle OPN = \angle OPM = 90°$

3. **Hint** AB and CD are two equal chords of circle with centre O and intersect at point P.

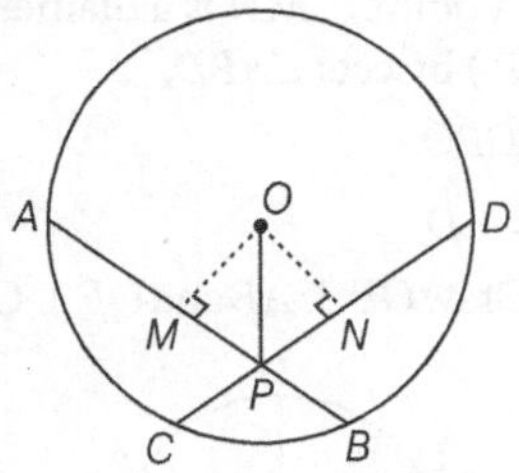

Draw $OM \perp AB$ and $ON \perp CD$

Here, $AM = MB = \frac{1}{2} AB$

and $\quad CN = ND = \frac{1}{2} CD$

[$\because$ perpendicular from centre on the chord bisects the chord]

$\Rightarrow \quad AM = MB = CN = ND \quad$ ...(i)

$\therefore \quad \Delta OPM \cong \Delta OPN \quad$ [by RHS congruence rule]

Then, $\quad MP = NP \quad$ [by CPCT] ...(ii)

On adding in Eq. (ii) AM both sides, we get

$MP + AM = NP + AM$

$\Rightarrow \quad MP + AM = NP + ND \quad$ [from Eq. (i)]

$\Rightarrow \quad AP = PD$

and on subtracting Eq. (ii) from MB, we get

$MB - MP = MB - NP$

$\Rightarrow \quad PB = CN - NP \quad$ [from Eq. (i)]

$\Rightarrow \quad PB = CP$

$\therefore AP = PD = 8$ cm and $PB = CP = 3$ cm

$\therefore AB = AP + PB = 8 + 3 = 11$ cm

$\because$ Chord AB = Chord $CD = 11$ cm

4. **Hint** Draw $OP \perp BC$

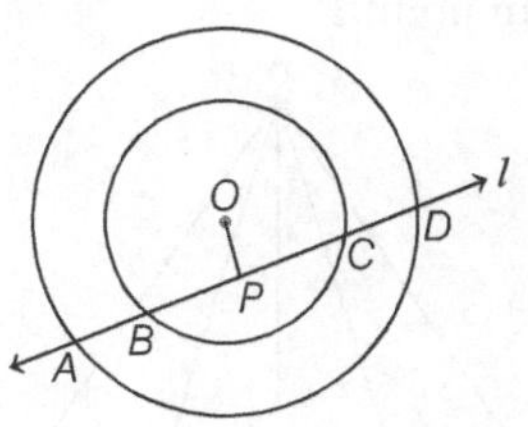

Also, $\quad OP \perp AD$

Then, $\quad BP = PC = \frac{BC}{2} = \frac{8}{2} = 4$ cm

and $\quad AP = PD = \frac{AD}{2} = \frac{12}{2} = 6$ cm

Hence, $AB = AP - BP = 6 - 4 = 2$ cm

Similarly, $CD = 2$ cm

5. **Hint** Solve as Example 1. **Ans.** = 17.32 cm

6. **Hint** Solve as Example 1. **Ans.** = 3 cm

7. **Hint** Solve as Example 2. **Ans.** = 51 cm

8. **Hint** Draw $OB \perp AC$ and $OE \perp DF$

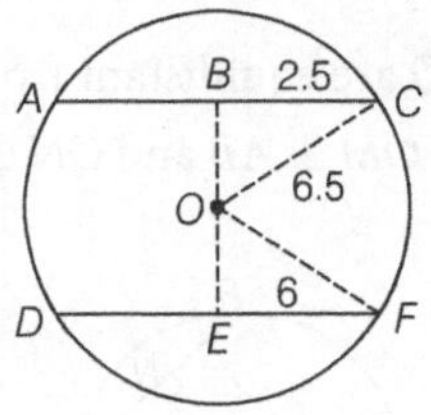

In ΔOBC,

$$OB = \sqrt{(6.5)^2 - (2.5)^2} = \sqrt{36} = 6 \text{ cm}$$

In ΔOEF,

$$OE = \sqrt{(6.5)^2 - (6)^2} = \sqrt{6.25} = 2.5 \text{ cm}$$

$\therefore \quad BE = 6 + 2.5 = 8.5$ cm

9. **Hint** Solve as Example 3. **Ans.** 7.25 cm

10. **Hint** Solve as Example 3. **Ans.** 5 cm

TOPIC 03 Equal Chords and Their Distances from the Centre

Distance of a Line from a Point

The length of the perpendicular from a point to a line is the distance of the line from the point.

Let AB be a line and P be a point. Since, a line has infinite number of points. So, by joining these points to P, we get infinite line segments as $PL_1, PL_2, PM, PL_3, PL_4$, etc. Out of these line segments, the perpendicular from P to AB say PM will be the least. This least length PM will be the distance of AB from point P.

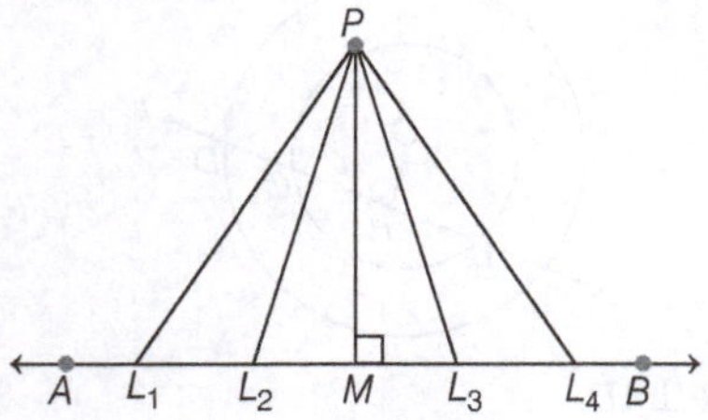

Note it

1. If the point lies on the line, then the distance of the line from the point is zero.
2. The longest chord of a circle is the diameter whose distance from the centre is zero.

Theorem 1 ***Equal chords of a circle (or of congruent circles) are equidistant from the centre (or centres).***

Given A circle with centre O and two equal chords; AB and PQ.

To prove AB and PQ are equidistant from the centre O.

Construction Draw $OM \perp AB$ and $ON \perp PQ$. Join OA, OB, OP and OQ.

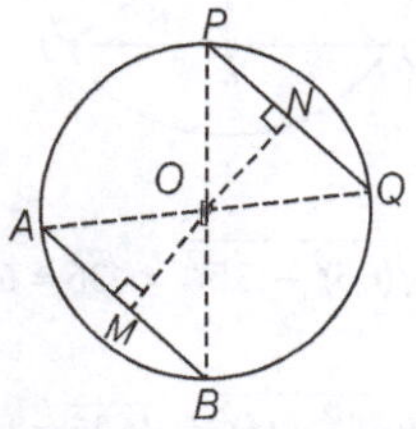

Proof We know that a perpendicular from the centre to a chord bisects the chord.

$\therefore \quad AM = MB = \frac{1}{2} AB \quad [\because OM \perp AB]$

and $\quad PN = NQ = \frac{1}{2} PQ \quad [\because ON \perp PQ]$

$\because \quad$ Chord AB = Chord PQ [given]

$\Rightarrow \quad \frac{1}{2} AB = \frac{1}{2} PQ$

Then, $\quad AM = MB = PN = NQ$

Now, in ΔOMA and ΔONQ, we have

$OA = OQ$ [radii of same circle]

$AM = NQ$ [proved above]

$\angle OMA = \angle ONQ$ [each 90°]

$\therefore \quad \Delta OMA \cong \Delta ONQ$ [by RHS congruence rule]

Then, $\quad OM = ON$ [by CPCT]

Hence, PQ and AB are equidistant from the centre O.

Hence proved.

Theorem 2 (Converse of Theorem 1) ***Chords equidistant from the centre of a circle are equal in length.***

Now, we take an example to illustrate the use of above results.

Example 1. **In the given figure, O is the centre of a circle and PO bisects $\angle APD$. Prove that $AB = CD$.**

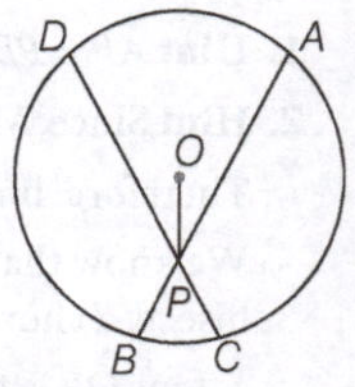

Or

If two intersecting chords of a circle make equal angles with the diameter passing through their point of intersection, then prove that the chords are equal.

Sol. Let AB and CD be two chords of a circle with centre O intersecting at a point P. MN is a diameter through P such that MN (or OP) bisects $\angle APD$,

i.e. $\angle APO = \angle DPO$.

To prove $AB = CD$

Construction Draw $OE \perp AB$ and $OF \perp CD$

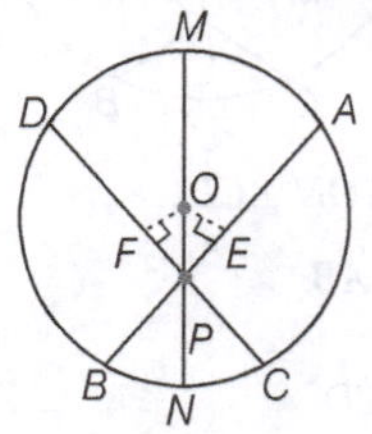

Proof In ΔOEP and ΔOFP,

$\angle OEP = \angle OFP$ [each 90°]

$OP = OP$ [common sides]

and $\quad \angle OPE = \angle OPF \quad [\because OP$ bisects $\angle APD]$

$\therefore \quad \Delta OEP \cong \Delta OFP$ [by AAS congruence rule]

Then, $\quad OE = OF$ [by CPCT]

Thus, chords AB and CD are equidistant from the centre O of the circle and we know that chords of a circle which are equidistant from the centre, are equal.

$\therefore \quad AB = CD$ **Hence proved.**

Example 2. In the following figure, equal chords AB and CD of a circle with centre O, cut at right angles at E. If M and N are the mid-points of AB and CD respectively, then prove that $OMEN$ is a square.

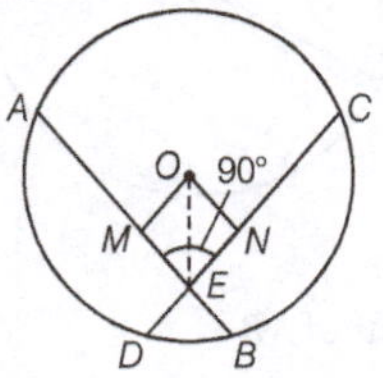

Sol. Given, M and N are the mid-points of AB and CD, respectively.

$\therefore \quad \angle OMB = \angle OND = 90°$

$\Rightarrow \quad \angle OME = \angle ONE = 90°$

Since, equal chords of a circle are equidistant from the centre.

$\therefore \quad OM = ON$

Thus, in ΔOME and ΔONE, we have

$OM = ON$

$\angle OME = \angle ONE$ [each 90°]

and $OE = OE$ [common sides]

$\therefore \quad \Delta OME \cong \Delta ONE$ [by RHS congruence rule]

So, $\angle MOE = \angle NOE = 45°$ [by CPCT]

and $\angle OEM = \angle OEN = 45°$ [by CPCT]

Thus, $\angle MON = \angle MOE + \angle NOE = 45° + 45° = 90°$

Similarly, $\angle MEN = 90°$

Also, $OM = ON$

Hence, $OMEN$ is a square.

Example 3. In the following figure, O is the centre of a circle. If AB and AC are chords of the circle such that $AB = AC$, $OP \perp AB$ and $OQ \perp AC$, then prove that $PB = QC$.

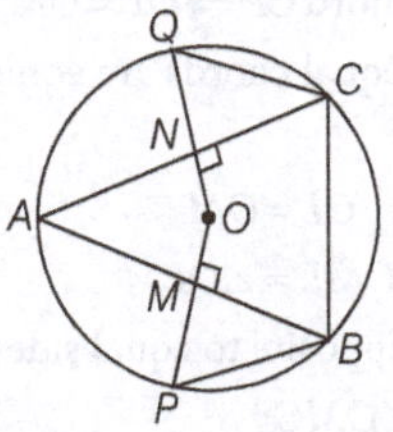

Sol. Given AB and AC be two equal chords of circle with centre O. Also, $OP \perp AB$ at M and $OQ \perp AC$ at N.

To prove $PB = QC$

Proof We know that the perpendicular from the centre of a circle to a chord bisects the chord.

$\therefore \quad AM = MB = \frac{1}{2}AB$ [$\because OP \perp AB$]

and $AN = NC = \frac{1}{2}AC$ [$\because OQ \perp AC$]

Since, $AB = AC$

$\therefore \quad \frac{1}{2}AB = \frac{1}{2}AC$

$\Rightarrow \quad AM = MB = AN = NC$ ...(i)

Now, in ΔPMB and ΔQNC, we have

$MB = NC$ [from Eq. (i)]

$\angle PMB = \angle QNC$ [each 90°]

$OM = ON$ ...(ii)

[$\because$ equal chords of a circle are equidistant from the centre]

$OP = OQ$ [radii of same circle]...(iii)

$\Rightarrow \quad OP - OM = OQ - ON$

[on subtracting Eq. (ii) from Eq. (iii)]

$\Rightarrow \quad PM = QN$ ...(iv)

$\therefore \quad \Delta PMB \cong \Delta QNC$ [by SAS congruence rule]

$\Rightarrow \quad PB = QC$ [by CPCT] **Hence proved.**

Try These 9.3

1. In the shown figure, find the shortest distance from the point P on line AB.

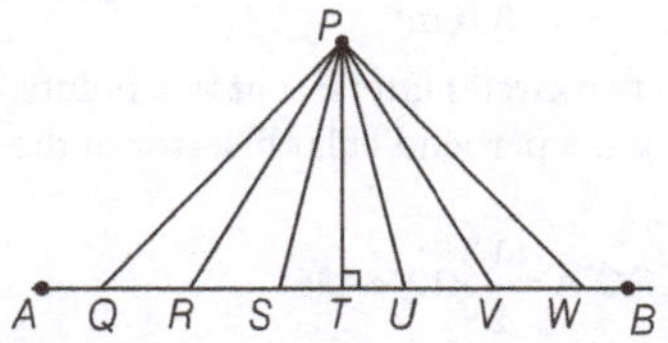

2. What will be the angles subtended by the equal chords at the centre of the same circle?
3. Two circles of radii 13 cm and 5 cm intersect at two points and the distance between their centres is 12 cm. Find the length of common chord.
4. In the shown figure, PQ and RS are two chords of a circle having its centre O. If $PQ = RS$ and $ON = 3$ cm, find OM.

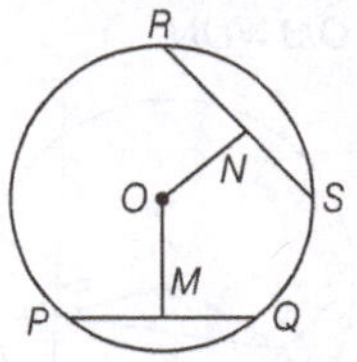

5. AB and CD are equal chords of a circle with centre O. If $OM \perp AB$ and $ON \perp CD$, then prove that $\angle OMN = \angle ONM$.
6. OD is perpendicular on chord AB of the circle with centre O. If BC is a diameter, then prove that $CA = 2OD$.
7. In figure, L and M are mid-points of two equal chords AB and CD of a circle with centre O.

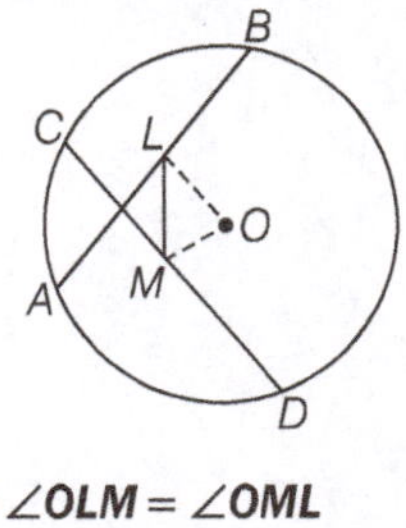

Prove that (i) $\angle OLM = \angle OML$ (ii) $\angle ALM = \angle CML$

Hints & Answers

1. Shortest distance is *PT*.
2. Equal angles will be subtended.
3. **Hint** Here, $AO'^2 + OO'^2 = 5^2 + 12^2$

$$= 25 + 144$$
$$= 169 = OA^2$$

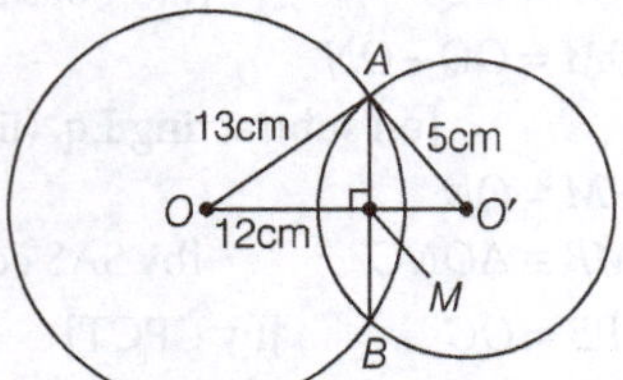

$\therefore$ $OO'A$ is a right angled triangle and right angled at O'.

$\therefore$ Area of $\Delta OO'A = \frac{1}{2} \times 12 \times 5$

$$= 30 \text{ cm}^2$$

Since, when two circles intersect at two points, then their centres lie on the perpendicular bisector of the common chord.

$\therefore$ Area of $\Delta OO'A = \frac{1}{2} \times 12 \times AM$

$\Rightarrow \quad 30 = 6\,AM$

$\Rightarrow \quad AM = 5$ cm

So, $AB = 2AM = 2 \times 5 = 10$ cm

4. **Hint** Since, equal chords of a circle are equidistant.

$\therefore$ $OM = ON = 3$ cm

5. **Hint** Since, two chords are equal, so both are at equidistant from the centre.

$\therefore \quad OM = ON$

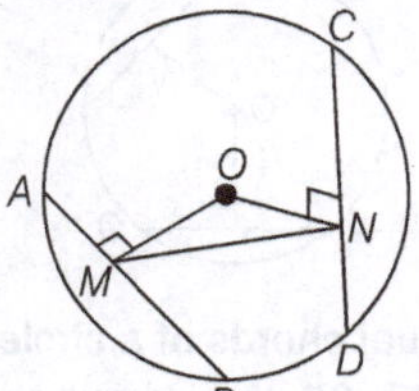

In ΔOMN, $\angle ONM = \angle OMN$

[opposite angles of equal sides are equal]

6.

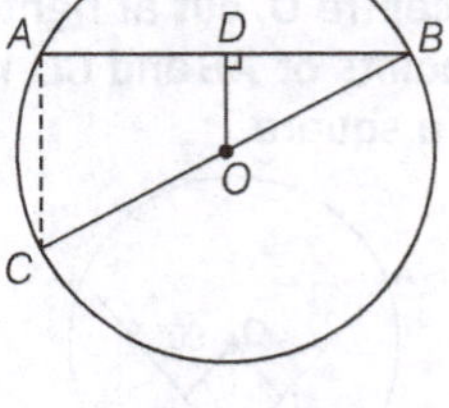

Since, $OD \perp AB$

$\therefore$ D is the mid-point of AB

i.e. $AD = BD$

Also, O is the mid-point of BC

i.e. $OC = OB$

Now, in ΔABC, we have D is the mid-point of AB and O is the mid-point of BC.

$\therefore$ By mid-point theorem, the line segment joining the mid-points of any two sides of a triangle is parallel to the third side and equal to half of it.

i.e. $OD \| AC$ and $OD = \frac{1}{2} AC \Rightarrow AC = 2OD$

7.

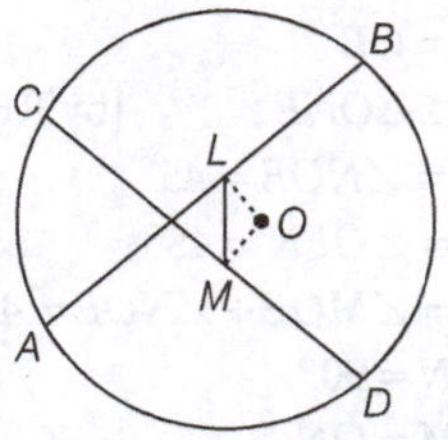

(i) AB and CD are two equal chords of a circle with center O. L is the mid-point of AB and M is the mid-point of CD.

$\therefore \quad OL \perp AB$ and $OM \perp CD$

But since,

Chord AB = Chord $CD \Rightarrow OL = OM$

[$\because$ equal chords are equidistant from the centre]

In ΔOLM,

Since, $\quad OL = OM$

$\therefore \quad \angle OML = \angle OLM \quad$ ...(i)

[angles opposite to equal sides of a triangle are equal]

(ii) But $\angle OLA = \angle OMC \quad$ [each 90°] ...(ii)

On subtracting Eq. (i) from Eq. (ii), we get

$$\angle OLA - \angle OLM = \angle OMC - \angle OML$$

$\Rightarrow \quad \angle MLA = \angle LMC$

TOPIC 04 Angle Subtended by an Arc of a Circle and Cyclic Quadrilaterals

Congruent Arcs of a Circle

Two arcs of a circle or two arcs of congruent circles are congruent if either of them can be superposed on the other completely.

Congruent Arcs Corresponding to Congruent Chords of a Circle

If two chords of a circle are equal, then their corresponding arcs are congruent and conversely if two arcs are congruent, then their corresponding chords are equal.

Angle Subtended by an Arc of a Circle

We know that a chord (other than diameter) of a circle cuts the circle into two different arcs i.e. major arc and minor arc.

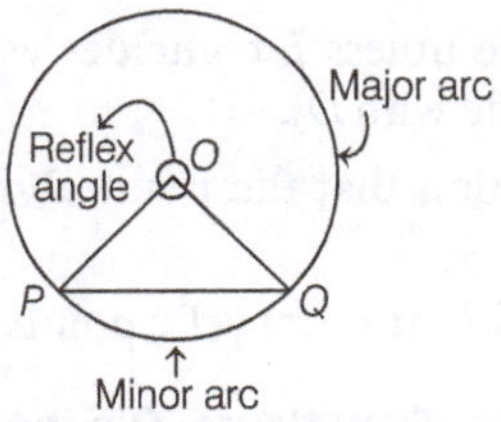

The angle subtended by an arc at the centre is defined as the angle subtended by the corresponding chord at the centre, in the sense that the minor arc subtends the angle and the major arc subtends the reflex angle. In the given figure, the angle subtended by the minor arc PQ at O is $\angle POQ$ and the angle subtended by the major arc PQ at O is reflex $\angle POQ$.

Note it Congruent arcs (or equal arcs) of a circle subtend equal angles at the centre.

Relation between the Angles Subtended by an Arc at the Centre and at a Point on the Circle

Let we have a circle with centre O and AB be its arc. Here, $\angle AOB$ is the angle subtended by an arc AB, (or $\overparen{AB}$) at the centre of the circle.

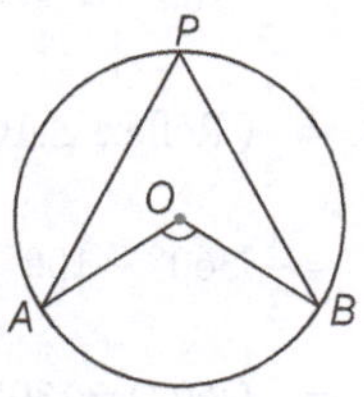

Also, $\angle APB$ is the angle subtended by arc AB ($\overparen{AB}$) at a point P on the remaining part of the circle (i.e. part of the circle, other than $\overparen{AB}$).

Theorem 1 ***The angle subtended by an arc at the centre is double the angle subtended by it at any point on the remaining part of the circle.***

Given A circle with centre O and let PQ be its arc. Arc PQ subtends $\angle POQ$ at the centre and $\angle PAQ$ at any point A on the remaining part of the circle. Here, from figure, we get three cases (i) when arc PQ is minor, (ii) when arc PQ is semi-circle and (iii) when arc PQ is major.

To prove $\angle POQ = 2\angle PAQ$ for cases (i) and (ii) and reflex $\angle POQ = 2\angle PAQ$ for case (iii).

Construction Join AO and extend it to a point B.

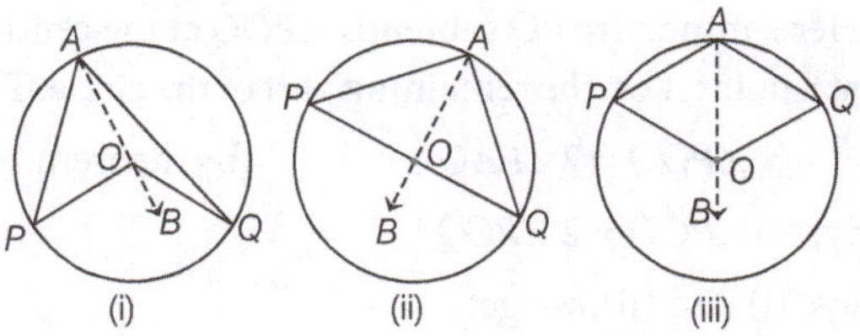

Proof We know that exterior angle of a triangle is equal to the sum of the two interior opposite angles.

So, for ΔOAQ, $\angle BOQ = \angle OAQ + \angle OQA$ ...(i)

and for ΔOAP, $\angle BOP = \angle OAP + \angle OPA$ ...(ii)

Now, in ΔOAQ, $OA = OQ$ [radii of same circle]

$\Rightarrow \angle OQA = \angle OAQ$

[$\because$ angles opposite to equal sides of a triangle are also equal]

Then, from Eq. (i), we get

$$\angle BOQ = \angle OAQ + \angle OAQ$$

$\Rightarrow \angle BOQ = 2\angle OAQ$ ...(iii)

Similarly, in ΔOAP, $\angle OAP = \angle OPA$

Then, from Eq. (ii), we get

$\angle BOP = 2\angle OAP$ ...(iv)

On adding Eqs. (iii) and (iv), we get

$$\angle BOQ + \angle BOP = 2\angle OAQ + 2\angle OAP$$

$\Rightarrow \angle POQ = 2\ [\angle OAQ + \angle OAP]$

$\Rightarrow \angle POQ = 2\angle PAQ$ ...(v)

For cases (i) and (ii), we have this result and for case (iii), replace $\angle POQ$ by reflex $\angle POQ$ in Eq. (v), we get reflex $\angle POQ = 2\angle PAQ$, as PQ is the major arc.

Hence proved.

Theorem 2 ***Angles in the same segment of a circle are equal.***

Given PQ is a chord of a circle with centre O which divides the circle in two segments and $\angle PAQ$ and $\angle PCQ$ are the angles of the same segment.

To prove $\angle PAQ = \angle PCQ$

Construction Join OP and OQ.

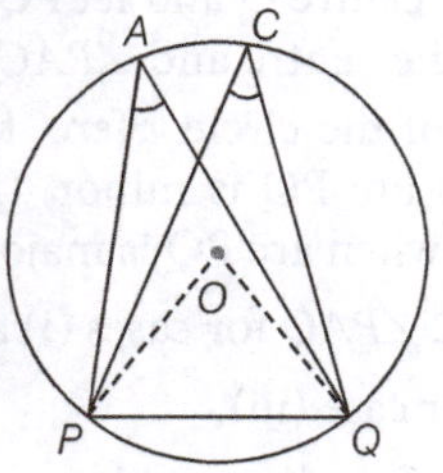

Proof Here, minor arc PQ subtends $\angle POQ$ at the centre and $\angle PAQ$ at a point A on the remaining part of the circle. Then,

$\angle POQ = 2\angle PAQ$ [by theorem 1] ...(i)

Similarly, $\angle POQ = 2\angle PCQ$ ...(ii)

From Eqs. (i) and (ii), we get

$2\angle PAQ = 2\angle PCQ$

$\Rightarrow \angle PAQ = \angle PCQ$ **Hence proved.**

Theorem 3 ***Angle in a semi-circle is a right angle.***

Given PQ is a diameter of a circle with centre O and $\angle PRQ$ be an angle in semi-circle.

To prove $\angle PRQ = 90°$

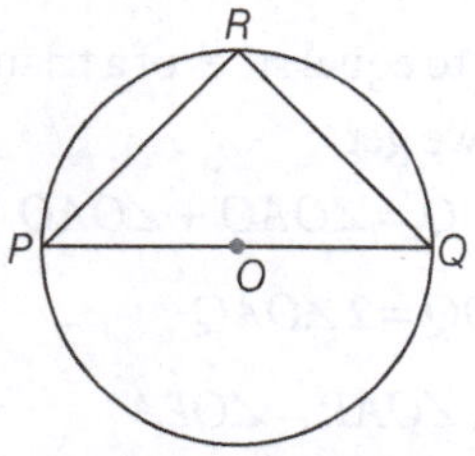

Proof We know that the angle subtended by an arc of a circle at its centre is twice the angle formed by the same arc at a point on the remaining part of circle.

So, $\angle POQ = 2\angle PRQ$

$\Rightarrow 180° = 2\angle PRQ$ [$\because POQ$ is a straight line]

$\Rightarrow \angle PRQ = 90°$ [dividing by 2]

Hence proved.

Theorem 4 ***If a line segment joining two points subtends equal angles at two other points lying on the same side of the line containing the line segment, the four points lie on a circle. (i.e. they are concyclic).***

Given AB is a line segment and C and D are two points lying on the same side of AB such that $\angle ACB = \angle ADB$

To prove Points A, B, C and D lie on a circle, i.e. concyclic.

Construction Draw a circle through the points A, C and B.

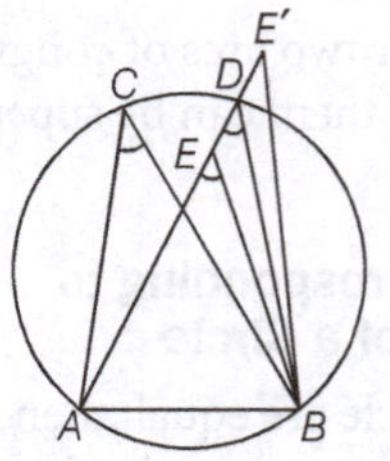

Proof Suppose, circle does not pass through the point D, then it will intersect AD (or extended AD) at a point say E (or E'). Join EB (or $E'B$).

Now, $\angle ACB = \angle AEB$ [angles of the same segment]

But $\angle ACB = \angle ADB$ [given]

$\therefore \angle AEB = \angle ADB$

This is not possible unless E coincides with D (similarly E' should also coincide with D).

Thus, our assumption that the point D does not lie on the circle, was wrong.

Hence, A, B, C and D are concyclic points. **Hence proved.**

Example 1. **In the given figure, O is the centre of the circle and the measure of $\angle AOC$ is $100°$. Determine $\angle ADC$ and $\angle ABC$.**

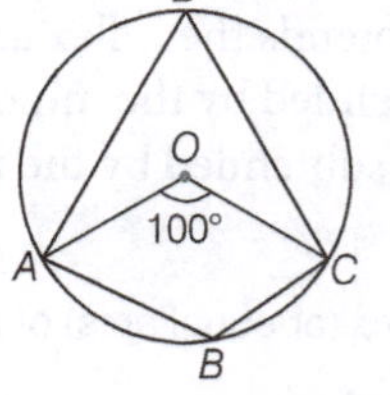

Sol. Given, arc ABC makes $\angle AOC = 100°$ at the centre of the circle and $\angle ADC$ at a point on the remaining part of the circle.

$\therefore \angle ADC = \frac{1}{2}(\angle AOC)$ [by theorem 1]

$= \frac{1}{2}(100°) = 50°$

Similarly, $\angle ABC = \frac{1}{2}(\text{Reflex } \angle AOC)$

$\Rightarrow \angle ABC = \frac{1}{2}(360° - 100°)$

$= \frac{1}{2}(260°) = 130°$

Hence, $\angle ADC = 50°$

and $\angle ABC = 130°$

Example 2. ***AB* is the diameter of the circle with centre *O* and radius *OD* is perpendicular to *AB*. If there is any point *C* on arc *DB*, then find $\angle BAD$ and $\angle ACD$.**

Sol. Given, *AB* is diameter of a circle with centre *O* and $OD \perp AB$.

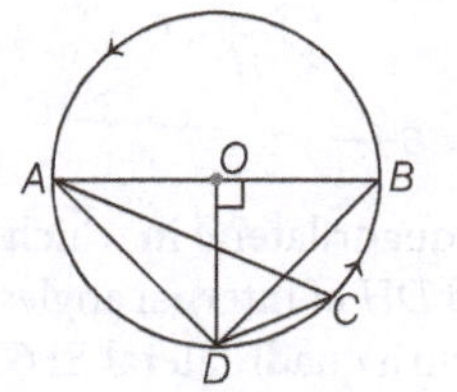

Clearly, $\angle AOD = \angle BOD = 90°$

Now, arc *BD* subtends $\angle BOD$ at the centre and $\angle BAD$ at a point on the remaining part of circle.

So, $\angle BOD = 2\,\angle BAD$ [by theorem 1]

$\Rightarrow \quad \angle BAD = \frac{1}{2}\angle BOD = \frac{1}{2} \times 90° = 45°$

$\Rightarrow \quad \angle BAD = 45°$

Similarly, arc *AD* subtends $\angle AOD$ at the centre and $\angle ACD$ at a point on the remaining part of circle.

So, $\angle AOD = 2\,\angle ACD$

$\Rightarrow \quad \angle ACD = \frac{1}{2}\angle AOD = \frac{1}{2} \times 90° = 45°$

Example 3. **In the adjoining figure, *AB* is a diameter of the circle, *CD* is a chord equal to the radius of the circle. *AC* and *BD* when extended intersect at a point *E*. Find the value of $\angle AEB$.**

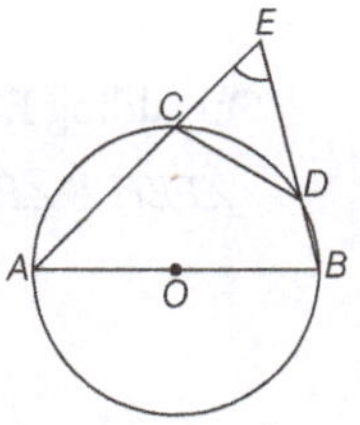

Sol. In the given figure,

Join *OC*, *OD* and *BC*.

Here, $OC = OD = CD = OA = OB$

ΔODC is an equilateral.

Therefore, $\angle COD = 60°$

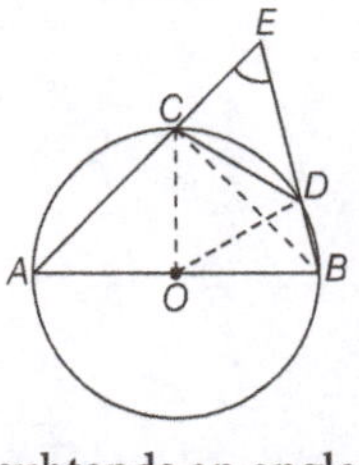

Now, $\angle CBD = \frac{1}{2}\,\angle COD$

[using the theorem, the chord subtends an angle at the centre is twice of the chord subtends at the remaining part of circle]

This gives, $\angle CBD = 30°$

Again, $\angle ACB = 90°$ [by theorem 3]

So, $\angle BCE = 180° - \angle ACB = 90°$

Now, in ΔCBE,

$\angle BCE + \angle CEB + \angle CBE = 180°$

$\Rightarrow \quad 90° + \angle CEB + 30° = 180°$ [$\because \angle CBD = 30°$]

$\Rightarrow \quad \angle CEB = 180° - 120° = 60°$

$\Rightarrow \quad \angle AEB = 60°$

Cyclic Quadrilaterals

A quadrilateral *ABCD* is called a cyclic quadrilateral if all the four vertices *A*, *B*, *C* and *D* are concyclic i.e. *A*, *B*, *C* and *D* lie on a circle. In figure, *ABCD* is a cyclic quadrilateral.

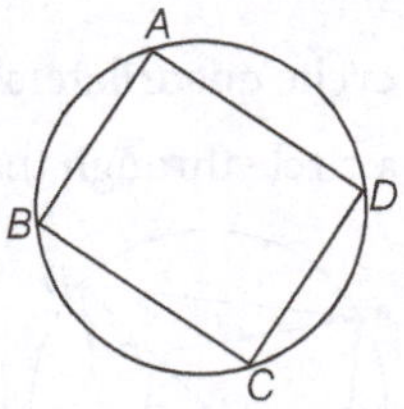

Theorem 5 ***The sum of either pair of opposite angles of a cyclic quadrilateral is 180°.***

Given A cyclic quadrilateral *ABCD* inscribed in a circle with centre *O*.

To prove $\angle A + \angle C = \angle B + \angle D = 180°$

Construction Join *OB* and *OD*.

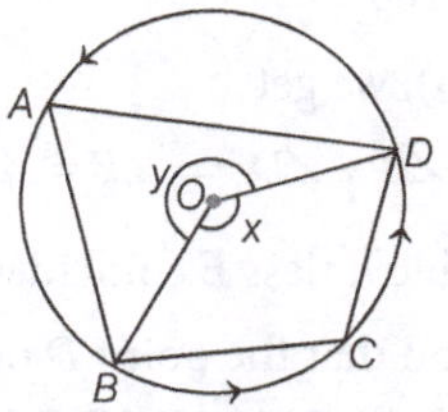

Proof Here, arc BCD subtends $\angle BOD$ at the centre and $\angle BAD$ at a point on the remaining part of circle.

Let $\angle BOD = x$

Then, $\angle A = \angle BAD = \frac{1}{2}x$ [by theorem 1] ...(i)

Similarly, $\angle C = \angle BCD = \frac{1}{2}y$ [by theorem 1]

[say reflex $\angle BOD = y$] ...(ii)

On adding Eqs. (i) and (ii), we get

$\angle A + \angle C = \frac{1}{2}x + \frac{1}{2}y = \frac{1}{2}(x + y)$

$= \frac{1}{2} \times 360° = 180°$

and $\angle B + \angle D = 360° - (\angle A + \angle C)$

[$\because$ sum of angles of a quadrilateral is 360°]

$= 360° - 180° = 180°$

Hence, $\angle A + \angle C = \angle B + \angle D = 180°$ **Hence proved.**

Theorem 6 ***If the sum of a pair of opposite angles of a quadrilateral is 180°, then quadrilateral is cyclic.***

Given A quadrilateral $ABCD$ in which

$$\angle A + \angle C = 180° \text{ or } \angle B + \angle D = 180°$$

To prove $ABCD$ is a cyclic quadrilateral.

Construction Draw a circle through the points A, B and C.

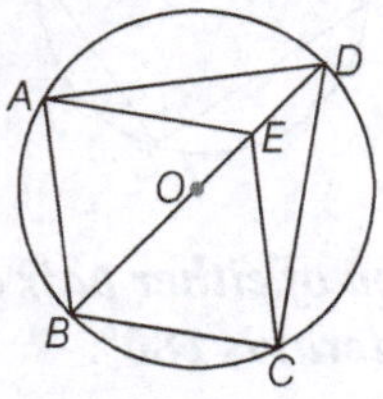

Proof Suppose, circle does not pass through the point D, then it will intersect BD at point E (or extended BD at E). Join EC and AE. Then, $ABCE$ is a cyclic quadrilateral.

$\therefore \quad \angle B + \angle E = 180° \quad$ ...(i)

Also, $\quad \angle B + \angle D = 180° \quad$ [given] ...(ii)

From Eqs. (i) and (ii), we get

$$\angle B + \angle E = \angle B + \angle D \Rightarrow \angle E = \angle D$$

But this is not possible unless E coincides with D.

Thus, our assumption that the point D does not lie on the circle, was wrong. So, point D lies on the circle.

Hence, $ABCD$ is a cyclic quadrilateral. **Hence proved.**

Example 4. **In the adjoining figure, if $\angle DBC = 80°$ and $\angle BAC = 40°$, then find $\angle BCD$. Further, if $AB = BC$, then find $\angle ECD$.**

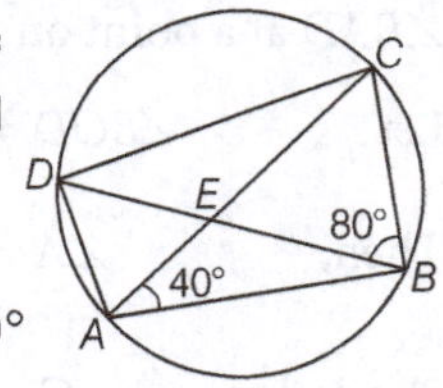

Sol. Given, $\angle DBC = 80°$ and $\angle BAC = 40°$

Consider, the chord CD, we find that $\angle CBD$ and $\angle CAD$ are angles in the same segment of the circle.

$\therefore \quad \angle CBD = \angle CAD \Rightarrow 80° = \angle CAD \Rightarrow \angle CAD = 80°$

Now, $\angle BAD = \angle BAC + \angle CAD$

$\Rightarrow \quad \angle BAD = 40° + 80° = 120° \quad$ ...(i)

Since, $ABCD$ is a cyclic quadrilateral.

$\therefore \quad \angle BAD + \angle BCD = 180°$

$\Rightarrow \quad 120° + \angle BCD = 180° \quad$ [using Eq. (i)]

$\Rightarrow \quad \angle BCD = 60°$

If $AB = BC$, then in ΔABC, we have

$$\angle ACB = \angle BAC$$

[$\because$ angles opposite to equal sides of a triangle are equal]

$\Rightarrow \quad \angle ACB = 40° \quad$ [$\because \angle BAC = 40°$]

$\therefore \quad \angle ECD = \angle BCD - \angle ACB = 60° - 40° = 20°$

Example 5. **Prove that the quadrilateral formed (if possible) by the internal angle bisectors of any quadrilateral is cyclic.**

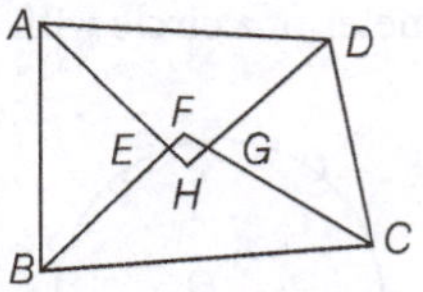

Sol. Let $ABCD$ be a quadrilateral in which the angle bisectors AH, BF, CF and DH of internal angles A, B, C and D respectively form a quadrilateral $EFGH$.

To prove $EFGH$ is a cyclic quadrilateral.

i.e. $\quad \angle E + \angle G = 180°$

or $\quad \angle F + \angle H = 180°$

Proof Since, $\angle FEH = \angle AEB = 180° - \angle EAB - \angle EBA$

[$\because$ in ΔAEB, $\angle EAB + \angle EBA + \angle AEB = 180°$]

$$= 180° - \frac{1}{2}(2\angle EAB + 2\angle EBA)$$

$$= 180° - \frac{1}{2}(\angle A + \angle B) \quad \text{...(i)}$$

[$\because$ AH and BF are bisectors of $\angle A$ and $\angle B$ respectively]

Similarly, $\angle FGH = \angle CGD = 180° - \angle GCD - \angle GDC$

$$= 180° - \frac{1}{2}(\angle C + \angle D) \quad \text{...(ii)}$$

On adding Eqs. (i) and (ii), we get

$$\angle FEH + \angle FGH = 180° - \frac{1}{2}(\angle A + \angle B) + 180° - \frac{1}{2}(\angle C + \angle D)$$

$$= 360° - \frac{1}{2}(\angle A + \angle B + \angle C + \angle D)$$

$$= 360° - \frac{1}{2} \times 360°$$

[$\because$ sum of angles of a quadrilateral is 360°]

$$= 360° - 180°$$

$$= 180°$$

Therefore, by theorem 6, the quadrilateral $EFGH$ is cyclic.

Hence proved.

Try These 9.4

1. **If $\angle AOB = 100°$ in the given figure, find the value of $\angle APB$.**

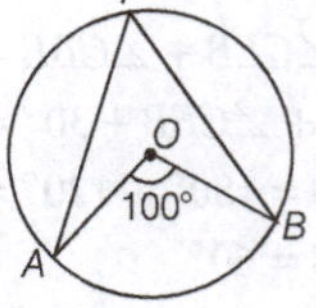

2. In the given figure, $\angle ABC = 125°$, where A, B and C are points on a circle with centre O. Find $\angle OAC$.

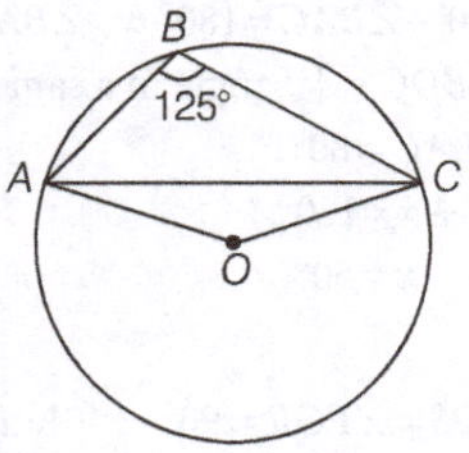

3. In the given figure, O is the centre of the circle with chords AP and BP being produced to R and Q, respectively. If $\angle QPR = 35°$, then find the measure of $\angle AOB$.

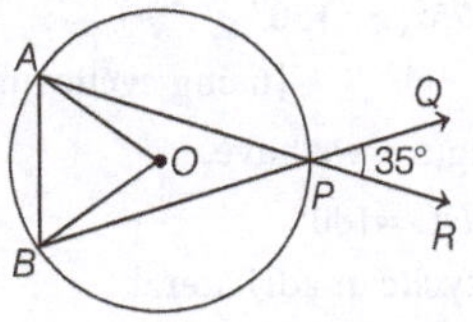

4. In the given figure, O is the centre of the circle and $BA = AC$. If $\angle ABC = 50°$, then find $\angle BOC$ and $\angle BDC$.

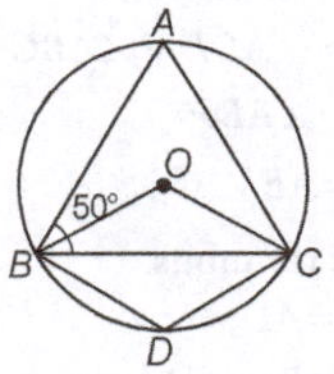

5. In the given figure, AB and CD are two chords of a circle intersecting each other at point E. Prove that

$\angle AEC = \frac{1}{2} \times$ (Angle subtended by arc CXA at the centre + Angle subtended by arc DYB at the centre)

NCERT Exemplar

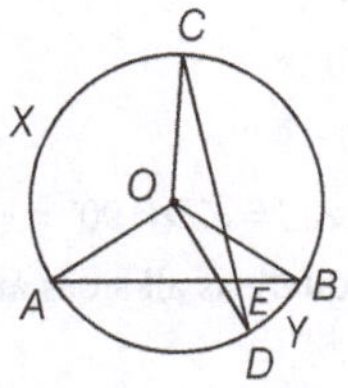

6. In the given figure, $\angle ACB = 70°$, then find $\angle ADB$.

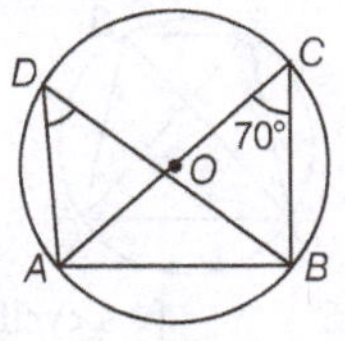

7. In the given figure, ΔABC is a triangle inscribed in a circle with centre O, such that $AB = AC$ and $\angle BEC = 100°$. Find the values of x and y.

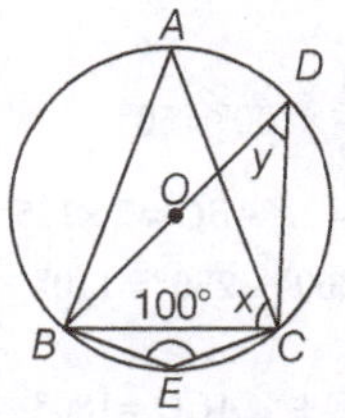

8. Two circles intersect at two points P and Q. PS and PR are diameters to the two circles (see figure). Prove that Q lies on the line segment SR.

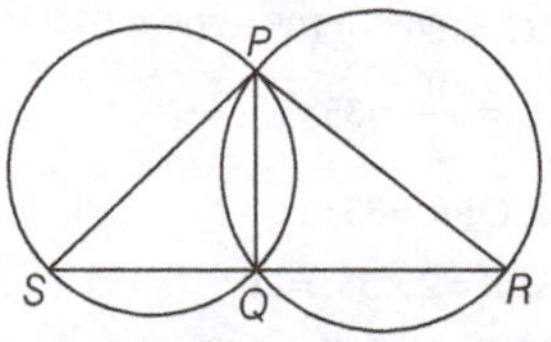

9. In the given figure, find the value of $\angle APB$.

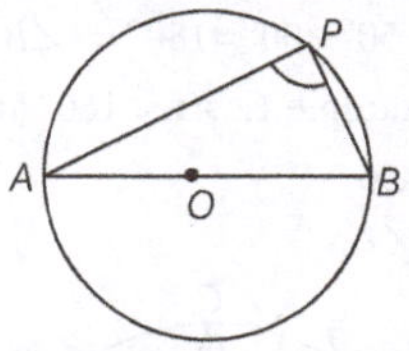

10. In the given figure, P and Q are centres of the two circles intersect at B and C. ACD is a straight line. Find the values of x, y and z.

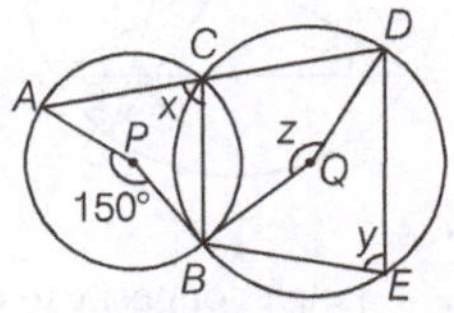

11. In the given figure, find the value of $x + y$.

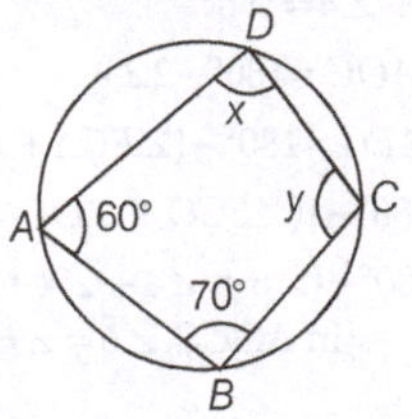

12. In the given figure, $ABCD$ is a parallelogram. A circle through A, B and C intersects CD produced at E. Prove that $AD = AE$.

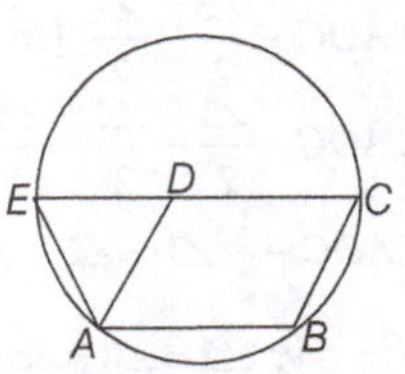

13. Prove that a cyclic rhombus is a square.

14. Prove that the diagonals of a cyclic trapezium are equal.

Hints & Answers

1. $\angle APB = \frac{1}{2}\angle AOB = \frac{1}{2}\times 100° = 50°$

2. **Hint** Reflex $\angle AOC = 2\angle ABC = 2\times 125° = 250°$

In ΔAOC, $\angle AOC = 360° - 250° = 110°$

In ΔAOC, we have

$\angle OAC + \angle AOC + \angle ACO = 180°$

$\because \quad \angle OAC = \angle ACO$

[angles opposite to the equal sides of triangle are equal]

$\therefore \quad \angle OAC + 110° + \angle OAC = 180°$

$\Rightarrow \quad 2\angle OAC = 180° - 110° = 70°$

$\Rightarrow \quad \angle OAC = \frac{70°}{2} = 35°$

3. Here, $\angle APB = \angle QPR = 35°$

$\therefore \angle AOB = 2\angle APB = 2\times 35° = 70°$

4. **Hint** Here, $\angle ABC = \angle ACB = 50°$

$\therefore \angle BAC + \angle ABC + \angle ACB = 180°$

$\Rightarrow \quad \angle BAC + 50° + 50° = 180° \Rightarrow \angle BAC = 80°$

Further solve as Example 1. **Ans.** 160° and 100°

5. **Hint** Here, $\angle 1 = 2\angle 6$ ...(i)

and $\angle 3 = 2\angle 7$ ...(ii)

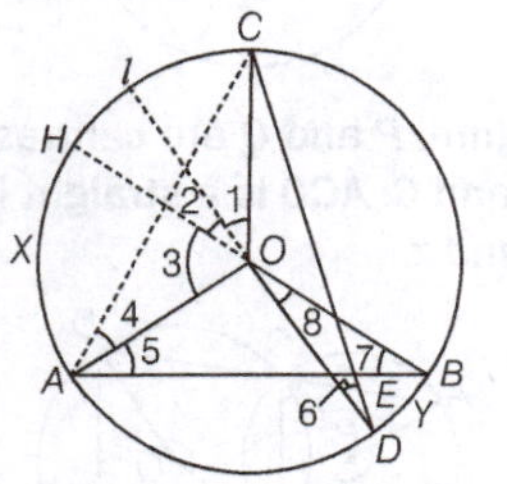

In ΔAOC, $OC = OA$ [radii of circle]

and $\angle OCA = \angle 4$ [angles opposite to equal sides are equal]

In ΔAOC, $\angle AOC + \angle OCA + \angle OAC = 180°$

$\Rightarrow \quad \angle AOC + \angle 4 + \angle 4 = 180°$

$\Rightarrow \quad \angle AOC = 180° - 2\angle 4$ ...(iii)

Now, in ΔAEC, $\angle AEC = 180° - (\angle ECA + \angle CAE)$

$\Rightarrow \quad \angle AEC = 180° - [(\angle ECO + \angle OCA) + \angle CAO + OAE]$

$= 180° - (\angle 6 + \angle 4 + \angle 4 + \angle 5)$

[in ΔOCD, $\angle 6 = \angle ECO$, angles opposite to equal sides are equal]

$= 180° - (2\angle 4 + \angle 5 + \angle 6)$

$= 180° - (180° - \angle AOC + \angle 7 + \angle 6)$

[from Eq. (iii) and in ΔAOB, $\angle 5 = \angle 7$]

$= \angle AOC - \frac{\angle 3}{2} - \frac{\angle 1}{2}$ [from Eqs. (i) and (ii)]

$= \angle AOC - \frac{\angle 1}{2} - \frac{\angle 2}{2} - \frac{\angle 3}{2} + \frac{\angle 2}{2}$

$= \angle AOC - \frac{1}{2}(\angle 1 + \angle 2 + \angle 3) + \frac{\angle 8}{2}$

[$\because \angle 2 = \angle 8$ (vertically opposite angles)]

$= \angle AOC - \frac{\angle AOC}{2} + \frac{\angle DOB}{2}$

$\Rightarrow \quad \angle AEC = \frac{1}{2}(\angle AOC + \angle DOB)$

6. $\angle ADB = \angle ACB = 70°$

7. **Hint** Here, $\angle BEC + \angle BAC = 180°$

$\Rightarrow \quad 100° + \angle BAC = 180° \Rightarrow \angle BAC = 80°$

Also, $\angle BAC = \angle BDC$ [$\because$ angle in a same segment of a circle]

$\therefore \quad y = \angle BAC = 80°$

In ΔABC, $80° + x + x = 180°$ [$\because AB = AC$]

$\Rightarrow \quad x = 50°$

8. **Hint** Join PQ.

$\angle PQS = \angle PQR = 90°$ [angles in a semi-circle]

So, $\angle PQS + \angle PQR = 90° + 90° = 180°$

$\therefore$ SQR is a line. Thus, Q lies on the line segment SR.

9. **Hint** $\angle APB = 90°$ [$\because$ angle in a semi-circle is right angle]

Ans. 90°

10. **Ans.** $x = 75°, y = 75°, z = 150°$

11. $x + y = 230°$ [using cyclic quadrilateral property]

12. **Hint** From the figure, we have

$\angle ADE + \angle ADC = 180°$ ... (i) [linear pair]

Also, $ABCE$ is a cyclic quadrilateral.

So, $\angle AED + \angle ABC = 180°$ ... (ii)

and $\angle ADC = \angle ABC$ ... (iii)

From Eqs. (i), (ii) and (iii), we get

$\angle AED + \angle ABC = \angle ADE + \angle ABC$

$\Rightarrow \quad \angle AED = \angle ADE$

$\therefore \quad AD = AE$

13. Let $ABCD$ be a cyclic rhombus.

$\therefore \quad AB = BC = CD = AD$

Also, $\angle A = \angle C$ and $\angle B = \angle D$

...(i) [$\because$ opposite angles of rhombus are equal]

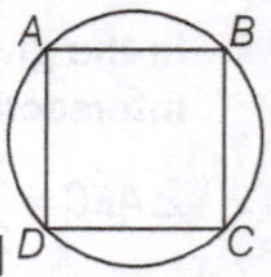

Now, $\angle A + \angle C = 180°$

[sum of opposite angles of cyclic quadrilateral is 180°]

$\Rightarrow \quad \angle A + \angle A = 180°$ [from Eq. (i)]

$\Rightarrow \quad \angle A = 90°$

$\therefore \quad \angle C = 90°$

Similarly, $\angle B = \angle D = 90°$

Hence, $\angle A = \angle B = \angle C = \angle D = 90°$

Hence, $ABCD$ is a square as all sides are equal and all the angles are equal to 90°.

14. **Hint** AC and BD are diagonals.

In ΔABD and ΔABC,

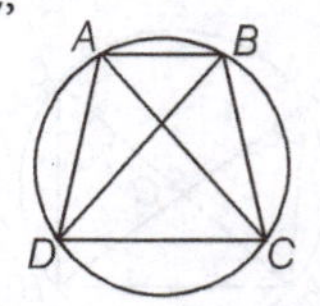

$AD = BC$ [$\because$ a cyclic trapezium is isosceles]

$AB = AB$ [common]

$\angle DAC = \angle DBC$ [angles in the same segment]

$\therefore \quad \Delta ABD \cong \Delta ABC$ [by SAS congruence rule]

Thus, $AC = BD$ [by CPCT]

NCERT FOLDER

Complete Solutions of All Exercises of NCERT Textbook

EXERCISE 9.1 (NCERT Page 118)

Q1. Recall that two circles are congruent if they have the same radii. Prove that equal chords of congruent circles subtend equal angles at their centres.

Sol. Let MN and PQ are two equal chords of two congruent circles with centres O and O' respectively i.e. $MN = PQ$.

To prove $\angle MON = \angle PO'Q$

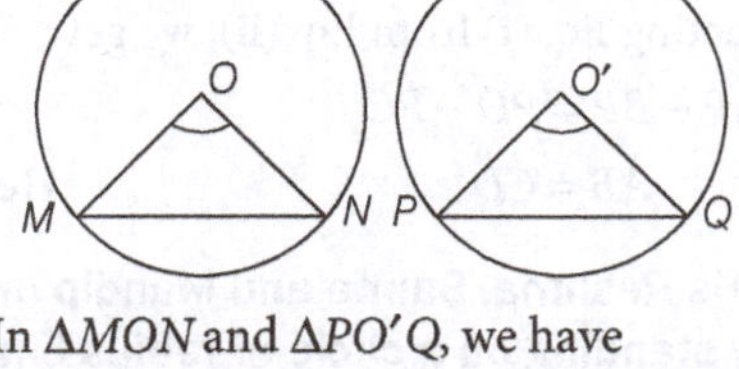

Proof In ΔMON and $\Delta PO'Q$, we have

$MO = PO'$ [radii of congruent circles]

$NO = QO'$ [radii of congruent circles]

and $MN = PQ$ [given]

$\therefore$ $\Delta MON \cong \Delta PO'Q$ [by SSS congruence rule]

So, $\angle MON = \angle PO'Q$ [by CPCT]

Hence, equal chords of congruent circles subtend equal angles at their centres. **Hence proved.**

Q2. Prove that if chords of congruent circles subtend equal angles at their centres, then the chords are equal.

Sol. Let MN and PQ be two chords of congruent circles such that angles subtended by these chords at the centres O and O' of the circles are equal i.e. $\angle MON = \angle PO'Q$.

To prove $MN = PQ$

Proof In ΔMON and $\Delta PO'Q$, we have

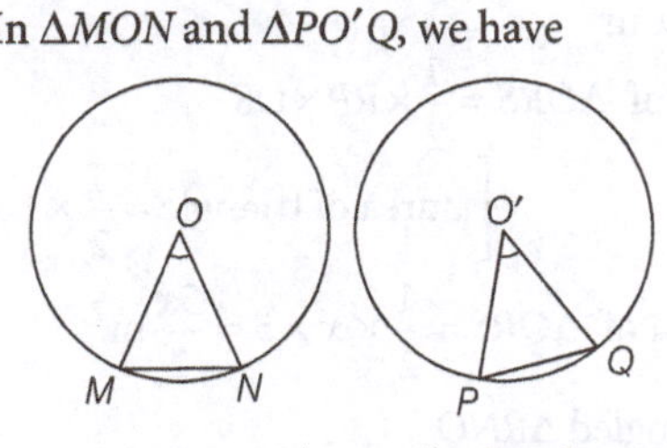

$MO = PO'$ [radii of congruent circles]

$\angle MON = \angle PO'Q$ [given]

and $NO = QO'$ [radii of congruent circles]

$\therefore$ $\Delta MON \cong \Delta PO'Q$ [by SAS congruence rule]

So, $MN = PQ$ [by CPCT]

Hence, chords are equal if they subtend equal angles at their centres. **Hence proved.**

EXERCISE 9.2 (NCERT Page 122)

Q1. Two circles of radii 5 cm and 3 cm intersect at two points and the distance between their centres is 4 cm. Find the length of the common chord.

Sol. Let O and O' be the centres of the circles of radii 5 cm and 3 cm, respectively. Let AB be their common chord.

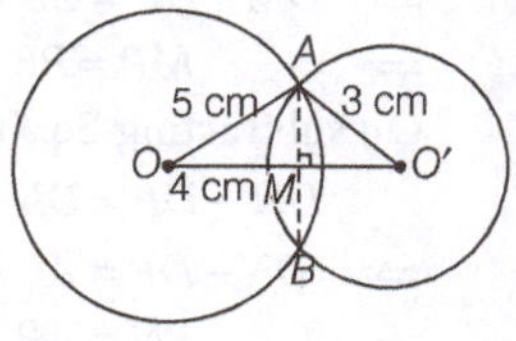

Given, $OA = 5$ cm, $O'A = 3$ cm and $OO' = 4$ cm

Then, $AO'^2 + OO'^2 = 3^2 + 4^2 = 9 + 16 = 25 = OA^2$

So, $\Delta OO'A$ is a right angled triangle and right angled at O'.

$\therefore$ Area of $\Delta OO'A = \frac{1}{2} \times O'A \times OO'$

$= \frac{1}{2} \times 3 \times 4 = 6 \text{ cm}^2$ ...(i)

Also, we know that when two circles intersect at two points, then their centres lie on the perpendicular bisector of the common chord.

$\therefore$ Area of $\Delta OO'A = \frac{1}{2} \times OO' \times AM$

$= \frac{1}{2} \times 4 \times AM = 2\,AM$ ...(ii)

From Eqs. (i) and (ii), we get

$2AM = 6 \Rightarrow AM = 3$ cm

$\therefore$ $AB = 2 \times AM = 2 \times 3 = 6$ cm

Q2. If two equal chords of a circle intersect within the circle, then prove that the segments of one chord are equal to corresponding segments of the other chord.

Sol. Let MN and AB be two chords of a circle with centre O. AB and MN intersect at P and $MN = AB$.

To prove $MP = PB$

and $PN = AP$

Construction Draw $OD \perp MN$ and $OC \perp AB$. Join OP.

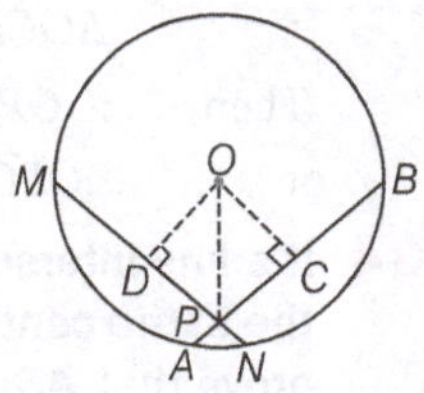

Proof Here, $DM = DN = \frac{1}{2} MN$

[$\because$ perpendicular from centre on the chord bisects the chord]

and $AC = CB = \frac{1}{2} AB$

[$\because$ perpendicular from centre on the chord bisects the chord]

Since, $MN = AB$, so we get

$$DM = CB = DN = AC \quad \ldots(i)$$

In right angled ΔODP and ΔOCP,

$OD = OC$ [$\because$ equal chords of a circle are equidistant from the centre]

$\angle ODP = \angle OCP$ [each 90°]

$OP = OP$ [common sides]

$\therefore \quad \Delta ODP \cong \Delta OCP$ [by RHS congruence rule]

Then, $\quad DP = PC$ [by CPCT] $\ldots$(ii)

On adding DM both sides, we get

$$DM + DP = DM + PC$$

$\Rightarrow \quad DM + DP = CB + PC$ [from Eq. (i)]

$\Rightarrow \quad MP = PB$

On subtracting Eq. (ii) from DN, we get

$$DN - DP = DN - PC$$

$\Rightarrow \quad DN - DP = AC - PC$ [from Eq. (i)]

$\Rightarrow \quad PN = AP$

Hence, $MP = PB$ and $PN = AP$ **Hence proved.**

Q3. If two equal chords of a circle intersect within the circle, then prove that the line joining the point of intersection to the centre makes equal angles with the chords.

Sol. Let RQ and MN be two equal chords of a circle with centre O. MN and RQ intersect at P and $MN = RQ$.

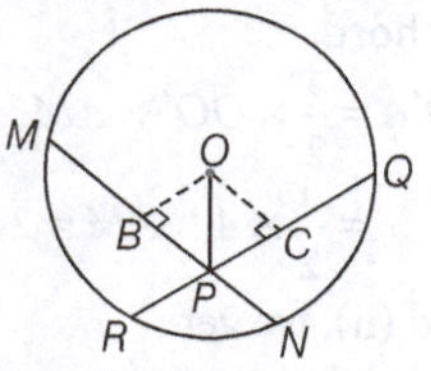

To prove $\angle OPM = \angle OPQ$

Construction Draw $OC \perp RQ$ and $OB \perp MN$. Join OP.

Proof In right angled ΔOCP and ΔOBP, we have

$\angle OCP = \angle OBP$ [each 90°]

$OP = OP$ [common sides]

$OC = OB$

[$\because$ equal chords of a circle are equidistant from the centre]

$\therefore \quad \Delta OCP \cong \Delta OBP$ [by RHS congruence rule]

Then, $\quad \angle OPC = \angle OPB$ [by CPCT]

or $\quad \angle OPQ = \angle OPM$ **Hence proved.**

Q4. If a line intersects two concentric circles (circles with the same centre) with centre O at A, B, C and D, then prove that $AB = CD$ (see figure).

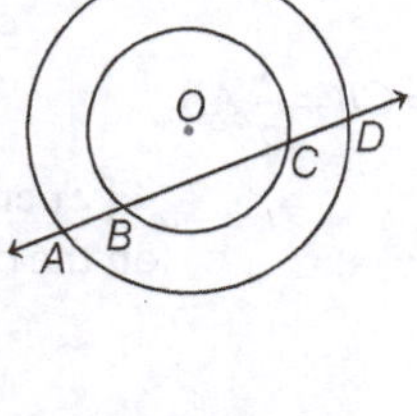

Sol. Let a line l intersects two concentric circles with centre O at A, B, C and D.

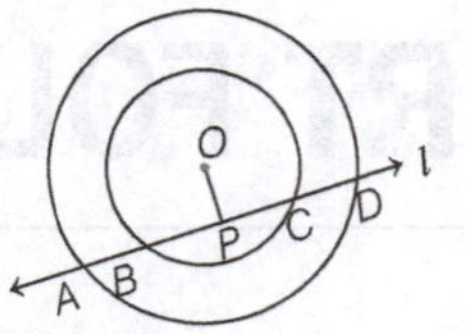

To prove $AB = CD$

Construction Draw OP perpendicular from O on line l.

Proof We know that the perpendicular drawn from the centre of a circle to a chord bisects the chord. Here, BC is the chord of the smaller circle and $OP \perp BC$.

$\therefore \quad BP = PC \quad \ldots$(i)

and AD is a chord of the larger circle and $OP \perp AD$.

$\therefore \quad AP = PD \quad \ldots$(ii)

On subtracting Eq. (i) from Eq. (ii), we get

$$AP - BP = PD - PC$$

$\Rightarrow \quad AB = CD$ **Hence proved.**

Q5. Three girls Reshma, Salma and Mandip are playing a game by standing on a circle of radius 5 m drawn in a park. Reshma throws a ball to Salma, Salma to Mandip, Mandip to Reshma. If the distance between Reshma and Salma and between Salma and Mandip is 6 m each, then what is the distance between Reshma and Mandip?

Sol. Let O be the centre of the circle and Reshma, Salma and Mandip are represented by the points R, S and M, respectively. Draw $OP \perp RM$ and $ON \perp RS$.

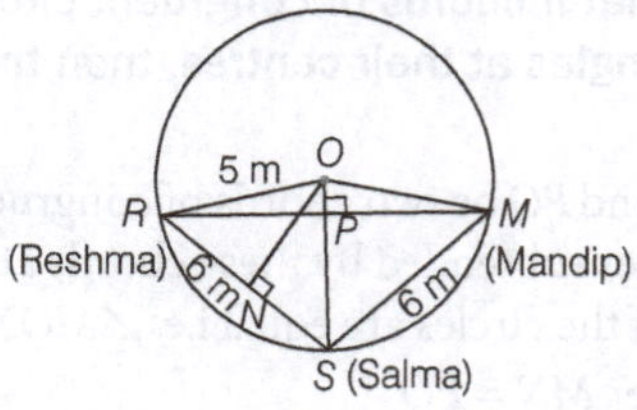

Let $RP = x$ m

$\therefore \quad$ Area of $\Delta ORS = \frac{1}{2} \times RP \times OS$

$\left[\because \text{area of triangle} = \frac{1}{2} \times \text{base} \times \text{height}\right]$

$\Rightarrow \quad$ Area of $\Delta ORS = \frac{1}{2} \times x \times 5 = \frac{5x}{2} \text{m}^2 \quad \ldots$(i)

In right angled ΔRNO,

$OR^2 = RN^2 + NO^2$ [by Pythagoras theorem]

$\Rightarrow \quad 5^2 = 3^2 + NO^2$

$\left[\because ON \perp RS, \text{ therefore } RN = SN = \frac{6}{2} = 3 \text{ m}\right]$

$\Rightarrow \quad NO^2 = 25 - 9 = 16$

$\Rightarrow \quad NO = 4$ m [on taking positive square root]

Again, area of $\Delta ORS = \frac{1}{2} \times RS \times ON$

$$= \frac{1}{2} \times 6 \times 4 = 12\,m^2 \quad \text{...(ii)}$$

From Eqs. (i) and (ii), we get

$$\frac{5x}{2} = 12 \Rightarrow x = \frac{24}{5} = RP$$

Here, P is the mid-point of RM.

[∵ perpendicular from centre to the chord, bisects the chord]

$\therefore \quad RM = 2RP = 2 \times \frac{24}{5} = \frac{48}{5} = 9.6$ m

Hence, the distance between Reshma and Mandip is 9.6 m.

Q6. A circular park of radius 20 m is situated in a colony. Three boys Ankur, Syed and David are sitting at equal distance on its boundary each having a toy telephone in his hand to talk each other. Find the length of the string of each phone.

Sol. Let Ankur, Syed and David be sitting on the points P, Q and R, respectively on the boundary of circular park.

Clearly, $PQ = QR = PR$, as they sitting at equal distance. Thus, ΔPQR is an equilateral triangle.

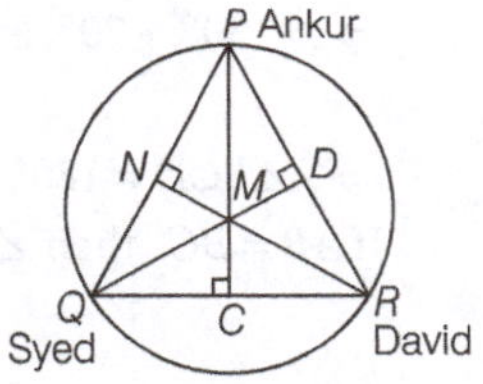

Let $PQ = QR = PR = x$ m

Now, draw altitudes PC, QD and RN from vertices to the sides of a triangle and these altitudes intersect at the centre of circle M.

[∵ altitudes of an equilateral triangle passes through the circumcentre of the equilateral triangle.]

As ΔPQR is an equilateral triangle, therefore these altitudes bisect their sides.

In right angled ΔPCQ, $PQ^2 = PC^2 + QC^2$

[by Pythagoras theorem]

$$\Rightarrow \quad x^2 = PC^2 + \left(\frac{x}{2}\right)^2 \quad \left[\because QC = \frac{1}{2}QR = \frac{x}{2}\right]$$

$$\Rightarrow \quad PC^2 = x^2 - \frac{x^2}{4} = \frac{3x^2}{4}$$

$$\therefore \quad PC = \frac{\sqrt{3}x}{2} \quad \text{[taking positive square root]}$$

Now, $\quad MC = PC - PM = \frac{\sqrt{3}x}{2} - 20$

[∵ PM = radius = 20 m]

In right angled ΔQCM, $QM^2 = QC^2 + MC^2$

[by Pythagoras theorem]

$$\Rightarrow \quad (20)^2 = \left(\frac{x}{2}\right)^2 + \left(\frac{\sqrt{3}x}{2} - 20\right)^2$$

[∵ QM = radius = 20 m]

$$\Rightarrow \quad 400 = \frac{x^2}{4} + \frac{3x^2}{4} - 20\sqrt{3}x + 400$$

$$\Rightarrow \quad x^2 - 20\sqrt{3}x = 0 \Rightarrow x(x - 20\sqrt{3}) = 0$$

$$\Rightarrow \quad x = 0 \text{ or } x - 20\sqrt{3} = 0 \Rightarrow x = 0 \text{ or } x = 20\sqrt{3}$$

But $x = 0$ is not possible because length of side of an equilateral triangle cannot be zero.

$\therefore \quad x = 20\sqrt{3}$ m

Thus, $PQ = QR = PR = 20\sqrt{3}$ m

Hence, the length of the string of each phone is $20\sqrt{3}$ m.

EXERCISE 9.3 (NCERT Page 127-129)

Q1. In figure, A, B and C are three points on a circle with centre O such that $\angle BOC = 30°$ and $\angle AOB = 60°$. If D is a point on the circle other than the arc ABC, then find $\angle ADC$.

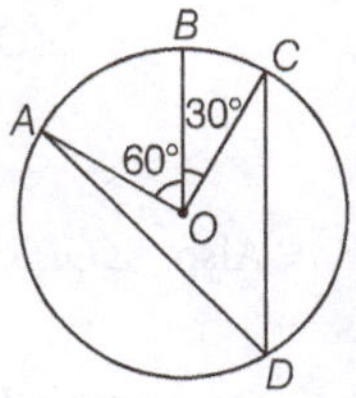

Sol. Here,

$\angle AOC = \angle AOB + \angle BOC = 60° + 30° = 90°$

Since, arc ABC makes an angle of 90° at the centre of the circle.

$$\therefore \quad \angle ADC = \frac{1}{2}\angle AOC$$

[∵ the angle subtended by an arc at the centre is double the angle subtended by it at any point on the remaining part of the circle]

$$= \frac{1}{2} \times 90° = 45°$$

Q2. A chord of a circle is equal to the radius of the circle. Find the angle subtended by the chord at a point on the minor arc and also at a point on the major arc.

Sol. Let BC be a chord, which is equal to the radius.

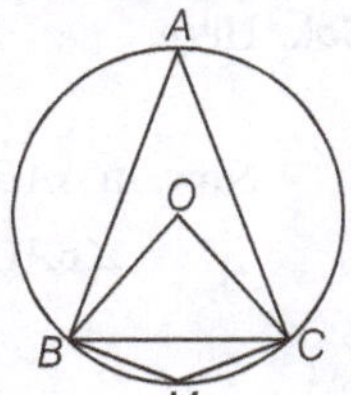

Join OB and OC.

Given, $BC = OB = OC$ [same radii]

So, ΔOBC is an equilateral triangle.

$\therefore \quad \angle BOC = 60°$

Then, $\angle BAC = \frac{1}{2}\angle BOC$

$$= \frac{1}{2} \times 60° = 30°$$

[∵ the angle subtended by an arc at the centre is double the angle subtended by it at any point on the remaining part of the circle]

Here, $ABMC$ is a cyclic quadrilateral.

$\therefore \quad \angle BAC + \angle BMC = 180°$

[∵ in a cyclic quadrilateral, the sum of any pair of opposite angles is 180°]

$\Rightarrow \quad \angle BMC = 180° - 30° = 150°$

Q3. In figure, $\angle PQR = 100°$, where P, Q and R are points on a circle with centre O. Find $\angle OPR$.

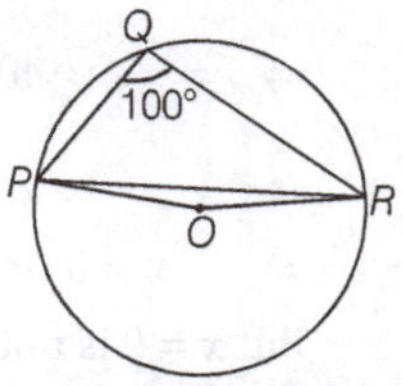

Sol. Here, reflex $\angle POR = 2\angle PQR$

$$= 2 \times 100° = 200°$$

[∵ the angle subtended by an arc at the centre is double the angle subtended by it at any point on the remaining part of the circle]

In ΔOPR, $\angle POR = 360° - 200° = 160°$ ...(i)

Again, in ΔOPR,

$OP = OR$ [radii of the same circle]

∴ $\angle ORP = \angle OPR$ ...(ii)

[∵ angles opposite to equal sides of a triangle are also equal]

Also, $\angle OPR + \angle ORP + \angle POR = 180°$

[by angle sum property of triangle]

On putting the values from Eqs. (i) and (ii), we get

$$\angle OPR + \angle OPR + 160° = 180°$$

$$\Rightarrow \quad 2\angle OPR = 180° - 160° = 20°$$

$$\Rightarrow \quad \angle OPR = \frac{20°}{2} = 10°$$

Q4. In figure, $\angle ABC = 69°$ and $\angle ACB = 31°$. Find $\angle BDC$.

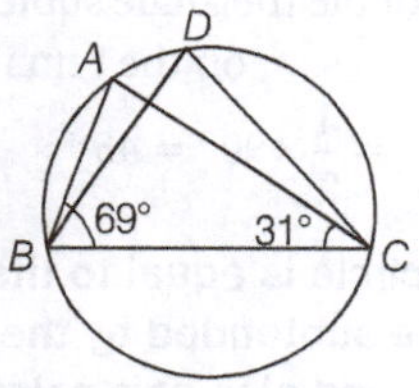

Sol. Here, $\angle BDC = \angle BAC$ ...(i)

[∵ the angles in the same segment are equal]

Now, in ΔABC, we have

$$\angle BAC + \angle ABC + \angle ACB = 180°$$

[angle sum property of triangle]

$$\Rightarrow \quad \angle BAC + 69° + 31° = 180°$$

$$\Rightarrow \quad \angle BAC + 100° = 180°$$

$$\Rightarrow \quad \angle BAC = 180° - 100°$$

$$\Rightarrow \quad \angle BAC = 80°$$

From Eq. (i), $\angle BDC = 80°$

Q5. In figure, A, B, C and D are four points on a circle. AC and BD intersect at a point E such that $\angle BEC = 130°$ and $\angle ECD = 20°$. Find $\angle BAC$.

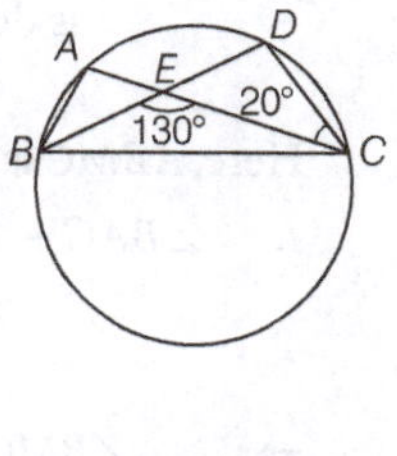

Sol. Given, $\angle BEC = 130°$ and $\angle ECD = 20°$

Here, AC is a straight line.

So, $\angle AEB + \angle BEC = 180°$ [linear pair]

$$\Rightarrow \quad \angle AEB = 180° - 130° = 50° \quad [\because \angle BEC = 130°]$$

$$\therefore \quad \angle CED = \angle AEB = 50°$$

[vertically opposite angles]

Now, in ΔEDC, $\angle CED + \angle EDC + \angle DCE = 180°$

[angle sum property of triangle]

$$\Rightarrow \quad \angle EDC = 180° - 20° - 50° = 110° \quad ...(i)$$

Also, $\angle BAC = \angle BDC$

[∵ the angles in the same segment are equal]

$$\Rightarrow \quad \angle BAC = \angle EDC = 110° \quad [\text{using Eq. (i)}]$$

Hence, $\angle BAC = 110°$

Q6. $ABCD$ is a cyclic quadrilateral whose diagonals intersect at a point E. If $\angle DBC = 70°$ and $\angle BAC = 30°$, then find $\angle BCD$. Further, if $AB = BC$, find $\angle ECD$.

Sol. We know that angles in the same segment are equal.

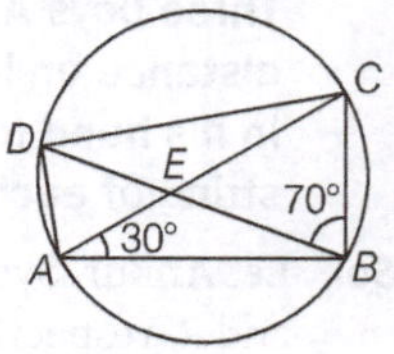

$$\therefore \quad \angle BDC = \angle BAC$$

$$\Rightarrow \quad \angle BDC = 30°$$

In ΔBCD, we have

$$\angle BDC + \angle DBC + \angle BCD = 180°$$

[angle sum property of triangle]

$$\Rightarrow \quad 30° + 70° + \angle BCD = 180°$$

$[\because \angle DBC = 70°$ and $\angle BDC = 30°]$

$$\Rightarrow \angle BCD = 180° - 30° - 70° = 80°$$

If $AB = BC$, then $\angle BCA = \angle BAC = 30°$

[∵ angles opposite to equal sides in a triangle are equal]

Now, $\angle ECD = \angle BCD - \angle BCA$

$$= 80° - 30° = 50°$$

$[\because \angle BCD = 80°$ and $\angle BCA = 30°]$

Hence, $\angle BCD = 80°$ and $\angle ECD = 50°$

Q7. If diagonals of a cyclic quadrilateral are diameters of the circle through the vertices of the quadrilateral, then prove that it is a rectangle.

Sol. Given Diagonals NP and QM of a cyclic quadrilateral $NQPM$ are the diameters of circle passing through the vertices M, P, Q and N.

To prove Quadrilateral $NQPM$ is a rectangle.

Proof Here, $ON = OP = OQ = OM$ [radii of same circle]

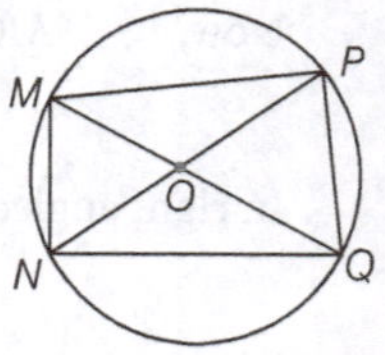

Then, $ON = OP = \frac{1}{2}NP$

and $OM = OQ = \frac{1}{2}MQ$

∴ $NP = MQ$

Hence, the diagonals of the quadrilateral $NQPM$ are equal and bisect each other.

So, quadrilateral $NQPM$ is a rectangle. **Hence proved.**

Q 8. If the non-parallel sides of a trapezium are equal, then prove that it is cyclic.

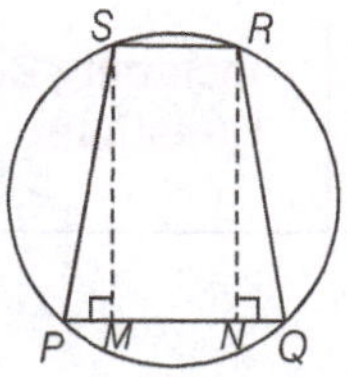

Sol. Given Non-parallel sides PS and QR of a trapezium $PQRS$ are equal.

To prove $PQRS$ is a cyclic trapezium.

Construction Draw $SM \perp PQ$ and $RN \perp PQ$.

Proof In ΔSMP and ΔRNQ, we have

$SP = RQ$ [given]

$\angle SMP = \angle RNQ$ [each 90°]

and $SM = RN$

[∵ distance between two parallel lines is always equal]

∴ $\Delta SMP \cong \Delta RNQ$ [by RHS congruence rule]

Then, $\angle P = \angle Q$ and $\angle PSM = \angle QRN$ [by CPCT]

Now, $\angle PSM = \angle QRN$

$\Rightarrow 90° + \angle PSM = 90° + \angle QRN$ [adding 90° both sides]

$\Rightarrow \angle MSR + \angle PSM = \angle NRS + \angle QRN$

[∵ $\angle MSR = \angle NRS = 90°$]

$\Rightarrow \angle PSR = \angle QRS$ i.e. $\angle S = \angle R$

Thus, $\angle P = \angle Q$ and $\angle R = \angle S$ ...(i)

Now, $\angle P + \angle Q + \angle R + \angle S = 360°$

[∵ sum of the angles of a quadrilateral is 360°]

$\Rightarrow 2\angle S + 2\angle Q = 360°$ [from Eq. (i)]

$\Rightarrow \angle S + \angle Q = 180°$

Hence, $PQRS$ is a cyclic trapezium. **Hence proved.**

Q 9. Two circles intersect at two points *B* and *C*. Through *B*, two line segments *ABD* and *PBQ* are drawn to intersect the circles at *A*, *D*, *P* and *Q* respectively (see figure). Prove that $\angle ACP = \angle QCD$.

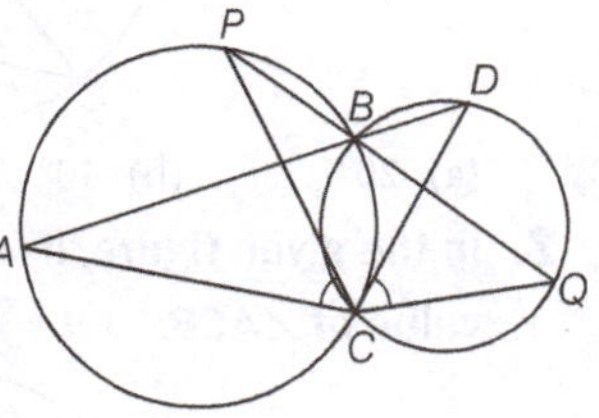

Sol. Given Two circles intersect at two points B and C. Through B, two line segments ABD and PBQ are drawn which intersect the circles at A, D, P and Q, respectively.

To prove $\angle ACP = \angle QCD$

Proof In circle I, $\angle ACP = \angle ABP$ ...(i)

[∵ angles in the same segment are equal]

In circle II, $\angle QCD = \angle QBD$ ...(ii)

[∵ angles in the same segment are equal]

Also, $\angle ABP = \angle QBD$ ...(iii)

[vertically opposite angles]

From Eqs. (i), (ii) and (iii), we get

$\angle ACP = \angle QCD$ **Hence proved.**

Q 10. If circles are drawn taking two sides of a triangle as diameters, then prove that the point of intersection of these circles lie on the third side.

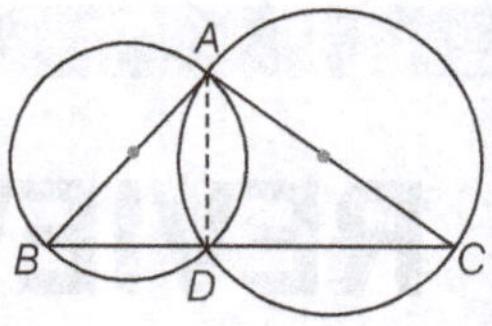

Sol. Given Two circles are drawn with sides AC and AB of ΔABC as diameters. Both circles intersect each other at D.

To prove D lies on BC.

Construction Join AD.

Proof Since, AC and AB are the diameters of the two circles.

∴ $\angle ADB = 90°$ ...(i) [angle in semi-circle]

and $\angle ADC = 90°$ ...(ii) [angle in semi-circle]

On adding Eqs. (i) and (ii), we get

$\angle ADB + \angle ADC = 90° + 90° = 180°$

$\angle BDC = 180°$

Hence, BDC is a straight line.

So, point of intersection D lies on the third side.

Hence proved.

Q 11. If ΔABC and ΔADC are two right angled triangles with common hypotenuse *AC*. Prove that $\angle CAD = \angle CBD$.

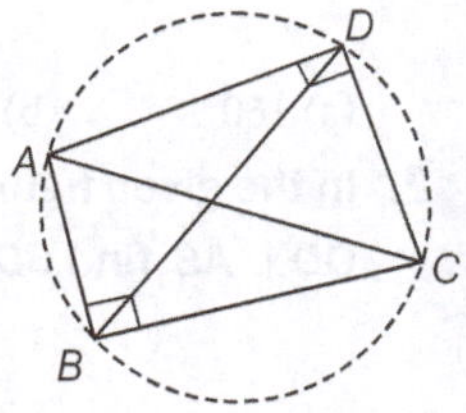

Sol. Given ΔADC and ΔABC are right angled triangles with common hypotenuse.

To prove $\angle CAD = \angle CBD$

Proof Since, $\angle ABC$ and $\angle ADC$ are 90°.

These angles are in the semi-circle.

Thus, both the triangles are lying in the semi-circle and AC is diameter of the circle.

∴ Points A, B, C and D are concylic.

Thus, CD is the chord.

$\Rightarrow \angle CAD = \angle CBD$

[∵ angles in the same segment of the circle]

Q 12. Prove that a cyclic parallelogram is a rectangle.

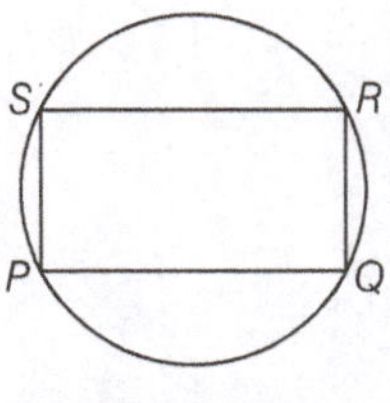

Sol. Given $PQRS$ is a parallelogram inscribed in a circle.

To prove $PQRS$ is a rectangle.

Proof Since, $PQRS$ is a cyclic quadrilateral.

$\angle P + \angle R = 180°$ ...(i)

[∵ sum of pair of opposite angles in a cyclic quadrilateral is 180°]

But $\angle P = \angle R$ ...(ii)

[∵ in a parallelogram, opposite angles are equal]

From Eqs. (i) and (ii), we get

$\angle P + \angle P = 180° \Rightarrow 2\angle P = 180° \Rightarrow \angle P = 90°$

∴ $\angle P = \angle R = 90°$

Similarly, $\angle Q = \angle S = 90°$

Thus, each angle of $PQRS$ is 90°.

Hence, $PQRS$ is a rectangle. **Hence proved.**

REVIEW EXERCISE

Including Competency Based Questions

Part I

Multiple Choice Questions

1. In the given figure, *O* is the centre of the circle and *CD* = *DE* = *EF* = *FG*. If the ∠*COD* = 40°, then reflex ∠*COG* is equal to

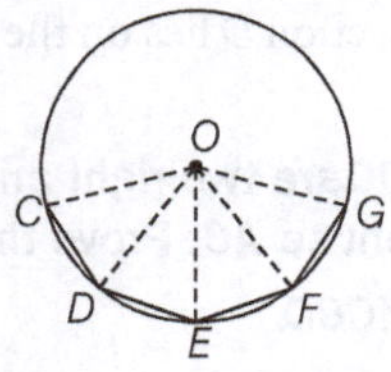

(a) 160° (b) 200° (c) 240° (d) 280°

2. In the given figure, if *OA* = 10 cm, *AB* = 12 cm and *OD* ⊥ *AB*, find *CD*.

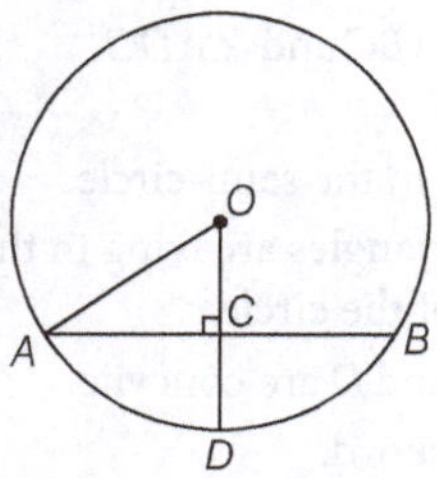

(a) 2 cm (b) 3 cm (c) 4 cm (d) 6 cm

3. In the given figure, *OD* is perpendicular to the chord *AB* of a circle whose centre is *O*. If *BC* is a diameter and *OD* = 4 cm, then *CA* equals Competency Based Question

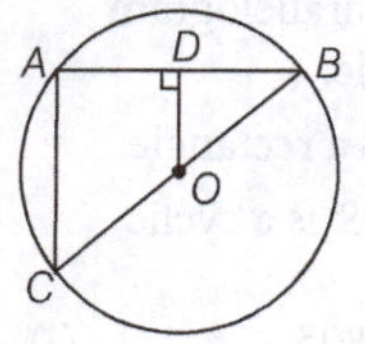

(a) 6 cm (b) 8 cm (c) 10 cm (d) 12 cm

4. In the given figure, a line intersect two concentric circles with centre *O* at *A*, *B*, *C* and *D*. If *AB* = 10 cm, find *CD*.

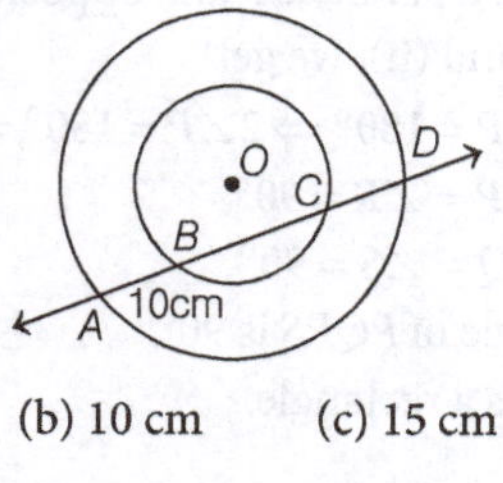

(a) 5 cm (b) 10 cm (c) 15 cm (d) 20 cm

5. In the given figure, *OA* and *OB* are respectively perpendiculars to chords *CD* and *EF* of a circle whose centre is *O*. If *OA* = *OB*, then

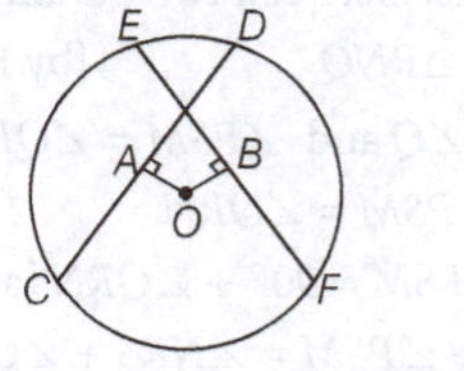

(a) *CE* = *DF* (b) *CE* > *DF*
(c) *CE* < *DF* (d) None of these

6. In the given figure, if ∠*ABC* = 20°, then ∠*AOC* is equal to Competency Based Question

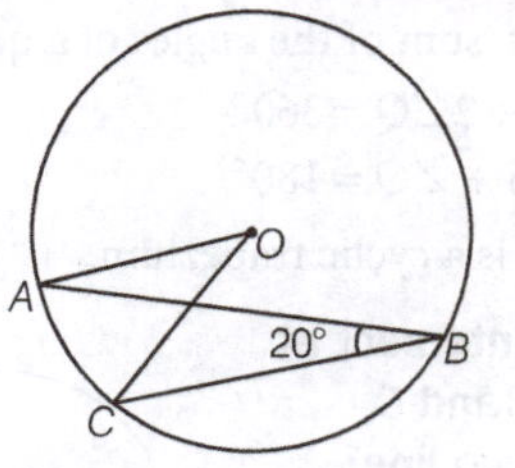

(a) 20° (b) 40° (c) 60° (d) 10°

7. In the given figure, if ∠*AOB* = 120°, then find the value of ∠*ACB*.

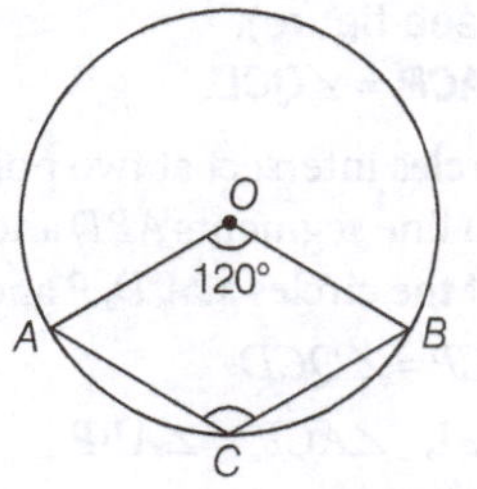

(a) 100° (b) 110° (c) 130° (d) 120°

8. In the given figure, if ∠*DAB* = 60°, ∠*ABD* = 50°, then ∠*ACB* is equal to Competency Based Question

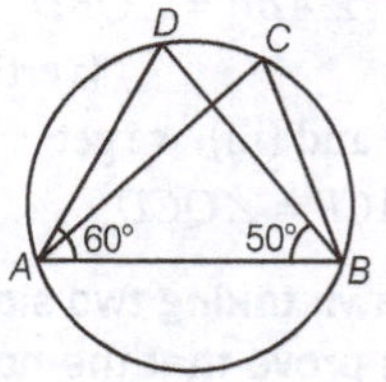

(a) 60° (b) 50° (c) 70° (d) 80°

9. In the given figure, BC is a diameter of the circle and $\angle BAO = 60°$. Then, $\angle ADC$ is equal to **Competency Based Question**

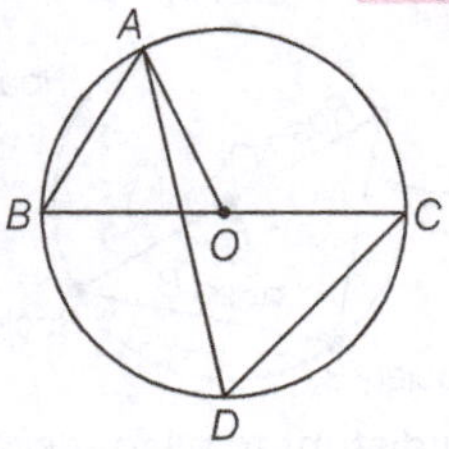

(a) 30° (b) 45° (c) 60° (d) 120°

10. In the given figure, O is the centre of the circle and chord AC and BD intersect at Q such that $\angle AQB = 140°$ and $\angle QBC = 25°$, find the value of $\angle ADB$. **Competency Based Question**

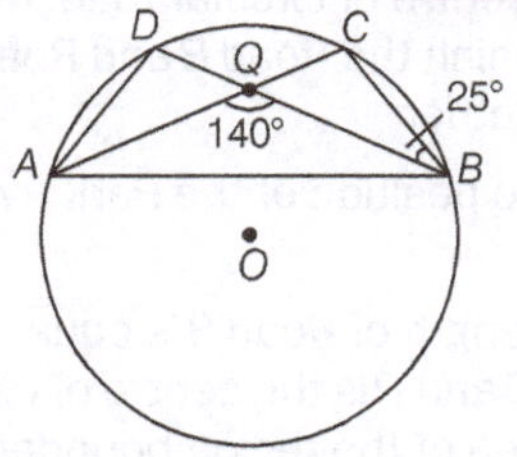

(a) 105° (b) 140° (c) 115° (d) 135°

11. In the given figure, $\angle ABC = 59°$, $\angle ACB = 40°$, find $\angle BDC$.

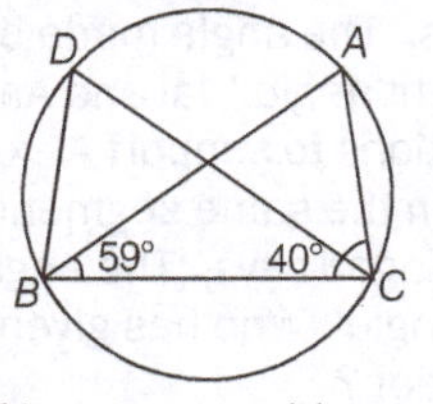

(a) 99° (b) 90° (c) 81° (d) 71°

12. In figure, if AOB is a diameter of the circle and $AC = BC$, then $\angle CAB$ is equal to **NCERT Exemplar**

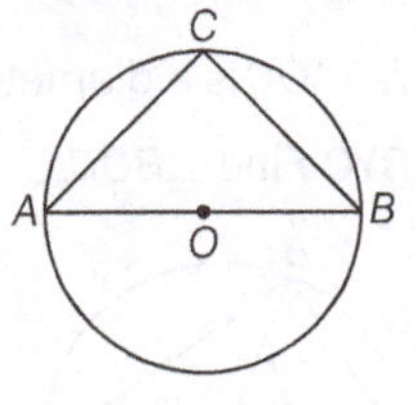

(a) 30° (b) 60° (c) 90° (d) 45°

13. The sum of opposite angles of a cyclic quadrilateral is

(a) 120° (b) 90° (c) 180° (d) 150°

14. In the given figure, $ABDC$ is a cyclic quadrilateral in which BC is diameter, then find $\angle BAC$.

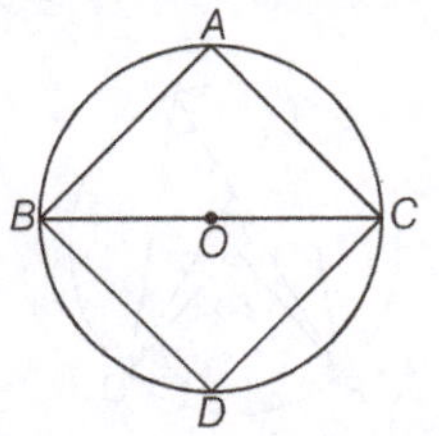

(a) 90° (b) 100° (c) 80° (d) 110°

Assertion-Reason Type Questions

15. Assertion The length of a chord which is at a distance of 5 cm from the centre of a circle of radius 10 cm is 17.32 cm.

Reason The perpendicular from the centre of a circle to a chord bisects the chord.

(a) Both Assertion and Reason are correct and Reason is the correct explanation of Assertion
(b) Both Assertion and Reason are correct but Reason is not the correct explanation of Assertion
(c) Assertion is correct but Reason is incorrect
(d) Assertion is incorrect but Reason is correct

16. Assertion Two diameters of a circle intersect each other at right angles. Then, the quadrilateral formed by joining their end-point is a rectangle.

Reason Angle in a semi-circle is a right angle.

(a) Both Assertion and Reason are correct and Reason is the correct explanation of Assertion
(b) Both Assertion and Reason are correct but Reason is not the correct explanation of Assertion
(c) Assertion is correct but Reason is incorrect
(d) Assertion is incorrect but Reason is correct

17. Assertion $ABCD$ is a cyclic quadrilateral. AB and DC are produced to meet in E. Then, $\angle ECB = \angle EDA$.

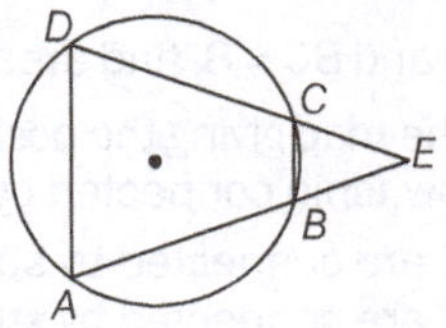

Reason Exterior angle in a cyclic quadrilateral is equal to opposite interior angle.

(a) Both Assertion and Reason are correct and Reason is the correct explanation of Assertion
(b) Both Assertion and Reason are correct but Reason is not the correct explanation of Assertion
(c) Assertion is correct but Reason is incorrect
(d) Assertion is incorrect but Reason is correct

Case Study Based Questions

18. Government of India is working regularly for the uplistment of handicapped persons by making them self dependent. For this, three STD booths to be operated by handicapped persons were installed at A, B and C as shown in the figure. These three booths are equidistant from each other as shown in the figure.

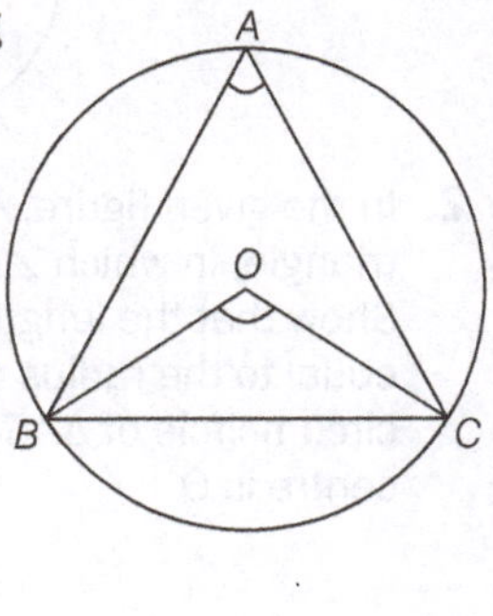

(i) Which type of ΔABC is given in the figure?

(ii) Find Measure of $\angle ABC$

(iii) (a) If $AB = 6$ cm, then find the value of $BC + CA$.

Or

(b) Find Measure of $\angle BOC$.

19. Given below is the figure of a circle with centre O. The measure of $\angle BOC = 88°$.

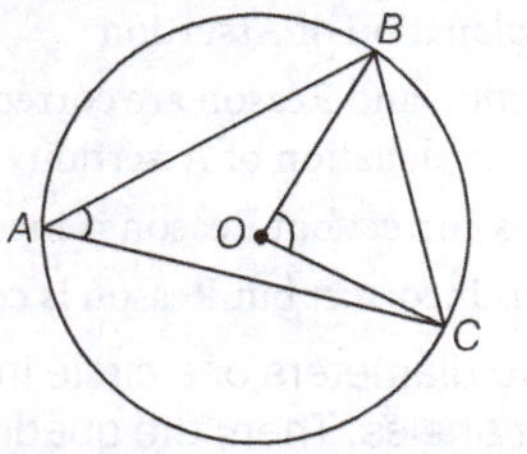

Based on the above information, answer the following questions.

(i) Find the measure of $\angle BAC$.

(ii) Priya claims, 'The length of OB is equal to the length of OC'. Siya and Aditi provide different justifications for Priya's claim. Siya says, 'OB and OC are radii of the same circle'. Aditi says, 'OC is the base of $\angle BOC$'. Who has given the correct justification for Priya's claim?

(iii) (a) Find the measure of $\angle OBC$.

Or

(b) If $OB = 5$ and $BC = 8$, find area of ΔBOC.

20. Given below is the map giving the position of four housing societies in a township connected by a circular Road A. Society 2 and 3 are connected by straight Road B, Society 4 and 2 are connected by straight Road C and Society 4 and 3 are connected by Road D. Point P denotes the position of a park.

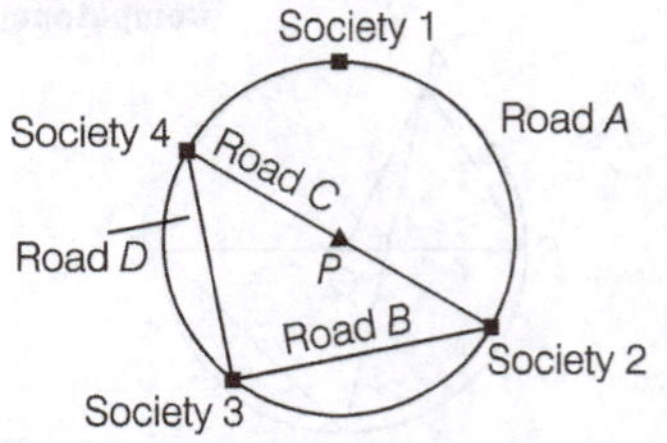

The park is equidistant to all four societies. Rubina claims that it is not possible to construct another circular road connecting all four societies.

Based on the above information, answer the following questions.

(i) If P is the centre of circular road, then find the angle at which the Road B and Road D connected with each other.

(ii) What is the position of the Park P with respect to Road A?

(iii) (a) If the length of Road B is equal to the length of Road D and P is the centre of circular road, then find area of the region bounded by Road B, Road D and Road C.

Or

(b) Alex says, 'The angle made by Road B on Road D is a right angle.' Jai and Angad give different justifications to support Alex's claim. Jai says, 'Angles in the same segment of a circle are equal.' Angad says, 'The angle in a semi-circle is a right angle'. Who has given the correct justification?

Part II

Very Short Answer Type Questions

1. In the given figure, chord AB subtends an angle equal to $60°$ at the centre of the circle. If $OA = 5$ cm, then find the length of AB.

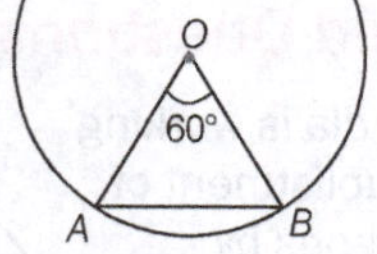

2. In the given figure, ABC is a triangle, in which $\angle BAC = 30°$. Show that the length of BC is equal to the radius of the circumcircle of ΔABC, whose centre is O.

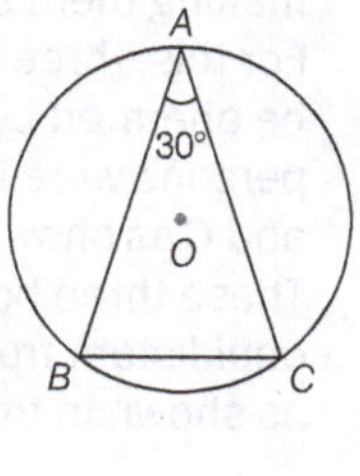

3. In the given figure, AOC is a diameter of the circle and arc $AXB = \frac{1}{2}$ arc BYC. Find $\angle BOC$.

NCERT Exemplar

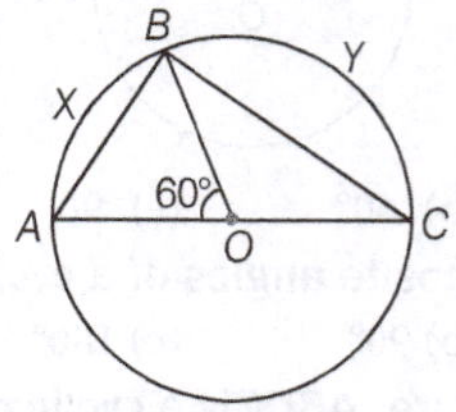

4. In the given figure, if $\angle POQ = 80°$, then find $\angle PAQ$ and $\angle PCQ$.

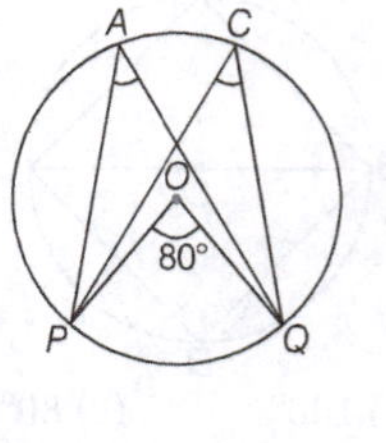

5. In the given figure, $\angle PQR = 100°$, where P, Q and R are the points on a circle with centre O. Find reflex $\angle POR$.

Competency Based Question

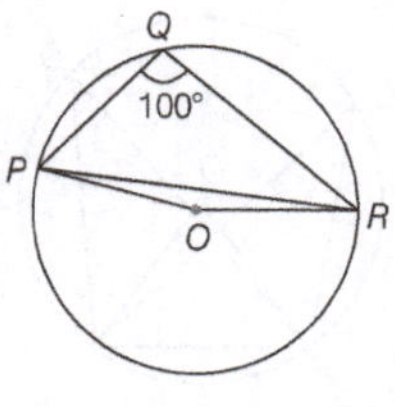

6. In the given figure, O is the centre of the circle and $\angle BDC = 42°$. Find the measure of $\angle ACB$.

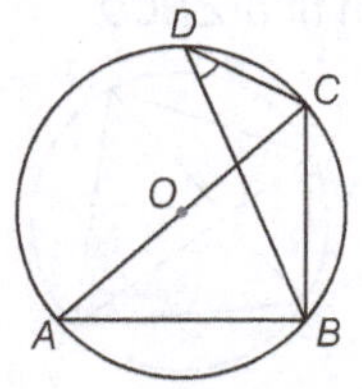

7. $ABCD$ is a cyclic quadrilateral whose diagonals intersect at a point O. If $\angle DBC = 85°$, $\angle BAC = 40°$, find $\angle BCD$. Further, if $AB = CD$, find $\angle OCD$.

8. In the given figure, $ABCD$ is a cyclic quadrilateral, in which AC and BD are its diagonals. If $\angle DBC = 60°$ and $\angle BAC = 30°$, then find $\angle BCD$.

Competency Based Question

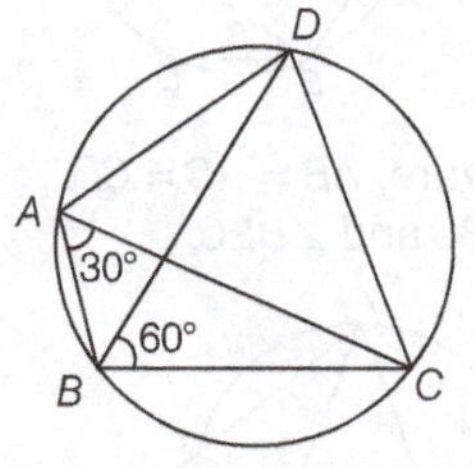

9. If $ABCD$ is a cyclic quadrilateral, in which $AD \parallel BC$, then prove that $\angle B = \angle C$.

Short Answer Type Questions

10. Two circles with centres O and O' intersect at two points A and B. A line PQ is drawn parallel to OO' through A (or B) intersecting the circles at P and Q. Prove that $PQ = 2\,OO'$.

NCERT Exemplar

11. If the length of a chord of a circle is 16 cm and is at a distance of 15 cm from the centre of the circle, then find the radius of the circle.

12. If the perpendicular bisector of a chord AB of a circle intersects the circle at P and Q, then prove that arc $PXA \cong$ arc PYB.

Competency Based Question

13. Prove that the right bisector of a chord of a circle bisects the corresponding arc of the circle.

14. Prove that the line joining the mid-points of two parallel chords of a circle passes through the centre.

15. AB and AC arc two equal chords of a circle. Prove that the bisector of the $\angle BAC$ passes through the centre of the circle.

16. If a line segment joining mid-points of two chords of a circle passes through the centre of the circle. Prove that the two chords are parallel.

NCERT Exemplar

17. If BM and CN are the perpendiculars drawn on the sides AC and AB of the ΔABC, then prove that the points B, C, M and N are concyclic.

NCERT Exemplar

18. Bisector AD of $\angle BAC$ of ΔABC passes through the centre O of the circumcircle of ΔABC, as shown in figure. Prove that $AB = AC$.

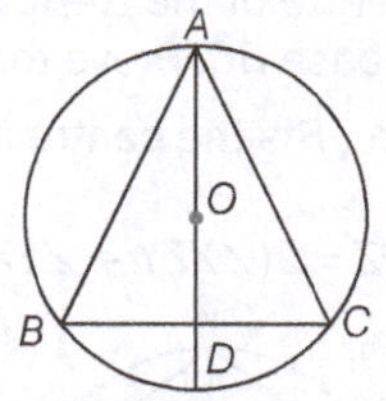

19. In the given figure, AB and AC are two equal chords of a circle whose centre is O. If $OD \perp AB$, $OE \perp AC$ and AO bisects $\angle DAE$, prove that ΔADE is an isosceles triangle and $\angle ABC = \angle ACB$.

Competency Based Question

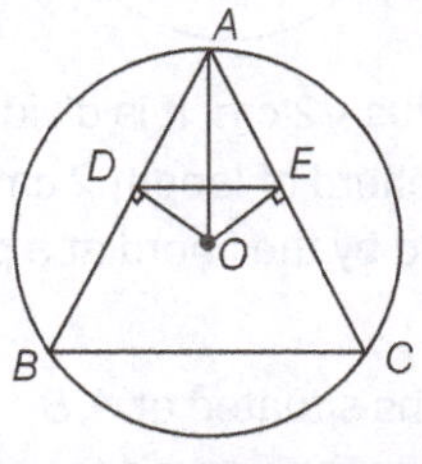

20. In following figure, O is the centre of the circle, $BD = OD$ and $CD \perp AB$. Find $\angle CAB$.

NCERT Exemplar

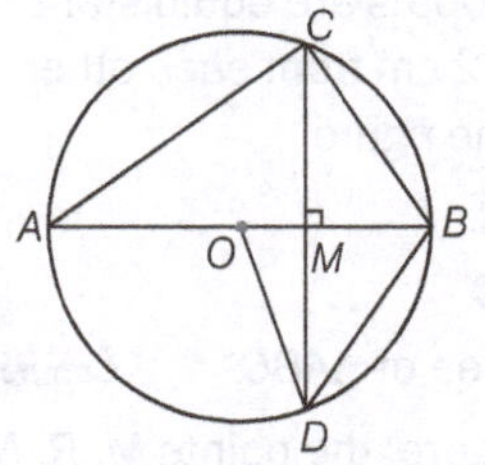

21. Three students Priyanka, Sonia and David are protesting against killing innocent animals for commercial purposes in a circular park of radius 20 m. They are standing at equal distances on its boundary by holding banners in their hands.

(i) Find the distance between each of them.

(ii) Find the area of triangle inscribed in a circle.

22. In the given figure, $\angle BAC = 55°$ and the altitude BE produced, meet the circle at D. Also, $\angle AOC = 100°$

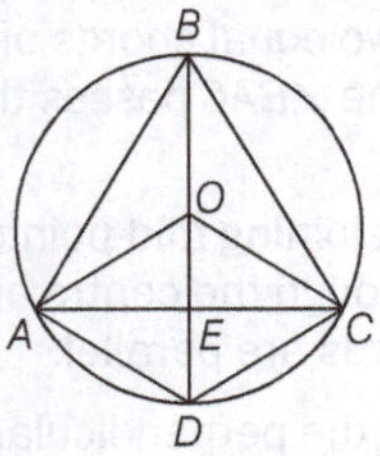

Determine

(i) $\angle ABE$. (ii) $\angle ABC$.

23. The circumcentre of the ΔABC is O. Prove that $\angle OBC + \angle BAC = 90°$. **NCERT Exemplar**

24. O is the circumcentre of the ΔABC and D is the mid-point of the base BC. Prove that $\angle BOD = \angle A$.

25. In the given figure, P is the centre of the circle. Prove that

$$\angle XPZ = 2(\angle XZY + \angle YXZ).$$

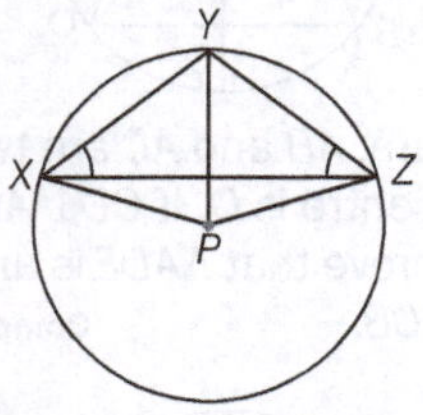

26. A circle has radius $\sqrt{2}$ cm. It is divided into two segments by a chord of length 2 cm. Prove that the angle subtended by the chord at a point in major segment is 45°. **NCERT Exemplar**

27. Three STD booths situated at A, B and C as shown in the figure are operated by handicapped persons. These three booths are equidistant having length 2 cm from each other as shown in the figure.

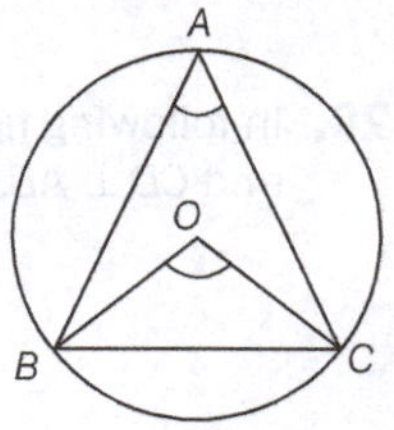

(i) Find $\angle BAC$.

(ii) Find $\angle BOC$.

(iii) Find the area of ΔABC. **Competency Based Question**

28. In the given figure, the points M, R, N, P, S and Q are concyclic. Find $\angle PQR + \angle OPR + \angle NMS + \angle OSN$ if O is the centre of the circle. **Competency Based Question**

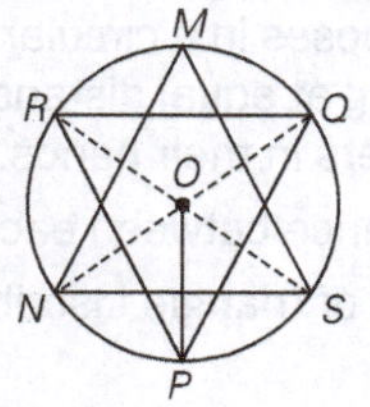

29. In the given figure, O is the centre of the circle, $\angle ADB = 30°$ and $\angle ABC = 40°$. Find the measure of $\angle CAB$. **Competency Based Question**

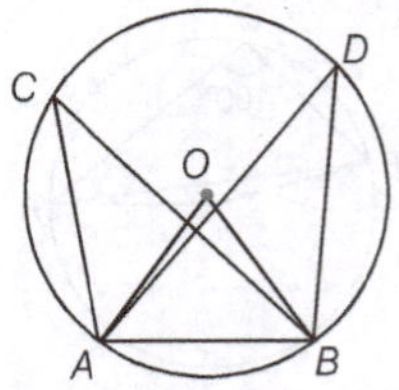

30. In the given figure, $ABCD$ is a cyclic quadrilateral, in which AC and BD are its diagonals. If $\angle DBC = 55°$ and $\angle BAC = 45°$, then find $\angle BCD$.

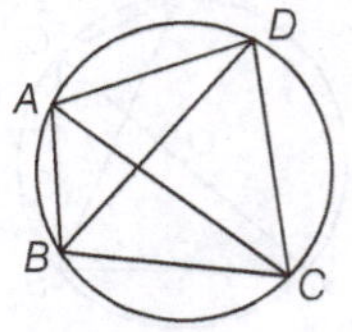

31. The chord ED is parallel to the diameter AC. Determine $\angle CED$. **Competency Based Question**

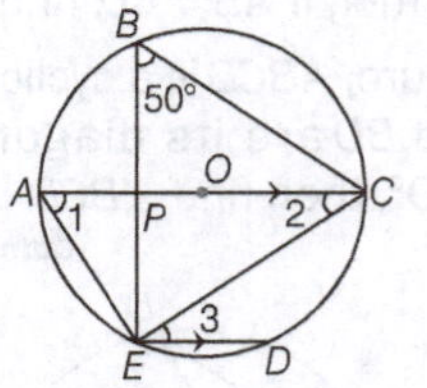

32. In the given figure, $AB = AC = CD$. Calculate $\angle ABC$ and $\angle BEC$.

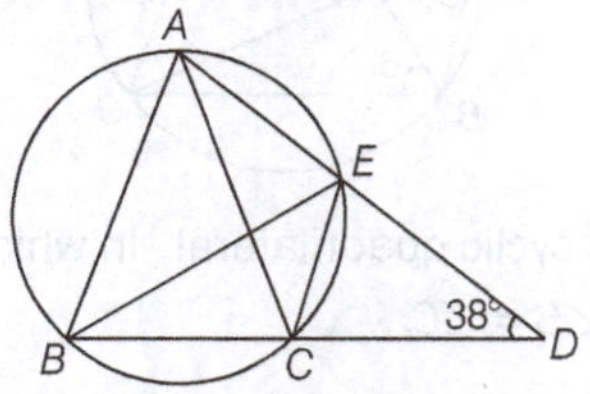

33. The Indian Hockey Federation organised a friendly hockey match between India and Pakistan on a circular ground. The sale proceeds of this match shall be donated to an orphanage. A rectangular turf is spread on the ground as shown in the figure.

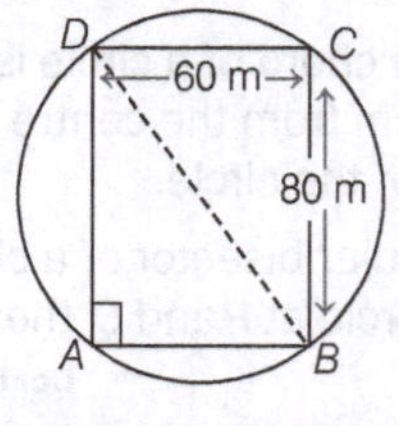

(i) Specify the name of the chord BD.

(ii) Find the radius of the stadium.

(iii) Find the area of ΔBCD. **Competency Based Question**

34. Two circles intersect at two points C and F. Through C, two line segments ACD and BCE are drawn to intersect the circle at A, D, B and E, respectively (see figure). If $\angle AFB = 48°$, find $\angle DFE$. **Competency Based Question**

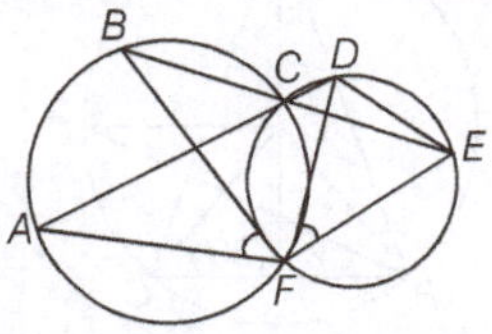

35. If a pair of opposite sides of a cyclic quadrilateral is equal, then prove that its diagonals are also equal. **NCERT Exemplar**

36. A quadrilateral $ABCD$ is inscribed in a circle such that AB is a diameter and $\angle ADC = 130°$. Find $\angle BAC$. **NCERT Exemplar**

37. On a common hypotenuse AB, two right angled triangles, ΔACB and ΔADB are situated on opposite sides. Prove that $\angle BAC = \angle BDC$. **NCERT Exemplar**

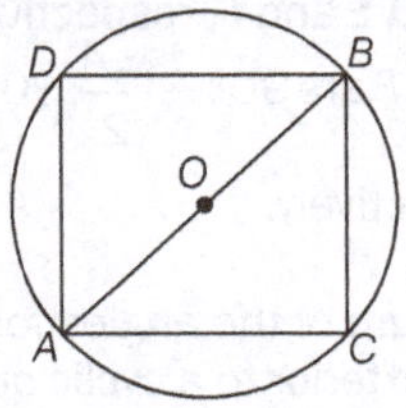

38. In the given figure, find the value of x.

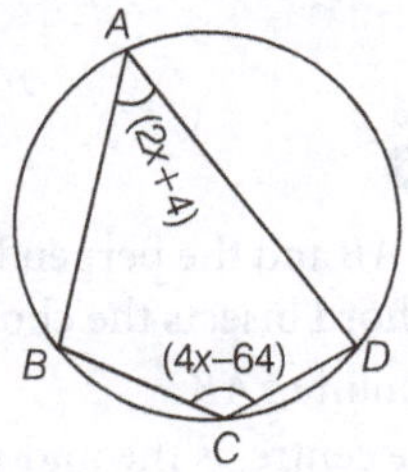

39. In the given figure, $ABCE$ is a cyclic quadrilateral and O is the centre of circle. If $\angle AEC = 110°$, then find $\angle ABC$ and $\angle ADC$.

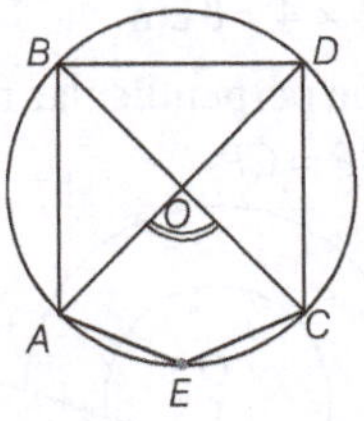

40. In the given figure, if $y = 3x$, then find the magnitude of x. **Competency Based Question**

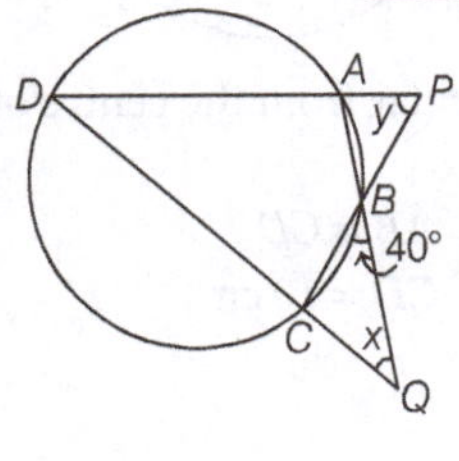

41. In the given figure, $\angle ADC = 130°$ and chord BC = chord BE. Find $\angle CBE$. **NCERT Exemplar**

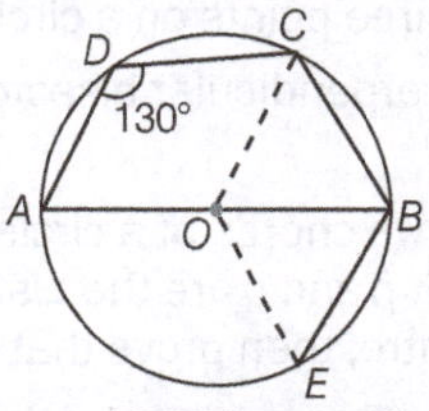

42. In the given figure, $ABCD$ is a cyclic quadrilateral and O is the centre of the circle. If $\angle BOD = 160°$, then find the measure of $\angle BPD$. **Competency Based Question**

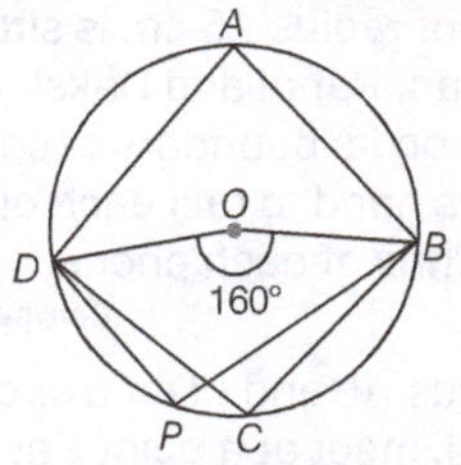

43. If a line is drawn parallel to the base of an isosceles triangle to intersect its equal sides, then prove that the quadrilateral so formed is cyclic. **NCERT Exemplar**

44. In the given figure, sides AB and DC of a cyclic quadrilateral $ABCD$ are produced to meet at E. Sides AD and BC are produced to meet at F. If $\angle ADC = 80°$ and $\angle BEC = 50°$, then find $\angle BAD$ and $\angle CFD$. **Competency Based Question**

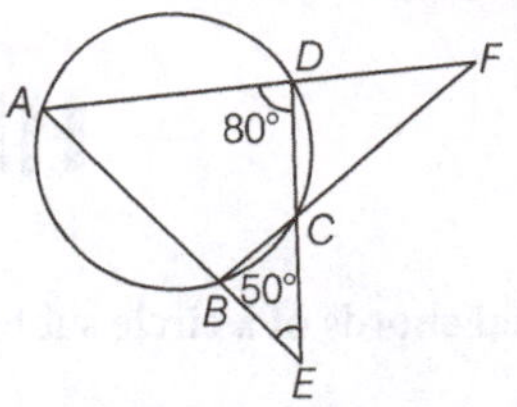

45. In the given figure, AOB is a diameter of the circle and C, D and E are any three points on the semi-circle. Find the value of $\angle ACD + \angle BED$. **NCERT Exemplar**

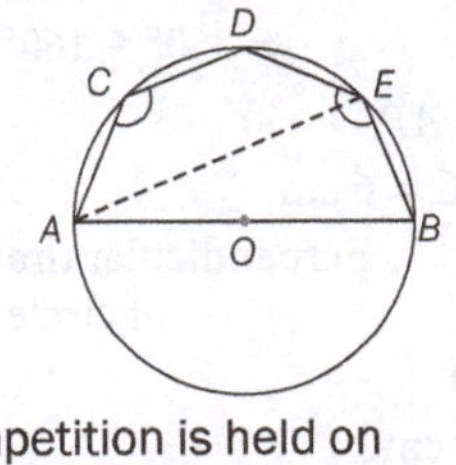

46. A rangoli competition is held on Delhi public school. In which the student make a different type of rangoli by using different colours. One of the student makes a rangoli which is shown in figure. **Competency Based Question**

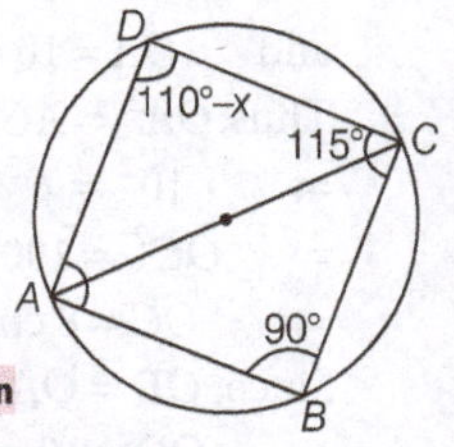

(i) Find the value of x. (ii) Find the value of $\angle A$.

(iii) Is it true that line joining points A and C passes through a centre?

Long Answer Type Questions

47. A, B and C are three points on a circle.

Prove that the perpendicular bisector of AB, BC and CA are concurrent. **NCERT Exemplar**

48. AB and AC are two chords of a circle of radius r such that $AB = 2AC$. If p and q are the distances of AB and AC from the centre, then prove that $4q^2 = p^2 + 3r^2$. **NCERT Exemplar**

49. Prove that the mid-point of the hypotenuse of a right angled triangle is equidistant from its vertices.

50. A circular park of radius 15 cm is situated in a colony. Three boys Aman, Rahul and Daksh are sitting at equal distance on its boundary each having a toy telephone in his hand to talk each other. Find the length of the string of each phone. **Competency Based Question**

51. Two equal chords AB and CD of a circle with centre O, when produced, meet at a point E as shown in figure. Prove that $BE = DE$ and $AE = CE$.

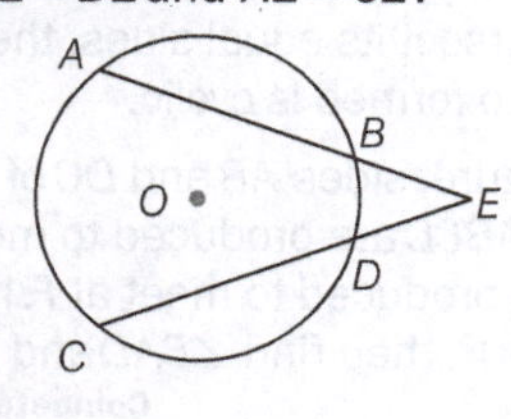

52. In the following figure, O is the centre of the circle and $\angle BCO = 30°$. Find x and y. **Competency Based Question**

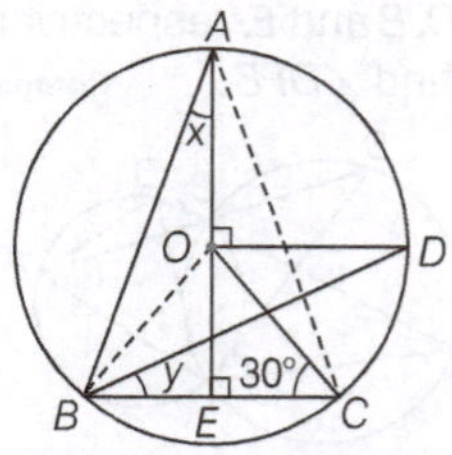

53. Prove that any angle subtended by a minor arc in the alternate segment is acute and any angle subtended by a major arc in the alternate segment is obtuse.

54. If bisectors of opposite angles of a cyclic quadrilateral $ABCD$ intersect the circle circumscribing it at the points P and Q, then prove that PQ is a diameter of the circle. **NCERT Exemplar**

55. Bisectors of angles A, B and C of a ΔABC intersect its circumcircle at D, E and F, respectively. Prove that the angles D, E and F are $90° - \frac{\angle A}{2}, 90° - \frac{\angle B}{2}$ and $90° - \frac{\angle C}{2}$ respectively.

56. Prove that the sum of the angles formed in the four segments exterior to a cyclic quadrilateral by the sides is equal to six right angles. **NCERT Exemplar**

HINTS & ANSWERS

Part I

1. (b) Since, equal chords of a circle subtend equal angles at the centre.

$\therefore \quad \angle COD = \angle DOE = \angle EOF = \angle FOG = 40°$

$\therefore \quad \angle COG = 4 \times 40° = 160°$

$\therefore \quad \text{Reflex } \angle COG = 360° - \angle COG = 360° - 160° = 200°$

2. (a) Since, $OD \perp AB$,

$\therefore \quad AC = BC = 6$ cm [$\because$ perpendicular drawn from the centre of circle bisects the chords]

and $\angle OCA = 90°$

and $OA = 10$ cm

Thus, $OA^2 = AC^2 + OC^2$ [by Pythagoras theorem]

$\Rightarrow \quad 10^2 = 6^2 + OC^2$

$\Rightarrow \quad OC^2 = 100 - 36 = 64$

$\Rightarrow \quad OC = 8$ cm

Since, $OD = OA$ [$\because OD$ is the radius of circle]

$\therefore \quad OD = 10$ cm

Thus, $CD = OD - OC = 10 \text{ cm} - 8 \text{ cm} = 2$ cm

3. (b) Since, $OD \perp AB$ and the perpendicular drawn from the centre to a chord bisects the chord.

$\therefore D$ is the mid-point of AB.

Also, O being the centre, is the mid-point of BC. Thus, in ΔABC, D and O are mid-points of AB and BC, respectively.

$\therefore OD \parallel AC$ and $OD = \frac{1}{2}CA$ [by mid-point theorem]

$\Rightarrow CA = 2OD = 2 \times 4 = 8$ cm

4. (b) **Hint** Let OP be perpendicular from O on line l.

$\therefore AP = DP$ and $BP = CP$

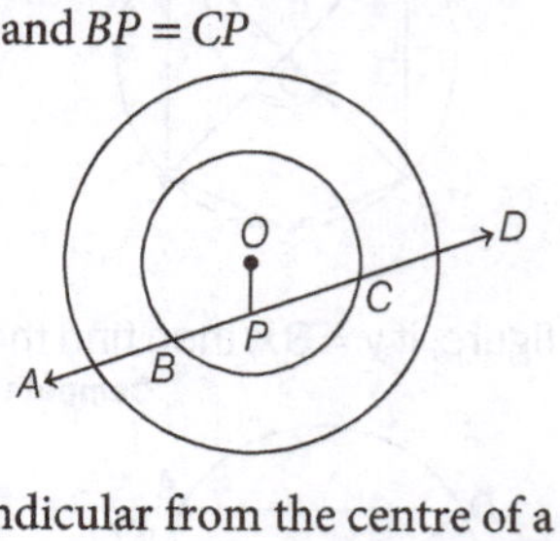

[$\because$ perpendicular from the centre of a circle to a chord, bisects the chord]

$\Rightarrow \quad AB = CD$

$\therefore \quad CD = 10$ cm

5. (a) We have, $OA \perp CD$ and $OB \perp EF$

$$OA = OB$$

$\Rightarrow$ Chords CD and EF are equidistant from O.

$\Rightarrow \quad CD = EF$

[$\because$ chords equidistant from the centre of a circle are equal in length]

arc CD = arc EF

On subtracting arc ED or ED from both sides,

$$\overset{\frown}{CD} - \overset{\frown}{ED} = \overset{\frown}{EF} - \overset{\frown}{ED}$$

$\Rightarrow \quad \overset{\frown}{CE} = \overset{\frown}{DF}$

$\Rightarrow \quad CE = DF$

6. (b) Given, $\angle ABC = 20°$

We know that angle subtended at the centre by an arc is twice the angle subtended by it at the remaining part of circle.

$\therefore \quad \angle AOC = 2\angle ABC = 2 \times 20° = 40°$

7. (d) Reflex $\angle AOB = 360° - 120° = 240°$

$\therefore \quad \angle ACB = \frac{1}{2}$ reflex $\angle AOB$

$\therefore \quad \angle ACB = \frac{1}{2} \times 240° = 120°$

8. (c) Given, $\angle DAB = 60°,\ \angle ABD = 50°$

Since, $\angle ADB = \angle ACB$ ...(i)

[angles in same segment of a circle are equal]

In ΔABD, $\angle ABD + \angle ADB + \angle DAB = 180°$

[by angle sum property of a triangle]

$\therefore \quad 50° + \angle ADB + 60° = 180°$

$\Rightarrow \quad \angle ADB = 180° - 110° = 70°$

From Eq. (i), $\angle ACB = \angle ADB = 70°$

9. (c) In ΔAOB, $OA = OB$ [both are the radius of circle]

$\Rightarrow \quad \angle OBA = \angle BAO$

[angles opposite to equal sides are equal]

$\Rightarrow \quad \angle OBA = 60°$ [$\because \angle BAO = 60°$, given]

We know that $\angle ABC = \angle ADC$

[angles in the same segment AC are equal]

$\therefore \quad \angle ADC = 60°$

10. (c) $\angle AQB = \angle QCB + \angle CBQ$ [exterior angle property]

$\Rightarrow \quad 140° = \angle QCB + 25°$

$\Rightarrow \angle QCB = 140° - 25° = 115°$

or $\angle ACB = 115°$

$\therefore\ \angle ADB = \angle ACB = 115°$ [angles in same segment]

11. (c) In ΔABC,

$$\angle ABC + \angle BAC + \angle ACB = 180°$$

$$59° + \angle BAC + 40° = 180°$$

$\Rightarrow \quad \angle BAC = 180° - 59° - 40°$

$= 180° - 99° = 81°$

$\therefore \quad \angle BDC = \angle BAC = 81°$

[angles in same segment]

12. (d) We know that diameter subtends a right angle to the circle.

$\therefore \quad \angle BCA = 90°$ ...(i)

Given, $AC = BC$

$\Rightarrow \quad \angle ABC = \angle CAB$ ...(ii)

[angles opposite to equal sides are equal]

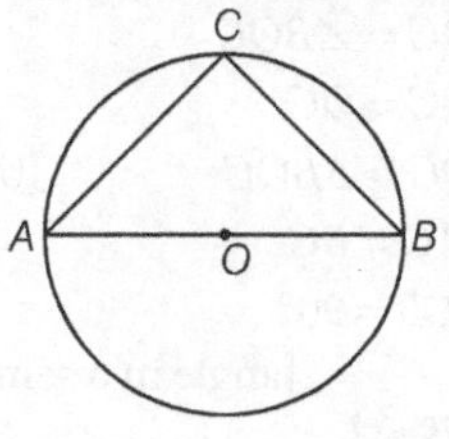

In ΔABC,

$\angle CAB + \angle ABC + \angle BCA = 180°$

[by angle sum property of a triangle]

$\Rightarrow \quad \angle CAB + \angle CAB + 90° = 180°$

[from Eqs. (i) and (ii)]

$\Rightarrow \quad 2\angle CAB = 180° - 90°$

$\Rightarrow \quad \angle CAB = \frac{90°}{2}$

$\therefore \quad \angle CAB = 45°$

13. (c) 180°

14. (a) Since, $ABDC$ is a cyclic quadrilateral and BC is diameter.

$\therefore \quad \angle BAC = 90°$ [angle of semi-circle]

15. (a) Let PQ be a chord of a circle with centre O and radius 10 cm. Draw $OR \perp PQ$.

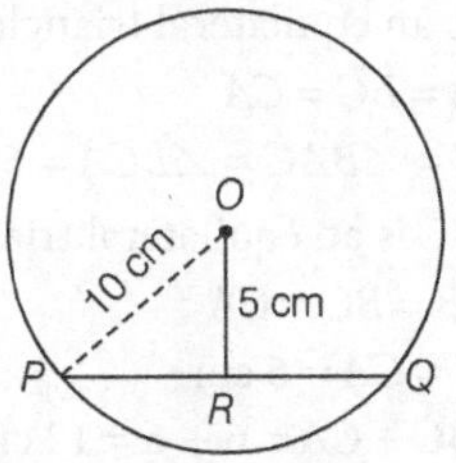

Now, $OP = 10$ cm and $OR = 5$ cm

In right angled ΔORP, we get

$$OP^2 = PR^2 + OR^2$$

$\Rightarrow \quad PR^2 = OP^2 - OR^2$

$\Rightarrow \quad PR^2 = 10^2 - 5^2 = 75$

$\Rightarrow \quad PR = \sqrt{75} = 8.66$ cm

Since, the perpendicular from the centre to a chord bisects the chord.

Therefore, $PQ = 2 \times PR = 2 \times 8.66 = 17.32$ cm

So, Assertion is correct. Also, Reason is correct and it is the correct explanation of Assertion.

16. (b) Let AB and CD be two perpendicular diameters of a circle with centre O.

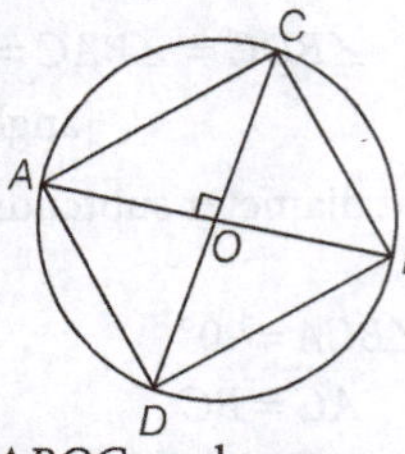

In ΔAOC and ΔBOC, we have

$OA = OB$ [O is the mid-point of AB]

$\angle AOC = \angle BOC$ [each equal to 90°]

and $OC = OC$ [common]

$\Delta AOC \cong \Delta BOC$ [by SAS congruence rule]

$\Rightarrow AC = BC$ [by CPCT]

Also, $\angle ACB = 90°$

[angle in a semi-circle is a right angle]

Similarly, we get

$BC = BD$ and $\angle CBD = 90°$

$DB = DA$ and $\angle BDA = 90°$

Hence, $ACBD$ is a square.

It implies that $ACBD$ is a rectangle.

Also, Reason is correct but it is not necessary that Reason is the correct explanation.

17. (d) $\angle ECB = \angle EAD$

[exterior angle in a cyclic quadrilateral is equal to interior opposite angle]

Assertion is incorrect but Reason is correct.

18. (i) Here, A, B and C represented three STD booths.

As A, B, C are equidistant from each other

$AB = BC = CA$

Hence, ΔABC is an equilateral triangle.

(ii) $\because$ ΔABC is an equilateral triangle.

$\therefore$ $AB = BC = CA$

So, $\angle ABC = \angle BAC = \angle BCA = 60°$

(iii) (a) $\therefore$ ΔABC is an equilateral triangle.

$\therefore$ $AB = BC = CA$

So, $BC = CA = 6$ cm

Now, $BC + CA = 6 + 6 = 12$ cm

Or

(b) We know that the angle substended by an arc at the centre of the circle is twice the angle subtended by it at any point on the remaining part of the circle.

$\therefore$ $\angle BOC = 2\angle BAC$

$\Rightarrow$ $\angle BOC = 2 \times 60° = 120°$

19. (i) (a) The angle subtended by the are at the centre is double the angle subtended by it on the remaining part of the circle.

$\therefore$ $\angle BOC = 2\angle BAC \Rightarrow 88° = 2\angle BAC$

$\Rightarrow$ $\angle BAC = \dfrac{88°}{2} = 44°$

$\therefore$ $\angle BAC = 44°$

(ii) OB and OC are the two radii of same circle, therefore OB and OC are equal.

Ans. Siya is correct.

(iii) (a) In ΔBOC, We have

$\angle BOC = 88°$,

$OB = OC$ [radii of same circle]

$\therefore$ $\angle OBC = \angle OCB$ [angles opposite to equal sides of triangle are equal]

Now,

$\angle BOC + \angle OBC + \angle OCB = 180°$

[angle sum property of a triangle]

$\Rightarrow$ $88° + \angle OBC + \angle OBC = 180°$

[$\because \angle OBC = \angle OCB$]

$\Rightarrow$ $88 + 2\angle OBC = 180°$

$\Rightarrow$ $2\angle OBC = 180° - 88°$

$\Rightarrow$ $2\angle OBC = 92°$

$\angle OBC = 46°$

Hence, $\angle OBC = 46°$

Or

(b) In ΔBOC, we have

$OB = OC$ [radii of same circle]

$\because$ $OB = 5$ cm [given]

$\therefore$ $OC = 5$ cm

and $BC = 8$ cm [given]

Then, area of ΔBOC

$= \sqrt{s(s - OB)(s - OC)(s - BC)}$

[by Heron's formula]

$\Rightarrow$ $s = \dfrac{OB + OC + BC}{2} = \dfrac{5 + 5 + 8}{2} = 9$

Now, area of ΔBOC,

$\Delta = \sqrt{9(9 - 5)(9 - 5)(9 - 8)}$

$= \sqrt{9 \times 4 \times 4 \times 1} = 3 \times 4 = 12 \text{ cm}^2$

20. (i) Since, P is the centre of circular road and Road C passing through P.

$\therefore$ Road C is the diameter of circular road.

$\therefore$ Road D and Road B are connected with each other at 90°. [angle in a semi-circle is a right angle]

(ii) The position of the Park P with respect to Road A is the centre of the circular Road A.

(iii) (a) Given, length of Road B = length of Road D

Let length of Road $B = a$

Then, length of Road $D = a$ and Road B and Road D are connected with each other at 90°.

[angle in a semi-circle is a right angle]

$\therefore$ Road B, Road D and Road C make a right triangular region.

Now, area of the region bounded by Road A, Road B and Road C

$$= \frac{1}{2} \times \text{base} \times \text{height} = \frac{1}{2} \times a \times a = \frac{1}{2} a^2 \text{ sq. units}$$

Or

(b) The angle made by Road B on Road D is a right angle lies in semi-circle. **Ans.** Angad is correct.

Part II

1. Hint ΔAOB is an equilateral triangle. **Ans.** $AB = 5$ cm

2. Hint Join OB and OC. Now, $\angle BOC = 2\angle BAC$

[$\because$ angle subtended by the chord at centre is double the angle subtended by it on any other point on the circle]

$\therefore \quad \angle BOC = 60°$

In ΔBOC,

$OB = OC$ [radii of circle]

$\therefore \quad \angle OBC = \angle OCB = 60°$

So, ΔBOC is an equilateral triangle.

$\therefore \quad BC = OB$ [radii of circle]

3. Hint arc $AXB = \frac{1}{2} \times$ arc BYC

$\therefore \quad \angle AOB = \frac{1}{2} \times \angle BOC$ **Ans.** 120°

4. Hint We know that the angle subtended by an arc at the centre is double the angle subtended by it at any point on the remaining part of the circle. **Ans.** 40°, 40°

5. Hint The angle subtended by an arc at the centre is double the angle subtended by it at any point of remaining part of circle.

Ans. Reflex $\angle POR = 200°$

6. Hint $\angle BDC = \angle BAC$ [angles in same segment]

$\angle ABC = 90°$ [angle in a semi-circle]

Ans. 48°

7. Hint $\angle BDC = \angle BAC$ [angles in same segment]

$\therefore \quad \angle BDC = 40°$

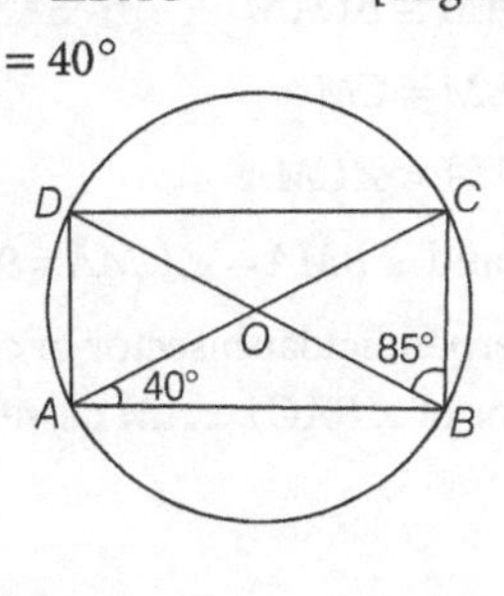

In ΔBCD, we have

$\angle BDC + \angle DBC + \angle BCD = 180°$ [angle sum property]

$\Rightarrow \quad 40° + 85° + \angle BCD = 180°$

$\Rightarrow \quad \angle BCD = 180° - 40° - 85°$

$= 180° - 125° = 55°$

If $AB = BC$, then $\angle BCA = \angle BAC = 40°$

[angles opposite to equal sides in a triangle are equal]

Now, $\angle OCD = \angle BCD - \angle BCA = 55° - 40° = 15°$

$\therefore \quad \angle BCD = 55°$ and $\angle OCD = 15°$

8. Hint $\angle DBC = \angle DAC$ [angles in same segment]

$\Rightarrow \quad \angle DAC = 60°$ [$\because DBC = 60°$]

$\therefore \quad \angle DAB = \angle BAC + \angle DAC$

$= 30° + 60° = 90°$

Now, $\angle DAB + \angle BCD = 180°$

[cyclic quadrilateral property]

Ans. 90°

9. Hint Given, $ABCD$ is a cyclic quadrilateral and $AD \parallel BC$.

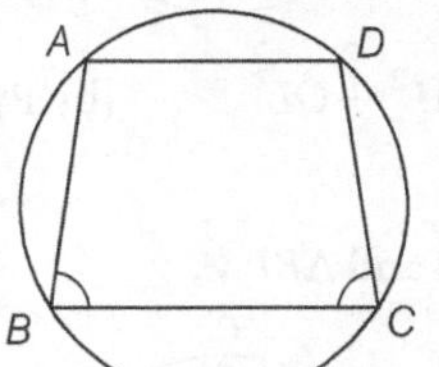

$\therefore \quad \angle A + \angle B = 180°$ ...(i)

[co-interior angles on the same side of transversal AB]

Also, $\angle A + \angle C = 180°$ ...(ii)

[sum of opposite angles of a cyclic quadrilateral]

On subtracting Eq. (ii) from Eq. (i), we get

$\angle A + \angle B - \angle A - \angle C = 0$

$\therefore \quad \angle B = \angle C$ **Hence proved.**

10. Draw two circles having centres O and O' intersecting at points A and B.

Draw parallel lines PQ and OO'.

Join OO', OP, $O'Q$, OM, $O'B$ and $O'N$.

In ΔOPB, $\quad BM = MP$ ...(i)

[since, perpendicular from the centre of a circle to a chord bisects the chord]

Similarly, in $\Delta O'BQ$, $BN = NQ$ ...(ii)

$\therefore \quad BM + BN = PM + NQ$

[adding Eqs. (i) and (ii)]

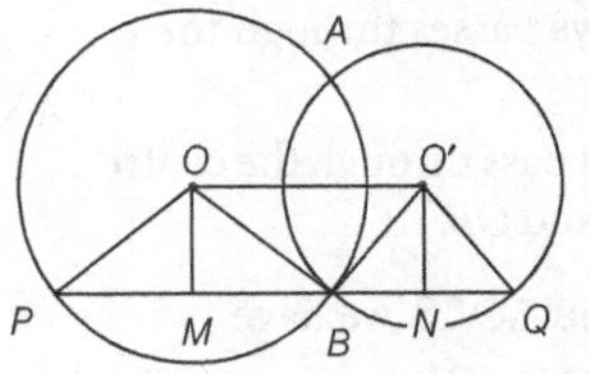

$\Rightarrow \quad 2(BM + BN) = BM + BN + PM + NQ$

[adding $BM + BN$ on both sides]

$\Rightarrow \quad 2OO' = (BM + MP) + (BN + NQ)$

$[\because OO' = MN = MB + BN]$

$= BP + BQ = PQ$

$[\because BP = BM + MP \text{ and } BQ = BN + NQ]$

$\Rightarrow \quad 2OO' = PQ$ **Hence proved.**

11. Hint Draw $OL \perp$ chord AB. Join OA.

Let radius $OA = r$

$\therefore \quad AL = \frac{AB}{2} = 8 \text{ cm}$ and $OL = 15$ cm

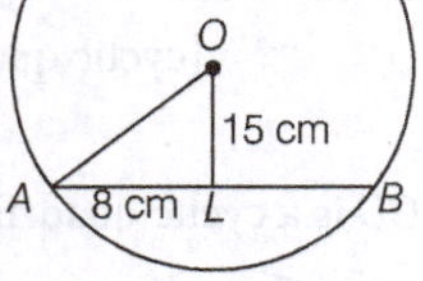

Now, $OA^2 = AL^2 + OL^2$ [by Pythagoras theorem]

Ans. 17 cm.

12. Hint In ΔAPM and ΔBPM,

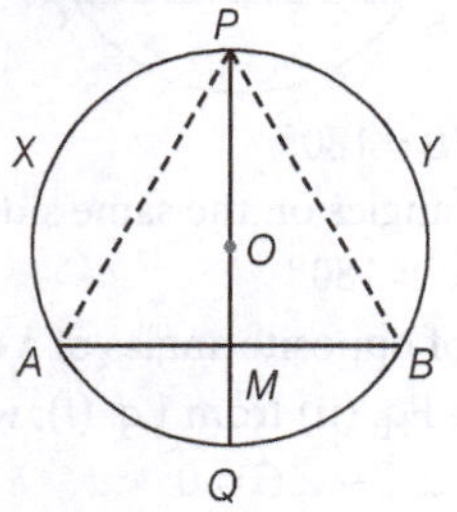

$AM = MB$ [PM bisects AB]

$PM = PM$ [common side]

$\angle AMP = \angle BMP$ [each 90°]

$\therefore \quad \Delta APM \cong \Delta BPM$ [by SAS congruence rule]

$\Rightarrow \quad PA = PB$ [by CPCT]

$\therefore \quad \text{arc } PXA \cong \text{arc } PYB$

13. Hint Let AB be a chord of a circle having its centre O. Let PQ be the right bisector of the chord AB, intersecting AB at L and the circle at Q. Since, the right bisector of a chord always passes through the centre.

So, PQ must pass through the centre O. Join OA and OB.

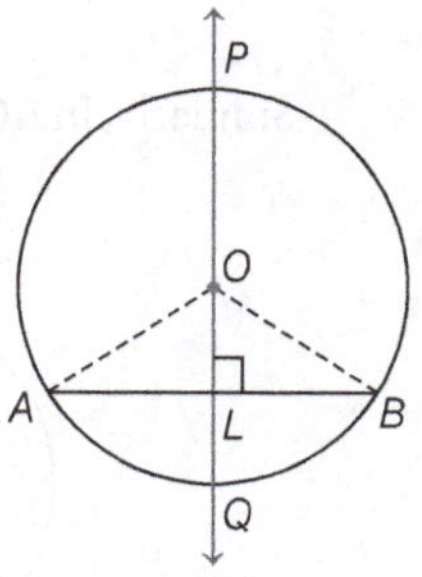

In ΔOLA and ΔOLB, we have

$OA = OB$ [radii of same circle]

$\angle ALO = \angle BLO$ [each 90°]

$OL = OL$ [common sides]

$\therefore \quad \Delta OLA \cong \Delta OLB$ [by RHS congruence rule]

Then, $\angle AOL = \angle BOL$ [by CPCT]

$\therefore \quad \widehat{AQ} = \widehat{BQ}$ **Hence proved.**

14. Hint Let AB and CD be two parallel chords having P and Q as their mid-points, respectively. Let O be the centre of the circle. Join OP and OQ and draw $OX \parallel AB \parallel CD$.

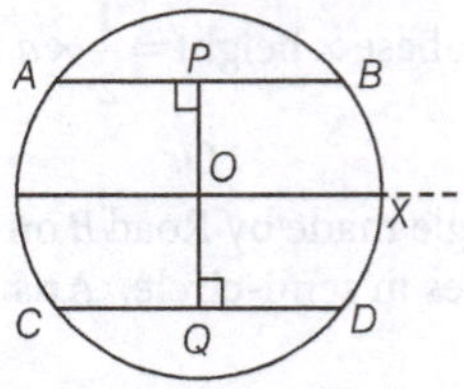

Now, P is the mid-point of AB.

Then, $OP \perp AB \Rightarrow \angle APO = \angle BPO = 90°$

But $OX \parallel AB$

$\therefore \quad \angle POX = \angle APO$ [alternate interior angles]

$\Rightarrow \quad \angle POX = 90°$

Similarly, $\angle XOQ = \angle CQO = 90°$

[alternate interior angles]

Now, $\angle POX + \angle XOQ = 90° + 90° = 180°$

So, POQ is a straight line.

Hence, PQ is a straight line passing through the centre of the circle. **Hence proved.**

15. Hint Given, AB and AC are two equal chords whose centre is O.

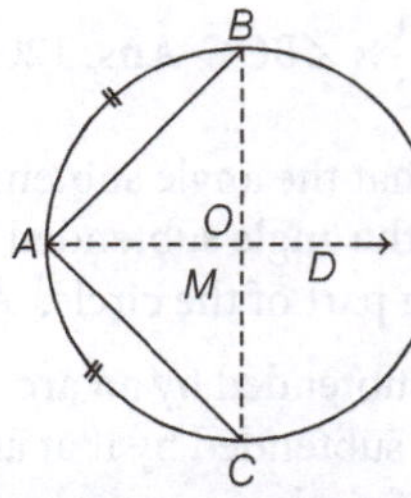

Join BC and draw bisector AD of $\angle BAC$.

In ΔBAM and ΔCAM, we have

$AB = AC$ [given]

$\angle BAM = \angle CAM$ [given]

and $AM = AM$ [common sides]

$\therefore \quad \Delta BAM \cong \Delta CAM$ [by SAS congruence rule]

$\Rightarrow \quad BM = CM$ [by CPCT]

and $\angle BMA = \angle CMA$ [by CPCT]

So, $BM = CM$ and $\angle BMA = \angle CMA = 90°$

$\therefore AM$ is the perpendicular bisector of chord BC.

Hence, bisector of $\angle BAC$ i.e. AM passes through the centre O. **Hence proved.**

16. Hint L is the mid-point of AB.

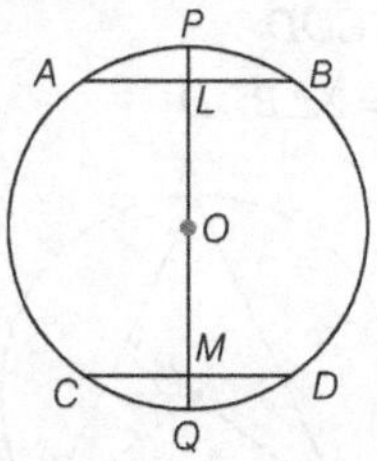

$\therefore \quad OL \perp AB$

[since, the line joining the centre of a circle to the mid-point of a chord is perpendicular to the chord]

$\therefore \quad \angle ALO = 90^\circ$ ...(i)

Similarly, $\quad OM \perp CD$

$\therefore \quad \angle OMD = 90^\circ$ ...(ii)

$\angle ALO = \angle OMD$ [alternate angles]

17. Hint Draw a circle passing through the points B, C, M and N.

$\therefore \ \angle BMC = \angle BNC = 90^\circ$

Since, if a line segment joining two points subtends equal angles at two other point lying on the same side of the line containing the line segment, then four points lie on a circle are concylic.

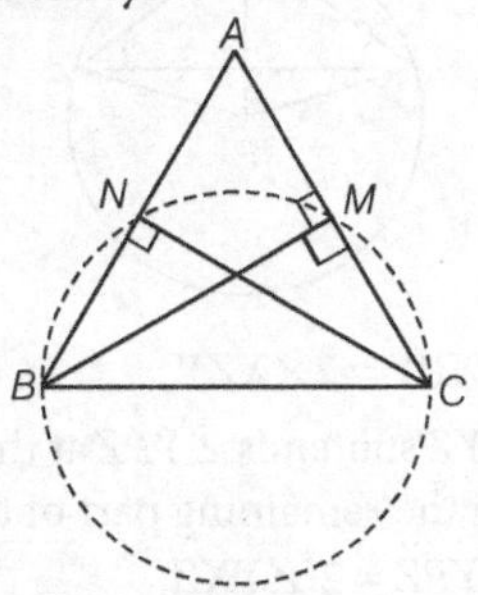

Hence, B, C, M and N are concylic.

18. Hint Draw $OP \perp AB$ and $OQ \perp AC$

In ΔAOP and ΔAOQ,

$\Rightarrow \quad \angle OPA = \angle OQA = 90^\circ$ [by construction]

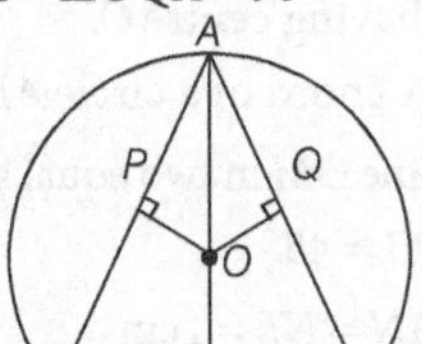

$\Rightarrow \quad \angle OAP = \angle OAQ$ [given]

$\Rightarrow \quad OA = AO$ [common side]

$\therefore \quad \Delta AOP \cong \Delta AOQ$ [by AAS congruence rule]

$\Rightarrow \quad OP = OQ$ [by CPCT]

$\therefore \quad AB = AC$

[$\because$ chords equidistant from the centre of circle are equal in length]

19. Hint $\because AB = AC$

$\Rightarrow \quad OD = OE$

[equal chords are equidistant from the centre]

In ΔAOD and ΔAOE,

$\Rightarrow \quad OA = AO$ [common]

$\Rightarrow \quad \angle ADO = \angle AEO$ [each 90°]

$\Rightarrow \quad OD = OE$

$\therefore \quad \Delta AOD \cong \Delta AOE$ [RHS congruence rule]

$\therefore \quad AD = AE$

Thus, ΔADE is an isosceles triangle.

Also, by congruent parts of congruent triangles,

$\angle ABC = \angle ACB$

20. Hint In $\Delta OBD, BD = OD$ [given]

$OD = OB$ [radii of same circle]

$\therefore \quad OB = OD = BD$

So, ΔODB is an equilateral triangle.

Then, $\angle BOD = \angle OBD = \angle ODB = 60^\circ$

In ΔBMC and ΔBMD, we have

$MB = MB$ [common side]

$\angle CMB = \angle BMD = 90^\circ$ [$\because CD \perp AB$]

$CM = MD$ [chord bisector]

$\therefore \quad \Delta BMC \cong \Delta BMD$ [by SAS congruence rule]

Then, $\angle MBC = \angle MBD = 60^\circ$ [$\because \angle OBD = 60^\circ$]

Since, AB is a diameter of the circle.

$\therefore \quad \angle ACB = 90^\circ$

In ΔACB, $\angle CAB + \angle CBA + \angle ACB = 180^\circ$

[by angle sum property of a triangle]

$\Rightarrow \quad \angle CAB + 60^\circ + 90^\circ = 180^\circ$

$\Rightarrow \quad \angle CAB = 180^\circ - (60^\circ + 90^\circ) = 30^\circ$

21. (i) Let us assume that A, B and C be the positions of Priyanka, Sonia and David respectively on the boundary of circular park with centre O.

Draw $AD \perp BC$.

Since, the centre of the circle coincides with the centroid of the equilateral ΔABC.

$\therefore$ Radius of circumscribed circle $= \dfrac{2}{3} AD$

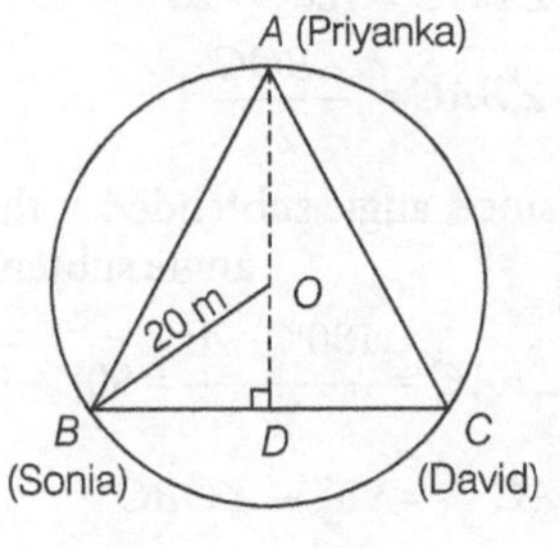

$\Rightarrow \quad 20 = \dfrac{2}{3} AD \Rightarrow AD = 20 \times \dfrac{3}{2}$

$\Rightarrow \quad AD = 30$ m

Now, $AD \perp BC$ and

Let $AB = BC = CA = x$ m

$\Rightarrow BD = CD = \frac{1}{2}BC = \frac{x}{2}$ m

In right angle ΔBDA, $\angle D = 90°$

$\therefore$ By Pythagoras theorem, we have

$$AB^2 = BD^2 + AD^2$$

$$\Rightarrow \quad x^2 = \left(\frac{x}{2}\right)^2 + (30)^2$$

$$\Rightarrow \quad x^2 - \frac{x^2}{4} = 900$$

$$\Rightarrow \quad \frac{3}{4}x^2 = 900 \Rightarrow x^2 = 900 \times \frac{4}{3}$$

$$x^2 = 1200$$

$$\Rightarrow \quad x = \sqrt{1200} = 20\sqrt{3}$$

Hence, distance between each of them is $20\sqrt{3}$ m.

(ii) Since, ΔABC is an equilateral triangle.

Therefore, area of $\Delta ABC = \frac{\sqrt{3}}{4}(\text{side})^2 = \frac{\sqrt{3}}{4} \times (20\sqrt{3})^2$

$$= \frac{\sqrt{3}}{4} \times 400 \times 3$$

$$= 300\sqrt{3} \text{ m}^2$$

22. Hint In ΔBAE

$$\angle ABE + \angle BAE + \angle AEB = 180°$$

[angle sum property]

$$\angle ABE = 180° - 90° - 55° = 35°$$

Now, $\angle ABC = \frac{1}{2}\angle AOC$

[$\because$ angle subtended at the arc is half of the angle subtended at the centre]

$\therefore \quad \angle ABC = \frac{1}{2} \times 100° = 50°$

Ans. $\angle ABE = 35°, \angle ABC = 50°$

23. Hint Let $\angle OBC = \angle OCB = \theta$

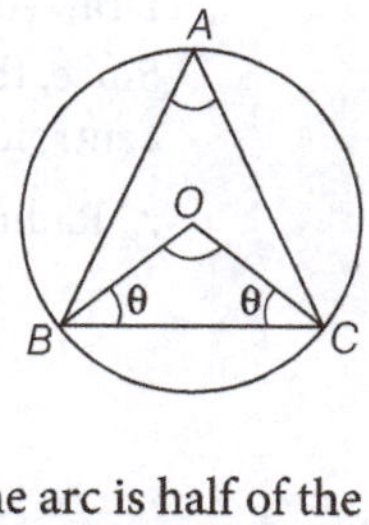

In ΔOBC,

$$\angle BOC + \theta + \theta = 180°$$

$$\Rightarrow \quad \angle BOC = 180° - 2\theta$$

$$\because \quad \angle BAC = \frac{\angle BOC}{2}$$

[since, angle subtended at the arc is half of the angle subtended at the centre]

$$\therefore \quad \angle BAC = \frac{180° - 2\theta}{2} = 90° - \theta$$

$\angle BAC = 90° - \angle OBC$ [$\because \angle OBC = \theta$]

$\Rightarrow \quad \angle BAC + \angle OBC = 90°$ **Hence proved.**

24. Hint Prove $\Delta ODB \cong \Delta ODC$ by SSS congruence rule, then $\angle BOD = \angle COD$

$\therefore \quad \angle BOC = 2\angle BOD$ ...(i)

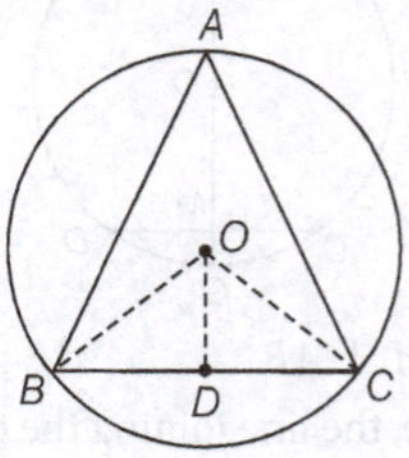

Also, $\angle BAC = \frac{1}{2}\angle BOC$

[since, the angle subtended by an arc at the centre is twice the angle subtended by it at any point on the remaining part of the circle]

$\Rightarrow \quad \angle BAC = \frac{2}{2}\angle BOD$

[from Eq. (i), $\angle BOC = 2\angle BOD$]

25. Hint Since, arc XY subtends $\angle XPY$ at the centre and $\angle XZY$ at a point Z in the remaining part of the circle.

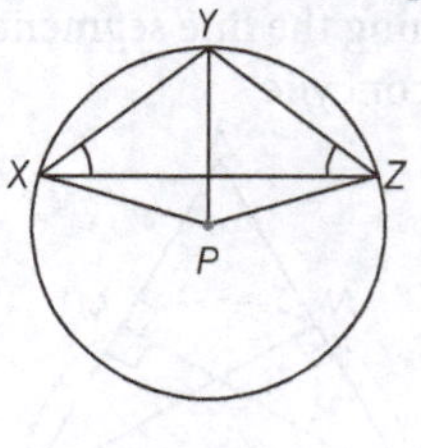

$\therefore \quad \angle XPY = 2\angle XZY$ ...(i)

Similarly, arc YZ subtends $\angle YPZ$ at the centre and $\angle YXZ$ at a point X in the remaining part of the circle.

$\therefore \quad \angle YPZ = 2\angle YXZ$ ...(ii)

On adding Eqs. (i) and (ii), we get

$$\angle XPY + \angle YPZ = 2\angle XZY + 2\angle YXZ$$

$\Rightarrow \quad \angle XPZ = 2(\angle XZY + \angle YXZ)$ **Hence proved.**

26. Given A circle having centre O.

Construction A chord of a circle $AB = 2$ cm, which is divided by the line OM in two equal segments.

To prove $\angle APB = 45°$

Proof Here, $AN = NB = 1$ cm

and $OA = OB = \sqrt{2}$ cm

In ΔONB, by Pythagoras theorem,

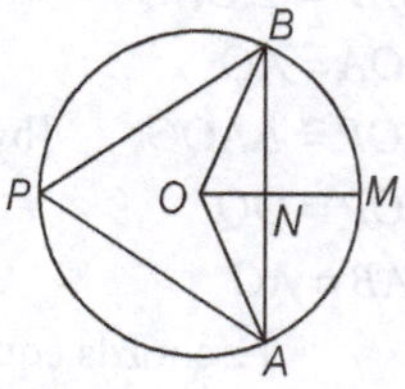

$$OB^2 = ON^2 + NB^2$$

$\Rightarrow \quad (\sqrt{2})^2 = ON^2 + (1)^2$

$\Rightarrow \quad ON^2 = 2 - 1 = 1 \Rightarrow ON = 1\text{cm}$

So, ΔONB is an isosceles triangle.

$\because \quad \angle ONB = 90°$

[since, ON is the perpendicular bisector of the chord AB]

$\therefore \quad \angle NOB = \angle NBO = 45°$

Similarly, $\quad \angle AON = 45°$

Now, $\quad \angle AOB = \angle AON + \angle NOB = 45° + 45° = 90°$

$\therefore \quad \angle APB = \frac{1}{2}\angle AOB$

[since, the angle subtended by an arc at the centre is twice the angle subtended by it at any point on the remaining part of the circle]

$\therefore \quad \angle APB = \frac{90°}{2} = 45°$ **Hence proved.**

27. Here, A, B and C represented 3 STD booths.

(i) As, A, B and C are equidistant from each other.

$\therefore \quad AB = BC = CA$

Then, ΔABC is an equilateral triangle.

Hence, $\angle BAC = \angle ABC = \angle BCA = 60°$

(ii) We know that the angle subtended by an arc at the centre of the circle is twice the angle subtended by it at any point on the remaining part of the circle.

$\therefore \quad \angle BOC = 2\angle BAC$

From part (i), $\angle BAC = 60°$

Hence, $\angle BOC = 2 \times 60° = 120°$

(iii) Since, ΔABC is an equilateral triangle.

$\therefore$ Area of $\Delta ABC = \frac{\sqrt{3}}{4}(\text{side})^2$

$= \frac{\sqrt{3}}{4} \times (2)^2 = \sqrt{3}\,\text{cm}^2$

28. Hint Given M, R, N, P, S and Q are concyclic.

Clearly, $\quad \angle PQR = \frac{1}{2}\angle POR \quad$ ...(i)

$\angle NMS = \frac{1}{2}\angle NOS \quad$ ...(ii)

[since, angle subtended by an arc at the centre is double the angle subtended by it at any point on the remaining part of the circle]

Let $\quad \angle OPR = x$

Then, $\quad \angle POR = 180° - 2x$

i.e. $\quad \angle POR = 180° - 2\angle OPR$

Similarly, $\quad \angle NOS = 180° - 2\angle OSN$

On substituting these values in Eqs. (i) and (ii), we get

$\angle PQR = \frac{1}{2}(180° - 2\angle OPR)$

$\Rightarrow \quad \angle PQR = 90° - \angle OPR \quad$ ...(iii)

and $\angle NMS = \frac{1}{2}(180° - 2\angle OSN)$

$\Rightarrow \angle NMS = 90° - \angle OSN \quad$ ...(iv)

On adding Eqs. (iii) and (iv), we get

$\angle PQR + \angle NMS + \angle OPR + \angle OSN = 180°$

29. Hint $\angle ACB = \angle ADB = 30°$ [same segment angle]

In ΔCAB, $\angle CAB + \angle ACB + \angle ABC = 180°$

[angle sum property]

$\Rightarrow \quad \angle CAB + 30° + 40° = 180°$ **Ans.** 110°

30. Hint $\angle DBC = \angle CAD = 55°$ [same segment angle]

Also, $\angle BAC = \angle BDC = 45°$ [same segment angle]

In ΔBCD, $\angle BCD + \angle DBC + \angle BDC = 180°$

[angle sum property of triangle]

$\Rightarrow \quad \angle BCD + 55° + 45° = 180°$ **Ans.** 80°.

31. Hint Join OE,

$\therefore \angle EOC = 2\angle EBC$

[$\because$ angle subtended by the arc at the centre is double the angle subtended by it at any point on the remaining part of the circle]

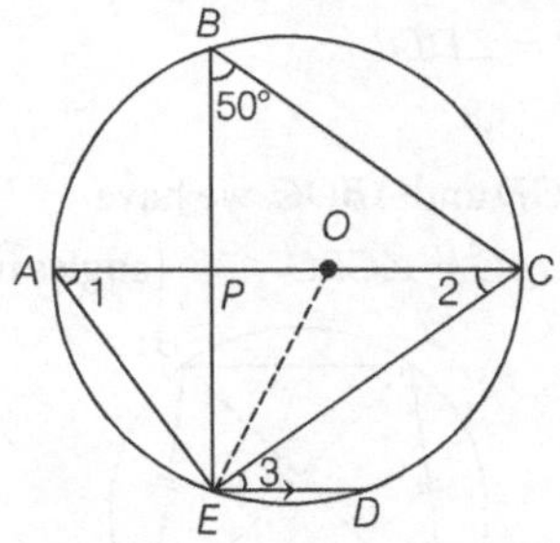

$\therefore \quad \angle EOC = 2 \times 50° = 100°$

In ΔOEC, $\angle OEC + \angle OCE + \angle EOC = 180°$

$\Rightarrow \quad \angle OCE + \angle OEC + 100° = 180°$

$\Rightarrow \quad \angle OCE + \angle OCE = 80°$

[$\because OE = OC$, radii]

$\therefore \quad \angle OCE = 40°$

$\therefore \quad AC \parallel ED$,

$\therefore \quad \angle CED = \angle OCE$ **Ans.** 40°

32. Hint $\angle CAD = \angle CDA = 38°$

[angles opposite to equal sides]

$\Rightarrow \quad \angle ACB = 180° - \angle ACD$ [linear pair]

$\because \quad AB = AC$

$\therefore \quad \angle ABC = \angle ACB$

Now, $\angle BAC = 180° - \angle ABC - \angle ACB$

$\angle BAC = \angle BEC$

[angles in the same segment are equal]

Ans. $\angle ABC = 76°$, $\angle BEC = 28°$

33. (i) As $ABCD$ is a rectangle, so each angle of a rectangle is 90°.

We know that if any chord subtends a right angle, then the chord BD is said to be the diameter of a circle.

(ii) Diagonal of the rectangular turf

$$= \sqrt{(60)^2 + (80)^2} = 100 \text{ m}$$

Since, rectangular turf is spread on the ground. So, its diagonal will be the diameter of the ground.

Hence, radius of circular ground $= \frac{100}{2} = 50$ m

(iii) $\therefore$ Area of $\Delta BCD = \frac{1}{2} \times BC \times CD$

$$= \frac{1}{2} \times 80 \times 60 = 2400 \text{m}^2$$

34. Hint $\angle AFB = \angle ACB$ ...(i)

[$\because$ angles in the same segment]

and $\angle DFE = \angle ECD$ ...(ii)

[$\because$ angles in the same segment]

Also, $\angle ACB = \angle ECD$ ...(iii)

[vertically opposite angles]

From Eqs. (i), (ii) and (iii), we get

$\angle AFB = \angle DFE$

$\therefore \quad \angle DFE = 48°$ [$\because \angle AFB = 48°$]

35. Hint In ΔAOD and ΔBOC, we have

$\angle DAO = \angle CBO$ [angles in same segment]

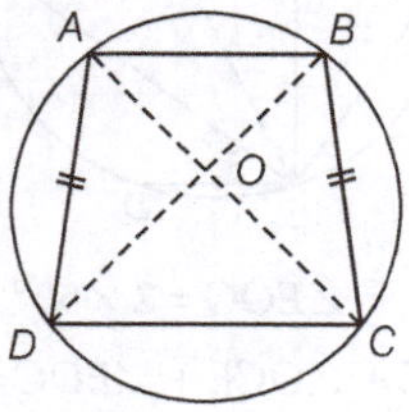

$\angle ODA = \angle OCB$ [angle in same segment]

$AD = BC$ [given]

$\therefore \quad \Delta AOD \cong \Delta BOC$ [by ASA congruence rule]

$\therefore \quad OA = OB$ ...(i)

and $\quad OC = OD$ ...(ii) [by CPCT]

On adding Eqs. (i) and (ii), we get

$OA + OC = OB + OD$

$\Rightarrow \quad AC = BD$ **Hence proved.**

36. Hint

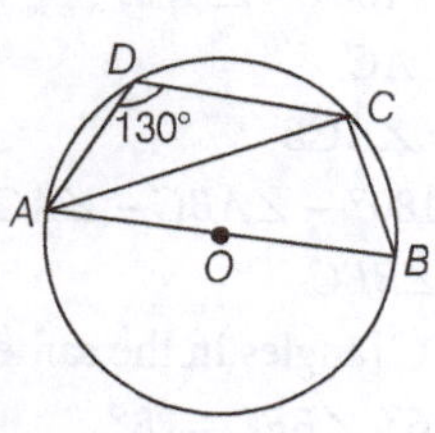

Here, $\angle ADC + \angle ABC = 180°$

[$\because$ sum of opposite angles of a cyclic quadrilateral is 180°]

$\Rightarrow \quad 130° + \angle ABC = 180°$

$\Rightarrow \quad \angle ABC = 50°$

$\therefore \quad \angle ACB = 90°$

In ΔABC,

$\angle BAC + \angle ACB + \angle ABC = 180°$

Ans. 40°

37. Hint Join CD

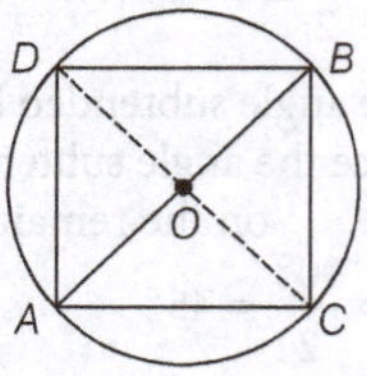

Let O be the mid-point of AB.

$\therefore OA = OB = OC = OD$

Since, mid-point of the hypotenuse of right triangle is equidistant from its vertices.

Therefore, O is the centre of circle passing through A, C, B and D.

$\therefore \quad \angle BAC = \angle BDC$ [angle in same segment]

Hence proved.

38. Hint In the given figure, $ABCD$ is a cyclic quadrilateral.

$\therefore (2x + 4) + (4x - 64) = 180°$

[$\because$ Sum of opposite angles of a cyclic quadrilateral is 180°]

Ans. $x = 40°$

39. Hint $\because$ Sum of opposite angles of cyclic quadrilateral is 180°.

$\therefore \quad \angle AEC + \angle ABC = 180°$

$\Rightarrow \quad 110° + \angle ABC = 180°$

$\therefore \quad \angle ABC = 70°$

and $\quad \angle ABC = \angle ADC$ [same segment angle]

Ans. 70°, 70°

40. Hint $\because \angle CBQ = \angle ABP = 40°$

$\therefore \angle DCB = x + 40°$ and $\angle DAB = y + 40°$

[exterior angle of a triangle is equal to the sum of interior opposite angles]

Now, use the property that sum of opposite angles of a cyclic quadrilateral is 180°.

Ans. 25°

41. Hint Let we consider the points A, B, C and D formed a cyclic quadrilateral. Then, sum of opposite angles of a quadrilateral is 180°.

$\therefore \quad \angle ADC + \angle OBC = 180°$ [$\because \angle ABC = \angle OBC$]

$\Rightarrow \quad 130° + \angle OBC = 180°$

$\Rightarrow \quad \angle OBC = 180° - 130° = 50°$

Now, in ΔBOC and ΔBOE,

$BC = BE$ [given]

$OC = OE$ [radii of the same circle]

$OB = OB$ [common side]

$\therefore \quad \Delta BOC \cong \Delta BOE$ [by SSS congruence rule]

Then, $\angle OBC = \angle OBE$ [by CPCT]

$\therefore \angle OBE = \angle OBC = 50°$ [from Eq. (i)]

$\therefore \quad \angle CBE = \angle OBC + \angle OBE$

$= 50° + 50° = 100°$

42. Hint $\angle BAD = \frac{1}{2}\angle BOD$ **Ans.** 100°

43. Hint Given ΔABC is an isosceles triangle such that $AB = AC$ and $DE \parallel BC$.

To prove Quadrilateral $BCDE$ is a cyclic quadrilateral.

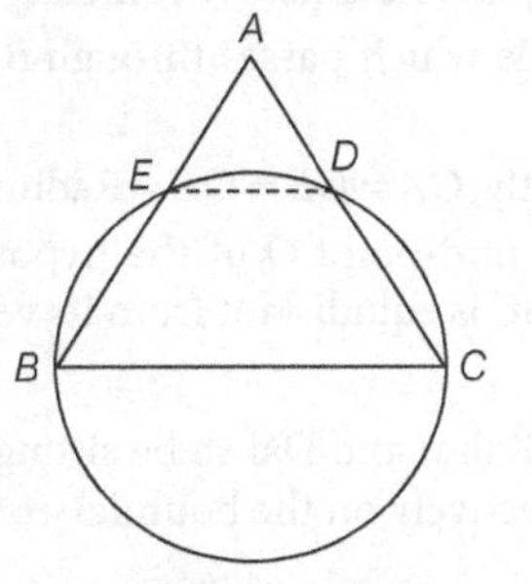

Construction Draw a circle passes through the points B, C, D and E.

Proof In ΔABC, $AB = AC$

[equal sides of an isosceles triangle]

$\Rightarrow \quad \angle ACB = \angle ABC$ ... (i)

[angles opposite to the equal sides]

$\because \quad DE \parallel BC$

$\Rightarrow \quad \angle ADE = \angle ACB$ ... (ii)

On adding $\angle EDC$ both sides in Eq. (ii), we get

$\angle ADE + \angle EDC = \angle ACB + \angle EDC$

$\Rightarrow \quad 180° = \angle ACB + \angle EDC$

$\Rightarrow \quad 180° = \angle ABC + \angle EDC$ [From Eq. (i)]

$\therefore$ $BCDE$ is a cyclic quadrilateral because the sum of opposite angles of quadrilateral is 180°.

44. Hint Sum of opposite angles of cyclic quadrilateral is 180°.

$\therefore \quad \angle ABC = 180° - 80° = 100°$

and $\quad \angle ABC + \angle CBE = 180°$ [linear pair]

$\Rightarrow \quad \angle CBE = 80°$ ... (i)

In ΔBCE,

$\angle CBE + \angle BCE + \angle CEB = 180°$

[angle sum property of triangle]

$\therefore \quad \angle BCE = 50°$ ... (ii)

Now, $\angle BCD + \angle BCE = 180°$ [linear pair]

$\Rightarrow \angle BCD = 180° - 50° = 130°$

and $\angle BAD + \angle BCD = 180°$

[sum of opposite angles of cyclic quadrilateral is 180°]

$\therefore \quad \angle BAD = 50°$

Now, $\angle CDF = 180° - \angle ADC$ [linear pair]

$= 100°$ ... (iii)

and $\angle DCF = \angle BCE = 50°$ [vertically opposite angles]

In ΔDCE,

$\angle CDF + \angle DCF + \angle CFD = 180°$

[angle sum property of triangle]

$\Rightarrow \quad \angle CFD = 30°$

45. Hint Since, $ACDE$ is a cyclic quadrilateral.

$\therefore \quad \angle ACD + \angle AED = 180°$ ...(i)

[$\because$ sum of opposite angles in a cyclic quadrilateral is 180°]

Also, $\angle AEB = 90°$ [angle in semi-circle] ...(ii)

On adding Eqs. (i) and (ii), we get

$\angle ACD + (\angle AED + \angle AEB) = 180° + 90°$

$\Rightarrow \quad \angle ACD + \angle BED = 270°$

Hence, the value of $(\angle ACD + \angle BED)$ is 270°.

46. (i) Since, points A, B, C and D lie on a circle. Therefore, $ABCD$ is cyclic quadrilateral.

In cyclic quadrilateral, sum of opposite angle is 180°.

$\therefore \quad \angle D + \angle B = 180° \Rightarrow 110° - x + 90° = 180°$

$\Rightarrow \quad x = 200° - 180°$

$\Rightarrow \quad x = 20°$

(ii) Also, $\angle A + \angle C = 180°$

$\angle A + 115° = 180°$

$\Rightarrow \angle A = 65°$

(iii) Here, $\angle D = 110° - 20° = 90°$

We know that if any chord subtends a right angle to the circumference, then that chord AC will be the diameter of circle.

Hence, chord AC passes through the centre of circle.

47. Given A, B and C are three points on a circle.

To prove The perpendicular bisectors of AB, BC and CA are concurrent.

Construction Join AB, BC and CA.

Draw ST, PM and QR perpendicular bisectors of AB, BC and CA respectively.

Proof

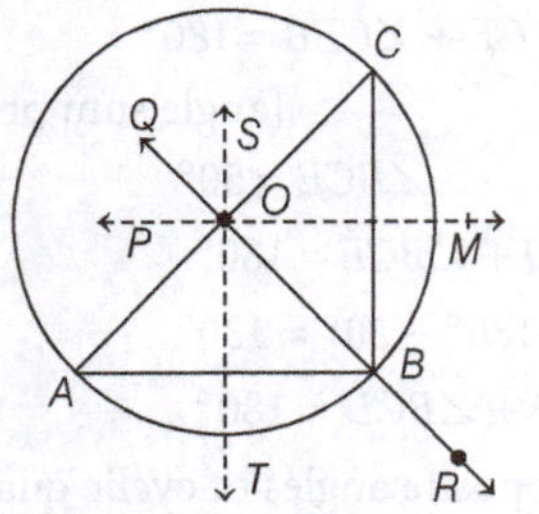

Since, O lies on ST, PM and QR perpendicular bisector of AB, BC and CA respectively.

$\therefore \quad OA = OB \quad \dots$ (i)

$\Rightarrow \quad OB = OC \quad \dots$ (ii)

$\Rightarrow \quad OC = OA \quad \dots$ (iii)

$\therefore \quad OA = OB = OC \quad$ [say r]

[from Eqs. (i), (ii) and (iii)]

Now, with O as centre and r as radius, draw circle which pass through A, B and C.

$\therefore$ Circle passing through the points A, B and C.

Since, ST, PM and QR can cut each other at O.

$\therefore$ O is the only point equidistant from A, B and C.

$\therefore$ The perpendicular bisectors of AB, BC and CA are concurrent.

48. Hint Let $AC = a$, then $AB = 2a$.

From centre O, perpendicular is drawn to the chords AC and AB at M and N, respectively.

$\therefore \quad AM = MC = \dfrac{a}{2}$ and $AN = NB = a$

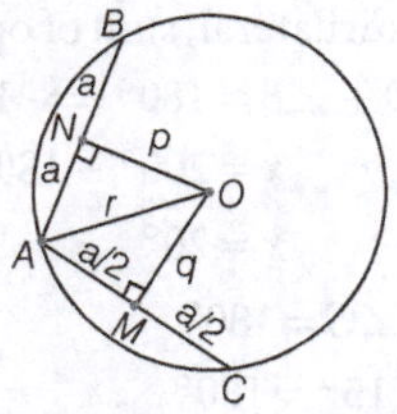

In ΔOMA and ΔONA, by Pythagoras theorem,

$$AO^2 = AM^2 + MO^2$$

$$\Rightarrow \quad AO^2 = \left(\frac{a}{2}\right)^2 + q^2 \quad \dots\text{(i)}$$

and $$AO^2 = (AN)^2 + (NO)^2$$

$$\Rightarrow \quad AO^2 = (a)^2 + p^2 \quad \dots\text{(ii)}$$

From Eqs. (i) and (ii), we get

$$\left(\frac{a}{2}\right)^2 + q^2 = a^2 + p^2$$

$$\Rightarrow \quad 4q^2 = 4p^2 + 3a^2 \Rightarrow 4q^2 = p^2 + 3r^2$$

[$\because$ in right angled ΔONA, $r^2 = a^2 + p^2$]

Hence proved.

49. Hint Let ΔABC be a right angled triangle such that $\angle BAC = 90°$.

Let O be the mid-point of the hypotenuse BC. Then, $OB = OC$. With O as centre and OB as radius, draw a circle.

Clearly, this circle passes through the points B and C.

If possible, suppose this circle does not pass through A. Let it meets BA or BA' produced at A'.

Then, $\angle BA'C = 90°$ [since, angle in a semi-circle is $90°$]

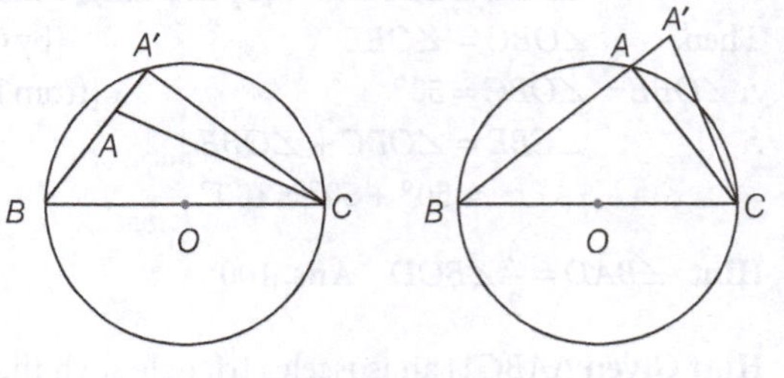

But $\quad \angle BAC = 90°$

$\therefore \quad \angle BA'C = \angle BAC$

This is not possible unless A coincide A'.

So, the circle which passes through B and C, also passes through A.

Consequently, $OA = OB = OC =$ Radius of the circle

Hence, the mid-point O of the hypotenuse BC of right angled ΔABC is equidistant from its vertices.

Hence proved.

50. Let Aman, Rahul and Daksh be sitting on the points A, B and C, respectively on the boundary of circular park.

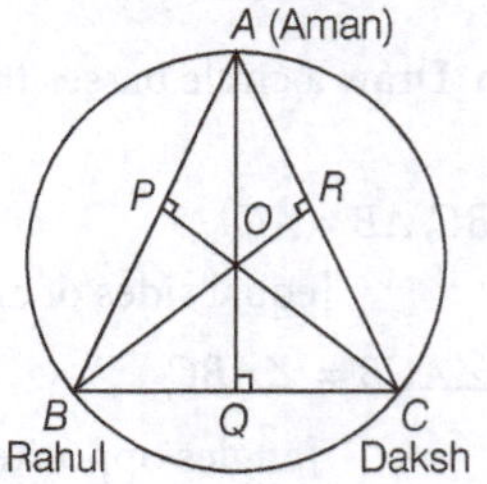

$\therefore \quad AB = BC = AC$

$\therefore$ ΔABC is an equilateral triangle.

Let $AB = BC = AC = x$ m

Now, draw altitude AQ, CP and BR from vertices to the sides of triangle and intersect at the centre O.

$\because$ ΔABC is an equilateral triangle, these altitudes bisect their sides.

In right angled ΔAQB,

$$AB^2 = AQ^2 + BQ^2 \quad \text{[by Pythagoras theorem]}$$

$$\Rightarrow \quad x^2 = AQ^2 + \left(\frac{x}{2}\right)^2$$

$$\Rightarrow \quad AQ = \frac{\sqrt{3}}{2}x$$

Now, $OQ = AQ - OA = \frac{\sqrt{3}}{2}x - 15$

[$\because AO$ = radius = 15 cm]

In right angled ΔBQO,

$$OB^2 = BQ^2 + OQ^2$$

$$\Rightarrow \quad 15^2 = \left(\frac{x}{2}\right)^2 + \left(\frac{\sqrt{3}}{2}x - 15\right)^2$$

$$\Rightarrow \quad 225 = \frac{x^2}{4} + \frac{3}{4}x^2 - 15\sqrt{3}x + 225$$

$\Rightarrow \quad x^2 - 15\sqrt{3}x = 0 \Rightarrow x(x - 15\sqrt{3}) = 0$

$\Rightarrow \quad x = 0$ or $x = 15\sqrt{3}$

But $x = 0$ is not possible.

$\therefore \quad x = 15\sqrt{3}$ m

Thus, $AB = BC = AC = 15\sqrt{3}$ m

51. Hint Join OE, draw $OL \perp AB$ and $OM \perp CD$.

In ΔOLE and ΔOME, $OL = OM$

[$\because$ equal chords are equidistant from the centre]

$OE = EO$ [common side]

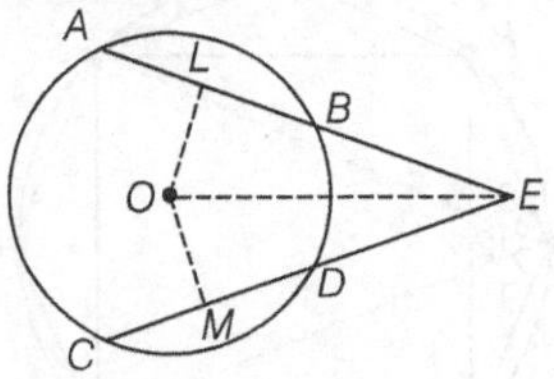

$\Rightarrow \quad \angle OLE = OME$ [each 90°]

$\therefore \quad \Delta OLE \cong \Delta OME$ [by RHS congruence rule]

$\Rightarrow \quad LE = ME$ [by CPCT] ... (i)

Since, $AB = CD$ ... (ii)

$\Rightarrow \quad \frac{1}{2}AB = \frac{1}{2}CD$

$\Rightarrow \quad BL = DM$ ... (iii)

On subtracting Eq. (iii) from Eq. (i), we get

$LE - BL = ME - DM$

$\Rightarrow \quad BE = DE$ ...(iv)

On adding Eqs. (ii) and (iv), we get

$AB + BE = CD + DE$

$\Rightarrow \quad AE = CE$ **Hence proved.**

52. Hint In ΔBOC,

$BO = CO$ [radii of a circle]

$\therefore \quad \angle OCB = \angle OBC = 30°$

[equal sides have corresponding equal angles]

$\therefore \quad \angle BOC = 180° - (\angle OBC + \angle OCB)$

[angle sum property of a triangle]

$= 180° - (30° + 30°) = 120°$ ...(i)

Also, $\angle BOC = 2\,\angle BAC$

[$\because$ angle subtended by the arc at the centre is double the angle subtended by it at any point on the remaining part of the circle]

$\therefore \quad \angle BAC = \frac{120°}{2} = 60°$ [dividing by 2]

Also, $\angle BAE = \angle CAE = 30°$

$\Rightarrow \quad \angle BAE = x = 30°$

Then, $\angle COE = \angle BOE = \frac{1}{2}\angle BOC$

$= \frac{1}{2} \times 120° = 60°$ [using Eq. (i)]

Now, $\quad \angle DOE = 90°$

$\Rightarrow \quad \angle DOC + \angle COE = 90°$

$\Rightarrow \quad \angle DOC + 60° = 90°$

$\Rightarrow \angle DOC = 90° - 60° = 30°$

We know that

$\angle DOC = 2\angle DBC$

[$\because$ angle subtended by the arc at the centre is double the angle subtended by it at any point on the remaining part of the circle]

$\Rightarrow \quad \angle DBC = \frac{1}{2} \times \angle DOC$

$\Rightarrow \quad y = \frac{1}{2} \times 30° \Rightarrow y = 15°$

53. Hint We know that, the angles subtended by an arc of a circle at its centre is twice the angle subtended by it at any point of the alternate segment of the circle.

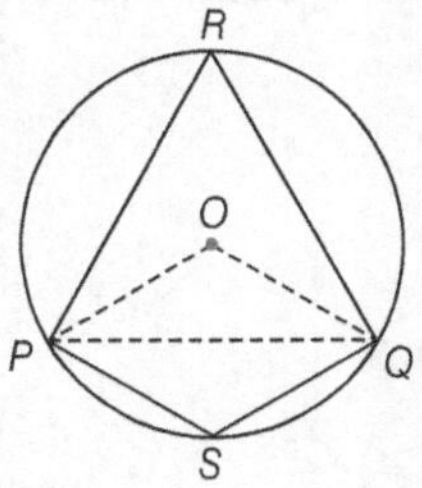

Since, $\widehat{PQ}$ is a minor arc and $\angle PRQ$ is the angle formed by it in alternate segment.

$\therefore \quad 2\angle PRQ = \angle POQ$

$\Rightarrow \quad 2\angle PRQ < 180°$

[since, $\angle POQ$ is an angle of ΔPOQ]

$\Rightarrow \quad \angle PRQ < 90°$

So, $\angle PRQ$ is an acute angle.

Now, $\widehat{QP}$ is a major arc and $\angle PSQ$ is the angle formed by it in the alternate segment.

$\therefore \quad 2\angle PSQ$ = reflex $\angle POQ$

$\Rightarrow \quad 2\angle PSQ = 360° - \angle POQ$

$\Rightarrow \quad 2\angle PSQ > 360° - 180°$ [$\because \angle POQ < 180°$]

$\Rightarrow \quad \angle PSQ > 90°$

Hence, $\angle PSQ$ is an obtuse angle. **Hence proved.**

54. Hint

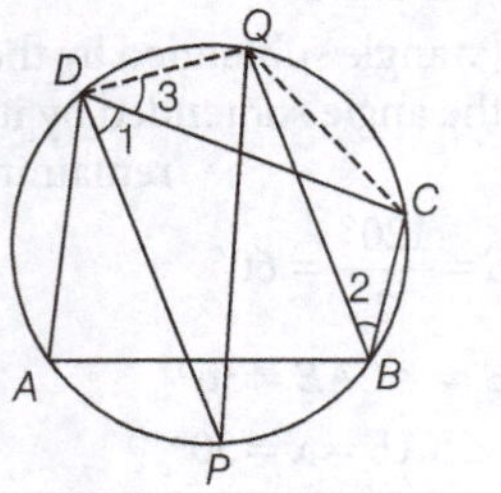

Since, $ABCD$ is a cyclic quadrilateral.

$\therefore \quad \angle CDA + \angle CBA = 180°$

[opposite angles of cyclic quadrilateral]

$\Rightarrow \quad \frac{1}{2}\angle CDA + \frac{1}{2}\angle CBA = \frac{1}{2} \times 180° = 90°$

[dividing by 2]

$\Rightarrow \quad \angle 1 + \angle 2 = 90°$

$\left[\because \angle 1 = \frac{1}{2}\angle CDA \text{ and } \angle 2 = \frac{1}{2}\angle CBA\right]$

But $\quad \angle 2 = \angle 3 \quad$ [angles in the same segment]

$\therefore \quad \angle 1 + \angle 3 = 90° \Rightarrow \angle PDQ = 90°$

Hence, PQ is a diameter.

[since, diameter subtends angle 90° in semi-circle]

Hence proved.

55. Hint We know that angles in the same segments are equal.

If is given that BE is the bisector of $\angle B$, AD is the bisector of angle $\angle A$ and CF is the bisector of $\angle C$

Thus, $ABE = \frac{\angle B}{2}$

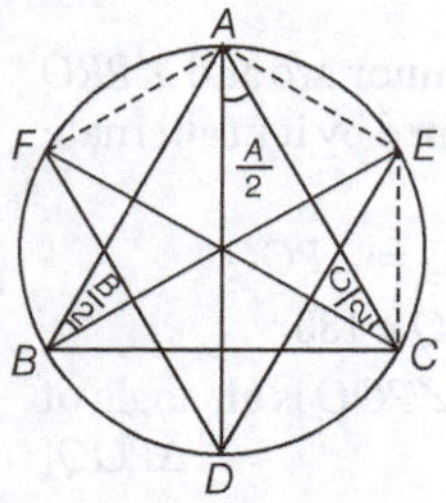

However, $\angle ADF = \angle ACF = \frac{\angle C}{2}$

[angles in the same segment for chord AF]

Thus, $\quad \angle ADE = \frac{\angle B}{2}$

Similarly, $\angle ADF = \angle ACF = \frac{\angle C}{2}$

[angles in the same segment for chord AF]

$\therefore \angle FDE = \angle ADE + \angle ADF = \frac{\angle B}{2} + \frac{\angle C}{2}$

$\left[\because \angle ADE = \frac{\angle B}{2}, \angle ADF = \frac{\angle C}{2}\right]$

$= \frac{(\angle B + \angle C)}{2} = \frac{180 - \angle A}{2} = 90° - \frac{\angle A}{2}$

[angle sum property]

Similarly, $\angle DEF = 90° - \frac{\angle B}{2}, \angle DFE = 90° - \frac{\angle C}{2}$

56. $PQRS$ is a cyclic quadrilateral and $\angle A, \angle B, \angle C$ and $\angle D$ are angles in the four exterior segments.

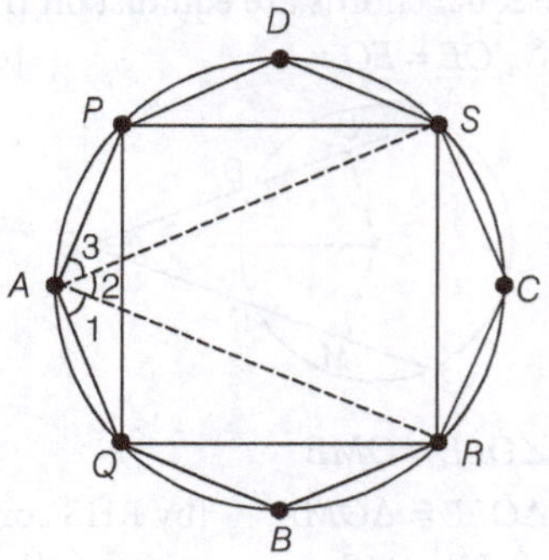

Join AS and AR.

In cyclic quadrilateral $AQBR$,

$\angle 1 + \angle B = 180° \quad$ ... (i)

In cyclic quadrilateral $ARCS$,

$\angle 2 + \angle C = 180° \quad$ ...(ii)

In cyclic quadrilateral $APDS$,

$\angle 3 + \angle D = 180° \quad$ ...(iii)

On adding Eqs. (i), (ii) and (iii), we get

$\angle 1 + \angle 2 + \angle 3 + \angle B + \angle C + \angle D$

$= 180° + 180° + 180°$

$\Rightarrow \angle A + \angle B + \angle C + \angle D = 540° = \text{Six right angles}$

Mind Map

CIRCLES

Angle Subtended by a Chord at a Point

Theorem 1
Equal chords of a circle subtend equal angles at the centre.

Theorem 2 (Converse of Theorem 1)
If the angles subtended by the chords of a circle at the centre are equal, then the chords are equal.

Cyclic Quadrilaterals

Theorem 1
The sum of either pair of opposite angles of a cyclic quadrilateral is 180°.

Theorem 2
If the sum of a pair of opposite angles of a quadrilateral is 180°, then quadrilateral is cyclic.

Perpendicular from Centre to the Chord

Theorem 1
The perpendicular from the centre of a circle to a chord bisects the chord.

Theorem 2 (Converse of Theorem 1)
The line drawn through the centre of a circle to bisect a chord is perpendicular to the chord.

Angle Subtended by an Arc of a Circle

Theorem 1
The angle subtended by an arc at the centre is double the angle subtended by it at any point on the remaining part of the circle.

Theorem 2
Angles in the same segment of a circle are equal.

Theorem 3
Angle in a semi-circle is a right angle.

Theorem 4
If a line segment joining two points subtends equal angles at two other points lying on the same side of the line containing the line segment, the four points lie on a circle. (i.e. they are concyclic).

Equal Chords and Their Distances from the Centre

The length of the perpendicular from a point to a line is the distance of the line from the point.

Theorem 1 Equal chords of a circle (or of congruent circles) are equidistant from the centre (or centres).

Theorem 2 (Converse of Theorem 1)
Chords equidistant from the centre of a circle are equal in length.

Topics to be Assessed Formatively

Terms Related to Circle

Chord

A line segment joining two points on the circumference of the circle is called a *chord* of the circle. In figure, PQ is a chord of the circle.

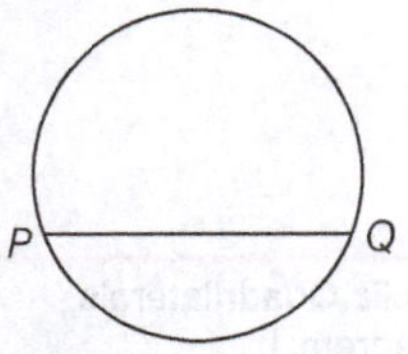

Diameter

A chord which passes through the centre of the circle is called a *diameter* of the circle. In figure, AB is the diameter of the circle. Diameter is the longest chord and all diameters have same length, which is equal to two times of the radius.

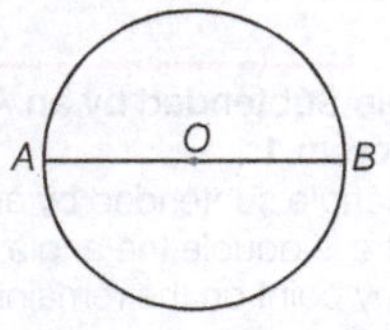

Note The word 'diameter' is also used in two senses, i.e. as a line segment and also as its length.

Circumference

The length of the complete circle is called its circumference.

Arc

A piece of a circle between two points on its circumference is called an *arc*. In other words, any part of the circumference of a circle is called an *arc* of that circle.

In adjoining figure, there are two pieces, one longer and the other smaller. The longer one is called the *major arc PRQ* and the smaller one is called the *minor arc PQ*. The minor arc $\widehat{PQ}$ is denoted by PQ and the major arc PRQ is denoted by $\widehat{PRQ}$, where R is a point on the major arc between P and Q.

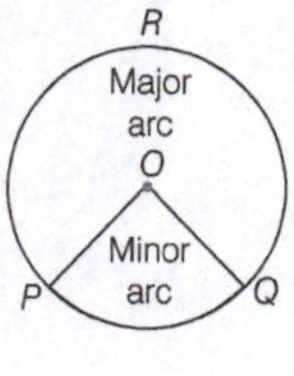

Semi-circle

A diameter of a circle divides the circle into two equal parts, i.e. into two equal arcs. Each of these two arcs is called a *semi-circle*.

Segment

The region between a chord and either of its arcs is called a *segment* of the circular region or simply a segment of the circle. This chord is called the base of the segment. The segment formed by minor arc along with chord, is called *minor segment* and the segment formed by major arc is called the *major segment*.

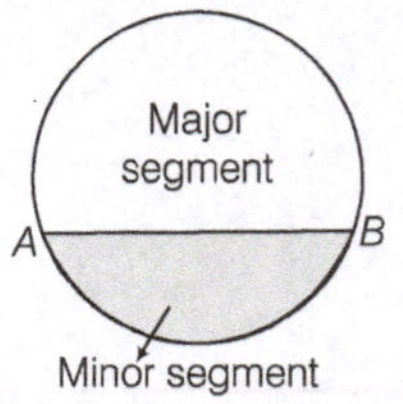

Note The major and minor segments of a circle are segments of a circular disc but these are generally called segments of a circle.

Sector

The region between an arc and the two radii joining the centre to the end points of the arc is called a *sector*. Sectors are of two types – *minor sector* and *major sector*. The sector corresponding to minor arc is called *minor sector* and the sector corresponding to major arc is called *major sector*.

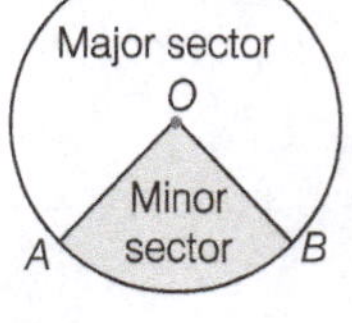

Semi-circular Region

When two arcs are semi-circles, then both segments and both sectors become same and each is known as a *semi-circular region*.

Angle Subtended

We know that, if we take a line segment PQ and a point R not lying on the line PQ, then by joining PR and RQ, we get $\angle PRQ$, which is called the angle subtended by the line segment PQ.

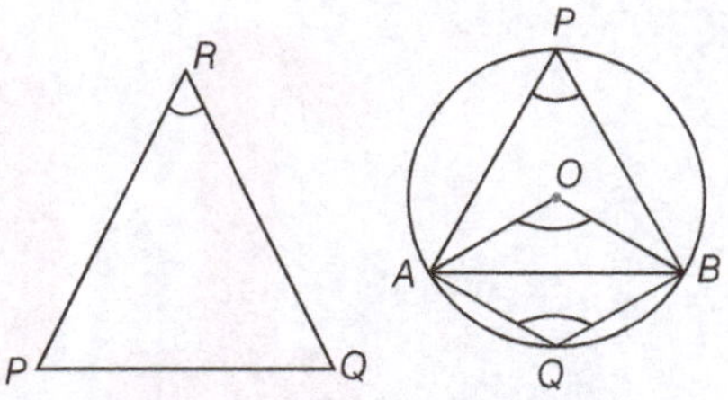

Similarly, in a circle with centre *O*, let *AB* be a chord and we take two points *P* and *Q* on the circle as shown in figure and join *PA*, *PB*, *QA* and *QB*. Then, we get $\angle APB$ and $\angle AQB$, which are called the angles subtended by the chord *AB* at the points *P* and *Q*, respectively. Also, $\angle AOB$ is the angle subtended by the chord *AB* at the centre *O*.

Circle Passing through Three Points

Suppose, we take a point *P*, then there may be as many circles as we like passing through this point.

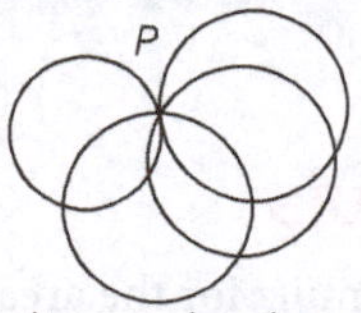

Circles passing through one point

Now, suppose we take two points *P* and *Q*, then through *P* and *Q*, infinite number of circles may be drawn.

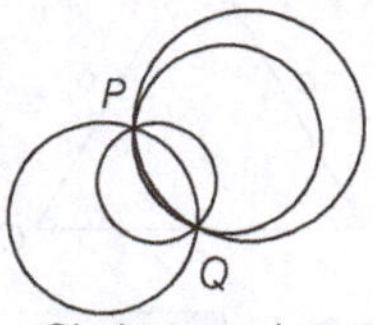

Circles passing through two points

Now, if we take three collinear points, then no circle can be drawn through these three points.

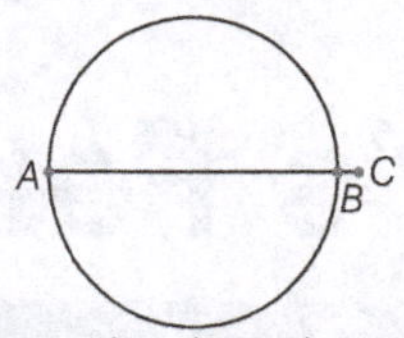

Circle passing through two out of three collinear points

If three points are on a line (collinear), then third point will be either inside or outside the circle which passing through the two points.

Now, suppose we take three non-collinear points *A*, *B* and *C*. (i.e. which are not on the same line). Then, draw perpendicular bisectors of *AB* and *BC* (say) *PQ* and *RS* respectively, which intersect each other at point *O*. Thus, *O* is a point which is at equal distances from points *A*, *B* and *C* because every point on the perpendicular bisector of a line segment is equidistant from its end points. If we draw a circle with centre *O* and radius *OA*, then it will also pass through points *B* and *C* which is a circle passing through three non-collinear points.

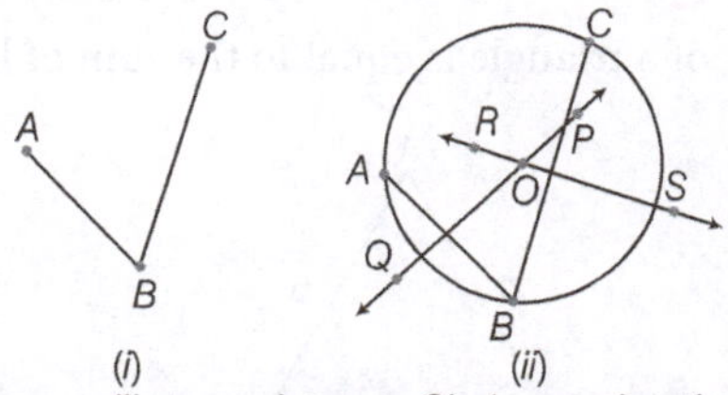

(*i*) Three non-collinear points

(*ii*) Circle passing through three non-collinear points

Theorem There is one and only one circle passing through three given non-collinear points.

CHAPTER 10

Heron's Formula

In earlier classes, we have studied about the area and perimeter of some specific types of triangles and quadrilaterals. In this chapter, we will study about the area and perimeter of specific and non-specific triangles, using Heron's formula.

Perimeter and Semi-perimeter of a Triangle

The perimeter of a triangle is equal to the sum of lengths of all three sides.

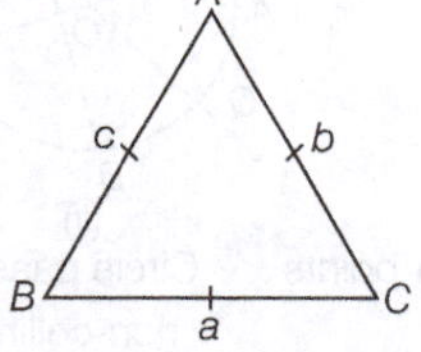

Let in ΔABC, $AB = c$, $AC = b$ and $BC = a$

Then, the perimeter of ΔABC is $(a + b + c)$ units and it is denoted by $2s$.

i.e. $$2s = a + b + c \text{ or } s = \frac{a+b+c}{2}$$

where, s denotes the semi-perimeter of ΔABC.

Example 1. If the perimeter of an isosceles triangle is 11 cm and its unequal side is 5 cm, then find the length of its equal sides.

Sol. Let equal sides of given isosceles triangle be b cm.

$\therefore$ Perimeter of the triangle,

$$2s = b + b + 5 \qquad [\because 2s = a + b + c]$$

$$\Rightarrow \quad 11 = 2b + 5 \qquad [\because 2s = 11 \text{ cm}]$$

$$\Rightarrow \quad 2b = 11 - 5$$

$$\Rightarrow \quad 2b = 6$$

$$\Rightarrow \quad b = \frac{6}{2} = 3 \text{ cm}$$

Heron's Formula

Heron derived the formula for the area of a triangle in terms of its three sides.

Let the lengths of the three sides of a ΔABC be a, b and c.

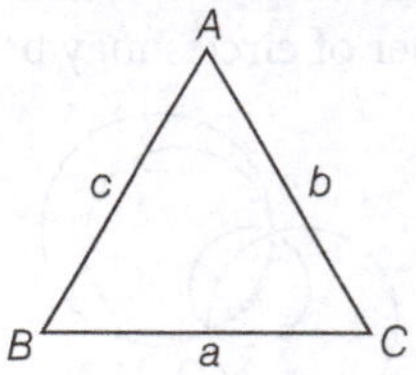

Then, $$\text{area of } \Delta ABC = \sqrt{s(s-a)(s-b)(s-c)}$$

This formula is given by Heron, that's why it is known as **Heron's formula**. This formula can be used for any triangle to calculate its area when height of the triangle cannot determined easily. Heron's formula is generally used for calculating area of scalene triangle.

Example 2. Find the area of a triangle whose sides are 12 cm, 16 cm and 20 cm, respectively.

Sol. Let the sides of triangle be $a = 12$ cm, $b = 16$ cm and $c = 20$ cm.

We know that semi-perimeter, $s = \dfrac{a+b+c}{2}$

$$\therefore \quad s = \frac{12 + 16 + 20}{2} = \frac{48}{2} = 24 \text{ cm}$$

By Heron's formula,

$$\text{Area of triangle} = \sqrt{s(s-a)(s-b)(s-c)}$$

$$= \sqrt{24(24-12)(24-16)(24-20)}$$

$$= \sqrt{24 \times 12 \times 8 \times 4} = \sqrt{9216} = 96 \text{ cm}^2$$

Hence, area of the given triangle is 96 cm^2.

Example 3. **Find the area of a triangle, two sides of which are 16 cm and 22 cm and the perimeter is 64 cm (as shown below)**

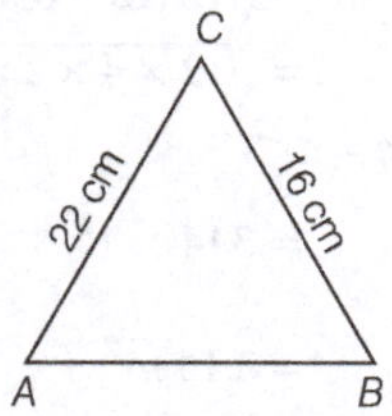

Sol. Here, we have perimeter of the triangle = 64 cm

$a = 16$ cm and $b = 22$ cm

Third side, $c = 64 - (16 + 22) = 26$ cm

So, $2s = 64$ i.e. $s = 32$ cm

$\therefore \quad (s - a) = 32 - 16 = 16$ cm

$\Rightarrow (s - b) = 32 - 22 = 10$ cm

and $(s - c) = 32 - 26 = 6$ cm

Therefore, area of the triangle

$= \sqrt{s(s-a)(s-b)(s-c)}$

$= \sqrt{32 \times 16 \times 10 \times 6}$

$= 32\sqrt{30}\ \text{cm}^2$

Example 4. **Find the area of an isosceles triangle, by using Heron's formula having base 4 cm and length of one of equal side as 6 cm.**

Sol. Let the given sides of isosceles triangle be $a = 4$ cm and $b = c = 6$ cm.

Then, semi-perimeter, $s = \frac{a+b+c}{2}$

$= \frac{4+6+6}{2} = \frac{16}{2}$

$= 8$ cm

Now, area of isosceles triangle

$= \sqrt{s\,(s-a)\,(s-b)\,(s-c)}$ [by Heron's formula]

$= \sqrt{8\,(8-4)\,(8-6)\,(8-6)}$

$= \sqrt{8 \times 4 \times 2 \times 2}$

$= \sqrt{128} = 8\sqrt{2}\ \text{cm}^2$

Hence, the area of isosceles triangle is $8\sqrt{2}\ \text{cm}^2$.

Example 5. **A triangular park *PQR* has sides 160 m, 100 m and 80 m (as shown below)**

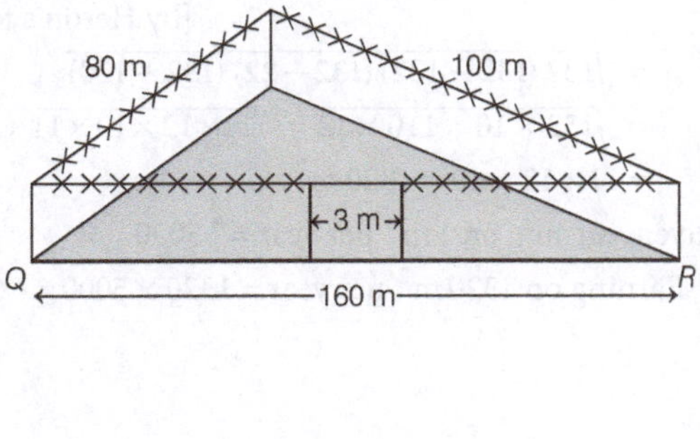

A gardner Sarita has to put a fence all around it and also plant grass inside. How much area does she need to plant grass? Find the cost of fencing it with barbed wire at the ratio of ₹ 16.25 per metre leaving a space 3m wide for a gate on one side.

Sol. For finding the area of given park *PQR*, we have

$a = 80$ m, $b = 100$ m and $c = 160$ m

We know that semi-perimeter,

$s = \frac{a+b+c}{2} = \frac{80+100+160}{2} = 170$ m

Therefore, area of the park

$= \sqrt{s(s-a)(s-b)(s-c)}$ [by Heron's formula]

$= \sqrt{170(170-80)(170-100)(170-160)}$

$= \sqrt{170 \times 90 \times 70 \times 10} = 300\sqrt{119}\ \text{m}^2$

Hence, Sarita needs the area to plant grass is $300\sqrt{119}\ \text{m}^2$.

Also, perimeter of the park $= PQ + QR + RP$

$= 340$ m

Therefore, length of the wire needed for fencing

$= 340 - 3$ [to be left for gate]

$= 337$ m

So, the cost of fencing $= ₹16.25 \times 337$

$= ₹5476.25$

Example 6. **The length of the sides of a triangle are in the ratio 3 : 4 : 5 and its perimeter is 144 cm. Find the area of the triangle.**

Sol. Given, perimeter = 144 cm

and ratio of the sides = 3 : 4 : 5

Sum of ratio terms = 3 + 4 + 5 = 12

$\therefore$ Ist side, $a = 144 \times \frac{3}{12} = 36$ cm

IInd side, $b = 144 \times \frac{4}{12} = 48$ cm

IIIrd side, $c = 144 \times \frac{5}{12} = 60$ cm

Now, semi-perimeter of the triangle,

$s = \frac{a+b+c}{2} = \frac{36+48+60}{2} = \frac{144}{2} = 72$ cm

$\therefore$ Area of triangle $= \sqrt{s\,(s-a)\,(s-b)\,(s-c)}$ [by Heron's formula]

$= \sqrt{72 \times (72-36)\,(72-48)\,(72-60)}$

$= \sqrt{72 \times 36 \times 24 \times 12}$

$= \sqrt{(36)^2 \times (24)^2}$

$= 36 \times 24 = 864\ \text{cm}^2$

Hence, the area of the given triangle is $864\ \text{cm}^2$.

Example 7. **The sides of a triangular park are 8 m, 10 m and 6 m, respectively. A small circular area of diameter 2 m is to be left out and the remaining area is to be used for growing roses. How much area is used for growing roses? [take $\pi = 3.14$]**

Sol. Let sides of a triangle be $a = 8\text{m}, b = 10\text{m}$ and $c = 6\text{m}$

Now, semi-perimeter of a triangle,

$$s = \frac{a+b+c}{2} = \frac{8+10+6}{2} = \frac{24}{2} = 12 \text{ m}$$

$\therefore$ Area of a triangle, $\Delta = \sqrt{s(s-a)(s-b)(s-c)}$ [by Heron's formula]

$$= \sqrt{12(12-8)(12-10)(12-6)}$$

$$= \sqrt{12 \times 4 \times 2 \times 6} = 24 \text{ m}^2$$

and area of a circle $= \pi r^2$

$$= 3.14 \times 1^2 \quad \left[\because r = \frac{d}{2} = \frac{2}{2} = 1\right]$$

$$= 3.14 \text{ m}^2$$

$\therefore$ Area for growing roses = Area of a triangle − Area of a circle

$$= 24 - 3.14$$

$$= 20.86 \text{ m}^2$$

NCERT FOLDER

Complete Solutions of All Exercises of NCERT Textbook

EXERCISE 10.1 (NCERT Page 134-135)

Q1. **A traffic signal board, indicating 'SCHOOL AHEAD' is an equilateral triangle with side a. Find the area of the signal board, using Heron's formula. If its perimeter is 180 cm, what will be the area of the signal board?**

Sol. Let side of signal board whose shape is an equilateral triangle be a.

$\therefore$ Semi-perimeter, $s = \dfrac{a+a+a}{2} = \dfrac{3a}{2}$

Now, area of signal board $= \sqrt{s(s-a)(s-a)(s-a)}$ [by Heron's formula]

$$= \sqrt{\frac{3a}{2}\left(\frac{3a}{2}-a\right)\left(\frac{3a}{2}-a\right)\left(\frac{3a}{2}-a\right)}$$

$$= \sqrt{\frac{3a}{2} \times \frac{a}{2} \times \frac{a}{2} \times \frac{a}{2}} = \frac{a^2\sqrt{3}}{2 \times 2} = \frac{\sqrt{3}}{4}a^2$$

Hence, area of signal board with side a, using Heron's formula, is $\dfrac{\sqrt{3}}{4}a^2$.

Now, if perimeter of a traffic signal board = 180 cm, then

$3a = 180$ [$\because$ perimeter of an equilateral triangle $= 3 \times a$]

$\Rightarrow \quad a = \dfrac{180}{3} = 60$ cm

Now, the area of signal board $= \dfrac{\sqrt{3}}{4}(60)^2 = \dfrac{\sqrt{3}}{4} \times 60 \times 60$

$$= 900\sqrt{3} \text{ cm}^2$$

Hence, the area of the signal board is $900\sqrt{3}$ cm^2, when its perimeter is 180 cm.

Q2. **The triangular side walls of a flyover have been used for advertisements. The sides of the walls are 122 m, 22 m and 120 m (see figure). The advertisements yield an earning of ₹ 5000 per m^2 per year. A company hired one of its wall for 3 months. How much rent did it pay?**

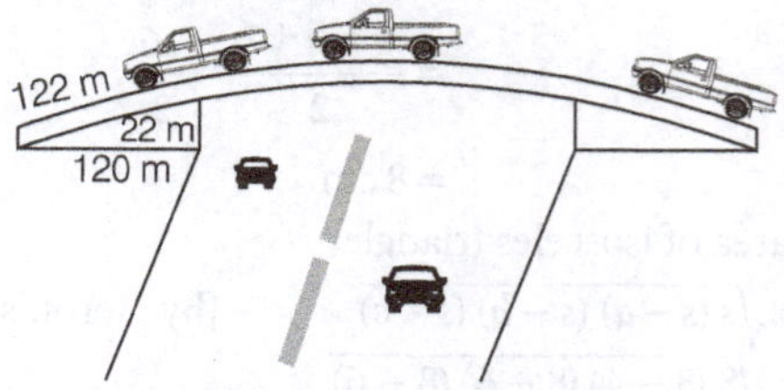

Sol. Let the sides of the wall be $a = 122$ m, $b = 22$ m and $c = 120$ m.

Then, semi-perimeter, $s = \dfrac{a+b+c}{2} = \dfrac{122+22+120}{2}$

$$= \frac{264}{2} = 132 \text{ m}$$

Now, area of the wall $= \sqrt{s(s-a)(s-b)(s-c)}$ [by Heron's formula]

$$= \sqrt{132(132-122)(132-22)(132-120)}$$

$$= \sqrt{132 \times 10 \times 110 \times 12} = \sqrt{11 \times 12 \times 10 \times 11 \times 10 \times 12}$$

$$= 11 \times 12 \times 10 = 1320 \text{ m}^2$$

Given, earning on 1 m^2 per year = ₹ 5000

$\therefore$ Earning on 1320 m^2 per year $= 1320 \times 5000 =$ ₹ 6600000

Now, earning in 12 months = ₹ 6600000

$\therefore$ Earning in 3 months $= \frac{6600000 \times 3}{12} =$ ₹ 1650000

Hence, the rent paid by the company for 3 months is ₹ 1650000.

Q 3. There is a slide in a park. One of its side walls has been painted in some colour with a message 'KEEP THE PARK GREEN AND CLEAN' (see figure). If the sides of the wall are 15 m, 11 m and 6 m, then find the area painted in colour.

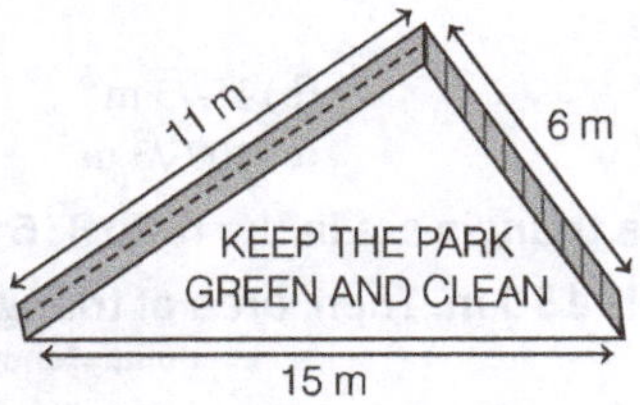

Note it Here, area painted in colour will be equal to the area of triangle with sides 15 m, 11 m and 6 m.

Sol. Let given sides of the wall be $a = 15$ m, $b = 11$ m and $c = 6$ m.

$\therefore$ Semi-perimeter, $s = \frac{a+b+c}{2} = \frac{15+11+6}{2} = \frac{32}{2} = 16$ m

Now, area of the wall $= \sqrt{s(s-a)(s-b)(s-c)}$ [by Heron's formula]

$= \sqrt{16(16-15)(16-11)(16-6)}$

$= \sqrt{16 \times 1 \times 5 \times 10}$

$= \sqrt{4 \times 4 \times 5 \times 5 \times 2}$

$= 5 \times 4\sqrt{2} = 20\sqrt{2}$ m^2

Hence, the area painted in colour is $20\sqrt{2}$ m^2.

Q 4. Find the area of a triangle two sides of which are 18 cm and 10 cm and the perimeter is 42 cm.

Sol. Given, perimeter of the triangle, $2s = 42$ cm ...(i)

$\therefore \quad s = \frac{42}{2} = 21$ cm

Let the given sides of the triangle be $a = 18$ cm, $b = 10$ cm and let $c = x$ cm.

Then, perimeter of the triangle,

$2s = a + b + c = 18 + 10 + x$ ...(ii)

From Eqs. (i) and (ii), we get $18 + 10 + x = 42$

$\Rightarrow 28 + x = 42 \quad \Rightarrow x = 42 - 28 = 14$

$\Rightarrow \quad c = 14$ cm

Now, area of a triangle $= \sqrt{s(s-a)(s-b)(s-c)}$ [by Heron's formula]

$= \sqrt{21(21-18)(21-10)(21-14)}$

$= \sqrt{21 \times 3 \times 11 \times 7}$

$= \sqrt{7 \times 3 \times 3 \times 11 \times 7}$

$= 7 \times 3\sqrt{11} = 21\sqrt{11}$ cm^2

Hence, the area of triangle is $21\sqrt{11}$ cm^2.

Q 5. Sides of a triangle are in the ratio of 12 : 17 : 25 and its perimeter is 540 cm. Find its area.

Sol. Given, sides of triangle are in the ratio 12 : 17 : 25 and perimeter = 540 cm

Let the sides of triangle be $a = 12x$, $b = 17x$ and $c = 25x$.

Then, perimeter of triangle $= a + b + c$

$\Rightarrow \quad 540 = 12x + 17x + 25x$

$\Rightarrow \quad 540 = 54x \Rightarrow x = \frac{540}{54} \Rightarrow x = 10$

and $\quad a = 12x = 12 \times 10 = 120$ cm

$b = 17x = 17 \times 10 = 170$ cm

and $\quad c = 25x = 25 \times 10 = 250$ cm

Now, semi-perimeter of a triangle,

$s = \frac{a+b+c}{2} = \frac{120+170+250}{2}$

$= \frac{540}{2} = 270$ cm

and area of triangle $= \sqrt{s(s-a)(s-b)(s-c)}$ [by Heron's formula]

$= \sqrt{270(270-120)(270-170)(270-250)}$

$= \sqrt{270 \times 150 \times 100 \times 20}$

$= \sqrt{\begin{pmatrix}2 \times 3 \times 3 \times 3 \times 5 \times 2 \times 3 \times 5 \times 5 \times 2 \times 2 \\ \times 5 \times 5 \times 2 \times 2 \times 5\end{pmatrix}}$

$= \sqrt{2^6 \times 3^4 \times 5^6} = 2^3 \times 3^2 \times 5^3$

$= 2 \times 2 \times 2 \times 3 \times 3 \times 5 \times 5 \times 5 = 9000$ cm^2

Hence, the area of triangle is 9000 cm^2.

Q 6. An isosceles triangle has perimeter 30 cm and each of the equal sides is 12 cm. Find the area of the triangle.

Sol. Given, perimeter of an isosceles triangle $(2s) = 30$ cm

Let the given sides be $a = 12$ cm, $b = 12$ cm and let $c = x$ cm

$\because$ Perimeter of a triangle $(2s) = a + b + c$

$\therefore \quad 30 = 12 + 12 + x \Rightarrow 30 = 24 + x$

$\Rightarrow \quad x = 30 - 24 \quad \Rightarrow x = 6$ cm

Thus, the sides of triangle are $a = 12$ cm, $b = 12$ cm and $c = 6$ cm.

Now, semi-perimeter of the triangle,

$s = \frac{1}{2} \times 2s = \frac{1}{2} \times 30 = 15$ cm

$\therefore$ Area of an isosceles triangle

$= \sqrt{s(s-a)(s-b)(s-c)}$ [by Heron's formula]

$= \sqrt{15(15-12)(15-12)(15-6)}$

$= \sqrt{15 \times 3 \times 3 \times 9}$

$= \sqrt{3 \times 5 \times 3 \times 3 \times 3 \times 3} = 9\sqrt{15}$ cm^2

Hence, the area of an isosceles triangle is $9\sqrt{15}$ cm^2.

REVIEW EXERCISE

Including Competency Based Questions

Part I

Multiple Choice Questions

1. **In Heron's formula $\sqrt{s\times(s-a)\times(s-b)\times(s-c)}$, s is equal to**

(a) $\frac{a+b+c}{4}$ (b) $\frac{a+b+c}{3}$

(c) $\frac{a+b+c}{2}$ (d) $a+b+c$

2. **The area of triangle with sides 5 cm, 12 cm and 13 cm in length is**

(a) 15 cm^2 (b) 30 cm^2

(c) 60 cm^2 (d) 120 cm^2

3. **Number of times area changed when sides of a triangle are doubled is** **Competency Based Question**

(a) Double (b) Four times

(c) Eight times (d) No change in the area

4. **The area of an equilateral triangle with side $2\sqrt{3}$ cm is ($\sqrt{3}=1.732$)** **NCERT Exemplar**

(a) 5.196 cm^2 (b) 0.866 cm^2

(c) 3.496 cm^2 (d) 1.732 cm^2

5. **The area of isosceles right angled triangle having each of equal sides a is**

(a) $\frac{1}{2}a^2$ (b) $2a^2$ (c) a^2 (d) $\frac{\sqrt{2}}{3}a^2$

6. **Each side of an equilateral triangle is 4 cm long. The height of triangle is**

(a) $10\sqrt{3}$ cm (b) $2\sqrt{3}$ cm

(c) $4\sqrt{3}$ cm (d) $\frac{\sqrt{3}}{2}$ cm

7. **An isosceles right angled triangle has area 8 cm^2. The length of hypotenuse is** **NCERT Exemplar**

(a) $\sqrt{32}$ cm (b) $\sqrt{16}$ cm (c) $\sqrt{48}$ cm (d) $\sqrt{24}$ cm

8. **The sides of a triangle are 25 cm, 17 cm and 12 cm. The length of the altitude on the longest side is equal to**

(a) 7.5 cm (b) 7.2 cm (c) 8.2 cm (d) 9.8 cm

9. **If area of equilateral triangle is $25\sqrt{3}$ cm^2, then its perimeter will be** **Competency Based Question**

(a) 10 cm (b) 20 cm

(c) 30 cm (d) 40 cm

10. **The perimeter of an equilateral triangle is 60 m. The area is** **NCERT Exemplar**

(a) $10\sqrt{3}$ m^2 (b) $15\sqrt{3}$ m^2

(c) $20\sqrt{3}$ m^2 (d) $100\sqrt{3}$ m^2

11. **If sides of a triangle are in the ratio 3 : 5 : 7 and its perimeter is 150 m. Then, area of triangle is** **Competency Based Question**

(a) $100\sqrt{2}$ m^2 (b) $375\sqrt{3}$ m^2

(c) $750\sqrt{3}$ m^2 (d) $375\sqrt{2}$ m^2

12. **The base of a right angled triangle is 24 cm and its hypotenuse is 26 cm long. The area of the triangle is**

(a) 120 cm^2 (b) 140 cm^2

(c) 312 cm^2 (d) 65 cm^2

13. **The difference between the semi-perimeter and the sides of ΔABC are 3 cm, 4 cm and 2 cm, respectively. The area of the triangle is**

(a) $6\sqrt{6}$ cm^2 (b) $3\sqrt{3}$ cm^2

(c) $5\sqrt{6}$ cm^2 (d) $3\sqrt{6}$ cm^2

14. **The length of hypotenuse of an isosceles right triangle with area 72 cm^2 is** **NCERT Exemplar**

(a) 12 cm (b) $12\sqrt{2}$ cm

(c) 24 cm (d) 12.5 cm

15. **The edges of a triangular board are 6 cm, 8 cm and 10 cm. The cost of painting it at the rate of 9 paise per cm^2 is** **NCERT Exemplar**

(a) ₹ 2.00 (b) ₹ 2.16

(c) ₹ 2.48 (d) ₹ 3.00

Assertion-Reason Type Questions

16. **Assertion** If the edges of a triangle are 7 cm, 9 cm and 12 cm, then the area of triangle is $14\sqrt{5}$ cm^2.

Reason If three sides of a triangle are given, then area triangle cannot always be determined by Heron's formula.

(a) Both Assertion and Reason are correct and Reason is the correct explanation of Assertion.

(b) Both Assertion and Reason are correct but Reason is not the correct explanation of Assertion.

(c) Assertion is correct but Reason is incorrect.

(d) Assertion is incorrect but Reason is correct.

17. **Assertion** The area of an equilateral triangle with side 2 cm is $\sqrt{3}$ cm.

Reason If the side of an equilateral triangle is a unit, then area of an equilateral triangle is $\frac{\sqrt{3}}{4}(a)^2$ sq units.

(a) Both Assertion and Reason are correct and Reason is the correct explanation of Assertion.

(b) Both Assertion and Reason are correct but Reason is not the correct explanation of Assertion.

(c) Assertion is correct but Reason is incorrect.

(d) Assertion is incorrect but Reason is correct.

Case Study Based Questions

18. Glass buildings can be strengthened using iron frames. A glass structure and its iron frame are shown below.

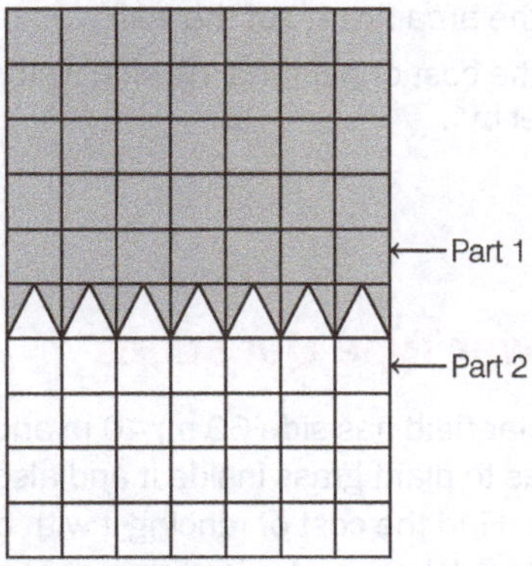

The frame consists of equal triangles. The dimensions of a triangle are shown below.

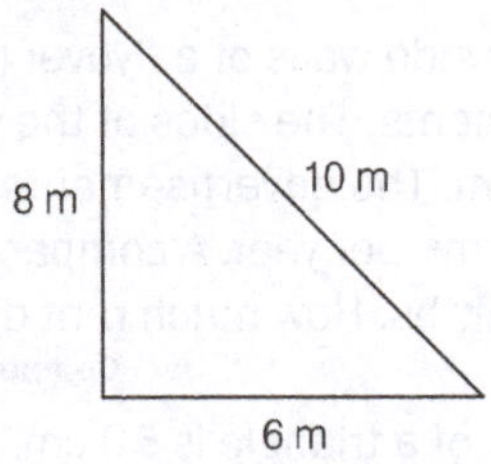

Based on the above information, answer the following questions.

(i) How much area is enclosed by one triangle?

(ii) What is the area of Part 1 of the frame?

(iii) (a) Is the area of Part 1 equal to the area of Part 2? Why?

Or

(b) Maintenance of the building's exterior is done by a company. The company charges ₹ 750 per sq m per month. Which of the following calculations represents the monthly maintenance charges?

19. The sides of a rectangular park are 20 m and 30 m respectively. A small triangular area of side 8 m, 10 m and 6 m respectively is to be left out at the park for growing flowering plants. The remaining area is be planted with natural grass.

(i) What is the semi-perimeter of the triangle for the above measurements?

(ii) Find the area used for growing flowering plants.

(iii) (a) If the cost of planting the flowering plant is ₹ 5.50 per m^2, then find the total cost of planting the flowering plants.

Or

(b) Find the area of the grass to be planted.

20. A zoo is in the shape of an isosceles trapezium. It is divided into three zones – Zone 1, Zone 2 and Zone 3. Animals are kept without cages in Zone 1. Zone 2 is for visitors and Zone 3 is reserved for park authorities. To avoid the entry of animals in zones 2 and 3, a 1.8 km long wired fencing is installed.

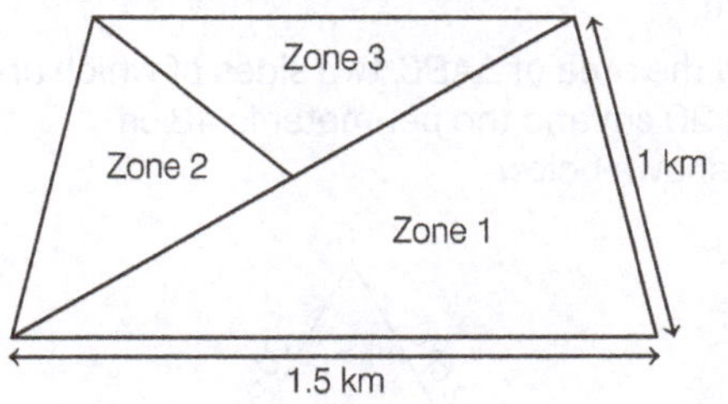

Based on the above information, answer the following questions.

(i) Find the area for animals

(ii) "The area reserved for animals is twice the area reserved for the zoo authorities." Do you have enough information to support this statement? Explain your answer.

(iii) (a) Find the cost of maintenance of animal zone at ₹ 1150 per km^2.

Or

(b) Find the total area reserved for visitors and park authorities if sum of paralled sides of the zoo is 2.4 km of distance between them is 0.8 km.

21. In the marriage of Raj's brother Rajesh, a conical tent is made by stitching 12 triangular pieces of cloth of two different colours red and white alternately, each piece measuring 10 cm, 20 cm and 20 cm.

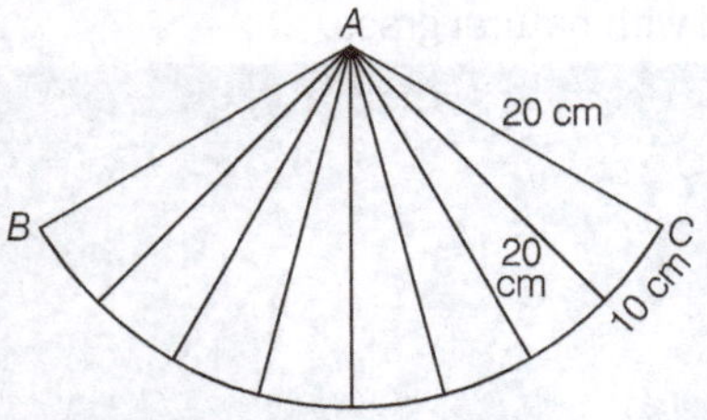

(i) Write the formula to find the area of triangle (by Heron's formula).

(ii) Find the semi-perimeter of one red colour triangle.

(iii) Find the area of one red colour triangle. (see in figure).

Or How much cloth of red colour is required to make a conical tent?

22. Green cleaning refers to cleaning methods and products that are environmentally friendly ingredients and procedures to preserve human health and environmental quality. To preserve the environment, Ramesh made a slide in the park of his society. One the side walls of the slide, there was a message 'TAKE SHORT WALK IN PARK DOWN A HAPPY TRAIL' (see figure). If the sides of the wall are 15m, 11m and 6m, then answer the questions by looking at the figure. $[\sqrt{2} = 1.41]$

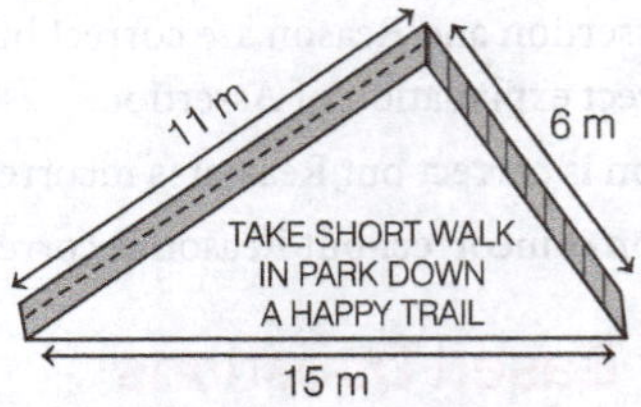

(i) Find the semi-perimeter of triangle.

(ii) Write the type of triangle given in question.

(iii) Find the area (in m^2) of the wall.

Or Find the cost of painting the side wall if the price is ₹ 8 per m^2.

Part II

Very Short Answer Type Questions

1. If the sides of a triangle are 13 cm, 14 cm and 15 cm. Then, find the area of the triangle. **CCE 2011**

2. Find the area of the triangle having perimeter 32 cm, one side 11 cm and difference of other two sides is 5 cm.

3. Find the area of ΔABC, two sides of which are 12 cm and 20 cm and the perimeter is 48 cm. (as shown below)

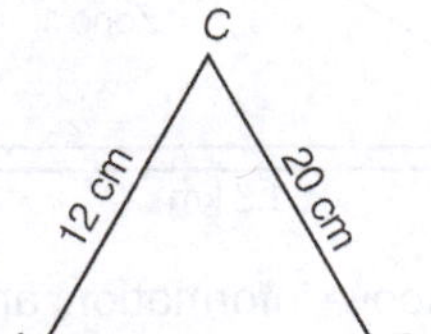

4. The perimeter of a triangular field is 450 m and its sides are in the ratio 13 : 12 : 5. Find the area of the triangle. **Competency Based Question**

5. The sides of a triangular ground are 5 m, 7 m and 8 m, respectively. Find the cost of levelling the ground at the rate of ₹ 10 per m^2. $[\sqrt{3} = 1.73]$ **CCE 2010**

6. The sides of a triangular field are 51 m, 37 m and 20 m. Find the number of flower beds that can be prepared if each bed is to occupy 9 m^2 of space. **Competency Based Question**

7. The sides of a triangle are x, $x+1$, $2x-1$ and its area is $x\sqrt{10}$. Find the value of x.

Short Answer Type Questions

8. A triangular field has side 60 m, 40 m and 30 m. Field owner has to plant grass inside it and also fence all around it. Find the cost of fencing it with barbed wire at the rate ₹ 12 per metre leaving a space 1.75 m wide for a gate on one side. Also, find the area of triangular field. **Competency Based Question**

9. The triangular side walls of a flyover have been used for advertisements. The sides of the walls are 13 m, 14 m and 15 m. The advertisements yield an earning of ₹ 2000 per m^2 per year. A company hired one of its walls for 6 months. How much rent did it pay? **Competency Based Question**

10. The perimeter of a triangle is 50 cm. One side of a triangle is 4 cm longer than the smaller side and the third side is 6 cm less than twice the smaller side. Find the area of the triangle. **Competency Based Question**

11. If each side of a triangle is doubled, then find the ratio of area of new triangle formed and the given triangle.

12. If every side of a triangle is doubled, then find the percentage increase in the area of the triangle.

13. The ratio of the equal sides to the base of an isosceles triangle is 3 : 1. If the perimeter of the triangle is 28 cm, then find its area.

14. The sides of a triangle are p, q and r. If $p+q=45$, $q+r=40$ and $p+r=35$, then find the area of the triangle.

HINTS & ANSWERS

Part I

1. (c) $s = \dfrac{a+b+c}{2}$

2. (b) **Hint** Area of triangle $= \sqrt{s(s-a)(s-b)(s-c)}$

$$s = \frac{5+12+13}{2} = 15$$

$$\text{Area} = \sqrt{15 \times 10 \times 3 \times 2} = 30 \text{ cm}^2$$

3. (b) **Hint** If $a_1 = 2a$

$$b_1 = 2b \text{ and } c_1 = 2c$$

$$s_1 = \frac{2a+2b+2c}{2} = 2s$$

$$\text{Area} = \sqrt{s_1(s_1-a_1)(s_1-b_1)(s_1-c_1)}$$

$$= \sqrt{2s(2s-2a)(2s-2b)(2s-2c)}$$

$$= 2 \times 2\sqrt{s(s-a)(s-b)(s-c)}$$

$$= 4\sqrt{s(s-a)(s-b)(s-c)}$$

4. (a) **Hint** Use Heron's formula to find the area, where $a = 2\sqrt{3}$ cm, $b = 2\sqrt{3}$ and $c = 2\sqrt{3}$

5. (a) **Hint** Here, sides are a, a, $\sqrt{2}a$.

$$s = \frac{a+a+\sqrt{2}a}{2}$$

Area $= \sqrt{s(s-a)(s-b)(s-c)}$

After solving, we get

Area $= \dfrac{1}{2}a^2$

6. (b) **Hint** Use Heron's formula,

Area of triangle $= 4\sqrt{3}$ cm^2

Also, area of triangle $= \dfrac{1}{2} \times b \times h$

$$\therefore \quad \frac{1}{2} \times 4 \times h = 4\sqrt{3}$$

$$\Rightarrow \quad h = 2\sqrt{3} \text{ cm}$$

7. (a) **Hint** Solve as Question 5.

Area of isosceles right triangle $= \dfrac{1}{2}a^2$

$$\therefore \quad \frac{1}{2}a^2 = 8 \Rightarrow a^2 = 16$$

$$\Rightarrow \quad a = 4$$

Hypotenuse of isosceles right triangle $= \sqrt{a^2 + a^2}$

$$= \sqrt{16+16} = \sqrt{32} \text{ cm}$$

8. (b) $\because s = \dfrac{a+b+c}{2} = \dfrac{25+17+12}{2} = 27$ cm

$\therefore$ Area of triangle $= \sqrt{27(27-25)(27-17)(27-12)}$

$$= \sqrt{27 \times 2 \times 10 \times 15} = 90 \text{ cm}^2$$

Also, area of triangle $= \dfrac{1}{2} \times 25 \times h = 90$

$$\Rightarrow \quad h = 90 \times \frac{2}{25} = 7.2 \text{ cm.}$$

9. (c) **Hint** Area of equilateral triangle $= \dfrac{\sqrt{3}}{4}a^2$

[Solve as Q-1 of NCERT Folder Exercise 10.1]

$$\therefore \quad \frac{\sqrt{3}}{4}a^2 = 25\sqrt{3}$$

$$\Rightarrow \quad a^2 = \frac{25 \times 4}{\sqrt{3}} \times \sqrt{3} = 100 \Rightarrow a = 10 \text{ cm}$$

Perimeter of equilateral triangle $= a + a + a$

$$= 3a = 3 \times 10 = 30 \text{ cm}$$

10. (d) **Hint** Perimeter of equilateral triangle = 60 m

$$\therefore \quad 3a = 60 \text{ m} \Rightarrow a = 20 \text{ m}$$

Area of equilateral triangle $= \dfrac{\sqrt{3}}{4}a^2$

[Solve as Q-1 of NCERT Folder Exercise 10.1]

$$= \frac{\sqrt{3}}{4} \times (20)^2 = \frac{\sqrt{3}}{4} \times 400 = 100\sqrt{3} \text{ m}^2$$

11. (b) **Hint** Sides of a triangle are given by $150 \times \dfrac{3}{15}$, $150 \times \dfrac{5}{15}$, $150 \times \dfrac{7}{15}$ i.e. 30 m, 50 m, 70 m

Using Heron's formula, we have area of triangle

$$= 375\sqrt{3} \text{ m}^2$$

12. (a) **Hint** By Pythagoras theorem,

$$P^2 = H^2 - B^2 = 26^2 - 24^2 = 100$$

$$\Rightarrow \quad P = 10 \text{ cm}$$

Using Heron's formula,

Area = 120 cm^2

13. (a) **Hint** We have, $s - a = 3$ cm, $s - b = 4$ cm and $s - c = 2$ cm

$$\Rightarrow 3s - (a+b+c) = 9 \text{ cm}$$

$$\Rightarrow \quad 3s - 2s = 9 \text{ cm}$$

$$\left[\because \frac{a+b+c}{2} = s \Rightarrow a+b+c = 2s\right]$$

$\Rightarrow \quad s = 9$ cm

$\therefore$ Area $= \sqrt{s(s-a)(s-b)(s-c)}$

$= \sqrt{9 \times 3 \times 4 \times 2} = 6\sqrt{6}$ cm^2

14. (b) **Hint** Area of isosceles right triangle with equal side a

$= \frac{1}{2}a^2$ [Solve as Q-5]

$\therefore \quad \frac{1}{2}a^2 = 72$

$\Rightarrow \quad a^2 = 72 \times 2 = 144$

$\Rightarrow \quad a = 12$ cm

Hypotenuse of an isosceles right angled triangle $= \sqrt{2}a$

$= 12\sqrt{2}$ cm

15. (b) Since, the edges of a triangular board are $a = 6$ cm, $b = 8$ cm and $c = 10$ cm.

Now, semi-perimeter of a triangular board,

$s = \frac{a+b+c}{2}$

$= \frac{6+8+10}{2} = \frac{24}{2} = 12$ cm

Now, area of a triangular board

$= \sqrt{s(s-a)(s-b)(s-c)}$ [by Heron's formula]

$= \sqrt{12(12-6)(12-8)(12-10)}$

$= \sqrt{12 \times 6 \times 4 \times 2}$

$= \sqrt{(12)^2 \times (2)^2}$

$= 12 \times 2 = 24$ cm^2

Since, the cost of painting for area 1 cm^2 = ₹ 0.09

$\therefore$ Cost of paint for area 24 cm^2 $= 0.09 \times 24 =$ ₹ 2.16

Hence, the cost of painting a triangular board is ₹ 2.16.

16. (c) **Assertion** Given sides of a triangle are $a = 7$ cm, $b = 9$ cm and $c = 12$ cm.

Now, $s = \frac{a+b+c}{2}$

$s = \frac{7+9+12}{2} = \frac{28}{2} = 14$

$\therefore$ Area of triangle using Heron's formula,

$\Delta = \sqrt{s(s-a)(s-b)(s-c)}$

$= \sqrt{14(14-7)(14-9)(14-12)}$

$= \sqrt{14 \times 7 \times 5 \times 2}$

$= 14\sqrt{5}$ cm^2

Reason If three sides of a triangle are given, then we can determine the area always by Heron's formula.

Thus, Reason is incorrect.

17. (a) **Assertion** Given side of an equilateral triangle is 2 cm.

$\therefore$ Area of an equilateral triangle $= \frac{\sqrt{3}}{4}(\text{side})^2$

$= \frac{\sqrt{3}}{4}(2)^2 = \sqrt{3}$ cm^2

Reason is also correct and it is the correct explanation of Assertion.

18. (i) Find area of triangle using Heron's formula;

Area $= \sqrt{s(s-a)(s-b)(s-c)}$

$\because \quad s = \frac{8+10+6}{2} = 12$ cm

$\therefore$ Area $= \sqrt{12 \times 4 \times 2 \times 6} = 24$ m^2

(ii) Area of Part 1 of frame = (Area of 1 triangle × 14) + (Area of 1 rectangular box × 35)

$= 24 \times 14 + (12 \times 8) \times 35$

$= 336 + 3360 = 3696$ m^2

(iii) (a) **Hint** The area of Part 2

= (Area of 1 rectangular box × 35) − (Area of 1 triangle × 14)

$= 3360 - 336 = 3024$ m^2

Ans. No

Or

(b) Area of frame = Area of Part 1 + Area of Part 2

$= 3696 + 3024$

$= 6720$ m^2

Monthly maintenance $= 750 \times 6720$

19. (i) Let sides of triangular area be $a = 8$ m, $b = 10$ m and $c = 6$ m, respectively.

Now, semi-perimeter of triangular area,

$s = \frac{8+10+6}{2} = \frac{24}{2} = 12$ m

(ii) Area used for growing flower planter

$= \sqrt{s(s-a)(s-b)(s-c)}$

$= \sqrt{12(12-8)(12-10)(12-6)}$

$= \sqrt{12 \times 4 \times 2 \times 6}$

$= 24$ m^2

(iii) (a) Cost of planting flowering plant = ₹ 5.50 per m^2

Then, total cost of planting flowering plants

$= 5.50 \times 24$

= ₹ 132

Or

(b) Area of the grass to be plated

$= $ Area of rectangular park

$-$ Area of triangular part

$= 20 \times 30 - 24$ [$\because$ area of rectangle $= l \times b$]

$= 600 - 24 = 576\ m^2$

20. (i) The third side for Zone 1 = 1.8 km

$\therefore \quad s = \dfrac{1.5 + 1 + 1.8}{2} = \dfrac{4.3}{2} = 2.15$ cm

$\therefore$ Area $= \sqrt{s(s-a)(s-b)(s-c)}$

$= \sqrt{2.15\,(2.15 - 1.5)\,(2.15 - 1.8)\,(2.15 - 1)}$

$= \sqrt{2.15(0.65)\,(0.35)\,(1.15)}\ km^2$

(ii) It is not clear that the area reserved for zones 2 and 3 are equal. So, we cannot say that area reserved for animals is twice the area reserved for zoo authorities.

Ans. No

(iii) (a) Cost of maintenance of animal zone

$= 0.7 \times 1150$

$= ₹\,851$ [area of zone $1 = 0.74\ km^2$]

Or

(b) Total area reserved for park authorities and visitor

$=$ Total area of zoo $-$ area of Zone 1

$= \dfrac{2.4 \times 0.8}{2} - 0.74 = 0.96 - 0.74 = 0.22\ km^2$

21. (i) $\therefore$ Area of triangle $= \sqrt{s(s-a)(s-b)(s-c)}$

(ii) In a conical tent, pieces are in the form of triangle, whose sides are 10 cm, 20 cm and 20 cm.

$\therefore \quad a = 10$ cm, $b = 20$ cm and $c = 20$ cm

So, $s = \dfrac{a+b+c}{2} = \dfrac{10+20+20}{2} = \dfrac{50}{2} = 25$ cm

(iii) (a) $\because s = 25$ cm

$\therefore$ Area of triangle $= \sqrt{s(s-a)(s-b)(s-c)}$

$= \sqrt{25(25-10)(25-20)(25-20)}$

$= \sqrt{25 \times 15 \times 5 \times 5}$

$= \sqrt{5 \times 5 \times 5 \times 3 \times 5 \times 5}$

$= 5 \times 5\sqrt{15}$

$= 25\sqrt{15}\ cm^2$

Or

(b) Since, area of one red colour triangular piece is $25\sqrt{15}\ cm^2$.

Since, tent is made of 12 triangular pieces of two colours. So, number of triangular pieces of red colour is 6. Hence, cloth of red colour required to make a conical tent is

$6 \times 25\sqrt{15} = 150\sqrt{15}\ cm^2$

22. (i) Given that $a = 15$ m, $b = 11$ m and $c = 6$ m

$\therefore$ Semi-perimeter $(s) = \dfrac{a+b+c}{2} = \dfrac{15+11+6}{2}$

$= \dfrac{32}{2} = 16$ m

(ii) Since, all three sides of triangle are unequal, so given triangle is a scalene triangle.

(iii) (a) $\because s = 16$ m

Now, area of the wall

$= \sqrt{16\,(16-15)\,(16-11)\,(16-6)}$

$= \sqrt{16 \times 1 \times 5 \times 10}$

$= \sqrt{4 \times 4 \times 1 \times 5 \times 5 \times 2}$

$= 4 \times 5\sqrt{2} = 20\sqrt{2}\ m^2$

Or (b) $\because$ Area of the wall $= 20\sqrt{2}\ m^2$

$\therefore$ Cost of painting $= 20\sqrt{2} \times 8 = 160\sqrt{2}$

$= 160 \times 1.41 = ₹\,225.6$

$= ₹\,226$ (approx.)

Part II

1. **Hint** Solve as Example 2. **Ans.** $84\ cm^2$
2. **Hint** Let the sides of triangle be 11, x and y cm.

   $\therefore \quad x + y + 11 = 32 \Rightarrow x + y = 21$

   and $\quad x - y = 5 \Rightarrow x = 13$ and $y = 8$

   Now, using Heron's formula calculate the area.

   Ans. $8\sqrt{30}\ cm^2$
3. **Hint** Solve as Example 3. **Ans.** $96\ cm^2$
4. **Hint** Solve as Example 6. **Ans.** $6750\ m^2$
5. **Hint** Cost = Area $\times$ Rate. **Ans.** ₹ 173
6. **Hint** Number of flower beds

   $= \dfrac{\text{Area of triangular field}}{\text{Space occupied by each flower bed}}$

   Ans. 34 flower beds can be prepared.
7. **Hint** Semi-perimeter, $s = \dfrac{x + x + 1 + 2x - 1}{2} = 2x$

   $\therefore$ Area of triangle $= \sqrt{2x(2x-x)(2x-x-1)(2x-2x+1)}$

   $\Rightarrow \quad x\sqrt{10} = \sqrt{2x \cdot x \cdot (x-1)(1)}$

   $\Rightarrow \quad x\sqrt{10} = x\sqrt{2(x-1)} \Rightarrow 10 = 2(x-1)$

   Ans. $x = 6$
8. **Hint** Solve as Example 5. **Ans.** ₹ 1539, $25\sqrt{455}\ m^2$
9. **Hint** Solve as Q.2 of NCERT folder Exercise 10.1.

   Ans. ₹ 84000.
10. **Hint** Let the smallest side be x cm. Then, the sides of the triangle are $x, x+4, 2x-6$.

    $\therefore \quad x + x + 4 + 2x - 6 = 50$

    $\Rightarrow \quad 4x = 52 \Rightarrow x = 13$

∴ Sides of triangle are 13, 17, 20.

Now, use Heron's formula to calculate area.

Ans. 109.54 cm^2.

11. Let a, b and c be the sides of the given triangle and s be its semi-perimeter.

Then, $s = \dfrac{a+b+c}{2}$ ...(i)

∴ Area of a triangle, $\Delta = \sqrt{s(s-a)(s-b)(s-c)}$ ...(ii)

[by Heron's formula]

According to the question, the sides of the new triangle are $2a, 2b$ and $2c$.

Let s' be the semi-perimeter of the new triangle.

Then, $s' = \dfrac{2a+2b+2c}{2} = a+b+c$ ...(iii)

From Eqs. (i) and (iii), we get $s' = 2s$

Now, area of new triangle,

$\Delta' = \sqrt{s'(s'-2a)(s'-2b)(s'-2c)}$

[by Heron's formula]

$= \sqrt{2s(2s-2a)(2s-2b)(2s-2c)}$

$= \sqrt{16s(s-a)(s-b)(s-c)}$

$= 4\sqrt{s(s-a)(s-b)(s-c)}$

$\Rightarrow \Delta' = 4\Delta$ [from Eq. (ii)]

$\Rightarrow \dfrac{\Delta'}{\Delta} = \dfrac{4}{1}$

Hence, the ratio of area of new triangle formed to the area of given triangle is 4 : 1.

12. Hint Solve as Q. 11.

Proceeding as is Q. 11, we get $\Delta' = 4\Delta$

where, Δ = Area of given triangle

and Δ' = Area of the new triangle

∴ Increment in the area of the triangle $= \Delta' - \Delta$

$= 4\Delta - \Delta = 3\Delta$

Now, percentage increase in the area of given triangle

$= \left(\dfrac{\text{Increase area of triangle}}{\text{Initial area of triangle}} \times 100\right)$

$= \dfrac{3\Delta}{\Delta} \times 100 = 300\%$

Hence, the percentage increase in the area of the triangle is 300%.

13. Hint Let equal sides be a and base b.

Now, $a : b = 3 : 1$

$\Rightarrow a = 3x, b = x$

Again, $a + a + b = 28$

$\Rightarrow 3x + 3x + x = 28 \Rightarrow x = 4$

$\Rightarrow a = 12, b = 4$

∴ Area $= \sqrt{14(14-12)(14-12)(14-4)}$

$= \sqrt{14 \times 2 \times 2 \times 10}$

Ans. $4\sqrt{35} \text{ cm}^2$

14. Hint $p + q = 45$, ...(i)

$q + r = 40$ ...(ii)

and $r + p = 35$ ...(iii)

On adding Eqs. (i), (ii) and (iii), we get

$p + q + r = 60$ ...(iv)

On solving, $r = 15, p = 20$ and $q = 25$

∴ Area of triangle $= \sqrt{s(s-p)(s-q)(s-r)}$

Ans. 150 sq units

Topics to be Assessed Formatively

Applications of Heron's Formula in Finding Areas of Quadrilaterals

Quadrilateral

A plane figure bounded by four line segments, is called a quadrilateral.

Let $ABCD$ be a quadrilateral. To find the area of a quadrilateral, we divide the quadrilateral into two triangular parts and use Heron's formula or any other suitable formula to calculate the area of these triangular parts.

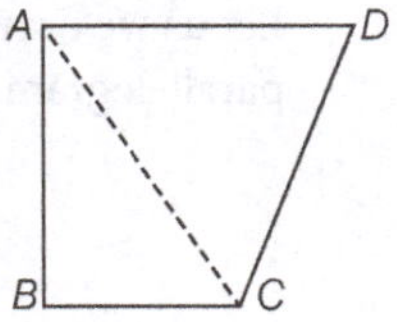

Area of quadrilateral $ABCD$
$= \text{Area of } \Delta ABC + \text{Area of } \Delta ADC$

Example 1. **Find the area of a quadrilateral $ABCD$, in which $AB = 5$ cm, $BC = 4$ cm, $CD = 4$ cm, $DA = 5$ cm and $AC = 7$ cm.**

Sol. Given, a quadrilateral $ABCD$ in which $AB = 5$ cm, $BC = 4$ cm, $CD = 4$ cm, $DA = 5$ cm
and $AC = 7$ cm

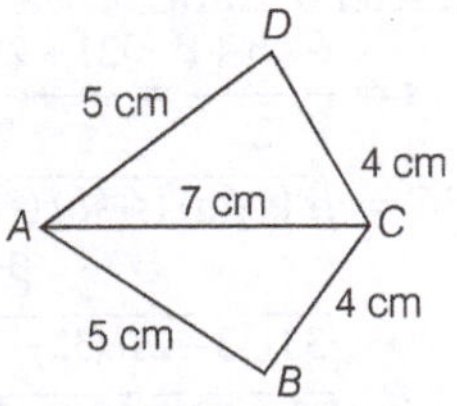

For ΔABC, let $a = 4$ cm, $b = 7$ cm and $c = 5$ cm

Then, semi-perimeter of ΔABC,

$$s = \frac{a+b+c}{2} = \frac{4+7+5}{2} = \frac{16}{2} = 8 \text{ cm}$$

$\therefore$ Area of $\Delta ABC = \sqrt{s(s-a)(s-b)(s-c)}$ [by Heron's formula]

$$= \sqrt{8(8-4)(8-7)(8-5)}$$
$$= \sqrt{8 \times 4 \times 1 \times 3} = \sqrt{96} = 9.80 \text{ cm}^2$$

The length of sides of ΔABC are same as length of sides of ΔCAD

$\therefore$ Area of ΔCAD = Area of ΔABC = 9.80 cm^2

Now, area of quadrilateral $ABCD$

$$= \text{ar}(\Delta ABC) + \text{ar}(\Delta CDA)$$
$$= 9.80 + 9.80 = 19.6 \text{ cm}^2$$

Hence, area of quadrilateral $ABCD$ is 19.6 cm^2.

Example 2. **The sides of a quadrilateral $ABCD$ are 6 cm, 8 cm, 12 cm and 14 cm (taken in order) respectively and the angle between the first two sides is a right angle. Find its area.**

Sol. The adjacent figure of quadrilateral $ABCD$.

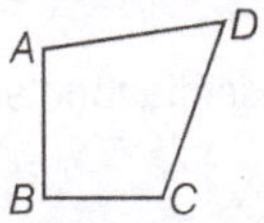

Here, $AB = 6$ cm, $BC = 8$ cm,
$CD = 12$ cm and $AD = 14$ cm

Also, $\angle ABC = 90°$

On joining the points A and C, we get the diagonal AC, which divides the quadrilateral into two triangles, namely ΔABC and ΔCAD.

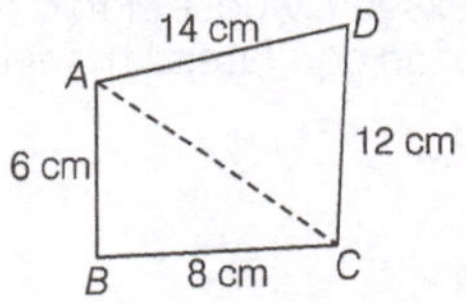

Now, in right angled ΔABC,

$$AC^2 = AB^2 + BC^2 \quad \text{[by Pythagoras theorem]}$$
$$\Rightarrow \quad AC = \sqrt{AB^2 + BC^2} = \sqrt{6^2 + 8^2} = \sqrt{36 + 64}$$
$$= \sqrt{100} = 10 \text{ cm}$$

Here, ΔABC is a right angled triangle.

$\therefore$ Area of $\Delta ABC = \frac{1}{2} \times \text{Base} \times \text{Height}$

$$= \frac{1}{2} \times 8 \times 6 = 24 \text{ cm}^2$$

In ΔCAD, let $a = 12$ cm, $b = 10$ cm and $c = 14$ cm

Then, semi-perimeter,

$$s = \frac{a+b+c}{2} = \frac{12+10+14}{2} = \frac{36}{2} = 18 \text{ cm}$$

$\therefore$ Area of $\Delta CAD = \sqrt{s(s-a)(s-b)(s-c)}$

$$= \sqrt{18(18-12)(18-10)(18-14)}$$
$$= \sqrt{18 \times 6 \times 8 \times 4} = \sqrt{3456} = 58.79 \text{ cm}^2$$

Now, add the areas of both triangles to get the required area of quadrilateral.

Now, area of quadrilateral $ABCD$

$$= \text{Area of } \Delta ABC + \text{Area of } \Delta CAD$$
$$= 24 + 58.79 = 82.79 \text{ cm}^2$$

Hence, the area of the quadrilateral $ABCD$ is 82.79 cm^2.

Useful Formulae

1. For a rectangle, whose length is l and breadth is b,
   - Area $= l \times b$
   - Perimeter $= 2(l + b)$
   - Length of diagonal $= \sqrt{l^2 + b^2}$
2. For a square, whose side is a,
   - Area $= a^2$
   - Perimeter $= 4a$
   - Length of diagonal $= \sqrt{2}\,a$
3. For a parallelogram, whose adjacent sides are a and b and altitude is h,
   - Area $= a \times h$
   - Perimeter $= 2(a + b)$
4. For a rhombus, whose diagonals are d_1 and d_2,
   - Area $= \frac{1}{2} \times d_1 \times d_2$
   - Perimeter $= 2\sqrt{d_1^2 + d_2^2}$ or $4(\text{Side})^2 = d_1^2 + d_2^2$
5. For a trapezium, whose parallel sides are a and b and the distance between them is h,
   - Area $= \frac{1}{2}(a + b) \times h$
6. For a regular hexagon, whose side is a,
   $= 6 \times$ Area of an equilateral triangle with side a
   - Area $= 6 \times \frac{\sqrt{3}}{4} a^2 = \frac{3}{2}\sqrt{3}\,a^2$
   - Perimeter $= 6a$

Example 3. **In the figure, *ABCD* is a rectangle of dimensions 4 cm and 6 cm. *E* and *F* are the mid-points of *AB* and *BC*, respectively. Find the area of the shaded portion.**

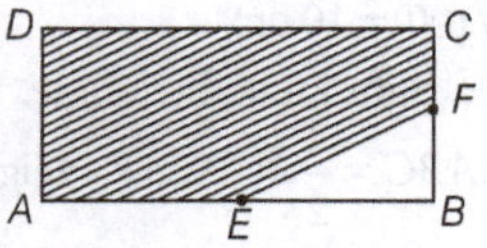

Sol. Given, $AB = 6$ cm and $BC = 4$ cm

Since, E and F are the mid-points of AB and BC, respectively.

$\therefore \quad AE = EB = 3$ cm and $CF = FB = 2$ cm

Now, area of rectangle $ABCD = AB \times BC$

$= 6 \times 4 = 24 \text{ cm}^2$

and area of $\Delta BEF = \frac{1}{2} \times BE \times BF$

$= \frac{1}{2} \times 3 \times 2 = 3 \text{ cm}^2$

$\therefore$ Area of shaded region = Area of rectangle $ABCD$ $-$ Area of $\Delta BEF = 24 - 3 = 21 \text{ cm}^2$

Hence, the area of shaded region is 21 cm^2.

Example 4. **Find the area of a field which is in the shape of trapezium having parallel sides are 20 m and 42 m and non-parallel sides are 21 m and 23 m.**

> Use the formula of area of a trapezium for which we require the height of trapezium. So, firstly divide the trapezium into a parallelogram and a triangle, find the area of triangle by two methods and equate them to get the height of triangle which will give the height of trapezium.

Sol. Let $ABCD$ be the given trapezium with $AB \parallel DC$.

Then, we have $AB = 42$ m, $CD = 20$ m
$AD = 21$ m and $BC = 23$ m

Let us we draw $CE \parallel DA$ and complete the parallelogram $AECD$.

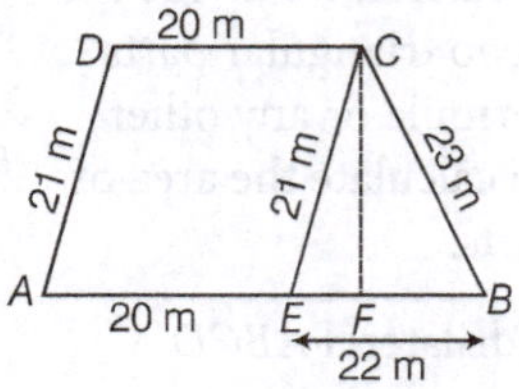

Then, $CE = 21$ m and $AE = 20$ m

[since, in a parallelogram, opposite sides are parallel and equal]

Now, $BE = AB - AE \Rightarrow BE = 42 - 20 = 22$ m

Let $CF \perp AB$ and $CF = h$ m

Now, in ΔEBC, let $a = 21$ m, $b = 23$ m and $c = 22$ m

Then, semi-perimeter of ΔEBC,

$$s = \frac{a+b+c}{2} = \frac{21+23+22}{2} = \frac{66}{2} = 33 \text{ m}$$

and area of $\Delta EBC = \sqrt{s(s-a)(s-b)(s-c)}$ [by Heron's formula]

$$= \sqrt{33(33-21)(33-23)(33-22)}$$
$$= \sqrt{33 \times 12 \times 10 \times 11} = 66\sqrt{10} \text{ m} \quad \text{...(i)}$$

Also, area of $\Delta EBC = \frac{1}{2} \times \text{Base} \times \text{Height} = \frac{1}{2} \times BE \times CF$

$$\Rightarrow \quad 66\sqrt{10} = \frac{1}{2} \times 22 \times h \quad \text{[from Eq. (i)]}$$

$$\Rightarrow \quad h = \frac{66\sqrt{10} \times 2}{22} \Rightarrow h = 6\sqrt{10} \text{ m}$$

Now, area of trapezium $ABCD$

$$= \frac{1}{2} \times [(\text{Sum of parallel sides}) \times \text{Height}]$$
$$= \frac{1}{2} \times (20 + 42) \times 6\sqrt{10} = \frac{62}{2} \times 6\sqrt{10}$$
$$= 186\sqrt{10} \text{ m}^2$$

Hence, area of the given trapezium is $186\sqrt{10} \text{ m}^2$.

Example 5. **Find the area of a parallelogram given in the figure. Also, find the length of the altitude from vertex *A* on the side *DC*.**

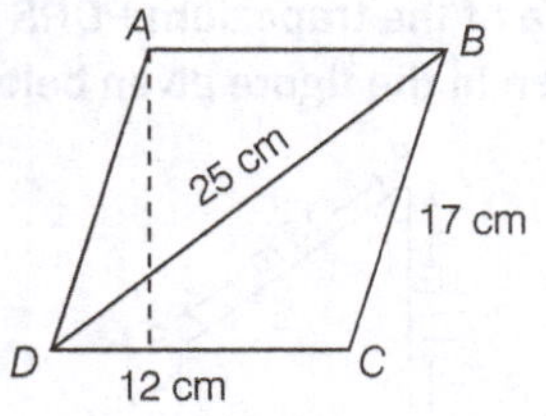

(*i*) Determine the area of ΔBCD by using Heron's formula.
(*ii*) Use relation,
Area of parallelogram $ABCD = 2$ (Area of ΔBCD)
(*iii*) Also, determine the area of parallelogram by using the formula, Area = Base × Altitude.
(*iv*) Further, equate the area of parallelogram obtained in (*ii*) and (*iii*) and get the required length of the altitude.

Sol. Clearly, area of parallelogram,

$$ABCD = 2\,(\text{Area of } \Delta BCD) \quad \text{...(i)}$$

Now, let the sides of ΔBCD be $a = 12$ cm, $b = 17$ cm and $c = 25$ cm.

Then, semi-perimeter of ΔBCD, $s = \dfrac{a+b+c}{2}$

$$= \frac{12+17+25}{2} = \frac{54}{2} = 27 \text{ cm}$$

And area of a $\Delta BCD = \sqrt{s(s-a)(s-b)(s-c)}$ [by Heron's formula]

$$= \sqrt{27\,(27-12)\,(27-17)\,(27-25)}$$
$$= \sqrt{27 \times 15 \times 10 \times 2}$$
$$= \sqrt{3 \times 3 \times 3 \times 3 \times 5 \times 5 \times 2 \times 2}$$
$$= 3 \times 3 \times 5 \times 2 = 90 \text{ cm}^2$$

From Eq. (i),
Area of parallelogram $ABCD = 2 \times$ Area of $\Delta BCD = 2 \times 90$

$$= 180 \text{ cm}^2 \quad \text{...(ii)}$$

Let altitude of the parallelogram be h cm.
Then, area of parallelogram $ABCD$ = Base × Altitude

$\Rightarrow \quad 180 = DC \times h$ [from Eq. (ii)]

$\Rightarrow \quad 180 = 12 \times h$

$\Rightarrow \quad h = \dfrac{180}{12} = 15$ cm

Hence, the area of parallelogram is 180 cm^2 and the length of altitude is 15 cm.

Example 6. **A conical tent is made by stitching 12 triangular pieces of cloth of two different colours red and white alternately, each piece measuring 10 cm, 20 cm and 20 cm.**

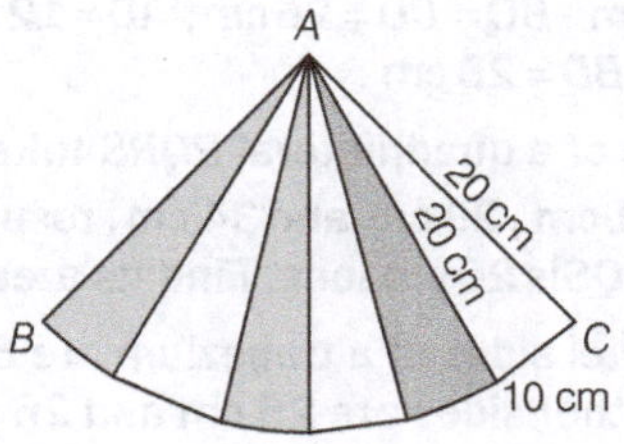

(*i*) How much cloth of red colour is required to make a conical tent?
(*ii*) Find the total length of triangular pieces of white colour.

Sol. (*i*) In a conical tent, pieces are in the form of triangle, whose sides are 10 cm, 20 cm and 20 cm.
Let $a = 10$ cm, $b = 20$ cm and $c = 20$ cm
Then, semi-perimeter of triangle,

$$s = \frac{a+b+c}{2} = \frac{10+20+20}{2} = \frac{50}{2} = 25 \text{ cm}$$

and area of triangle

$$= \sqrt{s(s-a)(s-b)(s-c)}$$ [by Heron's formula]

$$= \sqrt{25(25-10)(25-20)(25-20)}$$
$$= \sqrt{25 \times 15 \times 5 \times 5}$$
$$= \sqrt{5 \times 5 \times 3 \times 5 \times 5 \times 5}$$
$$= 5 \times 5\sqrt{15} = 25\sqrt{15} \text{ cm}^2$$

Thus, area of one red colour triangular piece is $25\sqrt{15}$ cm^2.
Since, tent is made of 12 pieces of two colours.
So, number of triangular pieces of red colour is 6.
Hence, cloth of red colour required to make a conical tent is $6 \times 25\sqrt{15} = 150\sqrt{15}$ cm^2.

(*ii*) The perimeter of one triangular piece,

$$2s = 10 + 20 + 20 = 50 \text{ cm}$$

$\therefore$ Total perimeter of 6 white colour pieces

$= 6 \times$ Perimeter of one triangular piece

$= 6 \times 50 = 300$ cm

Exercise

1. Find the area of a quadrilateral $ABCD$ in which $AB = 16$ cm, $BC = CD = 26$ cm, $AD = 12$ cm and the diagonal $BD = 20$ cm.
2. The sides of a quadrilateral $PQRS$ taken in order are 42 cm, 21 cm, 29 cm and 34 cm, respectively and the diagonal QS is 20 cm long. Find its area.
3. Two parallel sides of a trapezium are 60 cm and 77 cm and other sides are 25 cm and 26 cm. Find the area of the trapezium.
4. A field in the form of a parallelogram has sides 60 m and 40 m and one of its diagonals is 80 m long. Find the area of the parallelogram.
5. The diagonals of a rhombus are 4 cm and 6 cm. Find the area of a rhombus.
6. If the area of a parallelogram is 64 cm^2, base is 12 cm, find the altitude of the parallelogram.
7. The base and the corresponding altitude of a parallelogram are 10 cm and 3.5 cm, respectively. Find the area of the parallelogram.
8. If the sides of a rhombus are 10 cm each and one diagonal is 16 cm, find the area of the rhombus.
9. The perimeter of a rhombus is 146 cm, one of its diagonal is 55 cm. Find the length of the other diagonal and area of the rhombus.
10. Find the area of a parallelogram, whose one diagonal is 6.8 cm and the perpendicular distance of the diagonal from an opposite vertex is 7.5 cm.
11. Find the area of a rhombus, one side of which measures 20 cm and one of whose diagonal is 24 cm.
12. In the following figure, $ABCD$ is a rectangle and DEC is an equilateral triangle. Find the area of the shaded region.

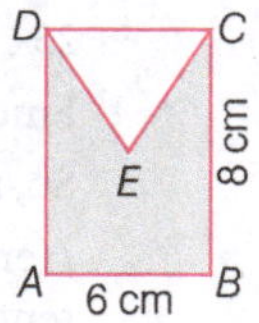

13. Find the area of the trapezium $PQRS$, with height PQ which is given in the figure given below.

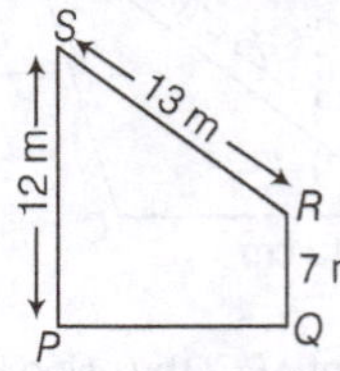

14. In the given figure, ΔABC has sides $AB = 7.5$ cm, $AC = 6.5$ cm and $BC = 7$ cm. On base BC, a parallelogram $DBCE$ of same area as that of ΔABC is constructed. Find the height DF of the parallelogram.

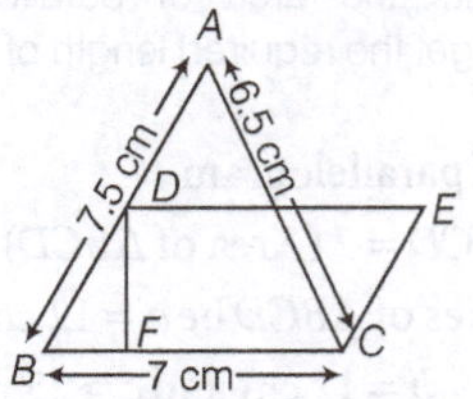

15. A kite is in the shape of a square with diagonal 40 cm and an isosceles triangle of base 6 cm and sides 4 cm. Find the area of the adjoining figure.

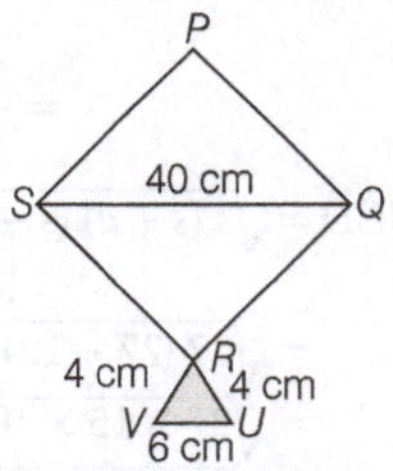

16. A triangle and a parallelogram have the same base and the same area. If the sides of the triangle are 13 cm, 14 cm and 15 cm and the parallelogram stands on the base 14 cm, then find the height of the parallelogram.

Answers

1. 336 cm^2
2. 546 cm^2
3. 1644 cm^2
4. $600\sqrt{15}$ m^2
5. Area of a rhombus = 12 cm^2
6. Altitude = 5.33 cm
7. Area of parallelogram = 35 cm^2
8. 96 cm^2
9. 48 cm, 1320 cm^2
10. 51 cm^2
11. 384 cm^2
12. Area of shaded region = $(48 - 9\sqrt{3})$ cm^2
13. Area of trapezium $PQRS$ = 114 m^2
14. DF = 3 cm
15. $(800 + 3\sqrt{7})$ cm^2
16. h = 6 cm

Surface Areas and Volumes

CHAPTER 11

In earlier classes, we have studied the surface areas and volumes of cube, cuboid and cylinder. In this chapter, we will study the surface areas and volumes of cone, sphere and hemisphere.

TOPIC 01 Surface Area and Volume of a Right Circular Cone

Right Circular Cone

A right circular cone is a solid generated by revolving a line segment which passes through a fixed point and makes a constant angle with a fixed line.

In other words, if a right angled triangle is revolved about one of the two sides forming a right angle, keeping the other side fixed in position, then the solid so obtained by segments is called a right circular cone.

In the figure given below, a right angled ΔOPA on revolving about the line segment OP, generates a right circular cone in which ABC is a circle.

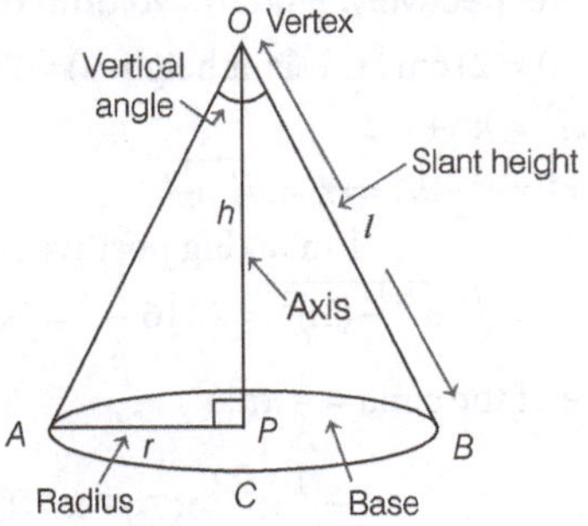

Terms Related to Cone

- **Vertex** O is called the vertex of the cone.
- **Axis** The fixed line OP is called the axis of the cone.
- **Base** The circle ABC is called the base of the cone.
- **Slant height** The length of the line segment joining the vertex O to the edge of the circular base of the cone, is called the slant height of the cone. Here, $OA = OB$ are the slant heights of the cone.
- **Vertical angle** $\angle AOB$ is called the vertical angle of the cone.
- **Height** The length of the line segment joining the vertex to the centre of the base is called the height of the cone. Here, OP is the height of the cone.
- **Radius** The radius AP of the base circle is called the radius of the cone.

Note It

- If the base of the cone is circular but the axis is not at right angle to the base, then cone is not right circular cone [see Fig. (i)].
- If the base of the cone is not circular, then cone is not right circular cone [see Fig. (ii)].

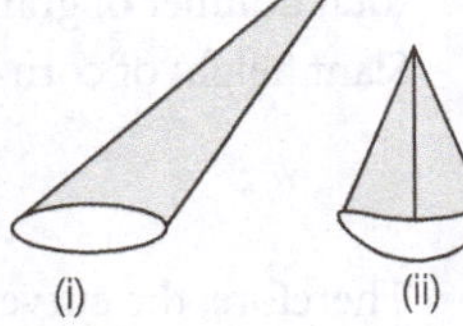

Relation between l, r and h

Let l be the slant height, r be the radius and h be the height of the cone. Then, relation between l, r and h is

$$l^2 = r^2 + h^2 \text{ or } l = \sqrt{r^2 + h^2} \text{ units}$$

[on taking positive square root]

Curved Surface Area of a Cone

For a cone having slant height l and base radius r, the curved surface area is given by

$$\text{Curved surface area of a cone} = \frac{1}{2} l \times 2\pi r$$

$\therefore$ Curved surface area of cone $= \pi rl$ sq units

Example 1. **Find the curved surface area of a right circular cone whose slant height is 32 cm and base radius is 14 cm.**

Sol. Given, slant height of cone $(l) = 32$ cm

and base radius $(r) = 14$ cm

Curved surface area $= \pi rl = \frac{22}{7} \times 14 \times 32 = 1408 \text{ cm}^2$

Example 2. **The diameters of two cones are equal. If their slant heights are in the ratio 5 : 4, then find the ratio of their curved surface areas.**

Sol. Given, diameters of two cones are equal.

So, radii of these cones are also equal.

Let r be the radius of each cone and slant height be $5x$ and $4x$.

We know that

Curved surface area of a cone $= \pi rl$

Then, curved surface area of first cone $= \pi r \times 5x$

and curved surface area of second cone $= \pi r \times 4x$

$\therefore$ Required ratio $= \frac{\pi r \times 5x}{\pi r \times 4x} = 5 : 4$

Example 3. **A corn cob (see figure below), shaped some what like a cone, has the radius of its broadest end as 3.5 cm and length (height) as 24 cm. If each 1 cm^2 of the surface of the cob carries an average of 3 grains. Find how many grains you would find on the entire cob.**

Sol. Here, we need to know the curved surface area of the corn cob to find the total number of grains on it.

Slant height of corn cob, $(l) = \sqrt{r^2 + h^2}$

$= \sqrt{(3.5)^2 + (24)^2} = \sqrt{12.25 + 576}$

$= \sqrt{588.25} = 24.25$ cm

Therefore, the curved surface area of the corn cob $= \pi rl$

$= \frac{22}{7} \times 3.5 \times 24.25 = 266.75 \text{ cm}^2$

$\because$ Number of grains of corn on 1 cm^2 of the surfaces of corn cob = 3

Therefore, number of grains on the entire curved surface of the cob $= 266.75 \times 3 = 800.25$

So, there would be approximately 800 grain of corn on the cob.

Total Surface Area of a Cone

If the base of the cone is to be closed, then a circular piece of paper of radius r is also required.

Total surface area of a cone = Curved surface area + Area of a base $= \pi rl + \pi r^2$

TSA of a cone $= \pi r(l + r)$ sq units

Example 4. **The height of a cone is 16 cm and its base radius is 12 cm. Find the curved surface area and the total surface area of the cone. (take, $\pi = 3.14$)**

Sol. Given, height of a cone $(h) = 16$ cm

and base radius $(r) = 12$ cm

We know that slant height of a cone, $l^2 = h^2 + r^2$

$\Rightarrow \quad l = \sqrt{h^2 + r^2}$

[on taking positive square root]

$\Rightarrow \quad l = \sqrt{(16)^2 + (12)^2} = \sqrt{256 + 144}$

$= \sqrt{400} = 20$ cm

Now, curved surface area of the cone $= \pi rl = 3.14 \times 12 \times 20$

$= 753.6 \text{ cm}^2$

and total surface area of the cone $= \pi rl + \pi r^2$

$= 753.6 + 3.14 \times 12 \times 12$

$= 753.6 + 452.16$

$= 1205.76 \text{ cm}^2$

Volume of a Cone

For a cone of base radius r and height h, the volume is given by

$$\text{Volume of a cone} = \frac{1}{3} \pi r^2 h \text{ cu. units}$$

Example 5. **The height and the slant height of a cone are 21 cm and 28 cm, respectively. Find the volume of the cone.**

Sol. Given, height $(h) = 21$ cm and slant height $(l) = 28$ cm

We know that $l^2 = h^2 + r^2$

$\Rightarrow \quad r^2 = l^2 - h^2 \Rightarrow r = \sqrt{l^2 - h^2}$

[on taking positive square root]

$= \sqrt{(28)^2 - (21)^2} = 7\sqrt{16 - 9} = 7\sqrt{7}$ cm

Hence, volume of the cone $= \frac{1}{3} \pi r^2 h$

$= \frac{1}{3} \times \frac{22}{7} \times 7\sqrt{7} \times 7\sqrt{7} \times 21$

$= 7546 \text{ cm}^3$

Example 6. **The radius and the height of a right circular cone are in the ratio 5 : 12, respectively. If its volume is 314 m^3, then find its slant height and the radius. [use $\pi = 3.14$]**

Sol. Let radius of cone $= 5x$ and height of the cone $= 12x$

Given, volume of the cone $= 314 \text{ m}^3$

$$\Rightarrow \frac{1}{3} \times 3.14 \times (5x)^2 \times (12x) = 314$$

$$\left[\because \text{volume of cone} = \frac{1}{3}\pi r^2 h\right]$$

$$\Rightarrow \quad 314x^3 = 314 \Rightarrow x^3 = 1$$

$$\Rightarrow \quad x = 1 \quad \text{[on taking cube root]}$$

$\therefore$ Radius $(r) = 5$ m and height $(h) = 12$ m

Now, slant height, $l = \sqrt{r^2 + h^2} = \sqrt{25 + 144} = \sqrt{169} = 13 \text{ m}$

Hence, radius $= 5$ m and slant height $= 13$ m

Example 7. **A conical tent is to accommodate 11 persons. Each person must have 4 sq m of the space on the ground and 20 cu m of air to breathe. Find the height of the cone.**

Sol. Let h m be the height, r m be the radius of base of the cone. Since, the tent can accommodate 11 persons and each person requires 4 sq m of the space on the ground and 20 cu m of air.

$\therefore$ Area of the base $= 11 \times 4 = 44 \text{ m}^2 \Rightarrow \pi r^2 = 44 \text{ m}^2$ ...(i)

$[\because \text{area of base} = \pi r^2]$

Volume of the cone $= 11 \times 20 = 220 \text{ m}^3$

$$\Rightarrow \quad \frac{1}{3}\pi r^2 h = 220 \text{ m}^3 \quad \text{...(ii)}$$

On dividing Eq. (ii) by Eq. (i), we get

$$\frac{\frac{1}{3}\pi r^2 h}{\pi r^2} = \frac{220}{44} \Rightarrow \frac{h}{3} = 5 \Rightarrow h = 15 \text{ m}$$

Hence, the height of the cone is 15 m.

Example 8. **Sarita has a piece of canvas whose area is 1498 m^2. She uses it to have a conical tent made, with a base radius of 14 m. Assuming that all the stitching margins and the wastage incurred while cutting, amounts to approximately 2 m^2. Find the volume of the tent that can be made with it.**

Sol. Since, the area of the canvas $= 1498 \text{ m}^2$

and area of the canvas lost in wastage $= 2 \text{ m}^2$

$\therefore$ The area of canvas available for making the tent

$$= (1498 - 2) \text{ m}^2 = 1496 \text{ m}^2$$

Now, surface area of the tent $= 1496 \text{ m}^2$

Radius of conical tent $= 14$ m

$$\therefore \quad \pi r l = 1496$$

$$\Rightarrow \quad \frac{22}{7} \times 14 \times l = 1496 \Rightarrow l = 34 \text{ m}$$

Now, $h = \sqrt{l^2 - r^2} = \sqrt{34^2 - 14^2} = \sqrt{1156 - 196} = \sqrt{960}$

$$\Rightarrow \quad h = 30.98 \text{ m}$$

So, the volume of conical tent

$$= \frac{1}{3}\pi r^2 h = \frac{1}{3} \times \frac{22}{7} \times 14 \times 14 \times 30.98$$

$$= 6361.22 \text{ m}^3$$

Try These 11.1

1. **The diameter of base and height of a cone is 14 cm and 24 cm, respectively. Find curved surface area of the cone.**
2. **Find the curved surface area of a cone whose circumference of the base and slant height are 88 cm and 2 cm, respectively.**
3. **Find the curved surface area of a cone whose area of the base and height are 154 cm^2 and 24 cm, respectively.**
4. **A conical tent is 12 m high and the radius of its base is 16 m. Find**
   (i) slant height of the tent.
   (ii) cost of the canvas required to make the tent, if the cost of 1 m^2 canvas is ₹ 70.
5. **A joker's cap is in the form of a right circular cone of base radius 8 cm and height 15 cm. Find the area of sheet required to make 25 such caps.**
6. **A taxi stand is barricaded from the remaining part of the road, by using 30 hollow cones made of recycled cardboard. Each cone has a base diameter of 48 cm and height 0.7 m. If the outer side of each of the cones is to be painted and the cost of painting is ₹ 24 per m^2, then what will be the cost of painting all these cones? [take $\pi = 3.14$]**
7. **Find the volume of the right circular cone whose**
   (i) $l = 24$ cm, $h = 21$ cm (ii) $l = 13$ cm, $h = 5$ cm
   (iii) $r = 5$, $h = 3$ cm (iv) $r = 2.5$, $h = 3$ cm
8. **If height and volume of a cone are 15 cm and $500\pi \text{ cm}^3$ respectively, then find the radius of base of the cone.**
9. **If the volume and the base area of a right circular cone are $48\pi \text{ cm}^3$ and $12\pi \text{ cm}^2$ respectively, then find the height of the cone.**
10. **If the height and the radius of a cone are tripled, then find the ratio of volume of new cone and that of original cone.**
11. **A right angled ΔABC with sides 6 cm, 8 cm and 10 cm is revolved about the side 8 cm. Find the volume of the solid so obtained.**
12. **If the ΔABC in Question 11 is revolved about the side 6 cm, then find the volume of the solid, so obtained. Also, find the ratio of volumes of the two solid obtained in Questions 11 and 12.**
13. **A heap of wheat is in the form of a cone whose diameter is 40 m and height is 15 m. Find its volume. The heap is to be covered by a canvas to protect it from rain. Find the area of the canvas required.**

Hints & Answers

1. Hint $l=\sqrt{(7)^2+(24)^2}=25$ cm.

Curved surface area $=\frac{22}{7}\times\frac{14}{2}\times 25$ **Ans.** 550 cm^2

2. Hint Circumference of base, $2\pi r=88\Rightarrow r=14$ cm

$\therefore$ Curved surface area $=\pi rl=\frac{22}{7}\times 14\times 2$ **Ans.** 88 cm^2

3. Hint Area of base, $\pi r^2=154\Rightarrow r^2=\frac{154\times 7}{22}\Rightarrow r=7$

$\Rightarrow\quad l=\sqrt{(24)^2+(7)^2}=25$ cm

Curved surface area $=\pi rl$. **Ans.** 550 cm^2

4. Hint (i) Slant height, $l=\sqrt{h^2+r^2}$ **Ans.** 20 m

(ii) Curved surface area of tent $=\pi rl$

$=\frac{22}{7}\times 16\times 20=1005.71\text{ m}^2$

Cost of the canvas required to make the tent

$=70\times 1005.71$ **Ans.** ₹ 70400

5. Hint $\because l^2=h^2+r^2\Rightarrow l=\sqrt{(15)^2+(8)^2}=17$ cm

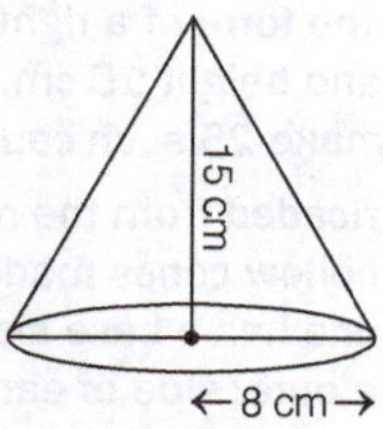

Curved surface area of a joker cap

= Curved surface area of cone

$=\pi rl=\frac{22}{7}\times 8\times 17=427.42\text{ cm}^2$ (approx.)

$\because$ The sheet required to make 1 cap $=427.42\text{ cm}^2$

$\therefore$ The sheet required to make 25 such caps

$=427.42\times 25$ **Ans.** 10686 cm^2

6. We have, diameter = 48 cm

$\therefore$ Radius = 24 cm = 0.24 m $\quad\left[\because 1\text{ cm}=\frac{1}{100}\text{ m}\right]$

and height (h) = 0.7 m

$\because\quad l=\sqrt{r^2+h^2}=\sqrt{(0.24)^2+(0.7)^2}$

$=\sqrt{0.0576+0.49}=\sqrt{0.5476}=0.74$ m

Curved surface area of a cone $=\pi rl=3.14\times 0.24\times 0.74$

$=0.55766\text{ m}^2$

$\because$ Cost of painting per m^2 = ₹ 24

$\therefore$ Cost of painting $0.55766\text{ m}^2=24\times 0.55766=$ ₹13.383

Thus, the cost of painting for 1 cone = ₹ 13.383

$\therefore$ Cost of painting 30 cones $=13.383\times 30=$ ₹ 401.49

7. Hint Solve as Example 5. **Ans.** (i) $945\pi\text{ cm}^3$

(ii) $240\pi\text{ cm}^3$ (iii) $25\pi\text{ cm}^3$ (iv) $6.25\pi\text{ cm}^3$

8. Hint Volume of cone $=\frac{1}{3}\pi r^2h=500\pi$

$\Rightarrow\frac{1}{3}r^2(15)=500\Rightarrow r^2=\frac{500}{5}=100$ **Ans.** $r=10$ cm

9. Hint Base area, $\pi r^2=12\pi\Rightarrow r^2=12$

Volume, $\frac{1}{3}\pi r^2h=48\pi\Rightarrow\frac{1}{3}\times 12\times h=48$

Ans. $h=12$ cm, $r=\sqrt{12}$ cm

10. Hint Volume of original cone $=\frac{1}{3}\pi r^2h$

Volume of new cone $=\frac{1}{3}\pi(3r)^2 3h=9\pi r^2h$,

$\therefore$ Required ratio $=\dfrac{9\pi r^2h}{\frac{1}{3}\pi r^2h}$ **Ans.** $\frac{27}{1}$ or 27 : 1

11. On revolving the right angled ΔABC about the side AB, we get a right circular cone as shown in the adjoining figure whose radius (r) = 6 cm and height (h) = 8 cm.

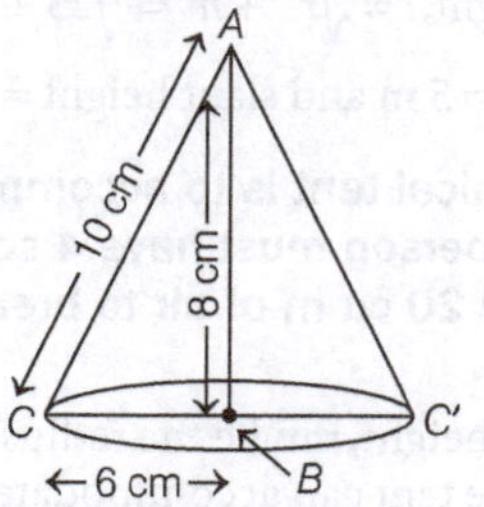

$\therefore$ Volume of the solid, so obtained $=\frac{1}{3}\pi r^2h=\frac{1}{3}\times\pi\times 6\times 6\times 8$

$=96\pi\text{ cm}^3$

12. On revolving the right angled ΔABC about the side, $BC=6$ cm, we get a cone as shown in the figure, whose radius (r) = 8 cm and height (h) = 6 cm.

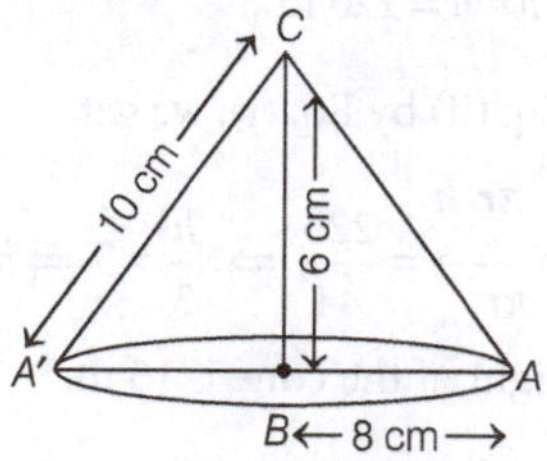

Volume of the solid so obtained, $V_1=\frac{1}{3}\pi r^2h=\frac{1}{3}\times\pi\times 8\times 8\times 6$

$=128\pi\text{ cm}^3$

In Question 11, the volume V_2 obtained by revolving the ΔABC about the side 8 cm i.e. $V_2=96\pi\text{ cm}^3$

Now, $\quad\frac{V_2}{V_1}=\frac{96\pi}{128\pi}=\frac{3}{4}\Rightarrow V_2:V_1=3:4$

Hence, the required ratio is 3 : 4.

13. Hint $\because l^2=h^2+r^2\Rightarrow l=\sqrt{(15)^2+(20)^2}$

$\Rightarrow l=\sqrt{225+400}=\sqrt{625}=25$ cm

$\therefore$ Volume of the heap of wheat $=\frac{1}{3}\pi r^2h=\frac{1}{3}\times\frac{22}{7}\times 20\times 20\times 15$

$=6285.71\text{ m}^3$

$\therefore$ Area of the canvas required = Curved surface area of the heap

$=\pi rl=\frac{22}{7}\times 20\times 25$ **Ans.** 1571.42 m^2

TOPIC 02 Surface Area and Volume of a Sphere and Hemisphere

Sphere

A sphere is three-dimensional figure (solid figure) which is made up of all points in the space, which lie at a constant distance from a fixed point, called the **centre** of the sphere and the constant distance is called its **radius**.

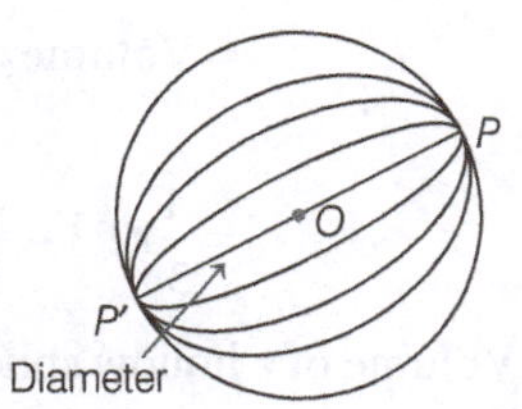

A line segment through the centre of a sphere and with the end points on the sphere is called a **diameter** of the sphere. In real life, we observe many objects such as a cricket ball, a round metallic ball, a fully blown football, etc., are examples of sphere.

Surface Area of a Sphere

For a sphere of radius 'r', the surface area is given by

Surface area of the sphere $= 4\pi r^2$ sq units

Example 1. **Find the surface area of a sphere having diameter 30 cm.**

Sol. Given, diameter of the sphere = 30 cm

$\therefore$ Radius of the sphere $= \frac{30}{2} = 15$ cm

Now, surface area of the sphere $= 4\pi r^2$

$$= 4 \times \frac{22}{7} \times (15)^2 = 4 \times \frac{22}{7} \times 15 \times 15 = 2828.57 \text{ cm}^2$$

Hemisphere

When a plane through the centre of a sphere divides the sphere into two equal parts, then these two equal parts are called **hemisphere.**

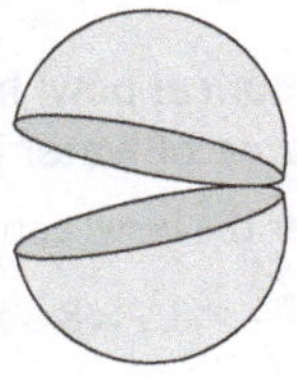

Surface Area of a Hemisphere

The curved surface area of a hemisphere is half the surface area of sphere.

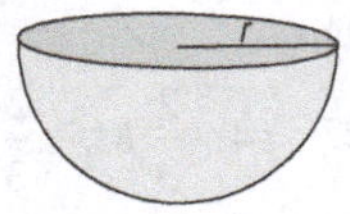

So, curved surface area of hemisphere $= \frac{1}{2} \times 4\pi r^2$

Curved surface area of hemisphere $= 2\pi r^2$ sq units

Where, r is the radius.

Also, area of base of the hemisphere $= \pi r^2$

So, total surface area of hemisphere

= Curved surface area of a hemisphere + Area of the base of hemisphere

$$= 2\pi r^2 + \pi r^2$$

TSA of hemisphere $= 3\pi r^2$ sq units

Where, r is the radius.

Example 2. **The hollow sphere, in which the circus motorcyclist performs his stunts, has a radius of 4.5 m. Find the area available to the motorcyclist for riding.**

Sol. Given, radius of sphere is 4.5 m.

So, the riding space available for the motorcyclist is the surface area of the sphere.

$\therefore$ The area available to the motorcyclist for riding $= 4\pi r^2$

$$= 4 \times \frac{22}{7} \times 4.5 \times 4.5 \text{ m}^2 = 254.57 \text{ m}^2$$

Example 3. **For a hemisphere of radius 28 m, find**

(i) the curved surface area of the hemisphere.

(ii) the total surface area of the hemisphere.

Sol. (i) The curved surface area of a hemisphere of radius 28 cm

$$= 2\pi r^2 = 2 \times \frac{22}{7} \times 28 \times 28$$

$$= 4928 \text{ cm}^2$$

(ii) The total surface area of the hemisphere

$$= 3\pi r^2 = 3 \times \frac{22}{7} \times 28 \times 28$$

$$= 7392 \text{ cm}^2$$

Example 4. **A hemispherical bowl is made from a metal sheet having thickness 0.3 cm. The inner radius of the bowl is 24.7 cm. Find the cost of polishing its outer surface at the rate of ₹ 4 per 100 cm². (take, $\pi = 3.14$)**

Sol. Given, inner radius of the hemispherical bowl = 24.7 cm

Thickness of metal sheet = 0.3 cm

Now, outer radius of the hemispherical bowl

$$= 24.7 + 0.3 = 25 \text{ cm}$$

$\therefore$ Outer surface area of the hemispherical bowl $= 2\pi r^2$

$$= 2 \times 3.14 \times (25)^2$$

$$= 157 \times 25 = 3925 \text{ cm}^2$$

Now, cost of polishing 100 cm² = ₹ 4

$\therefore$ Cost of polishing 3925 cm² $= \frac{4 \times 3925}{100} =$ ₹ 157

Example 5. **A hemispherical dome of building needs to be painted (see figure). If the circumference of the base of the dome is 17.6 m, then find the cost of painting it, given that cost of painting is ₹ 5 per 100 cm².**

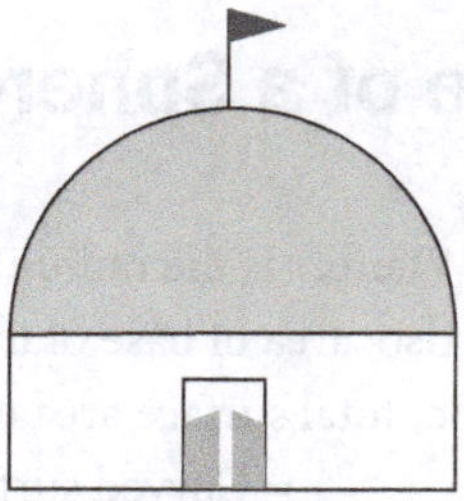

Sol. Let r be the radius of the dome.

Given, circumference of the base of the dome

= Circumference of a circle = 17.6 m

$\Rightarrow \quad 2\pi r = 17.6 \Rightarrow r = 17.6 \times \frac{7}{2 \times 22} = 2.8$ m

Curved surface area of the dome

= Curved surface area of a hemisphere = $2\pi r^2$

$= 2 \times \frac{22}{7} \times 2.8 \times 2.8 = 49.28$ m²

Now, cost of painting 100 cm² = ₹ 5

Then, cost of painting 1 m² = ₹ 500 $\quad [\because (100 \text{ cm})^2 = 1 \text{m}^2]$

∴ Cost of painting the whole dome = 500 × 49.28

= ₹ 24640

Volume of a Sphere

For a sphere of radius r, the volume is given by the formula

$$\text{Volume of a sphere} = \frac{4}{3}\pi r^3 \text{ cu units}$$

Example 6. **Find the volume of a sphere of radius 4.2 cm.**

Sol. Required volume $= \frac{4}{3}\pi r^3$

$= \frac{4}{3} \times \frac{22}{7} \times 4.2 \times 4.2 \times 4.2 \text{ cm}^3 \quad [\because r = 4.2 \text{ cm (given)}]$

$= 310.46 \text{ cm}^3$

Example 7. **How many balls each of radius 2 cm can be made by melting a big ball whose radius is 8 cm?**

Sol. Given, radius of big ball $(R) = 8$ cm

and radius of small ball $(r) = 2$ cm

∴ Volume of big ball $= \frac{4}{3}\pi R^3 = \frac{4}{3}\pi (8)^3 \text{cm}^3$

Volume of small ball $= \frac{4}{3}\pi r^3 = \frac{4}{3}\pi (2)^3 \text{cm}^3$

∴ Required number of balls $= \frac{\text{Volume of big ball}}{\text{Volume of small ball}}$

$= \frac{\frac{4}{3}\pi (8)^3}{\frac{4}{3}\pi (2)^3} = \frac{8 \times 8 \times 8}{2 \times 2 \times 2}$

= 64 balls

Volume of Hollow Sphere (Spherical Shell)

If R and r are the external and internal radii of a sphere respectively, then

Volume of hollow sphere (spherical shell)

= Volume of the external sphere

− Volume of the internal sphere

$= \frac{4}{3}\pi R^3 - \frac{4}{3}\pi r^3 = \frac{4}{3}\pi (R^3 - r^3)$

Volume of a hollow sphere (spherical shell)

$= \frac{4}{3}\pi (R^3 - r^3)$ cu. units

Example 8. **Volume of a hollow sphere is $\frac{11352}{7}$ cm³. If the outer radius is 8 cm, then find the inner radius of the hollow sphere.**

Sol. Let R and r be the outer and inner radii of the hollow sphere, respectively.

Then, volume of hollow sphere $= \frac{4}{3}\pi(R^3 - r^3)$

$\therefore \quad \frac{4}{3}\pi (8^3 - r^3) = \frac{11352}{7}$

$\Rightarrow \quad \frac{4 \times 22}{3 \times 7}(8^3 - r^3) = \frac{11352}{7}$

$\Rightarrow \quad 512 - r^3 = 387$

$\Rightarrow \quad r^3 = 125 \Rightarrow r = 5$ cm

Hence, the inner radius of the hollow sphere is 5 cm.

Volume of Hemisphere

Since, a hemisphere is half of a sphere, then

Volume of hemisphere $= \frac{1}{2} \times \frac{4}{3}\pi r^3 = \frac{2}{3}\pi r^3$ cu. units

Example 9. **A hemispherical bowl has a radius of 8.4 cm. What would be the volume of water it would contain?**

Sol. The volume of water the bowl can contain

$= \frac{2}{3}\pi r^3 = \frac{2}{3} \times \frac{22}{7} \times 8.4 \times 8.4 \times 8.4 = 1241.85 \text{ cm}^3$

Example 10. **The volume of two hemispheres are in the ratio 8 : 27. What is the ratio of their radii?**

Sol. Let volume of two hemispheres be V_1, V_2 and their radii be r_1, r_2, respectively.

Given, $V_1 : V_2 = 8 : 27 \Rightarrow \frac{2}{3}\pi r_1^3 : \frac{2}{3}\pi r_2^3 = 8 : 27$

$\left[\because \text{volume of hemisphere} = \frac{2}{3}\pi r^3\right]$

$\Rightarrow \quad r_1^3 : r_2^3 = 8 : 27 \Rightarrow r_1 : r_2 = 2 : 3$

Try These 11.2

1. **Find the surface area of a sphere of following diameters.**
   (i) 12 cm (ii) 22 m (iii) 7.5 m (iv) 14 m
2. **A toy is in the form a hemisphere of radius 3.5 cm. Find the curved surface area and total surface area.**
3. **The radius of the Moon is approximately one-fifth of the radius of the planet. Find the ratio of their surface areas.**
4. **A dome of a building is in the form of a hemisphere. From inside, it was white washed at the cost of ₹ 776.16. If the cost of white washing is ₹ 3.5 per sq m, then find the**
   (i) inside surface area of the dome.
   (ii) volume of the air inside the dome.
5. **A hemispherical bowl is made of steel 0.35 cm thick. The inner radius of the bowl is 6.65 cm. Find the cost of tin plating it on the outer side at the rate of ₹ 25 per 100 cm^2.**
6. **Find the volume of the sphere of the following diameters.**
   (i) 2.1 cm (ii) 32 cm (iii) 8 cm (iv) 12 m (v) 9 m
7. **A capsule of medicine is in the shape of a sphere of diameter 4.2 mm. How much medicine (in mm^3) is needed to fill this capsule?**
8. **A shopkeeper has one laddoo of diameter 10 cm. With the same material, how many laddoos of diameter 5 cm can be made?**
9. **If the radius of a sphere is doubled, then find the ratio of volume of the new sphere that of the original sphere.**
10. **A shot-put is a metallic sphere of radius 5.4 cm. If the density of metal is 8.4 g per cm^3, find the mass of the shot-put.**
11. **Find the volume of the hemisphere whose diameter is**
    (i) 22 cm (ii) 14 cm (iii) 9 m (iv) 25 m
12. **The circumference of the edge of a hemispherical bowl is 132 cm. Find the volume of the bowl.**
13. **The volume of two hemispheres are in the ratio 27 : 125. Find the ratio of their radii.**

Hints & Answers

1. **Hint** Solve as Example 1. **Ans.** (i) 452.57 cm^2
   (ii) 1521.14 m^2 (iii) 176.79 m^2 (iv) 616 m^2
2. **Hint** Curved surface area $= 2\pi r^2 = 2\pi(3.5)^2$
   $\therefore$ Total surface area $= 3\pi r^2 = 3\pi(3.5)^2$ **Ans.** 77 cm^2, 115.5 cm^2
3. **Hint** Let radius of planet be x. Then, radius of moon $= \dfrac{x}{5}$
   $\therefore$ Required ratio $= \dfrac{4\pi(x^2)}{4\pi(x/5)^2} = \dfrac{25}{1}$. **Ans** 25:1
4. (i) Inside surface area of the dome
   $= \dfrac{\text{Cost of white washing}}{\text{Cost of white washing per sq m}}$
   $= \dfrac{₹776.16}{₹3.5} = 221.76 m^2$

   (ii) Let r be the radius of the dome.
   $\because$ Inside surface area = 221.76 sq m
   $\Rightarrow \quad 2\pi r^2 = 221.76 \Rightarrow 2 \times \dfrac{22}{7} \times r^2 = 221.76$
   $\Rightarrow \quad r^2 = 35.28 \Rightarrow r = 5.9$ m (approx.)
   $\therefore$ Volume of the air inside the dome
   $= \dfrac{2}{3}\pi r^3 = \dfrac{2}{3} \times \dfrac{22}{7} \times 5.9 \times 5.9 \times 5.9 = 430.32 m^3$ (approx.)
5. **Hint**

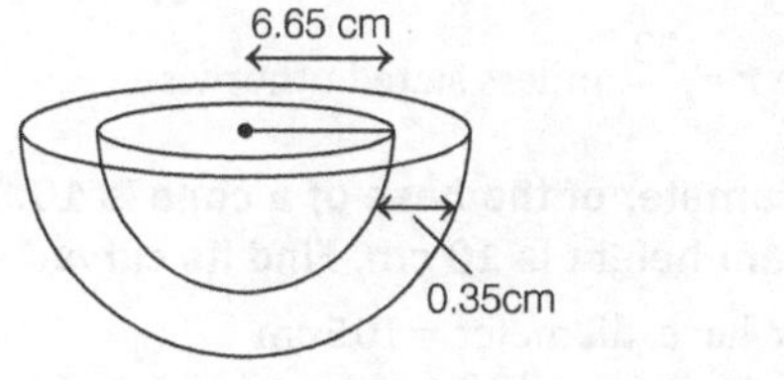

   $\because$ Outer radius of the bowl = Inner radius + Thickness
   $= 6.65 + 0.35 = 7$ cm.
   Outer curved surface area of the bowl $= 2\pi r^2$
   $= 2 \times \dfrac{22}{7} \times 7 \times 7 = 308 cm^2$
   $\because$ Cost of plating on outside for 100 cm^2 = ₹ 25
   $\therefore$ Cost of tin plating on outer side for 308 cm^2 $= \dfrac{25 \times 308}{100} =$ ₹77
6. **Hint** Volume of the sphere $= \dfrac{4}{3}\pi r^3$
   Ans. (i) 4.851 cm^3 (ii) 17164.19 cm^3 (iii) 268.19 cm^3
   (iv) 905.14 m^3 (v) 381.86 m^3
7. **Hint** Radius $(r) = \dfrac{4.2}{2} = 2.1$ mm
   Now, the volume of capsule $= \dfrac{4}{3}\pi r^3 = \dfrac{4}{3} \times \dfrac{22}{7} \times 2.1 \times 2.1 \times 2.1$
   Ans. 38.80 mm^3
8. **Hint** Solve as Example 7. **Ans.** 8
9. **Hint** Volume of original sphere $= \dfrac{4}{3}\pi r^3$
   Volume of new sphere $= \dfrac{4}{3}\pi(2r)^3$
   $\therefore$ Required ratio $= \dfrac{4/3\pi(2r)^3}{4/3\pi r^3} = \dfrac{8}{1}$. **Ans.** 8:1
10. $\because$ Volume of the sphere $= \dfrac{4}{3}\pi r^3 = \dfrac{4}{3} \times \dfrac{22}{7} \times 5.4 \times 5.4 \times 5.4$
    [$r = 5.4$ cm, given]
    $= 659.85 cm^3$
    Further, mass of 1 cm^3 of metal is 8.4 g.
    Therefore, mass of the shot-putt $= 8.4 \times 659.85$ g
    $= 5542.74$ gm $= 5.54$ kg [nearly]
11. **Hint** Volume of hemisphere $= \dfrac{2}{3}\pi(r)^3$
    Ans. (i) 2788.76 cm^3 (ii) 718.67 cm^3 (iii) 190.93 m^3
    (iv) 4092.26 m^3
12. **Hint** Circumference of bowl,
    $2\pi r = 132 \Rightarrow r = \dfrac{132 \times 7}{2 \times 22} = 21$ cm
    $\therefore$ Volume of bowl $= \dfrac{2}{3}\pi(21)^3$. **Ans.** 19404 cm^3
13. **Hint** Solve as Example 10. **Ans.** 3 : 5

NCERT FOLDER

Complete Solutions of All Exercises of NCERT Textbook

EXERCISE 11.1 (NCERT Page 140-141)

Assume $\pi = \frac{22}{7}$, unless stated otherwise.

Q1. Diameter of the base of a cone is 10.5 cm and its slant height is 10 cm. Find its curved surface area.

Sol. We have, diameter = 10.5 cm

$\therefore$ Radius $(r) = \frac{10.5}{2} = 5.25$ cm and slant height $(l) = 10$ cm

Now, curved surface area of the cone $= \pi r l = \frac{22}{7} \times 5.25 \times 10$

$= 165 \text{ cm}^2$

Q2. Find the total surface area of a cone if its slant height is 21 m and diameter of its base is 24 m.

Sol. We have, slant height $(l) = 21$ m and diameter = 24 m

$\therefore$ Radius $(r) = \frac{24}{2} = 12$ m

Now, total surface area of the cone $= \pi r(l + r)$

$= \pi \times 12(21 + 12) = \pi \times 12 \times 33 = 396\pi$

$= 396 \times \frac{22}{7} = \frac{8712}{7} = 1244.57 \text{ m}^2$

Q3. Curved surface area of a cone is 308 cm² and its slant height is 14 cm. Find

(i) radius of the base.

(ii) total surface area of the cone.

Sol. We have, slant height $(l) = 14$ cm

Curved surface area of a cone = 308 cm²

$\Rightarrow \quad \pi r l = 308$

[$\because$ curved surface area of a cone $= \pi r l$]

$\Rightarrow \frac{22}{7} \times r \times 14 = 308$

$\Rightarrow \quad r = \frac{308}{22 \times 2} = 7$ cm

(i) Radius of the base $(r) = 7$ cm

(ii) Total surface area of the cone $= \pi r(r + l)$

$= \frac{22}{7} \times 7(7 + 14) = 22 \times 21 = 462 \text{ cm}^2$

Q4. A conical tent is 10 m high and the radius of its base is 24 m. Find

(i) slant height of the tent.

(ii) cost of the canvas required to make the tent, if the cost of 1 m² canvas is ₹ 70.

Sol. We have, height $(h) = 10$ m and radius $(r) = 24$ m

(i) We know that $l^2 = h^2 + r^2 \Rightarrow l = \sqrt{r^2 + h^2}$

[on taking positive square root]

$\Rightarrow \quad l = \sqrt{(24)^2 + (10)^2} = \sqrt{576 + 100}$

$= \sqrt{676} = 26$ m

Hence, the slant height of the canvas tent is 26 m.

(ii) Canvas required to make the tent

= Curved surface area of tent

$= \pi r l = \pi \times 24 \times 26 = 624\pi \text{ m}^2$

$\because$ Cost of 1 m² canvas = ₹ 70

$\therefore$ Cost of 624π m² canvas $= 70 \times 624\pi$

$= 70 \times 624 \times \frac{22}{7} = 10 \times 624 \times 22 =$ ₹137280

Hence, required cost of the canvas is ₹ 137280.

Q5. What length of tarpaulin 3 m wide will be required to make conical tent of height 8 m and base radius 6 m? Assume that the extra length of material that will be required for stitching margins and wastage in cutting is approximately 20 cm. (take, $\pi = 3.14$)

Sol. Let r, h and l be the radius, height and slant height of the tent, respectively.

Given, $r = 6$ m and $h = 8$ m

We know that, $l^2 = h^2 + r^2 \Rightarrow l = \sqrt{r^2 + h^2}$

[on taking positive square root]

$\Rightarrow \quad l = \sqrt{(6)^2 + (8)^2} \Rightarrow l = \sqrt{36 + 64}$

$\Rightarrow \quad l = \sqrt{100} = 10$ m

Area of the canvas used for the tent

= Curved surface area of the cone

$= \pi r l = 3.14 \times 6 \times 10 = 188.4 \text{ m}^2$

$\therefore$ Length of tarpaulin required

$= \frac{\text{Area of tarpaulin required}}{\text{Width of tarpaulin}} = \frac{188.4}{3}$

[$\because$ width of tarpaulin = 3 m, given]

$= 62.8$ m

The extra material required for stitching margins and cutting

$= 20 \text{ cm} = 0.2 \text{ m} \quad \left[\because 1 \text{ cm} = \frac{1}{100} \text{ m}\right]$

Hence, the total length of tarpaulin required

$= 62.8 + 0.2 = 63$ m

Q6. The slant height and base diameter of a conical tomb are 25 m and 14 m, respectively. Find the cost of white-washing its curved surface at the rate of ₹ 210 per 100 m^2.

Sol. We have, slant height $(l) = 25\text{m}$ and diameter $= 14\text{m}$

$\therefore$ Radius $(r) = \dfrac{14}{2} = 7\text{m}$

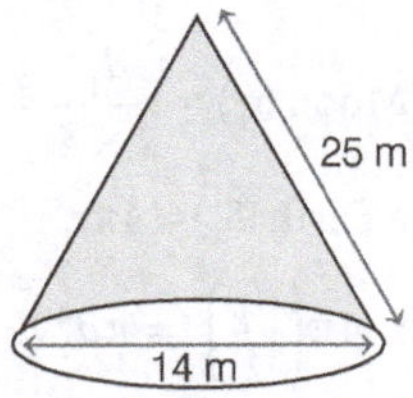

Curved surface area of the conical tomb

$= $ Curved surface area of a cone $= \pi r l$

$= \dfrac{22}{7} \times 7 \times 25 = 22 \times 25 = 550\ \text{m}^2$

Given, cost of white-washing per $100\ \text{m}^2 = ₹\,210$

$\therefore$ Cost of white-washing per $1\ \text{m}^2 = ₹\,\dfrac{210}{100}$

Then, cost of white-washing $550\ \text{m}^2 = \dfrac{210 \times 550}{100} = ₹1155$

Q7. A joker's cap is in the form of a right circular cone of base radius 7 cm and height 24 cm. Find the area of the sheet required to make 10 such caps.

Sol. We have, radius $(r) = 7\text{cm}$ and height $(h) = 24\text{cm}$

We know that, $l^2 = h^2 + r^2$

$\Rightarrow \quad l = \sqrt{h^2 + r^2}$

[on taking positive square root]

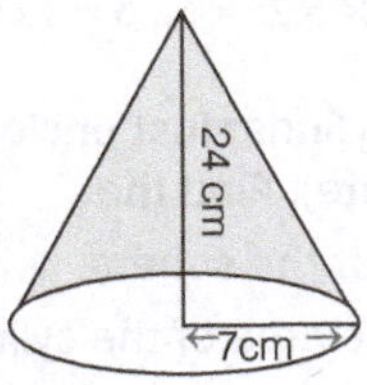

$\Rightarrow \quad l = \sqrt{(24)^2 + 7^2} = \sqrt{576 + 49} = \sqrt{625}$

$\Rightarrow \quad l = 25\,\text{cm}$

Curved surface area of a joker's cap

$= $ Curved surface area of a cone $= \pi r l$

$= \dfrac{22}{7} \times 7 \times 25 = 22 \times 25 = 550\ \text{cm}^2$

$\because$ The sheet required to make 1 cap $= 550\ \text{cm}^2$

$\therefore$ The sheet required to make 10 such caps $= 550 \times 10$

$= 5500\ \text{cm}^2$

Q8. A bus stop is barricaded from the remaining part of the road, by using 50 hollow cones made of recycled cardboard. Each cone has a base diameter of 40 cm and height 1 m. If the outer side of each of the cones is to be painted and the cost of painting is ₹12 per m^2, then what will be the cost of painting all these cones? (take, $\pi = 3.14$ and $\sqrt{1.04} = 1.02$)

Sol. We have, diameter $= 40$ cm

$\therefore$ Radius $(r) = \dfrac{40}{2} = 20$ cm

$= \dfrac{20}{100}\ \text{m} = 0.2\ \text{m} \qquad \left[\because 1\ \text{cm} = \dfrac{1}{100}\ \text{m}\right]$

and height $(h) = 1$ m

We know that $l^2 = h^2 + r^2 \Rightarrow l = \sqrt{r^2 + h^2}$

[on taking positive square root]

$\Rightarrow \quad l = \sqrt{(0.2)^2 + 1^2} = \sqrt{0.04 + 1}$

$= \sqrt{1.04} = 1.02$ m

$[\because \sqrt{1.04} = 1.02$, given$]$

Curved surface area of a cone $= \pi r l$

$= 3.14 \times 0.2 \times 1.02 = 0.64056\ \text{m}^2$

Now, cost of painting per $\text{m}^2 = ₹12$

$\therefore$ Cost of painting $0.64056\ \text{m}^2 = 12 \times 0.64056$

$= ₹\,7.68672$

Thus, cost of painting for 1 cone $= ₹\,7.68672$

$\therefore$ Cost of painting 50 cones $= 7.68672 \times 50$

$= 384.336 = ₹\,384.34$

EXERCISE 11.2 (NCERT Page 144-145)

Assume $\pi = \dfrac{22}{7}$, unless stated otherwise.

Q1. Find the surface area of a sphere of radius

(i) 10.5 cm (ii) 5.6 cm (iii) 14 cm

Sol. (i) We have, $r = $ Radius of the sphere $= 10.5$ cm

$\therefore$ Surface area of a sphere $= 4\pi r^2$

$= 4 \times \dfrac{22}{7} \times 10.5 \times 10.5$

$= 88 \times 1.5 \times 10.5 = 1386\ \text{cm}^2$

(ii) Solve as part (i). **Ans.** $394.24\ \text{cm}^2$

(iii) Solve as part (i) **Ans.** $2464\ \text{cm}^2$

Q2. Find the surface area of a sphere of diameter

(i) 14 cm (ii) 21 cm (iii) 3.5 m

Sol. (i) We have, diameter $= 14\text{cm}$

$\therefore$ Radius $(r) = \dfrac{14}{2} = 7\text{cm}$

$\therefore$ Surface area of a sphere $= 4\pi r^2 = 4 \times \dfrac{22}{7} \times 7^2$

$= 4 \times 22 \times 7 = 616\ \text{cm}^2$

(ii) **Hint** Solve as part (i). **Ans.** $1386\ \text{cm}^2$

(iii) **Hint** Solve as part (i). **Ans.** $38.5\ \text{m}^2$

Q3. Find the total surface area of a hemisphere of radius 10 cm. (take, $\pi = 3.14$)

Sol. We have, radius of a hemisphere $(r) = 10$ cm

$\therefore$ Total surface area of a hemisphere $= 3\pi r^2$

$$= 3 \times 3.14 \times (10)^2 = 9.42 \times 100$$
$$= 942 \text{ cm}^2$$

Q4. The radius of a spherical balloon increases from 7 cm to 14 cm as air is being pumped into it. Find the ratio of surface areas of the balloon in the two cases.

Sol. Let initial radius $(r_1) = 7$ cm

After increased radius $(r_2) = 14$ cm

Surface area of balloon with initial radius, $A_1 = 4\pi r_1^2$

$$= 4 \times \frac{22}{7} \times 7 \times 7 = 88 \times 7$$

$\Rightarrow$ $A_1 = 616 \text{ cm}^2$

Surface area of balloon with increased radius, $A_2 = 4\pi r_2^2$

$$= 4 \times \frac{22}{7} \times 14 \times 14 = 88 \times 28$$

$\Rightarrow$ $A_2 = 2464 \text{ cm}^2$

$\therefore$ Required ratio $= A_1 : A_2 = 616 : 2464 = 1 : 4$

Q5. A hemispherical bowl made of brass has inner diameter 10.5 cm. Find the cost of tin plating it on the inside at the rate of ₹ 16 per 100 cm².

Sol. We have, inner diameter $= 10.5$ cm

$\therefore$ Inner radius $(r) = \frac{10.5}{2} = 5.25$ cm

Curved surface area of hemispherical bowl of inner side

$$= 2\pi r^2 = 2 \times \frac{22}{7} \times (5.25)^2$$
$$= 2 \times \frac{22}{7} \times 5.25 \times 5.25 = 173.25 \text{ cm}^2$$

$\because$ Cost of tin plating on inside for 100 cm² = ₹ 16

$\therefore$ Cost of tin plating on the inside for 173.25 cm²

$$= \frac{16 \times 173.25}{100} = ₹\ 27.72$$

Q6. Find the radius of a sphere whose surface area is 154 cm².

Sol. Let the radius of the sphere be r cm.

Surface area of the sphere $= 154 \text{ cm}^2$

$\therefore$ $4\pi r^2 = 154$ [$\because$ surface area of a sphere $= 4\pi r^2$]

$\Rightarrow$ $4 \times \frac{22}{7} \times r^2 = 154$

$\Rightarrow$ $r^2 = \frac{154 \times 7}{22 \times 4} = 12.25$

$\Rightarrow$ $r = \sqrt{12.25} = 3.5$ cm

Hence, the radius of the sphere is 3.5 cm.

Q7. The diameter of the Moon is approximately one-fourth of the diameter of the Earth. Find the ratio of their surface areas.

Sol. Let diameter of the Earth $= d_1$

Then, diameter of the Moon $= \frac{1}{4} d_1$

$\therefore$ Radius of the Earth $(r_1) = \frac{d_1}{2}$

and radius of the Moon $(r_2) = \frac{d_1}{2 \times 4} = \frac{d_1}{8}$

Surface area of the Earth $(S_1) = 4\pi r_1^2$

$\Rightarrow$ $S_1 = 4\pi \left(\frac{d_1}{2}\right)^2 = \pi d_1^2$

Surface area of the Moon,

$$S_2 = 4\pi \left(\frac{d_1}{8}\right)^2 = 4\pi \frac{d_1^2}{64} \Rightarrow S_2 = \frac{\pi d_1^2}{16}$$

$\therefore$ Required ratio, $S_1 : S_2 = \frac{\pi d_1^2}{1} : \frac{\pi d_1^2}{16} = 16 : 1$

Q8. A hemispherical bowl is made of steel, 0.25 cm thick. The inner radius of the bowl is 5 cm. Find the outer curved surface area of the bowl.

Sol. The inner radius of the hemispherical bowl = 5 cm

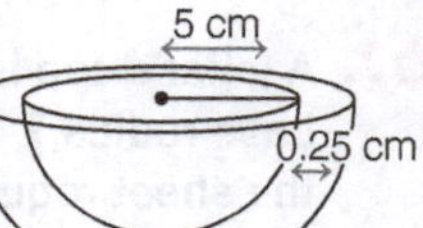

Thickness of the hemispherical bowl = 0.25 cm

We know that

Outer radius of the bowl

$$= \text{Inner radius} + \text{Thickness} = 5 + 0.25 = 5.25 \text{ cm}$$

Outer curved surface area of the bowl $= 2\pi r^2$

$$= 2 \times \frac{22}{7} \times 5.25 \times 5.25 = 173.25 \text{ cm}^2$$

Q9. A right circular cylinder just encloses a sphere of radius r (see figure). Find the

(i) surface area of the sphere.

(ii) curved surface area of the cylinder.

(iii) ratio of the areas obtained in (i) and (ii).

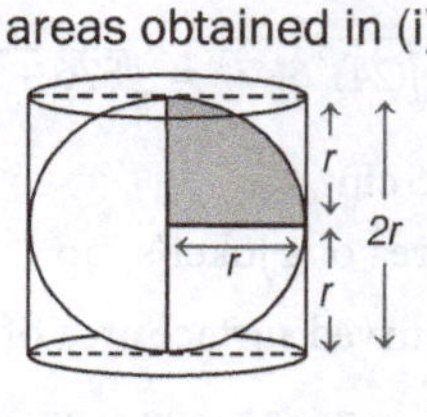

Sol. Given, radius of the sphere $= r$

$\therefore$ Radius of the cylinder = Radius of the sphere $= r$

and height of the cylinder = Diameter $= 2r$

(i) Surface area of the sphere $(A_1) = 4\pi r^2$

(ii) Curved surface area of the cylinder $(A_2) = 2\pi rh$

$\Rightarrow A_2 = 2\pi \times r \times 2r \Rightarrow A_2 = 4\pi r^2$

(iii) Required ratio, $A_1 : A_2 = 4\pi r^2 : 4\pi r^2 = 1 : 1$

EXERCISE 11.3 (NCERT Page 147)

Assume $\pi = \frac{22}{7}$, unless stated otherwise.

Q1. Find the volume of the right circular cone with
(i) radius 6 cm, height 7 cm.
(ii) radius 3.5 cm, height 12 cm.

Sol. (i) Given, radius $(r) = 6$ cm and height $(h) = 7$cm

$\because$ Volume of the right circular cone $= \frac{1}{3}\pi r^2 h$

$$= \frac{1}{3} \times \frac{22}{7} \times (6)^2 \times 7 = \frac{22}{3} \times 6 \times 6$$
$$= 22 \times 12 = 264 \text{ cm}^3$$

(ii) Do same as part (i). **Ans** 154 cm^2

Q2. Find the capacity (in litre) of a conical vessel with
(i) radius 7 cm and slant height 25 cm.
(ii) height 12 cm and slant height 13 cm.

Sol. (i) Given, radius $(r) = 7$cm
and slant height $(l) = 25$cm
We know that $l^2 = r^2 + h^2$

$\Rightarrow \quad h = \sqrt{l^2 - r^2}$ [on taking positive square root]
$$= \sqrt{(25)^2 - (7)^2}$$
$$= \sqrt{625 - 49} = \sqrt{576} = 24 \text{ cm}$$

Now, capacity of conical vessel $= \frac{1}{3}\pi r^2 h$
$$= \frac{1}{3} \times \frac{22}{7} \times 7 \times 7 \times 24$$
$$= 22 \times 7 \times 8 = 1232 \text{ cm}^3$$
$$= \frac{1232}{1000} \text{L} = 1.232 \text{ L} \quad \left[\because 1 \text{ cm}^3 = \frac{1}{1000} \text{L}\right]$$

(ii) Given, height $(h) = 12$ cm
and slant height $(l) = 13$ cm
We know that $l^2 = h^2 + r^2$

$\Rightarrow \quad r = \sqrt{l^2 - h^2}$
[on taking positive square root]
$$= \sqrt{(13)^2 - (12)^2} = \sqrt{169 - 144}$$
$$= \sqrt{25} = 5 \text{ cm}$$

Now, capacity of conical vessel $= \frac{1}{3}\pi r^2 h$
$$= \frac{1}{3} \times \frac{22}{7} \times 5 \times 5 \times 12 = \frac{22 \times 100}{7} \text{ cm}^3$$
$$= \frac{22 \times 100}{7 \times 1000} \text{L} \quad \left[\because 1 \text{ cm}^3 = \frac{1}{1000} \text{L}\right]$$
$$= \frac{11}{35} \text{L}$$

Q3. The height of a cone is 15 cm. If its volume is 1570 cm^3, then find the radius of the base. (take, $\pi = 3.14$)

Sol. Let radius of the base be r cm.
Given, volume of a cone $= 1570$ cm^3

$$\Rightarrow \quad \frac{1}{3}\pi r^2 h = 1570$$
$$\left[\because \text{volume of cone} = \frac{1}{3}\pi r^2 h\right]$$
$$\Rightarrow \quad \frac{1}{3} \times 3.14 \times r^2 \times 15 = 1570$$
$$\Rightarrow \quad r^2 = \frac{1570}{3.14 \times 5} = \frac{15700}{157} \Rightarrow r = 10 \text{ cm}$$

Hence, radius of the base is 10 cm.

Q4. If the volume of a right circular cone of height 9 cm is 48π cm^3, then find the diameter of its base.

Sol. Let r be the radius of the base.
Given, volume of a right circular cone $= 48\pi$ cm^3

$$\therefore \quad \frac{1}{3}\pi r^2 h = 48\pi$$
$$\left[\because \text{volume of a right circular cone} = \frac{1}{3}\pi r^2 h\right]$$
$$\Rightarrow \quad \frac{1}{3} \times r^2 \times 9 = 48 \quad [\because h = 9 \text{ cm, given}]$$
$$\Rightarrow \quad r^2 = 16 \Rightarrow r = 4 \text{ cm}$$
[on taking positive square root]

Hence, diameter of the base $= 2r = 2 \times 4 = 8$ cm

Q5. A conical pit of top diameter 3.5 m is 12 m deep. What is its capacity (in kilolitres)?

Sol. Given, diameter of the top of conical pit $= 3.5$ m

$\therefore$ Radius $(r) = \frac{3.5}{2}$ m and height of conical pit $(h) = 12$ m

Capacity of a conical pit = Volume of a cone $= \frac{1}{3}\pi r^2 h$
$$= \frac{1}{3} \times \frac{22}{7} \times \left(\frac{3.5}{2}\right)^2 \times 12$$
$$= \frac{1}{3} \times \frac{22}{7} \times \frac{3.5}{2} \times \frac{3.5}{2} \times 12$$
$$= 22 \times 0.5 \times 3.5 = 38.5 \text{ m}^3$$
$$= 38.5 \text{ kL} \quad [\because 1\text{m}^3 = 1\text{kL}]$$

Q6. The volume of a right circular cone is 9856 cm^3. If the diameter of the base is 28 cm, then find
(i) height of the cone.
(ii) slant height of the cone.
(iii) curved surface area of the cone.

Sol. Given, diameter of the base $(d) = 28$cm

$\therefore$ Radius of the base $(r) = 14$ cm $\left[\because \text{radius} = \frac{\text{diameter}}{2}\right]$

(i) Let h be the height of the cone.

Also given, volume of a right circular cone

$= 9856 \text{ cm}^3$

$\therefore \quad \frac{1}{3}\pi r^2 h = 9856$

$\left[\because \text{volume of right circular cone} = \frac{1}{3}\pi r^2 h\right]$

$\Rightarrow \frac{1}{3} \times \frac{22}{7} \times (14)^2 \times h = 9856$

$\Rightarrow \quad h = \frac{9856 \times 3 \times 7}{22 \times 14 \times 14} = \frac{448 \times 3}{28} = 48 \text{ cm}$

(ii) We have, $h = 48$ cm and $r = 14$ cm

$\therefore \quad l = \sqrt{h^2 + r^2} = \sqrt{(48)^2 + (14)^2}$

$= \sqrt{2304 + 196} = \sqrt{2500}$

$\Rightarrow \quad l = 50 \text{ cm}$

Hence, slant height of the cone is 50 cm.

(iii) Curved surface area of the cone $= \pi r l$

$= \frac{22}{7} \times 14 \times 50 = 44 \times 50 = 2200 \text{ cm}^2$

Q7. A right angled ΔABC with sides 5 cm, 12 cm and 13 cm is revolved about the side 12 cm. Find the volume of the solid so obtained.

Sol. On revolving the right angled ΔABC about the side AB, we get a right circular cone as shown in the adjoining figure, whose radius $(r) = 5$ cm and height $(h) = 12$ cm.

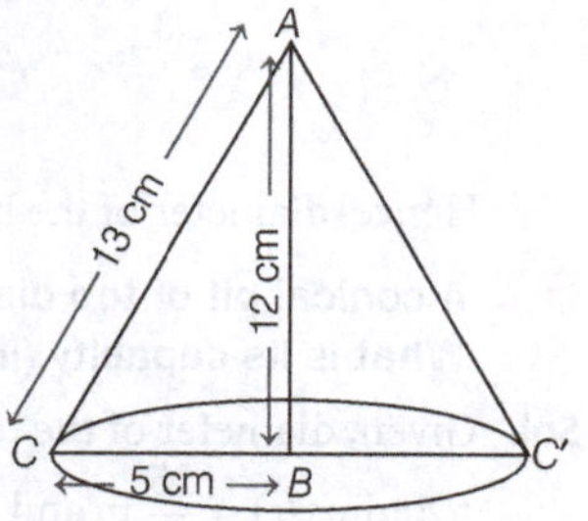

$\therefore$ Volume of the solid so obtained $= \frac{1}{3}\pi r^2 h$

$= \frac{1}{3} \times \pi \times 5 \times 5 \times 12$

$= \pi \times 5 \times 5 \times 4$

$= 100\pi \text{ cm}^3$

Hence, the volume of the solid so obtained is $100\pi \text{ cm}^3$.

Q8. If the ΔABC in the Question 7 is revolved about the side 5 cm, then find the volume of the solid so obtained. Also, find the ratio of volumes of the two solids obtained in Questions 7 and 8.

Sol. On revolving the right angled ΔABC about the side $BC (= 5 \text{ cm})$, we get a cone as shown in the figure whose radius $(r) = 12$ cm and height $(h) = 5$ cm.

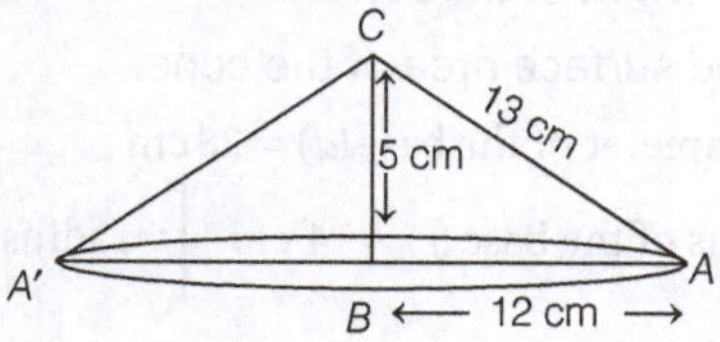

Volume of solid so obtained, $V_1 = \frac{1}{3}\pi r^2 h$

$= \frac{1}{3} \times \pi \times 12 \times 12 \times 5 = 240\pi \text{ cm}^3$

In Question 7, the volume V_2 obtained by revolving the ΔABC about the side 12 cm.

i.e. $V_2 = 100\pi \text{ cm}^3$

Now, $\frac{V_2}{V_1} = \frac{100\pi}{240\pi} = \frac{10}{24} = \frac{5}{12}$

Hence, the required ratio is 5 : 12.

Q9. A heap of wheat is in the form of a cone whose diameter is 10.5 m and height is 3 m. Find its volume. The heap is to be covered by canvas to protect it from rain. Find the area of the canvas required.

Sol. Given, diameter $(d) = 10.5$ m, then

Radius $(r) = \frac{10.5}{2} = 5.25$ m and height $(h) = 3$ m

We know that $l^2 = h^2 + r^2$

$\Rightarrow \quad l = \sqrt{r^2 + h^2}$

[on taking positive square root]

$= \sqrt{(5.25)^2 + (3)^2} = \sqrt{27.5625 + 9}$

$= \sqrt{36.5625}$

$= 6.047 \simeq 6.05 \text{ m}$

Volume of the heap of wheat $= \frac{1}{3}\pi r^2 h$

$= \frac{1}{3} \times \frac{22}{7} \times 5.25 \times 5.25 \times 3 = 86.625 \text{ m}^3$

$\therefore$ Area of the canvas required

= Curved surface area of the heap

$= \pi r l = \frac{22}{7} \times 5.25 \times 6.05 \text{ m}^2$

$= 22 \times 0.75 \times 6.05 \text{ m}^2$

$= 99.825 \text{ m}^2$

EXERCISE 11.4 (NCERT Page 150)

Assume $\pi = \frac{22}{7}$, unless stated otherwise.

Q1. Find the volume of a sphere whose radius is

(i) 7 cm (ii) 0.63 m

Sol. (i) We have, $r = 7$ cm

$\therefore$ Volume of a sphere $= \frac{4}{3}\pi r^3 = \frac{4}{3} \times \frac{22}{7} \times (7)^3$

$= \frac{88 \times 7 \times 49}{3 \times 7} = \frac{4312}{3} = 1437\frac{1}{3} \text{ cm}^3$

(ii) **Hint** Solve as part (i). **Ans.** 1.0478 m^3

Q2. Find the amount of water displaced by a solid spherical ball of diameter
(i) 28 cm. (ii) 0.21 m.

Sol. (i) We have, diameter $(d) = 28$ cm

$\therefore$ Radius $(r) = \frac{28}{2} = 14$ cm $\left[\because \text{radius} = \frac{\text{diameter}}{2}\right]$

Amount of water displaced by a solid spherical ball

$= \text{Volume of spherical ball} = \frac{4}{3}\pi r^3$

$= \frac{4}{3} \times \frac{22}{7} \times (14)^3$

$= \frac{4}{3} \times \frac{22}{7} \times 14 \times 14 \times 14$

$= 11498.67 \text{ cm}^3$

(ii) **Hint** Solve as part (i).

Ans $= 0.004851 \text{ m}^3$

Q3. The diameter of a metallic ball is 4.2 cm. What is the mass of the ball, if the density of the metal is 8.9 g/cm³?

Sol. We have, diameter $(d) = 4.2$ cm

$\therefore$ Radius $(r) = \frac{4.2}{2} = 2.1$ cm

Volume of the metallic ball $= \frac{4}{3}\pi r^3$

$= \frac{4}{3} \times \frac{22}{7} \times (2.1)^3 = \frac{4}{3} \times \frac{22}{7} \times 2.1 \times 2.1 \times 2.1$

$= 88 \times 0.3 \times 0.7 \times 2.1 = 38.808 \text{ cm}^3$

Given, the density of the metal per $\text{cm}^3 = 8.9$ g

$\therefore$ The mass of the ball $= 38.808 \times 8.9 = 345.39$ g

Hence, the mass of the ball is 345.39 g.

Q4. The diameter of the Moon is approximately one-fourth of the diameter of the Earth. What fraction of the volume of the Earth is the volume of the Moon?

Sol. Let diameter of the Moon and Earth be d_1 and d_2, respectively.

According to the question,

Diameter of Moon $(d_1) = \frac{1}{4} \times$ Diameter of the Earth

$\Rightarrow \quad d_1 = \frac{1}{4} d_2$

Hence, the radius of the Moon $= \frac{d_1}{2} = \frac{d_2}{8}$

and radius of the Earth $= \frac{d_2}{2}$

$\therefore$ Volume of the Earth $(V_1) = \frac{4}{3}\pi\left(\frac{d_2}{2}\right)^3 = \frac{4}{3}\pi \times \frac{d_2^3}{8}$

and volume of the Moon $(V_2) = \frac{4}{3}\pi\left(\frac{d_2}{8}\right)^3 = \frac{4}{3}\pi \times \frac{d_2^3}{512}$

Now, required fraction $= \frac{V_1}{V_2} = \frac{\frac{4}{3}\pi\left(\frac{d_2^3}{8}\right)}{\frac{4}{3}\pi\left(\frac{d_2^3}{512}\right)} \Rightarrow \frac{V_1}{V_2} = \frac{512}{8}$

$\Rightarrow \quad \frac{V_1}{V_2} = \frac{64}{1} \Rightarrow V_2 = \frac{1}{64}V_1$

Hence, volume of the Moon is $\frac{1}{64}$ of the volume of Earth.

Q5. How many litres of milk can a hemispherical bowl of diameter 10.5 cm hold?

Sol. Given, diameter = 10.5 cm

$\therefore$ Radius $(r) = \frac{10.5}{2} = 5.25$ cm

Volume of a hemisphere $= \frac{2}{3}\pi r^3$

$= \frac{2}{3} \times \frac{22}{7} \times 5.25 \times 5.25 \times 5.25 = 303.1875 \text{ cm}^3$

Quantity of milk that hemispherical bowl can hold

$= \frac{303.1875}{1000}$ L $\left[\because 1 \text{ cm}^3 = \frac{1}{1000} \text{ L}\right]$

$= 0.303$ L (approx.)

Q6. A hemispherical tank is made up of an iron sheet 1 cm thick. If the inner radius is 1 m, then find the volume of the iron used to make the tank.

Sol. Given, inner radius $(r_1) = 1 \text{ m} = 100$ cm

and thickness = 1 cm

$\therefore$ Outer radius $(r_2) = (100 + 1) = 101$ cm

[$\because$ outer radius = inner radius + thickness]

and outer volume $= \frac{2}{3}\pi(101)^3 \text{ cm}^3$

$\left[\because \text{volume of hemisphere} = \frac{2}{3}\pi r^3\right]$

Inner volume $= \frac{2}{3}\pi(100)^3 \text{ cm}^3$

Hence, volume of the iron used to make the tank

= Outer volume − Inner volume

$= \frac{2}{3}\pi[(101)^3 - (100)^3]$

$= \frac{2}{3} \times \frac{22}{7}(101 - 100)[(101)^2 + 101 \times 100 + (100)^2]$

$[\because a^3 - b^3 = (a-b)(a^2 + ab + b^2)]$

$= \frac{2}{3} \times \frac{22}{7}(10201 + 10100 + 10000) = \frac{44}{21}(30301)$

$= 63487.81 \text{ cm}^3 = \frac{63487.81}{100 \times 100 \times 100} \text{ m}^3 \quad \left[\because 1 \text{ cm} = \frac{1}{100} \text{ m}\right]$

$= 0.063 \text{ m}^3$ (approx.)

Q7. Find the volume of a sphere whose surface area is 154 cm².

Sol. Let r be the radius of the sphere.

Given, surface area of a sphere = 154 cm²

$\therefore \quad 4\pi r^2 = 154$

[$\because$ surface area of sphere $= 4\pi r^2$]

$\Rightarrow \quad 4 \times \frac{22}{7} \times r^2 = 154$

$\Rightarrow \quad r^2 = \frac{154 \times 7}{22 \times 4} \Rightarrow r = \frac{7}{2}$ cm

Hence, volume of a sphere $= \frac{4}{3}\pi\left(\frac{7}{2}\right)^3$

$\left[\because \text{volume of sphere} = \frac{4}{3}\pi r^3\right]$

$= \frac{4}{3} \times \frac{22}{7} \times \frac{7}{2} \times \frac{7}{2} \times \frac{7}{2}$

$= \frac{11 \times 7 \times 7}{3}$

$= 179.667 = 179.67 \text{ cm}^3$

Q8. A dome of a building is in the form of a hemisphere. From inside, it was white-washed at the cost of ₹ 4989.60. If the cost of white-washing is ₹ 20 per sq m, then find the

(i) inside surface area of the dome.

(ii) volume of the air inside the dome.

Sol. Given, cost of white-washed = ₹ 4989.60

and cost of white-washing per sq m = ₹ 20

(i) Inside surface area of the dome

$= \frac{\text{Cost of white-washed}}{\text{Cost of white-washing per sq m}}$

$= \frac{₹\, 4989.60}{₹\, 20} = 249.48$ sq m

(ii) Let r be the radius of the dome.

$\because$ Inside surface area = 249.48 sq m

$\Rightarrow \quad 2\pi r^2 = 249.48$

[$\because$ surface area of hemisphere $= 2\pi r^2$]

$\Rightarrow \quad 2 \times \frac{22}{7} \times r^2 = 249.48$

$\Rightarrow \quad r^2 = \frac{249.48 \times 7}{44}$

$\Rightarrow \quad r^2 = 39.69$

$\Rightarrow \quad r = 6.3$m

$\therefore$ Volume of the air inside the dome $= \frac{2}{3}\pi r^3$

$= \frac{2}{3} \times \frac{22}{7} \times (6.3)^3$

$= 523.908 \text{ m}^3$

Q9. Twenty seven solid iron spheres, each of radius r and surface area S are melted to form a sphere with surface area S'. Find the

(i) radius r' of the new sphere.

(ii) ratio of S and S'.

Sol. (i) Given, r be the radius of each solid iron sphere and r' be the radius of new solid iron sphere, then

Volume of new sphere $= \frac{4}{3}\pi r'^3$

and volume of old sphere $= \frac{4}{3}\pi r^3$

Then, volume of 27 solid iron spheres

$= 27 \times \text{volume of old sphere} = 27 \times \frac{4}{3}\pi r^3 = 36\pi r^3$

$\because$ Twenty seven solid iron spheres are melted to form a new sphere with radius r'.

$\therefore \quad \frac{4}{3}\pi r'^3 = 36\pi r^3$

$\Rightarrow \quad r'^3 = \frac{36 \times 3r^3}{4}$

$\Rightarrow \quad (r')^3 = 27r^3 = (3r)^3$

$\therefore \quad r' = 3r$ ...(a)

Radius (r') of the new sphere $= 3r$

(ii) Surface area (S) of solid iron sphere $= 4\pi r^2$

Surface area (S') of new sphere $= 4\pi(r')^2$

$= 4\pi(3r)^2 = 36\pi r^2$ [from Eq. (a)]

$\therefore$ Required ratio $= S : S' = 4\pi r^2 : 36\pi r^2 = 1 : 9$

Q10. A capsule of medicine is in the shape of a sphere of diameter 3.5 mm. How much medicine (in mm³) is needed to fill this capsule?

Sol. Given, diameter of capsule = 3.5 mm

$\therefore$ Radius (r) $= \frac{3.5}{2}$ mm $\left[\because \text{radius} = \frac{\text{diameter}}{2}\right]$

Now, volume of capsule

$= \frac{4}{3}\pi r^3 = \frac{4}{3} \times \frac{22}{7} \times \frac{3.5}{2} \times \frac{3.5}{2} \times \frac{3.5}{2}$

$= \frac{11 \times 0.5 \times 3.5 \times 3.5}{3} = 22.45833 = 22.46 \text{ mm}^3$

Hence, 22.46 mm³ medicine is needed to fill this capsule.

REVIEW EXERCISE

Including Competency Based Questions

Part I

Multiple Choice Questions

1. The radius of a cone is 3 cm and vertical height is 4 cm. Then, the area of the curved surface is

(a) 47.14 cm^2 (b) 42.15 cm^2

(c) 41.74 cm^2 (d) 44.17 cm^2

2. The diameter of a cone whose height and slant height are respectively 12 cm and 20 cm is

(a) 28 cm (b) 32 cm (c) 36 cm (d) 42 cm

3. The radius and slant height of a cone are in the ratio of 4:7. If its curved surface area is 792 cm^2. Then, its radius is

(a) 12 cm (b) 3 cm (c) 24 cm (d) 6 cm

4. The total surface area of a cone whose radius is $\frac{r}{2}$ and slant height $2l$ is NCERT Exemplar

(a) $2\pi r(l + r)$ (b) $\pi r\left(l + \frac{r}{4}\right)$

(c) $\pi r(l + r)$ (d) $2\pi rl$

5. If the volume of a right circular cone of height 9 cm is 27π cm^3, then the diameter of its base is

(a) 12 cm (b) 9 cm (c) 6 cm (d) 5.4 cm

6. A semi-circular sheet of metal of diameter 28 cm is bent into an open conical cup. Then, the capacity of the cup is Competency Based Question

(a) 522.26 cm^3 (b) 622.16 cm^3

(c) 722.26 cm^3 (d) 822.26 cm^3

7. A right angled ΔABC with sides 9 cm, 12 cm and 15 cm is revolved about the side 12 cm. The volume of the solid, so obtained is

(a) 702.57 cm^3 (b) 652.57 cm^3

(c) 1018.28 cm^3 (d) 702.57 cm^3

8. This is the picture of an ice-cream cone. The radius of the cone is 4 cm and the height is 15 cm. An ice-cream seller keeps $\frac{1}{4}$th of its empty. What is the volume (in cm^3) of the empty part of the cone?

Competency Based Question

(a) 12 π (b) 15 π (c) 19 π (d) 20 π

9. The surface area of sphere of radius 4.9 m is

(a) 100.61 m^2 (b) 224.01 m^2

(c) 201.22 m^2 (d) 301.84 m^2

10. If the radius of a sphere is doubled, then its surface area will be

(a) 2 times (b) 3 times

(c) 4 times (d) 1.5 times

11. A hemispherical bowl is made of steel, 0.25 cm thick. If the inner radius of the bowl is 3.75 cm, then the outer surface area of the bowl is

(a) 100.57 cm^2 (b) 105.37 cm^2

(c) 137.5 cm^2 (d) 105.57 cm^2

12. If the radius of a sphere is $2r$, then its volume will be Competency Based Question

(a) $\frac{4}{3}\pi r^3$ (b) $4\pi r^3$ (c) $\frac{8\pi r^3}{3}$ (d) $\frac{32}{3}\pi r^3$

13. The volume of a sphere whose surface area is 616 cm^2 is

(a) 1179.67 cm^3 (b) 1473.33 cm^3

(c) 1437.33 cm^3 (d) 1237.33 cm^3

14. The volume of hemisphere of radius 3.5 cm is

(a) 98.83 cm^3 (b) 80.83 cm^3

(c) 88.93 cm^3 (d) 89.83 cm^3

15. If the volume of two hemisphere are in the ratio $1 : 2\sqrt{2}$, then the ratio of their radii, is Competency Based Question

(a) 1 : 2 (b) $\sqrt{2} : 1$ (c) 2 : 1 (d) $1 : \sqrt{2}$

Assertion-Reason Type Questions

16. Assertion A semi-circular sheet of metal of diameter 28 cm is bent into an open conical cap. Then, the depth and capacity of cap is 12.12 cm and 622.16 cm^3, respectively.

Reason When the semi-circular sheet is bent into an open conical cap, the radius of the sheet becomes the slant height of the cap and the circumference of the sheet becomes the circumference of the base of the cone.

(a) Both Assertion and Reason are correct and Reason is the correct explanation of Assertion.

(b) Both Assertion and Reason are correct but Reason is not the correct explanation of Assertion.

(c) Assertion is correct but Reason is incorrect.

(d) Assertion is incorrect but Reason is correct.

17. Assertion A shot put in a metallic sphere of radius 4 cm. If the density of the metal is 10 g per cm^3, then the mass of the shot put is 2 kg.

Reason Volume of sphere of radius r is $\frac{4}{3}\pi r^3$.

(a) Both Assertion and Reason are correct and Reason is the correct explanation of Assertion.

(b) Both Assertion and Reason are correct but Reason is not the correct explanation of Assertion.

(c) Assertion is correct but Reason is incorrect.

(d) Assertion is incorrect but Reason is correct.

Case Study Based Questions

18. A farmer Ramesh grows a corn cob in his farm. Corn cob contains valuable vitamin B, antioxidants, carotenoids, lutein and zeaxanthin which are useful for body grow.

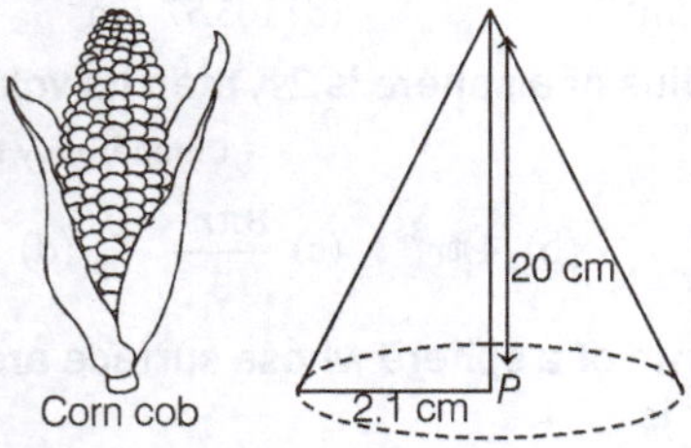

A corn cob (above figure). Shaped somewhat like a cone, has the radius of its broadest end as 2.1 cm and length as 20 cm.

Then, answer the following questions, which are based on above data.

(i) Find slant height of the conical corn cob.

(ii) Write the formula to find the curved surface area of cone.

(iii) (a) What is the curved surface area of the corn cob?

Or

(b) If each 1 cm^3 of the surface of the cob carries an average of four grains, then find how many grains you would find on the entire cob?

19. On his birthday, team leader Mr. Rakesh distributed ice-cream cones to his team members. The radius of ice-cream cone is 3 cm and the height of ice-cream cone is $6\sqrt{6}$ cm.

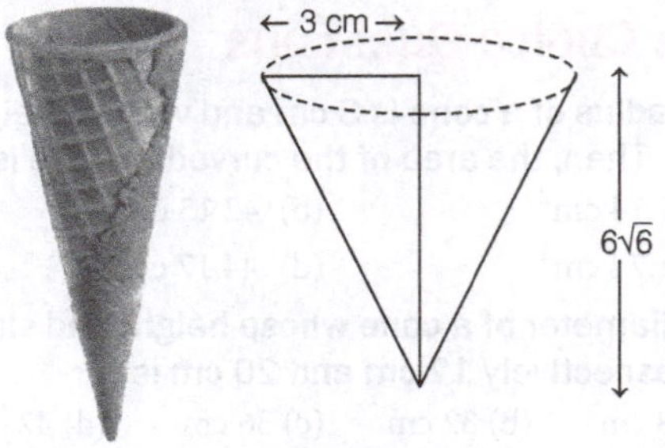

On the bases of above information, answer the following questions.

(i) Find the slant height of the ice-cream cone.

(ii) What is the curved surface area of a ice-cream cone?

(iii) (a) If ice-cream seller keeps $\frac{1}{6}$ th of its empty, then find the volume (in cm^3) of the empty part of the cone.

Or

(b) If ice-cream seller keeps $\frac{1}{4}$ th of its empty, then find the volume (in cm^3) of the filled part of the cone.

Part II

Very Short Answer Type Questions

1. How many square metres of canvas is required for a conical tent whose height is 3.5 m and the radius of whose base is 12 m? (take, $\pi = 3.14$)

2. If the radius of a right circular cone is halved and height is doubled, then what is the volume of new cone?

3. The diameter and height of a right circular cone are 6 cm and 7 cm, respectively. Find the volume of the right circular cone.

4. If surface area of a sphere is $676\ \pi\ cm^2$, then find its radius.

5. The radius of a spherical balloon is inflated from 1.5 cm to 2.5 cm by pumping more air in it. Find the ratio of surface area of resulting balloon to the original balloon. **Competency Based Question**

6. The volume of a sphere is $905\frac{1}{7}\ cm^3$. Determine its diameter.

7. If volume and surface area of a sphere is numerically equal, then find its radius.

8. A cone is 8.4 cm high and the radius of its base is 2.1 cm. It is melted and recast into a sphere. Then, what is the radius of the sphere? **Competency Based Question**

Short Answer Type Questions

9. Find the ratio of the curved surface areas of two cones, if the diameters of their bases are equal and slant heights are in the ratio 3 : 4.

10. The height and base diameter of a conical tent is 16 m and 24 m, respectively. Find the cost of canvas required to make it at the rate of ₹ 210 per m^2? **Competency Based Question**

11. How many metres of 5 m wide cloth will be required to make a conical tent, the radius of whose base is 3.5 m and height is 12 m?

12. Find the area of the metal sheet required to make two closed hollow cones each of height 24 cm and slant height 25 cm.

13. Curved surface area of a cone of radius 4 cm is 20π cm^2. Find total surface area of the same cone in terms of π. **Competency Based Question**

14. A right angled triangle with sides 3 cm, 4 cm and 5 cm is revolved about the side 4 cm. Find the volume and the curved surface area of the solid so formed.

15. The radius and height of a cone are in the ratio 3 : 4. If its volume is 301.44 cm^3, then what is its slant height? (take, $\pi = 3.14$)

16. Shashi has a piece of canvas whose area is 1102 m^2. She uses it to make a conical tent with base radius 14 m. Wastage in stitching margin and cutting amounts is 2 m^2. Find the volume of the tent that can be made with it. (take, $\sqrt{429} = 20.71$)

17. If the height of a cone is doubled, then find the percentage increase in its volume.

18. If the volume of a sphere is divided by it surface area, then the result is 27. Find the radius of sphere.

19. Metallic spheres of radii 6 m, 8 m and 10 m, respectively are melted to form a single solid sphere. Find the radius of the resulting sphere.

20. Find the amount of water displaced by a solid spherical ball of diameter 4.2 cm, when it is completely immersed in water. **NCERT Exemplar**

21. 27 solid iron spheres, each of radius 2 cm are melted to form a new solid sphere. What will be the surface area of the new sphere?

22. The radius of sphere is 5 cm. If the radius is increased by 20%, then find by how much per cent volume is increased?

23. If the radius of a sphere is doubled, then find the percentage increase in its volume.

24. The volumes of two spheres are in the ratio 64 : 27. If the sum of their radii is 21 cm. Find their radii.

25. A shopkeeper has one spherical laddoo of radius 5 cm. With the same amount of material, how many laddoos of radius 2.5 cm can be made? **NCERT Exemplar**

26. Two solid spheres made of the same metal have weights 5920 g and 740 g, respectively. Determine the radius of the larger sphere, if the diameter of the smaller one is 5 cm. **NCERT Exemplar**

27. Two hemispherical domes are to be painted as shown in the given figure. If the circumferences of the bases of the domes are 17.6 cm and 70.4 cm respectively, then find the cost of painting at the rate of ₹ 10 per cm^2. **Competency Based Question**

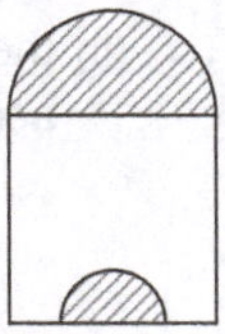

28. To maintain beauty of a monument, the students of the Delhi Public School cleaned and painted the dome of the monument. The monument is in the form of a hemisphere. From inside, it was white washed by the students, whose area is 997.92 m^2, then find the volume of the air inside the dome. If white washing costs ₹ 2 per m^2, how much does it costs? **Competency Based Question**

Long Answer Type Questions

29. Volume of a right circular cone is $\frac{2200}{7}$ cm^3 and its diameter is 10 cm. Find its curved surface area. $\left(\text{take, } \pi = \frac{22}{7}\right)$

30. Along a path, 100 conical pillars are constructed. Each pillar has base radius 14 cm and height 18 cm. Find the total cost of painting these pillars at the rate of ₹ 120 per m^2. (take, $\pi = 22/7$)

31. A right circular cone is 5.4 cm high and radius of its base is 2 cm. It is melted and recast into another right circular cone with radius of base as 1.5 cm. Find the height of the new cone formed.

32. The height and the base diameter of a conical tomb are 24 m and 14 m, respectively. Find the cost of white-washing its curved surface at the rate of ₹ 210 per 100 sq m. Also, find volume of air inside the tomb.

33. Calculate the curved surface area and total surface area of a cone, whose radius of the base and height are in the ratio 5 : 12 and its volume is 2512 cu cm. (take, $\pi = 3.14$) **Competency Based Question**

34. A cloth having an area of 165 m^2 is shaped into the form of a conical tent of radius 5 m.

(i) How many students can sit in the tent, if a student on an average occupies $\frac{5}{7}$ m^2 on the ground?

(ii) Find the volume of the cone. **NCERT Exemplar**

35. The volume of the two spheres are in the ratio 64 : 27. Find the ratio of their surface areas. **NCERT Exemplar**

36. The internal and external radii of a hollow hemispherical bowl are 15 cm and 16 cm, respectively. Find the cost of painting the bowl at the rate of 35 paise per cm^2, if

(i) the area of the edge of the bowl is ignored.

(ii) the area of the edge of the bowl is taken into account. **Competency Based Question**

37. A hemispherical bowl is made of 0.50 cm thick brass. The inner radius of the bowl is 6 cm. Find the inner and outer curved surface areas and volume of the bowl.

38. To maintain beauty of a monument, the students of the school cleaned and painted the dome of the monument. The monument is in the form of a hemisphere. From inside, it was white washed by the students whose area is 249.48 m^2.

(i) Find the volume of the air inside the dome.

(ii) If white washing costs ₹ 2 per m^2, how much does it costs? **Competency Based Question**

HINTS & ANSWERS

Part I

1. (a) We have, $r = 3$ cm and $h = 4$ cm

Let l cm be the slant height of the cone

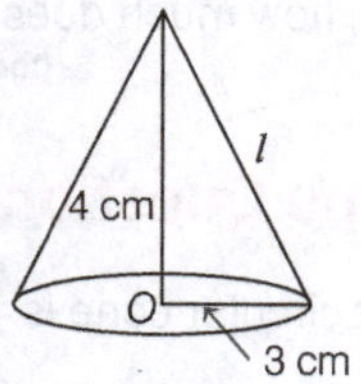

Then, $l^2 = r^2 + h^2 = (3)^2 + (4)^2 = 25$

$\Rightarrow \quad l = \sqrt{25} = 5$ cm

$\therefore$ Area of the curved surface $= \pi rl = \frac{22}{7} \times 3 \times 5$

$= 47.14 \text{ cm}^2$

2. (b) Here, $h = 12$ cm and $l = 20$ cm

We know

$l^2 = r^2 + h^2$

$\Rightarrow \quad 20^2 = r^2 + 12^2$

$\Rightarrow \quad r^2 = 256 \Rightarrow r = 16$ cm

$\therefore$ Diameter of the cone $= 2 \times 16 = 32$ cm

3. (a) Let r cm be the radius and l cm be the slant height of the cone.

Then, $r : l = 4 : 7$

$\Rightarrow \quad r = 4x$ cm and $l = 7x$ cm

Now, curved surface area $= 792 \text{ cm}^2$

$\Rightarrow \quad \pi rl = 792$

$\Rightarrow \quad \frac{22}{7} \times 4x \times 7x = 792$

$\Rightarrow \quad x^2 = 9 \Rightarrow x = 3$

$\therefore \quad r = 4x = 4 \times 3 = 12$ cm.

Hence, the radius of the base of the cone is 12 cm.

4. (b) Given, radius, $R = \frac{r}{2}$ and slant height, $L = 2l$

$\therefore$ Total surface area of a cone $= \pi R (L + R)$

$= \pi \times \frac{r}{2}\left(2l + \frac{r}{2}\right)$

$= \pi r\left(l + \frac{r}{4}\right)$

Hence, the total surface area of a cone is $\pi r\left(l + \frac{r}{4}\right)$.

5. (c) Let r be the radius of base.

Given, volume of cone $= 27\pi \text{ cm}^3$

$\Rightarrow \quad \frac{1}{3}\pi r^2 h = 27\pi$

$\Rightarrow \quad \frac{1}{3} \times \pi \times r^2 \times 9 = 27\pi$

$\Rightarrow \quad r^2 = 9 \Rightarrow r = 3$

Hence, diameter of cone is 6 cm.

6. (b) When the semi-circular sheet is bent into an open conical cup, then radius of the sheet becomes the slant height of the cup and the circumference of the sheet becomes the circumference of the base of the cone.

$\therefore l =$ slant height of the conical cup $= 14$ cm

Let r cm be the radius and h cm be the height of the conical cup.

Then, circumference of the base of the conical cup

= Circumference of the sheet

$\Rightarrow \quad 2\pi r = \pi \times 14$

$\Rightarrow \quad r = 7$ cm

Now, $\quad l^2 = r^2 + h^2$

$\Rightarrow \quad h = \sqrt{l^2 - r^2} = \sqrt{14^2 - 7^2}$

$= 7\sqrt{3}$ cm

$= 12.12$ cm

$\therefore$ Capacity of the cup = Volume of the cup

$$= \frac{1}{3}\pi r^2 h$$

$$= \frac{1}{3} \times \frac{22}{7} \times 7 \times 7 \times 12.12$$

$$= 622.16 \text{ cm}^3$$

7. (c) When a right angled triangle is revolved about the side 12 cm, we obtain a right circular cone with radius 9 cm and height 12 cm.

Volume of cone $= \frac{1}{3}\pi r^2 h = \frac{1}{3} \times \frac{22}{7} \times 9 \times 9 \times 12$

$$= 1018.28 \text{ cm}^3$$

8. (d) Volume of ice-cream cone $= \frac{1}{3}\pi r^2 h$

$$= \frac{1}{3} \times \pi \times 4 \times 4 \times 15 = 80\pi \text{ cm}^3$$

$\because$ Seller keeps $\frac{1}{4}$ th of its empty.

$\therefore$ Volume of the empty part of the cone

$$= \frac{1}{4} \times \text{Volume of cone}$$

$$= \frac{1}{4} \times 80\pi = 20\pi \text{ cm}^3$$

9. (d) Surface area of the sphere $= 4\pi r^2$

$$= 4 \times \frac{22}{7} \times 4.9 \times 4.9$$

$$= 88 \times 0.7 \times 4.9$$

$$= 301.84 \text{ m}^2$$

10. (c) Surface area of sphere $= 4\pi r^2$

When radius is doubled, then

New surface area $= 4\pi(2r)^2 = 4(4\pi r^2)$

$= 4 \times$ Original Surface area

$\therefore$ Surface area becomes 4 times.

11. (a) Outer radius of the bowl = Inner radius + Thickness

$$= 3.75 + 0.25 = 4 \text{ cm}$$

Outer curved surface area of the bowl $= 2\pi r^2$

$$= 2 \times \frac{22}{7} \times 4 \times 4 = 100.57 \text{ cm}^2$$

12. (d) Given, radius of a sphere $= 2r$

Volume of a sphere $= \frac{4}{3}\pi(\text{Radius})^3 = \frac{4}{3}\pi(2r)^3$

$$= \frac{4}{3}\pi \cdot 8r^3 = \frac{32\pi r^3}{3} \text{ cu units}$$

Hence, the volume of a sphere is $\frac{32\pi r^3}{3}$ cu units

13. (c) Given, surface area of sphere $= 616 \text{ cm}^3$

$\therefore$ $4\pi r^2 = 616$

$\Rightarrow$ $4 \times \frac{22}{7} \times r^2 = 616$

$\Rightarrow$ $r^2 = 49 \Rightarrow r = 7 \text{ cm}$

$\therefore$ Volume of sphere $= \frac{4}{3}\pi(7)^3 = \frac{4}{3} \times \frac{22}{7} \times 7 \times 7 \times 7$

$$= 1437.33 \text{ cm}^3$$

14. (d) We know that the volume of hemisphere of radius r is given by

$$V = \frac{2}{3}\pi r^3 = \frac{2}{3} \times \frac{22}{7} \times 3.5 \times 3.5 \times 3.5$$

$$= 89.83 \text{ cm}^3$$

15. (d) Let volume of two hemisphere be V_1 and V_2.

Given, $V_1 : V_2 = 1 : 2\sqrt{2}$

$\Rightarrow$ $\frac{2}{3}\pi r_1^3 : \frac{2}{3}\pi r_2^3 = 1 : 2\sqrt{2}$

$\Rightarrow$ $r_1^3 : r_2^3 = 1 : 2\sqrt{2}$

$\therefore$ $r_1 : r_2 = 1 : \sqrt{2}$

16. (a) **Assertion** When the semi-circular sheet is bent into an open conical cap, the radius of the sheet becomes the slant height of the cup and the circumference of the sheet becomes the circumference of the base of the cone.

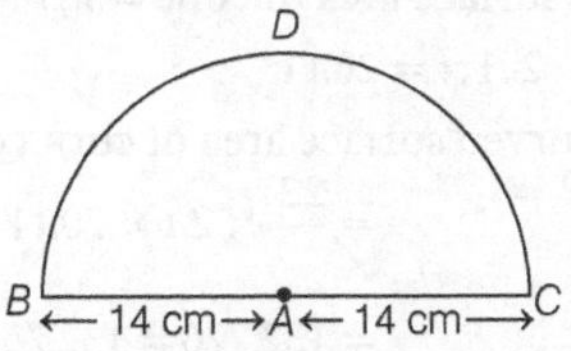

$\therefore l$ = Slant height of the conical cup = 14 cm

Let r cm be the radius and h cm be the height (depth) of the conical cup.

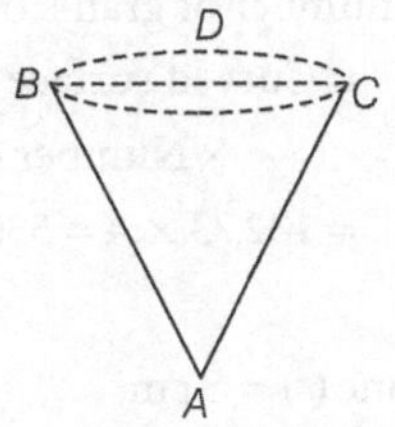

Then, circumference of the base of the conical cup

= Circumference of the sheet

$\Rightarrow$ $2\pi r = \pi \times 14 \Rightarrow r = 7 \text{ cm}$

Now, $l^2 = r^2 + h^2$

$\Rightarrow$ $h = \sqrt{l^2 - r^2}$

$\Rightarrow$ $h = \sqrt{(14)^2 - (7)^2} = 7\sqrt{3} \text{ cm}$

$\Rightarrow$ $h = (7 \times 1.732) = 12.12 \text{ cm}$

$\therefore$ Depth of the cup = 12.12 cm.

Now, capacity of the cup = Volume of the cup

$\therefore$ Capacity of the cup $= \frac{1}{3}\pi r^2 h = \frac{1}{3} \times \frac{22}{7} \times 7 \times 7 \times 12.12$

$= 622.16 \text{ cm}^3$

Reason is also correct and Reason is the correct explanation of Assertion.

17. (d) **Assertion** Given, radius of sphere is $r = 4$ cm

Now, volume of metallic sphere $= \frac{4}{3}\pi r^3 = \frac{4}{3}\pi(4)^3$

$= \frac{256}{3}\pi \text{ cm}^3$

Given, density of metal $= 10 \text{ g/cm}^3$

$\therefore$ Mass of shot put $=$ Density $\times$ Volume

$= 10 \times \frac{4}{3}\pi(4)^3 = \frac{2560}{3} \times 3.14$

$= 2679.5 \text{ g} = 2.68 \text{ kg} \neq 2 \text{ kg}$

Thus, Assertion is incorrect but Reason is correct.

18. (i) Given, radius of the broadest end $(r) = 2.1$ cm and length $(h) = 20$ cm

Then, $l = \sqrt{r^2 + h^2} = \sqrt{(2.1)^2 + (20)^2}$

$= \sqrt{4.41 + 400} = \sqrt{404.41} = 20.11$ cm

(ii) Curved surface area of cone $= \pi rl$

(iii) (a) $\because r = 2.1, l = 20.11$

$\therefore$ Curved surface area of corn cob $= \pi rl$

$= \frac{22}{7} \times 2.1 \times 20.11$

$= 132.726 = 132.73 \text{ cm}^2$

Or

(b) Since, the grains of corn are found on the curved surface of the corn cob.

So, total number of grains on the corn cob

$=$ Curved surface area of corn cob $\times$ Number of grains on 1 cm^2

$= 132.73 \times 4 = 530.92 = 531$

19. (i) Given,

Radius of cone $(r) = 3$ cm

Height of cone $(h) = 6\sqrt{6}$ cm

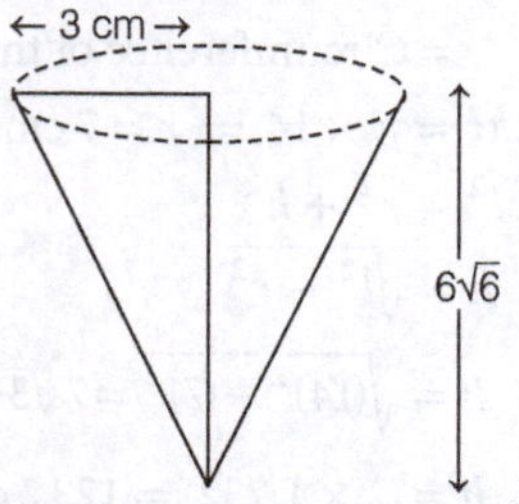

Let l be the slant height of ice-cream cone.

Then,

$l = \sqrt{r^2 + h^2}$

$= \sqrt{(3)^2 + (6\sqrt{6})^2} = \sqrt{9 + 216} = \sqrt{225}$

$\Rightarrow \quad l = 15$ cm

Hence, the slant height of the ice-cream cone is 15 cm.

(ii) From part (i), we have

Slant height $(l) = 15$ cm, $r = 3$ cm.

$\therefore$ Curved surface area of cone $= \pi rl$

$= \pi \times 3 \times 15$

$= \frac{22}{7} \times 45 = 141.42 \text{ cm}^2$

(iii) (a) Volume of a ice-cream cone $= \frac{1}{3}\pi r^2 h$

$= \frac{1}{3} \times \frac{22}{7} \times 3 \times 3 \times 6\sqrt{6}$

$= \frac{66}{7} \times 6\sqrt{6} \text{ cm}^3$

$\because$ Seller keeps $\frac{1}{6}$ th of its empty.

$\therefore$ Volume of the empty part of cone

$= \frac{1}{6} \times$ Volume of cone

$= \frac{1}{6} \times \frac{66}{7} \times 6\sqrt{6} = \frac{66}{7}\sqrt{6} = 23.09 \text{ cm}^3$

Hence, the volume of empty part of the cone is 23.09 cm^3.

Or

(b) We have, from part (a),

Volume of a cone $= \frac{66}{7} \times 6\sqrt{6}$

$\because$ Seller keeps $\frac{1}{4}$ th of its empty.

Therefore, seller filled $\left(1 - \frac{1}{4}\right)$ th of its.

i.e. $\frac{3}{4}$ th part filled of ice-cream cone.

$\therefore$ The volume of the filled part of a ice-cream cone $= \frac{3}{4} \times$ Volume of cone

$= \frac{3}{4} \times \frac{66}{7} \times 6\sqrt{6}$

$= 103.92 \text{ cm}^3$

Hence, the volume of the filled part of a ice-cream cone is 103.92 cm^3.

Part II

1. Hint Slant height, $l^2 = h^2 + r^2$

$\Rightarrow \quad l = 12.5$ m

$\therefore$ Canvas required $=$ Curved surface area of the cone $= \pi rl$

Ans. 471 m^2

2. Hint Given, radius of new cone $= \frac{r}{2}$

[$\because r =$ radius of old cone]

and height of new cone $= 2h$ [$\because h =$ height of old cone]

$\because$ Volume of old cone $= \frac{1}{3}\pi r^2 h$

$\therefore$ Volume of new cone $= \frac{1}{3}\pi\left(\frac{r}{2}\right)^2 (2h)$

$= \frac{1}{3} \times \pi \times \frac{r^2}{4} \times (2h)$

$= \frac{1}{3} \times \pi \times \frac{r^2}{2} \times h = \frac{1}{2}\left(\frac{1}{3}\pi r^2 h\right)$

$= \frac{1}{2}$ (volume of old cone)

Hence, volume of new cone is half of volume of old cone.

3. Hint Volume of the right circular cone $= \frac{1}{3}\pi r^2 h$

Ans. 66 cm^3

4. Hint Surface area of a sphere $= 4\pi r^2$. **Ans.** 13 cm

5. Hint Solve as Q. 4 of NCERT Folder Exercise 11.2.

Ans. 25 : 9

6. Hint Given, volume of a sphere $= 905\frac{1}{7}$ cm^3

$$\Rightarrow \quad \frac{4}{3}\pi r^3 = \frac{6336}{7}$$

$$\left[\because \text{volume of a sphere} = \frac{4}{3}\pi r^3\right]$$

$$\Rightarrow \quad \frac{4}{3} \times \frac{22}{7} \times r^3 = \frac{6336}{7}$$

$$\Rightarrow 8r^3 = \frac{6336 \times 3}{11} = 576 \times 3$$

$$\Rightarrow \quad (2r)^3 = 1728 = (12)^3 \quad \text{[on taking cube root]}$$

$$\Rightarrow \quad 2r = 12$$

$\therefore$ Diameter of the sphere is 12 cm.

7. Hint Volume of sphere = Surface area of sphere

$\Rightarrow \frac{4}{3}\pi r^3 = 4\pi r^2$ **Ans.** 3 cm

8. Volume of cone $= \frac{1}{3}\pi r_1^2 h$

$= \frac{1}{3} \times \pi \times 2.1 \times 2.1 \times 8.4$

$= 12.348\ \pi\ cm^3$

Let radius of sphere be r_2.

According to the question,

Volume of cone = Volume of sphere

$\Rightarrow \quad 12.348\pi = \frac{4}{3}\pi(r_2)^3 \Rightarrow (r_2)^3 = 9.261$

$\Rightarrow \quad r_2 = 2.1$ cm [taking cube root on both sides]

Hence, radius of sphere is 2.1 cm.

9. Hint Solve as Example 2 of Topic 1. **Ans.** 3 : 4

10. Hint Solve as Q. 4 (ii) of NCERT Folder Exercise 11.1.

Ans. ₹ 158400

11. Hint Length of cloth required to make conical tent

$= \frac{\text{Curved surface area of conical tent}}{\text{Width of the cloth}}$

[$\because$ curved surface area of tent = area of cloth]

Ans. 27.5 m

12. Hint Radius of cone, $r = \sqrt{l^2 - h^2} \Rightarrow r = 7$ cm

Total surface area of two cones $= 2\pi r(l + r)$

Ans. 1408 cm^2

13. Hint Given, curved surface area of a cone $= 20\pi\ cm^2$

$\Rightarrow \quad \pi r l = 20\pi \Rightarrow l = 5$ cm

Now, total curved surface area of cone $= \pi r(l + r)$

Ans. $36\pi\ cm^2$

14. Hint Solve as Question 7 of NCERT Folder Exercise 11.3. **Ans.** $12\ \pi\ cm^3$, $15\ \pi\ cm^2$

15. Hint Solve as Example 6 of Topic 1. **Ans.** 6 cm.

16. Hint Solve as Example 8 of Topic 1. **Ans.** 4252.45 m^3.

17. Hint Let r and h be the radius and height of the cone, respectively.

$\therefore$ Original volume $= \frac{1}{3}\pi r^2 h = V$

New radius $= r$ and new height $= 2h$

Then, new volume $= \frac{1}{3}\pi r^2 \times 2h = 2V$

$\therefore$ Increase in volume $= 2V - V = V$

So, percentage increase of volume

$= \left(\frac{\text{Increase in volume}}{\text{Original volume}} \times 100\right)$

$= \left(\frac{V}{V} \times 100\right)$ **Ans.** 100%

18. Hint Given, $\frac{\text{Volume of sphere}}{\text{Surface area of sphere}} = 27$

$\Rightarrow \quad \frac{\frac{4}{3}\pi r^3}{4\pi r^2} = 27$ **Ans.** 81 units.

19. Hint The sum of the volumes of three spheres is equal to volume of new spheres.

$\therefore \quad \frac{4}{3}\pi r_1^3 + \frac{4}{3}\pi r_2^3 + \frac{4}{3}\pi r_3^3 = \frac{4}{3}\pi R^3$

Ans. 12 m

20. Hint Diameter of the solid spherical ball = 4.2 cm

$\therefore$ Radius of the solid spherical ball, $r = 2.1$ cm

Now, volume of water displaced by a solid spherical ball when it is completely immersed in water

$$= \text{Volume of the solid spherical ball}$$

$$= \frac{4}{3}\pi r^3$$

Ans. 38.81 cm^3

21. Given, radius of one solid iron sphere = 2 cm

Volume of 27 solid iron sphere $= 27 \times \frac{4}{3}\pi \times 2 \times 2 \times 2$

$$= 288\,\pi\ cm^3$$

Let new sphere's radius be R.

Then, $\frac{4}{3}\pi R^3 = 288\pi \Rightarrow R^3 = 216$

$\Rightarrow \quad R = 6$ cm [taking cube root on both sides]

Therefore, the surface area of new sphere

$$= 4\,\pi R^2 = 4 \times \pi \times 6 \times 6 = 144\pi\ cm^2$$

22. Hint Radius of the sphere $(r_1) = 5$ cm

New radius $(r_2) = r_1 + 20\%$ of $r_1 = 5 + 20\%$ of 5

$$= 5 + \frac{20 \times 5}{100} = 6 \text{ cm}$$

Now, find volumes of sphere with radii r_1 and r_2 and find their difference percentage. **Ans.** 72.8%

23. We have, a sphere of radius r.

Volume of the sphere $= \frac{4}{3}\pi r^3$

Now, radius is doubled i.e. $2r$.

$\therefore$ Volume of new sphere $= \frac{4}{3}\pi(2r)^3$

$$\% \text{ of increase in volume} = \frac{\frac{4}{3}\pi(2r)^3 - \frac{4}{3}\pi r^3}{\frac{4}{3}\pi r^3} \times 100$$

$$= (8 - 1) \times 100 = 700\%$$

24. Let r_1 and r_2 be the radius of two spheres.

Given, ratio of volume of spheres $= \frac{64}{27}$

$$\Rightarrow \quad \frac{\frac{4}{3}\pi r_1^3}{\frac{4}{3}\pi r_2^3} = \frac{64}{27}$$

$$\Rightarrow \quad \frac{r_1^3}{r_2^3} = \frac{64}{27} \Rightarrow \frac{r_1}{r_2} = \frac{4}{3}$$

$$\Rightarrow \quad \frac{r_1}{4} = \frac{r_2}{3} = x \quad \text{[say]}$$

$$\Rightarrow \quad r_1 = 4x, r_2 = 3x$$

Also given, sum of radii = 21

$$\Rightarrow \quad r_1 + r_2 = 21$$

$$\Rightarrow \quad 7x = 21 \Rightarrow x = 3$$

$$\therefore \quad r_1 = 4x = 12 \text{ m}$$

$$r_2 = 3x = 9 \text{ cm}$$

25. Hint Solve as Example 7 of Topic 2. **Ans.** 8.

26. Let the radius of larger sphere be r_1.

Given, diameter of smaller sphere = 5 cm

$\therefore$ Radius of smaller sphere $(r_2) = \frac{5}{2}$ cm

We have, weight of larger sphere $(m_1) = 5920$ g

and weight of smaller sphere $(m_2) = 740$ g

We know that

$$\text{Volume } (V) = \frac{\text{Mass } (m)}{\text{Density } (D)}$$

$$\therefore \quad V_1 = \frac{5920}{D}\ cm^3 \quad \text{...(i)}$$

$$\text{and} \quad V_2 = \frac{740}{D}\ cm^3 \quad \text{...(ii)}$$

On dividing Eq. (i) by Eq. (ii), we get

$$\frac{V_1}{V_2} = \frac{\frac{5920}{D}}{\frac{740}{D}} \Rightarrow \frac{\frac{4}{3}\pi r_1^3}{\frac{4}{3}\pi r_2^3} = \frac{5920}{740}$$

$$\Rightarrow \quad \left(\frac{r_1}{r_2}\right)^3 = \frac{592}{74}$$

$$\Rightarrow \quad \left(\frac{r_1}{5/2}\right)^3 = \frac{592}{74}$$

$$\Rightarrow \quad \left(\frac{r_1 \times 2}{5}\right)^3 = \frac{592}{74}$$

$$\Rightarrow \quad \frac{8r_1^3}{125} = \frac{592}{74}$$

$$\Rightarrow \quad r_1^3 = \frac{592}{74} \times \frac{125}{8}$$

$$\Rightarrow \quad r_1^3 = \frac{74000}{592} = 125$$

$\therefore \quad r_1 = 5$ cm [taking cube root]

27. Hint Solve as Example 5 of Topic 2.

Here, find curved surface area of both domes separately and then add them to get the total area for painting. **Ans.** ₹ 8377.60

28. Here, dome of the monument is hemispherical in shape, which was white washed by the students.

Now, total area to be white washed = 997.92 m^2

Cost of white washing = ₹ 2 per m^2

$\therefore$ Total cost of white washing = ₹ 2 × 997.92 = 1995.84

Also, $2\pi r^2 = 1995.84$

$$\Rightarrow \quad r^2 = \frac{1995.84 \times 7}{2 \times 22}$$

$$\Rightarrow \quad r^2 = 317.52 \Rightarrow r = 17.8 \text{ m}$$

Volume of the air inside the dome

$= \text{Volume of hemisphere} = \frac{2}{3}\pi r^3$

$= \frac{2}{3} \times \frac{22}{7} \times 17.8 \times 17.8 \times 17.8 = 11816.62 \text{ m}^3$

29. **Hint** Solve as Q. 6 (iii) of NCERT Folder Exercise 11.3.

Ans. 204.29 cm^2

30. Radius of cone = 14 cm = 0.14 m

Height = 18 cm = 0.18 m

Slant height, $l = \sqrt{h^2 + r^2} \Rightarrow l = 0.2280$

CSA of cone $= \pi rl = \frac{22}{7} \times 0.14 \times 0.228 = 0.10032 \text{ m}^2$

Cost of painting of 1 m^2 area = ₹ 120

Cost of painting of 1 pillar = 120 × 0.10032

= ₹ 12.0384

∴ Cost of painting of 100 pillars = 100 × 12.0384

= ₹ 1203.84

31. **Hint** Volume of original cone = Volume of new cone

Ans. 9.6 cm

32. Given, height of conical tomb = 24 m

Diameter of conical tomb = 14 cm

Radius = 7 m

∴ Slant height, $l = \sqrt{(24)^2 + 7^2}$

$l = 25$ m

Now, curved surface area $= \pi rl = \frac{22}{7} \times 7 \times 25 = 550 \text{ m}^2$

Cost of the white washing at ₹ 210 per 100 m^2

$= \frac{210}{100} \times 550 =$ ₹ 1155

and volume of air inside the tomb $= \frac{1}{3}\pi r^2 h$

$= \frac{1}{3} \times \frac{22}{7} \times 7 \times 7 \times 24 = 1232 \text{ m}^3$

33. **Hint** Let radius of the base = $5x$

and height of the cone = $12x$

Given, volume of the cone = 2512 cm^3

$\therefore \quad \frac{1}{3}\pi r^2 h = 2512$

$\Rightarrow \quad \frac{1}{3}\pi (5x)^2 \cdot 12x = 2512$

$\Rightarrow \quad x^3 = 8 \Rightarrow x = 2$

∴ Radius = 10 cm, and height = 24 cm

Ans. 816.4 cm^2, 1130.4 cm^2

34. (i) **Hint** Number of students

$$= \frac{\text{Area of the base of a conical tent}}{\text{Area occupied by a student on the ground}}$$

Ans. 110

(ii) **Hint** Curved surface area of conical tent

= Area of cloth is used to form conical tent

Now, height of conical tent,

$$h = \sqrt{l^2 - r^2} = \sqrt{(10.5)^2 - (5)^2}$$

and Volume of the conical tent = Volume of a cone

Ans. 241.7 m^3.

35. **Hint** Volume of sphere $= \frac{4}{3}\pi r^3$

Let r_1 and r_2 be the radius of two spheres.

Then,

$$\frac{\frac{4}{3}\pi r_1^3}{\frac{4}{3}\pi r_2^3} = \frac{64}{27} \Rightarrow \frac{r_1}{r_2} = \frac{4}{3}$$ **Ans.** 16 : 9

36. **Hint** Internal radius of hollow hemispherical bowl

$r = 15$ cm

external radius of hollow hemispherical bowl

$R = 16$ cm

(i) Surface area of the bowl (edge of the bowl is ignored)

$= 2\pi r^2 + 2\pi R^2 = 2\pi(R^2 + r^2)$ **Ans.** ₹ 1058.20

(ii) The area of the bowl (edge of the bowl is taken into account)

$= 2\pi r^2 + 2\pi R^2 + \pi(R^2 - r^2)$ **Ans.** ₹ 1092.29

37. **Hint** Thickness of a hemispherical bowl = 0.50 cm

Inner radius of bowl = 6 cm

∴ Outer radius of bowl = 6.50 cm

Ans. $72\pi \text{ cm}^2, 84.5\pi \text{ cm}^2, 144\pi \text{ cm}^3$

38. Given, CSA of dome = 249.48 m^2

$\therefore \quad 2\pi r^2 = 249.48$

$\Rightarrow \quad r^2 = 39.69 \Rightarrow r = 6.3 \text{ m}$

(i) Volume of the air inside the dome

= Volume of hemisphere

$= \frac{2}{3}\pi r^3 = \frac{2}{3} \times \frac{22}{7} \times (6.3)^3 = 523.908 \text{ m}^3$

(ii) Here, dome of the monument is hemispherical in shape, which was white washed by the students.

Now, total area to be white washed = 249.48 m^2

Cost of white washing = ₹ 2 per m^2

∴ Total cost of white washing = ₹ 2 × 249.48

= ₹ 498.96

Mind Map

SURFACE AREAS AND VOLUMES

Right Circular Cone

A right circular cone is a solid generated by revolving a line segment which passes through a fixed point and makes a constant angle with a fixed line.

Let l be the slant height, r be the radius and h be the height of the cone. Then, relation between l, r and h is

$l^2 = r^2 + h^2$

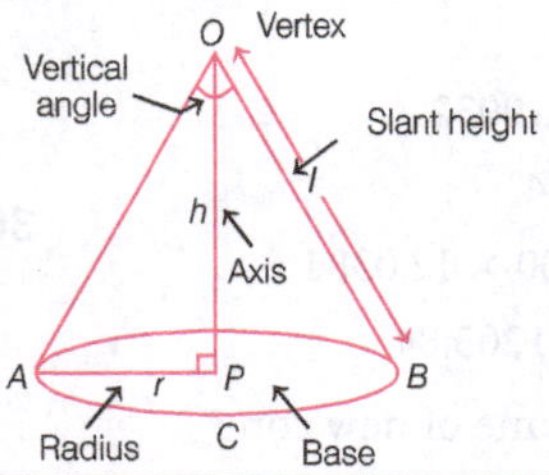

Curved Surface Area of a Cone

For a cone having slant height 'l' and base radius 'r', the curved surface area is given by

Curved surface area of a cone $= \frac{1}{2}\, l \times 2\pi r$

$\therefore$ Curved surface area of a cone $= \pi rl$ sq units

Total Surface Area of a Cone

If the base of the cone is to be closed, then a circular piece of paper of radius r is also required.

Total surface area of a cone

= Curved surface area + Area of a base

$= \pi rl + \pi r^2$

$\therefore$ TSA of a Cone $= \pi r(l + r)$ sq units

Volume of a Cone

For a right circular cone of base radius 'r' and height 'h', volume is given by

Volume of a Cone $= \frac{1}{3}\pi r^2 h$ cu units

Volume of a Sphere

For a sphere of radius 'r', the volume is given by the formula

Volume of a sphere $= \frac{4}{3}\pi r^3$ cu units

Volume of a Hemisphere

Volume of a hemisphere is half of the volume of a sphere.

$\therefore$ Volume of a Hemisphere

$= \frac{2}{3}\pi r^3$ cu units

Volume of Hollow Sphere (Spherical Shell)

If R and r are the external and internal radii of a sphere, then volume of hollow sphere (spherical shell)

= Volume of the external sphere – Volume of the internal sphere

$= \frac{4}{3}\pi R^3 - \frac{4}{3}\pi r^3 = \frac{4}{3}\pi(R^3 - r^3)$ cu units

Sphere

A sphere is three-dimensional figure (solid figure) which is made up of all points in the space, which lie at a constant distance from a fixed point, called the centre of the sphere and the constant distance is called its radius.

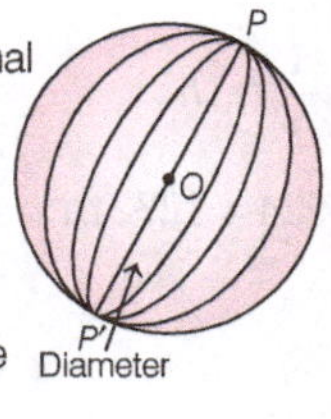

Hemisphere

When a plane through the centre of a sphere divides the sphere into two equal parts, then these two equal parts are called hemisphere.

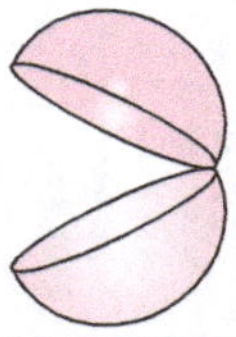

Surface Area of a Sphere

For a sphere of radius 'r', the surface area is given by

Surface area of the sphere $= 4\pi r^2$ sq units

Curved Surface Area of Hemisphere

The curved surface area of a hemisphere is half the surface area of sphere.

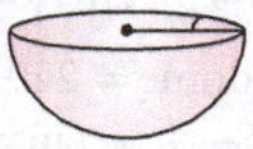

So, curved surface area of hemisphere

$= \frac{1}{2} \times 4\pi r^2 = 2\pi r^2$ sq units

Total Surface Area of Hemisphere

Area of base of the hemisphere $= \pi r^2$

$\therefore$ Total surface area of hemisphere

= Curved surface area of a hemisphere + Area of the base of hemisphere $= 2\pi r^2 + \pi r^2$

$\therefore$ TSA of hemisphere $= 3\pi r^2$ sq units

Topics to be Assessed Formatively

Surface Area of a Cuboid

Let the length of the cuboid be l units, breadth b units and height h units. Then,

(*i*) **Total surface area** Surface Area (SA) or Total Surface Area (TSA) of the cuboid

$= \text{Sum of areas of six rectangular faces}$

$= lb + lb + bh + bh + hl + hl$

$\Rightarrow$ $\boxed{\text{SA or TSA} = 2(lb + bh + hl) \text{ sq units}}$

i.e. SA or TSA = 2(Length × Breadth + Breadth × Height + Height × Length)

(*ii*) **Lateral surface area** If out of the six faces of a cuboid, we do not include the bottom and top faces, then the area of remaining four faces is called the lateral surface area of the cuboid. So,

Lateral surface area = Sum of area of four rectangular faces excluded the top and bottom faces

$= bh + bh + lh + lh = 2(l + b)h$

$\boxed{\text{Lateral surface area of a cuboid} = 2(l + b)h \text{ sq units}}$

or

$\boxed{\text{Lateral surface area of a cuboid} = (\text{Perimeter of the base}) \times \text{Height}}$

(*iii*) **Diagonal of a cuboid**

$\boxed{\text{Diagonal of a cuboid} = \sqrt{l^2 + b^2 + h^2} \text{ units}}$

Note (i) Area of the four walls of a room = Lateral surface area of a cuboid = $2(l + b)h$.

(ii) Total length of cuboid = Length of all 12 edges of the cuboid = Sum of semi-perimeter of all faces of the cuboid. $= 4(l + b + h)$ units

Example 1. **The length, breadth and height of a cuboid are 8 m, 6 m and 4 m, respectively. Find its total surface area, diagonal and area of four walls.**

Sol. Given, length of cuboid (l) = 8 m, breadth (b) = 6 m and height (h) = 4 m

$\therefore$ Total surface area of cuboid $= 2(lb + bh + hl)$

$= 2(8 \times 6 + 6 \times 4 + 4 \times 8) = 2(48 + 24 + 32)$

$= 2 \times 104 = 208 \text{ m}^2$

Diagonal of cuboid $= \sqrt{l^2 + b^2 + h^2} = \sqrt{(8)^2 + (6)^2 + (4)^2}$

$= \sqrt{64 + 36 + 16} = \sqrt{116} = 10.77 \text{ m}$

and area of the four walls of cuboid $= 2(l + b)h = 2(8 + 6) \times 4$

$= 2 \times 14 \times 4 = 112 \text{ m}^2$

Example 2. **The dimensions of a cuboid are in the ratio 1 : 2 : 3 and its total surface area is 88 m². Find the dimensions of the cuboid.**

Sol. Given, the dimensions of the cuboid are in the ratio 1 : 2 : 3.

So, let the dimensions of cuboid be x m, $2x$ m and $3x$ m.

Then, total surface area $= 2(lb + bh + hl)$

$= 2(x \times 2x + 2x \times 3x + 3x \times x)$

But given surface area $= 88 \text{ m}^2$

$\therefore \quad 2(x \times 2x + 2x \times 3x + 3x \times x) = 88$

$\Rightarrow \quad 2(2x^2 + 6x^2 + 3x^2) = 88 \Rightarrow 2 \times 11x^2 = 88$

$\Rightarrow \quad 22x^2 = 88 \Rightarrow x^2 = \frac{88}{22}$

$\Rightarrow \quad x^2 = 4 \Rightarrow x^2 = 2^2 \Rightarrow x = 2 \text{ m}$

[on taking positive square root]

$\therefore \quad 2x = 2 \times 2 = 4 \text{ m}$ and $3x = 3 \times 2 = 6 \text{ m}$

Hence, the dimensions of cuboid are 2 m, 4 m and 6 m.

Example 3. **The dimension of a rectangular box are in the ratio 2 : 3 : 4 and the difference between the cost of covering it with sheet of paper at the rate of ₹ 4 and ₹ 4.50 per sq m is ₹ 416. Find the dimensions of the box.**

Sol. Let the dimensions of the rectangular box be $2x$, $3x$ and $4x$ m.

$\therefore$ Surface area $= 2(2x \times 3x + 3x \times 4x + 4x \times 2x)$

[$\because$ surface area $= 2(lb + bh + hl)$]

$= 2(6x^2 + 12x^2 + 8x^2) = 2 \times 26x^2 = 52x^2$

Cost of covering the box with sheet of paper at the rate of ₹ 4 per m² $=$ ₹ $52x^2 \times 4 =$ ₹ $208x^2$

And cost of covering the box with sheet of paper at the rate of ₹ 4.50 per m² $=$ ₹ $4.50 \times 52x^2 =$ ₹ $234x^2$

According to the question,

Difference of the cost at different rate = 416

$\Rightarrow 234x^2 - 208x^2 = 416 \Rightarrow 26x^2 = 416$

$\Rightarrow \quad x^2 = 16 \Rightarrow x = 4$ [on taking positive square root]

Hence, the dimension of the box are 8 m, 12 m and 16 m.

Surface Area of a Cube

Let each edge of the cube be 'a' units. Then,

(*i*) Total surface area of the cube

$= \text{Sum of areas of six faces}$

$= 2(aa + aa + aa) = 2(a^2 + a^2 + a^2)$

$\Rightarrow \quad \boxed{\text{TSA} = 6a^2 \text{ sq units}}$

(*ii*) Lateral surface area of the cube = Sum of areas of four faces excluded the top and bottom faces

$= 2(aa + aa)$

$\Rightarrow \quad \boxed{\text{Lateral surface area} = 4a^2 \text{ sq units}}$

(*iii*) Diagonal of a cube $= \sqrt{a^2 + a^2 + a^2} = \sqrt{3a^2}$

$\Rightarrow$ **Diagonal of a cube $= \sqrt{3}a$ units**

Note Total length of a cube = Length of all 12 edges of a cube $= 12a$ units, where edge of cube is a units.

Example 4. **The total surface area of a cube is 486 cm^2. Find its lateral surface area and diagonal of the cube.**

Sol. Given, total surface area of the cube = 486 cm^2

But we know that, total surface area of cube $= 6a^2$ [$\because a =$ edge of the cube]

$\therefore \quad 6a^2 = 486$

$\Rightarrow \quad a^2 = \frac{486}{6} = 81$

$\Rightarrow \quad a = \sqrt{81} = 9$ cm [on taking positive square root]

We know that lateral surface area of cube

$= 4a^2 = 4(9)^2$

$= 4 \times 81 = 324$ cm

Diagonal $= \sqrt{3}a = \sqrt{3}(9) = 9\sqrt{3}$ cm

Volume of a Cuboid

Let length of the cuboid is l units, breadth is b units and height is h units, then

Volume of the cuboid = Length × Breadth × Height

or **Volume of the cuboid = lbh cu units**

Also, **Volume of the cuboid = Base area × Height**

The unit of measurement of volume is cubic unit.

Example 5. **A cuboidal water tank is 4 m long, 5 m wide and 8 m deep. How many litres of water can it hold?**

Sol. Given, the cuboidal water tank have length = 4 m, breadth = 5 m and height = 8 m

Volume of the tank = Capacity of the tank

= Length × Breadth × Height

$= 4 \times 5 \times 8 = 160 \text{ m}^3$

Quantity of water which the tank can hold

$= 160 \times 1000$ [$\because 1\text{m}^3 = 1000\text{L}$]

$= 160000$ L

Example 6. **The areas of three adjacent faces of a cuboid are x, y and z. If its volume is V, then find its volume.**

Sol. Let the dimensions of cuboid be l, b and h.

Given, area of three adjacent faces of a cuboid are x, y and z.

$\therefore \quad x = lb, y = bh$ and $z = hl$ ...(i)

and volume of cuboid $= V$

$\therefore \quad V = lbh$

On squaring both sides, we get $V^2 = l^2b^2h^2 = (lb)(bh)(hl)$

$\Rightarrow \quad V^2 = xyz$ [from Eq. (i)]

$\Rightarrow \quad V = \sqrt{xyz}$ [on taking positive square root]

Volume of a Cube

We know that, cube is a cuboid whose length, breadth and height are all equal. So, if one side (or edge) of a cube be a units, then Volume of cube $= l \times b \times h = a \times a \times a$

$\Rightarrow$ **Volume of cube $= a^3 = (\text{Side})^3$ cu units**

Example 9. **Find the surface area and the length of the diagonal of a cube, if the volume of a cube is 2197 cu cm.**

Sol. Given, volume of cube = 2197 cu cm

$\Rightarrow (\text{Side})^3 = 2197$ [$\because$ volume of cube $= (\text{side})^3$]

$\Rightarrow$ Side of cube $= \sqrt[3]{2197} = 13$ cm

[on taking cube root both sides]

Now, surface area of cube $= 6(\text{Side})^2$

$= 6(13)^2$ sq cm $= 1014$ sq cm

And length of the diagonal of cube $= \sqrt{3} \times$ Side

$= \sqrt{3} \times 13 = 22.517$ cm

Surface Area of a Right Circular Cylinder

We know that, right circular cylinder is generated by revolution of a rectangular sheet about one of its side, so the area of the rectangular sheet gives us the curved surface area of the cylinder and length of the rectangular sheet is equal to the circumference of the circular base.

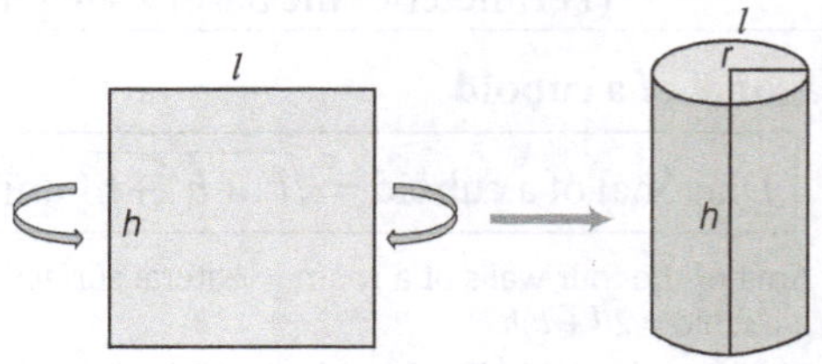

$\therefore$ Curved surface area of the cylinder

= Area of rectangular sheet

= Length of rectangular sheet × Height

= Circumference of the base of the cylinder × Height

[$\because$ length of rectangular sheet = circumference of the base]

Curved surface area of cylinder $= 2\pi rh$ sq units

where, circumference of the base of the cylinder $= 2\pi r$, r is the radius of the base and h is the height of the cylinder.

Total Surface Area of a Right Circular Cylinder

For total surface area of a cylinder, we also take area of both circular bases with curved surface area of the cylinder. So,

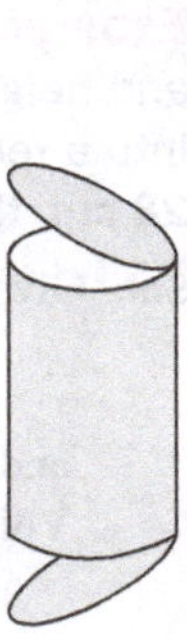

Total surface area of cylinder

= Curved surface area of cylinder + Area of both circular ends

$= 2\pi rh + \pi r^2 + \pi r^2 = 2\pi rh + 2\pi r^2$

TSA of cylinder $= 2\pi r(h + r)$ sq units

Where, r = radius of base and h = height of cylinder

Note For cylinder, unless stated otherwise, 'radius of a cylinder' shall mean 'base radius of the cylinder'.

Surface area of Hollow Cylinder

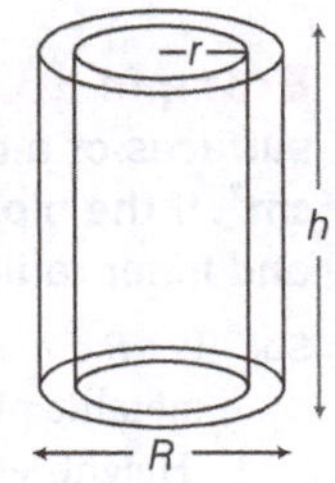

A solid bounded by two coaxial cylinders of the same height and different radii is called a hollow cylinder.

Let a hollow cylinder whose external and internal radii are R and r, respectively with h as height. Then,

Surface area of each base $= \pi(R^2 - r^2)$ sq units

Curved surface area = External surface area + Internal surface area

$= 2\pi Rh + 2\pi rh = 2\pi h(R + r)$ sq units

Total surface area = Curved surface area + 2 (surface area of each base)

$= 2\pi h(R + r) + 2\pi(R^2 - r^2)$

TSA of hollow cylinder $= 2\pi(R + r)(h + R - r)$ sq units

Example 10. **The ratio between the curved surface area and the total surface area of a right circular cylinder is 1 : 3. Find the ratio between the height and radius of the cylinder.**

Sol. Let radius of the cylinder $= r$ and height $= h$.

Then, curved surface area $= 2\pi rh$

and total surface area $= 2\pi r(h + r)$

According to the question,

Curved surface area : Total surface area = 1:3

$\Rightarrow \quad \dfrac{2\pi rh}{2\pi r(h+r)} = \dfrac{1}{3} \Rightarrow \dfrac{h}{h+r} = \dfrac{1}{3}$

$\Rightarrow \quad 3h = h + r \Rightarrow 2h = r$

$\Rightarrow \quad \dfrac{h}{r} = \dfrac{1}{2}$ or $h : r = 1 : 2$

Hence, required ratio between height and radius of the cylinder is 1 : 2.

Example 11. **A rectangular sheet of paper44 cm × 18 cm is rolled along its length and a cylinder is formed. Find the radius of the cylinder.**

Sol. Given, measures of a rectangular sheet = 44 cm × 18 cm

Here, length = 44 cm and breadth = 18 cm

Let radius of base of cylinder $= r$

On revolving it about its length, a cylinder is formed.

∴ Circumference of base of cylinder = Length of sheet

∴ $\quad 2\pi r = 44$

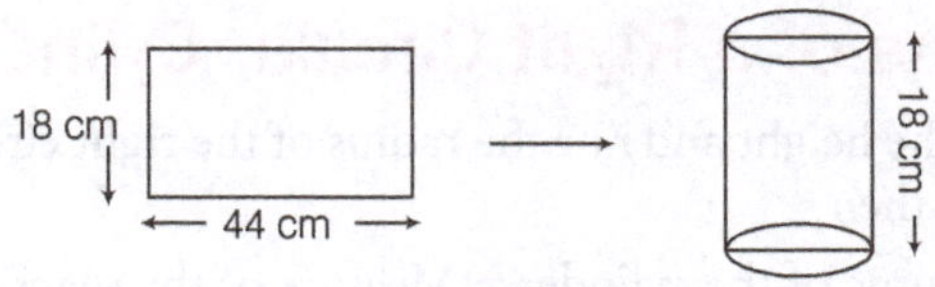

$\Rightarrow \quad 2 \times \dfrac{22}{7} \times r = 44 \Rightarrow r = \dfrac{44 \times 7}{2 \times 22} = 7$

Hence, radius of the cylinder is 7 cm.

Example 12. **An iron pipe 20 cm long has exterior diameter equal to 25 cm. If the thickness of the pipe is 1 cm, then find the whole surface area of the pipe.**

Sol. Given, length of the pipe (h) = 20 cm

Exterior diameter = 25 cm

$\Rightarrow$ Exterior radius $(R) = \dfrac{25}{2} = 12.5$ cm

Thickness of the pipe = 1 cm

∴ Internal radius (r) = External radius − Thickness

$= 12.5 - 1 = 11.5$ cm

Now, whole surface area of the pipe

= External curved surface + Internal curved surface + 2 (Area of the base of the pipe)

$= 2\pi Rh + 2\pi rh + 2(\pi R^2 - \pi r^2) = 2\pi(R + r)(h + R - r)$

$= 2 \times \dfrac{22}{7} \times (12.5 + 11.5) \times (20 + 12.5 - 11.5)\text{ cm}^2$

$= 2 \times \dfrac{22}{7} \times 24 \times 21\text{ cm}^2 = 3168\text{ cm}^2$

Example 13. **The cost of painting the outer curved surface of a cylinder at ₹ 1.50 per cm² is ₹ 660. If the height of the cylinder is 2 m. Then, find the curved surface of the base of cylinder.**

Sol. Given, height of the cylinder = 2m = 200 cm

[∵ 1m = 100 cm]

The total cost of painting = ₹ 660

Rate of painting the outer curved surface area of the cylinder = 1.50 per cm²

Total cost of painting = Curved surface area of the cylinder × Rate of painting the curved surface area

$\Rightarrow \quad 660 = \text{Curved surface area} \times 1.50$

$\Rightarrow$ Curved surface area $= \dfrac{660}{1.50}$

$\Rightarrow \quad 2\pi rh = 440$

[∵ curved surface area of cylinder $= 2\pi rh$]

$$\Rightarrow 2\times\frac{22}{7}\times r\times 200=440$$

$$\Rightarrow \quad r=\frac{440\times 7}{2\times 22\times 200}$$

$$\Rightarrow \quad r=\frac{35}{100}\text{ cm}$$

$\therefore$ Curved surface of the base of cylinder

= Circumference of the base of cylinder $=2\pi r$

$$=2\times\frac{22}{7}\times\frac{35}{100}=2.2\text{ cm}$$

Volume of a Right Circular Cylinder

Let h be the height and r be the radius of the right circular cylinder, then

Volume of the cylinder = Measure of the space occupied by the cylinder

= Area of circular base × Height

Volume of the cylinder = $\pi r^2 h$ cu units

Volume of a Hollow Cylinder

For volume of the material used for making a hollow cylinder will be obtain by subtracting the interior volume from exterior volume i.e.

Volume of the material = Exterior volume – Interior volume

$$=\pi R^2 h-\pi r^2 h$$

Volume of hollow cylinder $=\pi(R^2-r^2)h$

Where, R and r are exterior and interior radius respectively, h is the height of that hollow cylinder.

Example 14. **Find the capacity of a cylindrical storage tank of height 4 m and base diameter 8 m.**

Sol. Given, the height of cylindrical tank = 4 m

and diameter = 8 m

$\therefore$ Radius $=\frac{8}{2}=4$ m

Capacity of the cylindrical tank = Volume of a cylinder

$=\pi r^2 h$ [r = radius, h = height]

$$=\frac{22}{7}\times(4)^2\times 4$$

$$=\frac{22\times 4\times 4\times 4}{7}$$

$$=\frac{1408}{7}=201.14\text{ m}^3$$

Example 15. **A cylindrical bucket of diameter 28 cm and height 12 cm is full of water. The water is emptied into a rectangular tub of length 66 cm and breadth 28 cm, then find the height of water rises in the tub.**

Sol. Given, diameter of bucket = 28 cm

$\therefore$ Radius $(r)=\frac{28}{2}=14$ cm

and height of water in bucket $(h)=12$ cm

Volume of water in the bucket $=\pi r^2 h$

$$=\frac{22}{7}\times 14\times 14\times 12=7392\text{ cu cm}$$

Let h be the height of water rises in the tub.

Then, volume of water in the tub $=(66\times 28\times h)$ cu cm

According to the question, volume of water in bucket = Volume of water in tube

$$\Rightarrow 66\times 28\times h=7392 \Rightarrow h=\frac{7392}{66\times 28}=4\text{ cm}$$

Hence, water rises to a height of 4 cm in the tub.

Example 16. **The difference between outside and inside surfaces of a cylindrical metallic pipe 14 cm long is 44 cm². If the pipe is made of 88 cm³ of metal. Find outer and inner radii of the pipe.**

Sol. Let R cm and r cm be the external and internal radii of the metallic pipe, respectively.

Height/length of the pipe $(h)=14$ cm

According to the question,

Outside surface area – Inside surface area = 44 cm²

$$2\pi Rh-2\pi rh=44$$

$$\Rightarrow 2\times\frac{22}{7}(R-r)\times 14=44 \Rightarrow R-r=\frac{1}{2} \quad \text{...(i)}$$

Volume of the metal used for making the pipe = 88 cm³

$$\pi R^2 h-\pi r^2 h=88$$

$$\Rightarrow \frac{22}{7}\times(R+r)(R-r)\times 14=88$$

$$\Rightarrow R+r=\frac{88}{22} \Rightarrow R+r=4 \quad \text{...(ii)}$$

On adding Eqs. (i) and (ii), we get

$$R-r+R+r=\frac{1}{2}+4=0.5+4=4.5$$

$$\Rightarrow 2R=4.5$$

$$\Rightarrow R=\frac{4.5}{20}=2.25\text{ cm.}$$

On putting $R=2.25$ cm in Eq. (ii), we get

$$r=4-2.25=1.75\text{ cm}$$

Hence, outer and inner radii of the pipe are 2.25 cm and 1.75 cm, respectively.

Exercise

1. Find the surface area of a box whose length is 40 cm, breadth 27 cm and height 10 cm.
2. Find the length of the longest rod that can be placed in a room 12 m long, 9 m broad and 8 m high.
3. Find the lateral surface area of the cuboid of dimensions 80 cm $\times$ 40 cm $\times$ 20 cm.
4. A box of dimensions (2 m $\times$ 1.25 m $\times$ 85 cm) is to be made. Determine the area of the sheet require when the box is open at the top.
5. A cuboid is 12 cm long, 9 cm broad and 8 cm high. Find its total surface area.
6. If the length of diagonal of a cube is $8\sqrt{3}$ cm, then find its surface area.
7. The lateral surface area of a cube is 512cm^2. Find the side of the cube.
8. The floor of a rectangular hall has a perimeter 15 m. If the cost of painting the four wall at the rate of ₹ 10 per m^2 is 15000, find the height of the hall.
9. Arun built a cubical water tank with lid and each outer edge is 2.5 m long. The outer surface of the tank excluding the base is covered with square tiles of side 25 cm long. Find the number of tiles required.
10. A cuboidal water tank is 8 m long, 4 m wide and 3 m deep. How many litres of water can it hold?
11. A cuboidal water tank can hold 50000 L of water. If the length and depth of tank are 250 cm and 10 m respectively, then find the breadth of the tank.
12. Volume of a cube is $648\sqrt{3}$ cm³. Find its total surface area.
13. The perimeter of one face of a cube is 40 m. Find the volume of the cube.
14. The volume of cube is 2744 cm^3. Find its total surface area.
15. Find the number of cubes of 3 cm side which can be made from cuboid of dimensions $l=18$ cm, $b=15$ cm, and $h=2$ cm.
16. If the curved surface area of a cylinder is 1760 cm^2 and its base radius is 14 cm. Then, find its height.
17. A cylinder is formed by rolling a sheet whose dimension is 8.8 cm $\times$ 2.8 cm. Find the radius of the cylinder.
18. An iron pipe 10 cm long has exterior diameter equal to 15 cm. If the thickness of the pipe is 2 cm, find the whole surface of the pipe.
19. The curved surface area of a right circular cylinder is 660 cm^2 and base radius is 5 cm. Find its height.
20. If the diameter of the base and height of a cylinder are 6 cm and 14 cm, respectively. Then, find its volume.
21. The heights of two cylinders are in the ratio 5 : 3 and their radii are in the ratio 2 : 3. Then, find the ratio of their curved surface area.
22. A metal pipe is 66 cm long. The inner diameter of a cross section is 3 cm, the outer diameter being 3.3 cm. Find its
    (i) Inner curved surface area
    (ii) Outer curved surface area
    (iii) Total surface area
23. A cylindrical pillar is 100 cm in diameter and 2.5 m in height. Find the cost of painting curved surface of the pillar at the rate of ₹ 12.50 per m^2.
24. If the lateral surface area of a cylinder is 100 cm^2 and its height 10 cm, then find
    (i) Radius of its base (ii) Its volume
25. A rectangular paper 11 cm by 8 cm can be exactly wrapped to cover the curved surface of a cylinder of height 8 cm. Find the volume of the cylinder.
26. The internal and external diameter of steel pipe of length 140 cm are 8 cm and 10 cm, respectively. Then, find the volume of steel.
27. In a cylinder, if radius is halved and height is doubled, then find its volume.

Hints & Answers

1. 3500 cm^2 2. 17 cm 3. 4800 cm^2
4. 8.03 m^2 5. 552 cm^2 6. 384 cm^2
7. $8\sqrt{2}$ cm 8. 10 cm 9. 500
10. 96000 L 11. 2 m 12. 648 cm^2
13. 1000 m^3 14. 1176 cm^2 15. 20
16. 20 cm 17. 1.4 cm 18. 980.57 cm^2
19. 21 cm 20. 396 cm^3 21. 10 : 9
22. (i) 621.72 cm^2 (ii) 683.89 cm^2 (iii) 1308.56 cm^2
23. ₹ 98.13 24. (i) 1.59 cm (ii) 793.82 cm^3
25. 77 cm^3 26. 3960 cm^3
27. Halved

Statistics

CHAPTER 12

'Statistics' is the main branch of Mathematics which deals with collection, classification and analysis of numerical data. In this chapter, we will study about graphical representation of data.

We know that study of data becomes much clear and convenient, with the help of pictures or graphs, even if the data is complex. To represent the data through the pictures or graph is called the **graphical representation of data.**

Some of the graphical representations of data are

1. Bar graph
2. Histogram
3. Frequency polygon

Bar Graph

A bar graph is a pictorial representation of data in which bars depicting the variable of uniform width are drawn with equal spacing between them on one axis (say X-axis) and heights of bars shown on another axis (say Y-axis) depend on the values of the variable or frequency of corresponding observation.

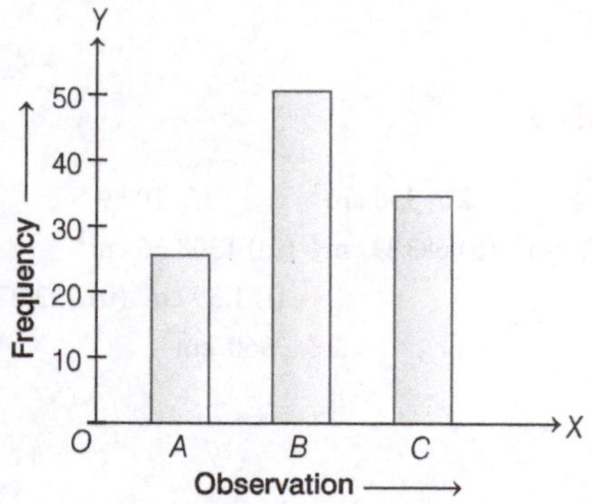

Example 1. **70 students from a locality, use different modes of transport to go to school as given below**

Modes of transport	Car	Bus	Moped	Bicycle	Rickshaw
Number of students	4	27	12	19	8

Draw a bar graph representing the above data.

Sol. Here, the variable is the mode of transport, so it has to be taken along the X-axis choosing any scale and the value of variable is the number of students taken along the Y-axis. All the bars should be of the same width and same space should be left between two consecutive bars.

These bars may be drawn as shown below

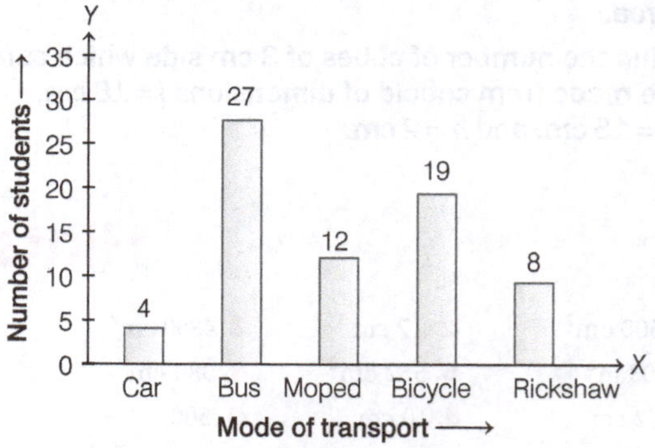

Note it Width of the bar is not important but for clarity, we take equal widths for all bars and maintain equal gaps in between them.

Example 2. **A survey conducted by WHO, for the cause of illness and death among the women between the ages 25-55 (in years) worldwide, found following figures (in %).**

	Causes	Female fatality rate (in %)
1.	Cardiovascular Conditions	15
2.	Neuropsychiatric Conditions	35
3.	Reproductive Health Conditions	10
4.	Injuries	20
5.	Other Causes	20

(i) Represent the information given above graphically.

(ii) Find out any two factors which play a major role in the causes of illness.

(iii) Which condition is the major cause of women's ill health and death worldwide?

Sol. (i) Here, we can choose the scale as 1 unit = 10%

To represent our first cause i.e. Cardiovascular Conditions, we draw a rectangle bar with width 1 unit and height 15 units.

Similarly, other causes are represented by having a gap of 1 unit in between two consecutive bars.

Required graph is as shown below.

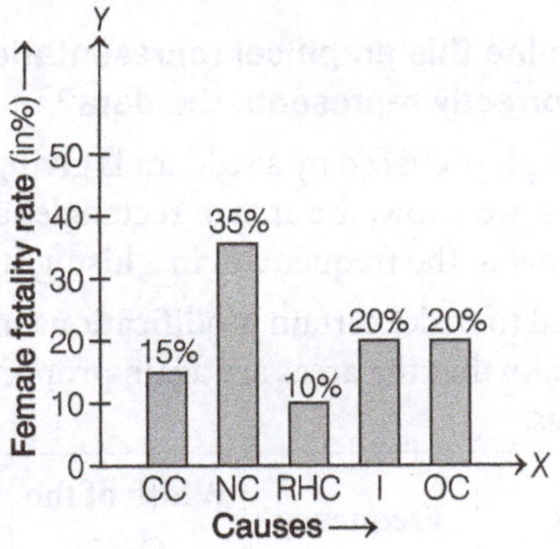

Scale : 1 unit = 10%

Here, CC = Cardiovascular Conditions

NC = Neuropsychiatric Conditions

RHC = Reproductive Health Conditions

I = Injuries

OC = Other Causes

(ii) Two factors can be as follow

(a) Lack of medical facilities.

(b) Lack of correct knowledge of treatment.

(iii) From the graph, we observe that 'Neuropsychiatric Condition' is the major cause of women's ill health and death worldwide because it has maximum % among the causes i.e. 35%.

Histogram

A histogram is the graphical representation of a grouped frequency distribution in exclusive form with continuous classes in the form of rectangles with class intervals as bases and the corresponding frequencies as heights. There is no gap between any two consecutive rectangles.

Example 3. **Represent the following frequency distribution by means of a histogram.**

Marks	10-20	20-30	30-40	40-50	50-60	60-70	70-80
Number of students	7	11	9	13	16	4	2

Sol. We represent the class intervals along the X-axis on a suitable scale and the corresponding frequencies along the Y-axis on a suitable scale. We construct rectangles with class intervals as bases and the corresponding frequencies as heights.

Thus, we obtain a histogram as shown below

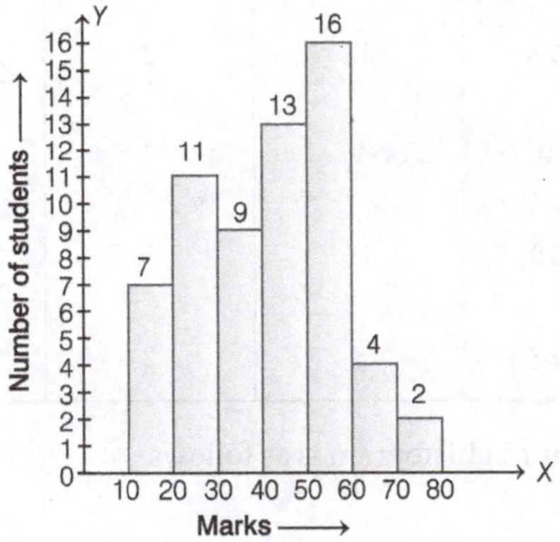

Histogram when Class Intervals are of Unequal Size

We know that in a histogram, the areas of the rectangles are proportional to the frequencies, but in this case the widths of the rectangles are varying. So, we need to make certain modifications in the lengths of the rectangles (i.e. frequencies), so that the areas are became proportional to the frequencies.

We calculate the adjusted frequency using the formula

$$\text{Adjusted frequency} = \frac{\text{Minimum class size}}{\text{Class size of that class}} \times \text{Frequency of that class}$$

Example 4. **A random survey of the number of children of various age groups playing football match in a park was found as follows**

Age (in years)	1-2	2-3	3-5	5-7	7-10	10-15	15-17
Number of children	5	4	10	12	9	10	8

Draw a histogram to represent the above data.

Sol. Here, minimum class size $= 2 - 1 = 1$

Adjusted frequency of a class

$$= \frac{\text{Minimum class size}}{\text{Class size of that class}} \times \text{Frequency of that class}$$

Frequency distribution after adjusting frequency

Age (in years)	Number of children (Frequency)	Width of the class	Adjusted frequency
1-2	5	1	$\frac{1}{1} \times 5 = 5$
2-3	4	1	$\frac{1}{1} \times 4 = 4$
3-5	10	2	$\frac{1}{2} \times 10 = 5$
5-7	12	2	$\frac{1}{2} \times 12 = 6$
7-10	9	3	$\frac{1}{3} \times 9 = 3$
10-15	10	5	$\frac{1}{5} \times 10 = 2$
15-17	8	2	$\frac{1}{2} \times 8 = 4$

The required histogram is as follows

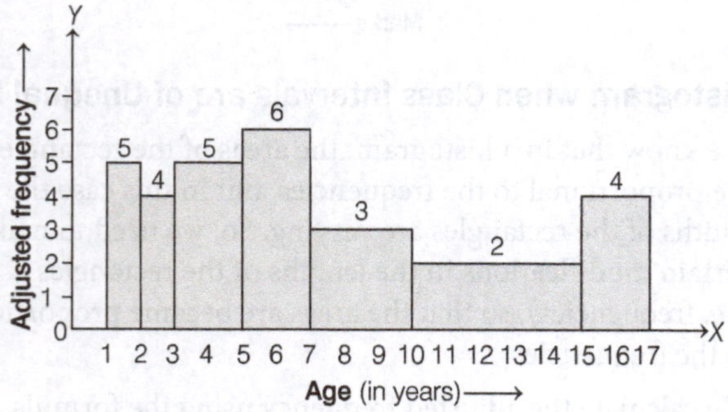

Example 5. **Sarita is a class teacher of Class IX in a school. She wanted to analyse the performance of two sections of students in a English test of 50 marks. Looking at their performance, she found that a few students got under 10 marks and a few got 35 marks or above. So, she decided to group them into intervals of varying size as follows**

0-10, 10-15, 15-20, 20-25, 25-30, 30-35, 35-50.

Then, she formed the following table.

Marks	Number of students
0-10	8
10-15	15
15-20	10
20-25	10
25-30	20
30-35	20
35-50	7

A histogram for the above data was prepared by a student as shown below.

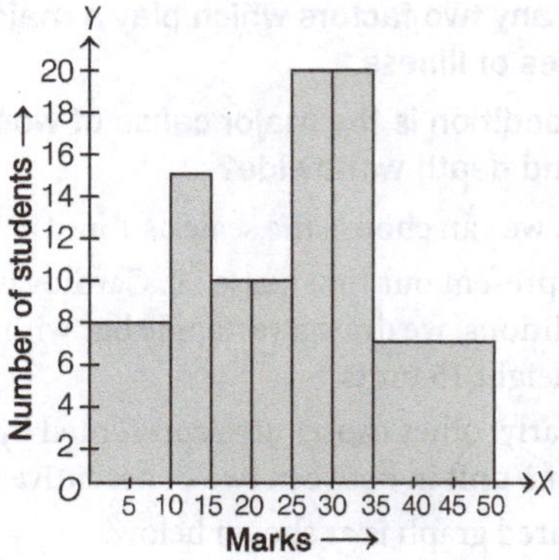

Carefully examine this graphical representation. Do you think that it correctly represents the data?

Sol. No, the graph prepared by a student is giving misleading picture. As, we know, the area of rectangles are proportional to the frequencies in a histogram.

So, we need to make certain modifications in the length of rectangles, so that the areas are again proportional to the frequencies.

Marks	Frequency	Width of the class	Length of the rectangle
0-10	8	10	$\frac{5}{10} \times 8 = 4$
10-15	15	5	$\frac{5}{5} \times 15 = 15$
15-20	10	5	$\frac{5}{5} \times 10 = 10$
20-25	10	5	$\frac{5}{5} \times 10 = 10$
25-30	20	5	$\frac{5}{5} \times 20 = 20$
30-35	20	5	$\frac{5}{5} \times 20 = 20$
35-50	7	15	$\frac{5}{15} \times 7 = 2.33$

Correct histogram for above table is given as

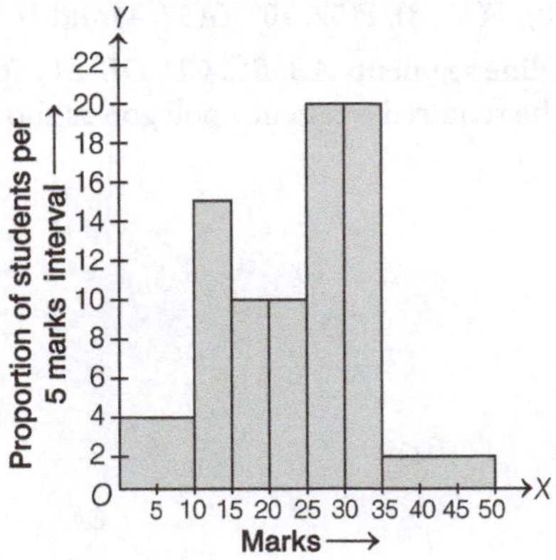

Frequency Polygon

A frequency polygon is the polygon obtained by joining the mid-points of upper horizontal sides of all the rectangles in the histogram.

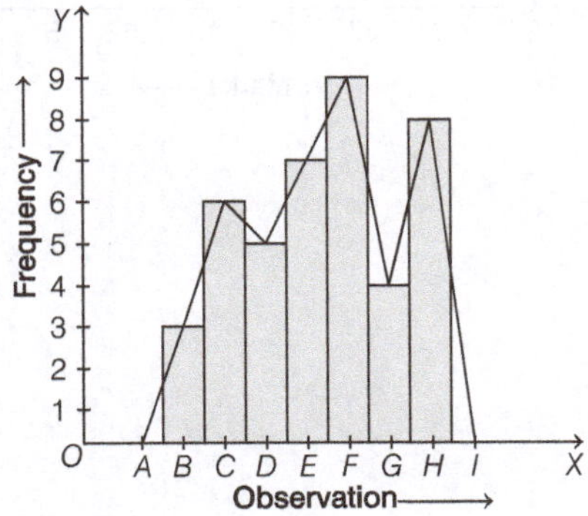

Example 6. **A random survey of the number of persons of various age groups present in a park was found as follows**

Age (in years)	4.5-9.5	9.5-14.5	14.5-19.5	19.5-24.5	24.5-29.5	29.5-34.5	34.5-39.5
Number of persons	10	28	32	40	50	35	12

Draw a frequency polygon corresponding to this frequency distribution table.

Sol. Let us first draw a histogram for this data and mark the mid-points of the top of the rectangles as *B, C, D, E, F, G, H*, respectively. Here, the first class is 4.5-9.5. So, the class preceeding 4.5 -9.5 is (0.5 -4.5). The first end point i.e. *B* join to the mid-point with zero frequency of (0.5 -4.5) as marked *A*. Let *I* be the mid-point of the class succeeding the last class of given data.

Thus, *ABCDEFGHI* is frequency polygon, which shown in figure below.

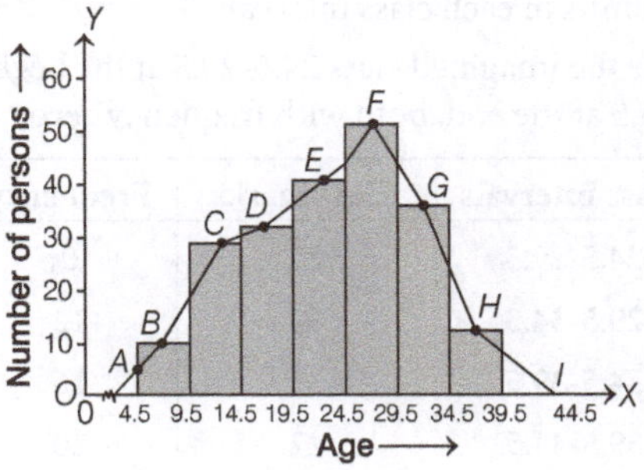

Frequency Polygon without Drawing Histogram

Frequency polygons can also be drawn independently without drawing histograms. For this, we first find class mark (i.e. the mid-points of the class intervals) of a class interval using the formula

$$\text{Class mark} = \frac{\text{Upper limit} + \text{Lower limit}}{2}$$

Now, take the class mark along the horizontal axis (i.e. *X*-axis) and frequencies along the vertical axis (i.e. *Y*-axis) and join all the class marks to get required frequency polygon.

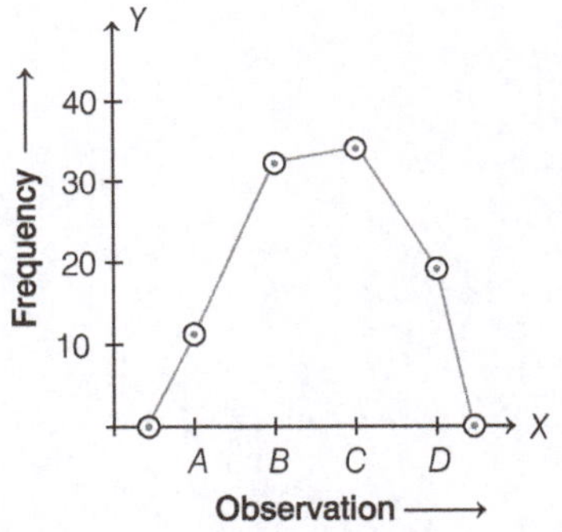

Note It To complete frequency polygon, we assume that there is a class interval with frequency zero before the first interval and after the last interval.

Example 7. **Draw a frequency polygon representing the following frequency distribution.**

Class intervals	30-34	35-39	40-44	45-49	50-54	55-59
Frequency	12	16	20	8	10	4

Sol. Given, class intervals are discontinuous, so we make continuous by subtracting and adding 0.5 in lower and upper limits of each class interval.

We take the imagined class 24.5-29.5 at the beginning and 59.5-64.5 at the end, both with frequency zero.

Class intervals	Class marks	Frequency
24.5-29.5	27	0
29.5-34.5	32	12
34.5-39.5	37	16
39.5-44.5	42	20
44.5-49.5	47	8
49.5-54.5	52	10
54.5-59.5	57	4
59.5-64.5	62	0

Along the X-axis, we take class marks 27, 32, 37, 42, 47, 52, 57 and 62 with a suitable scale.

Along the Y-axis, we take corresponding frequencies 0, 12, 16, 20, 8, 10, 4 and 0 with a suitable scale.

Now, plot the points $A(27, 0)$, $B(32, 12)$, $C(37, 16)$, $D(42, 20)$, $E(47, 8)$, $F(52, 10)$, $G(57, 4)$ and $H(62, 0)$.

We join line segments AB, BC, CD, DE, EF, FG and GH to obtain the required frequency polygon as shown below

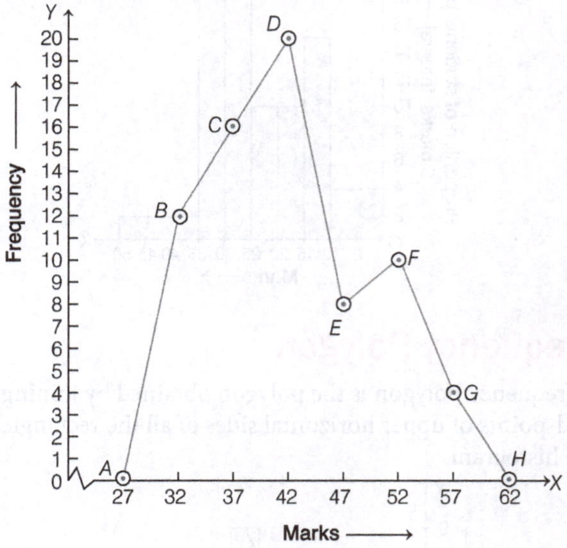

NCERT FOLDER

Complete Solutions of All Exercises of NCERT Textbook

EXERCISE 12.1 (NCERT Page 163-166)

Q1. A survey conducted by an organisation for the cause of illness and death among the women between the ages 15-44 (in years) worldwide, found following figures (in %).

S.No.	Causes	Female fatality rate (in %)
1.	Reproductive health conditions	31.8
2.	Neuropsychiatric conditions	25.4
3.	Injuries	12.4
4.	Cardiovascular conditions	4.3
5.	Respiratory conditions	4.1
6.	Other causes	22.0

(i) Represent the information given above graphically.

(ii) Which condition is the major cause of women's ill health and death worldwide?

(iii) Try to find out, with the help of your teacher, any two factors which play a major role in the cause of illness.

Sol. (i) We draw the bar graph of this data according to the following steps (The unit in second column is percentage.)

(a) We represent the causes on the horizontal axis choosing any scale, since width of the bar is not important but for clarity, we take equal widths for all bars and maintain equal gaps in between them. Let one cause be represented by one unit.

(b) We represent the female fatality rate (value) on the vertical axis. Here, we can choose the scale as 1 unit = 4%.

(c) To represent our first cause i.e. reproductive health conditions, we draw a rectangle bar with width 1 unit and height 31.8 units.

(d) Similarly, other causes are represented by leaving a gap of 1 unit in between two consecutive bars.

Now, the required graph is as shown below

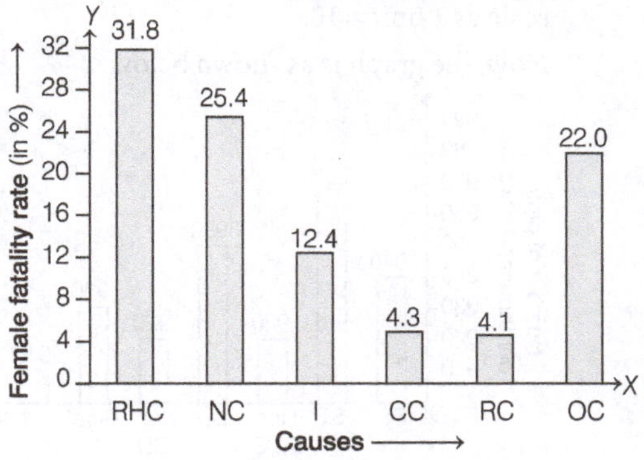

Here, we denote

RHC = Reproductive health conditions

NC = Neuropsychiatric conditions

I = Injuries

CC = Cardiovascular conditions

RC = Respiratory conditions

OC = Other causes

(ii) From the graph, we observe that 'reproductive health conditions' is the major cause of women's ill health and death worldwide because it has maximum percentage among the causes i.e. 31.8%.

(iii) The factors are as follow

(a) Lack of medical facilities.

(b) Lack of correct knowledge of treatment.

Q2. The following data on the number of girls (to nearest ten) per thousand boys in different sections of Indian society is given below

Sections	Number of girls per thousand boys
Scheduled Caste (SC)	940
Scheduled Tribe (ST)	970
Non-SC/ST	920
Backward districts	950
Non-backward districts	920
Rural	930
Urban	910

(i) Represent the information above by a bar graph.

(ii) In the classroom, discuss what conclusions can be arrived at from the graph.

Sol. (i) We draw the bar graph of this data, note that the unit in the second column is number of girls per thousand boys.

(a) We represent the section on the horizontal axis choosing any scale. Let one section be represented by one unit.

(b) We represent the number of girls per thousand boys on the vertical axis. Here, we can choose the scale as 1 unit = 10.

Now, the graph is as shown below

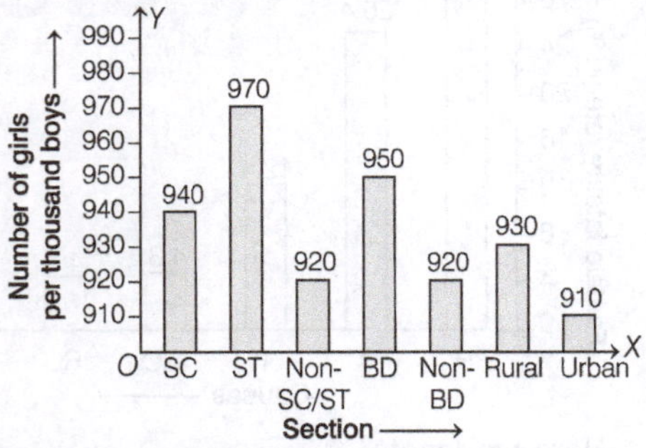

(ii) From the graph, we observe that the highest ratio of girls to boys per thousand is found in the ST community (970), while the lowest ratio is observed in Urban areas (910).

Furthermore, we observe that Rural areas, backward districts and SC/ST groups have a higher number of girls per thousand boys compared to Urban areas, non-backward districts and non SC/ST groups.

Q3. Given below are the seats won by different political parties in the polling outcome of a state assembly elections

Political party	A	B	C	D	E	F
Seats won	75	55	37	29	10	37

(i) Draw a bar graph to represent the polling results.

(ii) Which political party won the maximum number of seats?

Sol. (i) Solve as Q. 2.

The graph is as shown below

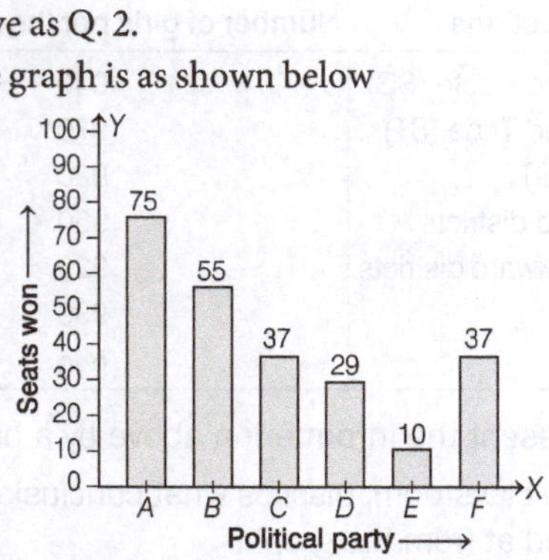

(ii) From the graph it is clear that party *A* won the maximum number of seats i.e. 75.

Q4. The length of 40 leaves of a plant are measured correct to one millimetre and the obtained data is represented in the following table.

Length (in mm)	Number of leaves
118-126	3
127-135	5
136-144	9
145-153	12
154-162	5
163-171	4
172-180	2

(i) Draw a histogram to represent the given data.

(ii) Is there any other suitable graphical representation for the same data?

(iii) Is it correct to conclude that the maximum number of leaves are 153 mm long and why?

Sol. (i) We know that the areas of the rectangles are proportional to the frequencies in a histogram.

Here, the given frequency distribution is not continuous. For continuous distribution, we take first interval as (118 − 0.5)-(126 + 0.5) = 117.5-126.5.

$$\left[\because \frac{127-126}{2} = 0.5\right]$$

The class width in this case is 9.

So, we get the following modified table of given data

Length (in mm)	Frequency	Width of the class
117.5-126.5	3	9
126.5-135.5	5	9
135.5-144.5	9	9
144.5-153.5	12	9
153.5-162.5	5	9
162.5-171.5	4	9
171.5-180.5	2	9

Now, we can draw the histogram for given data

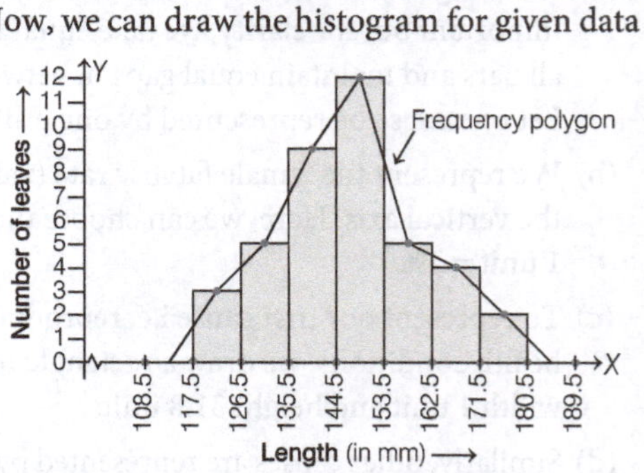

(ii) Yes, other suitable graphical representation for the same data is frequency polygon.

(iii) No, because the maximum number of leaves have their lengths lying in the interval 145-153. It is not necessary that all have their lengths as 153 mm.

Q5. The following table gives the lifetimes of 400 neon lamps

Lifetime (in hours)	Number of lamps
300-400	14
400-500	56
500-600	60
600-700	86
700-800	74
800-900	62
900-1000	48

(i) Represent the given information with the help of a histogram.

(ii) How many lamps have a lifetime of more than 700 h?

Sol. (i) The histogram for given table is

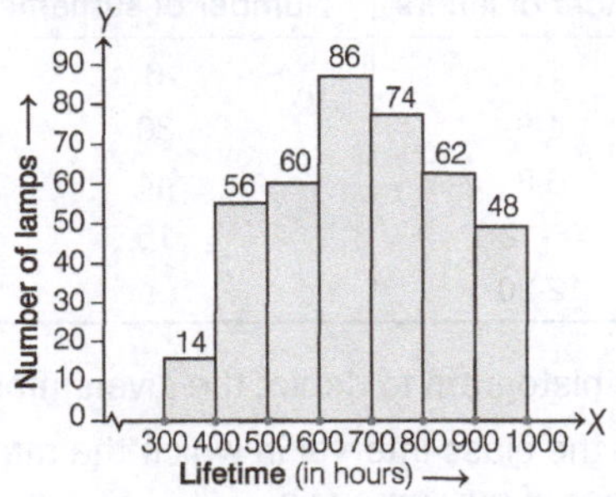

(ii) Number of lamps have a lifetime of more than 700 h

$= 74 + 62 + 48 = 184$

Q6. The following table gives the distribution of students of two sections according to the marks obtained by them

Section A		Section B	
Marks	**Frequency**	**Marks**	**Frequency**
0-10	3	0-10	5
10-20	9	10-20	19
20-30	17	20-30	15
30-40	12	30-40	10
40-50	9	40-50	1

Represent the marks of the students of both the sections on the same graph by two frequency polygons. From the two polygons compare the performance of the two sections.

Sol. We make modified table by given data as shown below

Classes	Class marks	Frequency (Section *A*)	Frequency (Section *B*)
0-10	5	3	5
10-20	15	9	19
20-30	25	17	15
30-40	35	12	10
40-50	45	9	1

Now, the required frequency polygons are as follows

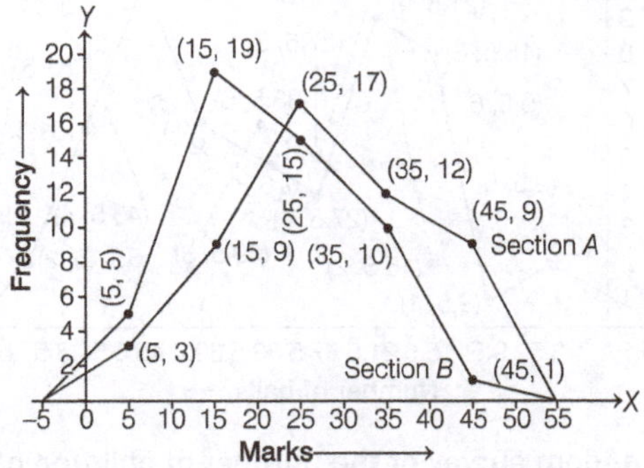

It is clear that from the polygon that the performance of section *A* is better in comparison of section *B* in term of good marks.

Q7. The runs scored by two teams *A* and *B* on the first 60 balls in a cricket match are given below

Number of balls	Team *A*	Team *B*
1-6	2	5
7-12	1	6
13-18	8	2
19-24	9	10
25-30	4	5
31-36	5	6
37-42	6	3
43-48	10	4
49-54	6	8
55-60	2	10

Represent the data of both the teams on the same graph by frequency polygons.

Sol. First, we make the class intervals continuous then modified table of given data is as shown below

Number of balls	Class marks	Runs scored by Team *A*	Runs scored by Team *B*
0.5-6.5	3.5	2	5
6.5-12.5	9.5	1	6
12.5-18.5	15.5	8	2
18.5-24.5	21.5	9	10
24.5-30.5	27.5	4	5
30.5-36.5	33.5	5	6
36.5-42.5	39.5	6	3
42.5-48.5	45.5	10	4
48.5-54.5	51.5	6	8
54.5-60.5	57.5	2	10

Now, frequency polygon for both teams are given below

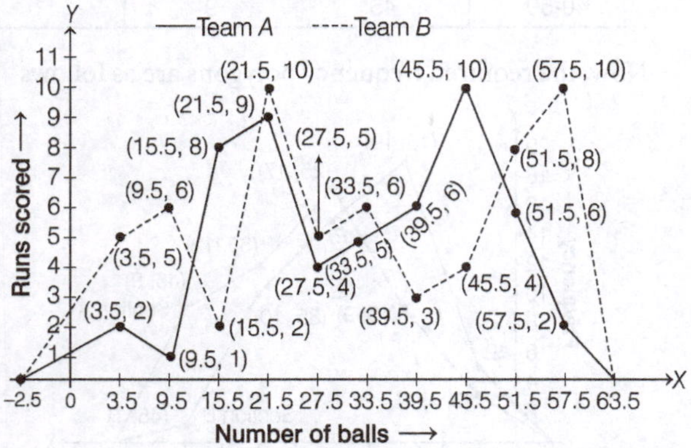

Q8. A random survey of the number of children of various age groups playing in a park was found as follows

Age (in years)	1-2	2-3	3-5	5-7	7-10	10-15	15-17
Number of children	5	3	6	12	9	10	4

Draw a histogram to represent the data above.

Sol. Here, the widths of the rectangles are varying. So, we need to make certain modifications in the lengths of the rectangles, so that the areas are became proportional to the frequencies.

The minimum class size is 1.

Length of rectangle (Adjusted frequency)

$$= \frac{\text{Minimum class size}}{\text{Class size of that class}} \times \text{Frequency of that class}$$

Then, modified table of given data is shown below

Age (in years)	Number of children (Frequency)	Width of the class	Length of the rectangle
1-2	5	1	$1/1 \times 5 = 5$
2-3	3	1	$1/1 \times 3 = 3$
3-5	6	2	$1/2 \times 6 = 3$
5-7	12	2	$1/2 \times 12 = 6$
7-10	9	3	$1/3 \times 9 = 3$
10-15	10	5	$1/5 \times 10 = 2$
15-17	4	2	$1/2 \times 4 = 2$

So, the histogram with varying width is given below

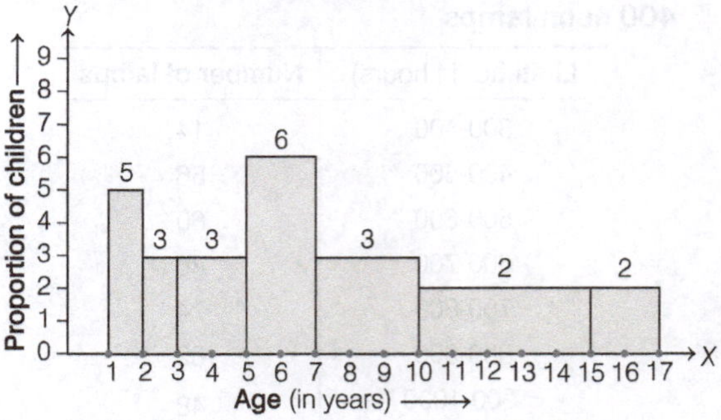

Q9. 100 surnames were randomly picked up from a local telephone directory and a frequency distribution of the number of letters in the English alphabet in the surnames was found as follows

Number of letters	Number of surnames
1-4	6
4-6	30
6-8	44
8-12	16
12-20	4

(i) Draw histogram to depict the given information.

(ii) Write the class interval in which the maximum number of surnames lie.

Sol. (i) Solve as Q. 8.

The histogram with varying width is as shown below

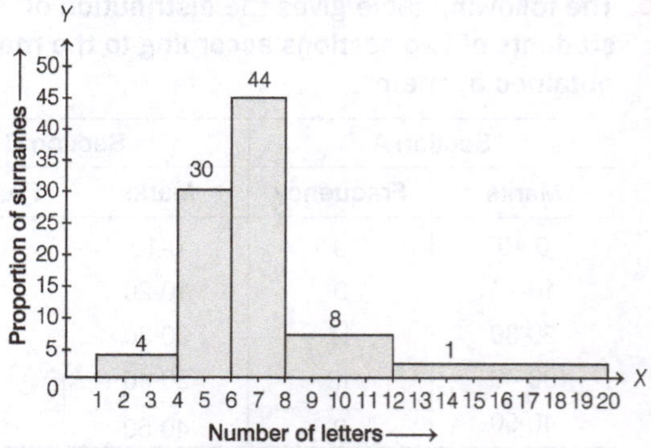

(ii) The class interval in which the maximum number of surnames lie, is 6-8.

REVIEW EXERCISE

Including Competency Based Questions

Part I

Multiple Choice Type Questions

1. The given figure shows the bar graph of the number of girls in a school from 2020 to 2023.

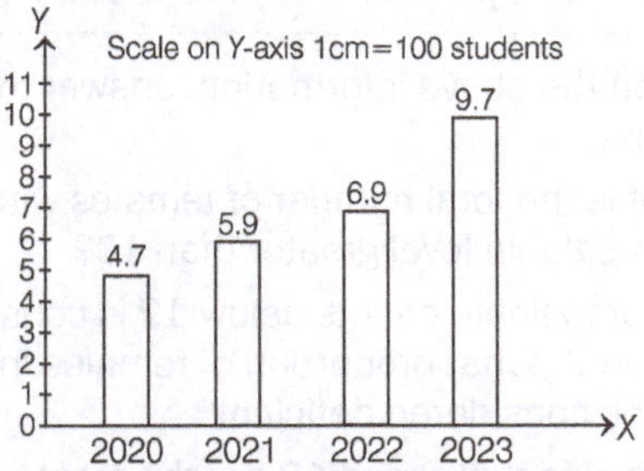

In which year, the number of girls was highest?

(a) 2020 (b) 2021 (c) 2022 (d) 2023

2. In a histogram, the area of each rectangle is proportional to

(a) the class mark of the corresponding class interval.

(b) the class size of the corresponding class interval.

(c) frequency of the corresponding class interval.

(d) cumulative frequency of the corresponding class interval.

3. Which of the following is correct?

(a) Adjust frequency $= \dfrac{\text{Class size of the class}}{\text{Frequency of the class}} \times \text{Minimum class size}$

(b) Adjust frequency $= \dfrac{\text{Minimum class size}}{\text{Class size of that class}} \times \text{Frequency of that class}$

(c) Adjust frequency $= \dfrac{\text{Class size of the class}}{\text{Minimum class size}} \times \text{Frequency of that class}$

(d) None of the above

4. To draw a histogram for the following frequency distribution.

Class interval	0-5	5-10	10-20	20-25	25-45
Frequency	6	8	9	24	40

The adjusted frequency for the class 25-45 is

(a) 5 (b) 15

(c) 20 (d) 10

5. The width of each of five continuous classes in a frequency distribution is 5 and the lower class limit of the lowest class is 10, then the upper class limit of the highest class is Competency Based Question

(a) 15 (b) 20 (c) 35 (d) 40

6. The width of each of six continuous classes in a frequency distribution is 8 and the upper class limit of the highest class is 48. The lower class limit of the lowest class is

(a) 40 (b) 48 (c) 8 (d) 0

7. A frequency polygon is constructed by plotting frequency of the class interval and the

(a) upper limit of the class (b) lower limit of the class

(c) mid-value of the class (d) any value of the class

8. For the class interval 39.5-49.5, the mid-value of the class interval is

(a) 29.5 (b) 34.5 (c) 44.5 (d) 47

9. The mid-value of a class interval is 25 and the class size is 8. The class interval is Competency Based Question

(a) 37-45 (b) 36.5-46.5 (c) 36.5-44.5 (d) 21-29

10. In a frequency distribution, the mid-value of the class is 10 and the width of the class is 6, then the lower limit of the class is

(a) 6 (b) 7 (c) 8 (d) 12

Case Study Based Questions

11. Rajasthan Government conducted a survey of 150 families of a town, the number of members in each family was recorded and the data has been represented by the following bar graph.

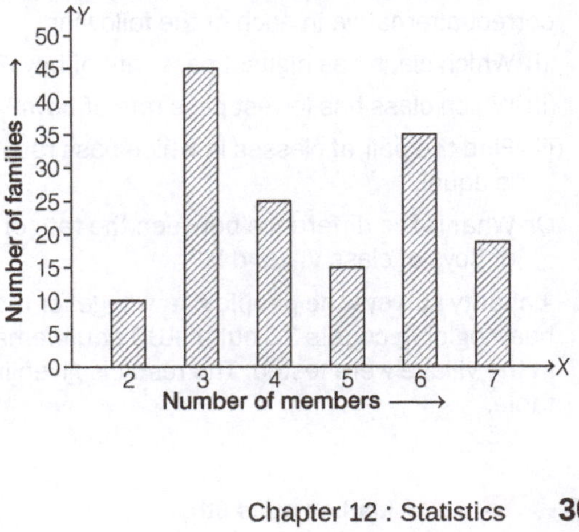

(i) What information does bar graph give?

(ii) How many families have 2 members each?

(iii) How many families have 6 members?

Or How many people live alone?

12. The following bar graph represents the budget allocation by Government of NCT of Delhi under Ladli scheme

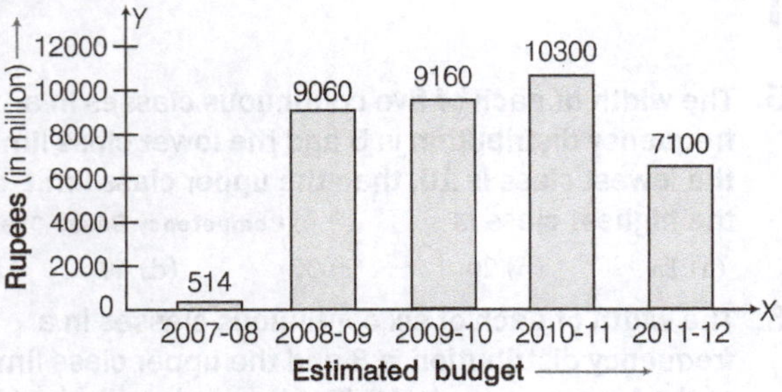

This scheme started in Jan 2008.

Study the above bar graph and answer the following questions.

(i) Find the year in which the budget was ₹ 514 million.

(ii) Find the year in which the budget was minimum.

(iii) Find the year in which the budget was maximum.

Or

Find the year in which the budget was ₹ 9160 million.

13. The following bar graph shows the results of annual examination in a secondary school.

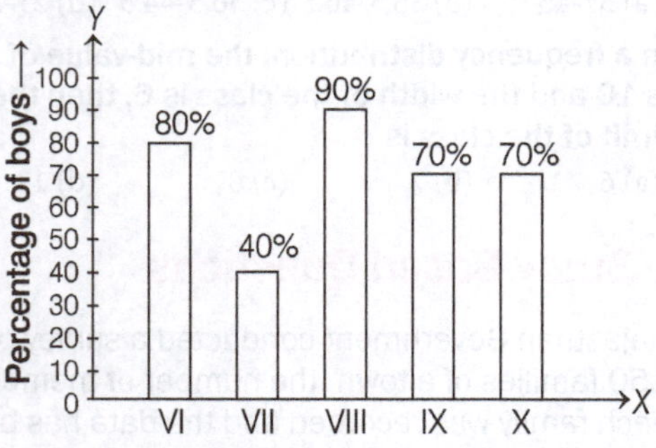

Read the bar graph (shown above) and choose the correct alternative in each of the following.

(i) Which class has highest pass rate of boys?

(ii) Which class has lowest pass rate of boys?

(iii) Find the pair of classes in which pass rate of boys is equal.

Or What is the difference between the rate of passing of boys of class VIII and IX?

14. A charity surveys the people of a village for their haemoglobin counts 25 out of 100 adult females in the village were tested. The result is given in this table.

Haemoglobin (mg/dl) counts	Number of females
5	3
6	3
7	2
8	5
9	1
10	1
11	3
12	4
13	2
14	1

Based on the above information, answer the following questions.

(i) What is the total number of females with a haemoglobin level greater than 10?

(ii) A haemoglobin counts below 12 is considered deficient. What proportion of females in the survey can be considered deficient?

(iii) Divya said that 8 and 12 are the most observed haemoglobin counts (mg/dl) among 25 females. Krishna said that 8 and 12 are the most observed haemoglobin counts (mg/dl) among 100 females in the village. Who is correct? Explain your answer.

Or

If the charity aims to provide additional nutritional support to those with a haemoglobin count below 9, how many females from the survey would be eligible for this support?

15. Five friends Anchal, Amisha, Mahi, Vishu and Sahar are living in a hostel. At the end of every month, they calculate the expenses on food and shopping. The table given below shows their monthly expenses for the month of November.

Name	Anchal	Amisha	Mahi	Vishu	Sahar
Expenditure (in ₹)	3000	5000	6000	4500	7000

Based on the above information, answer the following questions.

(i) Which graphical representation method would best represent the given data?

(ii) Which two friends had an expenditure of more than 5000?

(iii) What is the average expenses of the friends for the month of November?

Or If the total expenses were split equally among all five friends, then how much more or less would Mahi need to pay compared to her actual expenditure?

Part II

Short Answer Type Questions

1. In a survey of 85 families of a colony, the number of members in each family was recorded and the data has been represented by the following bar graph

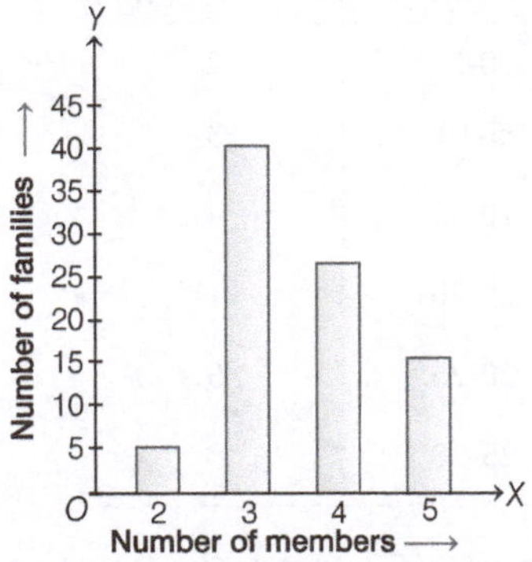

Read the bar graph carefully and answer the following questions.

(i) What information does bar graph give?

(ii) How many families have 3 members?

(iii) How many people live alone?

(iv) Which type of family is most common?

2. Shilpi, a Class IX student received cash award of ₹ 10000 (Ten thousand) in the singing competition. Her father advised her to make a budget plan for spending this amount. She made the following plan

S. No.	Head	Amount
1.	Donation in temple	200
2.	Tuition fee to needy child	100
3.	Welfare of senior citizens	500
4.	Welfare of street children	800
5.	Saving in bank	4000
6.	Books for family library	2000
7.	Picnic for family	1000
8.	Gift to grand parents	1100
9.	Tea party to friends	300
	Total	10000

Based on the above information, answer the following questions **Competency Based Question**

(i) Make a bar graph for the above data.

(ii) Which mathematical concepts have been covered in this?

(iii) Under which head Shilpi spend maximum amount?

3. The distribution of weights (in kg) of 100 people is given below

Weight (in kg)	Frequency
40-45	13
45-50	25
50-55	28
55-60	15
60-65	12
65-70	5
70-75	2

(i) For the class interval 45-50, find the mid value of the class interval.

(ii) Is it correct to conclude that the maximum number of weights is 55 kg and why?

(iii) Construct a histogram for the above distribution.

4. In the given figure, there is a histogram depicting daily wages of workers in a factory. Construct the frequency distribution table. **Competency Based Question**

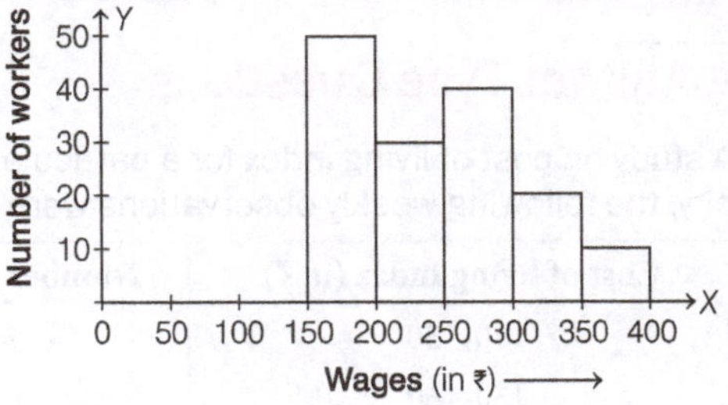

5. The frequency distribution has been represented graphically as follows

Marks	0-20	20-40	40-60	60-100
Number of students	10	15	20	25

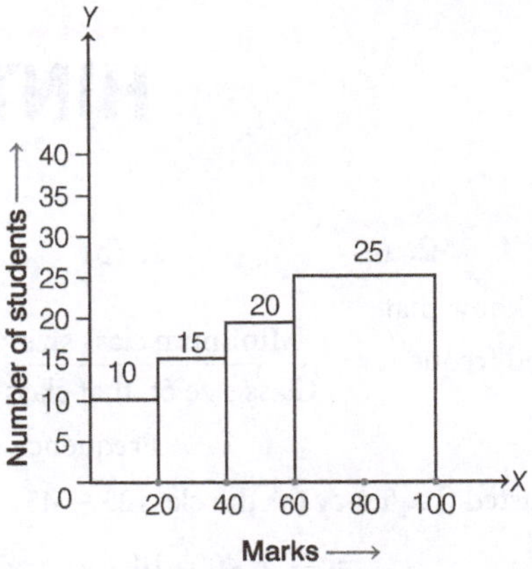

Do you think this representation is correct? Why?

6. The following table shows the number of literate females in the age group (10-57 yr) in a village

Age group (in years)	10-17	18-25	26-33	34-41	42-49	50-57	Total
Number of females (Frequency)	300	980	740	580	260	140	3000

Draw a histogram to represent the given data.

7. The class marks of a frequency distribution are 47, 52, 57, 62, 67, 72, 77, 82, 87, 92, 97 and 102. Find the class size and class limits.

8. Prepare a continuous grouped frequency distribution from the following data.

Mid-point	Frequency
5	4
15	8
25	13
35	12
45	6

Also, find the size of class intervals.

Competency Based Question

Long Answer Type Questions

9. A study on cost of living index for a particular year in a city, the following weekly observations were made.

Cost of living index (in ₹)	Number of weeks
140-150	5
150-160	10
160-170	20
170-180	9
180-190	6
190-200	2

(i) Draw a histogram and a frequency polygon on the same scale.

(ii) Write the class interval in which the maximum number of weeks lie.

10. Make a frequency polygon for given frequency table.

Class interval	Frequency
0-5	2
5-10	3
10-15	4
15-20	1
20-25	5
25-30	3

11. In a T-20 Cricket match (which is played for 20 overs), runs scored by two teams *A* and *B* are given below

Number of balls	Team *A*	Team *B*
1-12	4	8
13-24	5	15
25-36	8	3
37-48	9	10
49-60	8	10
61-72	12	6
73-84	6	9
85-96	14	6
97-108	8	10
109-120	4	14

Represent the data of both the team on the same graph by frequency polygons. **Competency Based Question**

HINTS & ANSWERS

Part I

1. (d) **2.** (c) **3.** (b)

4. (d) We know that

$$\text{Adjusted frequency} = \frac{\text{Minimum class size}}{\text{Class size of that class}} \times \text{Frequency of that class}$$

$\therefore$ Adjusted frequency for the class 25 − 45

$$= \frac{5}{20} \times 40 = 10$$

5. (c) Lower class limit of lowest class is 10. As the width of each of five continuous classes is 5, the class can be listed as given below.

10-15, 15-20, 20-25, 25-30, 30-35

$\therefore$ Highest class is 30-35.

Thus, the upper class limit of the highest class is 35.

6. (d) For the given data, the class can be listed as given below.

0-8, 8-16, 16-24, 24-32, 32-40, 40-48

∴ Lowest class is 0-8.

Thus, the lower limit of the lowest class is 0.

7. (c) Frequency polygon is the plot of frequencies v/s the mid-value of the classes.

8. (c) Mid-value of a class interval

$$= \frac{\text{Lower limit} + \text{Upper limit}}{2}$$

$$= \frac{39.5 + 49.5}{2} = 44.5$$

9. (d) Class marks = 25, class size = 8

Let upper class limit = U

and lower class limit = L

Then, $\frac{L+U}{2} = 25$

$\Rightarrow \quad L + U = 50 \quad \ldots(i)$

and $\quad U - L = 8 \quad \ldots(ii)$

On solving Eqs. (i) and (ii), we get

$U = 29$ and $L = 21$

Hence, interval of class is 21-29.

10. (b) Let x be the upper limit and y be the lower limit.

Since, the mid-value of the class is 10.

$\therefore \quad \frac{x+y}{2} = 10$

$\Rightarrow \quad x + y = 20 \quad \ldots(i)$

and $\quad x - y = 6 \quad$ [∵ width of class = 6] ...(ii)

By solving Eqs. (i) and (ii), we get

$y = 7$

Hence, the lower limit of the class is 7.

11. (i) The bar graph shown the number of members in each of the 150 families of a colony.

(ii) Clearly, 10 families have 2 members each.

(iii) Clearly, 35 families have 6 members each.

Or Clearly, there is no person who live alone.

12. (i) In the year 2007-08 the budget was ₹ 514 million.

(ii) The budget was minimum in 2007-08.

(iii) The budget was maximum in 2010-11.

Or In the year 2009-10, the budget was ₹ 9160 million.

13. (i) Class VIII has highest pass rate of boys i.e. 90%.

(ii) Class VII has lowest pass rate of boys i.e. 40%.

(iii) From graph it is clear that in class IX and X pass rate of boys are equal i.e. 70%.

Or In class VIII and class IX, the rate of passing of boys are 90% and 70%, respectively.

∴ Required difference = 90 − 70 = 20%

14. Hint

(i) **From the table**

- 11 mg/dl : 3 females
- 12 mg/dl : 4 females
- 13 mg/dl : 2 females
- 14 mg/dl : 1 female

∴ Required number of females = 3 + 4 + 2 + 1 = 10

(ii) Women below haemoglobin 12 = 18

Total females = 25

∴ Required proportion of females in the survey = $\frac{18}{25}$

(iii) Since, only 25 females were tested.

Ans. Divya is correct.

Or **From the table**

- 5 mg/dl : 3 females
- 6 mg/dl : 3 females
- 7 mg/dl : 2 females
- 8 mg/dl : 5 females

∴ Required number of females = 3 + 3 + 2 + 5 = 13

15. Hint

(i) Bar graphs are great for comparing value or convey information. It makes visual representations of data easy to spot. Bar graphs are best when changes are larger.

Ans. Bar graph

(ii) Mahi (₹ 6000) and Sahar (₹ 7000) had an expenditure of more than ₹ 5000.

(iii) Average expense

$$= \frac{3000 + 5000 + 6000 + 7000 + 4500}{5}$$

Ans. ₹ 5100

Or

Mahi's actual expenditure was ₹ 6000 and the equal share would be ₹ 5100 (average expense)

Difference = ₹ 6000 − ₹ 5100 = ₹ 900

∴ Mahi would need to pay ₹ 900 more.

Part II

1. (i) The bar graph shows the number of members in each of the 85 families of a colony.

(ii) Clearly, 40 families have 3 members each.

(iii) Clearly, there is no person which live alone.

(iv) Most common family is a family having 3 members.

2. (i) The bar graph of given data is given below

In the graph, head is taken on X-axis and amount is taken on Y-axis.

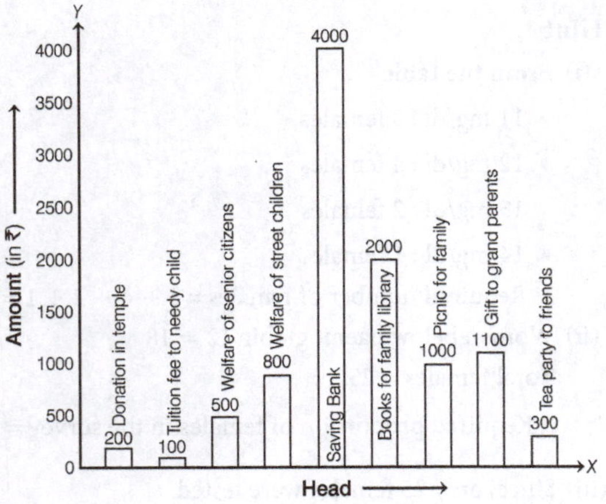

(ii) Representation of data using bar graph.

(iii) Shilpi spend maximum amount under saving bank scheme.

3. Hint

(i) Mid-value of class interval $= \dfrac{45+50}{2}$

$= 47.5$

(ii) No. Since, for the weight 50-55 kg, the frequency is 28.

∴ The maximum number of weights lies between 50-55.

(iii) The required histogram is as follows

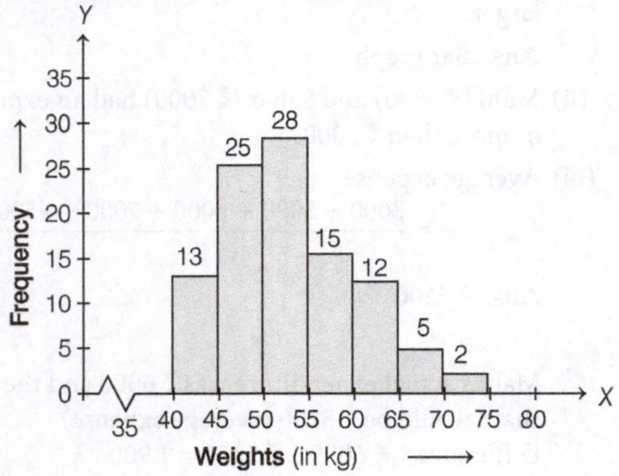

4. Hint It is clear from the given histogram that class interval start from 150 having width 50.

The frequency distribution table is given below

Wages (in ₹)	Number of workers
150-200	50
200-250	30
250-300	40
300-350	20
350-400	10
Total	150

5. No, because the width of the rectangles are varying, so we need to make certain modifications in the length of the rectangles so that the areas are proportional to the frequencies.

6. The given frequency distribution is in inclusive form. So, first we convert it into exclusive form.

For continuous distribution, take

first interval as $(10-0.5)-(17+0.5)=9.5\text{-}17.5$

Then, modify frequency distribution table is

Age group (in years)	Frequency
9.5-17.5	300
17.5-25.5	980
25.5-33.5	740
33.5-41.5	580
41.5-49.5	260
49.5-57.5	140
Total	3000

Now, the required histogram is as follows

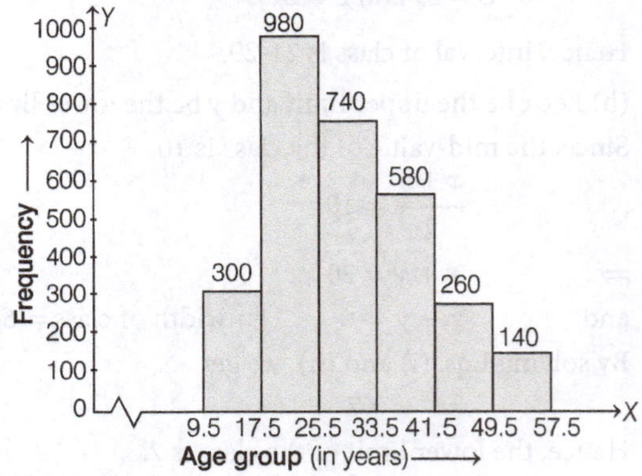

7. Hint Class size $= 52 - 47 = 5$

$\therefore$ Lower limit $= 47 - \dfrac{5}{2} = 47 - 2.5 = 44.5$

and upper limit $= 47 + \dfrac{5}{2} = 47 + 2.5 = 49.5$

Ans. The first class is 44.5- 49.5.

The other class limits are 49.5-54.5, 54.5-59.5, 59.5-64.5, 64.5-69.5, 69.5-74.5, 74.5-79.5, 79.5-84.5, 84.5-89.5, 89.5-94.5, 94.5-99.5, 99.5-104.5.

8. Required continuous grouped frequency distribution table is

Mid-point	Class interval	Frequency
5	0-10	4
15	10-20	8
25	20-30	13
35	30-40	12
45	40-50	6

Ans. Class size $= 10 - 0 = 10$

9. Hint

(i) We represent the class intervals along the horizontal line on a suitable scale and the corresponding frequencies along the vertical line on a suitable scale. We construct rectangles with class intervals as the bases and the respective frequencies as the heights.

Thus, we obtain the histogram as shown below

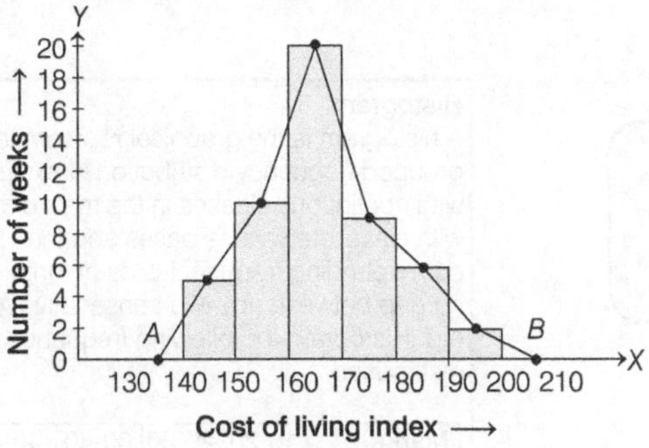

Now, we join the mid-points of the tops of adjacent rectangles by line segments.

Also, we take the imagined classes 130-140 and 200-210, each with frequency 0. We join *A* with the mid-point of the top of the first rectangle and join *B* with the mid-point of the top of the last rectangle. Thus, we obtain a complete frequency polygon.

(ii) The class interval in which the maximum number of weeks lie is 160-170.

10. Hint The given frequency table is as follows

Class interval	0-5	5-10	10-15	15-20	20-25	25-30
Class marks	2.5	7.5	12.5	17.5	22.5	27.5
Frequency	2	3	4	1	5	3

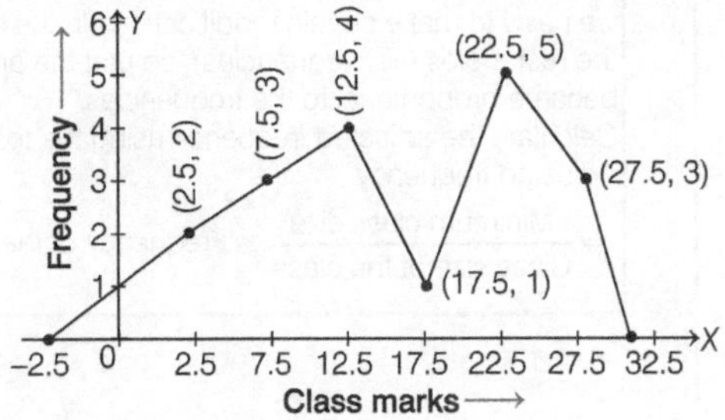

which is the required frequency polygon.

11. Hint Firstly, make the class intervals continuous, then modified table of given data as below

Number of balls	Class marks	Team *A*	Team *B*
0.5-12.5	6.5	4	8
12.5-24.5	18.5	5	15
24.5-36.5	30.5	8	3
36.5-48.5	42.5	9	10
48.5-60.5	54.5	8	10
60.5-72.5	66.5	12	6
72.5-84.5	78.5	6	9
84.5-96.5	90.5	14	6
96.5-108.5	102.5	8	10
108.5-120.5	114.5	4	14

Frequency polygon for both teams are given below as

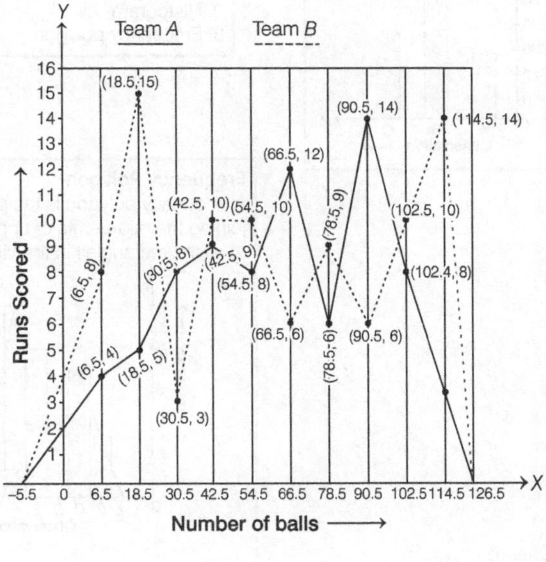

Mind Map

STATISTICS

Statistics means numerical facts or observations collected with definite purpose.

Graphical Representation Of Data

Representation of the data through the pictures or graphs is called the graphical representation of data.

Some of the graphical representations of data are

1. Bar graph
2. Histogram
3. Frequency polygon

Bar Graph

In a bar graph, bars of uniform width are drawn with equal spacing between them on one axis with various heights.

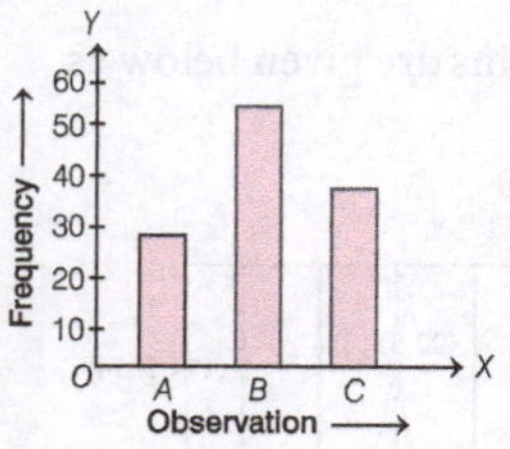

Histogram

A histogram is the graphical representation of a grouped frequency distribution in exclusive form with continuous classes in the form of rectangles with class intervals as bases and the corresponding frequencies as heights. There is no gap between any two consecutive rectangles.

e.g. Histogram for following frequency distribution.

Marks	10-20	20-30	30-40	40-50	50-60
Number of students	7	11	9	13	4

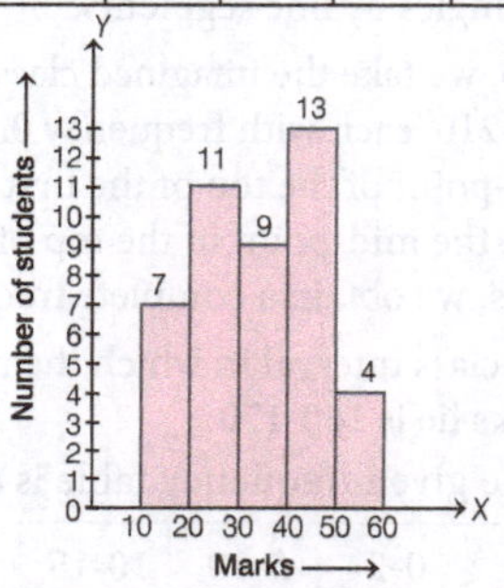

Histogram when Class Intervals are of Unequal Size

In this case, the width of the rectangles are varying. So, we need to make certain modifications in the lengths of the rectangles (i.e. frequencies), so that the areas are became proportional to the frequencies.

Calculate the adjusted frequency using the formula

Adjusted frequency

$$= \frac{\text{Minimum class size}}{\text{Class size of the class}} \times \text{Frequency of the class}$$

Frequency Polygon

A frequency polygon is the polygon obtained by joining the mid-points of upper horizontal sides of all the rectangles in the histogram.

e.g.

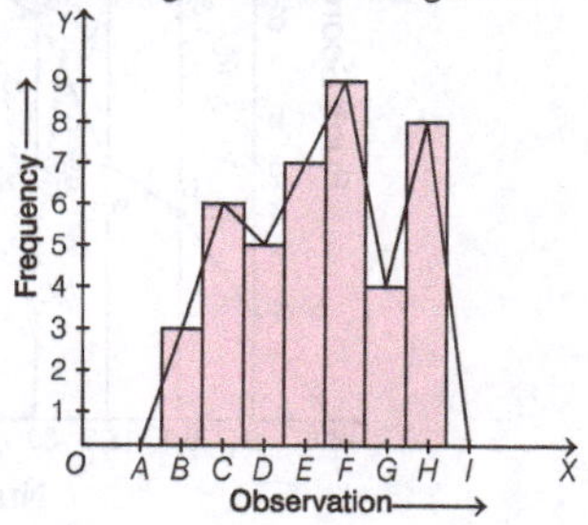

Frequency polygons can also be drawn independently without drawing histograms. For this, we first find class mark of a class interval using the formula

$$\text{Class mark} = \frac{\text{Upper limit} + \text{Lower limit}}{2}$$

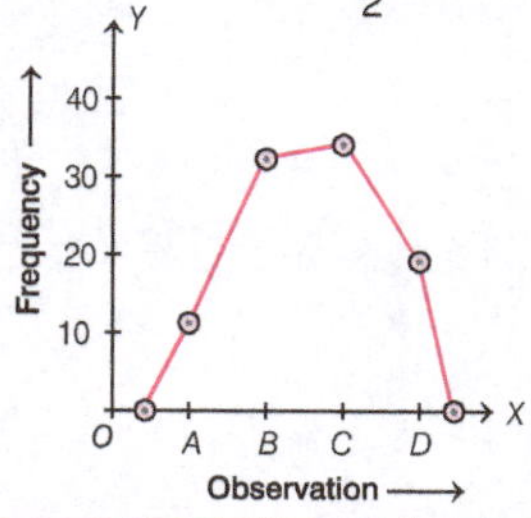

Topics to be Assessed Formatively

Collection and Presentation of Data

Collection of Data

Data The facts or figures (i.e. observation/information) which are numerical or otherwise; collected with a definite purpose, are called *data.*

We can define the types of data on the basis of their sources in two types

- **Primary data** The data collected by the investigator himself for a definite plan or purpose, is known as *primary data.*
- **Secondary data** The data which are not collected directly but obtained from some other sources (published or unpublished), is known as *secondary data.*

Presentation of Data

Presentation of data means to present or organise the collected data in a simple form which can be easily analysed and interpreted by the user of data. There are various ways to represent a collected data.

Some of them are given below

Presentation of Data in Ascending or Descending Order

Consider the marks obtained by 10 students in a Mathematics test as given below

55, 36, 95, 73, 60, 42, 25, 78, 75, 62

The data in this form is called **raw data.**

Now, arrange this raw data in ascending order as

25, 36, 42, 55, 60, 62, 73, 75, 78, 95

Now, we can clearly see that the lowest mark is 25 and the highest mark is 95. The difference of the highest and the lowest values in the data, is called the **range of the data.**

Here, range $= 95 - 25 = 70$

Presentation of Data in the Form of Ungrouped Frequency Distribution

If the number of observations (in a data) is large, then it takes much time to arrange them in increasing or decreasing order.

In this case of observations, data can be easily presented by using frequency distribution method. To present given data in the form of ungrouped frequency distribution or simply a frequency distribution table, we write observations in one column and the corresponding frequency in second column.

Example 1. Consider the marks obtained (out of 100 marks) by 30 students of Class IX of a school

10 20 36 92 95 40 50 56 60 70
92 88 80 70 72 70 36 40 36 40
92 40 50 50 56 60 70 60 60 88

Represent this data in the form of a frequency distribution table.

Sol. Required frequency distribution table is

Marks	Number of students (Frequency)	Marks	Number of students (Frequency)
10	1	60	4
20	1	70	4
36	3	72	1
40	4	80	1
50	3	88	2
56	2	92	3

Presentation of Data in the Form of Grouped Frequency Distribution

When a data has a large number of values (entries) as $x_1, x_2, \ldots, x_n$ and most of them are distinct, it becomes inconvenient to present this data in the form of ungrouped frequency distribution.

Here, we condense the data into finite number of groups as 20-29, 30-39, ..., etc.

These groupings are called **classes** or **class intervals.** In each of these classes, the least number is called the **lower class limit** and the greatest number is called the **upper class limit.**

The difference between the upper class limit and lower class limit is called **class size** or **class width.**

The number of entries of the data having their values lying in a class is defined as the frequency of the class. The table in which the corresponding frequencies are written against each class, is called the **frequency distribution** of given data.

Types of Grouped Frequency Distribution

1. **Exclusive form** (*Continuous form*) A frequency distribution in which upper limit of each class is excluded and lower limit is included, is called an *exclusive form.*

   e.g. In class 0-10, we include 0 and exclude 10 and in class 10-20, we include 10 and exclude 20.

2. **Inclusive form** (*Discontinuous form*) A frequency distribution in which each upper limit as well as lower limit are included, is called an *inclusive form.*

   e.g. In 0-10, both 0 and 10 are included; in class 11-20, both 11 and 20 are included, etc.

Example 2. **Consider the marks obtained by 20 students out of 50 marks of Class IX of a school in a test**

42, 40, 41, 6, 8, 30, 34, 37, 14, 12,
47, 43, 49, 21, 23, 4, 10, 17, 35, 36

Present this data as a grouped data

(i) in exclusive form **(ii) in inclusive form.**

Sol. We can classify the given data into group as given below

(*i*) In exclusive form

Marks (Class interval)	Tally marks	Number of students (Frequency)
0-10	𝍷𝍷𝍷	3
10-20	𝍷𝍷𝍷𝍷	4
20-30	𝍷𝍷	2
30-40	𝍸	5
40-50	𝍸𝍷	6

(*ii*) In inclusive form

Marks (Class interval)	Number of students (Frequency)
0-10	4
11-20	3
21-30	3
31-40	5
41-50	5

To Convert Discontinuous Form in Continuous Form

To convert the intervals in continuous form, firstly we find the difference between the upper limit of a class and the lower limit of its succeeding class, then add and subtract half of this difference to upper limit and lower limit, respectively.

e.g. Consider the intervals 11-20 and 21-30.

Here, lower limit of 21-30 = 21

and upper limit of 11-20 = 20

Now, difference = 21 − 20 = 1

$\therefore$ Half of the difference $= \frac{1}{2} = 0.5$

So, the new class interval formed from 11-20 is

(11 − 0.5)-(20 + 0.5), i.e. 10.5-20.5

Similarly, the new class interval formed from 21-30 is (21 − 0.5)-(30 + 0.5), i.e. 20.5-30.5.

Thus, we get the continuous classes as 10.5-20.5 and 20.5-30.5.

Example 3. **Following distribution table gives the weights of 38 passengers of a bus**

Weights (in kg)	Number of passengers	Weights (in kg)	Number of passengers
31-35	10	51-55	1
36-40	6	56-60	4
41-45	12	Total	38
46-50	5		

If two new passengers of weights 35.5 kg and 40.5 kg are boarded in the bus, then in which interval will we include them? If we cannot include them in given table, then construct the new table to include them.

Sol. We cannot add them in the classes end with 35 or 40, because intervals are in discontinuous form

Now, for classes 31-35 and 36-40, Lower limit of 36-40 = 36 and upper limit of 31-35 = 35

Difference between upper and lower limits = 36 − 35 = 1

$\therefore$ Half of difference $= \frac{1}{2} = 0.5$

Now, we can construct continuous class of given interval as follows

30.5-35.5, 35.5-40.5, 40.5-45.5, 45.5-50.5, 50.5-55.5, 55.5-60.5

By convention, we consider 35.5 in the classes 35.5-40.5. Similarly, 40.5 is consider in the classes 40.5-45.5.

Now, we can construct new frequency distribution table which include weights 35.5 kg and 40.5 kg as follows

Weights (in kg)	Tally marks	Number of passengers
30.5-35.5	𝍸 𝍸	10
35.5-40.5	𝍸𝍷𝍷	7
40.5-45.5	𝍸 𝍸 𝍷𝍷𝍷	13
45.5-50.5	𝍸	5
50.5-55.5	𝍷	1
55.5-60.5	𝍷𝍷𝍷𝍷	4
Total		40

Example 4. **A class test was held for 40 students and their marks out of 60 are as under**

4, 7, 9, 8, 9, 10, 8, 15, 16, 33, 15, 23, 27, 35, 38, 18, 20, 25, 28, 32, 43, 48, 36, 39, 24, 42, 45, 47, 28, 19, 39, 29, 34, 49, 50, 23, 34, 42, 32, 18

Construct a grouped frequency distribution table.

Sol. Here, we condense the data into groups 0-10, 10-20, ..., 50-60. Then, the required grouped frequency distribution table is as follows

Class intervals	Tally marks	Number of students (frequency)
0-10	𝍸 I	6
10-20	𝍸 II	7
20-30	𝍸 IIII	9
30-40	𝍸 𝍸	10
40-50	𝍸 II	7
50-60	I	1
Total		40

Measures of Central Tendency

The value of the variable which describes the characteristics of the entire data in the associated frequency distribution is called average of the data. Since, average represents the entire data, so it is also called **central value** or **measure of central tendency**.

Commonly used measures of central tendency are mean or arithmetic mean, median and mode. Here, we will study the measures of central tendency in ungrouped data.

Arithmetic Mean

The average of a given set of numbers, is called the arithmetic mean or simply the mean of the given numbers.

The mean (or average) of a number of observations is the sum of the values of all the observations divided by the total number of observations. It is generally denoted by $\bar{x}$.

$$\text{Mean, } \bar{x} = \frac{\text{Sum of all observations}}{\text{Number of observations}}$$

(*i*) **Arithmetic Mean of Simple or Individual Series**

The mean of n observations $x_1, x_2, x_3, \ldots, x_n$ is

given by $\quad x = \dfrac{(x_1 + x_2 + \ldots + x_n)}{n} = \dfrac{\sum_{i=1}^{n} x_i}{n}$

Note **Instead of writing $x_1 + x_2 + \ldots + x_n$, we write $\sum_{i=1}^{n} x_i$ or Σx.**

Here, greek symbol 'Σ' is called sigma, which is used for summation.

Example 5. **If following are the marks obtained by 5 students of a class, then find their mean.**

10, 5, 20, 25, 15

Sol. Mean, $\bar{x} = \dfrac{\Sigma x}{n} = \dfrac{10 + 5 + 20 + 25 + 15}{5} = \dfrac{75}{5} = 15$

(*ii*) **Mean of Ungrouped Frequency Distribution**

If $x_1, x_2, \ldots, x_n$ are n observations whose corresponding frequencies are $f_1, f_2, \ldots, f_n$, then mean is given by

$$\bar{x} = \frac{x_1 f_1 + x_2 f_2 + \ldots + x_n f_n}{f_1 + f_2 + \ldots + f_n} = \frac{\sum_{i=1}^{n} f_i x_i}{\sum_{i=1}^{n} f_i}$$

Example 6. **Find the mean of the following distribution.**

Variable	5	6	7	8	9
Frequency	4	8	14	11	3

Sol. Mean $= \dfrac{\Sigma f_i x_i}{\Sigma f_i} = \dfrac{5 \times 4 + 6 \times 8 + 7 \times 14 + 8 \times 11 + 9 \times 3}{4 + 8 + 14 + 11 + 3}$

$= \dfrac{20 + 48 + 98 + 88 + 27}{40} = \dfrac{281}{40} = 7.025$

Properties of Arithmetic Mean

Let $\bar{x}$ be the arithmetic mean of n observations $x_1, x_2, x_3, \ldots, x_n$. Then,

(*i*) $(x_1 - \bar{x}) + (x_2 - \bar{x}) + (x_3 - \bar{x}) + \cdots + (x_n - \bar{x}) = 0$

(*ii*) If each observation is increased by p then mean of new observations is $(\bar{x} + p)$.

(*iii*) If each observation is decreased by p then mean of new observations is $(\bar{x} - p)$.

(*iv*) If each observation is multiplied by a non-zero number p then mean of new observations is $p\bar{x}$.

(*v*) If each observation is divided by a non-zero number p, then mean of new observations is $\left(\dfrac{\bar{x}}{p}\right)$.

Example 7. **The mean of 24 numbers is 12. If 2 is added to every number, what will be the new mean?**

Sol. Let the given numbers be $x_1, x_2, \ldots, x_{24}$.

$\therefore$ Mean $= \dfrac{x_1 + x_2 + \ldots + x_{24}}{24}$

According to the question, $\dfrac{x_1 + x_2 + \ldots + x_{24}}{24} = 12$

$\Rightarrow \quad x_1 + x_2 + \ldots + x_{24} = 288 \quad \ldots(i)$

$\because$ 2 is added to every number.

$\therefore$ New numbers are $(x_1 + 2), (x_2 + 2), \ldots, (x_{24} + 2)$.

Mean of the new numbers$= \dfrac{(x_1 + 2) + (x_2 + 2) + \cdots + (x_{24} + 2)}{24}$

$$= \frac{(x_1 + x_2 + ... + x_{24}) + 48}{24} = \frac{288 + 48}{24} \text{ [from Eq. (i)]}$$

$$= \frac{336}{24} = 14$$

Hence, the new mean is 14.

Alternate Method By using the properties of arithmetic mean, we can easily and quickly find or check our answer. Since, each observations is increased by 2, then mean of new observations is $(\bar{x} + 2)$.

$\therefore$ New mean of 24 numbers $= 12 + 2 = 14$

Example 8. **The mean of 16 numbers is 50. If 5 is subtracted from each number, what will be the new mean?**

Sol. Let the given numbers be $x_1, x_2, ..., x_{16}$.

$$\therefore \text{Mean} = \frac{x_1 + x_2 + ... + x_{16}}{16}$$

According to the question, $\frac{x_1 + x_2 + ... + x_{16}}{16} = 50$

$\Rightarrow \quad x_1 + x_2 + ... + x_{16} = 50 \times 16 = 800$

$\because$ 5 is subtracted from each number.

$\therefore$ New numbers are $(x_1 - 5), (x_2 - 5), ..., (x_{16} - 5)$.

Mean of the new numbers

$$= \frac{(x_1 - 5) + (x_2 - 5) + ... + (x_{16} - 5)}{16}$$

$$= \frac{(x_1 + x_2 + ... + x_{16}) - 80}{16} = \frac{800 - 80}{16} = \frac{720}{16} = 45$$

Hence, the new mean is 45.

Median

The median is that value of the variable which divides the distribution into two equal parts such that the number of observations above is equal to the number of observations below it. Thus, after arranging the given data in an ascending or a descending order of magnitude, the value of the middle most observation, is called the median of the data.

Median of Ungrouped or Individual Series

Suppose, there are n observations, first arrange the given observations in ascending or descending order.

1. If n is odd then Median = Value of $\left(\frac{n+1}{2}\right)$th observation
2. If n is even, then Median

$$= \frac{1}{2}\left[\text{Value of } \left(\frac{n}{2}\right)\text{th and } \left(\frac{n}{2} + 1\right)\text{th observations}\right]$$

Example 9. **Find the median of the following observations.**

15, 40, 25, 16, 28, 32, 36, 42, 16, 19, 28

Sol. On arranging the given data in ascending order, we get

15, 16, 16, 19, 25, 28, 28, 32, 36, 40, 42

Hence, the number of observations, $n = 11$, which is odd.

$$\therefore \text{Median} = \text{Value of } \left(\frac{n+1}{2}\right)\text{th term}$$

$$= \text{Value of } \left(\frac{11+1}{2}\right)\text{th term}$$

$$= \text{Value of } \left(\frac{12}{2}\right)\text{th term}$$

$$= \text{Value of 6th term} = 28$$

Example 10. **The percentage of marks obtained by students of a class in Mathematics are 65, 35, 37, 23, 0, 18, 82, 92, 72, 32, 10, 5. Find the median.**

Sol. First, we write the given data in ascending order.

0, 5, 10, 18, 23, 32, 35, 37, 65, 72, 82, 92

Here, the number of observations is even, i.e. $n = 12$

$\therefore$ There are two middle terms $\frac{12}{2}$ th and $\left(\frac{12}{2} + 1\right)$th,

i.e. 6th and 7th term.

So, the median is the mean of the values of the 6th and 7th terms.

$$\therefore \text{Median} = \frac{32 + 35}{2} \quad [\because \text{6th term} = 32, \text{7th term} = 35]$$

$$= \frac{67}{2} = 33.5$$

Mode

For an individual data, mode is the value of the variable which occurs most frequently, i.e. an observation with the maximum frequency, is called the mode of the data.

Or

The value around which there is greatest concentration, is called the mode of the data.

Example 11. **Find the mode of the following marks (out of 10) obtained by 20 students.**

4, 6, 5, 9, 3, 2, 7, 7, 6, 5, 4, 9, 10, 10, 3, 4, 7, 6, 9, 9

Sol. On arranging the given data in ascending order, we get

2, 3, 3, 4, 4, 4, 5, 5, 6, 6, 6, 7, 7, 7, 9, 9, 9, 9, 10, 10

Here, 9 occurs most frequently, i.e. four times.

So, the required mode is 9.

Example 12. **Calculate the mean, median and mode for the following data.**

23, 25, 28, 25, 16, 23, 17, 22, 25, 25

Sol. Firstly, write the given data in ascending order.

16, 17, 22, 23, 23, 25, 25, 25, 25, 28

We can represent above data in the following table.

Item (x)	Frequency (f)	fx
16	1	16
17	1	17
22	1	22
23	2	46
25	4	100
28	1	28
Total	$N = \Sigma f = 10$	$\Sigma fx = 229$

Now, $\Sigma fx = 229$ and $\Sigma f = 10$

$$\therefore \text{Mean} = \frac{\Sigma fx}{\Sigma f} = \frac{229}{10} = 22.9$$

Here, $n = 10$ [even]

$$\therefore \text{Median} = \frac{1}{2}\left[\text{Value of}\left(\frac{n}{2}\right)\text{th term} + \text{Value of}\left(\frac{n}{2}+1\right)\text{th term}\right]$$

$$= \frac{1}{2}[\text{Value of 5th term} + \text{Value of 6th term}]$$

$$= \frac{1}{2}(23 + 25) = 24$$

Mode = Value of variable which occurs most frequently
= 25

Exercise

1. Find the range of the following data.
   36, 34, 48, 56, 72, 82
2. Find the range of the following array of data.
   70, 66, 71, 38, 55, 62, 63, 41, 40, 39, 34
3. In a group, frequency data class interval are 0-20, 20-40, 40-60, ..., then find the class width.
4. Write down the frequency of the class 20-25 in the following data.
   18, 19, 12, 13, 21, 27, 29, 22, 23, 26, 21, 17, 23, 24
5. Convert the given frequency distribution into a continuous grouped frequency distribution.

Class intervals	Frequency
100-103	8
104-107	8
108-111	17
112-115	10
116-119	5
120-123	6

6. The weights (in grams) of 20 mangoes picked at random from a basket are as follows
   22, 28, 32, 15, 12, 18, 26, 32, 36, 34, 33, 34, 39, 31, 33, 28, 29, 30, 27, 22
   Construct a grouped frequency distribution table with equal classes of equal width 5 for the given data above taking the first interval as 10-15 (it is not included).
7. Consider the marks obtained (out of 30 marks) by 20 students of class IX of a school.
   22, 24, 20, 18, 17, 15, 20, 25, 29, 23, 21, 18, 12, 13, 19, 22, 24, 27, 13, 19
   Represent this data in the form of a frequency distribution table.
8. The following data gives marks out of 50, obtained by 30 students of a class in a test
   40, 13, 38, 16, 27, 30, 7, 3, 24, 19, 39, 26, 7, 33, 19, 21, 13, 41, 17, 19, 17, 12, 7, 10, 1, 9, 21, 14, 47, 45
   Represent the above data as a grouped data in inclusive form.
9. What is the mean of the data 48, 42, 39, 46, 51, 57, 59, 42, 43, 47?
10. If the weight of 10 students (in kg) are 15, 17, 18, 20, 19, 17, 22, 24, 18, 20, then find the average weight of 10 students.
11. Suppose the mean of 20 observations is 11. If 3 is added to every number, then find the new mean of 20 observations.
12. The mean of 12 observations is 24. If each observation is divided by 3, then find the new mean.
13. Obtain the mean of the following distribution.

Frequency (f_i)	Variable (x_i)
4	4
8	6
14	8
11	10
3	12

14. If 12 is the mean of 10 observations and 10 is added to each observation, then what is the new mean?

15. The mean of a set of observations is *a*. If each observation is multiplied by *b* and each product is decreased by *c*, then find the mean of new set of observations.

16. The weight (in kg) of 7 students are given below

32.5, 36.4, 39.2, 41.3, 42.9, 37.2, 41.2

Then, find its median.

17. Find the median of the following data.

2.0025, 2.0205, – 2.06, – 2.206, – 2.006

18. Find the mode of the following marks obtained by 15 students (out of 30).

20, 22, 26, 15, 22, 24, 14, 16, 18, 30, 22, 23, 25, 26, 22

19. Find the mode of the following data.

Item (x)	Frequency (f)
10	5
12	6
13	3
14	4
17	8

20. Find the mean, median and mode of the following data.

10, 8, 7, 10, 5, 14, 10, 8, 14, 17

Answers

1. 48 **2.** 37 **3.** 20 **4.** 6

5.

Class intervals	Frequency
99.5 – 103.5	8
103.5 – 107.5	8
107.5 – 111.5	17
111.5 – 115.5	10
115.5 – 119.5	5
119.5 – 123	6

6.

Class intervals	Frequency
10 - 15	1
15 - 20	2
20 - 25	2
25 - 30	5
30 - 35	8
35 - 40	2

7.

Class intervals	Frequency
10 - 15	3
15 - 20	6
20 - 25	8
25 - 30	3

8.

Class intervals	Frequency
0 - 10	7
11 - 20	10
21 - 30	6
31 - 40	4
41 - 50	3

9. 47.4 **10.** 19 kg **11.** 14

12. 8 **13.** 8.05 **14.** 22

15. $ab - c$ **16.** 39.2 **17.** –2.006

18. 22 **19.** 17 **20.** 10.3, 10, 10

CHAPTERS TO BE ASSESSED FORMATIVELY

Areas of Parallelograms and Triangles (To be Assessed Formatively)

CHAPTER 13

The part of the plane enclosed by a simple closed figure is called a planar region corresponding to that figure. The magnitude or measure of this planar region is called its area. Area is always expressed with the help of a number in some unit.

We have also learnt some formulae for finding the areas of different plane figures such as triangle, rectangle, square, parallelogram, circle, etc. In this chapter, we shall discuss relationship between the areas of these geometric figures under the condition that they lie on the same base and between the same parallels.

Congruent Figures

Two figures are called congruent, if they have the same shape and the same size.

In other words, if two figures A and B are congruent, then using a tracing paper, we can superpose one figure over the other such that it will cover the other completely.

Thus, if two figures A and B are congruent, then they must have equal areas.

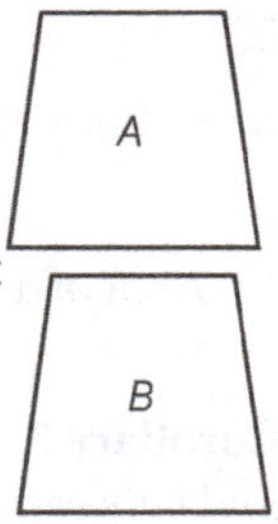

The converse of this statement is not true, i.e. two figures having equal areas need not to be congruent.

e.g. Area of a rectangle (C) having sides 16 cm and 4 cm

$= 4\times16 = 64\text{ cm}^2$

and area of a square (D) having side 8 cm $=(8)^2 = 64\text{cm}^2$

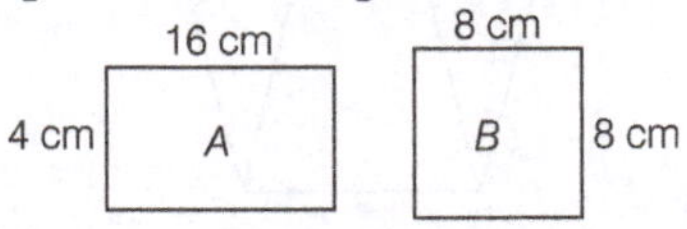

Here, area of rectangle and square are same but their shape is not same, so these are not congruent.

TOPIC 01 Parallelograms on the Same Base and Between the Same Parallels

Figures on the Same Base and between the Same Parallels

Two figures are said to be on the same base and between the same parallels, if they have a common base (or side) and the vertices (or vertex) opposite to the common base of each figure lie on a line parallel to the base.

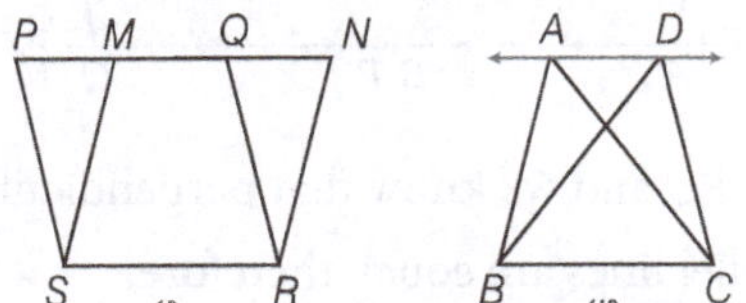

e.g. In figure (i), parallelogram $PQRS$ and trapezium $MQRS$ are on the same base SR. The vertices M and Q of trapezium $MQRS$ opposite to base SR and vertices P and Q of parallelogram $PQRS$ opposite to base SR lie on the line PN parallel to SR. So, both are on the same base SR and between the same parallels SR and PN.

Similarly, in figure (ii), ΔABC and ΔDBC lie on the same base BC and between the same parallels BC and AD.

Note In the adjoining figure, ΔDQR and ΔPQR lie on the same base QR but not lie between the same parallels QR and PM, because vertex D does not lie on PM.

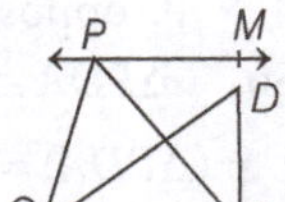

Example 1. **Which of the following figures is an example of figure having same base and same parallels?**

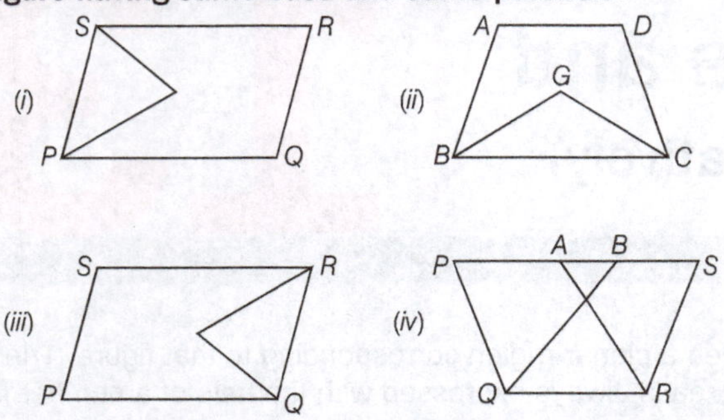

Sol. Only figure (iv) is an example of figures having same base QR and between same parallels QR and PS.

Areas of Parallelograms on the Same Base and between the Same Parallels

Let us construct two parallelograms having same base and between same parallels. The areas of these two parallelograms will be same. It can be proved with the help of following theorem.

Theorem ***Parallelograms on the same base and between the same parallels are equal in area.***

Let $ABCD$ and $PQCD$ be two parallelograms on same base DC and between same parallels PB and DC.

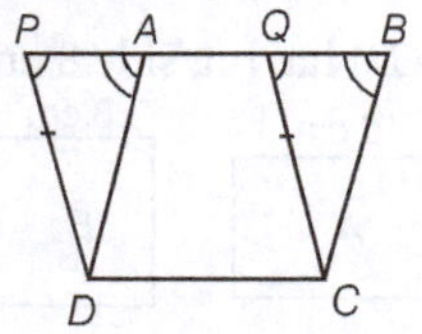

To prove Area of parallelogram $ABCD$

= Area of parallelogram $PQCD$

or $\quad$ $ar(\|gm\ ABCD) = ar(\|gm\ PQCD)$

Proof In ΔPDA and ΔQCB,

$\angle DPA = \angle CQB$ [corresponding angles from $PD \parallel QC$ and transversal PB] ...(i)

$\angle PAD = \angle QBC$ [corresponding angles from $AD \parallel BC$ and transversal PB] ...(ii)

Then, $\angle PDA = \angle QCB$

[by angle sum property of a triangle] ...(iii)

Also, $\quad PD = QC$

[$\because$ opposite sides of the parallelogram are equal] ...(iv)

So, $\quad \Delta PDA \cong \Delta QCB$ $\quad$ [by ASA congruence rule]

$\therefore$ $ar(\Delta PDA) = ar(\Delta QCB)$

[$\because$ congruent figures have equal areas] ...(v)

Now, adding area of trapezium $AQCD$ on both sides of Eq. (v), we get

$ar(\Delta PDA) + ar(\text{trapezium } AQCD)$

$= ar(\Delta QCB) + ar(\text{trapezium } AQCD)$

$\Rightarrow \quad ar(\|gm\ PQCD) = ar(\|gm\ ABCD)$

Hence, parallelograms on the same base and between the same parallels are equal in area. **Hence proved.**

Corollary 1. *The area of a parallelogram is equal to the product of its base and corresponding altitude height.*

Let $ABCD$ be a parallelogram in which AB is the base and AL is the height.

To prove $ar(\|gm\ ABCD) = AB \times AL$

Construction Draw $BM \perp DC$ and $AL \perp CD$ extended, so that rectangle $ABML$ is formed.

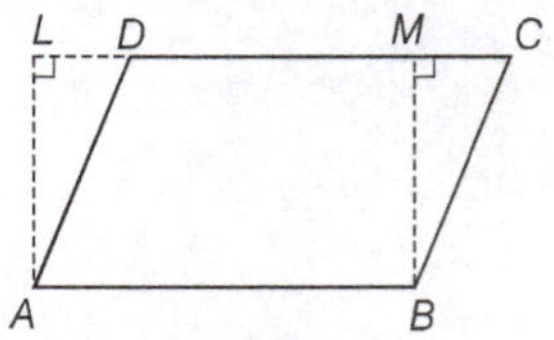

Proof Clearly, $\|gm\ ABCD$ and rectangle $ABML$ are on the same base AB and between the same parallel lines AB and LC.

$\therefore$ $ar(\|gm\ ABCD) = ar(\text{rectangle } ABML)$

$= AB \times AL$

$\therefore$ Area of a parallelogram = Base $\times$ Height

Hence proved.

Corollary 2. *Parallelograms on equal bases (or same base) and between the same parallels are equal in area.*

Let $ABCD$ and $PQRS$ be two parallelograms with equal bases AB and PQ and between the same parallels AQ and DR.

To prove $ar(\|gm\ ABCD) = ar(\|gm\ PQRS)$

Construction Draw $DL \perp AB$ (produced) and $RM \perp PQ$ (produced).

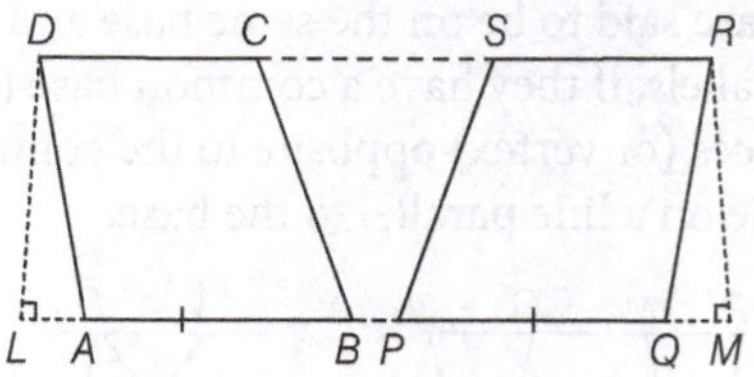

Proof $\because$ $AB = PQ$ and we know that perpendicular distance between parallel lines are equal, therefore

$DL = RM$

Now, ar (||gm $ABCD$) = $AB \times DL$

and ar (||gm $PQRS$) = $PQ \times RM = PQ \times DL$

[∵ area of a parallelogram = base × height]

⇒ ar (||gm $ABCD$) = ar (||gm $PQRS$) **Hence proved.**

Corollary 3. *If a triangle and a parallelogram are on the same bases and between the same parallels, then area of the triangle is equal to half of the area of parallelogram.*

Let ΔABP and ||gm $ABCD$ be on the same base AB and between the same parallels AB and PC.

To prove ar $(\Delta ABP) = \frac{1}{2}$ ar (||gm $ABCD$)

Construction Draw $BQ \parallel AP$ to get another parallelogram $ABQP$.

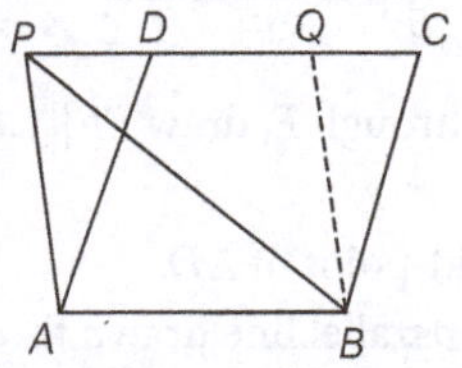

Proof Since, parallelograms $ABCD$ and $ABQP$ lie on the same base AB and between the same parallels AB and PC.

So, by the theorem, ar (||gm $ABCD$) = ar (||gm $ABQP$) ...(i)

Now, as diagonal PB of parallelogram $ABQP$ divides it into two congruent ΔABP and ΔQPB.

∴ ar (ΔABP) = ar (ΔQPB) ...(ii)

∵ ar (ΔABP) + ar (ΔQPB) = ar (||gm $ABQP$)

⇒ ar (ΔABP) + ar (ΔABP) = ar (||gm $ABQP$)

[using Eq. (ii)]

⇒ 2ar (ΔABP) = ar (||gm $ABQP$)

⇒ ar $(\Delta ABP) = \frac{1}{2}$ ar (||gm $ABQP$)

⇒ ar $(\Delta ABP) = \frac{1}{2}$ ar (||gm $ABCD$)

[using Eq.(i)]

Hence proved.

Alternate Method

Construction Draw $PL \perp AB$ and $CM \perp AB$, meeting AB produced at L and M.

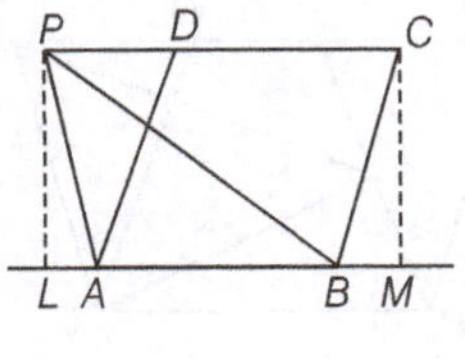

Proof Since, L, A, B and M are collinear and $AB \parallel PC$.

∴ $PL = CM$ ...(i)

[∵ perpendicular distance between parallel lines is always same]

Now, ar $(\Delta ABP) = \frac{1}{2} \times AB \times PL$

$\left[\because \text{area of a triangle} = \frac{1}{2} \times \text{base} \times \text{height}\right]$

⇒ ar $(\Delta ABP) = \frac{1}{2} \times AB \times CM$ [from Eq.(i)]

⇒ ar $(\Delta ABP) = \frac{1}{2}$ ar (||gm $ABCD$)

[∵ area of a parallelogram = base × height]

Hence proved.

Note

- Area of a triangle = $\frac{1}{2}$ × Base × Height
- Area of a trapezium = $\frac{1}{2}$ (Sum of length of parallel sides) × (Distance between parallel sides)
- Diagonal of a parallelogram divide it into four triangles of equal areas.

Types of Problems

There are mainly two types of problems related to area of parallelograms on the same base and between the same parallels, which are given below

Type I Problems Based on Calculating the Numerical Values of Different Terms

In this type of problems, numerical values of some terms of parallelogram are given and we have to find other terms, like sides of parallelogram, area, ratio of area etc. by using the given informations.

Example 2. In the following figure, *ABCD* is a parallelogram, $AE \perp DC$ and $CF \perp AD$. If $CD = 18$ cm, $AE = 9$ cm and $CF = 10$ cm, then find *AD*.

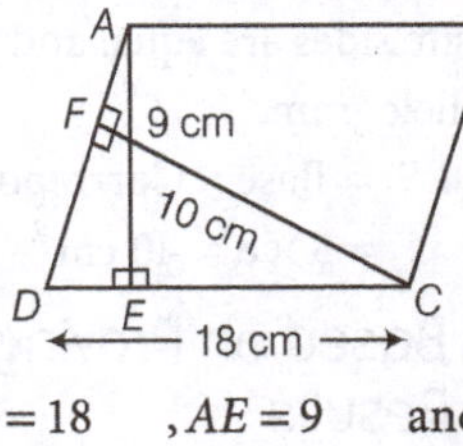

Sol. We have, $CD = 18$, $AE = 9$ and $CF = 10$ cm

We know that,

Area of a parallelogram = Base × Height

∴ ar (||gm $ABCD$) = $CD \times AE$ [∵ base = CD, height = AE]

$= 18 \times 9 = 162$ cm ...(i)

Again, area of a parallelogram $ABCD = AD \times CF$

[$\because$ base $= AD$, height $= CF$]

$\Rightarrow \quad 162 = AD \times 10$ [using Eq. (i)]

$\therefore \quad AD = \dfrac{162}{10} = 16.2$ cm

Example 3. **The perimeter of an isosceles triangle is 32 cm and its base is 12 cm. One of its equal side forms the diagonal of a parallelogram. Find the area of parallelogram.**

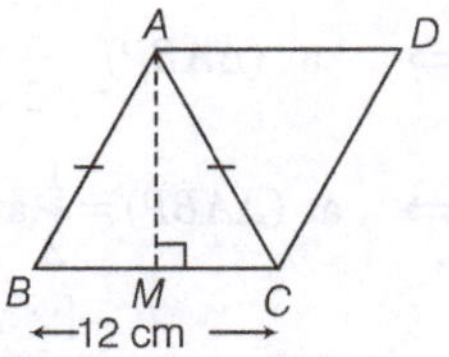

Sol. Let ABC be an isosceles triangle with base $BC = 12$ cm, perimeter $= 32$ cm and AC is a diagonal of a parallelogram $ABCD$.

Draw $AM \perp BC$.

So, $BM = CM = \dfrac{12}{2} = 6$ cm

Also, $AB = AC = \dfrac{32-12}{2} = 10$ cm

[$\because AB + BC + AC = 32$]

Now, $AM = \sqrt{AC^2 - CM^2} = \sqrt{10^2 - 6^2}$

$= \sqrt{100-36} = \sqrt{64} = 8$ cm

$\therefore$ Area of a parallelogram $ABCD = BC \times AM$

$= 12 \times 8 = 96\ \text{cm}^2$

Example 4. **In the adjacent figure, *PQRS* is a quadrilateral such that diagonal $QS \perp SR$ as well as $QS \perp PQ$. Find out ar(quad. *PQRS*).**

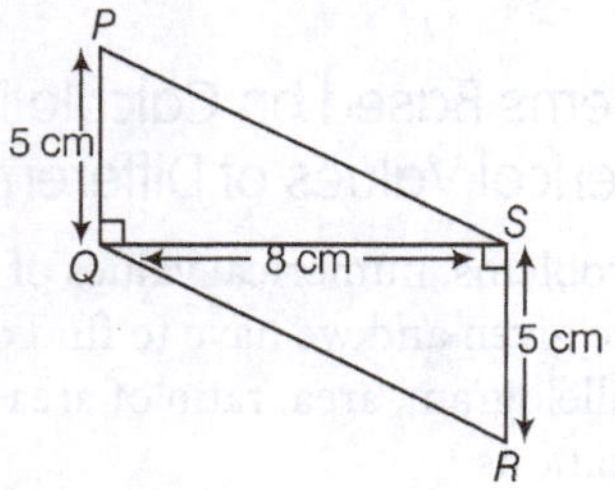

Sol. We observe that, $\angle PQS = \angle QSR$ [each 90°, given]

But these are alternate angles.

$\therefore \quad PQ \parallel SR$ ...(i)

Also, $PQ = SR$ [each 5 cm, given] ...(ii)

i.e. a pair of opposite sides are equal and parallel.

So, $PQRS$ is a parallelogram.

Hence, ar($\parallel$gm $PQRS$) = Base × Corresponding altitude

$= 5 \times 8 = 40\ \text{cm}^2$

Type II Problems Based on Proving/Showing the Given Results

In this type of problem, some informations about the figures are given and we have to prove/show the given results with the help of given informations.

Example 5. **In the adjacent figure, *ABCD* is a parallelogram and E is mid-point of *BC*. prove that *ar* (Δ*DEC*) = $\frac{1}{4}$ *ar* (∥gm *ABCD*).**

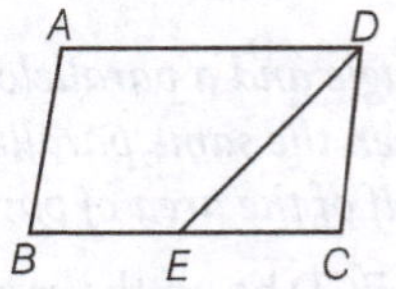

Sol. ***Given*** $ABCD$ is a parallelogram and E is mid-point of BC.

To prove ar (ΔDEC) $= \dfrac{1}{4}$ ar ($\parallel$gm $ABCD$)

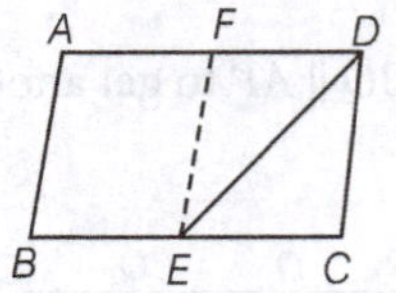

Construction Through E, draw $EF \parallel CD$, which meets AD at F.

Clearly, F is a mid-point of AD.

[$\because$ a parallel line drawn through the mid-point of a side of a parallelogram, bisect the opposite side]

Thus, $ABEF$ and $FECD$ are parallelograms.

[$\because$ opposite sides are parallel]

Now, as the parallelograms $ABEF$ and $FECD$ lie on the equal bases AB and CD, and between the same parallel AD and BC.

$\therefore \quad$ ar ($\parallel$gm $ABEF$) = ar ($\parallel$gm $FECD$)

$\Rightarrow \quad$ ar ($\parallel$gm $FECD$) $= \dfrac{1}{2}$ ar ($\parallel$gm $ABCD$)

[$\because$ ar ($\parallel$gm $ABCD$) = ar ($\parallel$gm $ABEF$) + ar ($\parallel$gm $FECD$)]

$\Rightarrow \quad$ ar (ΔEDF) + ar (ΔDEC) $= \dfrac{1}{2}$ ar ($\parallel$gm $ABCD$)

$\Rightarrow \quad$ 2 ar(ΔDEC) $= \dfrac{1}{2}$ ar ($\parallel$gm $ABCD$)

[$\because$ diagonal of a parallelogram divides it into two congruent triangles, so ar (ΔEDF) = ar (ΔDEC)]

$\Rightarrow \quad$ ar (ΔDEC) $= \dfrac{1}{4}$ ar ($\parallel$gm $ABCD$)

Hence proved.

Example 6. **In the given figure, parallelogram ABCD and PBCQ are given. If R is a point on PB, then show that ar (ΔQRC) = $\frac{1}{2}$ ar (∥gm ABCD).**

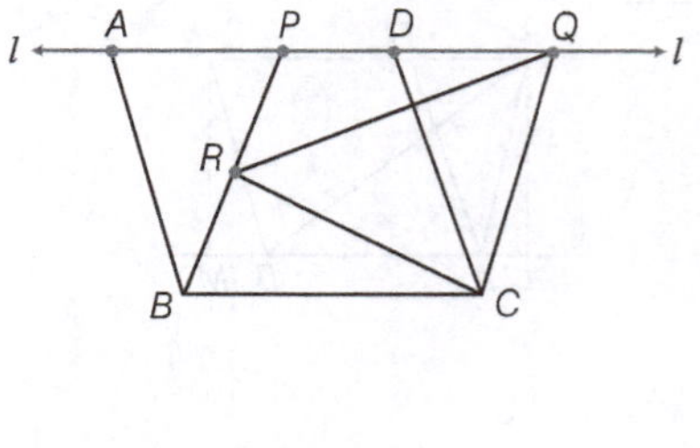

Sol. ***Given*** $ABCD$ and $PBCQ$ are two parallelograms, and R is a point on PB.

To prove $\text{ar}(\Delta QRC) = \frac{1}{2}\text{ar}(\|\text{gm } ABCD)$

Proof Here, parallelograms $PBCQ$ and $ABCD$ lie on the same base BC and between the same parallels BC and AQ.

So, $\text{ar}(\|\text{gm } PBCQ) = \text{ar}(\|\text{gm } ABCD)$ ...(i)

Now, ΔQRC and parallelogram $PBCQ$ lie on the same base CQ and between the same parallels CQ and BP.

So, $\text{ar}(\Delta QRC) = \frac{1}{2}\text{ar}(\|\text{gm } PBCQ)$ ...(ii)

From Eqs. (i) and (ii), we get

$\text{ar}(\Delta QRC) = \frac{1}{2}\text{ar}(\|\text{gm } ABCD)$ **Hence proved.**

Example 7. The diagonals of a parallelogram *ABCD* intersect at point *O*. Through *O*, a line is drawn to intersect *AD* at *P* and *BC* at *Q*. Show that *PQ* divides the parallelogram into two parts of equal areas.

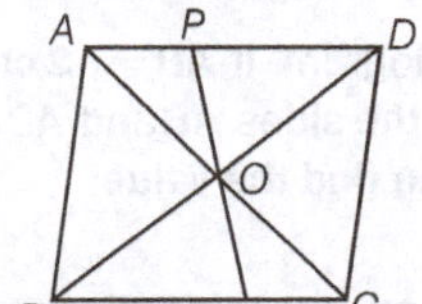

Sol. ***Given*** A parallelogram $ABCD$ whose diagonals AC and BD intersect at point O. Also, a line PQ intersects BC at Q and AD at P.

To prove PQ divides the parallelogram $ABCD$ into two parts of equal areas, i.e. $\text{ar}(ABQP) = \text{ar}(QPDC)$.

Proof Here, AC is the diagonal of the parallelogram $ABCD$. [$\because$ diagonal of a parallelogram divide it into two triangles of equal areas]

$\therefore$ $\text{ar}(\Delta ABC) = \text{ar}(\Delta ADC) = \frac{1}{2}\text{ar}(\|\text{gm } ABCD)$ ...(i)

In ΔAOP and ΔCOQ, $OA = OC$

[$\because$ diagonals of a parallelogram bisect each other]

$\angle AOP = \angle COQ$ [vertically opposite angles]

$\angle OAP = \angle OCQ$ [alternate interior angles]

So, $\Delta AOP \cong \Delta COQ$ [by ASA congruence rule]

$\therefore$ $\text{ar}(\Delta AOP) = \text{ar}(\Delta COQ)$

[since, areas of two congruent figures are equal]

On adding $\text{ar}(OPDC)$ both sides, we get

$\text{ar}(\Delta AOP) + \text{ar}(OPDC) = \text{ar}(\Delta COQ) + \text{ar}(OPDC)$

$\Rightarrow$ $\text{ar}(\Delta ADC) = \text{ar}(QPDC)$

$\Rightarrow$ $\frac{1}{2}\text{ar}(\|\text{gm } ABCD) = \text{ar}(QPDC)$ [from Eq. (i)]

$\Rightarrow$ $\text{ar}(QPDC) = \frac{1}{2}\text{ar}(\|\text{gm } ABCD)$ ...(ii)

Similarly, $\text{ar}(ABQP) = \frac{1}{2}\text{ar}(\|\text{gm } ABCD)$ ...(iii)

From Eqs. (ii) and (iii), we get

$\text{ar}(ABQP) = \text{ar}(QPDC)$

Hence, PQ divides the parallelogram into two parts of equal areas. **Hence proved.**

Example 8. *ABCD* is a trapezium with parallel sides *AB* = *a* cm and *DC* = *b* cm. *E* and *F* are the mid-points of the non-parallel sides. Find the ratio of ar (*ABFE*) and ar (*EFCD*).

Sol. Given, $AB = a$ cm, $DC = b$ cm and $AB \parallel DC$

Also, E and F are the mid-points of AD and BC, respectively.

So, distance between DC, EF and AB, EF will be same say h.

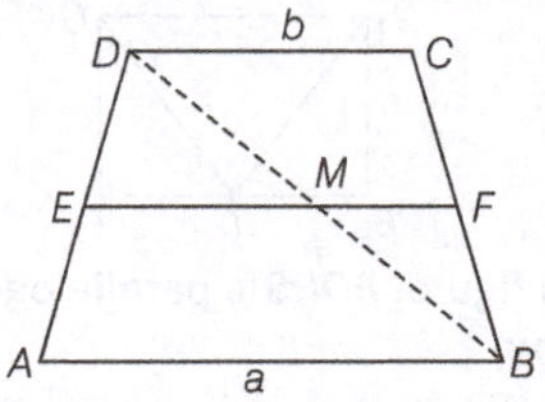

Join BD which intersects EF at M.

Now, in ΔABD, E is the mid-point of AD and $EM \parallel AB$.

So, M is the mid-point of BD.

Also, $EM = \frac{1}{2}AB$ [by mid-point theorem] ...(i)

Similarly, in ΔCBD, $MF = \frac{1}{2}CD$ ...(ii)

On adding Eqs. (i) and (ii), we get

$$EM + MF = \frac{1}{2}AB + \frac{1}{2}CD$$

$\Rightarrow$ $EF = \frac{1}{2}(AB + CD) = \frac{1}{2}(a+b)$

$\therefore$ Area of trapezium $ABFE$

$= \frac{1}{2}$ (Sum of lenght of a parallel sides) $\times$ (Distance between parallel sides)

$$= \frac{1}{2}\left[a + \frac{1}{2}(a+b)\right] \times h = \frac{1}{4}(3a+b)\,h$$

and area of trapezium $EFCD$

$$= \frac{1}{2}\left[b + \frac{1}{2}(a+b)\right] \times h = \frac{1}{4}(3b+a)h$$

$\therefore$ Required ratio $= \dfrac{\text{Area of } ABFE}{\text{Area of } EFCD}$

$$= \frac{\frac{1}{4}(3a+b)h}{\frac{1}{4}(3b+a)h}$$

$$= \frac{(3a+b)}{(a+3b)} \text{ or } (3a+b):(a+3b)$$

Try These 13.1

1. Identify the following figures, in which have same base and same parallels.

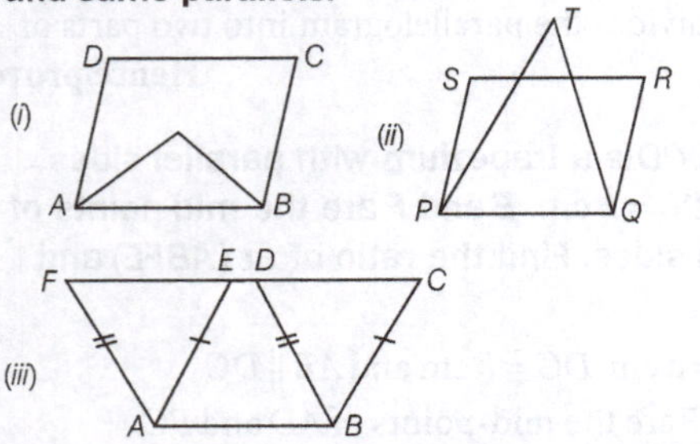

2. In the given figure, area of rectangle *EFGH* is 400 cm². If *L* is any point on *EF*, then find the area of ΔLGH.

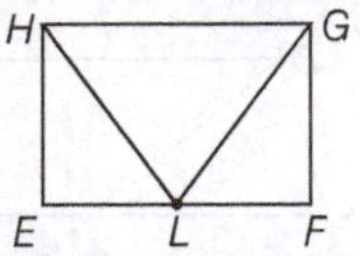

3. In the given figure, *PQRS* is parallelogram, then find the area of ΔPQX.

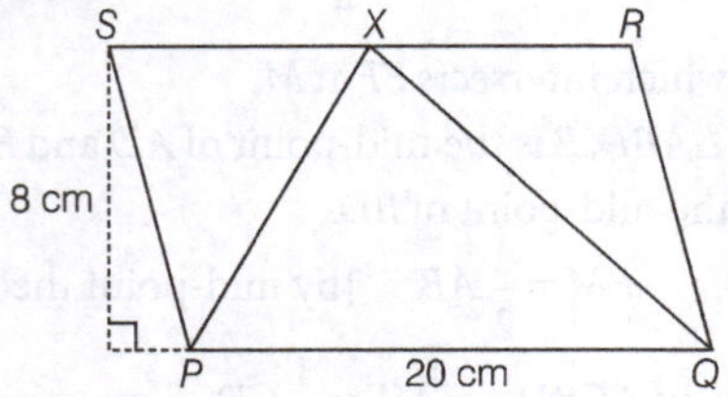

4. If the area, base and corresponding altitude of a parallelogram are x^2, $x-3$ and $x+4$ respectively, then find the value of *x*.

5. A rectangle and a parallelogram are on the same base and between same parallels. If the height of parallelogram is 4 cm and the length of base of rectangle is 8 cm, then find the area of parallelogram.

6. In the given figure, *ABCD* is a parallelogram, $AL \perp BC$, $AM \perp CD$, $AL = 4$ cm and $AM = 5$ cm. If $BC = 6.5$ cm, then find the value of *CD*.

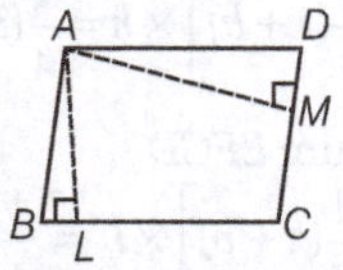

7. In the given figure, *AD* is the median and *E* is any point on *AC*, such that ar (ΔADE):ar (ΔABD) = 2 : 3, then find the ratio of ar (ΔEDC):ar (ΔABC).

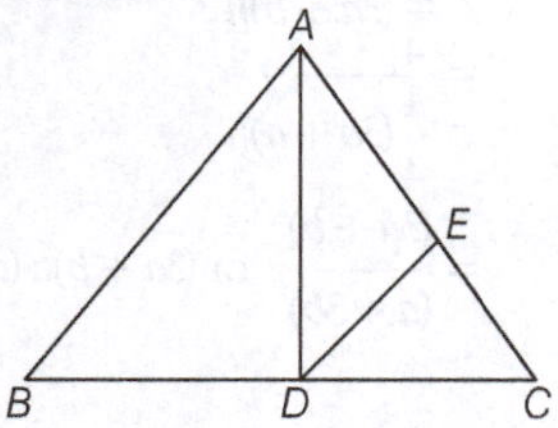

8. In the given figure, *D* is the mid-point of *BC* and *L* is the mid-point of *AD*. If ar (ΔABC) = *x* ar (ΔBDL), then find the value of *x*.

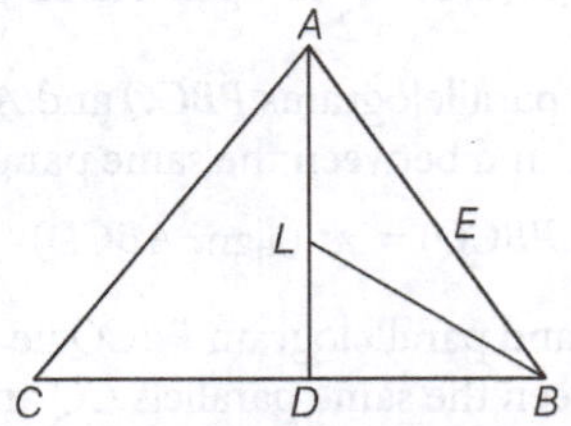

9. In a parallelogram *PQRS*, *PQ* = 8 cm and *PS* = 3 cm. If ar (||gm *PQRS*) = 48 cm², then find *SM* and *QT* (see the figure shown below).

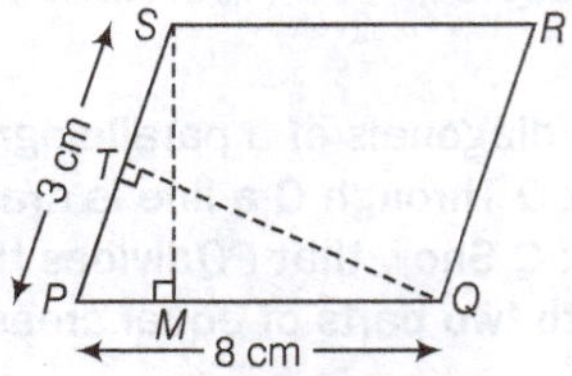

10. *ABCD* is a parallelogram. If *AB* = 7.2 cm and the altitudes corresponding to the sides *AB* and *AD* are respectively 10 cm and 8 cm, then find the value of *AD*.

11. The perimeter of an isosceles triangle is 16 cm and its base is 6 cm. One of its equal side forms the diagonal of a parallelogram. Find the area of parallelogram.

12. *ABCD* is a suqare. *E* and*F* are respectively the mid-points of *BC* and *CD*. If *R* is the mid-point of *EF*. Prove that ar (ΔAER) = ar (ΔAFR).

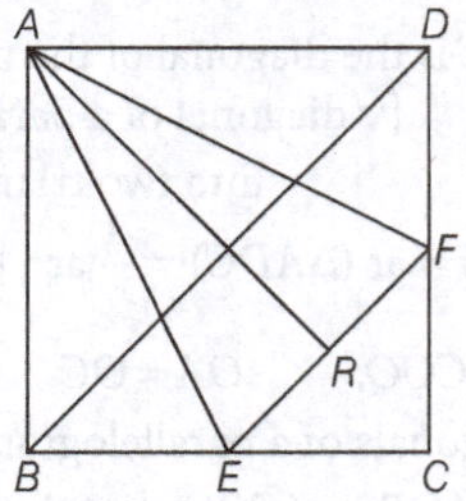

13. In the given figure, *ABCD* is a parallelogram and *EFCD* is a rectangle, $AL \perp CD$ and $CF \perp AB$. Prove that ar (||gm *ABCD*) = ar(*EFCD*).

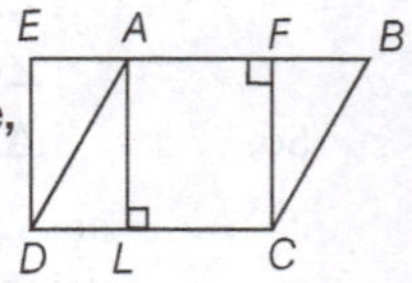

14. In the given figure, if *l* || *m* and quadrilaterals *ABCD*, *CDEF* and *EFGH* are parallelograms, then prove that ar (||gm *ABCD*) = ar (||gm *EFGH*).

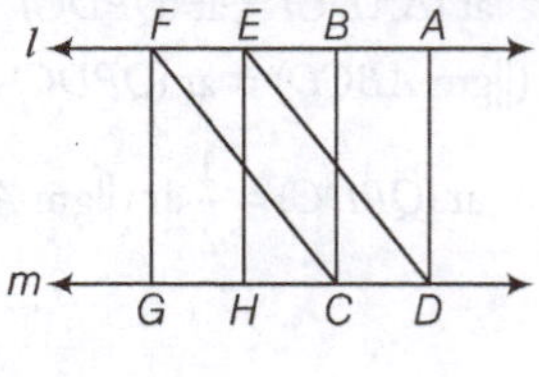

15. **Show that the line segment joining the mid-points of a pair of opposite sides of a parallelogram divides it into two parallelograms of equal areas.**

16. **In trapezium *ABCD*, *AB* || *DC* and *L* is mid-point of *BC*. Through *L*, a line *PQ* || *AD* has been drawn which meets *AB* in *P* and *DC* produced in *Q*.**
Prove that ar (*ABCD*) = ar (*APQD*). NCERT Exemplar

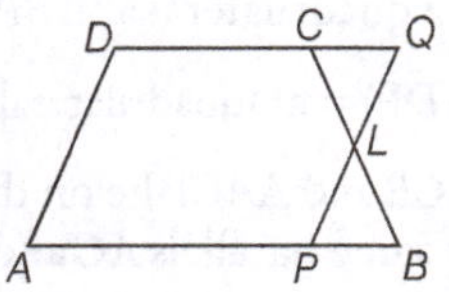

Hints & Answers

1 (*iii*) *ABCE* and *ABDF* are on same base *AB* and between same parallel *AB* and *FC*.

2 **Hint** Since a triangle and a parallelogram are on the same bases and between the same parallels, therefore area of the triangle is equal to the half of the area of parallelogram.

$\therefore$ Area of triangle $= \frac{1}{2}(400) = 200 \text{ cm}^2$

3 Solve as Q2, **Ans.** 80 cm^2

4 **Hint** $\because$ Area of a parallelogram = base × altitude

$\therefore \quad x^2 = (x-3)\times(x+4)$

$\Rightarrow \quad x^2 = x^2 + x - 12 \Rightarrow x = 12$

5 **Hint** Area of rectangle = area of parallelogram

$= 4\times 8 = 32$ cm

6 Solve as Example 2 **Ans.** 5.2 cm

7 **Hint** $\frac{\text{ar}(\Delta ADE)}{\text{ar}(\Delta ABD)} = \frac{2}{3} \Rightarrow \frac{\text{ar}(\Delta ADE)}{\text{ar}(\Delta ADC)} = \frac{2}{3}$

$\Rightarrow 3\,\text{ar}(\Delta ADE) = 2\,\text{ar}(\Delta ADC)$

$\Rightarrow 3[\text{ar}(\Delta ADC) - \text{ar}(\Delta EDC)] = 2\text{ar}(\Delta ADC)$

$\Rightarrow \text{ar}(\Delta EDC) = \frac{1}{3}\text{ar}(\Delta ADC) = \frac{1}{3}\times\frac{1}{2}\text{ar}(\Delta ABC)$

$\Rightarrow \text{ar}(\Delta EDC) = \frac{1}{6}\text{ar}(\Delta ABC)$ **Ans.** 1 : 6

8 Solve as Q7. **Ans.** $x = \frac{1}{4}$

9 Solve as Example 2 **Ans.** $SM = 6$ cm, $QT = 16$ cm

10 Solve as Example 2. **Ans.** 9 cm

11 Solve as Example 3. **Ans.** 24cm

12 **Hint** Since, *R* is is the mid-point of *EF*.

$\therefore$ *AR* is the median in ΔAEF.

As, a median of a triangle divides it into two triangles of equal area.

$\therefore \quad \text{ar}(\Delta AER) = \text{ar}(\Delta AFR)$.

13 **Hint** Since parallelograms on same base and between the same parallels are equal in area.

14 **Hint** Since parallelograms on same base and between the same parallels are equal in area.

15 Solve as Example 7.

16 **Hint** In ΔCLQ and ΔBLP,

$CL = BL$ [since, *L* is the mid-point of *BC*]

$\angle LCQ = \angle LBP$

[alternate interior angles as *BC* is a transversal]

$\angle CQL = \angle LPB$

[alternate interior angles as *PQ* is a transversal]

$\therefore \quad \Delta CLQ \cong \Delta BLP$ [by AAS congruence rule]

Then, $\text{ar}(\Delta CLQ) = \text{ar}(\Delta BLP)$ ...(i)

[since, congruent triangles have equal area]

Now,

$\text{ar}(ABCD) = \text{ar}(APQD) - \text{ar}(\Delta CQL) + \text{ar}(\Delta BLP)$

$= \text{ar}(APQD) - \text{ar}(\Delta BLP) + \text{ar}(\Delta BLP)$ [from Eq. (i)]

$\Rightarrow \quad \text{ar}(ABCD) = \text{ar}(APQD)$

TOPIC 02 Triangles on the Same Base and Between the Same Parallels

Triangles are said to be on the same base and between the same parallels, if their bases are common (same) and the vertices opposite to common base lie on a line parallel to the common base.

Areas of Triangles on the Same Base and between the Same Parallels

Theorem 1 ***Two triangles on the same base (or equal bases) and between the same parallels are equal in area.***

Let ΔPQR and ΔSQR be on the same base *QR* and between the same parallels *PS* and *QR*.

To prove $\text{ar}(\Delta PQR) = \text{ar}(\Delta SQR)$

Construction Draw *AR* || *PQ* and *BR* || *SQ*. Thus, we get two parallelograms *PQRA* and *SQRB*.

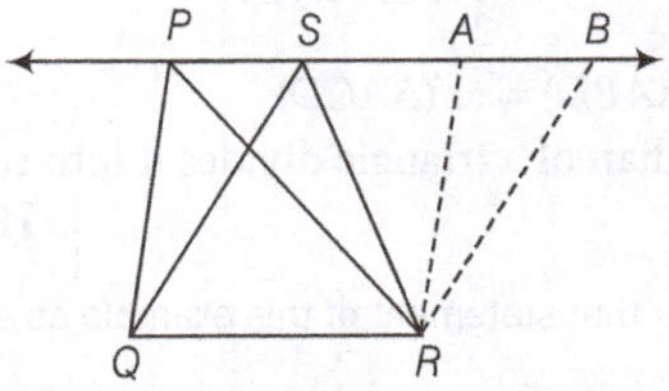

Proof Here, parallelograms *PQRA* and *SQRB* lie on the same base *QR* and between the same parallels *QR* and *PB*.

$\therefore \quad \text{ar}(\|\text{gm}PQRA) = \text{ar}(\|\text{gm}SQRB)$ ...(i)

Now, in parallelogram $PQRA$, diagonal PR divides it into two congruent triangles.

$\therefore \qquad \Delta PQR \cong \Delta PRA$

So, $\qquad ar(\Delta PQR) = ar(\Delta PRA)$

$\Rightarrow \qquad ar(\Delta PQR) = \frac{1}{2} ar(||gm PQRA) \qquad ...(ii)$

Similarly, in parallelogram $SQRB$, diagonal SR divides it into two congruent triangles.

$\therefore \qquad \Delta SQR \cong \Delta SRB$

So, $\qquad ar(\Delta SQR) = ar(\Delta SRB)$

$\Rightarrow \qquad ar(\Delta SQR) = \frac{1}{2} ar(||gm SQRB) \qquad ...(iii)$

Now, from Eqs. (i), (ii) and (iii), we get

$ar(\Delta PQR) = ar(\Delta SQR)$

Hence, the triangles on same base and between same parallels are equal in area.

Note
- Area of a triangle is half the product of its base (any side) and the height (perpendicular distance between vertex and base).
- Two triangles with same base (equal bases) and equal areas will have equal heights.

Theorem 2 **(Converse of Theorem 1)** ***Two triangles having the same base (or equal bases) and equal areas lie between the same parallels.***

Example 1. **Show that a median of a triangle divides it into two triangles of equal areas.**

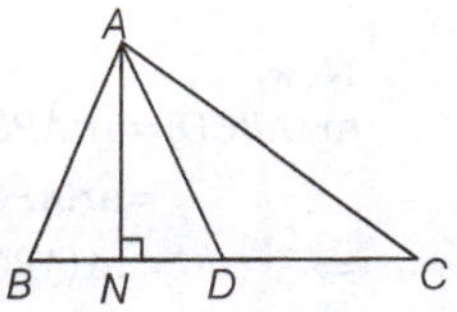

Sol. Let AD be a median of ΔABC.

To prove $\quad ar(\Delta ABD) = ar(\Delta ACD)$

Construction $\quad$ Draw $AN \perp BC$.

Proof $\quad$ Since, AD is a median of ΔABC. So, D is the mid-point of BC.

$\therefore \qquad BD = CD \qquad ...(i)$

Now, $ar(\Delta ABD) = \frac{1}{2} \times BD \times AN$

$\left[\because \text{area of a triangle} = \frac{1}{2} \times \text{base} \times \text{height}\right]$

$= \frac{1}{2} \times CD \times AN \qquad$ [from Eq. (i)]

$\Rightarrow \qquad ar(\Delta ABD) = ar(\Delta ACD)$

Hence, median of a triangle divides it into two triangles of equal areas. **Hence proved.**

Note Remember that statement of this example as a result.

Example 2. **In the adjacent figure, ABCD is a quadrilateral. BP is drawn parallel to AC and BP meets DC (produced) at P. Prove that ar(ΔADP) = ar(quadrilateral ABCD).**

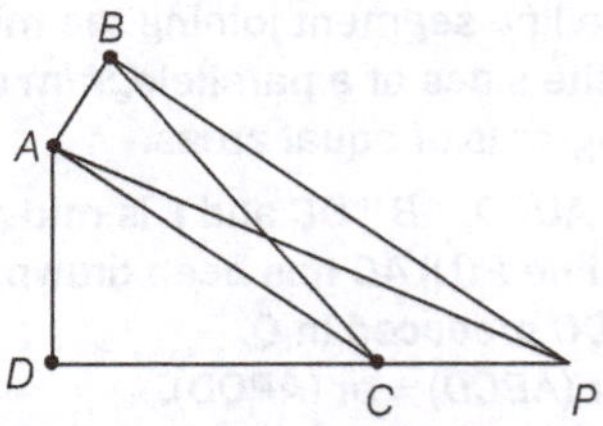

Sol. ***Given*** $ABCD$ is a quadrilateral and $BP \parallel AC$.

To prove $\quad ar(\Delta ADP) = ar(\text{quadrilateral } ABCD)$

Proof Here, ΔACB and ΔACP lie on the same base AC and between the same parallels AC and BP.

So, by the theorem, $ar(\Delta ACB) = ar(\Delta ACP)$

On adding $ar(\Delta ADC)$ both sides, we get

$ar(\Delta ACB) + ar(\Delta ADC) = ar(\Delta ACP) + ar(\Delta ADC)$

$\Rightarrow \qquad ar(ABCD) = ar(\Delta ADP)$ **Hence proved.**

Example 3. **ABCD is a parallelogram in which BC is produced to E such that CE = BC. AE intersects CD at F. If ar(ΔDFB) = 3 cm^2, then find the area of the parallelogram ABCD.**

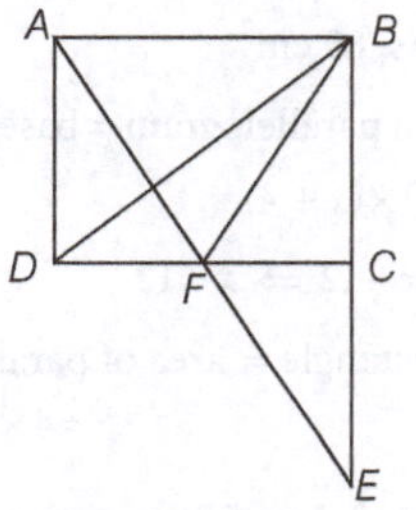

Sol. Given, $ABCD$ is a parallelogram and $CE = BC$ i.e. C is the mid-point of BE.

Also, $\qquad ar(\Delta DFB) = 3 \text{ cm}^2$

Since, ΔDFB and ΔADF are on same base DF and between same parallels AB and DF.

$\therefore \qquad ar(\Delta ADF) = ar(\Delta DFB) = 3 \text{ cm}^2 \qquad ...(i)$

Now, in ΔABE, by converse of mid-point theorem,

$EF = AF$

[$\because C$ is the mid-point of BE]...(ii)

In ΔADF and ΔCFE,

$\angle AFD = \angle CFE \qquad$ [vertically opposite angles]

$AF = EF \qquad$ [from Eq. (ii)]

and $\qquad \angle DAF = \angle CEF \qquad$ [alternate interior angles]

$\therefore \qquad \Delta ADF \cong \Delta ECF \qquad$ [by ASA congruence rule]

$\Rightarrow \qquad ar(\Delta ADF) = ar(\Delta CFE)$

[$\because$ congruent figures have equal area]

$\therefore \quad ar(\Delta CFE) = ar(\Delta ADF) = 3 \text{ cm}^2 \qquad$ [from Eq. (i)] ...(iii)

Now, in ΔBFE, C is the mid-point of BE, i.e. CF is the median of ΔBFE.

$\therefore \qquad ar(\Delta CEF) = ar(\Delta BFC)$

[$\because$ median of a triangle divides it into two triangles of equal area]

Using Eq. (iii), we get

$$\text{ar}(\Delta BFC) = 3 \text{ cm}^2 \quad \text{...(iv)}$$

Now, we have

$$\text{ar}(\Delta BDC) = \text{ar}(\Delta DFB) + \text{ar}(\Delta BFC)$$
$$= 3 + 3 = 6 \text{ cm}^2$$

[using Eqs. (i) and (iv)]

In parallelogram $ABCD$,

$$\text{ar}(\Delta ABD) = \text{ar}(\Delta BDC)$$

[∵ diagonal of a parallelogram divides it into two triangles of equal area]

or $\text{ar}(\Delta BDC) = \frac{1}{2} \text{ar}(\|\text{gm } ABCD)$

∴ $\text{ar}(\|\text{gm } ABCD) = 2 \text{ ar}(\Delta BDC)$
$= 2 \times 6 = 12 \text{ cm}^2$

Hence, the area of parallelogram $ABCD$ is 12 cm^2.

Example 4. In the given figure, $ABCD$ is a parallelogram. Points P and Q on BC trisect BC in three equal parts. Prove that

$$\text{ar}(\Delta APQ) = \text{ar}(\Delta DPQ) = \frac{1}{6} \text{ar}(\|\text{gm } ABCD).$$

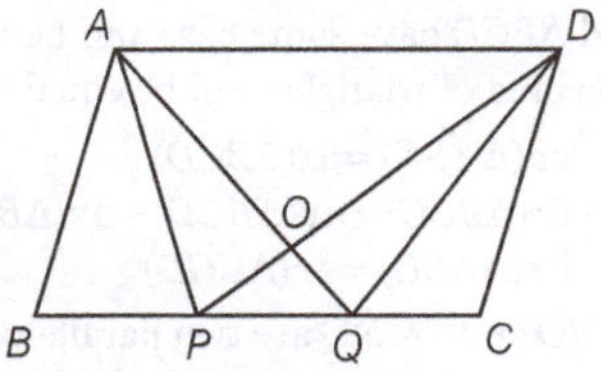

Sol. ***Given*** $ABCD$ is a parallelogram and points P and Q on BC trisect BC in three equal parts, i.e. $BP = PQ = QC$.

To prove

$$\text{ar}(\Delta APQ) = \text{ar}(\Delta DPQ) = \frac{1}{6} \text{ar}(\|\text{gm } ABCD)$$

Construction Join diagonal BD.

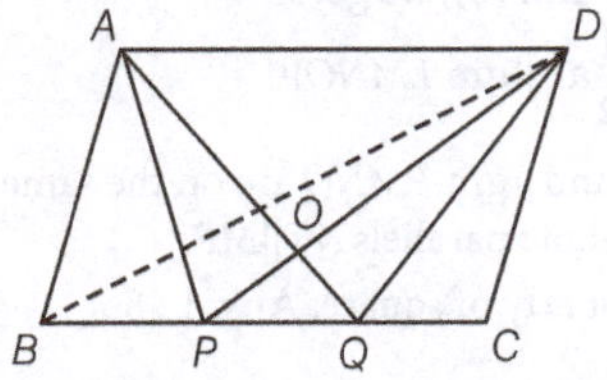

Proof Since, ΔAPQ and ΔDPQ are on the same base PQ and between same parallels AD and PQ.

∴ $\text{ar}(\Delta APQ) = \text{ar}(\Delta DPQ)$ ...(i)

In ΔDBQ, $BP = PQ$ [given]

i.e. P is mid-point of BQ and DP is median of ΔDBQ.

So, $\text{ar}(\Delta DBP) = \text{ar}(\Delta DPQ)$ ...(ii)

[∵ median of a triangle divides it into two triangles of equal area]

Similarly,

$$\text{ar}(\Delta DPQ) = \text{ar}(\Delta DQC) \quad \text{...(iii)}$$

From Eqs. (ii) and (iii), we get

$$\text{ar}(\Delta DBP) = \text{ar}(\Delta DPQ) = \text{ar}(\Delta DQC)$$

⇒ $\text{ar}(\Delta DPQ) = \frac{1}{3} \text{ar}(\Delta DBC)$ ...(iv)

Also, we know that

$$\text{ar}(\Delta DBC) = \frac{1}{2} \text{ar}(\|\text{gm } ABCD) \quad \text{...(v)}$$

[since, diagonal of parallelogram divide it into two triangles of equal area]

From Eqs. (iv) and (v), we get

$$\text{ar}(\Delta DPQ) = \frac{1}{3}\left[\frac{1}{2} \text{ar}(\|\text{gm } ABCD)\right]$$
$$= \frac{1}{6} \text{ar}(\|\text{gm } ABCD) \quad \text{...(vi)}$$

From Eqs. (i) and (vi), we get

$$\text{ar}(\Delta APQ) = \text{ar}(\Delta DPQ) = \frac{1}{6} \text{ar}(\|\text{gm } ABCD)$$

Hence proved.

Try These 13.2

1. **$ABCD$ is a parallelogram and O is the point of intersection of its diagonals (see the figure). If $\text{ar}(\Delta AOD) = 4 \text{ cm}^2$, then find $\text{ar}(\Delta AOB)$.**

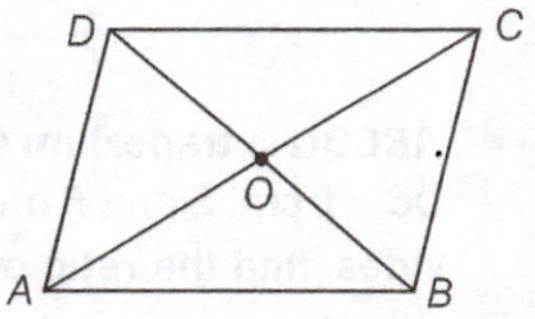

2. **ΔPQR is an equilateral triangle with $PM \perp QR$. Show that $\text{ar}(\Delta PQM) = \text{ar}(\Delta PRM)$.**
3. **If a triangle and a square are on the same base and between the same parallels, then find the ratio of triangle to the area of square.**
4. **In the adjoining figure, ΔABC and ΔEBC are on the same base BC and on the opposite sides of BC. Line segment AE bisects the line segment BC at the point D. Prove that $\text{ar}(\Delta ABE) = \text{ar}(\Delta ACE)$.**

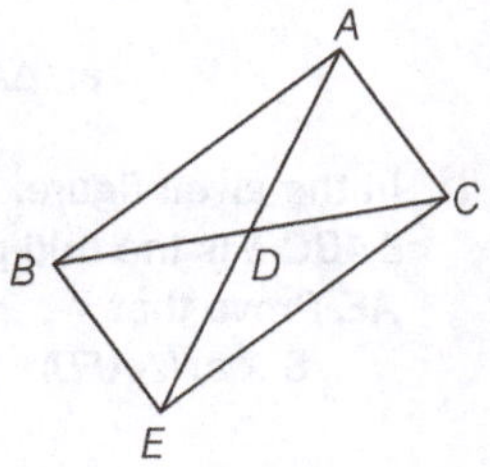

5. **In the given figure, it is given that $AD \| BC$. Prove that $\text{ar}(\Delta CGD) = \text{ar}(\Delta ABG)$.**

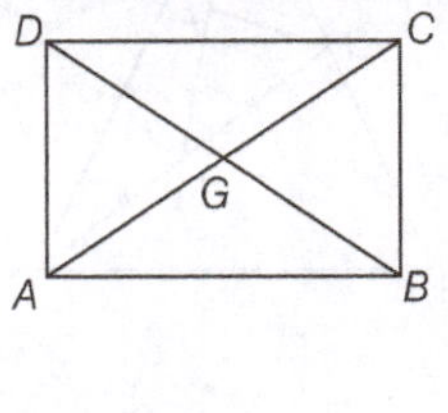

6. **In the given figure $\angle MNO$ and $PMNQ$ are two parallelograms. R is any point on side MP. Show that $ar(\Delta NRQ) = \frac{1}{2} ar(||gm\ LMNO)$**

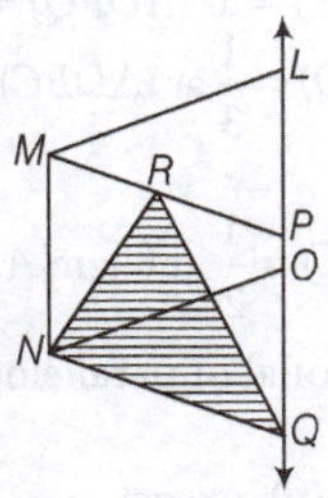

7. **$PQRS$ is a square. N and M are the mid-points of sides SR and QR respectively. O is a point on diagonal PR such that $OP = OR$. Show that $ONRM$ is a square. Also, find the ratio of ar(ΔORM) and ar$(PQRS)$.**

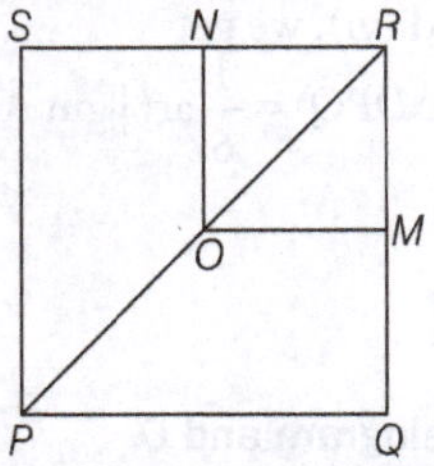

8. **$ABCD$ is a trapezium with parallel sides $AB = a$ cm and $DC = b$ cm, E and F are the mid-points of the non-parallel sides, find the ratio of ar$(ABFE)$ and ar$(EFCD)$.**

9. **$PQRS$ is a trapezium having PS and QR as parallel sides. A is any point on PQ and B is a point on SR such that $AB || QR$. If area of ΔPBQ is $17\ cm^2$, then find the area of ΔASR.**

10. **$ABCD$ is a parallelogram. X and Y are the mid-points of BC and CD, respectively. Prove that**

$$ar(\Delta AXY) = \frac{3}{8} ar(||gm\ ABCD).$$

11. **In the given figure, D is the mid-point of side AB of the ΔABC. E is the mid-point of CD and F is the mid-point of AE. Prove that**

$$8 \times ar(\Delta AFD) = ar(\Delta ABC).$$

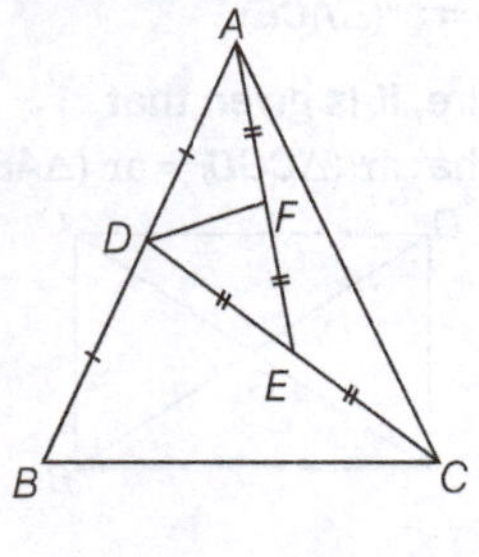

12. **In the given figure, X and Y are the mid-points of AC and AB respectively, $QP || BC$ and CYQ and BXP are straight lines. Prove that ar(ΔABP) = ar(ΔACQ).** NCERT Exemplar

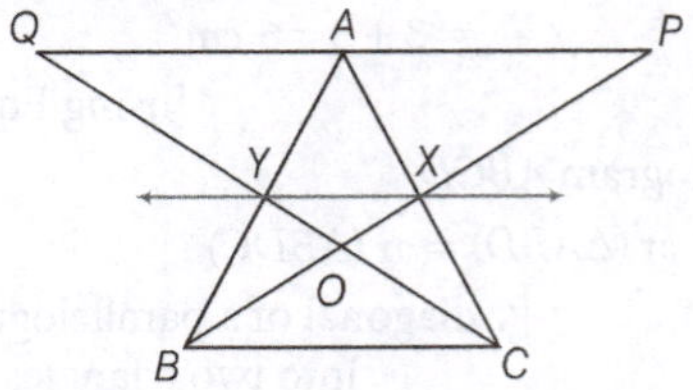

Hints & Answers

1 **Hint** Diagonals of a parallelogram divides equal in areas.

$\therefore$ ar(ΔAOD) = ar$(\Delta AOB) = 4\ cm^2$

2 **Hint** In an equilateral triangle, perpendicular line QR is a median line.

Thus, median of a triangle divides equal in area.

3 **Hint** If a triangle and a parallelogram are on same base and between same parallel lines, then area of triangle will be half of that parallelogram. **Ans.** 1 : 2

4 **Hint** Use property of median of a triangle.

5 **Hint** ΔABC and ΔBCD have same base and between same parallel lines. So area of triangles will be equal.

$\therefore$ ar(ΔABC) = ar(ΔBCD)

$\Rightarrow$ ar(ΔABC) − ar(ΔBCG) = ar(ΔBCD) − ar(ΔBCG)

$\Rightarrow$ ar(ΔABG) = ar(ΔCGD)

6 **Hint** Here, $LMNO$ and $PMNQ$ are two parallelograms on the same base MN and lie between the same parallels $MN || LQ$

$\therefore$ ar(||gm $LMNO$) = ar(||gm $PMNQ$) ...(i)

Also, ΔNRQ and ||gm $PMNQ$ are on the same base NQ and lie between the same parallels $NQ || MP$.

$\therefore$ ar$(\Delta NRQ) = \frac{1}{2}$ ar(||gm $PMNQ$) ...(ii)

From Eqs. (i) and (ii), we get

ar$(\Delta NRQ) = \frac{1}{2}$ ar(||gm $LMNO$)

Also, ΔNRQ and ||gm $PMNQ$ are on the same base NQ an lie between the same parallels $NQ || MP$.

7 **Hint** Use property of square. **Ans.** 1 : 8

8 **Hint**

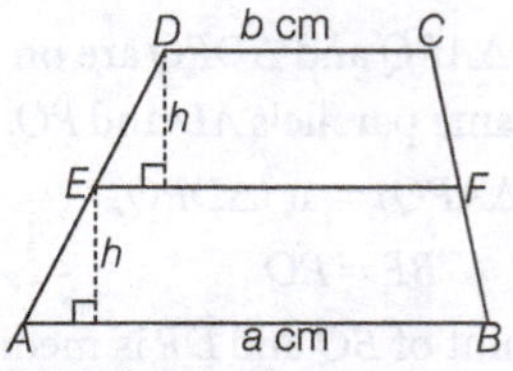

$$EF = \frac{AB + DC}{2} = \frac{a+b}{2}$$

[As E and F are the mid-points of AD and BC]

Now, ar$(ABFE)$:ar$(EFCD)$

$$\frac{1}{2}\left(a+\frac{a+b}{2}\right)h:\frac{1}{2}\left(b+\frac{a+b}{2}\right)h$$

$$(3a+b):(3b+a)$$

9 Now, ar (ΔSAR) = ar (ΔSAB) + ar (ΔABR) ...(i)

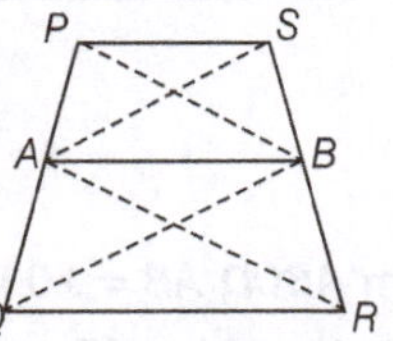

and ar (ΔPBQ) = ar (ΔPBA) + ar (ΔABQ) ...(ii)

Also, ar (ΔABQ) = ar (ΔABR) ...(iii)

and ar (ΔPBA) = ar (ΔSAB) ...(iv)

On adding Eqs (iii) and (iv), we get

ar (ΔABQ) + ar (ΔPBA) = ar (ΔABR) + ar (ΔSAB)

$\therefore$ ar (ΔPBQ) = ar (ΔSAR)

or ar (ΔSAR) = ar (ΔPBQ) = 17 cm^2

10 **Hint** $\because$ ar $(\Delta CYX) = \frac{1}{4}$ ar(ΔDBC) and

ar $(\Delta DBC) = \frac{1}{2}$ ar (||gm $ABCD$)

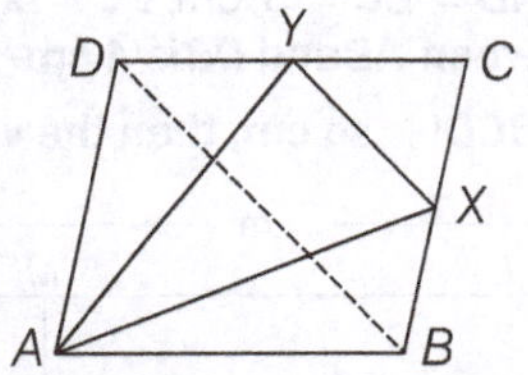

$\therefore$ ar $(\Delta CYX) = \frac{1}{8}$ ar(||gm $ABCD$)

Similarly, ar (ΔAYD) = ar(ΔABX)

$= \frac{1}{4}$ ar (||gm $ABCD$)

Now, ar (ΔAYX) = ar(||gm $ABCD$) − [ar(ΔABX) + ar(ΔAYD) + ar(ΔCYX)]

11 **Hint** Since DF is median of a ΔADE. Therefore

ar $(\Delta AFD) = \frac{1}{2}$ ar (ΔADE)

$= \frac{1}{2} \times \frac{1}{2}$ ar(ΔADC)

$= \times \frac{1}{4} \times \frac{1}{2}$ ar(ΔABC)

$\Rightarrow$ 8 ar(ΔAFD) = ar(ΔABC)

12 **Hint** Here, ΔBYC and ΔBXC lie on same base BC and between the same parallels BC and XY.

So ar(ΔBYC) = ar(ΔBXC)

$\Rightarrow$ ar(ΔBYC) − ar(ΔBOC) = ar(ΔBXC) − ar(ΔBOC) [subtracting ar (ΔBOC)]

$\Rightarrow$ ar(ΔBOY) = ar(ΔCOX)

$\Rightarrow$ ar (ΔBOY) + ar(ΔXOY) = ar(ΔCOX) + ar(ΔXOY) [adding ar (ΔXOY)]

$\Rightarrow$ ar(ΔBYX) = ar(ΔCXY) ...(i)

Hence, we observe that quadrilaterals $XYAP$ and $YXAQ$ are on the same base XY and between the same parallels XY and PQ.

$\therefore$ ar $(XYAP)$ = ar$(YXAQ)$ ...(ii)

On adding Eqs. (i) and (ii), we get

ar (ΔBYX) + ar$(XYAP)$ = ar (ΔCXY) + ar$(YXAQ)$

$\Rightarrow$ ar (ΔABP) = ar (ΔACQ)

REVIEW EXERCISE

Including Competency Based Questions

Part I

Multiple Choice Type Questions

1. The median of a triangle divides it into two

(a) triangles of equal area
(b) congruent triangles
(c) right angled triangles
(d) isosceles triangles

2. Two parallelograms are on equal bases and between the same parallels. The ratio of their areas is

(a) 1 : 2 (b) 1 : 1
(c) 2 : 1 (d) 3 : 1

3. *ABCD* is a quadrilateral whose diagonal *AC* divides it into two parts, equal in area, then *ABCD*

(a) is a rectangle
(b) is always a rhombus
(c) is a parallelogram
(d) need not be any of (a), (b) or (c)

4. If a triangle and a parallelogram are on the same base and between same parallels, then the ratio of the area of the triangle to the area of parallelogram is

(a) 1 : 3 (b) 1 : 2
(c) 3 : 1 (d) 1 : 4

5. In the given figure, $\angle BAD$ and $\angle ADC$ are right angles and $AX \parallel BC$. If $AB = BC = 5$ cm and $DC = 8$ cm, then the area of *ABCX* is

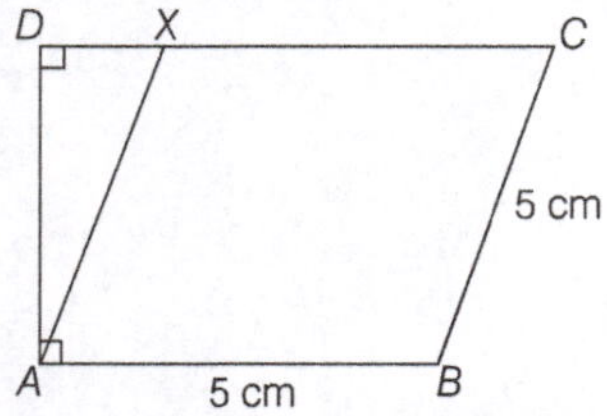

(a) 20 cm^2 (b) 64 cm^2
(c) 32 cm^2 (d) 42 cm^2

6. A point *D* is taken on the side *BC* of a ΔABC such that $BD = 2DC$, then ar (ΔABD) is equal to

(a) ar (ΔADC)
(b) 2 ar (ΔADC)
(c) 3 ar (ΔADC)
(d) 4 ar (ΔADC)

7. In parallelogram *ABCD*, $AB = 10$ cm. The altitudes corresponding to the sides *AB* and *AD* are respectively 7 cm and 8 cm. If *AD* is *K*, then the value of $K - 0.75$ is

(a) 6 cm (b) 7 cm
(c) 8 cm (d) 9 cm

8. *D* is the mid-point of side *BC* of ΔABC and *E* is the mid-point of *BD*. If *O* is the mid-point of *AE*, then ar $(\Delta BOE) = \frac{1}{k}$ ar (ΔABC), then *k* equals

(a) 6 (b) 7
(c) 8 (d) 9

9. In the given figure, *ABCD* is a trapezium in which $AB = 7$ cm, $AD = BC = 5$ cm, $DC = x$ cm and distance between *AB* and *DC* is 4 cm. If the area of trapezium *ABCD* is sq cm, then the value of $\frac{x}{8}$ is

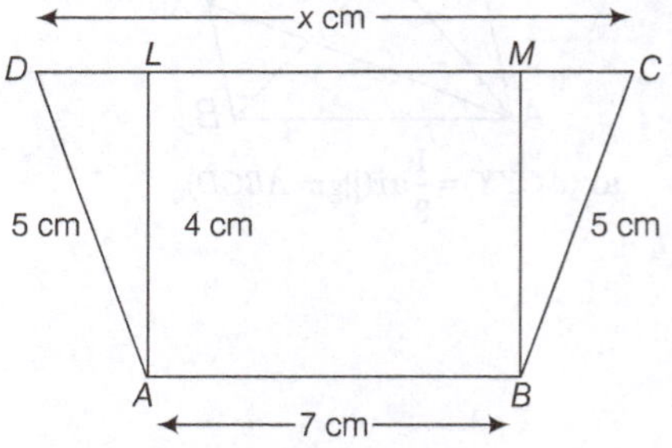

(a) 4 (b) 6
(c) 7 (d) 5

10. In the given figure, if *PQRS* is a quadrilateral such that diagonal $QS \perp SR$ as well as $QS \perp PQ$, then ar (quadrilateral *PQRS*) is

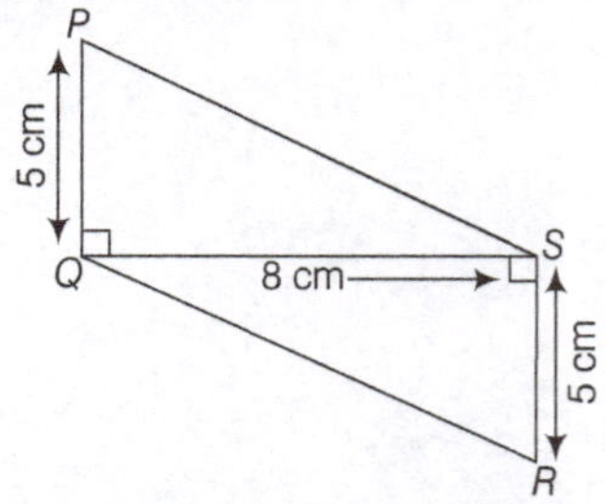

(a) 20 cm^2 (b) 40 cm^2
(c) 60 cm^2 (d) 80 cm^2

Very Short Answer Type Questions

11. Two parallelograms are on same base and between the same parallels. What is the ratio of their areas?

12. If a triangle and parallelogram are on the same base and between same parallels, then find the ratio of the area of the triangle to the area of parallelogram.

13. In parallelogram $ABCD$, $AB = 10$ cm and the altitude corresponding to the sides AB and AD are respectively 7 cm and 8 cm. Find AD.

14. In the given figure, the area of parallelogram $ABCD$ is 120 cm^2, then find the length of BC.

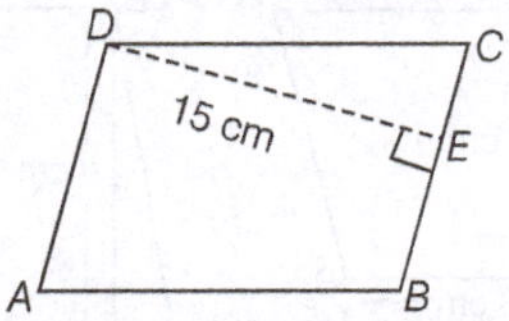

15. In the given figure, $ABCD$ is a rectangle in which $CD = 6$ cm and $AD = 8$ cm. Find the area of parallelogram $CDBF$.

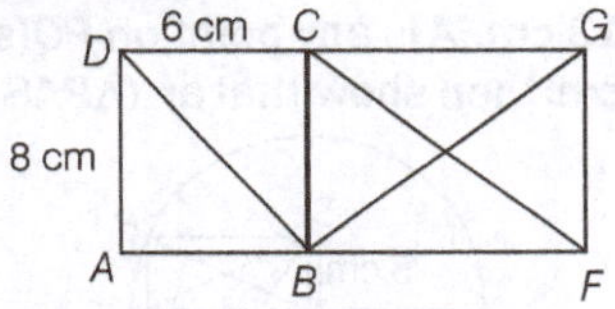

16. $ABCD$ is a parallelogram and Q is any point on the side AD. If ar (ΔQBC) = 10cm^2, then find ar (ΔQAB) + *ar* (ΔQDC).

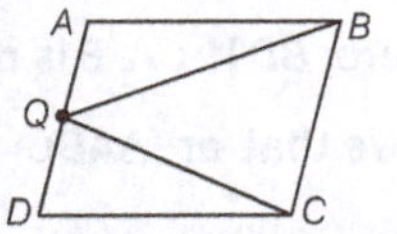

17. BD is one of the diagonals of a quadrilateral $ABCD$. AM and CN are the perpendiculars from A and C, respectively on BD. Show that ar (quadrilateral $ABCD$) $= \frac{1}{2} BD(AM + CN)$.

18. $PQRS$ is a parallelogram, whose area is 180 cm^2 and A is any point on the diagonal QS. Then, the area of $\Delta ASR = 90$ cm^2. This statement is true or false. Why?

Short Answer I Type Questions

19. In a quadrilateral $PQRS$, diagonals PR and QS intersect each other at O such that ar (ΔPOS) = ar (ΔQOR). If distance between sides PQ and SR is 4 cm, $PQ = 3$ cm and $SR = 7$ cm, then find ar ($PQRS$).

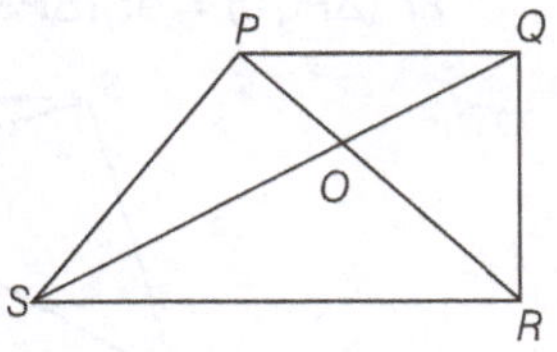

20. In a quadrilateral $ABCD$, it is being given that M is the mid-point of AC. Prove that ar (quadrilateral $ABMD$) = ar (quadrilateral $DMBC$).

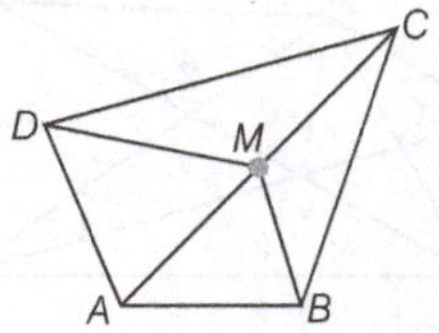

21. $ABCD$ is a parallelogram and X is the mid-point of AB. If ar (ΔADC) = 24 cm^2, then find ar ($AXCD$).

22. XD is a median of ΔXYZ. E is a point on XD such that $XE = ED$. Find ar (ΔYXD) : ar ΔXEZ

23. The medians BE and CF of a ΔABC intersect at G. Prove that ar (ΔGBC) = ar (quadrilateral $AFGE$).

24. In the given figure, area of parallelogram is 80 cm^2. Find

(*i*) ar (||gm $ABEF$)

(*ii*) ar (ΔABD)

(*iii*) ar (ΔBEF).

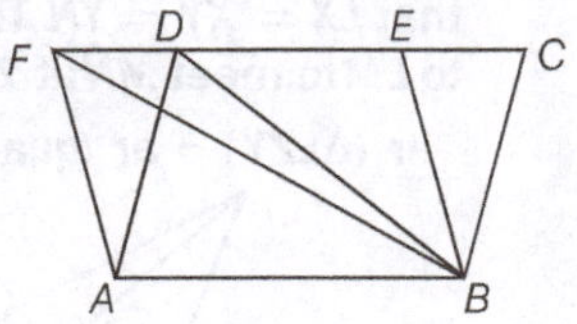

25. $ABCD$ is a trapezium with E being any point on side AB. If AD || EC and DE || BC, then find the ratio ar (ΔDAE) : ar (ΔBEC).

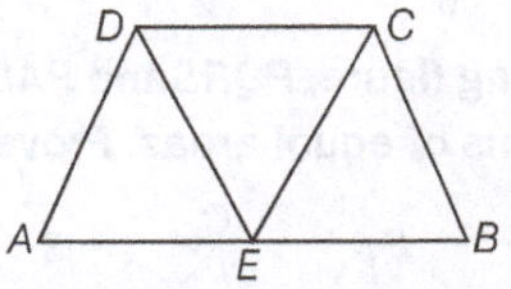

26. ΔABC and ΔDBC are on the same base BC with A and D on opposite sides of line BC, such that ar (ΔABC) = ar (ΔDBC). Show that BC bisects AD.

27. ΔABC and ΔBDE are two equilateral triangles such that D is the mid-point of BC. Then, prove that ar (ΔBDE) $= \frac{1}{4}$ ar (ΔABC).

28. In ΔABC, if L and M are the points on AB and AC, respectively such that LM || BC, then prove that ar (ΔLOB) = ar (ΔMOC), where O is point of intersection of MB and LC.

29. In the given figure, $ABCD$ and $AEFD$ are two parallelograms. Prove that ar (ΔPEA) = ar (ΔQFD).

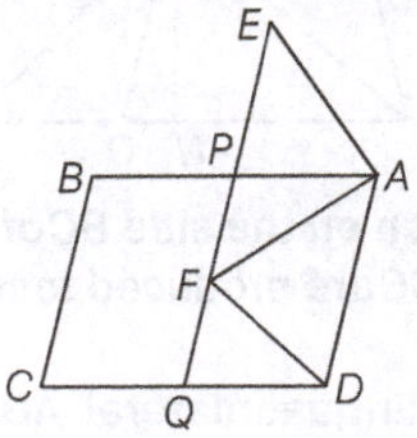

30. In the following figure, $CD \parallel AE$ and $CY \parallel BA$. Prove that ar (ΔCBX) = ar (ΔAXY).

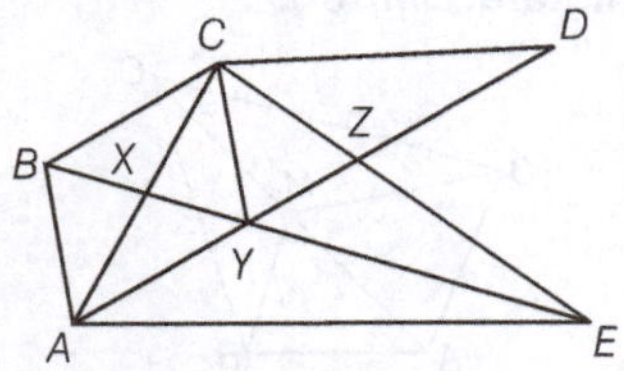

31. Prove that of all the parallelograms of given sides, the parallelogram which is a rectangle has the greatest area.

32. *ABCD* is a rectangle inscribed in a quadrant of a circle of radius 10 cm. If *AD* is $2\sqrt{5}$ cm, then find the area of the rectangle.

33. *X* and *Y* are points on the side *LN* of the ΔLMN such that $LX = XY = YN$. Through *X*, a line drawn parallel to *LM* to meet *MN* at *Z* (see the figure). Prove that ar (ΔLZY) = ar (quadrilateral *MZYX*).

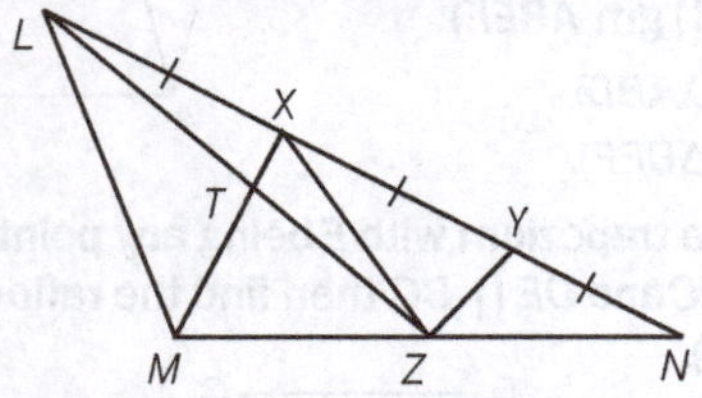

34. In the following figure, *PQRS* and *PABC* are two parallelograms of equal areas. Prove that $QC \parallel BR$.

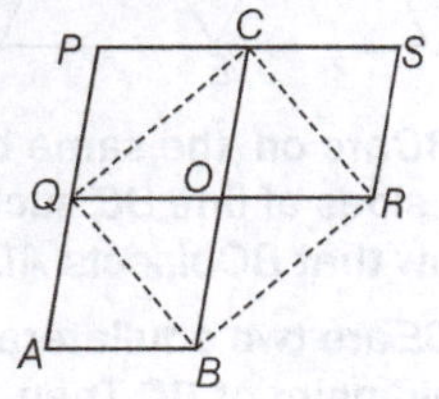

Short Answer II Type Questions

35. *ABCD* is a trapezium in which $AB \parallel DC$. *DC* is produced to *E* such that $CE = AB$ (see the figure). Prove that ar (ΔABD) = ar (ΔBCE).

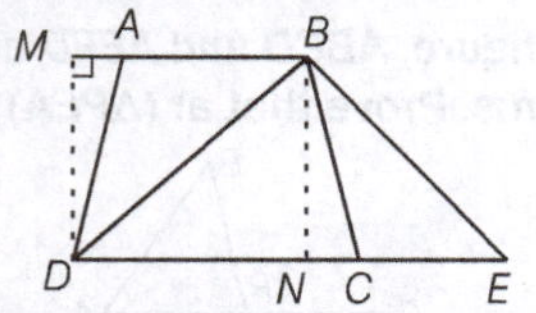

36. A point *E* is taken on the side *BC* of a parallelogram *ABCD*. *AE* and *DC* are produced to meet at *F*. Prove that

ar (ΔADF) = ar(quadrilateral *ABFC*).

37. The area of the parallelogram *ABCD* is 90 cm^2. Find

(*i*) ar (||gm *ABEF*)

(*ii*) ar (ΔABD)

(*iii*) ar (ΔBEF)

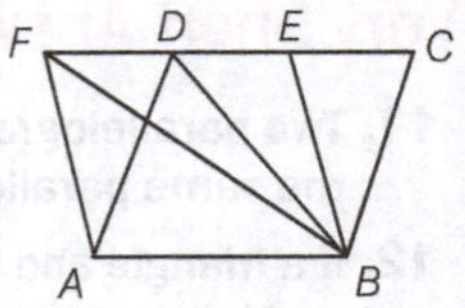

38. In a class, teacher gave two identical cardboard pieces which are in the shape of a parallelogram to two groups. First group was asked to find area of parallelogram using *AB* as base. Then, another group was asked to find height *h* of the parallelogram with *AD* as base. How will they find value of *h*?

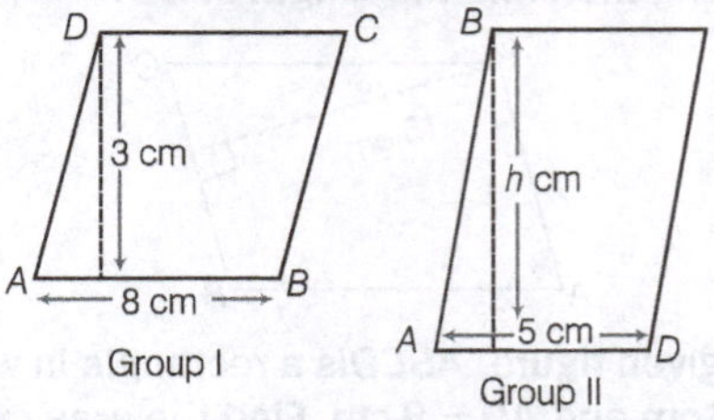

39. *PQRS* is a rectangle inscribed in a quadrant of a circle of radius 13 cm. *A* is any point on *PQ* (see the figure). If $PS = 5$ cm, then show that ar (ΔPAS) ≤ 30 cm^2.

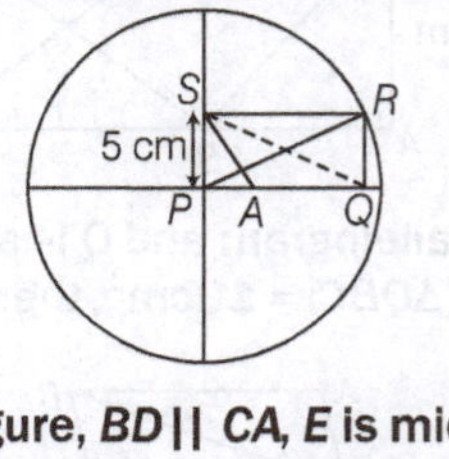

40. In the given figure, $BD \parallel CA$, *E* is mid-point of *CA* and $BD = \frac{1}{2}CA$. Prove that ar (ΔABC) = 2 ar (ΔDBC).

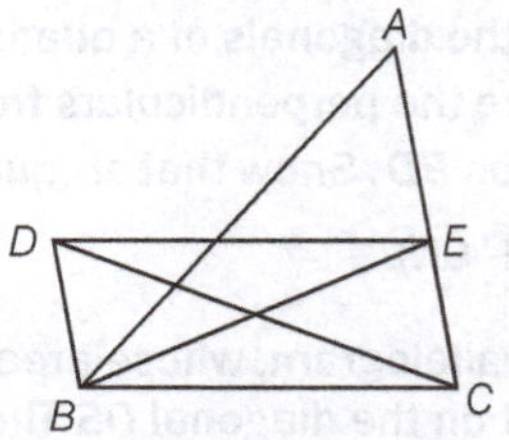

41. In ΔDEF, *M* and *N* are mid-points of sides *EF* and *DE*, respectively. If ar (ΔENM) = 4 cm^2, find ar (ΔDEF).

42. *O* is any point on the diagonal *PR* of a parallelogram *PQRS* (see the figure). Prove that ar (ΔPQO) = ar (ΔPSO)

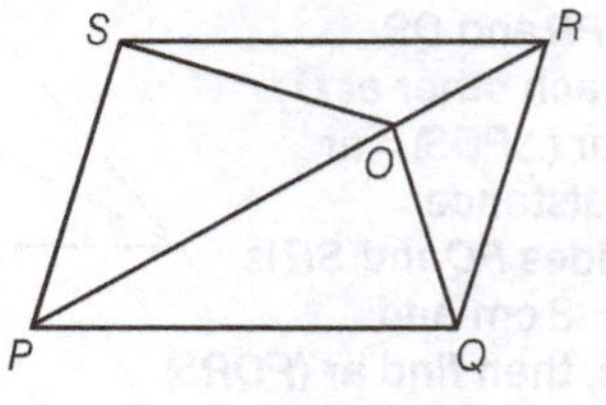

43. In the adjoining figure, $ABCDE$ is any pentagon. BP drawn parallel to AC meets DC produced at P and EQ drawn parallel to AD meets CD produced at Q. Prove that ar $(ABCDE)$ = ar (ΔAPQ).

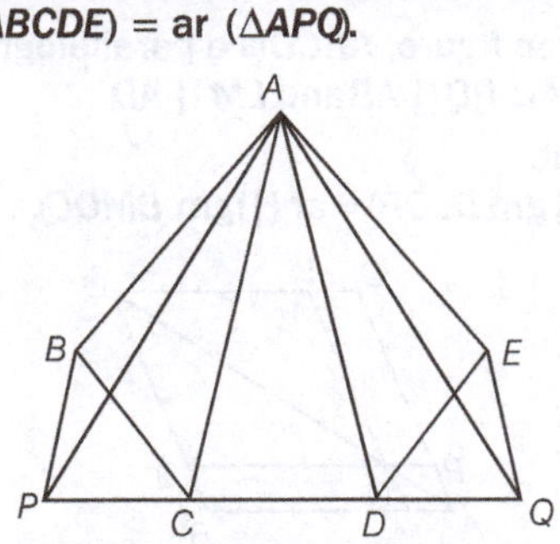

44. The medians of a ΔABC intersect each other at point G. If one of its median is AD, then prove that

(*i*) ar $(\Delta ABD) = 3 \times$ ar (ΔBGD)

(*ii*) ar $(\Delta ACD) = 3 \times$ ar (ΔCGD)

(*iii*) ar $(\Delta BGC) = \frac{1}{3} \times$ ar (ΔABC)

Long Answer Type Questions

45. $ABCD$ is a square. A is joined to a point P on BC and D is joined to a point Q on AB. If $AP = DQ$, then prove that AP and DQ are perpendicular to each other.

46. In the given figure, $ABCD$ and $EFGD$ are two parallelograms and G is the mid-point of CD. Then, prove that ar (ΔDPC) = ar $(EFGD)$.

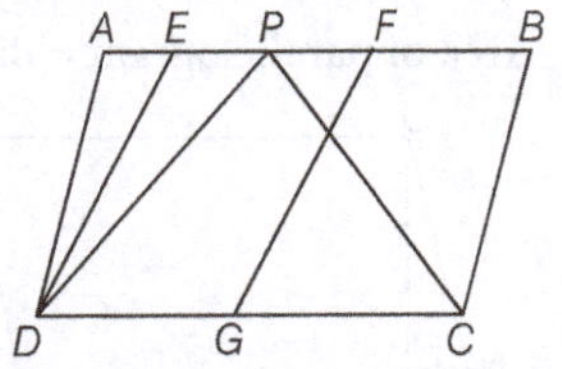

47. $ABCD$ is a parallelogram. P is the mid-point of AB. BD and CP intersect at Q such that $CQ : QP = 3 : 1$. If ar $(\Delta PBQ) = 10 \text{ cm}^2$, then find the area of parallelogram $ABCD$.

48. ABC is a triangle in which D is the mid-point of BC. E and F are mid-points of DC and AE, respectively. If area of ΔABC is 16 cm^2, then find the area of ΔDEF.

49. In the adjoining figure, $PSDA$ is a parallelogram. Points Q and R are taken on PS such that $PQ = QR = RS$ and $PA \parallel QB \parallel RC$. Prove that ar$(\Delta PQE)$ = ar(ΔCFD).

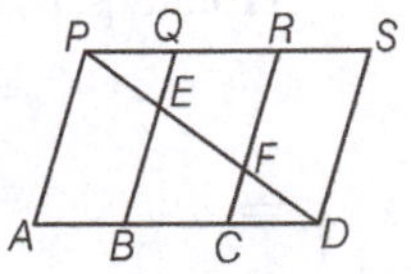

50. $ABCD$ is a trapezium in which $AB \parallel DC$, $DC = 30$ cm and $AB = 50$ cm. If X and Y are respectively the mid-points of AD and BC, then prove that

ar $(DCYX) = \frac{7}{9}$ ar $(XYBA)$.

51. $PQRS$ is a trapezium with $PQ \parallel RS$. X and Y are points on PS and RQ such that $SX = XP$ and $RY = YQ$. If $SR = 40$ cm and $PQ = 60$ cm, find the ratio ar $(SRYX)$: ar $(PQRS)$.

52. $ABCD$ is a trapezium in which $AB \parallel DC$ and $DC = 40$ cm, $AB = 60$ cm. If X and Y are the mid-points of AD and BC respectively, then prove that

(*i*) $DCYX$ is a trapezium.

(*ii*) ar (trapezium $DCYX$) $= \frac{9}{11}$ ar (trapezium $XYBA$).

53. In the following figure, $ABCD$ is a square, and T and U are respectively the mid-points of AD and BC. Find the area of ΔOTD, if $AB = 12$ cm.

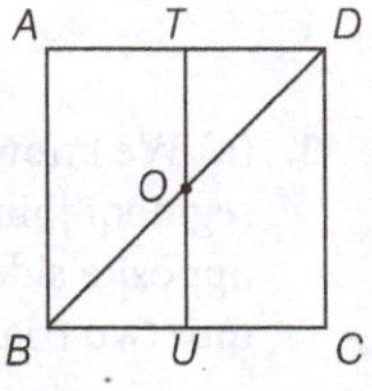

54. In ΔABC, AD is a median and P is a point on AD such that $AP : PD = 1 : 3$. Find the area of ΔABP.

55. In the given figure, P is any point on the diagonal AC of a parallelogram $ABCD$. Line segments EF and GH are drawn through P parallel to AB and CB, respectively. Prove that ar (ΔAEP) = ar (ΔAHP).

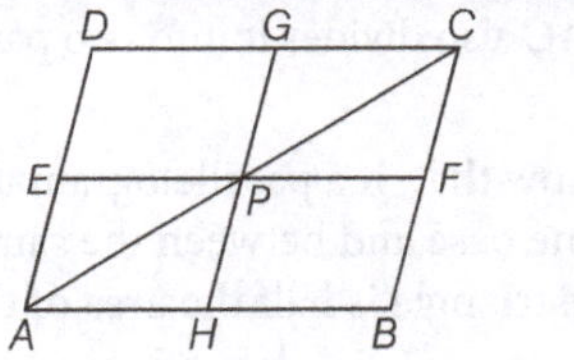

56. In the given figure, if $APCQ$ and $PBQD$ are parallelogram and $AD \parallel BC$, then show that

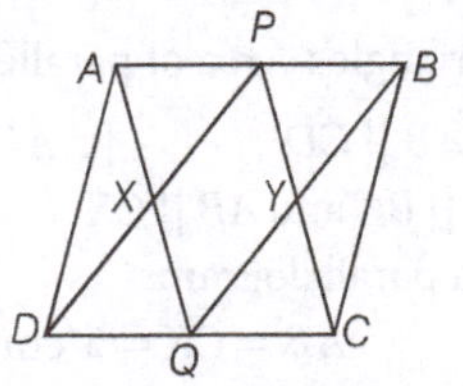

(*i*) quadrilateral $ABCD$ is a parallelogram.

(*ii*) ar (ΔPXQ) = ar (ΔPYQ).

57. In the given figure, $PQRS$ is a square and T and U are respectively the mid-points of PS and QR. Find the area of ΔOTS, if $PQ = 8$ cm.

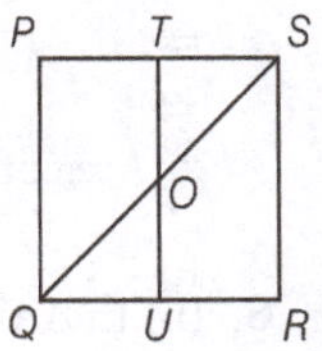

58. **In the adjoining figure, *ABC* is a triangle and *D* is the mid-point of *AB*. *P* is any point on *BC*. Line *CQ* is drawn parallel to *PD* to intersect *AB* at *Q*. *PQ* is joined. Show that ar (ΔBPQ) = $\frac{1}{2}$ ar (ΔABC).**

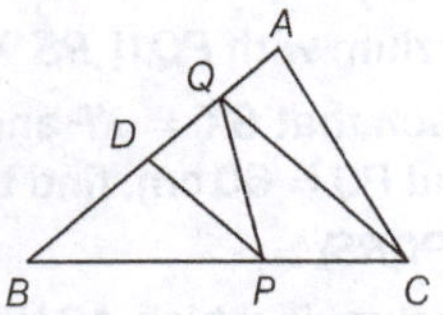

59. **In the given figure, *l*, *m*, *n* are straight lines such that *l* || *m* and *n* intersects *l* at *P* and *m* at *Q*. *ABCD* is a quadrilateral such that its vertex *A* is on *l*. The vertices *C* and *D* are on *m* and *AD* || *PQ*. Show that ar (*ABCQ*) = ar (*ABCDP*).**

60. **In the given figure, *ABCD* is a parallelogram, *O* is any point on *AC*, *PQ* || *AB* and *LM* || *AD*.**

Prove that:

ar (||gm *DLOP*) = ar (||gm *BMOQ*).

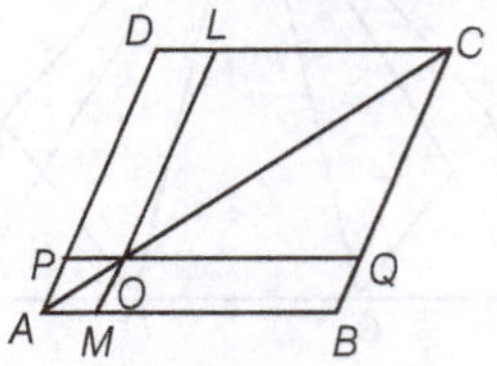

HINTS & ANSWERS

1. (a) We know that, a median of a triangle is a line segment joining a vertex to the mid-point of the opposite side. Thus, a median of a triangle divides it into two triangles of equal area.

2. (b) We know that, parallelogram on the equal bases and between the same parallels are equal in area. So, ratio of their areas is 1 : 1.

3. (d) Here, *ABCD* need not be any of rectangle, rhombus and parallelogram because if *ABCD* is a square, then its diagonal *AC* also divides it into two parts which are equal in area.

4. (b) We know that, if a parallelogram and a triangle are on the same base and between the same parallels, then area of the triangle is half the area of the parallelogram.

i.e., Area of triangle = $\frac{1}{2}$ Area of parallelogram

$$\Rightarrow \quad \frac{\text{Area of triangle}}{\text{Area of parallelogram}} = \frac{1}{2}$$

$\therefore$ Area of triangle : Area of parallelogram = 1 : 2

5. (a) Clearly, $AB \parallel CD$ $\quad [\because AD \perp CD$ and $AD \perp AB]$

Now, as $AX \parallel BC$ and $AB \parallel CX$

$\therefore$ *AXBC* is a parallelogram.

$\Rightarrow \quad AB = CX = 5$ cm

and $\quad AX = BC = 5$ cm

In ΔAXD,

$$AD^2 = AX^2 - XD^2$$

$$\Rightarrow \quad AD^2 = 5^2 - 3^2 = 25 - 9 = 16 \text{ cm}$$

$$\Rightarrow \quad AD = 4 \text{ cm}$$

$\therefore$ Area of parallelogram $ABCX = AB \times AD$

$$= 5 \times 4 = 20 \text{ cm}^2$$

6. (b) In ΔABC, we have $BD = 2DC$

Let *E* be the mid-point of *BD*.

Then, $BE = ED = DC$

Since, *AE* and *AD* are medians of ΔABD and ΔAEC, respectively.

$\therefore \quad$ ar $\Delta ABD) = 2$ ar $\Delta AED)$

and $\quad$ ar $\Delta ADC) =$ ar $\Delta AED)$

$\Rightarrow \quad$ ar $\Delta ABD) = 2$ ar $\Delta ADC)$

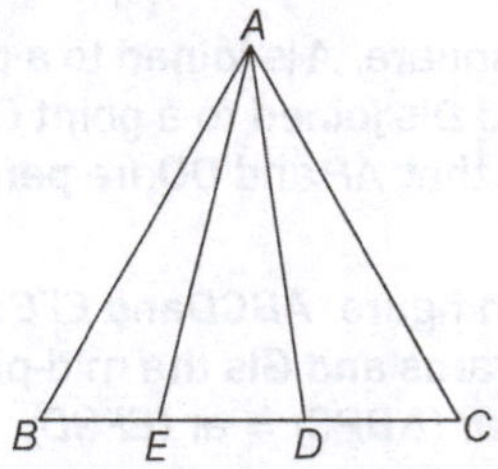

7. (c) We have, Area of parallelogram = Base × Height

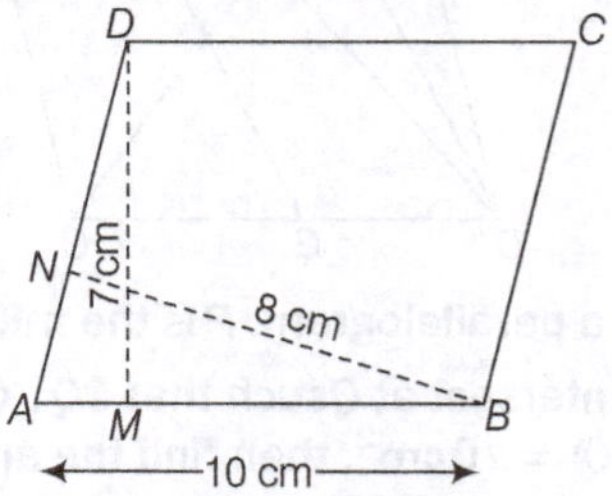

$\therefore$ ar (parallelogram $ABCD$) $= AB \times DM$

$$= (10 \times 7) \text{ cm}^2 \quad \ldots\text{(i)}$$

Also, ar (parallelogram $ABCD$) $= AD \times BN$

$$= (AD \times 8) \text{ cm}^2 \quad \ldots\text{(ii)}$$

From Eqs. (i) and (ii), we have

$$10 \times 7 = AD \times 8 \Rightarrow AD = \frac{10 \times 7}{8} \text{ cm}$$

$$\Rightarrow \quad AD = \frac{35}{4} = 8.75 \text{ cm}$$

$$\Rightarrow \quad K = 8.75 \text{ cm}$$

$\therefore$ Value of $K - 0.75 = 8.75 - 0.75 = 8$ cm

8. (c) Since AD and AE are medians of ΔABC and ΔABD, respectively.

$\therefore \quad \text{ar}(\Delta ABD) = \frac{1}{2}\text{ar}(\Delta ABC) \quad \ldots\text{(i)}$

and $\quad \text{ar}(\Delta ABE) = \frac{1}{2}\text{ar}(\Delta ABD) \quad \ldots\text{(ii)}$

OB is a median of ΔABE.

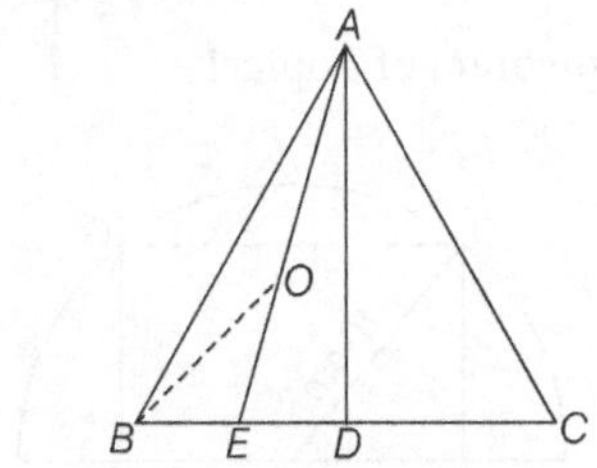

$\therefore \quad \text{ar}(\Delta BOE) = \frac{1}{2}\text{ar}(\Delta ABE) \quad \ldots\text{(iii)}$

From Eqs. (i), (ii) and (iii), we have

$\text{ar}(\Delta BOE) = \frac{1}{8}\text{ar}(\Delta ABC)$

$\therefore \quad k = 8$

9. (d) Here, $AL = BM = 4$ cm and $LM = 7$ cm.

In ΔADL, we have $AD^2 = AL^2 + DL^2$

$\Rightarrow \quad 25 = 16 + DL^2 \Rightarrow DL = 3$ cm

Similarly,

$MC = \sqrt{BC^2 - BM^2} = \sqrt{25-16} = 3$ cm

$CD = CM + ML + LD$

$= (3 + 7 + 3)$ cm $= 13$ cm

$\text{ar}(\text{trapezium } ABCD) = \frac{1}{2}(AB + CD) \times AL$

$= \frac{1}{2}(7 + 13) \times 4 \text{ cm}^2 = 40 \text{ cm}^2$

$\therefore$ Value of $\frac{l}{8} = \frac{40}{8} = 5.$

10. (b) Here, $\angle PQS = \angle QSR$ [each 90°, given]

But these are alternate angles.

$\therefore \quad PQ \parallel SR \quad \ldots\text{(i)}$

Also, $\quad PQ = SR \quad$ [each 5 cm, given] ...(ii)

i.e. a pair of opposite sides are equal and parallel.

So, $PQRS$ is a parallelogram.

Hence, ar (parallelogram $PQRS$)

$= \text{Base} \times \text{Corresponding altitude}$

$= 5 \times 8 = 40 \text{ cm}^2$

11. **Hint** If two parallelogram are on same base and between same parallel lines, then they have equal areas.

Ans: 1:1

12. **Hint** If a triangle and a parallelogram are on the same base and between same parallel lines, then the area of triangle is half that of parallelogram. **Ans:** 1 : 2

13. Solve as Example 2 of Topic 1. **Ans.** 8.75 cm

14. **Hint** Area of || gm = Base × Height. **Ans:** $BC = 8$ cm

15. **Hint** ar(|| gm $CDBF$) = ar(rectangle $ABCD$)

Ans. 48 cm^2

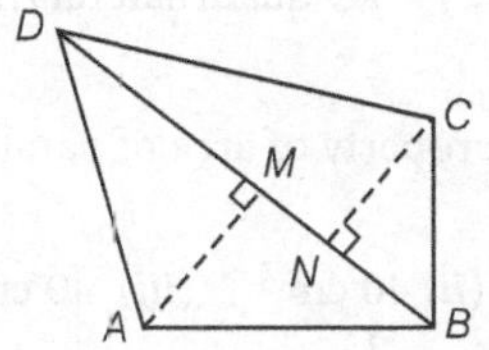

16. **Hint** ar(QAB) + ar(QDC) = ar(QBC) **Ans.** 10 cm^2

17. **Hint**

ar (quadrilateral $ABCD$) = ar (ΔABD) + ar (ΔBCD)

$= \frac{1}{2}(BD \times AM) + \frac{1}{2}(BD \times CN)$

$= \frac{1}{2}BD \cdot (AM + CN)$ **Hence proved.**

18. False

19. **Hint** $PQRS$ is a trapezium. **Ans.** 20 cm^2

20. We know that median of a triangle divides it into two triangles of equal areas. So, median BM divides ΔABC into two triangles of equal areas.

$\therefore \quad \text{ar}(\Delta ABM) = \text{ar}(\Delta BMC) \quad \ldots\text{(i)}$

Similarly, median DM divides ΔDAC into two triangles of equal areas.

$\therefore \quad \text{ar}(\Delta AMD) = \text{ar}(\Delta DMC) \quad \ldots\text{(ii)}$

On adding Eqs. (i) and (ii), we get

$\text{ar}(\Delta ABM) + \text{ar}(\Delta AMD) = \text{ar}(\Delta BMC) + \text{ar}(\Delta DMC)$

$\Rightarrow$ ar (quadrilateral $ABMD$) = ar (quadrilateral $DMBC$)

Hence proved.

21. **Hint** Use diagrams of a || gm divides it into 2 equal areas and then Use median divides the triangle into 2 equal areas. **Ans.** 36 cm^2

22. Solve as Q.7, of **Try these** 13.1. **Ans.** 2 : 1.

23. **Hint** Given, BE and CF are medians of a ΔABC.

We know that median of a triangle divides it into two parts of equal area.

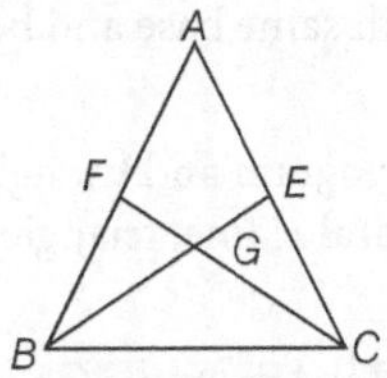

$\therefore \quad \text{ar}(\Delta FBC) = \text{ar}(\Delta AFC)$

$\Rightarrow \quad \text{ar}(\Delta FBC) = \frac{1}{2}\text{ar}(\Delta ABC) \quad \text{...(i)}$

Similarly, $\text{ar}(\Delta AEB) = \frac{1}{2}\text{ar}(\Delta ABC) \quad \text{...(ii)}$

From Eqs. (i) and (ii), we get

$$\text{ar}(\Delta FBC) = \text{ar}(\Delta AEB)$$

On subtracting ar (ΔGBF) from both sides, we get

$$\text{ar}(\Delta FBC) - \text{ar}(\Delta GBF) = \text{ar}(\Delta AEB) - \text{ar}(\Delta GBF)$$

$\Rightarrow$ ar (ΔGBC) = ar (quadrilateral $AFGE$)

Hence proved.

24. Hint use the property of area of parallelogram and triangle.

(*i*) 80 cm^2 (*ii*) 40 cm^2 (*iii*) 40 cm^2

25. Hint $\text{ar}(\Delta DAE) = \frac{1}{2}\text{ar}(||\text{gm}\, AECD)$

and $\text{ar}(\Delta BEC) = \frac{1}{2}\text{ar}(||\text{gm}\, BCDE)$

Also, ar (||gm $AECD$) = ar (||gm $BCDE$)

Ans. 1 : 1

26. Hint Use property of median of triangle and theorem of Topic-2

27. Given, ΔABC and ΔBDE are two equilateral triangles.

$\therefore$ Area of $\Delta ABC = \frac{\sqrt{3}}{4} \times (BC)^2$ ...(i)

$\left[\because \text{area of an equilateral triangle} = \frac{\sqrt{3}}{4}(\text{side})^2\right]$

and D is the mid-point of BC.

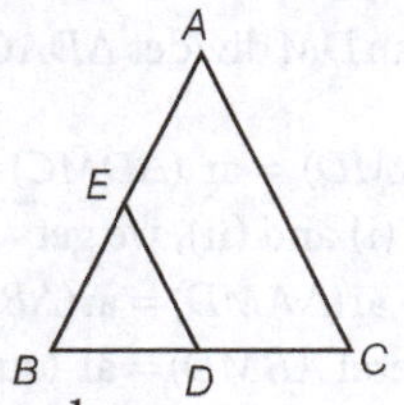

$\therefore$ $BD = CD = \frac{1}{2}BC$

$\therefore$ Area of $\Delta BDE = \frac{\sqrt{3}}{4}(BD)^2 = \frac{\sqrt{3}}{4}\left(\frac{BC}{2}\right)^2$

$= \frac{\sqrt{3}}{4} \cdot \frac{(BC)^2}{4}$ ...(ii)

From Eqs. (i) and (ii), we get

$\text{ar}(\Delta BDE) = \frac{1}{4}\text{ar}(\Delta ABC)$ **Hence proved.**

28. Hint Use Δ's with same base and between parallel lines are equal.

29. Hint Use parallelogram and triangle same base and between same parallel line, triangle has half area that of parallelogram.

30. Hint *Given* $CD \parallel AE$ and $CY \parallel BA$.

To prove ar (ΔCBX) = ar (ΔAXY)

Proof Since, ΔABC and ΔBAY both lie on the same base AB and between the same parallel AB and CY.

$\therefore$ ar (ΔABC) = ar (ΔBAY)

$\Rightarrow$ ar (ΔABX) + ar (ΔCBX) = ar (ΔABX) + ar (ΔAXY)

$\Rightarrow$ ar (ΔCBX) = ar (ΔAXY)

[eliminating ar (ΔABX) from both sides]

Hence proved.

31. Hint Use theorem of Topic-1

32. Hint

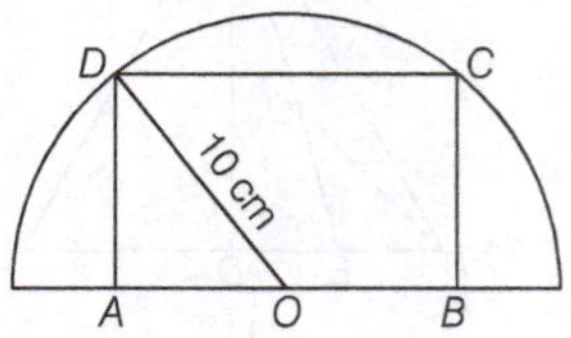

Ans. 40 cm^2

33. Hint Since, ΔXMZ and ΔZLX are on same base XZ and between same parallel LM and XZ.

$\therefore$ Their areas will be equal.

Add ar (ΔXYZ) on both triangles ΔXMZ and ΔZLX.

34. Hint *Given* ar(||gm $PQRS$) = ar(||gm $PABC$)

To prove $QC \parallel BR$

Proof $\because$ ar (||gm $PQRS$) = ar (||gm $PABC$)

On subtracting ar (||gm $QOCP$) from both sides, we get

ar (||gm $PQRS$) − ar (||gm $QOCP$)

= ar (||gm $PABC$) − ar (||gm $QOCP$)

$\Rightarrow$ ar (||gm $ORSC$) = ar (||gm $ABOQ$)

$\Rightarrow$ 2 × ar (ΔORC) = 2 × ar (ΔOBQ)

[$\because$ diagonal of a parallelogram divides it into two triangles of equal area]

$\Rightarrow$ ar (ΔORC) = ar (ΔOBQ)

Adding ar (ΔOBR) on both sides, we get

ar (ΔORC) + ar (ΔOBR) = ar (ΔOBQ) + ar (ΔOBR)

$\Rightarrow$ ar (ΔBRC) = ar (ΔBRQ)

Now, as ΔBRC and ΔBRQ being on the same base BR and equal in area, therefore they must be between the same parallels.

$\Rightarrow$ $QC \parallel BR$ **Hence proved.**

35. Hint $\text{ar}(\Delta ABD) = \frac{1}{2}AB \times DM$

and $\text{ar}(\Delta BCE) = \frac{1}{2}CE \times BN$

Also, $CE = AB$ and $DM = CN$

$\therefore$ ar (ΔABD) = ar (ΔBCE)

36. Hint Triangles on the same base and between the same parallels are equal in area.

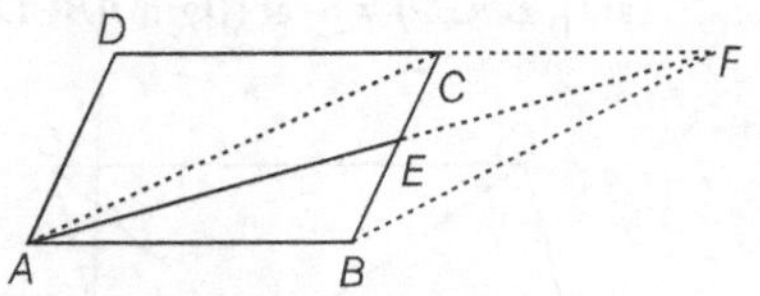

$\therefore \quad \text{ar}(\Delta ACB) = \text{ar}(\Delta AFB)$ ...(i)

Also, $\text{ar}(\Delta ACB) = \text{ar}(\Delta ADC)$ ...(ii)

[$\because$ diagonal of parallelogram divides it into two triangles of equal area]

From Eqs. (i) and (ii), we get

$$\text{ar}(\Delta ADC) = \text{ar}(\Delta AFB)$$

On adding ar (ΔACF) both sides, we get

$$\text{ar}(\Delta ADC) + \text{ar}(\Delta ACF) = \text{ar}(\Delta AFB) + \text{ar}(\Delta ACF)$$

37. Hint Use theorem 1 of Topic 2.

Ans. (i) 90 cm^2 (ii) 45 cm^2 (iii) 45 cm^2

38. Hint Put areas of both cardboard equal as they are identical. **Ans.** $h = 4.8$ cm

39. Hint Given, $PS = 5$ cm and radius of circle $= (PR) = 13$ cm

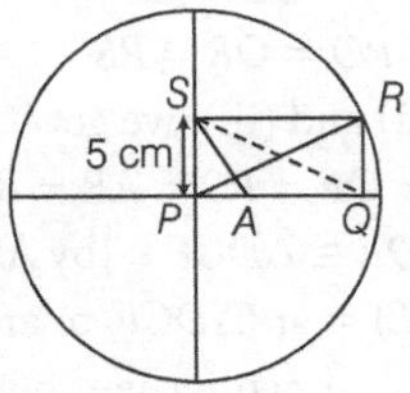

In ΔPQR,

$PR^2 = PQ^2 + RQ^2$ [by Pythagoras theorem]

$\Rightarrow PQ^2 = PR^2 - RQ^2$

$= (13)^2 - (5)^2$ [given, $PS = 5$ cm, $PR = 13$ cm]

$PQ = 12$ cm

Now, area of rectangle $PQRS = 12 \times 5 = 60 \text{ cm}^2$

$\Rightarrow$ Area of $\Delta PSQ = \frac{1}{2} \times 60 = 30 \text{ cm}^2$

[$\because$ diagonal of a rectangle bisect it into two triangles of equal area]

Now, A is any point on PQ. So, area of ΔAPS depends on the position of A.

If A is at point Q, then area will be 30 cm^2.

$\therefore \quad \text{ar}(\Delta PAS) \le 30 \text{ cm}^2$ **Hence proved.**

40. Hint *Given* $BD \parallel CA$, E is mid-point of CA, i.e. BE is median of ΔABC, also $BD = \frac{1}{2} CA$.

To prove $\quad \text{ar}(\Delta ABC) = 2\text{ar}(\Delta DBC)$

Proof We know that median of a triangle divides it into two triangles of equal area.

$\therefore \quad \text{ar}(\Delta ABE) = \text{ar}(\Delta EBC)$

$\Rightarrow \quad \text{ar}(\Delta EBC) = \frac{1}{2} \text{ar}(\Delta ABC)$ ...(i)

Also, $\quad \text{ar}(\Delta DBC) = \text{ar}(\Delta EBC)$ ...(ii)

[$\because$ triangles on same base and between same parallel lines are equal in area]

From Eqs. (i) and (ii), we get

$$\text{ar}(\Delta DBC) = \frac{1}{2} \text{ar}(\Delta ABC)$$

$\Rightarrow \quad \text{ar}(\Delta ABC) = 2\,\text{ar}(\Delta DBC)$ **Hence proved.**

41. Hint

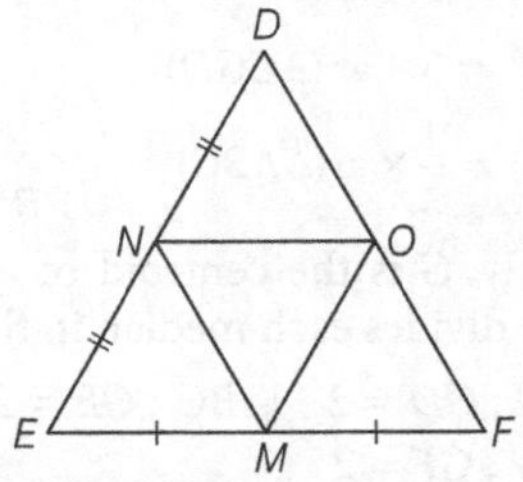

Joint M and N with mid-point of DF.

Now, $\text{ar}(\Delta ENM) = \frac{1}{4} \text{ar}(\Delta DEF)$ **Ans.** 16 cm^2

42. Hint *Given* $PQRS$ is a parallelogram and O is any point on the diagonal PR.

To prove $\text{ar}(\Delta PSO) = \text{ar}(\Delta PQO)$

Construction Join SQ, which intersect PR at B.

Proof We know that diagonal of a parallelogram bisect each other, so B is the mid-point of SQ.

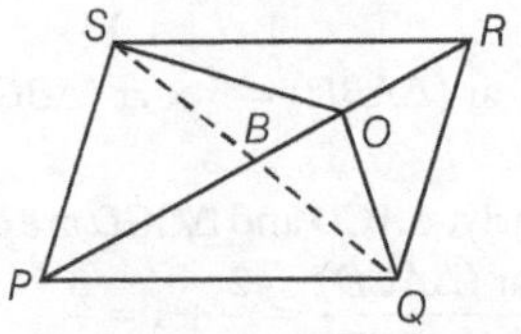

Thus, PB is a median of ΔQPS and median of a triangle divides it into two triangles of equal area.

$\therefore \quad \text{ar}(\Delta BPQ) = \text{ar}(\Delta BPS)$ ...(i)

Also, OB is a median of ΔOSQ.

$\therefore \quad \text{ar}(\Delta OBQ) = \text{ar}(\Delta OBS)$ ...(ii)

On adding Eqs. (i) and (ii), we get

$$\text{ar}(\Delta BPQ) + \text{ar}(\Delta OBQ) = \text{ar}(\Delta BPS) + \text{ar}(\Delta OSB)$$

$\Rightarrow \quad \text{ar}(\Delta PQO) = \text{ar}(\Delta PSO)$ **Hence proved.**

43. Hint We know that triangles on the same base and between the same parallels are equal in area.

Thus, $\text{ar}(\Delta ADE) = \text{ar}(\Delta ADQ)$ ...(i)

$\text{ar}(\Delta CAB) = \text{ar}(\Delta CAP)$ ...(ii)

On adding Eqs. (i) and (ii), we get

$\text{ar}(\Delta ADE) + \text{ar}(\Delta CAB) = \text{ar}(\Delta ADQ) + \text{ar}(\Delta CAP)$

On adding ar(ΔCDA) both sides, we get the required result.

44. Hint Let in ΔABC, AD, BE and CF are its median, which intersect each other at G.

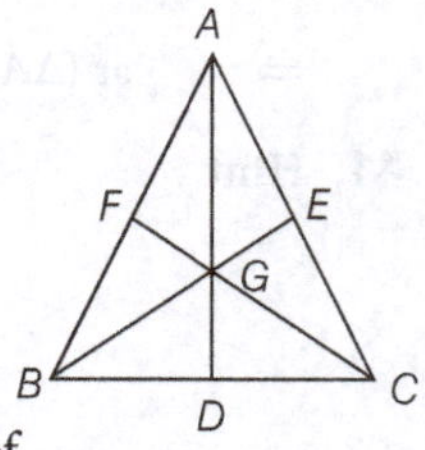

To prove

(i) $\text{ar}(\Delta ABD) = 3 \times \text{ar}(\Delta BGD)$

(ii) $\text{ar}(\Delta ACD) = 3 \times \text{ar}(\Delta CGD)$

(iii) $\text{ar}(\Delta BGC) = \frac{1}{3} \times \text{ar}(\Delta ABC)$

Proof Clearly, G is the centroid of ΔABC, which divides each median in the ratio 2 : 1.

We have, $AG : GD = 2 : 1$, $BG : GE = 2 : 1$

and $CG : GF = 2 : 1$ ...(i)

(i) Since, ΔABD and ΔBGD are along the same base and same height.

$$\therefore \frac{\text{ar}(\Delta ABD)}{\text{ar}(\Delta BGD)} = \frac{\frac{1}{2} \times BD \times AD}{\frac{1}{2} \times BD \times GD}$$

$$\Rightarrow \frac{\text{ar}(\Delta ABD)}{\text{ar}(\Delta BGD)} = \frac{AD}{GD}$$

$$= \frac{AG + GD}{GD} = \frac{AG}{GD} + 1$$

$$= \frac{2}{1} + 1 = \frac{3}{1} \quad \text{[from (i)]}$$

$\Rightarrow \text{ar}(\Delta ABD) = 3 \times \text{ar}(\Delta BGD)$ ...(ii)

Hence proved.

(ii) Similarly, ΔACD and ΔCGD are along the same base.

$$\therefore \frac{\text{ar}(\Delta ACD)}{\text{ar}(\Delta CGD)} = \frac{2}{1} + 1 = \frac{3}{1} \quad \text{[from (i)]}$$

$\Rightarrow \text{ar}(\Delta ACD) = 3 \times \text{ar}(\Delta CGD)$ ...(iii)

Hence proved.

(iii) On adding Eqs. (ii) and (iii), we get

$\text{ar}(\Delta ABD) + \text{ar}(\Delta ACD) = 3\ \text{ar}(\Delta BGD) + 3\ \text{ar}(\Delta CGD)$

$\Rightarrow \text{ar}(\Delta ABC) = 3\ \text{ar}(\Delta BGC)$

$\Rightarrow \text{ar}(\Delta BGC) = \frac{1}{3}\ \text{ar}(\Delta ABC)$

Hence proved.

46. Hint $\text{ar}(\Delta DPC) = \frac{1}{2}\text{ar}(||\text{gm } ABCD)$

and $\text{ar}(||\ EFGD) = \frac{1}{2}\text{ar}(||\text{gm } ABCD)$

47. Hint

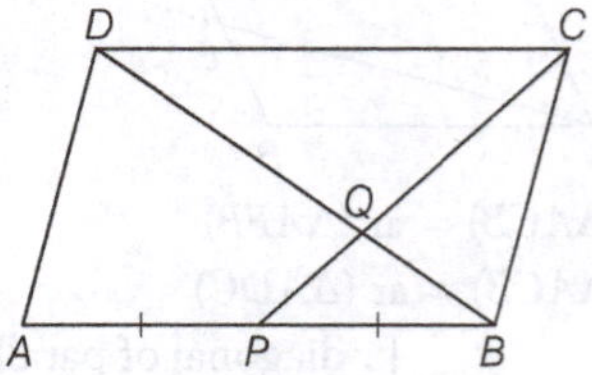

Ans. 160 cm^2

48. Solve as Q.41. **Ans.** 2 cm^2

49. Hint In quadrilateral $PABQ$,

$PQ \,||\, AB$ [$\because PS \,||\, AD$]

and $PA \,||\, QB$ [given]

So, $PABQ$ is a parallelogram.

$\therefore PQ = AB$ ...(i)

Similarly, $QBCR$ is also a parallelogram.

$\therefore QR = BC$ ...(ii)

and $RCDS$ is also a parallelogram.

$\therefore RS = CD$ ...(iii)

But $PQ = QR = RS$ [given]

From Eqs. (i), (ii) and (iii), we get

$PQ = QR = RS = AB = BC = CD$ ...(iv)

Now prove $\Delta PQE \cong \Delta DCF$ [by ASA congruence rule]

Then, $\text{ar}(\Delta PQE) = \text{ar}(\Delta DCF)$ or $\text{ar}(\Delta CFD)$

[$\because$ congruent figures have equal area]

50. Solve as Example 8 of Topic 1.

51. Solve as Example 8 of Topic 1. **Ans.** 9 : 20

Hint Height of parallelogram $PQRS = 2h$

52. Solve as Example 8 of Topic 1.

53. Hint $TD = OT = 6$ cm **Ans.** 18 cm^2

54. Hint Use property of median of a triangle.

Ans. $\frac{1}{8}$ ar(ΔABC).

55. Hint Prove that $AHPE$ is a parallelogram.

56. Hint Use the properties of parallelogram.

57. Hint Prove $\Delta TOS \cong \Delta UOQ$ using ASA congruence rule from there, $OS = QO$

Then find TS and OT and then area ΔOTS

58. Use property of area. **Ans.** 8 cm^2

CHAPTER 14

Constructions

(To be Assessed Formatively)

In the earlier classes, we have learnt how to construct a circle, the perpendicular bisector of a line segment, angles of 30°, 45°, 60°, 90°, 120° and the bisector of a given angle without giving any justification for these constructions. In this chapter, we shall learn the procedure of some of these constructions with reasoning behind, why these constructions are valid.

TOPIC 01 Some Basic Constructions

Construction 1

To construct the bisector of a given angle

If an angle (say $\angle ABC$) of any measure is given to us and we have to draw the bisector of this angle, then we use the following steps of construction and its justification.

Steps of Construction

Step I First, draw the given $\angle ABC$ and draw an arc of any radius taking B as centre (say). This arc intersects BA and BC at E and D, respectively.

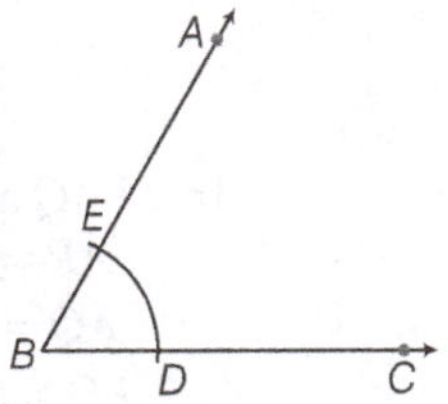

Step II Now, taking E and D as centres and with the radius more than $\frac{1}{2}ED$, draw two arcs which intersect each other at F (say).

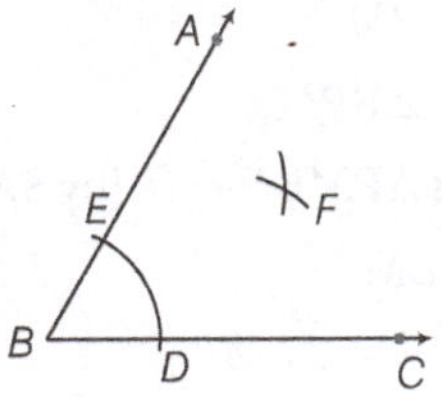

Step III Draw the ray BF, which is the required bisector of the $\angle ABC$.

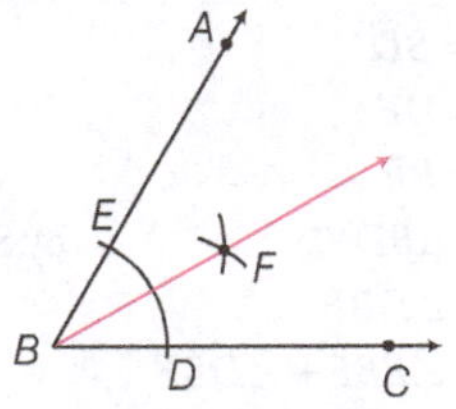

Justification Join DF and EF.

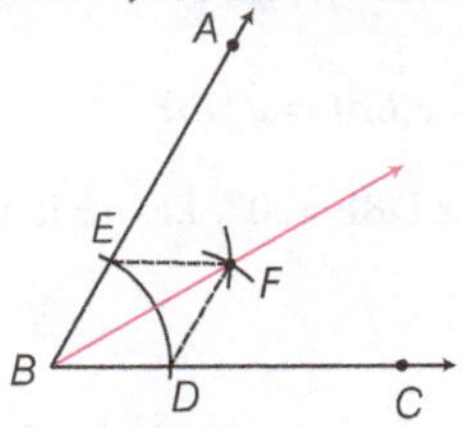

In ΔBEF and ΔBDF,

$BE = BD$ [radii of the same arc]

$EF = DF$ [arcs of equal radii]

$BF = BF$ [common sides]

$\therefore$ $\Delta BEF \cong \Delta BDF$ [by SSS congruence rule]

Then, $\angle EBF = \angle DBF$ [by CPCT]

Hence, BF is the bisector of a given $\angle ABC$.

Example 1. **Draw the angle bisector of 60° and justify the construction.**

Sol. ***Steps of Construction***

(*i*) First, draw a line segment *BC*, and make the $\angle ABC = 60°$ and draw an arc of any radius taking *B* as centre (say). This arc cuts arms *BA* and *BC* at *E* and *D*, respectively.

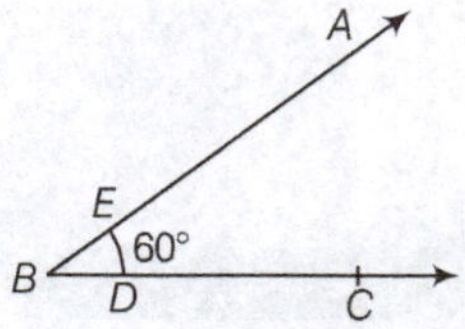

(*ii*) Now, taking *E* and *D* as centres and with the radius more than $\frac{1}{2}ED$, draw two equal arcs which cut each other at *F* (say).

(*iii*) Draw the ray *BF*.

Here, *BF* is the angle bisector of 60°.

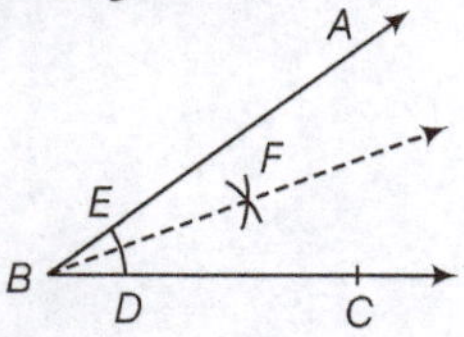

Justification Join *EF* and *DF*.

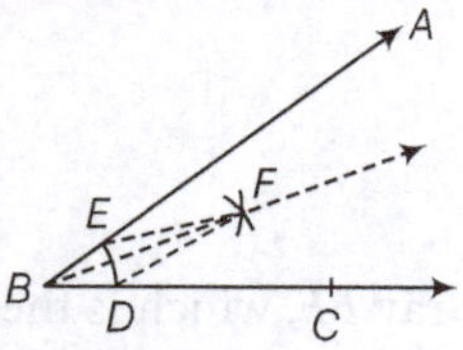

In ΔBEF and ΔBDF,

$BE = BD$ [radii of same arc]

$EF = DF$ [arcs of equal radii]

$BF = BF$ [common sides]

$\therefore \quad \Delta BEF \cong \Delta BDF$ [by SSS congruence rule]

$\angle EBF = \angle DBF$ [by CPCT]

$\because \quad \angle EBD = \angle EBF + \angle DBF$

So, $\quad \dfrac{\angle EBD}{2} = \angle EBF = \angle DBF$

$\Rightarrow \quad \dfrac{60°}{2} = \angle EBF = \angle DBF$

Hence, $\angle EBF = \angle DBF = 30°$, i.e. *BF* is the angle bisector of $\angle ABC$.

Construction 2

To construct the perpendicular bisector of a given line segment

If a line segment of any length is given to us and we have to draw the perpendicular bisector of this line segment, then we use the following steps of construction and its justification.

Steps of Construction

Step I First, draw the given line segment, say *AB*. Then, taking *A* and *B* as centres and with the radius more than $\frac{1}{2}AB$, draw arcs on both sides of the line segment *AB*, which intersect each other.

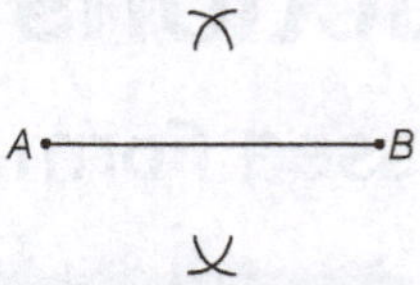

Step II Let arcs drawn in step I intersect each other at *P* and *Q*. Then, join *PQ*.

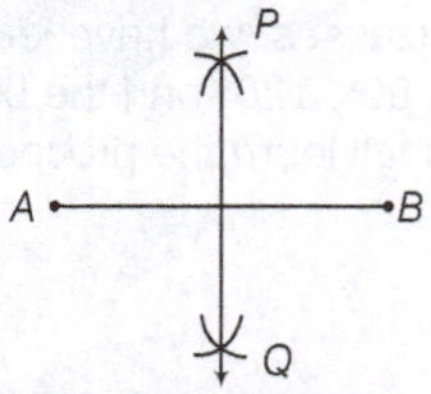

Step III *PQ* intersects *AB* at a point, *M* (say). Then, line *PMQ* is the required perpendicular bisector of *AB*.

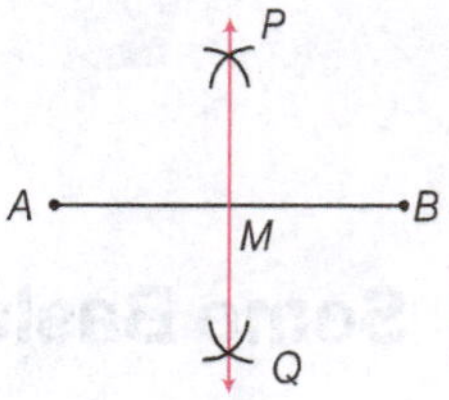

Justification

First, join *AP*, *AQ*, *BP* and *BQ*.

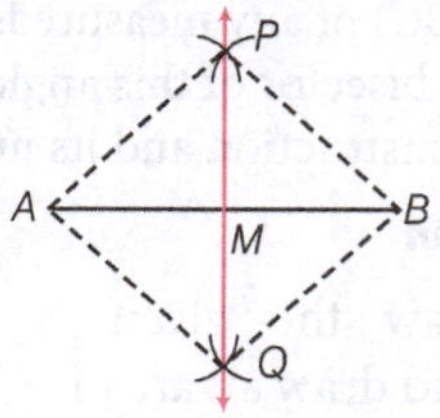

In ΔPAQ and ΔPBQ,

$AP = BP$ [arcs of equal radii]

$AQ = BQ$ [arcs of equal radii]

$PQ = PQ$ [common sides]

$\therefore \Delta PAQ \cong \Delta PBQ$ [by SSS congruence rule]

$\therefore \angle APM = \angle BPM$ [by CPCT]

Now, in ΔPMA and ΔPMB,

$AP = BP$ [arcs of equal radii]

$PM = PM$ [common sides]

$\angle APM = \angle BPM$ [proved above]

$\therefore \Delta PMA \cong \Delta PMB$ [by SAS congruence rule]

$\therefore \quad AM = BM$ [by CPCT]

and $\angle PMA = \angle PMB$ [by CPCT] ...(i)

Now, $\angle PMA + \angle PMB = 180°$ ...(ii)

[linear pair axiom]

From Eqs. (i) and (ii), we get

$\angle PMA = \angle PMB = 90°$

Hence, PM, i.e. PMQ is the perpendicular bisector of AB.

Example 2. Draw the perpendicular bisector of a line segment of length 7 cm and justify the construction.

Sol. ***Steps of Construction***

(*i*) Draw line segment $AB = 7$ cm. Then, draw two arcs on both sides of the line segment AB of radius more than $\frac{1}{2}AB$ (i.e. more than 3.5 cm) taking A and B as centre, respectively.

(*ii*) Let arcs drawn in step (i) intersect each other at points P and Q.

(*iii*) Join PQ which intersect AB at M.

Thus, line PQ or PMQ is the required perpendicular bisector of AB.

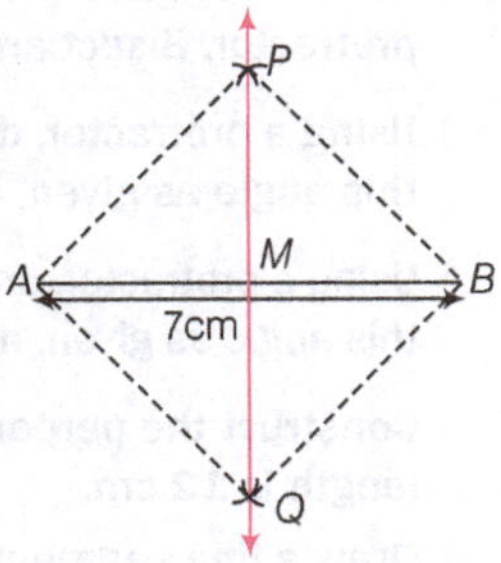

Justification Join AP, AQ, BP and BQ.

In ΔPAQ and ΔPBQ,

$AP = BP$ [arcs of equal radii]

$AQ = BQ$ [arcs of equal radii]

$PQ = PQ$ [common sides]

$\therefore$ $\Delta PAQ \cong \Delta PBQ$ [by SSS congruence rule]

$\therefore$ $\angle APM = \angle BPM$ [by CPCT] ...(i)

Now, in ΔPMA and ΔPMB,

$PM = PM$ [common sides]

$\angle APM = \angle BPM$ [from Eq. (i)]

$AP = BP$ [arcs of equal radii]

$\therefore$ $\Delta PMA \cong \Delta PMB$ [by SAS congruence rule]

$AM = BM$ [by CPCT]

and $\angle AMP = \angle BMP$ [by CPCT] ...(ii)

Now, $\angle AMP + \angle BMP = 180°$ [linear pair axiom]...(iii)

From Eqs. (ii) and (iii), we get $\angle AMP = \angle BMP = 90°$

Hence, PMQ is the required perpendicular bisector of the given line segment $AB (= 7 \text{ cm})$.

Construction 3

To construct an angle of 60° at the initial point of a given ray

Suppose, a ray AB (say) with initial point A is given and we have to draw an angle of 60° at the initial point A of AB, then we use the following steps of construction and its justification.

Steps of Construction

Step I First, draw a ray AB with initial point A.

Step II With some suitable radius, draw an arc of a circle taking A as centre which intersects AB at D.

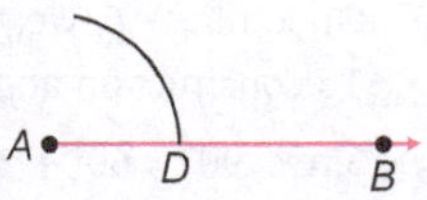

Step III Taking D as centre, draw an arc with same radius as before to intersect previously drawn arc at a point, E (say).

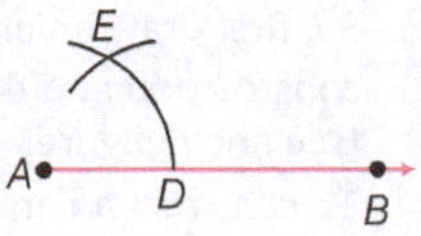

Step IV Draw the ray AC passing through E.

Then, $\angle CAB$ will be the required angle of 60°.

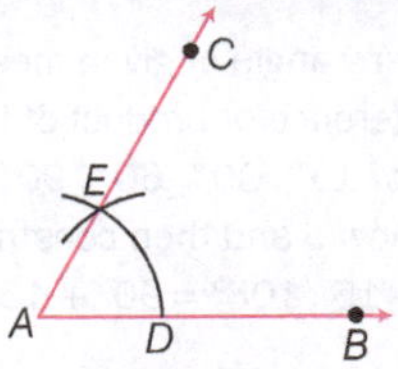

Justification Join DE.

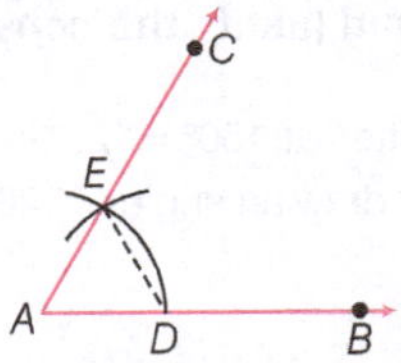

By construction, we have $AE = AD = ED$

So, ΔAED is an equilateral triangle.

Then, $\angle AED = \angle EAD = \angle ADE = 60°$

Hence, $\angle CAB = \angle EAD = 60°$

Constructions of Some Angles Other than 60°

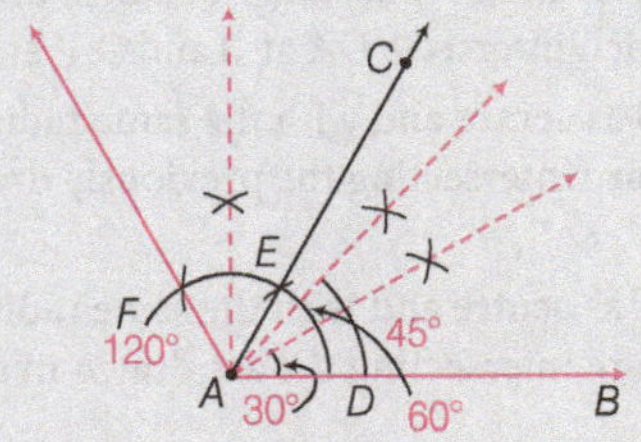

- To construct an angle of 30°

  First, draw an angle of 60° and then bisect it.

- To construct an angle of 15°. Since, $15° = \frac{30°}{2}$

  So first draw an angle of 30° and then bisect it.

- To construct an angle of 120°
  Since, $120° = 60° + 60°$
  So, after step III of construction 3, we take E as centre and draw an arc with same radius as before, such that it intersects the arc drawn in step II at a point, say F.
  On joining AF, we get the required angle of 120°.
- To construct an angle of 90°
  Since, $90° = 60° + 30° = 60° + \frac{60°}{2}$
  So, first draw an angle of 120° with the help of above construction and then bisect the $\angle FAC$.
  [see above figure]
- To construct an angle of 45°
  Since, $45° = \frac{90°}{2}$
  So, first draw an angle of 90° with the help of above construction and then bisect it to get an angle of 45°.

Note For constructing any angle of given measure, we first write it as the sum or difference or product of two or more angles in which one is out of 15°, 30°, 60°, 90° or 120°, etc. (whose construction is known) and then construct the angle.
e.g. $75° = 60° + 15°, 105° = 90° + 15°$

Example 3. Construct an angle of 150° at the initial point of a given ray and justify the construction.

Here, 150° can be written as 150° = 120° + 30°. So, to draw an angle of 150°, we first draw an angle of 120° and then add an angle of 30°.

Sol. *Steps of Construction*

(i) First, draw a ray OA with initial point O.

(ii) Produce AO to A' to form ray OA'.

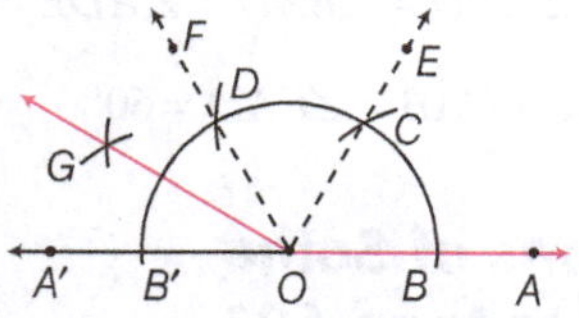

(iii) Taking O as centre and suitable radius, draw an arc of a circle which intersects OA at B and OA' at B'.

(iv) Taking B as centre and with the same radius as before, draw an arc intersecting the previously drawn arc at a point C.

(v) Taking C as centre and with the same radius as before, draw an arc intersecting the arc drawn in step (iii) at a point D.

(vi) Draw the ray OE passing through C and ray OF passing through D.
Then, $\angle EOA = 60°$, $\angle FOE = 60°$ and $\angle FOA' = 60°$

(vii) Now, taking D and B' as centres and with radius more than $\frac{1}{2}B'D$, draw two arcs to intersect each other at a point say G.

(viii) Draw the ray OG, which is the bisector of $\angle B'OF$.
Hence, $\angle GOA$ is the required angle of 150°.

Justification

$$\angle B'OG = \angle FOG = \frac{1}{2}\angle B'OF = \frac{1}{2}(60°) = 30°$$

Thus, $\angle GOA = \angle FOG + \angle FOE + \angle EOA$
$= 30° + 60° + 60° = 150°$

On measuring the $\angle GOA$ by protractor, we find that $\angle GOA = 150°$. Thus, the construction is justified.

Try These 14.1

1. **Draw an angle of measure 108° with the help of protractor and bisect it.**
2. **Draw an angle of measure 40° with the help of protractor. Bisect and justify it.**
3. **Using a protractor, draw an angle of measure 130°. With this angle as given, draw an angle of measure 65°.**
4. **Using a protractor, draw an angle of measure 68°. With this angle as given, draw an angle of measure 17°.**
5. **Construct the perpendicular bisector of a line, whose length is 12 cm.**
6. **Draw a line segment $AB = 10$ cm and using ruler and compass, divide it into two parts.**
7. **Construct a pair angle of 90° at both end of a line segment.**
8. **Construct an angle of $52\frac{1°}{2}$ using ruler and compasses.**
9. **An angle of 37.5° can be constructed by ruler and compass. If constructed then give its steps of construction.**

Hints & Answers

1. Solve as Example 1.
2. Solve as Example 1.
3. Solve as Example 1.
4. Solve as Example 1. **Hint** first bisect the angle of 68° to get an angle of 34° and then again bisect it to get an angle of 17°
5. Solve as Example 2.
6. Solve as Example 2.
7. **Hint** First draw an angle of 60°, say $\angle ABC$. Again, draw an angle of 60° at the point B of ray BA such that $\angle DBA = 60°$ and $\angle DBC = 120°$. Now, bisect $\angle DBA$ to get $\angle MBA = 30°$. Thus, $\angle MBC = 90°$ is constructed.
   Repeat the same procedure at the point C to draw an angle of 90°.

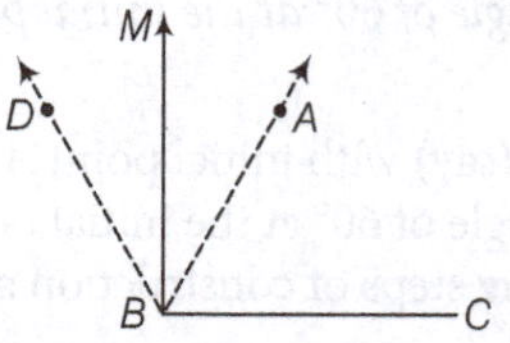

8. **Hint** First, draw the angle of $120°$ say $\angle ABC$, and of $90°$, say $\angle DBC$, so that $\angle ABD = 120° - 90° = 30°$

Bisect $\angle ABD$ to get $\angle EBD = \frac{30°}{2} = 15°$ and

$\angle EBC = 15° + 90° = 105°$, Now bisect $\angle EBC$ to get $\angle MBC = \frac{105°}{2} = 52\frac{1}{2}°$

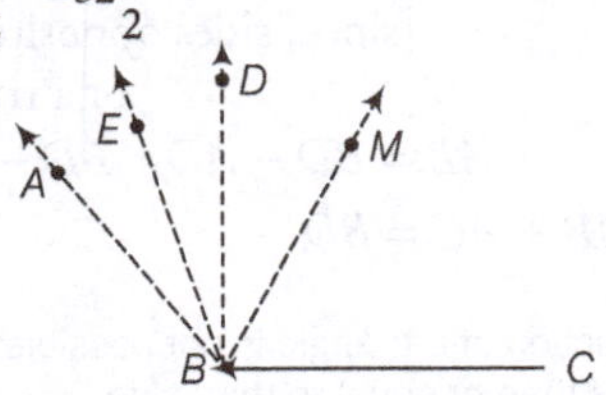

9. **Hint** First, draw an angle of $150°$ as drawn in Example 3. Let it be $\angle ABC$.

Now, bisect it to get $\angle DBC = \frac{150°}{2} = 75°$

Again, bisect $\angle DBC$ to get $\angle MBC = \frac{75°}{2} = 37.5°$

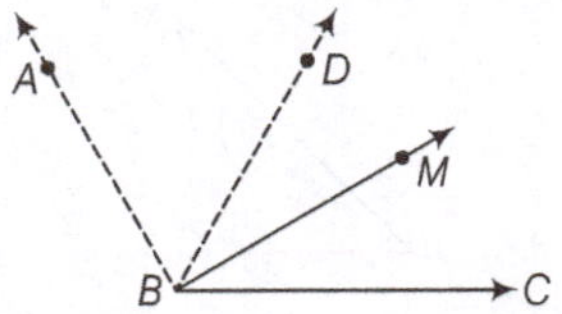

TOPIC 02 Some Constructions of Triangle

We know that there are six elements of a triangle, namely three angles and three sides. In order to construct a triangle, atleast three parts must be given, but all the combinations of three parts out of six parts are not sufficient to construct a triangle. e.g. If two sides and an angle (not included angle) are given, then it is not always possible to construct such a triangle uniquely.

Some Basic Constructions of a Triangle in Different Cases

Some basic constructions of a triangle in different cases are given below. This will be further helpful for our construction of unique triangle.

Case I *When two sides and angle between them are given*

Let the two sides of ΔABC be $AB = a$ cm, $BC = b$ cm and angle between them, i.e. $\angle ABC = x°$.

Steps of Construction

(*i*) Draw base $AB = a$ cm (say).

(*ii*) Draw a ray BX making an angle $x°$ at B

(*iii*) Cut-off $BC = b$ cm from BX.

(*iv*) Join AC.

Thus, ΔABC is the required triangle.

Case II *When three sides of a triangle are given*

Let three sides of ΔABC be $AB = a$ cm, $BC = b$ cm and $CA = c$ cm.

Steps of Construction

(*i*) First, draw the base $BC = b$ cm (say).

(*ii*) By taking B and C as centres, draw two arcs of radius a cm and c cm respectively, which intersect each other at A.

(*iii*) Join AB and AC.

Thus, ΔABC is the required triangle.

Case III *When one side and two angles are given*

Let one side of ΔABC be $AB = a$ cm (say) and angles be $\angle A = x°$ and $\angle B = y°$.

Steps of Construction

(*i*) Draw base $AB = a$ cm.

(*ii*) Draw two rays AX and BY making an angle $x°$ at A and $y°$ at B, which intersect each other at C.

(*iii*) Join AC and CB.

Thus, ΔABC is the required triangle.

Case IV *When base and altitude of a triangle are given*

Let the base of ΔABC be $BC = m$ cm and altitude be n cm.

Steps of Construction

(*i*) Draw base $BC = m$ cm and its perpendicular bisector OQ (say), which intersects BC at P (say).

(*ii*) Along PO, cut-off $PA = n$ cm.

(*iii*) Join AB and AC. Thus, ΔABC is the required triangle.

Constructions of Triangles in Some Special Cases

Construction 1

To construct a triangle, given its base, a base angle and sum of other two sides

Sometimes, base angle (say B), base (say BC) and sum of other two sides of a triangle (say $AB + AC$) are given to us and we have to construct the triangle (say ΔABC), then for this construction, *we use the following steps of construction*

Step I First, draw the given base (say BC) and make base angle (say $\angle XBC$) equal to given $\angle B$..

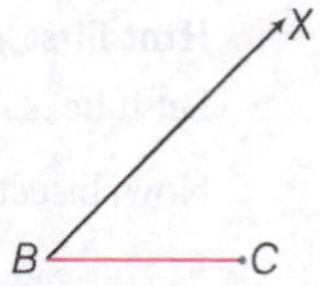

Step II Cut a line segment (say BD) equal to $AB + AC$ from the ray BX.

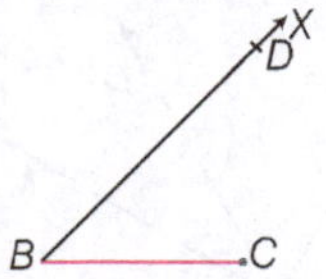

Step III Join DC.

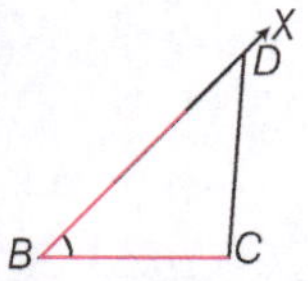

Now, we can use following two methods

Method I

Step IV Draw the perpendicular bisector of DC, say PQ.

Step V Let PQ intersects BD at a point A. Then, join AC. Thus, ABC will be the required triangle.

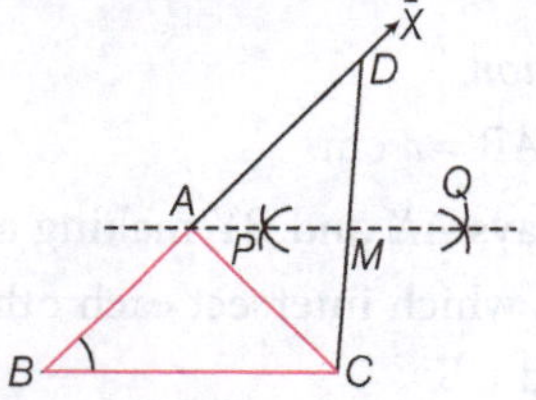

Justification

Base BC and $\angle B$ are drawn as given.

Since, PQ is the perpendicular bisector of CD and A lies on it.

So, $AD = AC$

$[\because \Delta AMD \cong \Delta AMC$, by SAS rule]

Now, $AB = BD - AD = BD - AC$

$\Rightarrow AB + AC = BD$

Method II

Step IV Make an $\angle DCY$ equal to $\angle BDC$ at C.

Step V Let CY intersects BX at A. Then, join AC. Thus, ABC will be the required triangle.

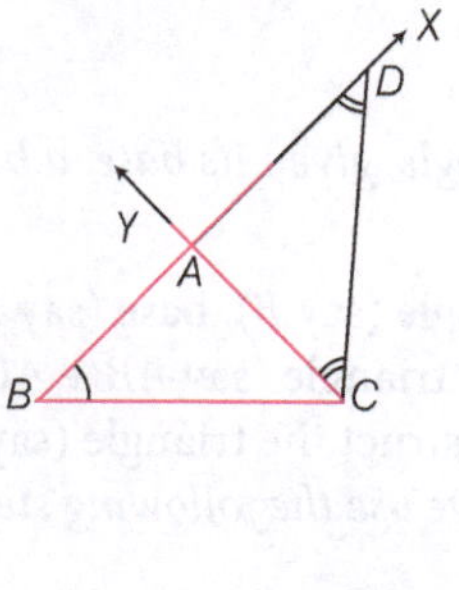

Justification

Base BC and $\angle B$ are drawn as given.

In ΔACD,

$\angle ACD = \angle ADC$ [by construction]

$\therefore AD = AC$

[since, sides opposite to equal angles of a triangle are equal]

Now, $AB = BD - AD = BD - AC$

$\Rightarrow AB + AC = BD$

Note The construction of a triangle is not possible, if the sum of two sides is less than or equal to third side.

Example 1. **Construct a ΔABC, in which $BC = 7$ cm, $AB + AC = 13$ cm and $\angle B = 60°$ and justify it.**

Sol. Given, $BC = 7$ cm, $AB + AC = 13$ cm and $\angle B = 60°$

Steps of Construction

(*i*) First, draw the base, $BC = 7$ cm. Now, draw a ray BX such that $\angle XBC = \angle B = 60°$.

(*ii*) Here, sum of two sides $= AB + AC$ $= 13$ cm

So, cut the line segment $BD = 13$ cm from ray BX.

(*iii*) Join DC.

(*iv*) Draw perpendicular bisector of DC, say PQ, which intersects BD at A.

(*v*) Now join AC. Thus, we get a ΔABC which is the required triangle.

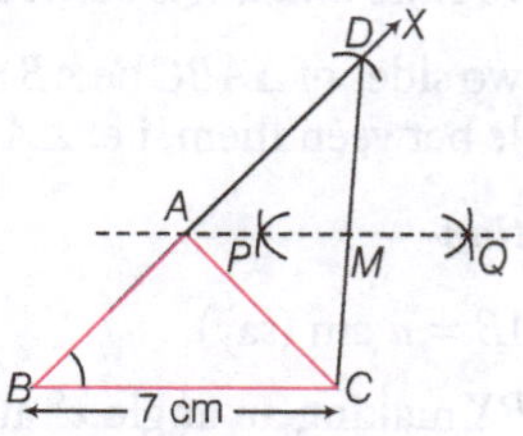

Justification

Base BC and $\angle B$ are drawn as given.

Since, PQ is the perpendicular bisector of CD and A lies on it.

$\therefore AD = AC$ $[\because \Delta AMD \cong \Delta AMC$, by SAS rule]

Now, $AB = BD - AD = BD - AC$

$\Rightarrow AB + AC = BD$

Thus, construction is justified.

Note Here, we can also apply method II from step III and then step IV and step V will be according to method II.

Construction 2

To construct a triangle, given its base, a base angle and the difference of the other two sides

Sometimes, base angle (say B), base (say BC) and difference of the other two sides (say $AB - AC$ or $AC - AB$) are given to us and we have to construct the triangle (say ΔABC), then for this construction, we use the following steps according to its case.

Case I *If $AB > AC$ i.e. $AB - AC$ is given.*

(*in other words, the side containing the base angle is greater than third side*)

Steps of Construction

Step I First, draw the base BC and draw a ray BX making an $\angle XBC$ equal to given angle B.

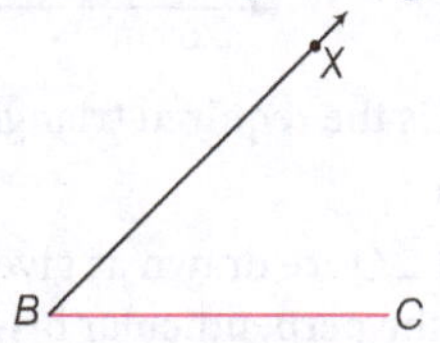

Step II Cut the line segment BD equal to given difference of sides, i.e. $AB - AC$ from the ray BX.

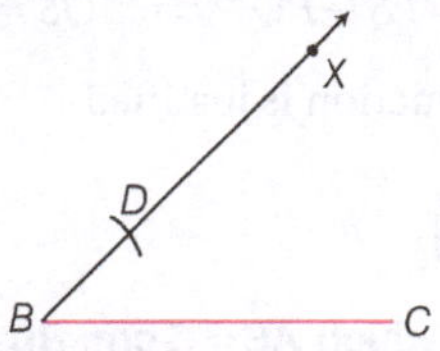

Step III Join DC and draw its perpendicular bisector say PQ, which bisects CD at M (say).

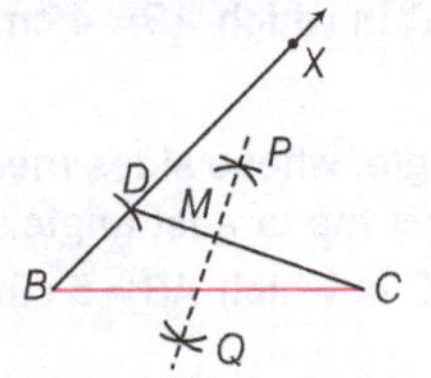

Step IV Let PQ intersects BX at a point A. Join AC.

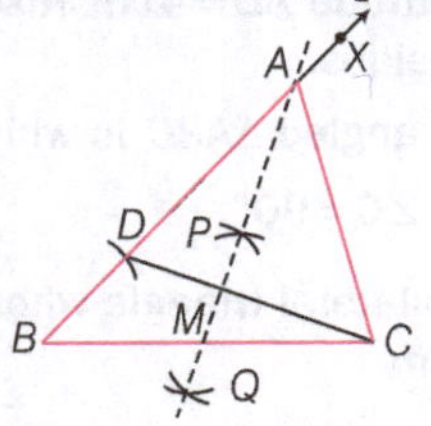

Thus, ABC is the required triangle.

Justification

Base BC and $\angle B$ are drawn as given.

Since, the point A lies on the perpendicular bisector of DC.

$\therefore \quad AD = AC$

$[\because \Delta AMD \cong \Delta AMC$, by SAS congruence rule$]$

So, $\quad BD = AB - AD = AB - AC$

Example 2. **Construct a ΔABC, in which $BC = 10$ cm $\angle B = 45°$ and $AB - AC = 5$ cm. Give justification.**

Sol. Given, $BC = 10$ cm, $\angle B = 45°$ and $AB - AC = 5$ cm

Steps of Construction

(*i*) First, draw the base, $BC = 10$ cm

At point B, draw a ray BX, which makes $\angle CBX = 45°$.

(*ii*) Here, $AB - AC = 5$ cm

$\therefore AB > AC$, i.e. The side containing the base $\angle B$ is greater than third side, so it is the case I.

Hence, cut line segment BD is equal to $AB - AC = 5$ cm from the ray BX.

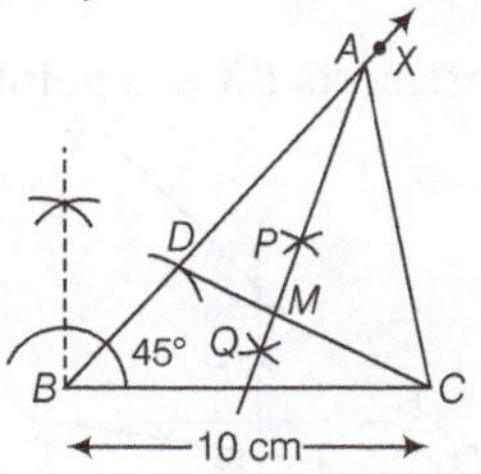

(*iii*) Now, join CD and draw its perpendicular bisector PQ, which bisects CD at M (say).

(*iv*) Let A be the intersection point of perpendicular bisector PQ and ray BX. Join AC. Thus, ΔABC is the required triangle.

Justification

Base BC and $\angle B$ are drawn as given. Since, the point A lies on the perpendicular bisector of DC.

$\therefore \quad AD = AC$

$BD = AB - AD \Rightarrow \quad BD = AB - AC$

Thus, the construction is justified.

Case II *If $AB < AC$ i.e. $AC - AB$ is given*

(*in other words, the side containing the base angle is less than third side*)

Steps of Construction

Step I First, draw the base BC and draw a ray BX making an $\angle XBC$ equal to given angle at B.

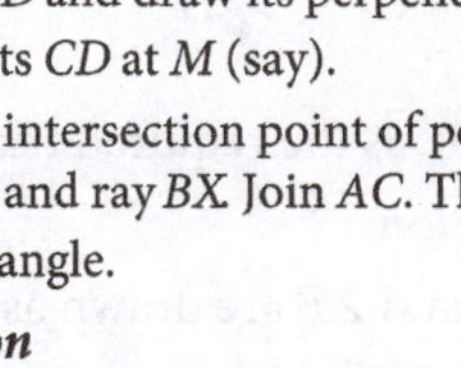

Step II Cut line segment BD equal to given difference of sides, i.e. $AC - AB$ from the ray BX extended on opposite side of base BC.

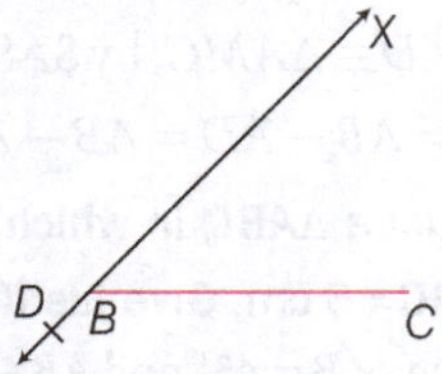

Step III Join DC and draw its perpendicular bisector, say PQ, which intersects DC at M (say).

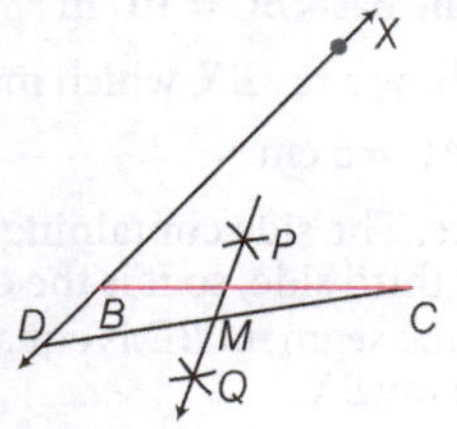

Step IV Let PQ intersects BX at a point A. Join AC.

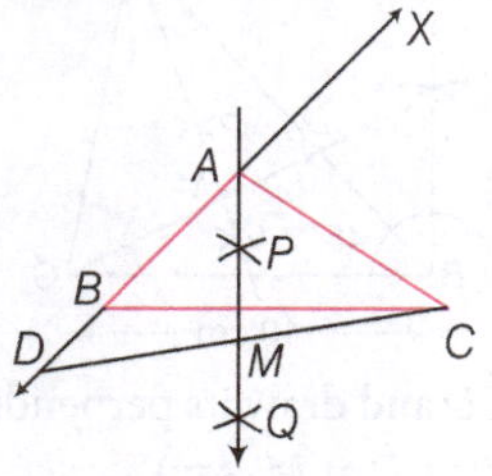

Thus, ABC is the required triangle.

Justification

Base BC and $\angle B$ are drawn as given.

Since, the point A lies on the perpendicular bisector of DC.

$\therefore \quad AD = AC$

$[\because \Delta AMD \cong \Delta AMC$, by SAS congruence rule$]$

So, $BD = AD - AB = AC - AB$

Note In above two cases, only step II of construction is differ, other steps are same in both cases.
The construction of the triangle is not possible, if difference of two sides is greater than or equal to third side.

Example 3. **Construct a ΔPQR, in which $QR = 6.5$ cm, $\angle Q = 60°$ and $PR - PQ = 1.5$ cm and justify it.**

Sol. Given, in ΔPQR, $QR = 6.5$ cm, $\angle Q = 60°$

and $\quad PR - PQ = 1.5$ cm

Steps of Construction

(*i*) Draw the base, $QR = 6.5$ cm.

At point Q, draw a ray QX making an $\angle XQR = 60°$.

Here, $\quad PR - PQ = 1.5$ cm

$\therefore \quad PR > PQ$

i.e. The side containing the base angle Q is less than third side, so it is the case II.

(*ii*) Cut line segment QS equal to $PR - PQ$, i.e. $QS = 1.5$ cm from the ray QX extended on opposite side of base QR.

(*iii*) Join SR and draw its perpendicular bisector ray AB, which intersects SR at M (say).

(*iv*) Let P be the intersection point of SX and perpendicular bisector AB. Then, join PR.

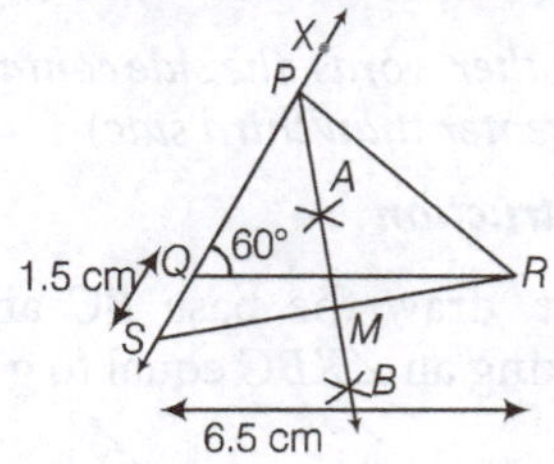

Thus, ΔPQR is the required triangle.

Justification

Base QR and $\angle Q$ are drawn as given.

Since, AB is the perpendicular bisector of SR and P lies on it.

$\therefore \quad PS = PR$

Now, $\quad QS = PS - PQ \quad \Rightarrow \quad QS = PR - PQ$

Thus, construction is justified.

Try These 14.2

1 Draw a ΔABC, in which $AB = 5$ cm, $BC = 4$ cm and $\angle B = 100°$. Draw the angle bisector of $\angle A$.

2 Construct a ΔABC, in which $AB = 4$ cm, $BC = 3$ cm and $AC = 5$ cm.

3 Construct a triangle, whose sides measure 4.5 cm, 5 cm and 5.3 cm. Bisect the largest angle.

4 Construct a ΔABC, in which $AB = 5$ cm, $\angle A = 45°$ and $\angle B = 60°$.

5 Construct an isosceles ΔABC, in which unequal side $BC = 6$ cm and altitude $AD = 4$ cm. Also, measure the lengths of equal sides.

6 Construct a right angled ΔABC, in which $AB = 5.6$ cm, $BC = 4.5$ cm and $\angle C = 90°$.

7 Construct an equilateral triangle whose altitude measure is 4.5 cm.

8 Construct an equilateral triangle of altitude 5 cm.

9 Construct a ΔABC, in which $BC = 4$ cm, $\angle C = 60°$ and $AB + AC = 8$ cm.

10 Construct a ΔABC, in which $AB = 6$ cm, $\angle A = 45°$ and $AC - BC = 2$ cm.

Hints & Answers

1. Solve as Case I of some basic constructions of a triangle.
2. Solve as case II of some basic constructions of a triangle.
3. Solve as Case II of some basic constructions of a triangle.

   Hint Since, angle opposite to largest side is largest, so bisect the angle opposite to the side of length 5.3 cm.
4. Solve as case III of some basic constructions of a triangle.
5. Solve as case IV of some basic constructions of a triangle.
6. Draw $BC = 4.5$ cm

   Make an angle of 90° at the point C of BC such that $\angle BCD = 90°$

   Draw an arc of 5.6 cm from point B which intersects CD at A.

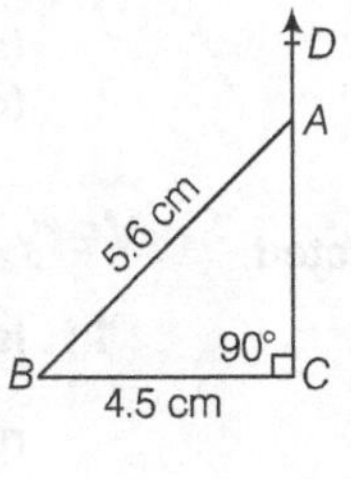

   Thus, ABC is the required triangle.
7. Draw a ray XY. Draw a perpendicular bisector PQ which intersects XY at M.

   Along MP, cut off $MA = 4.5$ cm. Draw an angle of 30° at point A on both sides of AM which intersect MX and MY at B and C, respectively. Thus, ABC is the required triangle.

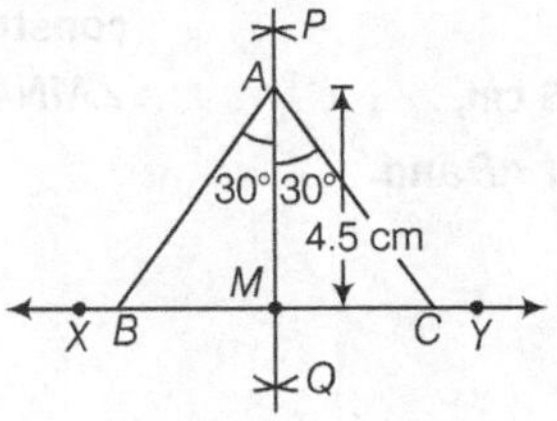

8. Solve as question no. 7.
9. Solve as Example 1.
10. Solve as Example 2.

REVIEW EXERCISE

Including Competency Based Questions

Part I

Multiple Choice Type Questions

1. With the help of a ruler and a compass it is not possible to construct an angle of

(a) 37.5° (b) 40°
(c) 22.5° (d) 67.5°

2. Which of the following angles cannot be constructed by using ruler and a pair of compasses only?

(a) $22\frac{1}{2}°$ (b) 45°
(c) 70° (d) 90°

3. The construction of a ΔLMN in which $LM = 8$ cm, $\angle L = 45°$ is possible when $(MN + LN)$ is

(a) 6 cm (b) 7 cm
(c) 9 cm (d) 5 cm

4. The construction of ΔABC, given that $BC = 6$ cm, $\angle B = 45°$ is not possible when difference of AB and AC is equal to

(a) 6.9 cm (b) 5.2 cm
(c) 5.0 cm (d) 4.0 cm

5. The construction of a ΔDEF in which $DE = 7$ cm, $\angle D = 75°$ is possible when $(EF - DF)$ is equal to

(a) 7.5 cm (b) 7 cm
(c) 8 cm (d) 6.5 cm

6. The construction of a ΔABC, given that $BC = 3$ cm, $\angle C = 60°$ is possible when difference of AB and AC is equal to

(a) 3.2 cm (b) 3.1 cm
(c) 3 cm (d) 2.8 cm

7. Which of the following angles can be constructed by using ruler and a pair of compasses only?

(a) 20° (b) 72°
(c) 105° (d) 130°

8. The construction of ΔABC, given that $BC = 6$ cm, $\angle B = 45°$ is not possible when difference of AB and AC is equal to

(a) 6.9 cm (b) 5.2 cm
(c) 5 cm (d) 4 cm

9. With the help of a ruler and a pair of compasses, it is not possible to construct an angle of

(a) 37.5° (b) 40°
(c) 22.5° (d) 67.5°

10. For what value of $(BC + AC)$, the construction of a ΔABC is possible, if $AB = 7$ cm and $\angle A = 45°$?

(a) 6.5 cm (b) 7 cm
(c) 6.9 cm (d) 7.3 cm

Very Short Answer Type Questions

11. Is this possible to construct an angle of $32\frac{1°}{2}$ using ruler and compass only?

12. Can an angle of 67.5° be constructed?

13. Write the angle bisector of 175°.

14. In the given figure, $\angle MNO = 60°$; by the help of construction

$\angle MNA = \angle ANB + \angle BNO$ and $\angle ANB = \angle BNO$

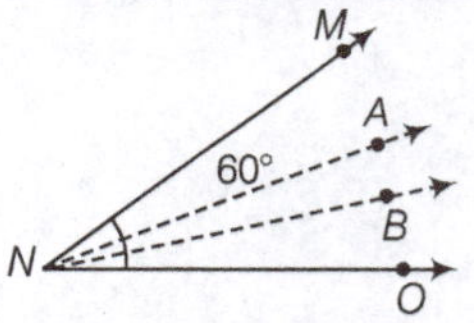

Then, find the measure of $\angle BNO$

15. For what value of $(BC + AC)$, the construction of a ΔABC is possible, if $AB = 6$ cm and $\angle A = 45°$?

16. Can a ΔABC be constructed, in which $AB = 5$ cm, $\angle A = 45°$ and $BC + AC = 5$ cm?

17. For what value of $(BC - AC)$, the construction of a ΔABC is possible, if $AB = 7$ cm and $\angle A = 75°$?

18. Can a ΔABC be constructed, in which $BC = 6$ cm, $\angle C = 30°$ and $AC - AB = 4$ cm?

19. Can a ΔABC can be constructed in which $\angle B = 105°$, $\angle C = 90°$ and $AB + BC + CA = 10$ cm?

Short Answer I Type Questions

20. Draw a line segment $AB = 12$ cm. Divide it into $\frac{3}{4}$th part. Measure the length of $\frac{3}{4}$th part of AB.

21. Construct a ΔABC, when $AB = 6.0$ cm, $BC = 8.0$ cm and $AC = 7.5$ cm.

22. Construct a ΔABC, when $AB = 5.2$ cm, $\angle A = 30°$ and $\angle B = 75°$.

23. Draw an angle of 110° with the help of a protractor and bisect it. Measure each angle.

24. Draw a line segment AB of length 4 cm. Draw a line perpendicular to AB through A and B, respectively. Are these lines parallel?

25. Construct an equilateral triangle, given its side $AB = 6$ cm and justify the construction.

26. Draw any exterior angle of a triangle and bisect it, using compass only.

Short Answer II Type Questions

27. Construct an equilateral triangle one of whose altitude measures 6 cm.

28. Draw a right angled triangle whose hypotenuse measures 6 cm and the length of one of whose sides containing the right angle is 4 cm.

29. Draw a line segment SR of length 10 cm. Divide it into 4 equal parts, using compass and ruler.

30. Construct an angle of $7\frac{1°}{2}$, using compass and ruler only.

31. Construct a ΔSTU, in which $\angle T = 150$, $TU = 3$ cm and $ST + US = 8$ cm.

32. Construct a ΔABC, in which $BC = 9$ cm, $\angle B = 75°$ and $AB + AC = 15$ cm.

33. Draw a Δ ABC in which $BC = 3.6$ cm, $\angle B = 30°$ and $AB - AC = 1.3$ cm.

34. Construct a ΔABC, in which $BC = 5$ cm, $\angle B = 30°$ and $AC - AB = 3$ cm.

35. Construct a ΔPQR, given that $QR = 3$ cm, $\angle PQR = 45°$ and $QP - PR = 2$ cm.

36. Construct a triangle, if the perimeter is 10.4 cm and two angles are 45° and 120°.

37. Construct a ΔABC, in which $BC = 5.2$ cm and $\angle B = 30°$ and the difference of the other two sides is 3.5 cm.

38. Construct a ΔABC whose perimeter is 12 cm and sides are in the ratio 3 : 4 : 5.

39. Construct a ΔPQR, whose perimeter is 12 cm and the length of whose sides are in the ratio 3 : 2 : 4.

40. Construct an isosceles triangle whose base is 4.8 cm and vertical angle is 75°.

41. Construct a triangle whose two sides are 6.0 cm and 3.3 cm and the angle opposite to the shorter side is 30°. How many triangles can be constructed?

42. Construct a triangle whose sides are 3.6 cm, 3.0 cm and 4.8 cm. Bisect the smallest angle and measure each part.

43. Construct a ΔABC, given that $BC = 6.8$ cm, $\angle B = 45°$ and $\angle C = 45°$. Draw the bisectors of $\angle B$ and $\angle C$. If these bisectors meet at I, then measure $\angle BIC$.

Long Answer Type Questions

44. Construct a ΔABC, whose perimeter is 12 cm, $\angle B = 60°$ and $\angle C = 45°$ and justify the construction.

45. Construct a triangle having sides of length 6.2 cm, 7.3 cm and 6 cm. Measure all the three angles. Bisect the smallest and the largest angles. Measure any acute angle formed by the bisecting rays at the point of intersection.

46. Construct an isosceles ΔABC in which base $BC = 4$ cm, sum of the perpendicular from A to BC and side $AB = 6.5$ cm.

HINTS & ANSWERS

1. (b) With the help of a ruler and a compass, we can construct the angels, 90°, 60°, 45°, 22.5°, 30° etc., and its bisector of an angle. So, it is not possible to construct an angle of 40°.
2. (c) 70° ; It cannot be constructed by using ruler and a pair of compasses only.
3. (c) We know that sum of two sides of a triangle is always greater than third side.
$\therefore \quad MN + LN > LM$ i.e. 8 cm.
4. (a) Given, $BC = 6$ cm and $\angle B = 45°$
We know that, the construction of a triangle is not possible, if sum of two sides is less than or equal to the third side of the triangle.
i.e., $\quad AB + BC \le AC$
$\Rightarrow BC \le AC - AB \Rightarrow 6 \le AC - AB$
So, if $AC - AB = 6.9$ cm, then construction of ΔABC with given conditions is not possible.
5. (d) We know that in a triangle the difference of two sides is never greater than any side,
i.e. $EF - DF < DE$ i.e. 7cm.
6. Given, $BC = 3$ cm and $\angle C = 60°$
We know that, the construction of a triangle is possible, if sum of two sides is greater than the third side of the triangle i.e.,
$$AB + BC > AC$$
$\Rightarrow BC > AC - AB \Rightarrow 3 > AC - AB$
So, if $AC - AB = 2.8$ cm, then construction of ΔABC with given conditions is possible.
7. (b) 105° ; It can be constructed by using ruler and a pair of compasses only.
8. (a) When, $AC - AB = 6.9$ cm, then the construction of a ΔABC, if $BC = 6$ cm and $\angle B = 45°$, is not possible.
Because for construction, we must have $AC - AB < BC$, i.e. $AC < AB + BC$.
9. (b) With the help of a ruler and a pair of compasses it is not possible to construct an angle of 40°. Because with the help of ruler and a pair of compasses, we generate the angles 60°, 90°, 45°, 22.5°, 30° etc. and compass generate only the bisects of an angle.
10. (c) The value of $(BC + AC)$ must be greater than 7 cm. Because the sum of any two sides of a triangle is always greater than the third side.
So, the value of $(BC + AC)$ can be 7.3 cm.
11. No, it is not possible, because $32.5° = \frac{1}{2} \times 65°$ and 65° cannot be constructed with the help of a ruler and compass. We can construct the angles 60°, 90°, 75°, 37.5°, 45°, 22.5°, 30° etc.
12. Yes, because $67.5° = \frac{135°}{2} = \frac{1}{2}(90° + 45°)$
13. Angle bisector of $175° = \frac{175°}{2} = 87.5°$
14. Given, $\angle MNO = 60°$
After bisector of 60, we get $\angle ANO = \frac{60°}{2} = 30°$
Again, bisector of $\angle ANO$, we get
$$\angle BNO = \frac{30°}{2} = 15°$$
15. The value of $(BC + AC)$ must be greater than 6 cm, because the sum of any two sides of a triangle is always greater than the third side.
16. No, the sum of any two sides of a triangle must be greater than third side and here it is equal to third side.
17. The value of $(BC - AC)$ must be less than 7 cm, because the difference of any two sides of a triangle is always less than the third side.
18. Yes, because the difference of any two sides of a triangle is less than the third side.
19. Given, $AB + BC + CA = 10$ cm
$\angle B = 105°$ and $\angle C = 90°$
$\because \quad \angle A + \angle B + \angle C = 180°$
Here, $\quad \angle B + \angle C = 105° + 90° = 195°$
$\Rightarrow 195° > 180°$, which can not be true.
Thus, ΔABC cannot be constructed.
20. ***Steps of Construction***
(i) Draw a line segment $AB = 12$ cm.
(ii) Draw the perpendicular bisector PQ of AB such that PQ will intersect AB at a point, M (say).
(iii) Now, draw the perpendicular bisector CD of MB. Thus, $AM + MN$ i.e. AN is the required line segment.

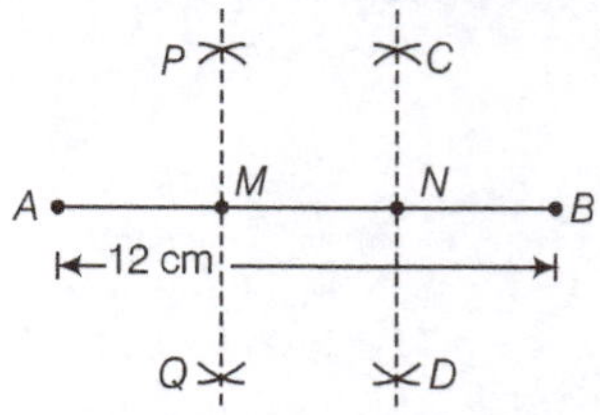

$\therefore AN = \frac{3}{4}AB = \frac{3}{4} \times 12$
$= 3 \times 3 = 9$ cm
Hence, the measure of AN is 9 cm.
21. Solve as Example 2 of Topic 2.
22. Solve as Example 4 of Topic 2.

23. Each angle measures 55°

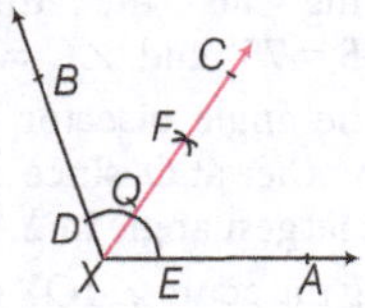

24. Yes, the lines are parallel.

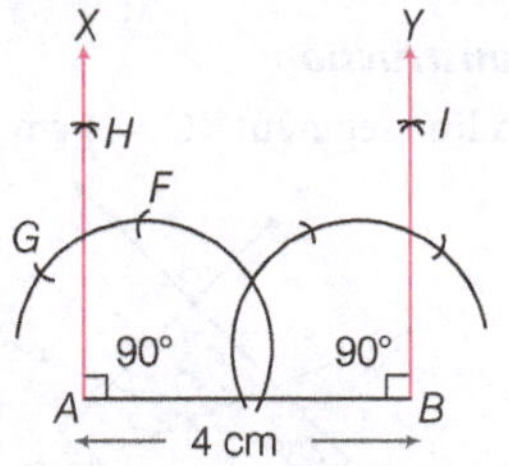

25. Solve as Q. 7 of Try These 14.2.

26. Draw any triangle and take any exterior angle and simply bisect it.

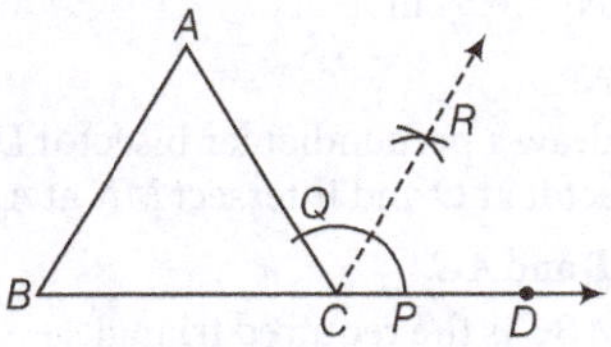

27. Solve as Q.7 of Try These 14.2.

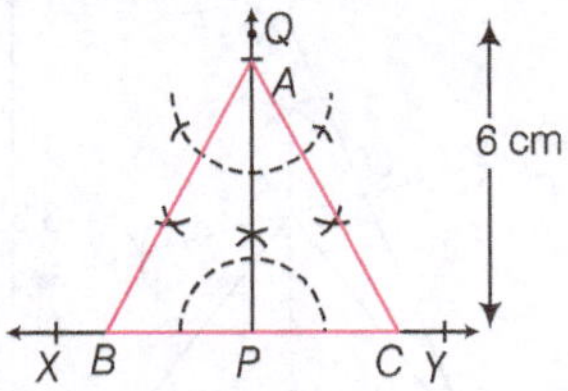

28. ***Steps of Construction***

(*i*) Draw a line segment $BC = 6$ cm.

(*ii*) Draw perpendicular bisector of BC which intersects BC at O.

(*iii*) Taking O as centre and radius OB, draw a semi-circle on BC.

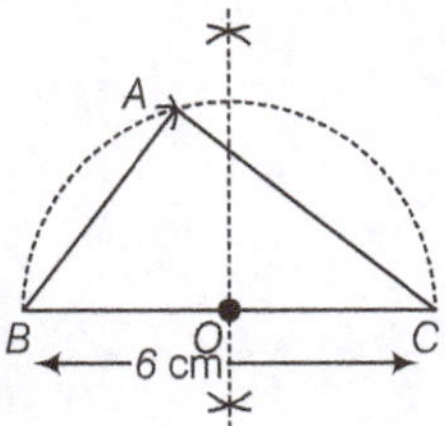

(*iv*) Taking B as centre and radius equal to 4 cm, draw an arc, cutting the semi-circle at A.

(*v*) Join AB and AC.

Thus, ABC is the required right angled triangle.

29. ***Steps of Construction***

(*i*) Draw a line segment $SR = 10$ cm.

(*ii*) Draw a perpendicular bisector of SR, which intersect it at M.

(*iii*) Again, draw a perpendicular bisector of MR, which intersects it at T.

(*iv*) Also, draw a perpendicular bisector of MS, which intersects it at N. Thus, SR has been divided into four equal parts SN, NM, TM, RT.

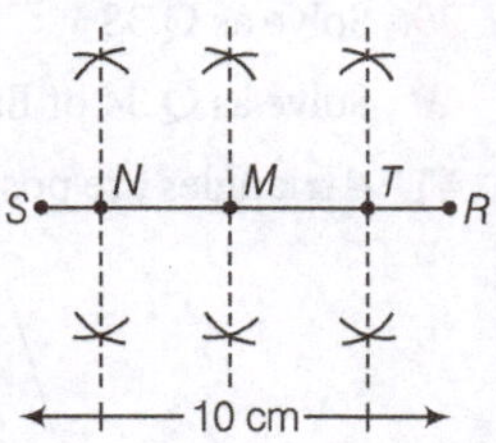

30. **Hint** Construct 60°, then 30°, then 15° and then $7\frac{1}{2}°$.

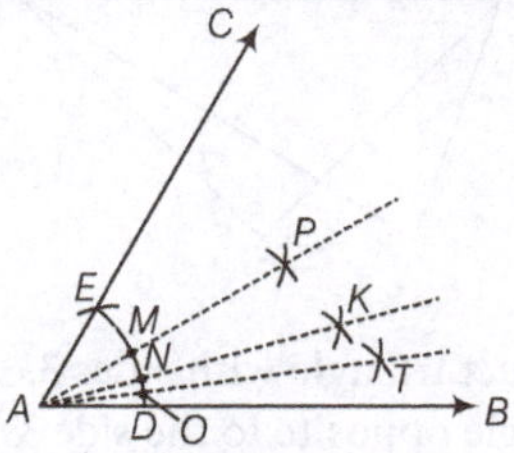

31. Solve as Example 1 of Topic 2.

32. Solve as Example 1 of Topic 2.

33. Solve as Example 2 of Topic 2.

34. Solve as Example 2 of Topic 2.

35. Solve as Example 2 of Topic 2.

36. Solve as Example 4 of Topic 2.

37. Solve as Example 2 of Topic 2.

38. ***Steps of Construction***

(*i*) Draw a line segment $PQ = 3 + 4 + 5 = 12$ cm.

(*ii*) Draw a ray PX in the downward direction making an acute angle with PQ.

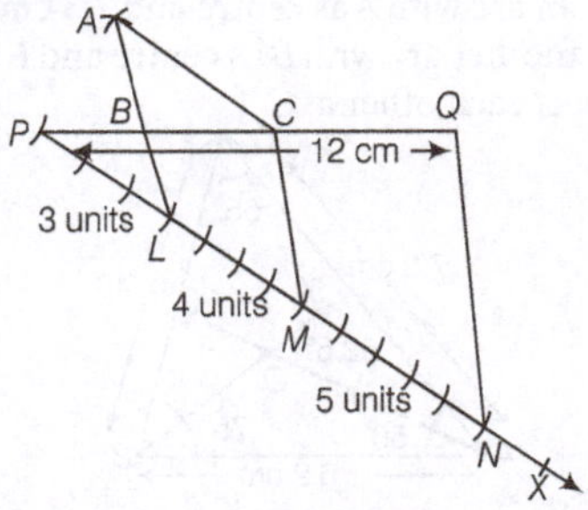

(*iii*) From P, cut $(3 + 4 + 5) = 12$, equal distance mark on PX.

(*iv*) Denote the points L, M and N on PX such that $PL = 3$ units $LM = 4$ units and $MN = 5$ units.

(*v*) Join NQ.

(*vi*) Through L and M, draw $LB \parallel NQ$ and $MC \parallel NQ$, cutting PQ at B and C, respectively.

(*vii*) With B as centre and radius BP, draw an arc and with C as centre and radius CQ, draw another arc cutting the previous arc at A on the upward side of PQ.

(*viii*) Join AB and AC. Thus, ABC is the required triangle.

39. Solve as Q.38

40. Solve as Q.34 of Exam Practice.

41. 4 triangles are possible, as shown

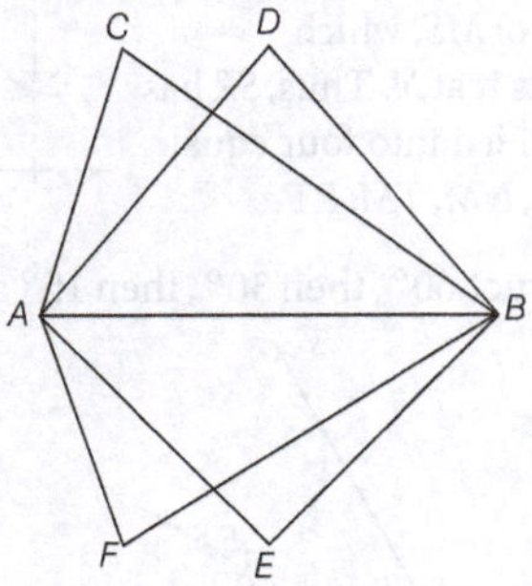

42. **Hint** Construct triangle with sides 3.6, 3.0, 4.8 cm. Then bisect the angle opposite to the side $3a$.

Ans. Each part measures 20°.

43. ***Steps of Construction***

(*i*) Draw a line segment $BC = 6.8$ cm.

(*ii*) Draw $\angle PBC = 45°$ at point B and draw $\angle QCB = 45°$ at point C.

(*iii*) Mark the point of intersection of ray BP and ray CQ at A.

(*iv*) Now, draw the angle bisectors of $\angle ABC$ and $\angle ACB$, let them to intersect each other at point O. On measuring the $\angle BOC$, we get the value 135°.

44. Solve as Example 4 of Topic 2.

45. ***Steps of Construction***

(*i*) Draw a line segment $AB = 6.2$ cm.

(*ii*) Draw an arc with A as centre and 7.3 cm as radius and draw another arc with B as centre and 6 cm as radius to intersect each other at C.

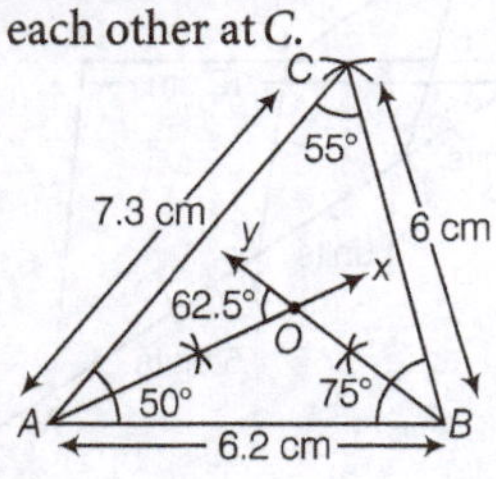

(*iii*) Join AC and BC. Thus, we get the required triangle ABC. On measuring all the three angles, we get $\angle A = 50°$, $\angle B = 75°$ and $\angle C = 55°$.

Now, draw the angle bisector of $\angle A$ and $\angle B$, which intersect each other at O, since $\angle A$ is the smallest angle and $\angle B$ is the largest angle in ΔABC.

(*iv*) On measuring the acute $\angle AOY$ formed by the bisecting rays AX and BY at the point of intersection O, we get $\angle AOY = 62.5°$

46. ***Steps of Construction***

(*i*) Draw a line segment $BC = 4$ cm.

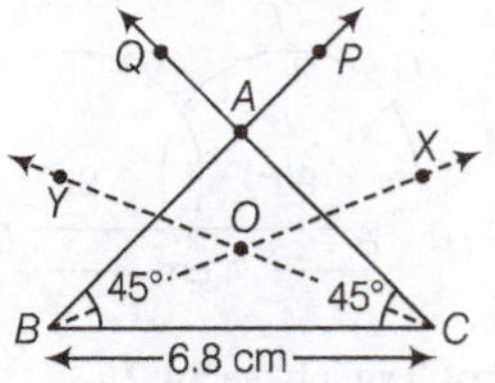

(*ii*) Draw a perpendicular bisector PQ of BC, which intersect it at M.

(*iii*) Cut $MN = 6.5$ cm.

(*iv*) Join BN.

(*v*) Now, draw a perpendicular bisector DE of BN which intersect it at O and intersect MN at A.

(*vi*) Join AB and AC.

Thus, ABC is the required triangle.

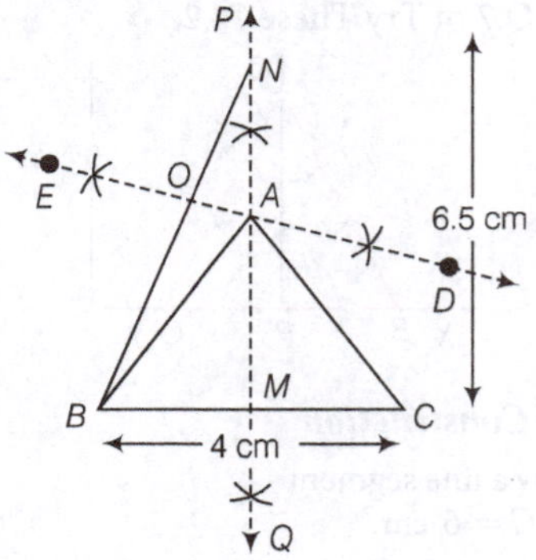

Probability

(To be Assessed Formatively)

CHAPTER 15

In our daily life, we come across some statements having words; chances, doubt, probably, most probably etc. e.g.

(*i*) There is 50% *chances* of Anil to crack the annual exam.

(*ii*) I *doubt* that he will pass the test.

(*iii*) *Most probably* it will rain today.

In all the above statements, the words 'chances', 'doubt', 'most probably' etc., are involve in an element of uncertainty. Here, in statement (i), 50% chances means it may or may not Anil crack the annual exam. We are predicting 50% chances of Anil to crack the annual exam, which based on his seriousness toward his study and hard work.

Similarly, in the other cases, the uncertainty can be measured numerically by means of probability. In this chapter, we will study the concept of probability as a measure of certainty or uncertainty.

Probability is the study of the chances of events happening. For understanding the concept of probability we have to know the some basic terms related to it.

Some Basic Terms

- **Experiment or Trial** An operation which can produce some well-defined outcomes, is called an experiment or trial.

  e.g. If a coin is tossed 20 times, then each toss is called an experiment or a trial and we get either head or tail as a result. Here, head and tail are called *outcomes*.

  The experiment can be divided into two types, which are given below

  1. **Random Experiment** An experiment, when repeated under identical conditions, do not produce the same outcomes every time but the outcomes produced is one out of the several possible outcomes, is known as a random or probabilistic experiment. e.g. Tossing a **fair** coin is a random experiment, because if we toss a coin, then either a head or tail will come up but if we toss a coin again and again, then the outcome each time will not be same but it will sure be either head or tail.
  2. **Deterministic Experiment** An experiment, when repeated under identical conditions, produce the same result or outcomes, is known as deterministic experiment. e.g. Tossing an **unfair** coin having either tail or head on both sides 20 times, we get the same result.

- **Event** A possible outcome or combination of outcomes is called an event. e.g. Getting head in the toss of a coin is an event.

- **Occurrence of an Event** An event E associated to a random experiment is said to be occur (or happen) in a trial, if the outcome of trial is one of the outcomes that favours E.

  e.g. If a die is rolled and the outcome of a trial is 4, then we say that each of the following events has happened (or occurred)

  (*i*) getting an even number.

  (*ii*) getting a number greater than 2.

  (*iii*) getting a number less than 5.

- **Elementary Event** An event having only one outcome of the random experiment is called an elementary event.

  e.g. In tossing of a coin, the possible outcomes are Head (H) and Tail (T).

  Therefore, if we define

  E_1 = Getting head (H) on the upper face of the coin

  and E_2 = Getting tail (T) on the upper face of the coin.

  Then, E_1 and E_2 are elementary events associated with the random experiment of tossing of a coin.

- **Compound Event** A collection of two or more elementary events associated with a random experiment is called a compound event.
e.g. In the random experiment of tossing of two coins simultaneously, if we define the event getting exactly one head, then it is a collection of elementary events (or outcomes) *HT* and *TH*. So, it is a compound event.

Note • Random toss is a phrase which means that the coin is allowed to fall freely without any bias or interference.
• Coin A coin has two sides, Head (*H*) and Tail (*T*).
• Die A die is a well-balanced cube with six faces marked with numbers 1, 2, 3, 4, 5 and 6. Sometimes, dots appear in place of numbers.

Probability— An Experimental Approach

If *E* is an event that happen when an experiment is performed, then the **experimental** or **empirical probability** of an event *E* is given by

$$P(E)=\frac{\text{Number of trials in which the event } E \text{ has happened}}{\text{Total number of trials}}$$

$$\text{or } P(E)=\frac{\text{Number of times in which the event } E \text{ has occurred}}{\text{Number of times the experiment has performed}}$$

The empirical probability depends on the number of trials undertaken and the number of times the outcomes you are looking for coming up in the trials.
In other words, percentage of occurrence or non-occurrence of an event is called the probability.

e.g. If a coin is tossed 1000 times and event E_1 = head occurs 455 times and event E_2 = tail occurs 545 times, then probability of occurrence of head, $P(E_1)=\frac{455}{1000}=0.455$

and probability of occurrence of tail, $P(E_2)=\frac{545}{1000}=0.545$

Important Points Related to Probability

1. The probability of happening of an event always lies from 0 to 1, i.e. $0 \le P(E) \le 1$. In percentage, it lies from 0% to 100%.
2. If probability of an event say *A* is 1, i.e. $P(A)=1$, then event *A* is called a **certain event** or **sure event.**
3. If probability of an event say *B* is 0, i.e. $P(B)=0$, then event *B* is called an **impossible event.**
4. The sum of all the probabilities of all possible outcomes of an experiment is 1.
5. $P(E)+P(\text{not } E)=1$ or $P(E)=1-P(\text{not } E)$
or $P(\text{not } E)=1-P(E)$
6. Experimental probability of an event can never be negative.

Example 1. **Two coins are tossed simultaneously 300 times and it is found that two heads appeared 135 times, one head appeared 111 times and no head appeared 54 times. If two coins are tossed at random, what is the probability of getting**

(i) 2 heads? (ii) 1 head? (iii) 0 head?

Sol. Here, two coins are tossed simultaneously 300 times.

So, total number of trials = 300

(*i*) Let E_1 be the event of getting 2 heads appeared 135 times.

∴ Number of trials in which 2 heads occur = 135

Hence, probability of getting 2 heads,

$$P(E_1)=\frac{135}{300}=0.45$$

(*ii*) Let E_2 be the event of getting 1 head appeared 111 times.

∴ Number of trials in which 1 head occur = 111

Hence, probability of getting 1 head,

$$P(E_2)=\frac{111}{300}=0.37$$

(*iii*) Let E_3 be the event of getting 0 head (no head) appeared 54 times.

∴ Number of trials in which 0 head occur = 54

Hence, probability of getting 0 head,

$$P(E_3)=\frac{54}{300}=0.18$$

Note If we toss two coins, then we get either 2 heads or 0 tail, 1 head or 1 tail, 0 head or 2 tails. So, probabilities of all possible outcomes in above example are calculated. Now, sum of all probabilities = 0.45 + 0.37 + 0.18 = 1.

Example 2. **The percentage of marks obtained by a student in the monthly unit tests are given below.**

Unit test	I	II	III	IV	V
Percentage of marks obtained	58	74	76	62	85

Find the probability that the student gets

(i) a first class, i.e. atleast 60% marks.
(ii) marks between 70% and 80%.
(iii) a distinction, i.e. 75% or above.
(iv) less than 65% marks.

Sol. Total number of unit tests held = 5

(*i*) Number of unit tests in which the student gets a first class, i.e. atleast 60% marks = 4

∴ Probability that the student gets a first class $=\frac{4}{5}=0.8$

(*ii*) Number of unit tests in which the student gets marks between 70% and 80% = 2

∴ Probability that the student gets marks between 70% and 80% $=\frac{2}{5}=0.4$

(*iii*) Number of unit tests in which the student gets distinction or marks equal and more than 75% = 2

$\therefore$ Probability that the student gets distinction $= \frac{2}{5} = 0.4$

(*iv*) Number of unit tests in which the student gets less than 65% marks = 2

$\therefore$ Probability that the student gets less than 65% marks $= \frac{2}{5} = 0.4$

Example 3. **A die is thrown 250 times and the outcomes are noted as given below.**

Outcome	1	2	3	4	5	6
Frequency	65	40	42	25	33	45

If a die is thrown at random, then find the probability of getting

(i) 1 (ii) 2 (iii) 3
(iv) 4 (v) 5 (vi) 6

Sol. Here, a die is thrown 250 times.

So, total number of trials = 250

In a random throw of a die, let E_1, E_2, E_3, E_4, E_5 and E_6 be the events of getting 1, 2, 3, 4, 5 and 6, respectively.

(*i*) Here, frequency of outcome 1 is 65, i.e. 1 occurs on a die 65 times.

$$\therefore P\text{ (getting 1)} = P(E_1) = \frac{\text{Number of times 1 occurs}}{\text{Total number of trials}}$$

$$= \frac{65}{250} = 0.26$$

(*ii*) Here, 2 occurs on a die 40 times.

$$\therefore P\text{ (getting 2)} = P(E_2) = \frac{\text{Number of times 2 occurs}}{\text{Total number of trials}}$$

$$= \frac{40}{250} = 0.16$$

(*iii*) Here, 3 occurs on a die 42 times.

$$\therefore P\text{ (getting 3)} = P(E_3) = \frac{\text{Number of times 3 occurs}}{\text{Total number of trials}}$$

$$= \frac{42}{250} = 0.168$$

(*iv*) Here, 4 occurs on a die 25 times.

$$\therefore P\text{ (getting 4)} = P(E_4) = \frac{\text{Number of times 4 occurs}}{\text{Total number of trials}}$$

$$= \frac{25}{250} = 0.10$$

(*v*) Here, 5 occurs on a die 33 times.

$$\therefore P\text{ (getting 5)} = P(E_5) = \frac{\text{Number of times 5 occurs}}{\text{Total number of trials}}$$

$$= \frac{33}{250} = 0.132$$

(*vi*) Here, 6 occurs on a die 45 times

$$\therefore P\text{ (getting 6)} = P(E_6) = \frac{\text{Number of times 6 occurs}}{\text{Total number of trials}}$$

$$= \frac{45}{250} = 0.18$$

Note Here, $P(E_1) + P(E_2) + P(E_3) + P(E_4) + P(E_5) + P(E_6)$
$= 0.26 + 0.16 + 0.168 + 0.10 + 0.132 + 0.18 = 1$

Example 4. **On one page of a telephone directory, there were 200 telephone numbers. The frequency distribution of their unit place digit (e.g. In the number 25828573, the unit place digit is 3) is given in table.**

Digit	0	1	2	3	4	5	6	7	8	9
Frequency	22	26	22	22	20	10	14	28	16	20

Without looking at the page, the pencil is placed on one of these numbers, i.e. the number is chosen at random. What is the probability that the digit in its unit place is 6?

Sol. Here, 200 telephone numbers are given on one page of a telephone directory.

$\therefore$ Total number of selected telephone numbers = 200

The frequency of digit 6 at unit place is 14. i.e. In 14 telephone numbers 6 is at unit place.

$\therefore$ Required probability

$$= \frac{\text{Frequency of 6}}{\text{Total number of selected telephone numbers}}$$

$$= \frac{14}{200} = 0.07$$

Example 5. **The record of a weather station shows that out of the past 250 consecutive days, its weather forecast were correct 175 times.**

(i) What is the probability that on a given day it was correct?

(ii) What is the probability that it was not correct on a given day?

Sol. Total number of days for which the weather forecast record is available = 250

(*i*) Here, 175 times the weather forecast were correct.

$\therefore$ Number of days when the forecasts was correct = 175

Hence, required probability $= \frac{175}{250} = 0.7$

(*ii*) Probability that forecast was not correct on a given day
= 1 – Probability that forecast was correct on a given day
$= 1 - 0.7 = 0.3$

Alternate Method

Number of days when the forecast was not correct
= Total number of days
– Number of days when forecast was correct
$= 250 - 175 = 75$

Hence, required probability $= \frac{75}{250} = 0.3$

Example 6. **A tyre manufacturing company kept a record of the distance covered before a tyre needed to be replaced. The table shows the results of 1000 cases.**

Distance (in km)	Less than 4000	4000 to 9000	9001 to 14000	More than 14000
Frequency	20	210	325	445

If you buy a tyre of this company, what is the probability that

(i) it will need to be replaced before it has covered 4000 km?

(ii) it will last more than 9000 km?

(iii) it will need to be replaced after it has covered somewhere between 4000 km and 14000 km?

Sol. Here, results of 1000 cases are given.

So, total number of trials = 1000

(*i*) The frequency of tyres that needs to be replaced before it covers 4000 km is 20.

So, P (tyre to be replaced before it covers 4000 km)

$$= \frac{20}{1000} = 0.02$$

(*ii*) The frequency of tyres that will last more than 9000 km is $325 + 445 = 770$.

So, P (tyre will last more than 9000 km) $= \frac{770}{1000} = 0.77$

(*iii*) The frequency of tyres that requires replacement between 4000 km and 14000 km is $210 + 325 = 535$.

So, P (tyre requiring replacement between 4000 km and 14000 km) $= \frac{535}{1000} = 0.535$

Example 7. **The probabilities of a student getting *A*, *B*, *C* and *D* grades are 0.35, 0.25, 0.35 and 0.05. Then, find the probability that**

(i) a student gets atmost grade C.

(ii) a student gets atleast grade C.

Sol. Let E_1, E_2, E_3 and E_4 denote the events getting grade A, B, C and D, respectively.

Then, $P(E_1) = 0.35, P(E_2) = 0.25,$

$P(E_3) = 0.35$ and $P(E_4) = 0.05$

(*i*) A student who gets atmost grade C can also get grade D.

$\therefore P$ (getting atmost grade C)

$= P$(getting grade C) $+ P$ (getting grade D)

$= 0.35 + 0.05 = 0.40$

Hence, the probability that a student gets atmost grade C is 0.40.

(*ii*) A student who gets atleast grade C can also get grades A and B.

$\therefore P$ (getting atleast grade C) $= P$ (getting grade A) $+ P$ (getting grade B) $+ P$ (getting grade C)

$= 0.35 + 0.25 + 0.35 = 0.95$

Hence, the probability that a student gets atleast grade C is 0.95.

Example 8. **Cards marked with the numbers 2 to 101 are placed in a box and mixed thoroughly. One card is drawn from this box. Find the probability that the number on the card is**

(i) an even number. (ii) a number less than 14.

(iii) a number which is a perfect square.

Sol. Since, the cards are marked from 2 to 101.

Therefore, total number of cards = 100

(*i*) There are 50 cards marked with even numbers from 2 to 101.

$\therefore P$ (getting an even number) $= \frac{50}{100} = \frac{1}{2}$

Hence, the probability of getting even number card is $\frac{1}{2}$.

(*ii*) There are 12 cards on which marked numbers are less than 14.

$\therefore$ P (getting a number less than 14) $= \frac{12}{100} = \frac{3}{25}$

Hence, the probability that the number on card is less than 14, is $\frac{3}{25}$.

(*iii*) The numbers from 2 to 101 which are perfect square are 4, 9, 16, 25, 36, 49, 64, 81, 100. i.e. squares of 2, 3, 4, 5, 6, 7, 8, 9 and 10, respectively.

Total number of cards having a number which is a perfect square = 9

$\therefore$ P (getting a number which is a perfect square)

$$= \frac{9}{100}$$

Hence, the probability that the number marked on the card which is a perfect square, is $\frac{9}{100}$.

REVIEW EXERCISE

Including Competency Based Questions

Part I

Multiple Choice Type Questions

1. A coin is tossed 100 times and head appears 46 times. Now, if we toss a coin at random, then what is the probability of getting a tail?

(a) $\frac{23}{50}$ (b) $\frac{27}{50}$ (c) $\frac{28}{50}$ (d) $\frac{26}{50}$

2. A Mathematics book contains 250 pages. A page is selected at random. What is the probability that the number on the page selected is a perfect square?

(a) $\frac{4}{25}$ (b) $\frac{3}{50}$ (c) $\frac{7}{50}$ (d) $\frac{9}{50}$

3. Three coins are tossed simultaneously 200 times with the following frequencies of different outcomes

Outcomes	3 heads	2 heads	1 head	No head
Frequency	23	72	77	28

The probability of getting two heads is

(a) 0.21 (b) 0.36 (c) 0.49 (d) 0.50

4. In a cricket match, if a batsman hits a boundary 8 times out of 40 balls he plays. Then, the probability that he did not hit a boundary, is

(a) 0.2 (b) 0.4 (c) 0.6 (d) 0.8

5. The record of a weather station shows that out of the past 250 consecutive days, its weather forecast were correct 175 times. Then, the probability that on a given day it was correct and it was not correct, is

(a) 0.1, 0.2 (b) 0.7, 0.3 (c) 0.9, 0.1 (d) 0.7, 0.5

6. The maximum temperature in Celsius of some cities on a day are given as below

Maximum temp (in °C)	10-15	16-20	21-25	26-30	31-35	36-40
Number of cities	1	2	18	21	19	18

The probability that maximum temperature lies between 16°C and 30°C, is

(a) $\frac{41}{79}$ (b) $\frac{56}{81}$ (c) $\frac{21}{53}$ (d) $\frac{1}{10}$

7. On one page of a telephone directory, there were 200 telephone number. The frequency distribution of their unit place digit (e.g. in the number 25828573 the unit's place digit is 3) is given in the following table

Digit	0	1	2	3	4	5	6	7	8	9
Frequency	22	26	22	22	20	10	14	28	16	20

Without looking at the page, the pencil is placed on one of these numbers, i.e. the number is chosen at random. What is the probability that the digit in its unit place is 6?

(a) 0.01 (b) 0.03
(c) 0.05 (d) 0.07

8. A die is thrown 250 times and the outcomes are noted as given below

Outcomes	1	2	3	4	5	6
Frequency	65	40	42	25	33	45

If a die is thrown at random, then the probabilities of getting 1 and 5 are respectively

(a) 0.26, 0.132
(b) 0.21, 0.139
(c) 0.20, 0.139
(d) 0.11, 0.112

Very Short Answer Type Questions

9. Can the experimental probability of an event be a negative number? If not, why?

10. Can experimental probability of an event be greater than 1? Justify your answer.

11. Check whether 8/7 can be empirical probability or not. Give reason.

12. Find the probability of Sun revolving around Earth.

13. A die is thrown 50 times and the outcomes are recorded as under

Outcomes	1	2	3	4	5	6
Number of times	11	9	8	5	7	10

If a die is thrown at random, then what is the probability of getting 8?

14. A die is thrown six times and number on it is noted as given below

Number of die	1	2	3	4	5	6
Frequency	1	1	1	1	1	1

What is the probability that it is a prime number?

15. Some families with 2 children were selected randomly and the following data recorded

Number of girls in a family	0	1	2
Number of families	111	714	375

If a family is chosen at random, then compute the probability that it has 1 girl.

16. In a cricket match, Shane Warne takes three wickets from every 27 balls he bowls. Find the probability of a batsman not getting out by Shane Warne's bowling.

17. 80 bulbs are selected at random from a lot and their lifetime (in hours) is recorded in the form of a frequency table given below

Lifetime (in hours)	300	500	700	900	1100
Frequency	10	12	23	25	10

One bulb is selected at random from the lot. Find the probability that its life is 1150 h.

18. A Mathematics book contains 250 pages. A page is selected at random. What is the probability that the number on the page selected is a perfect square?

19. What is the probability of an event that Monday is the first day of a week?

20. As the number of tosses of a coin increases the ratio of the number of heads to the total number of tosses will be $\frac{1}{2}$. Is it correct? If not, write the correct one.

21. The probabilities of a student getting grades *A*, *B*, *C* and *D* are 0.2, 0.3, 0.15 and 0.35 respectively, then find the probability that a student gets atleast *C* grade.

Short Answer I Type Questions

22. In a survey of 364 children aged 19-36 months, it was found that 91 liked to eat potato chips. If a child is selected at random, then find the probability that he/she does not like to eat potato chips.

23. A die was rolled 200 times and the number of times, 6 came up was noted. If the experimental probability calculated from this information is $\frac{2}{5}$, then how many times 6 came up?

24. In a medical examination 40 students of a class, their blood groups are recorded as follow

Blood group	A	AB	B	O
Number of students	10	13	12	5

A student is selected at random from the class. Find the probability that he/she has blood group B.

25. In a survey of 400 youngsters aged 16-20 yr, it was found that 191 have their Voter ID card. If an adult is selected at random, find the probability that he/she does not have his/her Voter ID card.

26. 12 packets of salt, each marked 2 kg, actually contained the following weights (in kg) of salt

1.950, 2.020, 2.060, 1.980, 2.030, 1.970, 2.040, 1.990, 1.985, 2.025, 2.000, 1.980

Out of these packets, one packet is chosen at random. What is the probability that the chosen packet contains more than 2 kg of salt?

27. Two coins are tossed 1000 times and the outcomes are recorded as below

Number of heads	2	1	0
Frequency	200	550	250

Based on this information, find the probability for atmost one head.

28. In a football match, a goalkeeper of a team can stop a goal 32 times out of 40 shots by a team. Find the probability that a team can make a goal.

29. On one page of a directory, there are 160 telephone numbers. The frequency distribution of the unit place digit is given as under

Unit place digit	0	1	2	3	4	5	6	7	8	9
Frequency	19	16	18	21	14	11	15	16	13	17

From this page, one of the number is chosen at random. What is the probability that the unit place digit in the chosen number is 7?

30. In 50 throws of a die, the outcomes were noted as under

Outcomes	1	2	3	4	5	6
Number of times	8	9	6	7	12	8

A die is thrown at random. What is the probability of getting an even number?

31. Teachers and students are selected at random to make two teams of 20 members each on sport day to participate in the event of 'Tug of War.' The numbers of volunteers are as follow

Teachers		Students	
Male	Female	Male	Female
12	18	20	10

Find the probability that the person chosen at random

(*i*) is a male teacher.

(*ii*) is a female student.

32. Three coins are tossed simultaneously 150 times with the following frequencies of different outcomes.

Number of tails	0	1	2	3
Frequency	25	30	32	63

Compute the probability of getting
(*i*) atleast 2 tails.
(*ii*) exactly 1 tail.

33. 80 bulbs are selected at random from a lot and their lifetime is recorded in the form of a frequency table given below

Lifetime (in hours)	300	500	700	900	1100
Frequencies	10	15	23	25	7

A bulb is chosen at random from the lot. What is the probability that the bulb chosen has lifetime less than 900 h?

34. A die is thrown 50 times and it shows the number 1, 23 times. Find the probability of getting a number other than 1 in the next throw of the die.

35. A 9th class English book contains 200 pages. A page is selected at random.What is the probability that the number on the page is divisible by 10?

36. The probability of guessing the correct answer to a certain question is $\frac{x}{5}$. If the probability of not guessing the correct answer is $\frac{2x}{3}$, then find the value of x.

37. At a hospital, a doctor compiled the following data about 400 patients whom he could cure of hepatitis

Time of cure	< 1 month	1-2 months	2-3 months	> 3 months
Number of patients	210	105	60	25

Another case of hepatitis is reported. What is the probability that this patient will be cured in
(*i*) less than 2 months?
(*ii*) 1 month or more but not more than 3 months?

38. A die is rolled 200 times and its outcomes are recorded as below

Outcome	1	2	3	4	5	6
Frequency	25	35	40	28	42	30

Find the probability of getting
(*i*) an even prime. (*ii*) a multiple of 3.

39. Following table shows the birth month of 80 students of Class XII

Jan	Feb	Mar	Apr	May	June
5	6	7	4	10	3
July	Aug	Sept	Oct	Nov	Dec
5	10	6	8	8	8

Find the probability that a student was born in a month in which the Independence day and Republic day are celebrated.

40. If the probability of winning a race of an athlete is $\frac{1}{6}$ less than twice the probability of losing the race, find the probability of winning the race.

41. If the difference between the probabilities of success and failure of an event is $\frac{3}{17}$, find the probabilities of success and failure of the event.

Short Answer II Type Questions

42. Two coins are tossed simultaneously 1000 times with the following frequencies of different outcomes.
(*i*) Two heads → 210 times
(*ii*) One head → 550 times
(*iii*) No head → 240 times

Find the probability of occurrence of each of these outcomes.

43. Probability of getting a blue ball is 2/3, from a bag containing 6 blue and 3 red balls. 12 red balls are added in the bag, then find the probability of getting
(*i*) a blue ball.
(*ii*) a red ball.

44. Some families with 2 children were selected randomly and the following data were recorded

Number of girls in a family	0	1	2
Number of families	109	706	204

If a family is chosen at random, compute the probability that it has
(*i*) exactly no girl.
(*ii*) exactly 1 boy.
(*iii*) exactly 2 girls.

45. A company selected 4000 households at random and surveyed them to find out a relationship between income level and the number of television sets in a home. The information, so obtained is listed in the following table

Monthly income (in ₹)	Number of televisions/households			
	0	1	2	Above 2
Less than 10000	20	80	10	0
10000-14999	10	240	60	0
15000-19999	0	380	120	30
20000-24999	0	520	370	80
25000 and above	0	1100	760	220

Find the probability

(i) of a household earning ₹ 10000-₹ 14999 per month and having exactly one television.

(ii) of a household earning ₹ 25000 and above per month and owning 2 televisions.

(iii) of a household not having any television.

46. While working out a question on probability, it was found that there were 286 letters of English alphabet. The following was observation of occurrence of each letter

a : 70, b : 14, e : 26, r : 40 and i : 36.

Others (not including vowels) = 100

Then, find the probability of

(i) a vowel letters.

(ii) non-vowel letters.

47. The maximum temperature in celsius of some cities on a day are given as below

Maximum temp (in °C)	10-15	16-20	21-25	26-30	31-35	36-40
Number of cities	1	2	18	21	19	18

(i) Find the probability that maximum temperature lies between 16°C and 30°C.

(ii) Find the probability that minimum temperature is less than 25°C.

48. The percentage of marks obtained by a student in monthly unit test are given below

Unit test	I	II	III	IV	V
Percentage of marks	70	72	65	68	85

Find the probability that the student gets

(i) more than 70% marks.

(ii) more than 90% marks.

49. The distances (in km) of 40 students from their residences to the school are given below

4, 19, 7, 13, 3, 10, 9, 14, 10, 12, 7, 2, 20, 13, 8, 9, 15, 19, 3, 5, 10, 10, 5, 15, 15, 11, 11, 15, 7, 16, 15, 7, 12, 16, 18, 6, 20, 2, 3, 2

Find the probability that a student selected at random

(i) lives at a distance atmost 15 km from their school.

(ii) lives within 1 km from their school.

50. If the difference between the probability of success and failure of an event is 5 / 19. Find the probability of success and failure of the event.

51. The table shows the marks (out of 150) obtained by a student in unit tests.

Unit test	I	II	III	IV	V	VI
Marks (out of 150)	72	96	105	80	125	139

Find the probability that the student gets 80% or more in the next unit test. Also, find the probability that the student gets less than 80% marks.

52. Three coins are tossed simultaneously 400 times and following frequencies of the outcomes were recorded

Outcomes	Frequencies
3 heads	103
2 heads	124
1 head	98
No head	x

(i) Find the probability of getting no head.

(ii) Find the probability of getting 1 head.

(iii) Find the probability of getting exactly 2 heads.

53. Fifty seeds were selected at random from each of 5 bags of seeds and were kept under standardised conditions favourable to germination. After 20 days, the number of seeds which had germinated in each collection were counted and recorded as follows

Bags	1	2	3	4	5
Number of seeds germinated	40	48	42	39	41

What is the probability of germination of

(i) more than 40 seeds in a bag?

(ii) 49 seeds in a bag?

(iii) more than 35 seeds in a bag?

54. Bulbs are packed in cartons each containing 40 bulbs, seven hundred cartons were examined for defective bulbs and the results are given in the following table.

Number of defective bulbs	0	1	2	3	4	5	6	More than 6
Frequency	400	180	48	41	18	8	3	2

One carton was selected at random. What is the probability that it has

(i) no defective bulb?

(ii) defective bulbs from 2 to 6?

(iii) defective bulbs less than 4?

Long Answer Type Questions

55. Three coins are tossed simultaneously 150 times and it is found that 3 tails appeared 24 times, 2 tails appeared 45 times, 1 tail appeared 72 times and no tail appeared 9 times. If three coins are tossed simultaneously at random. Find the probability of getting

(*i*) 3 tails. (*ii*) 2 tails.

(*iii*) 1 tail. (*iv*) 0 tail.

56. Given below is the frequency distribution of daily wages (in ₹) of 30 workers in a certain factory

Daily wages (in ₹)	110-130	130-150	150-170	170-190	190-210	210-230	230-250
Number of workers	3	4	5	6	5	4	3

A worker is selected at random. Find the probability that his wage is

(*i*) less than ₹ 150.

(*ii*) atleast ₹ 210.

(*iii*) more than or equal to ₹ 150 but less than ₹ 210.

(*iv*) in the interval ₹ 190 - ₹ 250.

57. A tyre manufacturing company kept a record of the distance covered before a tyre was replaced.

Distance (in km)	More than 1500	1100-1500	700-1100	300-700	Less than 300
Number of tyres	250	150	120	200	80

If you buy a tyre of this company, what is the probability that

(*i*) it will need a replacement before it has covered 700 km?

(*ii*) it will last more than 1100 km?

(*iii*) it will need to be replaced between 300 km to 1500 km?

(*iv*) it will need to be replaced, after 1500 km?

58. The table shows the number of people visiting the 'Good-living pavilion' in a trade fair during different times of the day.

Time	Number of people
9 am - 11 am	175
11 am - 1 pm	125
1 pm - 3 pm	225
3 pm - 5 pm	200
5 pm - 7 pm	120

Find the probability that the randomly chosen person visited the pavilion

(*i*) after 1 pm but before 5 pm.

(*ii*) between 9 am to 1 pm.

(*iii*) after 5 pm.

(*iv*) between 3 pm and 5 pm.

59. Over the past 200 working days, the number of defective parts produced by a machine is given in the following table

Number of defective parts	0	1	2	3	4	5	6	7	8	9	10	11	12	13
Days	50	32	22	18	12	12	10	10	10	8	6	6	2	2

Determine the probability that tomorrow's output will have

(*i*) no defective part.

(*ii*) atleast 1 defective part.

(*iii*) not more than 5 defective parts.

(*iv*) more than 13 defective parts.

60. Two dice are thrown simultaneously 500 times. Each time the sum of two numbers appearing on their tops is noted and recorded as given in the following table

Sum	2	3	4	5	6	7	8	9	10	11	12
Frequency	14	30	42	55	72	75	70	53	46	28	15

If the dice are thrown once more, what is the probability of getting a sum

(*i*) 3?

(*ii*) more than 10?

(*iii*) less than or equal to 5?

(*iv*) between 8 and 12?

61. A survey of 200 people was conducted about their preference of visiting various pavilion during trade fair.

Pavilion	Good living	Delhi pavilion	Toy pavilion	Defence pavilion
Number of people	95	45	40	20

Find the probability that a randomly selected person visited

(*i*) both good living and Delhi pavilion.

(*ii*) only the defence pavilion.

(*iii*) only the toy pavilion.

(*iv*) both toy pavilion and defence pavilion.

HINTS & ANSWERS

1. (b) Given, a coin is tossed 100 times, therefore total number of trials = 100

Also, head appears 46 times.

Now, tail appears 100 − 46 = 54 times

$\therefore P(\text{getting a tail}) = \frac{54}{100} = \frac{27}{50}$

2. (b) $\because$ Total number of pages = 250 [given]

Now, numbers on the page which are perfect square are 1, 4, 9, 16, 25, 36, 49, 64, 81, 100, 121, 144, 169, 196, 225.

So, the total number on the pages which are perfect square = 15

$\therefore$ Required probability $= \frac{15}{250} = \frac{3}{50}$.

3. (b) Let us define the event

A = Getting two heads

Total number of trials = 200

Number of trials in which we get two heads in which event A happens = 72

Hence, $P(A) = \frac{72}{200} = 0.36$

4. (d) Let A denote the event that the batsman did not hit a boundary, we have total number of trials = 40

Number of trials in which the event A happened

$= 40 - 8 = 32$

$\therefore \quad P(A) = \frac{32}{40} = \frac{4}{5} = 0.8$

5. (b) We have, total number of days for which the weather forecast was made = 250

Number of days for which the weather forecast was correct = 175

Number of days for which the forecast was not correct = 250 − 175 = 75

Therefore, probability that the forecast was correct on a given day

$= \frac{\text{Number of days for which the forecast was correct}}{\text{Number of days for which the forecast was made}}$

$= \frac{175}{250} = 0.7$

and probability that the forecast was not correct on a given day

$= \frac{\text{Number of days for which the forecast was not correct}}{\text{Number of days for which the forecast was made}}$

$= \frac{75}{250} = 0.3$

6. (a) Total number of cities

$= 1 + 2 + 18 + 21 + 19 + 18 = 79$

Let E be the event, which show maximum temperature of cities.

Number of cities whose maximum temperature lies between 16°C and 30°C = 2 + 18 + 21 = 41

$\therefore$ Probabilities that the temperature of cities lies between 16°C and 30°C $= \frac{41}{79}$

7. (d) Here, 200 telephone numbers are given on one page of a telephone directory.

$\therefore$ Total number of selected telephone numbers = 200

The frequency of digit 6 at unit place is 14 i.e. in 14 telephone numbers 6 is at unit place.

$\therefore$ Required probability

$= \frac{\text{Frequency of 6}}{\text{Total number of selected telephone numbers}}$

$= \frac{14}{200} = 0.07$

8. (a) Here, a die is thrown 250 times.

So, total number of trials = 250

In a random throw of a die, let E_1 and E_2 be the events of getting

1 and 5, respectively.

Here, frequency of outcomes 1 is 65, i.e. 1 occurs on a die 65 times.

$\therefore \quad P(\text{getting } 1) = P(E_1) = \frac{\text{Number of times 1 occur}}{\text{Total number of trials}}$

$= \frac{65}{250} = 0.26$

and here 5 occurs on a die 33 times.

$\therefore \quad P(\text{getting } 5) = P(E_5)$

$= \frac{\text{Number of times 5 occurs}}{\text{Total number of trials}}$

$= \frac{33}{250} = 0.132$

9. No; As probability lies from 0 to 1.

10. Solve as Q.9. **Ans.** No.

11. Solve as Q.9. **Ans.** No

12. 0

13. **Hint** Here, number of times 8 occurs = 0

Hence, required probability $= \frac{0}{50} = 0$

14. **Hint** From the given table, prime numbers are 2, 3 and 5.

So, the probability of getting a prime number (2 or 3 or 5)

$$= \frac{1+1+1}{6} = \frac{3}{6} = \frac{1}{2}$$

15. **Hint** Required probability $= \frac{714}{1200} = 0.595$

16. **Hint** The probability of batsman getting out by Shane Warne's bowling $= \frac{3}{27} = \frac{1}{9}$

Now, the probability of batsman not getting out by Shane Warne's bowling

$= 1 - P$ (batsman getting out) $= 1 - \frac{1}{9} = \frac{8}{9}$ **Ans.** $\frac{8}{9}$

17. **Hint** The number of bulbs whose life is 1150 h = 0

∴ Probability of selected bulb having life 1150 h

$= \frac{0}{80} = 0$ **Ans.** 0

18. **Hint** Total number of pages = 250 [given]

Now, numbers on the pages which are perfect square, are 1, 4, 9, 16, 25, 36, 49, 64, 81, 100, 121, 144, 169, 196, 225.

So, the total numbers on pages which are perfect square, = 15

∴ Required probability $= \frac{15}{250} = \frac{3}{50}$ **Ans.** $\frac{3}{50}$

19. 1

20. No, nearer to $\frac{1}{2}$

21. **Hint** Required probability = P (A Grade) + P (B Grade) + P (C Grade) **Ans.** 0.65

22. The number of children who do not like to eat potato chips = 364 − 91 = 273

∴ The probability that he/she does not like to eat potato chips $= \frac{273}{364} = 0.75$ **Ans.** 0.75

23. Since, a die was rolled 200 times.

Let 6 came up x times.

Probability of getting 6 $= \frac{2}{5}$

Then, probability of an event

$$= \frac{\text{Frequency of the event occurring}}{\text{Total number of trials}}$$

$$\Rightarrow \frac{2}{5} = \frac{x}{200} \Rightarrow x = \frac{400}{5} = 80$$

24. Solve as Example 4. **Ans.** $\frac{3}{10}$

25. Solve as Example 4. **Ans.** $\frac{209}{400}$

26. **Hint** Total number of packets of salt = 12 [given]

Number of packets containing more than 2 kg of salt = 5

∴ Required probability $= \frac{5}{12}$

27. **Hint** The number of trials in which atmost one head obtained = 550 + 250 = 800

∴ The probability for atmost one head $= \frac{800}{1000} = \frac{4}{5}$

28. Solve as Q. 22. **Ans.** $\frac{1}{5}$

29. Solve as Example 4. **Ans.** $\frac{1}{10}$

30. Solve as Q.13. **Ans.** $\frac{12}{25}$

31. **Hint** (*i*) Total number of teachers = 12 + 18 = 30

Number of male teachers = 12

∴ Probability that the person is a male teacher

$= \frac{12}{30} = \frac{2}{5}$

(*ii*) Total number of students = 20 + 10 = 30

Number of female students = 10

∴ Probability that the person is a female student

$= \frac{10}{30} = \frac{1}{3}$

32. **Hint** (*i*) Number of atleast 2 tails = 32 + 63 = 95

Probability of getting atleast 2 tails $= \frac{95}{150} = \frac{19}{30}$

(*ii*) Probability of getting exactly 1 tail $= \frac{30}{150} = \frac{1}{5}$

33. **Hint** Number of bulbs having life less than 900 h = 10 + 15 + 23 = 48

∴ Required probability $= \frac{48}{80} = \frac{3}{5}$

34. **Hint** Probability of getting 1 $= \frac{23}{50}$

So, probability of getting a number other than 1

$= 1 - \frac{23}{50} = \frac{50-23}{50} = \frac{27}{50}$

35. Solve as Q.18. **Ans.** $\frac{1}{10}$

36. **Hint** $P(A) + P(\overline{A}) = 1 \Rightarrow \frac{x}{5} + \frac{2x}{3} = 1$ **Ans.** $x = \frac{15}{13}$

37. Solve as Example 2. **Ans.** (*i*) $\frac{63}{80}$ (*ii*) $\frac{33}{80}$

38. Solve as Q.13. (*i*) $\frac{7}{40}$ (*ii*) $\frac{7}{20}$

39. **Hint** Required probability = $P(\text{Jan}) + P(\text{Aug})$

$$= \frac{5}{80} + \frac{10}{80} = \frac{15}{80} = 0.1875$$

40. **Hint** $P(\text{Win}) = 2P(\text{Loose}) - \frac{1}{6}$

$$\Rightarrow P(\text{Win}) = 2[1 - P(\text{Win})] - \frac{1}{6}$$

$$\Rightarrow 3P(\text{Win}) = \frac{11}{6} \Rightarrow P(\text{Win}) = \frac{11}{18}.$$

41. Solve as Q.40. **Ans.** $\frac{10}{17}$ and $\frac{7}{17}$ or $\frac{7}{17}$ and $\frac{10}{17}$

42. Solve as Example 1. **Ans.** (*i*) 0.21 (*ii*) 0.55 (*iii*) 0.24

43. Then, total number of balls in a bag = 6 + 3 = 9

After adding 12 red balls,

Total number of balls became = 9 + 12 = 21

Number of blue balls = 6

Number of red balls = 3 + 12 = 15

(*i*) P (getting a blue ball)

$$= \frac{\text{Number of blue balls}}{\text{Total number of balls}} = \frac{6}{21} = \frac{2}{7}$$

(*ii*) P (getting a red ball)

$$= \frac{\text{Number of red balls}}{\text{Total number of balls}} = \frac{15}{21} = \frac{5}{7}$$

44. Solve as Q.32.

Ans. (*i*) $\frac{109}{1019}$ (*ii*) $\frac{706}{1019}$ (*iii*) $\frac{204}{1019}$

45. **Hint** (*i*) The number of households earning ₹ 10000 - ₹ 14999 per month and having exactly one television = 240

$\therefore$ Required probability $= \frac{240}{4000} = \frac{6}{100} = 0.06$

(*ii*) The number of households earning ₹ 25000 and above per month and owning 2 televisions = 760

$\therefore$ Required probability $= \frac{760}{4000} = 0.19$

(*iii*) The number of households not having any television = 20 + 10 = 30

$\therefore$ Required probability $= \frac{30}{4000} = \frac{3}{400}$

46. **Hint** Given, number of occurrence of letter a = 70

Number of occurrence of letter b = 14

Number of occurrence of letter e = 26

Number of occurrence of letter r = 40

Number of occurrence of letter i = 36

Number of occurrence of others = 100

Here, a, e and i are vowels.

(*i*) Number of occurrence of a, e and i

$$= 70 + 26 + 36 = 132$$

Total number of letters = 286

$$\therefore P(\text{getting a vowel}) = \frac{132}{286} = \frac{6}{13}$$

(*ii*) Now, number of occurrence of non-vowel letters

$$= 14 + 40 + 100 = 154$$

$$\therefore P(\text{getting non-vowel letters}) = \frac{154}{286} = \frac{7}{13}$$

47. **Hint** Total number of cities

$$= 1 + 2 + 18 + 21 + 19 + 18 = 79$$

Let E_1 and E_2 be the event, which show maximum temperature of cities.

(*i*) Number of cities whose maximum temperature lies between 16°C and 30°C = 2 + 18 + 21 = 41

$\therefore$ Probability that the temperature of cities lies between 16°C and 30° C $= \frac{41}{79}$

(*ii*) Number of cities whose maximum temperature is less than 25°C = 1 + 2 + 18 = 21

$\therefore$ Probability that the temperature of cities is less than 25° C $= \frac{21}{79}$

48. Solve as Example 2. Ans. (*i*) $\frac{2}{5}$ (*ii*) 0

49. Solve as Q.26.

Ans. (*i*) $\frac{33}{40}$ (*ii*) 0

50. **Hint** Let p be the probability of success and q be the probability of failure.

Here, we have, $p - q = \frac{5}{19}$ ...(i)

Also, we know $p + q = 1$ ...(ii)

On solving Eqs. (i) and (ii), we get

$$2p = \frac{5}{19} + 1 \Rightarrow p = \frac{24}{2 \times 19} = \frac{24}{38} = \frac{12}{19}$$

From Eq. (ii), $\frac{12}{19} + q = 1 \Rightarrow q = 1 - \frac{12}{19} = \frac{7}{19}$

51. **Hint** The marks obtained by the student out of 150 marks = 80% of 150 $= \frac{80}{100} \times 150 = 120$ marks

Total number of unit test in which the student get 80% or more marks = 2

Probability that the student gets 80% or more marks in the next unit test $= \frac{2}{6} = \frac{1}{3}$

Probability that the student gets less than 80% marks

$$= 1 - \frac{1}{3} = \frac{2}{3}$$

52. **Hint** Given, total number of outcomes = 400

Now, outcomes for getting no head.

$$= 400 - (103 + 124 + 98) = 75$$

(*i*) Probability of getting no head $= \frac{75}{400} = \frac{3}{16}$

(ii) Probability of getting 1 head $= \frac{98}{400} = \frac{49}{200}$

(iii) Probability of getting exactly 2 heads $= \frac{124}{400} = \frac{31}{100}$

53. Solve as Q.52. **Ans.** (i) 0.6 (ii) 0 (iii) 1

54. Solve as Q.17. **Ans.** (i) $\frac{4}{7}$ (ii) $\frac{59}{350}$ (iii) $\frac{669}{700}$

55. Hint (i) Number of trials in which 3 tails appeared = 24

$\therefore \quad P(A) = \frac{24}{150} = 0.16$

(ii) Number of trials in which 2 tails appeared = 45

$\therefore \quad P(B) = \frac{45}{150} = 0.30$

(iii) Number of trials in which 1 tail appeared = 72

$\therefore \quad P(C) = \frac{72}{150} = 0.48$

(iv) Number of trials in which no tail appeared = 9

$\therefore \quad P(D) = \frac{9}{150} = 0.06$

56. Hint The total number of workers = 30 [given]

(i) Number of workers whose wage is less than ₹ 150 $= 3 + 4 = 7$

$\therefore$ Probability that a worker gets wage less than ₹ 150 $= \frac{7}{30}$

(ii) Number of workers whose wage is atleast ₹ 210 $= 4 + 3 = 7$

Probability that a worker gets wage of atleast ₹ 210 $= \frac{7}{30}$

(iii) Number of workers whose wage is more than or equal to ₹ 150 but less than ₹ 210 = 5 + 6 + 5 = 16

$\therefore$ Probability that a worker gets wage is more than or equal to ₹ 150 but less than ₹ 210 $= \frac{16}{30} = \frac{8}{15}$

(iv) Number of workers whose wage lies in the interval ₹ 190 - ₹ 250 = 5 + 4 + 3 = 12

$\therefore$ Probability that a worker gets wage lies in the interval ₹ 190 - ₹ 250 $= \frac{12}{30} = \frac{2}{5}$

57. Solve as Example 6.

Ans. (i) $\frac{7}{20}$ (ii) $\frac{1}{2}$ (iii) $\frac{47}{80}$ (iv) $\frac{5}{16}$

58. Hint Total number of people visited

$= 175 + 125 + 225 + 200 + 120 = 845$

(i) Number of people visited after 1 pm before 5 pm

$= 225 + 200 = 425$

Probability that the people visited after 1 pm before 5 pm $= \frac{425}{845} = 0.50$

(ii) 0.355 (iii) 0.142 (iv) 0.236

59. Hint (i) Number of days in which no defective part produced = 50

$\therefore$ The probability that tomorrow's output will have no defective part $= \frac{50}{200} = \frac{1}{4} = 0.25$

(ii) Number of days in which atleast one defective part produced $= 32 + 22 + 18 + 12 + 12 + 10 + 10 + 10 + 8 + 6 + 6 + 2 + 2 = 150$

$\therefore$ Probability that tomorrow's output will have atleast one defective part $= \frac{150}{200} = \frac{3}{4} = 0.75$

(iii) Number of days in which not more than 5 defective parts produced

$= 50 + 32 + 22 + 18 + 12 + 12 = 146$

$\therefore$ Probability that tomorrow's output will not have more than 5 defective parts $= \frac{146}{200} = 0.73$

(iv) Number of days in which more than 13 defective parts produced = 0

$\therefore$ Probability that tomorrow's output will have more than 13 defective parts $= \frac{0}{200} = 0$

60. Solve as Q.14.

Ans. (i) 0.06 (ii) 0.086 (iii) 0.282 (iv) 0.254

61. Solve as Q.52.

Ans. (i) 0.7 (ii) 0.1 (iii) 0.2 (iv) 0.3

Let's Investigate

ACTIVITY 1

To verify the algebraic identity
$(x+y+z)^2 = x^2 + y^2 + z^2 + 2xy + 2yz + 2zx.$

Prior Knowledge

1. Rectangle and its area.
2. Square and its area.

Materials Required

1. Hardboard
2. Coloured papers
3. Adhesive
4. White paper
5. A pair of scissors
6. Geometry Box

Theory

1. A **rectangle** is a parallelogram whose opposite sides are equal and each angle is equal to 90°.
   Area of rectangle = Length × Breath
2. A **square** is a rectangle whose all sides are equal.
   Area of square = $(\text{Side})^2$

Procedure

1. Take a hardboard of suitable size and paste a white paper on it.
2. From a coloured paper, cut out a square of side x units. (see Fig. 1.1)
3. Further, cut out a square of side y units $(y < x)$ from another coloured paper. (see Fig. 1.2)
4. Also, cut out a square of side z units $(z < y)$ from same coloured paper as in step 2. (see Fig. 1.3)

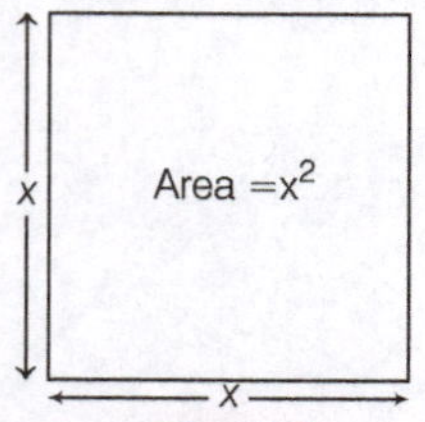

Figure 1.1

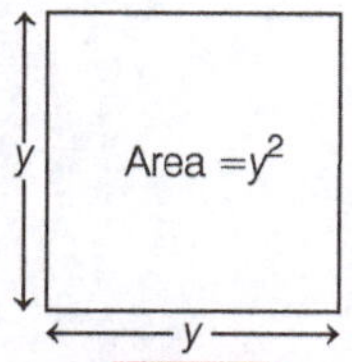

Figure 1.2

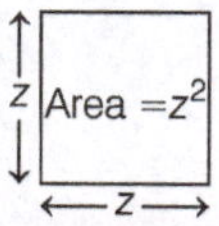

Figure 1.3

5. Cut out two rectangles of dimensions $x \times y$ from same coloured paper as in step 3. (see Fig. 1.4)
6. Also, cut out two rectangles of dimensions $y \times z$ from same coloured paper as in step 2. (see Fig. 1.5)
7. Now further, cut out two rectangles of dimensions $x \times z$ from same coloured paper as in step 3. (see Fig. 1.6)

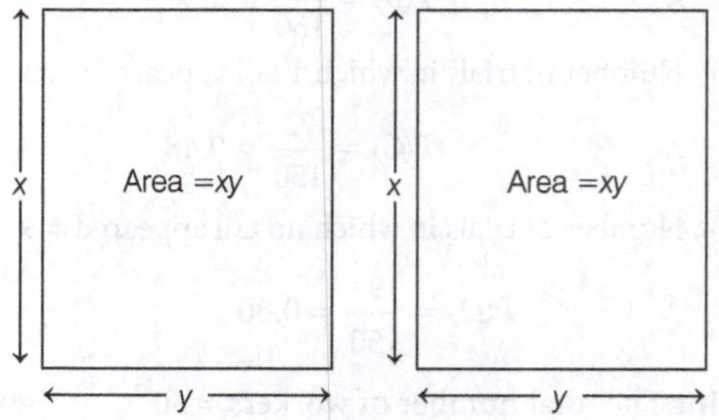

Figure 1.4

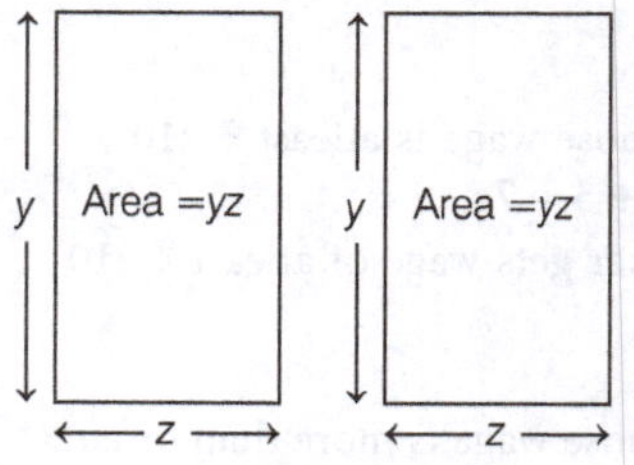

Figure 1.5

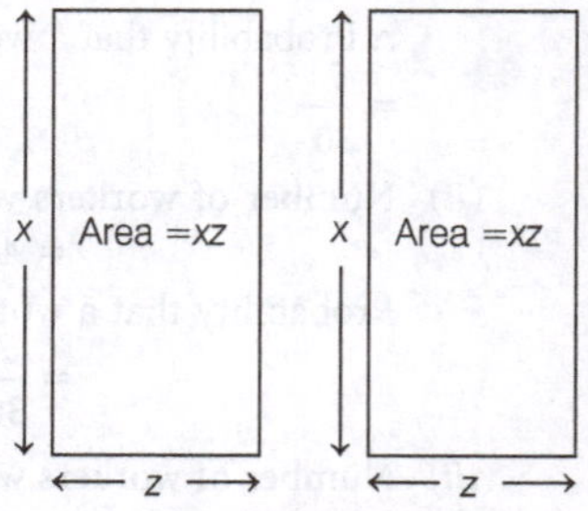

Figure 1.6

8. Paste the squares and rectangles on the hardboard as shown in Fig. 1.7.

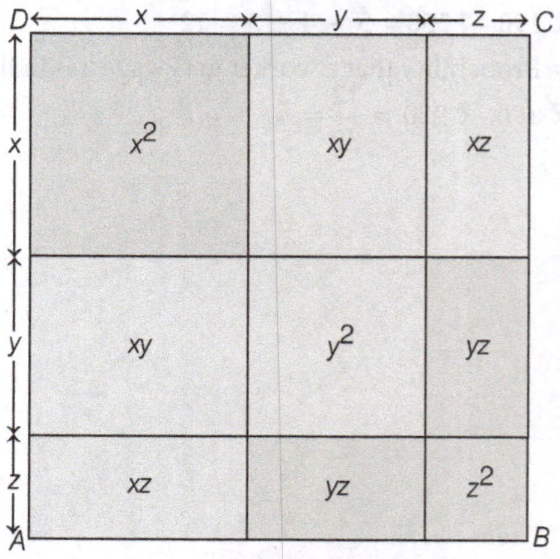

Figure 1.7

Observation

From Fig. 1.7, it is clear that from the arrangement of sqaures and rectangle, square $ABCD$ of side $(x+y+z)$ units is obtained.

$\therefore$ Area of square $ABCD = (x+y+z)^2$

[$\because$ area of square = (side)^2] ...(i)

Also, area of square $ABCD$ = Sum of the areas of all the squares and rectangles, which are used to make the square $ABCD$

$= x^2 + y^2 + z^2 + xy + xy + yz + yz + zx + zx$

$= x^2 + y^2 + z^2 + 2xy + 2yz + 2zx$ ...(ii)

From Eqs. (i) and (ii), we have

$(x+y+z)^2 = x^2 + y^2 + z^2 + 2xy + 2yz + 2zx$

Here, area is in square units.

On actual measurement, we get

$x = \ldots\ldots,\quad y = \ldots\ldots,\quad z = \ldots\ldots,$

So, $x^2 = \ldots\ldots,\quad y^2 = \ldots\ldots,\quad z^2 = \ldots\ldots,$

$2xy = \ldots\ldots,\quad 2yz = \ldots\ldots,\quad 2zx = \ldots\ldots,$

$x+y+z = \ldots\ldots$ and $(x+y+z)^2 = \ldots\ldots$

Hence, $(x+y+z)^2 = x^2 + y^2 + z^2 + 2xy + 2yz + 2zx$

Result

Identity $(x+y+z)^2 = x^2 + y^2 + z^2 + 2xy + 2yz + 2zx$ has been verified.

Applications

This identity may be used for

1. calculating the square of a number which can be expressed as a sum of three convenient numbers.
2. simplification and factorisation of algebraic expressions.

VIVA-VOCE

1 What do you mean by a polynomial?

Ans An algebraic expression, in which the variables have only non-negative integral power, is called a polynomial.

2 What do you mean by zeroes of a polynomial?

Ans If $p(x)$ is a polynomial, then a real number k is said to be zero of the polynomial $p(x)$, if $p(k) = 0$.

3 What do you mean by a trinomial?

Ans A polynomial with three terms is called a trinomial.

4 Is the expansion of $(x+y+z)^2$, trinomial?

Ans No, because on expanding $(x+y+z)^2$, we get six terms.

5 Is the identity $(a+b+c)^2 = a^2 + b^2 + c^2 + 2ab + 2bc + 2ca$, holds for all real values of x, y, z?

Ans Yes

6 Which identity should be used to expand $(3x - \sqrt{y} + z)^2$?

Ans $(a+b+c)^2 = a^2 + b^2 + c^2 + 2ab + 2bc + 2ca$

7 Write the condition that the three variables in identity $(a+b+c)^2 = a^2 + b^2 + c^2 + 2ab + 2bc + 2ca$ should be written in two variables form $(x+y)^2 = x^2 + y^2 + 2xy$.

Ans Anyone of the variable in the identity $(a+b+c)^2 = a^2 + b^2 + c^2 + 2ab + 2bc + 2ca$ should be zero.

8 If we take all the variables equal in the identity $(a+b+c)^2 = a^2 + b^2 + c^2 + 2ab + 2bc + 2ca$, then it will give us a cube of one variable. Is it true? Justify your answer.

Ans No, if $a = b = c$ then $(a+b+c)^2 = (a+a+a)^2 = 9a^2$, which is square of one variable.

ACTIVITY 2

To verify the algebraic identity $(x+y)^3 = x^3 + y^3 + 3x^2y + 3xy^2$.

Prior Knowledge

1. Concept of cuboid and its volume.
2. Concept of cube and its volume.

Materials Required

1. Acrylic sheets
2. Adhesive/Adhesive tape
3. A pair of scissors
4. Geometry Box
5. Cutter

Theory

1. **Cuboid** A cuboid is a solid bounded by six rectangular plane surfaces. e.g. Match box, brick, box, etc., are cuboid. (see Fig. 2.1)

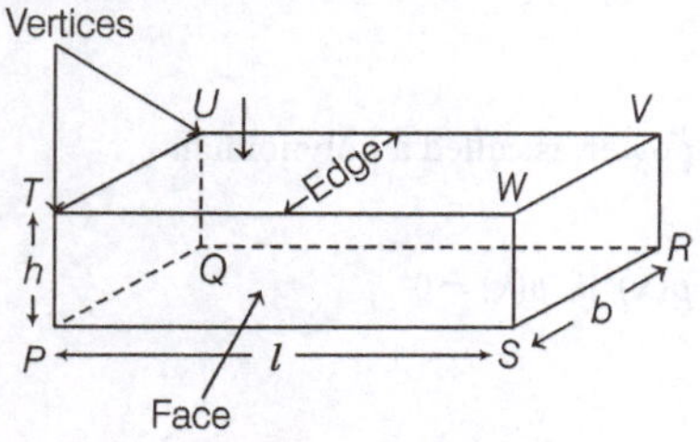

Figure 2.1

Properties of cuboid are

(i) In a cuboid, there are 6 faces, 12 edges and 8 corners (four at bottom and four at top face) which are called vertices.

(ii) Opposite faces of a cuboid are equal and parallel.

Volume of cuboid = lbh

where, l = length, b = breadth and h = height

2. **Cube** A cuboid whose length, breadth and height are same, is called a cube. (see Fig. 2.2)

Properties of cube are

(i) In a cube, there are 6 faces, 12 edges and 8 corners (four at bottom and four at top face) which are called vertices.

(ii) All the six faces of a cube are congruent square faces.

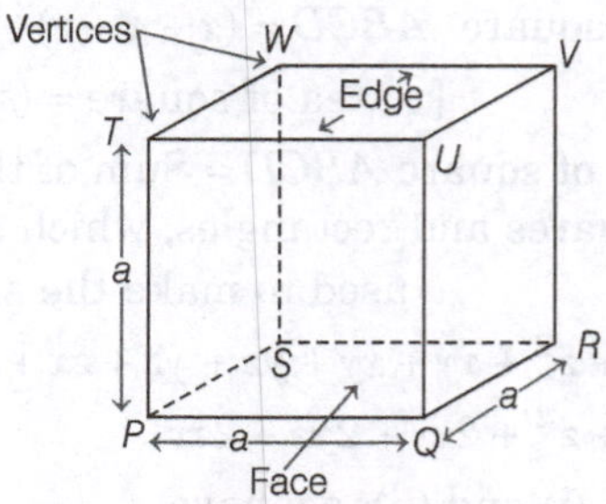

Figure 2.2

(iii) Each edge of a cube have same length.

Volume of cube = a^3

where, a is side of cube.

Procedure

1. Cut six squares of equal side x units from acrylic sheet. Paste all of them to form a cube by using adhesive tape/adhesive. (see Fig. 2.3)
2. Cut six squares of equal side y units ($y < x$) from acrylic sheet. Paste all of them to form a cube by using adhesive tape/adhesive. (see Fig. 2.4)

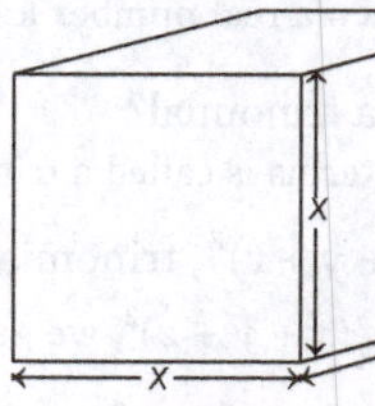

Figure 2.3

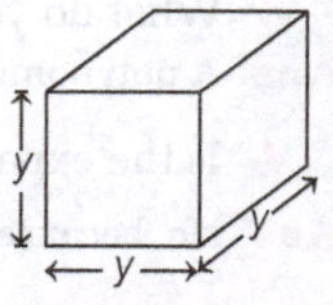

Figure 2.4

3. Also, cut 12 rectangles of length x units and breadth y units and 6 squares of side x units. Paste all of them to form three cuboids. (see Fig. 2.5)

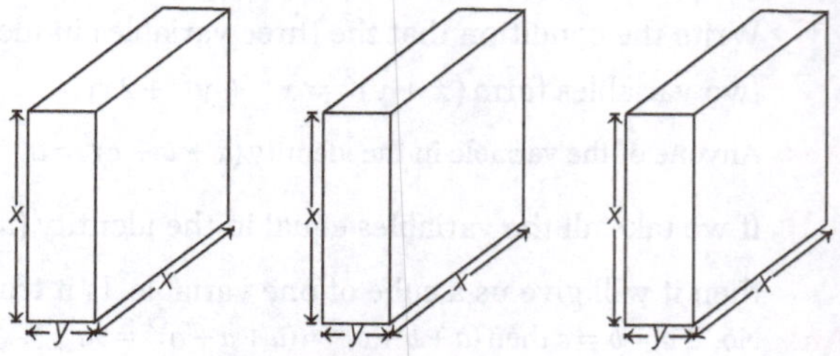

Figure 2.5

4. Cut 12 rectangles of length x units and breadth y units and 6 squares of side y units. Paste all of them to form another three cuboids. (see Fig. 2.6)

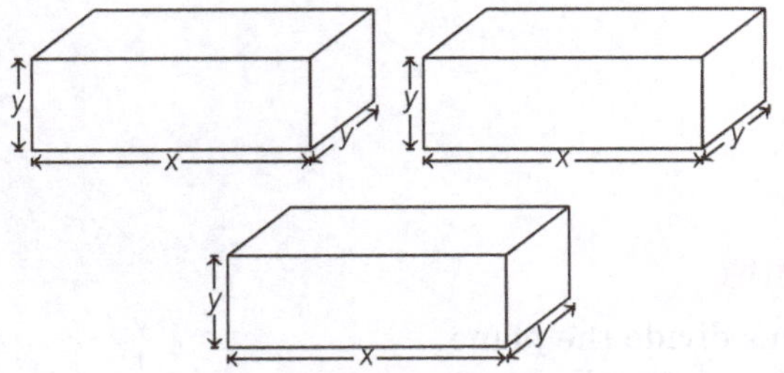

Figure 2.6

5. Arrange the cubes obtained in Fig. 2.3 and Fig. 2.4 and the cuboids obtained in Fig. 2.5 and Fig. 2.6, as shown in Fig. 2.7.

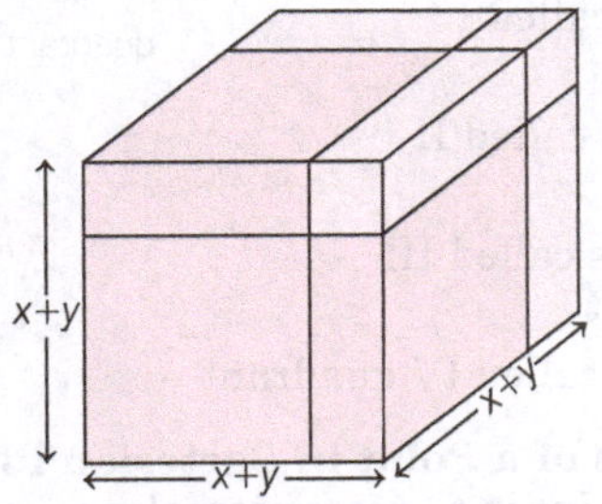

Figure 2.7

Observation

For Fig. 2.3, volume of cube of side x units = x^3

For Fig. 2.4, volume of cube of side y units = y^3

For Fig. 2.5, volume of a cuboid of dimensions
$x \times x \times y$ units = x^2y

So, volume of all three such cuboids
$x^2y + x^2y + x^2y = 3x^2y$

For Fig. 2.6, volume of a cuboid of dimensions
$x \times y \times y$ units = xy^2

So, volume of all three such cuboids
$xy^2 + xy^2 + xy^2 = 3xy^2$

In Fig. 2.7, we have obtained the cube of side $(x + y)$ units.

So, volume of cube = $(x + y)^3$ ...(i)

As, volume of cube of Fig. 2.7 = (Volume of cube of Fig. 2.3) + (Volume of cube of Fig. 2.4)
+ (Volume of three cuboids of Fig. 2.5)
+ (Volume of three cuboids of Fig. 2.6)

$= x^3 + y^3 + 3x^2y + 3xy^2$ ...(ii)

From Eqs (i) and (ii) we have,

$$(x + y)^3 = x^3 + y^3 + 3x^2y + 3xy^2$$

Here, volume is in cubic units.

On actual measurement, we get

x = ..., y = ...,

So, x^3 = ..., y^3 = ...,

$3x^2y$ = ..., $3xy^2$ =........,

$(x + y)^3$ = ...

Hence, $(x + y)^3 = x^3 + y^3 + 3x^2y + 3xy^2$

Result

The algebraic identity $(x + y)^3 = x^3 + y^3 + 3x^2y + 3xy^2$ has been verified.

Applications

The identity is useful for

1. calculating the cube of a number which can be expressed as the sum of two convenient numbers.
2. simplification and factorisation of algebraic expressions.

VIVA-VOCE

1 Is $(a + b)^3$ a trinomial? Justify.

Ans No, because $(a + b)^3$ has four terms.

2 What is the degree of expansion of polynomial $(x + 2y)^3$?

Ans 3, because the highest power of variable in the expansion of $(x + 2y)^3$ is 3.

3 In the identity $(a + b)^3$, what do you mean by a^3 and $3a^2b$?

Ans a^3 means volume of cube of side a and $3a^2b$ means volume of three cuboids of dimensions a, a and b.

4 What is the maximum number of zeroes that a cubic polynomial can have?

Ans Three

5 What is the expanded form of $(a + b)^3$?

Ans $(a + b)^3 = a^3 + b^3 + 3a^2b + 3ab^2$

6 For evaluating $(101)^3$, which identity would you use?

Ans We should use $(a + b)^3 = a^3 + b^3 + 3a^2b + 3ab^2$ by taking $a = 100$ and $b = 1$.

7 Write the standard form of cubic polynomial in one variable?

Ans $ax^3 + bx^2 + cx + d, a \neq 0$

ACTIVITY 3

To find the values of abscissa and ordinate of various points given in a cartesian plane.

Prior Knowledge

1. Knowledge of cartesian coordinate system.
2. To locate/plot a point in cartesian plane.

Materials Required

1. Cardboard 2. White paper
3. Graph paper with various given points
4. Geometry box 5. A pair of scissors
6. Glue

Theory

1. **Cartesian Coordinate System**

   The system used to describe the position of a point in a plane, is called **cartesian system.**

   In cartesian system, there are two perpendicular directed straight lines XX' and YY' which intersect at point O, then line XX' will be **horizontal line** and YY' will be **vertical line**, as shown in figure 3.1 (a).

   The point of intersection of these lines is called **origin** and it is denoted by O. The horizontal line XOX' is called **X-axis** and the vertical line YOY' is called **Y-axis**. Directions OX and OY are called the **positive directions** of X-axis and Y-axis, respectively and directions OX' and OY' are called the **negative directions** of X-axis and Y-axis, respectively.

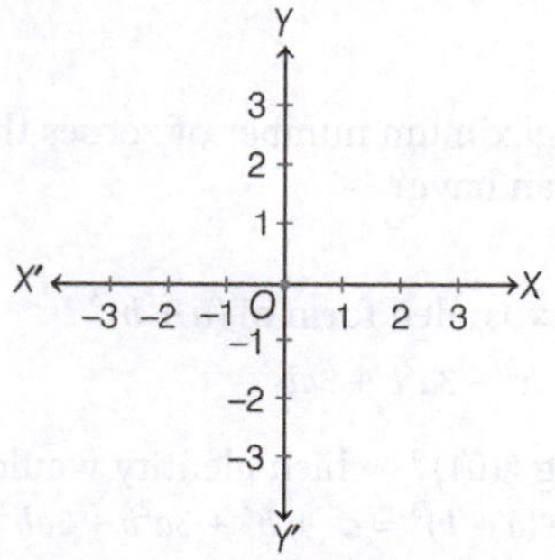

Figure 3.1 (a)

Quadrants

The axes divide the plane into four parts called quadrants. The quadrants are numbered I, II, III and IV anti-clockwise from OX. Thus

(i) XOY is called I quadrant
(ii) $X'OY$ is called II quadrant
(iii) $X'OY'$ is called III quadrant
(iv) XOY' is called IV quadrant

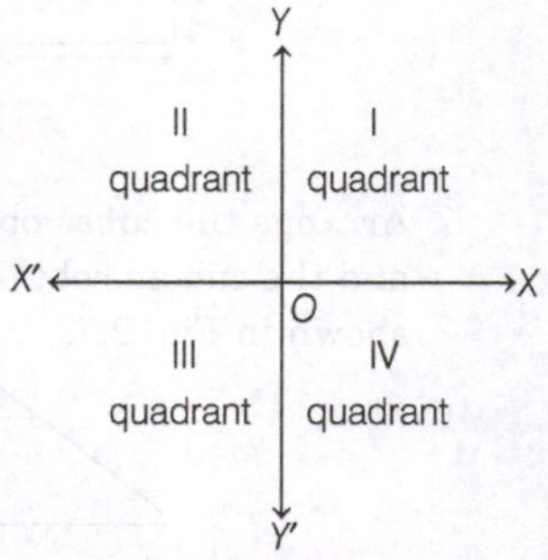

Figure 3.1 (b)

2. **Coordinates of a Point in Cartesian Plane**

   To locate a point in the cartesian plane, its perpendicular distances from X-axis and Y-axis are required, these distances are called **coordinates** of the point. Each point in cartesian plane has two coordinates; x-coordinate and y-coordinate.

   (i) The x-coordinate of a point is the perpendicular distance from the Y-axis measured along the X-axis (positive, along the positive direction of the X-axis and negative, along the negative direction of X-axis). The x-coordinate is also called the **abscissa**.

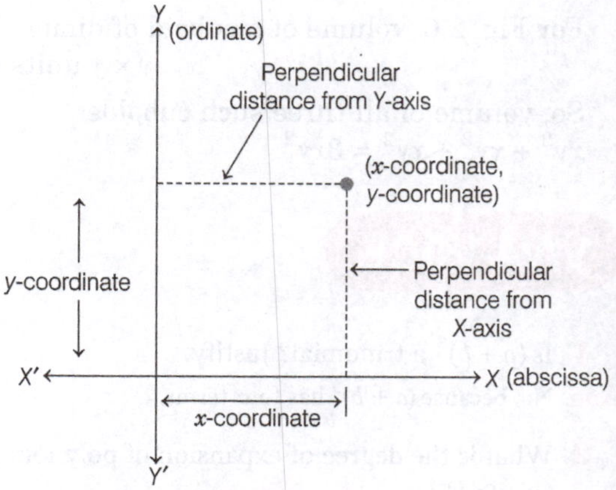

Figure 3.2

   (ii) The y-coordinate of a point is the perpendicular distance from the X-axis measured along the Y-axis (positive, along the positive direction of the Y-axis and negative, along the negative direction of Y-axis). The y-coordinate is also called the **ordinate**.

x-coordinate and y-coordinate taken together are called **cartesian coordinates** or **coordinates of a point** and are denoted by (x, y). Here, the x-coordinate comes first and after this y-coordinate comes, then (x, y) is also called an **order pair**.

The order of x and y is important in (x, y). Position of (y, x) will be different from (x, y).

Sign Conventions

The sign of coordinates of a point in a quadrant are given in following table.

Quadrant	Nature of X-axis & Y-axis	Sign of x/abscissa	Sign of y/ordinate	Coordinates of a point
I	$x>0, y>0$	+	+	(+,+)
II	$x<0, y>0$	−	+	(−,+)
III	$x<0, y<0$	−	−	(−,−)
IV	$x>0, y<0$	+	−	(+,−)

Procedure

1. Take a cardboard of suitable size and paste a white paper on it.
2. Now, paste the graph paper with various points drawn on it in the middle of white paper.
3. Now, look at the graph paper and the points whose abscissae and ordinates are to be found.

Observation

If L is a point plotted on graph paper and we have to find the abscissa and ordinate of point L.

Draw perpendiculars LE and LD from L to Y-axis and X-axis, respectively.

LE = – 2 units (distance from Y-axis, i.e. x-coordinate or abscissa)

LD = 9 units (distance from X-axis, i.e. y-coordinate or ordinate)

As point L lies in second quadrant.

So, the coordinates of L are (–2, 9).

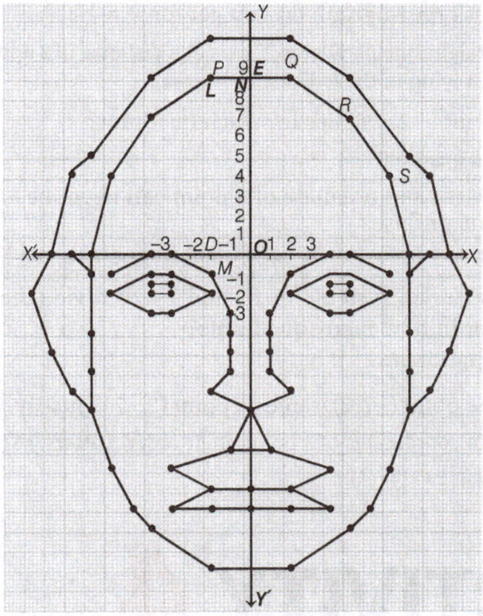

Note *Care should be taken while reading the coordinates, otherwise the location of the object will differ.*

Fill the given table for different points on the given graph.

Points	Abscissa	Ordinate	Quadrant	Coordinates
M				
N				
P				
⋮				

Result

The coordinates of the points plotted on the graph paper have been found.

Application

This activity is very useful in locating the position of a particular country/city or a place on map.

VIVA-VOCE

1 What do you understand by a cartesian system?

Ans The system used to describe the position of a point in a plane, is called cartesian system.

2 What is the ordinate of point lying in third quadrant at a distance of 2 units from X-axis and 5 units from Y-axis?

Ans – 2, because in third quadrant y-coordinate is negative.

3 What type of graph do you get for $y = -2$?

Ans A straight line parallel to X-axis at a distance of 2 units from origin below the X-axis.

4 What is the image of (– 3, – 1) in 2nd quadrant?

Ans (– 3, 1)

5 What type of graph do you get for $x = -2$?

Ans A straight line parallel to Y-axis at a distance of 2 units from origin lying in the left side of Y-axis.

6 A point $(-2, -6)$ lies in which quadrant?

Ans Third quadrant

7 Abscissa and ordanate of a point can never be equal. Is it true or false.

Ans False, as a point can be equidistant from X-axis and Y-axis.

8 In cartesian system, X-axis and Y-axis divide the graph paper in how many quadrants?

Ans Four quadrants

9 Is the point $(-7, 2)$, same as point $(2, -7)$? Justify.

Ans No, in coordinates of a point, their order matters, so $(-7,2)$ is not same as $(2,-7)$.

10 Find the new coordinates of a point (2, 3), when we rotate the axes at 180° in anti-clockwise direction.

Ans When we rotate the axes, the positive X and Y-axes will become negative. So, the new coordinates will be $(-2, -3)$.

11 In cartesian plane, the angle between two axes is not always 90°. Is it true or false.

Ans False, the angle between two axes is always 90°.

12 In which quadrant a point lies whose ordinate is negative?

Ans Either III or IV quadrant.

13 Is it correct that if any point on the X-axis, then the y-coordinate will be zero?

Ans Yes, because the distance from X-axis is zero.

ACTIVITY 4

To verify experimentally that if two lines intersect each other, then

(i) the vertically opposite angles are equal.

(ii) the sum of two adjacent angles is 180°.

(iii) the sum of all the four angles is 360°.

Prior Knowledge

1. Basic knowledge of lines and angles.
2. Pair of angles, adjacent angles, linear pair of angles and vertically opposite angles.

Materials Required

1. Cardboard
2. White sheet of paper
3. A full protractor
4. A nail
5. Two transparent strips marked as PQ and RS
6. Adhesive

Theory

1. **Lines and Angles**

(i) **Line Segment** A part of a line with two end points, is called a line segment. Line segment PQ is denoted by $\overline{PQ}$.

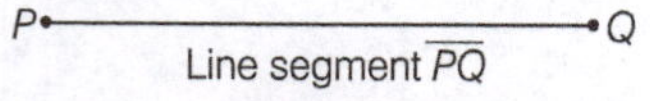

Figure 4.1

A line segment has a definite length, which can be measured. The line segment $\overline{PQ}$ is the same thing as the line segment $\overline{QP}$.

(ii) **Angle** The figure formed by two rays with the same initial point, is called an angle. In Fig. 4.2, the common initial point Q is known as the **vertex** of the angle and the rays ($\overrightarrow{QP}$ and $\overrightarrow{QR}$) forming the angle are called its **arms** or **sides**.

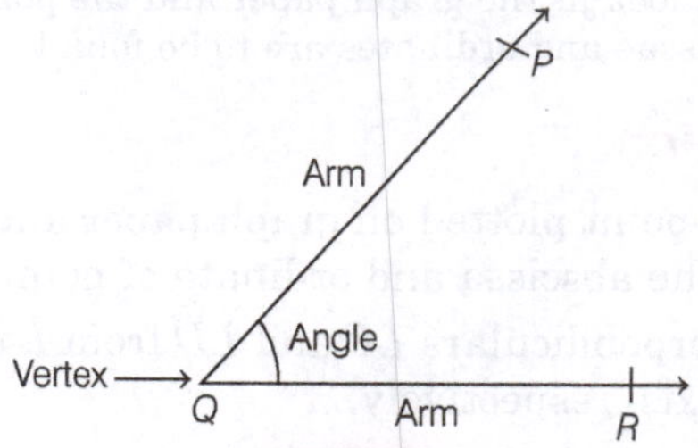

Figure 4.2

There are different types of angles such as acute angle, right angle, obtuse angle, straight angle, reflex angle and complete angle, which are discussed below :

(a) **Acute Angle** An angle whose measure is more than 0° but less than 90°, is called an acute angle.

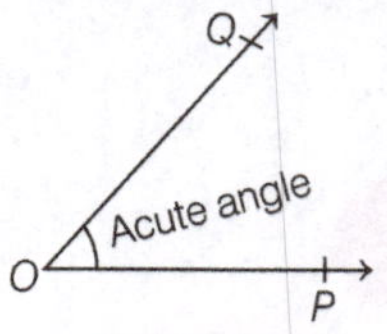

Figure 4.3

In Fig. 4.3, $\angle POQ$ is an acute angle.

Since, $0° < \angle POQ < 90°$

(b) **Right Angle** An angle whose measure is 90°, is called a right angle.

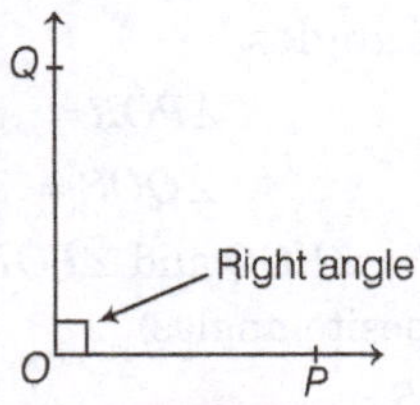

Figure 4.4

In Fig. 4.4, $\angle POQ$ is a right angle and $OQ \perp OP$.

(c) **Obtuse Angle** An angle whose measure is more than 90° but less than 180°, is called an obtuse angle.

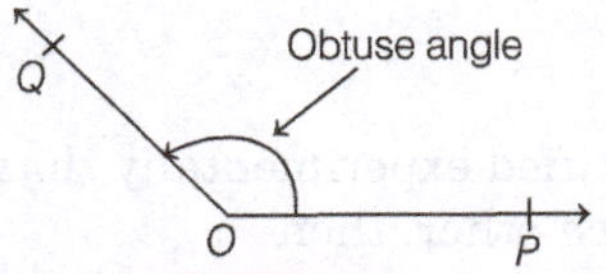

Figure 4.5

In Fig. 4.5, $\angle POQ$ is an obtuse angle.

Since, $90° < \angle POQ < 180°$

(d) **Straight Angle** An angle whose measure is 180°, is called a straight angle.

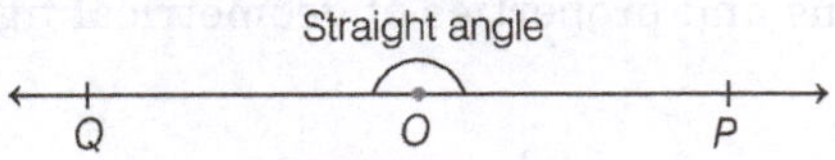

Figure 4.6

In Fig. 4.6, $\angle POQ = 180°$ is a straight angle.

A straight angle has two right angles.

(e) **Reflex Angle** An angle whose measure is more than 180° but less than 360°, is called a reflex angle. In Fig. 4.7 and Fig. 4.8, $\angle POQ$ and $\angle DEF$ are reflex angles.

- $180° <$ reflex $\angle POQ < 360°$

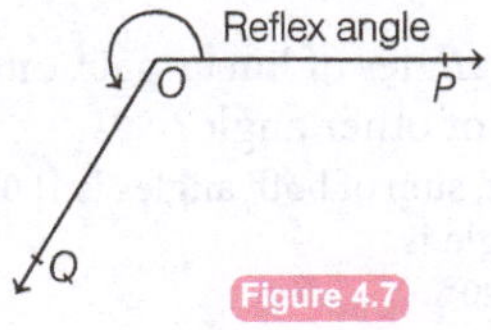

Figure 4.7

- $180° <$ reflex $\angle DEF < 360°$

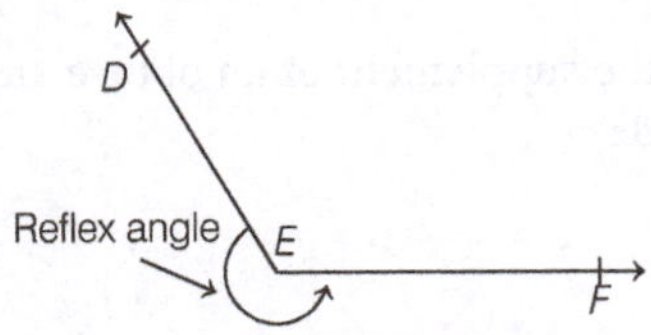

Figure 4.8

(f) **Complete Angle** An angle whose measure is 360°, is called a complete angle.

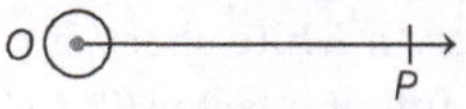

Figure 4.9

In Fig. 4.9, $\angle POP = 360°$ is a complete angle.

2. **Pair of Angles**

There are some relations between the angles which are described below:

(i) **Adjacent Angles** Two angles are called adjacent angles, if

(a) they have a common vertex,

(b) they have a common arm and

(c) their non-common arms are on different sides of the common arm.

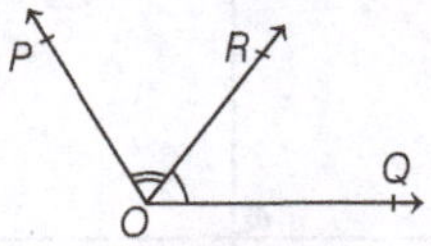

Figure 4.10

In Fig. 4.10, $\angle POR$ and $\angle ROQ$ are adjacent angles because these angles have a common vertex O, a common arm OR and non-common arms OP and OQ. When two angles are adjacent, then their sum is always equal to the angle formed by the two non-common arms. So, here

$\angle POQ = \angle POR + \angle ROQ$.

Note *Here, $\angle POQ$ and $\angle POR$ are not adjacent angles because their non-common arms OR and OQ lie on the same side of the common arm OP.*

(ii) **Linear Pair of Angles** If the non-common arms of two adjacent angles form a line, then adjacent angles are called linear pair of angles.

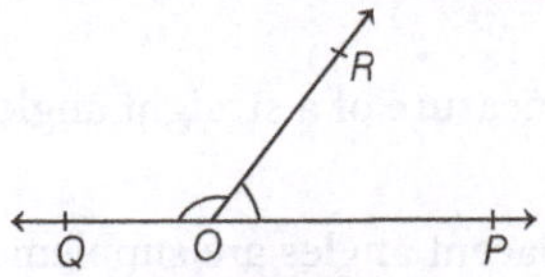

Figure 4.11

In Fig. 4.11, $\angle POR$ and $\angle QOR$ form a linear pair of angles.

(iii) **Vertically Opposite Angles** Two angles are called a pair of vertically opposite angles, if their arms form two pairs of opposite rays.

In other words, when two lines intersect each other at a point, then there are two pairs of vertically opposite angles.

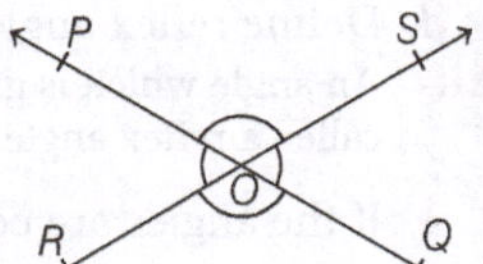

Figure 4.12

In Fig. 4.12, lines PQ and RS intersect each other at O. So, $\angle POR$ and $\angle QOS$ are vertically opposite angles. Also, $\angle POS$ and $\angle QOR$ are vertically opposite angles.

Procedure

1. Take a cardboard of suitable size and by using adhesive, paste a white sheet of paper on it.
2. Also, paste a full protractor (0° to 360°) with the help of adhesive on the cardboard. (see Fig. 4.13)
3. Mark the centre of protractor as O.
4. Now, make a hole in the middle of both transparent strips which contain two intersecting lines.
5. Fix both strips at O by putting a nail. (see Fig. 4.13)
6. Set the different positions of the strips PQ and RS, and measure the angles $\angle POS$, $\angle POR$ $\angle ROQ$ and $\angle SOQ$.

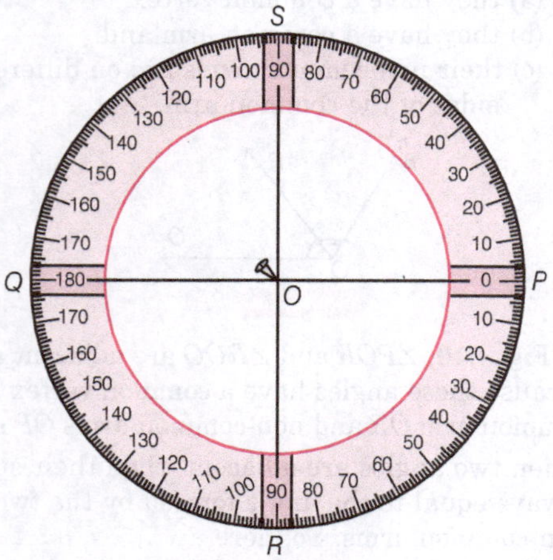

Figure 4.13

Observations

In one position of the strips, by actual measurement of angles

1. $\angle POS = ...$, $\angle POR = ...$

   $\angle ROQ = ...$, $\angle QOS = ...$

   Hence, $\angle POS = \angle ROQ$ and $\angle POR = \angle QOS$ (vertically opposite angles)
2. $\angle POR + \angle POS = ...$,

   $\angle POR + \angle QOR = ...$,

   $\angle ROQ + \angle QOS = ...$,

   $\angle POS + \angle QOS = ...$ (linear pairs)
3. $\angle POS + \angle POR + \angle ROQ + \angle QOS = ...$ (angles formed at a point)

Results

We have verified experimentally that if two lines intersect each other, then

1. the vertically opposite angles are equal.
2. the sum of two adjacent angles is 180°.
3. the sum of all the four angles is 360°.

Application

These properties are very useful in proving some theorems and properties of geometrical figures.

VIVA-VOCE

1 What is the measure of a straight angle?

Ans 180°

2 If the two adjacent angles are supplementary, then what does that mean?

Ans It means that they form a linear pair or sum of two angles is 180°.

3 Define reflex angle?

Ans An angle which is greater than 180° but less than 360° is called a reflex angle.

4 If the angles are complementary, then what does that mean?

Ans Sum of the angles is 90°.

5 What is the measure of the angle made at the centre of the circle?

Ans 360°

6 If two angles are vertically opposite angles, where the measure of one of the angles is 30°, then what is the measure of other angle?

Ans 30° because vertically opposite angles are equal.

7 If out of two angles of linear pair, one is 60°, then what is the measure of other angle?

Ans In a linear pair, sum of both angles is 180°, so if one angle is 60°, then other angle is

$180° - 60° = 120°$.

8 What is the angle between two parallel lines?

Ans 0°

9 What is the supplement of an obtuse angle?

Ans Acute angle

Sample Question Paper 1 (Unsolved)
Mathematics

Time : 3 hrs	M.M. : 80

General Instructions

1 This Question Paper has 5 Sections A, B, C, D and E.
2 Section A has 18 Multiple Choice Questions (MCQs) and 02 Assertion Reason Questions carrying 1 mark each.
3 Section B has 5 Very Short Answer type questions carrying 2 marks each.
4 Section C has 6 Short Answer type questions carrying 3 marks each.
5 Section D has 4 Long Answer type questions carrying 5 marks each.
6 Section E has 3 Case Based integrated units of assessment (4 marks each) with sub-parts of the values of 1, 1 and 2 marks each respectively.
7 All Questions are compulsory. However, an internal choice in 2 Qs of 2 marks, 2 Qs of 3 marks and 2 Questions of 5 marks has been provided. An internal choice has been provided in the 2 marks question of Section E.
8 Draw neat figures wherever required. Take $\pi = 22/7$ wherever required if not stated.

Section A

Section A consists of 20 Questions of 1 mark each.

Part I

1. If $x=2$ and $y=4$, then the value of $\left(\dfrac{x}{y}\right)^{x-y}+\left(\dfrac{y}{x}\right)^{y-x}$ is

(a) 2 (b) 6 (c) 4 (d) 8

2. If $x^2+\dfrac{1}{x^2}=14$, then the positive value of $x+\dfrac{1}{x}$ is

(a) 1 (b) 4 (c) 12 (d) 6

3. The measure of the angle between the coordinate axes is

(a) 90° (b) 180° (c) 0° (d) 360°

4. If $x-\dfrac{1}{x}=\dfrac{1}{2}$, then the value of $4x^2+\dfrac{4}{x^2}$ is

(a) 5 (b) 9 (c) 7 (d) 11

5. If $a+b+c=7$ and $ab+bc+ca=21$, then the value of $a^2+b^2+c^2$ is

(a) 6 (b) 18 (c) 7 (d) 9

6. In the given figure, AOB is a straight line and $\angle AOC+\angle BOD=95°$. Then, the value of $\angle COD$ is

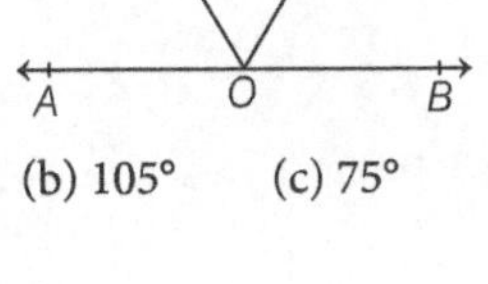

(a) 45° (b) 105° (c) 75° (d) 85°

7. The height of a cone is 21 cm and its slant height is 28 cm. Then, the volume of the cone is

(a) 7546 cm^3 (b) 8624 cm^3
(c) 7236 cm^3 (d) 5434 cm^3

8. In the given figure AB is a mirror, PQ is the incident ray and QR is the reflected ray. Then, $\angle AQP$ is

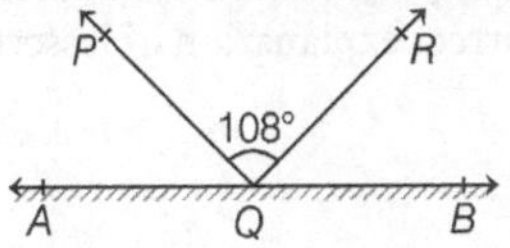

(a) 54° (b) 72° (c) 36° (d) 108°

9. The coefficient of x^2 in the polynomial, $p(x)=2x-1$ is

(a) 1 (b) -1 (c) 2 (d) 0

10. Zeroes of $q(x)=3x+5$ is/are

(a) -3 (b) $-\dfrac{5}{3}$ (c) 0 (d) $-\dfrac{3}{5}$

11. The taxi fare in a city is as follow. For the first kilometre, the fare is ₹ 18, for the subsequent distance, it is ₹ 11 per km. Taking the distance covered as x km and total fare as ₹ y, choose the correct linear equation for this information.

(a) $y=7x+11$ (b) $x=11y+7$
(c) $y=11x+7$ (d) $x=7y+11$

12. **In the given figure, *AOB* is a straight line. Then, $\angle AOC$ is**

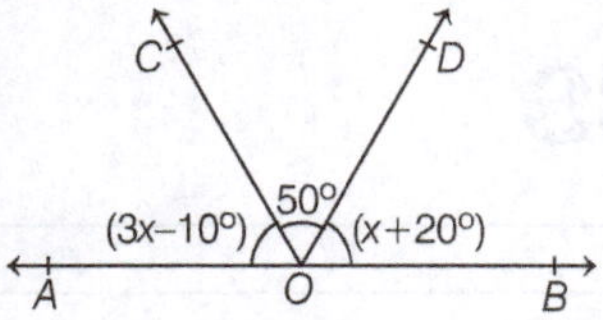

(a) 80° (b) 40° (c) 60° (d) 100°

13. **The volume of a sphere whose radius is 2r is**

(a) $\frac{4}{3}\pi r^3$ (b) $\frac{16}{3}\pi r^3$ (c) $\frac{2}{3}\pi r^3$ (d) $\frac{32}{3}\pi r^3$

14. **The total surface area of a right circular cone is**

(a) $\pi r(l+h)$ (b) $\pi r(l+r)$
(c) $\pi r(h+r)$ (d) $\pi r^2(l+r)$

15. **The class mark of the class 110-120 is**

(a) 100 (b) 110 (c) 120 (d) 115

16. **The surface area of a sphere having diameter 30 cm is**

(a) 2887.67 cm^2 (b) 2667.37 cm^2
(c) 2828.57 cm^2 (d) 2989.68 cm^2

17. **In the given figure, *AOB* is a straight line and $x:y:z=4:5:6$. Then, the value of y is**

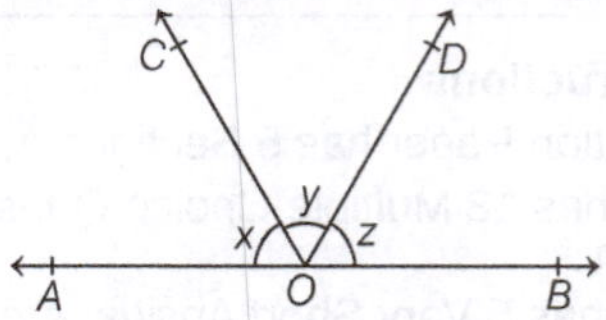

(a) 60° (b) 12° (c) 80° (d) 48°

18. **If a linear equation has solutions (–2, 2), (0, 0) and (2, –2) then it is of the form**

(a) $y-x=0$ (b) $x+y=0$
(c) $-zx+y=0$ (d) $-x+2y=0$

Part II

Directions (Q.Nos. 19-20) *In question numbers 19 and 20, a statement of Assertion (A) is followed by a statement of Reason (R). Choose the correct option.*

19. **Assertion** (A) If diameter of a sphere is decreased by 25%, then its curved surface area is decreased by 43.75%.

Reason (R) Curved surface area is increased when diameter decreases.

(a) Both Assertion and Reason are correct and Reason is the correct explanation of Assertion.
(b) Both Assertion and Reason are correct but Reason is not the correct explanation of Assertion.
(c) Assertion is correct but Reason is incorrect.
(d) Assertion is incorrect but Reason is correct.

20. **Assertion** (A) Decimal expansion of every rational number is only terminating.

Reason (R) Decimal expansion of every irrational number is non-terminating non-recurring.

(a) Both Assertion and Reason are correct and Reason is the correct explanation of Assertion.
(b) Both Assertion and Reason are correct but Reason is not the correct explanation of Assertion.
(c) Assertion is correct but Reason is incorrect.
(d) Assertion is incorrect but Reason is correct.

Section B

Section B consists of 5 Questions of 2 marks each.

21. If $x+\frac{1}{x}=4$, then find the value of $x^2+\frac{1}{x^2}$.

22. Simplify $\sqrt[5]{243a^{10}b^5c^{10}}$.

Or Factorise $9x^2+16y^2+25z^2+24xy-40yz-30xz$.

23. In the given figure, if *AOB* is a straight line, then find the value of *x*.

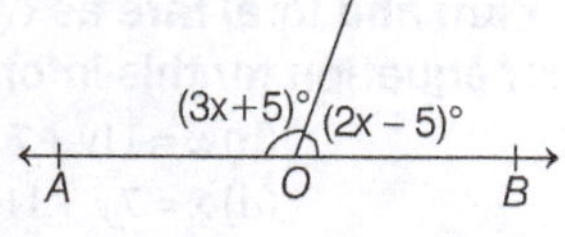

24. The mid-value of a class interval is 42 and the class size is 10. Find the lower and upper limits.

25. Two cones have their heights in the ratio 1 : 3 and the radii of their bases are in the ratio 3 : 1. Show that their volumes are in the ratio 3 : 1.

Or

If volume and surface area of a sphere is numerically equal, then find its radius.

Section C

Section C consists of 6 Questions of 3 marks each.

26. Find three rational numbers between $\frac{3}{7}$ and $\frac{2}{7}$.

27. Simplify $\left(\frac{5^{-1} \times 7^2}{5^2 \times 7^{-4}}\right)^{7/2} \times \left(\frac{5^{-2} \times 7^3}{5^3 \times 7^{-5}}\right)^{-5/2}$.

28. If $x - \frac{1}{x} = 7$, then find $x^2 + \frac{1}{x^2}$ and $x^4 + \frac{1}{x^4}$.

Or

Find the value of k, so that $2x + 1$ be a factors of $x^4 + 4x^3 - 16x^2 + 10x + k$.

29. In the adjoining figure, $y = ?$

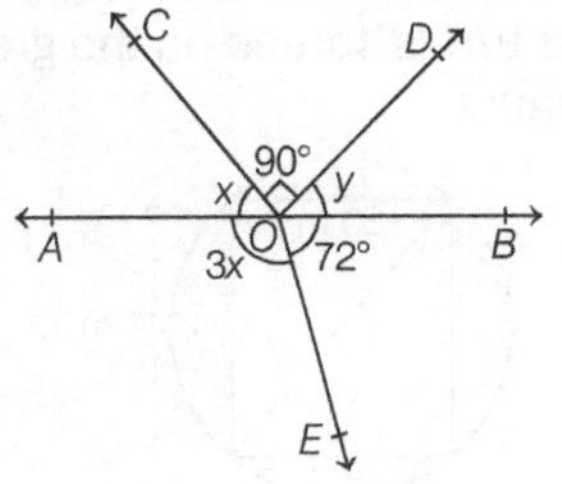

30. 70 students from a locality use different modes of transport to go to school as given below

Mode of transport	Car	Bus	Moped	Bicycle	Rickshaw
Number of students	4	27	11	20	8

Draw the bar graph representing the above data.

Or Represent the following frequency distribution by means of a histogram.

Marks	10-20	20-30	30-40	40-50	50-60	60-70	70-80
Number of students (Frequency)	7	11	9	13	16	4	2

31. The radius of sphere is 5 cm. If the radius is increased by 20%, then find by how much percent volume is increased?

Section D

Section D consists of 4 Questions of 5 marks each.

32. A hemispherical bowl is made of steel 0.5 cm thick. The inside radius of the bowl is 4 cm. Find the volume of steel used in making the bowl.

Or

A right-angled triangle of which the sides containing the right angle are 6.3 cm and 10 cm in length, is made to turn round on the longer side. Find the volume of the solid, thus generated. Also, find its curved surface.

33. Factorise

$$x^4 + 10x^3 + 35x^2 + 50x + 24$$

34. In the given figure, O is the centre of the circle, $BD = OD$ and CD intersect AB at 90°.

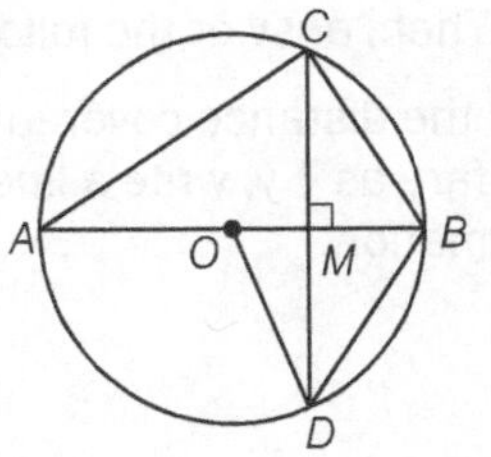

Find $\angle CAB$.

Or Two congruent circles intersect each other at points A and B. Through point A, any line segment PAQ is drawn, so that P and Q lie on the two circles. Prove that $BP = BQ$.

35. Prove that diagonals of a square are equal and perpendicular to each other.

Section E

Section E consists of 3 Questions of 4 marks each.

36. Case Study-1

An orphanage is an institution that takes care of orphans. An orphanage cares for small babies and also older children until they are placed in homes and adopted. A survey was conducted, it was found that 5 out of every 7 households are donating some amount of their income to an orphanage or old age home or institution for physically handicapped.

Then answer the following questions

(i) Find the fraction of households which are donating.

(ii) Write the type of decimal expansion in $\frac{5}{7}$.

(iii) Write the decimal form of $\frac{2}{7}$.

Or Write the decimal form of $\frac{5}{7}$.

37. Case Study-2

Rohan, a student of Class IX book an ola cab for travelling the tourist places of Jaipur city. The taxi fare in a city is as follows. Fare for the first km is ₹ 8 and for the subsequent distance it is ₹ 5 per km. Then, answer the following questions.

(i) Consider the distance covered as x km and the total fare as ₹ y, write a linear equation for this information.

(ii) Compare the above equation with $ax + by + c = 0$, and find the value of $(a + b + c)$.

(iii) If total fare is ₹ 93, then find the total distance.

Or If the distance covered is 11 km, then find total fare.

38. Case Study-3

The American Hockey Federation organised a friendly hockey match between America and Australia on a circular ground. The income of this match shall be donated to an orphanage. A rectangular turf is spread on the ground as shown in figure.

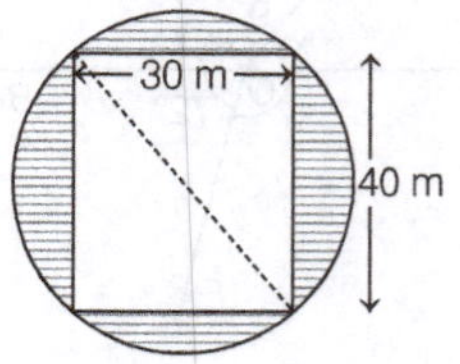

Answer the following questions

(i) Find the diagonal of the rectangular turf.

(ii) Find the radius of circular ground.

(iii) Find the area of rectangular ground.

Or Find the area (in m^2) of stadium.

Answer Key

1. (d) **2.** (b) **3.** (a) **4.** (b) **5.** (c)

6. (d) **7.** (a) **8.** (c) **9.** (d) **10.** (b)

11. (c) **12.** (a) **13.** (d) **14.** (b) **15.** (d)

16. (c) **17.** (a) **18.** (b) **19.** (c) **20.** (d)

21. 14 **22.** $3a^2bc^2$ or $(3x+4y-5z)(3x+4y-5z)$ **23.** 36° **24.** 37 and 47

25. or 3 units **26.** $\frac{11}{28}, \frac{10}{28}, \frac{9}{28}$ **27.** 175 **28.** 51 and 2599 or $\frac{151}{16}$ **29.** 54

31. 72.8% **32.** 56.83 cm^3 or 415.8 cm^3 and 234.03 cm^2 **33.** $(x+1)(x+2)(x+3)(x+4)$ **34.** 30°

36. (i) $\frac{5}{7}$ (ii) Non-terminating repeating (iii) $0.\overline{285714}$ or $0.\overline{714285}$

37. (i) $5x - y + 3 = 0$ (ii) 7 (iii) 18 km or ₹ 58

38. (i) 50 m (ii) 25 m (iii) 1200 m^2 or 625 π m^2

Sample Question Paper 2 (Unsolved)

Mathematics

Time : 3 hrs	M.M. : 80

General Instructions

See Sample Question Paper 1

Section A

Section A consists of 20 Questions of 1 mark each.

Part I

1. If 0.142857142857 ... express in the form of $\frac{m}{n}$, then the value of $(2m+n)$ is

(a) 1 (b) 2 (c) 7 (d) 9

2. $\sqrt[4]{\sqrt[3]{2^2}}$ equals

(a) $2^{-\frac{1}{6}}$ (b) 2^{-6} (c) $2^{\frac{1}{6}}$ (d) 2^6

3. The value of $249^2 - 248^2$ is

(a) 1^2 (b) 477 (c) 487 (d) 497

4. A point both of whose coordinates are negative will lie in

(a) I quadrant (b) II quadrant
(c) III quadrant (d) IV quadrant

5. If the coordinates of two points are $A(4,5)$ and $B(-3,6)$, then (abscissa of A) – (abscissa of B) is

(a) 3 (b) 5 (c) 7 (d) 9

6. If the point (3, 4) lies on the graph of the equation $3y - ax - 7 = 0$, then the value of a is

(a) $\frac{3}{5}$ (b) $\frac{4}{5}$ (c) $\frac{5}{3}$ (d) $\frac{7}{3}$

7. Simplify $\frac{2^{n+4} - 2(2^n)}{3(2^{n-3})}$

(a) $2^{n+1} - \frac{1}{8}$ (b) -2^{n+1}
(c) $1 - 2^n$ (d) $\frac{112}{3}$

8. If $a+b+c=9$ and $ab+bc+ca=40$, then the value of $a^2+b^2+c^2$ is

(a) 1 (b) $\frac{4}{5}$ (c) $\frac{5}{3}$ (d) $\frac{7}{3}$

9. If $x^2 + \frac{1}{x^2} = 23$, then the positive value of $\left(x + \frac{1}{x}\right)$ is

(a) –5 (b) 5 (c) ±5 (d) 25

10. In the given figure, find the value of $x + y$.

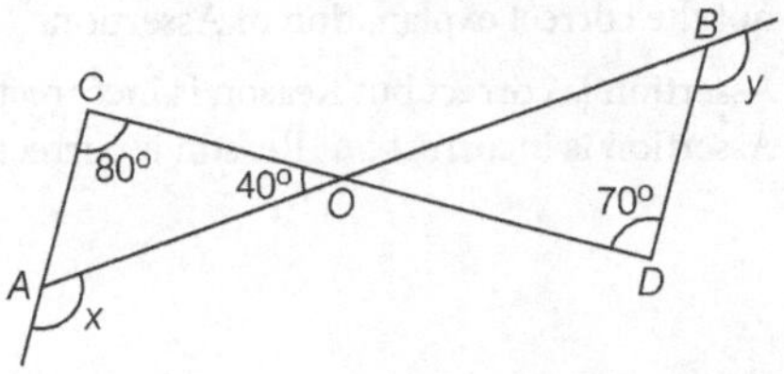

(a) 210° (b) 240° (c) 110° (d) 230°

11. The volume of a cone is 1570 cm³ and its height is 15 cm. What is the radius of the cone? [use $\pi = 3.14$]

(a) 5 cm (b) 15 cm
(c) 10 cm (d) 100 cm

12. D and E are the mid-points of sides AB and AC, respectively of ΔABC. If the perimeter of $\Delta ABC = 38$ cm, then find the perimeter of ΔADE is

(a) 19 cm (b) 38 cm
(c) 9.5 cm (d) 28.5 cm

13. The coefficient of x^2 in $(3x + x^3)\left(x + \frac{1}{x}\right)$.

(a) 3 (b) 1 (c) 2 (d) 4

14. If two supplementary angles are in the ratio 3 : 2, then the value of its angles are

(a) 144°, 36° (b) 108°, 72°
(c) 72°, 108° (d) 54°, 36°

15. If $\Delta ABC \cong \Delta FDE$ and $AB = 5$ cm, $\angle B = 40°$, $\angle A = 80°$, then find $\angle E$ is

(a) 60° (b) 120°
(c) 40° (d) 80°

16. The class mark of the class 35-55 is

(a) 40 (b) 55
(c) 35 (d) 45

17. The volume of two hemispheres are in the ratio 216 : 512. What is the ratio of their radii?

(a) 2 : 3 (b) 3 : 4 (c) 4 : 5 (d) 3 : 2

18. In ΔABC, $AB = 15$ cm, $BC = 24$ cm and $CA = 20$ cm. If D and E are respectively the mid-point of AB and BC, then the length of DE is

(a) 10 cm (b) 8 cm (c) 40 cm (d) 15 cm

Part II

Directions (Q.Nos. 19-20) *In question numbers 19 and 20, a statement of Assertion (A) is followed by a statement of Reason (R). Choose the correct option.*

19. **Assertion** (A) For all values of k, $\left(-\frac{3}{2}, k\right)$ is a solution of the linear equation $2x + 3 = 0$.

Reason (R) The linear equation $ax + b = 0$ can be expressed as a linear equation in two variables as $ax + y + b = 0$.

(a) Both Assertion and Reason are correct and Reason is the correct explanation of Assertion.
(b) Both Assertion and Reason are correct but Reason is not the correct explanation of Assertion.
(c) Assertion is correct but Reason is incorrect.
(d) Assertion is incorrect but Reason is correct.

20. **Assertion** (A) $ABCD$ is a cyclic quadrilateral, AB and DC are produced to meet in E, then $\angle ECB = \angle EDA$.

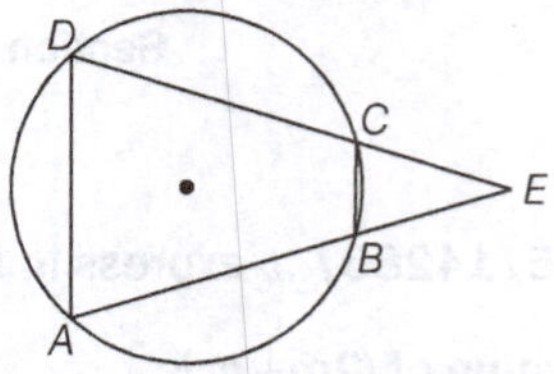

Reason (R) Exterior angle in a cylic quadrilateral is equal to opposite interior angle.

(a) Both Assertion and Reason are correct and Reason is the correct explanation of Assertion.
(b) Both Assertion and Reason are correct but Reason is not the correct explanation of Assertion.
(c) Assertion is correct but Reason is incorrect.
(d) Assertion is incorrect but Reason is correct.

Section B

Section B consists of 5 Questions of 2 marks each.

21. The radius of a circle is 10 cm and the length of one of its chords is 12 cm. Find the distance of the chord from the centre.

22. In the given figure, what value of x will make AOB, a straight line?

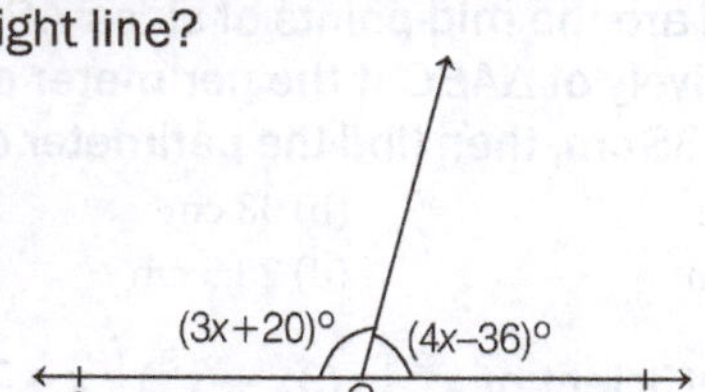

Or To improve the practical knowledge and awareness about the social life Directorate of Education announces a visit in a Delhi Public School. Girls are asked to prepare a rangoli in triangular shape as shown in figure.

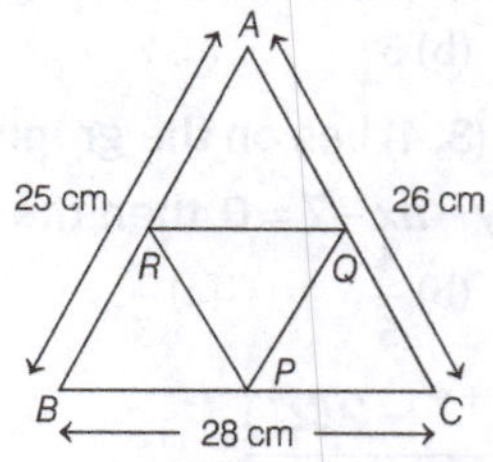

Dimensions of rangoli (ΔABC) are 25 cm, 28 cm, 26 cm. Garland is to be placed along the side of ΔPQR, which is formed by joining the mid-points of sides of ΔABC, then find the length of garland.

23. If the diagonals of a parallelogram are equal and intersect at right angles then prove that the parallelogram is a square.

24. If surface area of a sphere is $676\,\pi\text{ cm}^2$, then find its radius.

25. Factorise $x^4 - 3x^2 + 2$.

Or Factorise $\frac{x^3}{8} - 64 - 3x^2 + 24x$ using suitable identity.

Section C

Section C consists of 6 Questions of 3 marks each.

26. Simplify $\left(\frac{\sqrt{3}+\sqrt{2}}{\sqrt{3}-\sqrt{2}} + \frac{\sqrt{3}-\sqrt{2}}{\sqrt{3}+\sqrt{2}}\right)$.

27. Factorise

$$3x^3 - 4x^2 - 12x + 16$$

28. In the given figures, two sides *AB*, *BC* and the median *AD* of ΔABC are corres- pondingly equal to the sides *PQ*, *QR* and the median *PM* of ΔPQR. Prove that $\Delta ABC \cong \Delta PQR$.

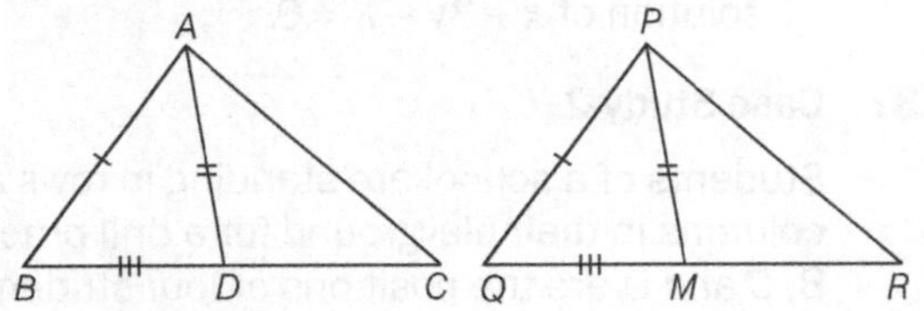

Or *ABCD* is a trapezium in which $AB \parallel CD$ and $AD = BC$. If *P*, *Q*, *R*, *S* be respectively, the mid-points of *BA*, *BD*, *CD* and *CA*, then show that *PQRS* is a rhombus.

29. The height and the slant height of a cone are 12 cm and 13 cm, respectively. Find the volume of the cone.

30. In the given figure, ray *OC* is the bisector of $\angle AOB$ and *OD* is the ray opposite to *OC*. Show that $\angle AOD = \angle BOD$.

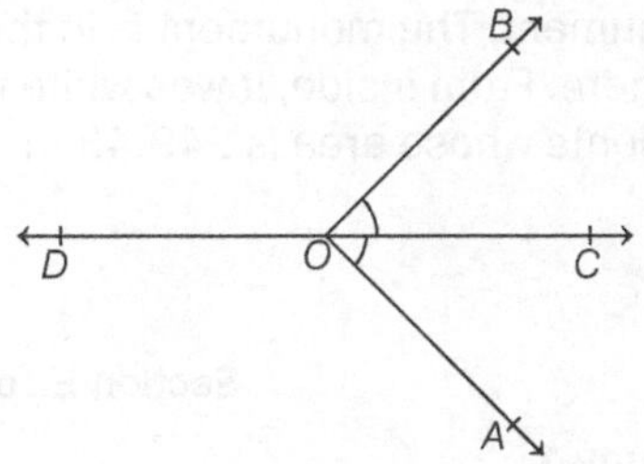

Or

Prove that the bisectors of a pair of vertically opposite angles are in the same straight line.

31. Given below are the seats won by different political parties in the polling outcome of a state assembly elections.

Political party	Seats won
BJP	85
CONGRESS	65
LJP	47
RJD	39
INC	20

(i) Draw a bar graph to represent the polling results.

(ii) Which political party won the maximum member of seats?

Section D

Section D consists of 4 Questions of 5 marks each.

32. If $a = \frac{1}{7-4\sqrt{3}}$ and $b = \frac{1}{7+4\sqrt{3}}$, find the value of the following

(i) $a^2 + b^2$

(ii) $a^3 + b^3$

Or

Simplify $\frac{-3}{\sqrt{3}+\sqrt{2}} - \frac{3\sqrt{2}}{\sqrt{6}+\sqrt{3}} + \frac{4\sqrt{3}}{\sqrt{6}+\sqrt{2}}$

33. In the given figure, *AB* is a line segment and *P* is its mid-point. *D* and *E* are points on the same side of *AB*, such that

$\angle BAD = \angle ABE$ and $\angle EPA = \angle DPB$.

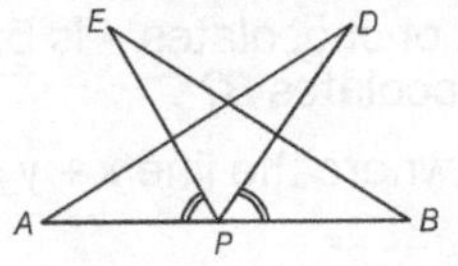

Show that

(i) $\Delta DAP \cong \Delta EBP$ (ii) $AD = BE$

34. The segment joining the mid-points M and N of parallel sides AB and DC, respectively of a trapezium $ABCD$ is perpendicular to both the sides AB and DC. Prove that $AD = BC$.

Or

To maintain beauty of a monument, the students of the school cleaned and painted the dome of the monument. The monument is in the form of a hemisphere. From inside, it was white washed by the students whose area is 249.48 m^2.

(i) Find the volume of the air inside the dome.

(ii) If white washing costs ₹ 2 per m^2, how much does it costs?

35. The internal and external radii of hollow hemispherical bowl is 15 cm and 16 cm respectively. Find the cost of painting the bowl at the rate of 35 paise per cm^2, if

(i) The area of the edge of the bowl is ignored.

(ii) The area of the edge of the bowl is taken into account.

Section E

Section E consists of 3 Questions of 4 marks each.

36. Case Study-1

Aditya purchased two types of chocolates A and B at the rate of ₹ x and ₹ y respectively. The total amount spent is ₹ 7. After reaching home, he forms a linear equation in two variables for two types of chocolates. He prepares a table and a graph of the linear equation as shown in given graph.

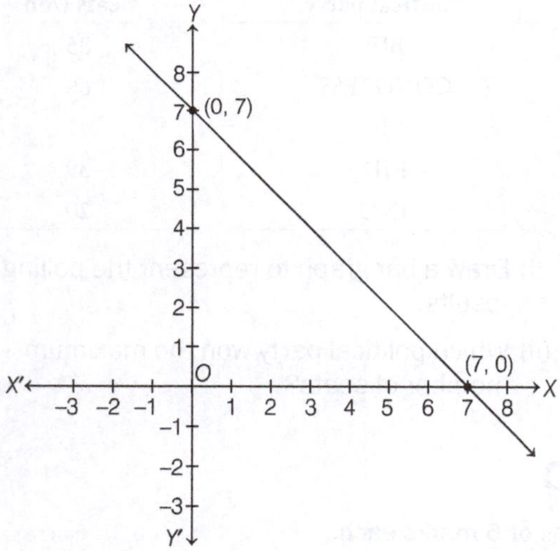

Now, answer the following questions.

(i) How to represent the above situation in linear equations in two variables?

(ii) If the cost of chocolates A is 5, then find the cost of chocolates B?

(iii) The point where the line $x + y = 7$ intersect y-axis is

Or

For what value of k, $x = 2$ and $y = -1$ is a solution of $x + 3y - k = 0$.

37. Case Study-2

Students of a school are standing in rows and columns in their playground for a drill practice. A, B, C and D are the positions of four students as shown in the figure.

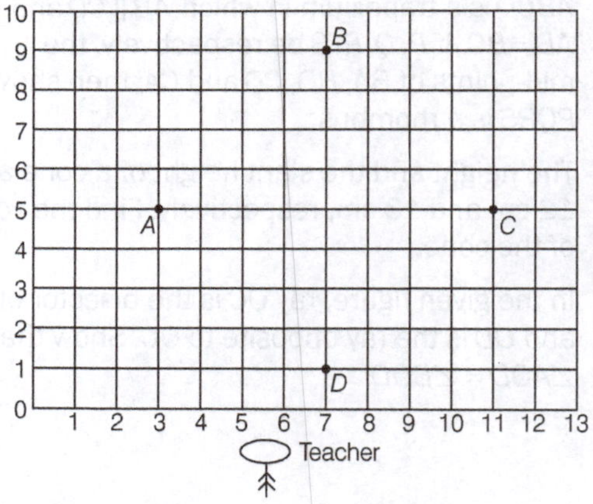

Now, answer the following questions.

(i) What are the coordinates of A and B respectively?

(ii) What are the coordinates of C and D respectively?

(iii) What is the distance between A and C?

Or

What are the coordinates of the point of intersection of AC and BD?

38. Case Study-3

Once four friends Rahul, Arun, Ajay and Vijay went for a picnic at a hill station. 'Due to peak season, they did not get a proper Hotel in the city. The weather was fine so they decided to make a conical tent at a park.

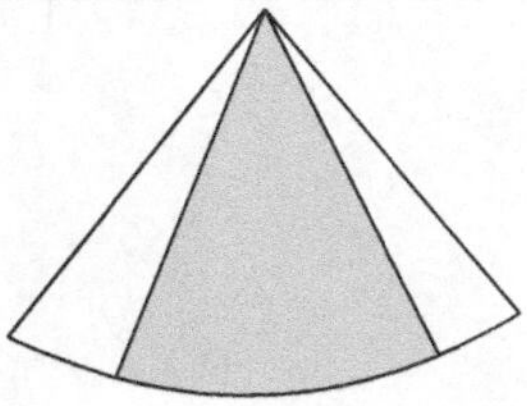

They were carrying 200 sq. m cloth with them. They made the conical tent with a height of 8 m and a diameter of 12 m. The remaining cloth was used for the floor.

Now, answer the following questions.

(i) What is the slant height of the tent?

(ii) How much cloth was used for the floor?

(iii) What was the area of the floor?

Or

What was the total surface area of the tent?

Answer Key

1. (d)	**2.** (c)	**3.** (d)	**4.** (c)	**5.** (c)
6. (c)	**7.** (d)	**8.** (a)	**9.** (b)	**10.** (d)
11. (c)	**12.** (a)	**13.** (d)	**14.** (b)	**15.** (a)
16. (d)	**17.** (b)	**18.** (a)	**19.** (c)	**20.** (d)
21. 8 cm	**22.** 28° or 39.5 cm	**24.** 13 cm		

25. $(x-\sqrt{2})(x+\sqrt{2})(x-1)(x+1)$ or $\frac{1}{8}(x-8)(x-8)(x-8)$ **26.** 10

27. $(x-2)(x+2)(3x-4)$ **29.** 314.29 cm^3 **31.** (ii) BJP **32.** (i) 194 (ii) 2702 or $6\sqrt{2}-5\sqrt{3}$

34. *Or* (i) 523.908 m^3 (ii) ₹ 498.96

35. (i) ₹ 1058.19 (ii) ₹ 1092.28

36. (i) $x+y=7$ (ii) 2 (iii) (0, 7) or $k=-1$

37. (i) $A(3,5)$; $B(7,9)$ (ii) $C(11,5)$, $D(7,1)$ (iii) 8 units or (7, 5)

38. (i) 10 cm (ii) 11.43 m^2 (iii) 113.14 m^2 or 301.71 m^2

Sample Question Paper 3 (Unsolved)

Mathematics

Time : 3 hrs | M.M. : 80

General Instructions

See Sample Question Paper 1

Section A

Section A consists of 20 Questions of 1 mark each.

Part I

1. Find the value of $\sqrt[4]{\sqrt[3]{2^4}}$.

(a) $2^{\frac{1}{9}}$ (b) $2^{\frac{1}{4}}$ (c) $2^{\frac{1}{6}}$ (d) $2^{\frac{1}{3}}$

2. If $x^2 + \dfrac{1}{x^2} = 7$, then find the value of $x + \dfrac{1}{x}$.

(a) 1 (b) 3 (c) 2 (d) 4

3. In the figure, POQ is a line. The value of x is

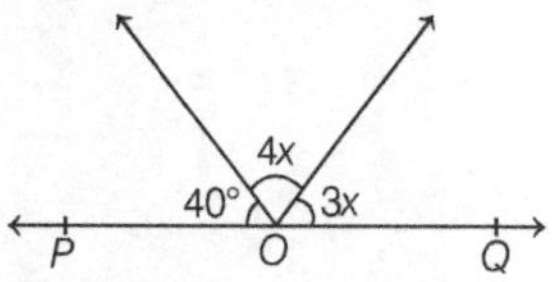

(a) 20° (b) 25° (c) 30° (d) 35°

4. The volume of hemisphere of radius 3.5 cm is

(a) 98.83 cm^3 (b) 80.83 cm^3
(c) 88.93 cm^3 (d) 89.83 cm^3

5. If $x = 2$, $y = 1$ is a solution of the equation $2x + 3y = k$, then the value of k is

(a) 3 (b) 5 (c) 8 (d) 7

6. The taxi fare in a city is as follows

For the first kilometre, the fare is ₹ 10 and for the subsequent distance, it is ₹ 6 per km. Taking the distance covered as x km and total fare as ₹ y. Then, the linear equation for this information is

(a) $4x - 10y + 6 = 0$ (b) $6x - y + 4 = 0$
(c) $x - 6y + 10 = 0$ (d) $10x + y - 4 = 0$

7. The radii of two right circular cones, are in the ratio 2 : 3 and their heights are in the ratio 5 : 4, then the ratio of their volumes is

(a) $\frac{2}{9}$ (b) $\frac{5}{9}$ (c) $\frac{6}{7}$ (d) $\frac{5}{22}$

8. If AB and CD are straight lines, then the value of x is

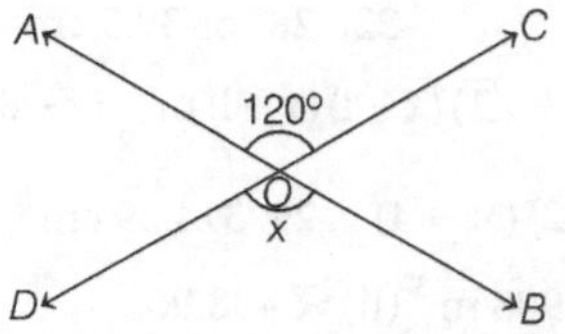

(a) 120° (b) 80° (c) 60° (d) 240°

9. The angle which is 24° more than its complement is

(a) 27° (b) 47° (c) 48° (d) 57°

10. The measure of an angle which is 34° more than its complementary is

(a) 62° (b) 78° (c) 56° (d) 17°

11. The class mark of the class 120-140 is

(a) 140 (b) 130 (c) 125 (d) 120

12. Complementary angle of 48° is

(a) 58° (b) 52° (c) 42° (d) 132°

13. The ratio of the total surface area of a sphere and a hemisphere of same radius is

(a) 4 : 3 (b) 3 : 2 (c) 2 : 3 (d) 2 : 1

14. The volume of a cone having radius of the base 35 cm and slant height 37 cm is

(a) 13200 cm^3 (b) 16600 cm^3
(c) 15400 cm^3 (d) 17800 cm^3

15. If $x^3 - 3x^2 + 3x + 7 = (x + 1)(ax^2 + bx + c)$, then the value of $a + b + c$ is

(a) 8 (b) 4 (c) 10 (d) 6

16. **If two supplementary angles are in the ratio 3:2, then their angles are**

(a) 108° and 72°
(b) 120° and 80°
(c) 120° and 60°
(d) 102° and 78°

17. **The total surface area of a cone of radius $\frac{r}{4}$ and slant height $4l$ is**

(a) $\pi r\left(l+\frac{r}{16}\right)$ (b) $4\pi r\left(3l+\frac{r}{4}\right)$
(c) $2\pi r\left(l+\frac{r}{16}\right)$ (d) $\pi r\left(2l+\frac{r}{8}\right)$

18. **The area of an equilateral triangle having a side of 20 m length is**

(a) $50\sqrt{3}\ m^2$ (b) $150\sqrt{3}\ m^2$
(c) $100\sqrt{2}\ m^2$ (d) $100\sqrt{3}\ m^2$

Part II

Directions (Q.Nos. 19-20) *In question numbers 19 and 20, a statement of Assertion (A) is followed by a statement of Reason (R). Choose the correct option.*

19. **Assertion** (A) An equation of the form $ax+by+c=0$, where a, b and c are real numbers, such that a and b are not both zero, is called a linear equation in two variables.

Reason (R) A linear equation in two variables has infinitely many solutions.

(a) Both Assertion and Reason are correct and Reason is the correct explanation of Assertion.
(b) Both Assertion and Reason are correct but Reason is not the correct explanation of Assertion.
(c) Assertion is correct but Reason is incorrect.
(d) Assertion is incorrect but Reason is correct.

20. **Assertion** (A) In ΔABC, $\angle C=\angle A$, $BC=4$ cm and $AC=5$ cm. Then, $AB=4$ cm.

Reason (R) In a triangle, angles opposite to two equal sides are equal.

(a) Both Assertion and Reason are correct and Reason is the correct explanation of Assertion.
(b) Both Assertion and Reason are correct but Reason is not the correct explanation of Assertion.
(c) Assertion is correct but Reason is incorrect.
(d) Assertion is incorrect but Reason is correct.

Section B

Section B consists of 5 Questions of 2 marks each.

21. If $a+b+c=15$ and $ab+bc+ca=71$, then find the value of $a^2+b^2+c^2$.

22. Express $0.\overline{3178}$ in the form of $\frac{p}{q}$, $q \neq 0$.

Or Find five rational numbers between $\frac{3}{5}$ and $\frac{4}{5}$.

23. Is 0.5015001500015 ...... is an irrational number?

24. Depict the following frequency distribution by a histogram.

Weekly wages (in ₹)	725-750	750-775	775-800	800-825	825-850
Number of workers (Frequency)	30	45	75	60	35

Or

Various modes of transport used by 1850 students of a school are given below.

School bus	Private bus	Bicycle	Rickshaw	By foot
640	360	490	210	150

Draw a bar graph to represent the above data.

25. A right circular cone is 3.6 cm high and the radius of its base is 1.6 cm. It is melted and recast into a right circular cone having base radius 1.2 cm. Find its height.

Section C

Section C consists of 6 Questions of 3 marks each.

26. Convert $23.\overline{43}$ into $\frac{p}{q}$ form.

27. Find $y^2 + \frac{1}{y^2}$ and $y^4 + \frac{1}{y^4}$, if $y - \frac{1}{y} = 9$.

28. If $x^2 + \frac{1}{x^2} = 62$, then find the value of $x^3 + \frac{1}{x^3}$.

Or Factorise $2x^2 - x + \frac{1}{12} + \frac{1}{6}x$.

29. The cost of a pencil is half of the cost of a pen. Write a linear equation in two variables to represent this statement. [take cost of a pen as x and cost of a pencil as y].

30. Draw a histogram to represent the following frequency distribution.

Class interval	10-15	15-20	20-30	30-50	50-80
Frequency	6	10	10	8	18

31. If $x = 2k - 1$, $y = k$ are the solution of the equation $3x - 5y - 7 = 0$, then find k.

Or

For what value of c, the linear equation $2x + cy = 8$ has equal values of x and y for its solution?

Section D

Section D consists of 4 Questions of 5 marks each.

32. (i) If $\sqrt{3} = 1.732$ and $\sqrt{2} = 1.4142$, then find the value of $\sqrt{\frac{\sqrt{3}-1}{\sqrt{3}+1}}$.

(ii) If $\left(\frac{2}{3}\right)^{2x}\left(\frac{3}{2}\right)^{x} = \frac{8}{27}$, then find the value of x.

Or Evaluate $\frac{15}{\sqrt{10}+\sqrt{20}+\sqrt{40}-\sqrt{5}-\sqrt{80}}$, is being given that $\sqrt{5} = 2.236$ and $\sqrt{10} = 3.162$.

33. In the given figure, AC is the diameter of a circle with centre O and chord BD intersect AC at 90° at point E. Find the values of p, q and r in terms of x.

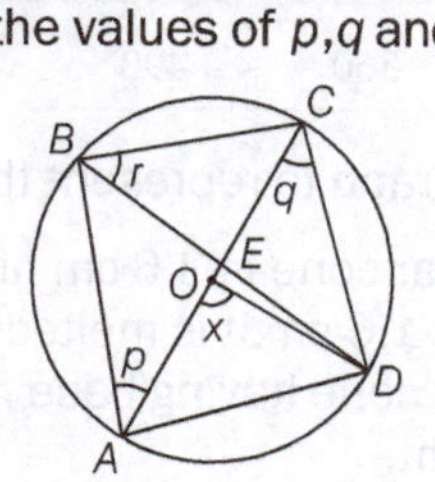

34. If $x + y + z = 1$, $xy + yz + zx = -1$ and $xyz = -1$, then find the value of $x^3 + y^3 + z^3$.

Or

Volume of a right circular cone is 2200/7 cm^3 and its diameter is 10 cm. Find its curved surface area. $\left(\text{take, } \pi = \frac{22}{7}\right)$

35. 70 students from a locality use different modes of transport to go to school as given below

Mode of transport	Number of students
Car	4
Bus	27
Moped	11
Bicycle	20
Rickshaw	8

Draw the bar graph of the above data.

Section E

Section E consists of 3 Questions of 4 marks each.

36. Case Study-1

With the increase in the fuel prices, the price of consumer products increases because oil is an essential component of the industrial and the manufacturing sectors, also petrol and diesel is used for the transportation of goods, thus creating an inflationary pressure. There are two statements based on petrol and CNG gas are given below.

Statement I Every six months, price of petrol increases at the rate of ₹ 4 per litre. Taking price of petrol in December, 2011 as x and present price of petrol as y.

Statement II Due to continuous rise in the petrol price, people are shifting towards CNG whose price increases at the rate of ₹ 3 per litre in a year.

So, give answer of the question by reading the above statements.

(i) According to first statement, form a linear equation showing amount spend on petrol in December 2012.

(ii) According to second statement, form a linear equation taking price of CNG in December 2011 as a and b in December 2012 as b.

(iii) If the price of petrol in December 2011 is ₹ 48, then find the price of petrol in December 2015.

Or

If the price of CNG in December 2011 is ₹ 22, then find the price of CNG in December 2015.

37. Case Study-2

Prime Minister's National Relief Fund (also called PMNRF in short) is the fund raised to provide support for people affected by natural and man-made disasters. Natural disaster that are covered under this include flood, cyclone, earthquake etc. Man-made disasters that are included are major accidents, acid attacks, riots. etc.

Two friends Sita and Gita, together contributed ₹ 200 towards Prime Minister's Relief Fund.

Answer the following.

(i) How to represent the above situation in linear equations in two variables? [take Sita's contribution as x and Gita's contribution as y]

(ii) Write the standard form of linear equations $x = -5$.

(iii) If Sita contributed ₹ 76, then how much was contributed by Gita?

Or If both contributed equally, then how much is contributed by each?

38. Case Study-3

The following bar graph represents the budget allocation by Government of NCT of Delhi under Ladli scheme

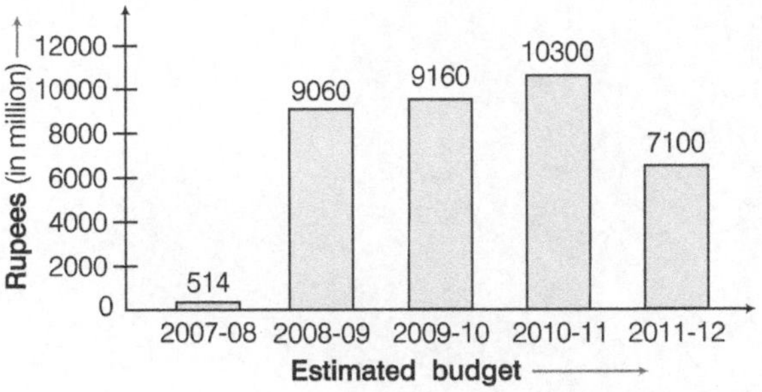

This scheme started in Jan 2008. Study the above bar graph and answer the following questions.

(i) Find the year, in which the budget was minimum.

(ii) Find the year, in which the budget was maximum.

(iii) Calculate the budget during the year of 2008-10.

Or Calculate the total budget during the year of 2009-12.

Answer Key

1. (d)	2. (b)	3. (a)	4. (d)	5. (d)
6. (b)	7. (b)	8. (a)	9. (d)	10. (a)
11. (b)	12. (c)	13. (a)	14. (c)	15. (b)
16. (a)	17. (a)	18. (d)	19. (b)	20. (b)
21. 83	22. $\frac{3178}{9999}$ or $\frac{19}{30},\frac{2}{3},\frac{7}{10},\frac{11}{15},\frac{23}{30}$		23. Yes	25. 6.4 cm
26. $\frac{2320}{99}$	27. 83 and 6887	28. 488 or $\frac{1}{12}(4x-1)(6x-1)$		29. $x-2y=0$

31. 10 or $\frac{8-2x}{x}$ 32. (i) 0.5176 (ii) 3 or 5.398 33. $p=90°-\frac{x}{2}, q=\frac{x}{2}, r=\frac{90°-x}{2}$

34. 1 or 65 π cm^2 36. (i) $y=x+8$ (ii) $b=a+6$ (iii) ₹ 80 or ₹ 34

37. (i) $x+y=200$ (ii) $1\cdot x+0\cdot y+5=0$ (iii) ₹ 124 or ₹ 100, ₹ 100

38. (i) 2007-08 (ii) 2010-11 (iii) ₹ 18220 million or ₹ 26560 million

Sample Question Paper 4 (Unsolved)
Mathematics

Time : 3 hrs	M.M. : 80

General Instructions
See Sample Question Paper 1

Section A

Section A consists of 20 Questions of 1 mark each.

Part I

1. If $a^x = c^q = b$ and $c^y = a^z = d$, then the value of xy is
(a) xq (b) qy (c) yz (d) qz

2. In the given figure, x is equal to

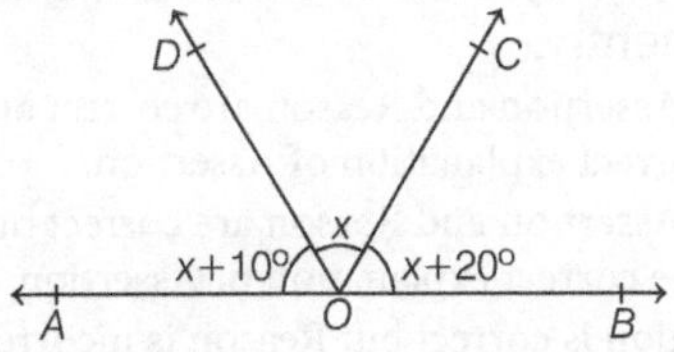

(a) 40° (b) 35° (c) 50° (d) 45°

3. Two supplementary angles are in the ratio 4 : 5. Then, the two angles are
(a) 80° and 100° (b) 60° and 75°
(c) 60° and 120° (d) 40° and 50°

4. Two complementary angles are in the ratio 4 : 5. The angles are
(a) 44° and 55° (b) 40° and 50°
(c) 30° and 60° (d) 80° and 100°

5. If x and y are the angles such that $x - y = 60°$ and $x + y = 80°$, then y is equal to
(a) 20° (b) 30° (c) 10° (d) 25°

6. A rectangular field has its length and breadth such that length is 3/4th of its breadth. If its area is equal to 25/3 sq units, then the length of the rectangular field is
(a) $\frac{5}{2}$ units (b) $\frac{10}{3}$ units (c) $\frac{12}{5}$ units (d) $\frac{7}{2}$ units

7. The measure of the supplement of an angle of 92° is
(a) 74° (b) 114° (c) 8° (d) 88°

8. If $x = 2$, $y = 1$ is the solution of equation $2x - 3y = k$, then find the value of k.
(a) 2 (b) 1 (c) -1 (d) 7

9. The formula to find the volume of the solid enclosed between two concentric spheres is
(a) $\frac{4}{3}\pi(R^3 - r^3)$ (b) $\frac{4}{3}\pi(R^2 - r^2)$
(c) $\frac{2}{3}\pi(R^3 - r^3)$ (d) $\frac{2}{3}\pi(R^2 - r^2)$

10. Radius of a sphere whose volume is 38808 cm^3 is
(a) 23 cm (b) 17 cm
(c) 21 cm (d) 19 cm

11. If the radius of its base is 7 cm and height is 15 cm. Then, the volume of a right circular cone is
(a) 650 cm^3 (b) 470 cm^3
(c) 750 cm^3 (d) 770 cm^2

12. If the area of an equilateral triangle is $9\sqrt{3}$ cm^2, then the side of the triangle is
(a) 6 cm (b) 2 cm (c) 5 cm (d) 3 cm

13. The volume and total surface area of a cone [where radius, height and slant height is r, h and l respectively] are
(a) $\frac{1}{3}\pi r^2 h$ cu units and $\pi r(h + r)$ sq units
(b) $\frac{1}{3}\pi r^2 h^2$ cu units and $\pi r(l + r)$ sq units
(c) $\frac{1}{3}\pi r^2 h$ cu units and $\pi r(l + r)$ sq units
(d) None of the above

14. The decimal expansion of $\frac{2}{11}$ is the type of

(a) Non-terminating
(b) terminating
(c) Non-terminating repeating
(d) Non-terminating non-repeating

15. The decimal number $0.3\overline{8}$ is the type of

(a) Terminating
(b) Non-terminating
(c) Non-terminating repeating
(d) Non-terminating non-repeating

16. If $p(x) = x^2 - 2\sqrt{2}x + 1$, then $p(2\sqrt{2})$ is equal to

(a) 0 (b) 1 (c) $4\sqrt{2}$ (d) $8\sqrt{2}+1$

17. If $49x^2 - b = \left(7x + \frac{1}{2}\right)\left(7x - \frac{1}{2}\right)$, then the value of b is

(a) 0 (b) $\frac{1}{\sqrt{2}}$ (c) $\frac{1}{4}$ (d) $\frac{1}{2}$

18. The coordinates of points P and Q are $(-5, 3)$ and $(-5, m)$, respectively. And if sum of abscissa and ordinate of both points are equal. Then, the possible value of m is

(a) -5 (b) -13 (c) -10 (d) 3

Part II

Directions (Q.Nos. 19-20) *In question numbers 19 and 20, a statement of Assertion (A) is followed by a statement of Reason (R). Choose the correct option.*

19. Assertion (A) 0.468 is a terminating decimal.

Reason (R) A decimal in which a digit or a set of digits is repeated periodically, is called a repeating or a recurring decimal.

(a) Both Assertion and Reason are correct and Reason is the correct explanation of Assertion.
(b) Both Assertion and Reason are correct but Reason is not the correct explanation of Assertion.
(c) Assertion is correct but Reason is incorrect.
(d) Assertion is incorrect but Reason is correct.

20. Assertion (A) The sum of two adjacent angle is $100°$ and one of them is $35°$, then other is $65°$.

Reason (R) Adjacent angle are always supplementry.

(a) Both Assertion and Reason are correct and Reason is the correct explanation of Assertion.
(b) Both Assertion and Reason are correct but Reason is not the correct explanation of Assertion.
(c) Assertion is correct but Reason is incorrect.
(d) Assertion is incorrect but Reason is correct.

Section B

Section B consists of 5 Questions of 2 marks each.

21. Find $0.\overline{23} + 0.\overline{22}$.

22. Rationalise $\frac{1}{\sqrt{5}+\sqrt{3}-\sqrt{2}}$.

Or

Simplify $\frac{6^{2/3} \times \sqrt[3]{6^7}}{\sqrt[3]{6^6}}$.

23. If $x^4 + \frac{1}{x^4} = 47$, then find the value of $x^3 + \frac{1}{x^3}$.

24. In the given figure, three coplanar lines AB, CD and EF intersect at a point O. Find the value of x. Hence, find $\angle AOD$, $\angle COE$ and $\angle AOE$.

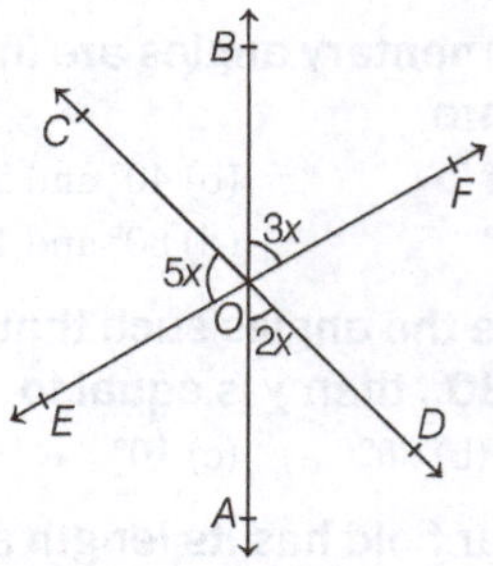

25. 24 solid iron spheres, each of radius r and surface area S are melted to form a sphere with surface area S'. Find the radius r' of the new sphere.

Or The curved surface area of a cone is $4070\ cm^2$ and its diameter is 70 cm. Find its slant height.

Section C

Section C consists of 6 Questions of 3 marks each.

26. For what value of c in terms of x, the linear equation $2x + cy = 8$ has equal values of x and y for its solution?

27. Find any four solutions of the equation $\pi x + y = 9$.

28. In the given figure, $\angle EBA = \angle EAB$ and $AC = BD$. Prove that $AD = BC$.

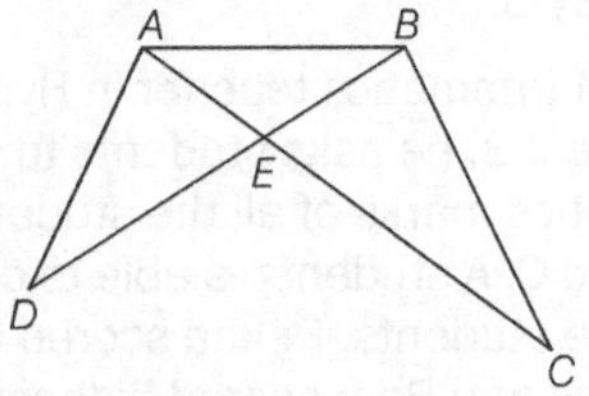

Or In figure, $\angle PQR = 110°$, where P, Q and R are points on a circle with centre O. Find $\angle OPR$.

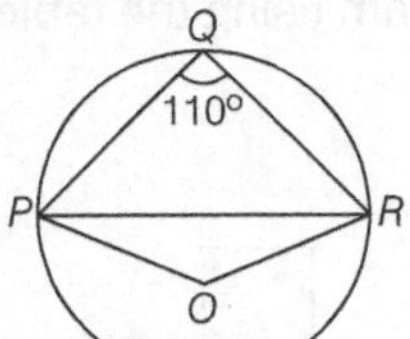

29. Three friends walk away from a point in three different directions, such that the path of each is equally inclined to those of the other two. Find the angles, their paths make with each other.

30. It is given that, $\angle XYZ = 70°$ and XY is produced to point P. Draw a figure from the given information, if ray YQ bisects $\angle ZYP$, then find $\angle XYQ$ and reflex $\angle QYP$.

Or If two equal chords of a circle intersect within the circle, then prove that the segments of one chord are equal to corresponding segments of the other chord.

31. There are 840 creatures in a zoo as per list given below

Beast animals	Other land animals	Birds	Water animals	Reptiles
120	345	165	135	75

Represent the above data by a chart.

Section D

Section D consists of 4 Questions of 5 marks each.

32. If $xyz = 1$, then show that

$$(1+x+y^{-1})^{-1} + (1+y+z^{-1})^{-1} + (1+z+x^{-1})^{-1} = 1.$$

Or

If $a = \dfrac{1}{9-4\sqrt{5}}$ and $b = \dfrac{1}{9+4\sqrt{5}}$, then find the values of the following

(i) $a^2 + b^2$ (ii) $a^3 + b^3$

33. Simplify $\dfrac{-3}{\sqrt{3}+\sqrt{2}} - \dfrac{3\sqrt{2}}{\sqrt{6}+\sqrt{3}} + \dfrac{4\sqrt{3}}{\sqrt{6}+\sqrt{2}}$.

34. Show that the diagonals of a parallelogram bisect each other.

Or

Prove that the quadrilateral formed (if possible) by the internal angle bisectors of any quadrilateral is cyclic.

35. The lengths of 62 leaves of a plant are measured (in mm) and the data is represented in the following table.

Length	Number of leaves
118-126	8
127-135	10
136-144	12
145-153	17
154-162	7
163-171	5
172-180	3

Draw a histogram to represent the given data.

Section E

Section E consists of 3 Questions of 4 marks each.

36. Case Study-1

To judge the preparation of students of class IX on topic 'Number System', Mathematics teachers write two numbers on blackboard and asks some questions about the two members, which are following, then answer the questions.

(i) Write the decimal form of $\frac{2}{11}$.

(ii) If $\frac{p}{q}$ form of $0.3\overline{8}$ is $\frac{m}{n}$, then value of $(m+n)$ is

(iii) Find the value of $0.\overline{18} + 0.3\overline{8}$.

Or

Determine the value of $0.\overline{3} + \frac{11}{3}$.

37. Case Study-2

To raise the fund for cancer patients, a charity race was organised on rectangular school ground *ABCD*. Lines have been drawn with chalk powder at a distance of 1 m each. 100 flower pots have been placed at a distance of 1 m from each other along *AD*. Niharika runs $\frac{1}{4}$ of the distance *AD* on the second line and posts a green flag. Preeti runs $\frac{1}{5}$ of the distance *AD* on the 8th line and posts a red flag as shown in below figure.

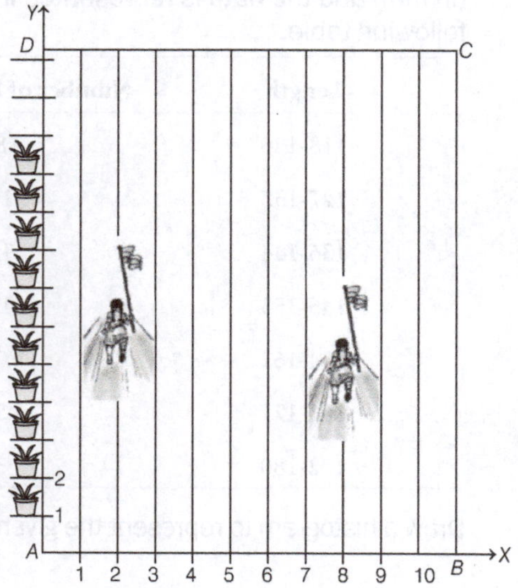

Then, give the answer of following questions.

(i) In which quadrant, the coordinates of green flag lies?

(ii) Write the name of quadrant, in which the red flag lies?

(iii) Write the coordinates of green flag.

Or Write the coordinates of red flag.

38. Case Study-3

Anil is a Mathematics teacher in Hyderabad. After Periodic test 3, he asks students to collect the Mathematics marks of all the students of Class IX-A, B and C. A students is able to collect marks from some students. Rekha scored least mark 6 in the class and Ram scored highest marks 59 out of 60 in the class. He prepares the frequency distribution table using the collected marks and draws Histogram using the table as shown in the figure.

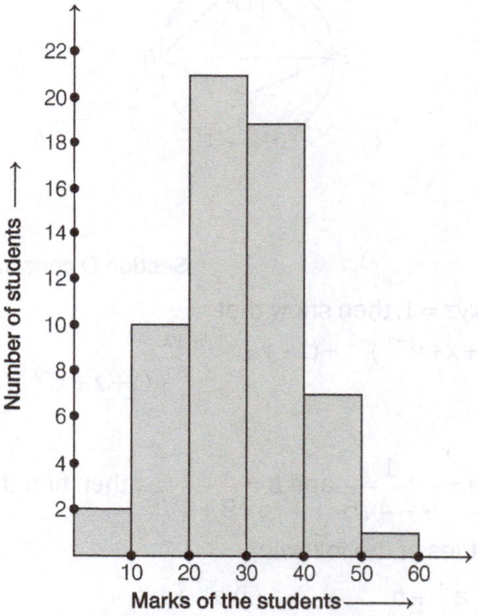

Now, answer the following questions.

(i) What is the width of the class?

(ii) What is the total number of students in Histogram?

(iii) How many students scored 50% and above marks?

Or

How many students scored less than 50% marks?

Answer Key

1. (d)	**2.** (c)	**3.** (a)	**4.** (b)	**5.** (c)
6. (a)	**7.** (d)	**8.** (b)	**9.** (a)	**10.** (c)
11. (d)	**12.** (a)	**13.** (c)	**14.** (c)	**15.** (c)
16. (b)	**17.** (c)	**18.** (b)	**19.** (b)	**20.** (c)

21. $0.\overline{45}$ **22.** $\dfrac{-2\sqrt{3}+3\sqrt{2}-\sqrt{30}}{12}$ or 6 **23.** 18

24. $x=18, \angle AOD=36°, \angle COE=90°, \angle AOE=54°$ **25.** $2(3)^{1/3}r$ or 37 cm

26. $\dfrac{8-2x}{x}$ **27.** $(0,9), \left(\dfrac{9}{\pi},0\right), (1,9-\pi), (2,9-2\pi)$

28. or 20° **29.** 120° **30.** $\angle XYQ=125°$ and reflex $\angle QYP=305°$

32. or (i) 322 (ii) 5778 **33.** $6\sqrt{2}-5\sqrt{3}$

36. (i) $0.1\overline{8}$ (ii) 25 (iii) $0.\overline{570}$ or 4

37. (i) 1st quadrant (ii) 1st quadrant (iii) (2, 25) or (8, 20)

38. (i) 10 (ii) 60 (iii) 27 or 33

Sample Question Paper 5 (Unsolved)

Mathematics

Time : 3 hrs	M.M. : 80

General Instructions

See Sample Question Paper 1

Section A

Section A consists of 20 Questions of 1 mark each.

Part I

1. The value of x in $\frac{x-\sqrt{6}}{\sqrt{3}+\sqrt{2}}=\frac{3\sqrt{3}-4\sqrt{2}}{1}$ is

(a) -1 (b) 0 (c) 1 (d) 2

2. Mohan has ₹ 25 in the form of 50 paisa and one rupee coins. He has half as many 50 paisa coins as he has one rupee coins. Then the number of one rupee coins is

(a) 20 (b) 25 (c) 5 (d) 30

3. In the given figure, AOB is a straight line. Then the value of x is

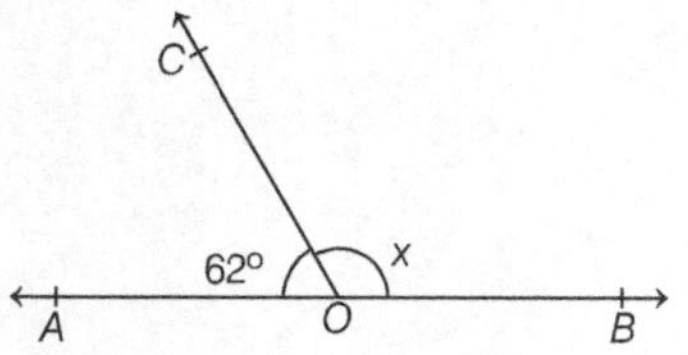

(a) 98° (b) 118° (c) 108° (d) 28°

4. The length of a chord of a circle with radius 10 cm is 16 cm, If $OD \perp AB$, then the length of OD (O is the centre) is

(a) 10 cm (b) 8 cm (c) 12 cm (d) 6 cm

5. In the following figure, O is the intersecting points of OA and OC and $OABC$ is a square of side 2 units. Then the position of points A, B and C are

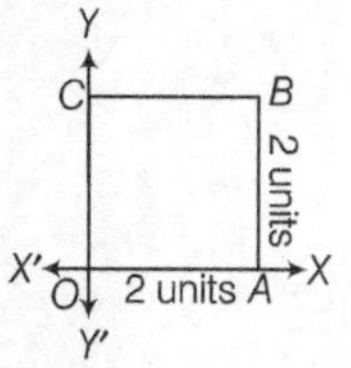

(a) $A=(2,0), B=(2,2)$ and $C=(0,2)$

(b) $A=(0,2), B=(2,2)$ and $C=(2,0)$

(c) $A=(2,2), B=(2,0)$ and $C=(0,2)$

(d) $A=(0,2), B=(1,1)$ and $C=(2,0)$

6. The name of an angle which is less than 360° and more than 180° is

(a) Obtuse angle

(b) Acute angle

(c) Reflex angle

(d) Supplementary angle

7. The coefficient of the highest power of x in the polynomial

$$3x^3-5x^4+7x^2-x^5+7 \text{ is}$$

(a) -5 (b) 0 (c) 3 (d) -1

8. Write the name of quadrilateral, in which the bisectors of the angle of a parallelogram enclose?

(a) Parallelogram (b) Rectangle

(c) Square (d) Rhombus

9. In the given figure AB, CD and PQ are three lines concurrent at O. If $\angle AOP=4y$, $\angle QOD=3y$ and $\angle BOC=2y$, then find the value of y.

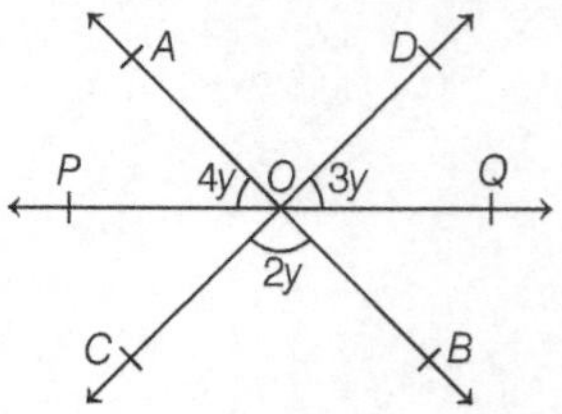

(a) 24° (b) 36° (c) 6° (d) 20°

10. A sphere and a cone are of the same radius and same height. Find the ratio of their curved surfaces.

(a) $2\sqrt{2}:1$ (b) $1:2\sqrt{2}$ (c) $2:\sqrt{5}$ (d) $\sqrt{5}:2$

11. **The base radii of two right circular cone of the same height are in the ratio 3 : 5, then find the ratio of their volumes.**
(a) 27 : 125 (b) 3 : 5 (c) 9 : 25 (d) 125 : 27

12. **Five years ago, Raju told Rita that he was 10 yr older than your age. Taking Raju's and Rita's present age as *x* yr and *y* yr, respectively. Then, form the linear equation which represents their age 5 yr ago.**
(a) $x+y=10$ (b) $x-y=10$
(c) $x-y=20$ (d) $x-y=0$

13. **The radius of a sphere is 3*r*, then its volume is**
(a) $108\,\pi r^3$ (b) $27\,\pi r^3$ (c) $18\,\pi r^3$ (d) $36\,\pi r^3$

14. **Find the class mark of the class 60-90.**
(a) 60 (b) 90 (c) 75 (d) 15

15. **The point whose ordinate is 4 and which lies on Y-axis is**
(a) (4, 0) (b) (0, 4) (c) (4, 2) (d) (1, 4)

16. **A lending library has a fixed charge for the first three days and an additional charge for each day thereafter. Roshni paid ₹ 35 for a book kept for seven days. Write a linear equation which satisfies this data.**
(a) $x+4y=35$ (b) $x+y=35$
(c) $x-y=35$ (d) $x-4y=35$

17. **Two circles with centre *A* and *B* intersect at *C* and *D*. If $\angle ACB = 60°$, then $\angle ADB$ is equal to**
(a) 60° (b) 120° (c) 30° (d) 150°

18. $x^2+\frac{1}{x^2}=7$, **then the value of** $x^3+\frac{1}{x^3}$ **is**
(a) 27 (b) 9 (c) 18 (d) 36

Part II

Directions (Q.Nos. 19-20) *In question numbers 19 and 20, a statement of Assertion (A) is followed by a statement of Reason (R). Choose the correct option.*

19. **Assertion** (A) If we draw triangles with angles 30°, 70° and 80° and the length of the sides of one triangle be different than that of the corresponding sides of the other then two triangles are not congruent.

Reason (R) If two triangles are constructed, which have all corresponding angles equal but have a pair of unequal corresponding sides, then two triangles cannot be congruent to each other.
(a) Both Assertion and Reason are correct and Reason is the correct explanation of Assertion.
(b) Both Assertion and Reason are correct but Reason is not the correct explanation of Assertion.
(c) Assertion is correct but Reason is incorrect.
(d) Assertion is incorrect but Reason is correct.

20. **Assertion** (A) Suppose the mean of 30 observations is 25. If each observation is multiplied by 5, then the new mean will be 120.

Reason (R) If we multiply each observation by any constant *k*, then the new mean will be equal to *k* times the original mean.
(a) Both Assertion and Reason are correct and Reason is the correct explanation of Assertion.
(b) Both Assertion and Reason are correct but Reason is not the correct explanation of Assertion.
(c) Assertion is correct but Reason is incorrect.
(d) Assertion is incorrect but Reason is correct.

Section B

Section B consists of 5 Questions of 2 marks each.

21. Find the value of *p*, if $(2x-1)$ is a factor of $2x^3+px^2+11x+p+3$.

22. (i) If $f(x)=x-7$, find the value of $f(x)-f(-x)$.

(ii) If $p(x)=4x^5-3x^4-5x^3+x^2-8$, then find $p(-2)$.

Or If $\sqrt{a}+\sqrt{b}+\sqrt{c}=0$, then prove that $(a+b-c)^2=4ab$.

23. In the given figure, *AB* is a mirror; *PQ* is the incident ray and *QR*, the reflected ray. If $\angle PQR = 112°$, find $\angle PQA$.

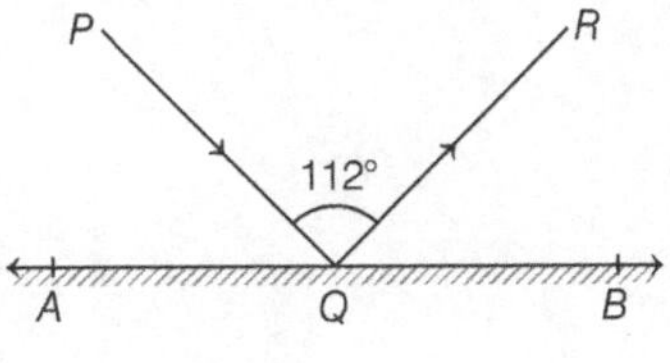

24. Find the value of x, if

$$\left(\frac{6}{5}\right)^{x}\left(\frac{5}{6}\right)^{2x}=\frac{125}{216}.$$

25. In the given figure, $\angle B=\angle E$, $BD=CE$ and $\angle 1=\angle 2$. Show that $\Delta ABC \cong \Delta AED$

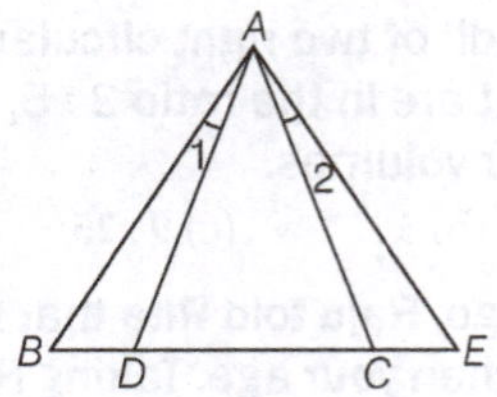

Or

Find the volume of a sphere whose radius is equal to $\sqrt{3}\,r$ (use $\pi=3.14$ and $\sqrt{3}=1.732$)

Section C

Section C consists of 6 Questions of 3 marks each.

26. In the given figure, two straight line PQ and RS intersect each other at O. If $\angle POT=75°$, then find the value of a, b and c.

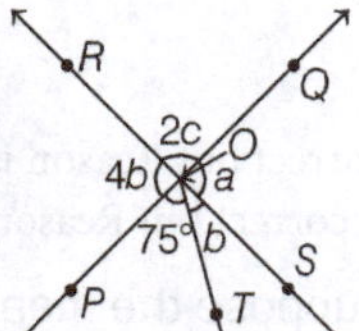

27. Two cones have their heights in the ratio 1 : 3 and the radii of their bases in the ratio 3 : 1. Show that their volumes are in the ratio 3 : 1.

28. Evaluate

(i) Evaluate $(106)^3$ by using suitable identity.

(ii) $\dfrac{8.73\times8.73\times8.73+4.27\times4.27\times4.27}{8.73\times8.73-8.73\times4.27+4.27\times4.27}$.

Or

If $x-y=6$ and $xy=88$, then find the value of x^3-y^3.

29. In the given figure, if $\angle AOB=90°$ and $\angle ABC=30°$, then find the measure of $\angle CAO$.

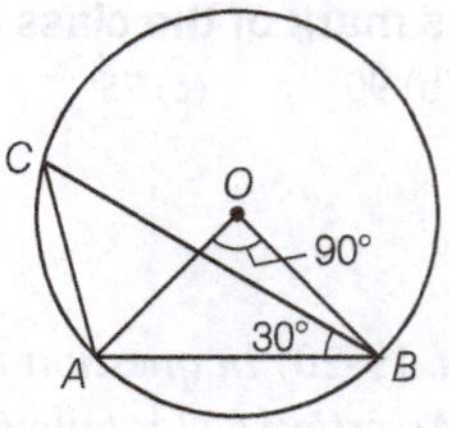

30. If p is any point in the square $ABCD$ and $DPQR$ is another square then prove that

$$AP=CR$$

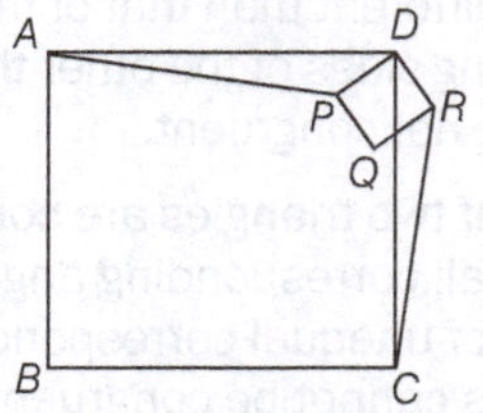

Or

Let y varies directly as x. If $y=12$ when $x=4$ then write a linear equation. What is the value of y when $x=5$?

31. Find the coordinates of the point

(i) which lies on X and Y-axes both.

(ii) whose ordinate is -4 and which lies on Y-axis.

(iii) whose abscissa is 5 and which lies on X-axis.

Section D

Section D consists of 4 Questions of 5 marks each.

32. In the given figure, *PQRS* is a square and $AB \parallel QS$. *M* is the mid-point of *AB*. Prove that *PM* bisects $\angle QPS$.

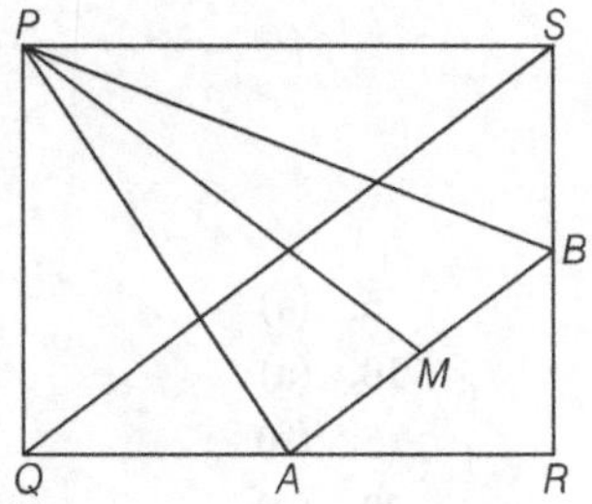

Or

ΔABC is an isosceles triangle in which $AB = AC$. *D*, *E* and *F* are the mid-points of the sides *BC*, *AC* and *AB*, respectively. Prove that $DE = DF$.

33. (i) Evaluate $\sqrt{5+2\sqrt{6}}+\sqrt{8-2\sqrt{15}}$.

(ii) If $2^x = 3^y = 6^{-z}$, then prove that

$$\frac{1}{x}+\frac{1}{y}+\frac{1}{z}=0.$$

34. Along a path, 100 conical pillars are constructed. Each pillar has base radius 14 cm and height 18 cm. Find the total cost of painting these pillars at the rate of ₹ 120 per m^2.
(take $\pi = 22/7$)

Or

A hemispherical bowl is made of 0.50 cm thick brass. The inner radius of the bowl is 6 cm. Find the inner and outer curved surface areas and volume of the bowl.

35. Prove that any angle substented by a minor arc in the alternate segment is acute and any angle substented by a major arc in the alternate segment is obtuse.

Section E

Section E consists of 3 Questions of 4 marks each.

36. Case Study-1

DAV school of Delhi decided to conducted different types of educational tours for the students. So, in class IX, $\frac{1}{12}$th times the square of the total number of students planned to visit historical monuments, $\frac{7}{12}$th times the member of students planned to visit old age homes while 15 students decided to teach poor children.

Based on the above information answer the following questions.

(i) Using above information, express the total numbers of students as a polynomial $p(x)$.

(ii) Find the coefficient of *x* in polynomial.

(iii) Find the value of $p(x)$ at $x = 2$.

Or At $x = -1$, find the value of $p(x)$.

37. Case Study-2

Car parking is a major problem in urban areas in both developed and developing countries. In the Jaipur City GT mall, the parking charges of a car in a parking lot is ₹ 30 for the first two hours and ₹ 10 per hour for subsequent hours.

Based on the above information answer the following questions.

(i) Taking total parking time to be *x* hour and total charges as ₹ *y*, write a linear equation.

(ii) If $y = 20$, then find the value of *x*.

(iii) If charges of a car in a parking lot is ₹ 50 for the first two hours, then write the linear equation.

Or If charges for subsequent hours is ₹ 8 per hour, then write linear equation.

38. Case Study-3

70 students from a locality, use different modes of transport to go to school as given below

Modes of transport	Car	Bus	Moped	Bicycle	Rickshaw
Number of students	4	27	12	19	8

Now, answer the following questions

(i) Which mode of transport used most by students?

(ii) Which mode of transport used less by students?

(iii) What is the difference in number of students who use Moped and Bus as a mode of transport?

Or

What is the percentage of number of student who used Rickshaw?

Answer Key

1. (c) 2. (a) 3. (b) 4. (d) 5. (a)
6. (c) 7. (d) 8. (b) 9. (d) 10. (a)
11. (c) 12. (b) 13. (d) 14. (c) 15. (b)
16. (a) 17. (a) 18. (c) 19. (a) 20. (d)
21. $p=-7$ 22. (i) $2x$ (ii) -140 23. $34°$ 24. 3 25. $21.75r^3$ cu. units
26. $a=84°, b=21°, c=48°$ 28. (i) 1191016 (ii) 13 or 1800 29. $60°$
30. $y=15$ 31. (i) (0, 0) (ii) (0, −4) (iii) (5, 0) 33. (i) $\sqrt{2}+\sqrt{5}$
34. ₹ 1204.025 or $72\pi\ cm^2$, $84.5\pi\ cm^2$, $\frac{469}{12}\pi\ cm^3$
36. (i) $p(x)=\frac{1}{12}x^2+\frac{7x}{12}+15$ (ii) $\frac{7}{12}$ (iii) $\frac{33}{2}$ or $\frac{29}{2}$
37. (i) $10x-y+10=0$ (ii) $x=1$ (iii) $10x-y+30=0$ or $8x-y+14=0$
38. (i) Bus (ii) Car (iii) 15 or 11.42%